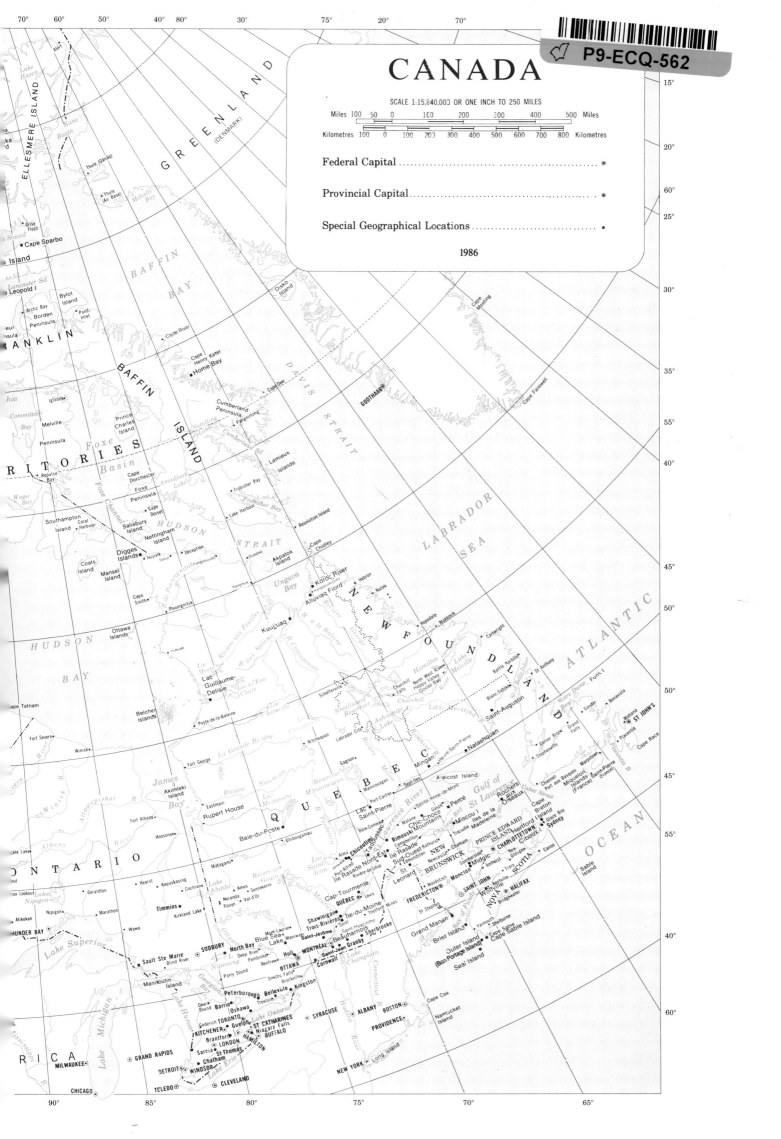

CANADA

SCALE 1:15,840,000 OR ONE INCH TO 250 MILES

Miles 100 50 0 100 200 300 400 500 Miles

Kilometres 100 0 100 200 300 400 500 600 700 800 Kilometres

Federal Capital .... ✶

Provincial Capital .... ✶

Special Geographical Locations .... ■

1986

The
Birds
of Canada
Revised Edition

The Birds

of Canada   Revised Edition

by W. Earl Godfrey

Colour Illustrations by
John A. Crosby

Line Drawings by
John A. Crosby and
S.D. MacDonald

National Museum of Natural Sciences
National Museums of Canada

©National Museums of Canada 1986

National Museum of Natural Sciences
National Museums of Canada
Ottawa, Canada K1A 0M8

Catalogue No. NM92-203/1986E

ISBN 0-660-10758-9

Printed in Canada

Edition française
Les oiseaux du Canada
ISBN 0-660-90265-6

Published by the
National Museums of Canada

Managing Editor
Bonnie Livingstone

Production Editor
Sandra Garland

Design
Gregory Gregory Limited

Typesetting
Nancy Poirier Typesetting Limited

Printing
D.W. Friesen & Sons Ltd

Colour Separations
Ashton-Potter/Prolith
Herzig Somerville Limited

Canadian Cataloguing in Publication Data

Godfrey, W. Earl
The Birds of Canada, revised edition

Issued also in French under title: *Les oiseaux du Canada, édition revisée*
Bibliography: p.
Includes indexes.
ISBN 0-660-10758-9
DSS cat. no. NM92-203/1986E

1. Birds — Canada — Identification. I. Crosby, John A.
II. MacDonald, S.D. III. National Museum of Natural Sciences (Canada).
IV. Title.

QL685.G62 1986   598.2971   C85-097101-2

To
P.A. Taverner
and
Robie W. Tufts
with appreciation

Contents

Topography of a Bird

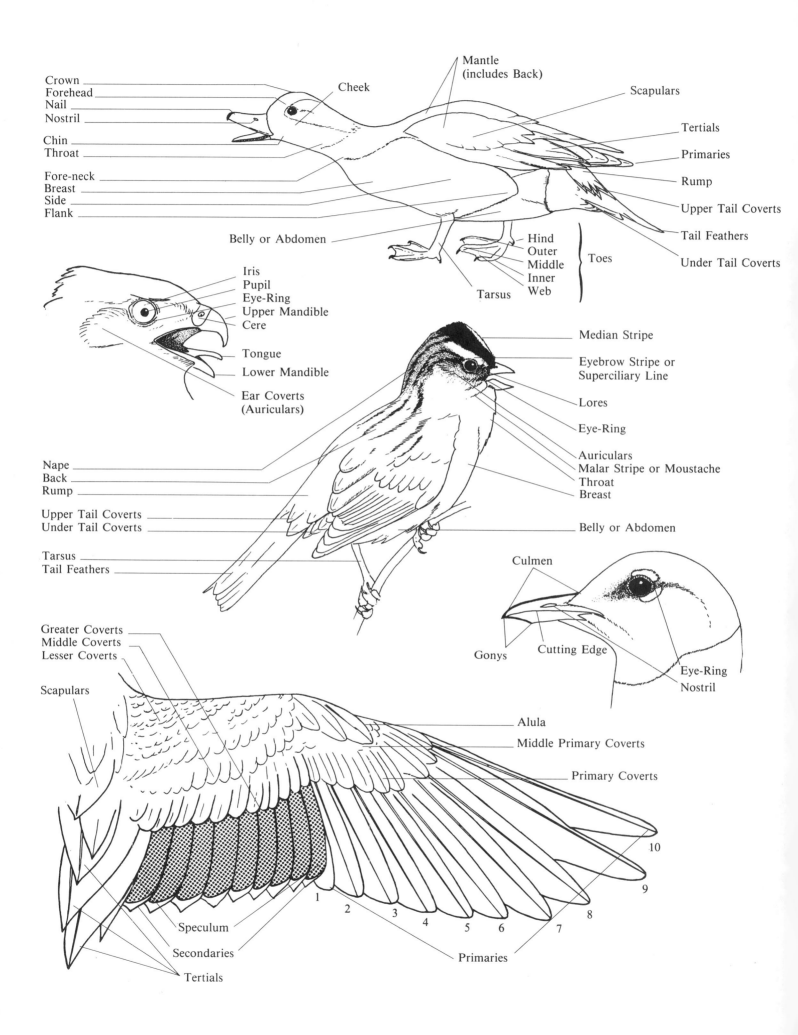

Crown
Forehead
Nail
Nostril

Chin
Throat

Fore-neck
Breast
Side
Flank

Cheek

Mantle (includes Back)

Scapulars

Tertials

Primaries

Rump

Upper Tail Coverts

Tail Feathers

Under Tail Coverts

Belly or Abdomen

Hind
Outer
Middle
Inner
Web

Toes

Tarsus

Iris
Pupil
Eye-Ring
Upper Mandible
Cere

Tongue
Lower Mandible

Ear Coverts (Auriculars)

Median Stripe

Eyebrow Stripe or Superciliary Line

Lores

Eye-Ring

Auriculars
Malar Stripe or Moustache
Throat
Breast

Nape
Back
Rump

Upper Tail Coverts
Under Tail Coverts

Tarsus
Tail Feathers

Belly or Abdomen

Culmen

Gonys

Cutting Edge

Eye-Ring
Nostril

Greater Coverts
Middle Coverts
Lesser Coverts

Scapulars

Alula

Middle Primary Coverts

Primary Coverts

Speculum

Secondaries

Tertials

Primaries

1 2 3 4 5 6 7 8 9 10

Introduction

The Value of Birds

There is no way of estimating in dollars and cents the total value of our bird life, but we do know that it is immense. Vast numbers of birds wage continuous warfare on the insect hordes that strive to devour our crops, devastate our forests, and annoy us generally. Others destroy countless tonnes of weed seeds annually. Hawks during the day and owls by night maintain a round-the-clock check on the numbers of rodent pests. Gulls and other birds perform a useful service as scavengers.

The study of birds as a hobby is an absorbing recreation that is enjoyed regularly by thousands of Canadians in all seasons and in all types of terrain. Their numbers are rapidly increasing. They use binoculars, spotting scopes, cameras, tape recorders, a large variety of bird books, outdoor apparel, and various forms of transportation. Many enthusiasts plan their vacation itineraries in the hope of satisfying their particular interest in birds, often joining one of the many elaborate bird tours to various parts of the world. Some of the provinces are well aware of this and have included a bird list in their tourist literature.

The hunting of game birds in season provides recreation to many thousands of Canadians. This is the nucleus of an industry involving guns, ammunition, hostelries, special apparel, and transportation.

Birds add immeasurably to the enjoyment of everyday life and contribute to a sense of well-being. Although one cannot put a price tag on the sight of the first spring Robin, the plunge of an Osprey, or the vesper carillon of a Hermit Thrush, these and the countless other aesthetic aspects of our birds are as real as the economic ones and fully as great.

Needless to say, most birds as well as their nests and eggs are protected by law, and it is illegal to kill or molest them. Open seasons are provided, however, for many game birds. A few species, such as starlings and crows, are considered harmful to man's interests and are not protected at all.

Bird Study as a Hobby

Estimates of the number of birdwatchers on this continent vary between two million and ten million people. Probably the former is fairly accurate. The study of birds is a fascinating hobby that can be pursued almost anywhere by men and women of all ages and in all walks of life. It may be carried on in one's backyard or in neighbouring fields and woods or be taken to distant lands. It need not be expensive, and one can put as much or as little time and energy into it as desired. Even the ill can watch birds at a backyard feeder or from a car. It is an avocation in which interest grows the more one pursues it. Regardless of where in the world bird students may be, they are never at a loss for something interesting to do in their leisure time.

Although man has an inherent interest in all wild animals, it is in birds that the greatest interest lies for the greatest number of people. The average person cannot, under ordinary circumstances, list an adequate daily variety of mammals, snakes, frogs, or fishes to sustain his or her interest. The reverse is true for insects, whose overwhelming numbers and variety discourage all but the serious student.

Birds are sufficiently numerous, varied, and elusive to challenge our ability to identify them, and yet they do not overwhelm us with difficulties. Their seasonal coming and going add interest to the changing year. Their colours, songs, graceful motions, intriguing habits, varied personalities, and mysterious migrations are additional reasons for the great popularity of bird study as a hobby.

The ability to identify birds accurately and efficiently in the field improves with practice and experience. Many people watch birds purely for recreation and do not want to go beyond that stage. They regard identification as a kind of game, the idea being to run up as high a score as possible in number of species identified in a day, a year, or in total experience. It is true that this activity may add little to the science of ornithology, but, like other outdoor sports, it does provide a great deal of healthful exercise and enjoyment for large numbers of people.

Although the science of ornithology is a well advanced one that keeps professionals continuously employed on a wide variety of problems, there always has been plenty of room for serious, competent amateurs. In fact, one of the reasons why ornithology is so well advanced today is that so many amateurs have contributed so much high-quality research toward a better understanding of birds and their biology. Some of the very best work in ornithology has been done by medical doctors, homemakers, lawyers, policemen, dentists, and business executives, to mention only a few. A glance at the list of acknowledgements in this book will show some of the many amateurs who contributed valuable information.

Kingdom — **Animalia**

Phylum — **Chordata**

Subphylum — **Vertebrata**

Class — **Aves**

Order — **Passeriformes**

Family — **Fringillidae**

Subfamily — **Carduelinae**

Genus — *Carduelis*

Species — *hornemanni*

Subspecies — *exilipes*

The Classification of Birds

Often people speak of "birds and animals" as though birds were something apart, different from animals. Birds, of course, *are* animals. All living things are either animals or plants—and birds certainly are not plants! Birds differ in many ways from other animals, but the most obvious difference is that birds—and only birds—possess feathers. Birds may be thought of, then, as feathered animals. All birds belong to the animal class Aves, which comprises only birds.

For the classification of all living things, biologists have devised an ingenious system, which is in use throughout the world. By this system the seemingly overwhelming variety of living things is broken down into an orderly arrangement.

Living things are first divided into two major categories called kingdoms: Animalia (animals) and Plantae (plants). These categories are subdivided into successively smaller groups according to relationships. In this way each unit is ultimately grouped with its nearest known relative. A specimen of the Hoary Redpoll breeding in northern Quebec, *Carduelis hornemanni exilipes*, for example, would be classified as shown at left.

Scientific Names

Scientific names are composed of Latin words or latinized words derived from Greek or, less often, from other languages. One of the main advantages of scientific names is that they are understood in all countries of the world regardless of language. They are made up of either two or three parts, and all are printed in italics.

The first part of the scientific name is the name of the genus (plural genera). It *always* begins with a capital letter. The second part is the name of the species, and the third (when present) is that of the subspecies. The species and subspecies parts of the scientific name *never* begin with a capital letter.

The genus contains from one to a number of closely related species, which have certain characters in common that separate them from species in other genera. Generic names therefore help us to recognize closely related species. They tell us, for instance, that *Carduelis hornemanni* (Hoary Redpoll) is more closely related to *Carduelis tristis* (American Goldfinch) than it is to *Loxia leucoptera* (White-winged Crossbill), because both *hornemanni* and *tristis* have the same generic name, *Carduelis*.

Breeding populations of some (not all) species have evolved differences in colour or size within geographically limited parts of the breeding range that distinguish the populations (subspecies) of those particular areas from other populations of that species. When this is the case, the scientific name has a third part, the name of the subspecies. For instance, the Hoary Redpoll populations breeding in the northeasternmost parts of the range in Canada are larger and paler than those nesting farther south in Canada and those in Eurasia. The species is, therefore divisible into two subspecies: *Carduelis hornemanni hornemanni* (Holböll) of the northeast and *Carduelis hornemanni exilipes* (Coues).

It will be noted that the surname of the author of a species or subspecies name follows that name without intervening punctuation and is not italicized. In cases where the species or subspecies is now placed in a genus other than that in which it was originally described, the surname of the author of the name is placed within parentheses.

Scope of the Book

The revised edition of this book includes all bird species known by the writer to occur, or to have occurred, in Canada and its coastal waters within a limit of 320 km off shore, up to December 1984, a total of 578 species. The occurrence of most of these species is documented by at least one specimen taken within the country. In some cases, however, no specimen is available but the species occurrence is usually supported by at least one identifiable photograph.

In addition, 37 species recorded in this country on the basis of sight records alone, unidentifiable photos, or other unsatisfactory evidence, are given hypothetical status and such species accounts are printed in small type and enclosed within brackets. Other species, such as the Red-faced Cormorant, have been previously recorded erroneously and are mentioned here in order to obviate further confusion concerning their status in this country. A few species mentioned in the literature are disregarded because obviously they either escaped from captivity or their presence here was otherwise assisted by man, and they were unable to establish an independent wild population for a minimum period of ten years in this country (e.g., Black-headed Parakeet, *Nandayus nenday*; Blue Tit, *Parus caeruleus*; Budgerigar, *Melopsittacus undulatus*, etc.).

At least 426 species are known to breed or to have bred in Canada. In addition, the extinct Labrador Duck almost certainly did so. Two more species, the Yellow-crowned Night-Heron and the American Oystercatcher, have been recorded in the literature as breeding in this country, but the evidence is not satisfactory.

Names of Birds

The English, French, and scientific names of species are provided from the most authoritative and up-to-date sources currently available. The scientific and English names are mostly those advocated by the American Ornithologists' Union's *Check-list of North American Birds* (Sixth Edition, 1983). The use of both English and French vernacular names for subspecies is, except in a few cases, discontinued. Species sequence is largely that of the *A.O.U. Check-list* (Sixth Edition).

The standard English names of bird species are capitalized. This helps to avoid ambiguity. For example, someone writes, "I saw a yellow warbler this morning but not a solitary vireo." One cannot be sure whether this correspondent had identified the particular species, the Yellow Warbler, or intended to say that he saw one of the several warblers that are yellow in colour but was not able to identify the particular species. Similarly any unaccompanied vireo of any species is a solitary vireo, but not necessarily a Solitary Vireo. Only the names of species are capitalized, not such general terms as "warblers" or "ducks." For example, "The Black Duck was the only duck identified."

French vernacular names used are those recommended by Henri Ouellet and Michel Gosselin (1983. Les noms français des oiseaux d'Amérique du Nord. Syllogeus no. 43. National Museum of Natural Sciences, National Museums of Canada, Ottawa).

Colour Plates

Four hundred and ninety-eight species are depicted in colour by artist J.A. Crosby. Not all plumages could, of course, be shown, but use of the plates in conjunction with the species descriptions in the text should help eliminate difficulty in making species identification. The number of the plate on which each illustrated species is shown is given at the beginning of the description of that species. The plates and descriptions supplement each other and should be used together in identifying unfamiliar species.

Descriptions of Species

The majority of bird species show variation in their plumages, which is correlated with age, sex, season, colour phases, or geography. In a few species there is very little variation (e.g., Black-capped Chickadee), but in some, variation is very great (e.g., Herring Gull, Snow Goose). Since not all plumages or plumage variations could be described in a book of this size, only those most frequently encountered are dealt with. Although simple descriptive terms are used as often as possible, technical words could not, and probably should not, be avoided. Most are defined in the glossary or are otherwise identified in the figure showing the topography of a bird (p. 8).

Beginners should keep in mind a few fundamentals concerning the plumages and moults of birds. In adults, the plumages of the male and female of some species, such as the Black-capped Chickadee and the Song Sparrow, look almost identical; in many others, the female is similar to the male but perceptibly duller, as in the American Robin or Dark-eyed Junco; in others, the female is strikingly different and decidedly less colourful, as in the Red-winged Blackbird, Brown-headed Cowbird, Williamson's Sapsucker, and White-winged Crossbill. In most species in which the male and female differ, it is usually the female that is duller coloured and smaller. Rarely is the female more brightly coloured and larger, but this is the case in the phalaropes. In our hawks and owls the female is usually larger than the male.

In some species, such as the Bobolink, Scarlet Tanager, and Lark Bunting, the adult male is far more brightly coloured in the nesting season, but in late summer he moults into an inconspicuous plumage similar to that of the female.

In most birds the first plumage is a natal down, worn at hatching or acquired shortly thereafter. The young individual then passes through a series of moults and plumages (the duration varying among species) until it attains fully adult (or definitive) plumage. Reference is frequently made in the descriptions in this book to juvenal plumage. This is the first plumage acquired after the natal down. The juvenal plumage is usually worn but a short time, and it is not to be confused with the term "juvenile," which is applied to any immature bird and its plumage at any stage.

Some birds, like the Horned Lark, acquire adult (or definitive) plumage in about three months, in their first late summer or early autumn; others, like the Bobolink, in their first late winter or early spring; many passerine birds such as the Rose-breasted Grosbeak acquire it late in their second summer. The Herring Gull requires about three and one-half years, and the Bald Eagle takes five or more years to acquire full adult plumage.

Most adult birds completely renew their plumage at least once a year in late summer or early autumn by moulting (this includes both the shedding and replacement of feathers). Many others have an additional partial moult in late winter or early spring, before the breeding season. In a very few species, of which the Sharp-tailed Sparrow and Bobolink are examples, there are two complete moults a year.

Abnormalities sometimes alter the appearance of birds. Albinism, the absence of colour in feathers that are normally coloured, is due to the failure of pigment to develop, and the result is white feathers. This may be complete or only partial. The opposite condition, caused by an

Figure 1
Length of wing

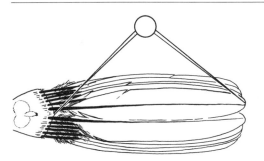

Figure 2
Length of tail

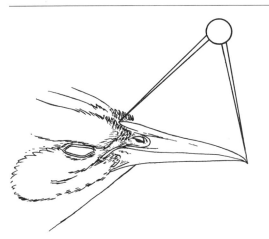

Figure 3
Length of exposed culmen

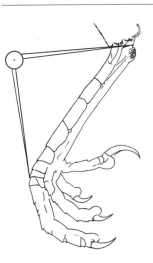

Figure 4
Length of tarsus

excess development of dark pigment, results in abnormally dark plumage; this is called melanism. It is much less common than albinism.

Measurements

Total length is given at the beginning of each species description. This is measured from the tip of the bill to the tip of the tail, with the bird flat on its back, its bill parallel with the ruler, its neck extended but not unduly stretched. This particular measurement should never be made from a dried skin. Although this measurement is not of great scientific value, it is useful in indicating relative size.

Measurements *in millimetres* of the closed wing, tail, exposed culmen, and tarsus are given for adult males; measurements usually of only the wing are given for adult females. In most cases ten males and ten females were measured. Small and large extremes of the series measured are given, with averages in parentheses. These measurements are useful as an aid to identification of the species. Unless otherwise credited, measurements were made mostly by Henri Ouellet from Canadian material in the National Museum of Natural Sciences, National Museums of Canada. In cases where more than one subspecies is found in Canada, the particular subspecies measured is indicated.

Methods used in taking these measurements are those advocated by S.P. Baldwin, H.C. Oberholser, and L.G. Worley (1931. Scientific Publications, Cleveland Museums Natural History, vol. 2, pp. i–ix, 1–165).

Wing: The length of the closed wing is the distance on the closed wing from the most anterior point of the wrist joint to the tip of the longest primary, unflattened (Figure 1).

Tail: The length of the tail is measured from that point between the two middle feathers where they emerge from the skin to the tip of the longest tail feather (Figure 2).

Exposed Culmen: This measurement is the distance from that point on the culmen where the feathers of the forehead cease to hide the culmen, forward in a straight line to the tip of the bill. It is really the chord of the exposed culmen. It is best taken with dividers (Figure 3).

Tarsus: This measurement, taken with dividers, is the distance from the middle point in the heel joint *behind* to the lower edge of the lowest undivided scute or to the junction with the base of the middle toe, in *front* (Figure 4).

Field Marks

Field marks are the points to look for to distinguish quickly and accurately in the field each species from those species most closely resembling it; for instance, how to tell a Common Loon from a Yellow-billed Loon, or a Double-crested Cormorant from a Pelagic Cormorant. It is assumed that the reader can tell a loon from a cormorant or a duck. The beginner should learn to distinguish members of one family from those of other families. By studying the coloured plates and the short accounts of each family, he will soon be able to tell at a glance loons from grebes, cormorants, or waterfowl (ducks, geese, and swans); or warblers from vireos or sparrows.

Voice

Voice is here included under Field Marks because the sounds of birds are an extremely useful aid to locating and identifying bird species in the field. In fact, for an experienced observer with good ears, most (not all) bird species are readily identifiable by voice alone. Needless to say, familiarity with bird sounds should be developed as rapidly as possible.

In print it is difficult to represent with any degree of clarity the songs of birds. The best that can be done is to suggest rhythms and syllables that may convey some idea of what to listen for. Only the commonest and most characteristic of bird sounds are given, mainly as an aid to identification.

Excellent recordings of the songs of most birds are readily available at reasonable prices. There is no quicker way to learn the songs of birds. Regardless of how it is done, learning them is important, for familiarity with bird sounds vastly increases the efficiency and enjoyment of the observer.

Habitat

Birds are by no means evenly distributed across their ranges. Each species has its particular likes concerning the type of surroundings it prefers, an ecological complex that best suits the requirements of that species as an environment in which to live. This environmental complex is its habitat. Particular habitat preferences are characteristic of each species and are inherited by each individual of that species. Thus all Horned Larks seek open areas and shun woodlands, while Brown Creepers inhabit woodlands and shun treeless areas. Distribution patterns within the range, then, are often intricate, and they, along with population densities, vary greatly according to the availability of suitable habitat.

In this book the habitat preferences of each species of regular occurrence in Canada are outlined. Of necessity, this is done in broad terms in such a vast and ecologically varied area as Canada. Such broad terms as "mature coniferous forest" or "second-growth deciduous woodland" have an additional advantage of being readily understood by everyone.

Nesting

In most cases, nesting data are given only for the species known to nest in this country. Incubation periods are credited to the author who published them or to persons who kindly furnished the writer with their unpublished data.

Range

A succinct outline of the extralimital range of the species has been given to indicate roughly the extent of the breeding range in the world and the winter range in the Western Hemisphere. It ties the Canadian part of the breeding range in with the general range in other parts of the world and indicates where the birds that leave this country in autumn spend the winter.

Range in Canada

This is a summary of the known distribution in this country. The text and breeding distribution maps have been thoroughly updated and revised to show the status and distribution in Canada of each bird species as it was known through 1983 and early 1984. The extent of the breeding range in the larger provinces and in the territories is indicated by citing selected breeding localities with emphasis on peripheral ones. From sections of the range where the species is common, only one or two sample localities could be cited. It will be understood, therefore, that no attempt could be made to cite all known breeding localities. Directional terms are explained in Figure 5.

Data used in delimiting these ranges were taken from a great many sources, most (but by no means all) of them published. All data were carefully considered before being used, and all are thought to be reliable. At the beginning, documentation of all the data was visualized, but it soon became apparent that this was not practicable in a one-volume book. The writer can furnish, upon request, the source of any particular distributional or other data.

Range maps show the breeding range in Canada of most of the birds that nest in the country. Areas in which breeding might occur but is not definitely known are indicated by question marks. For the species with a very restricted breeding range in this country no map is provided.

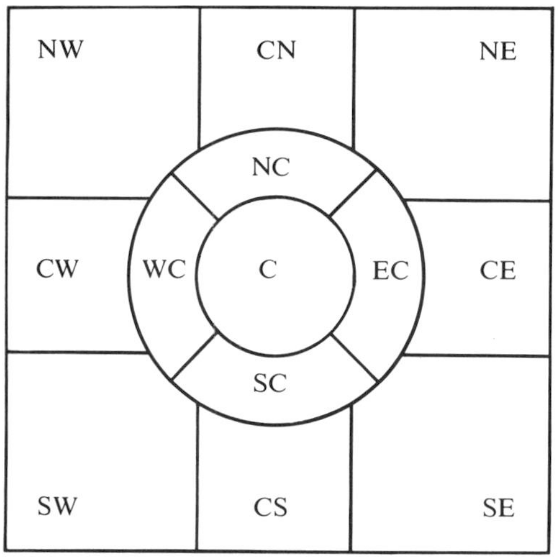

Figure 5
Explanation of directional terms used in range summaries:

CE: central eastern; CN: central northern; CS: central southern; CW: central western; EC: eastern central; NC: north central; NE: northeastern; NW: northwestern; SC: south central; SE: southeastern; SW: southwestern; WC: west central.

It should be borne in mind that the breeding range maps show the extent of those parts of Canada within which the species is known to nest *provided that a complex of ecological requirements peculiar to that species is met*. There will be, therefore, areas of various extent within the breeding range outlined where breeding will be absent because of lack of suitable habitat, for instance. Thus within the range shown, the Sora will breed only in marshy areas, Horned Larks will be absent from areas of forested habitat whether small or vast, and Pileated Woodpeckers will not be found nesting in expanses of treeless country.

In this new edition, a number of geographical names used in the range summaries were altered to conform with changes adopted by the Canadian Permanent Committee on Geographic Names in their *Gazetteer of Canada* series published by Surveys and Mapping Branch, Department of Energy, Mines and Resources, Ottawa. Some of these name changes involve geographical names long familiar to birders.

Species Numbers

Throughout the range summaries such terms as "common," "fairly common," etc., are used to indicate roughly the species' numerical status. The terms used are relative. It would be desirable to define them with mathematical precision. Although such precision may be possible in dealing with smaller well-censused areas, such uniformity is not practicable for a country of such vast geographic extent and ecological diversity as Canada. Indeed it is difficult to be sure of the application of even relative terms to much of the Arctic and Subarctic. It is felt that the relative terms used should not be confusing or difficult to understand. Moreover, experience has shown that the accuracy of even precise terms may in some areas be evanescent, to say the least!

Subspecies

In accordance with current practice, vernacular names for subspecies have been abolished.

In species divisible into subspecies that occur in Canada regularly, a paragraph deals briefly with the subspecies found in this country. In the case of casual or accidental species, the subspecies, if known, is given under Status in Canada.

Bird-Banding

Bird-banding, the marking of the individual bird by placing a numbered band on its leg, is directed in Canada by the Canadian Wildlife Service in cooperation with the United States Fish and Wildlife Service. By thus marking birds, a great mass of valuable information on various aspects of birds such as migration and longevity is being accumulated that could be secured in no other way.

If you find a *dead* wild bird with a band on its leg, remove the band and send it to Bird-Banding Office, Canadian Wildlife Service, Ottawa, Ontario K1A 0E7. Should the bird be uninjured, do not remove the band; merely record the complete band number and release the bird. In all cases give the date and place of capture, the manner in which it was secured, and the name of the person who secured it. You will be notified in due course as to where, when, and by whom the bird was banded.

Bands or band numbers on Rock Doves (domestic pigeons) are not wanted.

Acknowledgements

I thank my colleagues at the National Museum of Natural Sciences for their help and encouragement: Artist John A. Crosby skilfully painted all the colour illustrations and produced many black-and-white drawings. For these, and for his cordial spirit of cooperation in all aspects of those important tasks, I am most appreciative.

Henri Ouellet, Chief, Vertebrate Zoology Division, and Curator of Birds, expertly translated the first English edition into the first French edition and made the specimen measurements (except those credited otherwise). He read the Quebec parts of the range summaries in the new edition, generously provided additional distributional data gathered in the course of his extensive field work in Quebec, and contributed important data from the coastal strip of northern Yukon. On French vernacular names he has been a perennial source of advice.

Stewart D. MacDonald, Curator of Vertebrate Ethology, has, since the inception of the first edition, shared his vast first-hand knowledge of birds in the Canadian Arctic. His personally gathered distributional data have greatly improved many erstwhile poorly known arctic parts of the range maps. Most of his fine black-and-white illustrations of the first edition are retained in the second.

The late Violet M. Humphreys, Registrar (Zoology), assisted in ways too numerous to mention but above all her meticulous maintenance of the bird distribution files greatly lightened the labour of delimiting many intricate patterns of bird distribution.

Richard M. Poulin, Curatorial Assistant, furnished useful data from his field work in northern Saskatchewan. Specimen material collected by him over a period of years has contributed to a better understanding of the plumages and affinities of several gull species.

Michel Gosselin, Curatorial Assistant, was an unfailing source of help in many ways, and especially in tracing obscure records and geographic names in the province of Quebec.

Mrs. Bonnie Livingstone, Coordinator of Publishing, is thanked for her expertise in seeing the manuscript through publication.

Of the many people in other parts of Canada and the United States who furnished useful information I am especially grateful to four colleagues who were particularly helpful over extended periods: the late Robie W. Tufts, Wolfville, Nova Scotia; Ross D. James, Royal Ontario Museum, Toronto, Ontario; R. Wayne Campbell, British Columbia Provincial Museum, Victoria, British Columbia; and Ian A. McLaren, Dalhousie University, Halifax, Nova Scotia.

I am truly grateful to the many additional people who furnished data of various kinds, manuscripts, photographs, or specimens: John W. Aldrich, C.R.K. Allen, A.E. Allin, Robert F. Andrle, James L. Baillie, Jr., A.W.F. Banfield, Fred G. Bard, C.O. Bartlett, Jean Bedard, Tony Bigg, J. Sherman Bleakney, G.J. Borradaile, A.E. Bourguignon, Monty Brigham, R.S. Brodey, N. Rae Brown, R.G.B. Brown, P.W.P. Browne, Dan F. Brunton, E.W. Calvert, A.W. Cameron, J.M. Campbell, Geoffrey Carpentier, Raymond Cayouette, Roland C. Clement, Cyril Coldwell, F. Graham Cooch, F.N. Cowell, I. McT. Cowan, Albert R. Davidson, Bruce Dilabio, Keith Denis, Thomas Dyke, Alex. Dzubin, Sylvia Edlund, R.Y. Edwards, R.D. Elliot, A.J. Erskine, Robert S. Ferguson, Davis W. Finch, G.R. Fitzgerald, Roger A. Foxall, Robert Frisch, Richard Fyfe, Mrs. L.A. Gibbard, David A. Gill,

J.B. Gollop, J.E.V. Goodwill, Clive L. Goodwin, Stanley W. Gorham, James Grant, C.J. Guiguet, Donald R. Gunn, Donald R. Gutoski, Joseph A. Hagar, Francis Harper, Ross Harris, R.D. Harris, E.O. Höhn, Eric Holdway, H.V. Hosford, C. Stuart Houston, Mary F. Jackson, J.R. Jehl, C.L. Johnston, Edgar T. Jones, John P. Kelsall, John Kristensen, Ernie Kuyt, Hamilton M. Laing, A.G. Lawrence, Louise de K. Lawrence, Louis Lemieux, Harrison F. Lewis, Jon Lien, Robert Lister, Hoyes Lloyd, T.M. Lothian, James K. Lowther, Harry G. Lumsden, R.H. MacKay, Andrew H. Macpherson, Lloyd B. Macpherson, C.D. MacInnes, Bruce Mactavish, C. Douglas McCallum, Verna McGiffen, Douglas McRae, T.H. Manning, William C. Mansell, Kathy Martin, Patrick W. Martin, W.J. Merilees, J.B. Miles, Eric L. Mills, Willett J. Mills, W.A. Montevecchi, R.I.G. Morrison, David H. Mossop, David A. Munro, M.T. Myres, Robert W. Nero, David N. Nettleship, John Nicholson, Jacques Normandin, Harry C. Oberholser, Reginald Ouellet, Ralph S. Palmer, David F. Parmelee, Peter A. Pearce, Theed Pearse, George K. Peck, Harold S. Peters, Stuart S. Peters, Hazel Petty, Bruce C. Pigot, Ronald Pittaway, Allan R. Phillips, G.A. Poynter, Helen R. Quilliam, Austin L. Rand, Wayne E. Renaud, Christopher C. Rimmer, Chandler S. Robbins, Kenneth Ross, J.F. Roy, Loris S. Russell, W. Ray Salt, Richard E. Salter, Douglas C. Sadler, Jack Satterly, D.B.O. Savile, F.H. Schultz, George W. Scotter, S.G. Sealy, David E. Sergeant, P.F. Sherrington, Donald A. Smith, Neal G. Smith, Peter C. Smith, Thomas G. Smith, W. John Smith, L.L. Snyder, J. Dewey Soper, J. Murray Speirs, W.A. Squires, John B. Steeves, David Stirling, George M. Stirrett, George M. Sutton, R.W. Sutton, Rev. René Tanguay, J.B. Tatum, Philip S. Taylor, John S. Tener, Lewis McI. Terrill, Leslie M. Tuck, C.E. Tull, Stanley E. Vass, Lawrence H. Walkinshaw, Sam Waller, W.J. Walley, Dan Welch, Ron D. Weir, Alexander Wetmore, A.L. Wilk, Audrey E. Wilson, V.C. Wynne-Edwards, and many others.

Measurements of a number of species not adequately represented in the National Museum of Natural Sciences are mostly those of Ridgway (1901–1946) and Friedmann (1950).

Nest record card programmes were a useful source of unpublished data, in particular the Quebec Nest Record Card Program, which is housed in the National Museum of Natural Sciences.

Order **Gaviiformes:**
Loons

Family **Gaviidae:**
Loons

Number of Species in Canada: 5

Large swimming birds usually seen on open water. They are frequent divers and have larger and longer bodies than grebes and most ducks, and shorter necks than geese. They fly with feet extended beyond the stubby tail, and the neck slanted slightly downward giving a somewhat hump-backed appearance. The bill is *sharply pointed*, thus very different from ducks and geese, and is never hooked at tip as in cormorants and mergansers. The head is never crested, and the plumage is hard and glossy, velvety about head and neck. The short and very stiff tail is much better developed than in grebes. There are four toes, the front three completely connected by webs (in cormorants, all four are connected by webs; in grebes, toes are lobed, not webbed).

Loons are excellent swimmers and divers, diving from the water surface with head lowered in a plunging motion accompanied by a forward thrust of the body. Progress under water is very rapid; the body is propelled usually by the feet only, but the wings sometimes are used, especially in spurts and turns. As in other diving birds certain physiological adaptations of blood and muscle chemistry enable loons to remain submerged for considerable periods. They can ride low in water or sink slowly out of sight by changing their specific gravity through compression of plumage and forcing of air from lungs. Fish, which make up a large part of their food, are caught by underwater pursuit.

Because the legs are attached far back on the body, loons move awkwardly on land, usually by either pushing along on the breast in frog-like leaps or assuming a semi-erect posture and shuffling forward with tarsi flat on the ground. They seldom come ashore except for nesting purposes. The nest is placed near the water's edge to permit return to the water with a minimum of time and effort. Three of the four species cannot fly from land; and even from water their take-off is laboured and space-consuming. Once in the air, however, they fly swiftly and directly. During the moulting of the flight feathers (the primaries and secondaries being shed simultaneously) loons are flightless. In adults of the Common, Yellow-billed, and Pacific loons, the flightless period usually occurs in late winter; in the Red-throated this takes place in autumn. This awkward period occurs away from the nesting grounds, on broad expanses of open water where they can secure food and escape potential enemies with ease.

Red-throated Loon

Huart à gorge rousse
Gavia stellata (Pontoppidan)
Total length: 61 to 69 cm
Plate 1

A small loon with a slender bill, which often appears uptilted because of the abrupt upward angle of its lower edge. *Summer adults* with dark-grey head, red throat patch, and plain (not checkered black-and-white) back are unmistakable. *Winter adults and immatures* are, like other loons, dark grey above and white below, but in the hand the Red-throated Loon is easily separable by its speckled back (other winter loons have either "scaly" or plain backs) (see Figure 6). *Juvenals in first autumn and winter* differ from winter adults in the pattern of the back feathers: the white spots are longer, narrower, forming V-marks, especially on scapulars and wing coverts; the spots are more greyish, less pure white.

Breeding Distribution of Red-throated Loon

Range in Canada. Breeds from Prince Patrick and northern Ellesmere islands (Alert) south to central Yukon (Ogilvie Mountains); southern Mackenzie (Great Slave Lake); northern Saskatchewan (Little Gull Lake, southern Reindeer Lake); Keewatin; northern Manitoba; James Bay (South Twin Island); northern Ontario (Hudson Bay coast); northern and southeastern Quebec (Bienville Lake, north shore of the Gulf of St. Lawrence, and Anticosti Island; perhaps Gaspé Peninsula); coast of Labrador; and locally in Newfoundland (Bell Island); also in coastal British Columbia (Queen Charlotte Islands, Swanson Bay; isolated nesting near Courtenay, Vancouver Island); isolated nesting also on north shore of Lake Superior (Thunder Cape, Rossport). Summer records for northern Alberta (south to Caribou Mountains).

Winters on the coast of British Columbia, Newfoundland, New Brunswick, and Nova Scotia; small numbers on the lower Great Lakes. Migration is mostly coastal. A rare transient in the southern interior of the country but has been recorded in all provinces.

Figure 6
Feathers from mantle of
a) juvenal Pacific Loon
b) juvenal Red-throated Loon

Measurements. *Adult male*: wing, 272.5–292.5 (280.2); tarsus, 68.5–78.1 (73.9); exposed culmen, 48.2–57.1 (52.4). *Adult female*: wing, 259.0–281.0 (270.4); tarsus, 65.5–73.1 (69.9); exposed culmen, 46.4–54.6 (51.0) mm.

Field Marks. A smallish loon with slightly uptilted bill. *Summer adults* with dark-grey head, red throat patch, and plain-brown back (not checkered black-and-white) are easily distinguished from other loons. *Winter adults and immatures* are more difficult, but the uptilted bill will usually separate them from Common and Pacific loons. Its smaller size and much slenderer bill distinguish it from the Yellow-billed. At close range, the back is speckled with white (instead of being "scaly" or all black); thus it differs from other winter loons.

Habitat. Adults in summer frequent freshwater ponds and lakes, generally smaller and shallower than those used by the Pacific Loon, mainly on tundra but to some extent in forested country as well. They often visit larger lakes, rivers, and salt water to feed. In winter, adults and young frequent the seacoast. On the West Coast they tend to favour more inshore ocean areas than the Pacific Loon. Most immatures at all seasons remain on salt water until mature.

Nesting. Nest, a depression in the ground or in a heap of moss or other vegetation on the shores or islands of ponds and lakes; very close to water's edge or in shallow water. *Eggs*, usually 2; varying in colour between olive and dark brown with spots and blotches of blackish brown. Incubation 27 days (W.H. Drury, Jr.), 29 days (G.M. Sutton), by both sexes, begins with laying of first egg. Only one brood a season.

Range. Circumpolar. Breeds from northern Alaska across northern Canada and Greenland, south to coastal British Columbia, southern Mackenzie, James Bay, Newfoundland (sparsely), and Miquelon Island; also across northern Eurasia. Winter range in North America extends mainly from the Aleutian Islands south along the Pacific Coast to northwestern Mexico; and from southern Newfoundland south to southern Florida and the Gulf of Mexico coast.

Remarks. Although the Red-throated Loon is similar to other loons, it differs from them in several respects. The red throat patch and plain uncheckered back are unique among adult summer plumages of loons. The flightless period of adults occurs in autumn instead of late winter or early spring. Its take-off from water, which is much quicker and less laboured than that of other loons, enables it to inhabit much smaller ponds, and it is the only loon known to be able to fly directly from land. It is inclined to be more sociable than most loons. Although seen usually in small loose flocks, ones, or twos, it sometimes gathers into larger groups on favourite feeding waters; migration flocks of up to 500 have been observed.

On the breeding grounds it has spectacular courtship and distraction displays. In summer its repertoire is weird and varied, in keeping with the wildness of the arctic tundra-ponds it frequents. A prolonged mournful wail is common, an impressive far-carrying *gayorworrk*; and in flight a rapid guttural *kwuk-kwuk-kwuk-kwuk*, much like that of the Pacific Loon.

Arctic Loon

Huart arctique
Gavia arctica (Linnaeus)
Total length: 59 to 75 cm

Status in Canada. Non-breeding visitor to
British Columbia (specimens: Comox, November
1891; Victoria, March 1906).

Pacific Loon

(formerly included in Arctic Loon)

Huart du Pacifique
Gavia pacifica (Lawrence)
Total length: 58 to 74 cm
Plate 1

Breeding Distribution of Pacific Loon

Range in Canada. Breeds from Banks, Victoria,
and Prince of Wales islands, Boothia Penin-
sula, northern Melville Peninsula, Prince
Charles and North Spicer islands, and northern
Baffin Island (Pond Inlet, Admiralty Inlet
region, Nettilling Lake, Cumberland Sound)
south to southern Yukon; extreme northern
British Columbia; northern Alberta (Leland
Lakes); northern Manitoba (Herchmer, possibly
Reindeer Lake); northern Ontario (Little Cape,
Cape Henrietta Maria); northwestern Quebec
(locally: 40 km north of Inoucdjouac; Koartac);
and southern Baffin Island (Big Island).
Recorded in summer in northern Saskatchewan
and northern Melville Island but breeding
evidence lacking.

Winters on the coast of British Columbia.
Scarce transient in southern interior British
Columbia (Okanagan Lake, Arrow Lakes);
southern Alberta (Brooks); southern Saskatchewan
(Regina); and central Manitoba (Cormorant
Lake). Accidental in southeastern Quebec (Île
de la tête à la Baleine, October 1923; between
Sainte-Flavie and Rimouski, July 1934) and in
southern Ontario (sight records only: Toronto,
La Salle Park). Hypothetical for Nova Scotia
(sight records of winter plumages only).

Like Pacific Loon but with greenish (instead of purplish) sheen on
throat; darker grey nape; and slightly larger size *(G. a. viridigularis)*.

Range. Breeds in eastern Siberia (east of Indigirka River and south
of the Arctic) southward to Amurland, Sakhalin, and Kamchatka, and
in western Alaska (Cape Prince of Wales region).

Subspecies. *Gavia arctica viridigularis* Dwight.

Bill straight, evenly tapered. *Summer adults* somewhat like the Common
Loon but *crown and hind-neck grey*; long white streaks down sides of
neck; size smaller. *Winter adults* like the Common Loon, dark grey
above, white below; but the back is plain black without light tips to the
feathers, size smaller *Juvenals in first autumn and winter* are like
winter adults, but feathers of back are brownish instead of blackish and
are narrowly tipped with light grey (Figure 6).

Measurements. *Adult male*: wing, 281–303.5 (293.7); tarsus,
70.2–78.5 (74.3); exposed culmen, 49.5–55.0 (51.9). *Adult female*: wing,
277–304 (290.7); tarsus, 67.2–75.0 (71.9); exposed culmen, 49.0–54.0
(50.8) mm.

Field Marks. A small loon with a straight bill. In *summer adults*
the grey hind-neck and black throat are a combination that readily identifies it. In *winter adults*, the plain blackish back (no grey feather tips)
is diagnostic at close range. *Autumn and winter juvenals* have faintly
"scaly" backs like those of the Common and Yellow-billed, but in any
plumage the Pacific is a smaller bird with less robust bill. Its straight
bill separates it from the Red-throated and Yellow-billed, both of which
have slightly uptilted bills.

Habitat. In summer, adults frequent freshwater lakes (usually
larger, deeper ones than the Red-throated Loon prefers), in terrain
varying from flat to mountainous in either treeless or wooded country,
both near the coast and far inland; in winter, they frequent coastal salt
water, tending to favour more offshore waters than the Red-throated
Loon.

Nesting. Nest near water's edge varies from a lined depression in
the ground to a mass of vegetation and mud, sometimes built up in
shallow water. *Eggs*, usually 2; varying from greenish olive to dark
umber, with blackish spots and blotches. Incubation period 23.5 to
24.5 days (Jehl and Smith 1970), 27 to 29 (Sjölander).

Range. Breeds from northeastern Siberia and Alaska east across
northern Canada to Baffin Island. Winters mainly along the Pacific
Coast from southeastern Alaska south to southern Baja California.

Remarks. Because of its remote summer home, few Canadians
have a chance to know this attractive loon. The Alaska Highway provides easy access to a few lakes in southern Yukon where its interesting
courtship and distraction displays may be seen. Its voice is varied.
Raven-like croaks and growls are frequent. A prolonged, mournful wail
is often given, particularly at dawn or evening. Under stress it has a
habit of emitting a doglike yelp just before it dives. A guttural *kwuk-
kwuk-kwuk* is uttered during flight.

Common Loon

Huart à collier
Gavia immer (Brünnich)
Total length: 71 to 89 cm
Plate 1

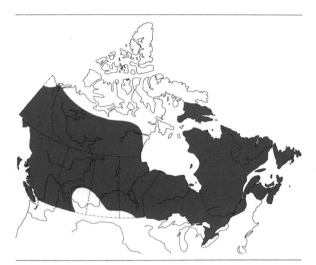

Breeding Distribution of Common Loon

Range in Canada. Breeds from northern Yukon (Old Crow Flats); western and southern Mackenzie (Mackenzie Delta, Great Bear Lake, Great Slave Lake); central Keewatin (Judge Sissons Lake ca. 70 to 80 km south of Schultz Lake); northern Saskatchewan; northern Manitoba; northern Ontario; central Baffin Island (Cumberland Sound); southward through southern British Columbia (but scarce on coastal islands north of Queen Charlotte Sound); southwestern and central-eastern Alberta (absent from southeastern corner); south-central Saskatchewan (Moose Mountain, Crescent Lake, but absent from most of the southern plains); southern Manitoba; southern Ontario (but now absent from many lakes in thickly settled southern parts); southern Quebec; New Brunswick; Prince Edward Island; Nova Scotia; and Newfoundland. Alleged nesting in northern Baffin Island requires confirmation. More definite data are needed to delimit the respective breeding ranges of this and the Yellow-billed Loon, where the ranges come together or overlap. Hybridization with *G. pacifica* has been recorded from northwestern Mackenzie (Ian Robertson and Mark Fraker, 1974. Canadian Field-Naturalist vol. 88, no. 3, p. 367).

Summer sight record for Southampton Island but no evidence of nesting.

Migrates through most of southern Canada and across northern Yukon (Porcupine River). Winters on the coast of British Columbia and on the Atlantic coast of Newfoundland, New Brunswick, Prince Edward Island, and Nova Scotia; uncommonly lower Great Lakes (Toronto).

Sexes alike. A large loon with straight, evenly tapered bill; culmen slightly convex (Figure 7). *Summer adults*: Head and neck black with greenish gloss, an incomplete white collar, white bar across throat, and black bill; back boldly checkered black-and-white; belly white. *Winter adults*: Upper parts dark grey, feathers of back tipped with pale grey; lower cheeks, throat, fore-neck, breast, and belly, white; bill greyish with blackish culmen (adults very often retain some summer plumage, which produces blotched black-and-white areas on head and neck). *Young in first winter*: Like winter adult but throat and fore-neck more or less speckled with browns; bill shorter; horn colour blackish on ridge (see Yellow-billed Loon).

Measurements. *Adult male*: wing, 339.0–381.0 (360.9); tarsus, 87.0–96.2 (92.9); exposed culmen, 72.5–90.1 (81.5). *Adult female*: wing, 315.8–360.0 (337.9); tarsus, 80.0–91.0 (86.3); exposed culmen, 73.0–86.0 (79.9) mm.

Field Marks. A large, heavy-headed loon. *Summer adult: All-black head* separates it from the Red-throated and Arctic, which have conspicuous areas of grey on the head. Very much like the Yellow-billed but has a straight *black* bill. *Winter adults and young*: All are similarly coloured dark grey above, white below. The Common Loon is a larger bird with noticeably heavier bill than the Pacific and Red-throated. Bill straight and robust, not apparently slightly upturned as in Red-throated and Yellow-billed.

Habitat. Adults in spring, summer, and autumn inhabit freshwater lakes and sometimes larger rivers while these are open; in winter, inshore seacoasts or larger bodies of fresh water near the coast are preferred. Immatures frequent coastal inshore salt water at all seasons, less often fresh water.

Nesting. Usually only one pair to a lake, but large lakes may have two or more pairs. Nest near water's edge, preferably on islands, also on shores of fresh water. It is usually a mass of decaying vegetation, sometimes a mere depression on a muskrat house; occasionally the eggs are laid on bare ground. *Eggs*, usually 2; vary in colour from olive green to olive brown with blackish or brownish spots. Incubation 29 days (Olson and Marshall), by both sexes. Chicks abandon the nest soon after natal down is dry.

Range. Breeds from northern Alaska, western and southern Mackenzie, central Keewatin, northern Manitoba, northern Ontario, central Baffin Island, Greenland, and Iceland south to northeastern California, northwestern Montana, North Dakota, northern Illinois, northern Ohio, northern New York, New Hampshire, and Maine. Winters mainly on the coasts from southern Alaska south to Baja California and from Newfoundland to Florida and Texas; also uncommonly on the lower Great Lakes; and from the British Isles to the western Mediterranean Sea.

Remarks. Soon after the winter ice breaks up on the interior lakes, the Common Loon returns to nest. Although it breeds over vast areas of Canada, it is now generally restricted to more remote waters where it is sparsely distributed. Usually there is only one pair to a lake, although larger lakes may have two or more pairs. On the breeding lakes, courtship and vocalizing are spectacular performances. Loons are devoted parents, and at least one of the pair remains with the young most of the time. Ten or eleven weeks elapse after hatching before the young can fly from their natal lake. Freeze-up forces both adults and young to the seacoasts where they winter. The following spring, the young remain on inshore salt water and do not return to the breeding waters until mature.

The voice is loud, resonant, and greatly varied. It has been variously described as maniacal, blood-curdling, horrible, beautiful, and thrilling. Three basic calls are (1) a laughing tremolo, (2) a weird yodel, (3) a wolflike wail.

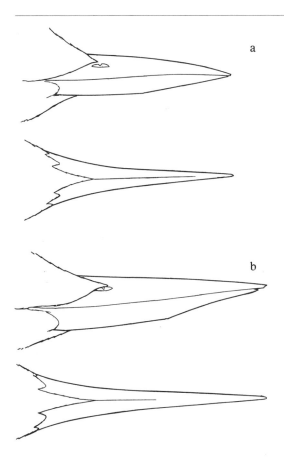

Figure 7
Lateral and ventral views of bill of (a) Common Loon (b) Yellow-billed Loon.

Note that in Yellow-billed Loon the feathering on the sides of the maxilla extends forward to touch the entire posterior end of the nostril and extends up and over the nostril to a point well anterior to the nasal tubercle. In Common Loon this feathering barely touches the posterior tip of the nostril and above the nostril usually does not project anteriorly beyond the nasal tubercle.

In ventral aspect, most of the bill anterior to the gonys is smooth, without a longitudinal groove; in Common Loon that part of the bill is longitudinally grooved to near the tip.

Like other loons, it is an excellent swimmer and diver. Fish are caught by underwater pursuit, the bird propelling itself usually by the feet only; but sometimes the wings also are used in spurts and turns. Ordinarily it does not stay under water more than a minute, but, under stress, submergences of three minutes or more have been recorded. Smaller fishes are eaten under water; larger, spiny ones may be brought to the surface before being swallowed. By compressing the plumage and forcing air from the lungs the Common Loon can ride low in the water and can even sink slowly out of sight. Because the legs are attached far back on the body, it moves awkwardly on land and therefore spends most of its time afloat. When undisturbed, loons often roll over on one side and preen vigorously, one foot waving slowly in the air. At such times the gleaming white under parts are visible for long distances. Often loons rear up on the water, flap wings, stretch neck, shake head, then settle back on the water.

Take-off for flight, which cannot be accomplished from land, is laboured. The bird half-flies, half-runs across the water for approximately 18 to 400 m. A breeze is a help but is not necessary. Flight is rapid, direct, and steady. Ground speeds up to 100 km/h have been recorded. Landing, at the end of a flat, low glide, is an impressive sight, the body impact leaving a long trail of spray on the water.

Away from the breeding grounds this loon is found in singles, pairs, small loose groups, and occasionally in considerable flocks. Sometimes it swims and dives in a well-spaced single file. Adults are flightless for a short time in late winter when all the flight feathers are moulted simultaneously. Sub-adults moult these feathers at other times depending on age.

Fishes are this loon's primary food, but its diet also includes crustaceans, molluscs, frogs, and vegetation. The fishes eaten are mainly ones of little economic importance, and some of the fishes taken compete with useful fishes for food and habitat. Loons are not frequenters of swift trout-streams; usually they are so sparsely distributed that they do no real harm. Occasionally, however, they concentrate about fishermen's nets and setlines, in which they get caught, and sometimes they damage them in their efforts to escape. Much persecuted in the past, they no longer nest in most of their former haunts in thickly settled country. Even on remoter waterways this loon is losing out to the summer cottager, the outboard motor, and the rifle. Wise laws now protect this picturesque bird at all seasons, but it is too late to restore it to many of its former lakes.

Yellow-billed Loon

Huart à bec blanc
Gavia adamsii (Gray)
Total length: 76 to 89 cm
Plate 1

Somewhat like the Common Loon but differs as follows: bill shape and feathering (Figure 7), especially about nostril; culmen almost straight, but lower edge of bill angles upward more abruptly, and commissural line of upper mandible curves a little below a straight line in posterior half of bill. Primary shafts always paler.

In body plumages similar to Common Loon but with some differences. *Summer adults*: Bill whitish yellow; head with purplish gloss, that of chin, throat, and lower neck sharply but not conspicuously defined against rest of head, which is duller with a suggestion of green; white patches of throat and sides of neck made up of fewer, coarser, vertical white streaks; white spots on back larger (especially on scapulars) and fewer, with those on rump sparser and not extending up lower back; shafts of primaries paler (pale brown above, becoming darker at tips; below, almost white to tips). *Winter adults*: Similar to Common Loon but cheeks and neck paler accenting a dark-brown auricular patch, this paleness extending upward to or above eye; shafts of primaries paler; bill shape different (Figure 7). When general bill-coloration is similar,

Breeding Distribution of Yellow-billed Loon

Range in Canada. Breeds from northern Banks Island, Victoria Island, Prince of Wales Island, and Melville Peninsula (probably) south to the barren grounds of northern and central-eastern Mackenzie (Hanbury River, Thelon River, but not in the Mackenzie valley) and south-central Keewatin (Angikuni Lake, Yathkyed Lake).

Migration to and from the wintering grounds apparently is mostly coastwise around northern Alaska, and northern Yukon, but some migrants occur as far south as Great Slave Lake. Casual in northwestern interior British Columbia (Atlin); Alberta; northwestern Saskatchewan (Fond du Lac); northern Manitoba (Churchill); and northeast to Devon Island, Jens Munk Island, and Pond Inlet, N.W.T. Sight records for Ontario (Ottawa; Grimsby).

Winters in small numbers in coastal British Columbia (Comox, Hardy Bay, Prince Rupert).

only the basal part of the culmen is dark in Yellow-billed; the entire culmen remains dark in Common. *Young in first autumn and first winter*: Similar to Common Loon of like age but upper parts paler, more greyish; white of cheek more extensive, reaching to or above eye. Bill at this age not very different in shape from Common Loon but the anterior third of culmen is pale instead of dark. Feathering at nostril as in Figure 7.

Measurements. *Adult male*: wing, 366.0–388.0 (376.4); tarsus, 90.0–99.0 (95.1); exposed culmen, 89.0–97.0 (91.3). *Adult female*: wing, 361.0–387.0 (368.7); tarsus, 88.0–96.0 (91.1); exposed culmen, 86.5–96.0 (89.5) mm.

Field Marks. Summer adults are separable from Common Loon by their whitish, slightly upturned bill. In winter, bill coloration is much more similar (see above). First autumn birds are very similar but the white area of the cheeks is more extensive in Yellow-bills, a dark-brown auricular patch is usually present in all greyish-brown plumages, colour of upper parts is slightly paler, and the smaller extent of dark coloration on the culmen may be helpful. In first autumn, bill shape is not obviously different in the two species. On water, the Common Loon generally carries the bill horizontally while the Yellow-billed is inclined to hold the tip higher, pointing upward some 20 degrees above horizontal. See L.C. Binford and J.V. Remsen, Jr. (1974. Western Birds, vol. 5, no. 4, pp. 111–126); D.M. Burn and J.R. Mather (1974. British Birds, vol. 67, no. 7, pp. 257–282).

Habitat. In summer adults inhabit tundra freshwater lakes, ponds, and rivers, especially those with ice-push islands, on which the nest is sometimes placed. Coastal bays and inlets are visited for feeding purposes. In winter both adults and immatures inhabit saltwater bays, inlets, and open ocean along the coast. Immatures apparently remain on salt water until mature.

Nesting. On shore or islands of tundra ponds, lakes, and rivers and not far from water's edge; nest varies from little or no material to a heap or mound of mud and marsh vegetation, or sometimes a considerable heap of vegetation. *Eggs*, 2; similar to those of the Common Loon, but in the small sample examined, the ground colour averages more brownish, less olive. Incubation period unknown.

Range. Breeds in northern Finland, Novaya Zemlya, northern Siberia, northern Alaska, and northwestern Canada. In North America it winters in southeastern Alaska, uncommonly off the coast of British Columbia, and casually south to California.

Remarks. This loon replaces its near relative, the Common Loon, in northwestern North America north of timberline. Because of the similarity of the two species and consequent confusion by observers, range details for this species are not very clear, but the ranges of the two species appear to be mainly but not completely allopatric. Some authors have treated these loons as mere races of the same species, but there seems to be no justification for this. The respective characters separating the two appear to be trenchant, and there is little or no evidence of intergradation shown in the considerable number of specimens seen by the writer. One probable hybrid specimen is known: a Common × Yellow-billed Loon taken at Port Credit, Ontario, 7 December 1956, is in the Royal Ontario Museum.

Order **Podicipediformes:** Grebes

Family **Podicipedidae:** Grebes

Number of Species in Canada: 6

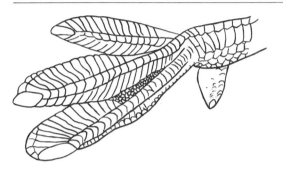

Figure 8
Foot of a grebe

Grebes are "tailless' water birds with smaller and shorter bodies than loons and, usually, straighter necks. They are excellent swimmers and divers. By altering their specific gravity they can lower themselves in the water until only the head or bill shows. In the breeding season adults of all but the Pied-billed have crests or ruffs, which loons never have. The bill is slender (except the Pied-billed with its stubby chicken-like bill) and pointed, thus very different from that of ducks and geese. In flight all Canadian species, except the Pied-billed, show a patch of white (absent in loons) in the wing. Grebes have lobed toes (Figure 8), not fully webbed ones. The tail feathers are vestigial, almost invisible. There is a narrow, bare strip in front of the eye. The feathers of the under parts have a peculiar silvery sheen. As in loons, the legs are attached far back on the body, and grebes therefore move awkwardly on land. Grebes have a habit of swallowing their own feathers, and the stomach often contains large numbers of them. The Prairie Provinces and southeastern British Columbia are richest in grebes, both in species and numbers, during the nesting season.

Pied-billed Grebe

Grèbe à bec bigarré
Podilymbus podiceps (Linnaeus)
Total length: 30.5 to 38.1 cm
Plate 2

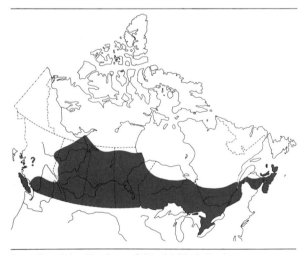

Breeding Distribution of Pied-billed Grebe

Range in Canada. Breeds in central and southern British Columbia (Williams Lake, perhaps Tachick and Ootsa lakes, southward including Vancouver Island); central-southern Mackenzie (Slave River Delta); Alberta; Saskatchewan (Lake Athabasca southward); Manitoba (Churchill southward); central Ontario (Sandy

A small grebe with a *very stout bill*, its ridge decidedly downcurved. In breeding plumage, adults have a black throat patch and a blackish band-like spot on the bill. In winter the black areas on throat and bill are lacking, but the stubby hen-like bill shape is always diagnostic. In flight it shows *no well-defined white patches* in the wing.

Measurements. *Adult male*: wing, 126–136 (129.3); tail, 35.5–43.5 (39.2); exposed culmen, 20–24.5 (22.8); tarsus, 40.5–43.5 (41.9). *Adult female*: wing, 112.5–127.5 (118.5) mm.

Habitat. In summer, freshwater ponds, sloughs, sluggish streams, shallow bays of lakes, all with margins or islands of emergent and aquatic vegetation. In winter, it inhabits fresh water where open, as well as saltwater tidal creeks, estuaries, and bays.

Nesting. Not colonial. Nest, a substantial structure of soft decayed marsh vegetation, either floating or built up from shallow water-bottom. *Eggs*, usually 5 to 7; dull bluish-white or greenish white, usually with buffy nest stains. Incubation, 21 to 24 days, probably averages 23 days, by both sexes. The young, like those of other grebes, leave the nest and take to the water soon after hatching.

Range. Western Hemisphere from southern Canada, south through Central America, the West Indies, and South America to Chile and southern Argentina. Winters from southwestern British Columbia and the Great Lakes (rarely) southward.

Subspecies. *Podilymbus podiceps podiceps* (Linnaeus) is the only race inhabiting Canada. Other races are found in the West Indies and in South America.

Lake, Fort Albany southward); southwestern Quebec (Saguenay River valley at Saint-Fulgence, Québec, Lac aux Loutres, Montréal; Madeleine Islands); New Brunswick (mainly southern, rarely north to Restigouche County); Prince Edward Island; and Nova Scotia (Falls Lake, Aylesford, Cape Breton Island).

Winters regularly in southwestern British Columbia (mainly on the coast; rarely in the southern interior: Okanagan Lake), rarely in southern Ontario (lower Great Lakes).

Casual in southern Yukon (Dezadeash Lake, Marsh Lake); James Bay (Moose Factory, Charlton Island); the north shore of the Gulf of St. Lawrence (Bonne-Espérance, Moisie River); and Newfoundland (various records, mostly in autumn). Accidental in northern Labrador (Ramah) and southern Baffin Island (Fair Ness).

Remarks. This is the grebe most often seen in most parts of eastern Canada. Soon after the ice leaves our freshwater ponds and marshes, this grebe puts in an appearance, and here it remains until ice begins to form again in autumn. Alert and rather shy, it often keeps out of sight in the marsh vegetation. It is noisy in spring, and its presence is frequently made known by its surprisingly far-carrying voice. The commonest call is a hollow *kow-kow-kow*, repeated perhaps a dozen times, speeding up and becoming *kow-uh* toward the end.

Horned Grebe

Grèbe cornu
Podiceps auritus (Linnaeus)
Total length: 31.5 to 38.1 cm
Plate 2

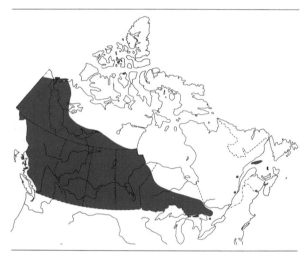

Breeding Distribution of Horned Grebe

Range in Canada. Breeds from northern Yukon (Old Crow); northwestern and southern Mackenzie (Anderson River, Great Slave Lake; recorded in summer on the Mackenzie Delta and Smart Lake); southern Keewatin (Simons Lake); southward through interior British Columbia, Alberta, Saskatchewan, and Manitoba; sporadically and locally eastward to Ontario (Fort Severn, Sandy Lake, Timmins south to Algonquin Provincial Park; reportedly locally to Eastbourne); southern Quebec (very locally: Lac-Sainte-Anne, Valcartier, Anticosti Island, and Madeleine Islands); and formerly New Brunswick (near Milltown).

Migrates through much of southern Canada but very rare in Newfoundland.

Winters in British Columbia (mainly on the coast, but small numbers are found occasionally in southern interior), the coasts of Nova Scotia, Prince Edward Island, and New Brunswick; occasionally on the lower Great Lakes.

A small grebe with short straight bill. Sexes alike. In flight shows a *single* white patch in wing. *Summer adults* with their broad *buffy ear-tufts*, conspicuous against black head, are likely to be mistaken only for the Eared Grebe. Its *chestnut neck* readily separates it from the Eared Grebe, which has a black neck, and it lacks the helmet head-shape of the Eared. *Winter plumages* are more difficult to identify since all grebes are more plainly and somewhat similarly attired. Smaller size, shorter neck, and much shorter bill distinguish it from the Red-necked and Western grebes, and the slender bill is very different from that of the Pied-billed. It closely resembles the Eared Grebe, but the blackish of the crown extends down only to the lower side of the eye where it gives way abruptly to white; in the Eared Grebe the transition from black to white is gradual, and the ear coverts are grey, not white. The sides of the neck are whiter (less greyish) in the Horned Grebe. In the hand, the two may be separated in any plumage by the bill. In the Horned, the height of the bill at the base is greater than its width; in the Eared, its width equals or exceeds its height (Figure 9).

Measurements *(P. a. cornutus)*. *Adult male*: wing, 135.5–146.5 (141.3); tail, 33.5–38.5 (36.1); exposed culmen, 23.3–25.6 (24.4); tarsus, 43.5–48.5 (46.6). *Adult female*: wing, 131–141 (136.9) mm.

Habitat. In summer, freshwater ponds, sloughs, and protected shallow bays of lakes, especially those with some emergent vegetation, in both the plains and wooded country. In winter, mainly inshore salt water, occasionally well off shore, sometimes larger freshwater lakes.

Nesting. Not colonial. Usually one pair to a pond; larger water bodies may have several pairs. Nest of soft or decayed, emergent or aquatic vegetation, floating and anchored or on broken-down marsh vegetation, either in the open or sheltered by emergent vegetation. *Eggs*, 3 to 8 (mean 5.9), most clutches contain 5, 6 or 7; incubation period 23 to 24 days, by both sexes (R.S. Ferguson).

Range. Breeds from central and southern Alaska and Canada (see Range in Canada) south to Idaho, northern South Dakota, northern Iowa, and central Wisconsin (sporadically farther east); also in Iceland, the Faeroe Islands, and Eurasia. In North America, it winters mainly on the coasts from the Aleutian Islands to southern California, and from Nova Scotia to Florida; less commonly in the interior from the Great Lakes southward. In the Old World, it winters south to the Mediterranean Sea, Iran, Turkestan, and Japan.

Subspecies. *Podiceps auritus cornutus* (Gmelin) is the North American race. It averages paler than the nominate race of the Old World.

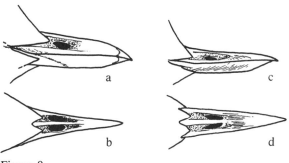

Figure 9
Bills of
Horned Grebe
a) lateral view
b) dorsal view
Eared Grebe
c) lateral view
d) dorsal view

Remarks. In early June, in full nuptial plumage, this little grebe is a handsome bird. Its rich chestnut neck and flanks look their best in bright sunshine, and the buffy ear-tufts glow against the jet-black head. By July, moult and fading have greatly dulled its beauty. Unlike the Eared Grebe, it does not nest in large colonies, but it has a wide distribution in the West, and many a small slough has its pair in summer. A small body of water is adequate; and if the water does not dry up, the birds will not often leave it. When the striped-headed young emerge from the egg, they soon take to water, and both parents care for them. The family spends the long summer days feeding, preening, dozing, or just floating. As with other grebes, the young often ride on the backs of their parents as they swim about.

J.A. Munro has studied the food eaten by this grebe in British Columbia. In the interior in summer, aquatic insects, particularly Odonata nymphs, water boatmen (Corixidae), and Coleoptera are the chief food of both adults and young. In winter on the coast, crustaceans are the most important food, with small fishes second in importance.

Red-necked Grebe

(Holboell's Grebe)

Grèbe jougris
Podiceps grisegena (Boddaert)
Total length: 46 to 52 cm
Plate 2

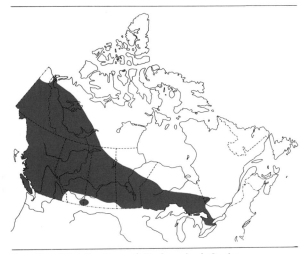

Breeding Distribution of Red-necked Grebe

Range in Canada. Breeds from northern Yukon (Old Crow); northwestern and southern Mackenzie (Mackenzie Delta; 80 km south of Fort Anderson; Great Slave Lake); northern Saskatchewan (Fond du Lac, Churchill River); central Manitoba (Thompson Junction, Thicket Portage); western and central Ontario (Sioux Lookout, Whitefish Lake, Sandy Lake, Lilla-belle Lake, Mildred); and recently extreme southwestern Quebec (Pelletier Lake) south through interior British Columbia (rarely also on Vancouver Island); southern Alberta (Brooks); southern Saskatchewan (Cypress Hills, Moose Mountain); southern Manitoba (Turtle Mountain Provincial Park); and southern Ontario (locally: Burlington; Lorne Park; and Luther Marsh, 35 km west of Orangeville).

A large grebe. Bill straight or slightly downcurved, tapering to a point, rather long and slender; yellowish in colour. In summer adults the conspicuous whitish cheeks and throat and chestnut-red neck are a combination that instantly separates this species from other grebes. The much smaller Horned Grebe also has a reddish neck in summer, but the cheeks and throat are black. *Winter plumage* is very different, and like most grebes the Red-necked has grey upper parts and white under parts. Its larger size and longer *yellowish* bill distinguish it from the Horned, Eared, and Pied-billed grebes. It is about the size of the Western Grebe, but it lacks the strong contrast of black and white on head and neck; it has grey instead of white on sides of neck, and the ridge of the bill is slightly downcurved instead of straight or slightly upcurved. In flight the wing shows two patches of white—one in front near where it joins the body, the other along the hind edge.

Measurements *(P. g. holbollii). Adult male*: wing, 187–203 (196.2); tail, 33.5–41 (37.5); exposed culmen, 43–58 (50.6); tarsus, 59.5–70 (64.4). *Adult female*: wing, 180.5–195 (188.7) mm.

Habitat. In summer, freshwater lakes, marshes, and sluggish rivers usually, but not necessarily, with margins or islands of emergent vegetation such as *Scirpus* or *Phragmites*. In winter, inshore coastal salt water, occasionally several kilometres from shore; sometimes freshwater lakes while they remain open.

Nesting. Either in single pairs or colonially. Nest, a low damp mass of aquatic vegetation often on a bed of broken-down marsh plants, often floating and attached to surrounding vegetation; occasionally on a muskrat house. *Eggs*, 3 to 8 (usually 4 or 5); plain bluish-white, generally nest-stained. Incubation 23 days (Heinroth and Heinroth), by both sexes. One brood annually.

Range. Breeds in Alaska, western and central-southern Canada and northwestern United States (Washington east to Minnesota); also in Europe and northern Asia. In North America it winters mainly along the coasts from the Aleutian Islands and southeastern Alaska south to central California and on the Atlantic Coast from Newfoundland south to central Florida.

Winters along the coast of British Columbia and on the Atlantic Coast north to Newfoundland, more rarely on the Great Lakes and in interior British Columbia. Migrates through much of the southern interior of the country but is rare in Labrador (Makkovik, Spotted Island). Not uncommon sometimes on the inner north shore of the Gulf of St. Lawrence (Moisie Bay) and is probably regular along the St. Lawrence River drainage and Chaleur Bay. Casual on Southampton Island.

Subspecies. *Podiceps grisegena holbollii* Reinhardt is the only subspecies known in Canada. It is slightly larger than the nominate race of the Old World.

Remarks. On its breeding grounds this large, handsome grebe is a noisy bird. Sometimes it breeds in small colonies, and when several call at the same time the result is a cacophony of wails, brays, and cackles. On the lakes of Manitoba its food is largely crayfish, salamanders, and aquatic insects. It also eats minnows and other small fishes, small crustaceans, molluscs, tadpoles, and some vegetation.

In autumn migration, concentrations build up at certain points along Lake Ontario. At Willow Beach, near Port Britain, approximately 5 km west of Port Hope, several hundred, more or less, may be seen in September and October.

Eared Grebe

Grèbe à cou noir
Podiceps nigricollis C.L. Brehm
Total length: 30.5 to 35.5 cm
Plate 2

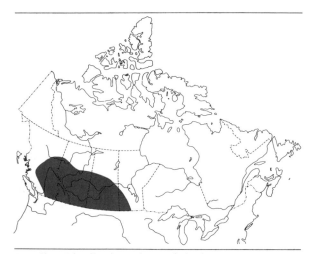

Breeding Distribution of Eared Grebe

Range in Canada. Breeds in central and southern interior British Columbia (Peace River District, Tachick Lake, Kleena Kleene, Okanagan valley); Alberta (Cardinal and Fairmont lakes, probably Birch River delta, southward); north-central and southern Saskatchewan (Kazan Lake, Nipawin southward); and southwestern Manitoba (Diamond Lake; old reports east to Shoal Lake).

Winters regularly on the coast of southern British Columbia.

Rare visitor to southern Mackenzie (Great Slave Lake) and southern Ontario (Niagara Falls, Lorne Park).

A small grebe with short slender bill, which appears slightly uptilted. Sexes similar. *Summer adults* with their buffy ear-tufts are likely to be confused only with the Horned Grebe from which they differ in having a *black neck* and a helmet-shaped head. In *winter*, smaller size and shorter, weaker bill separate it from the Red-necked and the differently marked Western Grebe. The slender bill is quite unlike that of the Pied-billed. Though very much like the Horned Grebe, the dark colour of the top of head is slightly more extensive, particularly behind the eye and on the ear region; the neck is more extensively greyish, and the shape of the head (J.A. Munro) is more triangular and the carriage more upright. In the hand, the bill dimensions (see Figure 9, Horned Grebe) are diagnostic.

Measurements *(P. n. californicus)*. *Adult male*: wing, 122.5–132 (128.1); tail, 26–39 (31.8); exposed culmen, 22.8–27.8 (25.8); tarsus, 40–44 (42.9). *Adult female*: wing, 119–127.5 (122.9) mm.

Habitat. In the breeding season, marshy, shallower parts of freshwater lakes and ponds in both wooded and treeless country. In winter, mostly coastal salt water in Canada, but also fresh water in the United States.

Nesting. Usually colonial, nesting in large or small colonies, small groups, or single pairs. Nest, a soggy heap of vegetation usually floating or built up from the bottom or on a dense bed of vegetation. It may be hidden in marsh vegetation or be completely exposed. *Eggs*, usually 3 or 4, but clutches variable 1 to 6; bluish or greenish white, generally nest-stained. Incubation period 20.5 to 21.5 days (Nancy McAllister) by both sexes.

Range. Breeds from southwestern Canada (east to Manitoba) south to northern Baja California, central Arizona, northern New Mexico, and southern Texas: also widely in Eurasia and Africa. In North America winters mainly from southern British Columbia to Colombia.

Subspecies. *Podiceps nigricollis californicus* Heermann is the race that inhabits North America. Additional races are found in the Old World.

Remarks. Marshy lakes in the western provinces are the summer home of this attractive grebe. Its commonest call-note is *co-eeeek*, given with a rising inflection and suggesting a contralto swamp tree-frog. It often nests in large communities, which are busy places in nest-building time. Usually only the female carries nesting material. This is secured either on the water surface or by diving. The bird swims with a beakful to the nest, drops it unceremoniously, then swims away for more. Occasionally the working bird hops awkwardly onto the flimsy nest and shapes it with her body. Although nests are often close together, relationships between the nesting pairs are mostly harmonious. Sometimes an intruder is driven off by a charge made with lowered head. Aquatic insects appear to be the chief summer food of both adults and young in interior British Columbia, with amphipods and terrestrial beetles eaten also in some numbers. On the coast in winter, mysids and amphipods are much relished (J A. Munro).

Western Grebe

Grèbe élégant
Aechmophorus occidentalis (Lawrence)
Total length: 56 to 73.5 cm
Plate 2

Breeding Distribution of Western Grebe

Range in Canada. Breeds in south-central and southern interior British Columbia (locally: Williams Lake, Swan Lake in Okanagan valley, Salmon Arm); north-central and southern Alberta (Peace River District, Christina Lake southward east of the mountains to Frank and Namaka lakes); central and southern Saskatchewan (Kazan Lake, Emma Lake southward); and southwestern Manitoba (north probably to northern Lake Winnipegosis, Lake St. Martin, Shoal Lake).

Winters commonly on the coast of British Columbia, occasionally in the southern interior (Okanagan Lake). A common spring and autumn migrant on lakes of southern interior British Columbia. Casual in southern Yukon (Teslin Lake), northeastern Alberta (Lake Athabasca). Rare visitant to southern Ontario and southwestern Quebec (well-documented sight record: Hudson, 31 May 1958).

A large grebe with long, very slender neck, sharply contrasted black-and-white coloration. Bill slender, sharp, slightly uptilted, greenish yellow with black culmen. Eye red. Very similar to Clark's Grebe but the black of crown extends down to below the eyes and lores (Figure 10) and the bill is greenish yellow instead of orange yellow.

Measurements. *Adult male*: wing, 190–205 (199.3); tail, 36.5–52.5 (41.8); exposed culmen, 65.3–80.5 (74.7); tarsus, 72–80 (77.2). *Adult female*: wing, 179–196.5 (186.6) mm.

Habitat. In the breeding season, freshwater lakes with some emergent vegetation, In winter, coastal saltwater bays and lagoons, sometimes open freshwater lakes.

Nesting. In colonies on borders of freshwater lakes. Nest, a mass of vegetation, floating and attached to nearby vegetation, or stationary; rarely on dry shore. *Eggs*, 3 to 5 or more; dull, plain bluish-white, usually nest-stained Incubation about 23 days (A.C. Bent), by both sexes.

Range. Breeds from western Canada (east to Manitoba) south to California, northern Utah, North Dakota, Nebraska (locally), and southwestern Minnesota. Winters mainly along the Pacific Coast from southeastern Alaska and British Columbia south to northwestern Mexico.

Remarks. On certain western lakes, this graceful grebe nests in colonies of various sizes, although the summer cottager with his outboard motor has driven it from some of the lakes it formerly favoured. Its plaintive, far-carrying, high-pitched *creek-creek*, given in twos, is easily recognizable. Some of its displays are spectacular, particularly when two birds rear up vertically and race side-by-side over the water's surface. This grebe is often more gregarious than other species both in summer and winter. Its diet is similar to that of other grebes but probably includes more small fishes.

Clark's Grebe

Grèbe à face blanche
Aechmophorus clarkii (Lawrence)
Total length: 56 to 73 cm

Range in Canada. Breeds in very small
numbers in southern Manitoba (probably),
southern Saskatchewan (Old Wives Lake),
southern Alberta, and perhaps in British
Columbia (range poorly known).

Figure 10
a) Western Grebe
b) Clark's Grebe

Extremely similar to Western Grebe in shape, colour, and size but the
black of the crown does not extend down to reach the eyes or the lores
(Figure 10). The bill is more orange yellow than greenish yellow. Advertising call a single *creek* (instead of double). Habitat and nesting similar
to Western Grebe and the two breed sympatrically with minimal interbreeding, Clark's Grebe being commoner in southern parts of the range,
Western commoner in the north.

Order **Procellariiformes:**
Albatrosses, Shearwaters, Petrels, and Allies

Birds of this order spend most of their lives at sea and ordinarily come ashore only to nest. In size they range from great albatrosses to swallow-like petrels. The wings are long and pointed, have ten primaries, and usually many secondaries. The tail is short or moderate in length. The bill covering is formed of horny plates, more or less clearly separated by sutures (Figure 11). The external nostrils are encased in well-formed tubes. The front toes are rather long and fully webbed; the hind toe is small and is not connected to the front toes by a web. A distinctive feature of birds of this order is a peculiar stomach oil, which can be ejected when the bird is disturbed. This has a strong, musky odour, which persists on museum specimens for decades.

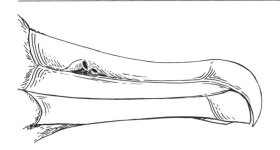

Figure 11
Bill of an albatross

Family **Diomedeidae:**
Albatrosses

Number of Species in Canada: 4

Large ocean birds, effortless flyers, possessing very long, very narrow wings, which are stiffly held in flight. The bill is strongly hooked at the tip and strongly plated (see Figure 11). There are *two nostril tubes*, one on each side of the bill near its base. Hind toe is rudimentary or absent. The seas of the Southern Hemisphere are richest in albatrosses. Thirteen species are known in the world. Only four have been recorded in Canada, and none of them nest in this country.

Short-tailed Albatross

Albatros à queue courte
Diomedea albatrus Pallas
Total length: about 94 cm
Plate 3

Status in Canada. Formerly of regular occurrence off British Columbia (reportedly common off Cape Beale in April 1894. A specimen taken at Esquimalt on 4 June 1893. Two specimens taken on Juan de Fuca Strait in 1889. One immature photographed within 64 km of Vancouver Island on 11 June 1960).

Adults: Head, body (including back), and bases of wings white. Rest of wings and tail dark brown. (Similar to adult Laysan Albatross but Laysan has a dark back like the wings.) *Immature*: All sooty. Like the Black-footed Albatross but lacks any pale area around the base of the bill; the bill is pale pinkish, the feet bluish white, not black.

Range. Breeds mainly on Torishima Island in the Seven Islands of Izu. Although this species is now greatly reduced and near extinction, there has been a recent small increase in its number to about 250 individuals.

Black-footed Albatross

Albatros à pattes noires
Diomedea nigripes Audubon
Total length: 72 to 91 cm
Plate 3

Status in Canada. A fairly common non-breeding visitor to offshore waters of British Columbia from March to autumn. Has been observed every month of the year.

Wingspread about 2.4 m. A dark-bodied albatross, blackish above and slightly lighter below, with a whitish area near the base of the dark bill. Adults have white tail coverts. In immature birds the whitish area at the base of the bill is often absent or poorly indicated, and there is little or no white in the tail coverts. The black feet and dark bill separate it in any plumage from immatures of the Short-tailed Albatross.

Measurements. *Adult male*: wing, 427–519 (474.9); tail, 146–153 (149.5); exposed culmen, 106–109 (107.4); tarsus, 95–99 (96.7). *Adult female*: wing, 413–454.5 (429) mm.

Habitat. The open ocean, usually well off shore.

Range. Bred, formerly at least, on Torishima, Bonin, Iwo Jima, Marshall, and Hawaiian islands in the Pacific Ocean, but no longer does so on some of these islands. The majority now nest on the Leeward chain of the Hawaiian Islands. Ranges over the Pacific north to southern Bering Sea.

Remarks. Like other albatrosses, this is an ocean wanderer. Since the decline of the Short-tailed Albatross, it is the only albatross that comes regularly in significant numbers into Canadian waters, but ordinarily it does not venture close to shore. To see it, one usually must travel some miles out to sea. Its effortless gliding flight, low over the wave troughs, is a source of wonder for the few who have a chance to observe it. This albatross feeds mainly on squid and fish but often follows fishing boats for scraps of offal. It nests in late autumn and winters on islands in the Pacific and is only a non-breeding visitor to Canadian waters.

Laysan Albatross

Albatros de Laysan
Diomedea immutabilis Rothschild
Total length: about 78 to 82 cm
Plate 3

Status in Canada. Recent observations, supported by photos, show this species to be a rare but probably regular winter visitor off the coast of British Columbia and of casual occurrence there at other seasons (R.W. Campbell and M.G. Shepard, 1973. Canadian Field-Naturalist, vol. 87, no. 2, p. 179).

A white-bodied albatross. *Adults (sexes similar)*: Head (except black patch in front of eye), neck, under parts, and rump white. Upper surface of wings *and back* blackish brown. Tail blackish. Under surface of wings patchy white. Bill varies from flesh to greyish; legs flesh to pinkish. *Immature*: All plumages worn by immatures capable of flight are similar to adults.

Field Marks. A white-bodied albatross resembling adults of the Short-tailed but with the dark coloration of the upper surface of the wings extending completely across the back.

Range. Breeding is now restricted to the Hawaiian Archipelago.

Black-browed Albatross

[**Black-browed Albatross**. Albatros à sourcil noir. *Diomedea melanophris* Temminck. Figure 12. Hypothetical. Sight record only. On 15 July 1980, an albatross superficially like *D. chlororhynchos* but with an all-yellow bill and heavy dark "eyebrow" mark was identified as this species in waters between southern Newfoundland and North Sydney, Nova Scotia, by D.E. Wolf and Bret Whitney. There is no Canadian specimen or photo.]

Figure 12
Black-browed Albatross

Yellow-nosed Albatross

Albatros à nez jaune
Diomedea chlororhynchos Gmelin
Total length: about 81 cm
Plate 3

Status in Canada. Accidental in Quebec (Moisie River, 20 August 1885) and New Brunswick (between Machias Seal Island and Grand Manan, 1 August 1913). Probably also Newfoundland (but specimen and data no longer extant). Sight record for Nova Scotia (64 km off Yarmouth, 20 August 1976).

This monotypic species is primarily a bird of the South Atlantic and Indian oceans.

Head and neck white, back of neck and cheeks tinged with grey. A blackish or greyish line from eye to base of bill. Back, upper side of wings, and tail, slaty brown. Underside of wings white with dark border. Rump, upper tail coverts, and under parts white. Bill of adults black *with a yellow ridge*; bill of immatures all black.

1 Common Loon, p. 22
a) summer adult
b) immature (first winter)

2 Yellow-billed Loon, p. 23
a) summer adult
b) winter adult

3 Red-throated Loon, p. 19
a) winter adult
b) summer adult

4 Pacific Loon, p. 21
a) summer adult
b) winter adult

Crosby

2

1 Red-necked Grebe, p. 27
a) summer adult
b) winter plumage

1a

1b

2a

2 Pied-billed Grebe, p. 25
a) juvenal
b) summer adult

2b

3a

3b

3 Eared Grebe, p. 28
a) summer adult
b) winter plumage

4a

4b

5

5 Western Grebe, p. 29

4 Horned Grebe, p. 26
a) winter plumage
b) summer adult

Crosby

3

1 Yellow-nosed Albatross, p. 32
a) immature
b) adult

1a

1b

3 Black-footed Albatross, p. 31
adult

3

4 Laysan Albatross, p. 32
a) adult, ventral view
b) adult, dorsal view

4a

4b

2a

2 Short-tailed Albatross, p. 31
a) adult
b) immature

2b

4

2 Pink-footed Shearwater, p. 43

1 Manx Shearwater, p. 45

6 Buller's Shearwater, p

6

2

1

5a

3 Greater Shearwater, p. 43

3

5b

4

4 Cory's Shearwater, p. 42

5 Audubon's Shearwater, p.
a) ventral view
b) dorsal view

Crosby

1 Flesh-footed Shearwater, p. 43

5

2 Short-tailed Shearwater, p. 45

3 Sooty Shearwater, p. 44

5 Fork-tailed Storm-Petrel, p. 48

4 Northern Fulmar, p. 41
a) light phase
b) dark phase

6 Leach's Storm-Petrel, p. 48

7 Wilson's Storm-Petrel, p. 47

8 British Storm-Petrel, p. 47

6

2 American White Pelican, p. 5
adult

1 Northern Gannet, p. 51
a) adult
b) first-year immature

1a

2

1b

3 Pelagic Cormorant, p. 56
a) immature
b) adult in fresh breeding plumage

3b

3a

4 Brandt's Cormorant, p. 56
a) immature
b) adult in fresh breeding plum

4a

4b

6 Great Cormorant, p. 54
a) adult in fresh breeding plumage
b) immature

6b

5a

6a

5b

5 Double-crested Cormorant, p. 55
a) immature
b) adult in fresh breeding plumage

Crosby

1 Cattle Egret, p. 65
adult in breeding plumage

2 Great Egret, p. 62
adult in breeding plumage

3 Green-backed Heron, p. 65
a) immature
b) adult

4 Black-crowned Night-Heron, p. 66
a) immature
b) adult in breeding plumage

5 Yellow-crowned Night-Heron, p. 67
a) immature
b) adult in breeding plumage

6 Great Blue Heron, p. 61
adult in breeding plumage

8

1 Least Bittern, p. 60
a) adult female
b) adult male

1a

4 Tricolored Heron, p. 64
fresh breeding plumage

1b

2 Snowy Egret, p. 63
adult

3a

3b

3 Little Blue Heron, p. 64
a) first-year immature
b) adult

6 White Ibis, p. 68
adult

7 Scarlet Ib[is]
adult

5 American Bittern, p. 59
adult

8 Glossy Ibis, p. 68
adult

9 White-faced Ibis, p. 69
adult

Family **Procellariidae**: Shearwaters and Fulmars

Number of Species in Canada: 14

a

b

Figure 13
Bill of Sooty Shearwater
a) lateral view
b) dorsal view

Shearwaters are smaller than albatrosses and, like them, are strictly marine. In flight they alternate rather rapid wing strokes with lengthy glides, the long narrow wings held stiffly at right angles to the body. Both the upper and lower mandibles are hooked. The two nostril tubes are situated on top of the bill (see Figure 13).

Fulmars are more robust in form and more gull-like than shearwaters, and they have a relatively stubby bill, of which only the upper mandible is hooked. The nostrils, which are enclosed in a conspicuous tube on top of the bill, are separated from each other by a narrow septum.

Northern Fulmar

Fulmar boréal
Fulmarus glacialis (Linnaeus)
Total length: 45.5 to 50.5 cm
Plate 5

Breeding Distribution of Northern Fulmar

Range in Canada. Breeds in colonies, some very large, mainly in the Arctic: Devon Island (Cape Vera, Cape Liddon, Hobhouse Inlet), Prince Leopold Island, Baffin Island (Admiralty Inlet, Buchan Gulf, Scott Inlet, Cape Searle, Reid Bay, Exeter Sound, Coburg Island); recently also in Newfoundland (Great, Funk, and Baccalieu islands; reportedly Witless Bay). Probably breeds in Labrador (Outer Gannet Island). Formerly bred on southern Ellesmere Island (Smith Island).

Found in summer in many other parts of the Canadian Arctic west to Banks Island (rarely), north to Ellesmere Island, and

Bill relatively much chunkier than that of any gull or shearwater. Conspicuous nostril tube over posterior part. Upper mandible strongly hooked. Neck short. Tail slightly rounded. Two colour phases. *Light Phase*: Head, neck, and under parts white. Back and upper surface of wings (tail paler) slaty grey, flight feathers darkest. Bill usually yellowish. *Dark Phase*: Entire plumage smoky grey; bill dark, becoming yellowish at tip. Many stages of intermediacy between the dark and light phases are common. Fulmars are somewhat gull-like in shape, but the wings, which are narrow, are stiffly held in flight. Wing beats differ from those of gulls, being more rapid and alternating with long glides. Dark phase resembles the Sooty Shearwater, but the Fulmar's bill is much chunkier, neck thicker.

Measurements *(F. g. minor). Adult male*: wing, 305–328 (319.2); tail, 119–128 (124.8); exposed culmen, 35–38.5 (36.8); tarsus, 50–58.5 (53.6). *Adult female*: wing, 258–310.5 (283.6) mm.

Habitat. The open ocean. At nesting time, frequents cliffs at or near salt water.

Nesting. In colonies, sometimes immense, on steep cliffs usually at salt water. The Cape Searle colony, Baffin Island, in 1950 was conservatively estimated at 200,000 birds (Wynne-Edwards). No actual nest is made, the egg being laid on bare rock or in a shallow hollow in soil, or in vegetation on cliff ledges. *Eggs*, one only; white. Incubation about 53 to 57 days (varies considerably), by both parents. The young fly six to seven weeks after hatching.

Range. Discontinuously circumpolar, breeding in the north Atlantic, north Pacific, and Arctic oceans. In North America it breeds in colonies along the coasts of Alaska, the Canadian Arctic, and in Greenland.

commonly southward to waters off Newfoundland, but not in Hudson Bay. Probably the commonest bird at sea in the eastern Canadian Arctic from late April to October. Winters off both the Pacific and Atlantic provinces, mostly well at sea. Casual or accidental in Ontario (Manitouwadge, 11 December 1970; near Moosonee, 8 December 1974; Arnprior, 3 May 1924; Ottawa River opposite Pointe-Fortune, Quebec, 15 November 1928) and southwestern Quebec (Beauport).

Subspecies. Three races occur in Canada. (1) *Fulmarus glacialis minor* (Kjaerbølling) is the only race that breeds in Canada.
(2) *F. g. glacialis* (Linnaeus), an Old World and east Greenland race, is a non-breeding frequent wanderer to eastern Canadian waters (specimens and banded birds in Labrador, Newfoundland, and Nova Scotia).
(3) *F. g. rodgersii* Cassin, nesting locally from Siberia to Alaska, is a regular non-breeding wanderer to offshore waters of British Columbia, but there is no record of it in the Canadian Arctic.

Black-capped Petrel

Diablotin errant
Pterodroma hasitata (Kuhl)
Total length: 35.5 to 40.5 cm

Status in Canada. Accidental. Three records, all for Ontario: a male found dead on Toronto Island, 30 October 1893; a specimen taken near Oakville about 1893; one found dead at Morgan's Point, Welland County, Ontario, on 21 August 1955. Canadian specimens of this species, which breeds in much-reduced numbers in the West Indies, are hurricane victims.

A rather heavy-bodied, stout-billed petrel with a dark cap, accentuated usually by a white collar and with white tail coverts and white at base of tail. Upper parts sooty becoming brown or greyish brown on back (feathers often with paler margins), darker on wings. End of tail similar to wings. *Base of tail and tail coverts white.* Forehead, sides of head, and neck white; with usually a white collar behind the dark cap. Under parts and wing linings white. Bill black, stout (fulmar-like but with tip of lower mandible downcurved). There is a dark colour-phase, which, however, retains the white upper tail coverts. See Mottled Petrel.

Mottled Petrel

(Scaled Petrel)

Diablotin maculé
Pterodroma inexpectata (Forster)
Total length: 33 cm

Status in Canada. Casual or accidental off British Columbia: a specimen that came aboard a ship about 24 km off Flores Island, Vancouver Island, on 24 February 1971, was photographed in the hand and released.

This and the Black-capped Petrel belong to the "gadfly petrel" group and are very different from the storm-petrels of the next family. In its largish size, heavy body, and stout bill, the Mottled Petrel is similar to the Black-capped. Upper parts of the Mottled Petrel, including crown, are medium grey (darkening along leading edge of wing) and lacking the white on nape and rump shown by Black-capped Petrel. Feathers of back have pale tips, those of rump dark tips. Face white with dark mark through eye. Under parts white with broad mottled grey area covering lower breast and belly. Underside of spread wing white with *a distinctive broad blackish bar across it* from mid-base to bend.

Habitat. The open ocean.

Range. Breeds in New Zealand. Wanders northward widely over the Pacific Ocean to the Aleutian Islands.

Cory's Shearwater

Puffin cendré
Calonectris diomedea (Scopoli)
Total length: 48.3 to 53.2 cm
Plate 4

Status in Canada. A non-breeding wanderer to waters off the Atlantic Coast. A specimen was collected about 65 km off Dover, Nova Scotia, 27 July 1916. Remains of one were found on Sable Island, Nova Scotia, 26 June 1970, but it had been dead for some time and might have floated there from outside Canadian waters. That it is commoner than generally realized off southern Nova Scotia is indicated by J.E.V. Goodwill's field notes, in which he recorded it at sea off various southern Nova Scotia localities on twenty-nine dates, July to October, 1960 and 1961. Hypothetical off western Newfoundland where one was reported on 11 August 1920 (Ludlow Griscom and E.R.P. Janvrin, 1922, Auk, vol. 39, no. 1, pp. 103–104).

A large, white-bellied shearwater of the Atlantic. Most like the slightly smaller, somewhat darker Greater Shearwater (Plate 4), but the grey on the top of the head extends farther down the sides of the face, blending into (not sharply contrasting with) the white of the throat; it usually has no well-defined white rump patch, and the bill (in *C. d. borealis*) is yellowish not blackish.

Habitat. The open ocean well off shore.

Range. The eastern Atlantic and western Indian oceans, the Mediterranean and Adriatic seas to Asia Minor.

Subspecies. *Calonectris diomedea borealis* (Cory), which breeds on the Azores, Madeira, Salvages, and Canary islands, is the only subspecies known to occur in Canada.

Pink-footed Shearwater

Puffin à pattes roses
Puffinus creatopus Coues
Total length: 48.2 cm
Plate 4

Status in Canada. A regular, non-breeding visitor to offshore waters of British Columbia, most numerous in late summer. Four specimens were collected on Swiftsure Banks, off Cape Flattery, British Columbia, 14 August 1946. Flocks of up to 20 individuals observed in August 1949, off Ucluelet. As many as 125 in a day have been reported (13 September 1969 off Tofino, British Columbia).

Upper parts, including sides of face and sides of neck, greyish brown. Under parts mostly white but chin and throat, sides of body, and wing linings with varying amounts of grey mottling. Under tail coverts greyish brown, more or less mottled with white. Bill mainly pale-yellowish flesh with dusky tip. Legs and feet, pale flesh.

Field Marks. A white-bellied shearwater of the Pacific, slightly larger than the Manx Shearwater, with grey-and-white wing linings (giving them a greyer appearance) and with a *pale* instead of dark bill. The light under parts separate it from the Sooty and Flesh-footed shearwaters.

Habitat. The ocean.

Range. Breeds on islands off the coast of Chile, wandering northward in the Pacific to southeastern Alaska.

Flesh-footed Shearwater

(formerly Pale-footed
Shearwater)

Puffin à pattes pâles
Puffinus carneipes Gould
Total length: 49.5 cm
Plate 5

Status in Canada. Patrick W. Martin first recognized the occurrence of this species off British Columbia on 31 July 1937, on the Goose Island Banks. He secured specimens there on 8 and 18 July 1939, and found the species locally rather numerous. He again visited the area on 14 July 1946, and secured two more specimens. Additional ones were taken there in 1947 and 1948. Martin observed two on La Pérouse Bank on 14 July 1946, and collected one there on 22 August 1949. He noted at least eight off Triangle Island on 28 and 29 June 1949.

Entire plumage sooty, including wing linings. Bill flesh coloured with dark tip. Legs and feet flesh coloured. In the field an all-dark shearwater resembling the Sooty but with flesh-coloured bill, legs, and feet, and with dark wing-linings.

Habitat. The open ocean.

Range. Breeds on islands in Australian and New Zealand seas. Wanders northward to waters off Japan and British Columbia.

Greater Shearwater

Puffin majeur
Puffinus gravis (O'Reilly)
Total length: 45.7 to 50.8 cm
Plate 4

Status in Canada. Non-breeding summer visitant (April to November) to pelagic and offshore waters, rarely near shore, of Nova Scotia, southern New Brunswick, Newfoundland, north to northern Labrador and southeastern Baffin Island. In summer, numerous in Strait of Belle Isle but scarce in the Gulf of St. Lawrence (Île de la tête à la Baleine, Quebec).

Head with sooty-brown cap extending somewhat below eyes and sharply marked off from white cheeks. Upper parts sooty brown, darkest on wings and tail, many feathers of back and wing coverts with pale-greyish margins. Posterior upper tail coverts white, forming a narrow white band across base of tail. Under parts white, the white extending up sides of neck to form an incomplete collar. Belly with small ashy patches. Under tail coverts ashy grey. Bill blackish. Legs and feet flesh-coloured, outer side of legs and outer toe blackish.

Measurements. *Adult male*: wing, 305.5–328 (318.2); tail, 105.5–120 (113.3); exposed culmen, 45.5–51 (47.7); tarsus, 56.5–62 (59.5) mm.

Field Marks. An Atlantic white-bellied shearwater. The white under parts readily separate it from the Sooty Shearwater, the only other common shearwater in Canadian Atlantic waters. Differs from the rarer Cory's Shearwater, also white-bellied, by a white band at the base of the tail, black bill, and by the black cap being sharply defined against white cheeks. Manx Shearwater, of accidental occurrence in eastern Canadian waters, is smaller, more contrastingly marked with black and white, and lacks the white band at the base of the tail.

Habitat. The open ocean.

Range. Known to breed only in the south Atlantic Ocean on islands in the Tristan de Cunha group. Wanders northward as far as Greenland and northern Europe; also to Africa and South America.

Remarks. To see shearwaters one usually must go 15 km or more out on the ocean, for ordinarily they do not come close to our shores. They are wonderful flyers, the long, stiffly held wings carrying them in effortless rapid glides over surprisingly long distances, especially when the wind is blowing. They fly low, often so close to the heaving water surface that one of the wing tips almost seems to drag as the bird banks gracefully. Shearwaters dive to pursue food, but usually alight on the water before doing so. In dead calm they experience great difficulty in taking off, flapping awkwardly for considerable distances with alternately paddling feet.

These greedy feeders flock to fishing boats for the offal thrown overboard during fish cleaning. They fight vigorously among themselves for possession of choice morsels, and emit squeals of delight or frustration. They feed on squids, caplin and other small fishes, offal, and similar sea food.

Wedge-tailed Shearwater

[**Wedge-tailed Shearwater**. Puffin à queue fine. *Puffinus pacificus* (Gmelin). Hypothetical. S.G. Jewett (1929. Auk, vol. 46, no. 2, p. 224) recorded a skin of this species labelled "Vancouver, B.C." with no other data, and the authority for the record is unknown.]

Buller's Shearwater

(New Zealand Shearwater)

Puffin de Buller
Puffinus bulleri Salvin
Total length: 38 to 45.5 cm
Plate 4

Status in Canada. A regular autumn visitor to waters off the British Columbia coast (mainly August to October). As many as 100 reported in a day (29 August 1968, 140 km off entrance to Juan de Fuca Strait). Specimen collected 26 September 1970, some 40 km off the British Columbia coast. Sight record of one north to Dixon Entrance, British Columbia, 2 November 1971.

Upper parts (including rump) bluish grey darkening to greyish black on crown, across upper side of wings, and tail. Under parts, including under surface of wings, mainly white. Bill bluish grey; feet flesh colour, blackish on outer sides.

Field Marks. A largish dark-capped white-bellied shearwater. Grey on upper parts, paler than in most shearwaters. Distinguished in flight by a broad, blackish M or inverted W across spread wings. The wedge-shaped tail is blackish, the upper tail coverts grey.

Habitat. The ocean.

Range. Breeds on islets off North Island, New Zealand. After nesting wanders northward on the Pacific Ocean.

Sooty Shearwater

Puffin fuligineux
Puffinus griseus (Gmelin)
Total length: 40.6 to 45.7 cm
Plate 5

Status in Canada. A non-breeding summer visitant to pelagic and offshore waters of both the Atlantic and Pacific coasts. Fairly common off the Atlantic Coast: from June to October off New Brunswick, Nova Scotia, Newfoundland, and Labrador north to eastern Hudson Strait; rare in the Gulf of St. Lawrence (Prince Edward Island; southeastern Quebec: Bonne-Espérance; Anticosti Island). Common to abundant off the British Columbia coast (occasionally common in Strait of Georgia), occurring from early March to October. In winter recorded twice near Victoria.

Upper and under parts sooty brown, becoming blackish on wings and tail. *Wing* linings greyish white. Bill dusky. Legs and feet blackish, purplish on inner sides of legs and webs.

Measurements. *Adult male*: wing, 255–298.5 (285.9); tail, 83.5–93 (88.8); exposed culmen, 39–43 (41.8); tarsus, 53.5–60.5 (56.8). *Adult female*: wing, 243.5–294 (270.8) mm.

Field Marks. An all-dark shearwater (including bill and feet) with whitish wing-linings. The only dark-bellied shearwater likely to be seen on the Atlantic Coast of Canada. On the Pacific, the Flesh-footed Shearwater is similar but has flesh-coloured bill, legs, and feet, and dark wing linings. The Short-tailed Shearwater has darker-grey wing linings and a shorter tail, and it is smaller.

Habitat. The open ocean but tending to approach shore more often than most shearwaters.

Range. Breeds on islands near Cape Horn, near New Zealand, and off the coast of Chile. Wanders widely over the great oceans: north to the Aleutian Islands in the Pacific, to northern Labrador and (casually) southern Greenland in the Atlantic.

Short-tailed Shearwater

(Slender-billed Shearwater)

Puffin à bec mince
Puffinus tenuirostris (Temminck)
Total length: 35.5 cm
Plate 5

Status in Canada. A late summer and autumn visitant to the pelagic waters off British Columbia, occasionally entering waters of the coast littoral. The numerical status of this species in British Columbia requires clarification.

Upper parts sooty or blackish. Under parts slightly paler. Wing linings usually greyish (sometimes whitish). Bill and feet dusky.

Field Marks. An all-dark shearwater of the Pacific. Its dark bill and legs distinguish it from the Flesh-footed Shearwater. Very difficult to distinguish from Sooty Shearwater; its smaller size usually not apparent; the underside of the wings is usually more greyish, less whitish than in the Sooty, but there is much overlapping.

Habitat. The open ocean.

Range. Breeds on islands off southeastern Australia. After the breeding season it wanders widely over the Pacific Ocean and northward to the Aleutian Islands.

Manx Shearwater

Puffin des Anglais
Puffinus puffinus (Brünnich)
Total length: 31 to 38 cm
Plate 4

Range in Canada. An uncommon visitor and recent local breeder on the Atlantic Coast. In 1977, it was discovered breeding in Newfoundland (Middle Lawn Island). Scarce visitor to Nova Scotia and New Brunswick; also sight records for the Gulf of St. Lawrence.

Upper parts, including flight feathers and tail, black. Under parts white, a few faint dusky markings on the flanks. Under tail coverts mostly white (only outer webs of outermost black). Wing linings white. Bill slender, black, the lower mandible paler.

Field Marks. Medium size. The black upper parts contrast sharply with white under parts, thus it is likely to be confused only with the very rare Little and Audubon's shearwaters, which are both decidedly smaller. Both Cory's and Greater shearwaters are obviously larger than Manx. Greater has a whitish area at the base of the tail which Manx lacks and Cory's has a yellowish bill (black in Manx).

Habitat. The ocean. Comes ashore only for nesting purposes.

Nesting. In a chamber at the end of a burrow in flat or sloping ground near the sea and usually lined with grasses and other vegetation. *Egg*, one only, white. Incubation, by both parents in turn, averages 51 days (R.M. Lockey).

Range. Breeds in Bermuda (formerly), Salvages Islands, Madeira Island, the Azores, locally northward to the British Isles, Faeroe Islands, and Iceland; recently on Penikese Island, Massachusetts, and in southern Newfoundland.

Subspecies. *Puffinus puffinus puffinus* (Brünnich).

Black-vented Shearwater

Puffin cul-noir
Puffinus opisthomelas Coues
Total length: 31 to 38 cm
Figure 14

Status in Canada. A rare visitor to coastal British Columbia: specimens from Albert Head taken on 24 October 1891, November 1891, February 1895. Sight records of one off Cape Scott, 15 July 1940, and on Goose Island Banks, 14 August 1948. Apparently it was more frequently observed before the turn of the century.

Upper parts, including flight feathers and tail, sooty brown becoming blackish on the rump. Under parts mainly white with brownish-grey wash on sides of neck, sometimes extending across upper breast. Under tail coverts dark brown. Wing linings mainly white.

Figure 14
Black-vented Shearwater

Field Marks. Most closely resembles the Pink-footed Shearwater, but Black-vented is much smaller, has a *dark* bill, the wing linings are white instead of grey, and the white of the under parts tends to be less greyish.

Habitat. The ocean.

Range. Breeds on islands off the west coast of Baja California. Wanders northward regularly, rarely to south coastal Alaska.

Little Shearwater

(Allied Shearwater)

Puffin obscur
Puffinus assimilis Gould
Total length: 28 cm

Status in Canada. Accidental. One specimen taken on Sable Island, Nova Scotia, on 1 September 1896.

A small shearwater with contrasting black upper parts and white under parts. Very similar to Audubon's Shearwater (see below) and to the nominate race of the Manx Shearwater, *Puffinus puffinus puffinus*, but much smaller than the latter. Wing, 18 cm instead of 23 cm.

Range. Breeds on islands in the Atlantic (Tristan da Cunha, Gough, Canary, Salvages islands; Madeira Island and the Azores) and in the south Pacific (off southwestern Australia, Chatham, Norfolk, Lord Howe, and Kermadec islands).

Subspecies. The above specimen is referable to *Puffinus assimilis baroli* Bonaparte.

Audubon's Shearwater

Puffin d'Audubon
Puffinus lherminieri Lesson
Total length: 30.5 cm
Plate 4

Status in Canada. Accidental. A female found dead on 8 September 1975, far inland near Almonte, Ontario! Reports of strays off Newfoundland and Nova Scotia require confirmation. Sight record of one on Western Bank, Nova Scotia, 7 October 1979; and in Gulf of Maine, Nova Scotia, 27 August 1980.

In its small size and general coloration, very similar to Little Shearwater but differs as follows: Under tail coverts mostly blackish (instead of mostly white); inner vanes of primaries with little or no white; upper parts more brownish black than slaty black; tail relatively and actually longer (average 86 mm); legs mostly flesh coloured.

Habitat. Ocean waters.

Range. Breeds on ocean islands (mainly tropical) from Bermuda (rarely) south to the Lesser Antilles, Guyana, and Cape Verde Islands; also widely in the tropical Pacific Ocean.

Subspecies. The one Canadian specimen agrees in size (wing 188; tail 86.5; exposed culmen 27.5 mm) with the eastern Panama form *Puffinus lherminieri loyemilleri* Wetmore!

Family **Hydrobatidae**: Storm-Petrels

Number of species in Canada: 5

Figure 15
Bill of Leach's Storm-Petrel

Small (length 15 to 23 cm) ocean birds, somewhat swallow-like in flight. Of the five species known to occur in Canada, four are dark sooty-brown (appearing blackish at a distance) with a white rump patch; the other is ashy grey. They spend most of their lives on the ocean, ordinarily coming to land only for nesting purposes. Flitting close to the surface of the ocean, often pattering up and down the waves as though walking on them, they are easily recognized as petrels. The upper mandible is decidedly hooked, the lower slightly so (see Figure 15). The single nostril-tube is situated on top of the bill at its base. They are the "Mother Carey's Chickens" of the sailors.

Wilson's Storm-Petrel

Pétrel océanite
Oceanites oceanicus (Kuhl)
Total length: 18 to 19 cm
Plate 5

Status in Canada. A fairly common to common non-breeding summer visitant, mainly to pelagic and offshore waters (but sometimes coming close to shore) of Nova Scotia, Prince Edward Island, New Brunswick, Newfoundland, and perhaps southern Labrador (sight records only). Sometimes found in the Gulf of St. Lawrence (near Bonne-Espérance, Quebec; Miscou Island, New Brunswick). Accidental in southwestern Quebec (Lake Deschênes, 23 September 1938) and southern Ontario (Long Beach, 14 August 1955; Lake Muskoka, 1897).

Tail not forked. General colour blackish brown, the secondary wing coverts greyish with narrow whitish margins. Upper tail coverts white, under tail coverts mainly white basally. Base of tail with more or less (concealed) white. Bill, legs, and toes black, webs yellowish.

Field Marks. In Canada an Atlantic species. It resembles the Leach's Storm-Petrel but has a square instead of a forked tail. The toes extend beyond the tip of the tail when the bird is flying. The yellow webs between the toes are diagnostic, if they can be seen. Often follows ships.

Habitat. The ocean.

Range. Ranges widely over the oceans except the north Pacific. Breeds on the South Orkneys, South Shetlands, Antarctica, and on islands near Cape Horn.

Subspecies. *Oceanites oceanicus oceanicus* (Kuhl).

Remarks. The Wilson's Storm-Petrel, like the Greater and Sooty shearwaters, nests and raises its young during our winters (its summers) in the Southern Hemisphere. It "winters" during our summers in the Northern Hemisphere on pelagic and offshore waters of the Atlantic Ocean, regularly from June to September.

British Storm-Petrel

Pétrel tempête
Hydrobates pelagicus (Linnaeus)
Total length: 15 cm
Plate 5

Status in Canada. Specimen taken on Sable Island, Nova Scotia, on 10 August 1970, is the first authentic North American record.

A small petrel, mostly sooty-black in colour, the upper wing coverts browner. Rump and upper tail coverts white, the latter with broad black tips. Under surface of wing sooty, this on the coverts mixed with white, thus forming a small white area. Tail square. Bill, legs, and feet (including webs) black.

Measurements. *Adult male*: wing, 119; tail, 53; exposed culmen, 11; tarsus, 22.5 mm (one specimen only).

Field Marks. A small, mostly sooty, white-rumped petrel. Smaller size and the presence of a *small whitish area on the underside of the spread wing* separate it from both the Leach's and Wilson's. Its square tail also distinguishes it from Leach's.

Habitat. Mostly salt water.

Range. Breeds in the North Atlantic and western and central Mediterranean.

Fork-tailed Storm-Petrel

Pétrel à queue fourchue
Oceanodroma furcata (Gmelin)
Total length: 20.5 to 23 cm
Plate 5

Breeding Distribution of Fork-tailed Storm-Petrel

Range in Canada. Common throughout the year on coastal waters off British Columbia. It nests in scattered colonies along the British Columbia coast (west coast of Vancouver Island; in Queen Charlotte Sound, and the Queen Charlotte Islands at Cox, Graham, and Langara islands).

A bluish-grey petrel, palest on throat and under tail coverts. Area about eye blackish. Wings more or less dusky or blackish on coverts, tips, and linings. Tail forked, bluish grey except whitish outer web of outermost feathers. Bill and legs black.

Measurements *(O. f. plumbea). Adult male*: wing, 145.3–155.9 (151.4); tail, 82.4–91.3 (86.5); exposed culmen, 13.9–15.2 (14.6); tarsus, 25.4–27 (26.2). *Adult female*: wing, 149.9–156.1 (153.2); tail, 82.6–96.5 (88.5); exposed culmen, 13.9–15.3 (14.6); tarsus, 24.4–27.5 (25.7) mm (Grinnell and Test).

Field Marks. A pearl-grey petrel of the West Coast with a decidedly forked tail and no white rump patch.

Habitat. Open sea. In breeding season comes to land, usually coastal islands, for nesting.

Nesting. In colonies. Nest usually at end of a shallow burrow in soil; occasionally in rock crevices. *Eggs*, one only; dull white, usually with a faint circle of tiny dark dots around the larger end. Incubation by both sexes.

Range. Breeds on the Kurile, Komandorskie, and Aleutian islands and southward along the North American Pacific Coast to northern California.

Subspecies. *Oceanodroma furcata plumbea* (Peale) is the only subspecies known to occur in Canada, although the slightly larger, slightly paler, more-northern nominate race might eventually be found as a visitant.

Remarks. Because of its colour, size, and habitat, this pretty petrel of the Pacific is not likely to be mistaken for any other bird. It is rather confiding and can readily be "chummed up" to a boat with small scraps of fish liver, and occasionally can even be caught in the hand. Vocally it has a variety of soft twitterings and high-pitched squeaks.

Leach's Storm-Petrel

Pétrel cul-blanc
Oceanodroma leucorhoa (Vieillot)
Total length: 19 to 23 cm
Plate 5

Tail forked. Plumage including wing linings mainly sooty blackish-brown. Wing coverts greyish brown. Upper tail coverts white (some middle ones greyish brown), creating a white rump patch. Bill, legs, and feet (including webs) blackish.

Measurements *(O. l. leucorhoa). Adult male*: wing, 145.5–159.5 (153.1); tail, 78.5–89.5 (84.2); exposed culmen, 15.5–17.5 (16.4); tarsus, 23.5–25.5 (24.3). *Adult female*: wing, 149.5–162 (154.3) mm.

Field Marks. A blackish petrel of both the East and West coasts with a white rump patch and a forked tail. Does not usually follow ships. On the East Coast it is likely to be confused with the similar Wilson's Storm-Petrel, but Wilson's has a square tail and (at very close range) yellow webs between the toes, and longer legs, which project slightly beyond the tail. The Fork-tailed Storm-Petrel of the West Coast is entirely different. See British Storm-Petrel.

Habitat. The ocean. At nesting time, coastal islands, or rarely mainland headlands, either wooded or grassy and treeless.

Nesting. In colonies, often dense. Nest in a chamber (sometimes with a few grasses or similar soft material) at the end of a shallow burrow in the ground excavated mainly by the male. *Egg*, one only; dull white, usually with a faint wreath of lilac dots about the larger end. Incubation, by both sexes, is long, variously given as 41 to 50 days, probably 41 to 42 days. Each bird may incubate for about 96 consecutive hours without food (at least up to 144 hours, according to W.A.O. Gross) and is relieved by its mate at night.

Breeding Distribution of Leach's Storm-Petrel

Range in Canada. Found on both the Pacific and Atlantic coasts. Breeds on the coastal islands of British Columbia where it is locally common but generally less numerous than the Fork-tailed Storm-Petrel. Occurs off the British Columbia coast throughout the year. On the Atlantic it nests on coastal islands (rarely the coastal mainland) from southern Labrador (Gannet Islands, St. Peter Islands); Newfoundland; Quebec (outer north shore of the Gulf of St. Lawrence at Perroquet Islands and off La Romaine; Bonaventure Island; Rochers aux Oiseaux); New Brunswick (Grand Manan Island); and Nova Scotia (Seal, Mud, Pearl, Ciboux, and St. Paul islands, and near Louisburg on the mainland of Cape Breton Island). Recorded in Nova Scotia from 11 April to 13 November; in New Brunswick, 23 April to December. Accidental in Ontario (Cornwall, 19 July 1939; near Kingston, 16 August 1955). Casual in northern Quebec (near Kuujjuaq, 12 July 1882) and probably eastern Baffin Island (Cape Mercy).

Range. Breeds locally in the north Pacific (northern Japan, the Kurile and Aleutian islands, and southeast along the Pacific Coast of North America to Baja California) and the north Atlantic (southern Labrador, Greenland, Iceland, and the Faeroe Islands south to Massachusetts and the British Isles).

Subspecies. (1) *Oceanodroma leucorhoa leucorhoa* (Vieillot) is the breeding form of the Atlantic; also on the coast of Japan and the Aleutian Islands. (2) *O. l. beali* Emerson, slightly smaller in size, breeds from southeast Alaska south along the coast of British Columbia to northern California.

Remarks. One could be standing in the middle of a petrel colony without knowing it. Although the ground below may be honeycombed with their burrows, the entrances are made inconspicuous by growing vegetation. During the daylight hours, the incubating birds do not stir, and their mates remain far out at sea. Even the faint musky odour exuded by these birds is recognizable only to the few who are familiar with it. When darkness comes on, however, the colony bustles with activity as these ocean foragers return to relieve their incubating mates. The air comes alive with sounds of flitting wings, eerie voices, and ghost-like forms. When daylight returns, the colony again appears deserted.

Like other petrels, this one spends most of its life on the trackless ocean, coming ashore only for nesting. Its food includes molluscs, crustaceans, small fishes, and oily materials gleaned from the ocean. It also takes refuse matter left by whales. This petrel can be lured close to a boat if bits of fish liver are thrown overboard. As in other petrels, the stomach contains an oily, orange-coloured liquid, which is ejected by the birds apparently as a protection. Its strong musky smell persists on museum specimens indefinitely.

This harmless gentle bird has many enemies. Cats, dogs, and rats introduced onto islands where it nests can soon wipe out whole colonies. Perhaps before the coming of the white man, it nested more frequently on the mainland, but it rarely does so today. It is probably significant that the nearest thing to a mainland colony ever seen by the writer (a small one near Louisburg, Cape Breton Island, Nova Scotia, where near-mainland conditions prevail) was made conspicuous by the wings of dead petrels left lying about by some predator. Larger gulls take a heavy toll by pursuing and capturing petrels, especially on moonlit nights. Lights at lighthouses lure others to their death.

Band-rumped Storm-Petrel

Pétrel de Castro
Oceanodroma castro (Harcourt)
Total length: 19.5 to 20.6 cm

Status in Canada. Accidental. One record. A female of the nominate subspecies *Oceanodroma castro castro* (Harcourt) was found alive on the Rideau River, near Ottawa, Ontario, on 28 August 1933. This race breeds on islands in the Atlantic Ocean from the Azores south to Ascension and St. Helena islands.

Like Leach's Storm-Petrel but tail less deeply forked, white rump patch not divided by a dark-grey median area, but the feathers of the rump patch have blackish tips, and the white of rump extends to and across the under parts near the base of the tail (not merely as a few white feathers).

Order **Pelecaniformes:**
Tropicbirds, Pelicans, Cormorants, Frigatebirds, and Allies

This order comprises fish-eating birds with all four toes connected by webs; a pouch extending from bottom of bill to throat; nostrils either small or absent; and the bill, except in tropicbirds, boobies, and gannets, with a hook at the tip.

Family **Phaethontidae:**
Tropicbirds

Number of Species in Canada: 1

Medium-sized marine birds, boldly marked in white and black, the adults with greatly elongated central tail feathers and with a bill gently tapered and pointed, not hooked (see Figure 16). Unlike gulls, they fly with quick wingbeats. Their streaming tail feathers separate them readily from both gulls and terns. They are birds of the tropical and subtropical seas and of accidental occurrence in Canada.

Figure 16
White-tailed Tropicbird

White-tailed Tropicbird

(Yellow-billed Tropicbird)

Petit Paille-en-queue
Phaethon lepturus Daudin
Total length: 72 to 82 cm

Status in Canada. Accidental. Five specimens for Nova Scotia (Schubenacadie, 6 September 1870; Wolfville, 27 August 1927; Brier Island, 7 October 1962; Cape Sable, 9 October 1962; Hillsborough, 26 July 1959. Also about six sight records in Nova Scotia).

Adults: Central tail feathers extremely elongated and slender (about 50 cm long). Plumage mainly white, often with a suggestion of pink. A broad black stripe through the eye. Outer webs of primaries, median wing coverts, and tertials, black. Flanks with greyish-black streaks. Bill gently tapering, pointed, *orange. Immatures:* Similar but central tail feathers only slightly elongated, back barred with black, and bill yellow.

    Habitat. Salt water, normally tropical.

    Range. Breeds in Bermuda, the Bahamas, the West Indies, the south Atlantic, southwest Pacific, and Indian oceans.

    Subspecies. *Phaethon lepturus catesbyi* Brandt.

Red-billed Tropicbird

[**Red-billed Tropicbird**. Grand Paille-en-queue. *Phaethon aethereus* Linnaeus. Hypothetical. References by authors to the occurrence of this species on the Newfoundland banks seem to be based on P.E. Freke's assertion that he "noticed" this bird there in August 1876 (see Peters and Burleigh 1951).]

Family **Sulidae:**
Boobies and Gannets

Number of Species in Canada: 2

Large, long-winged marine birds with a small inconspicuous throat pouch. On the wing, they frequently interrupt their flapping with short glides and often dive from the air. Their bills are rather long, tapered, straight (but more or less decurved at tip, not hooked). Although marine, they are not usually found far at sea, preferring the vicinity of the coast. Only the Northern Gannet is boreal in distribution.

Brown Booby

(White-bellied Booby)

Fou brun
Sula leucogaster (Boddaert)
Total length: 78 cm

Status in Canada. Accidental. One record only. A specimen was found alive near Blanche, Shelburne County, Nova Scotia, on 28 July 1941, by A.D. Simmons. Mr. Simmons' photograph and description of it are readily identifiable. The subspecies could not be determined, but it probably was *Sula leucogaster leucogaster* (Boddaert).

Adults: Head, neck, chest, and upper parts brown. Lower breast and belly white, contrasting sharply with brown of chest. Bill and feet yellowish. Juvenals are greyish brown, palest on the belly.

Range. Breeds in the West Indies and widely in tropical and subtropical parts of the Atlantic, Pacific, and Indian oceans.

Northern Gannet

Fou de Bassan
Sula bassanus (Linnaeus)
Total length: 88 to 102 cm
Plate 6

Breeding Distribution of Northern Gannet

Range in Canada. Fairly common in spring, summer, and autumn on the Altantic Coast (recorded March to December). Breeds in southeastern Quebec (Anticosti Island, Bonaventure Island, Madeleine Islands; formerly Perroquet Island, Mingan group, until about 1887); Newfoundland (Funk Island, Baccalieu Island, Cape St. Mary's); formerly in New Brunswick (Gannet Rock, south of Grand Manan, until about 1866); and Nova Scotia (Gannet Rock, until about 1880; perhaps also Harbourville). Recorded in summer along the Atlantic Coast at points far distant from the actual breeding colonies, regularly in small numbers off Prince Edward Island, and north to northern Labrador (Ramah Bay). Casual inland at various localities in the upper St. Lawrence River valley, Ottawa River, Lake Ontario, and Lake Erie (e.g. Montréal region, Ottawa, Kingston, Toronto, Niagara River). Accidental near Holman, Victoria Island, N.W.T.: specimen, 14 September 1975.

Bill somewhat longer than head, tapering, sharp-pointed (upper mandible slightly decurved near tip, but not hooked). *Adults*: Mainly white, the head and neck with a yellowish suffusion. Wing tips and bare skin about eye, black. Bill greyish. Iris pale grey. *Immature in first year*: Head, neck, and upper parts dark greyish-brown or slate with white triangular spots, particularly numerous on head and neck. Belly white with grey feather margins. Various stages of immaturity occur between the first-year birds, just described, and the adults, one stage presenting a rather striking piebald appearance.

Measurements. *Adult male*: wing (flattened), 487–511.5 (501.1); tail, 189.5–225.5 (214.5); exposed culmen, 93.5–107 (99.1); tarsus, 59–65 (62.5). *Adult female*: wing (flattened), 485–503 (495.9) mm.

Field Marks. A large marine bird. Adults might be confused with gulls, but the black of the wing tips is more extensive and is more sharply cut off from the white than in large gulls. Even at considerable distances Gannets are whiter-backed than the gulls that usually associate with them. In any plumage the longer bill, head, and neck of Gannets project farther ahead of the body than in gulls. This silhouette in flight, as well as the pointed tail, gives Gannets a characteristic "pointed at both ends" look.

Habitat. Coastal salt water, but not often far at sea. Accidental inland. In the breeding season, for nesting, rocky islands usually with steep cliffs; sometimes mainland cliffs.

Nesting. In colonies, sometimes very large, on coastal islands. Nest is placed on ledges of cliffs and sometimes on the flat top of coastal islands above the cliffs. Nest is mainly of seaweed (sometimes sticks and other debris are added), nest material varying from bulky to little or none. Nests usually close together. *Egg*, one only; white with pale-bluish tinge, generally nest-stained. Incubation variously given 42 to 46 days, one instance of 46 days (W. Duval); average for 220 eggs, 43.9 days (J.-M. Poulin) by both sexes. One brood annually.

Range. Breeds very locally along the northern Atlantic Coast from Nova Scotia (formerly) north to Newfoundland; also in Iceland, the Faeroe Islands, and the British Isles. Winters along the coasts from Virginia to Florida and from the British Isles to the Azores.

Remarks. Some three miles off the picturesque village of Percé, Quebec, the famous Bonaventure Island Gannet colony provides thousands of visitors each year with one of the most spectacular and readily accessible ornithological sights on this continent. As the boat rounds a projecting corner of the island, the great Gannet ledges come into view, all snowy-white with birds. In passing slowly along the base of the 120 m cliffs, the motor boat disturbs the birds, and they leave the ledges like snow before a wind. Thousands of glistening white Gannets scale and wheel in every direction, and all the while a dull roar persists, the united voices of the additional thousands still on the ledges.

Since the island became a sanctuary, the colony has flourished and has overflowed to the flat top of the island above the cliffs, a veritable snowfield of birds. There Gannets can be studied at close range, for they are extremely tame. Within a short time their fighting, courting, nest building, incubation, displays, feeding of the young, and weird flight take-offs may be seen. The Bonaventure colony apparently peaked in numbers about 1966 at 21,215 pairs but by 1973 was down to 17,281 pairs. By 1979 there was an impressive increase to 42,000 pairs.

Although Gannets are usually silent elsewhere, the breeding grounds are a bedlam of harsh, loud *kar-uck, kar-uck, kar-uck*, which often sounds like "get out, get out, get out." The nests are placed close together, and there is a good deal of quarrelling. Although the bill is powerful, with serrated sharp cutting edges that can easily cut to the bone a human hand or finger, the birds do not often injure one another seriously in these encounters.

Take-off from a crowded colony is an intriguing procedure. The bird wanting to leave for a flight solemnly raises the head and points the bill tip skyward, partly spreads the wings, and depresses the tail. With weird moans it waddles and hops its way toward the cliff edge or a less crowded part of the colony. Each time it passes too close to a neighbour, a furore is created with many a bill thrust and vocal threat received. Using both legs and wings, it rushes ahead and becomes airborne. Once in the air its flight is easy and graceful, alternating flaps and glides.

In midsummer, some nests contain young of various sizes; others have eggs still being incubated. During incubation the two large webbed feet are placed over the single egg. Gannets have no incubation patch. The newly hatched young are greyish black, almost naked, and very ugly. Later they grow a woolly white covering of down.

Gannets secure their fish food by diving from heights up to 30 m in the air. When a fish is sighted, the bird checks its speed momentarily, half closes its wings, and drops headfirst like an arrow, vertically or on a slight plane. As it hits the water it sends the spray high into the air. A flock of diving Gannets is a fascinating sight. They are useful to fishermen in providing the location of fish schools. Gannets do not remain long under water but almost invariably they manage to swallow their prey before emerging. Gannets in the breeding season eat herring, mackerel, capelin, and squid.

Family **Pelecanidae:** Pelicans

Number of Species in Canada: 2

Very large water birds with long, flattened bill, conspicuous gular pouch, long wings, short tail, robust legs, and fully webbed toes. Upper mandible is hooked at tip; lower mandible has a large naked pouch, which is connected with the throat and is capable of great distension.

American White Pelican

Pélican blanc d'Amérique
Pelecanus erythrorhynchos Gmelin
Total length: 150 to 188 cm
Plate 6

Wingspread 2.4 to 3.0 m. *Adults*: Bill long, flattened, with very conspicuous pouch, and in the breeding season an upright horny process on the culmen. Plumage mostly white with wing tips (primaries and many secondaries) black. Breast and lesser wing coverts with narrow lanceolate feathers tinged yellow. Bill and pouch yellow with reddish tinge. Bare skin around eyes orange; eyelids red. Feet orange-red. *Immatures*: Similar, but feathers on back of head ashy grey, bill and feet duller.

Measurements. *Adult male*: wing, 586–614 (602.5); tail, 157–162 (158.5); exposed culmen, 332–365 (347.3); tarsus, 119.5–124.5 (121.8). *Adult female*: wing, 533.5–543 (538.3) mm.

Field Marks. Unmistakable pelican outline. A very large white water bird with black wing-tips and a conspicuous yellow throat-pouch. Flies with neck doubled back against the shoulders. The Whooping Crane, Snow Goose, and Gannet also are large white birds with black

Breeding Distribution of American White Pelican

Range in Canada. Local summer resident in the western provinces. Breeds locally from southern interior British Columbia (Stum Lake); extreme southern Mackenzie (Mountain Rapids near Fort Smith); northern Alberta; northwestern Saskatchewan (Preston Lake); central Manitoba (Talbot Lake); and western Ontario (Lake of the Woods) south through the International Boundary. Recorded in summer on Great Slave Lake, District of Mackenzie. A common and fairly regular transient through the Nicola and Kamloops regions of British Columbia. One winter record (Cowichan Bay, British Columbia, 28 February 1947). Stragglers recorded from northern Mackenzie (Liverpool Bay, June or July 1900); northern Ontario (Hannah Bay, June 1943); southern Ontario and southern Quebec (various records); New Brunswick (Grand Manan; Pointe du Chêne; Cape Spencer; and near St. Stephen); Nova Scotia (Kings County, about fifty were recorded between 27 September and 15 October 1948); and Newfoundland (Raleigh, early June 1983).

wing-tips, but they fly with outstretched neck. North American swans are all-white with no black in the wings; they too fly with outstretched neck.

Habitat. In breeding season, interior lakes in both treeless and forested country. In winter, the seacoast and freshwater lakes.

Nesting. In colonies, on islands of interior lakes. Nest, a depression on the ground usually with various kinds of debris scraped up about the rim; sometimes on matted-down vegetation. *Eggs*, usually 2; white, usually nest-stained. Incubation is by both sexes.

Range. Breeds locally from southwestern Canada south to southern California, northern Utah, southern Montana, and South Dakota. Winters from southern United States to Guatemala.

Remarks. Canadian bird life offers few more spectacular sights than a long line or V of precisely spaced White Pelicans flying majestically across the prairie sky. The snowy whiteness of the great birds, enhanced by the jet-black wing-tips and enriched by the yellow bill and feet, stands out oddly, even far in the distance. They flap in unison half a dozen times, glide, flap again, then glide. Every motion is easy, unhurried, graceful, even in the strongest prairie gales. They are excellent gliders and often spend considerable time high in the air. In an amazingly short time after take-off, these ponderous birds, with wing-spreads up to nearly 3 m, can become mere tiny white specks in the sky overhead. Occasionally their descent is highly spectacular, for sometimes they drop down like meteors, the wind rushing like thunder through their half-closed wings. They are highly gregarious; feeding, roosting, flying, and nesting in flocks.

On the water they float with surprising buoyancy. Take-off, while briefly laboured, is rapid for such large birds. Unlike Brown Pelicans, they do not often dive from the air, but catch their food on or near the water surface while swimming or wading. They eat fishes, frogs, and salamanders. Competent studies show that the fishes taken include vast numbers of minnows and that most of the larger species that they catch are slow-moving non-game fish of little interest to man. Judging by the number of inquiries received from prospective visitors to the Prairie Provinces as to where pelicans may be seen, they are one of the attractions the Prairies have for Easterners. Although its numbers have decreased in many of its prairie haunts, the White Pelican is one of few large birds that still can be seen in something resembling former numbers. This magnificent bird should not be destroyed for petty or imaginary reasons.

Brown Pelican

Pélican brun
Pelecanus occidentalis Linnaeus
Total length: 118 to 147 cm
Figure 17

Figure 17
Brown Pelican in breeding plumage

Bill and pouch shape similar to that of White Pelican. *Adults in summer*: Head mainly white (yellowish on top), this extending down neck, framing the pouch; rest of neck and hind-head dark chestnut-brown. Upper parts dark brown. *Adults in winter*: Similar to adults in summer but hind-head and hind-neck white. *Immature*: Head and neck dark brown. Under parts whitish, the sides tinged with brownish grey.

Field Marks. Great pouched bill, large size, pelican outline. Brown and grey coloration is very different from that of the White Pelican. Unlike the White Pelican, it dives from the air.

Range. Breeds from South Carolina and California southward along the coasts to Central and South America; also the Greater and Lesser Antilles.

Status in Canada. Casual visitant to the coast of British Columbia (Queen Charlotte Strait, 18 July 1913; Race Rocks, January 1898, August 1939; Burrard Inlet, November 1880; Esquimalt Harbour, 24 November 1904; Victoria, 19 December 1932, 7 to 16 November 1935). Accidental in Nova Scotia (Prospect, December 1896; Three Fathom Harbour, June 1899; Clark's Harbour, June 1924; Louisburg, 19 May 1904; River John, 31 May 1885; Pictou Island, 15 May 1892) and Ontario (Waverly Beach, 25 September 1971, and sight records on Niagara River).

Subspecies. British Columbia specimens are referred to *Pelecanus occidentalis californicus* Ridgway. I have not been able to examine Nova Scotia specimens, which probably are *P. o. carolinensis* Gmelin, but there is a possibility of the occurrence of the West Indian race, *P. o. occidentalis*, there also.

Family **Phalacrocoracidae**: Cormorants

Number of Species in Canada: 4

Large water birds, 63 to 101 cm long, the adults shiny black. Bill slender, upper mandible strongly hooked. Adults have no external nostrils and therefore breathe through the mouth. They have a small naked throat pouch, a bare space about the eyes, and a stiff and rather long tail. All four toes are connected by webs. They inhabit both salt and fresh water. Their food is mainly fishes, which are taken by underwater pursuit; sometimes amphibians and crustaceans.

Field Marks. Adults are big black water birds, generally larger and longer than ducks. Cormorants often fly in lines or V-formation, like geese, but the all-blackness of adults distinguishes them, and the longer, slenderer tail of cormorants is diagnostic in any plumage. Loons lack the long tail, and have gleaming white under parts. When cormorants perch, they sit very upright, sometimes with half-spread wings. On the water they hold the bill higher than loons or geese.

Great Cormorant

(European Cormorant)

Grand Cormoran
Phalacrocorax carbo (Linnaeus)
Total length: 86 to 101 cm
Plate 6

Breeding Distribution of Great Cormorant

Range in Canada. Breeds locally along the Atlantic Coast in Newfoundland (Port au Port peninsula, Guernsey Island, Lewis Point); Quebec (Anticosti Island; Madeleine Islands;

Bill slender, rather long, hooked. Feathers of throat impinge in a point on the throat pouch. Tail feathers, fourteen in number. *Spring and summer adults*: Mainly shiny bluish-black or greenish-black, but feathers of upper back, scapulars, and wing coverts bronzy-brown with broad black margins. In spring, white hairlike feathers (lost by early summer) are scattered over head and neck, and there is a white patch on the flanks (also lost by early summer). Throat pouch dull yellow, bare, bordered behind by white feathers. Iris green. *Winter adults*: Similar but white feathers on head, neck, and flanks wanting. *Immatures*: Mainly brownish-black with more or less white on belly and breast, the light areas of under parts thus usually more extensive than in the Double-crested.

Measurements. *Adult male*: wing, 340–366 (355.7); tail, 150–169.5 (156.9); exposed culmen, 70–82.2 (77.8); tarsus, 67–74 (71.7). *Adult female*: wing, 326–346.5 (341.9) mm.

Field Marks. As this cormorant is confined in Canada to the Atlantic Coast, the slightly smaller Double-crested Cormorant is the only other cormorant likely to be seen with it. Adult Greats in summer have a white hind border to the throat pouch, and in late winter and in spring a small white patch on the flanks. The adult Double-crested, on the Atlantic Coast, has no white patch. The Great has a yellowish throat pouch, not *orange*-yellow, as in the Double-crested. Immature Greats usually (not always) have white bellies, this white extending to the base of the tail; thus the pale areas of under parts are usually more extensive than in Double-crests of similar age. *Voice*: Usually silent, but on nesting ledges adults have a variety of growls, croaks, and chucks. Downy young have high-pitched whining notes, a little like a Semipalmated Plover.

Baie des Loups, Sainte-Marie Islands, Percé); Prince Edward Island (Cape Tryon, East Point, McKinnon Point, Durell Point); Nova Scotia (Hertford Island; Crystal Farm, Antigonish County; and other localities mostly on Cape Breton Island and along the south coast to Shelburne County); and formerly on Grand Manan Island, New Brunswick. Anticosti Island has the largest breeding population (16 known colonies, but recent evidence indicates that some are no longer extant). Winters in southern Canadian waters north to Newfoundland and the outer north shore of the Gulf of St. Lawrence, but many individuals move somewhat farther south into United States waters. Casual far inland (Toronto, Ontario, 21 November 1896; photo records: Port Credit, January 1978 and winter 1979; Amherst Island, 22 May 1982).

Habitat. Frequents coastal salt water, usually not venturing seaward beyond sight of land. Sometimes visits fresh waters near the coast. Rests on coastal islands, rocks, shore cliffs, piling, and sandbars. Nests on coastal cliffs, sometimes trees.

Nesting. In colonies, often mixed with Double-crested Cormorants on coastal cliffs and islands, preferring the higher ledges. Nest, a rather bulky pile of seaweed and sticks usually on cliff ledges or flat cliff-tops, rarely (McKinnon Point and Durell Point, Prince Edward Island) in low trees. *Eggs*, usually 3 or 4; bluish green or bluish white with chalky covering. Incubation, about 28 to 31 days (Witherby) by both sexes. One brood annually.

Range. Breeds in Europe, Asia, Africa, and Australia, southern Atlantic Coast of Canada.

Subspecies. *Phalacrocorax carbo carbo* (Linnaeus) is the race inhabiting Canada, Iceland, and northern Europe. Seven additional races are found in other parts of the world.

Remarks. In 1940, the known breeding population of the Great Cormorant in Canada was 2172 birds. Since then, active census work and an increasing population have substantially expanded that figure as shown by A.J. Erskine (1972. Canadian Wildlife Service, Occasional Paper 14) and by Brown et al. (1975). In Nova Scotia alone, A.R. Lock and P.K. Ross (1973. Canadian Field-Naturalist, vol. 87, no. 1, pp. 43–49) have censused about 2050 pairs in 23 colonies.

Double-crested Cormorant

Cormoran à aigrettes
Phalacrocorax auritus (Lesson)
Total length: 73 to 89 cm
Plate 6

Breeding Distribution of Double-crested Cormorant

Range in Canada and Subspecies. (1) *Phalacrocorax auritus auritus* (Lesson) is a locally distributed spring, summer, and autumn resident breeding locally from Alberta east to the Atlantic Coast, north to northern Alberta (very locally: Wadlin Lake, Lac la Biche); central Saskatchewan (Peter Pond Lake, Churchill Lake, Suggi Lake); central Manitoba (Talbot Lake); southern James Bay (Way Rock); the north shore of the Gulf of St. Lawrence, and Newfoundland southward; formerly southern Labrador. Accidental on southern Baffin Island (Frobisher Bay). (2) *Phalacrocorax auritus*

Bill rather long, 5 to 6.4 cm, slender, hooked. Tail feathers, twelve. Feathers of hind edge of throat pouch not impinging in a point on its bare skin. *Adults*: Mainly shiny greenish-black, the feathers of upper back and wing coverts bronzy with black margins. Naked throat pouch and skin around and in front of eye, orange-yellow. Spring adults have an inconspicuous tuft of feathers on either side of head (shed early in nesting season), which is black in eastern race, largely white in western races. Bill dusky, sometimes mixed with yellow; iris green; legs and feet black. *First-year immatures*: Mostly dark sooty-brown, paler below with much buff streaked with brown, the belly darker than the breast. Feathers of back and wing coverts with dark margins.

Measurements *(P. a. auritus)*. *Adult male*: wing, 301–321 (309.2); tail, 132–154.5 (140.2); exposed culmen, 59–64.5 (61.2); tarsus, 62–69 (66.3). *Adult female*: wing, 273–313 (292.5) mm.

Field Marks. The only cormorant likely to be seen in the interior. On the Atlantic Coast likely to be confused with only one species (see Great Cormorant). On the Pacific Coast, the Double-crested's orange-yellow throat pouch separates it from the other cormorants found there. *Voice*: Usually silent except on nesting grounds. In courtship a series of *oak, oak, oak* sometimes dwindling to *tick, tick, tick*; a loud *hawk*; a louder *r-r-r-o-o-o-p*; a variety of croaks; young during and shortly after hatching *weet-weet-weet*; more mature young have a variety of high-pitched squeaking notes.

Habitat. Freshwater lakes and rivers, estuaries, coastal salt water but usually not far at sea. Nests on cliff ledges and their flat tops, and in trees near water. Rests on cliffs, rocks, gravel bars, and piling near water.

Nesting. In colonies, sometimes in association with other cormorants, gulls, etc., near either fresh or salt water. Nests placed on bare rock or soil on rocks, islets, cliff ledges and tops, or in trees near water. Nest is moderately bulky; composed usually of sticks, weed stalks, seaweed and other available materials. *Eggs*, usually 3 or 4 (2 to 7 recorded); pale greenish-blue with chalky covering, soon becoming nest-stained. Incubation averages about 28 days (van Tets *in* Drent and Guiguet 1961), 24.5 to 29 days (various authors), by both parents.

albociliatus Ridgway breeds on the coast of southern British Columbia (Bare Island, near Sidney, Vancouver Island; Ballingall Islets) and winters in the same general region. (3) *Phalacrocorax auritus cincinatus* (Brandt) winters commonly about Vancouver Island but is not known to breed in Canada. The species (subspecies not determined) has been recorded in summer in interior British Columbia and is of casual occurrence in southern Yukon (Dawson).

Range. Breeds from southwestern Alaska, central Alberta, James Bay, and Newfoundland south to Mexico and the Bahamas.

Remarks. On the water, cormorants ride low with the tail submerged. They are excellent swimmers and divers. Dives are made from the water's surface and are usually of 20 to 30 seconds' duration but sometimes longer. Ordinarily underwater propulsion is by the feet alone, but sometimes the wings are used also. Take-off from water requires considerable paddling, flapping, and splashing. Once in the air, they fly well with steady flaps. Occasionally there are glides over short distances. Often they fly low over the water, but occasionally, particularly when in flocks, they fly at considerable heights. Flying flocks may be in single-line formation, in more or less asymmetrical V's, or without obvious formation. On land they walk rather awkwardly. When perched, they have a characteristic habit of often partly extending both wings, holding them stationary in that position or sometimes waving them gently.

Cormorants are fish-eaters. Extensive studies of the food of this species made by H.F. Lewis in eastern Canada revealed that it usually does little economic harm, however.

Brandt's Cormorant

Cormoran de Brandt
Phalacrocorax penicillatus (Brandt)
Total length: 71 to 89 cm
Plate 6

Range in Canada. Rather common winter visitant and local breeder on the coast of British Columbia. Breeds on small islands on west side of Vancouver Island, between Tofino and Ucluelet (Sartine Island, Sea Lion Rock, White Island, Starlight Reef, Great Bear Rock).

Throat pouch with a narrow finger of feathers extending forward from mid-throat onto throat pouch. Head never crested. *Adults*: Black with greenish or bluish iridescence. Throat pouch dull-blue. Small patch behind throat pouch pale-brown contrasting with rest of head and on shoulders. In nuptial plumage with long white hairlike feathers on sides of head. *Immatures*: Mainly dark brown (blackish on top of head, hindneck, rump, and tail) and with a very pale patch behind throat pouch.

Measurements. *Adult male*: wing, 272.5–284 (279.9); tail, 106.5–129 (116.2); exposed culmen, 68–71.5 (69.9); tarsus, 62.5–67 (65). *Adult female*: wing, 257.5–267.5 (262.8) mm.

Field Marks. A Pacific Coast species. The dull-blue throat pouch is often not discernible but is very different from the yellow one of the Double-crested Cormorant in all plumages. The small pale-brown area at the base of the bill is lacking in the Pelagic, a slightly smaller species with less heavy head and bill. In spring, Pelagics show a white flank patch when flying, which Brandt's never have.

Habitat. Coastal salt water, nesting and roosting on rocky islands.

Nesting. In colonies, usually on rocky islands. Nest of seaweed, moss, and grass. *Eggs*, usually 4; pale bluish-white.

Range. Breeds along the Pacific Coast from southern British Columbia to Baja California. Some winter in southern coastal British Columbia.

Pelagic Cormorant

Cormoran pélagique
Phalacrocorax pelagicus Pallas
Total length: 63.5 to 66 cm
Plate 6

Throat pouch small, the bare part much restricted. Bare skin on face and throat dull red. Head crested in nesting season. *Adults*: Mainly black with purplish iridescence on head and neck, greenish and purplish gloss on back. In nuptial plumage with a crest on forehead, another on crown; narrow white feathers on sides of neck; a white patch on each flank, but these are lost by early summer. *Immatures*: Pale sooty-brown, slightly paler below.

Measurements *(P. p. pelagicus)*. *Adult male*: wing, 271–290 (276.5); exposed culmen, 45–55 (50.2). *Adult female*: wing, 247–274 (260.7) mm (Palmer 1962).

Field Marks. In spring (February to July) shows white flank patches in flight, lacking in other Pacific Coast species. Its dull-red throat pouch is difficult to see but is very different from the yellow one of the Double-crested. It lacks the pale area behind the throat pouch shown by Brandt's and is smaller (with slenderer neck and bill) and glossier. *Voice*: On the breeding cliffs various groans, but usually the bird is silent.

Breeding Distribution of Pelagic Cormorant

Range in Canada. Common permanent resident along the British Columbia coast, nesting there.

Habitat. Coastal salt water. Reported to dive more deeply than other cormorants. Rests on sandbars, rocky islands, cliffs, logs, piling, etc.; for nesting, it tends to use the narrow ledges of precipitous cliffs more extensively than other cormorants.

Nesting. In colonies, often with other bird species. Nests on narrow ledges of steep cliffs facing the sea, on islands, and sometimes even on lighthouses; nest rather bulky, composed of seaweed, grass, sticks, and moss. *Eggs*, usually 3 or 4; pale bluish with chalky deposit, often nest-stained. Incubation averages 31 days, by both parents (G.F. van Tets *in* Drent and Guiguet 1961).

Range. The north Pacific from northeastern Siberia to Japan and southern China; Bering Sea; and from Alaska to Baja California.

Subspecies. (1) *Phalacrocorax pelagicus resplendens* Audubon breeds commonly along the south coast of British Columbia (near Victoria and for an undetermined distance northward). (2) *P. p. pelagicus* Pallas averages larger with a comparatively heavier bill, breeds on the Queen Charlotte Islands, and visits the coast of southern British Columbia in winter.

Red-faced Cormorant

[**Red-faced Cormorant**. Cormoran à face rouge. *Phalacrocorax urile* (Gmelin). Erroneously recorded (1945. P.A. Taverner, *Birds of Canada*, p. 59; 1927. Auk, vol. 44, no. 2, pp. 219–220). The writer has examined the specimen (NMC 4066, Departure Bay, B.C., 7 April 1910) on which rests the supposed evidence of occurrence in Canada of this Siberian and Alaskan species. It is unquestionably *P. auritus*.]

Family **Anhingidae**: Darters

Number of Species in Canada: 1

Long-necked, long-tailed fish-eating birds. They show affinities with cormorants in their totipalmate (all four toes joined by webs) feet, nostrils without outer openings, and their feathers which, while suitable for water contact, are by no means entirely waterproof. Unlike cormorants, the bill is sharply pointed for spearing fish which are taken by diving from the water surface, from overwater flight, or from a perch.

Anhinga

Anhinga d'Amérique
Anhinga anhinga (Linnaeus)
Total length: 86 to 91 cm
Figure 18

Figure 18
Anhinga

Status in Canada. Accidental in Ontario (specimens: Wellington, 7 September 1904; Garden River, about 1881).

Cormorant-like but much slenderer, with snakier neck, much longer tail, and unhooked, heron-like, sharply pointed bill. In adults, the outer webs of the two middle tail feathers are decidedly crimped. *Adult male*: Mainly black with greenish iridescence. Back and scapulars streaked and spotted with silvery grey; wing coverts white. Tail with brownish-grey tip. *Adult female*: Similar but head, neck, and breast brownish. *Immature*: Mainly brownish.

Range. Tropical and subtropical Americas.

Subspecies. *Anhinga anhinga leucogaster* (Vieillot).

Family **Fregatidae**:
Frigatebirds

Number of Species in Canada: 1

Frigatebirds are found throughout the tropical seas. They have a greater wingspread in proportion to their body weight than probably any other bird and are marvellous flyers. Facing the wind, they can remain in the air for long periods, as motionless as a child's kite. When feeding, they perform swift, ineffably graceful darts as they catch fish near the water surface or pursue gulls and terns, forcing them to give up their prey. They have extremely long forked tails, tiny feet, and rather long bills, both mandibles of which are decidedly hooked at the tip. They have a small throat pouch, which is capable of great distension.

Magnificent Frigatebird

(Man-o'-war-bird)

Frégate superbe
Fregata magnificens Mathews
Total length: 95 to 114 cm;
wingspread: 213 to 244 cm
Figure 19

Figure 19
Magnificent Frigatebird

Status in Canada. Accidental in Nova Scotia (Halifax Harbour, 16 October 1876; off Devil's Island, June 1891; Pennant Bay, 5 December 1932; Lower Wedgeport, 14 July 1949, and for several succeeding days; Freeport, 4 August 1949); Newfoundland (Bonavista Bay, about 1932); Quebec (a specimen taken at Île Dupas in September a few years prior to 1936 is said to have been examined by Victor Gaboriault but the specimen apparently cannot now be found; sight record: Godbout, 13 August 1884); Ontario (sight record: Port Rowan, 13 October 1949); British Columbia (photo record: Langara Island, 25 August 1981).

Bill rather long with both mandibles hooked. Tail very long, deeply forked. Feet and throat pouch small. *Adult male*: Black, with bronzy or purplish gloss on upper parts, scapulars lanceolate. *Adult female*: Similar but breast and upper belly white, lesser wing coverts greyish brown; rest of plumage duller and more brownish. *Immature*: Like adult female but head and neck white.

Field Marks. Large size combined with long narrow wings, long deeply forked tail (tail is often closed in gliding flight), and coloration, described above. Sometimes glides for long periods on motionless wings. Does not swim or sit on the water.

Range. In the Atlantic, from the Bahamas to coastal Brazil, the Cape Verde Islands and coast of Gambia; in the eastern Pacific from Baja California south to the Galapagos Islands, coastal Ecuador and Peru. Wanders to the coasts of southern United States.

Subspecies. *Fregata magnificens rothschildi* Mathews.

Order **Ciconiiformes:**
Herons, Storks, Ibises, and Allies

The long-legged, long-necked, short-tailed wading birds comprising this order feed in the shallow water of marshes, swamps, and shores. They have long, rather broad wings with rounded tips; rather long bills, straight in most species, curved in some; long, slender toes that are never completely webbed.

Family **Ardeidae:**
Herons and Bitterns

Number of Species in Canada: 12

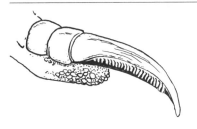

Figure 20
Middle toenail of Great Blue Heron

Wading birds with long legs, long necks, and short tails; rather long straight bills that taper to a point; and long, broad, round-tipped wings. Plumage rather long and loose. Crests and plumes are usually present in the breeding season. Small area in front of eyes (lores) is always bare. Toes are long and slender, with a small web connecting the base of the outer and middle ones, hind toes on same level as the others (not elevated); middle toenail pectinate (comblike) on inner border (see Figure 20). They fly with the neck doubled back against the shoulders and thus are easily separable in flight from cranes.

American Bittern

Butor d'Amérique
Botaurus lentiginosus (Rackett)
Total length: 61 to 86 cm
Plate 8

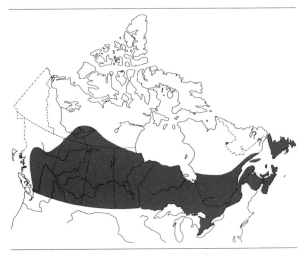

Breeding Distribution of American Bittern

Range in Canada. Breeds in central and southern interior British Columbia (probably north to Kispioux valley and Swan Lake; possibly Vancouver Island: Middle Quinsam Lake where present in the breeding season); southwestern Mackenzie (Great Slave Lake); Alberta; Saskatchewan; Manitoba (north to Churchill); Ontario (north to Moose Factory and Hudson Bay coast); Quebec (north to Fort-George, the

Adults: Upper parts yellowish brown with irregular small spots, bars, streaks, and freckles of darker browns and buffs. Yellowish streak over eye. Throat whitish with a brown stripe down its centre. Black streak down sides of neck. Breast, sides, and abdomen yellowish white broadly streaked with brown. Primaries brownish slate. Bill yellowish with blackish ridge. Legs and feet greenish yellow. *Immatures*: Similar to adults but without black stripe on sides of neck and more lightly marked generally.

Measurements. *Adult male*: wing, 259–275 (268.9); tail, 76.5–101 (90.2); exposed culmen, 70–86 (75.2); tarsus, 84.5–98 (89.5). *Adult female*: wing, 236–275 (244.8) mm.

Field Marks. Most likely to be confused with immature night-herons, but it is a generally more yellowish bird. In flight, its wing tips are darker than the rest of the wing. Its black neck-stripe, when seen, is diagnostic, but it is sometimes hard to see and is lacking in immatures; consequently its absence is not diagnostic. Its remarkable voice, once learned, is unmistakable. Rarely alights in trees. Night-Herons do so regularly. *Voice*: A hollow deep *pump-er-lunk*, repeated several times and heard most often in the evening or dawn of spring and early summer. At the height of the breeding season often heard any time of day, particularly in cloudy weather. It is audible for considerable distances. In flight, especially when startled, a croaking *ok-ok-ok-ok*; also a single harsh croak.

Habitat. Fresh and salt marshes, swamps, moist meadows, wet alder or willow thickets, less often drier fields.

Nesting. Nest, a platform of marsh vegetation in cattails, bulrushes, and similar marsh vegetation; occasionally in dry fields. *Eggs*, 4 to 6; olive brown or olive buff. Incubation period about 24 days (Mousley), by the female.

Range. Breeds from southern Canada south to southern California, southern Colorado, Missouri, western and central Texas, Pennsylvania,

Schefferville region, and the inner north shore of the Gulf of St. Lawrence; Anticosti and Madeleine islands); Newfoundland; New Brunswick; Prince Edward Island; and Nova Scotia. Recorded north to near Fort Norman, Mackenzie; Nueltin Lake, Keewatin; Grande rivière de la Baleine, Quebec; and Hamilton Inlet, Labrador.

Winters in southwestern British Columbia (Lulu Island, Ladner, Courtenay: rarely the Queen Charlotte Islands), and occasionally in extreme southern Ontario.

and Maryland. Winters from the middle and southern United States and southwestern British Columbia southward.

Remarks. In the evenings of late spring and early summer the deep hollow vocalizing of the American Bittern adds a pleasant mysteriousness to the marshlands of most parts of southern Canada. The "song" to some ears resembles the sucking sounds made by an old-fashioned water pump or those of a stake being driven into the mud by a wooden hammer; hence the bird's local names "Thunder Pump" and "Stake Driver."

The streaked breast and general coloration of this bittern blend perfectly with the marsh vegetation it inhabits. When alarmed it draws in its plumage tightly, points the bill straight up in the air, and "freezes." Thus, motionless, it is very difficult to see—an excellent example of protective coloration. If approached too closely, however, it springs awkwardly into the air with a rush of wings, dangling legs, and harsh croaks. Once in the air, it is a good flyer.

Most of this bittern's motions are deliberate. In capturing prey, however, the javelin-like beak is thrust out with flashlike speed. When used in self-defence, the beak also is a vicious weapon, capable of destroying a human eye. One jab has been known to repel a large steer (Tufts 1973).

This bittern does little harm and probably considerable good. In the marshes, it feeds on frogs, snakes, small fishes, crayfish, and other water animals. Sometimes it visits open fields to catch grasshoppers and mice.

Least Bittern

Petit Butor
Ixobrychus exilis (Gmelin)
Total length: 28 to 35.5 cm
Plate 8

Breeding Distribution of Least Bittern

Range in Canada. Breeds locally in southern Manitoba (Delta: nest with four eggs collected on 7 June 1949, by R.W. Sutton, in litt.); southern Ontario (north to near Sault Ste. Marie, Lake Nipissing, Ottawa); southern Quebec (Montréal, Saint-Lambert, Magog, possibly Québec); southern New Brunswick (Little River); and, rarely, Nova Scotia (Amherst Point Bird Sanctuary). In Nova Scotia, specimens have been taken at Upper Prospect, 16 March 1896; Cape Island, 25 April 1907; Little Hope Light, 1 September 1935; and the species has been reliably reported in summer near the Nova Scotia border (Squires 1952), but

Adult male: Top of head, back, and tail, black. Back of neck, larger wing coverts, and outer webs of inner secondaries, chestnut. Rest of wing coverts brownish yellow. Primaries slaty. Throat whitish. Sides of head, sides of neck, and under parts, pale buff with a blackish-brown patch on either side of breast. Wing lining yellowish white. Bill mostly yellow with dark ridge. Legs greenish. *Adult female*: Similar, but the blacks of the upper parts are mostly replaced by dark chestnut. Two buffy lines down back. Throat and under parts streaked with brown. *Immatures*: Similar to adult female, but feathers of back have buffy tips.

Colour Phase. An uncommon, local colour phase in which the creams and whites are replaced by chestnut. It was formerly thought to be a different species and was called Cory's Least Bittern, *Ixobrychus neoxena*.

Measurements. *Adult male*: wing, 111.5–115.3 (113.5); tail, 38.5–44 (43.9); exposed culmen, 39.5–47.5 (44.7); tarsus, 39–41 (40). *Adult female*: wing, 110–116 (113.2) mm.

Field Marks. Tiny size separates it from other herons. Its contrasting colour pattern is very different from that of the rails. *Voice*: A series of five or six low cooing sounds. When disturbed, a cackling *ca-ca-ca*.

Habitat. Cattail marshes and marshy vegetation of ponds or sluggish streams.

Nesting. In freshwater marshes. Nest, a rather frail structure built in and supported by a clump of marsh vegetation usually from 16 cm to 0.75 m above water. *Eggs*, usually 4 or 5; bluish white or greenish white. Incubation 17 to 18 days (M.W. Weller), by both sexes.

Range. From southern Canada and northern United States, south to the West Indies and through Mexico and Central America to Brazil and Paraguay. Winters from southern United States southward.

no proof of nesting in Nova Scotia is yet known. In Newfoundland three autumn records: St. John's, early October 1882, and 8 September 1953; off Cape St. Francis, 5 August 1933. Casual in southern Saskatchewan where an undated specimen was taken at Moon Lake (C.S. Houston, F.G. Bard, R.W. Nero, Blue Jay, vol. 16, no. 2, pp. 64–65), there is a sight record from Crane Lake; and British Columbia (Vernon, 30 July 1955; Vancouver, 16 June 1974). Old reports of a specimen taken at York Factory, northern Manitoba, cannot now be verified.

This diminutive heron remains mostly within the dense vegetation of the marshes. It is rather quiet and secretive. Consequently, for some parts of its range where it is thought to be rare or absent, it may be commoner than the records show.

Subspecies. *Ixobrychus exilis exilis* (Gmelin). There is a possibility that the British Columbia records might be referable to the race *hesperis*, which has not been identified in Canada.

Great Blue Heron

(Incorrectly "Crane")

Grand Héron
Ardea herodias Linnaeus
Total length: 108 to 132 cm
Plate 7

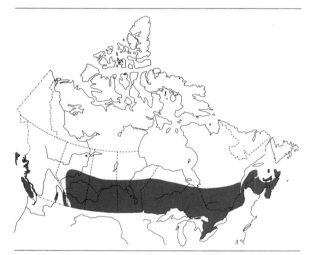

Breeding Distribution of Great Blue Heron

Range in Canada. Breeds in British Columbia (the coast from Vancouver Island to the Queen Charlotte Islands; and very locally in the interior at Enderby and along Kootenay River); Alberta (Pelican Lake and Lesser Slave Lake southward; also recently on Birch River at latitude 58°27′, longitude 112°17′ — John Kristensen in litt.); central and southern Saskatchewan (Churchill Lake, Suggi Lake); central and southern Manitoba (Talbot Lake, Stull River); central and southern Ontario (unnamed lake at 54°12′N, Moosonee, southward); southern Quebec (Basque Island, Gaspé, Madeleine Islands); New Brunswick; Prince Edward Island; and Nova Scotia.

Wanders farther northward in summer to southern Yukon (Carcross, Teslin); southern Keewatin (Nueltin Lake); northern Manitoba (Churchill); northern Ontario (Forts Severn and Albany); Hudson Bay, northern Quebec

Bill about 12.7 cm, rather stout at base tapering to a sharp tip. *Adults (breeding plumage)*: Head white with a broad black stripe on either side, extending from above the eye to the nape and projecting behind the head in a slender black crest. Neck greyish brown with a double row of black down the fore-neck. Lower neck and back with long slender plumes. Upper parts mainly greyish-blue. Under parts variously streaked and marked with black and white. Bill yellowish (to almost orange in breeding period), sometimes with a dusky ridge. Legs brownish green, often with reddish hue in mating season. *Immatures*: Similar but with entire crown dark-slate and with no crest or plumes.

Measurements *(A. h. herodias)*. *Adult male*: wing, 444–475.5 (463.1); tail, 171–188.5 (180); exposed culmen, 125–152 (143.1); tarsus, 171–186 (179.3). *Adult female*: wing, 444–459 (450) mm.

Field Marks. Our largest heron. Its colour and large size separate it from other Canadian herons. In the West, the Sandhill Crane is of similar size, but its plumage is plain grey without streaks, and adult cranes have a red bare area on the forehead. In flight, herons carry the neck doubled back with head against the shoulders; cranes carry the neck straight out. *Voice*: Under stress, various squawks and croaks; also a slightly goose-like *onk* but harsher.

Habitat. Feeds in and about open shallow water, either fresh or salt; edges of bays, streams, river margins, sloughs, lakes, ponds, ditches, mud flats, and marshes. Nests in deciduous, coniferous, and mixed woodland sometimes at considerable distances from water.

Nesting. Nests in various-sized colonies. Nest, a flattish structure of sticks usually in the upper strata of tall trees; sometimes in bushes or even on the ground where trees are wanting. Nests are repaired and used in successive years. *Eggs*, commonly 3 to 5, usually 4; pale greenish-blue. Incubation by both sexes lasts about 28 days (A.C. Bent), 26 to 27 days (Kees Vermeer). One brood annually.

Range. Southeastern Alaska east to the Gaspé Peninsula and Nova Scotia and south to Mexico, the West Indies, and Galapagos Islands. Winters from southern British Columbia and the northern United States south to Panama, Colombia, and Venezuela.

Subspecies. (1) *Ardea herodias herodias* Linnaeus breeds in eastern Canada and westward at least to Alberta. (2) *A. h. fannini* Chapman, a darker race, breeds on the Pacific Coast. In the interior of British Columbia few breeding records are known, but Munro and Cowan (1947) suggest that specimens from the Okanagan valley and Edgewood, perhaps wanderers from areas farther south, are referable to *A. h. treganzai* Court, a subspecies that has the neck and upper parts paler than in the two races known in Canada.

(Kuujjuaq); and Newfoundland. Accidental on southern Baffin Island (Cape Dorset). Winters commonly on the British Columbia coast, occasionally in the Maritimes and southern Ontario.

Remarks. This is the largest, most widely distributed, and most numerous heron in most parts of Canada. It is often mistakenly known as "crane," but it is not related to the cranes. Whether standing motionless or in stately slow-measured flight, this is among the most picturesque of birds. It is particularly numerous, especially in late summer, about the tidal bays and mud flats in parts of the Maritimes.

Its stilt-like legs enable it to wade well out in the water shallows. There, motionless and with infinite patience, it waits until a fish or frog ventures close by. A quick thrust of the long neck and spear-like bill captures the prey. When this is eaten, the bird again assumes its motionless posture. Often food is secured by slow stalking.

This heron eats fishes, frogs, salamanders, water snakes, large insects, including grasshoppers, and mice and other small rodents. Most of the fishes it takes are of little interest to man. Ordinarily it does not frequent trout streams, except where the occasional stream crosses an open meadow. At open pools of fish hatcheries it can be destructive, and where herons are common, such pools are best screened in. Otherwise it does little harm and indeed considerable good as a destroyer of water snakes, small rodents, and insects. Although alert and wary, it formerly was much persecuted by the thoughtless and uninformed. Today the federal Migratory Birds Convention Act makes it illegal to destroy this picturesque bird.

Great Egret
(Common Egret)

Grande Aigrette
Casmerodius albus (Linnaeus)
Total length: 88 to 107 cm
Plate 7

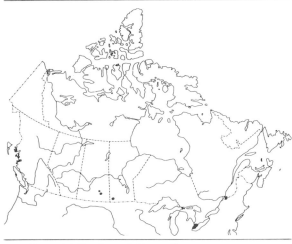

Breeding Distribution of Great Egret

Range in Canada. Breeds locally in southern Saskatchewan (Craven, Middle Quill Lake); Manitoba (Pipestone, Riding Mountain National Park); southern Ontario (Essex and Kent counties); and recently southern Quebec (Dickerson's Island).

An irregular non-breeding visitant to Quebec, New Brunswick, Nova Scotia, and Prince Edward Island. Recorded west to southwestern British Columbia (Cowichan Bay, Pritchard, mouth of Sooke River, Pitt Meadows) and Alberta (Cowley, Banff, and near Edmonton). Recorded north to northern

No crest. *Adults*: Plumage all white. In the breeding season a cascade of slender plumes sweeps down from the back and beyond the tail. Bill orange-yellow. Legs and feet black. *Immatures*: Similar but without plumes.

Field Marks. A very large white heron, almost as big as the Great Blue Heron, with *yellow* bill, black legs and feet. Snowy Egrets and immature Little Blue Herons are also white but have dark bills and are much smaller. The Cattle Egret is also a white heron with a yellow bill, but it is very much smaller and its stockier build is obvious. *Voice*: A harsh rattling croak.

Nesting. Nests usually in colonies, sometimes with other species. Nest, of sticks, usually in a tree at various heights. *Eggs*, 3 to 5; pale bluish-green. Incubation period (in Old World): 25 to 26 days.

Range. Inhabits all continents. In the New World, breeds from Oregon, southern Idaho, southern Saskatchewan, southern Manitoba, southern Minnesota, extreme southern Ontario, and New Jersey south through the West Indies, Mexico, Central and South America. Winters from southern United States southward.

Subspecies. *Casmerodius albus egretta* (Gmelin).

Remarks. In the southern United States this graceful large heron is common. In the early 1900s it was sadly reduced in numbers by hunters who killed it for its long plumes for the millinery trade. Wise laws now make it illegal in both the United States and Canada to destroy it. Under this protection it has regained much of its original numbers and range.

Ontario (Winisk), central-eastern Quebec (Petit Mécatina River), and Newfoundland (Harbour Main, Pass Island, Bell Island).

Intermediate Egret

[**Intermediate Egret**. Aigrette intermédiaire. *Egretta intermedea* (Wagler). Hypothetical. A specimen allegedly collected at Burrard Inlet, British Columbia, might actually have been secured elsewhere.]

Little Egret

Aigrette garzette
Egretta garzetta (Linnaeus)
Total length: 55 to 68 cm

Status in Canada. Accidental. A female was collected at Flatrock, Conception Bay, Newfoundland, on 8 May 1954, by Robert Emerson and was donated to the National Museum of Canada by L.M. Tuck. One also at Bay Roberts, Newfoundland (photograph taken 30 May 1983 by Bruce Mactavish leaves no doubt of identification). A single very wary bird, apparently of this species, appeared in Quebec in spring 1980: first on 14 May at Rimouski; on 17 May at Bic; and on 19 May it was at Cacouna where it remained until at least 6 September and where it was seen by many observers and was photographed.

Adults in breeding plumage: Plumage all white. Head with two very long (140 to 160 mm), extremely narrow, pointed crest-feathers. Upper breast with a number of longer feathers very narrow at tip but broad and loose at base. Back with numerous loose plumes. Bill and lores black, base of lower mandible greenish grey. Legs black, toes (in nominate race) yellow. *Adults in autumn and winter*: Similar, but lack head plumes, and the plumes of the back are fewer and shorter.

This Old World species resembles the Snowy Egret. It lacks the yellow lores of the Snowy Egret and in the breeding season possesses two very long, narrow crest-feathers, which are quite unlike any crest-feathers of the Snowy.

Range. Southern Europe and Asia, Africa, Sumatra, Java, and Australia. Accidental in North America.

Subspecies. *Egretta garzetta garzetta* (Linnaeus).

Snowy Egret

Aigrette neigeuse
Egretta thula (Molina)
Total length: 50 to 68 cm
Plate 8

Status in Canada. Rare non-breeding wanderer to British Columbia (Pitt Meadows, Victoria); Alberta (Pincher Creek, Sandy Lake); Saskatchewan (sight records: Good Spirit Lake; near Craven; Qu'Appelle valley); Manitoba (sight record: Steinbach); Ontario (rare in south, northward to near Uhthoff, Kingston; accidental north to mouth of Attawapiskat River); Quebec (Rigaud, Berthierville, Forillon National Park); New Brunswick (Grand Manan, Saint John. In 1973, up to 12 reported in province); Nova Scotia (Halifax, Windsor, Lower Clark's Harbour); Newfoundland (St. John's; Trepassey, Traytown).

Adults in breeding plumage: White, with crest of loosely webbed feathers and long filamentous plumes (shed later) growing from back and forming a train over back and tail. Bill black. Lores yellow. Legs black, toes yellow. *Immatures*: Similar but without plumes and more or less yellowish up the back of the legs.

Measurements (*E. t. thula*). *Adult male*: wing, 240–289 (259.9); culmen, 74–89 (83.3); tarsus, 83–106 (97.1). *Adult female*: wing, 233–273 (251.2) mm (A.M. Bailey).

Field Marks. A small white heron with *black bill, black legs*, and *yellow feet*. The black bill separates it from the similar-sized Cattle Egret and the much larger Great Egret. The uniformly coloured bill differs from the two-coloured bill of immature Little Blue Herons.

Habitat. Margins of both fresh and salt water of marshes, ponds, bays, wet meadows; sometimes fields and beaches.

Range. Breeds from southern United States (along the Atlantic Coast north to New Jersey) south through the West Indies and Central America to South America (Chile and Argentina). Wanders farther northward, especially in late summer. Winters from southern United States southward.

Subspecies. Eastern Canadian specimens are referable to *Egretta thula thula* (Molina). British Columbia and Alberta material probably belongs to the larger western subspecies *E. t. brewsteri* Thayer and Bangs but the writer has not examined western specimens.

Little Blue Heron

Aigrette bleue
Egretta caerulea (Linnaeus)
Total length: 50 to 74 cm
Plate 8

Status in Canada. Rare non-breeding spring, summer, and autumn wanderer to eastern Canada, most records being for late summer and autumn. Recorded north to southern British Columbia (rarely: Abbotsford); Saskatchewan (Last Mountain Lake, Arcola, Yorkton); Manitoba (near Hodgson); southern Ontario (north to French River, Sudbury District; and Winisk); Quebec (Moisie Bay, August 1928); southern Labrador (L'Anse-au-Loup, 23 May 1900); Newfoundland (various records June to December); Nova Scotia (specimens taken as early as 18 March as late as 23 October; sight records to mid-November); New Brunswick (recorded rarely from March to early December); and Prince Edward Island (Ellerslie, 20 August 1958; Brackley, 29 April 1962).

Adults: Head (crested with a few long feathers from nape) and neck dark purplish-red. Body dark slaty-blue. Numerous plumes extend down back and beyond tail. Lower neck with a tuft of elongated feathers. Eye yellow or greyish. Bill black at tip, bluish at base. Legs and feet bluish black. *Immatures*: Mainly white in first year but with variable small amounts of slate colour on wing tips. Bill black-tipped, pale-bluish basally. Legs dark greenish. Immatures eventually acquire a patchy white-and-blue aspect. They wear this during much of their second year.

Field Marks. The blackish-looking adults might be confused with the somewhat smaller Green-backed Heron, but the latter has yellow legs. The white immatures somewhat resemble egrets, but the dark bill is different from the yellow bill of the large Great Egret or the Cattle Egret, and the greenish legs are unlike those of the Snowy Egret. Older immatures have a patchy white-and-blue aspect that is unmistakable.

Habitat. Margins of lakes and ponds, marshes. More often on fresh than on salt water.

Range. Breeds in the southern Atlantic and Gulf states, north along the coast to Massachusetts (casually), and south through Central America to Peru and Uruguay. Wanders northward occasionally to southeastern Canada.

Subspecies. *Egretta caerulea caerulea* (Linnaeus).

Tricolored Heron

(Louisiana Heron)

Aigrette tricolore
Egretta tricolor (Müller)
Total length: 63.5 cm
Plate 8

Status in Canada. Accidental in Alberta (photo record: near Bashaw, 22 May 1981); Manitoba (photo record: Patricia Beach, 18 April 1976); Ontario (photo record: Rondeau Provincial Park, 21 April 1974; also various sight records); Quebec (photo record: Paspébiac, 18 May 1976; sight records: Île-du-Moine, 16 June 1974 and 5 June 1976); New Brunswick (specimen records: near Nauwigewauk, April 1895; Little River, April about 1920; Saint John, 13 April 1970; also several sight records); Nova Scotia (specimen record: Brier Island, 14 May 1978; photo records: Cape Sable Island, 15–17 April 1972; Seal Island, 18 May 1975; Sable Island, 15 May 1979; also sight records); Newfoundland (one found dead at Rushoon in June 1982).

Adults: Upper parts mainly dark blue. Nape and hind-neck feathers longer with a purplish sheen (in breeding plumage with a white occipital crest). Throat whitish, more or less tinged with chestnut, this continuing in a narrow line down front of neck. Lower back and rump whitish, but in the breeding season this is obscured by brownish-grey plumes, which reach to or beyond the tail. Neck and breast bluish-slate, on the breast mixed with purplish feathers. Abdomen and under wing coverts white. *Immatures*: Mainly dull brown or bluish above, with chestnut neck, white throat and abdomen. In the field, the white abdomen contrasting with dark breast and upper parts makes recognition rather easy.

Range. Baja California, the Gulf Coast of United States, and southern Maryland south to the West Indies and northern South America.

Subspecies. *Egretta tricolor ruficollis* Gosse.

Cattle Egret

Héron garde-bœufs
Bubulcus ibis (Linnaeus)
Total length: 48 to 51 cm
Plate 7

Range in Canada. A very recent arrival, first known occurrence in 1952. Breeds in southern Ontario (first nested in 1962 at Luther Marsh and Presqu'ile Provincial Park. Now nests sparsely from Pelee Island northeast to Kingston) and southern Saskatchewan (recently: one nest at Old Wives Lake in 1981). Wanders north to Thunder Bay and Ottawa and in Quebec north to Taschereau.

A spring, summer, and autumn wanderer to other parts of southern Canada; to date found more frequently in the East but with increasing frequency in the West, particularly in British Columbia.

First occurrence records known to the writer for the following provinces are: Newfoundland (Grand Banks, about 31 October 1952; St. Anthony, 27 October 1964); Nova Scotia (East Sable River, 23 November 1957); New Brunswick (near St. Stephen, 29 April 1961); Quebec (Lake Saint-Pierre, 15 August 1960); Ontario (Port Rowan, 3 May 1956; Lake St. Clair, 26 May 1956); Manitoba (near Brandon, 27 May 1961); Saskatchewan (near Eyebrow, 14 June 1974); Alberta (near Iron Springs, 12 November 1964); British Columbia (Sooke, 19 November 1973); Mackenzie (Fort Smith, 26 May 1971).

Adults: In breeding plumage mainly white with elongated pinkish-buff feathers on crown, back, and lower neck. Bill yellow, orange, or reddish. Legs greenish yellow to dull reddish. In winter, similar but buffy areas much paler, less extensive, and elongated feathers much shorter. Bill yellow; legs greenish, dark brown, or blackish. *Immatures*: Plumage all white, the feathers of crown, back, and lower neck not elongated.

Measurements. *Adult male*: wing, 231–251 (241.7); tail, 86–94.5 (91); exposed culmen, 53–63 (57); tarsus, 72–87 (77.2). *Adult female*: wing, 230–247 (239.5); tail, 81–93 (87.9); exposed culmen, 50–60 (55.2); tarsus, 70–78 (73.1) mm (adapted from Friedmann).

Field Marks. A small, stocky, mainly white heron with short neck and heavy chin. The buffy areas of adults, when visible, distinguish the species from other white herons ordinarily found in Canada. The Cattle Egret's yellow bill separates it from the slightly larger Snowy Egret and immature Little Blue Herons. Our only other white heron with a yellow bill is the Great Egret, an obviously very much larger bird with long neck and legs. Cattle Egrets often associate with grazing cows in pastures, but this habit is sometimes shared by the Snowy Egret.

Habitat. Forages frequently on grassland, often associating with cattle, whose grazing activities stir up insects, which form a large proportion of its food; also found in marshes.

Nesting. Usually in bushy shrubbery or low in a tree. Nest is of twigs, grasses, and leaves. *Eggs*, 4 to 6; very pale green or blue. Incubation period 22 to 26 days, average 23.7 days (D. Blaker), by both sexes.

Range. Widely distributed in the Old World, but only recently became established in the New World (noted in Surinam between 1877 and 1882 and in British Guiana in 1911–1912). It was first collected in North America on 23 April 1952, at Wayland, Massachusetts, but evidence suggests it appeared in Florida in the early 1940s. In 1957 it was breeding in Florida, Louisiana, and North Carolina. By 1962, it was nesting in Canada (southern Ontario).

Subspecies. *Bubulcus ibis ibis* (Linnaeus).

Green-backed Heron

(Green Heron)

Héron vert
Butorides striatus (Linnaeus)
Total length: 40.6 to 55.8 cm
Plate 7

Breeding Distribution of Green-backed Heron

Range in Canada. Local summer resident. Breeds in southwestern British Columbia (recently and locally: near Fort Langley, Dun-

Adults: Top of head and crest, black with greenish gloss. Sides of head and whole neck, rich chestnut. Throat and stripe down front of neck, white with brown streaks. Back glossy green with elongated bluish-grey plumes. Wing coverts glossy green, finely edged with buff. Belly bluish grey. Eye yellow. Bill greenish black, paler on lower mandible, yellowish at base. Legs and feet yellow. *Immatures*: Similar but plumes wanting; under parts are whitish, heavily streaked with brown. Bill and legs duller and paler than in adults.

Measurements *(B. s. virescens)*. *Adult male*: wing, 176.5–186.5 (181.9); tail, 60.5–70 (65.4); exposed culmen, 56.5–64 (60.5); tarsus, 51–53.5 (52). *Adult female*: wing, 171.5–178 (175.7) mm.

Field Marks. Small size, dark colour (looks blackish at a distance), and yellow legs combine to distinguish it. Back looks bluish in certain lights, sometimes causing confusion with adult Little Blue Heron, which, however, has dark legs. When nervous, it raises crest and twitches tail. *Voice* A harsh, explosive *keow*. Various clucks, squawks, and grunts.

Habitat. Edges of water, such as sluggish streams, ponds, and marshes sheltered by bushes and trees; alder thickets on drowned land.

Nesting. Usually nests are solitary but sometimes are in small colonies. Nest, a rather flimsy structure of sticks, generally 3 to 6 m up in a tree; sometimes on the ground. *Eggs*, usually 4 or 5; greenish or greenish blue. Incubation about 20 days (E.G. Cooley), by both parents.

can); southern Ontario (Barrie, Ottawa, perhaps North Bay); southern Quebec (Papineauville, Rigaud, Montréal, Saint-Mathieu); and southern New Brunswick (rare but eggs were collected many years ago at Washademoak).

Has been recorded outside its known breeding range in southern Manitoba (sight records: Brandon, Turtle Mountain Provincial Park, Delta Beach); northern Ontario (specimen: Moosonee, 18 August 1974); Quebec (Upper Razade, Rimouski); Newfoundland, (Harricott, St. John's, Port au Port); and Nova Scotia (Lawrencetown, Westport, Prospect). Casual in Saskatchewan (photo records: Regina, 20 May 1975, and 28–31 May 1979; also sight record for Saskatoon, 8 September 1977).

Range. Southwestern British Columbia, Nevada, Texas, central Minnesota, southern Ontario, and southern New Brunswick south to the West Indies, Central America, and Colombia. Winters from southern United States southward.

Subspecies. *Butorides striatus virescens* (Linnaeus) is the only race known to occur in eastern Canada. Undoubtedly, however, the British Columbia records refer to the western race *B. s. anthonyi* (Mearns) but I have not examined specimens.

Black-crowned Night-Heron

Bihoreau à couronne noire
Nycticorax nycticorax (Linnaeus)
Total length: 58 to 71 cm
Plate 7

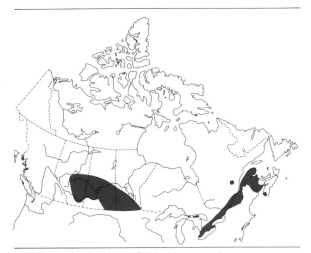

Breeding Distribution of Black-crowned Night-Heron

Range in Canada. Locally distributed spring, summer, and autumn resident, breeding locally in Alberta (Lower Thérien Lake south to Pakowki Lake, Brooks, and Strathmore); southern Saskatchewan (Prince Albert, Yorkton, Moose Mountain, Qu'Appelle valley, Deep Lake, and near Davidson); southern Manitoba (southern Lake Manitoba, southern Lake Winnipeg, Coulter); southern Ontario (Pelee Island, Port Weller, Luther Marsh, possibly Ottawa); southern Quebec (Montréal, Lake Saint-Pierre, Basque Island, Laterrière, Saint-Anne-de-la-Pocatière; probably near Gaspé); New Brunswick (Tracadie, Woodstock, Nantucket Island, Long Island); and Nova Scotia (locally: Outer Island). Uncommon visitor to Prince Edward Island, and rarely to British Columbia (Summerland). Has wandered north to central Quebec (Lake Mistassini, 6 August 1885 and Madeleine Islands) and Newfoundland (Come-by-Chance, 17 March 1947).

Bill, neck, and legs stout. No long plumes on back. *Adults*: Crown and back black with greenish gloss. Forehead white. Two to four slender long white feathers extending back from hind-head. Neck, wings, rump, and tail grey. Under parts white, tinged (except throat) with grey. Bill blackish. Legs and feet yellow to reddish. *Immatures*: Upper parts greyish brown with streaks of buffy white, and with spots of white on wings. Outer edge of primaries often tinged with rusty. Neck and under parts white, heavily streaked with brown.

Measurements *(N. n. hoactli). Adult male*: wing, 295–324 (308.5); tail, 118–125 (122.8); exposed culmen, 75.5–79.5 (78.1); tarsus, 81–84 (82.8). *Adult female*: wing, 289–307.5 (297.5) mm.

Field Marks. Rather stout with relatively heavy neck and short legs. The contrasting black back and all-white under parts identify the adult. Immatures look somewhat like the American Bittern but lack its yellowish tendency in general colour and the black streak down side of neck; the wing tip of this heron is not more blackish than the rest of the wing. This heron often alights in trees; the bittern very rarely does so. Immatures are very difficult to distinguish in the field from young Yellow-crowned Night-Herons (see following species). *Voice*: In flight, a single characteristic *kwok*. In breeding colonies, various squawks.

Habitat. Salt- and freshwater marshes, tidal estuaries, mud flats, edges of lakes, ponds, and sluggish streams, sometimes fields. Roosts and nests in trees.

Nesting. In colonies. Nest of sticks, usually in trees, occasionally in bushes, rarely on the ground. *Eggs*, usually 3 to 5; pale bluish-green. Incubation by both sexes, 24 to 26 days (A.O. Gross). One brood yearly.

Range. Widely distributed in both New and Old World. In New World from Washington, southern Idaho, and southern Canada south through the West Indies, Central and South America to northern Chile and central Argentina.

Subspecies. *Nycticorax nycticorax hoactli* (Gmelin).

Remarks. As its name implies, this stocky, short-legged heron is active at night. During the daylight hours it is more inclined to roost in trees. About sunset and in the gathering dusk it makes its steady way on broad wings to its feeding marshes. Often the characteristic flight calls, a throaty *qwock*, serve to direct one's eyes to its dim silhouette. It is not entirely nocturnal and crepuscular, however, for in areas where it is common it not infrequently is active during the daylight hours, particularly when the weather is dull. It feeds largely on fishes but takes also frogs, crayfish and other crustacea, and small rodents.

Yellow-crowned Night-Heron

Bihoreau violacé
Nycticorax violaceus (Linnaeus)
Total length: 55.8 to 71 cm
Plate 7

Status in Canada. Reported unsatisfactorily to have bred formerly at East Sister Island, west end of Lake Erie, Ontario, where apparently a nest was discovered on 23 May 1954 (J.L. Baillie, 1954. Audubon Field-Notes, vol. 8, no. 4, p. 310). Otherwise a rare wanderer to southern Manitoba (specimen: St. François Xavier, 7 May 1959; photo records: Oak Hammock, 16 August 1978 and Winnipeg, 15 May 1963; and several sight records); southern Ontario (Toronto, 15 August 1898; near Kitchener, 26 April 1954; Ottawa, 28 April 1970); southern Quebec (Île-du-Moine and Madeleine Islands); southern New Brunswick (Grand Manan, 2 April 1931; Saint John, May 1973); Nova Scotia (Cape Island, late March 1902; near Wolfville, 13 September 1932, and 28 July and 12 August 1937; Cole Harbour, 14 September 1925; McNab Island, 28 September 1919); and Newfoundland (Petites, about 26 March 1940; also a specimen with no data other than Newfoundland). Sight records for Saskatchewan (Lebret) and Prince Edward Island (Brackley Marsh).

Adults: Top of head, two long crest feathers, and white patch on side of face tinged with yellow. Feathers of back black broadly margined with grey. Flight feathers slate. Breast and belly grey. Bill black. Legs and feet yellow. *Immatures*: Very similar to immature Black-crowned Night-Heron but darker (more slaty, less brownish). Crown slightly darker than back. Flight feathers slate with no traces of rust, which is often present in the Black-crown. In the Yellow-crown, the tarsus is longer than the combined length of middle toe and nail (about equal in the Black-crown).

Measurements. *Adult male*: wing, 281–300 (294); tail, 102.0–118.7 (109.2); culmen (from base), 64.5–75.6 (70.9); tarsus, 93.6–106.2 (99.4). *Adult female*: wing, 271–305 (290) mm (A. Wetmore).

Field Marks. Stocky build, white cheek patch, and streaked back characterize the adults. Immatures very difficult to separate from young Black-crowns in the field. In flight the longer legs of the Yellow-crown extend the feet well beyond the tail. Under excellent close-range conditions, the somewhat darker general colour and the slightly stouter bill may be discerned. Immatures might be confused with the American Bittern, but they lack its rich brown colouring and its black line down the side of the neck. Voice quite similar to that of the Black-crown.

Nesting. Usually in small to large colonies; sometimes single pairs. Nest is of sticks, in trees or bushes. *Eggs*, 2 to 6, usually 3 to 5; pale bluish-green.

Range. Breeds from southern United States (and north along the Atlantic seaboard to Massachusetts and sporadically north to Indiana, Ohio, and perhaps extreme southern Ontario), south through the West Indies, Central America, and northern South America.

Subspecies. *Nycticorax violaceus violaceus* (Linnaeus).

Family **Threskiornithidae**: Ibises and Spoonbills

Number of Species in Canada: 3

Heron-like birds mostly with slender, long, downcurved bill. Upper mandible has a deep groove extending along both sides almost to the tip. The family is distributed widely in the warmer parts of the world.

White Ibis

Ibis blanc
Eudocimus albus (Linnaeus)
Total length: 61 to 68.5 cm
Plate 8

Status in Canada. Accidental in Ontario (specimens: Clayton, 13 October 1955; Long Point, summer 1965. Sight record: Point Pelee, 27 September 1970); Quebec (specimen: Nicolet, September 1934); Nova Scotia (specimen: Outer Island, 15 July 1959). Sight records for Newfoundland (near Cape Broyle and Ramea).

Bill long, slender, downcurved. *Adults*: White except the tips of four wing-primaries, which are black. Bill, legs, and bare skin in front of eye, orange to red. *Immatures*: Head, neck, and back brownish streaked with white. Rump, breast, and abdomen white.

Field Marks. Adults are white heron-like birds with narrowly black wing-tips, a long downcurved red or orange bill, and a reddish face. Wood Storks also are white but with a black tail, a black area along the hind part of the spread wing, and dark bill. Immature White Ibises differ from young Glossy and White-faced ibises in having a white rump and white under parts.

Range. From southern United States south to the West Indies, Peru, and Venezuela.

Scarlet Ibis

[**Scarlet Ibis**. Ibis rouge. *Eudocimus ruber* (Linnaeus). Plate 8. Hypothetical. One competently observed in Point Pelee National Park, Ontario, 11 September to 2 October 1937, by G.M. Stirrett (1941. Canadian Field-Naturalist, vol. 55, no. 1, p. 13) and others in other parts of the country, almost certainly escaped from captivity.]

Glossy Ibis

Ibis falcinelle
Plegadis falcinellus (Linnaeus)
Total length: 55.8 to 63.5 cm
Plate 8

Status in Canada. Rare wanderer to Ontario (some earlier records: Hamilton, two specimens collected, May 1857; Lake Simcoe, two collected, autumn 1828; Lake St. Clair, sight record, 23 May 1954; records north to Georgian Bay and Kingston); Quebec (Montréal, specimen taken 27 May 1900; Île aux Grues, 17 September 1956; Missisquoi Bay, sight record of two, 14 May 1956; specimen: Saint-Paul-du-Nord, 15 May 1970); Prince Edward Island (several reported, August 1878); Nova Scotia (Pictou County, specimen taken about 1865; Pictou, two taken from small flock about 1910; White Point Beach, one collected from flock of seven, 10 May 1946); New Brunswick (specimen: St. Andrews, 25 April 1965 and various sight records again in 1966, 1967, 1968, 1972, and 1973); and Newfoundland (Cape Broyle, sight record of six by Stuart Peters, 25 April 1956; Torbay, flock of seven, 24 and 26 May 1958, by L.M. Tuck; specimen taken at Cappahayden, 10 October 1958).

Bill slender, long, downcurved with a groove along either side. Skin around and in front of eye, bare. *Adults*: Mainly rich chestnut with greenish and purplish iridescence on crown, back, rump, tail, and wings. Bare skin in front of eye bluish. *Immatures*: Head and neck greyish brown or brownish black streaked with white. Upper parts with greenish gloss. Under parts dull brownish-grey.

Measurements. *Adult male*: wing, 256.5–278 (268.6); tail, 93.5–104.5 (99.9); exposed culmen, 128.5–148 (134.3); tarsus, 103.5–112.5 (107.2). *Adult female*: wing, 240.5–249 (244.8) mm.

Field Marks. The long evenly downcurved bill obviates confusion with all but the curlews and other ibises. The Glossy Ibis is obviously darker (looks black at a distance) and larger than any curlew. It closely resembles the White-faced Ibis, but adults of the latter in breeding plumage have a narrow white margin at the front of the face. In immature plumages the two cannot be safely separated in the field.

Range. In the New World, from southeastern United States (north to New Jersey and Virginia) to Cuba and Hispaniola. Found also in southern Europe, southern Asia, Africa, and Australia.

Subspecies. *Plegadis falcinellus falcinellus* (Linnaeus).

White-faced Ibis

(White-faced Glossy Ibis)

Ibis à face blanche
Plegadis chihi (Vieillot)
Total length: 55.8 to 63.5 cm
Plate 8

Status in Canada. Casual straggler to British Columbia (an immature collected in summer 1902, at Sardis; photo record of two near Cranbrook, May 1968; sight record near Saanich, Vancouver Island, 24 May 1982); Alberta (photos of several at Pakowki Lake on 3 July 1975, where it may nest. Photo record of two at Frank Lake on 11 May 1975); Saskatchewan (sight records only: near Stalwart, 29 May 1976; Valeport, 13 October 1976); Manitoba (two sight records: Oak Hammock Marsh, St. Ambroise Beach).

Adults in breeding plumage: Like the Glossy Ibis but with a narrow whitish area extending from forehead to behind eye and down along base of bill to the throat (absent in autumn and winter). Bare skin in front of eye reddish. *Immatures*: Very similar to the immature Glossy Ibis, but head and neck average slightly paler brown.

Range. From central California, eastern Oregon, Colorado, Nebraska, southwestern Louisiana, and Florida (locally), south to Argentina and Chile.

Family **Ciconiidae:**
Storks

Number of Species in Canada: 1

Long-legged heron-like birds, their bills stout at the base tapering to the tip. In the Wood Stork, the bill is decurved near the tip (see Figure 21). The family is widely distributed in the world, and the Common Stork, *Ciconia ciconia*, of the Old World is probably the most familiar species.

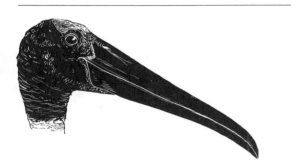

Figure 21
Head of Wood Stork

Wood Stork

(formerly Wood Ibis)

Tantale d'Amérique
Mycteria americana Linnaeus
Total length: 89 to 114 cm
Figure 21

Status in Canada. Casual or accidental visitant. Northern British Columbia (specimen: Telegraph Creek, 15 September 1970). Southern Ontario (near Simcoe, November 1892; Glengarry County, 2 August 1948; Kingston, September 1954; Hamilton, 9 November 1950; Dorcas Bay: desiccated specimen found in 1965; also Thorndale and Algonquin Provincial Park). New Brunswick (near Saint John East, 3 June 1911).

Bill very stout at base, tapered, downcurved near tip. *Adults*: Head and part of neck bare, dark grey or blackish grey. Plumage mainly white. Flight feathers greenish black. Tail bluish black. Legs blackish. *Immatures*: Similar but head and neck more or less feathered. Plumage greyish, with less green in the black of the flight feathers.

Field Marks. A larger white heron-like bird, with black flight feathers and tail and long stout bill, downcurved at tip. Flies with neck outstretched like a crane, showing a large amount of black along entire hind edge of spread wing. The long, trailing legs separate it from the White Pelican. On the ground the combination of the colour pattern, the heavy downcurved bill, and the dark bare head and neck make it unmistakable.

Range. Southern United States to South America.

Order **Phoenicopteriformes:** Flamingos

Flamingos are large, long-legged, long-necked wading birds, mostly pinkish in coloration with black flight feathers. Their large abruptly down-bent bill is different from that of other birds and is remarkably specialized for capturing the crustaceans, insects, and fishes that make up their diet. Because of this and other anatomical peculiarities, ornithologists have long differed over how to classify flamingos and they are now placed in an order of their own.

Family **Phoenicopteridae:** Flamingos

Number of Species in Canada: hypothetical

The six species of the world are mainly tropical and most, if not all, occurrences in Canada are probably escapees from captivity. Most of our records concern the Greater Flamingo *(P. ruber)*. Records of the South American *P. chilensis* are certainly based on escaped individuals and have no place in the Canadian avifauna.

Greater Flamingo

[**Greater Flamingo**. Flamant rose. *Phoenicopterus ruber* Linnaeus. Hypothetical. Single specimens have been captured in Newfoundland (Woodstock, 7 November 1977); Nova Scotia (Cape John, 15 October 1969); New Brunswick (Dorchester, November 1973); Quebec (Île aux Grues, 16 September 1972); Ontario (Dorion, 20–22 October 1978); and British Columbia (Aleza Lake, 23 September 1969). There is no way of ascertaining that any of these were wild birds and not escapees from captivity. However, the Nova Scotian specimen is said to retain the rich coloration characteristic of wild birds and it was first noted in Nova Scotia shortly after a hurricane that originated in the Bahamas. The Newfoundland specimen also was richly coloured. A 1973 Saskatchewan specimen is known to have been an escapee from a zoo and two Ontario records in autumn 1978 at Thunder Bay and Prince Edward County, respectively, are almost certainly escapees. Several flamingos, photographed in Quebec in 1981, have proved to be the South American *P. chilensis*, certainly escapees.]

Order **Anseriformes:**
Screamers, Swans, Geese, and Ducks

This order contains two families: (1) the widely distributed waterfowl family Anatidae (Swans, Geese, and Ducks) and (2) the Anhimidae (Screamers) in which there are three species, all confined to South America.

Family **Anatidae:**
Swans, Geese, and Ducks

Number of Species in Canada: 49

Water birds with lamellate, flattened (except in mergansers), round-tipped bill; narrow pointed wings; usually (not always), short tail; short to medium legs set rather far apart; four toes, the front ones webbed, the hind one slightly elevated and free. They have dense, waterproof plumage heavily underlain with down. Although swans, geese, and ducks appear superficially to be very different, they are similar in general structure and behaviour, thus are all included in one family.

Subfamily **Anserinae:**
Whistling-Ducks, Swans, and Geese

In species of this group plumages of adult male and female are similar and the pair bond tends to be relatively permanent. The tarsi are reticulated.

Tribe **Dendrocygnini:**
Whistling-Ducks

Smallish, rather long-legged, long-necked waterfowl, somewhat gooselike in shape. Feet are large with sharp claws. They differ from geese in their unducklike whistled vocalizations which give them their name. The eight species are tropical or subtropical.

Fulvous Whistling-Duck

(Fulvous Tree Duck)

Dendrocygne fauve
Dendrocygna bicolor (Vieillot)
Total length: 52 cm
Plate 9

Status in Canada. Casual visitant to British Columbia (specimens: 5 shot from flock of 11 near Alberni, September 1905; sight record: 100 Mile House); Ontario (specimens: Frenchman Bay, 27 November 1962; Mitchell Bay, 8 December 1960; photo record: Niagara R.M., 20 August 1962); Quebec (specimens: 6 shot by hunter from flock of 25, autumn 1955; specimen near Montmagny, 3 November 1973; sight record: Thurso); New Brunswick (specimens: Grand Manan: one shot from flock of 21, 4 November 1961; near Evansdale, 5 of 6 shot by hunters, 21 November 1961); Nova Scotia (specimen: Outer Island, 15 January 1976); and Prince Edward Island (photo record: Little Tignish Run, 17 August 1975).

Adults (sexes alike): Legs long for a duck, reaching beyond tail. Hind-toe much elongated. Tarsus reticulated in front. Mainly plain cinnamon or fulvous in coloration with reddish-brown crown; blackish line down back of neck; front and sides of neck dull white streaked with brown; wing coverts mainly chestnut; flanks with creamy-white stripes; back and wings dark brown with many rust-tipped feathers; upper tail coverts creamy white. Bill slaty grey. Legs bluish grey. *Immatures*: Similar but with little chestnut on wings.

Range. Southern United States south to Mexico; from Panama to the Guianas, and central Brazil to northern Argentina; also eastern Africa, India, and Ceylon.

Subspecies. *Dendrocygna bicolor helva* Wetmore and Peters.

Tribe **Cygnini**:
Swans

Large graceful waterfowl with very long necks, a narrow patch of bare skin in front of eye. In North American species the adults have all-white plumage. There are seven species in the world.

Tundra Swan

(Whistling Swan)

Cygne siffleur
Cygnus columbianus (Ord)
Total length: 121 to 140 cm
Plate 9

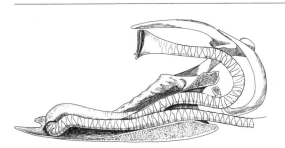

Figure 22
Longitudinal section through sternum of Tundra Swan. Note that windpipe does not make a high vertical loop over a bony hump. Compare Trumpeter Swan, Figure 23.

Breeding Distribution of Tundra Swan

Range in Canada. Breeds in the low and middle Arctic from southern Banks Island (near Sachs Harbour), southern Victoria Island (Cambridge Bay), King William Island, and central-western Baffin Island (Nuwata), south to northern Yukon (Old Crow); Mackenzie (Mackenzie Delta, Mason River, Thelon Sanctuary); northeastern Manitoba (Churchill); northern Ontario (Cape Henrietta Maria); Southampton Island; Hudson Bay (Mansel, Belcher, and Nottingham islands); and northwestern Quebec (Inoucdjouac to Cape Wolstenholme). Reports of breeding in northern Baffin Island (Mala River) are not completely satisfactory.

An isolated breeding site of one or two pairs situated ca. 90 km north of North Battleford,

Adults: Plumage all white, usually more or less rust-stained about head and neck. Bill, legs, and feet black. Bare skin in front of eye black, usually (not always) with a yellow or orange spot of variable size. *Immatures*: Pale ashy-grey, darkest on head and neck. In first autumn, bill is purplish flesh, becoming black toward tip, cutting edges, nostrils, and base. Space in front of eye lacks yellow spot and is more or less covered with fine feathers. In spring, the bill has become mostly black but sometimes with some ruddy flesh colours and the loral spot indicated in pale flesh.

Measurements. *Adult male*: wing, 517–552 (539.4); tail, 138–187 (168.3); exposed culmen, 85.5–97 (91.0); tarsus, 114–121 (116.8). *Adult female*: wing, 510–558 (533) mm.

Distinctions. Very similar to the larger Trumpeter Swan. Any native swan with a wing length under 560 mm and weight, unless very thin, under 9 kg is probably a Tundra Swan. Sometimes in winter, Trumpeter Swans become very thin and may weigh less than 9 kg. Positive identification of these two similar swans is provided by differences in convolutions of the windpipe in the breast bone (see Figure 22).

Field Marks. Because of large size and all-white plumage (no black wing-tips) it is likely to be mistaken only for the even larger, locally distributed Trumpeter Swan. When the yellow spot in front of the eye is observed, this marks it as a Tundra Swan, but not all Tundra Swans possess this spot. *Voice*: In chorus suggests a flock of Canada Geese but is more musical and often has a quavering quality. A common three-note call is strongly accented in the middle. The voice is less deep and far-carrying than that of the Trumpeter Swan, and the differences, when learned, make one of the best field marks.

Habitat. In spring and autumn migration it frequents lakes, sloughs, rivers, and sometimes fields. In summer, marshy lakes and ponds on low tundra of the North are popular, but the immediate vicinity of water is not necessary; large lakes for moulting.

Nesting. Nest, a mound of moss or grass on the ground, frequently near water. *Eggs*, 3 to 5; creamy white. Incubation period averages about 32 days (Banko and Mackay).

Range. Breeds in Alaska and the Canadian low Arctic. Winters mainly on the Pacific and Atlantic coasts of the United States from Washington to California and from Maryland to North Carolina.

Saskatchewan, may have become established through injury to one of a pair in spring migration (D.J. Nieman, J.K. Godwin and J.R. Smith, 1983. Blue Jay, vol. 41, no. 2, pp. 92–98).

Spring and autumn migrant through both coastal and interior British Columbia, the Prairie Provinces, and Ontario (but scarce east of the Great Lakes). Rare transient in extreme eastern Ontario and southwestern Quebec. Casual in New Brunswick, Nova Scotia, Prince Edward Island, Newfoundland, and Bathurst Island, N.W.T. Winters in southern British Columbia (south Thompson River, Fraser River delta, Victoria).

Remarks. Tundra Swans may be observed in numbers on spring migration at Long Point, Lake Erie, Ontario, between 20 March and 10 April.

Subspecies. *Cygnus columbianus columbianus* (Ord) is the North American subspecies. There is a photographic record of a "Bewick's" Swan, *C. c. bewickii* (Yarrell), a Eurasian race, near Regina, Saskatchewan, 27 October to 11 November 1978, but whether it was wild or an escapee is not known; also sight records for southern Ontario; others were reported in Alberta (Calgary, Strathmore) in March 1981.

Whooper Swan

[**Whooper Swan**. Cygne sauvage. *Cygnus cygnus* (Linnaeus). Hypothetical. Three immature birds spent the late winter of 1978–1979 along the west end of Lake Ontario, Hamilton to Oakville, Ontario. Two individuals, apparently the same as in 1978–1979, reappeared on 3 February 1980, at Bronte, Ontario. The evidence suggests that these were escapees from captivity.]

Trumpeter Swan

Cygne trompette
Cygnus buccinator Richardson
Total length: 137 to 168 cm
Plate 9

Range in Canada. Breeds locally in southern Yukon (Ortell Lake, upper Stewart River, Toobally Lakes region); extreme southwestern Mackenzie (Nahanni National Park); British Columbia (Terrace, Peace River region); central-western and southern Alberta (Peace River district, near Brooks, Hand Hills, Cypress Hills); extreme southwestern Saskatchewan (Cypress Hills).

Formerly ranged more widely, breeding north to northern Mackenzie (Franklin Bay, lower Anderson River, Rae); Manitoba (Norway House, Shoal Lake); probably northern Saskatchewan (Fond du Lac), and perhaps east to Eastmain, Quebec.

Formerly occurred sparingly in migration in southern Ontario (St. Clair Flats, 20 November 1875, and November 1884; also Toronto and Long Point) and southwestern Quebec (Longueuil).

Winters in western British Columbia (coastal islands including Queen Charlotte and Vancouver islands; and on certain lakes and open water in the interior, e.g. Lonesome Lake).

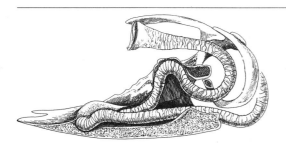

Figure 23
Longitudinal section through sternum of Trumpeter Swan showing the high vertical loop made by the windpipe over a bony hump.

Similar to Tundra Swan but larger, heavier, with relatively longer bill and slightly straighter culmen. Any native swan with a total length of 140 cm or more, and a folded wing of 58.4 cm or more is probably this species. *Adults (sexes similar)*: Similar to Tundra Swan but larger, bare skin in front of eye plain-black, cutting edge of lower mandible reddish posteriorly (see also Figure 23). *Immatures*: Similar to Tundra Swan but larger. In first autumn plumage grey above, darkest on crown and back of neck; bill pinkish, blackish at tip, base, and about nostrils; legs and feet olive buff, webs yellowish to greyish becoming dusky with age (Tundra Swan does not have yellow in the feet).

Measurements. *Adult male* (five measured): wing, 564–628 (596.5); tail, 182.5–200 (189.3); exposed culmen, 93–111.5 (104.0); tarsus, 118–128.5 (123.1). *Adult female* (four measured): wing, 565–636 (592.8) mm.

Field Marks. Swans are very large, long-necked, all-white birds with no black in the wing-tips. They fly with neck straight. Under most circumstances, the Trumpeter and the Tundra Swan are difficult to distinguish in the field because the larger size of the Trumpeter is rarely obvious. Adults lack a yellow spot in front of the eye, *usually* shown by the Tundra Swan, but mere absence of it does not necessarily indicate a Trumpeter Swan because some Tundra Swans lack it. *Voice*: When learned by the observer, it is probably the best way to distinguish the two at a distance. Deeper and more far-carrying than that of the Tundra Swan; a loud, trumpet-like, slightly guttural *ko-hoh* uttered from one to a number of times.

Habitat. Lakes, large sloughs, rivers; sometimes feeds in fields and grain stubbles. In winter, the mouths of rivers on the coast also are frequented.

Nesting. On a small island or muskrat house in a marshy freshwater lake or pond. Nest is a bulky platform of aquatic vegetation lined with down. *Eggs*, usually 5 to 8; dull white, often nest-stained. Incubation period about 32 days (R.H. Mackay), 33 to 37 days (W.E. Banko) by the female alone.

Range. Breeds locally in southern Alaska, southern Yukon, extreme southwestern Mackenzie, British Columbia, Alberta, southwestern Saskatchewan, Oregon, eastern Idaho, southwestern Montana, and Wyoming; formerly over a wider area. Winters in southeastern Alaska, western British Columbia, Idaho, Montana, and Wyoming.

Mute Swan

Cygne tuberculé
Cygnus olor (Gmelin)
Total length: 147 cm
Plate 9

Status in Canada. This native of temperate Eurasia is kept in captivity in many parts of North America. Some have escaped and are now living in a wild or semi-wild state as permanent resident, breeding birds in southwestern British Columbia (Elk Lake, Thetis Lake, Qualicum Beach, Cowichan Bay, Quamichan Lake, etc.); southern Saskatchewan (Regina); and southern Ontario (St. Thomas, Bradley's Marsh, Georgetown, Durham, Thunder Bay).

Adults: Plumage white. Bill orange or pinkish with black base and a *black knob on forehead* (larger in male). *Immatures*: Whitish, mottled and tinged with greyish brown, darkest on crown, lightest on breast; bill dusky flesh or pinkish, dark at base, no knob on forehead of first-year birds.

Tribe **Anserini**: Geese

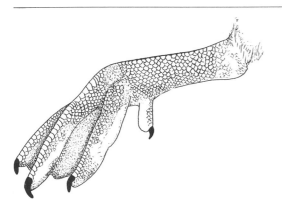

Figure 24
Reticulate tarsus of a goose

Geese inhabiting Canada are intermediate in size and neck length between swans and ducks. Compared with swans they are smaller, have shorter necks, the plumage of the neck is furrowed vertically, and there is no bare patch in front of the eye. Unlike most ducks, the sexes are coloured alike, there is no iridescent wing patch or speculum, and they have no eclipse plumage. They are much better walkers than ducks and feed more often on land. Tarsi are reticulate, not scutellate (Figure 24).

Bean Goose

Oie des moissons
Anser fabalis (Latham)
Total length: 71 to 89 cm

Status in Canada. Accidental in Quebec (Cap-Tourmente, 14–21 October 1982, when shot by a hunter and mounted).

Very similar to Pink-footed Goose but somewhat larger, more brownish, the bill black marked with *yellow*, the legs orange-yellow.

Range. Breeds in Scandinavia, northern Russia (including Novaya Zemlya), and northern Siberia south to northern Mongolia, Lake Baikal, and northern Amurland.

Subspecies. Specimen not examined by the writer but reportedly *Anser fabalis rossicus* Buturlin.

Pink-footed Goose

Oie à bec court
Anser brachyrhynchus Baillon
Total length: 60 to 74 cm
Plate 11

Status in Canada. Accidental in Newfoundland: A single individual, sufficiently well photographed for subspecific identification, was observed at St. Anthony from about 10 May to early June 1980, by Robert J. Walker, Bruce Mactavish, and others. Because the bird was not banded, was wary, arrived coincidentally with three other Eurasian vagrants, frequented a locality rather remote from game farms and waterfowl parks from which it could have escaped, and was apparently in excellent physical condition, it is thought to have been wild.

A brown-necked goose. *Adults*: Similar in general coloration to the Greater White-fronted Goose but lacks the conspicuous white areas of that species at the base of the bill (some Pink-footed Geese may show a very small white area at the base of the bill but it is never conspicuous); has no blackish markings on the under parts; has pink legs; and the bill is variably marked with black and pink (black base and tip with variable extent of pink between). Nail of bill black. First-autumn Pink-footed Geese are very difficult to distinguish in the field from Greater White-fronted of similar age unless the somewhat smaller size of the Pink-footed is apparent or pinkish leg-coloration is developed.

Range. Breeds in eastern Greenland, Iceland, and Spitsbergen. It winters mainly in the British Isles.

Greater White-fronted Goose

Oie rieuse
Anser albifrons (Scopoli)
Total length: 66 to 76 cm
Plate 11

Breeding Distribution of Greater White-fronted Goose

Range in Canada. Breeds from northern Yukon (Old Crow Flats), northern Mackenzie (Mackenzie Delta, Franklin Bay, Anderson River, Coronation Gulf, mouth of Perry River), southern Victoria Island (Cambridge Bay), northern Keewatin (Sherman Basin), south to middle-eastern Mackenzie (MacKay Lake, Outram River, and headwaters of the Hanbury River), and Keewatin (Angikuni Lake, Thelon River, Hyde Lake). A spring and autumn transient in Manitoba, Saskatchewan, Alberta, and British Columbia (common along coast). Of rare or casual occurrence in migration east of the Prairie Provinces in Ontario, Quebec, New Brunswick, Prince Edward Island, Nova Scotia, Newfoundland, and Labrador (near Hopedale) and north to Melville Island, N.W.T. Winters occasionally in southwestern British Columbia (Vancouver Island, Reifel Island).

Adults: Head, neck, back, rump, and wings, greyish brown. Forehead and narrow area behind base of bill, white. Tail dark brown edged with white. Upper tail coverts mostly white, creating white band across base of tail. Breast and belly greyish, heavily and irregularly blotched with blackish brown. Bill mostly pinkish (yellowish in one race). Legs and feet orange. *Immatures*: Similar to adults but lack white face patch (which begins to develop late in first autumn) and are without black blotches on under parts. Legs yellowish grey, becoming orange with age.

Measurements *(A. a. frontalis)*. *Adult male*: wing, 378–445 (412); tail, 117–127 (121); exposed culmen, 48–53 (51.2); tarsus, 73–77 (74.9). *Adult female*: wing, 388–421 (403.9) mm.

Field Marks. A brownish goose with no black on head or neck. Adults with narrow, white face patch, black blotches on under parts, and yellow or orange feet. Immatures lack the diagnostic markings about face and under parts; they thus resemble immature blue-phase Snow Geese, but the under parts are whiter and there is a narrow *white* band at base of tail, which contrasts with dark rump. In young "Blues" the rump and upper tail coverts are uniform pale *grey*. The White-front's yellow legs are diagnostic, as, in Canada, only the otherwise very different Emperor Goose has yellow legs. The blue phase of the Snow Goose at close range shows a "grinning patch" (see Figure 25), lacking in White-fronted. *Voice*: Rapidly repeated, usually in pairs, clanging laughlike *wah-wah, wah-wah,* or *kow-yow.* When feeding, a conversational gabbling.

Habitat. In breeding season the arctic tundra: edges of lakes; grassy flats; valleys, islands and deltas of streams. In migration, marshes, lakes and ponds, grassy fields, and grainfields.

Nesting. Often nests gregariously. Nest on ground, of mosses, grasses, tundra rubbish, lined with down and feathers. *Eggs*, usually 4 to 6; creamy white, often nest-stained. Incubation, by female while male stands guard, 22 to 28 days (various authors).

Range. Circumpolar (but absent as a breeder in eastern North America), Alaska, western Canada, eastern Greenland, Iceland, Scandinavia, and Spitsbergen. Winters in western North America (from southern British Columbia and southern Illinois south to Mexico), North Africa, India, China, and Japan.

Subspecies. (1) *Anser albifrons frontalis* Baird is the breeding race of most of the Canadian breeding range. (2) *Anser albifrons gambelli* Hartlaub with somewhat darker coloration of head, neck, and upper parts, and somewhat longer legs, is said by Delacour and Ripley (1975. American Museum Novitates 2565, pp. 1–4) to breed in taiga marshes of northwestern Canada east of the Richardson Mountains and south of the open tundra. (The only such skin available to the writer is an adult male from Old Crow River. In its darker coloration and longer tarsus (79 mm) it supports the validity of *gambelli*, although the culmen length (52.5 mm) is small and wing measurements, because of moulting, could not be made.) (3) *Anser albifrons flavirostris* Dalgety and Scott, similar to *frontalis* but with the bill yellow, breeds in western Greenland and normally winters in the British Isles. Its occurrence in Canada is shown by records from Quebec (near Matane, late September 1946; Henryville, 3–16 April 1977; near Rimouski, 20 June 1959); Prince Edward Island (Black Banks, 21 October 1961); Nova Scotia (Debert, 12 November 1949); and Newfoundland (St. Bride's, 10 October 1952).

The very large dark birds known as Tule Goose have recently been renamed *Anser albifrons elgasi* Delacour and Ripley. Their breeding range is unknown but is thought to be in the taiga zone in Alaska.

Snow Goose

(including "Blue Goose")

Oie des neiges
Anser caerulescens (Linnaeus)
Total length: 63.5 to 76 cm
Plate 10

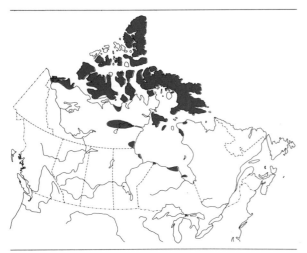

Breeding Distribution of Snow Goose

Range in Canada. Breeds in colonies of various sizes in the Arctic from Banks, Melville, Bathurst, Axel Heiberg islands, and northern Ellesmere Island (Hilgard Bay) south to northern Mackenzie (Mackenzie Delta, Anderson River, Perry River); Keewatin (Beverly Lake, Kazan Falls, Southampton Island, Coats Island, McConnell and Tha-anne rivers); northeastern Manitoba (La Pérouse Bay); northern Ontario (Cape Henrietta Maria); James Bay (Akimiski Island); northwestern Quebec (Povungnituk, Déception Bay); and southern Baffin Island. Reported without confirmation to have bred formerly on Twin Islands, James Bay. Migrates spring and autumn through British Columbia (white phase); Alberta (mainly white phase); Saskatchewan (mainly white phase); and Manitoba (in early spring, dark phase common with percentage of whites increasing as season advances; autumn, 75 per cent whites; F.G. Cooch). Large autumn con-

Sides of mandibles with blackish "grinning patch" (Figure 25). *White Phase*: *Adults*: Mainly white but often rust-stained on head, neck, and under parts. Wing tips black, the primaries grey at their bases. Bill pinkish, blackish at cutting edges. Legs and feet reddish. *Immatures*: Head and hind-neck more or less greyish, chin and throat whitish (often rust-stained). Back, scapulars, and wing coverts grey with paler feather-edges. Secondaries dusky with whitish edges. Primaries blackish becoming grey at their bases. Rump and upper tail coverts white. Tail variable grey and white. Under parts white, the sides sometimes lightly washed with grey. Bill brownish or blackish. Legs and feet purplish grey. *Blue Phase*: *Adults*: Head and neck white (often rust-stained), frequently with variable blotches of blackish brown on hind-neck. Upper back and scapulars dark brown, feather tips pale brown. Upper wing coverts bluish grey. Primaries and secondaries blackish with greyish bases. Tertials blackish with white edges, grey basally. Lower back, rump, and upper tail coverts vary from bluish grey to whitish. Tail feathers greyish brown with pale edges. Breast, belly, and sides usually dark greyish-brown but often variable, occasionally almost all white. Abdomen and under tail coverts usually grey or whitish. Bill and legs as in white phase. *Immatures*: Somewhat variable but usually head, neck, back, and under parts slaty grey; chin white; otherwise similar to adults. Bill and legs dark grey during first autumn. They become like adults during their second summer.

Measurements *(A. c. atlanticus)*. *Adult male*: wing, 430–485 (450); tail, 135–160 (140); exposed culmen, 59–73 (67); tarsus, 86–97 (92). *Adult female*: wing, 425–475 (445) mm (Kennard).

(A. c. caerulescens). *Adult male*: wing, 395–460 (430); tail, 115–165 (130); exposed culmen, 51–62 (58); tarsus, 78–91 (84). *Adult female*: wing, 380–440 (420) mm (Kennard).

Field Marks. Both phases have pink feet and a dark "grinning patch" on side of bill. *Blue Phase*: Adult would be confused only with the rare Emperor Goose of the Pacific Coast, but the latter has black fore-neck and throat, and orange legs. *White Phase*: White or greyish-white geese with black wing tips, they are likely to be confused with Ross's Goose (see Ross's Goose). *Immatures* of the blue phase resemble immature White-fronted but have dark legs and bill, grey instead of white upper tail coverts. *Voice*: A rather high-pitched falsetto monosyllabic *kowk*, somewhat musical in chorus, which is given both in flight and on the ground. While feeding, emits gabbling and groaning sounds. In nesting season, a sheep-like *kha-ah* is an alarm call.

Habitat. In migration (mostly avoids forested habitat), stops on fresh- or saltwater marshes, lakes, wet fields, grainfields, sandbars. In summer, frequent low, hummocky coastal plains with ponds, shallow lakes, or streams, less often higher drier terrain as well; also more rarely

centrations build up in southern James Bay. Autumn migration southwestwardly across Ontario is usually made non-stop in late October, although in rare years large numbers sometimes stop for a short time in settled parts. Usually a few stop regularly on the south shore of Georgian Bay. In spring there is a considerable migration northeastward over northwestern Ontario (Rat Rapids) toward James and Hudson bays. In Quebec, large numbers, mostly *atlanticus*, converge in spring and autumn on Cap-Tourmente (near Saint-Joachim, 50 km below Québec on the St. Lawrence River). East of central Quebec and in Labrador and the Maritime Provinces, the species is of casual occurrence in migration. Winters in Canada only in southwestern British Columbia (mouth of Fraser River).

Figure 25
Bill of Snow Goose showing "grinning patch"

far in the interior as at Beverly Lake, N.W.T. The race *atlanticus* on Bylot Island breeds also on protected slopes of ravines.

Nesting. Nests mainly in loose colonies (occasionally in single pairs) sometimes associated with Brant. Nest, on the ground, a mass of mosses or other tundra vegetation lined with down. *Eggs*, usually 3 to 5, most often 4; white to creamy but usually nest-stained. Incubation 20 to 25 days, usually 22 to 23 days (F.G. Cooch); in *atlanticus* 23 to 25 days (L. Lemieux), by female only, male standing guard.

Range. Northeastern Siberia, northern Alaska, arctic Canada, and northern Greenland. Winters mainly from southern British Columbia south to California; along the Gulf Coast from Mexico (Veracruz) and Texas to western Florida; on the Atlantic Coast, New Jersey to South Carolina.

Subspecies. (1) *Anser caerulescens atlanticus* (Kennard) (Greater Snow Goose), a larger race in which the blue colour phase is rare, is a high-arctic form that breeds on Ellesmere, Axel Heiberg, Devon, Somerset, Bathurst, Melville, and northern Baffin islands (south to approximately Baird Peninsula). In spring and autumn migration, most individuals of this race converge on Cap-Tourmente, Quebec, and spend some time there. (2) *A. c. caerulescens* (Linnaeus), smaller in size and with two colour phases (described above). It breeds in the low Arctic (south of *A. c. atlanticus* and west to Banks Island). In migration it is the race most likely to be encountered in settled country west of Quebec.

Apparently most of the population of the subspecies *atlanticus* stops at Cap-Tourmente and vicinity, in Quebec, and there has been a very substantial increase in numbers since the turn of the century. In autumn, the first geese arrive there usually in early September, and there is a gradual buildup of numbers until about mid-October. They remain until the marshes freeze, usually in late November. Spring arrival is, as a rule, in the latter part of March, and the geese spend about one and one-half months there before resuming their northward flight toward their high-arctic breeding grounds. Louis Lemieux (1959. Canadian Field-Naturalist, vol. 73, no. 2, pp. 117–128) provides additional detailed information on the breeding biology of this subspecies on Bylot Island, N.W.T.

Ross's Goose

Oie de Ross
Anser rossii Cassin
Total length: 53 to 58 cm
Plate 10

Figure 26
Ross's Goose

No "grinning patch" on side of bill. *Adults*: Mainly white. Wing tips black, greyish at base. Bill pinkish with greenish or bluish area near base; has *warty protuberances between base and nostrils* (see Figure 26), which are lacking in young birds and in some females. Legs and feet pink. *Immatures*: Similar to immature Snow Goose but much smaller and with shorter bill, the upper parts more whitish.

Measurements. *Adult male*: wing, 355–386 (372.4); tail, 106–129 (118.3); exposed culmen, 37.5–42 (40.3); tarsus, 68–73 (69.7). *Adult female*: wing, 338–385 (359.7) mm.

Field Marks. The smallest mainly white goose. A diminutive edition of the Snow Goose, scarcely larger than a large duck. Lacks black "grinning patch." At very close range, warty protuberances at base of bill may be discerned. *Voice*: A double-noted *luk-luk*, different from that of the Snow Goose, higher pitched, almost squeaky.

Breeding Distribution of Ross's Goose

Range in Canada. Breeds in northeastern
Mackenzie (Perry River region and adjoining
Queen Maud Gulf); southeastern Keewatin
(McConnell River); Southampton Island (Boas
River Delta, East Bay); northeastern Manitoba
(Cape Churchill); and northern Ontario (Cape
Henrietta Maria). Recorded in summer also
from Banks Island, N.W.T.

Main migration is in a southwest-northeast
direction with spring and autumn concentra-
tions on the Peace–Athabasca deltas of western
Lake Athabasca. Most pass through eastern
Alberta (Stettler, Sullivan Lake, Coronation,
and Hanna vicinities), and western Saskatche-
wan (Kindersley, Kerrobert, Macklin, Alsask
vicinities). Scarce transient in central-southern
and southeastern Saskatchewan (Caron, Regina,
Last Mountain Lake, Gainsborough); Manitoba
(The Pas, Killarney, Portage la Prairie,
Winnipeg, probably Churchill); northern
Ontario (Fort Severn; foot of James Bay); and
British Columbia (Stuart Lake, Comox, Kuper
Island, Rawlings Lake). Rare migrant in southern
Quebec (specimen: Cap-Tourmente, 30 September
1974; photo record: Beauport, 3 May 1975;
sight record: Cap-Tourmente, 19 October 1975;
Rivière-Ouelle, 10 May 1981). In western
Mackenzie it is a scarce visitor to Great Slave
Lake, and there are unconfirmed old reports from
the mouth of Horton River and Fort Anderson.

Habitat. On breeding grounds, tundra and low islands of freshwater lakes, floodplain marshes of rivers. In migration across eastern
Alberta, frequents large lakes, ponds, and stubble fields.

Nesting. In colonies. Nest varies from a scrape in the ground,
lined with down, to a considerable mound of moss and other material.
Eggs, most often 4 but varying from 2 to 9; dull white. Incubation
period 19 to 25, average 22 days (J.P. Ryder).

Range. Breeds very locally in the Canadian low Arctic. Winters
mainly in the Sacramento and San Joachim valleys of California and
rarely elsewhere in southern United States (Louisiana, eastern Texas).

Remarks. The breeding grounds of this small goose remained a
complete mystery until discovered in 1938 by Angus Gavin on Perry
River along the Mackenzie–Keewatin boundary. For some time, its total
numbers were thought to be about 2000. In 1965, estimates, based on
censuses on the wintering grounds in California, were decidedly more
optimistic and placed its total numbers at about 31,880. In 1983 estimates
were in excess of 100,000 individuals (F. Graham Cooch, pers. comm.).

Emperor Goose

Oie empereur
Anser canagicus (Sevastianov)
Total length: ca. 91 cm
Plate 11

Status in Canada. Rare winter visitant to the
coast of British Columbia. Most frequently
recorded from Masset, Queen Charlotte
Islands, but has occurred also at Chemainus,
Tlell, Cape Scott, Discovery Island, Triple
Island, White Rock, and Victoria.

Adults: Head and back of neck white; throat and fore-neck black.
Back, breast, and sides bluish grey, each feather with a blackish subterminal bar and a white tip, creating a barred effect. Secondaries and
tertials with wide white margins. Tail white. Belly grey, each feather
with a whitish tip. Bill pinkish or purplish with whitish tip. Legs and
feet orange-yellow. *Immatures*: Somewhat like adults but entire head
mottled with grey and body plumage duller. The white head is attained
at the first autumn moult. It is more or less flecked with black.

Field Marks. Most closely resembles the "blue goose" phase of the
Snow Goose but has a black throat and fore-neck and a dark rump. At
close range, the barred upper parts are obvious.

Range. Breeds on the coast of northeastern Siberia, St. Lawrence
Island, and coastal northwestern Alaska. Winters mainly in the Aleutian
Islands but wanders also down the North American coast casually as far
as California.

Brant
(includes Black Brant)

Bernache cravant
Branta bernicla (Linnaeus)
Total length: 58.4 to 76.2 cm
Plate 11

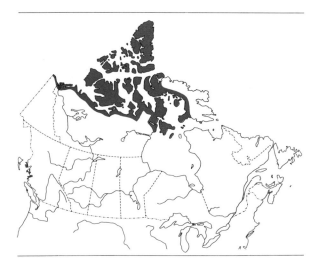

Breeding Distribution of Brant

Range in Canada. Breeds locally in maritime areas throughout the Arctic Archipelago north to Prince Patrick, Ellef Ringnes, and northern Ellesmere islands (Cape Columbia) and south to northern Yukon (Nunaluk Spit) and the arctic mainland of Mackenzie (Mackenzie Delta, Perry River); Keewatin (Cape Fullerton, Southampton Island); and southern Baffin Island (Cape Alberta, West Foxe Islands). An unconfirmed isolated breeding record has been reported from Copper Cliff, Ontario (J.L. Baillie, 1955. Audubon Field Notes, vol. 9, no. 1, p. 23).

Migrates along the British Columbia coast, the east coast of Hudson and James bays, also overland between Ungava Bay and the lower St. Lawrence River and inner north shore of the Gulf of St. Lawrence, and is a locally common transient on the coasts of New Brunswick, Prince Edward Island, Nova Scotia (particularly Cumberland, Colchester, and Pictou counties), and the Madeleine Islands. In recent years transients in southern Ontario (Ottawa River; lower Great Lakes) have become more or less regular. Otherwise scarce in the interior but recorded from southern Keewatin; Alberta (Grande Prairie, Jasper, Cooking Lake); Saskatchewan; Manitoba; and interior Quebec (although it migrates regularly across the interior of Ungava, flight appears to be usually non-stop between Ungava Bay and the lower St. Lawrence River; see H.F. Lewis, 1937. Auk, vol. 54, no. 1, pp. 73–95). Scarce and irregular on Labrador coast (Nain, Big (Jack Lane) Bay) and in Newfoundland. In Canada, winters mainly on the coast of British Columbia (mostly southern Strait of Georgia and adjacent waters) and rarely in extreme southern Ontario and the Maritimes.

Branta bernicla hrota. Adults: Head, neck, chest, and fore-neck black, contrasting with belly. Narrow white crescent on either side of neck. Back and upper sides of wings brown, the margins of the feathers paler. Wing tips blackish. Rump and tail black. Tail coverts white, the upper ones producing a broad white band at base of tail. Belly and sides brownish grey with paler feather-tips, giving a barred effect to the flanks. Bill and legs black. *Young in first autumn*: Like adults but white crescent on sides of neck wanting or poorly indicated; no barring on flanks; breast feathers narrower, softer, not square-tipped. Wing coverts, tail feathers (usually), and secondaries tipped with white.

Branta bernicla nigricans (Black Brant). *Adults*: Similar to *hrota*, but belly dark slaty-brown or blackish brown with little or no contrast with chest. White crescents usually meet in front of neck but not on hind-neck. Young similar to young *hrota* but belly much darker.

Measurements *(B. b. hrota). Adult male*: wing, 321–351 (333.9); tail, 96–105 (99.7); exposed culmen, 32–34 (32.9); tarsus, 60–69 (63.2). *Adult female*: wing, 296–336 (314) mm.

Field Marks. Like the Canada Goose, it has a black head and neck but lacks its white cheeks. Black of neck extends down to include breast (breast is pale in Canada Goose). Adult has narrow white patch on sides of neck, which the Canada lacks. On the water, hind parts ride higher. *Voice*: hoarse *r-r-r-ronk, car-r-rup,* or *ruk-ruk*; when feeding, chattering sounds.

Habitat. In winter and migration, mainly along saltwater bays, rocky shores, and tidal flats, particularly where eel grass *(Zostera)* is present. When occasionally it stops at inland points, it frequents lake and river shores, sometimes cultivated fields. In summer, arctic coastal islands, deltas, broad river-valleys, well-vegetated uplands, and tundra lakes, usually near the coast.

Nesting. Nests in loose colonies or singly. Nest on the ground, well lined with down, the foundation varying from a mere hollow in the ground to a mound of mosses and lichens. *Eggs*, usually 3 to 5, often more; creamy white. Incubation by female while male stands guard, usually 23 to 24 days but varying between 22 and 26 days (T.W. Barry).

Range. Circumpolar, breeding in arctic North America and Eurasia. In North American winters along the Pacific Coast from Queen Charlotte Islands to Baja California and along the Atlantic Coast from Massachusetts to North Carolina.

Subspecies. Two well-marked subspecies (described above) are found in Canada; and a third, intermediate in colour between them, occurs in the Old World. (1) *Branta bernicla nigricans* (Lawrence) breeds in the western Arctic along the coast of Mackenzie and northward on Banks and Prince Patrick islands; intergrading on the latter with *hrota*; winters along the Pacific Coast; casual in migration in southern Yukon and southern Saskatchewan. (2) *B. b. hrota* (Müller) breeds in the eastern Arctic and westward to the Adelaide Peninsula, probably Prince of Wales Island; intergrades with *nigricans* on Melville and Prince Patrick islands, and in the Perry River region. No specimens are available from Victoria Island.

Remarks. This small goose is primarily a saltwater bird and is a favourite with gunners along the coasts. It does not ordinarily fly in the familiar V-pattern of its near relative, the Canada Goose, but in long wavering lines or formationless flocks. Brant like company and usually are seen in groups. Spring migration is late, and in the Maritimes, many Brant linger at favourite feeding places until the first week of June. In migration and on the wintering grounds, Brant feed mainly on eel grass *(Zostera)* uncovered by the receding tide, or in shallow water by tipping up, like ducks.

Barnacle Goose

Bernache nonnette
Branta leucopsis (Bechstein)
Total length: 63.5 to 71.1 cm
Plate 11

Status in Canada. Casual visitant to Baffin Island, N.W.T. (Boas Lake, August 1924); Labrador (Okak); Quebec (Cap-Tourmente, 26 October 1925, and October 1953; Rupert-House; Lake Saint-Pierre, autumn 1926; Vieux-Comptoir River, 5 April 1944); Ontario (photo record: Long Point, 23 November 1970; sight record: Kingsville, autumn 1955); Manitoba (Croll, 3 May 1981); New Brunswick (sight record: McGowans Corner, 10 May 1972); Nova Scotia (sight record: Port Hebert Harbour, 20 November 1969); and Newfoundland (two shot by a hunter at Ladle Cove in late autumn 1981, one of which was a male banded at 2+ years of age on 19 July 1977 on Spitsbergen). The possibility exists that some of the foregoing were escapees from captivity.

Adults: Head mainly white with a black bar extending from eye to base of bill, the black of neck reaching up over nape and hind-crown (leaving broad white forehead). Neck and breast black. Back bluish grey, the feathers with broad blackish subterminal bars and brownish-white tips. Rump and tail black. Upper and under tail coverts white. Belly greyish white, contrasting sharply with black breast. Flanks bluish grey, barred with brownish white. Bill, legs, and feet black. *Immatures*: Similar but duller, the neck more greyish, the back more brownish.

Field Marks. Suggests a small Canada Goose but with a conspicuous white forehead.

Range. Breeds in eastern Greenland, Spitsbergen, and Novaya Zemlya.

Canada Goose

Bernache du Canada
Branta canadensis (Linnaeus)
Total length: 55.8 to 101.6 cm
Plate 11

Breeding Distribution of Canada Goose

Range in Canada. Breeds from northern Yukon (Herschel Island), northern Mackenzie (Richards Island, lower Anderson River), Victoria Island (Walker Bay, Cambridge Bay), King William Island, Boothia Peninsula (Felix Harbour), Melville Peninsula, Southampton Island, and Baffin Island (Foxe Peninsula, probably Cumberland Peninsula; according to P. Chagnon nesting in northern Baffin Island at Admiralty Inlet, nest found), south through Yukon, Mackenzie, and Keewatin; and south through southern British Columbia (including Queen Charlotte and Vancouver islands);

Varies greatly geographically, the subspecies *minima* being the smallest goose in Canada, *maxima* the largest. Although there is considerable geographic variation in colour also, all the subspecies have similar colour patterns. *Adults (B. c. interior)*: Head and neck black, with a large white patch on each cheek, the two cheek patches meeting under the throat; upper parts of body and wings greyish brown, the feathers narrowly tipped with brownish white; rump blackish; upper tail coverts white; tail black; under body brownish grey with paler feather-tips, the sides and flanks usually darkest, lower belly and under tail coverts white; feathers of breast broad and square-tipped; bill and legs black; eye brown. *Immatures (first autumn and winter)*: Similar to adults but breast feathers are narrower, softer, less conspicuously tipped; outer primaries with more pointed, less rounded tips.

Measurements *(B. c. interior*, one of the larger races). *Adult male*: wing, 430–473 (456.8); tail, 131–149 (143.9); exposed culmen, 46–55.5 (50.7); tarsus, 81–91.5 (89.1). *Adult female*: wing, 427–467 (445.5) mm (J.W. Aldrich).

Field Marks. Varies geographically from near Mallard size to large, but is always readily recognizable as a Canada Goose by the combination of long black neck and black head with large *white cheek patches*. Brant are similar in appearance but have a narrow white collar on the black neck and no white cheek patch on the all-black head. High-flying flocks in migration travel in a V-formation. *Voice*: the "honk" is a sonorous, two-syllabled nasal *ka-ronk* slightly up-slurred at the end and with a break in the voice between the two syllables. The small races have higher-pitched voices.

Habitat. Breeds over vast, ecologically varied areas in both treeless and forested country varying from prairies and plains in the West and coastal plains in the Arctic to mountains. Nests in the vicinity of water near lakes, ponds, and larger streams, marshes, muskegs, and hummocky coastal plains in the Arctic. Often forages on berry-bearing tundra, feeding especially on fruit of *Vaccinium* and *Empetrum*. In migration, lakes, rivers, coastal and freshwater marshes, bays, grassy fields, and grain stubbles.

Nesting. Usually on the ground near water, particularly islets or muskrat or beaver houses. Occasionally in a tree nest of a hawk or other large bird, an artificial platform, or on a cliff ledge. Nest is a

southern Alberta; southern Saskatchewan; southern Manitoba; north-central Ontario (coast of Hudson Bay and inland 95 km or more; Mattagami River; locally farther south); southern James Bay (North and South Twin and Charlton islands); central and southeastern Quebec (Lake Albanel, Natashquan, Anticosti Island, Blanc-Sablon; reportedly formerly in the Madeleine Islands until about 1858); southern Labrador (Sawbill, L'Anse-au-Clair); and Newfoundland.

In recent years local breeding derived from escapees from captivity, known releases, and in some cases, feral birds, has greatly increased and expanded the breeding range. Thus the breeding range now extends southward through southern Ontario (Toronto, Kingston, Nairn Island); southern Quebec (Granby, Grandes-Bergeronnes, Matagami, Franquelin); Prince Edward Island; New Brunswick (McAdam; formerly Miscou Island); and Nova Scotia (Amherst).

Winters on the coast of British Columbia; southern Alberta (small numbers: Bow River); southern Saskatchewan (small numbers: Regina); extreme southern Ontario; Prince Edward Island; Nova Scotia (Port Joli, Port Hebert, Sable River estuary, Barrington Bay, Cole Harbour); and Newfoundland (Stephenville. About 1000 winter in the province— L.M. Tuck).

Casual on Banks, Melville, Bylot, and Devon islands, N.W.T.

depression lined (sometimes bulkily, sometimes scantily) with sticks and various vegetal materials obtainable in the vicinity, and with an inner lining of down. *Eggs*, most often 4 to 6; white but often nest-stained. Incubation period 24 to 25 days (C.D. MacInnes), 25 to 28 days (C.W. Kossack), 28 to 33 days (J.S. Dow). Incubation by the female, the male guarding

Range. Breeds from the Komandorskie and Kurile islands (formerly) and from western Alaska eastward to Labrador and Newfoundland and south to northeastern California, Utah, Kansas, and rarely to Maine and Massachusetts. Winters from southern Canada (locally) south to northern Mexico and the Gulf Coast of United States. Introduced in the British Isles, Iceland, and New Zealand.

Subspecies. The subspecies of this goose are at present imperfectly understood. (1) *Branta canadensis canadensis* (Linnaeus), a large palish form: eastern Quebec, Labrador, Newfoundland. (2) *B. c. interior* Todd, a large form but darker and browner than *canadensis*: Manitoba, Ontario, western Quebec, southern Baffin Island. (3) *B. c. maxima* Delacour, (almost extirpated) the largest form and slightly paler than *canadensis*: formerly perhaps southern Manitoba. (4) *B. c. moffitti* Aldrich, coloured like *maxima* but somewhat smaller, especially bill and tarsus: interior southern and central British Columbia (Lac la Hache), southern Alberta, southern Saskatchewan. (5) *B. c. parvipes* (Cassin), colour similar to *moffitti* but size much smaller: interior Yukon, District of Mackenzie, District of Keewatin, northern British Columbia (Tuya Lake). (6) *B. c. fulva* Delacour, a large form much darker above and below than any of the above-mentioned races: coastal British Columbia. (7) *B. c. hutchinsii* (Richardson), a very small short-billed form similar in coloration to *parvipes*: Victoria Island, Adelaide Peninsula, Melville Peninsula, Southampton Island, and coast of western Baffin Island, N.W.T. (8) *B. c. minima* Ridgway, even smaller than *hutchinsii* and very much darker: migrant to coastal British Columbia. (9) *B. c. leucopareia* (Brandt), of the Aleutian Islands, now greatly reduced in numbers, formerly occurred in winter in coastal British Columbia. (10) *B. c. taverneri* Delacour is postulated to be the breeding form of coastal northern Yukon and northwestern District of Mackenzie (Mackenzie Delta).

Remarks. The Canada Goose is *the* wild goose to most Canadians. The majority of people see it in its spring or autumn migration flying high overhead. This is a thrilling and inspiring sight. When the geese are on the move and their resonant honking drifts down to us, there are few who do not pause and gaze upward as the big birds in V-formation move majestically across the sky. Despite their size they fly swiftly and soon pass out of sight.

This splendid goose is extremely popular as a game bird, but despite heavy hunting-pressure it has managed to increase its numbers substantially in recent years and has certainly profited by man's grain and grass fields. It is wary and sagacious, but courageous and formidable in defence of its nest or young. Family ties are very strong. Pairs usually mate for life, but when one of the pair dies, the other may take another mate. The young fly south in autumn with their parents and do not separate from them until they return in spring to the nesting grounds. Migrating flocks often comprise several families.

Subfamily **Anatinae**: Ducks

A large and varied group of waterfowl, mostly of medium body size, differing from geese in possessing scutellated tarsi, shorter necks, and more flattened bodies. In most species there are well-marked differences between plumages of the adult male and female. The legs of ducks are positioned more toward the rear of the body than in geese and ducks are therefore poorer walkers.

Tribe **Tadornini:**
Shelducks

Although these rather large, somewhat gooselike ducks are widely distributed in the world, they are not known to occur in North America in the wild.

Ruddy Shelduck

[**Ruddy Shelduck**. Tadorne roux. *Tadorna ferruginea* (Pallas). Hypothetical. Two were reported at Grandes-Bergeronnes, Quebec, 27–30 June 1978. Again in June 1979, two (thought to be the same individuals) were at the same locality. In late June–early July 1980, three individuals were present there. Although close observation showed that at least two of the three were not banded, and the possibility exists that they might have been wild stragglers from the Old World, the likelihood that they were escapees from captivity seems strong. A single at Glace Bay, Nova Scotia, in September 1982 was almost certainly an escapee.]

Tribe **Cairinini:**
Perching Ducks

There is great variation in size and plumage coloration among the 14 species of this tribe. Iridescent coloration is present in most of them and the group includes two of the most beautiful ducks in the world: the Wood Duck of North America and the Mandarin Duck of Asia. Members of the tribe nest mostly in holes, especially in trees, and they are equipped with sharp claws to assist in perching and climbing. Only one species, the Wood Duck, is native to Canada.

Wood Duck

Canard branchu
Aix sponsa (Linnaeus)
Total length: 43 to 53 cm
Plate 13

Breeding Distribution of Wood Duck

Range in Canada. Breeds in southern British Columbia (Vancouver Island, Graham Island, Sumas Prairie, Chilliwack, Okanagan valley, East and West Kootenay valleys); southern Alberta (Midnapore, Turner Valley); central Saskatchewan (Cumberland House, Emma Lake, Hudson Bay Junction; reportedly Qu'Appelle valley); southern Manitoba (Delta; probably north to Pike Lake, near The Pas and Cedar Lake); southern Ontario (north to Sault Ste. Marie, Pimisi Bay, Ottawa); southwestern Quebec (north to Île-aux-Coudres, Cap-Tourmente, Falardeau, Rimouski); New Brunswick; the peninsula of Nova Scotia (locally),

Head crested. *Adult male (breeding plumage)*: Head iridescent green and blue, deepening to purplish black below eye with a narrow white line above the eye and another extending back from it; chin, throat, and fore-neck white with a conspicuous spur of white extending up onto cheek and another around side of neck. Back, rump, and upper tail coverts bronze-green. Tail dark glossy-green above. Fore-wing greyish brown, greater coverts metallic green and purple; speculum bluish green, bordered behind by a thin white line. Upper breast reddish chestnut with small white markings. A vertical white bar on shoulder, bordered behind by a black one. Sides buffy, crossed by fine black wavy lines, bordered above and behind by black and white. Patch of purplish chestnut on either side near base of tail. Eye orange-red to vermilion. Bill, nail, ridge, and lower mandible blackish, sides of bill pinkish, base red with narrow yellow border behind. Legs and feet dull yellow or orange with dusky webs. *Adult female*: Crest shorter. Head brownish grey with greenish gloss. Chin, throat, line at base of bill, and small patch around eye, white. Rest of upper parts greyish brown with bronzy gloss on upper tail coverts and tail. Wing similar to male but duller. Neck grey; breast and flanks mottled grey, brown, and buff. Belly white, sparsely spotted with dusky. Eye blackish brown. Eyelids yellow. Legs and feet dull yellow. *Immature*: Somewhat like adult female but in male a spur of white extends up onto cheek as in adult male.

Measurements. *Adult male*: wing, 215–232 (223); tail, 91.5–110 (102.3); exposed culmen, 31–36 (33.1); tarsus, 34.5–37.5 (35.8). *Adult female*: wing, 203–225 (213.8) mm.

Field Marks. White face-markings of male unmistakable. Crest and small white patch around the eye identify female. When swimming the head bobs with each foot stroke. In flight the large tail and down-pointed bill are noticeable. Often the narrow white line on hind edge of spread wing is visible. The Pintail also has such a wing marking, but the Pintail's very long neck is quite different from that of the Wood Duck. *Voice*: A squealing *oo-eek, oo-eek, oo-eek* is uttered when the bird is flushed from the water in alarm, a good means of field identification when, as so often happens, it cannot be seen in its woodland habitat.

Habitat. Woodland lakes, ponds, and streams.

and Cape Breton Island (rarely: River Denys, Nyanza); and Prince Edward Island (locally: Schooner Pond). Has been recorded north in Manitoba to Churchill (one specimen record); in Ontario to Albany River and Moose Factory; in Quebec to the north shore of the Gulf of St. Lawrence (one banded in early autumn at Johan-Beetz Bay; recorded at Longue-Pointe); Newfoundland (Burin, Spruce Brook, Bowring Park, Cape Broyle, Ferryland). A few winter in southwestern British Columbia and extreme southern Ontario (Lake Erie, rarely north to Kingston).

Nesting. Nests in a hollow trunk or limb of a tree, sometimes in a hollow made by a large woodpecker or in a nesting box. Entrance may be anywhere from several to 15 m above ground, often (but not necessarily) near water. *Eggs*, 8 to 15; pale buffy-white. Incubation variable, 27 to 35 days, average 30 days, by the female. One brood annually. Downies leave the nest by climbing (for which their very sharp claws are well adapted) to the nest hole and dropping lightly to the ground.

Range. Breeds from southern British Columbia and northwestern Montana, south to central California; and from southern Manitoba east to Nova Scotia and south to the eastern Dakotas, eastern Kansas, east-central Texas, the Gulf Coast, Florida, and Cuba. Winters south to central Mexico.

Tribe **Anatini:**
Surface-feeding Ducks

Figure 27
Foot of surface-feeding duck

Ducks of this large tribe do not ordinarily dive. Food is commonly secured under shallow water by submerging perpendicularly the head, neck, and most of the body, leaving the tail sticking straight up above water. They feed also on the water surface and on land. Anatomically they are rather similar to the perching ducks, but lack their sharp claws and perching ability. They nest mostly on the ground. Unlike that of the diving ducks, the hind toe has no lobe (Figure 27). The speculum (wing patch) is more or less brightly coloured and iridescent. In most species, adult males have a well-marked "eclipse" plumage.

Green-winged Teal
(includes Common Teal)

Sarcelle à ailes vertes
Anas crecca Linnaeus
Total length: 36.5 cm
Plate 13

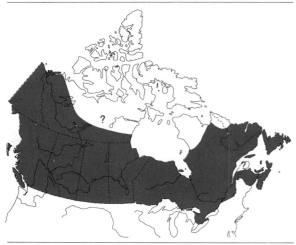

Breeding Distribution of Green-winged Teal

Range in Canada. Breeds from northern Yukon (Herschel Island); northwestern and western Mackenzie (Aklavik; Tuktoyaktuk; near Norman Wells, Nahanni National Park; Great Slave Lake; Grassy Island marshes on Thelon River); southern Keewatin (near Simon's Lake, Windy Bay, Eskimo Point); northern Manitoba (Churchill); coast and lowlands of southern

Our smallest duck. Size distinguishes it from all other ducks of regular occurrence in Canada except the Blue-winged and Cinnamon teals, the Bufflehead, and the Ruddy Duck. The bright-green speculum separates it from the latter two, and a complete absence of blue on the fore-wing from the first two.

Measurements. *Adult male*: wing, 172–189 (180.7); tail, 61–74 (68); exposed culmen, 36–40.5 (38.1); tarsus, 30–33 (31.4). *Adult female*: wing, 164–176.5 (170.5) mm.

Field Marks. Adult male's small size and markings in winter and spring are unmistakable. In flight the lack of any large bluish patch on the fore-wing separates it from other North American teals. *Voice*: Female, a weak quack. Male, a short high-pitched whistle.

Habitat. Freshwater ponds, marshes, shallow edges of lakes; also in migration and winter, shallow salt and brackish water and shores.

Nesting. Nest on the ground, usually near fresh water but sometimes some distance from it, generally concealed by grass or shrubbery. *Eggs*, usually 10 to 12, sometimes more or less; white to pale olive-buff. Incubation, 20 to 23 days, usually 21, is by the female.

Range. Breeds from middle Alaska and the northwestern and middle Canadian mainland south to California, northern New Mexico, northern Nebraska, Minnesota, northern Ohio, western New York, Maine, and Nova Scotia. Winters mainly in the United States. Another subspecies ranges widely in the Old World.

Hudson Bay; James Bay (Raft River, Roggan River); northern Quebec (Leaf Bay); north-central Labrador (Nain, Henley Harbour) and Newfoundland; south through British Columbia (but locally on Vancouver Island); Alberta, Saskatchewan, and Manitoba; middle and southern Ontario (very locally: Orangeville, Rainy River district, Cochrane, Ottawa, near Kingston, Niagara Peninsula, and Elgin County); central and southern Quebec (Lake Saint-Jean, Pointe-des-Monts, Anticosti Island, near Sorel, Oka, Madeleine Islands; in the interior locally: Schefferville); Labrador (Nain); New Brunswick (Maugerville; Grand Manan); Prince Edward Island; and Nova Scotia (including Cape Breton and Sable islands).

Has wandered north to Perry River, Repulse Bay, and Cape Dorset, N.W.T. Migrates through most of southern Canada.

Winters in British Columbia (commonly on the coast; in small numbers in Okanagan valley), and sparingly in southern Ontario, Nova Scotia, and Newfoundland.

Subspecies. (1) *Anas crecca carolinensis* Gmelin is the only subspecies breeding in Canada and is described above. (2) *A. c. crecca* Linnaeus of the Old World is similar to *carolinensis* but the adult males lack a vertical white bar in front of wing; the long, pointed scapulars are white with black outer borders; vermiculations on back coarser; and the whitish border to the green area on side of head more extensive. It is a casual visitant to Nova Scotia, New Brunswick, Newfoundland, Labrador, Quebec (sight records), and Ontario (sight record). Rare but more or less regular visitor to southwestern coastal British Columbia.

Baikal Teal

Sarcelle élégante
Anas formosa Georgi
Total length: 40.6 cm
Plate 9

Status in Canada. An immature male was collected by James Hatter at Ladner, British Columbia, on 20 December 1957. It was flying with a flock of Northern Pintails. An adult male was carefully observed by competent people at Carlsbad Springs, Ontario, on 31 March 1979 but was not seen again. The Ontario bird was probably an escapee from captivity.

Adult male: Crown, back of neck, throat, and stripe across the face from eye to throat, black; line along sides of crown and another bordering black of hind-neck, white; sides of face buffy; a broad metallic-green patch extending from above eye, back to nape and down sides of neck. Body with a crescentic white line on side of breast and at base of tail. Wing with green speculum. *Adult female*: Similar to female Green-winged Teal but with round whitish patch at base of bill and with the dark colour of crown extending in a spur down to eye.

Range. Breeds in Siberia. Winters from China, Korea, and Japan to India. Casual or accidental in North America.

Falcated Teal

[**Falcated Teal**. Sarcelle à faucilles. *Anas falcata* Georgi. Hypothetical. An adult male observed near Vernon, British Columbia, 15 April 1932, by Allan Brooks (1942. Condor, vol. 44, no. 1, p. 33).]

American Black Duck

Canard noir
Anas rubripes Brewster
Total length: 53.3 to 61 cm
Plate 12

Figure 28
Feathers from sides of breast of American Black Duck
a) adult female
b) adult male

Adults: Crown, nape, and line through eye, dark brown. Rest of head brownish grey, finely streaked with a dusky hue, the chin and throat usually immaculate. Body mainly dark brown, the feathers with buffy borders. Wing patch purple, bordered in front and behind by black, the hind bar often with a very narrow white edge. Wing linings white. Feathers of sides of breast of male and female usually differ (Figure 28), the buffy interior markings U-shaped in male, V-shaped in female. Bill greenish yellow in male, more olive in female and often blotched with a dusky colour (but variable). Legs reddish, orange, or greenish. *Juvenal*: Similar to adults, but bill and feet duller, under parts more streaky, breast feathers lack U- or V-shaped markings.

Measurements. *Adult male*: wing, 243–290 (267.9); tail, 81.5–94.5 (90.7); exposed culmen, 49.5–60 (53.8); tarsus, 45–48.5 (46.7). *Adult female*: wing, 244–280 (265.9) mm.

Field Marks. Dark brown above and below (in flight, white wing-linings flash contrastingly), darker than Mallard and lacking Mallard's whitish outer tail-feathers and wing bars. *Voice*: A *quack* or series of them, that of male lower, softer, and shorter.

Breeding Distribution of American Black Duck

Range in Canada. Commonest breeding duck in most of southeastern Canada. Breeds in Manitoba, (common summer resident at Churchill, a few breeding, although apparently many are post-breeding males; scarce local summer resident in southern Manitoba at Lake St. Martin, Seven Sisters dam); Ontario (commonly throughout eastern half and northward to James and Hudson bays, scarcer westward, rare and local near Manitoba border); Quebec (common throughout south and central parts, including Anticosti and Madeleine islands, and northward to about tree limit, occurring farther north coastwise after breeding); Labrador (mostly away from the outer coast, near Sandwich Bay, upper Hamilton River, Okak, Rigolet, Davis Inlet, Alliuk Bight), and throughout Newfoundland, New Brunswick, Nova Scotia, and Prince Edward Island. In recent years has nested very locally in Alberta (near Kelsey and Hanna) and Saskatchewan (Maidstone, Watson).

Rare in Mackenzie (a few in summer on Thelon and Finnie rivers; recorded, perhaps erroneously, from Anderson River); British Columbia (sight record of two at Cecil Lake, Peace River area, 4 May 1982); Keewatin (summer records from Windy River; Chesterfield Inlet); Franklin (Cape Dorset, Baffin Island, three collected on 8 June 1934).

Winters in southern Ontario (north to Sault Ste. Marie and Ottawa), southern Quebec (Montréal; Saguenay River mouth), and on the coasts of Nova Scotia, Prince Edward Island, New Brunswick, and southern Newfoundland. Recorded in winter at Cartwright, Labrador.

Habitat. Shallow margins of lakes, ponds, pools, quiet streams, coves, bays, mud flats, marshes, wet fields, grainfields, and open water. Frequents both salt and fresh water. During nesting, both dry and wet woodland.

Nesting. Usually on ground often in wooded areas (sometimes some distance from water), in bushy or grassy fields, on islands, or along brooks. Sometimes in a hole or fork in a tree, occasionally in an abandoned crow's or hawk's nest. Nest of twigs, stalks, grasses, leaves, with down lining. *Eggs*, 6 to 12, average 9; greenish buff to creamy white, unspotted. Incubation 23 to 33 (average 27) days.

Range. Breeds from northern Manitoba east to Labrador and Newfoundland and south to northern Minnesota, Wisconsin, Ohio, Pennsylvania, Maryland, and eastern Virginia. In winter from southeastern Canada to Texas, the Gulf States, Florida, and Bermuda.

Subspecies. None recognized. For years the large red-legged winter adults were thought to belong to a separate subspecies, supposedly breeding in the northern part of the range and migrating southward with the advent of cold weather. These characters have been shown by T.M. Shortt (1943. Wilson Bulletin, vol. 55, no. 1, pp. 3–7) to be a product of age, sex, and season. That they are not peculiar to birds of any one geographical area has been well demonstrated by bird banding. The myth of a "northern" race of Black Duck is still prevalent, however, among sportsmen.

Remarks. The Black is *the* wild duck to the sportsmen of eastern Canada, where it takes the place of the equally famous Mallard of the West. Wary and swift on the wing, it taxes the marksmanship of even the most experienced gunner. As a table bird it is a favourite on account of its good size and usually excellent flavour. In coastal areas, when much-hunted, Blacks spend most of the daylight hours on salt water or on remote mud flats exposed by the tide. In the evening or after dark they fly in to the grain stubbles or freshwater marshes and leave them again at dawn. Even when undisturbed in late summer they are inclined to be more active in the evening than at other times, and they then regularly build up considerable assemblages in certain favourite feeding places.

Mallard

Canard colvert
Anas platyrhynchos Linnaeus
Total length: 50 to 68.5 cm
Plate 12

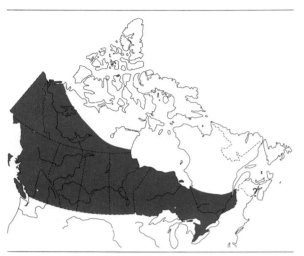

Breeding Distribution of Mallard

Range in Canada. Common breeder in the western provinces, progressively scarcer farther east, but recently numbers and range have substantially expanded eastward. Breeds in Yukon (across the southern part, and north to the arctic coast); Mackenzie (near Aklavik, Fort Anderson, near Fort Norman, Fort Simpson, and at various points on Great Slave Lake; recorded in summer on Great Bear Lake and various points south of it and in the Thelon Game Sanctuary); southern Keewatin (Windy River; recorded in summer off Tavani); through British Columbia; Alberta; Saskatchewan; Manitoba; Ontario; and southwestern Quebec (eastern James Bay, Lake Saint-Jean southward). Formerly only a scarce transient in the Maritimes, it now breeds in New Brunswick (Saint John River valley, Moncton, Dawsonville); Nova Scotia (Wolfville); and Prince Edward Island (Indian River, Clarke's Pond), but its breeding status in the Maritimes is complicated by heavy liberation of imported stock. Despite some nesting in the Maritimes and Madeleine Islands there is no sure evidence that a permanent breeding population is being built up at this date there.

Scarce transient in Newfoundland. Recorded in migration on the coast of Labrador and on Ungava Bay. Casual on Victoria Island, N.W.T. (sight records: Cambridge Bay, Albert Edward Bay, Holman).

Winters commonly in southern British Columbia (north to Stuart Lake); locally in southern Alberta (Calgary); southern Saskatchewan (Regina, rarely elsewhere); southern Ontario (north to Ottawa); southwestern Quebec (Montréal); Newfoundland; and the Maritimes.

Adult male in breeding plumage, with green head and neck, narrow white collar, chestnut lower neck and breast, and violet wing patch (speculum) bordered *both in front and behind* by a white bar; needs no further description. Bill greenish yellow. Legs orange. In summer, an eclipse plumage similar to the female is assumed, and moult into breeding plumage requires most of the autumn. *Adult female*: Top and sides of head buff streaked with dark brown. Throat usually unmarked, sometimes spotted or streaked. Upper parts dark brown, the feathers broadly edged with buff. Wing patch as in male but more greenish. Wing linings white. Breast and abdomen, buff marked with blackish brown and with U-shaped markings on breast feathers. Sides and flanks darker with buffy feather edges. Tail dark greyish-brown, much paler (whitish) on outer edges. Bill yellowish or greenish, more or less mixed with black. Legs and feet reddish orange. *Juvenal*: Similar to adult female but slightly duller and without U-shaped markings on breast feathers.

Measurements. *Adult male*: wing, 273–290 (282); tail, 78–94 (86.3); exposed culmen, 52.5–59.5 (56.1); tarsus, 44–49 (46.3). *Adult female*: wing, 230–276 (259) mm.

Field Marks. *Adult male*: Green head, narrow white collar, chestnut breast. Male Shoveler has chestnut sides and under parts but white breast. *Female and Immatures*: Resemble Black Duck but general colour lighter. Wing with *two* white bars, one in front and one behind wing patch, which are visible for considerable distances in flight. Whitish outer sides of Mallard's tail are visible over some distance in flight. In the Black Duck, the tail is uniformly dark. *Voice*: A rather loud *quack* is given by the female. The male's voice is similar but softer and higher pitched.

Habitat. One of the most adaptable of ducks, frequenting marshes, sloughs, ponds, small and large lakes, quiet waters of rivers, and flooded land in both treeless and wooded country. Also forages on land, especially grainfields, and can get along with very little water. Prefers fresh to salt water, but does frequent coastal salt water, especially in winter.

Nesting. Nest, usually on ground, generally near water but sometimes far from it; rarely in a tree. Nest of grasses, reeds, leaves, well lined with down. *Eggs*, 5 to 15 (usually 8 to 12); dull greenish or greyish buff to nearly white. Incubation, 28 ± 3 days (Girard) but usually 27 to 28 days, by the female, begins after laying of last egg.

Range. North America, Europe, and Asia.

Subspecies. *Anas platyrhynchos platyrhynchos* Linnaeus. As Austin (1932) and Todd (1963) have suggested for Labrador, some East Coast visitors may be of the Greenland race, *A. p. conboschas* Brehm.

Remarks. Doubtless no other duck in the world is so widely known as the Mallard. In the wild it is found in much of the earth's north-temperate zone. In captivity it is the ancestor of most varieties of domestic ducks, several of which still resemble it closely. Handsome and swift, it is a favourite with sportsmen, particularly in the West. In the Atlantic Provinces and Ungava its place is taken by a close relative, the Black Duck. Its food is varied, consisting of succulent aquatic vegetation, seeds, insects, and small aquatic animals. It is very fond of grains, wild rice, and corn. It is said to perform a useful function in devouring large numbers of mosquito larvae.

Northern Pintail

Canard pilet
Anas acuta Linnaeus
Total length: male, 66 to 76 cm;
female, 51 to 61 cm
Plate 12

Breeding Distribution of Northern Pintail

Range in Canada. Breeds from Yukon (arctic coast, Old Crow Flats, Dawson, and Lapierre House); northern Mackenzie (Mackenzie Delta, Anderson River, Bathurst Inlet, perhaps Perry River); southern Victoria Island (probably Cambridge Bay); southern Keewatin (Simon's Lake, Beverly Lake, Chesterfield Inlet; Southampton Island); northern Ontario (Hudson and James Bay coasts and lowlands, e.g., Shagamu River, Cape Tatnum, Cape Henrietta Maria, Raft River); northern and central Quebec (Lake Aigneau and False River, probably Povungnituk; Roggan River, Schefferville but rare or absent from much of the interior); south through interior British Columbia (west to Fraser delta); southern Alberta; Saskatchewan; Manitoba; southern Ontario (locally, Thunder Bay, Erieau, Kingston, Ramsayville); southern Quebec (locally: East-Templeton, Pointe Saint-Denis, Soeurs Island; Malbaie on the Gaspé Peninsula, Madeleine Islands, Anticosti Island, and north shore of the Gulf of St. Lawrence); New Brunswick (locally, Midgic, Saint John valley); Prince Edward Island (Hillsborough River); and Nova Scotia (Amherst Bog, Point Michaud, Sable Island).

Two isolated breeding records for District of Franklin (Ellesmere Island: Lake Hazen, 1966; and Banks Island: near Sachs Harbour, 1981).

Recorded in summer from Adelaide Peninsula, Baffin Island (Aitken Lakes, Koukdjuak River, Cape Alberta), and Newfoundland (possibly breeds). Uncommon transient in Labrador and Newfoundland. Abundant transient on the coast of British Columbia and decidedly more common in migration in eastern Canada than at other times.

Winters on the coast of British Columbia (particularly southern parts but north to Queen Charlotte Islands), extreme southern Ontario, and uncommonly in the Maritimes; north rarely to southern Newfoundland.

Adult male (winter, spring, early summer): Head and neck brown with a white line extending up either side of neck to near ear region. Back with fine vermiculations of a blackish hue and white producing a grey effect. Scapulars long, pointed, black with contrasting whitish margins. Forewing grey. Speculum varying between metallic green and bronze-purple, preceded in front by a band of chestnut and bordered behind by black, then white. Two long, black central tail feathers. Outer tail feathers dark brown, edged with white. Under parts mainly white, the sides finely barred with black giving grey effect. Under tail coverts with whiter outer margins. Bill bluish grey, blackish on ridge and nail. Legs and feet bluish grey to olive grey with dusky webs. A complete moult in summer produces a female-like eclipse plumage, and the breeding plumage is not assumed until mid or late autumn. *Adult female*: Top of head buffy brown, heavily streaked with black. Sides of head and neck buffy white streaked with dusky. Throat similar but only lightly streaked or immaculate. Upper back, dark brown with U-shaped buffy markings. Wing browner than in male, speculum duller, often speckled with black. Tail pointed, somewhat elongated, dark brown, marked with buffy white. Under parts dingy white, more or less mixed with dusky, about equally on breast; sides brownish with whitish V-shaped markings. Bill mainly dark greyish-blue. Legs and feet greyish blue to greenish grey with dusky webs. *Immatures*: Resemble adult female but under parts are more heavily streaked.

Measurements. *Adult male*: wing, 262–279 (271); tail, 158–205.5 (180.7); exposed culmen, 48.5–54 (51.7); tarsus, 42–47 (44.1). *Adult female*: wing, 230–266 (251.3) mm.

Field Marks. Adult male unmistakable. In all plumages the long very slender neck, pointed tail, and a narrow but conspicuous white line along the rear edge of the spread wing. *Voice*: Female, a low *quack*; male, a low two-syllable whistle, usually given in display.

Habitat. Shallow bodies of fresh water and marshes, large and small; also outside breeding season, salt and brackish waters of the coast. Frequently feeds on grain stubbles.

Nesting. Nest on the ground, frequently near water and often some distance from it. Nest sometimes well hidden in vegetation but is frequently placed in the exposed open prairie. *Eggs*, usually 7 to 10; vary in colour from pale olive-green to pale buff. Incubation, by the female, averages 23 days but may require 21 to 25 days.

Range. Inhabits both the New and Old worlds. In North America breeds in Alaska, Canada, western Greenland, and the western United States and winters from southern Canada southward.

Garganey

Sarcelle d'été
Anas querquedula Linnaeus
Total length: 38 cm
Plate 9

Status in Canada. Casual visitor to Alberta (an adult male observed at Two Hills, 24–26 June 1961; photo: one at Strathmore, 12 June 1982); Manitoba (photos: St. Ambroise, 23 May 1971); British Columbia (Iona Island, 17 May 1977); Yukon (sight record of adult male on 27 May 1976, at Old Crow Flats); Quebec (photo: male at Bergeronnes, 2 May, and at Trois-Pistoles, 4–6 May 1983); and New Brunswick (photo: Saint John, 3–19 May 1979). Although we cannot be completely sure that some of these were not escapees from captivity, the species is widely distributed in Eurasia and is known to wander.

Body size and bluish upper wing coverts suggest Blue-winged or Cinnamon teals but the blue is paler and more greyish. Adult male (except in eclipse plumage) is readily separable by a conspicuous white narrow curved area extending from above eye back to the nape, by lack of white crescent in front of eye, and by sharp contrast between dark breast and white belly. Females are very difficult to distinguish from North American teals but facial pattern of Garganey is heavier, more definite. In both sexes the grey, instead of yellowish, legs of the Garganey distinguish it from Blue-winged and Cinnamon teals.

Blue-winged Teal

Sarcelle à ailes bleues
Anas discors Linnaeus
Total length: 35.5 to 40.6 cm
Plate 13

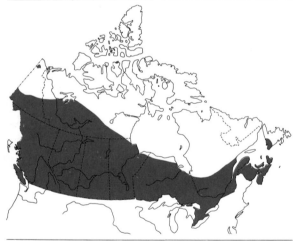

Breeding Distribution of Blue-winged Teal

Range in Canada. Summer resident, scarcer on the Pacific and Atlantic coasts. Breeds across southern Canada from Vancouver Island (Victoria) east to Cape Breton Island and Madeleine Islands, and southwestern Newfoundland (Doyles, Grand Codroy River), and north to northern British Columbia (Atlin); Yukon (rarely: Whisker Creek, possibly Pelly River; rarely at Old Crow); southwestern Mackenzie (Chick and Redrock lakes); northern Manitoba (Churchill); northern Ontario (Sandy Lake, southern James Bay); southern Quebec (Lake Saint-Jean, Madeleine Islands).

Recorded in summer north to Anticosti Island; rarely the north shore of the Gulf of St. Lawrence (Pointe-des-Monts, Moisie Bay, Gull Island, Saint-Augustin); and very rarely southern Labrador (specimens: Battle Harbour, 13 May 1937).

Adult male (breeding plumage): Head and upper neck lead grey with purplish tinge and with large white crescent in front of eye. Chin blackish. Back, rump, and tail dark brown; the feathers margined and otherwise marked with buff. Fore-wing chalky blue, a narrow white border separating the blue area from a bright-green speculum. Breast, abdomen, and sides brown, thickly crossed and spotted with black. On either side of base of tail a conspicuous white patch. Under tail coverts black. Eye brown. Bill bluish black or bluish grey, blackish on ridge. Legs and feet dull yellow. *Adult female*: Head and neck greyish white streaked with dusky, darkest on crown and with dusky line through eye. Chin and throat whitish. Back, rump, and tail dark brown, the feathers marked with buff. Wings as in male but speculum dull blackish with greenish gloss. Breast and sides brown, feathers edged with buff. Abdomen whitish mottled with brown. *Immature (first autumn)*: Resembles adult female, but richer green speculum distinguishes young males from young females. Later, further changes occur toward maturity.

Measurements *(A. d. discors)*. *Adult male*: wing, 176–193 (185.8); tail, 66–74 (70.4); exposed culmen, 40–42 (41.2); tarsus, 31–33.5 (32.1) mm. *Adult female*: wing, 160–182.5 (174.3) mm.

Field Marks. Small size. Large white crescent in front of eye and blue fore-wing easily distinguish adult male. In other plumages the blue fore-wing, conspicuous in flight, separates this teal from all other ducks but the Cinnamon Teal and Shoveler. The latter is larger and has a huge bill. Adult male Cinnamon Teal is cinnamon red. Females and young Blue-winged and Cinnamon teals are not distinguishable in the field, but the latter is not likely to be seen in eastern Canada. When at rest the female resembles the female Green-winged Teal, and both have a green speculum in the wing, but the presence of blue in the wing, best seen in flight, distinguishes the Blue-winged. *Voice*: Female, a weak, high-pitched *quack*; male, a sibilant, high-pitched *seep-seep*.

Habitat. Freshwater ponds, lakes, sloughs, marshes, weedy margins of sluggish rivers, even tiny streams. Not often a bird of salt or brackish water.

Nesting. Nest, on the ground, usually concealed in grass or other vegetation (but sometimes exposed), generally near water. Nest of grasses and other soft vegetation, lined with down. *Eggs*, usually 9 to 12; buffy white. Incubation, by female alone, 23 to 24 days (J. Delacour).

1 Tundra Swan, p. 72
a) adult
b) "Bewick's" Swan, an Old World
   race of Tundra Swan

1a

2a

2b

1b

2 Trumpeter Swan, p. 73
a) immature
b) adult

3 Mute Swan, p. 74
a) adult
b) immature

3a

3b

4 Fulvous Whistling-Duck, p. 71
adult

6b

5b

5a

6a

5 Baikal Teal, p. 84
a) adult male, breeding plumage
b) adult female

6 Garganey, p. 88
a) adult male, breeding plumage
b) adult female

sly 80

1a

1b

1c

1d

1e

1a

2

1 Snow Goose, p. 76
a) adult, intermediate between
   blue and white phases
b) first-year white phase
c) adult white phase
d) adult blue phase
e) first-year blue phase

2 Ross's Goose, p. 77

1a

3 Pink-footed Goose, p. 75
adult

3

2a

1 Canada Goose, p. 80
a) adult (*interior* race)
b) adult (*hutchinsii* race)

2 Brant, p. 79
a) *hrota* race
b) *nigricans* race

2b

2a

1a

4a

4 Greater White-fronted Goose,
p. 75
a) adult
b) immature

4b

5 Barnacle Goose, p. 80
adult

5

1b

6

6 Emperor Goose, p. 78
adult

Crosby/80

12

1a

1 Northern Pintail, p. 87
a) adult male in breeding plumage
b) adult female

1b

3 Mallard, p. 86
a) female
b) adult male in breeding plumage

3a

2

2 American Black Duck, p. 84

3b

4a

4 American Wigeon, p. 101
a) male in breeding plumage
b) female

6a

4b

5 Eurasian Wigeon, p. 100
adult male in breeding plumage

5

6

4b

4a

6a

6 Gadwall, p. 99
a) adult male in breeding plumage
b) female

Crosby

2 Cinnamon Teal, p. 97
a) adult male in breeding plumage
b) female

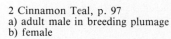

1 Green-winged Teal, p. 83
a) female (*carolinensis* race)
b) adult male in breeding plumage
   (*carolinensis* race)
c) adult male in breeding plumage,
   Eurasian subspecies (*crecca* race)

5 Northern Shoveler, p. 98
a) female
b) adult male in breeding plumage

3 Blue-winged Teal, p. 88
a) adult male in breeding plumage
b) female

4 Wood Duck, p. 82
a) female
b) adult male in breeding plumage

Crosby

14

1 Tufted Duck, p. 105
a) male in breeding plumage
b) female

2 Ring-necked Duck, p. 104
a) adult male in breeding plumage
b) female

3 Lesser Scaup, p. 106
a) immature male
b) adult male in breeding plumage
c) adult female

4 Greater Scaup, p. 105
a) adult male
b) adult female

5 Canvasback, p. 102
a) adult male in breeding plumage
b) female

6 Redhead, p. 103
a) adult male in breeding plumage
b) female

Crosby

1 Oldsquaw, p. 111
a) male in summer
b) female in summer
c) male in winter
d) female in winter

2 Harlequin Duck, p. 110
a) adult male in breeding plumage
b) male in "eclipse" plumage
c) female

3 Black Scoter, p. 112
a) adult male
b) female

4 Surf Scoter, p. 113
a) adult male
b) female

5 White-winged Scoter, p. 114
a) immature
b) adult female
c) adult male

6 Common Eider, p. 107
a) female
b) adult male in breeding plumage

7 King Eider, p. 108
a) adult male in breeding plumage
b) female

Crosby

1 Ruddy Duck, p. 121
a) female
b) male in winter
c) adult male in breeding plumage

2 Bufflehead, p. 117
a) adult male in breeding plumage
b) female

3 Common Goldeneye, p. 115
a) adult male in breeding plumage
b) female

4 Barrow's Goldeneye, p. 116
a) adult male in breeding plumage
b) adult female in breeding plumage

Range. Breeds from southern Canada south to southern California, New Mexico, middle Texas, Louisiana, and North Carolina. Winters from southern United States south to Ecuador, Brazil, and the West Indies.

Subspecies. (1) *Anas discors discors* Linnaeus is the breeding form of all of Canada except the Maritimes. (2) *Anas discors orphna* Stewart and Aldrich, a very slightly darker subspecies, breeds in Nova Scotia, probably New Brunswick and Prince Edward Island, and perhaps the Madeleine Islands (only Nova Scotia specimens examined).

Cinnamon Teal

Sarcelle cannelle
Anas cyanoptera Vieillot
Total length: about 40 cm
Plate 13

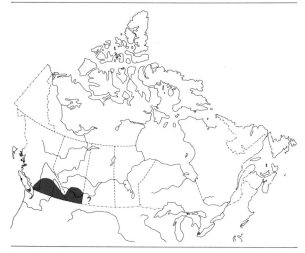

Breeding Distribution of Cinnamon Teal

Range in Canada. Uncommon local summer resident in southwestern Canada. Breeds locally in southern British Columbia (north to Williams Lake, west to Victoria); southern Alberta (Brooks; Mountain View, Tofield); and probably southwestern Saskatchewan (see summer records below). One breeding record for Ontario (a pair with nest and eggs at Amherstburg in 1983).

Recorded in breeding season, but not known to breed, north to Quesnel, British Columbia; Edmonton, Alberta; and in Saskatchewan (Crane Lake; Moose Jaw area; near Val Marie; Old Wives Lake, Leech Lake, Regina). Rare in southern Manitoba (Shoal Lake, Oak Lake). Casual in Ontario (Mitchell Bay, three males shot in October 1939; Big Point marsh: male shot on 14 November 1953). Sight records for Quebec (Laprairie, Soeurs Island, and Lake Saint-Pierre); Nova Scotia (Brier Island, 28–30 August 1980) and Yukon (Swan Lake, 21 May 1978).

Adult male (breeding plumage): Head, neck, breast, sides, and flanks dark cinnamon-red. Crown and chin blackish. Back, rump, and tail dark brown. Shorter scapulars cinnamon and black, longer scapulars brown with buffy medial stripes and blue outer vanes. Fore-wing blue, the ends of greater coverts white. Speculum iridescent green with black inner and outer borders. Abdomen usually dusky brown. Under tail coverts blackish. Eye orange. Bill blackish. Legs and feet dull orange-yellow; webs dusky. *Adult female*: Like the female Blue-winged Teal, but with slightly longer bill. *Immature (first autumn)*: Like adult female, but young male has much richer green speculum.

Measurements. *Adult male*: wing, 174–196 (186.3); tail, 64–75 (67.6); exposed culmen, 41.5–48 (46.1); tarsus, 31.5–35 (33.4). *Adult female*: wing, 169–189 (177.6) mm.

Field Marks. Small size, dark-red colour, and blue fore-wing of adult male are unmistakable. Females and young can be distinguished from all but Blue-winged Teal and Shoveler by blue fore-wing. The huge bill of the Shoveler, a larger bird, is very different. Females of Cinnamon and Blue-winged Teal cannot usually be separated in the field. *Voice*: Apparently much more silent than most ducks. I have never heard its voice. Male is said to have a "low, rattling, chattering note" (Wetmore). Female has a weak *quack*.

Habitat. Shallow fresh water: lakes, sloughs, sluggish streams, particularly those with margins of emergent vegetation and muddy shores.

Nesting. Nest on the ground. *Eggs*, 6 to 13, usually 10 to 12; whitish to pale pinkish-buff. Incubation 21 to 25 days (H.E. Spencer), by the female.

Range. Breeds from southwestern Canada south to central Mexico; also in South America. North American birds winter from southwestern United States south to Costa Rica, Panama, and northern Colombia.

Subspecies. *Anas cyanoptera septentrionalium* Snyder and Lumsden.

Northern Shoveler

Canard souchet
Anas clypeata Linnaeus
Total length: 43 to 53 cm
Plate 13

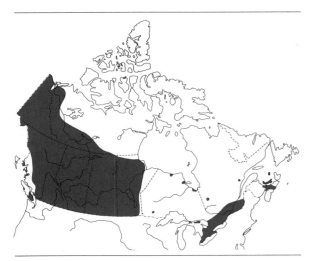

Breeding Distribution of Northern Shoveler

Range in Canada. Breeds from Yukon (locally, arctic coastal plain, Old Crow, Pine Lake, Sulphur Lake, Sheldon Lake); western Mackenzie (Aklavik, Great Slave Lake); northern Saskatchewan (Lake Athabasca); northern Manitoba (rarely, Churchill); south through British Columbia; Alberta; Saskatchewan; and Manitoba; locally in Ontario (Grand River, near Toronto; near Dunnville, Ottawa, Kingston, Atikokan, and at least four localities in Kent County; Shagamu River mouth, 55°51′N, 86°46′W. Probably also on west coast of James Bay: Opinnagau River, Hook Point, Big Pisquamish Point); Quebec (Lake Saint-Pierre, Lake Saint-François, Île-Verte, Lake Saint-Jean, Amos, Madeleine Islands). Also in New Brunswick (near Sackville); Prince Edward Island (Mount Stewart); and Nova Scotia (Three Fathom Harbour, Missaguash Bog).

Spring and autumn migrant through British Columbia (including coast), Alberta, Saskatchewan, and Manitoba; less commonly but regularly in southern Ontario and southeastern Quebec. Rare migrant in New Brunswick, Prince Edward Island, Nova Scotia, and Newfoundland (St. John's, 5 October 1957). Recorded rarely: Lake Saint-Jean (specimen: Saint-Gédéon, 9 September 1961); the north shore of the Gulf of St. Lawrence (La Romaine, 1 June 1915); Anticosti Island (11 October 1938); and Madeleine Islands (Grindstone Island, September 1906), Quebec. Some winter in southwestern British Columbia and occasionally in southern Ontario.

Bill longer than head, much wider at end than at base. *Adult male (breeding plumage)*: Head and most of neck dark green with purplish reflections. Breast and shoulders white. Middle back dark slaty-brown, feathers tipped paler. Rump and upper tail coverts blackish with greenish gloss. Most scapulars white, longer ones blue. Fore-wing blue; speculum green, bordered in front by a white line and above by black. Abdomen, sides, and flanks chestnut. Patch on either side of tail, white. Under tail coverts black. Eye orange or yellow. Legs and feet vermilion. *Adult female (breeding plumage)*: Head and neck greyish buff, streaked with dusky, darkest on crown. Back, scapulars, rump, and upper tail coverts dark brown; the feathers with buffy markings and margins. Wing similar to male but duller and with little or no black. Breast, abdomen, and under tail coverts buffy, streaked and mottled with dusky. Bill variable, greyish to brownish, tending to orange along cutting edges. Legs and feet orange. *Juvenals*: Similar to adult female, but breast and belly of young male tinged with chestnut. Young female like adult female, but fore-wing is slaty, green of speculum absent or much reduced.

Measurements. *Adult male*: wing, 231–252 (238.9); tail, 75.5–89 (83.9); exposed culmen, 63–66.5 (65.4); tarsus, 36–40.5 (38.2). *Adult female*: wing, 217–245 (225.7) mm.

Field Marks. The long bill is distinctive in both males and females at all seasons. The unique markings of the adult male can be seen in flight at long distances, the white breast contrasting markedly with dark head and abdomen. Blue-winged and Cinnamon Teal also have blue fore-wings but are much smaller and have much shorter bills. *Voice*: A rather silent species. Male has deep *woh, woh, woh*. Female, weak *quacks*.

Habitat. In breeding season, shallow, often muddy freshwater lakes, marshes, sloughs, and pot-holes, especially those providing good cover and food.

Nesting. Nest of grasses and similar material, lined with down; on the ground and usually not any great distance from water. *Eggs*, 6 to 14, usually 10 to 12, clutches tending to be smaller in re-nesting attempts; dull very pale olive-buff to very pale greenish-grey. Incubation variously recorded from 21 to 25 days, probably 23 to 25, by the female.

Range. Holarctic. In North America breeds mainly from Alaska east to Manitoba and south to California, New Mexico, Nebraska, and western Iowa, locally farther east. Winters from coastal southern British Columbia, Arizona, the Gulf Coast, and coastal Georgia and South Carolina south to Costa Rica and the West Indies.

Gadwall

Canard chipeau
Anas strepera Linnaeus
Total length: 45.7 to 55.8 cm
Plate 12

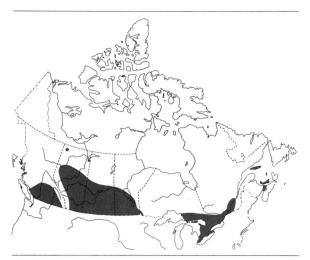

Breeding Distribution of Gadwall

Range in Canada. Breeds locally in southern British Columbia (Fraser Delta, Swan and Goose lakes, Okanagan valley, 150 Mile House, Caribou); Alberta (east of the mountains, and north to Hay and Zama lakes, delta of the Athabasca River); southern and central Saskatchewan; southern and central-western Manitoba (north to about Saskatchewan River Marshes); and in southern Ontario (north to Wawa, Lillabelle Lake, Ottawa); Quebec (locally Richelieu and Yamaska counties, formerly Anticosti Island); New Brunswick–Nova Scotia border; and Prince Edward Island (Indian River). Has been introduced into Lunenburg County, Nova Scotia, and some are said to have nested for a time.

Has been recorded north of its breeding range in British Columbia (Driftwood valley); northern Saskatchewan (Fond du Lac); and northern Manitoba (Churchill).

In migration in southern British Columbia it is more common in autumn than in spring, with a relatively large autumn population in the Okanagan valley. A more or less regular migrant in southern Ontario. Rare migrant in southwestern Quebec (Senneville, Amos, Kamouraska). In Nova Scotia, two specimen records, both on the Grand Pré meadows, 14 November 1931, and 11 November 1947. Rare transient in New Brunswick (Germantown Marsh, Queenstown).

Winters regularly but not abundantly on the coast of British Columbia from Victoria to Masset, Queen Charlotte Islands, and sometimes in the southern interior (Okanagan Landing).

Adult male (winter and spring): Head and neck grey, speckled with blackish, paler on chin and throat. Back dark grey, vermiculated with white, some scapulars broadly edged with yellowish brown. Upper and under tail coverts black. Tail brownish grey, the feathers with paler margins. Folded wing greyish at bend, then chestnut (on middle coverts), then black (greater coverts). Wing patch (speculum) white, bordered in front by black. Breast brownish black with numerous white or buffy crescentic marks (feathers white at base). Sides dark grey, crossed by narrow wavy white lines. Belly and wing linings white. Bill dark grey. Legs and toes yellow or orange with blackish webs. In summer a complete moult produces a female-like eclipse plumage. This is gradually moulted, and by November the adult nuptial plumage of winter and spring is again almost complete. *Adult female*: Head and neck similar to male. Back, scapulars, rump, upper tail coverts, breast, and sides, dusky with buffy edges and markings. Wing somewhat as in male's, but chestnut much reduced in extent or lacking. Lower breast, belly, and wing linings white. Bill dull orange with dusky culmen and spots. Legs dull yellow. *Young in first autumn*: Similar to female but belly streaked with dusky and general colour somewhat darker.

Measurements. *Adult male*: wing, 259–276 (266); tail, 78–91 (81.4); exposed culmen, 40.5–46.5 (43.5); tarsus, 40.5–43 (41.3). *Adult female*: wing, 241–251 (245.8) mm.

Field Marks. Adult male is a grey medium-sized duck showing (especially in flight) a small white wing patch and a black rump. The white wing patch, when it can be seen, separates females and immatures from similar-appearing Mallards and Pintails. American Wigeons also usually show a white area in the wing, but it is situated on the fore-wing. On the Gadwall it is a patch near the rear edge of the wing. *Voice*: Female's *quack* is usually softer than that of Mallard and slightly higher pitched. Male has loud *kack, kack*, a shrill whistled call (Wetmore), and a croaking note usually preceding a whistled note in display.

Habitat. In summer prefers sloughs and shallow margins of lakes bordered by good cover (see also Nesting). Sometimes feeds on grain-stubble fields. It does not often occur on salt water.

Nesting. Nest on the ground usually near water (often on low islands) but on drier ground than most ducks and usually concealed by vegetation; sometimes on open prairie at some distance from water. Nest is of grasses, weed stalks, and other vegetation and is lined with down. *Eggs* usually 10 to 12; dull creamy-white. Incubation 25 to 28 days, by the female (various authors).

Range. Western North America, Europe, and Asia.

Remarks. Despite its wide distribution in the world, the Gadwall is not very numerous. A bird of temperate climates, it seems reluctant to venture very far north. Its flesh is not highly prized by most sportsmen.

Eurasian Wigeon

Canard siffleur d'Europe
Anas penelope Linnaeus
Total length: 43 to 51 cm
Plate 12

Figure 29
Axillars of
a) Eurasian Wigeon
b) American Wigeon

Status in Canada. Scarce autumn and spring transient; local winter resident. British Columbia (scarce but regular winter resident on coast, 30 October to 30 March; rare in the interior). Alberta (Valhalla Lake; Jasper). Ontario (specimen taken at Long Point, 12 October 1914. Sight records for London, 4 April 1937; Port Colborne, 26 March 1935; Port Credit, 20 March 1957; Hamilton, 20 May 1957 and 31 March 1935; near Barrie, 26 April 1942; Humber Marsh, 5 and 8 December 1943; Simcoe County, April 1942). Quebec (two specimens taken at Lochaber, one in autumn 1926, one on 27 October 1934; a third near Johan-Beetz Bay; a fourth at Bonne-Espérance, November 1919, together with a sight record at Esquimaux Point, 13 June 1923; a fifth specimen was taken near Cap-Tourmente, 28 October 1933; also various sight records). Labrador (specimen shot at Seal Cove, October 1900). Newfoundland (specimens from Stephenville Crossing, 5 October 1927, and near St. John's, 20 October 1935, and from Conception Bay, 20 October 1953). New Brunswick (specimen taken near Grand Manan Island on 1 November 1927). Prince Edward Island (specimen shot 26 September 1936). Nova Scotia (specimens taken at Cape Sable, December 1926; near Yarmouth, 9 January 1912; Grand Pré, 28 October 1929, and 10 November 1944; Wallace, 4 November 1953; west Lawrencetown, 14 November 1957; Masstown, early November 1947). Single individuals banded in Iceland have been taken in Newfoundland, Prince Edward Island, and Nova Scotia.

Sight records only for Manitoba (Hartney, 3 June 1949; near Aubigny, 16 April 1977; also three sight records for Churchill); Saskatchewan (Cypress Lake, Cumberland House); and Yukon (Yukon Game Farm, 3 May 1981).

Adult male: Similar to American Wigeon but head and neck rusty-red; forehead and crown creamy buff; flanks vermiculated black-and-white. *Adult female and immatures* are very much like American Wigeon and are best distinguished by the colour of the axillars (Figure 29), which are thickly but finely speckled or marbled with dark grey instead of being pure white (or mainly so).

Field Marks. Adult male readily distinguished from American Wigeon by rusty-red head and buffy crown. Females of the two species are very similar, but the head of the Eurasian female is often tinged reddish; that of the American is always grey.

Range. Breeds in Iceland and across northern Europe and northern Asia (mostly between latitudes 71° and 48°N). Winters south to northern Africa, Asia Minor, Indochina, Taiwan, and Japan. Straggles regularly to North America (southern Canada and the United States).

American Wigeon

(Baldpate)

Canard siffleur d'Amérique
Anas americana Gmelin
Total length: 46 to 56 cm
Plate 12

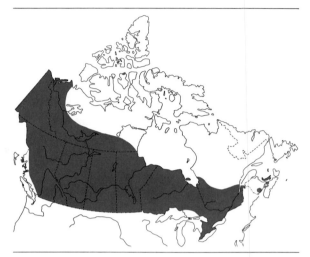

Breeding Distribution of American Wigeon

Range in Canada. Breeds from Yukon (north to Babbage River); northwestern and middle Mackenzie (Mackenzie Delta, Anderson River, Nahanni National Park, Great Slave Lake); southern Keewatin (Windy River, Old Post); northern Manitoba (occasionally, Churchill); south through interior British Columbia (Mile 85 Haines Road, Kleena Kleene, Swan Lake in Peace River area, Nulki Lake, Swan Lake in Okanagan); Alberta; Saskatchewan; and Manitoba; also locally in Ontario (Fort Severn, Cape Henrietta Maria, Nikip Lake, Leith, Garson, Luther Marsh, Toronto, Mud Lake, Cornwall); western Quebec (Moar Bay, Taschereau, Blue-Sea-Lake, Nicolet, Saint-Gédéon, Cap-Tourmente); and recently locally in Nova Scotia (Debert, Amherst Point); New Brunswick (Saint John valley); Prince Edward Island (Deroche Pond, Indian River); and southwestern Newfoundland (Grand Codroy River). Migrates commonly through British Columbia, Alberta, Saskatchewan, and Manitoba; regularly but less commonly in most of Ontario and southwestern Quebec. Has been recorded along the outer north shore of the Gulf of St. Lawrence (Mécatina Island, Mingan, Parsons Island). Accidental on Banks Island (Raddi Lake), N.W.T. Winters regularly in southwestern British Columbia, rarely in southern Ontario and Nova Scotia.

Adult male: Forehead and top of head, white; broad green patch from eye to nape; rest of head creamy, thickly speckled with black. Upper back pinkish brown, finely crossed with wavy black lines. Middle upper tail coverts greyish, finely barred with blackish; outer ones mainly black. Fore-wing with large white patch. Speculum greenish bordered by black. Breast and sides pinkish brown. Axillars white (sometimes lightly shaft-streaked). Belly white. Under tail coverts black. Bill greyish blue with black tip. Feet pale greyish-blue with dusky webs. *Adult female*: Head and neck creamy, heavily streaked with dusky. Back greyish brown, feathers edged with yellowish brown. Speculum mostly black, often with traces of green. Fore-wing with poorly defined whitish area. Axillars white, occasionally shaft-streaked. Breast and sides reddish brown. Belly white. Under tail coverts mixed brown and white. Bill and feet duller than in male. Wigeons have but 14 tail feathers compared with 16 in the Gadwall.

Measurements. *Adult male*: wing, 252–280 (263); tail, 95–124 (107.8); exposed culmen, 36–39 (37.4); tarsus, 38–41 (39.3). *Adult female*: wing 209–244 (233.3) mm.

Field Marks. Conspicuous white crown of adult male. In flight, white patch on front of wing of adult male and female (but much less noticeable in female). Immatures, before acquiring the white wing patch, otherwise generally resemble the adult female. In all plumages the white belly contrasts sharply with the dark breast in flight overhead (see Eurasian Wigeon). *Voice*: Male has pleasing mellow whistled notes usually grouped in threes. Female, a rather hoarse *quack*. On the water their appearance is often distinctive. They ride high and sometimes pivot lightly as they daintily peck at the surface for food.

Habitat. Breeds about freshwater sloughs, ponds, and marshy borders of lakes. In migration frequents also shallow coastal bays.

Nesting. Nest of grasses and weeds, lined with down, placed in a hollow on dry ground not always near water. *Eggs*, 7 to 12; creamy white. Incubation 24 to 25 days (J. Delacour), by the female.

Range. Breeds mainly from Alaska east to Hudson Bay, and south (east of the coast ranges) to northeastern California, Colorado, and Nebraska. Winters from southern Alaska, southern Illinois, and southern New England south to Central America and the West Indies.

Tribe **Aythyini**
Freshwater Diving Ducks

Figure 30
Foot of a diving duck

Medium-sized diving ducks, primarily frequenting fresh water in the breeding season (but found on salt water at other times). Compared with surface-feeding ducks the bill is rather broad, tail short, legs set farther back on the body, toes longish, the hind one broadly lobed (Figure 30). They are excellent divers, feed under water. Take-off from water is more difficult than in surface-feeders. No iridescent speculum but some species have a white or pale area in the secondaries.

Canvasback

Morillon à dos blanc
Aythya valisineria (Wilson)
Total length: 48 to 66 cm
Plate 14

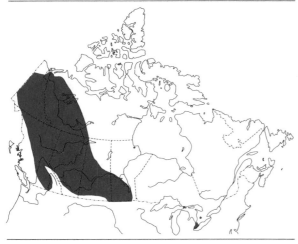

Breeding Distribution of Canvasback

Range in Canada. Common breeder, scarcer than formerly, in western Canada. Local winter resident. Breeds in interior British Columbia (Atlin, Cariboo, Peace River parklands, and Richter Pass); Yukon (Old Crow, Sulphur Lake, Pelly valley, Marsh Lake); western Mackenzie (Aklavik, Anderson River, and Fort Resolution); Alberta (except Rocky Mountains); Saskatchewan (Kazan Lake, Candle Lake, and Nipawin, probably northwest to Lake Athabasca, and south to Crane Lake and Redvers); middle and southern Manitoba (The Pas, Lake St. Martin, Riding Mountain, southern Lake Winnipeg, Killarney; in 1980, one nest at Churchill); and extreme southern Ontario (very rarely and locally: Walpole Island, Luther Marsh).

Migrates through southern parts of western Canada including southwestern British Columbia; also regularly in southern Ontario (especially Lake Erie) but scarcer in extreme eastern parts. Scarce and irregular in southwestern

Bill long, forehead sloping. *Adult male (winter and breeding)*: Head and neck chestnut, darkening to blackish on crown, base of bill, and throat. A broad, sharply defined black area extending completely around fore-part of body in front of wings. Back, scapulars, and sides white crossed by fine wavy dusky lines. Rump and tail coverts black. Tail blackish. Wing coverts grey, tertials white, all crossed by fine wavy lines; secondaries, including speculum, grey. Abdomen white, its hind part crossed by wavy fine lines. Eye red. Bill blackish. Legs and feet greyish blue. *Adult female (winter and breeding)*: Head and neck dark reddish-brown to buffy brown, darkest on crown and back of neck, paling to nearly white on chin and throat and around eye. Upper breast and fore-back dark brown with paler feather edges. Scapulars, rump, and upper tail coverts brown crossed with whitish. Tail greyish brown. Wing coverts dusky brown, finely dotted and streaked with white. Primaries brownish, secondaries and speculum grey. Sides and flanks brown, with light feather edges producing barred effect. Belly whitish, more or less mottled with greyish brown. Eye brown. *Immature*: In early autumn it resembles adult female, but the under parts are more decidedly mottled. Sexes differentiate in September and October.

Measurements. *Adult male*: wing, 222–231 (227.2); tail, 52–60 (57.6); exposed culmen, 59–65 (62.2); tarsus, 44–46 (45.5). *Adult female*: wing, 210–226 (217.4) mm.

Field Marks. Long bill combined with sloping forehead makes a profile unlike that of any other duck. The white back of the male separates it at some distance from the male Redhead, which has a grey one. *Voice*: Male (usually silent) has courtship notes rendered as *ick, ick, cooo* (A.A. Allen), first two parts quick and high pitched, not far-carrying; the last part is louder and at a distance may be the only part heard. Female has a coarse *kurr*; also a *quack*.

Habitat. Deeper waters of marshes, larger sloughs, deep-water lakes with pondweed and vegetated margins. In migration and winter also salt and brackish bays; large lakes; and (where open) sluggish parts of larger rivers.

Nesting. Nest, a bulky structure of marsh vegetation, lined with down, usually in shallows near open water, sometimes on dry ground; occasionally at some distance from water. *Eggs* are greyish olive or greenish drab and average 10 to a clutch. Incubation 23 to 28 days usually 24 days (H.A. Hochbaum), by the female.

Quebec (Montréal, Québec, Trois-Rivières); casual in New Brunswick (French Lake, Coles Island); and in Nova Scotia (Clark's Harbour, Little Harbour Lake, Voglers Cove). Winters in fluctuating numbers in southwestern British Columbia and extreme southern Ontario (mainly Lake Erie from Rondeau Provincial Park west; smaller numbers farther east: upper Niagara River, Toronto, Kingston).

Redhead

Morillon à tête rouge
Aythya americana (Eyton)
Total length: 43 to 58 cm
Plate 14

Breeding Distribution of Redhead

Range in Canada. Breeds in interior British Columbia (north at least to Nulki Lake; recorded in breeding season north to Peace River region); southwestern Mackenzie (Fort Resolution); Alberta (Wood Buffalo National Park, Peace River, Lesser Slave Lake, Flat Lake, Buffalo Lake, Astotin Lake, Belvedere, Brooks; not mountainous southwestern corner); Saskatchewan (north at least to Kazan Lake); central-western and southern Manitoba (north to Cedar Lake, Lake St. Martin); southern Ontario (rarely and locally: Lake St. Clair; Charter Island, Lennox–Addington County; Luther Marsh; formerly Toronto Island); southwestern Quebec (very locally: Lake Saint-François, Île-du-Moine); New Brunswick (very rarely: Middle Island, St. John River; formerly probably near St. Croix); and recently Nova Scotia (locally: Amherst Point Bird Sanctuary, Wallace). Recorded in breeding season in southern Yukon (Teslin Lake) and southwestern Mackenzie (Nahanni National Park). Migrates through southern parts of the western provinces including southwestern British Columbia; regularly (locally common but scarce in extreme east) in southern Ontario where formerly it was much commoner; uncommonly in southwestern Quebec; rarely in New Brunswick, Prince Edward Island, and Nova Scotia. Winters in southern British Columbia in small numbers (formerly abundantly in Okanagan valley), southern Ontario (Lake Erie, Lake Ontario), and very rarely Nova Scotia.

Range. Breeds from interior-central Alaska and western continental Canada south to northern California, western Nevada, Utah (locally), northern Colorado, and northern Minnesota. Winters mainly from northern and middle United States south to the Gulf States and Mexico.

Adult male (winter and breeding plumage): Head and upper neck chestnut with slight purplish gloss. Breast, lower neck, fore-back, rump, upper and under tail coverts, black. Back and scapulars, sides and flanks, finely barred black-and-white, giving grey appearance. Wing coverts grey. Speculum paler grey with narrow white border. Forepart of abdomen white, hind part crossed by fine greyish lines. Eye yellow. Bill pale bluish with whitish ring behind black tip. Legs and feet bluish grey. *Adult female (winter and breeding plumage)*: Head and neck brown, darkest on crown and back of neck, paling to whitish brown at base of bill and on chin. Faint pale streak behind eye. Back, scapulars, and rump dark brown; feathers with paler edges. Tail and tail coverts brown. Wing similar to male's. Belly whitish. Fore-neck, breast, and sides brownish, feathers tipped with ashy. Eye brown. Bill and feet duller than male's.

Measurements. *Adult male*: wing, 223–242 (231.6); tail, 50.5–66 (58.5); exposed culmen, 46–52.5 (49.4); tarsus, 41–43 (41.8). *Adult female*: wing, 202–231 (219.2) mm.

Field Marks. Resembles the Canvasback, but head profile is very different—the Redhead has an abruptly rising forehead and slightly concave bill; the Canvasback has a long sloping forehead. The back of the male Redhead is decidedly more greyish, less whitish. Female Redheads resemble female scaups and Ring-necks. In flight the *grey* wing-patch of the Redhead separates it from both species of scaups, which have white areas in the wings. The female Redhead has only a buffy suggestion of a lighter area at the base of the bill where female scaups have a well-marked white one. Female Ring-necks are darker and have a more definite eye-ring and a ring on the bill. *Voice*: Male has a cat-like *mee-ow*; female a coarse *kurr-kurr-kurr*; also purring and growling notes.

Habitat. Freshwater lakes and their shallow edges. In migration often rafts well out on lakes coming in to shallower margins in the evening. Not usually a saltwater duck, it frequents fresh or brackish water even when near the seacoast.

Nesting. Nest, a mass of vegetation, well cupped and lined with down (also very often lays eggs in nests of other ducks). Nest is usually placed among emergent vegetation of shallow water, but sometimes on dry land, in some areas commonly. *Eggs*, (average clutch size 9) are pale olive-buff or creamy buff. Incubation 24 to 28 days, by female.

Range. Breeds in southern Alaska and from southern parts of western Canada south to southern California, central Arizona, northwestern New Mexico, western Nebraska, northern Iowa, and southern Wisconsin. Winters in middle and southern United States and Mexico, in smaller numbers farther north.

Ring-necked Duck

Morillon à collier
Aythya collaris (Donovan)
Total length: 38 to 46 cm
Plate 14

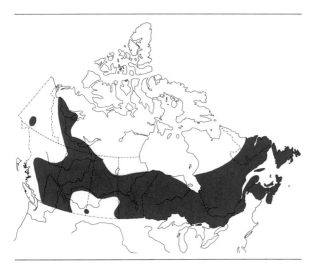

Breeding Distribution of Ring-necked Duck

Range in Canada. Breeds in central and southern interior British Columbia (north at least to Bulkley valley; commonly in Cariboo parklands; locally in East Kootenay near Invermere; former breeding reported at Chilliwack); southern Yukon (Swan Lake); northwestern Mackenzie (Arctic Red River, Chick Lake); Alberta (northern and central parts; very locally in southern parts); Saskatchewan (northwest to Lake Athabasca and south to about the southern edge of the aspen parklands, locally to Redvers area; and the Cypress Hills); middle and southern Manitoba (north at least to The Pas and Pikwitonei region); Ontario (locally; northward to near Hudson Bay in Fort Severn area; Kenora, Thunder Bay, Geraldton, and Cochrane districts; Peterborough; and eastward in the area between Lake Ontario and the Ottawa River); Quebec (Lac du Vieux-Comptoir, Messines, Lochaber Bay on the Ottawa River, Lake Magog, Lake Edmond, Rush and Green lakes, Lake Saint-Jean, Anticosti Island, Piashti River near north shore of Gulf of St. Lawrence); Labrador (near Hopedale); New Brunswick (mainly southern part); Prince Edward Island; Nova Scotia (commonly Cape Breton Island, locally elsewhere); and Newfoundland (Gander, Codroy, and Upper Humber rivers, Goobies, Whitbourne). Winters in southwestern British Columbia; occasionally southern Ontario (Great Lakes); rarely Nova Scotia (Lockeport, Port Hebert Harbour, Sable River). Has greatly extended its range in eastern Canada in recent years.

Adult male (breeding plumage): Crown feathers rather long and erect, giving head a triangular shape. Head and neck black glossed with purple and green; chin white; neck with narrow inconspicuous chestnut collar about lower neck. Back, scapulars, rump, upper and under tail coverts, tail, and breast, black. Belly white, hind part crossed by fine blackish lines. Sides and flanks white, crossed by fine blackish lines giving a grey effect. A spur of white extends upward in front of folded wing. Wing coverts sooty; speculum pearl grey; tertials slightly glossed greenish; under wing coverts white and brownish grey. Eye yellow. Bill dark slate with bluish-white band near end and a narrow whitish margin at base and edges. Legs and feet greyish blue to grey. *Adult female*: Head and neck greyish brown, darkest on crown; area behind base of bill, narrow eye-ring, and chin, whitish. No collar. Back, scapulars, rump, tail coverts, and tail, dark brown, the feathers with paler edges. Wing similar to male's but coverts duller. Breast and sides brownish with paler feather margins. Belly mottled brown and white. Eye (variable) yellowish to brownish. Bill dark-lead colour with light band near tip less prominent than in male and lacking markings at base and edges. Legs and feet similar to male's. *Immatures*: In early autumn both sexes similar to adult females, but in September and October sexes begin to differentiate, the blackish feathers of males appearing among the brownish feathers of head and back. In any plumage the greenish gloss to the tertials distinguishes the Ring-necks from similar Redheads.

Measurements. *Adult male*: wing, 188.5–201 (195.6); tail, 53–62.5 (57.9); exposed culmen, 44.5–54 (48.2); tarsus, 34–37 (35.3). *Adult female*: wing, 176–191 (184.1) mm.

Field Marks. The triangular head shape is different from that of other species. Males somewhat resemble scaups but have *black* backs, a spur of white extending up in front of the folded wing, and a white ring near end of the bill. The female's whitish ring around the eye separates it from scaups and the Redhead, which it closely resembles. Its light area near base of bill is less well-defined than in scaups. Back and head are somewhat darker than in the Redhead. The grey speculum, if visible, separates it from the scaups, which have a white one. *Voice*: Male is generally silent but in breeding season has a low-pitched hissing whistle which is not far-carrying. Female has scaup-like notes and growls.

Habitat. Mainly shallow fresh water (often acid) of marshes, sedge meadows, and bogs; occasionally tidal estuaries and bays. Unlike most diving ducks, it is not often found far out on large expanses of open water. In migration, also rivers and larger lakes, particularly those with marshy edges. Not often found on strictly salt water at any time.

Nesting. Nest, on low vegetated margins of open water of bogs, ponds, and sloughs, is of marsh vegetation found at the nest site and is lined with down. *Eggs*, 6 to 14 (average 9); olive grey, olive brown, or buffy brown. Incubation, 25 to 29 days, is by female (H.L. Mendall).

Range. Breeds in southern Alaska and from Canada south to northeastern Washington, Michigan, northeastern New York, northern Vermont, central New Hampshire, and southern Maine with isolated or sporadic breeding south to southern Oregon, northeastern Nevada, northwestern Montana, southern Colorado, central Nebraska, northwestern Indiana, northwestern Pennsylvania, and eastern Massachusetts. Winters mainly from southern United States (north on the coasts to southern British Columbia and Massachusetts) south through Mexico to Guatemala and in the West Indies.

Tufted Duck

Fuligule morillon
Aythya fuligula (Linnaeus)
Total length: 40.5 to 45.6 cm
Plate 14

Status in Canada. Since about 1961 has become a rare but more or less regular visitor to British Columbia, mostly in the Vancouver, Victoria, and Ladner regions, some occurrences supported by photos. Sight records for Ontario (Hamilton, March 1956 and winter 1981; photo: Oakville, 25 January 1983) and Quebec (Saint-Pierre-d'Orléans, 3 May 1976). While some records may be of escapees from captivity, there is little reason to doubt that most of the British Columbia records, at least, are of wild birds.

Similar to Ring-necked Duck but the male Tufted Duck's drooping crest separates it. Females and eclipse males lack the light eye-ring of the Ring-neck and usually show less white at the base of the bill. The wing stripe of the Tufted Duck is white in all plumages (grey in the Ring-neck); see Greater and Lesser scaups.

Range. Eurasia.

Greater Scaup

Grand Morillon
Aythya marila (Linnaeus)
Total length: 43 to 53 cm
Plate 14

Breeding Distribution of Greater Scaup

Range in Canada. Full extent of breeding range uncertain owing to confusion in literature with Lesser Scaup. Breeds in Yukon (Old Crow Flats perhaps north to arctic coast; widely recorded in summer in southern parts); north-western British Columbia (Haines Road); Mackenzie (Mackenzie Delta, Anderson River, Great Slave Lake, Ptarmigan Lake); southern Keewatin (Rankin Inlet, Windy River; probably McConnell River); northern Manitoba (Churchill, northern Lake Winnipeg); northern Ontario (Hudson Bay coast); central-western, northern, and southeastern Quebec (Moar Bay, Grande rivière de la Baleine, Leaf Bay–Kuujjuaq region, Anticosti Island, Madeleine Islands); Newfoundland (Browsey Island); and Prince Edward Island. Perhaps also Labrador (Nain; south of Lake Melville) and at Ellice River and Coppermine, N.W.T. Reports of flightless young in New Brunswick (Tabusintac), and Nova Scotia (Cape Breton Highlands National Park) are unfortunately not supported by specimens or photographs.

Adult male (winter and breeding plumage): Head, neck, breast, shoulders, fore-back, rump, tail coverts, and ventral area, black; head and neck with *greenish* gloss. Middle back and scapulars white crossed by wavy black lines. Wing coverts slaty brown, finely marked with white. Tail and primaries dark brown. Speculum white, bordered in front, above, and behind with black. Belly white, sharply cut off from black breast, the hind part crossed by zig-zag narrow blackish lines; sides and flanks white, finely vermiculated with black. Eye yellow. Bill greyish blue with black nail. Legs and feet bluish grey. *Adult female (winter and breeding)*: Head dark brown with well-defined whitish area at base of bill and chin. Back, rump, upper tail coverts, and tail dark brown. Upper side of wing dark brown, speculum as in male. Upper breast, sides, and flanks greyish brown with buffy feather tips. Belly white, mottled with dusky. Eye dark yellow. Bill dull bluish-grey, nail black. *Immatures*: In September both sexes resemble the adult female, but the white face-patch is more restricted. In October and November the sexes differentiate, and by February the head of the male closely resembles that of the adult.

Measurements. *Adult male*: wing, 213–229 (222.4); tail, 51.5–59 (56); exposed culmen, 41.5–48 (45.2); tarsus, 36.5–41.5 (39.5). *Adult female*: wing, 197–219 (209.9) mm.

Field Marks. Very difficult to separate in life from the slightly smaller Lesser Scaup. In good light and at close range the Greater has a greenish gloss to the head; that of the Lesser is dark purple. In flight the white wing-stripe of the Greater extends farther toward the tip. There is, however, much overlapping, and only extremes can be recognized with certainty. This *white* wing-stripe separates the scaups in all plumages from the similar Ring-necked and Redhead, which have a grey one. The well-defined whitish patch at the base of the female's bill also is characteristic of the scaups, but see the Ring-necked and the Redhead, which have less well-defined similar markings. Scaups have yellow eyes. *Voice*: Male, generally silent, is said to have a cooing note in courtship; also a low whistle. Female has a harsh *kerr* or *kerr-urr*.

Habitat. In breeding season, lakes, ponds, and more sluggish rivers. In migration and winter, saltwater bays and coasts, large freshwater lakes. Generally it is less partial to smaller bodies of water than the Lesser Scaup.

Nesting. Nest on ground, usually near shore of lake or pond or on islands in lakes; sometimes covererd by grasses. Nests may at times be relatively close together. Nest, a hollow in ground or tussock, lined with surrounding vegetation, down, and feathers. *Eggs*, usually 8 to 10; olive-grey to olive-buff. Incubation, by the female, lasts 23 to 27 days (J. Delacour).

Rare migrant in Alberta (La Saline, Beaverhill Lake) and Saskatchewan (Indian Head; sight records at Regina and Gainsborough). Winters in British Columbia (regularly on the coast, sometimes on Okanagan Lake, South Thompson River); southern Ontario (commonly on Lake Ontario and Lake Erie); southern Quebec (occasionally Montréal); and the Maritime Provinces (north to Newfoundland).

Range. Holarctic. Breeds in Iceland; the Orkney and Hebrides islands; Norway; Sweden; northern Russia, and Siberia mostly north of latitude 60°; on Bering Island; and in Alaska and Canada. In North America it winters on the Pacific Coast (southern Alaska to California); on the Atlantic Coast to the Gulf States and Mexico; and on Lakes Erie and Ontario.

Subspecies. *Aythya marila nearctica* Stejneger.

Lesser Scaup

Petit Morillon
Aythya affinis (Eyton)
Total length: 38 to 45.5 cm
Plate 14

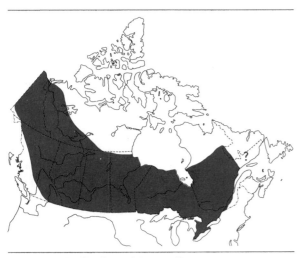

Breeding Distribution of Lesser Scaup

Range in Canada. Breeds in Yukon (north to Old Crow); western Mackenzie (Mackenzie valley north to wooded parts of Mackenzie Delta, Anderson River, Great Slave Lake); interior British Columbia (Atlin and southward to Columbia Lake and Vernon); Alberta (throughout, but locally in the south about larger lakes and irrigation projects; commonly in the northern half); Saskatchewan; Manitoba (north to Churchill); Ontario (widely but sparsely: Fort Severn, Lake River, Keezhik Lake, Lillabelle Lake, Kenora, Luther Marsh, Lake St. Clair, mouth of Nottawasaga River, Denbigh, Ottawa); and central Quebec (Moar Bay region, Schefferville, Lake Saint-Jean, upper St. Lawrence valley).

Migrates more or less commonly through the western provinces (including western British Columbia) and Ontario; fairly commonly in southwestern Quebec (St. Lawrence River; occasionally east to Johan-Beetz Bay and Anticosti Island); uncommonly in New Brunswick, Nova Scotia, and Prince Edward Island; rarely Newfoundland. Winters in small numbers in coastal British Columbia and southern Ontario (Lake Erie).

Very similar to Greater Scaup but slightly smaller. In the hand, the relatively smaller nail of the bill is usually diagnostic in any plumage. *Adult male (winter and breeding)*: Like the Greater Scaup but head with mainly purple gloss (instead of mainly greenish). Sides and flanks more heavily vermiculated (less whitish). White in wings usually does not extend far into primaries. *Adult female*: Like Greater Scaup but smaller and with the white stripe in wing more restricted.

Measurements. *Adult male*: wing, 193–209 (199.8); tail, 48.5–57.5 (51.9); exposed culmen, 39.5–43.5 (41.7); tarsus, 35.5–37.5 (36.3). *Adult female*: wing, 187–200.5 (192.9) mm.

Field Marks. Separable from Greater Scaup only under good observation conditions. Although the present species is smaller, this is useless in the field. Adult male Lesser Scaups have a purplish (instead of greenish) gloss to the head and also more greyish (less whitish) sides. Females usually cannot be distinguished on the water. In flight both sexes can often be separated from the Greater Scaup by the shorter white wing-stripe (Plate 14), which in the Lesser does not extend far, if at all, onto the primaries. For separation from other ducks, see Greater Scaup. *Voice*: Similar to Greater Scaup.

Habitat. In the breeding season, the vicinity of interior lakes and ponds; low islands; moist sedge meadows. In migration and winter, it inhabits *smaller* interior lakes, ponds, and rivers to a greater extent than the Greater Scaup but, like it, frequents also coastal bays, estuaries, and large lakes.

Nesting. Nest is a hollow in dry ground lined with grass and feathers. It is often hidden by grass or bushes and usually is not very far from water. *Eggs*, 8 to 12; olive-buff. Incubation 23 to 26 days (R.D. Harris), by female.

Range. Breeds in interior northwestern North America from central Alaska and western Canada (north to about tree limit) south to northern Idaho, northeastern Colorado, Nebraska, and Iowa. Winters mainly from southern British Columbia, Colorado, Arkansas, southern Illinois, and eastern Maryland south to northern South America and the West Indies.

Tribe **Mergini:**
Sea Ducks and Mergansers

A rather motley assemblage of diving ducks, most of them more strikingly patterned than the freshwater divers. The mergansers are unique as a group in possessing a slender cylindrical bill hooked at the tip, and equipped with backward-directed lamellae, ideal for catching and holding slippery fish (Figure 36). In fact, the mergansers are so different that some systematists place them in a separate tribe.

Common Eider

(American Eider)

Eider à duvet
Somateria mollissima (Linnaeus)
Total length: 53 to 71 cm
Plate 15

Breeding Distribution of Common Eider

Range in Canada. Breeds locally and commonly on the coastal islands and shores of Yukon. Banks Island; Victoria Island (Simpson Bay, Walker Bay, Finlayson Islands); Jenny Lind Island; and the coasts of Mackenzie (east at least to Bathurst Inlet); and from middle Ellesmere Island; Seymour Island; Devon Island (Grinnell Peninsula, Croker Bay); Somerset Island (Port Leopold); Cornwallis Island (Resolute Bay); Baffin Island; Southampton Island; Hudson and James bays; Hudson Strait (east of Cape Weggs); Ungava Bay; Labrador; Newfoundland; north shore of the Gulf of St. Lawrence; lower St. Lawrence River (Rivière-Ouelle, Gaspé Peninsula, Île aux Coudres); and the Maritime Provinces (but breeding on Prince Edward Island not established). It winters from southern Baffin Island and islands north of Hudson Bay southward along the Atlantic Coast to the Maritimes and in Hudson and James bays. Some inhabiting the western part of the arctic range move westward around northern Alaska to winter in Bering Sea; a few may remain (Taylor Island, N.W.T.). Rare in British Columbia (late autumn records: Vancouver Island, Queen Charlotte Islands, Prince George, 31 October 1949). Casual in southern Ontario (Niagara River, Lake Simcoe, Mimico); and in southern Manitoba (specimens: Giroux, November 1911; Lake Manitoba, 23 October 1911).

Forehead profile rather flat. Feathering at base of bill extends forward to below nostril (Figure 31). Southeastern subspecies *S. m. dresseri* (see also Subspecies): *Adult male (winter and breeding)*: Two bare frontal processes with rounded ends extend backward on either side of forehead. Plumage mostly black and white. Top of head black, this cap divided almost in two by a median white streak; rest of head white with green wash on back of head, nape, and below border of cap. Neck, breast, back, fore-wing, scapulars, spot on either side of rump, white. Tertials curved outward. Middle of rump, tail coverts, greater wing coverts, belly, and sides, black. Eye brown. Bill in spring, orange-yellow, otherwise varying from grey to green. Legs and feet yellowish or greenish. *Adult female*: A brownish duck. Bill processes narrower than in male. Head and neck brown streaked with black, darkest on crown. Upper parts dark brown to blackish brown, the feathers barred or edged with buff. Breast and sides buffy, the feathers barred with blackish and tipped with greyish buff. Belly sooty-brown with vague dark bars. Greater wing coverts greyish brown lightly tipped with white forming two narrow wing bars. Secondaries and tertials brown with buffy outer edges. Tertials curved outward. Eye brown. Bill duller and greener than in winter male, sometimes yellowish.

Measurements *(S. m. dresseri)*. *Adult male*: wing, 262–291 (274); tail, 82.5–102 (92.4); exposed culmen, 52–58.5 (56.4); tarsus, 49–56 (53.4). *Adult female*: wing, 250–293 (271.5) mm.

Field Marks. Contrasting solid areas of black and white with a black belly mark the males as eiders. Adult male separable from King Eider by all-white back and flat forehead profile. Brown females and immatures separable from Black Duck by their flat forehead profile and barred flanks. Females closely resemble female King Eider, but Common Eider has barred flanks (flank markings crescent-shaped in King Eider), somewhat longer bill, and an extension of the feathering on side of bill, forward to below the nostril. In fresh plumage, female Common Eider is slightly less rich brown. In flight this eider often alternates flapping with short glides. *Voice*: Male has drawn-out cooing *ah-hoo* or *ah-ee-oo* of various intensities, used especially in display; also moaning notes. Female: hoarse *kuk-kuk-kuk* notes, like other diving ducks.

Habitat. A marine species. Is fond of low-lying rocky coasts and large and small rocky islands but is found also along other types of shore, especially where mussel beds and reefs provide feeding grounds. Occasionally uses fresh water near the coast. Sometimes occurs well off shore on salt water.

Nesting. Often highly colonial. Nest, foundation of plant material. Sometimes, perhaps frequently, old nest sites are re-used (F.G. Cooch). Down lining is added as egg-laying progresses. On the ground, usually near salt water in rock-sheltered situations or in depressions in low vegetation. *Eggs*, usually 4 to 6; olive to olive-buff. Incubation, by the female, lasts 28 to 29 days (F.G. Cooch); 25 to 26 days (D. Guignion).

Range. Holarctic. Breeds from Iceland, Spitsbergen, Novaya Zemlya, south to the British Isles, Denmark, France, and the Baltics, also northern Siberia; and in North America from the Arctic south coastally to Kodiak Island and Maine. In winter somewhat farther south.

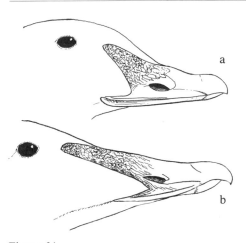

Figure 31
Bill of
a) King Eider female
b) Common Eider female

Subspecies. (1) *Somateria mollissima dresseri* Sharpe, described above, occupies the southeast Atlantic part of Canada north to about the Hamilton Inlet area of Labrador. (2) *S. m. borealis* (Brehm) has the bill frontal processes narrower, terminating in sharp points instead of broad rounded ones, and the male has a less-extensive greenish wash on head; breeds from about Hamilton Inlet, Labrador, northward, and westward in the Arctic to Somerset, Cornwallis, and Southampton islands. Many winter farther south in the breeding range of *dresseri*. (3) *S. m. sedentaria* Snyder resembles *dresseri* and has similar bill frontal processes, but adult females and immatures are noticeably paler and greyer; breeds and winters on Hudson and James bays (south of Southampton, Coats, and Mansel islands). (4) *S. m. v-nigra* Bonaparte: male has large black V on throat (this occasionally occurs also in other races), and in both sexes anterior end of feathered area on side of bill is more rounded than in other races; the bare frontal processes average narrower and more sharply pointed than in even *borealis*; breeding range from Bathurst Inlet and Jenny Lind Island westward, and apparently separated from the ranges of the eastern races by a hiatus.

King Eider

Eider à tête grise
Somateria spectabilis (Linnaeus)
Total length: 53 to 63 cm
Plate 15

Breeding Distribution of King Eider

Range in Canada. Breeds along the arctic coast and islands from the high Arctic (Prince Patrick, Lougheed, and northern Ellesmere islands; recorded rarely on Ellef Ringnes Island but not known to nest); south to the coast of northern Yukon (very sparsely: Herschel Island); northern Mackenzie; and Keewatin (mainly coasts but also in interior at Garry Lake and 80 km north of Schultz Lake); Southampton Island; Hudson and James bays (Chesterfield Inlet, McConnell River, Cape Henrietta Maria, Belcher Islands, South Twin Island); northern Quebec (Stupart Bay, Kogaluc River); and probably northern Labrador (but evidence unsatisfactory).

Winters on open water off Labrador, the Gulf of St. Lawrence, and Newfoundland (regularly, especially southwest coast). Recorded rarely in New Brunswick and Nova Scotia. Apparently the western arctic population migrates westward to winter in the Bering

Feathers on side of bill do not extend forward as far as nostril (Figure 31). *Adult male (winter and breeding)*: Top of head, nape, and sides of upper neck pale bluish-grey. Bill processes broadened into a knoblike yellow frontal shield. Greenish patch on cheeks bordered above by narrow white line. Border about bill processes, small patch about eye, and large V on throat, black. Rest of head, neck, fore-back, upper breast, shoulders, patch on either side of base of tail, white. White of breast tinged pinkish. Lower back, scapulars, rump, tail coverts, lower breast, belly, and sides, black. Tail brownish black. Anterior lesser wing coverts and greater coverts blackish, rest white. Remainder of wing blackish. Some tertials (erectile in life) out-curved with purplish-black outer webs. Legs and feet yellowish to orange with dusky webs. Eye brown. Bill processes rich yellow, bill red to orange with purplish nail. *Adult female*: Very similar to female Common Eider but has slightly warmer brown coloration, unstreaked chin, more decidedly *crescentic* black markings on sides. Feathers on *top* of bill extend forward to above nostrils but those on *sides* of bill fall far short of nostril (reverse of Common Eider).

Measurements. *Adult male*: wing, 264–283 (273); tail, 81–87.5 (83.7); exposed culmen, 26–30 (28.9); tarsus, 46.5–50 (48.1). *Adult female*: wing, 245–274 (263.4) mm.

Field Marks. Adult male is unmistakable. Female closely resembles female Common Eider, but at very close range differently shaped feathered areas of bill may be discerned (see above). Sides, and sides of breast, have more decidedly *crescentic* black markings in present species. King Eider is usually a more warmly brown bird, particularly compared with the Hudson Bay race of Common Eider, *sedentaria*, but this is not always reliable compared with other races of the Common Eider. *Voice*: Male, in courtship, a low musical *coo uur-aaa-oo* with emphasis on last syllable; female, coarse grunting croaks (S.D. MacDonald).

Habitat. In breeding season much less marine than Common Eider, preferring the vicinity of tundra freshwater ponds, lakes, and streams for nesting, usually not at any great distance from the coast, which is frequently visited for feeding purposes. Rarely considerably inland (Garry Lake, District of Keewatin). At other seasons, the habitat is mainly marine, like the Common Eider's. Its more frequent occurrence on the Great Lakes probably reflects its greater tolerance for fresh water.

Sea. Individuals, however, from as far west as King William and Southampton islands help swell large August migration concentrations off west Greenland. Casual in British Columbia (Victoria, 11 January 1942; Hardy Bay, 18 October 1938; Queen Charlotte Islands, 16 January 1972), and rare on the upper St. Lawrence River and tributaries and Great Lakes (Montréal, Ottawa, Toronto, Niagara River, etc.). Accidental in Alberta (Calgary, 4 November 1894) and at Lake Mistassini, Quebec.

Nesting. Unlike the Common Eider, it is not colonial and the nest is usually near fresh water but sometimes on flat tundra at considerable distance from water. Nest, on the ground, often partly protected by sparse vegetation or rocks, is lined with down (noticeably darker than that of Common Eider). *Eggs*, usually 3 to 6; resemble those of Common Eider in colour but average smaller. Incubation by female; period 22 to 23 days (David F. Parmelee). Young are inclined to form packs with adult females in charge.

Range. Breeds on islands in Bering Sea, in arctic Alaska, across arctic Canada, Hudson and James bays, Greenland, and the northern coasts and islands of Europe and Asia, from the Kanin Peninsula of northern Russia, Spitsbergen and Novaya Zemlya, east to Anadyr. In western North America, it winters north to the limit of open water in Bering Sea, south to the Aleutian and Kodiak islands, with stragglers south to California (very rarely), and in eastern North America mainly from southern Greenland to Newfoundland, with smaller numbers south to Massachusetts, New York, and New Jersey.

Spectacled Eider

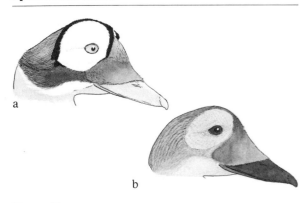

Figure 32
Spectacled Eider
a) adult male
b) adult female

[**Spectacled Eider**. Eider à lunettes. *Somateria fischeri* (Brandt). Figure 32.

Field Marks. Adult male has a large white area surrounding the eye. This is framed with a narrow black border (hence the name "spectacled"). The black under parts extend forward across the breast almost to base of neck, thus differing from other eiders. Female resembles other eiders, but in good light one can discern a paler-brown area, the counterpart of male's "spectacles."

Status in Canada. Hypothetical. No specimen has yet been taken in Canada, but as the species is known to occur more or less regularly on Barter Island and Demarcation Point, Alaska, near the Yukon border, it probably occurs at least occasionally on the poorly known Yukon coast. Manning, Höhn, and Macpherson (1956) provide a convincing sight record of a male on Sachs River, Banks Island, on 20 June 1952. C.J. Guiguet (in litt.) observed a male "in full or near full plumage" at 18 to 21 m, off southern Vancouver Island (James Island) on 22 September 1962.]

Steller's Eider

Eider de Steller
Polysticta stelleri (Pallas)
Total length: 43 to 49 cm
Figure 33

Figure 33
Steller's Eider, male

Status in Canada. Casual visitor to coastal British Columbia (specimen: Masset, 15 October 1948; photo records: Mitlenatch Island Nature Park, 17 June 1970, and Sidney, 13 February 1976). Accidental in Quebec (specimens: two near Pointe-des-Monts, February and March 1898). Casual in Mackenzie (specimen: Colville River Delta, 18 June 1909).

Adult male (winter and breeding): Head and part of upper neck shiny white with greenish tuft of feathers on forehead and back of head. Ring about eye, spot on back of head, and entire chin and throat, black. Collar about neck bluish black. Middle of back, entire rump, tail coverts, and tail, black. Long scapulars purplish with white inner webs. Wing coverts white. Speculum blue, bordered by white. Inner secondaries and tertials curved outward, inner webs white, outer webs mostly metallic blue. Middle of belly blackish brown, paling to cinnamon-buff on breast and sides. Black spot on sides near front of folded wing. Eye brown. Bill greyish blue. Legs and feet dark bluish-grey. *Adult female*: Head and neck brown mixed with buff, darkest on crown. Body blackish brown cross-marked with buff, becoming blackish on belly. Speculum blue, bordered in front and behind with white. Eye brown. Bill dusky bluish. Legs and feet dark bluish-grey.

Measurements. *Adult male*: wing, 210–225; bill, 37–42; tarsus, 36–40. *Adult female*: wing, 210–218 mm (J.C. Phillips).

Field Marks. The smallest, trimmest, and most "uneiderlike" of the eiders. Markings of adult male are unmistakable. Female's dark, rich-brown general coloration and *Mallard-like speculum* identify it.

Range. Breeds in northeastern coastal Siberia from the Lena Delta and New Siberian Islands east to Chukotski Peninsula and Anadyr Bay, and in Alaska east probably to Barter Island and Humphrey Point, and south to St. Lawrence Island and Hooper Bay, perhaps to the Aleutian Islands and Alaska Peninsula. In winter it ranges somewhat farther south, in North America to the Aleutian Islands, south coast of the Alaska Peninsula, Kodiak Island, and rarely to Queen Charlotte Islands.

Labrador Duck

Canard du Labrador
Camptorhynchus labradorius (Gmelin)
Total length: 48 to 59 cm
Figure 34

Figure 34
Labrador Duck, adult male

Status in Canada. Extinct. Presumed, on unsatisfactory evidence, to have bred in southern Labrador and in that part of Quebec formerly included under the name "Labrador." Three specimens mentioned by William Dutcher (1891. Auk, vol. 8, no. 2, pp. 203–204) from "Labrador" may have come from either Quebec or Labrador. In migration and winter it occurred in Nova Scotia (Pictou, Halifax Harbour) and New Brunswick (Grand Manan). Recorded also from southwestern Quebec (Laprairie, spring 1862: specimen) where its occurrence was probably rare or casual. The last specimen known to be taken in Canada was shot on Grand Manan, New Brunswick, in April 1871.

Bill rather long and broadened toward tip. Lamellae of lower mandible long. Feet large. Anterior part of cheek with stiff feathers. *Adult male*: Head and neck, white with black longitudinal stripe through crown and a narrow black collar around lower neck. Back, rump, tail and tail coverts, primaries, and under parts, black. Scapulars and wings (except primaries) mostly white. Basal part of bill and around nostrils yellow; rest blackish. *Adult female*: Mostly brownish grey with paler area on cheeks. Chin and throat whitish. Upper breast mottled grey and whitish. Wings with white speculum.

Range. Extinct. Breeding range unknown but presumed to have been in Labrador. In winter occurred south probably to Chesapeake Bay. Last record of a living bird, 12 December 1878, at Elmira, New York.

Remarks. The Labrador Duck became extinct before much was recorded about it. Details of its life history and even the reasons for its extinction are largely unknown and are likely to remain so. It does not seem to have been numerous anywhere within its restricted range. As it was not especially good to eat, hunters did not often seek it on its wintering grounds. Authors have suggested that its breeding grounds may have been restricted to a few islands in "Labrador." In that case it would have been more susceptible than other species of wider distribution to the havoc wrought on bird populations there by mid-eighteenth century plumage hunters and eggers. Others have suggested that its peculiarly specialized bill may have been correlated with feeding on particular food, which later became unavailable in adequate quantity. Its diet is known to have included mussels and small surf clams, however. The most plausible explanation of its passing seems to be that the already small numbers were singly unable to withstand persecution by man, particularly on its restricted breeding grounds.

Harlequin Duck

Canard arlequin
Histrionicus histrionicus (Linnaeus)
Total length: 38 to 45 cm
Plate 15

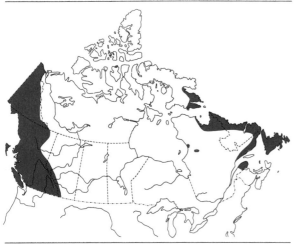

Breeding Distribution of Harlequin Duck

Range in Canada. Breeding range divided into two widely separated parts. Western part: Yukon (arctic coast southward); British Colum-

Adult male (winter and breeding plumage): Head and neck mainly dark leaden-blue. A crescentic white patch at base of bill, an oval white ear patch, and another white patch down side of neck. A black median stripe through centre of crown with chestnut on either side of it. Narrow white collar around neck, incomplete in front and behind. Back slaty blue. Tail black, slender and pointed. Long bar on side of breast, white bordered with black. Speculum metallic blue. Inner secondaries extensively white. Wing linings brown. Upper breast bluish. Belly dark brown often with bluish wash. Sides chestnut. Eye reddish brown. Bill bluish grey to bluish black. Legs and feet bluish grey. *Adult female*: Head and neck dark brown with three white areas, one behind eye, one below the eye, and one in front of eye reaching the forehead. Rest of plumage blackish brown, more greyish below and becoming whitish on abdomen. Bill, legs, and feet paler and duller than in male. *Immature*: In first autumn resembles adult female. Young male begins to resemble adult in late autumn but is not completely like adult until second year.

Measurements. *Adult male*: wing, 188–202 (196.4); tail, 77–101.5 (91.6); exposed culmen, 25–27 (25.8); tarsus, 36.5–38.5 (37.8). *Adult female*: wing, 179–201 (188.6) mm.

bia (Atlin, McDonald Creek on Alaska High-
way, Glacier National Park, Nicola, Likely,
Penticton region, Wise Island); southwestern
Alberta (Rocky Mountains: Valley of the Ten
Peaks). Eastern part: southeastern Baffin
Island (Crook's Inlet to Cumberland Sound);
Labrador; Quebec (Lake Guillaume-Delisle,
Lake Minowean, Hutte sauvage Lake, Bienville
Lake; probably Ungava Bay and outer north
shore of the Gulf of St. Lawrence; Gaspé
Peninsula); and Newfoundland (Gros Morne
National Park).

Recorded in summer in western Mackenzie
(Mackenzie valley, Great Slave Lake). Migrates
mainly to and from the coasts. Rare transient
in the interior east of the Rockies in Alberta
(Lake Athabasca, Beaverhill Lake); Saskatche-
wan (Saskatchewan Landing, Regina); Mani-
toba (Pike Lake, north of The Pas; Shoal
Lake, Winnipeg, Churchill); Ontario (Hamil-
ton, Niagara River, Toronto); southwestern
Quebec (Lachine Rapids, Sainte-Anne-de-
Bellevue). Winters along the coast of British
Columbia and on the Atlantic Coast in south-
ern Labrador, Newfoundland, the coast of the
Maritimes, and rarely in southern Ontario
(Thunder Bay, Niagara River, Ottawa).

Field Marks. Pattern of adult male is unmistakable. Female might
be confused with female Bufflehead or Surf Scoter. It has usually three
(sometimes only two) whitish areas on the head, whereas the female
Bufflehead has but one, and in flight lacks the Bufflehead's white wing
patch. Its small size and short-bill profile separate it from the female
Surf Scoter. When swimming it bobs its head slightly with each stroke.
Voice: Usually rather silent. A low whistle beginning with two longer
notes and ending in a trill, on a descending scale. A series of harsh
croaks.

Habitat. In breeding season, swift rivers and streams. In other
seasons, coasts and islands, often the roughest and rockiest of shores
where the water is highly turbulent and the surf breaks constantly.

Nesting. Nest is placed on the ground, usually near fast streams,
often in a clump of bushes or in recesses in rocks. Reports of nesting in
hollow trees require confirmation. *Eggs*, usually 4 to 7; cream to pale
buff. Incubation 28 to 29 days (S. Bengtson) is by the female.

Range. Breeds in eastern Siberia, southern and middle Alaska
(north probably to Anaktuvuk Pass) and southern Yukon south in the
mountains to central California and Colorado; and from southern
Baffin Island, Greenland, and Iceland south to Newfoundland. Winters
from breeding range south to Korea, southern Japan, central-western
California, and Massachusetts; rarely farther south.

Oldsquaw

Canard kakawi
Clangula hyemalis (Linnaeus)
Total length; 43 to 59 cm
Plate 15

Breeding Distribution of Oldsquaw

Range in Canada. Breeds throughout the Arctic
from Prince Patrick and northern Ellesmere
islands south to southern parts of the tundra in
northern Yukon (Old Crow; probably tundra
areas in Ogilvie Mountains where fairly
common in summer); northwestern British
Columbia (80 km west of Atlin); southwestern
and middle Mackenzie (Great Slave Lake, probably Chick Lake); southern Keewatin (Windy
River); northeastern Manitoba (Churchill);
coast and islands of Hudson and James bays

Bill short, rather high at base. *Adult male (autumn, winter, early
spring)*: Head and neck mainly white with grey cheeks and a large dark-
brown patch extending from rear of cheek to side of upper neck. Back,
rump, upper tail coverts, and breast brownish black. Wing blackish with
brown speculum. Scapulars slender, pointed, pearl grey. Wing linings
greyish brown. Lower belly to tail white becoming grey on sides and
flanks. Tail with two central feathers very long, slender, pointed; rest of
tail feathers dusky, edged with white, outermost with increasing extent
of white. Eye variable, brown to reddish brown. Bill, basal half and
nail blackish, pinkish near tip. Legs and feet bluish grey. *Adult male
(late spring, early summer)*: Head and neck brown with large, sharply
defined patch of grey on sides of head and small white area behind and
above eye. Back and scapulars brown with russet edges. *Adult female
(autumn, winter, early spring)*: Head and neck mainly white, but crown,
throat, and patch on side of upper neck brownish black. Back, upper
tail coverts, tail, and wings blackish brown. Tail greyish brown, central
tail feathers only slightly elongated. Breast mixed grey and brown. Belly
white. *Adult female (summer plumage)*: Head and neck mostly brown
with white distributed as follows: ring about eye, line extending back
from eye, spot at base of bill, and area on side of neck. Rest of
plumage similar to winter but more bleached and abraded. Bill greyish
brown to greenish, darkening toward tip. Legs bluish grey. *Immatures*:
Adult plumage not attained until second year. Young until late summer
resemble adult female in summer, but head and neck are brownish grey
and scapulars have no grey edges. In late autumn, young male begins to
resemble adult male about the head.

Measurements. *Adult male*: wing, 209–228 (220.4); tail, 165–237
(194.9); exposed culmen, 26–30 (27.5); tarsus, 34–38 (35.8). *Adult
female*: wing, 152–219 (194.1) mm.

Field Marks. In winter plumage, the large dark patch on the sides
of the white head makes recognition of both sexes easy. In summer, the
adult male's large white patch on the sides of the otherwise dark-brown
head is unlike that of any other duck. The male's long tail could be
confused only with that of the differently marked Pintail. In flight no

(Cape Henrietta Maria, Bear Island, Grey Goose Island, South Twin Island); northern Quebec (Payne Lake, Kuujjuaq, Hutte sauvage Lake); and south along the coast of Labrador to southeastern Quebec (Brador Bay; perhaps westward as far as Kégashka). Reportedly nesting in Newfoundland (Terra Nova National Park). Winters along the coast of British Columbia, on open water of the Great Lakes and James Bay, and along the Atlantic Coast from southern Labrador and northern Newfoundland (Hare Bay) southward through the Maritimes.

other extensively white duck has all-dark wings. *Voice*: A noisy duck with a variety of calls of several syllables, often rather musical and easily recognized once learned. The voice is far-carrying and in chorus at a distance somewhat suggests the baying of hounds. Courting male calls a throaty *ah, ah, ungha*.

Habitat. In summer, tundra lakes and ponds; also coasts and islands. In other seasons, coastal waters and large freshwater lakes and rivers.

Nesting. Nest in a depression in the ground often in grasses or dwarf willow near a tundra pond or lake, on an island, or near salt water. *Eggs*, usually 6 to 8; olive to yellowish buff. Incubation period 26 ± 0.8 days (R.M. Alison), by the female.

Range. Breeds in the Arctic of both the New and Old Worlds. In North America, winters mainly on the coasts from the Aleutian Islands to Washington and from northern Greenland to South Carolina; in the interior mainly on the Great Lakes but also (irregularly, in smaller numbers) on other lakes and rivers of the United States.

Black Scoter

(formerly Common Scoter)

Macreuse à bec jaune
Melanitta nigra (Linnaeus)
Total length: 43 to 54 cm
Plate 15

Range in Canada. Widely but locally distributed in summer. Definite breeding records are few: southern Keewatin (Windy River); northern Quebec (Bienville Lake, Feuilles Bay); and Newfoundland (Avalon Peninsula; Mizzen Topsail; and near Grand Lake). Probably northern Manitoba (North Knife River). Summers regularly on the British Columbia coast, Hudson and James bays (abundantly), southern Hudson Strait and Ungava Bay, Labrador, Newfoundland, Gulf of St. Lawrence, but is scarce off the southern Maritimes. Rarely recorded in Yukon (except regular in small numbers on arctic coast), much of Mackenzie (recorded rarely on Great Slave Lake), interior British Columbia, Alberta, and Saskatchewan, southern Manitoba. Winters along the coast of British Columbia and on the Atlantic Coast from Newfoundland south; a few irregularly on the Great Lakes.

Feathers at base of bill do not extend nearly to nostrils either along the ridge or sides of bill. *Adult male*: Plumage entirely black except under surface of flight feathers, which is grey (contrasting with black under wing coverts). Eye brown. Bill black with swollen basal part yellow to orange. Legs brownish black. *Adult female*: Top of head and nape dark brown, rest of head greyish with indistinct brown mottling. Rest of upper parts sooty brown often with paler feather-edges. Belly lighter brown. Eye and legs as in male. Bill (lacks basal swelling of male) blackish often with yellow streaks. Young in first autumn similar to adult female but paler, more whitish on abdomen and breast.

Measurements. *Adult male*: wing, 213–233 (225.4); tail, 83–97 (88.5); exposed culmen, 42–45.5 (43.7); tarsus, 45–48.5 (46.5). *Adult female*: wing, 210–230 (220.4) mm.

Field Marks. Adult male our only scoter without a patch of white either in wing or on head. Female has plain light cheeks (females of other scoters usually show two light patches on side of head), against which brown cap is well defined. Also female White-winged has white patch in wing (conspicuous in flight), which Black Scoter lacks.

Habitat. Similar to White-winged Scoter.

Nesting. Nest, a depression in the ground lined with grass and down, near freshwater pools, lakes, and rivers in either tundra or wooded country. *Eggs*, 6 to 10; light to pinkish buff. Incubation by female.

Range. Circumpolar. Breeds in Alaska and northern continental Canada; also from Iceland, Spitsbergen, northern parts of Norway, Russia, and Siberia, south to Scotland and north-central Siberia. In North America, winters on the Pacific Coast from the Aleutian Islands to southern California; the Atlantic Coast from Newfoundland to South Carolina; and in small numbers on the Great Lakes.

Subspecies. *Melanitta nigra americana* (Swainson).

Surf Scoter

Macreuse à front blanc
Melanitta perspicillata (Linnaeus)
Total length: 48 to 58 cm
Plate 15

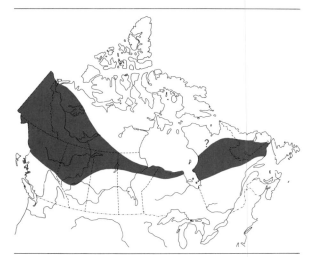

Breeding Distribution of Surf Scoter

Range in Canada. *Summers* regularly from northern Yukon, the arctic coast of western Mackenzie, and southern Keewatin south through the coast and middle interior of British Columbia, northern Alberta, northern Saskatchewan, and northern Manitoba, the coasts and islands of southern Hudson and James bays, the coast and interior of Labrador, and the coasts of the Atlantic provinces (scarce in Newfoundland). Actual breeding data are few: Breeds in Yukon; western Mackenzie (Mackenzie Delta, Anderson River, Great Bear Lake, Great Slave Lake); Alberta (Elk Island National Park, Wentzel Lake); northern Saskatchewan (Lake Athabasca, Little Gull Lake, Wollaston Lake); northern Manitoba (Churchill); James Bay (Charlton and Shepard islands); Ontario (Shagamu and Aquatuk lakes; Sutton Ridges); Labrador (Petitsikapau Lake, Churchill Falls); and Quebec (Wakuach Lake, near Otelnuk Lake, Bienville Lake). According to Bent (1925), eggs and the parent female were collected on Akpatok Island, Ungava Bay.

Winters commonly on the coast of British Columbia (rarely in southern interior) and on the Atlantic Coast from Newfoundland and the Gulf of St. Lawrence southward; occasionally on Lakes Erie and Ontario. Migration is mainly coastwise, but small irregular numbers are recorded in southern parts of the interior provinces. Common migrant at Lake Mistassini, interior Quebec, perhaps indicating an overland route between James Bay and the Atlantic Coast.

Casual north to Repulse Bay, District of Keewatin.

Feathers extend forward on ridge of bill to form a blunt point, in male almost or quite to nostril; no feathers on side of bill. *Adult male*: Plumage black with white triangle on forehead and another on nape. Bill with base swollen and elevated along ridge abruptly descending over nostrils; a roundish or squarish black patch on sides of bill near base, bordered behind and above by orange or red and in front and below by white; ridge and nasal area reddish; nail yellowish. Eye white. Legs reddish on outer side, orange inner side with blackish blotches; webs blackish. *Adult female*: Crown to just below eye brownish black; rest of head and neck brown with two vague whitish areas, one in front of cheek, the other over ear; nape with vague greyish or whitish patch. Body blackish brown, paler below. Wings plain brown. Eye brown. Bill blackish with roundish black spot on sides near base faintly indicated. *Immatures*: In first autumn, they resemble adult females, but the two whitish areas on sides of head are better defined, under parts whiter, and the whitish patch on nape is lacking.

Measurements. *Adult male*: wing, 232–244 (236.3); tail, 79–86 (81.8); exposed culmen, 35–42 (37.7); tarsus, 43–47 (44.8). *Adult female*: wing, 203–230.5 (221.5) mm.

Field Marks. Male has solid black colour and contrasting white head markings. Female and immatures have two vaguely defined whitish areas on sides of head like the White-winged Scoter, but Surf Scoter has no white wing patch.

Habitat. Similar to White-winged Scoter.

Nesting. Nest similar to that of White-winged Scoter but said to use less grass in its construction. *Eggs*, 5 to 7; pinkish or buffy-white. Incubation by the female.

Range. Breeds in Alaska and locally in northern continental Canada. Winters mainly on the salt water of coasts from the Aleutian Islands and southeastern Alaska to the Gulf of California and from southern Newfoundland to Florida. Also in small numbers on the Great Lakes and more rarely at other interior points in the United States.

White-winged Scoter

Macreuse à ailes blanches
Melanitta fusca (Linnaeus)
Total length: 48 to 58 cm
Plate 15

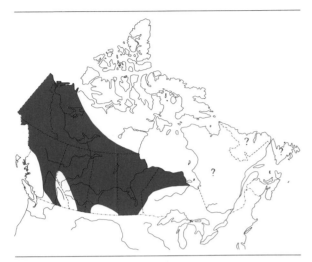

Breeding Distribution of White-winged Scoter

Range in Canada. The commonest scoter in most areas. Breeds widely in Yukon; western Mackenzie (Mackenzie Delta, Stanton); southern Keewatin (Nueltin Lake); and southward in interior British Columbia (Atlin, François Lake, Nicola and Quesnel regions, Swan Lake in Peace River District; Cariboo parklands); Alberta (on most larger lakes, except in mountainous southwestern part, commonest in central parts); Saskatchewan (Flotten Lake, Emma Lake, lakes north of Nipawin, York Lake region, Cypress Lake, Last Mountain Lake, Quill Lake, Lake Athabasca); Manitoba (Churchill, Lake St. Martin, Shoal Lake); and northern Ontario (Ney Lake, Sutton Lake). Widely distributed in summer also on coasts of eastern Canada (James Bay, Labrador coast, Gulf of St. Lawrence, Newfoundland, and the Maritimes) and the coast of British Columbia, but without satisfactory evidence of breeding. Recorded in summer north to northeastern Mackenzie (Cape Bathurst and mouth of Coppermine River; sight records, Bathurst Inlet); Ungava Bay, and more rarely Hudson Strait, West Foxe Islands, and a sight record of two on Melville Island. Winters commonly along the coast of British Columbia and on the Atlantic Coast north to Newfoundland and the Gulf of St. Lawrence; and in irregular small numbers on the Great Lakes.

Feathers on sides of bill extend forward almost to nostril. *Adult male (winter and breeding plumage)*: Mainly black; a white spot extending backward and upward below the eye; and a wing patch formed by the white of the secondaries. Eye pale grey or whitish. Bill with black swollen base, red or purplish sides becoming orange near base, ridge white, edges black, nail reddish. Legs purplish pink on outer sides, tending to orange on inner sides. *Adult female*: Head and neck brownish black, often with two vague whitish patches, one on ear, one in front of eye. Rest of plumage sooty brown, some feathers with paler edges. Wing patch formed by white secondaries. Eye brown.

Measurements *(M. f. deglandi)*. *Adult male*: wing, 262–285 (274.1); tail, 77.5–87 (81.6); exposed culmen, 37–44 (39.6); tarsus, 49.5–52.5 (51.1). *Adult female*: wing, 254–271 (259.9) mm.

Field Marks. Scoters are good-sized, thick-necked, heavy-headed ducks, the males mostly black, females dark sooty-brown. They are often seen in rafts of various sizes or flying in groups low over the water. This is the only scoter with a white wing patch that is conspicuous in flight but it usually is not visible while the birds are resting. Young and some adult females show two lighter patches on the sides of the head, similar to the female Surf Scoter but different from the Black Scoter.

Habitat. Salt water of coasts (usually not far from shore), freshwater lakes inland, and larger rivers. Rarely comes to land except for nesting. Nest, usually near fresh water in shrubby tangles and woodland, often on an island, more rarely at some distance from water. Many, perhaps mostly post-breeding males and non-breeders, are found on coastal salt water even during the nesting season.

Nesting. Nest, on the ground, usually well hidden in shrubbery, a depression lined with grasses, dark down, and a few feathers. *Eggs*, 6 to 16; pale ochraceous pink. Incubation by female requires 26 to 29 days (Bauer and Glutz).

Range. Breeds from northwestern Alaska and the interior of the western Canada mainland, mostly south of tree limit (summers commonly in eastern Canada, but definite evidence of breeding needed), south to northeastern Washington and central North Dakota. Winters on the Pacific Coast (Aleutian Islands and Alaska Peninsula to Baja California) and on the Atlantic Coast (Gulf of St. Lawrence to South Carolina) and sporadically in the interior to Colorado, Nebraska, Louisiana, and in small numbers on the Great Lakes.

Subspecies. *Melanitta fusca deglandi* (Bonaparte) is the breeding bird of Canada.

Common Goldeneye

(American Golden-eye)

Garrot à oeil d'or
Bucephala clangula (Linnaeus)
Total length: 40.5 to 51 cm
Plate 16

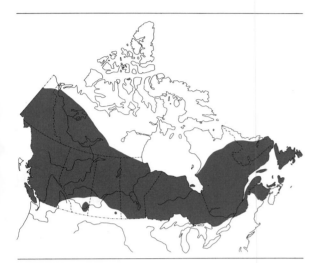

Breeding Distribution of Common Goldeneye

Range in Canada. Breeds north to near tree limit in Yukon, western and southern Mackenzie (Mackenzie Delta, Mackenzie valley, Great Slave Lake, Rocknest Lake); southwestern Keewatin (Nueltin Lake); northern Manitoba; northern Ontario; northern Quebec (Hutte sauvage Lake); middle Labrador; and Newfoundland; south to southern British Columbia (locally: Swan Lake in Okanagan, Burnaby Lake, Duncan); Alberta and Saskatchewan (southeast to Moose Mountain, and except in southernmost parts where suitable trees are lacking); southern Manitoba (Turtle Mountain); southern Ontario (at least to Orillia and Cornwall); southern Quebec; New Brunswick; Prince Edward Island; and Nova Scotia (mainly Cape Breton Island). Wanders in summer somewhat north of nesting grounds. Winters where open water permits, in coastal and southern British Columbia; middle and southern Alberta (small numbers at Edmonton, Banff, Calgary, Drumheller); southern Ontario; southern Quebec (north at least to Pointe-des-Monts); Newfoundland; New Brunswick; Prince Edward Island; and Nova Scotia.

Adult male (winter and breeding plumage): Head and upper neck black with green and purple reflections and a large *round* white spot behind base of bill. Back, rump, and upper tail coverts black. Tail dark grey. Inner scapulars black, the outer ones white with black edges. Middle and greater wing coverts and most of secondaries, white. Lesser coverts near bend of wing, black. Primaries and wing linings blackish brown. Lower neck (all round), breast, and sides, white. Flanks white with black feather edges. Eye yellow. Bill blackish. Legs and feet yellow or orange with dusky webs. *Adult female (winter and breeding)*: Head brown. Neck with white collar incomplete behind. Back, scapulars, and upper tail coverts bluish grey, feathers edged with pale grey. Rump blackish. Upper tail coverts dark brown tipped with grey. Tail greyish brown. White of wing less extensive than in male. Speculum white, crossed by a dark bar. Upper breast grey with white feather tips. Belly white. Sides and flanks grey, feather tips whitish. Under tail coverts white mixed with dark grey. Eye pale yellow. Feet yellowish or orange. Bill dusky with yellowish band near tip (sometimes more extensively yellow). *Immatures*: In early autumn resemble adult females but lack white collar.

Measurements. *Adult male*: wing, 215–235 (225.4); tail, 77–95 (87); exposed culmen, 35–43.5 (38.4); tarsus, 39–42 (40.1). *Adult female*: wing, 188–220 (204.2) mm.

Field Marks. A medium-sized chunky duck with large areas of white in wings. Male has large *round* white spot behind base of bill. In females the dark head-colour extends only partly down neck, leaving lower neck white. Wings whistle more loudly in flight than in most ducks. For distinctions from Barrow's Goldeneye, see next species. *Voice*: Generally silent in autumn and early winter. In courtship, male has a harsh vibrating double-noted *zzee-at*. Female has a variety of harsh, low-pitched *grrk* notes. The characteristic musical whistle heard in take-off or in flight is not vocal but is produced by the wings.

Habitat. In nesting season, woodland lakes and muskeg ponds. In other seasons it frequents the seacoast, tidal estuaries, freshwater lakes and rivers. Wintering in numbers on rivers where current is adequate to keep water open, it is one of the characteristic winter ducks of the interior.

Nesting. Nests in natural cavities in trees or large woodpecker holes. Will use nest boxes, occasionally chimneys. Nest heights, from 1.5 to 18 m above ground. Perhaps in local absence of suitable trees may resort to rock cavities. *Eggs*, 6 to 15 (average 10); pale bluish-green. Incubation by the female, variably reported 26 to more than 30 days. Young flutter from nest to ground or water.

Range. Breeds north to or near tree limit in Europe, Asia, and North America. In North America from Alaska to Newfoundland and southward to southern Canada and northern United States (northwestern Montana, northern parts of Minnesota, Michigan, Vermont, and Maine). Winters from southeastern Alaska and southern Canada south to California, the Gulf Coast, and Florida.

Subspecies. *Bucephala clangula americana* (Bonaparte).

Barrow's Goldeneye

Garrot de Barrow
Bucephala islandica (Gmelin)
Total length: 41 to 52 cm
Plate 16

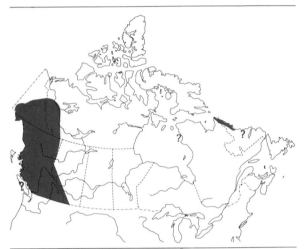

Figure 35
Bill of
a) Common Goldeneye
b) Barrow's Goldeneye

Breeding Distribution of Barrow's Goldeneye

Range in Canada. Breeds (in two widely separated areas): southern Yukon (Canol Road, Takhini River, Kathleen River, Burwash Landing); Mackenzie (Chick Lake, probably Nahanni National Park); British Columbia (widely: Atlin, Parker Lake, Peace River area, Alta Lake; densest population in dry belt of Okanagan, Nicola, Kamloops, Chilcotin, and Cariboo districts; alleged breeding on Vancouver Island not yet conclusive); and southwestern Alberta (mountains and foothills); also in Labrador (probably Killinek). Recorded in summer at McCormack Island, eastern Hudson Bay. Definite nesting records for eastern Canada are needed.

Winters in coastal British Columbia but rarely in the interior to Exshaw and Calgary, Alberta; and from the north shore of the Gulf of St. Lawrence (Bonne-Espérance, Piashti Bay) southward coastally along Anticosti Island, Gaspé Peninsula, New Brunswick, Prince Edward Island, and Nova Scotia, and on lower St. Lawrence River; more rarely on the Great Lakes, upper St. Lawrence drainage (Ottawa; Sherbrooke, Montréal), and Lake Saint-Jean.

Adult male (winter and breeding): Similar to Common Goldeneye, but the head is highly glossed with purple or violet and with large white *crescent* behind base of bill. Body similar to Common Goldeneye but with less white in wings and scapulars. White of scapulars a mere row of large dots over folded wings. White of fore-wing greatly reduced and completely separated from white speculum by a black bar. Eye yellow. Bill black. Legs and feet orange-yellow with dusky webs. *Adult female (winter and breeding)*: Very similar to Common Goldeneye, but head is usually slightly darker brown. Feathers of hind-neck usually longer, giving the head a more puffy appearance. Eye pale yellow. Bill usually more extensively yellow (especially from February to May) than in the Common Goldeneye.

Measurements. *Adult male*: wing, 225–243 (235.3); tail, 85–91 (88.8); exposed culmen, 31–38 (34.5); tarsus, 41–43 (46.3). *Adult female*: wing, 201–214 (207.2) mm.

Distinctions. Females and immatures closely resemble Common Goldeneyes but have shorter, stubbier bills, which taper more abruptly toward the tip (Figure 35). Males have a more abrupt forehead, which in immature males often can readily be felt as a lump under the plumage by stroking the forehead with the finger. The windpipe of both young and old males (not females) of the Common Goldeneye has a conspicuous bulbous enlargement that is lacking in Barrow's Goldeneye.

Field Marks. A white *crescent* at the base of the bill, instead of a round white patch, separates adult males from those of the Common Goldeneye. The more extensive black of the body of Barrow's Goldeneye, which extends as a black spur close to the waterline in front of the wing, also is diagnostic. The vertically rising forehead of the present species is a useful character, too. Females of the two species are often extremely difficult to separate in life, but Barrow's has a stubbier, more extensively yellow bill (February to May).

Habitat. In British Columbia in nesting season, lakes and ponds, either acid or alkaline, usually near the nesting tree but sometimes up to at least 0.8 km from it. In spring, concentrations occur on large lakes, but most disperse to smaller lakes and ponds as the latter become ice-free. In winter, mostly coastal rivers, estuaries, and lakes. Usually does not favour highly saline water (J.A. Munro). Habitat of eastern populations poorly known, but winter habitat includes coastal freshwater rivers and estuaries and saltwater bays. Nesting in much of the eastern population is independent of trees.

Nesting. Nest when in timbered country usually in hollows in trees; otherwise mostly in holes in rocks; rarely in a Crow's nest. *Eggs* similar to those of Common Goldeneye; in British Columbia and Alberta mean *clutch* size is 9, range 4 to 15; incubation period averages 32.5 days, standard deviation ± 1.5 days, range 30 to 34 days, counted from time last egg is laid (Mary F. Jackson).

Rarely reported from Newfoundland (specimen: Notre Dame Bay, 9 March 1956; sight records at Gander and Marysville), and non-mountainous parts of Alberta (Camrose, Elk Island National Park, Beaverhill Lake); sight records for Saskatchewan (Semans) and Manitoba (various sight records: Oak Lake north to Churchill).

Range. Breeds in widely separated areas: from southern Alaska and southern Yukon south to eastern Washington and California (high central Sierra Nevada); also in Labrador, southwestern Greenland, and Iceland. In winter it is found somewhat farther south.

Bufflehead

Petit Garrot
Bucephala albeola (Linnaeus)
Total length: 30 to 38 cm
Plate 16

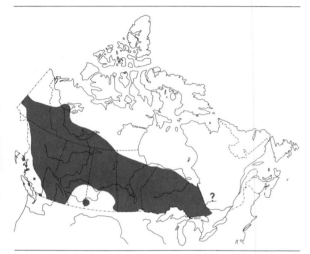

Breeding Distribution of Bufflehead

Range in Canada. Breeds (in the vicinity of woodland) in southern Yukon (Kluane, Big Salmon and Sheldon lakes); western Mackenzie (Jungle Ridge Creek, Chick Lake, Great Slave Lake, Fort Simpson, probably Fort Norman); British Columbia (widely east of the Cascade Mountains, but locally farther west: middle Quinsam and Sumas lakes, Kleena Kleene); Alberta; Saskatchewan; middle and southern Manitoba. Absent as a breeder in treeless southern parts of the Prairie Provinces but breeds in Moose Mountain and Cypress Hills; sparsely and locally in Ontario (Favourable Lake, Winisk; and rarely as far south as Sudbury). Said to be present in breeding season in western Quebec, but no evidence of breeding.

In migration found commonly also in western British Columbia, southern parts of the Prairie Provinces; fairly commonly in southern Ontario and southwestern Quebec, and less commonly in New Brunswick, Nova Scotia (including Cape Breton Island), Prince Edward Island, and Newfoundland. Winters in coastal and southern British Columbia (entire length of coast; Okanagan Lake); southern Alberta (very locally: Calgary); southern Ontario (Lake Erie, Lake Ontario); southern New Brunswick; Nova Scotia; and southern Newfoundland (regularly off Traytown and Gambo).

Adult male (winter and breeding): Head dark with strong green, purple, and bronze gloss and with a large triangle of white, starting below the eye and broadening upward over back of head. Neck white. Back and rump black, paling to grey on upper tail coverts. Tail grey. Inner scapulars black, outer ones white with fine black outer edge. Wing coverts mainly white with black along front edge of wing. Primaries blackish. Secondaries mainly white. Tertials black. Wing linings dusky mixed with white. Breast and sides white, becoming pale greyish on abdomen. Eye brown. Bill leaden blue, usually yellowish along edge of upper mandible. Legs and feet pinkish flesh. *Adult female (winter and breeding)*: Head and neck dark greyish-brown with a narrow white cheek patch extending backward from below the eye. Back, scapulars, rump, upper tail coverts sooty brown. Tail sooty grey. Upper sides of wings similar to back but with white patch in secondaries. Sides grey. Breast and belly white. Eye brown. Bill dusky or dark lead-grey. Legs grey with pinkish or bluish tinge. *Immatures*: In first autumn closely resemble female.

Measurements. *Adult male*: wing, 163–173 (167.7); tail, 67.5–78 (73.9); exposed culmen, 27–30.5 (28.9); tarsus, 33–35 (33.9). *Adult female*: wing, 141–167 (152.6) mm.

Field Marks. A small duck with a white patch in the wing, which distinguishes it from the teals. Male in breeding plumage, with a large wedge of white on the head; looks a little like the male Hooded Merganser but may be distinguished even at long distances by its white flanks, and at closer range also by its stubbier bill. Females and immatures are small dark ducks with a small white patch on the side of the head and a small white area in the wing especially noticeable in flight. *Voice*: Male, a squeaky whistle; also a guttural rolling note. Female, a hoarse croak somewhat like the Common Goldeneye but weaker.

Habitat. In breeding season, ponds and lakes in or near open woodland. At other seasons freshwater and alkali lakes, and rivers of the interior; and saltwater bays and estuaries on the coast.

Nesting. Nests in cavities in trees, preferably those made by large woodpeckers; will use nesting boxes. Nest cavity lined with down and feathers. *Eggs* buffy to creamy white. *Clutch size* in British Columbia 5 to 16 (perhaps those over 12 are a product of more than one bird), usually 7 to 10; incubation period 29 to 31 days (A.J. Erskine), by the female.

Range. Breeds from west-central and southern Alaska and forested parts of western Canada south to southern British Columbia, northern Montana, and central Manitoba; locally in Oregon and northeastern California. Winters from the Aleutian Islands, Alaska Peninsula, the Great Lakes, and the Maritime Provinces south to Mexico and the Gulf Coast.

Smew

Harle piette
Mergellus albellus (Linnaeus)
Total length: ca. 40.5 cm
Plate 17

Status in Canada. Accidental visitor to British Columbia (Vancouver region: photo records 28 February to 31 March 1974, and 14 January to 30 March 1975. Sight record 14, 18, 23 November 1970); Ontario (photo record: Niagara River, 26 February to 6 March 1960; sight record: Normandale, 9 and 10 December 1973). Sight records only for Quebec (Montréal region, 12 February 1967; and 11 December 1976).

A small merganser with shorter, more "duck-like" bill than other mergansers and a drooping, not conspicuous, crest. *Adult male*: Mainly white with dark patch from around eye to base of bill; at closer range its black middle back, small black-and-white crest, and two narrow dark lines up sides of breast can be seen. *Females and immatures*: Have conspicuous pure-white cheeks and throat sharply contrasted against the chestnut-red rest of head; back, breast, and flanks, grey; belly white. Both sexes have white wing patches (female's smaller) conspicuous in flight.

Hooded Merganser

Bec-scie couronné
Lophodytes cucullatus (Linnaeus)
Total length: 43 to 58 cm
Plate 17

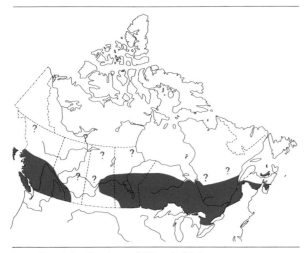

Breeding Distribution of Hooded Merganser

Range in Canada. Northern limits of range poorly known. Breeds in British Columbia (north to Queen Charlotte Islands and in the interior at least to Vanderhoof and perhaps the Topley areas); Alberta (breeding records for the mountains at Banff, Crowsnest Pass, and Waterton Lakes; recorded in summer at Barrhead); Saskatchewan (Brightwater Reservoir, Big Quill Lake, Tobin Lake); Manitoba (southern and middle wooded parts, recorded in summer north to Churchill and Misty Lake); Ontario (north to southern James Bay, Kenora region, Lake Nipigon, Kapuskasing, Gogama); southern Quebec (Montréal, Saint-Cyrille in L'Islet County, La Mauricie National Park, perhaps north to Baie-du-Poste); southern New Brunswick (St. Croix and St. John rivers); Prince Edward Island (Warren Grove Creek); and Nova Scotia (rarely: Kejimkujik National Park).

Species has been recorded north to southern Mackenzie (Great Slave Lake); southern Keewatin (Fourhill Lakes); northern Ontario; northern Quebec (Clearwater Lake, Bienville

Head crested in both sexes. *Adult male (winter and breeding)*: Head and neck black with large triangle of white extending backward from behind eye and with narrow black border along nape. Back black becoming brownish on rump and tail. Two spurs of black reach down onto sides of breast. Fore-wing grey. Speculum white, divided by black bar. Inner secondaries and tertials black striped with white. Sides and flanks reddish brown crossed by fine blackish lines. Breast and belly white. Eye yellow. Bill blackish. Legs and feet pale yellowish-brown. *Adult female*: Head and neck greyish brown, throat much paler, crest brownish and shorter than in male. Back, scapulars, rump, and tail, dark brown. Wings brown with restricted white wing patch. Breast and sides brownish grey. Belly white. Eye brown. Bill dusky above, yellowish below. Legs brownish. *Young* resemble female, but they are paler, and the crest is poorly developed.

Measurements. *Adult male*: wing, 188–197 (192.8); tail, 87.5–99.5 (93.2); exposed culmen, 32–43 (39.3); tarsus, 31–39 (33). *Adult female*: wing, 172–188 (182.6) mm.

Field Marks. Adult male's large white head-patch could be confused with that of the Bufflehead, but its slender merganser bill and coloured flanks are very different. The female Hooded Merganser is identified as a merganser by the slender bill. Its small size and darker coloration separate it from other mergansers.

Habitat. Primarily a freshwater duck. In nesting season, freshwater ponds, lakes, and rivers in or near woodland. In migration and winter, similar freshwater bodies. Sometimes frequents saltwater bays, but much less often than the Red-breasted and Common mergansers.

Nesting. Nests in a hole in a tree. *Eggs*, usually 5 to 12; larger numbers recorded, probably a product of more than one female. Incubation period 29 to 37 days, averaging 32.6 days (T.E. Morse et al.).

Lake). Rare visitor in Newfoundland (Trepassey; also sight records: Cape Broyle and La Manche), and Labrador (Lake Melville). Winters in small numbers in southern British Columbia and occasionally on the southern Great Lakes.

Range. Breeds from southern Alaska and across southern Canada, south mainly to Oregon, Wyoming, Iowa, eastern Missouri, eastern Arkansas, and western Tennessee. Winters from southern British Columbia, the Great Lakes, and Massachusetts south to the Gulf Coast and Mexico.

Common Merganser

(formerly American Merganser)

Grand Bec-scie
Mergus merganser Linnaeus
Total length: 53 to 68.5 cm
Plate 17

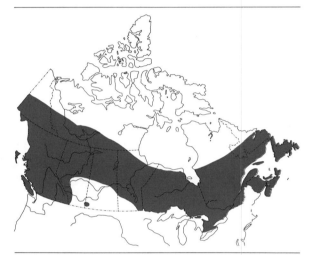

Breeding Distribution of Common Merganser

Range in Canada. Breeds in southern Yukon (north at least to Sheldon Lake and Dawson); southern Mackenzie (Great Slave Lake, Gagnon Lake); British Columbia; Alberta (mountainous southwest and Lake Athabasca regions; locally the Cypress Hills; otherwise only a migrant in southern prairies); Saskatchewan (wooded parts: Lake Athabasca, Churchill River, Hasbala Lake, Flotten Lake, Torch River, Kingsmere Lake, Cypress Hills region); Manitoba (Cormorant Lake, Moose and Cedar lakes, Oxford Lake, northern Lake Winnipegosis, Waterhen Lake, Lake St. Martin, Riding Mountain. Reported as breeding on Nelson River); Ontario (Moose River and Sioux Lookout south to southern Lake Huron and Peterborough County); central and southern Quebec (north to Lake Saint-Jean and Lake Mistassini; reportedly Lake Bienville); Labrador (Churchill Falls, Flatwaters Cove); Newfoundland; New Brunswick; Nova Scotia; and Prince Edward Island. Recorded in summer, but not known to breed, north to central Mackenzie (Thelon River); southern Keewatin, and northern Quebec. Winters in British Columbia (coast; small numbers in southern interior); southern Alberta (a few regularly near Calgary); southern Ontario (Great Lakes, lower Ottawa and St. Lawrence valleys); southern Quebec (north to Lake Saint-Jean); Newfoundland; and the Maritime Provinces.

Nostrils nearer to middle of bill than to base (Figure 36) thus different from Red-breasted Merganser. *Adult male*: Head and upper neck blackish, strongly glossed with green. Upper back and scapulars black. Rump, upper tail coverts, and tail, grey. Fore-wing mainly white, greater coverts crossed by a dark bar. Primaries and outermost secondaries blackish brown, others mainly white. Lower neck, breast, belly, sides, and under tail coverts, white faintly suffused with pinkish. Eye variable, red to brown. Bill red, dusky on ridge and tip. Legs and feet red. *Adult female*: Head conspicuously crested. Head and upper neck tawny brown. Chin and throat white. Lower hind-neck, back, scapulars, rump, tail, and sides, grey. Upper side of wings grey with white speculum. Abdomen and under tail coverts white. Eye reddish or yellowish. Bill dull reddish with dusky ridge and nail. Legs dull red. *Young in first winter*: Resemble adult female but have shorter crests.

Measurements. *Adult male*: wing, 267.5–281 (273.8); tail, 100.5–111.5 (104.1); exposed culmen, 54.5–59 (56.5); tarsus, 47.5–54.5 (51.9). *Adult female*: wing, 236–274 (249.9) mm.

Field Marks. Long slender bill marks it as a merganser. Adult male is likely to be confused only with the Red-breasted Merganser but lacks the conspicuous crest and reddish breast-band of that species. Females of the two are more difficult to identify, but in the Common Merganser the white throat is more sharply defined and the red of the neck is sharply cut off from (not blended into) the whitish breast.

Habitat. Primarily fresh water. In summer frequents freshwater lakes and rivers, usually in or near woodland. In winter mostly freshwater rivers and the open water, when available, of lakes; less often coastal salt water. Clear water is preferred and is probably necessary for feeding.

Nesting. Nest is usually in tree cavities but sometimes in holes in banks, in rock piles, and on the ground among bushes; rarely on cliffs or even in a chimney. *Eggs*, usually 8 to 12; creamy white. Incubation by the female, reportedly lasts 28 to 35 days (various authors).

Range. Holarctic: southern Alaska, and across southern Canada, Iceland, Scotland, Norway, Sweden, Russia, and Siberia, south to California, Arizona, South Dakota, Minnesota, Michigan, central New York, Maine, the Netherlands, Germany, and south-central Russia. In North America winters south to southern California, northern Mexico, the Gulf Coast, and Florida.

Subspecies. *Mergus merganser americanus* Cassin.

Red-breasted Merganser

Bec-scie à poitrine rousse
Mergus serrator Linnaeus
Total length: 51 to 64 cm
Plate 17

Breeding Distribution of Red-breasted Merganser

Range in Canada. Breeds from Yukon (north to the arctic coast); Mackenzie (north to Mackenzie Delta and Fort Anderson, perhaps Perry River); southeastern Victoria Island; southern Keewatin (Angikuni Lake, Thlewiaza River; summer sight records for Southampton Island); and Baffin Island (Nettilling Lake; Cumberland Sound; also very sparsely north to Utuk Lake (female with 10-day-old young); sight record of single birds at Oliver Sound and near Arctic Bay); south to northern British Columbia (Atlin region); northern Alberta (Lake Athabasca; reports of breeding farther south require confirmation); northern and central Saskatchewan (Reindeer, Kazan, Flotten, and Namew lakes); Manitoba (Churchill, Cochrane River, Lake St. Martin, Seven Sisters dam); southern Ontario (Bay of Quinte, Brothers Island, Kingston); central and, locally, southeastern Quebec (Lake Mistassini, Anticosti Island, Gaspé Peninsula, Madeleine Islands); Labrador; Newfoundland; New Brunswick; Nova Scotia (including Sable Island); and Prince Edward Island. Winters in British Columbia (regularly all along coast; occasionally in southern interior); the Great Lakes (small numbers); St. Lawrence valley (Basque Island); Newfoundland; and the Maritimes.

Head crested. Nostrils nearer base of bill than in Common Merganser (Figure 36). *Adult male (winter and spring)*: Head and upper neck black glossed with green; conspicuous crest. Back, most of scapulars, and tertials, black. Wing black and white. Rump, upper tail coverts, and sides, grey finely crossed with wavy black lines. Breast pale cinnamon, streaked and mottled with black. Lower neck and abdomen white. Eye, legs, and feet, red. Bill red with dusky ridge. *Adult female*: Head and neck cinnamon brown, darkest on top of head, blending into whitish on throat. Rest of upper parts grey. Wing with white speculum crossed by black bar. Sides brownish grey. Abdomen white. Eye and bill red; legs dull reddish.

Measurements. *Adult male*: wing, 231–251 (244.1); tail, 78.5–87 (82.3); exposed culmen, 55–63.5 (58); tarsus, 45–50 (46.9). *Adult female*: wing, 205.5–246 (221.3) mm.

Field Marks. Adult male, with its greenish-black crested head and reddish breast-band, is easy to recognize. Females and young similar to Common Merganser, but brown of head *blends* into whitish throat and into grey of lower neck (not sharply cut off as in Common Merganser).

Habitat. Generally more marine than Common Merganser; preferring coastal salt water in winter. In breeding season both salt and fresh water: bays, lagoons, estuaries; also freshwater lakes and rivers.

Nesting. Nest on ground, under bushes, sometimes in rock piles or under logs or tree roots, usually near water. It is a depression, often with some grasses or leaves, lined with down (down darker than that of Common Merganser). *Eggs*, 7 to 12, variable; greenish buff to buffy, more richly coloured than in Common Merganser. Incubation, 29 to 35 (average 31.8) days (P. Curth) by the female.

Range. Holarctic. Breeds from Alaska, Mackenzie, southern Baffin Island, Greenland, Iceland, Scandinavia (from 71°N), and Russia, south to British Columbia, southern Manitoba, central Michigan, eastern Maine, Scotland, Ireland, northern Germany, Poland, and middle Russia. In North America, winters (especially along the coasts) from southern Canada to southern United States.

Subspecies. *Mergus serrator serrator* Linnaeus.

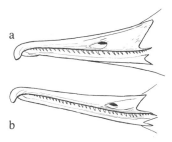

Figure 36
Bill of
a) Common Merganser
b) Red-breasted Merganser

Tribe **Oxyurini:**
Stiff-tailed Ducks

Small to medium-sized diving ducks with peculiar stiff, elongated, narrow-vaned tail which is unlike that of any other group of ducks. The body plumage is shiny and dense, thus superficially resembling that of grebes. Like grebes, too, they are capable of sinking slowly under the water surface with scarcely a ripple. Of the eight species only one is found in Canada.

Ruddy Duck

Canard roux
Oxyura jamaicensis (Gmelin)
Total length: 35.5 to 43 cm
Plate 16

Figure 37
Ruddy Duck

Breeding Distribution of Ruddy Duck

Range in Canada. Breeds in central and southern British Columbia (north at least to Nulki and Tachick lakes and Peace River parklands; mainly in the interior but locally also on Vancouver Island); Alberta (except southwestern part); southwestern Mackenzie (probably Canol Road near Norman Wells: female with young carefully observed by S.D. MacDonald and W.J. Smith; Great Slave Lake); central and southern Saskatchewan (north at least to Kazan and Emma lakes); and southwestern Manitoba (north to near Moose and Cedar lakes, east at least to Red River valley); very locally and sporadically farther east in southern Ontario (Lake St. Clair; Luther Marsh; Wainfleet Marsh; near Mitchell Bay, Lansdowne, Thunder Bay, Blenheim, Mud Lake); southern Quebec (Rouyn, Lake Saint-Pierre); New Brunswick; and Nova Scotia (Amherst Point Bird Sanctuary).

Bill broad, with concave ridge, the nail small and slightly turned back under end of bill (Figure 37). Tail feathers stiff, narrow, rather long, their coverts short. *Adult male (breeding plumage)*: Top of head to below eye, and nape, black. Large cheek patch and chin white. Neck, sides of breast, and all upper parts (except wings, rump, and tail) chestnut. Upper side of wing brown, secondaries tipped white. Rump and tail brown. Wing linings mixed white and brown. Under tail coverts white. Abdomen silvery white mixed with dusky. Eye brown or reddish brown. Bill blue. Legs and feet bluish grey with dusky webs. *Adult male (autumn and winter)*: Crown duller and browner; chestnut areas replaced by dark brown and grey. *Adult female*: Top of head to below eye, and a poorly defined streak across cheeks, dark brown. Back, scapulars, rump, upper tail coverts, and upper side of wings, blackish brown irregularly crossed with buffy or greyish lines. Under parts silvery white mixed with dusky. Eye brown. Bill dusky. Legs bluish grey. Young in first autumn resemble adult female.

Measurements. *Adult male*: wing, 133–147.5 (141.4); tail, 67–79 (72.2); exposed culmen, 38.5–41 (40.3); tarsus, 33–38 (34.2). *Adult female*: wing, 134–145.5 (139.5) mm.

Field Marks. On the water often cocks tail up like a wren, but this is not unique as other ducks sometimes do it too. Adult male in breeding plumage has large white cheek patch, black cap, and extensive reddish chestnut on upper parts and sides; in autumn and winter, it lacks chestnut colouring, but black cap and white cheek patch are obvious. Female has dark cap and light cheek, the latter crossed by a poorly defined horizontal line; might be confused with female Black Scoter, but the Ruddy is much smaller with entirely different buzzy flight.

Habitat. Essentially a freshwater duck. In summer, freshwater lakes, ponds, sloughs, with margins of emergent vegetation. In migration prefers similar fresh or brackish water bodies, often extensive; but will frequent saltwater bays on occasion.

Nesting. Nest, a well-concealed woven mass of marsh vegetation attached to growing marsh plants, usually a few inches over water. *Eggs*, 5 to 10; extremely large for so small a duck, with thick, rough shell, dull white in colour. Incubation 27 days (T.E. Randall), 25 to 26 days (J.B. Low).

Regular migrant in southern parts of western Canada, east to the Great Lakes, scarcer farther east, rare in the Maritimes and Newfoundland.

Casual north to southern Yukon (Alaska Highway at Takhini River; Sulphur Lake); northeastern Manitoba (Churchill, York Factory); and eastern Hudson Bay (Grande rivière de la Baleine). Winters in small numbers in southern British Columbia and southern Ontario (Lakes Erie and Ontario).

Range. Southern part of western (mainly) Canada south to Guatemala, the West Indies; also central and eastern Andes of Colombia. Winters mainly from southern British Columbia and middle United States southward.

Subspecies. *Oxyura jamaicensis rubida* (Wilson).

Order **Falconiformes:** Diurnal Birds of Prey

A large and complex group of diurnal flesh-eating birds, world-wide in distribution. The bill is hooked and the toes are equipped with sharp claws for holding and tearing flesh (but in some groups the claws are relatively blunt, e.g. American vultures).

Family **Cathartidae:** American Vultures

Number of Species in Canada: 2

Large, long-winged birds *with the head bare of feathers*; a strongly hooked bill with large open nostrils; toes rather long (the hind one elevated), but weakly hooked and unsuitable for grasping and holding prey. They feed on dead animals and thus serve a useful purpose as scavengers. Flight, on long, broad wings, with much protracted sailing and circling, is extremely graceful.

Black Vulture

Urubu noir
Coragyps atratus (Bechstein)
Total length: 61 to 69 cm
Plate 23

Status in Canada. Casual or accidental in southern Ontario (specimen: 21 July 1947, 6.4 km north of Niagara Falls; also sight records); southwestern Quebec (specimens: both from Beauport, 28 October 1897; 20 March 1932); New Brunswick (about 12 records: Spruce Lake, Grand Manan, Campobello Island, Escuminac); and Nova Scotia (specimens: Pugwash, 12 January 1896; Owl's Head, Halifax County, 1 December 1918). Sight record for Prince Edward Island (Cape Wolfe, 22 November 1981). Additional sight records have been reported for eastern Canada.

For western Canada there is a photo record for southwestern Yukon (Kluane Lake, 2 July 1982) and a sight record for British Columbia (Okanagan Falls, 25 June 1981).

Bare head and neck mark it as a vulture. Differs from Turkey Vulture in somewhat smaller size; black instead of red head, long narrow nostrils; relatively shorter wing (longest primaries little longer than largest secondaries); shorter tail (less than half the length of the folded wing instead of more than half); and square instead of rounded tail. In flight the Black Vulture shows a light area near end of each wing and a shorter square-tipped (not rounded) tail; also its flaps are more rapid.

Range. Southern United States south through Mexico and Central America to Argentina and Chile.

Turkey Vulture

Urubu à tête rouge
Cathartes aura (Linnaeus)
Total length: 67 to 81 cm
Plates 18 and 23

Head and extreme upper neck bare except for sparse hairlike bristles. Bill rather long, hooked, with very large broad nostrils. Wings long. *Adults*: Naked head and upper neck, red. Upper body, wings, and tail black, the feathers of back and wing coverts edged with brown. Neck and under parts black. Eye brown. Bill whitish, red basally. Legs, flesh colour. *Juvenal*: Similar to adults but bare skin of head blackish.

Measurements *(C. a. septentrionalis). Adult male*: wing, 518–550 (535.9); tail, 252–298 (271); culmen (from cere), 24–25 (24.4); tarsus, 65–71 (68.1). *Adult female*: wing, 527–559 (545.8) mm (Friedmann).

Breeding Distribution of Turkey Vulture

Range in Canada. Breeds locally in small numbers in southern British Columbia (Comox, Pender Island, Harrison Mills, Vernon, Columbia Lake); central and southern Alberta (locally north to near Ashmont); central Saskatchewan (Moose Jaw, Rush Lake, Old Wives Lake, Qu'Appelle valley, north to Biggar, Chitek and Murray lakes); southern Manitoba (Riding Mountain, Elk Island, Long Lake); western Ontario (Poplar Bay, Kenora); southern Ontario (north to Bruce Peninsula, Manitoulin Island, Credit Forks, Georgetown and Frontenac County; locally north to North Bay, White Lake and Calabogie).

Uncommon visitor to southern Quebec (Montréal area, Lake Raymond, Wright, Barrington, Hatley, Pointe-des-Monts); New Brunswick; and Nova Scotia (well-spaced records at various points including Cape Breton Island). Casual in northern Ontario (Fort Severn, Moose Factory). Accidental in Labrador (Nain, West St. Modeste) and Newfoundland (St. Anthony, Renews). Winters occasionally in southern British Columbia (Comox, Oyster River, Okanagan Landing).

Field Marks. A large long-winged (wingspread to 183 cm) black bird with small red (blackish in young) head and longish hooked bill. In flight it soars effortlessly for long periods with wings held definitely above horizontal in a broad V; often tilts gracefully from side to side; black under wing coverts contrast with paler flight feathers.

Habitat. Inhabits various types of terrain, except heavy unbroken forest. Spends long periods on the wing, often at considerable heights.

Nesting. No nest. The two eggs are laid on the ground among rocks, under logs, on cliffs, or in caves. They are yellowish white with bold irregular blotches of browns and often sparse spots of pale lavender. Incubation period variously reported: 30 to 41 days (*in* Bent 1937).

Range. Southern Canada, south through the United States to the West Indies, Central America, and to southern South America.

Subspecies. (1) *Cathartes aura septentrionalis* Wied is the breeding subspecies of southern Ontario and eastern United States. Most wanderers to other parts of eastern Canada are probably referable to it. (2) *C. a. teter* Friedmann, with an average shorter tail and wings, inhabits western Canada including western Ontario. (Alexander Wetmore, 1964. Smithsonian Miscellaneous Collections, vol. 146, no. 6, pp. 1–18, maintains that *meridionalis* is an older name for *teter* Friedmann.)

California Condor

[**California Condor**. Condor de Californie. *Gymnogyps californianus* (Shaw). Hypothetical. According to Beebe (1974), there are old sight records for Burrard Inlet, British Columbia.]

Family **Accipitridae**:
Ospreys, Kites, Eagles, Hawks, and Allies

Number of Species in Canada: 15

A large family widely distributed in the world and containing a great variety of both large and small species. The bill is strongly hooked (but lacks the well-formed toothlike projection found in the falcons) and has a membranous covering on its base called a *cere*. The strong feet are equipped with sharp, curved talons for catching and holding prey. The sexes are usually (not always) coloured similarly; the female is larger than the male.

Subfamily **Pandioninae:** Ospreys

This subfamily contains but a single species, the Osprey. The bird subsists entirely on fishes, which are captured by diving from the air. Bill is strongly hooked and feet are peculiarly adapted for catching and holding fish. Talons long and sharp, outer toe is reversible, and the soles of the feet have horny spicules (Figure 38).

Osprey

Balbuzard
Pandion haliaetus (Linnaeus)
Total length: 53 to 62 cm;
wingspread: 135 to 183 cm
Plates 19 and 23

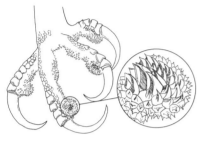

Figure 38
Foot of Osprey showing spiny processes on soles

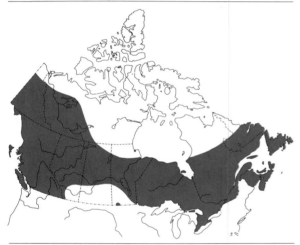

Breeding Distribution of Osprey

Range in Canada. Breeds in Yukon (locally north to Bell River area, perhaps Old Crow Flats); southern Mackenzie (Great Slave Lake; perhaps farther north, for it has been observed in summer north to Great Bear Lake, Fort Norman, and Inuvik); British Columbia; Alberta (except extreme southeastern part); northern and central Saskatchewan (Lake Athabasca; Île-à-la-Crosse; Big River; Nipawin area); Manitoba (Overflowing River; Hayes River between Swampy Lake and Fox River; near York Factory; Churchill; Lake St. Martin; Hillside Beach; Indian Bay; Turtle Mountain); Ontario (Stull Lake, Moose Factory, and Lake Abitibi south to Simcoe County, and the east end of Lake Ontario); southern and central Quebec (north to near mouth of Grande rivière de la Baleine, Bienville Lake and the Schefferville region; probably Hutte sauvage Lake); southern and central Labrador (north to Flowers Bay and inland along Hamilton River); Newfoundland; New Brunswick; Prince Edward Island; and Nova Scotia. Migrates through all of southernmost Canada.

A large, very long-winged hawk. Legs heavy and bare except for a short way down front; soles of feet equipped with sharp horny processes for holding slippery fish (Figure 38). Plumage rather stiff. *Adults*: Head mostly white, streaked brown on crown and with broad blackish-brown stripe down side of neck from eye to back. Rest of upper parts dark brown. Under parts white, the breast more or less spotted with brown. *Young, first autumn*: Similar to adult but brown feathers of upper parts have whitish tips, and the crown is more heavily streaked.

Measurements. *Adult male*: wing, 457–488 (469.7); tail, 197–215 (204.2); culmen (from cere), 31–33.5 (32.4); tarsus, 56.5–62.5 (61). *Adult female*: wing, 488–518 (493.3) mm.

Field Marks. Large size separates it from most hawks, and its white under parts distinguish it from eagles and vultures. Its facial markings and slight crest are also distinctive. Habitually hunts over water, often hovering in the air, and dives in spectacular manner into water for fish. In flight, the long slender wings are angled backward, noticeably at the bend, and a black wrist mark shows on their undersides.

Habitat. The vicinity of lakes, large rivers, and coastal bays.

Nesting. Nest, a massive structure of sticks, is placed at various heights usually in isolated trees, either dead or living; sometimes on telephone poles, cliff pinnacles, even on an abandoned Indian tepee, or on the ground. It is used and added to year after year. Sometimes nests in scattered colonies. *Eggs*, 2 to 4; buffy white, handsomely blotched very heavily to lightly with rich browns. Incubation 35 to 38 days in Europe, 32 to 33 days in America; mainly or solely by female.

Range. Cosmopolitan, occurring in tropical and temperate parts of all continents. In the Western Hemisphere breeds from Alaska and central Canada south to the Bahamas, Mexico, and British Honduras; winters from southern United States south to the West Indies, northern Argentina, Paraguay, and Peru.

Subspecies. *Pandion haliaetus carolinensis* (Gmelin).

Remarks. Ospreys subsist entirely on fish, which they capture by spectacular dives from the air. They hit the water with a resounding splash and occasionally disappear momentarily below the surface. Then, with a few flaps of their powerful wings they clear the water, shrug off the excess water, and continue flying. If successful in catching a fair-sized or large fish, this is carried, in both claws, parallel with the bird's body, head first. Most of the fish it takes, such as tomcod and flounders on the coast, and suckers, perch, and sunfish on freshwater lakes and rivers, are of little economic importance.

Subfamily **Accipitrinae:**
Kites, Hawks, Eagles, Harriers

The accipiters (Goshawk, Sharp-shinned, and Cooper's hawks) have short rounded wings and a long tail thus showing a characteristic flight silhouette (Plate 23). The buteos (Red-tailed, Red-shouldered, Broad-winged, Swainson's, Rough-legged, and Ferruginous hawks) are heavily built hawks with broad rounded wings and broad rounded tails (Plate 22).

Most hawks perform a useful service in curbing the numbers of harmful rodents. A few do take small birds (Goshawk, Cooper's, and Sharp-shinned hawks) but because of the depredations of a small minority the tendency has been all too general to condemn the whole family, and consequently all hawks have been slaughtered indiscriminately, often by persons who should know better. The law now protects these beautiful, valuable, and exciting birds.

Certain pesticides, notably DDT, are another peril and several species, especially the Bald and Golden eagles, have been sadly reduced to a point where their very existence in this world has been gravely threatened in recent years.

American Swallow-tailed Kite

Milan à queue fourchue
Elanoides forficatus (Linnaeus)
Total length: 61 cm including very long tail

Status in Canada. Accidental. Single specimens support its occurrence in Ontario (specimen said to be "certainly an Ontario record," probably Toronto, taken many years prior to 1907, recorded by J.H. Fleming, 1907. Auk, vol. 24, no. 1, p. 87. Photo record: Point Pelee, 20 May 1978; Buckhorn, 14–24 June 1982) and Nova Scotia (Lower East Pubnico, extant specimen, August 1905). There are unconfirmed additional (mostly old) sight records for Saskatchewan, Manitoba, and Ontario. Formerly when more numerous within its normal range it probably strayed to Canada more frequently than it does today. Canadian records are presumably referable to the nominate race *E. f. forficatus* (Linnaeus).

Almost unmistakable. A medium-sized hawk, strikingly marked with contrasting black and white, with very long deeply forked tail (outer feathers project 23 cm beyond middle ones) and long pointed wings. Wings and tail solid black except mainly white tertials. Rest of plumage including head, shoulders, and under parts white. Under wing coverts white, contrasting with black flight feathers.

Range. From South Carolina, Georgia, Florida, and the Gulf Coast southward through eastern Mexico and Central America to northern Argentina and Bolivia.

Mississippi Kite

Milan du Mississippi
Ictinia mississippiensis (Wilson)
Total length: 35.5 to 38 cm
Plate 23

Status in Canada. Accidental in Ontario (photo record: Point Pelee, 16 May 1979; sight records: Toronto, 19 September 1951; Point Pelee, May 1971 and 20–21 May 1982).

Adult male: Head pale grey with small black area in front of eye. Mantle dark slate-grey passing into blackish at bend of wing. A broad band across secondaries pale grey, becoming almost white at feather tips. Primaries blackish, their webs with inconspicuous small areas of rufous. Tail plain black, slightly notched. Under parts neutral grey. Iris red; legs orange or orange-red. *Adult female*: Similar to male but darker and somewhat larger. *Immatures* have heavily brown-streaked under parts and the black tail has white barring.

Measurements. *Adult male*: wing, 286–305 (295); tail, 149–166 (157.1); culmen (from cere), 14.5–15.5 (15.1); tarsus, 35–37. *Adult female*: wing, 300–315 (309) mm.

Field Marks. Adults are graceful, falcon-shaped greyish hawks with *unmarked* black tail (slightly notched), a slaty-grey mantle, a broad pale-grey (almost whitish) trailing edge to the secondaries. *Immatures* have the upper parts much mixed with brown, heavily brown-streaked under parts, and the blackish tail has about three whitish bars underneath.

Range. Breeds locally from northeastern Kansas, Missouri, and Iowa (formerly southern Illinois and Indiana) and South Carolina, south to Texas and northern Florida. Winters from southeastern United States south to Guatemala.

Bald Eagle

Pygargue à tête blanche
Haliaeetus leucocephalus (Linnaeus)
Total length: male, 76 to 86 cm;
wingspread, 175 to 210 cm;
female, 89 to 94 cm;
wingspread, 198 to 225 cm
Plate 18

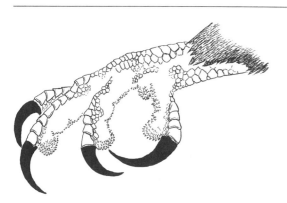

Figure 39
Foot of Bald Eagle

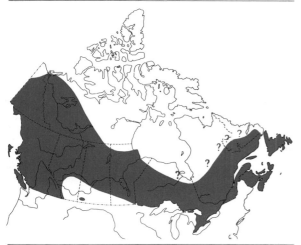

Breeding Distribution of **Bald Eagle**

Range in Canada. Locally distributed breeder
and, in southern parts, winter resident; com-
monest along the Pacific and (decidedly less so)
Atlantic coasts. Breeds locally in Yukon (Aishihik
Lake, Johnson's Crossing probably north to
Porcupine River); Mackenzie (Mackenzie Delta,
Lockhart and Anderson rivers, Lake Hardisty,
Great Bear River, Rae, Hornby Channel);
British Columbia (commonest on coast; locally
but widely distributed in interior); Alberta
(northern half and in southwestern mountains);
Saskatchewan (mainly northern half: Lake
Athabasca, Reindeer Lake, Candle Lake,
Emma Lake, Grove Lake, Middle Lake;
formerly at least in southwestern corner: Little
Frenchman Creek); Manitoba (Eyrie Lake,
Landing Lake, Churchill, Cedar Lake, Moose
Lake); north-central and southern Ontario
(north at least to Stull and Swan lakes); southern and central Quebec (north at least to Anticosti Island, Mascanin, or Jalobert, Bay);
southern Labrador (Petitsikapau Lake; adults
in summer reported on Churchill River below

Legs only partly feathered (Figure 39). Bill relatively longer than in
Golden Eagle. *Adults*: Dark brown with pure-white head, neck, tail, and
upper tail coverts. Bill and feet yellow. *Immature*: Requires about four
years to attain pure-white head and tail. In first year very dark brown
all over, but white bases of feathers of under parts show through,
giving mottled effect. White on head and tail increases with successive
plumages until pure-white head and tail are attained. Separable from
Golden Eagle, in any plumage, by legs, which are not feathered
completely to toes.

Measurements *(H. l. alascanus). Adult male*: wing, 561–577
(568.4); tail, 277.5–283.5 (282.2); culmen (from cere), 48.5–53 (50.1);
tarsus, 84–91 (88.5). *Adult female*: wing, 600–614.5 (605.6) mm.

Field Marks. Great size and markings of adult are unmistakable.
Immatures are more difficult. Osprey has white under parts. Vultures
have unfeathered head. Longer bill and superior size separate it from
the dark buteos. Most likely to be confused with Golden Eagle (see
Plates 18 and 23).

Habitat. Usually the vicinity of water: larger rivers, lakes, seacoasts, and the adjacent countryside.

Nesting. Mostly in trees, frequently near the top; more rarely on
cliff ledges. Nest, a large structure of sticks and weeds with a wide
variety of trash as lining material. As nests are used for many years,
they may become huge. *Eggs*, usually 2 (sometimes 1 or 3); dull white
and small for so large a bird. Incubation about 35 days (F.H. Herrick)
by both sexes.

Range. Breeds from northwestern Alaska and central Canada
south to southern United States and Baja California. Winters from
Alaska and southern Canada southward to, or beyond, southern limits
of breeding range.

Subspecies. (1) *Haliaeetus leucocephalus alascanus* Townsend is the
breeding subspecies all across Canada. (2) *H. l. leucocephalus*
(Linnaeus), a slightly smaller subspecies, is a non-breeding visitor to
Quebec (Sainte-Germaine; Lake Saint-Jean County); New Brunswick
(Léger Brook, Millbank, Chipman), Nova Scotia (Halifax, East
Jeddore), and Prince Edward Island (Kings County) between 6 May and
18 October.

Churchill Falls; headwaters of Eagle River)
Newfoundland; New Brunswick; Nova Scotia;
and Prince Edward Island (Brudenell River).

Recorded in summer north to Old Crow and
arctic coastal plain (Blow River), Yukon;
Windy River, Keewatin; Cocos Lake and
Moose Factory, Ontario; Lake Waswanipi,
Lake Mistassini, Schefferville, and near Ungava
Bay, Quebec. Winters north to northern British
Columbia, Alberta, southern Ontario, southern
Quebec, southern Newfoundland (Baccalieu
Island, Notre Dame Bay), and the Maritime
Provinces.

Remarks. The Bald Eagle is a large majestic bird which has
declined alarmingly in recent years. It is a scavenger more than a predator, subsisting mainly on fish. It is commonest along the seacoasts,
where castups from the sea supply most of its food requirements. Occasionally it makes its own kills and sometimes it robs the Osprey of its
finny prey. On occasion, usually when fish food is not available, it may
take a few birds.

White-tailed Eagle

[**White-tailed Eagle** (formerly Gray Sea Eagle). Pygargue à queue blanche. *Haliaeetus albi-
cilla* (Linnaeus). Hypothetical. Sight records on Cumberland Sound, Baffin Island,
October 1877; and in spring 1878, when a pair allegedly nested there (Ludwig Kumlien,
1879. U.S. National Museum Bulletin 15, p. 82). Birds resembling this species at Pangnirtung, Baffin Island, were described by a policeman, no date, to Soper (1928). Said to have
bred at Okak, Labrador, by Samuel Weiz (1866. Proceedings Boston Society Natural
History 10, p. 267). An immature male dated 18 March 1898, said by a taxidermist to
have been taken on Vancouver Island, British Columbia (L.B. Bishop, 1905. Auk, vol. 22,
no. 1, pp. 79–80). Although some of these records, particularly those from Cumberland
Sound, seem convincing, unfortunately none is completely satisfactory.]

Northern Harrier

(Marsh Hawk)

Busard Saint-Martin
Circus cyaneus (Linnaeus)
Total length: male, 45 to 51 cm;
female, 48 to 61 cm
Plate 18

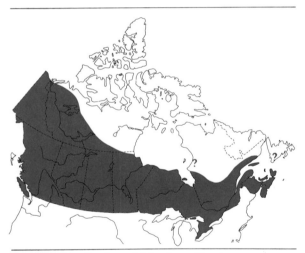

Breeding Distribution of Northern Harrier

Range in Canada. Breeds in Yukon (north to
the coastal plain); Mackenzie (Mackenzie Delta,
lower Anderson River, Rae, Fort Resolution,
Fort Providence, Fort Simpson); British
Columbia (throughout interior and on Van-
couver Island: Middle Quinsam River, Comox);
Alberta; Saskatchewan (breeding records
needed from northern part); Manitoba;
Ontario; southern Quebec (north at least to
Lake Saint-Jean and to Natashquan on north
shore of Gulf of St. Lawrence; also Madeleine
Islands); and the Maritime Provinces; probably

Head with partial facial disc slightly suggestive of an owl. Legs long
and slender; wings and tail long in proportion to body size. Well-
defined white rump patch (upper tail coverts) present in all plumages
except downy. *Adult male*: Head, neck, and upper parts bluish grey
becoming blackish on wing tips; contrasting *white rump patch* (upper
tail coverts); tail grey with narrow dusky bands. Breast, abdomen, and
thighs white, sparsely spotted with rusty. Under wing coverts mainly
white, contrasting with blackish tips. Eye and legs yellow. *Adult female*:
Upper parts dark brown with intermixture of cinnamon on scapulars
and some wing coverts; neck streaked brown and buffy; conspicuous
white rump patch; tail crossed by five to seven dusky bars. Under parts
buffy white streaked with brown, mainly on throat and breast. Underside of flight feathers with alternating light and dusky bars. Eye pale
yellowish to greyish brown; legs yellow. *Immature (first autumn and
winter)*: Resembles adult female but darker and more richly coloured.
Light markings on wing coverts, head, neck, and outer tail feathers,
deeper cinnamon. Tail crossed by four or five bars. Under parts rich
rusty-brown and less extensively, less heavily streaked. Eye dark brown.

Measurements. *Adult male*: wing, 329–351 (340.9); tail, 201–225
(213.7); culmen (from cere), 16.5–17.3 (16.9); tarsus, 71–79.5 (75.4).
Adult female: wing, 355–398 (376.7) mm.

Field Marks. Readily recognizable. A slender, long-winged, long-
tailed, medium-sized hawk (gull-grey in adult male, reddish brown
in female and young) with a conspicuous white rump patch in all
plumages. Most often seen quartering low over open country with alternating flaps and glides. When gliding, wings are held a little above
horizontal, somewhat like a vulture. It is widely distributed and not
uncommon in southern Canada.

Habitat. Hunts over broader fields, meadows, marshes (both fresh
and salt) and similar open country.

Nesting. Nest, composed of weeds, sticks, grasses, and rushes, is
placed on the ground among low bushes or other low vegetation,
usually in a moist meadow or marshy place but sometimes, especially on
the prairies, in dry areas. *Eggs*, 4 to 6 (usually 5); bluish white sometimes sparsely spotted or smeared with pale brown. Incubation variously
reported 21 to 31 days, probably about 29 to 31 days, by the female.

1 Hooded Merganser, p. 118
a) adult female
b) adult male in breeding plumage

2 Smew, p. 118
a) adult male in breeding plumage
b) adult female

3 Red-breasted Merganser, p. 120
a) female
b) adult male in breeding plumage

4 Common Merganser, p. 119
a) adult male in breeding plumage
b) female

Crosby

1 Northern Harrier, p. 128
a) adult male
b) adult female
c) first-year immature

2 Turkey Vulture, p. 123
adult

4 Golden Eagle, p. 145
a) adult
b) adult (flying)

3 Bald Eagle, p. 127
a) adult
b) immature

Crosby

1 Northern Goshawk, p. 138
a) first-year immature
b) adult

2 Broad-winged Hawk, p. 140
a) adult
b) first-year immature

3 Sharp-shinned Hawk, p. 137
a) first-year male
b) adult male

4 Cooper's Hawk, p. 138
a) adult female
b) adult male

5 Osprey, p. 125
adult

Crosby

1 Ferruginous Hawk, p. 143
adult, pale phase

2 Red-tailed Hawk, p. 142
adult

5 Rough-legged Hawk, p. 144
a) adult male, pale phase
b) adult female, pale phase

3 Red-shouldered Hawk, p. 139
adult

4 Swainson's Hawk, p. 141
adult, pale phase

Crosby

1 Prairie Falcon, p. 152
adult

2 Peregrine Falcon, p. 150
a) first-year immature
b) adult

3 Gyrfalcon, p. 151
a) immature, dark phase
b) adult, white phase

4 Merlin, p. 148
a) first-year immature
b) adult male

5 American Kestrel, p. 148
a) male
b) female

Crosby

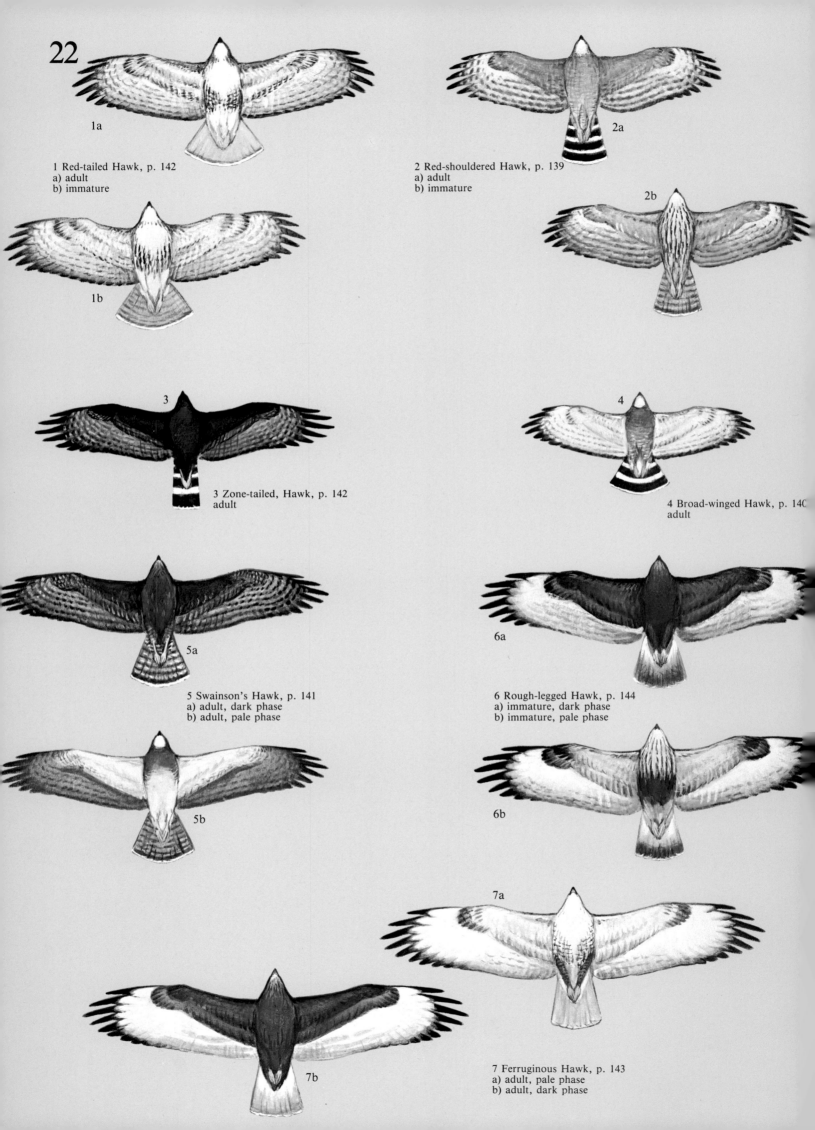

22

1a

1 Red-tailed Hawk, p. 142
a) adult
b) immature

1b

2a

2 Red-shouldered Hawk, p. 139
a) adult
b) immature

2b

3

3 Zone-tailed, Hawk, p. 142
adult

4

4 Broad-winged Hawk, p. 140
adult

5a

5 Swainson's Hawk, p. 141
a) adult, dark phase
b) adult, pale phase

5b

6a

6 Rough-legged Hawk, p. 144
a) immature, dark phase
b) immature, pale phase

6b

7a

7 Ferruginous Hawk, p. 143
a) adult, pale phase
b) adult, dark phase

7b

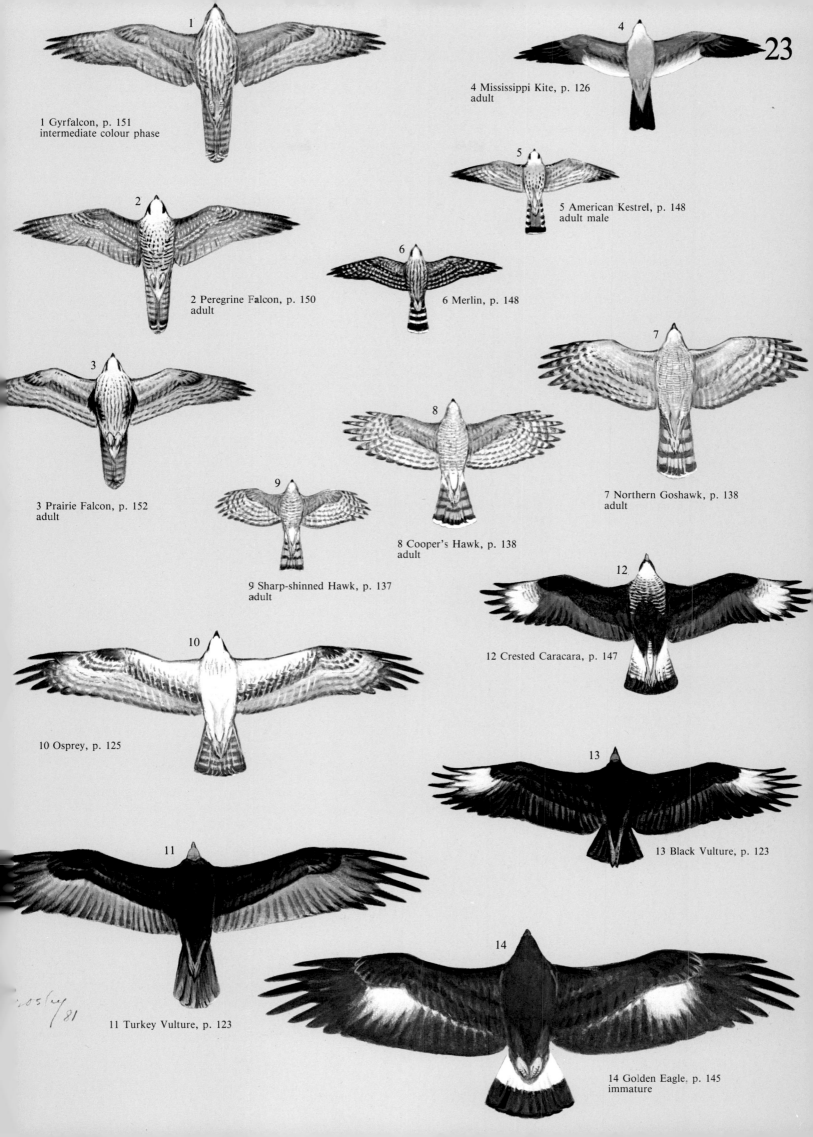

23

1 Gyrfalcon, p. 151
intermediate colour phase

2 Peregrine Falcon, p. 150
adult

3 Prairie Falcon, p. 152
adult

4 Mississippi Kite, p. 126
adult

5 American Kestrel, p. 148
adult male

6 Merlin, p. 148

7 Northern Goshawk, p. 138
adult

8 Cooper's Hawk, p. 138
adult

9 Sharp-shinned Hawk, p. 137
adult

10 Osprey, p. 125

11 Turkey Vulture, p. 123

12 Crested Caracara, p. 147

13 Black Vulture, p. 123

14 Golden Eagle, p. 145
immature

24

1 Ruffed Grouse, p. 160
a) grey phase (flying)
b) red phase

1a

1b

2 Sharp-tailed Grouse, p. 163

2

3

3 Greater Prairie-Chicken, p. 162

4a

4b

4 Ring-necked Pheasant, p. 155
a) female
b) male

5a

5b

5 Sage Grouse, p. 162
a) female (flying)
b) male in autumn

Crosby

Newfoundland (a few occur in summer but definite breeding evidence lacking).

Recorded north to southern Keewatin (Windy River); Repulse Bay, N.W.T.; Grande rivière de la Baleine mouth, Feuilles River, Quebec; and Dead Islands Harbour, Labrador.

Migrates through breeding range. Winters in small numbers in southern parts of British Columbia, Alberta, southern Ontario, and Nova Scotia.

Range. Holarctic. Breeds from western Alaska east across central Canada and south to southwestern United States, western Oklahoma, southern Illinois, Ohio, and southeastern Virginia; also from Norway, Sweden, Russia, and Siberia, south to Portugal, Spain, and central Asia. In North America it winters from southern Canada south to Colombia and the West Indies.

Subspecies. *Circus cyaneus hudsonius* (Linnaeus).

Sharp-shinned Hawk

Epervier brun
Accipiter striatus Vieillot
Total length: male, 25 to 30 cm;
female (larger than male), 30 to 36 cm,
therefore the smallest of our accipiters.
Plates 19 and 23

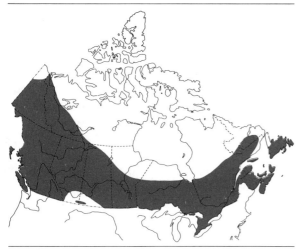

Breeding Distribution of Sharp-shinned Hawk

Range in Canada. Breeds in woodland in central and southern Yukon (presumably north to Old Crow); central-western and southern Mackenzie (Forts Resolution and Simpson; Grandin River near Mazenod Lake; occurs in summer northwest to Aklavik Range); British Columbia; Alberta (except treeless southeast); Saskatchewan (north to Stoney Rapids and southeast to near Regina); central and southern Manitoba; central and southern Ontario (recorded in summer north to Moose Factory); southern and middle Quebec (north probably to Lake Mistassini and Pointe-des-Monts; sight records in summer near Matamec and Natashquan; Anticosti Island); Labrador (Goose Bay); Newfoundland; New Brunswick; Prince Edward Island; and Nova Scotia. Migrates through most of southern Canada with large September concentrations passing through Point Pelee, Ontario. Winters in small numbers in coastal and southern British Columbia, southern Ontario, southern Newfoundland, and the Maritimes.

Accidental on Victoria Island (Holman).

An accipiter less than 35.5 cm in total length is likely to be this species. Adults have upper parts dark blue; breast and abdomen, barred dull reddish-brown and white. First-year birds have brown upper parts; whitish, heavily brown-streaked breast and abdomen. Thus very similar to Cooper's Hawk, but usually decidedly smaller, with relatively slenderer and longer legs and square-tipped tail and with cap not appreciably darker than back. Easily distinguished from the similar-sized Merlin and American Kestrel by its lack of a toothlike projection on the upper mandible and its short, rounded wings.

Measurements *(A. s. velox)*. *Adult male*: wing, 152.5–173.5 (167.3); tail, 124.5–139.5 (132.5); culmen (from cere), 10–10.9 (10.5); tarsus, 47–53.5 (49.5). *Adult female*: wing, 188–206 (199.7) mm.

Field Marks. Short, rounded wings and long tail mark it as an accipiter. Almost identical with Cooper's Hawk but usually smaller; however, a large female Sharp-shin is of about the same size as a small male Cooper's Hawk. The Cooper's Hawk has the tip of the tail slightly rounded (that of the Sharp-shin is square), and the Cooper's cap is darker than the back. The similar-sized American Kestrel and Merlin have longer, pointed wings of falcons, and the American Kestrel, in addition, has a reddish back and tail.

Habitat. Woodland and wood edges; also, particularly in migration, hedges, bushy clearings, and shores frequented by other bird migrants.

Nesting. Nest is placed in a tree, preferably coniferous, 3 to 21 m up. It is rather large (crow size), is made of small sticks and lined with twigs and bark. *Eggs*, usually 3 to 6; dull white or bluish white, irregularly and handsomely blotched with browns. Incubation 34 to 35 days (Nice), by both parents.

Range. Breeds from northwestern Alaska and forested parts of Canada south to northern Mexico, the Gulf Coast of United States, and Greater Antilles. Winters from extreme southern Canada to Costa Rica.

Subspecies. *Accipiter striatus velox* (Wilson) is the breeding subspecies of all of Canada, except the Queen Charlotte Islands (and perhaps other coastal parts of British Columbia), where its place is taken by *A. s. perobscurus* Snyder, a somewhat darker subspecies.

Remarks. The Sharp-shinned and Cooper's hawks, as well as the Goshawk, feed largely on other birds and are among the few hawks that deserve the "blame" that unfortunately has been heaped on hawks in general.

Cooper's Hawk

Epervier de Cooper
Accipiter cooperii (Bonaparte)
Total length: male, 35 to 46 cm;
female, 43 to 51 cm
Plates 19 and 23

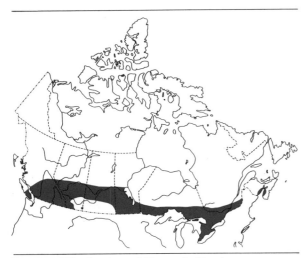

Breeding Distribution of Cooper's Hawk

Range in Canada. Breeds in southern British Columbia (Quamichan Lake, Okanagan Landing, Burnaby, Nita Lake, Lac la Hache); southern Alberta (Seebe, Banff and Jasper national parks, Cypress Hills north probably to Lesser Slave Lake); southern and central Saskatchewan (Spirit Lake, Yorkton, Fort Qu'Appelle, Armley, Carlton); southern Manitoba (Lyleton, Hillside Beach, Winnipeg, Fort Garry); southern Ontario (definite breeding records north to Ottawa, Port Sydney, Thunder Bay, and Rainy River; recorded, but not known to breed, north to Casummit Lake and Timmins); southern Quebec (Lake Saint-Louis, Bernierville, Île Jésus); rarely in New Brunswick (Bayswater); and very rarely Nova Scotia (Black River).

Winters in southern British Columbia and occasionally in southern Ontario, rarely north to Ottawa.

Accipiter outline. Similar to the Sharp-shinned Hawk in all plumages but decidedly larger with relatively stouter legs and a rounded tail; in adults the blackish cap is more or less well-defined against the colour of the back and lower neck. The Goshawk, which is decidedly larger and in adults differently coloured below, is separable by the tarsus, more than half of which is feathered, less than half in Cooper's. The Broad-winged Hawk is of about the same size as Cooper's, and immatures are similarly coloured, but the Broad-wing lacks the Cooper's heavy barring on the underside of the flight feathers and has only three outermost primaries emarginate (five in Cooper's).

Measurements. *Adult male*: wing, 217–258.5 (234.2); tail, 181–215.5 (191.5); culmen (from cere), 15–19.5 (16.9); tarsus, 60.5–70.5 (66.4). *Adult female*: wing, 241–268 (256.1) mm.

Field Marks. Accipiter outline. Intermediate in size between Sharp-shinned and Goshawk. Rounded tail and, in adults, usually somewhat darker cap separate it under good conditions from the usually smaller Sharp-shin. The Goshawk is larger and heavier, the bluish-backed adults with greyish (not reddish) under parts. Young Broad-wings have a buteo outline and lack heavy barring on underside of flight feathers.

Habitat. Similar to Sharp-shinned Hawk but, according to Palmer (1949), found more often in woodland and less in forest edges than its smaller relative.

Nesting. Nest, constructed of sticks and often lined with bark and sometimes a little moss or grass, is placed 6 to 18 m up in a coniferous or deciduous tree. *Eggs*, generally 3 to 5; greenish white, either unmarked or slightly spotted with brown. Incubation period 35 to 36 days (Brown and Amadon).

Range. Breeds from southern Canada south to northwestern Mexico, south-central Texas, central Alabama, and central Florida. Winters mainly from northern United States south to Costa Rica.

Northern Goshawk

Autour des palombes
Accipiter gentilis (Linnaeus)
Total length: 51 to 66 cm
Plates 19 and 23

A robust, long-tailed, relatively short-winged hawk. Feathers extend halfway down front and sides of tarsus. Tail somewhat rounded. *Adults*: Upper parts dark bluish-slate becoming blackish on top of head and behind eye. A light stripe extends from base of bill backward over eye to back of head. Under parts grey to whitish with dusky shaft-streaks and numerous grey vermiculations. Tail crossed by three or four poorly defined blackish bars and tipped greyish. Eye red; feet yellow. *First-year immatures*: Upper parts dusky brown mixed with buffy. Light streak over eye. Tail crossed by four or five dusky bars and tipped whitish. Under parts buffy to whitish, prominently streaked with dark brown. Eye yellowish grey.

In any plumage, separable from other similar hawks, except the Cooper's Hawk, by five emarginate primaries; and from Cooper's Hawk by the extension of feathering halfway down the tarsus. Any Canadian accipiter over 51 cm in length is almost certainly a Goshawk.

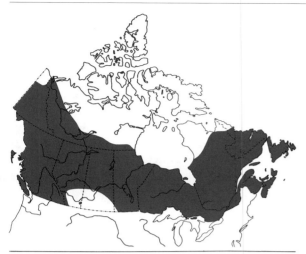

Breeding Distribution of Northern Goshawk

Range in Canada. Breeds in wooded parts of Yukon (north to Old Crow Flats); western Mackenzie (Mackenzie Delta, Grandin River, Wood Buffalo National Park); British Columbia; Alberta (except southern prairies south of Rosedale but including Cypress Hills); northern and middle Saskatchewan (south at least to Beaver, Spruce, and Carrot rivers, locally Cypress Hills); Manitoba (except extreme southwestern part; breeds south to Aweme); Ontario (south to Thunder Bay District; Mount Albert, north of Toronto; and Mallorytown Landing on St. Lawrence River); Quebec (near Kuujjuaq, Grande rivière de la Baleine, Pointe-des-Monts, Old-Chelsea, Île Jésus); Labrador (Hopedale; probably north to near tree limit); Newfoundland; New Brunswick; Prince Edward Island; and Nova Scotia; possibly southwestern Keewatin (Nueltin Lake).

Stragglers (north of breeding range) to Horton River, and southeastern Baffin Island. Winters in the breeding range (north to Mackenzie Delta; and Kuujjuaq, Quebec) and southward in varying numbers.

Measurements *(A. g. atricapillus)*. *Adult male*: wing, 308–330 (319.1); tail, 216.5–235.5 (226.3); culmen (from cere), 21–23 (21.6); tarsus, 70–82.5 (78.4). *Adult female*: wing, 324.5–356 (347.1) mm.

Field Marks. Long tail and short rounded wings, habit of flying with short rapid flaps then sailing briefly mark it as one of our three accipiters. Large size immediately separates it from the Sharp-shinned Hawk. The Cooper's Hawk more closely approaches it in size. Adults of both Cooper's and the Goshawk have blue backs, but the light *stripe over the eye and grey under parts* identify the Goshawk. Immatures of the two are similar in colour, but the Cooper's Hawk is always somewhat smaller and slenderer.

Habitat. Forests and woodlands, perhaps preferring mixedwood types; also forest edges and clearings; hunts at low levels.

Nesting. Nest, a bulky structure of sticks with bark lining and often a few fresh twigs of evergreen, is placed 5 to 23 m up in a tree, either deciduous or coniferous, the former preferred. Often uses same nest in successive years. *Eggs* usually 2 to 4; pale bluish-white. Incubation probably about 36 to 38 days.

Range. Breeds in forested parts of Europe and Asia; and in North America from forested parts of Canada south to northwestern Mexico, Colorado, Minnesota, and western Maryland. In winter, ranges somewhat farther south.

Subspecies. (1) *Accipiter gentilis atricapillus* (Wilson) is the form inhabiting all of Canada except western British Columbia. (2) *A. g. laingi* (Taverner), a darker-coloured race, inhabits Vancouver Island and Queen Charlotte Islands and is probably a permanent resident there, although breeding has not yet been conclusively shown.

A specimen taken at Red Bay, Labrador, on 11 November 1925, has been provisionally identified as an example of the Old World race, *A. g. gentilis* (Linnaeus), according to Todd (1963). It has not been examined by the writer.

Red-shouldered Hawk

Buse à épaulettes
Buteo lineatus (Gmelin)
Total length: male, 45 to 58 cm;
female, 48 to 61 cm
Plates 20 and 22

Buteo outline. Intermediate in size between Red-tailed and Broad-winged hawks. Four outermost primaries emarginate (inner web abruptly cut away near tip) thus separating it from other buteos, except the Red-tailed Hawk. Separable from the Red-tail by the tarsus (half-feathered in the Red-tail, much less than half in Red-shoulder). *Adults*: Upper parts brown mixed with buffy and whitish, "shoulder" of wing (lesser coverts) mainly reddish-brown. Tail above, blackish crossed by five or more narrow white bars and tipped with white; below, whitish or greyish inconspicuously banded. Breast and abdomen barred and streaked with reddish brown and white, many feathers with black shaft streaks. *Immatures*: Upper parts darker brown than in adults and lacking most of the reddish-brown colour (also much restricted on lesser coverts). Tail above, brown crossed by numerous inconspicuous lighter bands, which are often mixed with rusty. Breast and abdomen whitish striped with brown.

Breeding Distribution of Red-shouldered Hawk

Range in Canada. Breeds in southern Ontario (north at least to Lake Panache, Lake Nipissing, and Ottawa region); southwestern Quebec (Gatineau Park, Montréal, Lennoxville, Hatley, Cap-Tourmente); and rarely southern New Brunswick (Washademoak Lake). Sight records without breeding evidence north to Algoma district, Timmins, and Low Bush, Ontario; and Blue-Sea-Lake, Quebec. Rare visitant to Nova Scotia (specimen: Louis Head, 1 March 1975; Seal Island, 11 October 1980; also sight records) and Manitoba (specimen: struck by a truck 4.8 km west of Clearwater, on 1 December 1978; photo record: St. Adolphe, 3–11 April 1979). One sight record for British Columbia (Hope, 8 June 1948). Occasional in winter in southern Ontario (Toronto, Hamilton, Point Pelee).

Measurements *(B. l. lineatus)*. *Adult male*: wing, 311–326 (318.3); tail, 194–208.5 (201.2); culmen (from cere), 20–22 (21.1); tarsus, 72–80 (77.3). *Adult female*: wing, 331–346 (340.1) mm.

Field Marks. Often seen (like the Red-tail) soaring slowly in wide circles. Buteo outline but less stocky with relatively longer tail than in Red-tail and Broad-wing. Adults, when perched, usually show a distinctive checkered blackish-and-white area on the side of the folded wing. Adults are reddish-breasted, and the upper side of the tail is crossed by several narrow but conspicuous white bars, thus differing from the Red-tail. An adult of the smaller Broad-winged Hawk is similarly marked, but the white bars across the tail are much broader. Young Broad-wings are smaller and stockier with a shorter tail. In flight overhead, Red-shoulders show a whitish area near the ends of the spread wings (see Plate 22), but this is not always a reliable diagnostic feature. The red "shoulders" are diagnostic but are hard to see in life.

Habitat. Woodland, particularly in low country; woodlots and groves near open fields and farming country.

Nesting. The nest, a bulky structure of sticks lined with bark strips, leaves, lichens, often green twigs with leaves attached, is placed from 7 to 18 m up in either a deciduous or coniferous tree. *Eggs*, 2 to 4; dull white, variously (sometimes boldly) marked with browns. Incubation variously reported 25 to 28 days, by both sexes.

Range. Northern California to northwestern Baja California; and from eastern Nebraska, Wisconsin, Michigan, southern Ontario, and southern Quebec south to the Florida Keys, Gulf Coast of United States, and eastern Mexico. In winter retreats from northernmost breeding grounds.

Subspecies. *Buteo lineatus lineatus* (Gmelin) is the only subspecies known to occur in Canada.

Broad-winged Hawk

Petite Buse
Buteo platypterus (Vieillot)
Total length: male, 34 to 42 cm;
female, 38 to 47 cm
Plates 19 and 22

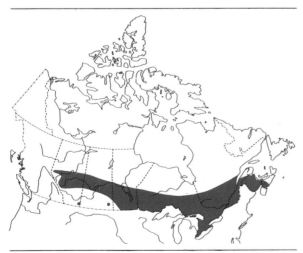

Breeding Distribution of Broad-winged Hawk

Shaped like a Red-tailed Hawk but much smaller, only three primaries emarginate, and tarsus less than half feathered. *Adults*: Dark brown above. Tail brownish black above with two visible light-grey or whitish bands across it (the one farther to the rear broadest) and narrowly tipped whitish. Dark streak down lower jaw. Breast reddish brown, usually with some white (but sometimes almost solid brown). Flanks and abdomen barred brown and white. (Note: A melanistic colour-phase is known in both adults and young, but it is very rare.) *First-year young*: Upper parts dark brown, head and neck streaked with buff, wing coverts and feathers of back edged with same. Upper tail coverts largely mixed with white. Tail above, greyish brown faintly crossed by five or six narrow dusky bars and narrowly tipped with white; tail underneath, pale grey narrowly barred with dusky, especially on inner webs. Under parts creamy white, streaked with dark brown, but brown streaks sparser or absent on mid-breast, mid-abdomen, and under tail coverts.

Measurements. *Adult male*: wing, 239–272.5 (263.4); tail, 149–162.5 (155.1); culmen (from cere), 17.5–20 (18.4); tarsus, 59.5–67.5 (63.4). *Adult female*: wing, 279–291.5 (284) mm.

Field Marks. A small crow-sized buteo. Resembles Red-shouldered Hawk, but in any plumage its shorter tail distinguishes it. In adults the whitish rear tail-band is much broader than in the Red-shoulder. The Broad-winged is a smaller hawk than the Red-tail. Its rather melancholy call, in a minor key, slightly suggestive of an Eastern Wood-Pewee, is readily recognizable among woodland hawks.

Range in Canada. Breeds in wooded parts of central Alberta (Miquelon Lakes north at least to Lesser Slave Lake region and Cold Lake; also Cypress Hills); central Saskatchewan (Niska Lake, Prince Albert, Nipawin, Moose Mountain); southern Manitoba (Turtle Mountain Provincial Park, Red River valley, Carman, Portage la Prairie, Lake St. Martin; probably north to about The Pas); southern and central Ontario (Favourable Lake and Fraserdale southward); southern Quebec (Amos, Lake Saint-Jean, Montréal, Hull, Blue-Sea-Lake); New Brunswick (Grand Manan, Saint John, Saint-Léonard); and rarely in Nova Scotia (Nappan, Halifax). Reported without evidence of breeding north to Lake Athabasca, Alberta and Saskatchewan; Moose Factory, Ontario; and eastern Gaspé Peninsula (Mount Saint-Alban, Cap Bon Ami) and Lake Sainte-Anne, Quebec. Recorded without evidence of breeding in British Columbia (photo: near Fort St. John, 28 August 1974; also several sight records).

In autumn migration, spectacular numbers are sometimes observable at Hawk Cliff, just east of Port Stanley, Ontario, and smaller numbers at other points on the north shore of Lake Erie and western Lake Ontario, especially between 18 and 23 September.

Habitat. Forests and woodlands.

Nesting. The nest, usually rather small and often poorly constructed (sometimes uses nest of crow or other large bird), is made of sticks and twigs, sparsely lined with bark and mosses; often twigs bearing green leaves are added. Generally 6 to 12 m up in either deciduous or coniferous tree. *Eggs*, 2 to 4; variable in colour but usually whitish, blotched and spotted with reddish brown and purple. Incubation 23 to 25 days (F.L. Burns), by both sexes. One brood annually.

Range. Breeds in woodland from Alberta east across southern Canada and south to eastern Texas, the United States Gulf Coast, southern Florida, and the West Indies. Winters mainly from southern Mexico to Colombia, Venezuela, Ecuador, northern Peru, and western Brazil. Occasionally farther north.

Subspecies. *Buteo platypterus platypterus* (Vieillot) is the only subspecies found in Canada.

Swainson's Hawk

Buse de Swainson
Buteo swainsoni Bonaparte
Total length: male, 47 to 52 cm;
female, 48 to 56 cm
Plates 20 and 22

Breeding Distribution of Swainson's Hawk

Slightly smaller than the Red-tailed Hawk, but separable from it and the Red-shouldered Hawk in any plumage by three (instead of four) emarginate outer primaries. The differently proportioned Northern Goshawk has five emarginate primaries. Rough-legged and Ferruginous hawks have completely feathered legs; those of Swainson are less than half-feathered. Plumage of adult extremely variable. *Adult male (pale phase)*: Upper parts dark brown usually with rusty feather-margins; crown and back of neck generally with white showing through. Tail above, greyish crossed by numerous narrow bands of dusky and tipped whitish. Outer upper tail coverts whitish barred with brown. Under parts with broad band of cinnamon or russet across breast; throat white; abdomen buffy white, its sides usually barred with brown. Feet yellow. *Adult female (pale phase)*: Similar to adult male but breast band often (not always) darker, less rufous. *Adults (dark phase)*: Upper and under parts brownish black, except under tail coverts, which are buffy white, barred with dark brown (many intermediate stages between these pale and dark extremes are common). A rufous phase occurs in which the under parts are heavily washed and barred with reddish brown. *Juvenal (apparently worn through first winter)*: Upper parts dark brown mixed with buff or white; forehead whitish; cheeks buffy with dusky streaks; crown, nape, and sides of neck streaked blackish, buffy, and whitish; outer upper tail coverts (except dark phase) with more or less white; tail similar to adult; under parts buffy, heavily spotted on breast and upper abdomen with blackish brown; throat whitish with sparse dusky streaks; thighs barred dusky. In dark phase the upper parts are darker, white of upper tail coverts much more restricted, and under parts blackish spotted with tawny.

Measurements. *Adult male*: wing, 360–396.5 (378.6); tail, 181–204.5 (189.5); culmen (from cere), 21.5–23 (22.4); tarsus, 62–73 (67.3). *Adult female*: wing, 390–418 (403.1) mm.

Range in Canada. Summer resident, spring and autumn transient. Breeds in British Columbia (very locally: Okanagan Landing, Dog Creek. Recorded in summer at Swan Lake, Okanagan valley; Chilcotin River; Telegraph Creek; Atlin); Yukon (no definite breeding record but occurs in summer sparsely near Whitehorse, Carcross, Morley River, Dawson, Porcupine River at Yukon–Alaska boundary); Mackenzie (range poorly known: old breeding record near Fort Anderson and on Onion River near Lockhart River); Alberta (commonly on prairies of southern part; occasionally Waterton Lakes National Park; observed in summer in Banff National Park, Joussard, Grouard, High Prairie, Saskatoon Lake, and La Glace); southern Saskatchewan (Carlton, Prince Albert); and southwestern Manitoba (Treesbank, Carberry, Aweme, Winnipeg, Stonewall). Recorded north to Bernard Harbour, Dolphin and Union Strait, District of Mackenzie, 9 September 1914. Casual on coast of British Columbia (Victoria, Union Bay) and in eastern Canada: Ontario (Moose Factory, Toronto, Ottawa) and southern Quebec. Specimens: Montréal, spring 1894; Sainte-Anne-de-la-Pérade, 17 September 1925; also sight records).

Field Marks. A large western open-country buteo, the commonest large hawk of the prairies. Similar to the Red-tailed Hawk in size but has narrower, more pointed wings and never a red tail. Extremely variable in appearance, but most (pale-phase) adults show a broad *band across the breast*, which is diagnostic (Red-tailed and Rough-legged hawks have band across *abdomen*). In flight a narrow whitish area is usually present on the sides of the rump (but very different from well-defined large white rump patch of the Northern Harrier); when gliding, wings are held slightly above horizontal (see also Northern Harrier and Turkey Vulture). Dark-phased and immature Swainson's resemble other dark buteos, but the shape and angle of its wings and whitish rump area, when discernible, are helpful.

Habitat. Open dry country of the West; plains, prairies, dry mountain valleys and foothills; less commonly, tundra of the low Arctic. Sparse woods or even single small trees or bushes are adequate for nesting purposes.

Nesting. The bulky nest of sticks, lined with finer materials, is built in either a large or small tree, usually deciduous (sometimes bushes), at heights varying from ground level to considerable heights depending on local conditions. The same nest is often used in successive years. *Eggs*, usually 2, sometimes 3; pale bluish to dull white, most frequently sparingly and irregularly marked with brown, less often immaculate. Incubation about 28 days, by both sexes (A.C. Bent).

Range. Breeds from Alaska (locally) east to northwestern Mackenzie and Manitoba; east to Illinois (rarely); and south to northern Mexico. Winters mainly in Argentina.

Remarks. This is the common hawk of the prairies. It is frequently seen perched on a roadside fence post or quartering leisurely over the grasslands in search of rodents, which make up most of its food. It is an efficient and tireless destroyer of gophers, mice, and, to some extent, grasshoppers. Like all our buteos, it is an extremely valuable bird.

Zone-tailed Hawk

[**Zone-tailed Hawk**. Buse à queue barrée. *Buteo albonotatus* Kaup. Plate 22. Hypothetical. Photos of a hawk, almost certainly of this species, at Musquadoboit Harbour, Nova Scotia, 24 September to 4 October 1976.]

Red-tailed Hawk
(includes Harlan's Hawk)

Buse à queue rousse
Buteo jamaicensis (Gmelin)
Total length: male, 48 to 56 cm;
female, 53 to 61 cm
Plates 20 and 22

Figure 40
Four emarginate primaries of Red-tailed Hawk

In parts of western Canada highly variable in appearance. Breeding populations from Ontario east are relatively uniform, and the following description applies to eastern birds (see also Subspecies). *Adults (B. j. borealis)*: Above dark brown variously intermixed with white and rufous. Upper surface of tail chestnut with narrow black subterminal band and whitish tip. From corner of mouth down side of neck a dusky stripe. Under parts whitish with broad (often poorly defined) band across abdomen, formed by blackish longitudinal markings of varying density and extent. Underside of tail greyish, sometimes faintly barred. *Immatures*: Similar to adults but upper side of tail pale brownish (sometimes tinged reddish), crossed by ten or more narrow dusky bars; general coloration darker, contrasting more with whites.

In the hand, separable in all plumages from Rough-legged and Ferruginous hawks by its half-feathered (instead of fully feathered) tarsus. Swainson's Hawk has three outermost primaries sharply emarginate, Red-tail four (Figure 40).

Measurements *(B. j. borealis)*. *Adult male*: wing, 340–390 (361.4); tail, 198.5–225.5 (208); culmen (from cere), 22–28 (24.5); tarsus, 81–86 (83.6). *Adult female*: wing, 354.5–384 (371.5) mm.

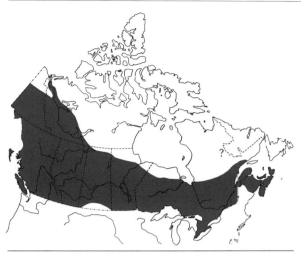

Breeding Distribution of Red-tailed Hawk

Range in Canada (includes *harlani*). Breeds from central Yukon (commonly southwestern part, scarcer farther east, breeding north to Forty Mile and Fort Selkirk); northwestern and southwestern Mackenzie (Aklavik; Fort Norman; Slave River; near Fort Smith); northern Saskatchewan (Reindeer Lake); north-central Manitoba (Ilford); central Ontario; and southwestern Quebec (north to Mistassini Lake and lower Sainte-Marguerite River; recorded in summer north to Schefferville); south through southern British Columbia, southern Alberta, southern Saskatchewan, southern Manitoba, southern Ontario, southern Quebec, New Brunswick, Prince Edward Island, and Nova Scotia. Recorded in summer on Churchill River, Labrador. Sight records for Newfoundland. Winters in small numbers in southwestern British Columbia, southern Ontario, and occasionally in the Maritimes.

Field Marks. The buteo outline with broad, rounded wings and broad tail shows well in flight. Adults, with upper side of tail chestnut, are the only large hawk species so marked. Both adults and immatures (except dark phase) show a more or less well-defined belt across the *abdomen*. Swainson's Hawk, of the West, also has a dark band on the under parts, but it is across the *breast*, and in soaring the wings tilt somewhat upward (held horizontal in Red-tail). Rough-legged Hawks with dark abdominal band have a conspicuous black crescent on the underside of the spread wing near the wrist. Dark-phased individuals of the Red-tail are often difficult to distinguish in life from dark-phased Rough-legged, Ferruginous, and Swainson's hawks, but red in the tail of the adult (often absent in *harlani* and *kriderii*) marks the Red-tail. Swainson's soars on slightly uptilted more-pointed wings.

Habitat. Both woodland and open country but usually in the vicinity of trees during the nesting season, although cliff ledges are used for nesting where trees are not available.

Nesting. Nest usually in trees, either deciduous or coniferous, and frequently well up. Will use low trees where large ones are not available; also cliff ledges. Nest a bulky structure of sticks, often lined with bark. *Eggs*, 2 to 4, occasionally more; whitish usually lightly spotted with browns. Incubation 28 to 32 days by both sexes.

Range. Central Alaska and Canada north to near limit of large forests (except Newfoundland), south through United States and Mexico to Panama and the West Indies.

Subspecies. (1) *Buteo jamaicensis borealis* (Gmelin), which breeds from western Ontario east, has a plain-red tail usually with black subterminal bar, as described above. (2) *B. j. calurus* Cassin is generally more heavily coloured, sometimes with dark reds intermixed, especially on breast, and has both dark and light phases with various intermediate stages. It breeds from middle Manitoba west to interior British Columbia. (3) *B. j. kriderii* Hoopes, of the southern prairies, is characterized by variable, often substantial, amounts of white in the plumage including the tail, and a dilution of colour of dark parts. (4) *B. j. harlani* (Audubon), of Yukon and northern British Columbia, is a heavily pigmented form, characterized especially by the tail, which is mottled and freckled with black, grey, white, and red in various proportions and with longitudinal streaks instead of transverse bars. Under parts vary from black to mainly white, and almost no two are coloured alike, there being also various admixtures of white in the upper plumage and tail. (5) *B. j. alascensis* Grinnell, of the Queen Charlotte Islands, resembles *calurus* but is smaller. (I have not seen adequate material to appraise *B. j. abieticola* Todd, Annals Carnegie Museum 31, p. 291.)

Ferruginous Hawk

Buse rouilleuse
Buteo regalis (Gray)
Total length: 56 to 61 cm
Plates 20 and 22

Figure 41
Bill (viewed from above) of
a) Ferruginous Hawk
b) Rough-legged Hawk

Tarsus feathered to toes, thus differing from other hawks except Rough-legged, from which it differs in its markedly wider bill (Figure 41) and in plumage. Both pale and dark colour-phases occur, the former commoner. *Adults (pale phase)*: Upper parts brown streaked with white on head and neck, much orange-cinnamon about shoulders, back, and on upper tail coverts. Tail white to greyish, often with ochraceous wash of variable extent, unbanded. Cheeks brown streaked with white. Throat, breast, and abdomen white, usually with sparse brown markings on abdomen and sides. Thighs ochraceous barred with dark brown. Wing lining white mixed with ochraceous and dark brown. *Adults (dark phase)*: Dark brown, some of the feathers edged with cinnamon. Tail similar to pale phase but often more heavily washed with dark brown. *First-year immatures (light phase)*: Somewhat like adults but orange-cinnamon of upper parts greatly reduced and confined to feather edges.

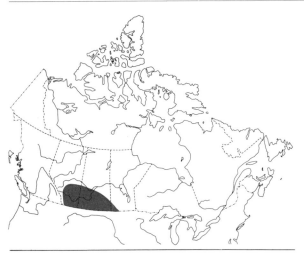

Breeding Distribution of Ferruginous Hawk

Range in Canada. Breeds (much scarcer than formerly) in southern Alberta (east of the Rocky Mountains, north to near Alliance); southern Saskatchewan (north, formerly at least, to vicinity of Carlton); and southwestern Manitoba (formerly: Aweme: photos taken by Talbot Criddle, of four large young in nest on 4 July 1917, seem to be the only definite breeding record for Manitoba. There are various other records of the occurrence of the species including recent sight records in southwestern parts).

Under parts white but with dark-brown streaks on breast (variable in extent, often absent) and brown spots, sometimes blotches on sides of abdomen. Thighs very different from adult: white, spotted with dark brown. Tail grey (white basally) and tipped whitish, the grey area indistinctly banded on upper side. *First-year immatures (dark phase)*: Somewhat like dark-phase adults but tail crossed by indistinct bars and tipped whitish.

Measurements. *Adult male*: wing, 415.5–439.5 (426.8); tail, 224.5–229 (226.5); culmen (from cere), 26.5–27.5 (27); tarsus, 82.5–89.5 (86). *Adult female*: wing, 415–465 (437.5) mm.

Field Marks. A large buteo of the southern prairies. Pale-phased adults are separable from similar buteos by the reddish-brown colour about the shoulders, back, and rump; extensively white under parts with *contrasting dark thighs*; and unbanded plain white or greyish tail. Dark-phase birds have uniformly dark bodies with whitish or greyish tail, usually definitely lighter than the back, and large areas of white on underside of the light feathers. In flight often shows flash of white near ends of upper side of wing. The Rough-leg shows this but is otherwise differently marked and is not likely to be on the southern prairies in summer. Pale-phase immatures are extensively white below but lack the diagnostic contrasting thigh colour of the adults.

Habitat. Plains, prairies, and badlands.

Nesting. Nest is of sticks, twigs, and sometimes sagebrush roots and is placed in trees, on ledges of badlands and river cutbacks, and on hillsides. Nests are used in successive years, sometimes becoming immense. *Eggs*, most often 3 to 5; white with usually bold blotches and spots of brown. Incubation said to last 28 days (A.C. Bent).

Range. Breeds from eastern Washington and southern parts of the Canadian Prairie Provinces south to Nevada, New Mexico, and northwestern Texas. Winters mainly from southwestern United States to central Mexico; casually farther north.

Rough-legged Hawk

Buse pattue
Buteo lagopus (Pontoppidan)
Total length: male, 50 to 56 cm;
female, 54 to 59 cm
Plates 20 and 22

Breeding Distribution of Rough-legged Hawk

Legs feathered to toes. Plumage extremely variable, including pale and dark phases and various intermediates. Separable in all plumages from other Canadian hawks except the Ferruginous (and obviously distinctive Golden Eagle) by its *completely feathered legs* to the base of the toes. In all plumages it is distinguishable from the Ferruginous Hawk by bill shape, the bill being markedly narrower at the gape in the Rough-legged Hawk, broader in the Ferruginous Hawk when viewed from above (Figure 41). In *Pale Phase* (commoner in most localities) the adult male generally (not always) differs from the adult female in having abdomen barred rather than blotched or patched with dark brown, and his tail tends to have several narrow dark bands on the posterior half alternating with whitish (female one or more broad bands). For detailed analysis of sexual dimorphism, see T.J. Cade (1955. Condor, vol. 57, no. 6, pp. 313–346). Immatures of the *pale phase* resemble adults but lack bars on the tibiae; have the terminal half of tail unbarred dark-brown; have a better-defined, more extensive abdominal band than even adult females; and the whitish of under parts is buffier. *Dark Phase*: Uniform blackish-brown above and below, but usually with some concealed white on basal third of tail and some light barring on rest of tail. Tail tipped whitish. Primaries usually have some white on inner webs, and there is considerable and variable white on under wing surface.

Range in Canada. Breeds in northern Yukon (Herschel Island, Old Crow); across the Arctic Archipelago; north rarely to Prince Patrick Island and Bylot Island, and east to Baffin Island; northern and eastern Mackenzie (Mackenzie Delta, Anderson River, Coronation Gulf, Bathurst Inlet, Perry River, Dickson Canyon, Helen Falls on Hanbury River, Artillery Lake); Keewatin (Back River, Baker Lake, Nueltin Lake, Beverly Lake); northern Manitoba (Churchill); northern Ontario (Cape Henrietta Maria); Southampton Island; east coast of Hudson Bay (Long Island, Christie Island); northern and southeastern Quebec (Grande rivière de la Baleine, Kuujjuaq, Seal Lake, Lake Aulneau, Hutte sauvage Lake; outer north shore of Gulf of St. Lawrence: Wolf-Bay eastward; reported formerly and doubtfully at Pointe-des-Monts); Labrador (Cape Chidley, Davis Inlet, near Hopedale, Aillik, and Red Bay); and Newfoundland (locally: Meagle Mountain, Partridgeberry Hills). Recorded in summer in southern Yukon, southern James Bay, northern Lake Superior, and Anticosti Island, but breeding data lacking.

Winters in irregular numbers in southern British Columbia, southern Prairie Provinces, southern Ontario, southern Quebec, Newfoundland, and the Maritime Provinces.

Measurements. *Adult male*: wing, 380–412.5 (401.5); tail, 195–223 (208.9); culmen (from cere), 21.5–24.5 (22.3); tarsus, 64.5–71.5 (68.1). *Adult female*: wing, 412–434 (422.8) mm.

Field Marks. A large, long-winged buteo of the open country (see also Ferruginous Hawk) with a habit of hovering in the air over one spot like an Osprey or American Kestrel. Light-phase (usually commoner) birds have a large dark wrist mark on underside of wing, white base to the tail, and (in immatures and most adult females) a conspicuous dark patch on the belly. Dark-phase birds are similar to other dark-phase buteos but show considerable white on the underside of wing and in spread wing tips; the habit of hovering is also helpful in recognition. Frequently when hovering the legs are dangled, showing *fully feathered legs*. The Ferruginous Hawk of the prairies is the only other hawk with legs feathered to toes (see Ferruginous Hawk). Dark-phase Swainson's lacks conspicuously white areas in the under surface of the wings.

Habitat. In summer inhabits the low Arctic and Subarctic, especially where escarpments, rocky outcrops, cliff ledges, ravines, steep riverbanks, or low trees provide nesting places. In migration and winter, it prefers open country such as fields and marshes.

Nesting. Nest is made of sticks, grasses, and weed stalks (depending on availability of material) and is placed on cliff ledges, boulders, shelves in steep riverbanks, and, when available, in trees at heights of 6 to 9 m; occasionally on flat ground. Nest is used in successive years, resulting sometimes in large accumulations of debris. *Eggs*, 2 to 6 (usually 3 to 5); greenish white, variously blotched, streaked, smeared, or spotted with browns. Incubation period 28 to 31 days (various authors).

Range. Panboreal. Breeds from Alaska eastward across low arctic and subarctic Canada; northern Scandinavia, northern Russia, and northern Siberia. In North America, it winters south to California, New Mexico, Oklahoma, Tennessee, and Virginia; casually farther south.

Subspecies. *Buteo lagopus sanctijohannis* (Gmelin) is the only subspecies of known occurrence in Canada.

Golden Eagle

Aigle royal
Aquila chrysaetos (Linnaeus)
Total length: male, 76 to 89 cm;
female, 89 to 104 cm
Wingspread: 187 to 230 cm
Plates 18 and 23

Separable in all plumages from the Bald Eagle by the legs, which are *feathered to the toes* (Figure 42). *Adults*: Mainly dark brown (fading paler), legs usually paler. Nape and hind-neck tawny or golden brown. Tail dark brown, base paler and with several poorly defined ashy bands. Bill dusky. Cere and feet yellow. *Immatures*: Similar to adults but with more white in tail. Juvenal is darker and has basal two-thirds of tail white and considerable white in the secondaries. Older immatures as they approach maturity have decreasing amounts of white in tail and wing.

Measurements. *Adult male*: wing, 555–610 (580.5); tail, 320–360 (337.4); culmen (from cere), 37–41 (39.5); tarsus, 101–122 (111.6) (one specimen 130). *Adult female*: wing, 620–666 (633.2) mm (Friedmann).

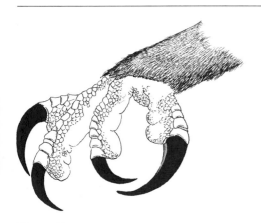

Figure 42
Foot of Golden Eagle

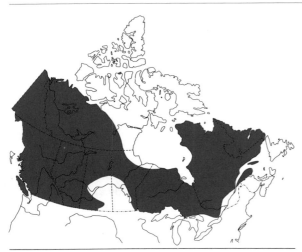

Breeding Distribution of Golden Eagle

Range in Canada. Scarce, local permanent resident. In the East, no longer occupies many of its former breeding localities. Less rare in mountains of the West. *Breeds* locally in Yukon (Sheep Creek Canyon and elsewhere in Kluane Game Sanctuary; widely distributed in southern half and north to the coast); Mackenzie (Mackenzie Delta; Anderson River; Horton River; near Reliance); British Columbia (mostly east of Coast Range: Tank Creek, near Merritt; Langley Lake; McIntyre Creek; rarely on coast: Upper Campbell Lake and Malahat, Vancouver Island); Alberta (mainly in mountains: Old Fort Point, Sheep Creek, Cascade Mountain, Lake Louise; also reported on Red Deer River in Brooks region; reported formerly from Edmonton region); Saskatchewan (Stone River, Beechy, Snakebite Coulee, Big Muddy valley, Killdeer Badlands); Manitoba (Cochrane River 64 km north of Brochet; Hell Gate Gorge); Ontario (Sutton Narrows, Cape Henrietta Maria; probably Pipestone Lake. Formerly Thunder Cape and near York branch of Madawaska River; Mazinaw Lake; Schooner Lake); Quebec (Saglouc Inlet; Wakeham Bay; Finger Lake-Feuilles Bay Region; Pointe-des-Monts, Anticosti Island, Bay Saint-Paul, Notre Dame Mountains; Dépôt Usborne, Pontiac County, Gaspé Peninsula); and Labrador (Lake Michikamau); probably Keewatin (recorded as occurring at Back River near Wolf Rapids; Repulse Bay; and inland from Eskimo Point). Very rare visitor to New Brunswick, Nova Scotia, and Prince Edward Island. Casual in Newfoundland (St. John's, 31 January 1951).

Winters in much of the breeding range.

Field Marks. Great size and much more massive bill separate it from dark-phase buteos. In soaring the wings are held horizontal, thus differing from vultures, and the eagle's head is feathered. Ospreys always have white under parts. The adult Bald Eagle, with its white head and tail, is readily separable from the Golden. Many immature Golden Eagles have a white tail with a sharply contrasting dark terminal band and show a white area in the spread wing (Plate 23). Adults are a bit difficult to distinguish from young Bald Eagles, but often the "golden" back of the neck of the Golden Eagle is visible. The fully feathered legs of the Golden are diagnostic but are hard to see in the field.

Habitat. Variable. Mountainous terrain, foothills with grassy areas inhabited by ground squirrels, the vicinity of cliffs in various situations from those on prairie river valleys to sea cliffs. In winter and migration, it hunts over various types of country, including plains.

Nesting. Nest, usually on a cliff, sometimes in a tree, is constructed of sticks and similar coarse material and lined with grasses, weeds, mosses, and leaves. When used for a number of years it may become very large. *Eggs*, usually 2; white or pale buffy, usually more or less spotted and blotched with brown. Incubation 43 days (Walker and Walker).

Range. Holarctic. Locally distributed in North America from Alaska and Canada south to southern United States and central Mexico; also found across Europe and Asia south to northern Africa.

Subspecies. *Aquila chrysaetos canadensis* (Linnaeus), the only race known in North America.

Family **Falconidae:** Caracaras and Falcons

Number of Species in Canada: 6

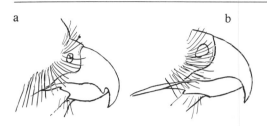

Figure 43
Bill of
a) a falcon
b) an accipiter

Falcons are among the swiftest and most picturesque of the diurnal birds of prey. Because of their spirit, power, and speed, they were the favourites of the old falconers for use in hunting. They have powerful taloned feet and a strong hooked bill with a membranous covering or cere at its base. On the cutting edge of the upper mandible toward the tip is a toothlike projection (absent in the caracaras) which distinguishes the falcons (Figure 43). They fly with quick, powerful wing strokes. In silhouette they have long pointed wings and medium to longish, somewhat tapered tail (Plate 23). As in most birds of prey, the female is larger than the male.

The Peregrine Falcon, of all birds of prey, has been hit hardest by the effects of pesticides and it has been extirpated from most of its North American range south of the Arctic. There is another threat. It and the Gyrfalcon are in great demand by falconers all over the world and an illegal market exists in which a single bird brings thousands of dollars.

Crested Caracara

[**Crested Caracara** (formerly Audubon's Caracara). Caracara huppé. *Polyborus plancus* (Miller). Plate 23. Hypothetical. Specimen taken near Thunder Bay, Ontario, on 18 July 1892 (H.H. Brown, 1893. Auk, vol. 10, no. 4, p. 364) was probably an escapee from captivity.]

Eurasian Kestrel

Faucon crécerelle
Falco tinnunculus Linnaeus
Total length: 32 to 35 cm (female larger than male)

Status in Canada. Accidental. A male was collected at Alkali Lake, British Columbia, on 10 December 1946 by Leo Jobin.

Resemblance to American Kestrel obvious but differing as follows. In males the upper wing coverts are chestnut (instead of blue) with black spots, thus like the back; the upper side of the tail is grey (not chestnut); the head much less variegated (black markings greatly restricted to smaller and much paler blackish moustache; chestnut crown patch lacking). Females resemble American Kestrel but black markings on sides of head much reduced and paler; blackish subterminal tail band more obvious.

Measurements *(F. t. tinnunculus)*. *Adult male*: wing, 230–258 (243.5); tail, 150–180 (166.5); tarsus, 38–41 (39.5). *Adult female*: wing, 235–270 (252.2); tail, 141–170 (157.3); tarsus, 40–42.5 (41.7) mm (Friedmann 1950).

Range. Breeds in much of Eurasia and south to southern Africa, India, China, and Japan.

American Kestrel

(formerly Sparrow Hawk)

Crécerelle d'Amérique
Falco sparverius Linnaeus
Total length: male, 22.5 to 27 cm;
female, 23 to 30.5 cm
Plates 21 and 23

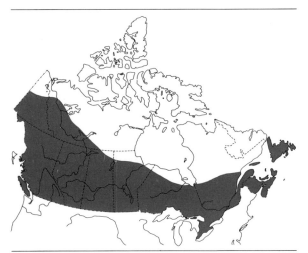

Breeding Distribution of American Kestrel

Range in Canada. Common summer resident across southern Canada. Small numbers winter locally. *Breeds* in southern Yukon (fairly common north to Dawson area; birds recorded north to Lapierre House and arctic coast); western Mackenzie (Forts Good Hope, Simpson, Providence, and Resolution; also Canol; birds recorded in breeding season along Mackenzie River north to Aklavik); British Columbia (except northern parts of heavily forested coast); Alberta; Saskatchewan (north to Lake Athabasca and Stony Rapids); Manitoba (north to Bird); Ontario (north to Sandy Lake, Moosonee); southern Quebec (north to Pointe-des-Monts and Lake Saint-Jean; probably Anticosti Island; possibly to Lake Mistassini and Lower Moisie River where recorded rarely); New Brunswick; Prince Edward Island; Nova Scotia; and southern Newfoundland.

Winters in small numbers in southern British Columbia, southern Ontario, southwestern Quebec, and Nova Scotia (occasionally).

Casual on Jenny Lind Island, N.W.T. (specimens: 1 and 23 June 1966; photo record: 27 April 1971).

Toothed upper mandible. The only Canadian hawk combining small size, much red in tail and upper parts, and conspicuous black face-markings. *Adult male*: Top of head blue with (usually) large chestnut crown patch. Face with narrow black patch from front of eye down along side of throat and another down across ear. Back reddish, barred with black. Tail chestnut with broad black subterminal bar. Upper wing coverts blue, more or less spotted with black. Breast and belly white to buffy, with large black spots. *Adult female*: Resembles male but back and tail duller and both heavily barred with black. Wing coverts similar to back. Breast and belly striped with brown. *Immatures* similar to adults of their respective sexes.

Measurements. *Adult male*: wing, 174.5–187 (181.9); tail, 113–122 (117.1); culmen (from cere), 11.5–13 (12); tarsus, 34.5–37.5 (36.3). *Adult female*: wing, 171.5–201 (186.3) mm.

Field Marks. Our only small hawk showing conspicuous red in the tail and back. At closer range the black face-marks are visible. Often hovers over one spot. Often noisy, repeating *killy-killy-killy*. When perching frequently flicks its tail.

Habitat. Hunts more open country: fields, meadows, burntlands, prairies, woodland openings, cities, in both flat and hilly terrain. Often perches on dead-topped trees, fence posts, poles, and buildings. In breeding season availability of nesting sites (see Nesting) is, of course, necessary.

Nesting. Nests (little or no attempt at nest building) in a natural cavity or woodpecker hole in a tree; sometimes also in a cliff cavity, magpie nest, bank burrow, bird box, or suitable recess in a building. *Eggs*, 3 to 7 (usually 4 or 5), white or pinkish variably marked with browns. Incubation 29 days (A. Sherman) mainly by the female.

Range. Central Alaska and much of forested Canada south through North, Central, and South America (including the West Indies) to Tierra del Fuego and San Fernandez Islands. Winters from northern United States and (locally in small numbers) southern Canada southward.

Subspecies. *Falco sparverius sparverius* Linnaeus.

Remarks. Like other birds of prey, the American Kestrel has remarkable eyesight. It spends much time searching for its prey from a vantage point of some treetop, telephone pole, fence post, or even a television antenna on a city apartment building. It is inclined to be sociable; often several will be found foraging harmoniously for grasshoppers in the same field.

Merlin

(formerly Pigeon Hawk)

Faucon émerillon
Falco columbarius Linnaeus
Total length: male, 25 to 27 cm;
female, 30.5 to 33 cm
Plates 21 and 23

Toothed bill separates it as a falcon. Obviously small size distinguishes it from all other Canadian falcons but the American Kestrel. Very different coloration (always lacks any red in upper parts and never has conspicuous face-markings found in all plumages of American Kestrel) distinguishes it from that species. *Adult male* (see Subspecies): Upper parts blue streaked with black; tail banded with black (subterminal band widest) and tipped with white. Throat white. Breast and abdomen buffy streaked with dark brown, often forming bars on sides, which sometimes have a bluish tinge. Narrow whitish line over eye. Under wing coverts crossed by alternating white and brown bands giving somewhat

Breeding Distribution of Merlin

Range in Canada. Widely distributed in summer; scarce in winter. Breeds in Yukon (north to Firth River); Mackenzie (Reindeer Depot; Rae; Forts Anderson, Providence, Resolution, McPherson; Soulier Lake); southwestern Keewatin (Ennadai Lake); British Columbia (widely distributed but not known on Queen Charlotte Islands); Alberta; Saskatchewan; Manitoba; Ontario (south at least to Muskoka District, Manitoulin Island, Cornwall); Quebec (north to Hutte sauvage Lake and Kuujjuaq); Labrador (Makkovik; probably north to Cape Chidley); Newfoundland (commonly throughout); Nova Scotia (rarely: New Glasgow, Halifax); and Prince Edward Island; probably New Brunswick (but sparsely).

Winters in southern British Columbia (not uncommon on south coast; more rarely in interior); occasionally in southern Alberta (Calgary, Edmonton, Millet); southern Saskatchewan (Skull Creek, Dodsland, Saskatoon); southern Manitoba (Brandon); southern Ontario; southwestern Quebec (Montréal, Québec); New Brunswick; Nova Scotia; and Newfoundland.

checkered appearance. *Adult female*: Similar to male but blue of upper parts replaced by dark brown (but often with a suggestion of bluish). *Immatures*: Resemble closely adult female but pure brown above with no suggestion of bluish; buffier below.

Measurements *(F. c. columbarius)*. *Adult male*: wing, 173–192 (184.5); tail, 111.5–117 (114.5); culmen (from cere), 12–13.5 (12.7); tarsus, 35.5–37 (36.2). *Adult female*: wing, 201–215 (206.9) mm.

Field Marks. Small size eliminates confusion with all but Sharp-shinned and American Kestrel. Pointed, longish wings distinguish it from the similarly coloured Sharp-shinned Hawk (which has short, rounded wings). Complete lack of reddish coloration in the tail or of conspicuous black face-markings separates it from the American Kestrel.

Habitat. Variable. In breeding season open (sometimes denser) woodland, either coniferous or deciduous; and woodland openings; wooded prairie coulees. Hunts in almost any type of country, especially outside breeding season, including marshes, beaches, mud flats, and fields, often far removed from trees.

Nesting. Nest is frequently an abandoned one of some other species, such as a crow or magpie, in either a coniferous or deciduous tree; occasionally in a tree cavity or on a cliff ledge; sometimes a hollow in the ground. *Eggs*, usually 4 to 6; the creamy-white ground colour much hidden by profuse markings and blotches of brown. Incubation period 29 to 31 days (G.A. Fox).

Range. Breeds in wooded parts of Alaska and Canada south to South Dakota, Michigan, and northern New York; also in forests of northern Europe and Siberia. In North America, it winters mainly from southern British Columbia and southern United States (small numbers north to southern Canada) south to the West Indies, Venezuela, and Peru.

Subspecies. In Canada, four. (1) *Falco columbarius columbarius* Linnaeus, a rather dark subspecies: eastern Canada intergrading with *bendirei* in northern Manitoba and with *richardsonii* in southwestern Manitoba. (2) *F. c. suckleyi* Ridgway, very dark coloration; breeds in coastal British Columbia (Owikeno Lake; Upper Campbell Lake; also apparently in interior (Redstone, Chilcotin—Munro and Cowan 1947), but limits of range imperfectly known). (3) *F. c. richardsonii* Ridgway, a very pale subspecies: prairie and aspen grove belt of southern Alberta (north at least to Lac la Nonne), southern Saskatchewan and extreme southwestern Manitoba. (4) *F. c. bendirei* Swann, intermediate in colour between *columbarius* and *richardsonii*: northern Saskatchewan, northern Alberta, Mackenzie, Yukon, eastern British Columbia (area of intergradation with *suckleyi* poorly understood), and probably mountainous southwestern Alberta.

Northern Hobby

[**Northern Hobby**. Faucon hobereau. *Falco subbuteo* Linnaeus. Hypothetical. A well-described observation of one individual apparently of this species near Merritt, in the Nicola valley, British Columbia, on 22 May 1982, is not supported by a photo.]

Peregrine Falcon

(Duck Hawk)

Faucon pèlerin
Falco peregrinus Tunstall
Total length: male, 38 to 46 cm;
female, 46 to 54 cm
Plates 21 and 23

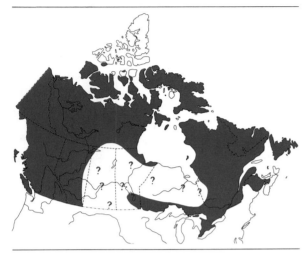

Breeding Distribution of Peregrine Falcon

Range in Canada. Range extent and numbers have been drastically reduced in recent years by pesticides. No longer breeds in most of south-eastern Canada and the prairie provinces but in 1979 and 1980 was again nesting very locally in southern Quebec. Breeds (or bred formerly) locally, depending on availability of nest sites and food, on Banks Island (Cape Lambton, Russell Point, Cape Kellett, Nelson Head; probably Sachs Harbour); Melville Island (Dundas Peninsula); Victoria Island (Minto Inlet, Holman Island, and near Washburn Lake and Cape Isabella); Somerset Island (Fort Ross); Devon Island (Cape Sparbo); Boothia Peninsula; and Baffin Island (Gibbs Fiord, Pangnirtung, head of Frobisher Bay, Dorset); south through Yukon (below Fort Selkirk, Old Crow, arctic coast); Mackenzie (Arctic Red River, Fort Good Hope, Liard River, Grandin River, Great Bear and Great Slave lakes, Anderson River including mouth, Timber River, Helen Falls, Bathurst Inlet); Keewatin (Adelaide Peninsula, Repulse Bay, Back River, Beverly Lake, Windy River, Angikuni Lake, Carr Lake); Southampton Island; Belcher Islands; Coats Island; British Columbia (commonest on north coast: Langara Island, Moore Islands, Scott Islands group; Okanagan Falls, Kalamalka Lake, Hanceville); Alberta (formerly: Athabasca Lake, Athabasca District, Rosebud, Red Deer River, Brooks region); Saskatchewan (formerly Cypress Hills and to Battle Creek region); Manitoba (formerly Gladstone); Ontario (formerly: north shore of Lake Superior, Algonquin Provincial Park, and Bruce Peninsula south to Leeds and Grey counties; nesting not known in northern Ontario); Quebec (Kuujjuaq, False River mouth; formerly: Gaspé Peninsula, Bic, Kamouraska, Mont-

Toothed upper mandible marks it as a falcon. Inner toe (without claw) does not quite reach penultimate joint of middle toe (extends to or beyond in Gyrfalcon and Prairie Falcon). Somewhat resembles Prairie Falcon, but see Field Marks. *Adults*: Crown, hind-neck, face, and well-defined moustache mark blackish; back, upper wings, and rump ashy blue barred with dark slate; tail barred with blackish and tipped whitish. Under parts buffy white to pinkish with blackish-brown bars on sides and thighs, usually spots on abdomen. Under wing coverts and axillars white barred with black. *Immatures*: Crown, face, and upper parts blackish brown edged with buffy. Moustache marks blackish. Tail dark brown, crossed by narrow buffy bars (often obsolescent or indicated by spots) and tipped buffy white. Under parts buffy, heavily streaked (except throat) with blackish brown.

Measurements *(F. p. anatum)*. *Adult male*: wing, 301.5–318 (311.1); tail, 137–146.5 (141.7); culmen (from cere), 18.5–20 (19.4); tarsus, 47–49.5 (48.2). *Adult female*: wing, 340–366 (356.2) mm.

Field Marks. A powerful crow-sized falcon. Conspicuous head-pattern visible for a considerable distance but resembles that of the Prairie Falcon. The Peregrine is much darker above (blackish or bluish instead of sandy brown) and lacks the contrasting axillars and flank patches shown in flight by the Prairie Falcon. Adult Peregrines are barred below, and the under parts of immatures are usually very much more heavily streaked than in Prairie Falcons.

Habitat. In breeding season the vicinity of cliffs and adjacent country, both coastal and inland; often about seabird colonies. At all seasons more open country is preferred, particularly shores and marshes frequented by shorebirds and waterfowl. Occasionally large cities.

Nesting. Little or no nest. Eggs laid on a cliff ledge (rarely cliff top); rarely in broken top of a great tree, or on a tall city building; occasionally on the ground. *Eggs*, usually 3 to 5; with creamy ground colour generally concealed by heavy markings of rich reddish-browns. Incubation 33 to 35 days (J.A. Hagar), 28 to 29 days for each egg (Brown and Amadon), by both sexes.

Range. Practically cosmopolitan. Breeds from Alaska, northern Canada, and Greenland south through the Americas (not in West Indies) to southern South America; also from northern Norway, Novaya Zemlya, and northern Siberia south to South Africa, India, Ceylon, Malay States, the Philippines, East Indies, Australia, and Tasmania (not New Zealand). In North America winters north to northern United States, southwestern British Columbia, and southern Ontario.

Subspecies. (1) *Falco peregrinus anatum* Bonaparte is the sub-specific name currently applied to most southern Canadian breeding populations (except those of islands along the British Columbia coast). (2) *F. p. pealei* Ridgway, inhabiting the Queen Charlotte Islands and Moore Island, British Columbia, differs from *anatum* in its darker coloration and slightly larger size. (3) *F. p. tundrius* White, of arctic Canada, is the palest of Canadian races and the black malar stripe is less extensive; size smaller.

Remarks. The streamlined, powerful Peregrine Falcon is one of the swiftest birds in the world, capable of overtaking flying prey with ease. Its victim is often struck such a powerful blow by the large taloned feet that it is killed in the air instantly. In a dive pursuing prey the Peregrine has been timed at speeds up to 290 km/h. Although its food is almost entirely made up of other birds, it is nowhere sufficiently numerous to have any appreciable ill-effect on any one species. In the 1960s, Peregrine Falcon populations of the subspecies *F. p. anatum*, the breeding

réal, Aylwin. In 1979 and 1980, resumed nesting very locally in south part of the province); Labrador (Cape Chidley, Okak, Nain, Pamiarluk, Makkovik, Gannet Islands); and formerly in New Brunswick (Grand Manan Island) and Nova Scotia (Diamond Island; Advocate). Recorded in summer north to Axel Heiberg Island but without evidence of breeding.

Definite breeding records lacking, but probably bred sparingly in Saskatchewan, Manitoba, and Newfoundland as species occurrence is recorded locally in summer. Migrates through all of southern Canada including Prince Edward Island. Winters in British Columbia (along coast), southern Ontario, and rarely Nova Scotia and New Brunswick. Very rarely elsewhere.

birds of the eastern United States and southeastern Canada, were virtually wiped out by pesticides, mainly the chlorinated hydrocarbon DDT. Recent programmes of captive breeding and release in the wild in both the United States and Canada are showing encouraging results and there has been some local nesting once more. In 1983 and 1984, for instance, the Peregrine nested in Montréal after 30 years' absence. DDT was banned in the United States and Canada in the early 1970s but is still used in many Latin American countries, and birds wintering there still pick up significant quantities of pesticides.

Gyrfalcon

Faucon gerfaut
Falco rusticolus Linnaeus
Total length: male, 53 to 57 cm;
female, 56 to 63 cm
Plates 21 and 23

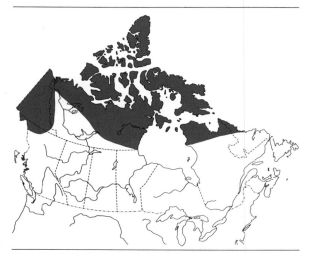

Breeding Distribution of Gyrfalcon

Range in Canada. Breeds sparsely across arctic Canada, but vast areas exist from which definite breeding records are wanting. Breeds from northern Banks Island (Mercy Bay); Ellesmere Island (Slidre Fiord, Bay Fiord, Cape Hayes); Bylot Island; Baffin Island (Admiralty Inlet, Abodyar Island, Clyde Inlet, Dorset); and Boothia Peninsula (Felix Harbour) south to northwestern British Columbia (Chilkat Pass, Atlin, Spatsizi Provincial Park); southern Yukon; northern Mackenzie (Mackenzie Delta, Anderson River, Redrock Lake, Point Lake, Thelon River, Lynx Lake); southern Keewatin (Edehon Lake, Digges Island); northern Quebec (Wakeham Bay, Ford Lake, Kuujjuaq); and northern Labrador (Nachvak Bay, perhaps Paul Island). Records of breeding at Fort Chipewyan, Alberta; and Brador, Quebec, are unsatisfactory. Wanders south of breeding range in winter.

Toothed upper mandible identifies it as a falcon. Large size, stout legs and feet, legs feathered in front more than halfway to toes, and markings, are all features that distinguish it from other falcons. Plumage variable. Pale phase mainly white, usually more or less barred, spotted and streaked with dark brown. Dark phase is mainly leaden blackish-brown, above and below; the under parts are narrowly streaked with white. Many intermediate stages with barred or unbarred tails are common. White (pale-phase) birds are commonest in the breeding season in the eastern high Arctic; darkest birds in the Ungava Peninsula. In adults the cere and feet are usually yellow; in immatures, bluish or greyish.

Measurements *(F. r. obsoletus). Adult male*: wing, 355–373 (364.1); tail, 190.5–206 (201.7); culmen (from cere), 21.5–23.5 (22.3); tarsus, 60.5–63 (61.2). *Adult female*: wing, 361.5–407 (384.4) mm.

Field Marks. Pale phase is unlike any other hawk. Easily separable from Snowy Owls by its smaller head, narrower pointed wings, and quicker wing beats. Darker birds are likely to be confused with the immature Peregrine Falcon, but are more uniformly coloured, and the moustache stripe is more obscure or lacking.

Habitat. In summer, arctic and subarctic open country near cliffs or mountains both inland and on rocky coasts; sometimes wooded country. In winter various types of open country, sometimes wooded.

Nesting. Nest usually placed on cliffs, often inaccessible. Usually no real nest is built beyond a few sticks, grasses, or moss, but as it is used in successive years, an accumulation of the remains of prey develops. Sometimes it nests also in trees. Nests of other birds, such as the Rough-legged Hawk, occasionally are used. *Eggs*, usually 3 or 4; creamy white with pale-rufous suffusion and (not always) spots and blotches of reddish browns. Incubation period 28 to 29 days (A.L.V. Manniche).

Range. Holarctic. Breeds in Alaska, northern Canada, Greenland, Iceland, northern Scandinavia, northern Russia, and northern Siberia. In North America, it winters from the breeding grounds irregularly southward to southern Canada and rarely to Washington, Montana, Ohio, New York, and Massachusetts.

Subspecies. (1) *Falco rusticolus obsoletus* Gmelin is the breeding subspecies across arctic Canada. The fourth primary from the outside is usually shorter than the outermost. (2) *F. r. uralensis* (Severtzov and Menzbier) is known in Canada only as a visitor to British Columbia. Fourth primary from outside equal to or longer than outermost. The writer has examined (courtesy British Columbia Provincial Museum) specimens from Alberni, 30 January 1917; Saanich, December 1904; Victoria, 10 November 1916.

Prairie Falcon

Faucon des Prairies
Falco mexicanus Schlegel
Total length: male, 43 to 45.5 cm;
female, 47 to 51 cm
Plates 21 and 23

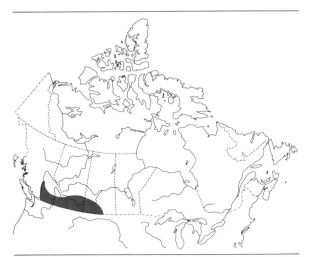

Breeding Distribution of Prairie Falcon

Range in Canada. Breeds in southern British Columbia (dry southern interior: Spences Bridge, Vaseux Lake, Napier Lake, Doc English Gulch, Dog Creek); southern Alberta (Rosebud, Rumsey, Little Sandhill Creek, Brooks); and southern Saskatchewan (Battle Creek; Frenchman River, 24 km east of Eastend; Big Muddy valley; Beechy).

Species has been recorded north to Nulki Lake, British Columbia; Edmonton and Battle River region, Alberta; and St. Louis, Saskatchewan; east to southern Manitoba (Whitewater Lake, Winnipeg) and Ontario (sight records: Hamilton, Point Pelee); and west to southern Vancouver Island. Winters in small numbers in southern British Columbia, Alberta, Saskatchewan, and Manitoba (very rarely).

Toothed upper mandible marks it as a falcon. Inner toe (without claw) reaches to or beyond penultimate joint of middle toe (contrary in Peregrine Falcon). Resembles Peregrine Falcon, but see Field Marks. *Adults*: Head with whitish line over eye and dark-brown moustache (malar) streak. Upper parts brown, feathers margined and incompletely barred with tawny; paler band across hind-neck. Central tail feathers plain, rest barred buff and brown. Throat white, rest of under parts streaked and otherwise marked with dark brown, these markings coalescing to a brownish patch on flanks. Axillars mainly brown contrasting with whitish under wing coverts. *Juvenal*: Resembles adults but upper parts darker and under parts more buffy.

Measurements. *Adult male*: wing, 301–349.5 (317.2); tail, 163–191 (173.3); culmen (from cere), 20–21.5 (20.9); tarsus, 51.5–54 (52.9). *Adult female*: wing, 330–358 (346.6) mm.

Field Marks. A crow-sized falcon. Most like Peregrine Falcon but decidedly paler and sandy brown above (not dark slate or blackish). In flight shows *dark axillars and flank patches*. The American Kestrel and Merlin are obviously smaller.

Habitat. Typically dry open country of the West; in breeding season the vicinity of cliffs, canyons, coulees, badlands, and rock outcrops; hunts over adjacent grasslands and sometimes high mountains and wooded country.

Nesting. Eggs are laid on bare rock or in a scrape or in the nest of other large birds. Prefers shallow cavities or ledges protected by an overhang. *Eggs*, 3 to 6; resemble those of the Peregrine Falcon but are much lighter in colour. Incubation 29 to 31 days, mostly by the female.

Range. Breeds from dry parts of southwestern Canada south to Baja California, southern parts of Arizona and New Mexico, and northern Texas. Winters from southwestern Canada to central Mexico.

Order **Galliformes:**
Megapodes, Curassows, Pheasants, Grouse, and Allies

Fowl-like, scratching ground birds make up this order, which has a vast distribution in the world and contains many of the important game birds. The Jungle Fowl is the ancestor of our domestic hen, and this and the Wild Turkey are important components of the poultry industry.

Family **Phasianidae:**
Partridges, Pheasants, Grouse, Turkeys, and Quail

Number of Species in Canada: 16

This large, widely distributed family contains some of the most useful and valuable birds in the world including many of the domestic fowls and a great variety of game birds, as well as some of the most beautiful ones such as the peacocks and other gorgeously feathered pheasants.

Subfamily **Phasianinae:**
Partridges and Pheasants

Fowl-like birds with legs, toes, and nostrils bare. In some species the legs are equipped with spurs. Some species have more or less extensive areas of bare skin on the head. Tail varies from short to very long and elaborate. The subfamily, which is widely distributed, contains some of the most beautiful fowl.

Gray Partridge

(European Partridge; Hungarian Partridge)

Perdrix grise
Perdix perdix (Linnaeus)
Total length: 30.5 to 33 cm
Plate 27

Breeding Distribution of Gray Partridge

Range in Canada. Introduced. Permanent resident, more or less well established in suitable southern parts of the country. Numbers subject to fluctuations, and range limits uncertain because of repeated introduction attempts on marginal or submarginal habitat. Resident in southern British Columbia (locally), including a small southern Vancouver Island population; southern and central Alberta; southern Saskatchewan (north about to Prince Albert,

The *unmarked reddish-brown* outer tail feathers distinguish it from other chicken-like game birds found in Canada except the Chukar (see Field Marks). The very finely vermiculated breast separates it from all others including the Chukar. The chestnut horseshoe-shaped patch on the abdomen, when present, is diagnostic, but it is smaller or absent in females. Crown in males has narrow pale streaks; in females the crown streaks are broadened into spots.

Measurements. *Adult male*: wing, 151–161.6 (154.2); tail, 77–86.8 (80.8); exposed culmen, 14.8–16.4 (15.6); tarsus, 40–43.1 (41.3). *Adult female*: wing, 144–158 (151.3) mm.

Field Marks. A smallish shortish-tailed partridge (but obviously larger than any quail) with plain, pale-brown eyebrow line, cheeks, and throat, greyish breast, chestnut-brown bars on the flanks, and (in male) a chestnut abdominal patch. Reddish-brown outer tail feathers, unmarked, separate it from all but Chukar (red-phase Ruffed Grouse show a conspicuous dark subterminal tail-band), but the present species differs from the Chukar in lacking a broad black head and neck stripe, in having no suggestion of red on bill or legs, and in possessing brown (not mainly black) flank bars. Voice in spring a raspy *tur-ip*.

Habitat. Open grassland and agricultural land.

Nesting. Nest, a hollow scraped in the ground and lined with grasses, usually in shelter of grass and low shrubs. *Eggs*, usually 9 to 20, are plain olive-brown. Incubation, 23 to 25 days (Witherby et al.), is by female.

Range. Native of western Eurasia from the British Isles, southern Norway, southern Sweden, and middle Russia south to northern Portugal, northern Spain, Italy, Rumania, and southern Russia, east about to western Mongolia. Widely introduced and established in parts of North America from southern Canada to northern and middle United States.

Carlton, Nipawin); southern Manitoba; southern and central Ontario (mostly east: locally north to Sault Ste. Marie, Timmins, Cochrane; also Thunder Bay district); extreme southwestern Quebec (north to Trois-Rivières, Plessisville, Aylmer); southern New Brunswick; Prince Edward Island; and Nova Scotia (locally).

Subspecies. Origin of imported stocks is poorly known, and probably several of the many subspecies recognized in its native range are intermixed.

Remarks. This little foreigner was imported into North America as a game bird and, as such, has proved to be a great success in many parts of its new home. It flushes warily with a clatter of wings and a rapid cackle. It flies and glides speedily but never very high above the ground. The reddish spread tail shows prominently in flight.

The Gray Partridge is a hardy species, able to withstand the cold and ordinary snow of winter in most southern parts of Canada. At times very heavy snows can cause high mortality, but even then the species manages to hold its own in marginal territory through its surprisingly high reproductive potential.

In midwinter, when snow lies deep over the land, coveys of Gray Partridge often appear about farmyards and even on the grounds about suburban dwellings.

Chukar

Perdrix choukar
Alectoris chukar (Gray)
Total length: 33 to 39.5 cm
Plate 27

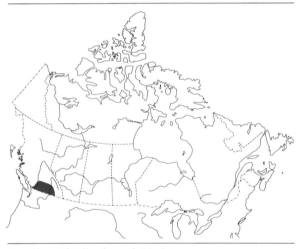

Breeding Distribution of Chukar

Range in Canada. Introduced to interior southern British Columbia (1950–1955) in the Similkameen valley: U.S. border to Keremeos; Okanagan valley: U.S. border to Penticton; Thompson valley: Shuswap Lake to Lytton; and Fraser valley: extent unknown but Lytton to probably mouth of Chilcotin River. Has been introduced into central and southern Alberta, southern Saskatchewan, and southern Ontario without success.

A medium-sized chicken-like bird. Sexes similar. Upper parts greyish brown with pinkish wash. Black band from forehead through eye, down side of neck, and broadening across upper breast. Rest of breast bluish grey. Throat patch and abdomen buff. Flanks boldly barred with black and chestnut. Outer tail reddish brown terminally. Bill, feet, and eyelids red to pink.

Measurements. *Adult male* (two specimens): wing, 166.5–167.9; tail, 97.5–101.2; exposed culmen, 21–21.9; tarsus, 47.5–49.1. *Adult female* (one specimen): wing, 153.5 mm.

Field Marks. Black border around throat patch, bold black bars on flanks, red bill and legs. In flight shows reddish outer tail like Gray Partridge, but Gray Partridge has no black on head, breast, or flanks and no red on legs and bill.

Habitat. Rugged steep terrain in areas of light precipitation, relatively snow-free in winter.

Range. Native to mountainous central and southern Europe and Asia. Introduced into drier mountainous western United States and north to extreme southern British Columbia and southern Alberta.

Ring-necked Pheasant

Faisan de chasse
Phasianus colchicus Linnaeus
Total length: male, 82 to 91 cm;
female, 45.5 to 57 cm
Plate 24

Breeding Distribution of Ring-necked Pheasant

Range in Canada. Introduced. Permanent resident but populations fluctuate, locally distributed across southern Canada: British Columbia (southern parts: notably successful in Osoyoos-Keremeos area; dry country north of Ashcroft and north at least to Alkali Lake and Pavilion; parts of southern Vancouver Island; established also on Queen Charlotte Islands); central Alberta (particularly successful on irrigated southern parts but ranging north to near Athabasca; introduced also in Grande Prairie district); southern Saskatchewan (north to about the Battleford and Carlton areas; introduced at Nipawin where in 1959 it was existing precariously); southwestern Manitoba; southern Ontario (mainly south of southern Bruce Peninsula, Lake Simcoe, and Kingston; especially successful on Pelee Island; locally in small numbers north to Ottawa and St. Joseph's Island; also Thunder Bay district); southwestern Quebec (Eastern Townships, Montréal; reported also from Hudson, Hull, and even Charlesbourg but presently confined mainly to the Montréal area); New Brunswick; Prince Edward Island; Nova Scotia (but rare on Cape Breton Island where status is uncertain); and Newfoundland (St. John's).

The gorgeous male with long (40.5 to 45.5 cm) tapering pointed tail, bill resembling that of a domestic rooster, and spurred tarsus, is quite unlike any other wild bird in Canada. The white ring about neck is variable in extent and sometimes lacking. Female very differently coloured: a dark-spotted, pale-brownish hen-like bird with very long (28 to 30.5 cm) slender, tapering, pointed tail. Females might be confused with the locally distributed Sage Grouse but lack the black abdominal patch of that species and have unfeathered legs (tarsi).

Measurements. *Adult male*: wing, 228.5–244.5 (236.6); tail, 428.5–514.5 (460.9); exposed culmen, 28.5–32 (30.7); tarsus, 66.5–75 (71). *Adult female*: wing, 198–224 (207.1) mm.

Habitat. Mainly farmland with fields of grain, corn, alfalfa, soybeans, grass, and weeds near cover, such as hedges, ditch shrubbery, ground-hugging shrub patches, marsh edges, ungrazed woodland borders, groves with underbrush. Irrigated areas on the prairies.

Nesting. Nest, a depression in the ground lined with grass or leaves, is usually in fields, wood edges, or under bushes. *Eggs*, 8 to 15, are plain olive-brown. Incubation 22.25 to 25 days, by female (various authors).

Range. It is native from the Ukraine east through central Asia to Manchuria and southern China; also in Japan and Taiwan. Introduced and widely established in Europe (including British Isles), New Zealand, and North America. In North America from southern Canada south locally to California, Utah, New Mexico, northwestern Texas, northwestern Oklahoma, southern Illinois, Pennsylvania, New Jersey, and Maryland.

Subspecies. Populations, introduced from several subspecies, now mingled and composite, are best referred to species only; hence *Phasianus colchicus* Linnaeus.

Subfamily **Tetraoninae**
Grouse and Ptarmigan

These fowl-like birds have completely or partly feathered legs (in ptarmigan, the toes also are feathered, Figure 44); species with unfeathered toes have in winter a fringe of horny pectinations on either side of the toes (Figure 45); feathers hide the nostrils; over the eye is a small bare stripe. On the sides of the neck in some species there are elongated feathers, and in others there is bare skin capable of distension.

Spruce Grouse

(includes Franklin's Grouse)

Tétras du Canada
Dendragapus canadensis (Linnaeus)
Total length: 38 to 43 cm
Plate 25

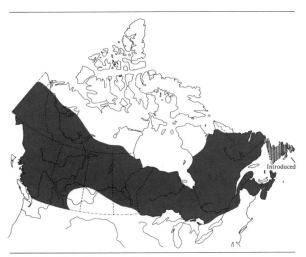

Breeding Distribution of Spruce Grouse

Range in Canada. Permanent resident, north to near tree limit, in coniferous forests. Extirpated in vicinity of thickly settled parts of range in the south but still common in remoter suitable parts of the country. Breeds in Yukon (north to Rampart House, Old Crow); western and southern Mackenzie (southern Mackenzie Delta, Norman Wells, Fort Franklin, Hardisty Lake, Fort Simpson, Great Slave Lake); southern Keewatin (Windy River); British Columbia (mainland, but not known from coastal islands); Alberta (except southeastern prairies); northern and south-central Saskatchewan (south to Nipawin and Fishing Lake); Manitoba (except southwest); Ontario (south to about Algonquin Provincial Park; formerly south to Peel and Leeds counties); northern, central, and southern Quebec (north to Lake Guillaume-Delisle, Kuujjuaq, Koroc River; extirpated from thickly settled southwestern parts; absent from Anticosti and Madeleine islands); Labrador; New Brunswick (but unknown from Grand Manan group); and Nova Scotia (including Cape Breton Island). Introduced into Newfoundland in 1964, and in 1978 was doing well near Gander Lake. Absent from Prince Edward Island, but possibly occurred formerly and was extirpated.

Legs feathered to toes. *Adult male*: Upper parts finely barred black and grey, often brownish especially on wings. Tail black, broadly tipped with pale brown (except in *franklinii* of the West, which has all-black tail and white-tipped upper tail coverts). Forehead, cheeks, throat, and upper breast black narrowly bordered with white. Lower breast black centrally, broadly barred with white laterally and on middle of abdomen. Sides mixed grey and black. Under tail coverts black tipped with white. *Adult female*: Very different. Upper parts irregularly barred black, grey, and rusty. Tail irregularly barred black and rusty (in *franklinii* upper tail coverts tipped with white). Under parts barred black, white, and rusty, rustiest on breast. *Immatures* resemble adults of their respective sex.

Measurements *(D. c. canadensis)*. *Adult male*: wing, 168–186.3 (177.1); tail, 113–131.8 (120.9); exposed culmen, 13.6–17 (15.2); tarsus, 34.9–39.8 (36.9). *Adult female*: wing, 161–178 (168.4) mm.

Field Marks. East of the Rocky Mountains, the black-breasted male is readily identifiable. In the western mountains, it might be confused with the Blue Grouse (q.v.). Females somewhat resemble Ruffed Grouse but have bars across the back and shorter tail without a black subterminal bar, and lack ruffs. Since Spruce Grouse are absurdly tame, they can be closely approached and studied.

Habitat. Usually coniferous and mixedwood forests, muskeg, forest edges, and openings; also older burntlands and blueberry barrens.

Nesting. Nest, a depression on the ground sparsely lined with grasses and leaves, often under a small isolated conifer sapling on dry ground near a wet bog. *Eggs*, (usually 4 to 7, occasionally more) are buffy, handsomely marked with rich browns. Incubation (period uncertain) by female, probably about 24 days (R.S. Palmer), 23.5 days (McCourt, Boag, and Keppe).

Range. Permanent resident in coniferous woodland from about tree limit in Canada and Alaska south to northeastern Oregon, western Montana, northwestern Wyoming, northern Minnesota, Michigan, northern New York, northern Vermont, northern New Hampshire, and Maine. Introduced in Newfoundland.

Subspecies. (1) *Dendragapus canadensis franklinii* (Douglas): inhabits southern two-thirds of mainland British Columbia (except Peace River; north at least to Ingenika River, and Hudson Hope) and mountainous southwestern Alberta. Male differs from other races in the all-black tail (no brown tips) and in both sexes having broadly white-tipped upper tail coverts. Until recently, regarded as a full species. (2) *D. c. osgoodi* (Bishop): Yukon and northern British Columbia (Atlin, Telegraph Creek, Fort Nelson) and western Mackenzie (Norman Wells; Canol Road between Carcajou and Mackenzie rivers; intergradation eastward not well understood). (3) *D. c. canadensis* (Linnaeus): central-eastern British Columbia (Peace River), central Alberta, central Saskatchewan, Manitoba, northern Ontario, northern and central Quebec, and Labrador. (4) *D. c. canace* (Linnaeus): southern Ontario (north to Temagami and Georgian Bay), southern Quebec (north to Lake Saint-Jean), New Brunswick, and Nova Scotia.

Remarks. The Spruce Grouse is deserving of its other name "Fool Hen." Unlike the Ruffed Grouse, it has never learned to fear man greatly. Ridiculously tame, it can often be killed with a stick or stone. Consequently it disappears rapidly with the advance of settlement and is now gone from most southern parts of its former range where man has thickly settled. It feeds to a large extent on the needles and buds of coniferous trees, especially in winter. Berries of various kinds are much relished when they are available.

Blue Grouse

(Dusky and Sooty grouse)

Tétras sombre
Dendragapus obscurus (Say)
Total length: male, 47 to 57 cm;
female, 43.5 to 47.5 cm
Plate 25

Breeding Distribution of Blue Grouse

Range in Canada. Permanent resident in western mountains: southern Yukon (locally north to Mayo Lake but rare or absent from the St. Elias range); extreme southwestern Mackenzie (near mouth of Nahanni River; mountains west of Fort Simpson); British Columbia (including Queen Charlotte and Vancouver islands, islands in Strait of Georgia, most of the interior but apparently absent locally from some quite large areas); and southwestern Alberta (Jasper, Banff, and Waterton Lakes national parks; Canmore, Coleman). Migrations local and vertical, many breeding in valleys and wooded plains and wintering at considerable altitudes in coniferous forests.

Tail square or slightly rounded. Legs feathered to base of toes. Large size separates it from most Canadian grouse, and square or slightly rounded tail feathers from the equally large Sage Grouse (which has pointed tail-feather tips). Coloration most similar to that of the much smaller Spruce Grouse, but the male's breast is uniformly slaty (no decidedly black patch); and adult female has the centre of abdomen plain slaty (barred in female Spruce Grouse). *Adult male*: Head and neck slaty, mixed on throat and sides of neck with white. Upper parts blackish, more or less finely mottled with grey or brown and with buffy brown on wings. Tail black with or without (see Subspecies) a well-defined terminal grey band. Under parts slaty with white markings on flanks and under tail coverts. *Adult female*: Similar to male but crown, scapulars, chest, and sides barred or otherwise marked with brown. Tail with indistinct tail band (individually variable regardless of subspecies).

Measurements. *Adult male*: wing, 223–239 (231.9); tail, 159–182 (169.9); exposed culmen, 18.5–21 (19.7); tarsus, 43–47.5 (45.5). *Adult female*: wing, 196–218 (206.1) mm.

Field Marks. Adult male a large, dark, slate-coloured grouse, most likely to be confused with the much-smaller male Spruce Grouse. In Canada, coastal males have a well-defined grey terminal tail-band, but this is lacking in interior males. Blue Grouse males have a uniformly slaty breast without the well-defined black patch of male Spruce Grouse (also a western race of the Spruce Grouse *franklinii* has white spots on upper tail coverts, always lacking in Blue Grouse). Females are similar to female Spruce Grouse but have a plain slaty patch in the middle of the abdomen, and the under parts are less extensively and less heavily barred.

Habitat. Varies seasonally. In breeding season many inhabit lowland burntlands, slashings, open mountainsides, meadows, forest edges and openings, although some, especially in northern British Columbia and Yukon, breed near tree limit. After the breeding season and during winter the species inhabits coniferous forests at higher altitudes. In winter it is largely arboreal, feeding mainly on needles of conifers.

Nesting. Nest, a depression on the ground lined with grasses, leaves (including conifers), and similar material available near the nesting site. Nest is often at foot of a tree or near a log or rock. *Eggs*, usually 7 to 10; creamy, finely dotted with browns. Incubation 24 to 25 days (J.F. Bendell).

Range. Southeastern Alaska, southern Yukon, and extreme southwestern Mackenzie south along the coast to northern California, and in the mountains south to southern California, northern Arizona, and central New Mexico; east to southwestern Alberta and the Black Hills, South Dakota.

Subspecies. In Canada, four. (1) *Dendragapus obscurus sitkensis* Swarth (Queen Charlotte Islands; islands in Queen Charlotte Sound, British Columbia): adult male with distinct terminal tail-band; females more reddish-brown, less blackish, than in *fuliginosus*. (2) *D. o. fuliginosus* (Ridgway) (mainland coast of British Columbia and Vancouver Island; inland to Lillooet): males with distinct grey terminal tail-band, like *sitkensis*; females duller brown more black in upper parts. (3) *D. o. pallidus* Swarth (drier parts of southern interior British Columbia: habitat adjoining Okanagan and Similkameen valleys and north at least to Chilcotin drainage): males without distinct tail-band, rectrices broader and more truncate than in *sitkensis* and *fuliginosus*; both sexes paler. (4) *D. o. richardsonii* (Douglas) (southern Yukon, southwestern Mackenzie, interior British Columbia except range of *pallidus*, and extreme southwestern Alberta): adult males with tail similar to that of *pallidus*, both sexes darker than *pallidus*, paler than *fuliginosus*, females less reddish than *sitkensis*.

Willow Ptarmigan

Lagopède des saules
Lagopus lagopus (Linnaeus)
Total length: 35.5 to 43 cm
Plate 25

Figure 44
Feathered foot of Willow Ptarmigan

Breeding Distribution of Willow Ptarmigan

Range in Canada. Breeds in the arctic islands north to Banks, southern Melville, Bathurst, and Baffin islands (north probably to southern Admiralty Inlet–Gifford Fiord but evidently absent from most of east coast); Yukon; northern Mackenzie (Kittigazuit, Anderson River, Great Bear Lake, Artillery Lake); Keewatin (south to Nueltin Lake) and Southampton Island; British Columbia (interior mountains south to Kleena Kleene region and Garibaldi Park; also Porcher Island); southwestern Alberta (northern Jasper National Park); northeastern Manitoba (Churchill, Herchmer); northern Ontario (very locally: Cape Henrietta Maria, Lake River); some James Bay islands; north and central Quebec (locally south in the interior to Lake Bienville and Irony Mountain, perhaps to Eastmain Hills; farther south along James Bay coast and small islands to Moar Bay; and on the outer north shore of Gulf of St. Lawrence: Bluff Harbour; Kégashka; Saint-Augustin); Labrador; and Newfoundland.

Recognizable as a ptarmigan by feathered toes and large amounts of white (wings white even in summer). Black tail feathers separate it from the White-tailed Ptarmigan. Most similar to Rock Ptarmigan but much red on neck and breast separates summer males. Females of Willow Ptarmigan separable by larger size and heavier, broader bill. In winter it never shows the black stripe through the eye, possessed by male Rock Ptarmigan, but as this is lacking in many female Rock Ptarmigan, its absence is not diagnostic, and larger size and heavier bill must be relied upon. *Adult male (summer)*: Head, neck, and upper breast chestnut; feathers about base of bill and chin, more or less white; eye-ring white; back, scapulars, rump, and upper tail coverts, mixed blacks, browns, and a little white; wings white with dusky shafts to the primaries (except in *L. l. leucopterus*); tail blackish, tipped narrowly with white; belly and legs white; comb red. *Adult male (early autumn)*: Similar to male in summer but reddish brown of head, neck, and breast paler; upper parts paler and more decidedly barred. *Adult male (winter)*: All white except most of tail feathers, which are black tipped with white; shafts of wing primaries dusky (except in *L. l. leucopterus*). *Adult female (summer)*: Upper parts intricately patterned with blacks, buffs, and white; under parts more decidedly barred with black; wings mostly white (except some wing coverts like the back) and dusky shafts of primaries (except *leucopterus*); tail blackish, tipped white; comb paler red than in male. *Adult female (early autumn)*: Similar to adult male in similar dress, the head, neck, and breast with more or less reddish-brown but usually enough of the heavily barred plumage of the summer female's under parts is retained to distinguish her. *Adult female (winter)*: Like adult male in winter, but the concealed bases of the crown feathers are often more greyish.

Measurements *(L. l. leucopterus). Adult male*: wing, 210.5–226 (217.9); tail, 129–140 (133.2); exposed culmen, 12.5–17.5 (14.1); tarsus, 34.5–38 (36.4). *Adult female*: wing, 196.5–205 (200.4) mm.

Field Marks. Ptarmigan are smallish arctic or alpine grouse, readily separable from other grouse by large amounts of white in the plumage (brown with white wings and abdomen in summer; mainly white in winter). Canada has three species, but the White-tailed is restricted to the western mountains. Willow and Rock Ptarmigan both have semi-concealed black tails, visible in flight, thus differing in all plumages from the White-tailed Ptarmigan. Summer adult male Willow Ptarmigan differ from the other two in the reddish brown of head, neck, and breast. Summer females are difficult to distinguish from other ptarmigan in the field, as are birds of both sexes in white winter dress. Willow Ptarmigan in white winter plumage never have the black eye-stripe shown by male Rock Ptarmigan, but as this is lacking in many females of the latter its absence is not diagnostic.

Habitat. In the Arctic, low tundra preferring moister better-vegetated country than the Rock Ptarmigan. In the western mountains frequents willow-grown meadows just above timberline, shrubby mountainsides, willow-bordered stream bottoms mostly near or just above timberline. In winter many descend to intermontane lowlands and from the arctic tundra to well south of tree limit, inhabiting muskegs, lake and river margins, and forest openings.

Nesting. Nest on the ground, a depression lined with grasses or leaves. *Eggs*, usually 7 to 10; yellowish, thickly and handsomely spotted and blotched with blackish brown. Incubation by female, probably about 22 days (Conover *in* Bent).

Range. Circumpolar. Breeds in Alaska, northern Canada, northern Europe, and northern Asia. Mainly permanent resident but somewhat migratory.

Introduced on Scatarie Island, Nova Scotia, in 1968 and reported to be doing well there in 1980.

Winters throughout much of breeding range north to Banks and southern Baffin islands but migrates irregularly south to south-central Alberta (Camrose, Sullivan Lake); south-central Saskatchewan (Qu'Appelle valley rarely); southern Manitoba (Gypsumville, Ashern, southern Lake Manitoba); central Ontario (rarely south to Whitby); and southern Quebec (Chelsea, and perhaps rarely south to Montréal).

Subspecies. (1) *Lagopus lagopus leucopterus* Taverner: arctic islands including southern Baffin and Southampton islands; also east coastal Mackenzie (Dolphin and Union Strait east) and north coast of Keewatin (Adelaide Peninsula). (2) *L. l. albus* (Gmelin): Yukon, west coastal and interior Mackenzie (north to mouth of Anderson River, Cape Dalhousie, Great Bear Lake), Keewatin (but replaced by *leucopterus* in extreme north), northeastern Manitoba, west coast of Hudson Bay (north at least to Chesterfield Inlet), British Columbia (except northwest, intergradation areas with *alexandrae* imperfectly understood), and southwest Alberta. (3) *L. l. alexandrae* Grinnell: northwestern British Columbia (Porcher Island; also according to *A.O.U. Check-list of North American Birds*, Atlin and Dease Lake). (4) *L. l. ungavus* Riley: Quebec and Labrador. (5) *L. l. alleni* Stejneger: Newfoundland.

Remarks. Ptarmigan are arctic grouse. They are found also at higher elevations in the western mountains. They have separate summer, autumn, and winter plumages. In winter they are mainly white, in summer largely brown and grey. Thus they are well camouflaged at all seasons—excellent examples of "protective coloration."

Rock Ptarmigan

Lagopède des rochers
Lagopus mutus (Montin)
Total length: 32.5 to 39.5 cm
Plate 25

Breeding Distribution of Rock Ptarmigan

Range in Canada. The most boreal ptarmigan. Breeds from Prince Patrick, Ellef Ringnes, and northern Ellesmere islands south through the Arctic Archipelago, through Yukon (including Herschel Island); north and middle interior British Columbia (Atlin, Ingenika River, probably to southern part: occurs in June near Bella Coola, Yule Lake, Mount Seymour near Vancouver); northern and middle Mackenzie (south to Cap Mountain and Artillery Lake; probably south to southwestern mountains); southern Keewatin (south to Alder Lake), Boothia and Melville peninsulas; Southampton Island; Belcher Islands; northern Quebec (south to Schefferville region); northern Labrador (Cape Chidley, Ramah); and Newfoundland. Perhaps bred formerly on Anticosti Island.

Winters mainly within breeding range (north at least to Melville and Devon islands but probably most withdraw from northernmost parts) and south to southern Mackenzie (Great Slave

Black tail instead of white separates it from White-tailed Ptarmigan. Similar to Willow Ptarmigan. Males in summer lack any suggestion of dull red on head and neck feathers; in late-summer plumage, upper parts of both sexes are more finely marked than in Willow. In white winter plumage, the black loral bar through eye (usually absent in females) instantly identifies Rock Ptarmigan. The slighter bill and smaller size of Rock Ptarmigan will help identify similar individuals of these two species.

Measurements *(L. m. rupestris). Adult male*: wing, 178–195.5 (187); tail, 101–117.5 (107.7); exposed culmen, 11.5–14.5 (12.8); tarsus, 31–33.5 (32.2). *Adult female*: wing, 173.5–188 (179) mm.

Field Marks. In white winter plumage, black bar at eye, when present (often absent), separates it from the other two ptarmigan. Black tail (often concealed) eliminates White-tailed Ptarmigan (see Willow Ptarmigan).

Habitat. In breeding season generally prefers higher, drier, barer country than Willow Ptarmigan; arctic and alpine highlands. In winter and during migration both species sometimes utilize similar habitats.

Nesting. Nest, a depression in ground or moss, lined with available vegetation and feathers, often sheltered by a rock, hummock, or low vegetation. *Eggs*, usually 6 to 9; very similar to those of Willow Ptarmigan but smaller, creamy to buffy, heavily spotted and blotched with blackish brown. Incubation, about 21 days (A. Pedersen), is by female.

Range. Circumpolar. Arctic Ocean islands and coasts south in Eurasia to Iceland and locally in the mountains to Scotland, France, Spain, Austria, central Asia, and northern Japan; and in North America south to southern Alaska, northern Canada, and southern Greenland.

Lake); northern Saskatchewan (Athabasca Lake); northern Manitoba (Lynn Lake, York Factory); northwestern Ontario (Fort Severn, Winisk); central Quebec (James Bay and high barren country 240 to 320 km inland from it; outer north shore Gulf of St. Lawrence); Labrador; and Newfoundland.

Casual in summer on Bonaventure Island, Quebec (9 July 1922). Accidental in Nova Scotia (Elmsdale, 20 April 1922).

Subspecies. (1) *Lagopus mutus nelsoni* Stejneger: northern Yukon. (2) *L. m. welchi* Brewster: Newfoundland. (3) *L. m. rupestris* (Gmelin): currently all Canadian populations except those of the two previously mentioned races are included in *rupestris*. (4) *L. m. captus* Peters: northern Ellesmere Island.

Remarks. Ptarmigan are notable for their remarkable seasonal plumage changes. The adults acquire no less than three different plumages annually, and in spring, summer, and autumn seem to be continuously moulting.

White-tailed Ptarmigan

Lagopède à queue blanche
Lagopus leucurus (Richardson)
Total length: 31.5 to 34.5 cm
Plate 25

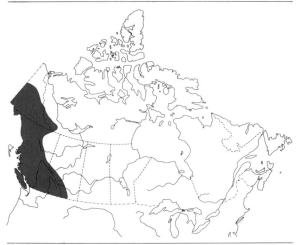

Breeding Distribution of White-tailed Ptarmigan

Range in Canada. Resident in higher mountains of Yukon (north at least to Lapierre House); southwestern Mackenzie (Nahanni Mountains); British Columbia (higher mountains of most of the mainland and Vancouver Island); and southwestern Alberta (Jasper, Banff, and Waterton Lakes national parks).

Smallest ptarmigan. A small grouse with white wings in summer; all-white plumage in winter identifies it as a ptarmigan. All-white tail separates adults in all seasons from other ptarmigan.

Measurements *(L. l. leucurus). Adult male*: wing, 168–181.7 (173.9); tail, 95–109 (101.6); exposed culmen, 11.6–14.9 (13.6); tarsus, 28.5–34.5 (30.9). *Adult female*: wing, 162.5–178.6 (169.8) mm.

Field Marks. Not an arctic grouse, it is to be expected only in mountains of the West. All-white tail and small size separate adults in all plumages from other ptarmigan. Other ptarmigan have a black tail.

Habitat. High altitudes of the western mountains from tree limit to the highest most barren tops preferring alpine rocky meadows and slide-rock slopes. Some descend to timber in winter.

Nesting. Nest, a depression in the ground sparsely lined with available grasses or grass-like vegetation, leaves, and feathers. *Eggs*, usually 6 to 8, buff, dotted, spotted, or small-blotched, leaving decidedly more ground colour exposed than in other ptarmigan. Incubation period probably about 22 days.

Range. South-central Alaska and Yukon, south through the Cascade Mountains to Washington; and in the Rockies through British Columbia and southwestern Alberta through Montana, Wyoming, and Colorado, to northern New Mexico.

Subspecies. (1) *Lagopus leucurus leucurus* (Richardson): British Columbia (except Vancouver Island) and southwestern Alberta. Yukon birds, included in this race by current authors, require further study. (2) *L. l. saxatilis* Cowan: Vancouver Island, British Columbia.

Ruffed Grouse

Gélinotte huppée
Bonasa umbellus (Linnaeus)
Total length: 40.5 to 48 cm
Plate 24

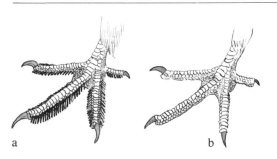

a   b

Figure 45
Foot of Ruffed Grouse
a) in winter
b) in summer

Head slightly crested. Tail, many-barred and with broad subterminal band. Separable from other grouse by black or reddish-brown ruff (soft, broad, longish feathers on sides of neck) and broad subterminal dark tail bar. Two colour phases occur regardless of age, sex, or season. Grey phase is commoner in interior western Canada, and both phases are more or less common in eastern Canada, but in extreme southwestern British Columbia reddish brown is predominant. Female smaller than male, with shorter ruffs and tail, and the tail band is usually incomplete across the two central tail feathers.

Measurements *(B. u. togata). Adult male*: wing, 174.5–187 (179.6); tail, 144–184 (157.2); exposed culmen, 14–16.5 (15.4); tarsus, 42–45 (43.3). *Adult female*: wing, 170.5–184.5 (176.6) mm.

Field Marks. A chicken-like woodland grouse with fan-like many-barred tail. Diagnostic *dark* subterminal tail band is noticeable, especially in flight. Ruffs diagnostic at close range. Springs suddenly from ground with noisy whirring rapid flight. Drumming of male, beginning with slow dull thuds, which quickly increase in tempo until they die away in a muffled roll, suggests the starting of a car in the distance.

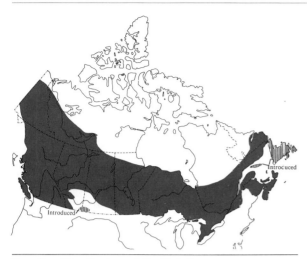

Breeding Distribution of Ruffed Grouse

Range in Canada. Permanent resident (numbers subject to periodic fluctuations) in southern and central Yukon (north to about Old Crow, Lapierre House); southwestern Mackenzie (Forts Resolution and Simpson, Wrigley; perhaps Rae and Roche-qui-Trempe-à-l'eau); British Columbia (except Queen Charlotte Islands, the islands in Queen Charlotte Sound, and apparently most of the northern mainland coast, although observed near head of Rivers Inlet); Alberta (except most of southeastern corner but introduced into the Cypress Hills); Saskatchewan (north at least to Lake Athabasca and Reindeer Lake, but absent from much of southwestern plains; introduced into Cypress Hills); southern and central Manitoba (north at least to Thicket Portage; probably York Factory); Ontario; southern and south-central Quebec (north to Lake Albanel and the north shore of Gulf of St. Lawrence; introduced on Anticosti Island); southern Labrador (north to Goose Bay, Hamilton Inlet); New Brunswick; Nova Scotia (including Cape Breton Island); and Prince Edward Island. Introduced into Newfoundland. Not found on Madeleine Islands.

Habitat. Mainly second-growth deciduous and mixed woodland, wood edges and openings, alder- and willow-bordered ravines and stream edges, old orchards. Much less partial to extensive stands of mature forest, but uses coniferous woods for shelter.

Nesting. Nest, a hollow in the ground lined with leaves and a few feathers, is usually in second-growth woodland, often at the base of a tree, rock, log, or bushpile. *Eggs*, usually 9 to 12; buffy, sometimes sparsely spotted with browns. Incubation, about 24 days (Bump et al.) by the female.

Range. Permanent resident from central Alaska and much of forested Canada (except Newfoundland where now introduced) south to northern California, central Idaho, central Utah, western South Dakota, Minnesota, central Arkansas, northern Georgia, and northeastern Virginia.

Subspecies. (1) *Bonasa umbellus yukonensis* Grinnell: Yukon, southwestern Mackenzie, northern Alberta. (2) *B. u. umbelloides* (Douglas): interior British Columbia (except certain southern parts; see *sabini, phaia*), southwestern and central Alberta, Saskatchewan (except southern part), and Manitoba (except southwestern part). Birds from much of interior British Columbia average somewhat darker than *umbelloides* and have been named *affinis* Aldrich and Friedmann; but for the present at least, I follow the *A.O.U. Check-list of North American Birds* (1957) and J.C. Dickinson, Jr. (1953. Bulletin Museum of Comparative Zoology, Harvard University, vol. 109, no. 2, pp. 123–205) in placing them with *umbelloides*. (3) *B. u. brunnescens* Conover: Vancouver Island and adjoining mainland from Vancouver north at least to Kingcome River. (4) *B. u. sabini* (Douglas): extends into Canada to Chilliwack region of Fraser valley (Munro and Cowan 1947). (5) *B. u. phaia* Aldrich and Friedmann: southeastern British Columbia; distribution poorly understood. (6) *B. u. incana* Aldrich and Friedmann: southern Saskatchewan, southwestern Manitoba. (7) *B. u. obscura* Todd: northern Ontario, central Quebec east at least to Lake Mistassini. Additional material needed farther east and from southern Labrador. (8) *B. u. togata* (Linnaeus): central Ontario (between *obscura* and *monticola*), southern Quebec including Gaspé Peninsula, New Brunswick, Nova Scotia, and Prince Edward Island. (9) *B. u. monticola* Todd: extreme southern Ontario south to Seaforth, Glen Morris, and Hamilton.

Remarks. The Ruffed Grouse is known to most people simply as "partridge." It is a great favourite with the sportsman because it makes a challenging target when flying and is a delicious table-bird. It bursts into the air with a startling clatter of wings, flies fast, takes advantage of any cover between it and the hunter, and before the startled novice can raise his gun, it is out of range. Its numbers are subject to drastic fluctuations periodically, the cause of which is poorly understood. Its drumming (see Field Marks) is one of the pleasantly mysterious sounds of the spring woodlands. This is produced by quick forward and upward strokes of the male's wings as he stands erect on his drumming log.

Sage Grouse

(Sage Hen)

Gélinotte des armoises
Centrocercus urophasianus (Bonaparte)
Total length: male, 66 to 73 cm;
female, 55 to 58 cm
Plate 24

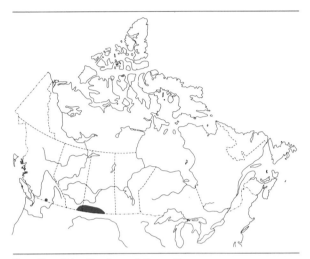

Breeding Distribution of Sage Grouse

Range in Canada. Permanent resident in south-eastern Alberta (commonest in Manyberries–Wild Horse region with recent peripheral sight records at Magrath, Milk River, and Champion) and southwestern Saskatchewan (plains between International Boundary and Cypress Hills east to Wood Mountain). Formerly southern British Columbia (locally: Osoyoos Lake) but now extirpated there.

Unmistakable. A very large grouse. Upper parts finely marked with browns, buff, dull white, and black. Abdomen with large black patch (somewhat smaller in female). Tail of peculiarly shaped feathers, each one narrow, tapering gradually to a sharp point.

Measurements *(C. u. urophasianus)*. *Adult male*: wing, 282–317.5 (299.4); tail, 241–285 (263.4); exposed culmen, 31.6–37 (35.1); tarsus, 52.4–58 (56.4). *Adult female*: wing, 247.5–279 (261.2) mm.

Field Marks. A very large greyish-brown grouse of the sagebrush plains with a large black patch on the abdomen, and a rather long tail composed of narrow pointed feathers (see Ring-necked Pheasant).

Habitat. Plains and intermontane valleys where sagebrush *(Artemisia)* flourishes.

Nesting. Nest, a shallow depression in the ground, usually sparsely lined with grass and usually sheltered by a sagebrush or clump of grass. *Eggs*, usually 7 to 9; olive-buff, evenly spotted with brown. Incubation probably 25 to 27 days (R.L. Patterson) is by the female.

Range. Locally distributed permanent resident, now reduced numerically, from central Washington, southern Idaho, Montana, south-eastern Alberta, southwestern Saskatchewan, and western North Dakota south to eastern California, Nevada, southern Utah, and western Colorado. Formerly extreme southern interior British Columbia and northern New Mexico.

Subspecies. *Centrocercus urophasianus urophasianus* (Bonaparte) is the only race known to occur in Canada today. Formerly *C. u. phaios* Aldrich occurred in southern British Columbia but is now extirpated.

Greater Prairie-Chicken

Grande Poule-des-prairies
Tympanuchus cupido (Linnaeus)
Total length: 42 to 47.5 cm
Plate 24

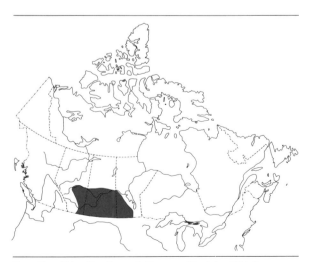

Breeding Distribution of Greater Prairie-Chicken

A medium-sized grouse with heavily barred body, short rounded tail, tarsi feathered to toes (bare behind), and in adults a group of stiff, narrow elongated feathers (poorly developed in female) over an inflatable sac on sides of neck. It is widely confused with Sharp-tailed Grouse, but the barred (instead of V-marked) under parts; the rounded, mostly dark (instead of pointed, mostly whitish) tail; and the elongated neck feathers (when present) readily mark the Greater Prairie-Chicken. Compared with the Ruffed Grouse, it has a shorter tail without a dark subterminal band, tarsi are feathered to toes, and the elongated neck feathers are very different from the soft, square-tipped ruffs of the Ruffed Grouse.

Measurements *(T. c. pinnatus)*. *Adult male*: wing, 215.5–234 (222.7); tail, 76.5–106 (95.7); exposed culmen, 15.8–19.9 (17.7); tarsus, 46.5–51 (49.8). *Adult female*: wing, 202.5–219 (213) mm.

Field Marks. The dark rounded tail (best seen in flight), *barred under parts*, and elongated neck feathers instantly separate it from the Sharp-tailed Grouse. The barred *upper parts* and shorter tail without a dark subterminal bar distinguish it from the Ruffed Grouse. Very different habitat preferences make confusion with female Spruce Grouse unlikely, but Spruce Grouse never have profuse whitish bars on secondaries and wing coverts.

Habitat. Natural grassland, broadly open to fairly brushy. Cultivated lands, especially grainfields, but near open to semi-brushy wild land. More extensive man-made clearings.

Range in Canada. In the interim between the disappearance of the bison from the prairies (about 1880) and the beginning of intensive settlement (about 1920), the natural prairie grasslands flourished as never before and probably never will again. Natural grassland is ideal for the Greater Prairie-Chicken and it too flourished in that period and declined rapidly when its habitat was destroyed by the settlements of man. Alberta (formerly ranged north to Lac la Biche. By the mid-1930s had practically disappeared. Recent sight records: near Coutts, 14 September 1965; near Mountain View, 5 March 1972). Saskatchewan (formerly north to Emma Lake and Nipawin regions. Now very rare: One shot at Leader, 3 November 1972. Sight records: Mortlach, 19 December 1971 and 16 April 1972; Avonlea, 20 September 1975; Ruthilda, 14 January 1976). Manitoba (formerly north to Peonan Point and Grand Rapids. Recent record: specimen killed near Langruth, autumn, about 1961). Ontario (formerly Essex County (1824–1836) and Kent County (until 1897). Reappeared about 1925 on St. Joseph's Island spreading to Manitoulin Island about 1938 but probably now extirpated there due to hybridization with Sharp-tailed Grouse. Has been reported in Thunder Bay area). For an interesting account of this species in the Prairie Provinces see A. Johnston and S. Smoliak (1976. Blue Jay, vol. 34, no. 3, pp. 153–156).

Nesting. Nest on the ground, a depression lined with grasses and similar available material, usually in tall grass clumps or low bushes. *Eggs*, average clutch 11 to 14; olive, lightly dotted or spotted with pale brown. Incubation (about 23 or 24 days) is by the female.

Range. Prairies of Alberta, Saskatchewan, and Manitoba, and southern Ontario south to northern Texas; also in southwestern Louisiana and coastal Texas. Formerly also on the Atlantic seaboard from eastern Massachusetts (possibly southern Maine) south to Maryland and Washington, D.C., and in Kentucky. Range now much less extensive than formerly.

Subspecies. *Tympanuchus cupido pinnatus* (Brewster).

Sharp-tailed Grouse

Gélinotte à queue fine
Tympanuchus phasianellus (Linnaeus)
Total length: 41.5 to 47 cm
Plate 24

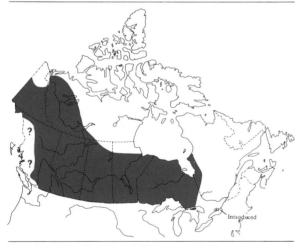

Breeding Distribution of Sharp-tailed Grouse

Range in Canada. Populations fluctuate numerically periodically. Breeding range peripheries subject to change and far from static: central and southern Yukon (north at least to Dawson, where sometimes common, and Mayo Landing); western Mackenzie (Fort Smith, Hay River, Fort Providence, Rae, Canol, St. Charles Rapids, Fort Good Hope; valley of

A medium-sized grouse with short pointed tail and V-marked under parts. It is widely miscalled "Prairie Chicken," but its V-marked under parts and pointed whitish (except central feathers) tail instantly distinguish it from the Greater Prairie-Chicken. Sage Grouse also has pointed tail but is much larger, tail is grey, and there is a large black patch on its abdomen. Other grouse have broader rounded tails.

Measurements *(T. p. phasianellus). Adult male*: wing, 199–212.5 (205.6); tail, 119–127.9 (124.4); exposed culmen, 14.2–19.6 (16.2); tarsus, 41.5–50 (44.9). *Adult female*: wing, 195–206 (198.9) mm.

Field Marks. A medium-sized grouse with short pointed tail. Separable from Greater Prairie-Chicken by V-marks (instead of conspicuous bars) on under parts, and in flight by white outer sides of tail (Greater Prairie-Chicken has dark rounded tail). Pointed white-sided tail separates it from most other grouse. Sage Grouse has a pointed grey tail, is much larger, and has a black belly patch. Ring-necked Pheasant has a long coloured (not white) tail.

Habitat. On the prairies: grassland, shrubby sandhills, coulees, creeks, brushy patches; in parklands: grassland and grain-bearing land near brush or open woodland; in coniferous areas: openings made by burns or man; muskegs and bogs.

Nesting. Nest on the ground, lined with grasses, is usually situated in a clump of grass or under or near a bush or tree in areas varying from open grassland to open woodland. *Eggs*, usually 10 to 13; brown or buff with or without fine dark-brown spots. Incubation probably lasts about 24 days and is by the female.

Range. Breeds from north-central Alaska and Yukon east to central-western Quebec and south through the western North American interior to eastern Oregon, northern Utah, Colorado, Minnesota, and northern Michigan. Formerly farther south. Northern populations irregularly migratory.

Lockhart and Anderson rivers, Conjuror Bay; occurrences reported north to Fort McPherson); northern and southern interior British Columbia (distribution local and poorly understood: Tagish Lake, Prophet River, and in southern interior west to Kleena Kleene region, north at least to Vanderhoof region, east to Baynes Lake and probably Elko); Alberta; Saskatchewan; Manitoba (Ilford, Amery, and probably Herchmer southward); western and northern Ontario (south to Lake of the Woods, Thunder Bay, Manitoulin Island, east to Lake Abitibi, and southeast very locally to Victoria, Lennox and Addington, and Prince Edward counties); and central-western Quebec (Rupert-House, probably north to Fort-George, breeding distribution poorly known).

Winters within much of breeding range but is partly migratory or nomadic in northernmost segment. Occasional irruptive movements occur involving large numbers as in autumn 1932 in eastern Ontario and western Quebec, when the species was recorded south to Gravenhurst, Ontario; and Pontiac and Papineau counties, Quebec (see L.L. Snyder, 1935. University of Toronto Studies, Biological Series 40). Old records east to Saguenay River and Québec.

Subspecies. (1) *Tympanuchus phasianellus phasianellus* (Linnaeus): central-western Quebec, north and central Ontario, northern Manitoba. (2) *T. p. kennicotti* (Suckley): western Mackenzie south to Great Slave Lake. (3) *T. p. caurus* (Friedmann): Yukon, northern and northwestern British Columbia, northern Alberta (to Peace River–Lesser Slave Lake region) and northwestern Saskatchewan (Lake Athabasca). Area of intergradation with *phasianellus* unknown. (4) *T. p. columbianus* (Ord): interior central and southern British Columbia. (5) *T. p. jamesi* (Lincoln): central and southern Alberta (except mountains), southern Saskatchewan, and extreme southwestern Manitoba (Whitewater Lake). (6) *T. p. campestris* (Ridgway): southern Manitoba (except southwest corner) north to northern Lake Winnipeg and The Pas, and contiguous parts of western Ontario (Lake of the Woods, Thunder Bay). No Manitoulin Island material available; therefore race unknown but probably *campestris*.

Remarks. The Sharp-tailed Grouse is the common grouse of the prairies. It is commonly miscalled "prairie chicken," but the Greater Prairie-Chicken is another species altogether, which has all but disappeared from the Canadian prairies.

In spring the Sharp-tails gather on ancestral dancing grounds, and at dawn the males perform a peculiar courtship dance, characterized by rapid stamping of the feet, lowered head, ruffled plumage, and a low booming sound, produced through the mouth by air from inflated purplish sacs on the sides of the neck.

Subfamily **Meleagridinae:** Turkeys

A small subfamily of two species confined to the New World. The domestic turkey, familiar to everyone, is derived from the Wild Turkey and illustrates the main characters of the group.

Wild Turkey

Dindon sauvage
Meleagris gallopavo Linnaeus
Total length: 91 to 122 cm
Figure 46

Range in Canada. Extirpated. Formerly a permanent resident (in fluctuating but sometimes fair numbers) in extreme southern Ontario, north to Lambton, Middlesex, Oxford, Brant, and Wentworth counties; also Simcoe County; range extended also eastward through parts of Halton, Peel, and York counties to Durham County. Apparently it was temporarily greatly reduced in unusually severe winters, as in 1842, but was able to recover while suitable habitat remained. Destruction of its timber habitat was undoubtedly the primary factor in its extirpation, and its decline kept pace with the depletion of the forests during the nineteenth century. Its final extirpation in Canada was completed probably about 1902 (C.H.D. Clarke, 1948. Sylva, vol. 4, no. 6, pp. 5–12; 24).

Reintroductions into southern Ontario have been mostly unsuccessful except perhaps at Ivy Lea. In Alberta, introductions in 1962 into Cypress Hills seem so far to have met with some success and have spread into the Saskatchewan side. Introduced locally in British Columbia (e.g. Sidney Island) and southern Manitoba (Pembina River valley and vicinity).

Like domestic turkey, but tail of Canadian wild birds tipped with brown instead of whitish or pale buff.

Measurements *(M. g. silvestris). Adult male*: wing, 480–550 (512.9); tail, 370–440 (397.2); culmen (from cere), 31–38 (34.8); tarsus, 146–181.5 (162.6). *Adult female*: wing, 382–438 (414.3) mm (Ridgway and Friedmann).

Habitat. Extensive mature deciduous forest.

Nesting. On the ground. *Eggs*, pale buff spotted with purplish grey. Incubation 28 days (A.C. Bent).

Range. Native to eastern and southwestern United States and Mexico; formerly southern Ontario. Now extirpated or reduced in much of former range.

Subspecies. *Meleagris gallopavo silvestris* Vieillot.

Remarks. Many people are surprised to learn that Wild Turkeys once inhabited even a small part of Canada. Here these large birds were on the northern periphery of their range, and their existence seems to have been somewhat precarious at best because of heavy mortality suffered in severest winters. As long as their hardwood-forest habitat remained and hunting pressure was light, the surviving population was able to recover from such winter kills. Once ever-widening settlement destroyed the forests, and as more and more unrestrained gunners roamed the land, the Wild Turkey in Ontario had no chance.

The Wild Turkey very closely resembles the domesticated variety. The latter originated from a Mexican subspecies, and can be distinguished from the wild bird by its whitish or pale-buffy tips to the upper tail coverts and tip of the tail. The Wild Turkey of Canada had the upper tail coverts and tail-tip rusty or chestnut.

In the Prairie Provinces, the Sandhill Crane is commonly miscalled "Wild Turkey," but the crane is an entirely different kind of bird.

Figure 46
Wild Turkey

Subfamily **Odontophorinae:** Quails

New World quails are small or smallish. They lack the spurs of pheasants, have a short bill in which the lower mandible has the cutting edge more or less serrated or "toothed." Some species have a conspicuous erect crown plume. All are non-migratory.

Northern Bobwhite

Colin de Virginie
Colinus virginianus (Linnaeus)
Total length: 24 to 27 cm
Plate 27

Breeding Distribution of Northern Bobwhite

Range in Canada. Permanent resident in extreme southern Ontario; north to southern Huron County, Hamilton. Range has fluctuated violently within historic times. With settlement and clearing of southern Ontario, it spread rapidly to a maximum in the 1840s (C.H.D. Clarke, 1954. Federation of Ontario Naturalists Bulletin 63, pp. 6–15) north to Kingston, Muskoka, and south Georgian Bay but now much decreased. Introduced into southwestern British Columbia (Huntingdon: where it persisted for a number of years before dying out). Introduced into many other parts of southern Canada, mostly without permanent success.

Male: White stripe above eye; throat patch white framed by black. In female the white of these areas is replaced by buff and the black by reddish brown. Upper parts predominantly reddish brown and flanks striped (not barred) in both sexes. Completely unfeathered tarsi and diminutive size separate it from Canadian grouse. Ruddy upper parts distinguish it from other quail. Striped (instead of barred) flanks eliminate confusion with the larger Chukar and the Gray Partridge.

Measurements *(C. v. virginianus)*. *Adult male*: wing, 109.8–116.2 (112.7); tail, 61.5–65.8 (63.4); exposed culmen, 13–14.9 (13.8); tarsus, 31.5–33.5 (32.6). *Adult female*: wing, 109.6–115 (112.5) mm.

Field Marks. Distinctive face markings and ruddy upper parts distinguish it from other quails; diminutive size from our grouse, partridges, and pheasants. Its whistled *bobwhite* is unmistakable.

Habitat. Cultivated areas growing grain and corn, or weedy abandoned farms near brushy patches or edges for shelter.

Nesting. Nest, a hollow in the ground, lined with grass and usually well concealed by an arch woven from the surrounding vegetation. *Eggs*, 14 to 16, more or less; plain dull-white. Incubation lasts about 23 to 24 days (various authorities) and is by both parents.

Range. Eastern Wyoming, southern Minnesota, central Michigan, extreme southern Ontario, New York, and Massachusetts south through eastern New Mexico and western Texas to Guatemala, southeastern United States and Cuba. Introduced in Washington.

Subspecies. *Colinus virginianus virginianus* (Linnaeus) is the native subspecies. Origin of British Columbia stock uncertain.

Remarks. As a destroyer of harmful insects, as a game bird, or just as a pleasant aspect of the countryside, the Bobwhite rates highly. Unfortunately it is not widely distributed in Canada.

California Quail

Colin de Californie
Callipepla californica (Shaw)
Total length: 24 to 27 cm
Plate 27

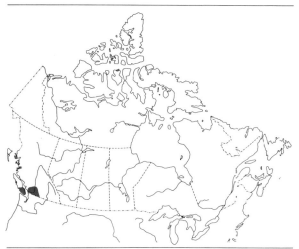

Breeding Distribution of California Quail

Range in Canada. Introduced and well established locally for many years in southern British Columbia: southern Vancouver Island (Victoria, Comox); Vancouver; Okanagan valley (Osoyoos to Vernon); Keremeos; Cache Creek to Twenty Mile House.

A small, chicken-like, brown and blue-grey bird with a black forward-curved plume standing up from the crown. To be looked for in Canada only in southern British Columbia. Male has jet-black throat with white border, white streaks on flanks, scaly abdomen with small chestnut patch. Female similar but lacks the black-and-white head pattern, has smaller crown plume, and shows little, if any, chestnut on abdomen. Bobwhite has no crown plume and is very differently coloured. Mountain Quail has chestnut throat-patch, conspicuously barred flanks, and the crown plume is longer, *straight*, not forward-curved.

Measurements. *Adult male*: wing, 105.6–114.5 (110.5); tail, 76–95.5 (85.6); exposed culmen, 11.8–13.8 (12.4); tarsus, 30–33.7 (31.9). *Adult female*: wing, 105.6–114 (110.1) mm.

Field Marks. As above.

Habitat. Tall shrubbery or low trees interspersed with less extensive open areas (grassy or weedy ground for foraging); hence frequent about man's dwellings, gardens, and parks; mainly in low country.

Nesting. Nest, a hollow in the ground lined with grass or leaves, usually more or less hidden by shrubbery. *Eggs*, usually 10 to 18 (average 14) are creamy white to buffy, more or less irregularly marked with brown. Incubation about 22 days, the greater part by the female.

Range. Oregon and western Nevada south to southern Baja California. Introduced into southern British Columbia, Washington, and Utah.

Subspecies. Parent stocks appear to include more than one race, now mixed. It seems best not to try to refer present stock to any one race.

Mountain Quail

Colin des montagnes
Oreortyx pictus (Douglas)
Total length: 27 to 29 cm
Plate 27

Breeding Distribution of Mountain Quail

Range in Canada. Scarce local resident in extreme southwestern British Columbia where probably introduced many years ago, possibly native, but history obscure. Vancouver Island (small numbers present for over a century, mainly in hills between Victoria and Sooke Harbour; reported north to Duncan). Formerly southwestern mainland (three shot on Vedder Mountain, 26 September 1921 but no recent reports, probably extirpated).

Unmistakable. A small chicken-like bird distinguished from other quail by a long *straight* crown plume, chestnut throat, bold white bars on chestnut flanks. Sexes similar.

Measurements *(O. p. palmeri)*. *Adult male*: wing, 129–136 (131.2); tail, 71–82 (76.5); culmen from base, 15.7–17.9 (16.9); tarsus, 35–37 (36.3). *Adult female*: wing, 125–134 (130.2) mm (Ridgway and Friedmann).

Habitat. Mountains and hills but little definite information is available on preferences of this introduced species in its restricted range in Canada.

Nesting. A depression in the ground scantily lined with grass or leaves. *Eggs*, 6 to 15 (average 9 to 10) in United States, are pale cream to buff, unmarked. Incubation period 24 to 25 days (P.A. Johnsgard).

Range. Washington and southwestern Idaho south to northern Baja California. Introduced to southwestern British Columbia and Washington.

Subspecies. *Oreortyx pictus palmeri* Oberholser.

Order **Gruiformes:**
Cranes, Rails, and Allies

Family **Rallidae:**
Rails, Gallinules, Coots

Number of Species in Canada: 10

Rails are predominantly marsh birds. They are expert skulkers and move among the marsh vegetation with mouselike dexterity. When approached, they usually prefer to run instead of fly. When they do fly, flight is weak and slow, and the bird quickly drops back into the cover of the marsh. They are often noisy, especially at night, and are far more often heard than seen. Their laterally compressed bodies, enabling them to pass through small spaces in dense marsh vegetation, have given rise to the expression "thin as a rail."

The legs are strong, the front toes long and slender; wings are short, rounded, and rather weak; tail short; bill variable from short to long in the different species. Food is largely seeds, insects, and snails.

Yellow Rail

Râle jaune
Coturnicops noveboracensis (Gmelin)
Total length: 15 to 19 cm
Plate 26

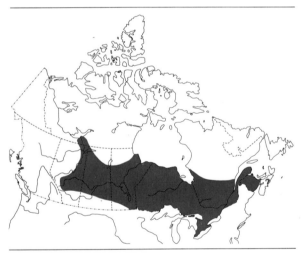

Breeding Distribution of Yellow Rail

Range in Canada. Breeds very locally in southern Mackenzie (Fort Resolution, Little Buffalo River, Salt River); Alberta (Red Deer, Driedmeat Lake, Lake Athabasca region); Saskatchewan (Jackfish Lake, Medstead, Scentgrass Lake, Maidstone, Lloydminster, Battleford, Last Mountain Lake, Qu'Appelle valley, possibly Regina); Manitoba (Churchill, York Factory, Reader Lake, Overflowing River, Brandon, Whitemouth, Rennie); Ontario (widely but very locally north to marshes bordering coasts of James and Hudson bays, including Ship Sands Island, south to Lake St. Clair and Holland Marsh, and perhaps Ottawa; apparently absent

A small short-billed buffy rail, similar in outline to the Sora. Breast buffy, throat light. Back marked with fine *white crossbars*. Separable from Sora by white tips of the secondaries and by fine white crossbarring on back (Sora has white longitudinal stripes). Downies are black but differ from downy Soras in lacking orange bristles on throat.

Measurements. *Adult male*: wing, 73–93 (86.7); tail, 27.5–38 (33.3); exposed culmen, 11.5–15.5 (13.9); tarsus, 21–27.5 (23.7). *Adult female*: wing, 75.5–89 (84.2) mm (Ridgway and Friedmann).

Field Marks. Short bill distinguishes it from other rails of regular occurrence in Canada except the Sora. Adult Soras have a grey breast and a black throat and face. Immatures of the two species are difficult to distinguish in the field except in flight during which the Yellow Rail shows a white wing patch (white tips to secondaries) or at close range when the fine white *crossbarring* on the upper parts of the Yellow can be seen. A common call is a clicking *tick-tick, tick-tick-tick* (in twos and threes) easy to recognize once learned.

Habitat. Grassy (or grasslike) marshes. In migration also grainfields and hayfields.

Nesting. Nest, in a grassy marsh, is a well-concealed cup of finer grasses or sedges in a tussock or on a mat of dead grass. *Eggs*, usually 8 to 10; a rich buff speckled mostly about larger end with reddish brown. Incubation period about 18 days (R.D. Elliot).

Range. Locally from Canada (see Range in Canada) south to North Dakota, Minnesota, Wisconsin, Michigan, Ohio, and Massachusetts; also eastern California and, apparently, in Valley of Toluca, Mexico. Winters from Oregon to California and in the Gulf States.

Subspecies. *Coturnicops noveboracensis noveboracensis* (Gmelin).

from large areas); southern Quebec (near Gaspé, Sainte-Anne-de-la-Pocatière; possibly north on James Bay to Fort-George); and New Brunswick (near Milltown, Midgic). Possibly breeds in Nova Scotia (Noel), but evidence not completely satisfactory.

Rarely reported migrant in Nova Scotia (Wolfville region, Meadowville, Little River, Glace Bay). Casual in Labrador (Hamilton Inlet).

Black Rail

[**Black Rail**. Râle noir. *Laterallus jamaicensis* (Gmelin). Hypothetical. Recorded from British Columbia, southern Ontario, southern Quebec, and Nova Scotia. Most supposed records are based on mistaken identifications of the black young of other rails or on old specimens, the origin of which is uncertain. Plausible sight records are from Rondeau, Ontario (J.L. Baillie, 1951. Audubon Field Notes, vol. 5, no. 4, p. 253), and Hatley, Quebec (H. Mousley, 1921. Auk, vol. 38, no. 1, pp. 56–57).]

Corn Crake

Râle de genêts
Crex crex (Linnaeus)
Total length: ca. 26.5 cm

Status in Canada. Accidental. A straggler from Europe. Specimens are from Baffin Island (Cape Dorset, 24 September 1928); Newfoundland (two evidently from St. Shotts: one in 1859; one 28 September 1928); and Nova Scotia (near Pictou, October, about 1874).

A short-billed buffy rail with blackish streaking on upper parts, chestnut wing coverts, and chestnut bars on flanks. Its much larger size and the extensive chestnut on its wing distinguish it from our native short-billed rails.

Clapper Rail

Râle gris
Rallus longirostris Boddaert
Total length: 35.5 to 40 cm
Plate 26

Status in Canada. Casual in New Brunswick (Grand Manan, 17 January 1952; Kent Island, 1 April 1953; near Alma, 4 October 1954); Nova Scotia (Lawrencetown, 10 May 1892, and October 1893. Sight records: Sable River, 2 September 1957; Brier Island, 23 September 1957); and Newfoundland (St. John's, 22 September 1969).

A large long-billed rail, likely to be confused only with the King Rail. The Clapper Rail's markings are similar but less conspicuous; colours usually considerably paler and more greyish; dimensions in average slightly smaller. These characters separate most specimens, but some individuals are perplexingly like King Rails and should be identified by specialists. Most races frequent salt marshes where King Rails are seldom found.

Measurements *(R. l. crepitans)*. *Adult male*: wing, 142.5–159.5 (151.1); tail, 55–69 (64.6); exposed culmen, 55–69.5 (63.3); tarsus, 48–56 (51.7). *Adult female*: wing, 135.5–160 (146.8) mm (Ridgway and Friedmann).

Range. Coasts from California south to Ecuador and northwestern Peru; and from Connecticut southward coastally through southern United States, Mexico, Central America to Sao Paulo, Brazil; also the West Indies and in freshwater marshes in Distrito Federal, Mexico, and the lower Colorado valley.

Subspecies. *Rallus longirostris crepitans* Gmelin. Possibly one or more other races are represented by the specimens, but they have not all been examined by the writer.

King Rail

Râle élégant
Rallus elegans Audubon
Total length: 39 to 48 cm
Plate 26

Range in Canada. Breeds in extreme southern Ontario (St. Clair flats, Point Abino, near Welland, Port Rowan, Long Point, Hamilton, Toronto, Terra Cotta). Non-breeding birds recorded in Ontario (Crane Lake on Bruce Peninsula; Port Perry; Nottawasaga River, Simcoe County; Kingston; Ottawa). Casual or accidental in Manitoba (Long Lake, 26 October 1921); Quebec (Sabrevois, October 1899, Contrecoeur, 3–4 June 1972; Île-Verte, 29 May 1973); New Brunswick (Point Lepreau, 21 September 1952); Prince Edward Island (Mount Stewart, 21 December 1957); and Newfoundland (near St. John's, 20 October 1935). Casual in winter in southern Ontario (Point Pelee, Toronto, La Salle, Kingston).

A large, long-billed rail. Similar in colour and outline to the Virginia Rail but cheeks not grey. The King Rail's much larger size separates it from all other rails of regular occurrence in Canada (but see Clapper Rail).

    Measurements. *Adult male*: wing, 159–177 (163.4); tail, 56–72.5 (65.9); exposed culmen, 58–65.5 (62.5); tarsus, 52–64 (58.4). *Adult female*: wing, 147–162 (154.3) mm (Ridgway and Friedmann).

    Habitat. Freshwater marshes, but more inclined than most rails to wander onto adjacent fields.

    Nesting. Nest, a well-made structure of marsh vegetation supported a few inches above water in clumps of marsh vegetation or bushes; sometimes a grass-lined scrape in moist ground in or near a marsh. *Eggs*, usually 5 to 11; pale buff with small spots of several shades of brown. Incubation 21 to 24 days, by both sexes.

    Range. Breeds from eastern Nebraska, central Minnesota, southern Michigan, southern Ontario, central New York, and (rarely) Massachusetts, south to southern Texas and Florida; also Cuba and Isle of Pines. Winters mainly in southern United States and Cuba; occasionally much farther north.

    Subspecies. *Rallus elegans elegans* Audubon.

Virginia Rail

Râle de Virginie
Rallus limicola Vieillot
Total length: 23 to 25.5 cm
Plate 26

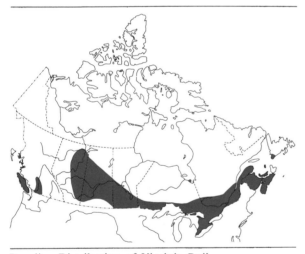

Breeding Distribution of Virginia Rail

Range in Canada. Breeds in southern British Columbia (Vancouver Island, Tatton Lake, 150 Mile House); Alberta (definitely breeding at Vermilion, Brooks, and Czar; observations at Glenevis, Many Island Lake, Millet, Lac Sainte-Anne, Spruce Grove; probably at Fort Chipewyan—specimen in breeding condition 30 June 1945); central and southern Saskatchewan (Regina, Moose Mountain, Yorkton district, Dafoe, Simpson, Kutawagan Lake, Kazan Lake, Prince Albert, Hudson Bay); southern Manitoba (Lyleton, Hillside Beach, Winnipeg, Dog Lake, Indian Bay, Riding Mountain;

A small cinnamon-breasted rail with long slender reddish bill and grey cheeks. Our other long-billed rails, the King and the Clapper, are obviously much larger with more than twice its body bulk. Our other small rails have stubby bills. Adult-size young in late summer are mostly black.

    Measurements. *Adult male*: wing, 101–107.9 (105.4); tail, 40–48.6 (44.5); exposed culmen, 35.3–41.8 (39.9); tarsus, 33.1–38.2 (36.4). *Adult female*: wing, 94.2–102.2 (98.1) mm.

    Field Marks. As above.

    Habitat. Freshwater, bulrush, cattail, or sedge marshes.

    Nesting. Nest, in a marsh, a loosely woven basket of marsh vegetation with grass lining, attached to stalks of a clump of vegetation a little above the mud or water. *Eggs*, 7 to 12; very pale-buff to whitish, sparingly spotted with reddish brown. They are paler and less heavily spotted than those of the Sora. Incubation 19 to 20 days (L.H. Walkinshaw) by both sexes.

recorded in summer and probably breeds north to Halcrow Lake near The Pas and to Moose and Cedar lakes); central and southern Ontario (north at least to Wabigoon, Maskinonge Bay, Thunder Bay, Bigwood, Ottawa; recorded in summer, probably breeds north to Kapuskasing, Timmins, Cochrane; one report of breeding at North Point); southern Quebec (Hatley; Montréal, Senneville, Québec, Saint-Fulgence on Saguenay River, Gaspé, Madeleine Islands); New Brunswick (Grand Manan; Midgic); Nova Scotia (sparingly: Cumberland County); Prince Edward Island (Boughton River); and southwestern Newfoundland (Codroy valley).

Winters in small numbers in southern (mainly southwestern) British Columbia, and casually southern Ontario and Nova Scotia.

Sora

Râle de Caroline
Porzana carolina (Linnaeus)
Total length: 20 to 30 cm
Plate 26

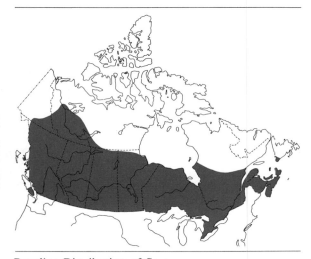

Breeding Distribution of Sora

Range in Canada. Breeds in southern Yukon (near Whitehorse); British Columbia (Comeau Lake near Atlin, southward and west to southern Vancouver Island); southern Mackenzie (Mills Lake; Great Slave Lake; Fort Simpson; Nahanni National Park; Willow Lake River. Probably farther north: sight records of three, Brackett Lake, 10 July 1958; of four, 32 km east of Fort Franklin, 15 July 1958; and of one east of Norman Wells); Alberta; Saskatchewan; Manitoba (north to Churchill); Ontario; central-western and southern Quebec (Rupert-House, Grande rivière de la Baleine, Lake Saint-Jean, Godbout, Montréal, Hatley, Gaspé, Madeleine Islands); New Brunswick; Nova Scotia; Prince Edward Island; and Newfoundland (Codroy valley, probably elsewhere).

Casual in southern Labrador (Sandwich Bay, Battle Harbour); southeastern Quebec (Harrington-Harbour); and Queen Charlotte Islands (Masset), British Columbia. Occasional in winter in southwestern British Columbia (Lulu Island, Pitt Meadows).

Range. Breeds from southern Canada south locally to southern South America (Straits of Magellan). Winters mainly from southern United States southward; irregularly farther north.

Subspecies. *Rallus limicola limicola* Vieillot.

A chunky small rail with short yellowish bill. *Throat and front of face, black. Breast grey.* Upper parts olive brown, inconspicuously streaked with black and narrowly (feather edges) with white. Young are similar but have no black on throat or face, and no grey on breast: throat white, breast light brown. Young Soras resemble Yellow Rail but are larger; white streaks on back are longitudinal (not transverse), and there is no white on the tips of the secondaries. Downies are black with orange bristles on throat.

Measurements. *Adult male*: wing, 100.4–108.9 (104.8); tail, 40.5–50.6 (45.7); exposed culmen, 21–24.1 (22.2); tarsus, 31.2–36.5 (33.8). *Adult female*: wing, 97.6–108.4 (101.9) mm.

Field Marks. Short yellow bill eliminates all rails of regular occurrence in Canada except Yellow Rail, but grey breast, black throat and face of adult Sora distinguish it. Vocally a far-carrying whinny on a descending scale is characteristic (see Yellow Rail).

Habitat. In breeding season freshwater or brackish marshes. In migration sometimes also salt marshes.

Nesting. Nest, a shallow basket woven of dead marsh vegetation attached to stalks of marsh plants; sometimes a heap of marsh vegetation; sometimes on ground in grass near marsh or pond. *Eggs*, usually 8 to 13; buffy spotted with browns. Eggs are darker and more heavily spotted than those of Virginia Rail. Incubation 16 to 20 days (L.H. Walkinshaw) by both sexes.

Range. Breeds from Canada south to northern Baja California, Nevada, southern New Mexico, northern Missouri, Ohio, West Virginia, and Pennsylvania. Winters mainly from southern United States south to the West Indies, Colombia, and Peru; occasionally farther north in the United States.

Purple Gallinule

Gallinule violacée
Porphyrula martinica (Linnaeus)
Total length: 30.5 to 35.5 cm
Plate 26

Status in Canada. Casual visitor to southeastern Canada: southern Ontario (near Toronto, 8 April 1892; Guelph; St. Clair flats; Moosonee, 18 October 1971; Ottawa, 29 December 1973 and 25 April 1974); southern Quebec (Québec, mid-September 1909, October 1930; Stoke, 18 October 1979); New Brunswick (near Saint John, 6 April 1881; Gagetown, September 1880; Quaco, September 1881; Grand Manan); Nova Scotia (Halifax: 30 January 1870, April 1889, January 1896; Chezzetcook: January 1896; Scaterie Island: ca. 1 July 1915; Canard: about 1 May 1927); and Newfoundland (Lamaline; Torbay, 24 May 1933; Burgeo, 10 May 1945; St. John's, May 1948; Iona, May 1948; Broad Cove, May 1933; Millertown, 17 April 1953; Badger, 8 November 1950; Rencontre West, 8 November 1951; Port Rexton, October 1959); and Labrador (Mud Lake, near Northwest River, 12 October 1970).

Adults somewhat similar to Common Moorhen (next species), but head, neck, and breast deep purple (looks black at distance), back and wing coverts glossy olive-green, under tail coverts *all* white. Frontal shield bluish. Autumn immatures have no purple on them; the head, neck, and breast being brownish, becoming whitish on throat and abdomen, but the upper body showing at least some olive green. Adults are unmistakable. Immatures differ from immature Common Moorhens in having more greenish colour of upper body, more oval-shaped (less elongated) nostrils, no black (all white) in under tail coverts, middle toe not longer than tarsus. Lack of scallops on toes separates them from coots.

Range. Breeds from the Gulf States and South Carolina south through Mexico, Central America, and the West Indies to Uruguay, northern Argentina, Brazil, and Peru.

Common Moorhen

(formerly Florida Gallinule)

Poule-d'eau
Gallinula chloropus (Linnaeus)
Total length: 30.5 to 37.5 cm
Plate 26

Figure 47
Foot of
a) American Coot
b) Common Moorhen

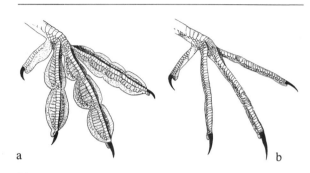

Breeding Distribution of Common Moorhen

Range in Canada. Summer resident and transient. Breeds from southern Ontario (Point Pelee north at least to southern Georgian Bay and Ottawa); southwestern Quebec (Sorel, Montréal, La Prairie, Magog); New Brunswick (rarely Germantown); and Nova Scotia (locally: Amherst Point Bird Sanctuary).

Casual in British Columbia (photo: Iona Island, May–June 1981); southern Manitoba (Sandy Bay Indian Reserve: 12 July 1931); central Ontario (north shore Lake Superior; Lake Nipissing); eastern Quebec (Gaspé, Anticosti Island); New Brunswick (Grand Manan, Dick's Lake, South Bay); Nova Scotia (Halifax, Canard River, Yarmouth, Sable Island); Newfoundland (St. John's, St. Shotts, Colinet); and Prince Edward Island (sight record: Mount Stewart 14 September 1972).

Adults: Head and neck black, becoming slate on breast and flanks. Flanks streaked with white. Back brown to brownish olive. Outer under tail coverts white, inner ones black. Middle of abdomen whitish. Frontal shield and bill red, bill tipped yellowish. Toes long (middle toe longer than tarsus), without webs or scallop-shaped lobes. Nostrils narrow, elongated. *Immatures*: Similar but paler and duller, throat whitish flecked with black, under parts more mixed with white, no red on bill. *Downies* are blackish with white beard and reddish bill. Gallinules and moorhens (see also Purple Gallinule) are separable from coots in any plumage by their unlobed toes (Figure 47).

Measurements *(G. c. cachinnans)*. *Adult male*: wing, 171.9–185 (177.9); tail, 68–77 (72.1); culmen (from base of frontal shield), 29.2–34.6 (31.9); tarsus, 55–58 (56.9). *Adult female*: wing, 162–172.5 (165.7) mm.

Field Marks. A blackish-grey freshwater marsh bird with chicken-like red bill and white line along flanks. The red bill distinguishes it from coots; the white flank-line separates it from both coots and Purple Gallinule. Its small head and the habit of bobbing the head in time with each foot stroke when swimming distinguish gallinules, moorhens, and coots from small ducks (except the very differently marked Wood Duck, which also characteristically bobs its head while swimming).

Habitat. Freshwater marshes of various sizes, usually where there is at least a small area of open water; waterside vegetation on edges of lakes, ponds, or slow rivers.

Nesting. More or less colonial. Nest, often a basket-like platform of marsh vegetation attached to living marsh plants above or at water-level. Usually other nestlike platforms are built nearby. *Eggs*, usually 9 to 12; buffy, irregularly dotted and spotted with browns. Incubation, about 21 days, by both sexes (A.C. Bent).

Range. Except for colder parts of the world, nearly cosmopolitan but not in Australia. In Western Hemisphere breeds in California (locally) and central Arizona; and from Nebraska, Iowa, lower Michigan, southern Ontario, southwestern Quebec, and Massachusetts south through Mexico, Central America, and the West Indies to northern Chile and Argentina. Winters mainly from the Gulf States and California and Arizona southward.

Subspecies. *Gallinula chloropus cachinnans* Bangs.

Eurasian Coot

(European Coot)

Foulque macroule
Fulica atra Linnaeus
Total length: 38 cm

Status in Canada. Accidental in Labrador
(Separation Point in Sandwich Bay, mid-
December 1927; Tangnaivik Island in Anakta-
lak Bay, December 1927), and Newfoundland
(Exploits Harbour, December 1927).

Similar to American Coot and most easily distinguished from it by
colour of all under tail coverts, which are slaty or blackish like rest of
under parts instead of mostly white.

  Range. Breeds across Eurasia, including Iceland; in northern
Africa, Australia, Tasmania, and New Guinea. Accidental in North
America.

  Subspecies. *Fulica atra atra* Linnaeus.

American Coot

Foulque d'Amérique
Fulica americana Gmelin
Total length: 33 to 40.5 cm
Plate 26

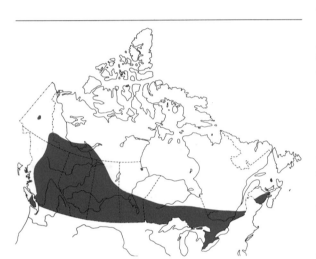

Breeding Distribution of American Coot

Range in Canada. Breeds in southeastern
Yukon (Swan Lake); British Columbia (north
to Vanderhoof and Fort Nelson region; west to
southern Vancouver Island); Alberta; southwestern Mackenzie (Nahanni National Park,
Little Buffalo River, 16 km north of Yellowknife); Saskatchewan (northern Lake Athabasca, Crean Lake, Cumberland House); Manitoba (north to Moose and Cedar lakes; recently
a few have nested at Churchill); western and
southern Ontario (western Lake Erie north to
Red Lake, Lillabelle Lake, and Ottawa;
summer records on southern James Bay);
southern Quebec (uncommon, local: near
Kilmar; Montréal region; Cap-Tourmente;
Madeleine Islands); southern New Brunswick
(scarce, local: Williamstown Lake, Harvey
Station; possibly Midgic); Prince Edward Island
(Conway Pond); and Nova Scotia (Cumberland
County: Missaguash Bog; Amherst Point Bird
Sanctuary).

  Winters in southern British Columbia
(Okanagan valley, Arrow Lake, and on
the coast including Vancouver Island) and
occasionally in southern Ontario.

Distinguished from gallinules and moorhens by broad scallop-like lobes
on toes (Figure 47). *Adults*: Body, even dark-slate becoming black on
head and neck. Wing edged narrowly with white and secondaries with
white tips (usually hidden by folded wing). Outer under tail coverts
white, inner ones blackish. Bill whitish with spot of chestnut near tip;
frontal shield mostly chestnut. *Immature (early autumn)*: Similar to
adults but paler; under parts more mixed with white. *Downies* blackish
with bristle-like orange down on throat, cheeks, neck, back, and wings.
Under plumage more or less grey-tipped. Bill reddish.

  Measurements. *Adult male*: wing, 189–199.8 (195.9); tail, 51.6–57.2
(54.7); culmen (from base of frontal shield), 31.9–39.2 (34.5); tarsus,
56–64.2 (58.1). *Adult female*: wing, 168–193 (182.5) mm.

  Field Marks. American Coot and Common Moorhen are dark-grey
(often look black) marsh birds, the size of small ducks but with
chicken-like bills, much smaller heads than ducks, and a habit of bobbing the head with each swimming stroke. American Coot's white bill
and lack of white line along the flanks separate it from Common
Moorhen. In flight the American Coot shows a white line on hind edge
(secondaries) of wing. The name "Coot" is often erroneously applied to
scoters.

  Habitat. Mainly freshwater marshes, ponds, sloughs, lakes, and
slow rivers. Although often frequenting the same marsh as moorhens,
coots tend to use broader expanses of open water.

  Nesting. Usually more or less colonial. Nest on a mass of marsh
vegetation, either floating and anchored to living marsh plants or resting
on the marsh. *Eggs*, usually 8 to 12 but often more or less; buffy to
greyish, thickly and evenly fine-spotted with dark brown. Incubation, 23
to 24 days (G.W. Gullion), is by both sexes.

Casual in northern Ontario (Fort Severn); central and eastern Quebec (Pierce Lake, Mingan, Tête-à-la-Baleine, Johan-Beetz Bay, Mécatina Island, Vieux-Fort, Anticosti Island); Labrador (Table Bay); Newfoundland (about seventeen specimen records through 1956, mostly autumn). Accidental in District of Franklin (Bellot Strait).

Range. Breeds from Canada southward through the United States, West Indies, Mexico, and Central America; in the northern Andes of South America; and on most of the Hawaiian Islands. Winters from Maryland and southern British Columbia southward.

Subspecies. *Fulica americana americana* Gmelin.

Family **Aramidae:** Limpkins

Number of Species in Canada: 1

This New World family is in many ways intermediate between the crane and the rail families. It contains only one species.

Limpkin

Courlan
Aramus guarauna (Linnaeus)
Total length: 66 to 71 cm

Status in Canada. Accidental in Nova Scotia: In 1954 or 1955, on Brier Island, one was rescued from a large house cat by Wickerson Lent. He carried the bird to his home in Westport, where he revived it and later released it. Thus Mr. Lent had a specimen in hand and I have no doubt as to his ability to identify it. There are two sight records, both of single birds on Sable Island, one on 12 September 1964 and the other on 27 November 1967.

Sexes similar. Bill twice as long as head. Culmen straight for basal two-thirds but gently downcurved toward the tip, thus suggesting an ibis. General coloration olive brownish, the head, neck, interscapulars, upper wing coverts, breast, and abdomen streaked with white. Legs blackish olive. Iris brown.

Distinctions. The general coloration and long legs might suggest an immature night-heron but night-herons never have a downcurved bill. The bold white streaking separates it from the North American ibises. In flight, the wing motion shows a cranelike upflicking of the wing tips.

Range. Southeastern Georgia through Florida to the Greater Antilles and from Mexico to central Argentina and Uruguay.

Subspecies. Undeterminable but probably the northern race *Aramus guarauna pictus* (Meyer).

Family **Gruidae:** Cranes

Number of Species in Canada: 3

Large, long-necked, long-legged birds with rather long straight bills. Superficially they resemble herons, but they differ from them in having no partition between the nostrils; shorter hind toe, which is elevated above the level of the other toes; middle toenail with no comb-like inner edge; adults (in Canadian species) with the forehead bare; plumage denser and firmer; tertials, very long and curving down over the primaries.

In flight, cranes carry the neck straight and extended; herons fold the neck in an S-shape.

Sandhill Crane

(Little Brown Crane)

Grue du Canada
Grus canadensis (Linnaeus)
Total length: 86 to 122 cm
Plate 26

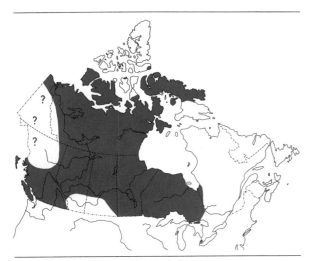

Breeding Distribution of Sandhill Crane

Range in Canada. Transient and summer resident. Breeds or formerly bred (extirpated from much of southern parts of former range) from Banks Island (Mercy Bay, Kellett River, Sachs Harbour), Victoria Island (Holman), and southeastern Devon Island (Dundas Harbour) southward through the Arctic Archipelago and southeast to Cumberland Peninsula of Baffin Island; northern Yukon (north coast, breeding unknown in interior); Mackenzie; Keewatin (south to McConnell River and mouth of Thlewiaza River); Southampton Island; southern and coastal British Columbia (Lulu Island; northern Vancouver Island; Queen Charlotte Islands; parklands of the Cariboo; Kleena Kleene region; Quesnel region; formerly Okanagan valley, Sumas Prairie, Pitt Meadows); Alberta (now mainly from Athabasca valley north; recently Rocky Mountain House. Formerly south to Innisfail, Spotted Lake, Sedgwick); Saskatchewan (now mostly central and northern parts; formerly south to Touchwood Hills, Saltcoats, Balgonie, Grayson, Wauchope; recently resumed breeding at Kutawagan Lake); Manitoba (formerly Shoal Lake, Sperling, Eden; Lake St. Martin in 1933, but present status unknown there; nesting not definitely known in northern Manitoba, but there are breeding season occurrences near Churchill and Ilford); and Ontario (Hudson Bay lowlands, Kinoje Lake, Rainy River district, Cochrane, Manitoulin Island; noted in summer between Kapuskasing and Moosonee, and near Big Sandy Lake; formerly bred in southern Ontario: Lake St. Clair); and western Quebec (Boatswain Bay). Recorded in summer on Melville Island (Bailey Point), N.W.T.

Migration primarily west of Hudson Bay. As a transient (in addition to breeding range) it is

A large heron-like bird of general slaty coloration, usually more or less stained with rusty (adventitious in adults), black wing tips, and in adults a bare (except for sparse black hairlike feathers) reddish patch on forehead and upper face. Young more brownish and without bare forehead patch. Most likely to be confused with Great Blue Heron (which is widely miscalled "crane"), but the Sandhill Crane is readily distinguished by (1) its more even grey coloration lacking any decided stripes or other pattern, (2) broad perforate nostrils (one can readily look through them to other side of bill), (3) the much shorter hind toe, which is elevated above the level of the others, and (4) the middle toenail, which is not pectinate (see Figure 20).

Measurements *(G. c. canadensis). Adult male*: wing, 427.5–474 (460.9); tail, 146–183.5 (170.3); exposed culmen, 88–102 (95.6); tarsus, 160–206 (187.9). *Adult female*: wing, 423–456 (440.3) mm.

Field Marks. Heron-like appearance, large size, even slaty coloration, and at closer range, reddish forehead. The Great Blue Heron is widely miscalled "crane," but true cranes including the present species are easily distinguished from all herons, even at great distances, by the crane habit of flying with outstretched neck and noticeably quicker wing upstrokes. The voice of the Sandhill also is distinctive—a vibrant, far-carrying *gar-oo-ooo*.

Habitat. In breeding season, marshes, bogs, broad flat arctic valleys, marshy tundra, and neighbouring vicinities. In migration it visits fields, marshes, and shallow-water edges of lakes.

Nesting. Nest, a mass of aquatic vegetation in shallow water or a depression in the ground, often lined with grass or willow sticks, on hummocks, sometimes on a muskrat house. *Eggs*, usually 2; buff to olive buff, spotted and blotched with browns. Incubation, by both parents, requires about 29 to 30 days (L.H. Walkinshaw), or perhaps a little more.

Range. Breeds from northeastern Siberia, northern Alaska, and middle arctic Canada (Banks and Devon islands), south locally to northeastern California, Nevada, Wyoming, Colorado, South Dakota, and Michigan; also from southern Mississippi, Alabama, and Georgia south through Florida to Cuba and the Isle of Pines. Winters from southern United States south to central Mexico and Cuba.

found through Yukon, interior British Columbia, and southern parts of the Prairie Provinces (locally large flocks). Spectacular concentrations at north end of Last Mountain Lake, Quill Lakes and Kindersley–South Saskatchewan River region, Saskatchewan, in southward migration. Rare transient in southern Ontario (e.g., Guelph, Toronto, Rondeau, Beaumaris; also Thunder Bay region) and southern Quebec (Lennoxville). Casual in Prince Edward Island (specimens: Alexandra, 22 September 1905; Earnscliffe, 25 October 1905), New Brunswick (sight record: Point Lepreau), Newfoundland (specimen: Pouch Cove, 20 September 1971), and Nova Scotia (Port Williams, Great Village, and Little Dover).

Subspecies. (1) *Grus canadensis canadensis* (Linnaeus), a small-sized race, breeds across the northernmost parts of the range. (2) *G. c. tabida* (Peters), the largest race, breeds mainly in northern U.S.A., but range extends northward into southern British Columbia. It bred formerly in extreme southern Ontario. (3) *G. c. rowani* Walkinshaw was recently described (1966. Canadian Field-Naturalist, vol. 79, no. 3, pp. 181–184). It is intermediate in size between the two foregoing subspecies but has disproportionately long legs in relation to the wings. Its breeding range is geographically between the ranges of (1) and (2) and is outlined preliminarily by J.W. Aldrich (1979. Proceedings 1978 Crane Workshop, pp. 139–148) as "the Aspen Parklands and Boreal Forest Life Areas at least from central southern Mackenzie District and central Alberta eastward through northern and middle Saskatchewan, middle Manitoba, and northern Ontario to James Bay."

Common Crane

Grue cendrée
Grus grus (Linnaeus)
Total length: about 104 cm
Plate 26

Status in Canada. Has appeared in Alberta on three occasions: one near Cavendish, 11–20 December 1957; Stirling Lake, south of Lethbridge, 20 March 1958; and near Athabasca, 19 September 1958 (W. Wishart and F. Sharp, 1959. Auk, vol. 76, no. 3, p. 358). Identifiable photographs were taken. It is not known whether these concerned the same individual or the same as that seen in Alaska on 24 April 1958 (B. Kessel and R.W. Kelly, 1958. Auk, vol. 75, no. 4, p. 465). Both Sharp and Wishart (in litt.) found the Alberta bird wary and there seems little to suggest that it was an escaped captive.

A slate-grey crane most likely to be mistaken for the Sandhill Crane. The Common is readily separable, however, by a conspicuous white stripe on the side of the head and upper neck, which contrasts with black face and throat; blackish tail.

Whooping Crane

Grue blanche d'Amérique
Grus americana (Linnaeus)
Total length: 127 to 142 cm
Plate 26

Adults: Mainly white; wing tips, alula, and a very small patch on back of head, black; crown, lores, and cheeks below and behind eye, bare (except for sprinkling of blackish hairlike feathers) and dull red. *Immatures (first autumn)*: Variable. Rusty brown, buffy, and white in various proportions, brown predominating on head and neck, white on under parts and back; no bare red face-patch.

Measurements. *Adult male*: wing, 550–630 (601.7); tail, 205–245 (223.8); exposed culmen, 129–147 (138.5); tarsus, 265–301 (276.5). *Adult female*: wing, 583–610 (one 535), (597.9) mm (Ridgway).

Field Marks. A very large long-legged, long-necked, heron-like bird, white in colour with black wing-tips (more or less hidden when wing is folded) and red face. In flight it carries neck outstretched, a characteristic that separates it from herons, and the upstroke of the wing is quicker than the downstroke. The Snow Goose and White Pelican also are large white birds with black wing-tips, but both have short legs; in addition, the pelican flies with neck folded back against the shoulders.

Habitat. For nesting, marshy or swampy slough country, formerly mainly in the aspen belt of the Prairie Provinces. In migration, it visits grainfields near sloughs or ponds.

Nesting. Nest, a flat-topped mound of marsh vegetation with a slight depression in the centre, usually in shallow water. *Eggs*, usually 2; buff marked with various browns. Incubation 34 to 35 days (R.P. Allen) by both sexes.

Range in Canada. Perilously close to extinction. The few wild individuals left are known to breed only in Wood Buffalo National Park, Mackenzie, and very recently just south of the Mackenzie border in extreme northern Alberta. Migrates through Saskatchewan and eastern Alberta.

Known former breeding range included southern Mackenzie (Fort Resolution, Salt River); Alberta (near Killam, Whitford Lake, Wainwright; probably elsewhere but records either lacking or uncertain); Saskatchewan (Battleford, Baliol, Bradwell, Muddy Lake, north of Davidson, Yorkton, Moose Mountain); and Manitoba (Oak Lake, Shoal Lake, Winnipeg region). In migration east rarely to southern Ontario (Yarker, 27 September 1871).

Reported former occurrences, without evidence of breeding, and mostly unsatisfactorily documented, north to northern Mackenzie (Fort Anderson, Mackenzie Delta); Keewatin (Baker Lake, Eskimo Point); and northern Manitoba (Churchill).

Range. Now precariously near extinction. Currently known to breed in southern Mackenzie and to winter in Aransas National Wildlife Refuge, coastal Texas. Formerly bred in southern Mackenzie, the Prairie Provinces, North Dakota, Minnesota, Iowa, Illinois, and Louisiana (White Lake). Formerly wintered from coastal Texas, Louisiana, Alabama, Georgia, and Florida south to central Mexico. Recently introduced (by placing of eggs in nests of *G. canadensis*) into Idaho (Grays Lake) but to date not yet known to breed there.

Remarks. The Whooping Crane, the tallest of Canadian birds, has for some years tottered on the brink of extinction. Formerly it ranged over a large part of western North America. Since the white man's coming to the Prairies, with his extensive agriculture and his gun, the Whooping Crane's numbers have dwindled. Now a pitiful remnant is all that stands between it and extinction. Needless to say, it is highly illegal to molest this fine species at any time. A large bird with a low reproductive potential, deprived of the greater part of its former breeding range, and with the added handicap of having to make a long, dangerous migration flight twice a year between Texas and Mackenzie, its chances of long survival seem poor.

Nevertheless, strictly enforced protection and a recent cooperative programme of the United States and Canadian governments of hatching eggs artificially and raising the young in captivity, and including the use of wild Sandhill Cranes as foster parents (by placing eggs of Whooping Cranes in nests of Sandhill Cranes), has resulted in a slow net numerical increase over the years. (See Table 1.)

Table 1
Whooping Crane Population (1941–1983)

Year	Wild Population	Number in Captivity	Total Population
1941	21 including 2 young	2	23
1955	28 individuals	3	31
1956	24 including 3 young	3	27
1957	26 including 3 young	5	31
1958	32 including 9 young	6	38
1959	33 including 2 young	6	39
1960	36 including 6 young	6	42
1961	38 including 5 young	7	45
1962	32 including no young	8	40
1963	33 including 7 young	7	40
1964	42 including 10 young	8	50
1966	43 including 5 young	8	51
1970	57 including 6 young	19	76
1971	59 including 5 young	21	80
1972	51 including 5 young	21	72
1973	48 including 1 young	21	69
1974	49 including 2 young	24	73
1975	61 including 8 young	24	85
1976	76 including 12 young	24	100
1977	76 including 9 young	25	101
1978	83 individuals	26	109
1979	91 individuals	25	116
1980	95 individuals	23	118
1981	86 individuals	23	109
1982	89 individuals	28	117
1983	107 individuals	37	144

Data supplied by F. Graham Cooch, Canadian Wildlife Service.

Order **Charadriiformes:**
Shorebirds, Gulls, Auks, and Allies

Family **Charadriidae:**
Plovers

Number of Species in Canada: 12

Plovers are plump-bodied shorebirds with short necks, rather large eyes, and short thickish bills (not longer than head). The bill is rather soft basally with a hard tip somewhat suggesting the bill of a pigeon (Figure 48). Hind toe usually absent or obsolete (present in Black-bellied Plover).

Figure 48
Bill of
a) a sandpiper
b) a plover

Northern Lapwing

Vanneau huppé
Vanellus vanellus (Linnaeus)
Total length: 30.5 to 33 cm
Plate 35

Status in Canada. Accidental. A great storm-borne flight in December 1927 accounts for most of the records: Baffin Island (Pangnirtung Fiord, October 1926); Labrador (the 1927 flight carried large numbers to the coast from Battle Harbour, Sandwich Bay, and Hamilton Inlet north to Hopedale); Quebec (Harrington-Harbour, Saint-Augustin); Newfoundland (large numbers at numerous localities between 17 December 1927 and 15 January 1928. One specimen had been banded in England. Specimens also from Quidi Vidi, 23 November 1905; St. Anthony, 19 November 1944; Glenwood, 7 January 1955; and Fogo Island, 30 January 1960); New Brunswick (in 1927 specimens were taken at Three Islands, Outer Wood Island, Hay Island, Saint John); Nova Scotia (Ketch Harbour, 17 March 1897; Upper Prospect, 12 December 1905; and from the 1927 flight, specimens were taken in Richmond, Antigonish, and Colchester counties).

In January 1966 another sizeable flight occurred bringing Lapwings to Newfoundland, Nova Scotia, New Brunswick, Prince Edward Island, and southern Quebec (Ruisseau-Vert).

There have been occasional occurrences in additional years in the Atlantic provinces, especially Newfoundland.

A rather large plover with long slender crest (shorter in young). Looks black and white at a distance, but at closer range upper parts show glossy green. Broad black band across breast (extends to throat in summer). Sides of head mainly whitish. Belly white. Under tail coverts chestnut. Tail white with broad black subterminal bar. The Northern Lapwing is not likely to be confused with any other bird of probable occurrence in Canada.

Range. Breeds in Eurasia: British Isles, the Faeroe Islands, northern Sweden, Russia (north to latitude 62°) and Siberia (north to latitude 57°), south to Spain, north Italy, northern China. Winters from southern parts of breeding range south to northern Africa, India, Indochina, Taiwan, and Japan.

Black-bellied Plover

Pluvier argenté
Pluvialis squatarola (Linnaeus)
Total length: 26.5 to 34.5 cm
Plate 28

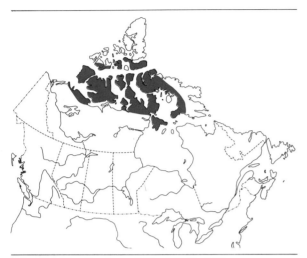

Breeding Distribution of Black-bellied Plover

Range in Canada. Breeds from Banks, Melville, Bathurst, Devon, and Bylot islands south to northern Mackenzie (Cape Bathurst, Cockburn Point, Perry River); southern Victoria Island (Cambridge Bay); northern Keewatin (Adelaide Peninsula); Melville Peninsula; Southampton Island; and southwestern Baffin Island (Bowman Bay).

Recorded in summer north to Axel Heiberg Island (Iceberg Glacier) and northern Ellesmere Island (Cape Belknap).

Scarce transient in Yukon (Dawson: in spring). Spring and autumn transient in southern Mackenzie (apparently local and uncommon: Forts Simpson and Resolution; Rae; Great Bear Lake), and southern Keewatin (mainly the coast; also locally in the interior: Aberdeen and Beverly lakes). Spring and autumn transient in British Columbia (common on coast; scarcer in interior where most records are for autumn; one spring record for Rolla, Peace River); Alberta; Saskatchewan; Manitoba; Ontario; southern and central-western Quebec (coast of Hudson and James bays and the north shore of the Gulf of St. Lawrence; scarce in the interior north of Lake Saint-Jean); the Maritime Provinces (common in autumn; scarcer in spring); and Newfoundland (fairly common in autumn; rare in spring). Scarce transient in Labrador (autumn records: Cartwright, Okak).

Spring migration from coastal northeastern United States appears to be mainly to James and Hudson bays. Perhaps many fly there non-stop. Smaller numbers pass northward farther east through the Maritimes. In autumn more birds spread farther east, and the species is common in Anticosti Island, eastern Gaspé, the Maritimes, and even Newfoundland. Evidence of any significant migration in northern Quebec and Labrador is lacking.

Winters regularly in small numbers in southwestern British Columbia (southern Vancouver Island; mouth of Fraser River).

A small hind toe usually present. Axillars black. Similar in all plumages to Lesser Golden-Plover, but in spring and summer the crown is mostly whitish, upper parts lack yellow speckles, and the black of under parts does not extend so far backward, thus leaving the rear abdomen and under tail coverts white. Autumn Black-bellies have much less yellow speckling on upper parts than do autumn Lesser Goldens. The presence of a small hind toe and the distinctions under Field Marks separate it from the slightly smaller Lesser Golden-Plover.

Measurements. *Adult male*: wing, 180.2–191 (187.8); tail, 71.2–79.7 (74.8); exposed culmen, 27.2–31.8 (29.9); tarsus, 45–50.2 (47.2). *Adult female*: wing, 182–199 (187.7) mm.

Field Marks. Likely to be confused only with the Lesser Golden-Plover but is easily recognizable in all plumages by its whitish tail and upper tail coverts and by its black axillars (armpits), which are visible in flight at some distance. In spring and summer its whitish crown and the white rear part of the abdomen are additional distinctions. Its flight call is a trisyllabic whistled *tee-yu-eee*, the middle syllable lowest.

Habitat. Although it often frequents short-grass fields, especially moist ones, it is more likely to be found on mud flats, muddy shores and pools, beaches, and sandbars, in the vicinity of either fresh or salt water. In the Arctic, dry gravel ridges are popular for nesting purposes, but wetter tundra areas also are used.

Nesting. Nest, a shallow depression in the ground lined with bits of lichen or moss. *Eggs*, usually 4; vary from light buff or greyish to pinkish, greenish, or brownish, spotted or blotched with blackish brown especially on larger end. Incubation 27 days (W.H. Drury).

Range. Breeds in Alaska and the middle and low Arctic of Canada; also in northern Russia (Kanin Peninsula eastward) and across northern Siberia. Winters from southwestern British Columbia southward along the Pacific coast to Chile; and on the Atlantic and other eastern coasts from New Jersey south to southern Brazil; also the West Indies. Winters also from the British Isles, the Mediterranean, southern China, and Hawaii south to South Africa, Australia, and New Zealand.

Greater Golden-Plover

Pluvier doré d'Eurasie
Pluvialis apricaria (Linnaeus)
Total length: 28 cm
Plate 35

Status in Canada. Accidental in Newfoundland: specimen received on 20 April 1961, by L.M. Tuck from Cappahayden, Avalon Peninsula. Others, presumably this species, reported to Tuck about the same time, suggest that a flight arrived in Newfoundland a few days earlier. Also sight records: Stephenville Crossing, 24 May 1963 (seven individuals).

Very similar to the slightly smaller Lesser Golden-Plover but axillars white in all plumages.

Range. Breeds in Iceland, the Faeroe Islands, and eastward across northern Europe through northern Scandinavia, northern Russia, and western Siberia (to Yenisei River), south to the British Isles, the Netherlands (formerly), Denmark, northern Germany, Poland, and the Baltics. In migration occurs regularly in southern Greenland.

Subspecies. The Newfoundland specimen is referable to *Pluvialis apricaria altifrons* (Brehm).

Lesser Golden-Plover

Pluvier doré d'Amérique
Pluvialis dominica (Müller)
Total length: 24.7 to 28 cm
Plates 28 and 35

Breeding Distribution of Lesser Golden-Plover

Range in Canada. Summer resident and transient. Breeds from Banks Island (De Salis Bay); Victoria Island (Cambridge Bay, Prince Albert Peninsula); Melville Island (Winter Harbour); Bathurst Island; eastern Devon Island; and Bylot Island, south through Yukon (Herschel Island, Keno Hill; probably mountains near Burwash Creek, Edith Creek, Tepee Lake; and near Klutlan Glacier) to northwestern British Columbia (Kliweguh Creek); central Mackenzie (Great Bear Lake; Artillery and Prairie lakes); Keewatin (Adelaide Peninsula, Whale Point; perhaps lower Back River; distribution poorly known); northeastern Manitoba (Churchill); Southampton Island; northern Ontario (Cape Henrietta Maria); and south-central Baffin Island (Amadjuak Lake, Cape Dorchester).

Spring and autumn migrant in British Columbia, Alberta, Saskatchewan, Manitoba; mainly autumn migrant in Ontario; and autumn migrant in Quebec, Labrador, Newfoundland, New Brunswick, Prince Edward Island, and Nova Scotia. Although Nova Scotia is frequently mentioned in the literature as the place where allegedly vast numbers rest and

Lacks hind toe. Axillars grey. *Adults (spring and summer)*: Upper parts, including crown and upper tail coverts, blackish or dusky, speckled with yellow and often a few white spots. Forehead, line over eye and down side of neck, white. Lower cheeks, throat, middle of breast, abdomen, sides and under tail coverts, black. Bill black. Legs dark bluish-grey. *Adults and young in autumn*: Upper parts duller, no black on face or under parts. Vague whitish line over eye but not down side of neck. Breast pale greyish-brown, faintly barred with dusky.

Measurements *(P. d. dominica)*. *Adult male*: wing, 175.1–188.4 (180.3); tail, 66–72.7 (68.9); exposed culmen, 22–24.5 (23.3); tarsus, 42.2–44.8 (43.5). *Adult female*: wing, 172–183 (179.6) mm.

Field Marks. Similar to Black-bellied Plover but in breeding plumage distinguishable from it by dark crown and consequent white line over eye and down side of neck; black of abdomen extends to under tail coverts. Both adults and young are separable from Black-bellied in any plumage by their grey (instead of black) axillars and dark (instead of whitish) rump and tail.

Habitat. Tends to prefer drier habitats than the Black-bellied Plover. In migration, short-grass and stubble fields, pastures, ploughed land; and to some extent beaches and shores of both fresh and salt water. In the Arctic, relatively dry uplands, ridges, slopes, and tundra knolls, both coastal and inland.

Nesting. Nest a shallow depression in lichens or soil, lined with pieces of lichen. *Eggs*, usually 4; buffy, boldly spotted and blotched with blackish. Incubation, 26 days (D.F. Parmelee), by both sexes.

Range. Breeds in northern Siberia, Alaska, and northern Canada. Winters on South American plains from southern Bolivia and southern Brazil south to central Argentina; also from India, southern China, and the Hawaiian Islands south to Australia, and New Zealand. Main migration in North America in spring is up the Mississippi valley over the Prairie Provinces and west of Hudson Bay. In autumn, southward both east and west of Hudson Bay, with a considerable proportion apparently flying over the Altantic Ocean from southeastern Canada and northeastern United States to South America.

fatten in preparation for the long transoceanic flight to South America, the writer is aware of no such concentrations there in the present century. The possibility of change in the eastern migration route has been suggested by some.

Subspecies. (1) *Pluvialis dominica dominica* (Müller) is the only subspecies known to breed in Canada. It migrates through most of the southern parts. (2) *P. d. fulva* (Gmelin), breeding from Siberia east to western coastal Alaska (Cape Lisburne to Kuskokwim River), a smaller bird with brighter, more profusely yellow colouring especially in autumn, is a scarce autumn transient on the coast of British Columbia and has been taken once in Alberta (Tofield, 9 September 1925).

Mongolian Plover

Pluvier de Mongolie
Charadrius mongolus Pallas
Total length: 19 to 21 cm
Figure 49

Figure 49
Mongolian Plover

Status in Canada. Accidental in Ontario (an adult in breeding plumage was discovered in Presqu'ile Provincial Park on 4 May 1984 by R.D. McRae who photographed and described it in detail) and Alberta (photos: of an adult at the Syncrude site, north of Fort McMurray, on 18 June 1984. The photos suggest that it belongs to one of the *mongolus* group of subspecies).

Slightly larger than Semipalmated Plover but with longer legs and bill. Brown above, mostly white below but adults in breeding plumage have a broad rufous breast band which in northern races is separated from the white throat by a thin blackish line. Abdomen white. Face has a black mask and there are varying amounts of white on forehead. Bill black. In all plumages this species is very similar to Greater Sand Plover, *C. leschenaulti* of the Old World. For distinctions in all plumages see A.J. Prater et al., 1977. *Guide to the identification and ageing of Holarctic waders* (British Trust for Ornithology, Beech Grove, Tring, Herts.).

Range. Breeds in central and northeastern Asia; has bred in northern and western Alaska. Winters in the Old World. Accidental in Oregon, California, Louisiana, and Ontario.

Subspecies. Not determinable without the specimen. However, photographs and description of the Alberta individual restrict it to a race of the *mongolus* group.

Snowy Plover

Gravelot à collier interrompu
Charadrius alexandrinus Linnaeus
Total length: 14.5 to 17.3 cm
Plate 28

Status in Canada. Casual. At Buck Lake, 30 km south of Regina, Saskatchewan, a male was collected on 31 May 1964. Sight records for southwestern British Columbia (Tofino, Denman Island, Iona Island; photo record: Sandspit, Queen Charlotte Islands, 12 July 1980).

Its status in Ontario is hypothetical. Although two specimens are alleged to have been taken in Toronto, one in July 1897, the other in May 1880, the records are unsatisfactory.

A diminutive plover (wing chord not over 107 mm) with relatively longish slender bill (culmen, 13 to 15.5 mm). Upper parts pale brown as in Piping Plover. Very narrow black bar above white forehead. No breast band, just a single dark patch on either side of chest. Rest of under parts white. Bill black. Legs grey. Distinguished from Piping Plover by smaller size, relatively (and actually) longer bill, and grey legs (Piping and Semipalmated plovers have yellow legs).

Subspecies. The Regina specimen has been referred to *Charadrius alexandrinus nivosus* (Cassin). The species breeds in many widely separated parts of the world including western and southern United States.

Wilson's Plover

Pluvier de Wilson
Charadrius wilsonia Ord
Total length: 18 to 20.5 cm

Status in Canada. Casual in Nova Scotia: on Brier Island one was collected on 28 April 1880; Halifax: a summer adult listed without date by R.B. Sharpe (1896. *Catalogue of birds in the British Museum*. Vol. 24, p. 216; photo records: Sable Island, 2 April 1972; Seal Island, 17 May 1975 and another there on 26–27 May 1984). Sight records for Ontario (Hamilton, Point Pelee).

Another brown-backed plover with single breast band, thus resembling Semipalmated and Piping Plover but readily distinguishable by its longer, thicker, all-black bill. Brown of upper parts darker than Piping Plover. Slightly larger than both.

Subspecies. *Charadrius wilsonia wilsonia* Ord, which breeds on the Atlantic coast of the United States from Virginia to Florida, along the entire coast of the Gulf of Mexico, and in the West Indies.

Common Ringed Plover

Grand Gravelot
Charadrius hiaticula Linnaeus
Average total length: 19 cm
Plate 28

Breeding Distribution of Common Ringed Plover

Range in Canada. Summer resident. Breeds from northern Ellesmere Island (Alert, Nansen Sound) south through Bylot Island and eastern Baffin Island (Clyde and Pond inlets, Admiralty Inlet. Possibly Cumberland Sound). Winters in the Old World.

Extremely like Semipalmated Plover but has no web between the basal parts of inner and middle toes (a small web between outer and middle toes is possessed by both species; Figure 50); it has a broader black breast band; and the white areas of head are slightly more extensive.

Field Marks. Not safely separable in the field from Semipalmated Plover except by direct comparison under excellent conditions.

Nesting. Nest a hollow in sand, gravel, or turf, often lined with small stones or bits of shell. *Eggs*, usually 4; pale buff spotted with blackish brown and small amounts of grey. Incubation, by both sexes, about 23 to 26 days.

Range. Breeds in northeastern arctic Canada, Greenland, Iceland, and across northern Eurasia east to Chukotski Peninsula. Winters from the British Isles, Mediterranean Sea, Asia Minor, and China south to southern Africa and India.

Subspecies. *Charadrius hiaticula hiaticula* Linnaeus.

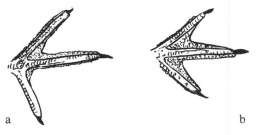

a   b

Figure 50
Foot of
a) Common Ringed Plover
b) Semipalmated Plover

Semipalmated Plover

Pluvier semipalmé
Charadrius semipalmatus Bonaparte
Total length: 16.5 to 19.5 cm
Plate 28

Breeding Distribution of Semipalmated Plover

Range in Canada. Summer resident and transient. Breeds from Banks Island (Sachs Harbour, Kellett River); Victoria Island (Cambridge Bay, perhaps Holman Post); Boothia Peninsula (Sagvak Inlet, Krusenstern Lake); northern Melville Peninsula (Fury and Hecla Strait); and central and southern Baffin Island (north at least to Clyde Inlet) south through Yukon (Old Crow, Carcross, Rose-Lapie Pass) to northwestern British Columbia (Mile 85 Haines Road; Atlin; Graham Island; and southward very locally to Le Blanc Lake and Vancouver); through Mackenzie (Mackenzie Delta, Anderson River, and the arctic coast, Great Slave Lake); throughout Keewatin; northern Alberta (Wood Buffalo National Park); northern Saskatchewan (Lake Athabasca); northern Manitoba (Churchill, Herchmer, Bird); northern Ontario (Big Piskwamish Point, Cape Henrietta Maria); Quebec (mainly coastal apparently, but locally also in the interior: north to Hudson Strait and Ungava Bay; south to southern James Bay, Lake Bienville, Schefferville, the north shore of the Gulf of St. Lawrence: Sainte-Marie and Fog islands; Madeleine Islands); Labrador (entire coast, and sparsely in the interior: Sandgirt and Menihek lakes); Newfoundland; Nova Scotia (very locally: near Englishtown; mouth of Chebogue River; Cooks Beach, Sable Island); and southern New Brunswick (Grand Manan, Waterside marsh, and Fundy National Park).

Transient, more or less common, through most of southern Canada (but scarce in south-interior of British Columbia and mountainous southwestern Alberta). In the Maritime Provinces much more numerous in autumn.

Bill short. No hind toe. Front toes partly webbed, including small web at base of inner and middle toes (Figure 50). *Adults (spring and summer)*: Narrow black patch from base of bill to cheeks. Black bar above white forehead. Upper parts brown. Black breast band on otherwise white under parts. Legs and base of bill, rich yellow. Tip of bill black. *Autumn adults and young*: Similar but black areas replaced by dark brown. Young have black bills.

Measurements. *Adult male*: wing, 114.9–123.9 (118.8); tail, 52.5–59.2 (56); exposed culmen, 11.9–14.4 (13); tarsus, 22–25.3 (23.9). *Adult female*: wing, 118–126 (121.3) mm.

Field Marks. A small short-billed brown-backed plover with well-defined single breast band. Similar to Piping Plover but upper parts much darker brown (like wet sand rather than dry sand) and with black (dark-brown in young) area extending from base of bill to cheeks. The much larger Killdeer has a double breast band. Semipalmated Plover often calls *pe-wit*, the second syllable higher pitched (see Common Ringed Plover).

Habitat. Both fresh and salt mud flats, beaches, flat open margins of ponds, lakes, and rivers. In nesting season inhabits also sparsely vegetated low gravel ridges, gravelly plains, beaches, and sand dunes.

Nesting. Nest a depression in sand, gravel, moss, or dead seaweed, sparsely, if at all, lined with bits of shell or plant material. *Eggs*, 3 to 4; buffy, variously spotted with blackish browns. Incubation, about 23 days, by both sexes.

Range. Breeds in Alaska (north to Colville Delta) and Canada (see Range in Canada). Winters from southern California, the Gulf of Mexico coast, and South Carolina south (including the West Indies) to southern Argentina and Chile.

1a

1 Blue Grouse, p. 157
(*D. o. fuliginosus*)
a) adult male
b) adult female

2a

2c

1b

2 Spruce Grouse, p. 156
a) adult female (*canadensis* race)
b) adult male (*canadensis* race)
c) adult male (*franklinii* race)

2b

3 Willow Ptarmigan, p. 158
a) head in winter
b) adult male, early summer
c) adult female, early summer
d) winter

3a

3b

3c

3d

4a

4b

4c

4d

4 Rock Ptarmigan,
p. 159
a) male in winter
b) adult female,
   summer
c) adult male,
   summer
d) male in winter

White-tailed Ptarmigan, p. 160
head in winter
adult male, early summer
adult female, summer
winter

5a

5b

5c

5d

Crosby

1 Whooping Crane, p. 177
adult

2 Sandhill Crane, p. 176
adult

3 Common Crane, p. 177
adult

4 Purple Gallinule, p. 172
adult in summer

5 Common Moorhen, p. 173
a) immature
b) adult in summer

6 American Coot, p. 174
adult in summer

7 Yellow Rail, p. 168
summer adult

8 Sora, p. 171
a) summer adult
b) autumn immature

9 King Rail, p. 170
summer adult

10 Virginia Rail, p. 170
summer adult

11 Clapper Rail, p. 169

Crosby

1 Gray Partridge, p. 153
adult male

2 Northern Bobwhite, p. 166
a) female
b) male

2a

2b

3 Chukar, p. 154

4

4 Mountain Quail, p. 167

5a

5b

5 California Quail, p. 167
a) adult female
b) adult male

6 Curlew Sandpiper, p. 237
a) adult in breeding plumage
b) winter plumage

6a

6b

7a

8

8 White-winged Redshank,
p. 201
adult in breeding plumage

7 Spotted Redshank, p. 202
a) adult in breeding plumage
b) winter plumage

7b

9a

9b

9 Rufous-necked Stint, p. 220
a) adult in breeding plumage
b) adult in winter plumage

10

10 Ruff, p. 239
male in winter

11 Spoonbill Sandpiper,
p. 238
a) winter plumage
b) breeding plumage

11a

11b

1 Killdeer, p. 194
adult

2 Lesser Golden-Plover, p. 181
a) adult in breeding plumage
b) autumn immature

2a

2b

2a

2b

3a

3b

3a

3b

4 Common Ringed Plover,
p. 183
adult in breeding plumage

3 Black-bellied Plover, p. 180
a) adult in breeding plumage
b) autumn immature

4

5

5 Semipalmated Plover, p. 184
adult in breeding plumage

8 Ruddy Turnstone, p. 213
a) adult in breeding plumage
b) autumn immature

8b

6 Piping Plover, p. 193
adult in breeding plumage

6

8a

7

7 Snowy Plover, p. 182
adult in breeding plumage

1 Hudsonian Godwit, p. 211
a) adult in breeding plumage
b) autumn plumage

1b

1a

2 Eskimo Curlew, p. 207

2

4

3 Whimbrel, p. 208

3

4 American Avocet, p. 198
adult in breeding plumage

5

5 Long-billed Curlew, p. 210
adult in breeding plumage

6

6 Marbled Godwit, p. 212
adult in breeding plumage

Crosby

30

1 Solitary Sandpiper, p. 202
a) autumn immature
b) adult in breeding plumage

2 Spotted Sandpiper, p. 205
a) autumn immature
b) adult in breeding plumage

3 Stilt Sandpiper, p. 237
a) adult in breeding plumage
b) autumn immature

4 Willet, p. 203
a) autumn immature (flying)
b) adult in breeding plumage

5 Greater Yellowlegs, p. 200

6 Lesser Yellowlegs, p. 201

1 Black Turnstone, p. 214
a) adult in breeding plumage
b) winter plumage
c) flight pattern

2 Surfbird, p. 215
a) flight pattern
b) winter plumage
c) adult in breeding plumage

3 Sharp-tailed Sandpiper, p. 234
a) adult in breeding plumage
b) autumn immature

5 American Black Oystercatcher,
p. 196
adult in breeding plumage

4 Wandering Tattler, p. 204
a) adult in breeding plumage
b) autumn and winter

32

2 Rock Sandpiper, p. 235
adult in breeding plumage

3 Purple Sandpiper, p. 234
a) autumn and winter
b) adult in breeding plumage

1 Dunlin, p. 236
a) adult in breeding plumage
b) autumn and winter

4 Red Knot, p. 216
a) adult in breeding plumage
b) autumn and winter

5 Short-billed Dowitcher, p. 240
a) autumn and winter
b) adult in breeding plumage

6 Long-billed Dowitcher, p. 241
a) adult in breeding plumage
b) autumn and winter

8 Common Snipe, p. 242

7 American Woodcock, p. 243

Crosby

Piping Plover

Pluvier siffleur
Charadrius melodus Ord
Total length: 15 to 19.5 cm
Plate 28

Breeding Distribution of Piping Plover

Range in Canada. Local summer resident and transient, becoming much scarcer; now absent from many parts of its range. Breeds in southeastern central Alberta (Bittern, Miquelon, Buffalo, Gull, Baxter, and Beaverhill lakes); southern Saskatchewan (Jackfish Lake, Bigstick, Quill, Johnston, and Last Mountain lakes; Indian Head); rarely on Lake Athabasca (Wolverine Point); southern Manitoba (Dawson Bay on Lake Winnipegosis, Lakes Manitoba and Winnipeg, Shoal Lake); southern Ontario (Point Pelee, Long Point, Hamilton, Toronto, Consecon, Rockport, Ipperwash Beach, Wasaga Beach, Manitoulin Island); southeastern Quebec (New-Carlisle, Madeleine Islands, probably Natashquan); southwestern Newfoundland (mouths of Grand and Little Codroy rivers; probably Stephenville Crossing); New Brunswick (Tabusintac, Neguak Beach; probably Miscou Island); Prince Edward Island (Stanhope, Howe Bay); and southern Nova Scotia (Cape Sable and various other "white" sand beaches on the South Shore; Sable Island).

Small web between outer and middle toes. Similar in size, proportions, and markings to Semipalmated Plover, but brown of upper parts much paler, more greyish; black on head confined to a bar above white forehead and lacking on cheeks; breast band often broken or (in autumn adults and immatures) very poorly defined or lacking.

Measurements *(C. m. melodus)*. *Adult male*: wing, 114.8–127 (121.3); tail, 48.2–56.8 (53.1); exposed culmen, 10.3–13 (12.1); tarsus, 22–22.9 (22.4). *Adult female*: wing, 110–122 (118.1) mm.

Field Marks. A very pale edition of the Semipalmated Plover from which it is readily separable by much paler upper parts (colour of dry, instead of wet, sand); and lack of any black or dark brown on the cheeks. Breast bar often broken; poorly defined or almost absent in autumn adults and young. Its whistled, ventriloquial *queep*, or *queeplo*, is very different from calls of the Semipalmated Plover.

Habitat. Sandy beaches on both salt and fresh water.

Nesting. Nest, a shallow depression in sand above the high-water mark of ocean or lake beaches, is either unlined or scantily lined with pebbles and bits of shell. *Eggs*, usually 4; light buff to whitish, sparsely but usually quite evenly dotted with blackish brown; ground colour paler, spots smaller and sparser than in Semipalmated Plover. Incubation, 27 to 31 days, by both sexes (L. Wilcox).

Range. Breeds from southern Canada (Alberta to Newfoundland) south to South Dakota, Nebraska, southern shores of Lakes Michigan and Erie, and on the Atlantic coast to Virginia. Winters on the Atlantic Coast from South Carolina to Florida and westward along the Gulf of Mexico to Texas.

Subspecies. (1) *Charadrius melodus melodus* Ord, characterized by having the black pectoral band more frequently broken, breeds from southeastern Quebec and Newfoundland south through the Maritimes. (2) *C. m. circumcinctus* (Ridgway), with usually an unbroken pectoral band, breeds from the Great Lakes westward.

Killdeer

Pluvier kildir
Charadrius vociferus Linnaeus
Total length: 23 to 28.5 cm
Plate 28

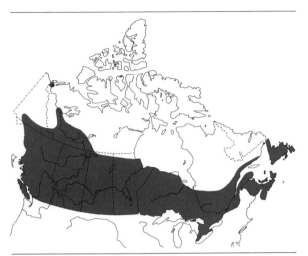

Breeding Distribution of Killdeer

Range in Canada. Common summer resident in much of southern Canada, scarcer east of southwestern Quebec. Has expanded its range and numbers eastward recently in Quebec, the Maritimes, and Newfoundland. Breeds in southern Yukon (recently at Kluane Lake); British Columbia (Mile 301 Alaska Highway, southward locally through the interior; also Vancouver Island); Mackenzie (Fort Simpson, Slave River; Fort Norman; Aklavik); Alberta; Saskatchewan; and Manitoba (north at least to Churchill); Ontario; southern Quebec (Mont-réal, Québec, Lake Saint-Jean, Pointe-des-Monts; Forillon Peninsula, Sainte-Marie Islands, Madeleine Islands; in 1980 nested at Blanc-Sablon); extreme southern Labrador (Forteau Bay); New Brunswick (in increasing numbers: near Bathurst, Riley Brook, St. Andrews, Jemseg); Nova Scotia (in increasing numbers); Prince Edward Island; and Newfoundland (Gros Morne National Park, Searston, Stephenville Crossing).

Recorded in summer in northern Yukon (Arctic coastal plain, Old Crow); southern Keewatin (Windy and McConnell rivers); Anticosti Island, and Kuujjuaq, Quebec. Accidental in northern Labrador (Nain).

Winters in small numbers in southern British Columbia (Vancouver, Okanagan Landing) and occasionally southern Ontario (Toronto).

The double black band across the breast and cinnamon-coloured rump and upper tail coverts readily identify it.

Measurements. *Adult male*: wing, 148.8–165 (158); tail, 86–99.6 (94); exposed culmen, 18.8–21.2 (20.3); tarsus, 35.1–38 (36.4). *Adult female*: wing, 153–167.8 (161.4) mm.

Field Marks. The double black band across breast and the cinnamon-buffy rump and upper tail coverts are unmistakable (other "ringed" plovers have only one breast band and are smaller and shorter-tailed). Its ringing *kill-dee*, rapidly and frequently repeated, is a common summer voice of upland fields in most of southern Canada west of the Maritimes.

Habitat. Open uplands. Pastured, mowed, or ploughed fields, bare gravel, golf courses, roadside ditches, and similar disturbed areas where grass is short, sparse, or absent. After nesting, it frequents margins of ponds and lakes, muddy and moist places. Rarely salt marshes.

Nesting. Nest, a shallow depression in the ground, sparsely lined with a few pebbles and bits of weeds. *Eggs*, usually 4; light buff, boldly blotched and spotted with blackish. Incubation, usually 24 to 26 days (W.P. Nickell), by both sexes.

Range. Breeds from southern Canada south to central Mexico, the Gulf Coast of the United States, south-central Florida, and the West Indies; also in Peru. Winters from southern British Columbia, Colorado, the Ohio valley, and Long Island south to northern South America.

Subspecies. *Charadrius vociferus vociferus* Linnaeus.

Remarks. The handsome, noisy Killdeer derived its name from one of its numerous calls. It is common in most of southern Canada except in the extreme east. Although a shorebird, it favours open interior uplands more often than the seashore. It is among the earliest of birds to appear in spring, soon after the first patches of bare ground begin to show in the fields.

Mountain Plover

Pluvier montagnard
Charadrius montanus Townsend
Total length: 21 to 23.5 cm
Figure 51

Figure 51
Mountain Plover

Status in Canada. Rare summer visitor and breeder to southeastern Alberta (near Wild Horse: four on 22 June 1941; also two observed approximately 32 km west of there on 5 July 1971; and two observed in the Cypress Hills on 12 June 1966) and southwestern Saskatchewan (near Bracken: one on 5 June 1939). J.D. Soper (1941. Canadian Field-Naturalist, vol. 55, no. 9, p. 137) suspected that the 1941 Alberta birds were nesting. A nest along Milk River, southern Alberta, was discovered in late May 1979. Sight record of eight near Val Marie, Saskatchewan, on 22 September 1977.

Bill rather slender. Legs rather long for a plover. *Adults (breeding plumage)*: Upper parts plain greyish-brown, some feathers margined with buffy. Front of crown and line from bill to eye, black. Forehead and superciliary stripes white. Under parts plain dull-white with buffy-greyish wash across breast. Bill black. Legs pale brownish-yellow. *Adults and young in autumn*: Similar to breeding adults but black head-markings absent. The Mountain Plover approaches the Killdeer in size but lacks black breast bands. Its plain back distinguishes it from autumn Lesser Golden and Black-bellied plovers. A bird of the dry short-grass plains of the United States, it is to be expected in Canada only in southern parts of the Prairie Provinces.

Family **Haematopodidae**: Oystercatchers

Number of Species in Canada: 2

Large shorebirds, coloured either in contrasting black and white or all blackish, with long, stout, laterally compressed bright-red bills. Their legs and feet are heavy, and they have no hind toe.

American Oystercatcher

Huîtrier d'Amérique
Haematopus palliatus Temminck
Total length: 43 to 50.5 cm
Figure 52

Status in Canada. Casual visitor. Ontario: one, presumably the same bird, in 1960 was first observed at Toronto, 22 May; it was photographed by D.R. Gunn at Presqu'ile Point on 29 May, and collected at Rose Hill on 21 July for the Royal Ontario Museum. Quebec (sight record: Cacouna, 19 May 1980). New Brunswick: Grand Manan (date unknown). Nova Scotia: one photographed at Matthews Lake, 25 April 1983. Another oystercatcher was carefully identified on 19 May 1957, at Grand Desert by Charles Allen, T.H. Morland, and John Comer, three competent observers. It was not collected, and the possibility of the occurrence of the similar European Oystercatcher was not completely ruled out. New Brunswick: six oystercatchers were observed on 31 May 1971 in Kouchibouguak National Park but the species was not certainly identified.

Audubon's assertion that in 1833 he found it breeding in the Bay of Fundy and northward to the north shore of the Gulf of St. Lawrence cannot now be corroborated.

Figure 52
a) American Oystercatcher
b) American Oystercatcher in flight
c) Eurasian Oystercatcher in flight
(note white rump and lower back)

Bill laterally compressed (height greater than width) and about twice as long as head. *Adults*: Head, neck, and upper chest, black. Back and most of wings, greyish brown. Broad band across wings, white. Upper tail coverts mostly white. Tail dark brownish-grey to blackish. Under parts (posterior to breast) white. Bill mainly red. Legs pale flesh. (See also American Black Oystercatcher.) The European Oystercatcher *(H. ostralegus)* is very similar to the American species, but the back (hidden when the wings are folded but visible in flight) is white, and the upper surface of the wings is black instead of brown.

Field Marks. A crow-sized black-and-white shorebird with a large reddish bill and conspicuous white wing patches. In flight shows dark back and white rump (both back and rump white in European Oystercatcher).

Range. Breeds from Massachusetts south on the Atlantic, Gulf, and Caribbean coasts to middle Argentina; some of the West Indies; and from Baja California on the Pacific coast to Chile; also the Galapagos Islands.

Subspecies. *Haematopus palliatus palliatus* Temminck.

American Black Oystercatcher

Huîtrier de Bachman
Haematopus bachmani Audubon
Total length: 43 to 45 cm
Plate 31

Breeding Distribution of American Black Oystercatcher

Range in Canada. Permanent resident on the outer coast and rocky coastal islands of British Columbia from southern and western Vancouver Island northward.

Bill as in American Oystercatcher. A crow-sized all-black shorebird with a red laterally compressed bill twice the length of the head. Unmistakable. *Young* similar, but more brownish; bill dusky, orange at base.

Field Marks. A crow-sized all-black shorebird with robust red bill and pinkish feet. *Voice*: a repeated loud *queep*.

Habitat. Rocky, outer saltwater shores and islands.

Nesting. Eggs are laid in a depression on a bare rock, often lined with bits of stone and shell chips, or in a hollow in beach gravel or other ground. *Eggs*, usually 2 to 3, are buffy and are uniformly spotted and scrawled with blackish browns and some bluish-grey. Incubation period 26 to 30 days, usually 27 days (J. Dan Webster). Incubation by both parents.

Range. Breeds on the Pacific coasts of North America from Attu Island, the Aleutian Islands, Alaska, eastward and southward to central-western Baja California.

Family **Recurvirostridae:**
Avocets and Stilts

Number of Species in Canada: 2

Large shorebirds with extremely long legs; long, very slender bill, slightly upcurved in avocets, nearly straight in the Black-necked Stilt; head smallish, neck rather long.

Black-necked Stilt

Echasse d'Amérique
Himantopus mexicanus (Müller)
Total length: 34.5 to 39.5 cm
Figure 53

Range in Canada. Very rare, erratic and local breeder in central Alberta (two nests at Beaverhill Lake, June 1977) and perhaps Saskatchewan (Qu'Appelle, June 1894, eggs in National Museum of Natural Sciences collection not certainly identifiable). Unusual drought conditions in much of the normal breeding range in 1977 presumably account for the breeding of the species in that year far north of its usual range, to Montana and Alberta.

A casual or accidental visitor to British Columbia (photo: Sea Island, 13 May 1971); Alberta (photos: Calgary, 12 May 1970; Irricana, 24 May 1972; see also breeding above); Saskatchewan (sight records: Arcola, three on 20 May 1955; one near Rosetown, 7 May 1971; see also breeding above); Manitoba (sight records: Delta region, 13 May 1969, and 9 August 1969; Oak Hammock Marsh, 21 October 1978); Ontario (sight records: Timmins, 1 September 1955; Smithville, 14 October 1979; Lake of the Woods, 7 June 1981); New Brunswick (old specimens no longer extant from St. Croix River and Maces Bay; sight record: Bay of Chaleur, 27 May 1972); Newfoundland (specimen: Trepassey, 23 June 1947); and Nova Scotia (Cape Sable: photos of two, 27 May 1979).

Bill twice as long as head, slightly upturned, very slender, sharp-pointed. Legs extremely long, slim, stilt-like, red in colour. *Adults* (female duller and more brownish than male): hind part of crown, back of head (to below eye), hind-neck, upper back, and wings, black. Forehead, spot above eye, front of face and lower cheeks, sides and front of neck, rump, and under parts white. Tail greyish. Immatures similar to female but still duller, the feathers of the dark upper parts margined with brownish or whitish.

Field Marks. A large shorebird contrastingly attired in black and white, with slender upturned bill (twice as long as head) and excessively long stilt-like red or pink legs. Wings solid black with no white stripe.

Range. Breeds locally from central Alberta, Montana, southern Oregon, northern Utah, southern Colorado, and the Gulf Coast of Texas south through the West Indies, Mexico, and Central America to northern Brazil, the Guianas, and northern Colombia.

Figure 53
Black-necked Stilt

American Avocet

Avocette d'Amérique
Recurvirostra americana Gmelin
Total length: 40.5 to 50.7 cm
(male larger than female)
Plate 29

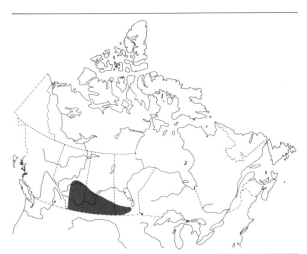

Breeding Distribution of American Avocet

Range in Canada. Breeds in southeastern British Columbia (very locally: near Creston) and on the prairies of central and southern Alberta (Beaverhill Lake, Edmonton, Lower Thérien Lake, High River, Milk River; formerly north to Lesser Slave Lake); southern Saskatchewan (Edam, Saskatoon, Big Quill Lake, Maple Creek, Yorkton; perhaps north to Wakaw); and southwestern Manitoba (Oak Lake, West Shoal Lake, Delta, Dog Lake). In 1980 was reported nesting in extreme western Ontario (very locally: Sable Island in Lake of the Woods). Formerly bred north to southern Mackenzie (Rae about 1861). That the species formerly ranged more widely is indicated by specimens taken in the nineteenth century at Rae and Fort Resolution, Mackenzie; Fort Chipewyan and Lesser Slave Lake, Alberta.

Scarce visitant in most of southern British Columbia (mouth of Fraser River, Arrow Lake, Okanagan Landing, Kootenay; rarely Vancouver Island); southern Ontario (Toronto, Erie Beach, Geraldton; also various sight records); Quebec (La Pocatière, Rimouski); New Brunswick (two old specimens from Charlotte County; also sight records: Saint John and near Sackville); and Nova Scotia (photo record: Cape Sable Island, 28 August 1969; also several sight records).

Bill extremely slender, long, and slightly flattened; usually upturned, often decidedly so (but sometimes the extreme tip is downcurved in a slight hook). Legs long, pale bluish, front toes webbed. The peculiar awl-like bill, large size, and striking coloration make it unmistakable. Winter adults and immatures are similar to adults in breeding plumage, but the pinkish-buff coloration of head, neck, and breast is largely replaced by white and some grey.

Measurements. *Adult male*: wing, 222–228.5 (224.6); tail, 76.5–89 (86.1); exposed culmen, 91.5–92 (91.8); tarsus, 95.5–102.5 (99.1). *Adult female*: wing, 214.5–236.5 (224.1) mm.

Field Marks. This very large, strikingly coloured shorebird with very slender upturned bill and very long legs is unmistakable. Young lack most of the vinaceous coloration on head, neck, and breast but are otherwise so similar to breeding adults that they are easily recognized. Common call when alarmed is a strident *kleep*, many times repeated.

Habitat. Shores and flats of sparsely vegetated lakes and sloughs, especially alkaline ones.

Nesting. Often in loose colonies. Nest, a depression in the ground usually on dried-out mud shores or islands of shallow lakes or sloughs. Nest lined with grasses, weeds, and similar available material, sometimes only sparsely but often forming a considerable structure. *Eggs* 3 to 5, usually 4; vary in colour from dark olive to light brown, rather profusely spotted and blotched with dark browns and a few spots of lavender. Nests are not infrequently found with up to eight eggs, but these are probably the product of more than one female. Incubation by both sexes. Period 22 to 24 days.

Range. Breeds from eastern Washington, southern Idaho, and southern parts of the Prairie Provinces of Canada south to southern California, southern Nevada, central Colorado, and southern Texas; perhaps also locally in central Mexico (San Luis Potosi). Winters from California and southern Texas south through Mexico to Guatemala.

Family **Scolopacidae:** Sandpipers, Phalaropes, and Allies

Number of Species in Canada: 51

This, the sandpiper family of the shorebirds, is a large and very widely distributed one. Members of the family show great differences in size and colour. The bill is slenderer than that of plovers, is soft and rather flexible throughout its length, and does not have the well-marked horny tip of plovers' (Figure 48). Bill is usually straight but sometimes down-curved (curlews) or somewhat upturned (godwits). Legs are slender, long or medium, and usually a hind toe is present (absent in Sanderling). Most are gregarious and are found in companies or flocks on shores and wet ground and in marshes with either fresh or salt water.

Subfamily **Scolopacinae:** Sandpipers and Allies

A large and varied group, widely distributed in the world. Its main characters are outlined above under the family Scolopacidae.

Common Greenshank

Chevalier aboyeur
Tringa nebularia (Gunnerus)
Total length: 33 to 38 cm
Figure 54

Very similar in size, colour, and markings to Greater Yellowlegs but (1) legs pale olive-green; (2) white of rump extends to include lower back; (3) shoulder of folded wing noticeably darker than rest of upper wing coverts, near colour of primaries; (4) general coloration paler, especially in winter plumages.

Range. Breeds in Scotland and from Scandinavia eastward across Russia and Siberia and south to Lake Baikal. Winters mainly from the Mediterranean and Black Sea regions, northern India, China, and Japan south to southern Africa, New Zealand, and Australia. In migration regularly visits the western Aleutian Islands.

Figure 54
Common Greenshank

Status in Canada. Accidental in Newfoundland. Photo record: one individual was at Riverhead, Conception Bay, from 3 to 11 December 1983. An individual of the same species was in exactly the same locality for some time in August 1984. Readily identifiable photos of the December bird were taken by Bruce Mactavish, one of several competent observers who studied the bird.

Greater Yellowlegs

Grand Chevalier
Tringa melanoleuca (Gmelin)
Total length: 32 to 38 cm
Plate 30

Breeding Distribution of Greater Yellowlegs

Range in Canada. Breeding range rather poorly known. Breeds in southern Mackenzie (Gagnon and Rutledge lakes; probably Nahanni National Park); south-central British Columbia (Fort St. James, Nukko Lake, Kleena Kleene, Mile 93 Caribou Road; possibly Peace River parklands); northern and central Alberta (Zama Lake, Lake Athabasca, Fawcett, Athabasca, Entrance, Nordegg, Rocky Mountain House, Sundre, Boggy Lake, Jasper National Park); northwestern and central Saskatchewan (Lake Athabasca, Hanson Lake, Wollaston Lake); north-central and central Manitoba (probably Ilford, Bird, Moose and Cedar lakes); northern Ontario (muskegs inland from James and Hudson bays: Hawley and Aquatuck lakes); central Quebec (Lake Mistassini, Schefferville region, south to the Gulf of St. Lawrence and Anticosti Island); central and southern Labrador (Hopedale, Cartwright); Newfoundland (Gaff Topsail); and northeastern Nova Scotia (Cape Breton Island).

Migrates through the southern interior and along the Pacific and Atlantic coasts. Stragglers north to southern Keewatin (probably: sight records 80 km below Eskimo Point; Windy River), and northern Quebec (Ungava Bay, Povungnituk). Casual on Southampton Island. Accidental in Baffin Island (Cumberland Sound). Irregularly a few winter in southwestern British Columbia (southern Vancouver Island).

A large shorebird with almost straight or very slightly uptilted bill (5 to 5.8 cm); marked with grey, black, and white (in autumn, adults and immatures have the black replaced by grey), rump more whitish than rest of upper parts, and long bright-yellow legs. Distinguished from Lesser Yellowlegs by much larger size.

Measurements. *Adult male*: wing, 182–197.5 (189.4); tail, 69–84.2 (77.2); exposed culmen, 53.3–59.5 (56.1); tarsus, 59.4–67 (63.4). *Adult female*: wing, 183–198.4 (188.6) mm.

Field Marks. A large, slim, grey-and-white shorebird with long *bright-yellow legs*. In flight it shows whitish rump and no wing stripe. A large edition of the Lesser Yellowlegs, and when, as often happens, the two are together they are readily distinguishable by size. Otherwise size is tricky. The bill of the Greater tends to turn up slightly. In migration its ringing whistled calls are in series of *three or four* on a descending scale, very different from the *one or two* softer whistles of the Lesser. On the ground, when disturbed, a loud long-continued monotonous series of *keks*. Both yellowlegs on the ground have frequent nodding motions (actually they begin with a backward jerk of the head).

Habitat. In migration, pools, sloughs, shallow margins of lakes and sluggish streams, flooded land; and on the coast, salt marshes, tidal pools, mud flats, and bays, but is not partial to outer wave-swept shores. In breeding season, wooded muskeg country, its bogs, ponds and lakes, low sparsely wooded ridges, and burntlands; also open woodlands, not necessarily very close to water.

Nesting. Nest, a depression or scrape in the ground or moss, lined with grasses, moss, or leaves, in boggy places or sparsely wooded ridges. *Eggs*, usually 4; buffy, spotted and blotched with browns. Nesting activities poorly known. Male takes active part in caring for the young.

Range. Breeds in southern Alaska and in wooded muskeg country across Canada (see Range in Canada). Winters from central California (rarely southern British Columbia), southern Arizona, the Gulf of Mexico coast, and South Carolina south to southern South America, including the West Indies.

Lesser Yellowlegs

Petit Chevalier
Tringa flavipes (Gmelin)
Total length: 23 to 28 cm
Plate 30

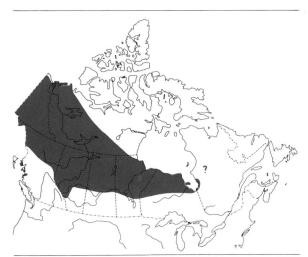

Breeding Distribution of Lesser Yellowlegs

Range in Canada. Breeds from northern Yukon (upper Firth River); northwestern and east-central Mackenzie (Mackenzie Delta, Fort Anderson, Artillery Lake, Redrock Lake); southern Keewatin (Nueltin Lake); northern Manitoba (Churchill); northern Ontario (Fort Severn); and central-western Quebec (Moar Bay); south to central British Columbia (Peace River District); south-central Alberta (Turner Valley, Buffalo Lake); central Saskatchewan (Amyot Lake, Whitefox River); central Manitoba (The Pas; unconfirmed reports near Mulvihill); and northern Ontario (Favourable Lake, Moosonee).

In southward migration common in most of extreme southern Canada from interior British Columbia to Nova Scotia, but spring migration is mainly through the interior, at which time the bird is much scarcer in British Columbia, Quebec, and the Maritimes. Rare to casual in Labrador and Newfoundland. Scarce on British Columbia coast.

Bill straight, 3.4 to 3.5 cm. Almost exactly like Greater Yellowlegs in all plumages, but decidedly smaller and lacks any suggestion of an uptilted bill. Lacks faint whitish marbling usually present on underside of the flight feathers of Greater Yellowlegs.

Measurements. *Adult male*: wing, 146.2–158.3 (152.1); tail, 58–66 (60.9); exposed culmen, 33.6–37 (35.4); tarsus, 46.8–53.6 (50.4). *Adult female*: wing, 150.1–158.5 (156.2) mm.

Field Marks. Long, bright-yellow legs, grey-and-white coloration, whitish rump and tail identify it as a yellowlegs. Its smaller size is obvious when compared directly with Greater Yellowlegs, but is less helpful otherwise. Bill straight, not slightly uptilted. On take-off, utters one or two call-notes, which are much softer, flatter and usually very different from the loud, ringing three or four of the Greater. Lesser Yellowlegs might be confused with autumn Stilt Sandpiper, a small bird with more-greenish legs and a whitish line extending completely over and behind the eye.

Habitat. In migration very similar to that of Greater Yellowlegs, often in company with that species. For nesting, open woodland and burntland in country interspersed with muskegs, ponds, and lakes, the wet areas used for feeding and raising of young.

Nesting. Nest, a depression in the ground lined with grasses and leaves, near a log, stump, small tree, or in the open. *Eggs*, usually 4; buffy, spotted and blotched with browns. Incubation by both parents. As in Greater Yellowlegs, the male apparently assumes a large part of caring for the young.

Range. Breeds in Alaska and much of western Canada east to James Bay. Winters from South Carolina, the Gulf States, and Mexico south to Chile and Argentina; also in the West Indies.

White-winged Redshank

[**White-winged Redshank** (The Redshank). Chevalier gambette. *Tringa totanus* (Linnaeus). Plate 27. Hypothetical. A careful observation in Halifax County, Nova Scotia, on 2 January 1960, by L.B. Macpherson and Fred Dobson (Tufts 1973) of a redshank was either this species or possibly the Spotted Redshank, *Tringa erythropus*. A redshank was observed also at Homeville, Nova Scotia, on 26 July 1974, by Sara and George MacLean and thought to be one of this species. In neither of the above cases, however, was a prominent white trailing edge to the spread wing observed. This character of the White-winged Redshank is difficult to miss in a flying bird and the possibility of the Spotted Redshank was by no means eliminated.

"The Redshank," as a name, is inadequate and presents difficulties when comparisons with Spotted Redshank are attempted. The new substitute name here proposed is not only descriptive but it obviates the other difficulties mentioned.]

Spotted Redshank

Chevalier arlequin
Tringa erythropus (Pallas)
Total length: 35 cm
Plate 27

Status in Canada. Casual in British Columbia
(photo record: one remained at the Reifel
Waterfowl Refuge, near Vancouver from
24 September through 11 November 1970. This
or another was at the same locality in the first
week of May 1971); several sight records for
British Columbia; Newfoundland (photo
record: Newman Sound in Terra Nova National
Park, 15 May to at least 21 May 1974). Sight
record for Ontario (St. Davids, 25 July 1976;
photo record: Lakefield, 7 May 1981).

Proportions similar to those of Lesser Yellowlegs but somewhat larger.
Adults in breeding season differ from all other shorebirds in their sooty-
black plumage (speckled with white) above and below; but with white
rump. In winter the species resembles Greater and Lesser yellowlegs but
the legs are red or orange, not yellow. White of rump in Spotted Redshank is more extensive, reaching far up the back. In winter plumages,
the Spotted Redshank resembles also the White-winged Redshank
(Tringa totanus) but lacks the prominent white wing bar shown by that
species.

Measurements. *Adult male*: wing, 157–167; tail, 60–67; tarsus,
52–59; exposed culmen, 54–58.5. *Adult female*: wing, 166–176; exposed
culmen, 56–64 mm.

Range. Breeds from northeastern Norway eastward through the
taiga of northern Russia and northern Siberia. Winters mainly in
southern Eurasia.

Solitary Sandpiper

Chevalier solitaire
Tringa solitaria Wilson
Total length: 19 to 23 cm
Plate 30

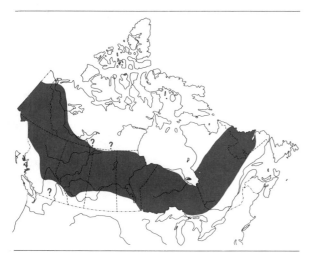

Breeding Distribution of Solitary Sandpiper

Range in Canada. Summer resident and tran-
sient. Breeds north to near tree limit from
Yukon (Old Crow, Kathleen River, Lapie
River); Mackenzie (Mackenzie Delta, Wood
Buffalo National Park; probably Fort Norman,
Brackett Lake, and possibly Thelon River);
south to central British Columbia (Peace River
District, Heart Lake, Moffat Lake); south-
central Alberta (Bragg Creek, Jasper National
Park, Bowden); central Saskatchewan (Emma
Lake, Hudson Bay, Torch River); Manitoba
(Churchill, Ilford, Herchmer south perhaps to
Lake St. Martin); northern and central Ontario
(Sutton Lake, Raft River, Moosonee, south to
Sault Ste. Marie, Mildred, Timmins); Quebec
(Schefferville and 145 km south, Hutte sauvage
Lake; Paul Bay; Chibougamau Park); and
Labrador (near Nain and Hopedale).

Spring and autumn transient through British
Columbia (scarcer on coast), Alberta, Saskatch-
ewan, Manitoba, Ontario, central and southern
Quebec, New Brunswick, Prince Edward Island,
Nova Scotia, and rarely Newfoundland. In the
Maritimes commoner in southward migration
than in spring.

Upper parts including rump very dark blackish-brown with slight green
sheen, speckled in summer adults with white, in immatures with buffy
white. Legs, dark olive-green. Heavy black-and-white barring of axillars
distinguishes it from similar small sandpipers. Yellowlegs have finer and
sparser barring on the axillars but are decidedly larger and have bright-
yellow legs and whitish upper tail coverts.

Measurements *(T. s. solitaria)*. *Adult male*: wing, 124.5–130
(127.2); tail, 53.2–58.5 (55.2); exposed culmen, 28–31 (29.3); tarsus,
29.8–33.5 (31.2). *Adult female*: wing, 126–135 (130.2) mm.

Field Marks. A rather slender, straight-billed, dark-backed sandpiper with dark-green legs and a habit of nodding. Both species of
yellowlegs also have a habit of nodding, but the Solitary Sandpiper's
dark legs, dark rump, and smaller size distinguish it. From the Spotted
Sandpiper, it is distinguished by its darker upper parts and legs,
streaked breast, and different nodding motions involving mainly the
front of the body instead of mainly the rear. In flight, it differs further
from the Spotted Sandpiper in showing no white wing stripe and much
more white in outer tail. Its full wing-stroke differs from the markedly
shallow stroke of the Spotted. Common call, *peet weet*, like that of the
Spotted Sandpiper but shriller.

Habitat. More inclined to frequent quiet woodland pools and tarns
than most sandpipers, but also inhabits more open places; shallow
muddy edges of fresh and brackish water, margins of lakes, rivers,
sloughs, open muddy parts of marshes, cattle wallows. In breeding
season, muskegs and shallow water edges in or near woodland.

Nesting. Eggs are laid in old nests, of tree-nesting birds, such as
American Robin, Rusty Blackbird, Gray Jay, and Cedar Waxwing, at
various heights in both coniferous and deciduous trees. The four *eggs*
are greenish or buffy, spotted and blotched with browns and a little
bluish-grey. Relatively little is known concerning its nesting habits.

Range. Breeds in central-eastern and southern Alaska and in more
northern wooded parts of Canada. Winters from Baja California, the
Gulf of Mexico, Florida, and southeastern Georgia south to Argentina.

Subspecies. (1) *Tringa solitaria solitaria* Wilson is the breeding
form throughout the eastern part of the range and in western Canada
north to southeastern Yukon (Lapie River) and north-central Manitoba
(Ilford). (2) *T. s. cinnamomea* (Brewster), with more ashy upper parts,
slightly larger size, and (usually) with white mottling near the base of
the underside of the outer primary, and in autumn immatures with
deeper buff spots on the back, breeds in the northern part of the range
in the West (east to northeastern Manitoba) and south to northwestern
British Columbia, Great Slave Lake, and Churchill, Manitoba.

Green Sandpiper

[**Green Sandpiper**. Chevalier cul-blanc. *Tringa ochrophus* Linnaeus. Hypothetical. W. Swainson and J. Richardson (1831. *Fauna Boreali-Americana*. Part 2. London: J. Murray) recorded a specimen of this Old World species from Hudson Bay, and T.M. Brewer (1878. Bulletin Nuttall Ornithological Club, vol. 3, no. 2, p. 49) discussed another specimen allegedly from Halifax, Nova Scotia. Neither record is satisfactory.]

Willet

Chevalier semipalmé
Catoptrophorus semipalmatus (Gmelin)
Total length: 35.5 to 43 cm
Plate 30

Breeding Distribution of Willet

Range in Canada. Locally common summer resident. Breeds in two disjunct areas: (1) southeastern and central-eastern Alberta (Miquelon Lakes, Brooks, Dominion Range Station on Milk River), southern Saskatchewan (Carlton, Maple Creek, Yorkton), and southwestern Manitoba; and (2) Nova Scotia (including Cape Breton Island) and recently in southern New Brunswick (Baie Verte, Cape Jourimain, Cormierville) and Prince Edward Island (Tracadie, Bayshore and Brackley marshes).

Rare migrant in southwestern British Columbia (Comox, Victoria); northern Manitoba (Churchill); southern Ontario (Toronto; sight records for Kenora, Niagara River, Ottawa); Newfoundland (Argentia, St. Andrews, Grand Banks); and southwestern Quebec (Godbout; sight records near Montréal, Île-du-Moine).

A large grey-and-white shorebird with bill straight and slightly longer than head, white upper tail coverts, and very broad white band across the wing, contrasting with the blackish flight feathers. The wing markings are diagnostic in any plumage. American Oystercatcher and Avocet are other large shorebirds with much white in the wings, but the bills and markings of both are very different.

Measurements *(C. s. inornatus). Adult male*: wing, 196.3–208.1 (203.9); tail, 74.9–81.8 (78.3); exposed culmen, 56.3–66 (61.1); tarsus, 64–71.4 (66.7). *Adult female*: wing, 202.2–213.1 (207.3) mm.

Field Marks. A large greyish straight-billed shorebird somewhat suggesting a robust Greater Yellowlegs but with grey-blue legs. In flight it flashes a very conspicuous black-and-white wing pattern, visible at considerable distances, a pattern unlike that of any other greyish straight-billed shorebird. Noisy on breeding grounds. Common call: when on ground in nesting season, a loud, long-continued series of *yips*; in flight *pil-willet, pil-willet,* or *pil-will-willet.*

Habitat. In the West, moist and wet meadows, grassy edges of prairie sloughs and lakes. In the East, salt marshes and beaches on the coast.

Nesting. Nest, a depression in the ground, lined with grass and weeds. *Eggs,* usually 4; olive-buff, spotted and blotched with browns. Incubation period about 22 days.

Range. Breeds from eastern Oregon, Idaho, and southern parts of the Prairie Provinces of Canada south to northeastern California, northern Colorado, and South Dakota; on the Atlantic Coast in Nova Scotia, and locally from New Jersey to Florida, Texas, and Tamaulipas, Mexico; also in the West Indies. Winters from southern United States south to Peru and Brazil.

Subspecies. (1) *Catoptrophorus semipalmatus semipalmatus* (Gmelin) breeds in the Maritimes. (2) *C. s. inornatus* (Brewster), a larger, decidedly paler race, is the bird of the interior, breeding in the Prairie Provinces.

Remarks. This large wader, with its noisy ways and showy wing pattern, is an impressive bird on its nesting grounds. In the Maritime Provinces it has substantially expanded its breeding range during recent years.

Wandering Tattler

Chevalier errant
Heteroscelus incanus (Gmelin)
Total length: 26.5 to 29 cm
Plate 31

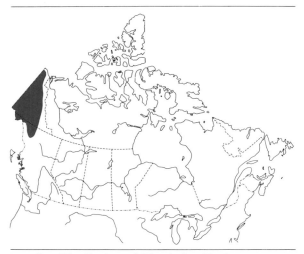

Breeding Distribution of Wandering Tattler

Range in Canada. Breeds (extent of breeding range poorly known) in high mountains of Yukon (British Mountains, upper Malcolm River; Rock River in the Richardson Mountains; probably Rose River at Canol Road; perhaps upper Macmillan River) and northwestern British Columbia (Chilkat Pass; probably Atlin and Dease Lake).

Migrant, fairly common, along outer coast and islands of British Columbia. Rare visitor to Alberta (specimen record: Swan Lake, 30 May 1938. Sight records: Jasper National Park, Beaverhill Lake, and near Edmonton). Casual in Ontario (photo record: Fort Erie, 8 June 1977; also two sight records) and Manitoba (photo: Churchill, 14 June 1981).

Bill straight. Upper parts plain slaty-grey, unrelieved from crown to tip of tail and without wing stripes. Adults in breeding plumage have the under parts heavily barred with dark grey and white. Winter adults and immatures lack bars on the under parts, these replaced by a grey suffusion over breast and sides. In all plumages a well-defined white eyebrow line is present. Legs yellow-green to dull orange-yellow.

Measurements. *Adult male*: wing, 161.2–179.9 (170.1); tail, 72.3–80 (74.9); exposed culmen, 34–40.3 (37.7); tarsus, 32.5–36.5 (33.9). *Adult female*: wing, 167.4–181.6 (173.8) mm.

Field Marks. A medium-sized shorebird of the far West with plain dark-grey upper parts, longish straight bill, well-defined white eyebrow line, and in migration showing a preference for outer coasts. The heavily barred under parts of breeding plumage are unlike those of other shorebirds, except the Stilt Sandpiper, which is a smaller, brownish-backed bird with a white rump. Winter-plumaged adults and immatures have plain-grey breast and sides, but the *uniform* dark grey of the upper parts distinguishes them from the Surfbird, Black Turnstone, Red Knot, and both yellowlegs, all of which show some white or whitish near the tail. In flight it shows no white wing stripe. It has the habit of teetering.

Habitat. In migration, usually outer rocky seacoasts and islands. In breeding season, mountain streams and meadows.

Nesting. The few nests known have been on gravel bars of high mountain streams. Nest, a depression in gravel, compactly lined with twigs and rootlets. *Eggs*, 4; greenish, spotted and blotched with browns. Incubation is said to be by both parents, lasting 23 to 25 days.

Range. Breeds in the mountains of interior Alaska, Yukon, and northwestern British Columbia; also evidently in northeastern Siberia. Winters on the Pacific Coast from southern California to Ecuador, on the Hawaiian Islands, and on many islands of the south Pacific south to Fiji, Tonga, and Society islands.

Spotted Sandpiper

Chevalier branlequeue
Actitis macularia (Linnaeus)
Total length: 17.7 to 20.5 cm
Plate 30

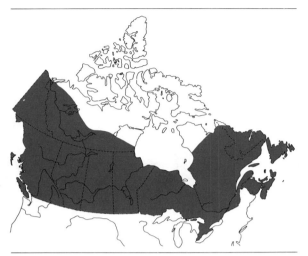

Breeding Distribution of Spotted Sandpiper

Range in Canada. Common and widely distributed summer resident and transient. Breeds from northern Yukon (north to arctic coast); northwestern and central Mackenzie (Mackenzie Delta, Lockhart and Anderson rivers, marshy parts of Thelon River); southwestern Keewatin (Windy River mouth); northern Quebec (Lake Guillaume-Delisle, Kuujjuaq, Koroc River); and northern Labrador (Okak); south through British Columbia (including southern Vancouver Island); and all the provinces.

Occasionally winters in southwestern British Columbia (Vancouver Island, Chilliwack).

Adults in breeding plumage are unmistakable with roundish black spots on the white under parts and a slightly metallic lustre to the greyish-brown upper parts. Autumn birds have unspotted white under parts, shading to grey on upper breast, and narrow dusky bars on wing coverts. Separable from Solitary Sandpiper by all-white axillars.

Measurements. *Adult male*: wing, 94–102.5 (99.7); tail, 47–53 (49.1); exposed culmen, 21.6–25 (23.1); tarsus, 23.3–25.1 (24.3). *Adult female*: wing, 99.3–108.3 (105.7) mm.

Field Marks. The common breeding sandpiper all across southern Canada. On the ground a pale-legged sandpiper with a pale area at base of lower mandible and a habit of teetering almost constantly, the tail figuring prominently in this. In flight the stiffly held, down-bowed wings and quick shallow wing-strokes with frequent short glides are characteristic. Black roundish spots on the under parts of spring and summer adults are unmistakable. Young and adults in autumn have plain-white under parts with grey shading on upper breast. Although less well marked, they have the same characteristic motions, pale legs, and pale area at base of lower mandible and usually show a whitish area just in front of the folded wing. Most likely to be confused with the Solitary Sandpiper, but the peculiar flight, white stripe in spread wing, much less white in tail, and yellowish or flesh-coloured legs mark the Spotted. Common call: a sharp *peet-weet*; a series of *weet*.

Habitat. Sandy, rocky, or muddy shores of interior lakes, ponds, rivers, and streams as well as on coastal salt water, usually in open to fairly open places. Often forages on floating logs.

Nesting. Nest, a hollow in the ground with a sparse lining of grass, moss, bits of weeds, or similar vegetation, usually not too far from water. *Eggs*, usually 4; buffy with spots and blotches of dark brown and often a few spots of bluish grey. Incubation 20 to 22 days (J.K. and J.T. Miller). Incubation is largely by male (Mousley) but in late clutches female may assist.

Range. Breeds from northwestern Alaska eastward across Canada and south to southern California (mountains), central Texas, northern Alabama, western North Carolina (mountains), and eastern Maryland. Winters from southwestern British Columbia, southern Texas, the Gulf States, and coastal South Carolina south to northern Chile and southern Brazil.

Terek Sandpiper

[**Terek Sandpiper**. Bargette de Térek. *Xenus cinereus* (Güldenstaedt). Hypothetical. One sight record only. A single individual was carefully observed at Churchill, Manitoba, on 13 July 1972, by James F. Akers.]

Upland Sandpiper

Maubèche des champs
Bartramia longicauda (Bechstein)
Total length: 28 to 32 cm
Plate 34

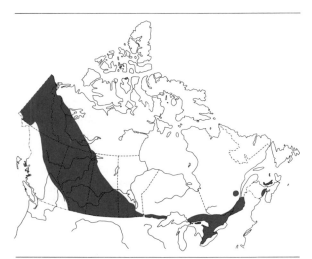

Breeding Distribution of Upland Sandpiper

Range in Canada. Breeds locally in Yukon (Firth valley, Old Crow, Duke Meadows, Wolverine Creek, Hutshi Lakes, Burwash Landing); southern Mackenzie (Norman Wells, Nahanni National Park); British Columbia (interior locally: Peace River District, Pinto Lake; 145 km west of Williams Lake; summer records for Newgate); Alberta; south-central and southern Saskatchewan (Prince Albert, Nipawin, Maple Creek, Grenfell); southern Manitoba (Garland, Aweme, probably Lake St. Martin); southern Ontario (north to about Thunder Bay, Sault Ste. Marie, Azilda); southern Quebec (Aylmer, Montréal, Hatley, Cap-Tourmente; probably Lake Saint-Jean region; possibly Mont-Joli); southern New Brunswick (Salisbury, Steeves Mountain); and Prince Edward Island (locally: St. Eleanors).

Migrates through the interior. Rare transient in coastal British Columbia (Comox, Victoria, Vancouver). Casual in eastern Quebec (Godbout). Scarce transient in Nova Scotia (Grand Pré, Canard, Sable Island); also southeastern Keewatin (80.4 km below Cape Eskimo). Accidental in Labrador (desiccated specimen found in Freytag Inlet, Hebron Fiord, 23 June 1981).

Bill (2.5 to 3.5 cm), straight but upper mandible slightly downcurved at tip. Inner web of outermost wing primary (often others also) with sawtooth-shaped markings, which distinguish it from our other shorebirds except the Whimbrel and the Long-billed Curlew (both larger birds with much longer, decidedly downcurved bills).

Measurements. *Adult male*: wing, 157.8–169.8 (163.4); tail, 76.4–88 (82.6); exposed culmen, 27.7–30.5 (28.9); tarsus, 47–51.3 (48.9). *Adult female*: wing, 161–177.9 (168.2) mm.

Field Marks. A rather large buffy upland sandpiper without any very conspicuous markings, but with slender neck, rather small head, straight shortish bill (slightly shorter than head), and rather long tail for a sandpiper. On alighting, it often extends wings straight up for a moment, exposing black-and-white barring of entire wing lining. In flight, blackish lower back is exposed. These points, combined with its habit, unlike most sandpipers, of frequenting upland habitats, make recognition easy.

Habitat. Open grassy uplands; hayfields, pastures, and prairies; also (in Yukon) sandy, sparsely vegetated flats and bogs up to timberline.

Nesting. Nest, a depression in the ground lined with grass and usually hidden in grass or other low vegetation. *Eggs*, usually 4, rather large for the size of the bird; pale buff, small-spotted with browns and a little bluish grey. Incubation 21 days, by both sexes (I.O. Buss and A.S. Hawkins).

Range. Breeds from southern Alaska and Canada (see Range in Canada) south to northeastern Oregon, southeastern Wyoming, northwestern Oklahoma, northern Texas, southern Illinois, central Virginia, and Maryland. Winters in southern South America.

Eskimo Curlew

Courlis esquimau
Numenius borealis (Forster)
Total length: 30.5 to 37 cm
(of which bill in adults is 5 to 6.5 cm)
Plate 29

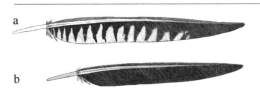

Figure 55
Outermost primary of
a) Whimbrel
b) Eskimo Curlew

Range in Canada. Now almost, if not completely, extinct. Formerly a locally very common transient and summer resident. Known to have bred in northwestern Mackenzie (Fort Anderson, Lac Rendez-vous, Franklin Bay, Point Lake). Breeding range probably larger but extent unknown.

Spring migration in North America was mainly through the interior, over the drainage of the Mississippi and Missouri rivers and west of the Great Lakes and Hudson Bay. Therefore it undoubtedly occurred as a spring transient in the Prairie Provinces, but definite data apparently were not recorded. Known as a spring migrant in southern Mackenzie (Forts Resolution and Simpson). In autumn, formerly an abundant transient on the coast of Labrador (numbers falling off sharply just prior to 1888–1890), the north shore of the Gulf of St. Lawrence, Newfoundland, Madeleine Islands, Nova Scotia, Prince Edward Island, and New Brunswick. Rare in southern Ontario (near Kingston, 10 October 1873; Toronto, 1864; and Hamilton), and in interior southwestern Quebec (Lake Saint-Pierre). Casual in southern Baffin Island.

The last recorded specimen taken in Canada was at Battle Harbour, Labrador, on 29 August 1932. There were unconfirmed sight records on James Bay in 1976, from Lake Manitoba in 1980, and near Monica Slough, south of Regina, Saskatchewan, 14 May 1982.

Similar to Whimbrel but considerably smaller with (usually) shorter, not so decidedly downcurved, bill; and with primaries plain brown, completely lacking the bars or sawtooth markings that characterize those of the Whimbrel. Crown somewhat mottled with buff, but light crown stripe less well defined than in the Whimbrel. The short bill is not always a reliable species criterion, as immature Whimbrels often have the bill almost or quite as short. The unmarked primaries are the best criterion (Figure 55).

Measurements. *Adult male*: wing, 200.5–214 (206.3); tail, 77–83.5 (80.1); exposed culmen, 48–53 (51.3); tarsus, 39.5–44 (42.1). *Adult female*: wing, 189.5–215 (203.8) mm (Ridgway).

Field Marks. The almost-extinct Eskimo Curlew cannot safely be separated from the Whimbrel in the field except under extremely favourable circumstances. A small-bodied curlew with short, slender, less decidedly decurved bill. Crown with no well-defined median stripe; dark line in front of eye poorly developed. Breast tends to have more definitely arrow-shaped markings than in the Whimbrel, and the under parts, especially in spring, are more buffy.

Nesting. Nest, a depression in the ground lined with a few dead leaves or a little dry hay. *Eggs*, usually 4; brownish green to olive blotched with brown. Little is known of its nesting habits.

Range. Extent of former breeding range now uncertain but known to have included northwestern Mackenzie and perhaps northern Alaska. Wintered from southern Brazil south to southern Argentina and Chile.

Remarks. Excessive shooting seems to have been the most plausible main reason for the decline of this little curlew. Migrating in flocks, often large ones, numbers could often be killed by a single shotgun blast. Sometimes the confused and decimated flocks returned to the decoys only to receive another barrage from the waiting hunters. One needs to look no further for a reason for this curlew's decline.

Sight records in recent years in the United States and Canada, as well as an unfortunate shooting of one in the West Indies, provide a basis for hope that at least a few Eskimo Curlews may still exist.

Whimbrel

(Hudsonian Curlew)

Courlis corlieu
Numenius phaeopus (Linnaeus)
Total length: 38 to 48 cm
(of which bill, in adults, is 7 to 10 cm)
Plate 29

Breeding Distribution of Whimbrel

Range in Canada. Breeding range apparently two disjunct areas. Breeds in Yukon (arctic coastal plain, Old Crow Mountains, probably Burwash Creek summit); and northwestern Mackenzie (Richards Island, Caribou Hills, Anderson River); also in southern Keewatin (upper Kazan River region, Boundary Lake); northeastern Manitoba (Churchill); and northern Ontario (Cape Henrietta Maria, Lake River). Recorded in the breeding season on Southampton Island and Banks Island.

Spring and autumn (including late summer) transient, mainly coastwise and on lower Great Lakes. In spring, up the Pacific Coast and the lower Great Lakes and west side of Hudson Bay with small numbers in the interior between. In late summer and autumn, southern Southampton Island, both coasts of Hudson Bay, spreading east to Newfoundland, the north shore of the Gulf of St. Lawrence, and the Maritimes. A spring and autumn transient in British Columbia (common on coast; very rare in interior); scarce spring transient in Alberta, Saskatchewan, and interior southern Manitoba. In interior Ontario it is locally fairly common in spring in extreme southern parts near Lakes Erie and Ontario, much scarcer there in autumn; scarce elsewhere; in extreme eastern parts (Ottawa) more frequently reported in autumn. Quebec (mainly autumn transient on Hudson and James bays; common on north shore of the Gulf of St. Lawrence, Anticosti and Madeleine islands, and the St. Lawrence River east of Québec; scarcer in interior west of Québec; scarce along Ungava Bay; not recorded from the northern interior). Labrador (uncommon autumn transient on coast). Newfoundland (common autumn transient). Locally common to very common autumn transient in the Maritimes, notably Cape Breton Island.

Accidental on northern Baffin Island (Arctic Bay).

Bill downcurved, slender but usually shorter than in Long-billed Curlew. Separable from that species also by Whimbrel's barred axillars, dark stripe through eye, light median crown stripe, more greyish (less pinkish-cinnamon) plumage, and smaller size. Both the Whimbrel and Long-billed Curlew have a characteristic saw-tooth colour pattern on the inner webs of the primaries, which is lacking in the smaller Eskimo Curlew.

Measurements *(N. p. hudsonicus)*. *Adult male*: wing, 223–241.5 (232.8); tail, 83.7–95.2 (91.3); exposed culmen, 74.4–88.2 (81.9); tarsus, 54.7–58.5 (56.4). *Adult female*: wing, 221.5–250.5 (240.7) mm.

Field Marks. Long, slender, downcurved bill, large size for a shorebird, and brownish coloration mark it as a curlew. Presence of head stripes and lack of conspicuous pinkish-cinnamon wing linings distinguish it from the larger Long-billed Curlew (see also Eskimo Curlew).

Habitat. Variable. For nesting, hummocky, grass-sedge, heath, and mossy tundras varying from wet tussocky lowland types to dry uplands of hills, sedge-hummocked alpine tundra, and moderately dry tundra ridges with scattered three-foot-high dwarf birch. In migration tidal mud flats, beaches, lakeshores, sparsely vegetated parts of marshes, short-grass fields and stubbles, and heaths, especially those with crowberry *(Empetrum)*.

Nesting. Nest, a depression in the ground or on a tussock of vegetation in either wet or dry tundra; nest lined with lichens, sedge leaves, or other vegetation. *Eggs*, 4, olive-buff to greenish, spotted and blotched with various browns and lavender. Incubation period 22 to 23.5 days (J.R. Jehl and D.J.T. Hussell).

Range. Breeds in Alaska, Canada, Iceland, the Faeroe Islands, and northern Eurasia east to Ob River, and from Yana River eastward across northeastern Siberia. Winters from coastal southern United States south to the Galapagos Islands, southern Chile, and Brazil; and elsewhere south to southern Africa, Australia, Tasmania, and islands in the south Pacific Ocean.

Subspecies. (1) *Numenius phaeopus hudsonicus* Latham is the only subspecies known to nest in Canada and is the common transient. (2) *N. p. phaeopus* (Linnaeus), of Europe and northwestern Siberia, is of accidental occurrence in southern Labrador (Red Bay, 14 May 1932). It has a whitish lower back and rump. (3) *N. p. islandicus* Brehm, of Iceland and the Faeroe Islands, is of accidental occurrence in Nova Scotia (Sable Island, 23 May 1906) and Newfoundland (Pistolet Bay, 27 June 1943). Similar to the nominate race but averages larger. There are sight records of Old World individuals (unidentified of course to subspecies) for Ontario and Nova Scotia.

Bristle-thighed Curlew

Courlis de Tahiti
Numenius tahitiensis (Gmelin)
Total length: 38 to 47 cm

Status in Canada. Accidental in British Columbia. A male collected at Grant Bay, northwestern Vancouver Island, on 31 May 1969. One photographed at Tofino, Vancouver Island, on 1 September 1982; sight record: one at Blackie Spit, 13–14 May 1983.

Very similar to the Whimbrel but decidedly more buffy, especially on rump and tail. In the hand, the feathers of the thighs are seen to have long bristle-like tips.

Measurements. *Adult male*: wing, 222–230 (226.9); tail, 84–96 (92.1); exposed culmen, 69–88 (78.7); tarsus, 51–58.5 (55.2). *Adult female*: wing, 227–252 (240.3); tail, 97–109 (100.9); exposed culmen, 83–96 (90); tarsus, 54.5–60 (56.7) mm (Ridgway).

Field Marks. Similar in size and markings to the Whimbrel but generally more buffy. Look for the buffy rump and tail.

Range. Breeds in western Alaska. Winters on islands of the Pacific Ocean from the Marshals and Hawaiians south to Fiji, Samoa, and Marquesas, etc.

Slender-billed Curlew

Courlis à bec grêle
Numenius tenuirostris Vieillot

Accidental. The taking of a specimen by I.L. Terry, Jr., at Crescent Beach, Ontario, in autumn about 1925 seems adequately documented by Beardslee and Mitchell (1965). The specimen is in the Buffalo Museum of Science.

Far Eastern Curlew

Courlis de Sibérie
Numenius madagascariensis (Linnaeus)
Total length: 56 to 59 cm

Status in Canada. Accidental in British Columbia (photo: one at Boundary Bay for a considerable period in early autumn 1984).

A large curlew. Similar in size and general appearance to Long-billed Curlew but lacks the pinkish-cinnamon in the wings and the strongly buffy tones of the under parts. Wings and their coverts more coarsely marked, especially the underside of wings. Axillars strongly barred. Greatly resembles Eurasian Curlew but shows no whitish rump patch, the rump being concolour with the back.

Range. Breeds in eastern Siberia eastward to Kamchatka and south to Transbaicalia, northeastern Mongolia, northern Manchuria, and Ussuriland.

Eurasian Curlew

[**Eurasian Curlew**. Courlis cendré. *Numenius arquata* (Linnaeus). Figure 56. Hypothetical. Sight records only. Nova Scotia (one well observed at Cherry Hill Beach, 6 May 1978) and Northwest Territories (Middle Cheyne Island, 21 June 1977).]

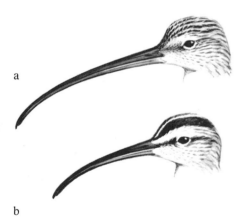

a

b

Figure 56
Head of
a) Eurasian Curlew
b) Whimbrel

Long-billed Curlew

Courlis à long bec
Numenius americanus Bechstein
Total length: 51 to 66 cm
(of which bill, in adults, is 12.7 to 19 cm)
Plate 29

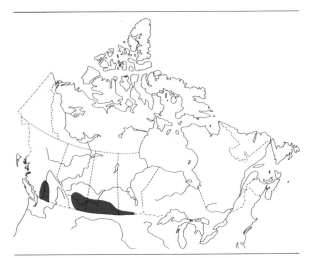

Breeding Distribution of Long-billed Curlew

Range in Canada. Summer resident in southern parts of western Canada. Breeds in southern interior British Columbia (Osoyoos, Kamloops, Riske Creek, Baldy Mountain, Dog Creek); southern Alberta (Sullivan Lake, Rosebud, Fort MacLeod, Brooks, Medicine Hat); southern Saskatchewan (north to Marsden, Struan, Big Quill Lake); and formerly southern Manitoba (Aweme and on the prairies of the Red and Souris rivers).

Casual in southern Mackenzie (Fort Simpson), on James Bay, and in New Brunswick. Records elsewhere in eastern Canada are unsatisfactory, but there is an uncertain record for southern Ontario (Ajax). Rare transient on British Columbia coast (Vancouver, very rarely Vancouver Island).

Bill extremely long, slender, downcurved. Larger size and sickle bill distinguish curlews from other shorebirds (see ibises). This, our largest shorebird, can always readily be distinguished from the Whimbrel, a slightly smaller curlew, and from the Eskimo Curlew by its plain, unbarred, cinnamon-coloured axillars.

Measurements *(N. a. parvus)*. *Adult male*: wing, 249–271 (258.6); tail, 92–105.5 (99.2); exposed culmen, 112–134 (123.4); tarsus, 73.6–81.5 (76). *Adult female*: wing, 265.5–284.5 (274.6) mm.

Field Marks. Large size for a shorebird, sickle bill, and brownish coloration mark it as a curlew (see also ibises). Most likely to be confused with the Whimbrel, a somewhat smaller curlew. Greater length of bill is not always a safe criterion as some immature Long-bills have bills as short as some adult Whimbrels or shorter. Its lack of a dark stripe through the eye and more pinkish-buff coloration, especially on the lining of the spread wing, distinguish it from the Whimbrel. Also it lacks any well-defined median crown stripe, but this is usually hard to ascertain in the field.

Habitat. Grasslands of the southern prairies and grassy intermontane valleys of southern interior British Columbia.

Nesting. Nest, a depression in the ground, lined (often sparsely but sometimes well) with grass and weeds. *Eggs*, usually 4; olive buff, more or less evenly spotted with browns and olive. Incubation, evidently by both sexes, requires about 20 days.

Range. Breeds from southern western Canada south to Utah, New Mexico, Texas (formerly east to Wisconsin and Illinois). Winters from California, western Nevada, Texas, and Louisiana south to Guatemala; also in South Carolina, Georgia, and Florida.

Subspecies. (1) *Numenius americanus parvus* Bishop is the only breeding subspecies known in Canada. (2) *N. a. americanus* Bechstein, a longer-billed race breeding farther south in the United States is a casual visitor to New Brunswick (one specimen).

Black-tailed Godwit

Barge à queue noire
Limosa limosa (Linnaeus)
Total length: 38 to 44.5 cm
Plate 35

Status in Canada. Accidental in Newfoundland (specimens: Placentia Bay, 20 May 1954; La Scie, one found dead in 1978; sight record: St. John's, 6 to 31 March 1970). In Quebec: a sight record of one at Saint-Fulgence, 22–23 May 1983; and one at Baieville, 6–7 June 1984.

Bill long, slender, slightly upturned or straight. Adults in breeding plumage have most of head, neck, breast, and sides pinkish cinnamon; the belly and under tail coverts white, broadly barred with dusky. Its mainly black tail, white upper tail coverts, and white wing stripe distinguish it from the Marbled and Bar-tailed godwits, but not from the Hudsonian. In any plumage it can be distinguished from the Hudsonian Godwit by its white axillars and extensively white wing lining (these are blackish in the Hudsonian).

Range. Breeds in Iceland and widely in Eurasia.
Subspecies. *Limosa limosa islandica* Brehm.

Hudsonian Godwit

Barge hudsonienne
Limosa haemastica (Linnaeus)
Total length: 37 to 42.5 cm
Plates 29 and 35

Breeding Distribution of Hudsonian Godwit

Range in Canada. Breeding range probably not fully known. Breeds in northwestern and south-central Mackenzie (inner deltas of Mackenzie and Anderson rivers; Fort Anderson region, West Mirage Islands in Great Slave Lake; reportedly Burnside River on Bathurst Inlet); northwestern British Columbia (Chilkat Pass); northeastern Manitoba (Churchill); northwestern Ontario (Sutton River, mouth of Brant River); and probably Akimiski Island in James Bay. Perhaps nests on Southampton Island.

Spring migration crosses western Ontario, the Prairie Provinces, and southern Mackenzie and is therefore somewhat dispersed. Southward movement in the autumn is remarkably concentrated, passing down the west coast of Hudson and James bays in a lane only a few kilometres wide. Main body of adults reaches James Bay in late July and early August, settling in large groups on tidal flats; at the same time a few hundred over-flying adults appear in the Madeleine Islands and in Prince Edward Island, Nova Scotia, and New Brunswick (J.A. Hagar). Exodus of adults from James Bay is in the last ten days of August, in flocks of 150 to 350. Since there are no observations of large flocks anywhere on the Atlantic coast or in the West Indies, a non-stop flight of at least 4850 km to some stopping place in northern South America seems likely (J.A. Hagar). Young of year begin to gather on the west coast of James Bay in early September and depart in much the same way as adults from mid-September to early October.

Except on main routes outlined above, the species is infrequent to casual, usually in very small numbers. Rare spring transient in British Columbia (Atlin, Peace River District, 150 Mile House) and in southern Ontario (near Toronto, Point Pelee). In autumn, recorded in small numbers on the east coast of James Bay (casually north to Grande rivière de la Baleine

A large shorebird with slightly upturned slender bill. This and the Marbled Godwit are the only godwits of regular occurrence in Canada. Its mainly black tail strongly contrasting with immaculate white upper tail coverts, solid blackish or dark-brown axillars, and white wing stripe readily separate it in any plumage from the larger Marbled Godwit. (For distinctions from the Bar-tailed and Black-tailed godwits, both of which are of accidental occurrence in Canada, see those species.)

Measurements. *Adult male*: wing, 195.5–208.5 (203.4); tail, 70–83.8 (74.9); exposed culmen, 68.2–81.2 (75.2); tarsus, 53.5–59.5 (56.6). *Adult female*: wing, 207–219 (212.8) mm.

Field Marks. Large size, long slender slightly upturned bill, and general coloration make it a godwit (Avocet and Black-necked Stilt also are large waders with upturned bills, but their coloration and markings are entirely different). The black tail and sharply contrasting white rump patch, white wing stripe, blackish axillars, and lack of bright cinnamon on the wing linings distinguish it at any season from the Marbled Godwit, the only other godwit of regular occurrence in Canada. Its blackish tail separates it from the Willet and Greater Yellowlegs, with which it might be confused in autumn. Its bluish-grey legs are very different from those of either species of yellowlegs.

Habitat. In autumn migration, largest concentrations on tidal mud flats, gently sloping beaches, and sandbars; smaller numbers (and in spring migration nearly the whole species), shores and shallow water of lakes, ponds, and rain pools. For nesting, wet grassy or sedge tundra seems to be preferred.

Nesting. Few detailed descriptions. What appears to be a typical nest is on a hummock or low mound in wet sedge or grass tundra with widely scattered small trees; nest proper, a shallow scrape usually in or under the edge of a prostrate dwarf birch, and unlined except for a few dead leaves, perhaps windblown (J.A. Hagar). *Eggs*, 4; olive buff, variously marked with darker spots and blotches of olive brown; general effect dark, markings obscure. Incubation period about 22 days (Hazel Ellis); 23.5 days (J.R. Jehl and D.J.T. Hussell).

on east Hudson Bay); in southern Ontario, the north shore of the Gulf of St. Lawrence (Bonne-Espérance); Gaspé, Quebec; and casually in Newfoundland. Sight records for southern Labrador (Flatwaters Cove). A regular autumn transient in small numbers in the Maritimes. Casual on Igloolik Island, southern Melville Peninsula (Repulse Bay), and southern Baffin Island (Cumberland Sound).

Range. Breeds locally in western subarctic Canada; also southern Alaska (Cook Inlet). Winters in southern South America.

Bar-tailed Godwit

Barge rousse
Limosa lapponica (Linnaeus)
Total length: 38 to 44.5 cm
Plate 35

Status in Canada. Accidental in British Columbia (Colebrook, 30 October 1931; Saanichton Bay, 9 September 1972; Reifel Island, 16 September 1972) and Newfoundland (sight record: St. John's, 26 October to 6 November 1972).

A large shorebird with slender slightly upturned bill. In breeding plumage, the under parts are plain cinnamon, this extending up on the sides of the neck and head. Upper tail coverts white, barred and spotted with dusky. Tail brownish, barred with white or buff. Adults in autumn and winter have dull-whitish under parts, and immatures have the breast greyish buff. Distinguished from Hudsonian Godwit by heavy bars and spots on the white of the upper tail coverts, barred axillars (instead of solid sooty-brown or blackish), lack of a white wing-stripe, and narrowly barred tail (no solid black masses). The narrowly barred tail, lack of a white wing stripe, and barred axillars (instead of plain white ones) distinguish it from the Black-tailed Godwit. The heavily black-and-white barred axillars and lack of pinkish cinnamon on the underside of the wing separate it from the larger Marbled Godwit.

Range. Breeds in northern Eurasia and western and northern Alaska. Winters from southern Eurasia south to Australia and New Zealand.

Subspecies. No specimens examined by the writer but presumably the Newfoundland bird was referable to *Limosa lapponica lapponica* (Linnaeus) and the British Columbia birds to *L. l. baueri* Naumann.

Marbled Godwit

Barge marbrée
Limosa fedoa (Linnaeus)
Total length: 42.5 to 50.5 cm
Plate 29

Breeding Distribution of Marbled Godwit

Range in Canada. Breeds in the grasslands of central and southern Alberta (Beaverhill Lake, Brooks, west to the foothills); southern Saskatchewan (17 km east of Nipawin, Crane Lake, Regina); central and southern Manitoba (Oak Lake, Lake St. Martin; probably The Pas); and northern Ontario (North Point). Rare transient in British Columbia (Clayoquot, Port

Godwits are very large shorebirds with very long slender bills (slightly upturned or straight) and long legs. (American Avocet and Black-necked Stilt are also large with upturned bills but are coloured entirely differently. Curlews have downcurved bills.) The Marbled Godwit, our largest godwit, is a buffy-brown bird with much pinkish cinnamon in the plumage, especially the wings. It is distinguished from the Hudsonian Godwit and the Black-tailed Godwit (of accidental occurrence in Canada) in any plumage by its lack of white upper tail coverts, lack of white wing stripe, and its larger size (see also Bar-tailed Godwit).

Measurements. *Adult male*: wing, 216.5–230.5 (223.5); tail, 77.2–84.4 (80.9); exposed culmen, 88.2–101.5 (95.9); tarsus, 64–73.6 (69.4). *Adult female*: wing, 221–242.5 (233.6) mm.

Field Marks. A very large buffy-brown shorebird with a very long, slightly upturned or straight bill. Shows much pinkish cinnamon on the underside of the wing in flight. In size and colour it resembles the Long-billed Curlew and, like it, inhabits the southern prairies in summer, but curlews have decidedly downcurved bills. Avocets and Black-necked Stilts are other large shorebirds that, like the godwits, have upcurved bills, but they are so differently coloured that they could not be confused with godwits. The Marbled Godwit is the breeding godwit of the Prairie Provinces, where it is a noisy and conspicuous bird. Its calls include a monotonous *carack* (sounds like *correct*) repeated loudly at varying speeds; *ack-ack* in couplets or triplets; and *karatica, ratica, ratica, ratica*.

Habitat. In breeding season, grasslands of the Prairies and the edges of prairie sloughs and lakes. In migration, also beaches and tide flats.

Simpson, Victoria, Columbia Lake); southern Ontario (Toronto, Rockhouse Point, Ottawa), southern Quebec (Montréal, Lake Saint-Pierre, Rivière-Ouelle, Métis; Madeleine Islands, August 1975, photographed); New Brunswick (Mace's Bay, autumn 1879); and Nova Scotia (near Halifax; reliable sight records at Sable River, Lawrencetown Beach, and elsewhere).

Nesting. Nest, a depression in either dry or moist grassland, sometimes at a considerable distance from water. It is sparsely lined with grass. *Eggs*, usually 4; buffy, rather sparingly blotched (mainly at the larger end) and spotted with browns.

Range. Breeds from southern parts of the Prairie Provinces of Canada south to central Montana, North Dakota, northeastern South Dakota, and west-central Minnesota. Winters from southern United States south to Guatemala and British Honduras, more rarely to South America.

Ruddy Turnstone

Tournepierre à collier
Arenaria interpres (Linnaeus)
Total length: 20.5 to 25 cm
Plates 28 and 35

Breeding Distribution of Ruddy Turnstone

Range in Canada. Breeds on Banks, Melville, Bathurst, Victoria, Prince of Wales, and King William islands, and perhaps Somerset Island; Boothia Peninsula, Igloolik Island, southwestern Baffin Island (Bowman Bay, Taverner Bay), Southampton Island (also Coats and Mansel islands); Ellesmere (Alert, Slidre Fiord) and Axel Heiberg islands, and southward (sparsely on Devon Island and perhaps Bylot Island). Also on Herschel Island, Yukon, and in northwestern coastal Mackenzie (Franklin and Liverpool bays, Cape Bathurst).

Recorded northwest to Prince Patrick Island (Wilkie Point) but evidence of breeding is lacking.

Spring and autumn transient in much of southern Canada but absent or rare in the mountains of Yukon, interior British Columbia, and southwestern Alberta. Much commoner in autumn from southern Quebec eastward than in spring. Generally commoner coastally than in the interior, but concentrations occur on the Great Lakes. Spring and autumn transient in British Columbia (mainly coast and islands, uncommon); Alberta (east of the mountains, scarce); Saskatchewan (scarce to locally fairly common); Manitoba (scarce to locally fairly common in interior; common on Hudson Bay coast); Ontario (common on James and Hudson bays and on the Great Lakes; elsewhere generally scarce); Quebec

Bill tapering to a point, hard, blackish, very woodpecker-like. Legs short, orange. Woodpecker-like bill identifies it as a turnstone. The peculiar black, white, and russet colour-pattern of spring and summer adults is unmistakable. Autumn adults and immatures are much duller, the blacks being replaced by greyish browns; the russet patches are lacking or reduced to buffy feather edges, and the sides of head and neck are heavily streaked with dusky. But the breast patches, although more brownish and somewhat obscured by whitish feather-tips, retain their characteristic shape, thus separating this species from the Black Turnstone. Bill shape and white lower back separate it from the Surfbird (which has only a white rump).

Measurements *(A. i. morinella). Adult male*: wing, 135.9–151.7 (146); tail, 56.9–64.6 (60.5); exposed culmen, 21.1–24 (22.6); tarsus, 24.8–27 (26.5). *Adult female*: wing, 140–156.3 (146.9) mm.

Field Marks. A stocky shorebird with shortish neck; short orange legs; pointed, often slightly upturned blackish bill; and in spring and summer a striking black, white, and russet colour-pattern. Autumn adults and immatures, although more brownish and without the russet patches, still show enough of the peculiar breast pattern to identify them. Both species of turnstone and the Surfbird have a broad dark band near the end of the tail, but in flight turnstones show a white lower back. The orange legs and peculiar breast patches separate this species from the Black Turnstone. The white lower back, dark rump band, white upper tail coverts, and dark hind half of the tail form a striking pattern that in flight separates the turnstones from the rest of our shorebirds.

Habitat. In migration, rocky shores, pebbly and sandy beaches, muddy places strewn with sea debris, kelp piles along saltwater tide lines; shores and beaches of freshwater lakes of the interior; sometimes crowberry flats. For nesting, in the Arctic, habitat varies from tundra, well-vegetated with willow and dryas, to rather bare and open places, and from the plateau tops of gravelly ridges to low, flat sandy islands and hummocky moist tundra.

Nesting. Nest, a shallow depression in the ground, usually (not always) lined with leaves of available vegetation. *Eggs*, usually 4; greyish green variously streaked and spotted with browns. Incubation 21 to 22 days (Parmelee and MacDonald), by both sexes but, until the approach of hatching, mainly by the female. Young leave the nest within a day after hatching.

Range. Circumpolar. Breeds (usually not far from coasts) in northern Alaska (south to the delta of Yukon River; St. Lawrence and St. Matthew islands), northern Canada, northern and central Greenland, Iceland, north coasts of Europe (locally south to islands in the Baltic), northern Siberia, and Wrangell Island. Winters from southern United States south to Chile and southern Brazil; and from southern Europe (north on the Atlantic Coast to the British Isles), coastal southern Asia, and the Hawaiian Islands south to southern Africa, the East Indies, Australia, and New Zealand.

(commoner on southeast coasts in autumn than in spring; scarce in southern interior; known to migrate on coasts of Hudson, James, and Ungava bays but extent and numbers poorly known; no records available from northern interior north of Lake Saint-Jean); Labrador (uncommon autumn migrant); Newfoundland (fairly common autumn migrant); Maritime Provinces (uncommon spring, common autumn migrant). Non-breeding birds occasionally are found in summer in widely scattered localities in the country south of the breeding range.

Subspecies. (1) *Arenaria interpres morinella* (Linnaeus) occupies most of the breeding range in Canada except the northeast part (see next subspecies). It is the common migrant race of all of southern Canada, but on the British Columbia coast it is scarce and the following race also occurs there. (2) *A. i. interpres* (Linnaeus) has more extensive black and less extensive paler russet in the upper parts. Breeds on Ellesmere and Axel Heiberg islands (perhaps also Devon Island) and winters in the Old World. More blackish migrants on the British Columbia coast are referred to this race, although in some specimens (three males, Clayoquot, 15 May 1907) the russet in the upper parts is darker than in Ellesmere Island and Greenland *interpres*. They doubtless originate in Alaska. Some authors consider Alaskan and Siberian birds separable from the nominate race, as *A. i. cinclus* (Pallas), but the writer has not seen adequate material to be sure of the validity of *cinclus*.

Black Turnstone

Tournepierre noir
Arenaria melanocephala (Vigors)
Total length: 22.5 to 25.5 cm
Plate 31

Range in Canada. Very common transient and winter resident on the coast of British Columbia. Casual in migration in the interior of British Columbia (Vanderhoof region) and Yukon (Teslin, Watson Lake).

Bill pointed, woodpecker-like, blackish as in Ruddy Turnstone. Legs short, dusky. *Adults in breeding plumage*: Head, neck, breast, and upper parts mainly sooty black. Lower back (partly concealed by folded wings) white, separated from white base of tail by blackish rump band as in Ruddy Turnstone. Hind half of tail black, narrowly margined white. In high plumage, forehead, sides of neck, and sides of breast, spotted with white. Line over eye and spot in front of eye, white. Wing stripe, belly, sides, and under tail coverts, white. *Adult and young in autumn*: Similar to above but without any white on head or neck.

Measurements. *Adult male*: wing, 144–150.8 (147.1); tail, 59–64.4 (61.8); exposed culmen, 21–24.9 (23); tarsus, 25–27.6 (26.3). *Adult female*: wing, 141.5–157 (150.9) mm.

Field Marks. A chunky, short-legged, black-and-white shorebird of the West Coast. In flight it shows the same white lower back and base of tail separated by dark band as in Ruddy Turnstone, but differs from the Ruddy in darker all black-and-white coloration, dusky instead of orange legs, and uniform (not patchy) dark breast. Surfbird also has base of tail and upper tail coverts white, but the lower back is dark and the spread wing shows much less white.

Habitat. Exposed, rocky, or kelp-covered ocean shores and wave-washed reefs.

Range. Breeds on the coast of western and southern Alaska (Cape Prince of Wales south to Chichagof Island). Winters along the Pacific Coast of North America from southeastern Alaska south to Baja California and Sonora, Mexico.

Surfbird

Bécasseau du ressac
Aphriza virgata (Gmelin)
Total length: 24 to 25.5 cm
Plate 31

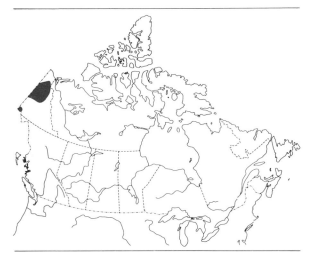

Breeding Distribution of Surfbird

Range in Canada. Breeds in Yukon at higher elevations in the Ogilvie Mountains (headwaters of south Tatonduk River; 80 km north of Dawson; and at other localities); Richardson Mountains (Rock River); in Kluane Game Sanctuary (Amphitheatre Mountain); and in the Ruby and Sifton ranges. Fairly common spring and autumn transient along the outer coasts and islands of British Columbia; winter resident on both coasts of Vancouver Island and probably elsewhere on the British Columbia coast. Casual visitant to Alberta (one photo record: Beaverhill Lake).

Bill plover-like, rather slender, with slightly enlarged horny tip. Legs short. *Adults (spring and summer)*: Head and neck streaked dark grey and white. Upper body and wing coverts dark grey, the back feathers with whitish margins; scapulars with admixture of chestnut. Base of tail and upper tail coverts white; rest of tail brownish black. Wing stripe white. Under parts white, the fore-neck streaked with dusky, breast heavily spotted and V-marked with greyish brown, the flanks V-marked with same. Legs and base of lower mandible yellowish. *Adults (autumn and winter)*: Similar to above but upper parts (except upper tail coverts) plain dark greyish-brown. Breast plain dark greyish-brown, the lower breast often inconspicuously spotted with dusky. *Immatures*: Similar to autumn adults, but scapulars and wing coverts narrowly margined with white, and breast much mixed with whitish.

Measurements. *Adult male*: wing, 160.5–173.4 (165.6); tail, 60.3–67.2 (63.9); exposed culmen, 21.5–25 (23.6); tarsus, 31–32 (31.1). *Adult female*: wing, 171–183.2 (176.9) mm.

Field Marks. A chunky, short-legged shorebird of the rocky West Coast, most likely to be confused with turnstones, Rock Sandpiper, or the autumn Red Knot. Its upper parts and breast are darker than those of the Red Knot, and its white rump patch contrasts sharply with its dark hind-tail and lower back (the Red Knot often shows lightish rump, but this is never conspicuous). The Surfbird has a tail pattern similar to that of turnstones, but flight exposes its dark lower back (turnstones show white on lower back and more white in wings). Its white rump patch separates it from the Rock Sandpiper.

Habitat. Rocky wave-swept ocean shores in migration and winter in British Columbia. Breeds in stony heaths of high alpine slopes and ridges (Robert Frisch).

Nesting. In Alaska, on barren rocky mountains above timberline. Nest a shallow depression in rocky ground. *Eggs*, 4; buff, boldly marked usually with bay and browns, thus in colour somewhat like eggs of certain falcons, although the pyriform shape is, of course, similar to the eggs of many other shorebirds. The nest and eggs were unknown until 1926 (Joseph Dixon, Condor, vol. 29, no. 1, pp. 2–16).

Range. Breeds in Alaska (Mount McKinley Park and the Fortymile River system) and Yukon. Winters along the Pacific Coast from southeastern Alaska south to the Straits of Magellan.

Red Knot

Bécasseau maubèche
Calidris canutus (Linnaeus)
Total length: 25 to 28 cm
Plate 32

Breeding Distribution of Red Knot

Range in Canada. Breeds very locally in the Arctic from Prince Patrick Island (Mould Bay), Ellef Ringnes Island (Isachsen), Axel Heiberg Island, and northern Ellesmere Island (Alert) south to southern Victoria Island (Cambridge Bay), and Southampton Island; probably Adelaide Peninsula and Mansel Island.

Spring migration is mainly west of Quebec and James and Hudson bays. In autumn it spreads farther east to the Maritimes and rarely to the coast of Labrador and Newfoundland. An uncommon spring and autumn transient on the coast of British Columbia (but not recorded from the interior), coastal Yukon, eastern Alberta, Saskatchewan, interior Manitoba, interior Ontario. Common transient on west coast of James and Hudson bays. Autumn transient, rare in spring, from southern Quebec east to the Maritimes. Birds from the northernmost parts of the breeding range (Bathurst and Ellesmere islands) winter in the Old World.

Bill straight, 3.0 to 3.8 cm, slightly longer than head. Legs short. In breeding plumage, unmarked robin-red throat and breast combined with a short straight bill distinguish it from all others. Dowitchers have long bills, and the accidental Curlew Sandpiper has a definitely downcurved bill. Autumn Red Knots have white under parts with fine dusky streaking on the breast; light-grey upper parts, the feathers of the back with faint white narrow margins and a fine black submarginal line, giving a semicircular pattern to the feather tips. Upper tail coverts white, barred with dusky. Legs yellowish olive.

Measurements *(C. c. rufa)*. *Adult male*: wing, 155.9–173.9 (162.5); tail, 58–66.5 (62.2); exposed culmen, 33.5–37.8 (35.4); tarsus, 31–32.8 (32). *Adult female*: wing, 166–172.1 (168.7) mm.

Field Marks. In spring, a sturdy sandpiper with brick-red breast and *short* straight bill (dowitchers and others with reddish breast have *long* bills; the accidental Curlew Sandpiper has definitely downcurved bill). In autumn, a chunky large sandpiper with light-grey upper parts; white under parts finely streaked with dusky on breast; short legs; and short straight bill. In flight it shows a narrow white wing stripe and a rump obviously lighter than the rest of the upper parts. On the West Coast, autumn Red Knots might be confused with the Surfbird or Wandering Tattler. The Red Knot has a poorly defined lighter rump compared with the rest of the upper parts. The Surfbird has a sharply defined white rump, and in the Wandering Tattler the rump is dark grey, exactly like the rest of the upper parts.

Habitat. In migration it favours beaches and mud flats, also rocks covered with seaweed. In breeding season (Ellesmere and Prince Patrick islands) favours well-vegetated moist tundra for nesting, feeding, and rearing of young; nests also on higher, stony ridges.

Nesting. Nest, a shallow depression in the ground, lined with willow twigs, dry leaves, grass, and bits of moss. May be located on hummocks in moist ground or in glacial gravel on higher, drier arctic hills. *Eggs*, usually 4; buffy, spotted and scrawled with brown. Incubation by both parents, and both care for the young. Incubation period for two nests: 21 days, 20.25 hours; 21 days, 6 hours, 12 minutes respectively (David A. Gill).

Range. Breeds locally in the Arctic of both the New and Old Worlds; in the New World in northern Alaska (Point Barrow), locally in the Canadian Arctic, and in northern Greenland. In the New World, winters from southern California and Massachusetts (rarely) south along the coasts to southern South America.

Subspecies. (1) *Calidris canutus canutus* (Linnaeus) breeds in the Old World and also occupies the northern part of the breeding range in North America on Prince Patrick, Ellef Ringnes, Melville, Bathurst, and Ellesmere islands; and probably northern Prince of Wales Island. Some migrate along the coast of British Columbia, but the writer has seen no evidence of its migration in eastern Canada south of Broughton Island, Baffin Island. (2) *C. c. rufa* (Wilson), a well-marked race characterized by paler coloration above and below and with the rufous of under parts decidedly less extensive posteriorly, occupies the southern part of the breeding range from southern Victoria Island east at least to Southampton Island, but its areas of intergradation with the nominate race are not known. It is the migrant through most of southern Canada east of the Pacific Coast. However, little material has been examined from the Prairie Provinces.

Sanderling

Bécasseau sanderling
Calidris alba (Pallas)
Total length: 18 to 22.5 cm
Plates 33 and 35

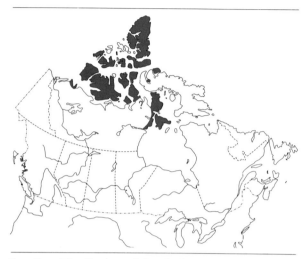

Breeding Distribution of Sanderling

Range in Canada. Breeds in the Arctic from Prince Patrick Island (Mould Bay), Lougheed Island, and northern Ellesmere Island (Lake Hazen, Fosheim Peninsula, probably Alert) south through Banks Island (Collinson Point, Sachs Harbour) to northwestern Mackenzie (rarely: near Franklin Bay), Victoria Island (De Haven Point), Prince of Wales Island, King William Island, Melville Peninsula, and Southampton Island, Cape Fullerton, Bylot Island, and northern Baffin Island (photo record: near Nanisivik, Strathcona Sound).

In migration it disperses widely and is a common transient in most of the country south of the breeding range and in all the provinces. Very scarce in Yukon (except on the coast) and interior British Columbia (mainly in autumn) but common on the British Columbia coast, Alberta, Saskatchewan, Manitoba. From Ontario eastward it is mainly an autumn transient, particularly in Quebec, Labrador, Newfoundland, and the Maritimes. Non-breeding birds occur in summer south of the breeding range.

Winters in small numbers in southwestern British Columbia (Fraser River mouth, Vancouver Island), and Nova Scotia.

Bill about as long as head, rather heavy, black. Toes three (hind toe lacking or very rarely rudimentary). Lack of a hind toe distinguishes it from other sandpipers.

Measurements. *Adult male*: wing, 114.5–121.6 (118.3); tail, 47.3–53 (50.6); exposed culmen, 22.5–26.6 (24.4); tarsus, 23.5–25.8 (24.7). *Adult female*: wing, 122.3–128.9 (124.4) mm.

Field Marks. A chunky sandpiper with short heavy black bill and (in flight) a conspicuous white wing stripe. In autumn more extensively white than other sandpipers. The short stout black bill and black legs contrast sharply with the nearly immaculate snowy whiteness of the under parts. Young birds show a faint buffy suffusion on sides of breast. In breeding plumage the feathers of the upper parts are edged with rusty; breast and sides of head and neck rusty, spotted and barred with dusky and white.

Habitat. In migration it favours sand beaches on either salt or fresh water, but sometimes one finds it on mud flats and other muddy places. In the nesting season, stony, sparsely vegetated, usually drier tundra and rock desert.

Nesting. Nest, a slight hollow on dry stony ground, usually in or at the edge of a patch of vegetation, and lined with grasses. *Eggs* usually 4; olive with brown spots, especially on the larger end, and sometimes a few blackish ones. Incubation period said to be 23 to 24 days (Manniche). Female incubates assisted by the male.

Range. Holarctic. Breeds on arctic tundra around the world. In North America: the Arctic of Canada and Greenland. Winters in many parts of the world: in North America from southern British Columbia, Massachusetts, and the Gulf Coast of the United States south to southern Chile and southern Argentina; also the West Indies. In the Old World winters south to South Africa, Australia, and New Zealand.

Semipalmated Sandpiper

Bécasseau semipalmé
Calidris pusilla (Linnaeus)
Total length: 14 to 17 cm
Plates 33 and 35

Breeding Distribution of Semipalmated
Sandpiper

Range in Canada. Breeds widely in the Arctic
and Subarctic: Banks Island (Sachs Harbour,
De Salis Bay); Victoria Island (Read Island;
Cambridge Bay); King William Island; and cen-
tral and southern Baffin Island (Frustration
Bay, Taverner Bay, Nettilling Lake, Frobisher
Bay, West Foxe Islands); coastal Yukon, north-
ern and central-eastern Mackenzie (islands
north of and coast east of Mackenzie Delta,
Baillie Island, shores of Dolphin and Union
Strait, Bathurst Inlet, Perry River; also in
the interior: Thelon River); northwest coastal
and southern Keewatin (Adelaide Peninsula,
Beverly Lake, Chesterfield Inlet, Windy River,
McConnell River); Southampton and Coates
islands; the Hudson Bay coast of Manitoba
(Churchill) and of northern Ontario (Cape
Henrietta Maria); northwestern Quebec
(Inoucdjouac, Bellin (Payne), Ungava Bay, and
south along the coast to Comb Islands); and
Labrador (Ramah and probably south to Seal
Island). Recorded in summer on southern
Somerset Island (Fort Ross), Bathurst Island,
Prince Leopold Island, N.W.T. Unconfirmed
reports of nesting on Melville Island.

Common to abundant in migration in most
parts of southern Canada except the coast of
British Columbia where rare (Sumas and
Calvert Island). Much scarcer in spring than
autumn in British Columbia and from eastern
Ontario eastward. In Newfoundland, a common autumn transient but has not been
recorded there in spring. In autumn it is
common to abundant in the Maritimes.

Bill rather short, straight, black. Front toes with small basal webs. Legs
black. Its very small size distinguishes it from all but the Least and
Western sandpipers. Small webs between the front toes separate it from
the Least. (For distinctions from Western Sandpiper, see next species.)

Measurements. See Table 2.

Field Marks. The Semipalmated, Least, and Western sandpipers
are our tiniest shorebirds (sparrow-sized). They are similar in appearance. The present species differs from the Least by black (not greenish
or yellowish) legs, slightly thicker bill, and greyer, paler upper parts. Its
bill is usually noticeably shorter than that of the Western and has no
tendency to be sligthly downcurved as in many Westerns. In breeding
plumage it has greyer upper parts, lacking the bright cinnamon shown
on head and back of the Western. Its breast is less heavily streaked, and
usually there are no V-marks on the breast or flanks. In autumn
plumages the two are very similar, and the shorter, straighter bill of the
Semipalmated is the best means of distinguishing them. There is some
overlapping, however, and only typical individuals of the two can be
safely identified in the field. Flight call: *chert*.

Habitat. In migration, sand beaches, mud flats, open edges of
pools, ponds, lakes, rivers, and shores, both fresh and salt. In nesting
season, moist or wet sedge-grass or heath tundra, sandy places along
arctic rivers, and pond-dotted sand dunes.

Nesting. Nest, a depression in a hummock or knoll in wet tundra
or in sand near ponds or rivers. It is lined with grass and willow leaves.
Eggs, usually 4; vary from dull white to olive-buff, speckled and spotted
with reddish browns, often coalescing into blotches on larger end. They
are similar to those of the Least and Western sandpipers. Incubation is
by both sexes; lasts 18 to 19 days (D.F. Parmelee).

Range. Breeds in northern Alaska (arctic coast south to Yukon
Delta) and across the low Arctic of Canada. Winters from South
Carolina and the Gulf Coast of the United States, the West Indies, and
eastern Mexico south to northern Chile and southern Brazil.

Table 2
Mensural characters of the Semipalmated
Sandpiper and the Western Sandpiper.
Measurements are in millimetres

	Semipalmated Sandpiper					Western Sandpiper				
	N	Range	Mean	Confidence limits for the mean	Confidence limits for individuals values	N	Range	Mean	Confidence limits for the means	Confidence limits for individual values
Culmen										
♂♂ adult	48	16.60–21.10	19.23	18.96–19.51	17.31– 21.15	17	20.80–26.20	22.52	21.88–23.17	19.54– 25.50
♂♂ immature	30	15.10–22.00	18.55	17.97–19.13	15.39– 21.71	11	21.00–24.00	22.45	21.83–23.06	20.33– 24.56
♀♀ adult	46	18.30–23.90	20.96	20.58–21.34	18.36– 23.55	25	23.40–28.80	26.54	26.03–27.04	23.97– 29.10
♀♀ immature	19	17.10–22.20	19.75	18.96–20.54	16.21– 23.29	8	24.40–27.70	26.31	25.39–27.23	23.54– 29.08
Distal corner of nostril to tip of bill										
♂♂ adult	46	13.70–18.10	15.73	15.47–15.99	13.97– 17.49	17	17.50–22.90	19.02	18.41–19.64	16.41– 21.63
♂♂ immature	30	12.70–17.50	15.34	14.89–15.78	12.90– 17.72	11	17.40–20.00	18.86	18.29–19.44	16.87– 20.86
♀♀ adult	46	14.50–19.80	17.24	16.88–17.59	14.84– 19.63	23	19.90–24.10	22.63	22.25–23.02	20.75– 24.51
♀♀ immature	18	13.80–18.60	16.47	15.70–17.23	13.13– 19.80	8	21.10–24.40	22.59	21.84–23.33	20.36– 24.82
Wing										
♂♂ adult	48	90.20–99.00	94.60	94.01–95.18	90.57– 98.63	18	90.70–95.30	93.52	92.75–94.28	90.19– 96.84
♂♂ immature	30	88.20–97.40	92.81	91.98–93.65	88.25– 97.38	11	91.00–97.00	93.47	92.17–94.78	88.93– 98.01
♀♀ adult	46	94.30–99.60	96.99	96.51–97.47	93.72–100.27	25	91.30–99.50	96.11	95.26–96.95	91.80–100.41
♀♀ immature	19	90.30–96.80	94.04	93.02–95.05	89.49– 98.58	7	94.80–98.20	96.99	95.96–98.01	94.09– 99.88
Tarsus										
♂♂ adult	48	19.50–23.40	21.15	20.92–21.37	19.56– 22.73	18	21.40–23.10	22.13	21.87–22.38	21.02– 23.24
♂♂ immature	30	20.00–22.70	21.28	21.03–21.53	19.90– 22.66	11	20.70–22.90	21.65	21.20–22.10	20.09– 23.22
♀♀ adult	45	20.50–23.70	22.04	21.83–22.26	20.59– 23.49	25	22.40–25.00	23.58	23.29–23.86	22.13– 25.03
♀♀ immature	18	20.40–23.10	21.80	21.44–22.16	20.22– 23.38	8	22.40–24.00	23.21	22.78–24.08	21.91– 24.51
Culmen length/ bill-width ratio										
♂♂ adult	46	8.83–15.44	12.39	11.84–12.94	8.62– 16.15	16	14.55–18.38	16.48	15.78–17.18	13.60– 19.36
♂♂ immature	30	9.74–13.78	11.68	10.89–12.47	7.28– 16.01	11	16.67–18.46	17.39	16.70–18.07	15.01– 19.76
♀♀ adult	44	8.98–16.36	12.84	12.11–13.57	7.93– 17.76	25	15.60–21.20	19.00	18.28–19.73	15.30– 22.71
♀♀ immature	18	10.23–15.86	12.61	11.52–13.70	7.86– 17.36	8	17.72–22.08	19.81	18.05–21.57	14.53– 25.09

After H. Ouellet, R. McNeil, and J. Burton (1973.
Canadian Field-Naturalist 87(3):296).

Western Sandpiper

Bécasseau d'Alaska
Calidris mauri (Cabanis)
Total length: 15 to 18 cm
Plate 33

Bill and legs blackish, the former often slightly downcurved. Front toes with small basal webs. Small size separates it from all but the Least and Semipalmated sandpipers. Presence of small webs at the base of the front toes distinguishes it from the Least in any plumage. It is less easily distinguished from the Semipalmated Sandpiper except in breeding plumage, at which time the Western has much more rusty (rather than buffy) in the upper parts and heavier streaking on the breast, *this often forming V-marks, which frequently extend to the sides.* In autumn plumages the two are very difficult to distinguish, but if a deep-rusty feather or two are still retained in the dorsum (such feathers are buffy in *pusilla*) they are diagnostic of *mauri*.

The longer bill of *mauri* will readily separate typical individuals. Bill measurements will separate most of more difficult ones. H. Ouellet, R. McNeil, and J. Burton (1973. Canadian Field-Naturalist, vol. 87, no. 3, pp. 291–300) found that specimens whose culmen lengths exceed 23.6 and 23.3 mm for adult and immature females respectively, and 21.2 and 21.7 mm for adult and immature males respectively are statistically referable to *mauri*. Similarly birds in which the distance from the distal corner of the nostril to the bill tip exceeds 19.6 and 19.8 mm for adult and immature females respectively, and 17.5 and 17.8 for adult and immature males respectively are *mauri*.

Status in Canada. Spring and autumn transient, common only in coastal British Columbia (scarce, mainly autumn transient in the interior). Rare transient in Alberta (specimen: near Calgary, 18 August 1972; photo records: Sturgeon Lake, Standard; also sight records) and Ontario (specimens: Port Franks, Long Point, Toronto, Fort Erie, Ottawa); Quebec (specimens: Lachine, 9 September 1970; Madeleine Islands, 15 September 1970; also sight records); and Nova Scotia (specimen: Sable Island, 9 September 1970; photo: Hartlen Point, 2 October 1981; also sight records). Sight records for Saskatchewan, Manitoba, New Brunswick, and southern Mackenzie.

Measurements. See Table 2.

Field Marks. One of our three tiniest sandpipers. Its blackish (not yellowish-green) legs and usually longer bill, when discernible, are sure distinctions from the Least Sandpiper. Compared with the Semipalmated Sandpiper, it shows much more rusty on crown and other upper parts in breeding plumage; also the breast streaks tend to be arrow-shaped. In autumn, however, the two are often very similar. In typical Westerns the bill is noticeably longer and is slightly downcurved, but many autumn individuals of the two cannot safely be identified in life. Flight call a high-pitched *cheep*.

Habitat. In migration similar to that of Semipalmated Sandpiper.

Range. Breeds on the coast of western and northern Alaska east at least to Camden Bay. Winters mainly from the coast of California, the Gulf Coast of United States, and North Carolina south to Venezuela, and in Peru; also the West Indies.

Rufous-necked Stint

Bécasseau à col roux
Calidris ruficollis (Pallas)
Total length: 13 to 17.5 cm
Plate 27

Status in Canada. Accidental in British Columbia (Iona Island, 24–25 June, 13–15 July and 25–26 August 1978. Photos examined by the writer conclusively establish the identification). Sight record for Ontario (Toronto, July 1976).

Similar in size to Least Sandpiper but wing and tail average longer. *Summer adults* have the *throat, foreneck and upper breast cinnamon-rufous*, this passing into a few dusky spots or streaks on sides of breast, and to a white abdomen; upper parts mostly dusky, the feathers edged with grey and with rufous or cinnamon, several scapulars often conspicuously edged with cinnamon; central upper tail coverts mostly blackish. *Winter plumages*: Upper parts brownish grey, the feathers of the back and scapulars with medial streaks of black; under parts white, the *sides* of chest more or less blotched with grey. Bill and legs blackish, the toes unwebbed.

Range. Breeds in northeastern Siberia and on Seward Peninsula and Barrow, western Alaska. Winters from southern China south to New Zealand and Australia.

Little Stint

Bécasseau minute
Calidris minuta (Leisler)
Total length: 14 to 16.5 cm
Plate 33

A very small straight-billed sandpiper closely resembling the Least, Semipalmated, and Western sandpipers, and Rufous-necked Stint in size and general coloration. Lack of palmations (small webs) between the front toes distinguishes it from the Semipalmated and Western sandpipers in all plumages. Its black (not greenish or yellowish) legs separate it from the Least Sandpiper.

In breeding plumage adults have extensive pale-rufous or orange-cinnamon coloration on the top and sides of head, nape, down sides of neck, and as a wash across the breast (where mixed with dusky spotting). *Throat and chin are white*.

Measurements. *Adult male*: wing (flattened), 92–99 (95.9); culmen, 17–19 (17.8); tarsus, 19–22 (20.5). *Adult female*: wing (flattened), 96–103 (99.5); culmen, 17–20 (19.0); tarsus, 21–22 (21.3) mm (Prater, Marchant, and Vuorinen).

Field Marks. Adults in summer plumage can be distinguished from the other North American tiny sandpipers (Least, Semipalmated, Western) by their decidedly lighter, brighter, more extensive orange-cinnamon suffusion on crown, cheeks, nape, sides of neck, and across the breast. In addition, the Little Stint's black legs separate it from the Least Sandpiper. Its usually shorter, perfectly straight bill distinguishes it from most Westerns. It has a noticeably slenderer bill than the Semipalmated Sandpiper and lacks palmations between the toes.

Two other species, both accidental in Canada, have extensive rufous coloration about head, neck, and breast in breeding plumage. The Rufous-necked Stint has this rufous coloration extending onto the throat (throat is white in Little Stint). The Spoonbill Sandpiper also is similarly coloured but the peculiar bill is diagnostic in all plumages.

Status in Canada. Accidental. An adult male was collected at North Point, James Bay, Ontario, on 10 July 1979, by R.I.G. Morrison who donated the specimen to the National Museum of Natural Sciences. Also reported from Nova Scotia (photo record: Hartlen Point, 23 October 1983); New Brunswick (sight record: Castalia, Grand Manan, 30 June–4 July 1980); and British Columbia (unconfirmed sight record: Iona Island, 21 July 1983).

Immature and winter Little Stints are much more difficult to recognize in the field.

Range. Breeds on tundra of northeastern Eurasia from northeastern Norway, northern Finland, and across northern Russia eastward to the lower Indigirka River and the Chukotski Peninsula, and northward to Novaya Zemlya and New Siberian Islands. Winters in Africa, islands in the Indian Ocean, Iran, India to Ceylon; more rarely farther north.

Temminck's Stint

Bécasseau de Temminck
Calidris temminckii (Leisler)
Total length: 13 cm
Figure 57

a   b

Figure 57
Tail of
a) Semipalmated Sandpiper
b) Temminck's Stint

Status in Canada. Accidental in British Columbia (one at Reifel Island, Ladner, 1–4 September 1982, was photographed at point blank range).

A tiny thin-billed sandpiper of accidental occurrence in Canada. *Autumn and winter plumages*: Upper parts rather uniformly grey or olive grey, the back feathers with vaguely darker shaft streaks. Head and cheeks grey, with poorly defined dull white supercilium confined anteriorly to eye. Tail with central feathers brown, the outer feathers *white*. Under parts white with dull grey suffusion on chest. *Breeding plumage*: Feathers of upper parts with blackish-brown centres and buffy fringes. Breast suffused with buff and streaked dusky. Rest of under parts white. Tail similar to winter aspect. Legs variable, yellow, yellowish brown, olive brown, rarely even blackish.

Field Marks. Not likely to be seen in Canada. Size of Least Sandpiper. In autumn and winter a thin-billed sandpiper with uniformly grey upper parts, and a grey suffusion on the breast reminiscent of that of an immature Spotted Sandpiper. When the *white* (not grey) outer tail feathers can be seen, they separate it from the Least and Semipalmated sandpipers. *Caution*: The grey outer tail feathers of the Least and Semipalmated may look white in certain lights and the white lateral tail coverts of those species are very easily mistaken for tail feathers, with consequent misidentification of the species.

Range. Breeds in northern Scandinavia, northern Russia, and northern Siberia eastward to the Chukotski Peninsula and Anadyrland. Winters from the Mediterranean Basin, Iran, India, and southeastern China south to central Africa and Indonesia.

Long-toed Stint

[**Long-toed Stint**. Bécasseau à longs doigts. *Calidris subminuta* (Middendorf). Hypothetical. Has been reported in British Columbia (Vancouver area) but without adequate documentation.]

Least Sandpiper

Bécasseau minuscule
Calidris minutilla (Vieillot)
Total length: 12.5 to 17 cm
Plate 33

Breeding Distribution of Least Sandpiper

Range in Canada. Breeds in Yukon (Babbage and Firth rivers, Old Crow, Lake Marsh); northwestern British Columbia (Queen Charlotte Islands, Chilkat Pass); northern Mackenzie (Franklin Bay, Coppermine, Aklavik, West Mirage Islands; Nahanni National Park; and probably Fort Norman and Thelon Sanctuary); central Keewatin (near Schultz Lake); Southampton Island (rarely: Coral Harbour); northern Saskatchewan (Milton Lake; probably Lake Athabasca; Hasbala and Reindeer lakes); northern Manitoba (Churchill, Herchmer); northern Ontario (coast of Hudson and James bays: Cape Henrietta Maria; perhaps south to Big Trout Lake); Quebec (Inoucdjouac, Bush Lake; Ford Lake, Lake Bienville; Schefferville; Blanc-Sablon; Anticosti and Madeleine islands; recorded in breeding season at numerous other northern localities north to Lake Aigneau and Kuujjuaq); Labrador (Indian Harbour, Goose Bay, Nain, possibly north to Ramah; and in the interior: upper Hamilton River); Newfoundland; and locally in Nova Scotia (Sable Island and Cape Sable Island). Alleged breeding on southern Victoria Island, N.W.T., requires confirmation.

A common to locally abundant spring and autumn transient through most southern localities coast to coast. Casual in southern Baffin Island.

The tiniest of our native sandpipers. Bill straight, rather slender. In the hand, small size separates this from all our native sandpipers except Semipalmated and Western. Its completely unwebbed (instead of partly webbed) toes distinguish it from them (see also Field Marks).

Measurements. *Adult male*: wing, 84.4–90.9 (86.7); tail, 37–40.4 (39.5); exposed culmen, 17–20 (18.2); tarsus, 18.2–20 (19.1). *Adult female*: wing, 82.3–91.2 (89) mm.

Field Marks. Our tiniest native sandpiper, but only slightly smaller than Semipalmated and Western. The Least is more ruddy above, has usually a buffier breast, slenderer bill, and greenish-yellowish legs (those of other two are blackish). The Least is coloured very much like Baird's but is smaller, with yellowish-green legs (black in Baird's). In flight its common call *queeeeeet* differs from that of the Semipalmated, which lacks the long *e*.

Habitat. In migration, muddy margins of fresh or salt water with or without low vegetation, mud flats, wet fields; sometimes beaches and dry fields. In breeding season, sedge, grass, and mossy bogs; hummocky marshes; sometimes also higher drier situations with low vegetation.

Nesting. On the ground. A shallow depression lined sparsely with dry leaves or grass. *Eggs*, usually 4; pale buff, spotted and blotched, sometimes very heavily, with various browns. The male takes a large part in incubation of the eggs. Incubation period 19.50 to 21.50 days (Jehl and Hussell).

Range. Breeds in southern Alaska and across subarctic Canada. Winters from southern United States south to central Peru and Brazil; also in the West Indies.

White-rumped Sandpiper

Bécasseau à croupion blanc
Calidris fuscicollis (Vieillot)
Total length: 18 to 20 cm
Plate 33

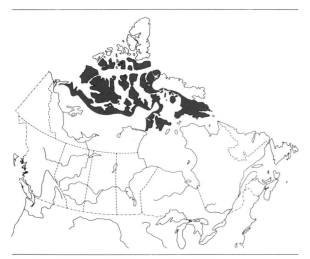

Breeding Distribution of White-rumped
Sandpiper

Range in Canada. Breeds across the Arctic
from Banks Island (Big River), Melville Island
(Winter Harbour), Bathurst Island, Devon
Island, and northwestern Bylot Island south to
northern Mackenzie (Franklin Bay; Cockburn
Point; 80 km east of Fort Anderson), northern
Keewatin (Adelaide Peninsula, Pelly Bay; prob-
ably Chesterfield Inlet; perhaps inland on Back
River), Southampton Island, and southern
Baffin Island (Jordan River, Cape Dorset).

Spring migration is mainly through the interior east of the Rockies and west of western
Quebec and Hudson Bay, much more rarely
farther east; in autumn, mainly down the
Atlantic Coast and the eastern interior. Transient, mainly in spring, in Alberta (rare), Saskatchewan, and interior Manitoba (common on
the Hudson Bay coast, in both spring and
autumn); an uncommon transient in spring and
autumn in eastern interior Ontario (but
common on coast of James and Hudson bays);
mainly autumn transient, rare in spring, in
Quebec (all the coasts and at least the southern
interior: Montréal, Saguenay–Lake Saint-Jean
region); Labrador (abundant in autumn along
coast); Newfoundland; New Brunswick; Prince
Edward Island; and Nova Scotia. In British
Columbia, a few spring records (Atlin,
Victoria, Peace River District). Casual on
Prince Patrick Island (Mould Bay) and Axel
Heiberg Island (Mokka Fiord).

A small sandpiper with straight bill about as long as head. The only
small, moderately short-legged sandpiper with a completely white rump
patch. Might be confused with Stilt Sandpiper, which also has a white
rump and is somewhat similar in autumn dress, but the Stilt Sandpiper's
longer bill is abruptly broadened near the tip, and its legs are much
longer than those of the White-rump, extending the feet well beyond the
tip of the folded wing.

Measurements. *Adult male*: wing, 117–126 (120.4); tail, 47.5–53.6
(51.4); exposed culmen, 20–23.6 (21.7); tarsus, 21–24.5 (22.9). *Adult
female*: wing, 117.5–124 (120.6) mm.

Field Marks. A small sandpiper with bill about as long as head,
dark legs, and with a white patch completely across the rump (often
hidden by wings when at rest, but readily noticeable in flight). Stilt
Sandpiper also has a white rump, and its autumn plumage is somewhat
like that of the White-rump, but the Stilt Sandpiper is a slender bird
with obviously longer legs and longish bill. Other white-rumped sandpipers are obviously larger or are otherwise very distinctive. Common
calls: in migration a distinctive high-pitched *jeet*.

Habitat. In migration, muddy shores, mud flats, and sand or
gravel beaches on both salt and fresh water. Also, in the breeding
season, wet and moist grassy tundra.

Nesting. Nest, usually on a tussock or mound in wet or moist
tundra, is a shallow depression in soil or moss, lined with grasses and
dead leaves. *Eggs*, usually 4; greenish to olive-buff, blotched and
spotted with browns. Incubation apparently is mainly, if not entirely, by
the female. Incubation period about 22 days.

Range. Nearctic. Breeds in northern Alaska (rarely) and in the
Canadian Arctic. Winters in southern South America.

Baird's Sandpiper

Bécasseau de Baird
Calidris bairdii (Coues)
Total length: 18 to 19.5 cm
Plate 33

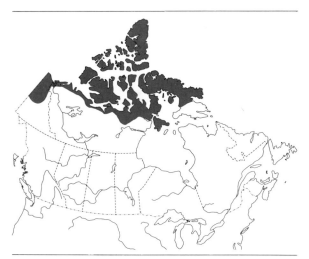

Breeding Distribution of Baird's Sandpiper

Range in Canada. Breeds from Prince Patrick Island (Mould Bay), Melville Island (Winter Harbour), Ellef Ringnes Island (probably), and northern Ellesmere Island (Fosheim Peninsula, Lake Hazen) south to northern and central Yukon (Herschel Island; Ogilvie Mountains: headwaters of south Tatonduk River); northern Mackenzie (barrens east of Anderson River; Dolphin and Union Strait); northern Keewatin (Adelaide Peninsula, Mount Meadowbank on lower Back River, Southampton Island); southern Melville Peninsula (Gore Bay); and south-central Baffin Island (Nettilling Lake).

Spring migration is mainly through the interior west of Hudson Bay. In autumn, largely over the spring route but also regularly in small numbers west to the Pacific Coast and much farther east, rarely to Newfoundland. Migrates spring and autumn through interior British Columbia (also in autumn west to the coast), commonly through Alberta, Saskatchewan, and Manitoba. Uncommon autumn migrant, rare in spring, in eastern interior Ontario and the Ontario coasts of James and Hudson bays. Uncommon autumn migrant in Quebec (Montréal, Québec, Arvida, Cape Weggs, Grande rivière de la Baleine, Cabbage Willows Bay). Scarce autumn migrant in New Brunswick (Campobello Island, St. Andrews) and Nova Scotia (Grand Pré). Very rare in Newfoundland (Argentia).

Bill rather short, straight, slender. A small sandpiper with rather buffy upper parts (in immatures, feathers of back with narrow white margins, giving back a scaly appearance), buffy band across the breast, lightly streaked with dusky. Rump sooty brown, the feathers narrowly edged with buffy brown. Bill blackish. Legs blackish with slight suggestion of olive. From the Pectoral Sandpiper it is distinguished by its smaller size, less well-defined and more lightly streaked breast band, blackish legs, and by the middle tail feathers, which are more obtuse, with tips extending little beyond the others; from the Least, by its blackish legs and larger size; from the Semipalmated and Western, by its completely unwebbed toes, larger size, and more decidedly buffy breast band; and from the White-rumped, by its dark rump and more buffy breast.

Measurements. *Adult male*: wing, 117.6–125.3 (121.5); tail, 50–57 (52.1); exposed culmen, 20.5–24.5 (22.4); tarsus, 21.3–24.2 (22.9). *Adult female*: wing, 120–128 (122.7) mm.

Field Marks. One of several similar small sandpipers collectively known as "peeps." Larger than the Least, Semipalmated, and Western sandpipers; about the same size as the White-rump; and smaller than the Pectoral. In addition to size differences, which usually are not too reliable in the field unless birds can be compared side by side, its blackish legs distinguish it from the Pectoral and the Least. These tend to have streaked upper parts, but Baird's, especially autumn immatures, has a faintly scaly pattern on the back.

Its more buffy breast band, less-greyish upper parts, and, in flight, lack of a white rump-patch distinguish it from the White-rump. Spring and summer Sanderlings show much rusty about head, neck, and upper breast, but at other times they are very different. The Sanderling shows a broad white wing stripe in flight; Baird's an obscure one. The Buff-breasted Sandpiper is entirely different with the entire under parts uniformly buffy and with yellow legs.

Adults in breeding plumage closely resemble Semipalmated Sandpiper but the back of Baird's is usually more heavily blotched with black and buff, the breast usually definitely buffier. In Baird's the tip of the folded wing extends beyond the tip of the tail. Under good conditions the tertials of Baird's can be seen to fall well short of the tip of the folded wing; in Semipalmated they almost reach the wing tip.

Habitat. In migration it tends to prefer drier parts of muddy areas (often with patches of grass or other low vegetation) near both fresh and salt water; also beaches; flooded and sometimes dry fields. Less inclined to feed in water than many other sandpipers. In the Arctic it nests usually in drier situations than many sandpipers; ridges, flats, and rocky slopes, both inland and coastal; occasionally in moister places.

Nesting. Nest, a shallow depression on the ground, lined with grass and perhaps a few willow leaves. *Eggs*, usually 4, sometimes 3; buffy, rather thickly spotted with browns. Incubation is by both sexes and lasts 21 days (W.H. Drury).

Range. Breeds in northeastern Siberia, northwestern Alaska, arctic Canada, and northwestern Greenland. Winters mainly in western and southern South America.

1 Semipalmated Sandpiper, p. 218
a) adult in breeding plumage
b) autumn immature

2 Least Sandpiper, p. 222
a) adult in breeding plumage
b) autumn plumage

3 Little Stint, p. 220
adult in breeding plumage

4 White-rumped Sandpiper, p. 223
a) adult in breeding plumage
b) adult in autumn plumage

5 Western Sandpiper, p. 219
a) adult in breeding plumage
b) autumn immature

6 Sanderling, p. 217
a) autumn immature
b) adult in breeding plumage

7 Baird's Sandpiper, p. 224
autumn plumage

Crosby

1 Red-necked Phalarope, p. 245
a) adult female in breeding plumage
b) winter plumage

2 Red Phalarope, p. 246
a) adult female in breeding plumage
b) adult winter plumage
c) autumn immature

3 Wilson's Phalarope, p. 244
a) adult female in breeding plumage
b) adult male in breeding plumage
c) autumn immature

4 Pectoral Sandpiper, p. 233

6 Upland Sandpiper, p. 206

5 Buff-breasted Sandpiper, p. 238

1 Ruddy Turnstone,
p. 213
summer adult

2 Dunlin, p. 236
autumn and winter

3 Semipalmated Sandpiper,
p. 218

5 Red-necked Phalarope,
p. 245
autumn and winter

6 Sanderling, p. 217
autumn

4 Red Phalarope, p. 246
autumn and winter

7 Greater Golden-Plover, p. 181
a) adult in breeding plumage
b) autumn plumage

8 Lesser Golden-Plover, p. 181
autumn plumage

9 Northern Lapwing, p. 179
adult in breeding plumage

10 Hudsonian Godwit, p. 211
adult in breeding plumage

11 Black-tailed Godwit, p. 210
a) adult in breeding plumage
b) autumn plumage

12 Bar-tailed Godwit, p. 212
a) autumn plumage
b) adult in breeding plumage

1 Ivory Gull, p. 273
a) adult
b) first winter
c) wing (adult)
d) wing (first year)

2 Glaucous Gull, p. 268
a) adult
b) first winter
c) second winter
d) wing (adult)

4 Iceland Gull, p. 263
("Kumlien's Gull")
(*kumlieni* race)
a) adult
b) first winter
c) second year
d) wing (adult)

3 Iceland Gull, p. 263
(*glaucoides* race)
a) adult
b) first winter
c) second year
d) wing (adult)

6 Herring Gull, p. 260
a) adult in summer
b) adult in winter
c) first winter
d) second year
e) third year
f) wing (adult)

5 Iceland Gull, p. 263
("Thayer's Gull")
(*thayeri* race)
a) adult
b) first winter pale extreme
c) first winter dark extreme
d) wing (adult)

7 California Gull, p. 259
a) head of adult
b) adult
c) first winter
d) wing (adult)

Crosby '82

1 Black-legged Kittiwake, p. 270
a) first year
b) adult in breeding plumage
c) adult in winter plumage

2 Heermann's Gull, p. 257
a) first year
b) adult
c) wing (adult)

3 Mew Gull, p. 257
a) wing (adult)
b) adult
c) first winter

4 Ring-billed Gull, p. 258
a) adult
b) first winter
c) wing (adult)

5 Lesser Black-backed Gull,
p. 265
a) first winter
b) second winter
c) adult *(L. f. graellsii)* in winter

6 Glaucous-winged Gull, p. 267
a) head of adult
b) adult
c) first winter
d) wing (adult)

7 Western Gull, p. 266
a) head of adult
b) adult
c) first winter
d) wing (adult)

8 Great Black-backed
Gull, p. 269
a) head of adult
b) adult
c) first winter
d) wing (adult)

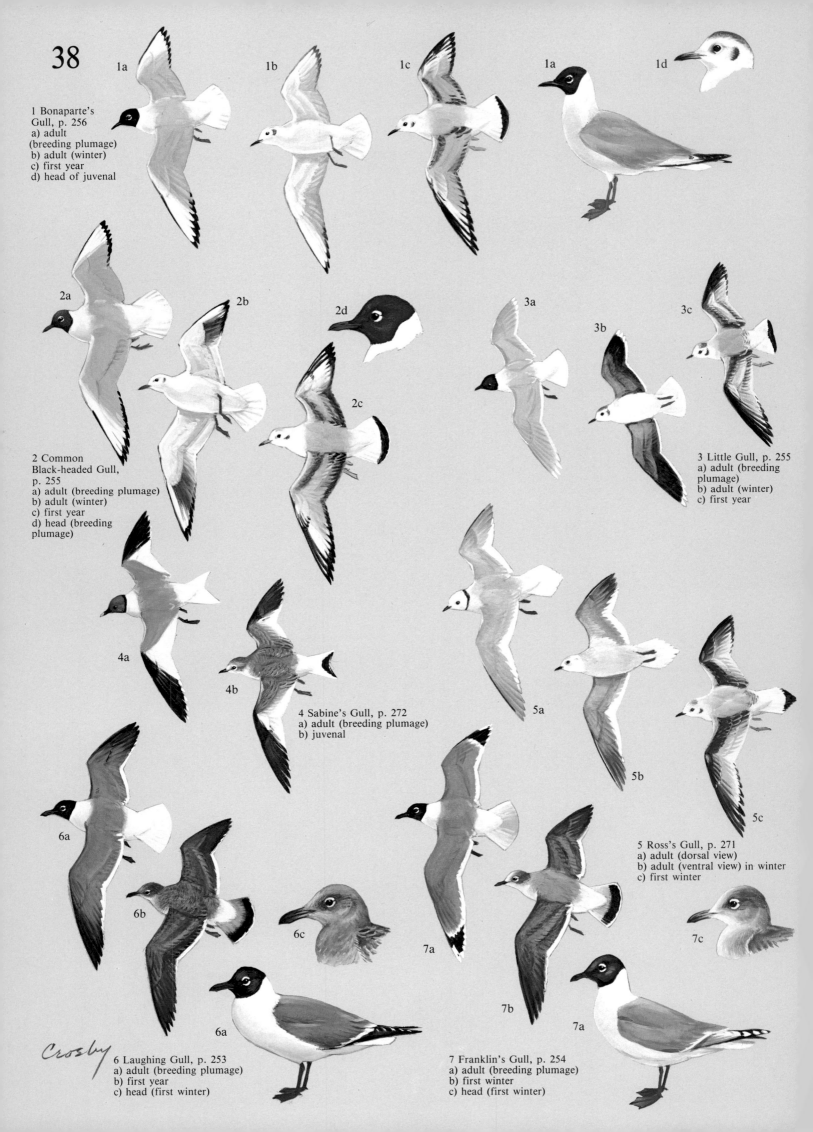

38

1 Bonaparte's
Gull, p. 256
a) adult
(breeding plumage)
b) adult (winter)
c) first year
d) head of juvenal

1a 1b 1c 1a 1d

2a 2b 2d 3a 3b 3c

2c

2 Common
Black-headed Gull,
p. 255
a) adult (breeding plumage)
b) adult (winter)
c) first year
d) head (breeding
plumage)

3 Little Gull, p. 255
a) adult (breeding
plumage)
b) adult (winter)
c) first year

4a 4b

4 Sabine's Gull, p. 272
a) adult (breeding plumage)
b) juvenal

5a 5b 5c

5 Ross's Gull, p. 271
a) adult (dorsal view)
b) adult (ventral view) in winter
c) first winter

6a 6b 6c 7a 7b 7c

Crosby

6 Laughing Gull, p. 253
a) adult (breeding plumage)
b) first year
c) head (first winter)

7 Franklin's Gull, p. 254
a) adult (breeding plumage)
b) first winter
c) head (first winter)

6a 7a

39

1

1 Great Skua, p. 252

2 Pomarine Jaeger, p. 248
adult (light phase)

2

3

3 Long-tailed Jaeger, p. 251
adult

4c

4a

4b

4 Parasitic Jaeger, p. 250
a) adult (light phase)
b) first autumn
c) adult (dark phase)

5 Common Tern, p. 278
a) summer adult (dorsal view)
b) head of first-autumn immature
c) summer adult (ventral view)

5c

5a

5b

6a

6b

6 Forster's Tern, p. 280
a) summer adult
b) head of first-autumn immature

7a

7 Arctic Tern,
p. 279
a) summer adult
(dorsal view)
b) summer adult
(ventral view)

7b

8a

8b

8 Caspian Tern, p. 274
a) adult in autumn
and winter
b) summer adult

10a

10 Black Tern, p. 283
a) summer adult
b) first autumn

11

9

10b

9 Royal Tern, p. 275
adult

11 Roseate Tern, p. 277
summer adult

Crosby

40

1 Common Murre, p. 286
a) winter plumage
b) summer adult
c) summer adult
("Ringed Murre" phase)

2 Thick-billed Murre, p. 287
a) winter plumage
b) summer adult

3 Razorbill, p. 288
a) first-winter immature
b) summer adult

4 Tufted Puffin,
p. 295
breeding plumage

5 Horned Puffin, p. 297
breeding plumage

6 Atlantic Puffin, p. 296
breeding plumage

7 Rhinoceros Auklet, p. 295
a) breeding plumage
b) immature

8 Cassin's Auklet, p. 293

9 Pigeon Guillemot, p. 291
a) breeding plumage
b) winter plumage

10 Black Guillemot, p. 290
a) breeding plumage
b) immature

11 Ancient Murrelet, p. 292
a) winter plumage
b) breeding plumage

12 Marbled Murrelet, p. 291
a) winter plumage
b) breeding plumage

13 Dovekie, p. 285
a) winter plumage
b) breeding plumage

Crosby

Pectoral Sandpiper

Bécasseau à poitrine cendrée
Calidris melanotos (Vieillot)
Total length: 20 to 24 cm
(male larger than female)
Plate 34

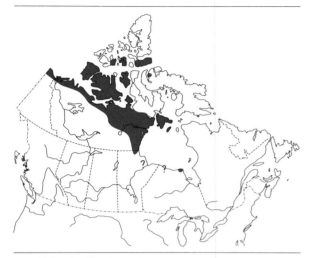

Breeding Distribution of Pectoral Sandpiper

Range in Canada. Breeds on the coast of Yukon (Babbage River); Mackenzie (Richards Island, Bernard Harbour, Perry River); Banks Island; Melville Island (Mecham River); Bathurst Island; Victoria Island (Cambridge Bay); Devon Island; northern Baffin Island (Arctic Bay); Prince of Wales Island, Keewatin (Adelaide Peninsula; 80 km north of Schultz Lake; probably McConnell River); Southampton Island; Manitoba (Churchill); and northern Ontario (Cape Henrietta Maria). Probably breeds very locally along the west coast of Hudson Bay. Summer records for Prince Patrick and Bylot islands without evidence of breeding.

Migration in spring is mainly through the interior west of Hudson Bay; in autumn, spreading eastward to the Atlantic and westward to the Pacific Coast. A spring and autumn migrant in British Columbia (but rare in spring on the coast), Alberta, Saskatchewan, Manitoba, and Ontario (but much scarcer in spring in eastern localities). Mainly an autumn transient in Quebec (along coast of Hudson and James bays, the north shore of the Gulf of St. Lawrence where it is uncommon to rare, the southern interior and coast), Labrador (coast; uncommon), Newfoundland (uncommon), and commonly in New Brunswick, Prince Edward Island, and Nova Scotia. Casual in winter in southwestern British Columbia (Chilliwack).

A medium-sized sandpiper with straight bill (2.5 to 3.4 cm). Tail with two middle feathers pointed and extending well beyond the others. Broad buffy band across the breast and fore-neck, heavily and evenly streaked with dusky, and sharply cut off from white belly. Throat white. Rump blackish brown. Bill greenish yellow at base becoming black at tip. Legs yellowish green or greenish yellow.

Measurements. *Adult male*: wing, 136–142.8 (138.7); tail, 60.4–63.9 (62.2); exposed culmen, 28.7–30 (29.3); tarsus, 27.8–30 (28.9). *Adult female*: wing, 123.9–129 (126.3) mm.

Field Marks. A medium-sized sandpiper with a broad, buffy, heavily streaked breast band, *sharply cut off from white of belly*. Baird's and White-rumped sandpipers have a similar streaked band on the breast, but it is less sharply defined. Pectoral's legs are greenish yellowish (black in the somewhat smaller Baird's), and it lacks the white rump shown in flight by the White-rumped Sandpiper. Least and Semipalmated sandpipers are much smaller birds. The neck of the Pectoral is longer than that of any of the others mentioned. Hunters often flush it in places frequented by Common Snipe, but as the Pectoral flies away it shows a broad black mark down lower back and rump, which the snipe lacks. On the arctic breeding grounds, males inflate the throat immensely in courtship, this giving them a different appearance from any of our other shorebirds. At the same time they emit grunting notes. On migration when flushed or flying, the common note is a grating *kriek*.

Habitat. In migration, grassy marshes, moist grassy edges of pools and ponds, flooded fields; sometimes short-grass drier fields. In the breeding season, sedge, grass, or shrub tundra and tundra meadows, especially moist or wet ones and with tussocks and hummocks; also mounds and ridges in such places; rolling tundra.

Nesting. Nest on the ground, often well hidden in the grass and sedge of a tussock or bunch of similar vegetation. It is substantially made of grasses and leaves. *Eggs*, usually 4; greenish to buffy, heavily blotched and spotted with browns. Incubation and care of the young are by the female. Incubation said to require 21 to 23 days (A.C. Bent).

Range. Breeds mainly along the coasts from eastern Siberia, northern and western Alaska, and locally in the low Arctic and Subarctic of Canada east to Southampton Island. Winters in southern South America and in small numbers south to Australia and New Zealand.

Sharp-tailed Sandpiper

Bécasseau à queue fine
Calidris acuminata (Horsfield)
Total length: 21.5 cm
Plate 31

Range in Canada. Scarce autumn transient on the coast of British Columbia (Masset, Queen Charlotte Islands; Comox and Victoria, Vancouver Island, Rivers Inlet. Two specimens from Masset, 27 December 1897, suggest occasional wintering). Casual visitor to Alberta (photo records: Beaverhill Lake, 21 September and 5 October 1975; Tofield, 23 May 1978) and Yukon (photo: Swan Lake, 13 September 1981). Accidental in Ontario (photo record: Hamilton, 29 November to 5 December 1975).

Similar to Pectoral Sandpiper, but tail feathers, especially outer ones, more sharply pointed at tips; *basal* part of outermost primary shaft brownish instead of white as in Pectoral (see Field Marks).

Field Marks. Closely resembles Pectoral Sandpiper, but breast markings never sharply cut off against white of under parts. Winter adults have the breast more lightly streaked and spotted (Pectoral's breast much more heavily and regularly streaked, not spotted). Immatures distinguishable from Pectoral by strong suffusion of cinnamon on breast; much finer and much more restricted dusky streaking on breast.

Habitat. Similar to Pectoral Sandpiper.

Range. Breeds in northern Siberia. Winters south to Australia and New Zealand, migrating mainly through eastern Siberia and along the Pacific coast of Asia; also along the Pacific coast of North America from about Kotzebue Sound, Alaska, south to Washington, rarely to California.

Purple Sandpiper

Bécasseau violet
Calidris maritima (Brünnich)
Total length: 20 to 30 cm
Plate 32

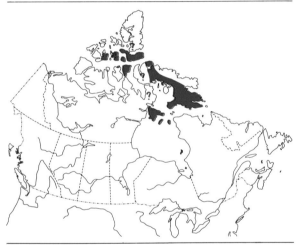

Breeding Distribution of Purple Sandpiper

Range in Canada. Breeds (more definite data are needed to show western and northern limits) from Melville Island (sparsely: Sabine River), Bathurst Island, and Devon Island (probably) and northern Bylot Island, south to Southampton Island, Belcher Islands, northern James Bay (North Twin Island), and southern Baffin Island (Cape Dorset, Amadjuak Lake, probably Cumberland Sound); west at least to central Melville and Somerset islands. Observed in summer west to Banks Island (Mercy Bay) and Prince Patrick Island (Mould Bay). On Prince of Wales Island, a fairly common spring and autumn migrant.

Bill slightly longer than head, nearly straight or slightly downcurved, yellowish or orange basally. Legs short, dull greenish-yellow to yellowish brown. In winter plumage, back is almost blackish *with purplish gloss*; head, neck, and breast dark grey, feathers of breast with white edges broader toward white belly; throat whitish; flanks with heavy grey streaks. In breeding plumage, blackish-brown back is variegated with buff and white, breast heavily spotted and streaked.

Measurements. *Adult male*: wing, 117.9–130 (124.9); tail, 55.9–63 (60.2); exposed culmen, 27.2–32 (29.2); tarsus, 22–23.8 (23.1). *Adult female*: wing, 122.6–132.6 (126.9) mm.

Field Marks. A chunky, often tame, short-legged sandpiper, typical of rocky Atlantic shores, the most likely *winter* sandpiper on the East Coast. In winter plumage, very dark-grey coloration, short dull-yellowish legs, and yellowish or orange basal part of bill. In flight shows, as do many others, a white wing-stripe and a dark rump.

Habitat. In migration and winter, rocky coastal shores; less often sand beaches and muddy pools. Even when it is found in the interior it is likely to be on the stones of breakwaters or similar stony situations. In breeding season, it nests on moss and lichen tundra, often at considerable elevations and sometimes far inland but often also on low tundra near shore and on coarse gravel-sand beaches along rivers. Many continue to use the shore for feeding.

Nesting. Nest, a depression in the ground or moss, well lined with leaves or dwarf birch or other available vegetation. The four *eggs* are said to be greenish or buffy, spotted and blotched with various browns. Apparently incubation is largely by the male, but more information is needed on this and most other phases of the breeding cycle. Incubation period about 21 to 22 days.

Winters on the Atlantic Coast in Newfoundland, New Brunswick, Prince Edward Island, and Nova Scotia. Casual migrant in southern Ontario (Niagara Falls, Crystal Beach, Toronto, Ottawa). Accidental in southern Manitoba (southwestern Lake Winnipeg). Rare in extreme southwestern Quebec (Aylmer, Montréal, Lake Saint-Pierre) becoming commoner below Québec on the St. Lawrence. Migration mainly east of Hudson Bay and presumably mostly coastal, where it is a common transient in autumn along the Labrador coast from Button Islands and southward.

Range. Breeds locally from eastern arctic Canada, Greenland, Iceland, and northern Eurasia from northern Scandinavia to Taimyr Peninsula and on Spitsbergen, Franz Josef Land, Novaya Zemlya, and the New Siberian Islands; formerly the Faeroe Islands. Winters in southwestern Greenland and Iceland, and on the Atlantic Coast from Newfoundland to Maryland; also in the British Isles and on shores of the North and Baltic seas.

Rock Sandpiper

(Aleutian Sandpiper)

Bécasseau des Aléoutiennes
Calidris ptilocnemis (Coues)
Total length: ca. 23 cm
Plate 32

Range in Canada. Common winter resident and transient on the coast of British Columbia. One record inland (Atlin, 29 October 1932).

Like Purple Sandpiper, but in breeding plumage the upper parts have much more rusty colouring, and the breast has a poorly defined dusky patch or extensive dusky blotches.

Measurements *(C. p. couesi). Adult male*: wing, 109–118.5 (114.3); tail, 50.8–55 (52.4); exposed culmen, 25.2–27.9 (26.8); tarsus, 22.3–24.2 (23.2). *Adult female*: wing, 116–125 (120.9) mm.

Field Marks. In winter plumage like Purple Sandpiper (q.v.). A bird of the West Coast likely to be found on rocky outer shores with Black Turnstones, Surfbirds, and Wandering Tattlers. It lacks the white rump of the Surfbird and the intricate white patterns shown in flight by the Black Turnstone. The Rock Sandpiper's white wing stripe, evident in flight, distinguishes it from the Wandering Tattler. In breeding plumage the rusty parts and dusky *breast* patch are a little suggestive of the Dunlin, but the Dunlin has dark (instead of yellowish) legs, and all-dark bill, and much more extensive black *abdominal* patch.

Habitat. In migration and winter, rocky ocean shores are the usual habitat.

Range. Breeds in northeastern Siberia, the Commander, Kurile, and Sakhalin islands, many islands in Bering Sea, and from central-western Alaska south to western Alaska Peninsula, the Shumagin and Aleutian islands. Winters within much of breeding range and south on the North American Pacific coast to Oregon and locally southern California and northwestern Baja California.

Subspecies. *Calidris ptilocnemis tschuktschorum* (Portenko).

Dunlin

(Red-backed Sandpiper)

Bécasseau variable
Calidris alpina (Linnaeus)
Total length: 19 to 23.5 cm
Plates 32 and 35

Breeding Distribution of Dunlin

Range in Canada. Breeding range poorly known. Breeds in northern Mackenzie (Baillie Island), southern Somerset Island (Fort Ross), Southampton Island, Keewatin (Karrack Lake, Baker Lake, Chesterfield Inlet, McConnell River), northeastern Manitoba (Churchill), and northwestern Ontario (Cape Henrietta Maria). Noted in summer in southwestern Baffin Island (West Foxe Islands, Bowman Bay), southern Melville Island, and southeastern Victoria Island, N.W.T. (probably breeding on the last).

Spring and autumn transient in British Columbia (abundant on coast, much scarcer in interior); Alberta (scarce); Saskatchewan (uncommon); Manitoba (locally common); Ontario (locally common); Quebec (mainly autumn: Montréal, Québec, Arvida, mouth of Kégashka River, Gaspé, Grande rivière de la Baleine); and in New Brunswick; Prince Edward Island; and Nova Scotia (locally scarce to common in autumn, rare in spring). Scarce transient in interior Yukon (Coal Creek, Dawson), and apparently very scarce in interior western Mackenzie. Casual in Newfoundland (Stephenville Crossing, 2 October 1946). Sight records only for Labrador.

Winters regularly and commonly on the coast of British Columbia.

Bill blackish, rather long and slightly downcurved. Legs greenish black. Spring and summer adults, with a large black patch on the abdomen contrasting with the white of the rest of the under parts, and much cinnamon on the back, are likely to be confused with only the Rock Sandpiper of the West Coast, which has vague black blotches on the lower breast, not on the abdomen. In winter dress, the grey of the back is uniform (but before the moult is complete a few black feathers with buffy borders may still be present), not streaked as in most sandpipers of similar or smaller size, and there is a greyish suffusion, faintly streaked, across the breast. Winter White-rumps and Sanderlings also have a clear grey back, but the former has a completely white rump and the latter has no hind toe. The longer, slightly decurved bill of the Dunlin is different from both. The Curlew Sandpiper of the Old World is very similar to the Dunlin in winter, but the former has a completely white rump. Juvenal Dunlins (seen mostly on or near the breeding grounds) are very buffy above, and the sides of the abdomen and lower breast have large spots and streaks of dusky brown.

Measurements *(C. a. pacifica). Adult male*: wing, 111.7–119.6 (114.9); tail, 41.5–53.7 (47.8); exposed culmen, 34–37.5 (35.9); tarsus, 26.1–27.8 (26.7). *Adult female*: wing, 112.5–121.2 (117.3) mm.

Field Marks. A medium-sized sandpiper with longish bill, noticeably downcurved near the tip. In spring and summer the reddish back and large black patch on the belly make it readily recognizable (Rock Sandpiper of the West Coast has some blackish blotches on the under parts, but they are on the lower breast not the belly, and its legs are yellowish not black). In autumn and winter: unpatterned grey back, grey suffusion across the breast, and longish downcurved bill. Western Sandpiper often has a slightly downcurved bill, but it is an obviously smaller bird with less uniformly grey back. White-rumps in winter plumage have a uniformly grey back but a white rump-patch. Sanderlings have snowy-white under parts in autumn and winter, thus lacking the grey suffusion of the Dunlin across the breast. The Curlew Sandpiper (of casual occurrence in Canada) in autumn and winter looks like a Dunlin but with a white patch across the rump.

Habitat. In migration, muddy margins of both salt and fresh water, mud flats, flooded grassland, sandy beaches and bars. On breeding grounds, usually moist to wet grassy or hummocky tundra; also coastal salt marshes.

Nesting. Nest on the ground, usually a grass-lined depression on a hummock or mound in moist grassy tundra or coastal salt marsh. *Eggs*, usually 4; greenish to buffy, with some gloss, spotted and blotched with browns. Incubation, by both sexes, 21 to 22 days.

Range. Holarctic, breeding southward from the Arctic Ocean to southwestern Alaska, the northern mainland of Canada east to Southampton Island and down the west coast of Hudson Bay; the British Isles, the Baltics, northern parts of Russia and Siberia; also Greenland, Iceland, Spitsbergen, and Novaya Zemlya. Winters from southern Alaska to Baja California and from Massachusetts to Florida and the Gulf Coast of the United States; and from the British Isles, Mediterranean and Red seas, south to northern Africa; also India, southern China, Japan, and Taiwan.

Subspecies. *Calidris alpina hudsonia* (Todd), a long-billed race with dark flank-streaks and dark shaft-streaks on the under tail coverts is the breeding form in most of Canada. *C. a. pacifica* (Coues) breeds in western Alaska and is found in British Columbia in migration and in winter.

Curlew Sandpiper

Bécasseau cocorli
Calidris ferruginea (Pontoppidan)
Total length: 18 to 23 cm
Plate 27

Status in Canada. Rare visitor to British
Columbia (Masset, Queen Charlotte Islands,
31 July 1936; also photo record: Iona Island,
24–25 June 1978); Alberta (photo record: Frank
Lake, 9 October 1975); Ontario (Toronto about
1886, near Port Maitland, 11 September 1965,
and near Essex, 14–17 May 1982 (photo). Also
sight records: Whitby, 21 October 1961, photographed; Waverly Beach, 18–19 July 1971;
Blenheim, 22 August 1976; Kapuskasing, May
1953; Dundas, October 1954; Hamilton,
October 1959; Niagara, July 1971; Amherst-
view, July 1974); Quebec (sight record: Saint-
Fulgence, 10 October 1974; photo: Saint-Blaise,
16 May 1982); New Brunswick (two collected at
Red Head, one on 3 August, one 31 August
1895; one found dead Grand Manan, 18 October
1966. Sight records at Castalia, 27 August, and
at Eel River Bar, 18 October 1973); and Nova
Scotia (photo record: Cherry Hill Beach, 2 July
1983; sight records at Port Morien Bar,
26 October 1969; Brier Island, 10 June 1971;
Three-Fathom Harbour, 31 October 1971, and
elsewhere).

In breeding plumage unmistakable: rich chestnut breast, white rump
with a few dark bars, and a rather long *downcurved* bill. Knots and
dowitchers also have reddish breasts, but their bills are straight. In
winter plumage the red of breast is lacking (although some immatures
have a faint rusty suffusion). The decidedly downcurved bill separates it
from other small and medium-sized sandpipers except the Dunlin. The
two are then similar in colour, but the Curlew Sandpiper has a white
patch completely across the rump.

Range. Breeds in northern Siberia. Winters from southern Eurasia
and the Philippines south to southern Africa, Australia, Tasmania, and
New Zealand.

Stilt Sandpiper

Bécasseau à échasses
Calidris himantopus (Bonaparte)
Total length: 19 to 23.5 cm
Plate 30

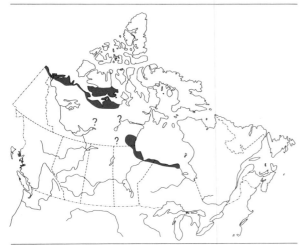

Breeding Distribution of Stilt Sandpiper

Range in Canada. Breeds in southern Victoria
Island (Cache Point, Cambridge Bay); coastal
Yukon (Clarence Lagoon, Blow River); north-
ern Mackenzie (mouth of Anderson River,
Cockburn Point, probably Perry River); south-
eastern Keewatin (McConnell River, Boundary
Lake); northeastern Manitoba (Churchill); and
north coastal Ontario (Cape Henrietta Maria,

Bill rather long, nearly straight but slightly depressed at tip, the tip
expanded and flattened. Legs relatively long, dull greenish-yellow or
yellowish olive (see Field Marks).

Measurements. *Adult male*: wing, 120–127 (123.9); tail, 48–55
(51.7); exposed culmen, 38.6–41.9 (39.6); tarsus, 36–45 (40.4). *Adult
female*: wing, 126.1–133.9 (131.4) mm.

Field Marks. A slender sandpiper with longish legs, longish bill
very slightly depressed at tip, and white patch across the rump, characters that distinguish it from most small and medium sandpipers. In
breeding dress, the heavily and closely barred under parts distinguish it
from all but the Wandering Tattler, a larger bird with no white rump
patch at any time. In autumn plumages the under parts are not barred,
but the longer legs and bill separate it from most other sandpipers.
Possibly it might be confused with the Lesser Yellowlegs, but smaller
size, a light line over the eye, and dull yellowish-green legs (yellowlegs
have bright-yellow legs) should distinguish it. It does not have the frequent bobbing motions of the yellowlegs. Its appearance and the habit
of plunging its long bill vertically into the mud or shallow water suggest
a dowitcher. If unsure, flush the bird. The Stilt Sandpiper has only the
rump white, but the dowitcher in flight shows a white lower back and a
white wing stripe. Stilt Sandpiper's long legs and bill readily distinguish
it from the obviously smaller White-rumped Sandpiper.

Habitat. In migration it prefers shallow quiet water and edges of
pools, ponds, sloughs, and lakes; sometimes beaches. In nesting season,
wet tundra and the vicinity of ponds, lakes, and marshes; occasionally
drier ridges.

Sutton River mouth). Found in summer in the interior of Mackenzie District but nesting not documented.

Migrates spring and autumn, mainly through the western provinces: Alberta, Saskatchewan, Manitoba, and in smaller numbers, British Columbia (mainly interior, rare on coast); uncommon mainly autumn transient in southern Ontario; rare autumn visitant to southern Quebec (Laprairie, Amos, Québec, Arvida, Madeleine Islands); New Brunswick (North Head, Kent Island, Saint John); and Nova Scotia (Sable Island, Lawrencetown Beach). Evidence of occurrence in Newfoundland is unsatisfactory.

Accidental on Bathurst Island, N.W.T. (specimen: 10 June 1975).

Nesting. Nest, a depression sparsely lined with a few leaves or grasses in tundra moss or ground. *Eggs*, apparently usually 4; pale buff with large irregularly shaped spots. Very little is known of the breeding cycle. Incubation period at least 21 days (Jehl and Hussell).

Range. Breeds in extreme northeastern Alaska and the low Arctic of western Canada east to western Hudson Bay. Winters in South America.

Spoonbill Sandpiper

Bécasseau spatule
Eurynorhynchus pygmeus (Linnaeus)
Total length: about 17 cm
Plate 27

Status in Canada. Accidental in British Columbia (one at the Iona Island sewage treatment plant, Richmond, 30 July to 3 August 1978, was superbly photographed leaving no possible doubt concerning the identification); Alberta (sight record by competent observers of two individuals at Keoma on 19 May 1984).

Resembles superficially the small calidrine sandpipers but in all plumages the terminal third of the bill (both upper and lower mandibles) is abruptly expanded to a flat, broad spatula. Summer adults have a rufous head, neck, and upper breast. Winter birds resemble the Western and Semipalmated sandpipers (including black legs) but have a whiter forehead. In any plumage the peculiar bill is diagnostic.

Range. Breeds in northeastern Siberia (Chukotski Peninsula). Winters in southeastern China, eastern Asam, and Burma. Casual in Alaska.

Buff-breasted Sandpiper

Bécasseau roussâtre
Tryngites subruficollis (Vieillot)
Total length: 19 to 22.5 cm
Plate 34

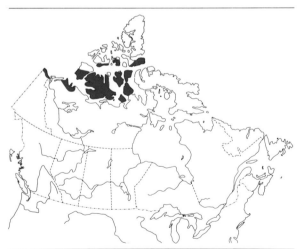

Breeding Distribution of Buff-breasted Sandpiper

Range in Canada. Breeds on Banks Island; Melville Island (Winter Harbour, perhaps Sabine Bay); Bathurst Island (Polar Bear Pass); Devon Island (near Cape Sparbo); Victoria Island (Cambridge Bay, Jenny Lind Island,

Bill shorter than head. A very buffy sandpiper, the buff coloration extending over all the under parts, darkest on breast becoming buffy white on abdomen and under tail coverts. In autumn the feathers of the back are narrowly margined with white. The extensive buff on the under parts combined with considerable dark marbling and spotting on inner webs of the flight feathers readily identifies it in the hand. Bill blackish, paler near base. Legs greenish yellow.

Measurements. *Adult male*: wing, 128.2–138.7 (133.4); tail, 56.8–61.4 (59); exposed culmen, 19.9–21.3 (20.5); tarsus, 31.8–34 (33.1). *Adult female*: wing, 120.4–127 (123.9) mm.

Field Marks. The extensive buffy coloration on the under parts, the dove-like head (short bill, high forehead), the unmarked buffy sides of head, and the yellowish legs make it one of the easy sandpipers to identify. The silvery-white wing linings are conspicuous in flight or when, as frequently happens in courtship, the wings are raised high. Because of the buffy coloration and, in autumn, "scaly" back, it might be confused with Baird's Sandpiper, but Baird's has black legs, the buff of the breast is cut off rather sharply from the white of the abdomen, and the sides of head are entirely different. Buff-breasts often assume an erect posture like the Upland Sandpiper.

Habitat. In migration short-grass prairies, fields, grain stubbles, and drier grassy places near water. On nesting grounds either drier grassy and mossy tundra or wet, marshy tundra.

Albert Edward Bay, probably Holman); Prince of Wales Island (Crooked Lake); King William Island; Boothia Peninsula (probably Wrottesley valley); northwestern Mackenzie (barrens between Horton River and Franklin Bay, Harrowby Bay); and northern Yukon (Firth and Babbage rivers).

Migration is mainly through Alberta, Saskatchewan, Manitoba, and southern Mackenzie (Fort Simpson, Great Slave Lake) and small numbers pass through southern Keewatin (McConnell River). Scarce in southern Yukon (Mayo Landing, Teslin) and British Columbia (coast and interior). Rare migrant in Ontario (occasionally east to Ottawa) and southern Quebec (Montréal, Lake Saint-Pierre, Godbout; casually east to Madeleine Islands). Casual in Labrador (Henley Harbour, perhaps Port Burwell, N.W.T.); Newfoundland (Argentia, Stephenville Crossing); Nova Scotia (photo records: Conrad Beach, 8 April 1976; Seal Island, 27 August 1971 and 3 September 1973; also various sight records); New Brunswick (Fredericton, 11 September 1966, photographed); and Prince Edward Island (sight records only).

Nesting. Nest, a slight depression in dry ground sparsely lined with grass and leaves. *Eggs*, usually 4; buff to dull white, marked especially at larger end with dark browns and with small spots or blotches over the entire egg. Its nesting routine is very poorly known but incubation is by the female alone.

Range. Breeds locally in northern Alaska (Point Barrow) and in the western Arctic of Canada. Winters in central Argentina.

Ruff

Bécasseau combattant
Philomachus pugnax (Linnaeus)
Total length: 21.5 to 29 cm
(male larger than female)
Plate 27

Status in Canada. A Eurasian visitor that occurs with some regularity in North America. A rare visitor to British Columbia (Reifel Refuge, 7 August 1972; and 29 June 1975; Victoria, 24 July 1975); Alberta (two males and two females near Calgary, 15 May 1967); Saskatchewan (male collected near Regina, 8 May 1965; sight record near Saskatoon, May 1970); Manitoba (Churchill, 23 June (1975?) photo; and sight record, 23 June 1970); Ontario (specimen records: Fort Severn, Toronto, Crystal Beach, Thunder Bay (Yacht Harbour) in Welland County; various sight records April–September); Quebec (Sept-Îles, 27 May 1933; Île-du-Moine, 23–25 July 1977; Cacouna, 5–21 May 1978; Henryville, 5 May 1979); New Brunswick (Grand Manan: old undated specimens; recent sight records at Jourimain Marsh); Nova Scotia (Cole Harbour, 27 May 1892; Sable Island, 29 May 1975; New Minas, 1 October 1928; various sight records); Prince Edward Island (sight records only: Brackley Marsh); and Newfoundland (photo: Gros Morne National Park, 16 May 1982; specimen: Quidi Vidi Lake, 9 April 1980).

Bill about as long as head, slightly tapering when viewed from the side. Adult male in breeding plumage is exceedingly variable in colour but is unmistakable by its extraordinary ruff (an erectile shield of feathers on the neck) and by two broad ear-tufts. The shield may be black (with purplish gloss), brown, white, and various combinations. These adornments are lacking in autumn and winter plumage when adult male resembles the full-coloured female. Autumn and winter birds are nondescript; the feathers of the upper parts have dark centres and sandy margins; breast is buffy, sometimes spotted with dusky; chin and belly white. Legs variable in colour. In any plumage a broad dark stripe extends down the rump and centre of tail. This stripe is bordered on either side by white, the white broadening to form an oval white patch on either side of the tail. These oval white patches are quite unlike anything shown by the Upland Sandpiper, Greater and Lesser yellowlegs, or any similar species.

Short-billed Dowitcher

Bécasseau roux
Limnodromus griseus (Gmelin)
Total length: 26.5 to 30.5 cm
Plate 32

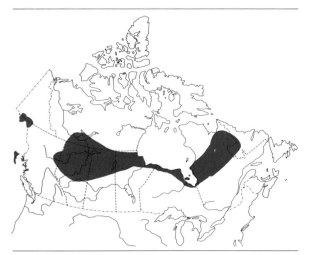

Breeding Distribution of Short-billed Dowitcher

Range in Canada. Breeding range poorly known. Breeds locally in southern Yukon (Kluane Game Sanctuary; Lake Laberge; Swan Lake); northwestern and probably central-eastern British Columbia (Queen Charlotte Islands, Chilkat Pass, probably Peace River District); southern Mackenzie (north to near Fort Simpson); Alberta (various localities: Edmonton north to Lesser Slave Lake); northern Saskatchewan (probably Montreal Lake and Doré Lake); northern Manitoba (Churchill); northwestern Ontario (Winisk); James Bay (North Twin and Akimiski islands); and northern Quebec (Schefferville region; probably Kuujjuaq).

Regular spring and autumn transient in British Columbia, southern Alberta, southern Saskatchewan, Manitoba, and on the west coast of Hudson and James bays, southern Ontario (but apparently very scarce in interior western localities), Quebec (locally: Montréal, Québec, Lake Saint-Jean, north shore of the Gulf of St. Lawrence, Percé), Labrador (rare: Turnavik West, Henley Harbour), Newfoundland (autumn transient, uncommon), and the Maritimes (uncommon in spring, more common in autumn).

Bill straight, twice as long as head. Dowitchers (there are two very similar species) have such long, straight bills that, in the hand, they are likely to be confused with only the Common Snipe and the Woodcock (see also Stilt Sandpiper). The whole lower back of dowitchers (concealed by the folded wings) is white, and the rump is white with a few black bars and spots. Woodcock and Common Snipe have no white on those parts. (For distinctions between the two species of dowitchers see Long-billed Dowitcher.)

Measurements *(L. g. griseus). Adult male*: wing, 132.8–145.3 (139.2); tail, 51.5–57.3 (53.4); exposed culmen, 51.9–57.5 (54.8); tarsus, 32.9–35.9 (34.1). *Adult female*: wing, 131–146.1 (139.8) mm.

Field Marks. Dowitchers are medium-sized sandpipers with long straight bills. The lower back (concealed by folded wings but conspicuous in flight) and rump are white. Common Snipe and the Woodcock also have long straight bills but no white on rump or lower back. Dowitchers in autumn resemble also the Stilt Sandpiper, a smaller bird that in flight shows a white rump but no white on the back and lacks the white wing stripe of the dowitchers. There are two species of dowitchers (see Long-billed Dowitcher).

Habitat. In migration, soft muddy margins of fresh, brackish, and salt water; mud flats; beaches. In nesting season, muskegs and similar boggy and marshy places with low vegetation.

Nesting. The nest is lined with grasses and moss and is usually a depression on or near a hummock in wet sedge or grassy meadows or muskegs. The *eggs*, usually 4, are greenish to olive-buff, spotted with browns. Incubation period 21 days (Jehl and Hussell).

Range. Breeds in southern Alaska and widely but locally in Canada. Winters from southern United States south through Central America and the West Indies to Brazil and Peru.

Subspecies. Three, all well marked. (1) *Limnodromus griseus griseus* (Gmelin): cinnamon of under parts pale and much restricted posteriorly with belly mainly white; spotting dense but mainly on breast; upper parts dark; white bars on tail narrow, thus closely approaching those of the Long-billed Dowitcher; bill shorter than in other races. Breeds in Quebec. (2) *L. g. hendersoni* Rowan: cinnamon of under parts darker and more extensive than in (1), spotting sparser but more extensive, often extending to belly; upper parts paler; white bars on tail broader; bill slightly longer. Breeds from eastern British Columbia to Manitoba; north to southern Mackenzie. (3) *L. g. caurinus* Pitelka: averages larger than (1) and (2) and intermediate between them in spotting and extent of cinnamon on under parts. Known breeding range, southern Alaska. Occurs in British Columbia as a transient.

Long-billed Dowitcher

Bécasseau à long bec
Limnodromus scolopaceus (Say)
Total length: 28 to 32 cm
Plate 32

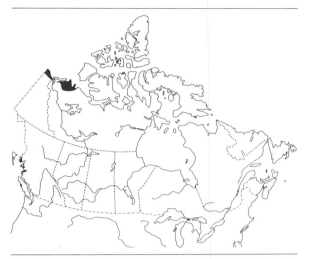

Breeding Distribution of Long-billed Dowitcher

Range in Canada. Breeds in northern Yukon (near Blow River, Babbage River, Firth River) and in extreme northwestern Mackenzie (Anderson River, Franklin Bay). Spring and autumn transient mainly in the western provinces: British Columbia (coast and interior), Alberta, Saskatchewan, and Manitoba. Less commonly in southern Ontario (Toronto, Hamilton, Rockhouse Point, Ottawa) and Quebec (Laprairie). Rare in Nova Scotia (specimen: Sable Island, 4 October 1897) and New Brunswick (Grand Manan).

Like Short-billed Dowitcher, but bill averages decidedly longer; in breeding plumage the cinnamon of the under parts consistently extends over belly and usually over under tail coverts; ventral spotting is dense and is restricted to upper breast and throat; markings of sides of breast are well-formed bars rather than spots; light bars on tail tend to be narrower than in western races of the Short-billed Dowitcher but there is much overlapping. Autumn Long-bills usually have unspeckled grey upper breasts; Short-bills have slightly paler, finely speckled (or lightly spotted) upper breast but this is not always dependable.

Measurements. *Adult male*: wing, 139–146.2 (141.2); tail, 52.1–57.9 (55); exposed culmen, 57–64 (61.5); tarsus, 36–41 (38.2). *Adult female*: wing, 139–148 (144.3) mm.

Field Marks. So similar to the Short-billed Dowitcher that many individuals cannot be safely distinguished in the field. Bill lengths overlap, and only extremes can serve as useful indicators. In breeding plumage however, birds with well-formed bars on the sides of the *breast* instead of spots (caution: both species have bars on sides and flanks) and with obviously longer bills can safely be called Long-bills. Individuals with extensive white on the belly, no bars on sides of breast, and short to moderate bills are Short-bills. Also the Long-bill's upper parts are darker than those of the Short-bills breeding in the Prairie Provinces (subspecies *hendersoni*), but the eastern nominate race of the Short-bill has the upper parts as dark as those of the Long-bill. Eastern Short-bills are best distinguished in breeding plumage from the Long-billed by their much more extensively white bellies. The common call of the Short-billed Dowitcher is a double or triple *tu*; that of the Long-bill is a thin *keek*. Needless to say, field identification of the two species should be attempted with caution.

Habitat. In migration, it favours freshwater situations more than the Short-billed Dowitcher.

Nesting. Apparently similar to the Short-billed Dowitcher but has not been closely studied.

Range. Breeds in northeastern Siberia, northwestern Alaska, and northwestern Mackenzie. Winters from southern United States (California to Florida) and south through Mexico (mainly western) to Guatemala.

Jack Snipe

Bécassine sourde
Lymnocryptes minimus (Brünnich)
Total length: 19 to 22.4 cm

Status in Canada. Accidental visitor from the Old World. Labrador (Makkovik Bay, specimen taken 24 December 1927).

Smaller than Common Snipe with much shorter bill (bill little more than 4 cm). Lacks median crown stripe. Flanks not barred. Tail has no brick-red colour; *middle tail feathers longest*.

Great Snipe

[**Great Snipe**. Bécassine double. *Gallinago media* (Latham). Hypothetical. The type specimen of *Scolopax leucurus* Swainson, later identified as this species, was alleged to have come from "Hudson's Bay" (W. Swainson and J. Richardson, 1831. *Fauna Boreali-Americana*. Part 2, p. 501. London: J. Murray).]

Common Snipe

(Wilson's Snipe)

Bécassine des marais
Gallinago gallinago (Linnaeus)
Total length: 26 to 30 cm
(including 6.5 to 7 cm bill)
Plate 32

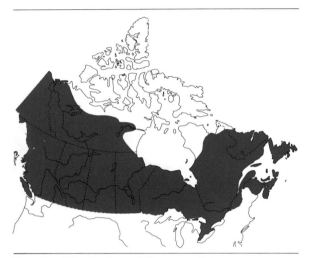

Breeding Distribution of Common Snipe

Range in Canada. Breeds from northern Yukon (north to arctic coastal plain); northwestern and central Mackenzie (Aklavik, Anderson River, Thelon River marshes); southern Keewatin (McConnell and Windy rivers); James Bay (North Twin Island); northern Quebec (Grande rivière de la Baleine, Feuilles River, Kuujjuaq and Koroc River); and central Labrador (Webb Bay) south through British Columbia (breeding records lacking from Queen Charlotte Islands), Alberta, Saskatchewan, Manitoba, Ontario, Quebec (including Madeleine Islands), Newfoundland, New Brunswick, Prince Edward Island, and Nova Scotia (including Sable Island).

Winters regularly in southern British Columbia (small numbers on coast and southern interior); casually and irregularly elsewhere (southern Ontario, New Brunswick, Nova Scotia, and Newfoundland).

Bill long, straight. Upper parts mixed browns, buff, ochre, and blackish with buff stripes down back. Crown with light-buff or whitish median stripe. Tail stubby, with subterminal area of brick-red crossed by narrow black bar near end and tipped buff or whitish. Breast buffy brown, variously marked with dusky. Belly white. Sides and flanks barred with blackish brown. Woodcock and dowitchers also have long straight bills, but American Woodcock is coloured very differently, and the outermost three primaries are extremely narrow. Dowitchers have the lower back (partly hidden by folded wings) mainly white, no brick-red in the tail, and no median crown stripe.

Measurements. *Adult male*: wing, 122.3–128.4 (125.2); tail, 53.2–58 (55.3); exposed culmen, 61–70.3 (65.2); tarsus, 31–35.6 (32.4). *Adult female*: wing, 121.9–132.5 (127) mm.

Field Marks. A long-billed shorebird that flies up, usually from low marshy places, with a peculiar zig-zag flight, uttering a characteristic raspy *scaipe* and showing at close range a little brick-red in the tail. In spring it is frequently detected by the hollow tremolo "winnowing" sound, produced by the tail and wings in the air overhead. The dowitcher is a long-billed shorebird of similar proportions, but in flight it shows a conspicuously white lower back and has no red in the tail and no light median crown stripe.

Habitat. In breeding season, various types of large and small freshwater marshes, bogs, marshy edges, moist meadows and similar places that provide soft mud and low cover. In migration, also ploughed and puddly fields, wet stubbles, ditches, and creeks; also edges of salt marshes. Water edges trampled into black mud by the hoofs of animals are often very inviting. Sometimes more open wet alder runs and occasionally even wet woodland. The few that winter in eastern Canada usually resort to springs.

Nesting. On the ground, in a slight depression lined with grass in or near a marsh, bog, slough, or lake, or sometimes in the grass of prairie or fields near by. *Eggs*, usually 4; greenish buff to brownish, heavily marked with dark browns. Incubation 18 to 20 days (L.M. Tuck), mainly if not entirely by the female.

Range. Holarctic. In North America breeds from northwestern Alaska and the northern mainland of Canada south to California, Arizona, Nebraska, central Iowa, northern Illinois, northwestern Pennsylvania, and northern New Jersey. Winters mainly from southern British Columbia, Utah, central Nebraska, Indiana, and North Carolina south to the West Indies, Colombia, Venezuela, and southern Brazil. Breeds also in Iceland, the Faeroe Islands, and widely across much of Eurasia, and winters south as far as central Africa, Ceylon, Java, and the Philippines.

Subspecies. (1) *Galinago gallinago delicata* (Ord) is the breeding subspecies of North America and the only subspecies likely to be encountered in Canada. (2) The Eurasian subspecies *G. g. gallinago* (Linnaeus) is of accidental occurrence in Labrador (Makkovik Bay, 24 December 1927).

Remarks. A common spring sound, high in the air, over low-lying areas is a hollow tremolo *who-who-who-who-who*. This is a courtship performance of the Common Snipe. The sound is produced in flight by the rush of air past the spread tail feathers, and the tremolo effect by the rapidly beating wings. Another common spring sound, produced vocally, usually while the bird is perched on the ground or on a fence post, is a harsh *kak-kak* repeated various times. At any season a harsh *scaipe* is given while the bird is in flight, especially when flushing.

Eurasian Woodcock

Bécasse des bois
Scolopax rusticola Linnaeus
Total length: 33 to 35.5 cm

Status in Canada. Accidental in Quebec (one
shot at Chambly, 11 November 1882) and in
Newfoundland (one taken near St. John's,
9 January 1862).

Decidedly larger than American Woodcock with greyer, distinctly barred
under parts. The three outermost primaries are not narrow as in American Woodcock. An Old World species which breeds across Eurasia from
the British Isles to northern Japan.

American Woodcock

Bécasse d'Amérique
Scolopax minor Gmelin
Total length: 25.5 to 30.5 cm
(including bill of 6.4 to 7.6 cm)
Plate 32

Figure 58
Emarginate outer primaries of American
Woodcock

Breeding Distribution of American Woodcock

Range in Canada. Breeds from southeastern
Manitoba (Red River valley, Reaburn, Birds
Hill Provincial Park, Piney, north to Manigota-
gan); southern and south-central Ontario (north
at least to Thunder Bay and Michipicoten
Island, northern Lake Superior; North Bay;
Cochrane District); southern Quebec (Hull,
Montréal, Magog, Québec, Rivière-du-Loup,
eastern Gaspé Peninsula; Forillon National
Park, and Bonaventure Island; La Motte, Lake
Saint-Jean, probably Anticosti Island); New-
foundland (Indian Head, Doyles, Squires
Memorial Provincial Park, Mummichog Park;

Bill long and straight; eyes large and set high in the head; wings short,
rounded, outer three primaries very much narrower than rest (Figure
58). General cinnamon coloration: "autumn leaf" patterns above, plain
below.

Measurements. *Adult male*: wing, 122–128 (125); tail, 53–61 (57.8);
exposed culmen, 63.9–67.7 (65.8); tarsus, 30–34.8 (31.5). *Adult female*:
wing, 129.6–139.6 (136) mm.

Field Marks. A plump, cinnamon-coloured shorebird of thickets,
with very long bill, large eyes set high in the head, short neck and tail.
Usually it is not seen until it flies up at close range, its short wings producing a *twittering whistle*. The Common Snipe, also a long-billed
shorebird, is very differently coloured, and the wings do not whistle in
flight. The wings of the Mourning Dove produce a distinct whistling
sound in flight, but is body proportions are very different (short bill,
long tail).

Habitat. In spring the singing grounds of the males are in clearings
and openings of various sizes in or near areas of low immature open
mixedwood or hardwood or alder-willow thickets. These young open
woodlands serve as nesting places and, along with alder thickets, as the
male's daytime territory. In autumn, alder runs and moist alder thickets
are popular, but dry open second growth is also frequented. Woodcock
feed largely on earthworms and are likely to be found in the vicinity of
soft moist soils suitable for the production of earthworms. Sometimes in
dusk or darkness the birds feed in open fields or roadside ditches at
considerable distances from woodland.

Nesting. On the ground in young open mixedwood or deciduous
woodland, alder thickets, or sometimes in brushy or weedy fields. Nest,
a depression in the ground sparsely lined with leaves. *Eggs*, usually 4;
less pear-shaped (more ovate) than those of most shorebirds; buffy,
rather sparingly spotted with brown and some grey. Incubation, 19 to
21 days (O.S. Pettingill, Jr.), by the female.

Range. Breeds from southeastern Canada south to Louisiana,
Mississippi, southern central Alabama, and central Florida; west to
southeastern Manitoba and extreme eastern Texas. Winters chiefly in
southeastern Arkansas, Louisiana, and southwestern Mississippi, and in
smaller numbers somewhat farther north and west.

Remarks. Although a shorebird, the Woodcock is found mostly in
moist brushy tangles and alder thickets. It sleeps during the day, and
when disturbed it springs from the ground with whistling wings, whirs
up over the alder tops, then soon drops back into cover.

It is one of the earliest birds to return in spring, while snow
patches still remain in the woods. When dusk settles over the alder
patches on a spring evening, the male's well-spaced nasal *peent* is a

singles, including one "ground calling," reliably reported north to St. Anthony); New Brunswick; Prince Edward Island; and Nova Scotia (including Cape Breton Island).

Casual on north shore of the Gulf of St. Lawrence (Johan-Beetz Bay, Havre Saint-Pierre). Sight records north to Fort Albany, Ontario.

Occasional winter occurrences in Canada may be wounded or otherwise unhealthy individuals.

common sound. It is similar to a call of the Common Nighthawk and is often mistaken for that bird long before the Common Nighthawk has returned from the south. This note is given by the Woodcock while on the ground. Every few minutes, however, it whirs up from the ground, wings whistling loudly, mounts high in the semi-darkness where it does a peculiar sky dance on wings, then plummets back to earth and resumes its ground calling.

The long slender bill has a flexible tip and is ideal for probing the ground for earthworms, which make up a large part of the Woodcock's food.

Subfamily **Phalaropodinae:** Phalaropes

Figure 59
Foot of Red Phalarope

Phalaropes are small swimming "sandpipers." Their toes are equipped with lobes (which sandpiper's toes lack), and there are small webs at their bases (Figure 59). The tarsi are laterally flattened. Plumage is dense and waterproof. They are the only small shorebirds that habitually swim. Often they feed by swimming in small circles, picking up bits of food as they go. The males are smaller and much duller in colour than the females. Females take the initiative in courtship, and the males incubate the eggs and care for the young.

Wilson's Phalarope

Phalarope de Wilson
Phalaropus tricolor (Vieillot)
Total length: 21 to 25.5 cm
Plate 34

Breeding Distribution of Wilson's Phalarope

Range in Canada. Breeds in southern Yukon (Swan Lake, Lake Laberge); interior central and southern British Columbia (Cowichan Bay, Vancouver, Nulki Lake, 149 Mile Lake, Dale Lake, Cranbrook; Peace River District); Alberta (north at least to Bear Lake in Grande Prairie region, Hay and Zama lakes, probably Athabasca delta); central and southern Saskatchewan (north at least to Nipawin and Prince Albert and probably to Niska Lake); central-western and southern Manitoba (north to Reader and Halcrow lakes near The Pas,

Female larger and more brightly coloured than male. Bill very slender and awl-like, not obviously flattened, thus different from that of Red Phalarope. Front toes with very narrow lateral membranes and very small basal webs. Differs from other phalaropes in larger size, lack of a white wing stripe, and absence of distinct scallops on the lateral membranes of the front toes.

Measurements. *Adult male*: wing, 116.5–128 (121.1); tail, 45.8–53.7 (51.3); exposed culmen, 28.4–33 (30.8); tarsus, 29.9–33.5 (31.7). *Adult female*: wing, 128.9–137.3 (132.5) mm.

Field Marks. Phalaropes are swimming sandpipers. However, the Wilson's Phalarope wades and walks on shore more often than the other two species. When on land its needlelike bill and slender neck distinguish it from sandpipers. Lack of a white stripe in the spread wing separates it from the two other phalaropes in any plumage. In breeding plumage the female, with a black stripe from the eye down the side of the neck merging posteriorly into chestnut, is easily recognized. The male is smaller and duller and, like the Red-necked Phalarope, has a cinnamon suffusion on sides of neck. It lacks the buffy streaks present on the back of the Red-necked and usually shows a small whitish area on the back of the neck, which the Red-necked lacks. Common call: harsh grunts seemingly out of keeping with the daintiness and relatively small size of the bird.

Habitat. In the breeding season, sloughs, shallow lakes, and freshwater marshes.

Nesting. Nest, a depression in the ground, sparsely to well lined with dry grasses, and usually near shallow water. *Eggs*, usually 4; pale buff, well spotted and blotched with blackish brown. Incubation, by the male, lasts about 20.2 days (D.F. Parmelee).

Range. Breeds from southern interior of western Canada south in the interior to south-central California, northern Utah, central Kansas, and northern Indiana; locally southern Ontario and southwestern Quebec. Winters mainly in Argentina and rarely Chile.

rarely and recently at Churchill); Ontario (North Point on James Bay, Richmond, Winchester, Russell, Luther Marsh near Orangeville; Kingston; Holland Marsh near Bradford; Dunnville, Haldimand County; West Lorne, Elgin County, probably Lake of the Woods); and southwestern Quebec (Soeurs Island, near Montréal; Île-du-Moine, Yamaska; possibly Lake Saint-Jean). Perhaps breeds rarely in southern New Brunswick (Sackville) and Nova Scotia (Amherst Point).

Rare transient in eastern Quebec (Anticosti Island, Madeleine Islands), and New Brunswick (Point Lepreau, probably Grand Manan; possibly may have nested near Sackville in 1978). There is a convincing sight record of ten seen off the coast of Nova Scotia, 19 June 1934 (A.O. Gross, 1937. Auk, vol. 54, no. 1, p. 27); also several subsequent sight records; photo record: Seal Island, 25 August 1971. Newfoundland (photo records: Terra Nova National Park, 31 May 1982; Stephenville Crossing, 15 August 1973). Sight records only for Prince Edward Island.

Remarks. This phalarope is a common summer inhabitant of the prairie sloughs and pools. On the water it rides as lightly as thistledown, often spinning in small circles and seizing by quick thrusts of its slender bill bits of food stirred up in the shallow water. It is more inclined, however, to feed on land than are the other phalaropes. Land and aquatic insects (especially the larvae of mosquitoes), brine shrimps, and amphipods provide a large part of its diet.

As in all phalaropes, the male is a "hen-pecked husband." He is smaller and plainer than the female. He builds the nest, incubates the eggs, and cares for the young. The female takes the initiative in courtship. The writer once saw a little male being ardently pursued by five females at one time!

Red-necked Phalarope

(Northern Phalarope)

Phalarope hyperboréen
Phalaropus lobatus (Linnaeus)
Total length: 16.5 to 20 cm
Plates 34 and 35

Breeding Distribution of Red-necked Phalarope

Range in Canada. Breeds in the low Arctic and Subarctic from southern Victoria Island (Simpson Bay, Cambridge Bay; reported in summer north to Holman); central Keewatin (Beverly Lake, Chesterfield Inlet, Coats Island, Southampton Island); and southern Baffin Island south to northwestern British Columbia (Atlin, Chilkat Pass); southern Yukon (Ogilvie Mountains); Mackenzie (barrens east of Mackenzie Delta, Franklin Bay, Coronation Gulf, Bathurst Inlet, probably Perry River and indefinitely southward; Nahanni National Park);

Female larger and in breeding plumage more brightly coloured than the male. A shorebird with lobed membranes along the sides of the front toes is a phalarope. White wing stripe separates it in all plumages from Wilson's Phalarope. Its very slender pointed bill distinguishes it from the Red Phalarope.

Measurements. *Adult male*: wing, 101–106.5 (104.6); tail, 45–51 (48.4); exposed culmen, 20.2–23.5 (21.8); tarsus, 19.8–21.6 (20.7). *Adult female*: wing, 106.7–114.9 (111.6) mm.

Field Marks. A small shorebird that swims for sustained periods, often with spinning motions, is a phalarope. In breeding plumage, lack of extensive red on the under parts easily distinguishes it from the Red Phalarope. In winter and immature plumages, these two species are very similar, but at close range the much slenderer needlelike bill of the Red-necked can often be discerned. Both Red-necked and Red phalaropes have a white wing stripe, visible in flight or when the wing is raised, which separates them from the Wilson's Phalarope at all times.

Habitat. In the breeding season low-arctic and subarctic freshwater pools and their low-vegetation margins. In migration, mostly the open ocean and seacoast, but interior lakes and ponds are also frequented to a smaller extent.

Nesting. Nest, a depression lined with grass or leaves in a tussock or mound in a marshy place with scattered ponds. *Eggs*, usually 4; olive buff, well spotted or blotched with brown. Incubation about 20 days (H.B. Conover), by the male; 22.5 days (Jehl and Hussell).

northern Alberta (locally: Caribou Mountains); northern Saskatchewan (Lake Athabasca); southern Keewatin (McConnell River); northeastern Manitoba (Churchill); northern Ontario (Cape Henrietta Maria, Little Cape); James Bay (North Twin Island, Grey Goose Island, Belcher Islands); northern Quebec (islands in Ungava Bay; Gregory Lake; Schefferville region and south on the Hudson and James Bay coasts to Rupert Bay); and Labrador coast (south to Battle Harbour). Non-breeding birds are found in summer south of the breeding range.

Migrates commonly along both the Atlantic and Pacific coasts and at sea, with good numbers also passing through interior British Columbia, Alberta, and Saskatchewan. Scarcer in interior Manitoba, infrequent to rare in the southern interior of Ontario and Quebec (mainly in autumn), but likely to turn up eventually almost anywhere. Occurs in all the coastal provinces, mostly as an offshore migrant.

Range. Breeds across the low Arctic or Subarctic of both the New and Old Worlds. Winters at sea in both hemispheres, mainly south of the equator.

Red Phalarope

Phalarope roux
Phalaropus fulicaria (Linnaeus)
Total length: 19.5 to 23 cm (female larger and more brightly coloured than the male)
Plates 34 and 35

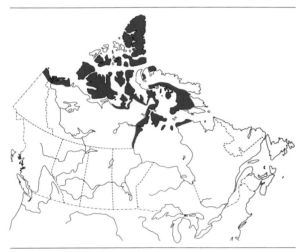

Breeding Distribution of Red Phalarope

A sandpiper-like shorebird with scalloped membranes along the sides of the front toes is a phalarope (Figure 59). Front toes half-webbed at bases. In breeding plumage the entire under parts (except blackish throat) are chestnut red, quite unlike any other phalarope. Adults and young in autumn are mainly white below and similar to the other species. In any plumage the broader, flattened bill of the Red Phalarope is diagnostic compared with the slender bill of the other two species.

Measurements. *Adult male*: wing, 121–132 (125.1); tail, 58.5–67.1 (63); exposed culmen, 21–23 (22.3); tarsus, 21.8–23 (22.3). *Adult female*: wing, 128–136.3 (131.9) mm.

Field Marks. A sandpiper-like bird with a persistent habit of swimming is a phalarope. In spring and summer the all-red under parts and yellow (with dark tip) bill readily distinguish this species. In autumn and winter it closely resembles the other two species. At close range its flatter, thicker bill, often with a small light area at the base of the lower mandible, distinguishes it from the other two. In flight its white wing stripe separates it from the Wilson's Phalarope.

Habitat. In migration mainly the open sea, where it swims buoyantly; comes closer inshore occasionally, especially during storms, occasionally coming to land; more rarely freshwater bodies of the interior. In the breeding season, grass, sedge, and moss tussocky tundra interspersed with shallow freshwater ponds and shallow lakes, generally not very far from the coast.

Nesting. Nest, often a depression in the ground, usually (not always) lined with grass or similar vegetation. Usually it is situated on a dry spot or tussock near a tundra pond; sometimes a cup-shaped structure attached to vegetation over water. *Eggs*, usually 4; dark to light greenish-buff, heavily and irregularly marked, most heavily at larger end, with dark browns. Incubation mainly by the male, but Herbert Brandt (1943. *Alaska Bird Trails*, p. 396) twice observed a female on eggs in Alaska, and Sutton (1932) suspected that the female may incubate to a limited extent. Incubation period 18 to 19 days (D.F. Parmalee).

Range in Canada. Breeds from Banks Island (Kellett River; probably Mercy Bay); Melville Island (Bailey Point, Sabine Bay); and Ellesmere Island (Fosheim Peninsula) south to northern Yukon (Clarence Lagoon); northern Mackenzie (Franklin Bay, Perry River); Keewatin (Adelaide Peninsula, Chesterfield Inlet, McConnell River); Southampton Island; Mansel Island (probably); near northern Quebec (Digges Island, N.W.T.); and probably northern Labrador. The species has been recorded on Prince Patrick, Ellef Ringnes and Axel Heiberg islands but without evidence of breeding.

Migrates mainly at sea and along both the Pacific and Atlantic coasts. Scarce in the interior, most records for autumn; in interior British Columbia (Swan Lake, Okanagan; Sirdar Lake); Alberta (Beaverhill Lake, Didsbury, Banff National Park, Stirling); Saskatchewan (Sandfly Lake on Churchill River); Manitoba (East Shoal Lake); Ontario (Rondeau; Toronto; Middlesex County; White Lake; Ottawa); and Quebec (Valleyfield, Brosseau, Disraeli, Beauport).

Range. Circumpolar. Breeds on tundra mostly near the coast across North America and Eurasia. Winters at sea, mainly in the Southern Hemisphere off both coasts of South America and western Africa; small numbers farther north.

Family **Laridae**:
Skuas, Gulls, Terns, and Skimmers

Number of Species in Canada: 42

Subfamily **Stercorariinae**:
Skuas and Jaegers

Gull-like, graceful, swift, and predatory sea birds that rob other birds of food. They spend most of the year on the ocean but nest on the arctic tundra. Bill is strongly hooked. Wings long and pointed. Front toes fully webbed, claws hooked and sharp. In flight they show more or less white at the base of the primaries on the underside of the wing. Adult jaegers have the central tail feathers elongated.

Their size and strongly hooked bills (gulls have only slightly hooked bills) combined with webbed feet distinguish them from most other birds of regular occurrence in Canada except cormorants, shearwaters, and petrels. The presence of open nostrils and of two instead of three webs on each foot distinguishes them from cormorants. The nostrils are not enclosed in tubes as in shearwaters, petrels, and albatrosses.

These dashing pirates commonly pursue gulls and terns, forcing them to disgorge their food. With a graceful swoop the jaegers snap up the disgorged fish or other item before it hits the water. They capture fish, small mammals, large insects, and sometimes adult birds for food, and they eat eggs and young of other birds as well as carrion.

Pomarine Jaeger

Labbe pomarin
Stercorarius pomarinus (Temminck)
Total length: 51 to 58.5 cm
Plate 39

Figure 60
Tail of adult Pomarine Jaeger

The most robust of the jaegers (although the extremely long tail of the smaller Long-tailed Jaeger gives it an almost equal total length) with decidedly heavier and longer bill and usually longer wing. Adults are distinguishable from adults of the other jaegers by the tips of the elongated central tail feathers, which are blunt and are usually twisted so that they are nearly or quite vertical (projection beyond other tail feathers 5 to 10 cm, Figure 60). There are two colour phases. *Adults (light phase)*: Top of head black. Wings and tail sooty greyish-brown. Primaries whitish at bases with whitish shafts. Throat, neck, and breast white, the sides of the neck suffused with golden yellow, and usually there is a more or less complete band of dusky mixed with white across the breast and more or less dusky markings on sides (dusky markings on breast and sides variable in extent, sometimes almost absent). Posterior abdomen and tail coverts greyish brown. Adults in *dark phase* are uniform greyish-brown above and below, but with whitish areas on wings as in light phase. *First-year Immatures (light phase)*: Upper parts dark brown with buff spots on scapulars and rump; head and neck dark brown; under parts barred buffy and dark brown. Central tail feathers project little beyond others. Young separable from those of other jaegers by larger size.

Measurements. *Adult male*: wing, 340–359.5 (346.4); tail, 174.5–238.5 (212.7); exposed culmen, 34.9–40.9 (36.9); tarsus, 49.4–55 (53.1). *Adult female*: wing, 355.5–367 (359.9) mm.

Field Marks. Adults separable from other jaegers in both colour phases by the tips of the central tail feathers, which are blunt and twisted to a vertical plane. Projecting central tail feathers much shorter (5 to 10 cm) than in adult Long-tailed. Young of all jaegers are almost impossible to distinguish in the field, but direct comparison may distinguish Pomarine by larger size and heavier bill (see also Great Skua).

Breeding Distribution of Pomarine Jaeger

Range in Canada. Breeds in the Arctic from Banks Island, Melville Island (Winter Harbour, Sherard Bay), Bathurst, Prince of Wales, Somerset, and Devon islands south to northwestern Mackenzie (Baillie Island); southern Victoria Island (abundantly Anderson Bay to Wellington Bay and elsewhere); Southampton Island (Itiuachuk); southern Baffin Island (Lake Amadjuak); and northwestern Quebec (Inoucdjouac, Povungnituk).

Non-breeding birds are found in summer off northern British Columbia (Goose Island Banks), in Hudson Bay, the coast of Labrador, Newfoundland, and the north shore of the Gulf of St. Lawrence.

Migrates mainly at sea and off both the Pacific and Atlantic coasts and has occurred in all the coastal provinces. Very rare in the interior of British Columbia (Chilcotin, exact locality unspecified; Canal Flats); southern Yukon (Teslin Lake); Saskatchewan (Yellow Grass, Prince Albert National Park); Manitoba (mouth of Red River); Ontario (Rock Point, Niagara River, Hamilton, Detroit River), and interior Quebec (Saint-Lambert).

Habitat. In the breeding season, low tundra interspersed with lakes, pools, or sluggish streams, often on coastal plains but also at variable distances (usually not great) inland. In migration the ocean, mainly well off shore; rarely large interior lakes.

Nesting. Nest, a slight depression, lined with grass or sometimes unlined, on a mound or other rise of ground in usually low tundra. *Eggs*, usually 2; brownish olive, spotted with browns. Incubation, by both sexes, lasts about 24 to 27 days.

Range. Breeds in northern Alaska, arctic Canada, Greenland, Spitsbergen, Novaya Zemlya, northern Russia, and northern Siberia. Winters at sea mainly from the latitude of North Carolina to the West Indies and off Africa, and from the latitude of southern California south to Peru, and off eastern Australia.

Parasitic Jaeger

Labbe parasite
Stercorarius parasiticus (Linnaeus)
Total length: 46 to 53.5 cm
Plate 39

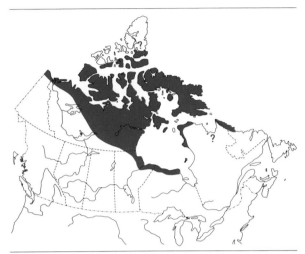

Breeding Distribution of Parasitic Jaeger

Range in Canada. Breeds in the Arctic and
Subarctic from Banks Island, southern Melville,
Bathurst, Cornwallis, and southern Ellesmere
islands south to southern Mackenzie (locally:
Great Slave Lake); southern Keewatin (Angikuni Lake, McConnell River); Southampton
Island; northeastern Manitoba (Churchill);
northern Ontario (Cape Henrietta Maria);
northern Quebec (Kogaluc River); and northern
Labrador (Metik Islands). Non-breeding birds
found in summer south of the breeding range.

Migration mainly at sea and along the Paci-
fic and Atlantic coasts, usually well off shore.
Scarce in the interior: Yukon (Old Crow);
British Columbia (Wells Gray Park); Alberta
(Beaverhill Lake; numerous sight records else-
where); Saskatchewan (Old Wives Lake, Last
Mountain Lake, Nipawin); southern Manitoba
(Scanterbury, Pelican Island); southern Ontario
(numerous records for the Great Lakes; also
recorded from Ottawa; sight records elsewhere);
and southwestern Quebec (La Ferme, near
Amos).

Figure 61
Tail of adult Parasitic Jaeger

Smaller than Pomarine Jaeger. Central tail feathers of adults pointed
and never twisted, thus differing from adult Pomarine Jaeger (Figure
61). Central tail feathers much shorter than in adult Long-tailed Jaeger
(projecting only 6.5 to 9 cm beyond others). There are two colour
phases, light and dark, both similar to Pomarine. The light phase of the
Parasitic is slightly paler above; breast band and markings on sides
when present are decidedly paler and more uniform (little or no white
mottling or bars); yellow suffusion on sides of head and neck less extensive and intensive; and the feathers at the base of the upper mandible
are whitish. Young of the year somewhat smaller than Pomarine and
have more decided streaking on the head (see also Long-tailed Jaeger).

Measurements. *Adult male*: wing, 317–334.5 (325); tail, 195–232.5
(209.7); exposed culmen, 28.6–32.8 (30.4); tarsus, 44–48.7 (45.8). *Adult
female*: wing, 305–335.5 (325.6) mm.

Field Marks. The pointed, untwisted central tail feathers distinguish it from the Pomarine. The shorter central tail feathers (extending
no more than 9 cm beyond the others) separate it from the adult Long-
tailed Jaeger, which has long streaming tail feathers (except of course
when moulting). Especially in the light phase, the Parasitic usually
shows a pale area at the base of the upper mandible, often a useful
character at close range. First-year birds are almost impossible to distinguish in the field from young of other jaegers.

Habitat. In nesting season, low grassy or mossy tundra interspersed with ponds or lakes; also low stony country. In migration open
ocean and coasts; rarely large lakes of the southern interior.

Nesting. Often tends to be colonial in nesting. Nest, a depression
in moss or grass, sometimes sparsely lined with available vegetation.
Eggs, usually 2; greenish or brownish, spotted and blotched with dark
brown; sometimes only lightly spotted or nearly immaculate. Incubation
period given by various authors as 23, 24, 25 to 26, and up to 28 days.
Incubation by both sexes.

Range. Holarctic. Breeds in the Arctic and Subarctic of Alaska,
Canada, Greenland, Iceland, northern Scotland, northern Norway,
Sweden, Finland, northern Russia, and northern Siberia south near the
coast to Kamchatka and the Sea of Okhotsk. Winters at sea in the
Atlantic offshore from Maine and the British Isles south to Argentina
and southern Africa; in the Pacific from Baja California south to
southern Chile, Australia, and New Zealand.

Long-tailed Jaeger

Labbe à longue queue
Stercorarius longicaudus Vieillot
Total length: 50.7 to 58.5 cm
(including long tail).
Plate 39

Breeding Distribution of Long-tailed Jaeger

Range in Canada. Breeds in the Arctic from Prince Patrick, Ellef Ringnes, Axel Heiberg, and northern Ellesmere islands south to southern Yukon (on alpine tundra: Ogilvie Mountains south to Gladstone Lakes 61°23′N, 138°12′W); northern Mackenzie (Baillie Island, Anderson River, Perry River); southern Keewatin (Aberdeen Lake; McConnell River); Southampton Island; northern Quebec (40 km north of Inoucdjouac, Povungnituk; perhaps George River).

Migrates mainly at sea, uncommon to rare at inshore coastal localities on the Pacific and Atlantic coasts. Very rare in the interior; British Columbia (Buffalo and Okanagan lakes); Alberta (Kananaskis Provincial Park); Saskatchewan (Last Mountain Lake); southern Manitoba (Lake Winnipeg); southern Ontario (Ottawa, Kempenfeldt Bay, Point Pelee; sight records for Algonquin Provincial Park and Kingston).

Figure 62
Tail of adult Long-tailed Jaeger

The smallest of the jaegers, although the extremely long tail gives it a total length equal to or exceeding that of the Parasitic. In adults the long slender tail feathers, projecting 12.7 to 23 cm beyond the others, distinguish it from other jaegers (Figure 62). Bill sheath (or false cere) is about equal to chord of remainder of upper mandible (in Parasitic, bill sheath longer than chord of remainder of upper mandible), and the bill of the Long-tailed, viewed dorsally, is actually and relatively slenderer. Similar in coloration to Parasitic Jaeger, but a dark phase in adult Long-tailed is excessively rare, if indeed it exists at all. Adult, like light-phase Parasitic but consistently lacks a breast band (some Parasitics and Pomarines also lack breast band); cap decidedly more blackish (less greyish); there is no whitish area at the base of the upper mandible; and the legs, but not feet, are bluish grey (blackish in other jaegers). Smaller size distinguishes it in any plumage from the Pomarine Jaeger.

Measurements. *Adult male*: wing, 294–315.5 (301); tail, 268–334.5 (289.9); exposed culmen, 26.4–28.5 (27.4); tarsus, 38.5–45.4 (42.2). *Adult female*: wing, 294–324 (307.5) mm.

Field Marks. Adults with fully developed, long, streaming central tail feathers are readily recognizable. Adults in moult with only partly developed tail resemble Parasitic Jaeger but have blacker (less brownish) cap, and bluish-grey instead of black legs. They have no band across the breast. First-year immatures are very difficult to separate from those of other jaegers but show less white in the spread wing.

Habitat. In nesting season, vegetated upland rolling tundra, often wet but by no means always on ponds and streams; stony plateaus; flat coastal tundra, tending to prefer better-drained areas than the Parasitic Jaeger. In migration, mainly the open ocean, rarely large freshwater lakes of the southern interior.

Nesting. Nest, a depression in the ground either unlined or sparsely lined with available vegetation. *Eggs*, 1 to 2; similar to those of the Parasitic Jaeger but averaging slightly smaller. Incubation 23 days, by both sexes (Manniche).

Range. Circumpolar. Breeds in the Arctic of Alaska, Canada, and Greenland; and in the Old World from Jan Mayen, Spitsbergen, and Novaya Zemlya south to northern Scandinavia, northern Russia, and northern Siberia including Kamchatka and the northeast coast of the Sea of Okhotsk. Winters at sea in the Atlantic and Pacific oceans, most commonly in more southern parts.

Great Skua

Grand Labbe
Catharacta skua Brünnich
Total length: 50.7 to 56 cm
Plate 39

Status in Canada. A non-breeding visitant to offshore coastal waters: Labrador (sight records only); Newfoundland (off Fogo and Funk islands, Cape Broyle, Argentia. Up to 20 per day on the Grand Banks, mid-September 1961 —S.W. Gorham. One banded in Iceland on 11 July 1952, was shot off Horse Island, Newfoundland, late October 1952—L.M. Tuck); and Nova Scotia (Lockeport, Yarmouth). A few sight records for New Brunswick. Alleged occurrences in the Canadian Arctic require confirmation.

A large dark-brown sea bird with robust 5 cm bill, strongly hooked at the tip, a large white patch at the base of the primaries, and white primary shafts. Larger and much more robust than jaegers. Unlike adult jaegers, it never has elongated central tail feathers. In adults the feathers of the head, neck, and back have yellowish or whitish tips. Immatures are more uniform brown and have less conspicuous white patches in the wing.

Measurements *(C. s. skua). Adult male*: wing, 367–389.5 (378.3); tail, 140.9–163 (149.8); exposed culmen, 44.8–48.3 (46); tarsus, 63.5–69.8 (66.9). *Adult female*: wing, 377–395.9 (387.8) mm.

Field Marks. A large dark sea bird with a conspicuous white patch at the base of the flight feathers and a robust hooked bill. Central tail feathers never elongated, thus differing from adult jaegers. A much larger and more robust bird than immature jaegers, and with a much larger white patch in its broader, more rounded wings.

Habitat. In Canada, the open ocean, usually well off shore, seldom coming within sight of land.

Range. Breeds in Iceland, the Faeroe, Shetland, and Orkney islands; wandering widely over the North Atlantic. Breeds also on the coasts of the antarctic continent, southern South America (southern Chile, Tierra del Fuego, Falkland Islands) and on islands in the southern seas; wandering widely over the ocean northward in the Pacific to British Columbia and Japan.

Subspecies. *Catharacta skua skua* Brünnich is the only race known to occur on our Atlantic Coast and its offshore waters (*C. s. loennbergi* has been erroneously attributed to birds taken on the British Columbia coast but this apparently is because of confusion with another species, *C. maccormicki*).

South Polar Skua

Labbe antarctique
Catharacta maccormicki (Saunders)
Total length: 50.7 to 56 cm

Status in Canada. Rare visitant to waters off British Columbia (two specimens, not seen by the writer: Goose Island Bank, 27 July 1948; 80 km west-southwest of Cape Culvert, 26 June 1938. The former has been erroneously recorded by authors as *C. s. loennbergi*, a larger brown form of the Great Skua with heavier bill and longer tarsus. (See Devillers, loc. cit.) Occasional visitor to waters off the East Coast (George's Banks, Grand Banks).

Similar to Great Skua but has two colour phases. In pale phase it is separable, even in the field, by its very pale head and nape from all other skuas. Dark-phase birds are more difficult. In the hand, measurements of the tarsus are helpful: *C. maccormicki* 58.5–70.0 (averages 63.8); *C. skua skua* 61.4–73.9 (68.5) mm (Pierre Devillers, 1977. Auk, vol. 94, no. 3, p. 422).

Range. Breeds in the Antarctic: Antarctic Peninsula, South Shetland Islands, Belleny Island, and inland on the antarctic continent. After the breeding season wanders far northward over the seas.

Subfamily **Larinae**: Gulls

Long-winged swimming birds with front toes more or less fully webbed, the hind toe small (absent rarely) and somewhat elevated. Adults are typically coloured in greys and white, often with black on wing tips, head, or elsewhere. Immatures are attired mostly in browns, greys, and white.

Gulls have a suggestion of a hook at the end of the upper mandible (but not a strong hook, and the bill is not divided into a horny tip and a long cere as in jaegers). Tail usually square or rounded (but forked in Sabine's Gull). Gulls usually pick their food up from the water or land surface and in flight they tend to hold the bill straight out in line with the body. Most species are decidedly larger than terns.

Laughing Gull

Mouette à tête noire
Larus atricilla Linnaeus
Total length: 38 to 43 cm
Plate 38

Range in Canada. Formerly bred (perhaps no longer does so) very locally in Nova Scotia (islands off Halifax County, perhaps also in Lunenburg and Yarmouth counties) and southern New Brunswick (Machias Seal Island).

Casual in Prince Edward Island (Wood Island); Newfoundland (Burnt Islands, Grey River, Isle aux Morts, Boswarlos, all in 1958); southern Quebec (Montréal region; sight records for Québec, Sept-Îles, and Madeleine Islands); and southern Ontario (various records on Lakes Ontario and Erie; one at Ottawa, 5 May 1983); accidental in northern Ontario (Winisk).

Adult a smallish, white-bodied, grey-mantled gull of the Atlantic Coast; in breeding plumage with black head; primaries black with *no white spots*, only narrowly tipped with white, *the outermost and usually the next* without white tip. Mantle darker than that of other small East Coast gulls. *First-autumn*: Upper parts greyish brown, feather edges pale; wing tips brownish black, all but outermost primaries tipped white; secondaries white tipped; rump and upper tail coverts white; tail with dark subterminal bar; throat and breast greyish brown blending into white on abdomen; bill blackish; legs brownish.

Measurements. *Adult male*: wing, 308–330 (321); tail, 113–133 (122.6); exposed culmen, 37–44 (40.2); tarsus, 50–54 (51.6). *Adult female*: wing, 295–326 (312.3) mm (J. Dwight).

Field Marks. Adult a small gull of the Atlantic Coast with dark-grey mantle, a white line along hind edge of spread wing, primaries appearing all black (adults of other gulls show light areas in primaries; Black-legged Kittiwake shows no white spots in primaries, but only the tips are black), reddish bill, and in breeding season a black head. Because of its black head it is most likely to be confused with Bonaparte's Gull but is a somewhat larger bird with darker mantle, dark-reddish bill. *First-autumn*: Slightly smaller than Ring-billed Gull, but darker; breast darker, uniform grey, not spotted.

Habitat. Coastal: harbours, river mouths, coastal islands, mud flats, occasionally wanders inland on rivers or lakes.

Nesting. Usually in colonies. Nest on the ground of grass and weeds. *Eggs*, usually 3; buffy to olive with spots and blotches of brown and some underlying grey or purplish. Incubation reportedly 20 to 23 days.

Range. Breeds from southern Nova Scotia south locally along the Atlantic Coast to Florida, the Bahamas, and Greater and Lesser Antilles; around the Gulf of Mexico in Florida, Louisiana, Texas, and Mexico; off northern Venezuela; and Salton Sea, southern California south to the coasts of Sonora and Sinaloa, Mexico. Winters on the coasts from North Carolina and the Gulf of Mexico south to northern South America and on the Pacific Coast from southern Mexico to Ecuador.

Franklin's Gull

Mouette de Franklin
Larus pipixcan Wagler
Total length: 34 to 39.5 cm
Plate 38

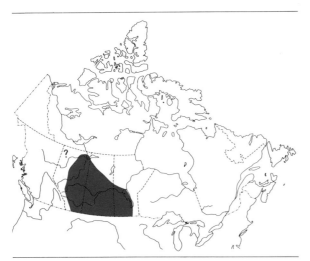

Breeding Distribution of Franklin's Gull

Range in Canada. Breeds commonly in Alberta (east of the mountains: Many Island Lake, Beaverhill Lake, Lake Athabasca; present in good numbers in summer at Hay and Zama lakes); central and southern Saskatchewan (north at least to Kazan and Torch lakes); and southwestern Manitoba (Overflowing River and Lake Winnipeg southward).

Recorded in summer in central-eastern British Columbia (Peace River District) and northeastern Manitoba (Hayes River). Migration from breeding grounds mainly southward. Formerly an uncommon transient in British Columbia (Okanagan Lake, Alta Lake, Sirdar Lake, Comox) but much more numerous and regular in recent years. Rare visitor to southern Ontario (Toronto, Ottawa: specimen, 19 October 1974) and Quebec (Montréal region, Québec). Casual in New Brunswick (Grand Manan, 6 December 1925; photo record: Dalhousie, 25 July 1974); Nova Scotia (photo record: Sable Island, 26 May 1973; Seal Island, 18–20 July 1983); and Newfoundland (Arnold's Cove, 14 June 1974). Accidental in northern Baffin Island, N.W.T. (Pond Inlet: 9–14 June 1979, photos of one adult).

Adults with basal part of central tail feathers grey, thus differing from other white-tailed gulls. In breeding season adults have a black head, thus resembling Bonaparte's and Laughing gulls (see Field Marks). Larger than Bonaparte's, slightly smaller than Laughing. First-year birds similar to those of Laughing Gull but smaller, usually paler on breast, and with subterminal dark tail band not extending to outer tail feathers.

Measurements. *Adult male*: wing, 262.5–290 (279.7); tail, 95.4–109.3 (104.9); exposed culmen, 28–31 (29.5); tarsus, 39.5–45 (42.8). *Adult female*: wing, 261–285 (273.1) mm.

Field Marks. A smallish gull of the prairies. Adults in breeding plumage with black head thus resembling Bonaparte's from which Franklin's differs in larger size, stouter *red* bill, and very different wing-tip pattern in flight (Plate 38). First-year birds of both species have dark tail band, but Franklin's has much grey on crown and face (Bonaparte's shows well-defined dark ear spot) and dark white-tipped primaries (Bonaparte's shows long tongues of white reaching to near primary tips). It closely resembles Laughing Gull, but the two are widely separated geographically except as wanderers to the Great Lakes. The large amount of white in the spread wing tip of Franklin's distinguishes adults from those of Laughing Gull. First-year birds of the two are more difficult to separate in the field, but Franklin's usually has a paler breast and forehead.

Habitat. In the breeding season, prairie lakes and marshes; foraging regularly on grassy fields and ploughed land, often in large numbers.

Nesting. In colonies. Nest, a floating anchored mass of marsh vegetation in lake or marsh. *Eggs*, usually 3; buffy or greenish brown, variously spotted and blotched with browns. Incubation, by both parents, lasts 24 days (Joanna Burger).

Range. Breeds from the Prairie Provinces of Canada south to eastern Oregon, northwestern Utah, south-central Montana, northeastern South Dakota, and northwestern Iowa. Winters in the Pacific from Guatemala south to the Gulf of Panama, the Galapagos Islands, and Chile; also coastal Louisiana and Texas.

Remarks. The swirling flocks and high-pitched cries of this pretty gull are a pleasant summer aspect of the prairies. In spring they descend on the freshly ploughed fields where they seek out myriads of cutworms and wireworms. Later in the season they feast on grasshoppers.

Little Gull

Mouette pygmée
Larus minutus Pallas
Total length: 28 cm
Plate 38

Breeding Distribution of Little Gull

Range in Canada. First known nesting in North America was in 1962 when nests were discovered at Oshawa, Ontario. Now breeds sporadically, locally and precariously along Lakes Erie and Ontario (Oshawa, Rondeau, Pickering), and Bassett Island. In 1980, discovered nesting on Georgian Bay (North Limestone Island). Recently found nesting at Churchill, Manitoba and at LaSalle, Quebec.

Elsewhere in Canada a scarce visitant to southwestern British Columbia, Saskatchewan, Manitoba (north to Churchill). Rare but regular in Ontario, April to November. Summer visitor to Quebec (especially the St. Lawrence River valley, Montréal to Baie-Comeau). Rare in New Brunswick, Nova Scotia, and Newfoundland (but regular in winter). Sight records for Prince Edward Island and for northern coastal Yukon (Komakuk Beach DEW Station).

Our smallest gull.

Measurements. *Adult male*: wing, 210–230 (220.5); tail, 85–95 (91.9); exposed culmen, 21–25 (23.2); tarsus, 25–28 (26.5). *Adult female*: wing, 212–227 (220.5) mm (J. Dwight).

Field Marks. Diminutive size. Smaller than Bonaparte's Gull, which it resembles and often associates with. Adults in summer with black head, reddish-brown bill; in winter, mainly white head with dark ear patch and often a slaty patch on hind crown. Adults at all seasons are identifiable in flight by dark undersurface of wings and plain-grey white-tipped upper side of primaries (occasionally one, perhaps not mature, has outermost web of outermost primary black, with black smudges on other primaries and with paler-grey wing linings). First-year birds have underside of wing white, a black ear-spot, and a black terminal band, thus very similar to Bonaparte's of similar age, but Little Gull shows in flight a blackish bar diagonally across the upper surface of wing, which *continues around the bend of wing to join the base of the black primaries*; also the Little Gull shows more extensive black in wing tips. Young Sabine's Gull and Black-legged Kittiwake also have a dark bar diagonally across upper wing, but Sabine's Gull has forked tail and the young Black-legged Kittiwake shows a black bar across back of neck.

Range. Breeds in Eurasia from Denmark, southern Sweden, Finland, northwestern Russia, and central Siberia south to northern Germany, eastern Poland, Turkestan, Altai, and Lake Baikal. Winters south to the Mediterranean, Black, and Caspian seas. Breeds very locally in Canada (southern Ontario), and in northern Wisconsin and Michigan.

Common Black-headed Gull

Mouette rieuse
Larus ridibundus Linnaeus
Total length: 35.5 to 38 cm
Plate 38

Status in Canada. Scarce visitor and very local breeder. In recent years it has become a regular visitor to Labrador and Newfoundland (Badger, Green Island, Chapel Arm, Placentia, Fermeuse, etc.); Nova Scotia (Halifax, Cole Harbour–Chezzetcook area, Port Hawkesbury, etc.); Quebec (Havre-Saint-Pierre, Madeleine Islands; photo record at Beauharnois, May 1975); Prince Edward Island; and New Brunswick. Rarer visitant to Ontario (specimen records: Oshawa, 29 July 1963; Fort Erie, 13 October 1966; Ottawa, 1 October 1975; also various sight records). Rare visitor to British

Adults (breeding plumage): Head dark brown, a narrow white border behind eye; mantle grey; wing pattern similar to that of Bonaparte's Gull but inner edge of inner webs of primaries blackish; rest of plumage white; bill and legs crimson. *Adults (winter)*: Similar to summer adults but head largely white with small dark patch in front of eye and a larger patch on ear coverts with varying amounts of greyish brown on hind crown and nape. *First-winter* birds similar to winter adults but with some brownish feathers in the grey mantle, a black band across the end of the tail, duller wing tips with white areas more restricted, bill flesh with dark tip, legs yellowish flesh. It is somewhat larger than Bonaparte's Gull.

Measurements. *Adult male*: wing, 284–315 (300); tail, 113–124 (117.5); exposed culmen, 31–37 (33.6); tarsus, 43–47 (44.7). *Adult female*: wing, 280–297 (288.2) mm (J. Dwight).

Columbia (photo record: Clover Point, October 1974; also sight records). Sight record for northern Manitoba (Churchill).

Recently has bred very locally in Newfoundland (Stephenville Crossing: at least two pairs of adults photographed in 1977 with three newly fledged young) and southeastern Quebec (Madeleine Islands: at least five nests in both 1981 and 1982).

Field Marks. Closely resembles Bonaparte's Gull (often accompanies it), with similar wing pattern but is larger with relatively longer, differently coloured bill. *Adults*: Similar to Bonaparte's Gull but bill reddish, underside of wing tip much more extensively blackish, with mainly the outermost primary showing white (Plate 38), head in breeding plumage dark brown instead of black. First-winter birds are similar to Bonaparte's Gull but bill slightly longer, flesh basally with blackish tip.

Nesting. In colonies either by the sea or inland. Nest, a loosely made assemblage of readily available plant materials, is placed either directly on the ground or on vegetation. *Eggs*, usually 3, vary from light to darker browns and are spotted and blotched with dark brown. Incubation is by both sexes, the usual period 22 to 24 days.

Range. Breeds in Iceland, the Faeroe Islands, and across Eurasia to Kamchatka. Recently in eastern Canada.

Subspecies. *Larus ridibundus ridibundus* Linnaeus. British Columbia birds have not been collected but there is a possibility of the occurrence there of another race, *L. r. sibericus* Buturlin.

Bonaparte's Gull

Mouette de Bonaparte
Larus philadelphia (Ord)
Total length: 30.3 to 37 cm
Plate 38

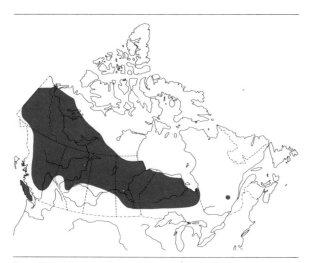

Breeding Distribution of Bonaparte's Gull

Range in Canada. Breeds from northern Yukon (Old Crow Flats, Canyon–Aishihik lakes, Lapie and Pelly rivers, Chapman Lake, Ogilvie Mountains); northwestern interior Mackenzie (Anderson River, Keith Arm); northern Saskatchewan (Black Lake, Hasbala Lake); and northeastern Manitoba (Churchill) south to southern British Columbia (Vancouver Island, Kleena Kleene, Bridge Lake); central Alberta (between Camrose and Edmonton); central Saskatchewan (16 km southwest of Glaslyn; Maidstone; Nipawin); south-central Manitoba (Riding Mountain); and central Ontario (Lake Miminiska, Rat Rapids, Cochrane); James Bay (near the Ontario–Quebec boundary); and Quebec (100 km up Eastmain River; Rouyn: nest found 31 May 1983; and Point Racine on Mistassini River according to Quebec Nest Record Card Programme).

More or less common migrant south of breeding range and on the Pacific Coast;

A small gull. *Adults* with grey mantle; mainly white wing tips with broad black ends and a narrow black border on outer side of outermost primary; head black in breeding plumage, mainly white with dusky ear spot in autumn and winter; rest of plumage white; bill black; legs red. *First-year* birds similar to winter adults but have dark subterminal tail band, more black in primaries, grey mantle mixed with brown; legs flesh. Adult plumage is assumed in second autumn. Wing-tip pattern (largely white, narrowly bordered by black) distinguishes it from other North American gulls. The mostly white *underside* of the wing tips distinguishes adults from Black-headed Gull.

Measurements. *Adult male*: wing, 251–273 (258.7); tail, 95.9–105.6 (101.9); exposed culmen, 27.9–30.6 (29.2); tarsus, 34.5–38.2 (36). *Adult female*: wing, 245.5–261.2 (251.5) mm.

Field Marks. A small gull. Adults in breeding plumage with black head thus resembling Franklin's, Laughing, and Black-headed gulls, but bill black instead of reddish. The largely white wing tip *with narrow black borders* flashes conspicuously in flight at considerable distances and distinguishes it at any season and age from terns and other gulls except the rare Black-headed. The underside of the wing tip in Bonaparte's is mostly white (in Black-headed, dark with the outer primary showing white). Winter adult and immature Bonaparte's have mainly white head with a conspicuous dark ear patch.

also in southern Ontario; southern Quebec (St. Lawrence River, inner north shore of the Gulf of St. Lawrence, Lake Saint-Jean, Gaspé Peninsula, Madeleine Islands); New Brunswick; Prince Edward Island; and Nova Scotia. Scarce visitant to Newfoundland (Bonavista, Stephenville Crossing, Chance Cove, Fermeuse). Records for Labrador require confirmation. Non-breeders are commonly found in summer outside the known breeding range. Rare or casual in winter in southwestern British Columbia (Strait of Georgia), and southern Ontario (Hamilton, Toronto).

Habitat. For nesting, the vicinity of muskegs, ponds, and lakes in coniferous woodland. Post-breeders and non-breeders frequent lakes, rivers, marshes, coastal bays and harbours, sandbars, and mud flats.

Nesting. Nest is placed usually in a coniferous tree in the vicinity of a muskeg lake or pond and is composed of twigs, grass, moss, and lichen; rarely on the ground or in marsh vegetation. *Eggs*, usually 3; buffy grey to buffy green, spotted and blotched with browns. Incubation period 23 days, 20 hours (D.F. Parmelee); 24 days (J.R. Jehl and D.J.T. Hussell).

Range. Breeds in western and central Alaska and in the coniferous belt of western and central Canada. Winters from southern British Columbia, Lakes Erie and Ontario, and Massachusetts south to northern Mexico, Bermuda, Cuba, and Haiti.

Heermann's Gull

Goéland de Heermann
Larus heermanni Cassin
Total length: 46 to 53 cm
Plate 37

Status in Canada. Fairly common non-breeding summer and early autumn visitor to south coastal British Columbia (Vancouver Island, commonest at southern end, from late June to late October or early November).

Measurements. *Adult male*: wing, 337–368 (347.3); tail, 138–154 (142.3); exposed culmen, 37–48 (43.7); tarsus, 52–58 (54.8). *Adult female*: wing, 329–344 (337.7) mm (J. Dwight).

Field Marks. An easily recognized medium-sized gull of the West Coast. *Adult:* Dark-grey coloration above and below with white head (much obscured by dusky in autumn), white trailing edge to spread wing, black tail with white tip, red bill, and black legs. *First year:* Even more uniformly dark with black wing tips, tail, and head; bill buffy or pinkish with dark tip; legs blackish.

Habitat. Saltwater coasts and islands.

Range. Breeds on islands on the west coast of Mexico (March–June). After breeding, it migrates northward along the Pacific Coast as far as southwestern British Columbia. Winters on the Pacific Coast from Oregon to Guatemala.

Mew Gull

(Short-billed Gull)

Goéland cendré
Larus canus Linnaeus
Total length: 40.5 to 46 cm
Plate 37

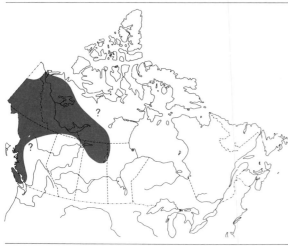

Breeding Distribution of Mew Gull

Range in Canada. Breeds in southern Yukon (commonly: north probably at least to Dawson and southern Ogilvie Mountains); Mackenzie (Mackenzie Delta, Fort Anderson, mouth of Horton River, Great Slave Lake, Fort Smith;

Adults: Grey mantle; black wing tips, the primaries tipped with white and the outermost two with a large white subapical spot; rest of plumage white (in winter, head and neck streaked with dusky); bill plain greenish-yellow; irides variable, brown to grey, often flecked with yellow; eye-ring red; legs yellowish green. Small size separates it from all similar gulls except Black-legged Kittiwake (which lacks white subapical spots on primaries and has no well-developed hind toe). *First-year* Mew Gull is similar in plumage coloration to first-year Herring or California gulls but has a dark terminal tail band, rather poorly defined against the grey basal two-thirds of tail. Compared with first-year Ring-billed, it has more uniformly coloured body plumage, especially the grey of the under parts, the wing coverts paler, contrasting less with their pale tips; and the basal part of the tail is darker grey. Adult plumage is acquired with assumption of third-winter dress.

Measurements. *Adult male*: wing, 324–360.5 (346.7); tail, 129–149 (139.9); exposed culmen, 32–36.3 (34.1); tarsus, 49–53.2 (50.8). *Adult female*: wing, 321–350.5 (335.5) mm.

Field Marks. A small gull of the Northwest and Pacific coasts with general Herring Gull type of plumage coloration. Adults with relatively small, plain, greenish-yellow bill without any red or black markings, thus different from Ring-billed and California gulls; Mew Gull also shows more white in wing tip and is smaller than those gulls. Obviously smaller than Herring and "Thayer's" gulls. The Black-legged Kittiwake, also a small gull, has no white spots in the black wing tip.

perhaps east to Thelon River marshes); north-western Saskatchewan (Lake Athabasca, Cree Lake, southern Reindeer Lake); and very locally in northern Manitoba (in 1980, two nests were discovered in Churchill; probably breeds also in the Manitoba part of Reindeer Lake); also northwestern and coastal British Columbia (Atlin Lake, Liard Hot Springs, and locally southward on the coast to Kennedy Lake and Lake Cowichan, Vancouver Island).

In migration, regularly through interior British Columbia, northern Alberta, and northern Yukon (Old Crow). Rare in southern Alberta (Brooks, Camrose, Jasper). Recorded in summer north to the arctic coast of Mackenzie (Baillie Island) and east to Thelon River marshes. Casual visitor to Ontario (Port Weller, Thorold), New Brunswick (Sheffield) and Newfoundland (Lock's Cove on Notre Dame Bay). Sight records for Quebec and Nova Scotia.

Winters commonly on British Columbia coast.

Habitat. In nesting season, marshes, lakes, and rivers. In migration and winter, marine outer coasts, harbours, bays, mud flats, beaches, garbage dumps, often with the larger gulls.

Nesting. Both in colonies and as solitary pairs. Nest usually on the ground about lakes or on islands in marshy places, sandpits, occasionally in trees. *Eggs*, usually 3, less often 2; buffy variously marked with browns. Incubation 22 to 23 days, probably sometimes longer (*in* Witherby) by both sexes.

Range. Breeds in central and southern Alaska, northwestern continental and west-coastal Canada; also across Europe and Asia from near the Arctic Circle south to the British Isles, Netherlands, the Black and Caspian seas, northern Mongolia, Kamchatka, and the Kurile Islands. Winters from southeastern Alaska to southern California; in Europe south to the Mediterranean Sea, and in eastern Asia on the coasts of China and Japan to Taiwan.

Subspecies. (1) *Larus canus brachyrhynchus* Richardson is the breeding form. (2) *L. c. canus* Linnaeus is a casual visitor (specimen at Lock's Cove, Newfoundland, 19 April 1956, had been banded as a chick on the White Sea).

Ring-billed Gull

Goéland à bec cerclé
Larus delawarensis Ord
Total length: 45.5 to 51 cm
Plate 37

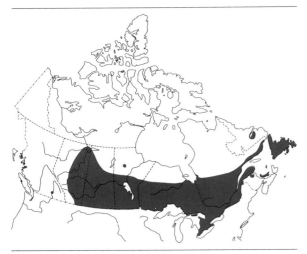

Breeding Distribution of Ring-billed Gull

Adult is a grey-mantled gull with black wing tips (two outermost primaries with a white subterminal spot), and with remainder of plumage white; decidedly smaller than the Herring and somewhat smaller than the California Gull. Adults, with black band across yellow bill, yellow iris, reddish eye-ring and gape, greenish-yellow legs. The black band on the bill with no red on lower mandible distinguishes adults from adults of other gulls. In the California Gull when black is present on the bill, a red spot also is present on lower mandible. Some immatures of other gulls (e.g., third-year Herring) often show a more or less well-marked black band on the bill but show signs of immaturity by presence of dusky feathers in tail, mantle, or under parts; such Herring Gulls often have a faint red spot on lower mandible, which the Ring-billed never has.

First-year Ring-billed, like most gulls of similar age, has much brown in the body plumage and dark-brown wing tips, but compared with Herring, Western, California, and Mew gulls it has a decidedly greater amount of white in the body plumage, especially in the under parts, which appear white mottled with brown, instead of rather uniform dark-brown or grey. Tail with usually a narrow, dark, sharply defined subterminal band of uniform width. (In some individuals, however, this band is poorly defined, and therefore, for identification purposes, this character cannot always be relied upon.) Iris brown; basal part of bill, flesh, tip dark; legs pinkish or greyish. The first feathers of the grey mantle appear in the first winter, and the bird assumes adult plumage early in its third year. In the hand, smaller size easily distinguishes otherwise doubtful specimens from Herring and Western gulls, and usually from the California Gull. The Ring-billed is only slightly larger than the Mew Gull, which is rather similar in first year. The Ring-billed has much whiter brown-mottled under parts (first-year Mew Gull more uniform dark-grey), and its upper parts have more whitish feather edges, thus contrasting more with the dark feather centres.

Range in Canada. Has greatly expanded its range and numbers in recent years. Breeds in interior British Columbia (locally: Whiskey Island in Okanagan Lake); Alberta (east of the mountains: Lake Athabasca, Lac la Biche, Buffalo Lake, Lake Newell); Saskatchewan (Kazan Lake, Redberry Lake, La Ronge, Maple Creek, Last Mountain Lake); Manitoba (north at least to Southern Indian Lake); Ontario (southern James Bay, Lake of the Woods, Black Bay on Lake Superior, North Channel, Georgian Bay, Lake Erie, Lake Ontario); southern Quebec (locally: north shore of the Gulf of St. Lawrence: Betchouane, Gull Island, Green Island, Parsons Island, La Romaine, Fog Island, Saint-Augustin; mouth of Eastmain River; also Lake Saint-Jean and near Saint-Lambert. Reports of breeding on Hudson Bay require confirmation); southern Labrador (Lake Melville); Newfoundland (Browsey Island, South Penguin Island); recently northeastern New Brunswick (Bathurst Harbour); and very recently Prince Edward Island (Sable Point, Poverty Beach).

Non-breeding birds are reported in summer in interior British Columbia, southern Mackenzie (Great Slave Lake), southern Keewatin (Nueltin Lake), and Hudson Bay.

In migration, found also in southern British Columbia (now common in winter about Fraser delta), Gaspé Peninsula, New Brunswick, Prince Edward Island, and Nova Scotia. Winters in extreme southern Ontario (lower Great Lakes, where water remains open); also Nova Scotia (Yarmouth, Cape Breton Island); and other parts of the Maritimes, where its numbers are increasing.

Measurements. *Adult male*: wing, 362–383.3 (369.9); tail, 139–152 (146.8); exposed culmen, 37.8–44 (40.9); tarsus, 53–62 (58.1). *Adult female*: wing, 339.5–377 (353.5) mm.

Field Marks. Smaller than Herring Gull, but size is useful only when the two are together. Black band on yellow bill (no red spot) and greenish-yellow legs distinguish adults from adults of other gulls. Third-year Herring Gull sometimes shows a black band-like area on bill, but the Herring is larger with pinkish legs. California Gull adult frequently shows a black area on bill but also a red spot on the lower mandible, which Ring-billed lacks. First-year Ring-billed Gull is more whitish, particularly in under parts, than other gulls of similar age with which it is likely to be confused. Tail with dark narrow band, usually of even width and very sharply defined (second-year Herring and California gulls show a dark tail band, but it is poorly defined and usually not of even width. However the occasional Ring-billed also has the tail band poorly defined, and this difference is by no means infallible). Paler, more spotted body coloration, especially under parts, separates it from first-year Mew Gull.

Habitat. Shores, islands, and water surfaces of freshwater lakes, ponds, and rivers, and saltwater shores on the coast; commonly frequents also garbage dumps and fields (especially newly ploughed ones); follows boats.

Nesting. In colonies often with other species, usually on islands (sometimes beaches, etc.) in fresh or alkaline waters in the interior and on islands in salt water off the coast. Nest on the ground, of grass, weeds, and rubbish. *Eggs*, usually 3; buffy, variously spotted and blotched with browns and some underlying purplish grey. Incubation period in incubator, 26 to 27 days (James Moffitt) but perhaps different in the wild.

Range. Breeds from southern Canada south to northeastern California, central Idaho, central Colorado, northeastern South Dakota, northern Michigan, southern Ontario, and northern New York. Winters from Oregon, the lower Great Lakes (where water remains open), and Maine south into Mexico.

Remarks. These gulls eat insects, grubs, worms, and occasionally mice or the eggs of other birds. They often congregate where grasshoppers abound and gorge themselves on the insects. They are useful scavengers.

California Gull

Goéland de Californie
Larus californicus Lawrence
Total length: 52 to 58.5 cm
Plate 36

Adults similar to Herring Gull *(L. argentatus smithsonianus)* but differ as follows: Legs greenish to yellowish; lower mandible with usually a black spot or bar in addition to a red spot; iris usually brown, sometimes grey or even straw; eye-ring reddish; gape orange to reddish; mantle averages darker grey; size averages smaller, sex for sex. Outermost primary more often with long all-white tip, but this often crossed by a subterminal black bar similar to that of Herring Gull. Similar also to the *thayeri* race of the Iceland Gull, but adult *thayeri* has different wing-tip pattern (grey tongue on two outermost primaries usually reaches the white mirrors), flesh-coloured legs, and lacks any black spot on the bill. *First-year* California Gull closely resembles Herring Gull of similar age, but by late summer the basal half of the bill becomes flesh coloured, contrasting with dark tip instead of remaining mostly dark as in first-year Herring. Resembles first year Ring-billed Gull, but the body plumage is darker and more uniform, the under parts less whitish and more uniform (less spotted). Like the Herring Gull, adult plumage is not attained until the fourth year (for details see W.H. Behle and R.K. Selander, 1953. Auk, vol. 70, no. 3, pp. 239–260).

Breeding Distribution of California Gull

Range in Canada. Breeds in southern Mackenzie (Great Slave Lake); southern British Columbia (locally: northern Okanagan Lake); Alberta (east of the mountains: Lake Athabasca, Lac la Biche, Lake Winnifred, Pakowki Lake, Lake Newell near Brooks; recorded in summer northwest to Zama Lake); Saskatchewan (Lake Athabasca, Redberry Lake, Last Mountain Lake, Bigstick Lake); and southern Manitoba (Dog Lake, Pelican Lake, Lakes Manitoba and Winnipegosis). Very rare in Ontario (Toronto: an adult female sat on a clutch of two eggs in 1981 and on a single egg in 1982).

In migration, spring and autumn, small numbers occur on the south coast and in the interior of British Columbia and in the mountains of southwestern Alberta (Jasper, Banff).

Measurements. *Adult male*: wing, 369–419.5 (391.7); tail, 142.8–171 (153.6); exposed culmen, 44.9–55 (49.5); tarsus, 55–64.5 (60.5). *Adult female*: wing, 361.5–386.5 (375) mm.

Field Marks. Adults similar to Herring Gull but distinguishable by greenish or yellowish legs, and often by the presence of a blackish area (not always present) in addition to the red one on the lower mandible. Ring-billed and Mew gulls both are similar to California Gull and, like it, have greenish legs, but the Ring-billed has a well-defined black band around the bill and no red spot, and the Mew Gull, a smaller species, has a plain greenish-yellow bill. First-year California Gull is a somewhat darker bird with less spotted under parts than first-year Ring-billed, and the tail is dark (the Ring-bill has a white tail with a sharply defined dark subterminal bar). In later plumages the California shows a dark bar across the end of the tail, but it is usually broader and less well defined than in the Ring-billed. Many immatures of the two species are difficult to separate in the field. The flesh-coloured base of the bill helps separate it from first-winter Herring Gulls.

Habitat. In nesting season the vicinity of inland freshwater and alkaline lakes, rivers, and marshes, but the birds also spread out over wide areas to fields, especially newly ploughed ones. In migration frequents also various coastal situations.

Nesting. Nests in colonies, often with Ring-billed Gulls and other birds, on islands of lakes, marshes, and rivers. Nest, a depression in the ground or on bare rock, lined with grass, weeds, and rubbish, often sparsely; but nest sometimes a substantial structure up to 30 cm high. *Eggs*, usually 3; similar to those of other large gulls but often more boldly marked. Variable from bluish white to buffy brown, spotted and often boldly marked with browns and some purplish grey. Average incubation time for first egg, 26.7 days; the second, 25; the third, 23.6 in Utah (Behle and Goates); by both sexes.

Range. Breeds from interior Mackenzie south through the Canadian Prairie Provinces to Washington (Benton County), southeastern Oregon, northeastern California, northwestern Utah, northwestern Wyoming, central Montana, and east-central North Dakota. Winters from southern Washington south along the Pacific Coast to Guatemala.

Herring Gull

Goéland argenté
Larus argentatus Pontoppidan
Total length: 58.5 to 66 cm
Plate 36

A large, broadly distributed gull, widely known as "sea-gull." *Adults (L. a. smithsonianus)*: Mantle pearl grey. Wing tips black, each feather tipped white; outermost primary with large white spot usually separated from white tip by a narrow, sometimes broken, black bar; ninth primary with or without a small white spot; a tongue of grey extends out from base of primaries usually not reaching white spot on either ninth or tenth primaries. Head, neck, tail, and under parts white (in winter head and neck more or less streaked dusky). Bill yellow with red spot on lower mandible; iris yellow, occasionally lightly freckled with brown; eye-ring yellow-orange; legs pinkish flesh. *First-year* birds are mottled brown in general colour with plain dark-brown wing tips, dark bill, and brown irides. *Second-winter* birds, paler brown more mixed with white, and with some grey beginning to show in the mantle; unevenly banded tail; basal part of the bill and extreme tip, flesh; remainder dark. *Third-winter* birds show extensive grey in the mantle, pale bill with enough dark coloration often remaining to form a dark band somewhat similar to that of adults of the smaller Ring-billed Gull.

Breeding Distribution of Herring Gull

Range in Canada. Breeds from northern interior Yukon; northern Mackenzie (wooded parts of Mackenzie Delta; inland 25 to 40 km from the coast at Perry River); southern and central Keewatin; Southampton Island (Bay of God's Mercy, Prairie Point); and central-western and southern Baffin Island (Straits Bay, Taverner Bay, Dorset, Frobisher Bay, Home Bay) south (except on the Pacific Coast) to south-central interior British Columbia (108 Mile Lake, Bridge Lake); northeastern Alberta (Bistcho Lake, Lake Athabasca, Caribou Mountains, Lower Thérien Lake); northern Saskatchewan (Lake Athabasca, Peter Pond Lake, Prince Albert National Park); southern Manitoba (Lake Winnipeg, Shoal Lake); southern Ontario (Lakes Erie and Ontario); southern Quebec (commonly in northern and eastern parts south to Madeleine Islands; locally in extreme southwest: Lac des Îles, Lac Simon, Rasades, Basques, and Pèlerin islands); Labrador; Newfoundland; New Brunswick; Nova Scotia; and Prince Edward Island.

Common to abundant in migration in most parts of southern Canada including the Pacific Coast but is not frequently reported from southern parts of Alberta or Saskatchewan. Winters on the coast of British Columbia, the southern Great Lakes, St. Lawrence River, and along the Atlantic Coast from Newfoundland through the Maritimes.

The combination of pearl-grey mantle, blackish wing tips, and flesh-coloured legs separates adults from those of other larger Canadian gulls except the *thayeri* race of the Iceland Gull, which has a different wing-tip pattern and a reddish eye-ring.

Measurements *(L. a. smithsonianus)*. *Adult male*: wing, 414–462 (432.7); tail, 167–192.5 (176.4); exposed culmen, 57–61.5 (59.4); tarsus, 66–70.9 (68.4). *Adult female*: wing, 400.5–430 (403.2) mm.

Field Marks. A largish gull. Adults with pearl-grey mantle, white-spotted black wing tips, and pinkish-flesh legs. The pearl-grey mantle distinguishes it from adults of the Great Black-backed and Western; blackish wing tips from Glaucous, Iceland, and Glaucous-winged; flesh-coloured legs from adult Ring-billed (which has a black band on the bill and no red spot), adult California (which often has a black spot on the bill in addition to the red one), Mew Gull (which is much smaller with no red spot on bill), and the smaller Black-legged Kittiwake. Very similar to "Thayer's" Gull and not always distinguishable in the field, unless the darker (more blackish) wing tips or yellowish eye-ring (instead of reddish) of the Herring can be discerned.

First-year bird is mottled brown, with dark bill and eye. The dark wing tips distinguish it from the Glaucous, the Iceland, and the Glaucous-winged; darker body colour, particularly below, distinguishes it from the first-year Great Black-backed. First-year Herring Gull has a darker body than first-year Ring-billed, and the all-dark tail is very different from the banded tail of immatures of that species, but leg colour is not reliable as young Ring-bills sometimes have pinkish legs also. Very similar to first-year Western Gull, but under excellent conditions the Herring's slenderer bill may help to distinguish it. Not usually safely separable from first-autumn California Gull in the field, although yearling California Gull shows a flesh-coloured base of the bill and a dark tip, while first-year Herring has a mainly dark bill. In succeeding plumages Herring Gull often shows a dark terminal band on the tail, suggestive of immature Ring-billed, but in the latter the band is usually (not always) narrower, more uniform in width, and more sharply defined. In doubtful cases the smaller size of the Ring-bill is apparent if the two are together. See also *thayeri* race of Iceland Gull.

Habitat. Various types of shores and islands on the coast as well as inland freshwater lakes and rivers. Often feeds at dumps, canneries, open fields; frequently follows ships but seldom to great distances from land.

Nesting. Mostly in colonies of various sizes, sometimes in single pairs, not infrequently with other species like cormorants, terns, and other gulls. Nest is usually on the ground, a depression lined (sometimes very sparsely) with grass, moss, seaweed, or sometimes vegetation and rubbish. Most often on coastal islands, or on islands and boulders in inland lakes and rivers, situations varying from low islets to the flat tops and ledges of high ones; also on cliff ledges and occasionally in trees. *Eggs*, usually 2 or 3; vary from bluish grey to brownish with irregular spots and blotches of dark brown and some lilac. Incubation, variously recorded, 25 to 28 days, the greater part by the female.

Range. In North America from central and north-central Canada and western Greenland south to western interior Canada, northern Minnesota, central Wisconsin, central Michigan, northern New York (south along the coast to Long Island), and casually to north coastal Virginia; also in Iceland, Europe, and northern Siberia. Winters from southern parts of the breeding range south to the West Indies, Panama, northern and central Africa, Indochina, and the northern Philippines.

Subspecies. (1) *Larus argentatus smithsonianus* Coues occupies the range outlined above. (2) *L. a. vegae* Palmén, characterized by somewhat larger size and darker mantle, is a casual visitant from Siberia to coastal British Columbia (one specimen record: Henderson Lake, Vancouver Island, 27 November 1922). *Larus thayeri* Brooks, treated as a subspecies of *L. argentatus* by many authors *(A.O.U. Check-list of North American Birds*, Fifth Edition), is here regarded as a subspecies of *L. glaucoides*.

Remarks. Although the name "sea-gull" has no official status, it has wide popular usage with reference to large gulls in general. Probably the Herring Gull is the species most often called "sea-gull"; this, despite the fact that it is widely distributed in the interior as well as on the coast and rarely travels very far out on the ocean.

The Herring Gull is largely a scavenger, often gathering in noisy numbers about fishing boats and fish-processing plants for the offal thrown on the water. It scavenges also at garbage dumps and sewer outlets, and along the shores it cleans up dead or stranded aquatic animals in great numbers. Its menu includes fishes and marine and freshwater invertebrates of many kinds, and occasionally eggs and young of other birds. Sometimes it flocks to the fields where it devours larger insects, especially grasshoppers; occasionally mice. Often it takes wild berries like blueberries or crowberries.

It is a lively and graceful addition to our waterways, and our shores would indeed be duller places without it and its numerous interesting congeners.

Iceland Gull

(includes Thayer's and Kumlien's gulls)

Goéland arctique
Larus glaucoides* Meyer
Total length: 57 to 63.5 cm
Plate 36

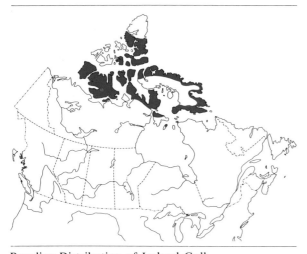

Breeding Distribution of Iceland Gull

*Includes *L. thayeri* of *The Birds of Canada* (1966), and of the 32nd Supplement to the *A.O.U. Check-list of North American Birds* (1973. Auk, vol. 90, no. 2, pp. 411–419). Studies made by Brian Knudsen for the National Museum of Natural Sciences in summers of 1975 and 1976 at Home Bay, Baffin Island (where in 1961 *thayeri* and *kumlieni* were thought by N.G. Smith (1966. Ornithological Monographs 4), to breed sympatrically with no observed interbreeding) produced no evidence of assortative mating of the morphs but indicated instead an area of widespread interbreeding among phenotypes of these two taxa. Additional reasons for treating *thayeri* here as a subspecies of *L. glaucoides* include abundant specimen evidence from widely separated localities that colour and pattern differences between *thayeri* and *kumlieni* are completely bridged by individual variation.

A medium-sized gull. Adults with white head and body, grey mantle, reddish-purplish eye ring, geographically and individually variable wing-tip coloration (immaculate white in one race; grey to black markings in two races), variable irides (clear yellowish to heavily speckled with brown), yellowish bill with reddish spot on lower mandible. First-winter birds vary in general coloration from greyish white with variable brownish markings *(L. g. glaucoides* and *L. g. kumlieni)* to mainly dull greyish brown with more or less whitish markings *(L. g. thayeri)*. There are three well-marked subspecies.

Two of the subspecies *(L. g. kumlieni* and *L. g. thayeri)* are individually highly variable and unstable, scarcely any two individuals exactly alike in the extent and intensity of wing tip and irides pigmentation.

Habitat. In nesting season arctic coastal or near coastal cliffs. In migration, shores of salt water and, less often, freshwater lakes and rivers.

Nesting. Nests in colonies, sometimes with other species. Nest of grasses, mosses, and seaweed is usually placed on cliff ledges at or near the coast. *Eggs*, 2 or 3, resemble those of Herring Gull in coloration.

Range. Breeds in arctic Canada and western Greenland. Winters mainly on the Pacific Coast of Canada and United States and the Atlantic Coast from southern Labrador south to Virginia; also on the Great Lakes; and from Iceland, the Faeroe Islands, Norway, and Sweden south to the British Isles, northern France, and the Baltic Sea. In migration variable numbers occur in the interior of Canada and the United States. For range in Canada see under subspecies accounts below.

Status of *Larus glaucoides glaucoides* **in Canada**. A non-breeding visitor, mostly in winter, to southeastern Canada from breeding grounds in southern Greenland.

Range of *L. g. kumlieni* **in Canada**. Breeds in coastal southern Baffin Island from southern Foxe Peninsula eastward, and northward on the East Coast to Home Bay. Reported to breed also in extreme northwestern Quebec (Erik Cove) and Digges Island, N.W.T.

Winters mainly on the Atlantic Coast in southern Labrador, Newfoundland, coasts of southern Quebec, and the Maritime Provinces; also in smaller numbers on the Great Lakes and the upper St. Lawrence River (Québec, Montréal). Transient in small numbers on the upper St. Lawrence River and its drainage. Reported from northern Hudson Bay, but to what extent it uses that bay in migration is not known. Casual in British Columbia (specimen: Departure Bay, 14 March 1928).

Range of *L. g. thayeri* **in Canada**. Breeds from Banks, northern Victoria, Bathurst, Axe Heiberg, and central Baffin islands south to southern Victoria Island, Kent Peninsula, northeastern Keewatin, northern Southampton Island, and northern and central-eastern Baffin Island (intergrading with *L. g. kumlieni* at Home Bay). Winters mainly in coastal British Columbia.

(1) Nominate (Greenland) subspecies
Larus glaucoides glaucoides Meyer. The palest and most stable of the subspecies. Adults with plain-white wing tips (no black or slaty) and clear pale-yellow irides. First-winter birds have pale mantle variously mottled with browns and whitish; the head and neck streaked with greyish browns; the primary tips whitish more or less tinged with brownish grey, often with faint subterminal darker markings; and tail variously marked and mottled with brown and white.

Field Marks. Herring Gull size or smaller, but with pale wing tips. A small edition of Glaucous Gull, but the bill decidedly (relatively and actually) smaller and slenderer, eye ring reddish-purplish (yellow in Glaucous). First-year birds closely resemble Glaucous Gulls but have all-dark bill (basal part contrastingly paler than tip in yearling Glaucous).

(2) "Kumlien's" Gull
Larus glaucoides kumlieni Brewster. An extremely unstable subspecies, very few individuals exactly alike. Intermediate between *L. g. glaucoides* and *L. g. thayeri*. Adults similar to *L. g. glaucoides* but wing tips more or less smudged with greys or greyish browns (extent of dark markings and their intensity varies greatly: extremes vary from immaculate-white primary tips as in *glaucoides* to slaty black as dark as in some *thayeri*). Irides vary from plain yellow to dark brown but usually yellowish with more or less brown speckling. First-year birds are very similar to *L. g. glaucoides*, averaging slightly darker but most are probably indistinguishable.

Measurements. *Adult male*: wing, 395.5–423 (408.4); tail, 167–177.5 (173.5); exposed culmen, 43–46.9 (44.9); tarsus, 58.2–62.9 (60.9). *Adult female*: wing, 372–415 (391.8) mm.

Field Marks. Pale wing tips separate adults from most similar gull species except Glaucous. Adults distinguishable from Glaucous as explained in *L. g. glaucoides* and additionally by greyish smudges on wing tips and in some individuals by the presence of dark irides. The all-dark bill distinguishes first-year birds from Glaucous Gulls of similar age.

Difficult to distinguish from *L. g. glaucoides* in the field but in adults the presence of grey smudges on the wing tips will separate some. First-year birds of the two races cannot be identified subspecifically in the field. See also *L. g. thayeri*.

(3) "Thayer's" Gull
Larus glaucoides thayeri Brooks. On average, the darkest subspecies but characterized by great individual variation (Figure 63). Size slightly larger especially the bill. In typical adults the dark areas of the wing tips are blackish with a pale-greyish or white tongue on the outermost primary closely approaching (or joining) a long white tip; and on the next a similar pale tongue usually joins a large white area near the tip (Plate 36). Mantle averages darker grey. Irides extremely variable, dark to clear yellow, but in average more heavily speckled with brown than in *kumlieni*. Legs pinkish flesh to decidedly pink. Distinguishable from Herring Gull adults by reddish-purplish eye ring and usually (not always) different wing-tip pattern (Figure 64), slightly darker mantle, and slightly smaller proportions. Similar to Glaucous-winged Gull but primary tips usually darker (more blackish), the whitish areas more extensive, especially on ninth primary; bill definitely slenderer.

a   b

Figure 63
Variation in pattern and pigmentation in
wing tips of adult "Thayer's" Gull
a) pale extreme
b) average

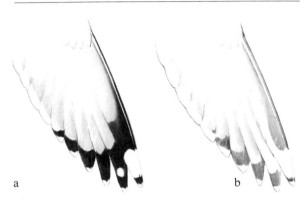

a   b

Figure 64
Wing tips (ventral view) of
a) Herring Gull adult
b) "Thayer's" Gull adult

Juvenal and first-winter birds are extremely variable, far more so than is generally realized, with some dark extremes as dark in general coloration as in average Herring Gulls of similar age and with occasional pale extremes similar to darker *kumlieni*! However most *thayeri* are decidedly darker than *kumlieni* with more solidly coloured (less whitish intermix) tail. They superficially resemble Herring Gulls of like age but in most cases (but by no means all) the wing tips are paler, little (if any) darker than the general coloration of the rest of the wing. In overall coloration they resemble first-year Glaucous-winged Gulls but they average smaller with decidedly less heavy bill. The dark extremes are fully as dark or darker than Herring Gulls of similar age and could easily be mistaken for that species. In the hand, these dark individuals can usually be distinguished from Herring Gulls by their more greyish (less brownish) general coloration, particularly that of tail and wing tips; also by the inner webs of the primaries, which are paler grey (more whitish) than in the Herring Gull.

Measurements. *Adult male*: wing, 397–425.5 (411.4); tail, 160.5–186 (172.3); exposed culmen, 47.1–52.7 (50.6); tarsus, 62.5–66.2 (64.5). *Adult female*: wing, 361.5–408.5 (390.1) mm.

Field Marks. Individual variation is much more extreme than is generally realized. *Adults*: Many differ from the Herring Gull in their obviously paler, less blackish wing tips. Those with definitely blackish wing tips are more difficult but the mantle averages darker grey, the legs are often more pinkish, the eye ring is purplish red (not yellowish orange), and the irides are very often obviously darker. Most are separable from the Glaucous-winged Gull by their more-blackish wing tips. The wing tips of Glaucous-winged look relatively more uniform pale-grey. (Caution: Some *thayeri* have wing tips fully as pale as Glaucous-winged, or even paler, and might be mistaken for that species unless the slenderer bill of *thayeri* can be ascertained.)

Juvenal and first-winter "Thayer's" Gulls resemble Herring Gulls of similar age but most have much paler wing tips and tail (intermediate between Herring Gull and "Kumlien's" Gull in colour) and the underside of the spread primaries in "Thayer's" is paler, showing more contrast with the under wing coverts. (Some "Thayer's" Gulls are as dark as Herring Gulls, or even darker overall, but the more silvery undersurface of the spread primaries will help distinguish them from Herring Gulls.)

Average first-year "Thayer's" are very similar to Glaucous-winged but the latter have a decidedly deeper, heavier bill.

A large proportion of "Thayer's" Gulls, both adult and first-year, can be distinguished from "Kumlien's" with considerable confidence in the field. However, there is so much individual variation, even complete overlapping of characters, that some individuals of one race are almost certain to be mistaken for the other. For instance, some (not all) reports of "Kumlien's" Gull occurrence on the West Coast may well be based on field observation of pale extremes of "Thayer's" Gull.

Lesser Black-backed Gull

Goéland brun
Larus fuscus Linnaeus
Total length: 53 to 61 cm
Plate 37

Status in Canada. In recent years a rare visitor to the Northwest Territories (Victoria Island: Albert Edward Bay, 17 July 1972); Mackenzie (northern Richardson Mountains, 3–4 July 1977); Manitoba (Churchill, 5 June 1968); Ontario (Hamilton, November 1971, Ottawa, 13 November 1971, and (specimen) 11 November 1974; Niagara Falls, 11 November 1973; Cobourg-Oakville—Toronto area, autumn 1972; Quebec (Beauharnois, 18–19 November 1972 and December 1976; Gatineau, early December 1978); New Brunswick (sight records: Grand Manan, 28 August 1968; Castalia, 18 September 1975); Nova Scotia (Digby: an adult, apparently the same individual, spent at least 11 consecutive winters there. It was first seen there in March 1970 and returned again each winter through 1979–1980); Prince Edward Island (photo record: Murray River, 2 January 1983); and Newfoundland (sight records only: Quidi Vidi Lake, St. John's Harbour). Probably Saskatchewan (sight record: Regina).

Although there were no valid Canadian records prior to 1968, this Old World gull has become in recent years a regular visitor to Canada in small but increasing numbers.

Adults: Sexes similar. Mantle dark slaty-grey *(L. f. graellsii)* to black *(L. f. fuscus)*. Head, neck, entire under parts, and tail white. Primaries black, the "tongues" dark grey and restricted in extent, and with usually a white mirror (white spot) on the outermost primary only. Bill yellow with red spot on lower mandible; iris yellow; eye-ring red; legs and feet most often yellow (but many adults have flesh-coloured legs!). First-year birds very similar to Herring Gull but the upper parts are more buffy, tail has larger, more definite whitish areas basally; under tail coverts with larger, heavier, but sparser dark markings. In all plumages the bill is relatively slender.

Measurements. *Adult male*: wing, 415–438 (425.6); tail, 152–169 (159.8); tarsus, 58–66 (63.6); exposed culmen, 49–55 (52.4); height of bill at angle, 16–19 (16.7). *Adult female*: wing, 394–410 (402.4); tail, 142–159 (150.1); tarsus, 57–60 (59.1); exposed culmen, 45–48 (46.2); height of bill, 14–17 (15.4) mm (J. Dwight).

Field Marks. A dark-mantled gull the size of Herring Gull. About two-thirds of the adults have yellow legs and this, when present, separates them from other dark-mantled gulls likely to be seen in Canada. Overall smaller size and slenderer bill distinguish it from Great Black-backed Gull and in winter, the more heavily streaked head separates it from adult Great Black-backs. Similar to Western Gull but bill definitely slenderer, iris yellowish grey (not amber), yellow of legs when present separates it from Canadian and U.S. subspecies of the Western Gull (but not from a Mexican race unlikely to be found in Canada). Yellow legs, when present, and slender bill always separate it from the rare Slaty-backed Gull. Caution: Hybrids between Great Black-backed and Herring gulls very closely resemble Lesser Black-backed Gull but most such hybrids are somewhat larger, have decidedly heavier bill, and the legs are never yellowish.

Habitat. Similar to Herring Gull.

Range. Breeds from Iceland, the Faeroe Islands, Scandinavia, and northern Russia south to the British Isles. Winters from the British Isles east to the Baltic southward to northern Africa and the Persian Gulf.

Subspecies. Most Canadian records are referable to the paler-mantled subspecies. *Larus fuscus graellsii*, but photos of the Victoria Island and Churchill birds suggest the darker-mantled nominate race in those instances.

Slaty-backed Gull

Goéland à manteau ardoisé
Larus schistisagus Stejneger
Total length: 61 to 70.5 cm

Status in Canada. Accidental. Good photos of an adult at Clover Point, British Columbia, March 1974. Evidence of occurrence at Harrowby Bay, Mackenzie District (Bent 1921) is unsatisfactory.

Adults (sexes similar): Similar enough in general appearance to be confusable with the Western, Lesser Black-backed, and Great Black-backed gulls. Mantle dark neutral-grey to slaty black. Head, neck, under parts, and tail white (in winter the head and neck somewhat streaked with dusky grey). Primary tips blackish, usually with white spot near the end of the ninth and tenth (outermost) primaries. The dark-grey tongues on each of the inner webs of eighth to fifth primaries pass into a *narrow white area* before fusing with the black tips. Iris yellowish grey; eye-ring pinkish to purplish pink; legs pinkish to reddish flesh.

Measurements. *Adult male*: wing, 430–477 (440.1); tail, 185–197 (190.5); tarsus, 63–72 (68.1); culmen 50–60. *Adult female*: wing, 405–426 (416) mm (J. Dwight).

Field Marks. Adults very similar to Western Gull but mantle usually somewhat darker; spread wing shows more white near primary tips. Iris yellowish grey (not amber); eye-ring reddish (not orange-yellow). Resembles Lesser Black-backed Gull but bill always noticeably heavier, legs pinkish (never yellowish). Obviously smaller in all dimensions than Great Black-backed Gull.

Range. Breeds from the Gulf of Anadyr, Kamchatka, and Komandorski islands south to Hokkaido, Japan.

Western Gull

Goéland d'Audubon
Larus occidentalis Audubon
Total length: 61 to 68.5 cm
Plate 37

Range in Canada. Regular winter visitor in small numbers to the coast of southern British Columbia (mainly Vancouver Island; also Seymour Inlet). Breeds rarely through hybridization with the Glaucous-winged Gull in southwestern British Columbia (near Tofino and Long Beach).

Adults: The dark mantle distinguishes it from other *common* Pacific Coast gulls except the otherwise very different Heermann's Gull (see Field Marks). Its wing tips (white mirror on only the outermost primary; inner webs of outermost primaries usually without grey tongues), yellowish eye-ring, usually darker (nominate race) irides distinguish it from the Slaty-backed Gull. *First-year*: The much darker primaries distinguish it from the Glaucous-winged; relatively deeper bill and more evenly dark tail (less light spotting or marbling) from the Herring Gull; heavier bill and darker general coloration from the California Gull in first-year dress.

Measurements. *Adult male*: wing, 400–420 (412.3); tail, 166–177 (170); exposed culmen, 52–58 (55.6); tarsus, 65–74 (69.2). *Adult female*: wing, 384–408 (397.6) mm (J. Dwight).

Field Marks. *Adults*: A large dark-backed gull with white head, tail, and under parts, yellow bill with red spot, and pinkish legs. The dark back and upper surface of the wings distinguish it from all other common Pacific Coast gulls except the Heermann's, from which it differs in its yellow bill, pink legs, white under parts, white tail, and much larger size. First-year Westerns are less easily distinguished, but they can be recognized from other large gulls of similar age by characters given in the first paragraph.

Habitat. Seacoasts of the Pacific.

Range. Breeds on the Pacific Coast from northern Washington (Destruction Island) south to Baja California and the coast of Sonora, Mexico. Winters in much of its breeding range and north to southern coastal British Columbia.

Subspecies. *Larus occidentalis occidentalis* Audubon is the only race so far ascertained to occur in Canada. Additional races breed in west coastal United States.

Glaucous-winged Gull

Goéland à ailes grises
Larus glaucescens Naumann
Total length: 61 to 71 cm
Plate 37

Breeding Distribution of Glaucous-winged Gull

Range in Canada. Breeds and winters along the entire coast of British Columbia. Very rare in the interior: Alberta (specimens: Therien and Bear Lake); Yukon (specimen: near Windy Pass on Dempster Highway, 15 June 1977); Manitoba (specimen: Churchill, 1 June 1964).

Hybridization with *L. argentatus* is reported at Okanagan Lake, British Columbia, by W.J. Merilees (1974. Canadian Field-Naturalist, vol. 88, no. 4, pp. 485–486).

A large, rather heavy-billed gull. Wing tips grey, similar in coloration to the mantle, not blackish as in most other large gulls of the Pacific Coast. Eye ring purplish pink, irides silvery to yellowish powdered with brown, giving a dark appearance. Adults of the geographically widely separated *kumlieni* race of the Iceland Gull often have similar pale grey on the wing tips, but the Glaucous-winged is a larger bird with much heavier bill, somewhat darker mantle, and the grey coloration of wing tips is more uniform and extensive, the white areas smaller. First-year Glaucous-winged, compared with yearling Herring, Western, and California gulls, are paler generally with grey wing tips instead of blackish brown. First-year Glaucous-winged Gulls are very similar to the *thayeri* race of Iceland Gull of similar age, but the former has a heavier bill.

Measurements. *Adult male*: wing, 393–443.5 (422.9); tail, 132.5–195 (173); exposed culmen, 50–61 (55.1); tarsus, 65–73 (69.6). *Adult female*: wing, 363.5–414 (396.3) mm.

Field Marks. A large pink-legged gull of the Pacific Coast. Adults with grey wing tips, not blackish as in most other large West Coast gulls. Some individuals of the *thayeri* race of the Iceland Gull also have grey wing tips but differ from Glaucous-winged in possessing more white in the tip; also *thayeri* has a slenderer bill. Yearlings have greyish-brown wing tips, not noticeably darker than the back. In very much worn immatures the wing tips sometimes bleach white.

Habitat. Primarily the vicinity of salt and brackish water along the Pacific Coast: bays, islands, estuaries, the ocean (usually not far off-shore), beaches, mud flats, wharves, dumps, fish canneries. Often follows boats. Follows rivers for various distances but is not normally found very far inland.

Nesting. Nests colonially. Nest, a heap of seaweed, kelp, rock-weed, and grasses, is often on flat low islands, rock ledges of higher islands or headlands. *Eggs*, 2 or 3; similar to those of other large gulls, but have buffy to olive-buff ground colour, spotted and blotched with darker browns and some lavender grey. Incubation period 26 to 28 days (R.H. Drent).

Range. Breeds from western and southern Alaska south to northwestern Washington; also on the Commander Islands, St. Lawrence Island, the Pribilof and Aleutian islands. Winters from southeastern Alaska south coastally to southern Baja California and casually to Sonora.

Glaucous Gull

Goéland bourgmestre
Larus hyperboreus Gunnerus
Total length: 66 to 76 cm
Plate 36

Breeding Distribution of Glaucous Gull

Range in Canada. Breeds on arctic coasts and islands from Prince Patrick, Ellef Ringnes, and northern Ellesmere islands south to northern Yukon (coast and Herschel Island); northern Mackenzie (arctic coast); northern Keewatin (Adelaide Peninsula, and in the interior near Garry Lake); Southampton Island, Coats Island, Digges Sound, and Belcher Islands in Hudson Bay; northern Quebec (Bellin, Lake Guillaume-Delisle); Payne Bay, N.W.T.; and northern Labrador (south to about Hopedale).

Winters from southern parts of the breeding range southward, mostly on the Atlantic and Pacific coasts and islands of southern Canada; also Hudson Bay and in small numbers on the Great Lakes and St. Lawrence River. In much of the southern interior, it is scarce and irregular even in migration. It is, however, regular in small numbers on the upper St. Lawrence River and its drainage system (including the Ottawa) and on the Great Lakes.

A very large heavy-billed gull with white wing tips in adults and nearly white in immatures. Adults with pale-grey mantle, rest of plumage including wing tips immaculate white (but in winter, head and neck are vaguely marked with brownish grey). First-year immatures are extensively marked with pale greys and buffs, the wing tips slightly paler (nearly white). Second-year birds are extremely pale, sometimes almost white. The white (or in immatures very pale) wing tips distinguish it from all but the Iceland Gull and the otherwise very different Ivory Gull. Larger size and very much heavier, longer bill separate it from the very similar Iceland Gull.

Measurements. *Adult male*: wing, 447–477.2 (459.2); tail, 188.5–201 (196.3); exposed culmen, 53–64.6 (60.4); tarsus, 67.3–76.6 (72.7). *Adult female*: wing, 411.5–437 (425.1) mm.

Field Marks. A very large gull without any dark colour on the wing tips, thus separable from other gulls except the Iceland and Ivory. The latter is so much smaller and otherwise different that confusion is unlikely. Adults likely to be confused only with Iceland Gull, but Glaucous is a larger bird than the Iceland with decidedly longer, heavier bill and yellowish eye-ring (reddish or purplish in Iceland Gull). First-year immatures have all the basal part of the bill pale, contrasting with the dark tip; whereas yearling Icelands have an almost uniformly dark bill. Second-year Glaucous are extremely pale or whitish all over.

Habitat. In winter and migration, seacoasts, bays, and harbours, and less often offshore waters; also, in small numbers, inland lakes and rivers. For nesting purposes, arctic cliffs near the coast, coastal islands, islands in freshwater lakes near the coast, edges of coastal lagoons.

Nesting. Usually colonial on cliffs (often shares cliffs with other species), solitary on islands, usually on or near coast, rarely considerably inland: Garry Lake, Keewatin (A.H. Macpherson). Nest, an accumulation of grass, seaweed, moss, and debris, often added to from year to year. *Eggs* 2 to 3 (usually 3); buffy brown to olive brown, spotted and blotched with dark browns and often with some grey or lavender grey. Incubation 27 to 28 days (Swenander), apparently by both sexes.

Range. Breeds on arctic coasts and islands from northern Alaska eastward across northern Canada, Greenland, Iceland, and across northern Europe to eastern Siberia. Winters from the southern part of the breeding range south to southern California and New York; also, in small numbers on the Great Lakes; and in the Old World south to the British Isles and coasts of western Europe, China, and Japan; casually farther south.

Subspecies. *Larus hyperboreus hyperboreus* Gunnerus is the subspecies of most of the breeding range in Canada. Populations breeding in northern Yukon and western Mackenzie (east to about Harrowby Bay) are closer to *L. h. barrovianus* Ridgway, characterized by somewhat smaller size, particularly of bill, and slightly darker mantle.

Great Black-backed Gull

Goéland à manteau noir
Larus marinus Linnaeus
Total length: 71 to 78.5 cm
Plate 37

Breeding Distribution of Great Black-backed
Gull

Range in Canada. Breeds mainly on or near the
coast from Ungava Bay (Leaf River mouth)
and northern Labrador (Cape Chidley,
N.W.T.) southward to south coastal Quebec
(entire north shore of the Gulf of St. Lawrence,
lower St. Lawrence River west at least to near
Montréal, also on Anticosti and Madeleine
islands), Newfoundland, and the Maritime
Provinces. Also rarely and very locally (but
increasingly) inland in southern Ontario (Little
Haystack Rock, Bruce Peninsula, Kingston
region, Presqu'ile Provincial Park) and southwestern Quebec (Montréal, Lake Champlain).
Non-breeding wanderers occur north at least to
southern Baffin Island (Bowman Bay, West
Foxe Island) and west to Hudson Bay (Chesterfield Inlet, Churchill, Grande rivière de la
Baleine). Sight records of black-backed gulls
reported from the high Arctic may refer to this
species.

Winters mainly on the East Coast from the
Strait of Belle Isle southward: Newfoundland,
coastal southern Quebec, New Brunswick,
Prince Edward Island, and Nova Scotia; also
increasingly in small to fair numbers on
St. Lawrence River (Québec, Montréal), and on
Lakes Ontario, Erie, and Huron.

Hybridizes occasionally with *L. argentatus*
as evidenced by specimens in museums
(J.R. Jehl, Jr., 1960. Auk, vol. 77, no. 3,
pp. 343–345; R.F. Andrle, 1973. Canadian
Field-Naturalist, vol. 87, no. 2, pp. 170–171;
W.E. Godfrey, 1973. Canadian Field-
Naturalist, vol. 87, no. 2, pp. 171–172).

A very large gull of the eastern part of the continent, the adult with a
distinctive black mantle, thus unlike any other gull likely to be found in
eastern Canada except the rare Lesser Black-backed Gull (q.v.). In
winter, white of head lightly streaked with dusky. Immatures are separable from other eastern gulls except the Glaucous by large size and
large heavy bill; distinguished from Glaucous Gull by much darker
general coloration and blackish-brown wing tips. First-year birds show
more white in the tail, particularly the outer feathers, than Herring Gull
of similar age, and the upper and under parts are paler. Full adult
plumage is not assumed until at least the fourth year, but the first few
black feathers begin to appear in the mantle the second year.

Measurements. *Adult male*: wing, 446–486.5 (471.6); tail, 191–199
(195.4); exposed culmen, 62.5–66 (64.3); tarsus, 76–82.5 (79.9). *Adult
female*: wing, 445.5–461.5 (455.5) mm.

Field Marks. A very large gull of the east, mainly the coast. Much
larger, with heavier bill, than the Herring Gull. Black mantle (see also
Lesser Black-backed Gull) and great size characterize adults. In winter,
the much less heavily streaked head of adults usually separates them
from adult Lesser Black-backs. First-year birds are separable from
Herring Gull of similar age by whiter under parts, usually whiter head,
paler back, larger size, and heavier bill. *Voice*: Notes varied and many
similar to those of other gulls, but a deep hoarse *err-ul* is distinctive.

Habitat. Nesting is on coastal islands and cliffs; sometimes on
islands of freshwater lakes usually (not always) near the coast. In other
seasons almost any shoreline situation, including coastal islands; also
freshwater lakes and rivers mostly near the coast, but some winter far
inland on large lakes with open water.

Nesting. Nests singly or in colonies on coastal islands and cliffs;
also less commonly on islands of freshwater lakes near the coast; rarely
far inland. Nest, a depression lined with grass and seaweed, a mound of
vegetable material, or sometimes an unlined depression. *Eggs*, usually 3,
sometimes 2; usually buff to olive brown, blotched and spotted with
browns and purplish greys. Incubation by both sexes, 26 to 30 days
(various authors).

Range. Breeds along the east coast of North America from Labra-
dor south to New York. Also southern Greenland, Iceland, the Faeroe
Islands, Spitsbergen, Bear Island, and northern Norway, south mainly
on the coast through the British Isles, northern France, and Denmark.
Winters south to North Carolina, and in the Old World south to the
Mediterranean, Black, and Caspian seas.

Black-legged Kittiwake

(Atlantic Kittiwake)

Mouette tridactyle
Rissa tridactyla (Linnaeus)
Total length: 40 to 46 cm
Plate 37

Breeding Distribution of Black-legged
Kittiwake

Range in Canada. Breeds on coasts and islands off eastern Canada: Prince Leopold, Cornwallis, Cobourg, Bylot, and eastern Somerset islands; eastern Hudson Strait (Resolution and Button islands); southeastern Quebec (north shore of the Gulf of St. Lawrence west to Corossol Island; Anticosti Island, Bonaventure Island, Percé Rock, Rochers aux Oiseaux); Newfoundland (commonly on cliffs on all coasts); and Nova Scotia (one colony on Green Island (= Bird Island) off Gabarus). Common in summer off Labrador but breeding known only at Outer Gannet Island.

Wanders widely over salt water outside breeding season to Hudson Bay, west to Victoria Island (Prince Albert Land), and north rarely to within 250 km of the Pole (Fletcher's Ice Island, between 85°15′N and 86°10′N and 75°00′W and 96°00′W). Transient and winter resident on the coast of British Columbia and from the Gulf of St. Lawrence southward off New Brunswick, Nova Scotia, and more rarely Prince Edward Island. Numerous individuals banded in Greenland, the British Isles, Russia, Iceland, and Denmark have been recovered in Newfoundland and elsewhere on the Atlantic Coast. Casual or accidental inland in southern Ontario (Kingston, Toronto, Lake Nipissing). Casual in Alberta (single specimens: Calgary, 13 November 1976; Wabamun Lake, 25 December 1979; sight record of one, Beaverhill Lake, 17 July 1977).

The rudimentary condition of the hind toe (a tiny fleshy lump with usually no toenail) separates it from all our other gulls except the Red-legged Kittiwake, which is of accidental occurrence in Canada. Tail slightly forked.

Measurements. *Adult male*: wing, 295–322 (305.1); tail, 124–136 (128.5); exposed culmen, 33–39 (35.7); tarsus, 32–36 (33.6). *Adult female*: wing, 285–314 (297.9) mm (Dwight).

Field Marks. *Adults*: A smallish grey-mantled saltwater gull with the extreme wing tips sharply black (as though dipped in ink) and without white spots, bill plain yellow without red spot, legs dark brown to blackish. *First-year*: Clear white below (thus unlike most gulls at that age), grey mantle with dark bar diagonally across wing coverts, dark band across back of neck, dark ear spot, dark tail tip, and blackish bill and legs. The black band across back of neck distinguishes it from other gulls except Red-legged Kittiwake (which, however, lacks both dark band across wing coverts and dark tail band).

Habitat. Marine. In breeding season rocky coasts where cliff ledges provide nest sites. In other seasons mostly offshore and pelagic waters. Rare or accidental inland.

Nesting. In colonies, often large. Nest, a neat well-cupped structure of seaweed, grass, moss, and so on, is placed on ledges or similar projections of cliffs beside or near the sea. *Eggs*, usually 2, sometimes 1 or 3; varying from buffy to greenish or bluish, spotted and blotched with browns and grey. Incubation by both sexes, said to be 21 to 24 days (Hantzsch); other authors 25 to 30 days.

Range. Circumpolar. Breeds on islands and shores of the Arctic Ocean south to the Aleutian Islands and southern Alaska, southern Newfoundland, France, the Kurile Islands, and Sakhalin. Winters south to Baja California, southern New Jersey, northwestern Africa, and Japan.

Subspecies. (1) *Rissa tridactyla tridactyla* (Linnaeus) is the only subspecies that breeds in Canada and the only one known from Canadian localities except the Pacific Coast. (2) *R. t. pollicaris* Ridgway (longer bill and slightly larger size, slightly better developed hind toe, and slightly more extensive black on primaries) is the subspecies known to visit British Columbia in migration and winter.

Red-legged Kittiwake

Mouette à pattes rouges
Rissa brevirostris (Bruch)
Total length: 35 to 40 cm

Status in Canada. Accidental. Specimen found
dead near Forty Mile, Yukon Territory,
15 October 1899.

Adult similar to Black-legged Kittiwake but with red legs and grey
(instead of white) wing linings. First-year bird similar to first-year
Black-legged Kittiwake but lacks dark diagonal bar across wing coverts
and has no black tip to the tail; smaller size.

Ross's Gull

Mouette rosée
Rhodostethia rosea (MacGillivray)
Total length: 32 to 35.5 cm
Plate 38

Range in Canada. Nested in 1977 and 1978 on
Cheyne Islands, east of Bathurst Island,
N.W.T.; also in 1980 at Churchill, Manitoba.
Species has been observed elsewhere in the
Arctic without evidence of breeding: Boothia
Peninsula (Felix Harbour), Melville Peninsula
(Igloolik), Cornwallis Island, Prince Leopold
Island, Meighen Island, Seymour Island,
Broughton Island, and Keewatin (McConnell
River). Casual in Newfoundland (specimen:
Fogo Island, 18 December 1976); southwestern
British Columbia (photo record: Clover Point,
autumn 1966); and Ontario (photo: one at
Moosonee, 14–23 May 1982).

Tail distinctly wedge-shaped. Adults (breeding plumage): Mantle grey,
secondaries white-tipped; primaries grey, but outer web of outermost is
black; wing linings bluish grey; fine black collar around neck; rest of
plumage white with distinct shrimp-pink tinge, strongest on breast and
belly; bill black, legs red. *Adults (winter plumage)*: Similar to breeding
plumage but lacks black neck ring; white parts less pinkish, more
washed with grey. First-year birds have considerable blackish in wing
coverts and wing tips, a black ear spot, black tip to the wedge-shaped
tail (except outermost feathers), and as in adults the wing lining is
bluish grey.

Measurements. *Adult male*: wing, 248–265 (255.1); tail, 121–138
(125.3); exposed culmen, 18–20 (19.3); tarsus, 30–33 (32.1). *Adult
female*: wing, 252–260 (256) mm (J. Dwight).

Field Marks. A small arctic gull with a variably wedge-shaped tail
in all plumages. Adults show a relatively *broad* white trailing edge to
the spread wing and in the breeding season a narrow black collar. The
shrimp-pink tinge of the body plumage varies and is often not very
apparent. In boldly marked wing pattern, first-year birds resemble other
small gulls of similar age but the blue-grey wing linings appear surprisingly dark (although much paler than in Little Gull). The combination
of dark wing linings and wedge-shaped tail is present in all plumages.

Habitat. In summer, shoal waters where ice floes are grounded for
extended periods thus trapping loose pack ice which tends to form rafts
of upthrust rough ice. Thus tidal action is diverted into upwelling
currents (S.D. MacDonald).

Nesting. In colonies on low, reef-like islets in or adjacent to poly-
nias where there is extensive open water in early spring (see Habitat).
Nest may be a well-formed scrape (in softer ground) or a barely perceptible depression (in coarse ice-pushed gravel) or on moss or other vegetation. Nests variably lined with feathers (mostly strawlike shafts of
eider primaries), strands of moss, stipes of *Laminaria*, grasses, sedges,
depending upon availability. *Eggs*, 1 to 3, dark greenish-olive with indistinct spotting of darker greenish-olive or brown; sometimes smears of
chalky-white deposit. Incubation by both parents (S.D. MacDonald).

Range. Poorly known. Breeds in northern Siberia and locally arctic
Canada; formerly Greenland (Disko Bay). Winter range poorly known
but probably mainly in open waters of the Arctic.

Sabine's Gull

Mouette de Sabine
Xema sabini (Sabine)
Total length: 33 to 35.5 cm
Plate 38

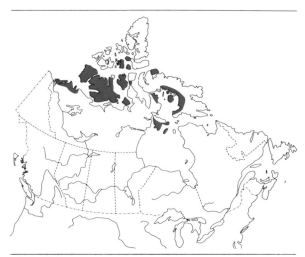

Breeding Distribution of Sabine's Gull

Range in Canada. Breeds on arctic coasts and islands from Banks Island (probably west coast), Bathurst Island, Grinnell Peninsula, Victoria Island (Austin Bay, Cambridge Bay), Prince of Wales Island (Little Browne Bay), and Bylot Island (Canada Point) south to northwestern Mackenzie (Richards Island, Cape Bathurst, Franklin Bay), King William Island, southern Southampton Island, and southwestern Baffin Island (northern Foxe Peninsula to Taverner Bay). Recorded in summer on Melville Island and Yukon coast.

Migration is mainly along the Pacific Coast: British Columbia (regular autumn transient on coast, less common in spring; rare in interior). Rare migrant in the Canadian interior but recorded in Alberta, Saskatchewan, Manitoba, Ontario, and Quebec. Rare autumn visitor to Labrador (Okak, Big Bay); casual in New Brunswick (Indian Island; Grand Manan). Various sight records for Nova Scotia.

Distinctly forked tail distinguishes it in all plumages from other Canadian gulls.

Measurements *(X. s. sabini)*. *Adult male*: wing, 259.2–278 (268.2); tail, 112.2–129 (120.4); exposed culmen, 22.4–25.4 (24.1); tarsus, 31.9–36 (33.8). *Adult female*: wing, 257–278.7 (262.8) mm.

Field Marks. No other Canadian gull has a *distinctly* forked tail (Black-legged Kittiwake shows just a suggestion of forked tail). Adult in breeding plumage with dark-grey hood narrowly bordered by black, black bill with yellow tip, black legs, and boldly patterned spread wing (unlike any tern) is unmistakable. Juvenal shows similar spread-wing pattern but has brown back and wing coverts, greyish-brown wash on crown and face, black-tipped tail. In the Arctic it is likely to be confused only with young of the rare Ross's Gull, but the forked tail, lack of sharply marked dark ear spot, and white (instead of bluish-grey) wing linings distinguish Sabine's Gull.

Habitat. In nesting season, low wet tundra and tundra lakes usually not very far inland, low coasts, and islands. Outside breeding season, mostly coastal waters, rarely on southern interior fresh water.

Nesting. Usually in small colonies, occasionally single pairs; sometimes in association with Arctic Terns. Nest a shallow depression in a tundra hummock, pond or lake edge or island, either unlined or lined with grasses and willow twigs. *Eggs*, 2 or 3; brown to olive-brown, rather faintly spotted and blotched with somewhat darker browns. Incubation, by both sexes, lasts about 21 days, 6 hours (D.F. Parmelee); also variously given by others as 23 to 26 days.

Range. Breeds on arctic coasts and islands in Alaska (south to Bristol Bay), arctic Canada, Greenland, Spitsbergen, and Siberia (south to Anadyr). Winter range poorly known but includes coastal Peru.

Subspecies. *Xema sabini sabini* (Sabine) is the only subspecies known to breed in Canada. On the Pacific coast of British Columbia, *X. s. woznesenskii* Portenko (averages slightly darker) is a migrant to and from its breeding grounds in western Alaska.

Ivory Gull

Mouette blanche
Pagophila eburnea (Phipps)
Total length: 39.5 to 48.5 cm
Plate 36

Breeding Distribution of Ivory Gull

Range in Canada. Breeds in the high Arctic. Range imperfectly known. Former breeding localities include: northern Prince Patrick Island (Cape Krabbé), and the Polynia Islands; reefs west to Meighen Island; a floating ice island at 79°13.2'N, 97°29.1'W on 20 June 1960. Present breeding localities include: Seymour Island; eastern Ellesmere Island (near Craig Harbour, Clarence Head, Talbot Inlet, Ekblaw Glacier; near Princess Marie Bay); Devon Island (Lady Ann Strait, Dundas Harbour); and breeding reported also on the Brodeur Peninsula (73°30'N; 86°45'W and at 72°57'N, 88°30'W). Present in summer on Prince Leopold Island. Reports of breeding at other localities are unsatisfactory.

Winters over arctic drift-ice south to the arctic coasts, Labrador, pack-ice off northeastern Newfoundland, and occasionally in numbers on the north shore of the Gulf of St. Lawrence (Harrington-Harbour, Tête-à-la-Baleine, Mutton-Bay, Anticosti Island), more rarely in Nova Scotia and New Brunswick. Very rare in British Columbia (Penticton, Dease Lake); interior Manitoba (Egg Lake, Woodlands); Ontario (Fort Albany, Oba, Toronto); and southwestern Quebec (Saint-Jean-Port-Joli, Saint-Raymond, Vandry, Beauharnois).

Measurements. *Adult male*: wing, 328–346 (338); tail, 141–160 (148.3); exposed culmen, 33–38 (35.9); tarsus, 37–42 (39.6). *Adult female*: wing, 320–340 (329.2) mm (J. Dwight).

Field Marks. *Adults*: The only gull having the *entire* plumage pure white with black legs. *First-year* birds also are easily recognized: a white gull with black legs, a narrow dark subterminal tail band, the flight feathers and many wing coverts tipped with blackish brown, and frequently a "dirty face" caused by dark smudges on face and throat. Under good conditions when the gull is perched, one may see that the feathering of tibia extends down to near the top of the tarsus, and the legs therefore appear short. Less inclined to alight on water than other gulls.

Habitat. In summer, mainly high-arctic coastal situations with both permanent ice and open water; also islands, including floating ice islands; uses both flat land and cliff ledges for nesting; often ranges inland for considerable distances. At other seasons, mainly edges of pack-ice and drift-ice.

Nesting. In colonies either on flat ground or on cliff edges; sometimes on nunataks well inland. Nest varies from a depression lined sparsely with only a few feathers to a bulky structure of moss, lichen, saxifrages, and grass. *Eggs*, 1 to 3, usually 2; buffy olive, spotted or blotched with dark brown and some ashy grey. Incubation (in Spitsbergen) 24.25 to 25.25 days, by both sexes (Bateson and Plowright).

Range. Breeds in the high Arctic of Canada, northern Greenland, Spitsbergen, Franz Josef Land, Novaya Zemlya, and Severnaya Zemlya. Winters over northern drift-ice and edges of pack-ice casually south in North America to the New England coast.

Subfamily **Sterninae**: Terns

Terns are usually smaller than gulls, have sharp-pointed bill, shorter legs, and usually decidedly forked tail. They dive from the air for food. In flight they tend to point the bill more downward than gulls.

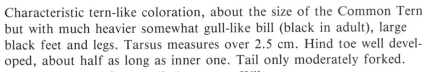

Gull-billed Tern

Sterne hansel
Sterna nilotica Gmelin
Total length: 33 to 38 cm
Figure 65

Status in Canada. Accidental in New Brunswick (specimen: Grand Manan, August 1879) and Nova Scotia (photo record: Halifax, 24 July 1979. Also sight records). It is normally found on warm temperate waters of both the New and Old Worlds.

Characteristic tern-like coloration, about the size of the Common Tern but with much heavier somewhat gull-like bill (black in adult), large black feet and legs. Tarsus measures over 2.5 cm. Hind toe well developed, about half as long as inner one. Tail only moderately forked.

    Subspecies. *Sterna nilotica aranea* Wilson.

Figure 65
Bill of Gull-billed Tern

Caspian Tern

Sterne caspienne
Sterna caspia Pallas
Total length: 48 to 58.4 cm
Plate 39

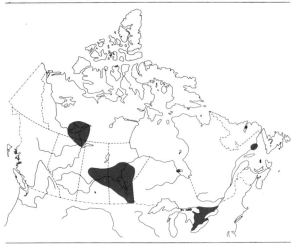

Breeding Distribution of Caspian Tern

A very large tern with heavy coral-red bill, black cap (only slightly crested, black nuchal feathers with blunt tips), black feet, and only slightly forked tail, the outermost feathers not greatly elongated. By late summer the forehead and crown become heavily streaked with white (winter plumage). Immatures similar to winter adults but upper parts mottled with dusky; bill, dull orange.

    Measurements. *Adult male*: wing, 400–422 (411.1); tail, 130–150 (137.9); exposed culmen, 65–75 (69.4); tarsus, 40.5–46 (43.2). *Adult female*: wing, 404–423 (416) mm (Ridgway).

    Field Marks. Large size (as big as the medium-sized gulls) and slower wingbeats in flight distinguish it from all other terns of regular occurrence in Canada. The pointed tapering red bill and dark cap eliminate confusion with any gull. Its hoarse voice is distinctive, a low *ca-arrr ka-ka-ka-kaow*, higher pitched in early autumn young.

    Habitat. Lakes and large rivers in the interior; also coasts. Often rests on sandbars and beaches. For nesting usually sandy or rocky islands in interior lakes; in Quebec coastal islands.

    Nesting. Usually in colonies often near other terns or gulls; sometimes single pairs. Nest, on the ground, may be a mere depression or be fairly well lined with vegetation. *Eggs*, 2 or 3; buffy, usually sparingly spotted with browns. Incubation 27 ± 0.4 days (Penland) by both sexes.

Range in Canada. Breeds very locally in southern Mackenzie (Great Slave Lake); northeastern Alberta (Lake Athabasca); central Saskatchewan (Doré Lake, Last Mountain Lake); south-central and southern Manitoba (Southern Indian Lake, God's Lake, Lakes Winnipeg and Winnipegosis, Whiteshell Lake); James Bay (Akimiski Strait); southern Ontario (Georgian Bay, North Channel of Lake Huron, Lake Ontario, Thousand Islands group in upper St. Lawrence River, Kingston); southeastern Quebec (Fog Island, probably Madeleine Islands); Labrador (Lake Melville); and probably Newfoundland (locally). Recorded in summer in western Ontario (Lake of the Woods).

Scarce transient in central and southern Alberta; Saskatchewan; southwestern Quebec (Montréal region); New Brunswick (Buctouche, Nantucket Island); Prince Edward Island (Tracadie Bay, Conway Inlet); and Nova Scotia (Cole Harbour, Cape Sable Island). Regular but scarce summer visitant to the coast of British Columbia; casual in the British Columbia interior. Wanders north to northern Manitoba (Churchill). A specimen taken at Boxey, Newfoundland, 30 September 1958, had been banded on 10 July 1958, at Rogers City, Michigan.

Range. Breeds locally in North America, Europe, Asia, Africa, Australia and New Zealand. In North America, locally from Canada to southern United States and central Baja California. In the Western Hemisphere, it winters from central California south through Baja California; the Gulf of Mexico, the Caribbean, and the West Indies.

Royal Tern

Sterne royale
Sterna maxima Boddaert
Total length: 45.5 to 53 cm
Plate 39

Status in Canada. Accidental in Nova Scotia (Brier Island: specimens, 1 October 1958; 13 September 1960; also sight records for Sable Island, Three Fathom Harbour, Chebucto Head, and off Yarmouth). Sight record of one for Newfoundland (Placentia, 10 July 1983) and for Ontario (near Kingsville, August 1974).

A large tern similar to Caspian Tern but smaller, with slenderer more orange (less deep red) bill, much more deeply forked tail (outer feathers reach to wing tips; Caspian has shorter, broader, outer tail feathers, which fall well short of wing tips), underside of primary tips much paler, black nuchal feathers of cap longer and pointed. Royal Tern has complete black cap for only a short period in spring, after which forehead and forecrown become white, only the hind part remaining black. Immatures are distinguishable from young Caspians by the more deeply forked tail.

Measurements. *Adult male*: wing, 360–382 (371); tail, 147.5–192 (171.9); exposed culmen, 59–68 (64.1); tarsus, 29.5–34.5 (31.8). *Adult female*: wing, 357–393 (374) mm (Ridgway).

Subspecies. *Sterna maxima maxima* Boddaert. The species breeds from Maryland southward on the Atlantic Coast as well as in other parts of the world.

Elegant Tern

Sterne élégante
Sterna elegans Gambel
Total length: 41 to 43 cm

Figure 66
Head of
a) Elegant Tern
b) Royal Tern

Status in Canada. Accidental in British
Columbia. In 1983, five appeared in the vicinity of Victoria on 23 August and at least two
remained there until 25 September. At the same
time, several were identified in the Vancouver
area where the species was present from
23 August through September. A photo was
taken at Crescent Beach (British Columbia Provincial Museum no. 864) on 24 August 1983.

Closely resembles Royal Tern but is somewhat smaller. The Elegant has
a slenderer, more downcurved bill (Figure 66) and a longer shaggier
black crest. In nonbreeding plumages of both species the forehead is
white, but in the Elegant Tern the black of the rear of the head usually
extends farther forward to enclose the eye while in the Royals of the
Pacific Coast the eye is surrounded by white and thus more conspicuous
(however as some Royals, at least on the Atlantic Coast, are similar to
Elegants in this respect, this character is not infallible in field identification). Call of the Elegant Tern a nasal *karreek karreek*.

Measurements. *Adult male*: wing, 292–320 (309.4); tail, 115–165
(140.2); exposed culmen, 59–65.5 (62.4); tarsus, 28–30.5 (29.5) mm
(Ridgway).

Range. Breeds on the Pacific Coast from extreme southern California (San Diego Bay) south along the coast of Mexico to Sinaloa.

Sandwich Tern

Sterne caugek
Sterna sandvicensis Latham
Total length: 35.5 to 40.5 cm

Status in Canada. Accidental in southern
Ontario (specimen: Bruce County, autumn
1881).

Another black-capped, grey-mantled tern with white under parts.
Somewhat resembles the Common Tern, but the bill is black with
yellowish tip and is much longer; legs black and longer; black nuchal
feathers longer and pointed. No other tern has a black, yellow-tipped
bill.

Subspecies. *Sterna sandvicensis acuflavida* Cabot. Nearest point of
breeding is Atlantic coastal United States (Carolinas).

Roseate Tern

Sterne de Dougall
Sterna dougallii Montagu
Total length: 35.5 to 43 cm
Plate 39

Range in Canada. Breeds locally in small numbers in southern Nova Scotia (Thrumcap Island, Guysborough County; Indian Island; Sable Island; Mud Island; Little Bald Tusket Island, but apparently no longer nests on most of these islands, except Sable), on Madeleine Islands, Quebec, and a single nest was located on Machias Seal Island, New Brunswick, by Reg Nevell, in July 1979 (Peter C. Smith, in litt.) There are sight records only for Ontario.

Similar to Common Tern but both webs of outer tail feathers white; bill of breeding adults usually black (sometimes with various extent of red at base); wing shorter, tail longer.

Measurements. *Adult male*: wing, 222–231.5 (230); tail, 166–214.5 (187.6); exposed culmen, 36–40.5 (38.1); tarsus, 18–20 (19). *Adult female*: wing, 218.5–233 (230) mm (Ridgway).

Field Marks. Most breeding Roseate Terns have a black bill, which distinguishes them from the Common, Arctic, and Forster's terns. Some, however, may show considerable red on the basal half of the bill, in which case the Roseate's longer, more deeply forked tail, and white, faintly rosy under parts (instead of greyish) will help separate it from breeding Common and Arctic terns.

Habitat. Coastal salt water, nesting on islands and shores.

Nesting. In colonies often with other species on coastal islands and shores. Nest, on the ground either unlined or sparsely lined. *Eggs*, 2 or 3; similar to those of Common Tern but average a little paler and slightly longer. Incubation variously recorded 21 to 26 days, by both sexes; 21 days (L. Jones).

Range. Breeds locally on coasts and islands on both sides of the Atlantic from Nova Scotia to Virginia and south to the West Indies and the north coast of Venezuela, and from the British Isles to southern Africa; also in the Indian Ocean; China and the Philippines to Australia and islands in the South Pacific. In North America winters from the West Indies to Brazil.

Subspecies. *Sterna dougallii dougallii* Montagu.

Common Tern

Sterne pierregarin
Sterna hirundo Linnaeus
Total length: 33 to 40.5 cm
Plate 39

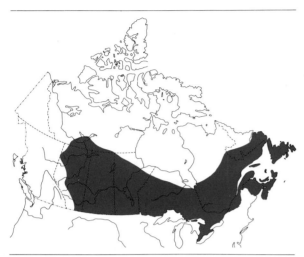

Breeding Distribution of Common Tern

Range in Canada. Locally common summer resident and transient. Breeds in southern Mackenzie (Great Slave Lake); Alberta (east of the Rocky Mountains: Lake Athabasca, Miquelon Lakes, Many Island Lake); Saskatchewan (Lake Athabasca, Flotten Lake, Crane Lake, Regina); north-central to southern Manitoba (Bird, Cedar Lake, Shoal Lake; probably northwest to Kasmere Lake); central and southern Ontario (Severn Lake and Moosonee south to Lake Erie, Lake Ontario, and St. Lawrence River); James Bay (Charlton Island); southern Quebec (Lake Mistassini, north shore of Gulf of St. Lawrence, Montréal, Madeleine Islands); southern Labrador (Lake Melville, Cartwright); Newfoundland; New Brunswick; Prince Edward Island; and Nova Scotia.

Transient in British Columbia (Strait of Georgia and the southern interior).

Adults (breeding): Crown and nape black; back and upper side of wings pearl grey; tips and outer webs of primaries dusky to silvery grey; tail forked, white with grey outer webs; under parts very pale greyish becoming white on chin, cheeks, under tail coverts, and wing linings; bill red, usually with black tip; legs reddish. *Adults (winter)*: Similar but forehead white, a broad black patch extends from in front of eye around back of head; bill dusky red. *Immature*: Head pattern similar to adult but feathers of mantle extensively tipped with blackish and buff; lesser wing coverts blackish; bill dusky, orange near base; legs pinkish or yellowish.

Measurements. *Adult male*: wing, 252.5–274 (262.6); tail, 133.4–149 (140.9); exposed culmen, 32.5–40.8 (37.1); tarsus, 19.6–22.5 (20.8). *Adult female*: wing, 245.8–268.2 (258.9) mm. Tarsus longer than in Arctic Tern (see Forster's and Roseate terns).

Field Marks. Very similar in all plumages to Arctic Tern and often very difficult to distinguish. Bill of summer adults more orange-red and usually tipped with dusky (Arctic has blood-red bill usually with no dusky tip); under parts less greyish, face whiter. Immatures extremely difficult to distinguish. When at rest the longer legs of both adult and immature Common Tern compared with those of Arctic Tern are often noticeable (see *also* Forster's and Roseate terns). *Voice*: A harsh *ke-ar-r-r*; also *kit, kit*.

Habitat. For nesting, open edges of sandy and gravelly beaches, flat areas on islands frequently near edges of sparse low vegetation, thus usually different from nesting habitat of Forster's Tern, although Common Tern occasionally nests in a similar marshy situation, even on muskrat houses. Forages over inshore coastal waters and interior lakes and larger rivers.

Nesting. Usually colonial, sometimes single pairs; often with other terns. Nest a shallow depression in sand, gravel, turf, or rock, variously lined with grass, twigs, pebbles, or bits of shell. *Eggs*, usuallly 3, often 2 or 4; variable, pale buff to brown or olive, spotted and blotched with darker browns and some purplish-grey. Incubation (by both sexes) 21 to 30, average 25.7, days (O.L. Austin, Jr.).

Range. Breeds widely in the Northern Hemisphere of both the New and Old Worlds. In North America, from Alberta east to Newfoundland and south to northeastern Montana, South Dakota, southern Michigan, northern Ohio, northern New York, and on the Atlantic Coast to North Carolina; also southeastern Texas and Florida. Does not breed on the Pacific Coast of North America. Winters from southern Baja California and South Carolina south to the Straits of Magellan and in the Old World south to southern Africa.

Subspecies. *Sterna hirundo hirundo* Linnaeus is the only subspecies known in North America.

Arctic Tern

Sterne arctique
Sterna paradisaea Pontoppidan
Total length: 35.5 to 43 cm
Plate 39

Breeding Distribution of Arctic Tern

Range in Canada. Breeds from northern Yukon (Herschel Island and arctic coast); northern Mackenzie (Mackenzie Delta, Baillie Island); Banks Island (Sachs Harbour); Melville Island; Lougheed Island; Bathurst Island; and northern Ellesmere Island (Ravine Bay); south through Yukon to northern British Columbia (Atlin, Chilkat Pass; probably Dease Lake); southern Mackenzie, (Nahanni National Park, Great Slave Lake); northwestern Saskatchewan (Lake Athabasca); southern Keewatin (Nueltin Lake); northern Manitoba (Churchill); northern Ontario (Cape Henrietta Maria, Hawley and Kinoje lakes); James Bay (Gasket Shoal); central and southeastern Quebec (James Bay coast, Boundary Lake, near Schefferville; north shore of the Gulf of St. Lawrence, Madeleine Islands); Labrador (coast; also interior: Attikamagen Lake); Newfoundland; and the coast of New Brunswick; Nova Scotia (Cape Breton Island, Sable Island, Mud Island); and Prince Edward Island. Occurs in summer and perhaps breeds in northeastern Alberta (Athabasca Lake).

In spring migration (late May to mid-June) varying numbers migrate up the upper St. Lawrence River and take a shortcut overland route to James Bay over extreme southwestern Quebec and southeastern Ontario (Ottawa), occasionally straying west to Bronte.

Postbreeding movements are to the Atlantic and Pacific oceans. Transient in southern British Columbia (coast and interior) and very rarely in central Alberta (Lac la Nonne).

Very similar to Common Tern but legs (tarsi) shorter; bill of breeding adults of a deeper red and without (usually) a dusky tip; under parts more distinctly grey, this extending farther up on lower face. Adults in winter plumage have forehead and front of crown whitish, under parts white, blackish bill and feet. Autumn immatures have shorter tarsi than Common Tern, but the plumage is very similar.

Measurements. *Adult male*: wing, 251.7–272.5 (264.2); tail, 147.3–197 (170.1); exposed culmen, 29.8–33.9 (31.5); tarsus, 15–16.7 (15.8). *Adult female*: wing, 251.5–273 (261) mm.

Field Marks. Very difficult to distinguish from Common Tern except under favourable conditions. Bill of Arctic is of darker blood-red, usually lacks dusky tip; lower face slightly more greyish. Autumn adults and immatures of the two usually are not separable. When on land or perched, however, the shorter legs of the Arctic are noticeable to those familiar with the two species. Roseate Tern in breeding plumage has a mostly black bill, white under parts (instead of distinctly grey), and longer tail and legs.

Habitat. For nesting, the vicinity of either salt or fresh water, on sandpits, dunes, deltas, sand and gravel beaches, rocky shores and islands, marshy tundra. Forages over either salt or fresh water. Outside nesting season it is marine.

Nesting. In colonies, sometimes single pairs; sometimes with other species. Nest, a depression in ground, moss, or rock, frequently unlined but sometimes lined with various amounts of grass. *Eggs*, usually 2 or 3; very similar to those of the Common Tern. Incubation 21 to 22 days (R. Dircksen), by both sexes; 20 to 21 days (D.F. Parmelee).

Range. Circumpolar, breeding in the Arctic and Subarctic of both the New and Old Worlds; in North America: Alaska, northern Canada, and Greenland, south on the Atlantic Coast to Massachusetts. Eastern North American populations in migration cross the north Atlantic and pass along the west coast of Europe and Africa. Winters in the oceans of the southern Hemisphere.

Remarks. The Arctic Tern makes one of the longest and most remarkable of all migratory journeys. Those that nest in eastern Canada start their autumn migration by launching out across the vast Atlantic Ocean. Once on the other side, they travel southward along the west coasts of Europe and Africa and thus reach their winter range in waters off South Africa and southward to the Antarctic Circle.

Probably this tern sees more daylight during its lifetime than any other animal. It summers in the North while up to 24 hours of daylight daily prevail and "winters" in the South where the periods of daylight greatly exceed the hours of darkness.

Bird banding has dispelled most of the secrets surrounding the long migrations of the Arctic Tern. One banded on 22 July 1927, in Labrador, was recovered near La Rochelle, France, on 1 October of the same year. Another banded in Labrador on 23 July 1928, was retaken in Natal, South Africa, on 14 November 1928. Additional similar recoveries of banded birds have revealed the major details of these great journeys. Banding also has provided information on the longevity of this tern. One banded as a flightless young in Norway died 27 years later in the same tern colony in which it was raised.

Forster's Tern

Sterne de Forster
Sterna forsteri Nuttall
Total length (including long tail):
35.5 to 38 cm
Plate 39

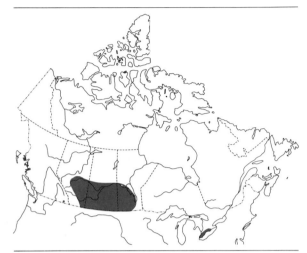

Breeding Distribution of Forster's Tern

Range in Canada. Breeds in southeastern British Columbia (very locally: Creston); south-central and southeastern Alberta (Buffalo and Driedmeat lakes, Wabamun Lake; probably Many Island Lake); southern Saskatchewan (Waterhen Lake, near Kinistino; Sled Lake, Regina); southern Manitoba (Lakes Winnipeg, Winnipegosis, and Manitoba, Shoal Lake; north to Moose and Cedar lakes); and locally southern Ontario (Rondeau, Long Point, formerly Lake St. Clair).

Scarce transient in southern Quebec (various sight records for Île-du-Moine and the Montréal region). Casual transient in most of British Columbia (Okanagan Lake, 24 June 1928) and Nova Scotia (near Dartmouth, 4 September 1924; also sight records).

Dark inner web (instead of outer web) of outermost tail feathers distinguishes it in all plumages from other similar terns.

Measurements. *Adult male*: wing, 250–265.5 (257.3); tail, 146–180.5 (169.1); exposed culmen, 36.5–41.8 (39.4); tarsus, 21.2–25.2 (24). *Adult female*: wing, 253–260 (256.5) mm.

Field Marks. Similar to Common Tern but adults in breeding plumage with tail greyish (instead of white); upper side of primaries paler, especially near their bases, than wing coverts; breast and belly white instead of slightly greyish; and bill more yellowish-orange. Adults in winter plumage and in first autumn are easily recognized by a well-defined but more limited dark bar extending from the eye across the ear *but not around back of head*. Voice also is somewhat different (more nasal) from other similar terns.

Habitat. Marshes (in Canada only inland), frequently those bordering lakes.

Nesting. On floating mats of aquatic vegetation, muskrat houses, or islets. *Eggs*, 2 to 4 (usually 3); buff to olive buff, marked with small spots and less often blotches of dark brown, and some purplish-grey. Incubation 23 to 25 days, probably by both sexes.

Range. Breeds from the Prairie Provinces of Canada south through eastern parts of Washington and Oregon to south-central California, central Idaho, northern Utah, southeastern Wyoming, eastern Colorado, eastern South Dakota, central Iowa, and southeastern Wisconsin; also from southeastern Maryland and eastern Virginia to southern Louisiana, and southeastern Texas. Winters from central California to Guatemala and from Virginia to northern Florida and along the Gulf of Mexico from western Florida to Mexico.

Least Tern

Petite Sterne
Sterna antillarum (Lesson)
Total length: 22 to 25 cm

Figure 67
Head of Least Tern (adult in breeding plumage)

Status in Canada. Accidental in Nova Scotia (specimens: Barrington, 28 August 1924; Grand Desert, 13 August 1970; and Alton, no data; photo record: Seal Island, early September 1983); and New Brunswick (a male found dead in Saint John on 11 April 1984). Sight records for Kent Island and Point Lepreau. For Quebec there is an uncertain mention by C.E. Dionne (1906) of a specimen thought to have been killed near Québec many years ago. There are sight records only for Ontario (Erie Beach, 26 June 1958), Saskatchewan (Regina, 26 May 1957), and New Brunswick (Kent Island; Point Lepreau).

A tiny tern similar in general coloration to the much larger Common Tern, but in breeding plumage bill and legs are orange-yellow, and the black cap has a large white forehead patch, leaving only a narrow black bar between eye and base of bill (Figure 67). In any plumage diminutive size distinguishes it from other terns.

Measurements. *Adult male*: wing, 163–178 (168.1); tail, 70–93 (81.2); exposed culmen, 26–31 (28.8); tarsus, 14–15.5 (14.5). *Adult female*: wing, 160–167 (162.9) mm (Ridgway).

Subspecies. Nova Scotia specimens are referable to *Sterna antillarum antillarum* (Lesson) but probably other races are involved in the inland records.

Bridled Tern

Sterne à collier
Sterna anaethetus Scopoli
Total length: 35.5 to 39 cm

a

b

Figure 68
Head of
a) Sooty Tern
b) Bridled Tern

Status in Canada. Accidental in Newfoundland: An immature now in the Museum of Comparative Zoology at Harvard College was taken at Custlett on 21 January 1891. On 6 and 7 September 1955, Tuck studied at close range at Fermeuse, Newfoundland, another immature which he identified as this species. The Newfoundland specimen of this tropical and subtropical species has been referred to the subspecies *S. a. recognita* (Mathews).

Adults resemble Sooty Tern but back more greyish brown, crown black and separated from the dark back by *whitish hind-neck*; white of forehead less extensive but white extension backward over eye reaching well past eye (Figure 68). Young resemble adults, but head mainly grey or dusky mottled brown, feathers of upper parts with pale edges. The under parts are greyish white (brown in young Sooty Tern).

Sooty Tern

Sterne fuligineuse
Sterna fuscata Linnaeus
Total length: 38 to 43 cm

Status in Canada. Accidental visitor from the tropics and subtropics where widely distributed in the world. Nova Scotia: specimen found dead near Wolfville, 28 August 1924, after a hurricane. Also sight record of one at Three Fathom Harbour, 21 October 1968, after Hurricane Gladys. The specimen mentioned above was not seen by the writer but probably is referable to the subspecies *S. f. fuscata* Linnaeus.

Contrasting black upper parts and white under parts are entirely unlike those of any tern of regular occurrence in Canada (see Black Tern, Black Skimmer, and Bridled Tern). Tail well forked. Forehead (and narrow extension back to top of eye) and under parts white; crown, hind-neck, broad line eye to bill, and rest of upper parts black (except outermost tail feathers *mostly* grey to whitish); bill and legs black. Young are brown above and slightly paler below; feathers of back, tipped white.

White-winged Tern

Guifette leucoptère
Chlidonias leucopterus (Temminck)
Total length: 23 to 25 cm
Figure 69

a   b

Figure 69
a) Black Tern
b) White-winged Tern

Summer adults are similar to Black Tern but "shoulders" (lesser wing coverts), upper tail coverts, and tail *white*; the wing linings mostly black. Winter adults and immature birds have *white upper tail coverts* and lack brown patches on sides of breast. In the hand the shorter bill of the White-winged is evident and tail of adult females is seen to be variously marked with greys.

    Field Marks. See above.

    Habitat. Similar to Black Tern.

    Range. *Palaearctic*. Breeds in southeastern Europe and central Asia south to Turkestan and northern Mongolia. Winters in Africa, southern Asia, and the Malay Archipelago to Australia.

Status in Canada. Accidental in New Brunswick. One, carefully observed by several competent observers, at Grand Point on Grand Lake, Queen's County, New Brunswick, from 27 to 30 July 1968. An adult female, collected on 10 July 1971, near Portobello Creek, Sunbury County, New Brunswick, by Peter Pearce, is in the National Museum of Natural Sciences. One, presumably the same individual, was earlier seen on 23 May 1971, at nearby McGowans Corner. On 19 August 1976, one was observed at Miscou Island, New Brunswick.

Black Tern

Guifette noire
Chlidonias niger (Linnaeus)
Total length: 23 to 26.5 cm
Plate 39

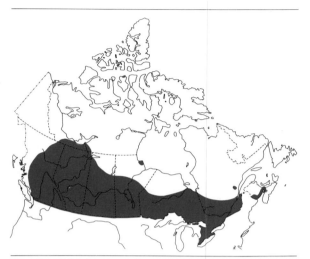

Breeding Distribution of Black Tern

Range in Canada. Summer resident, commonest in the Prairie Provinces. Breeds in southwestern Mackenzie (Buffalo Lake, probably Nahanni National Park and Slave River Delta); interior-central and southern British Columbia (Nukko Creek; Swan Lake, Peace River; near Fort Nelson, Pitt Lake, Kleena Kleene, Cranbrook); Alberta; Saskatchewan (north to Lake Athabasca, Lac la Ronge Provincial Park); Manitoba (north regularly to The Pas and Pikwitonei Lake; also locally near Churchill); Ontario (north to Sandy Lake; near Fort Albany; perhaps Lake Abitibi); southwestern Quebec (Île aux Noix, Lakes Saint-Pierre and Saint-Louis, Lake Trois Saumons, probably Lake Abitibi and Lake Saint-Jean); southern New Brunswick (very locally: Timber Lake, Sackville); and Nova Scotia (very locally: Missaguash Bog).

Rare transient (mainly in autumn) in Prince Edward Island (Tignish); Madeleine Islands; and Nova Scotia (Sable Island, Cape Sable Island, Barrington Passage, Devils Island, Crescent Beach). Sight records for Newfoundland.

A small dark tern with slightly forked tail. Colour and small size are diagnostic.

Measurements. *Adult male*: wing, 195.5–214.5 (207.5); tail, 73–83.9 (79.9); exposed culmen, 26.7–29.5 (27.9); tarsus, 15.3–17 (16.5). *Adult female*: wing, 193.3–215 (205.7) mm.

Field Marks. Adults in breeding plumage, with all-black head, neck, and under body (except white under tail coverts) and with dark-slate mantle, rump, and tail, are easily identified. Adults in winter plumage and young are mainly white below but have the characteristic slaty mantle and tail, and head markings shown in Plate 39. They are darker above than other terns of regular occurrence in Canada and have the tail uniformly dark-grey.

Habitat. In Canada, mainly interior watery marshes, lakes, ponds, sloughs, and rivers in either treeless or wooded country.

Nesting. Nest, a hollow on rafts or mats of marsh vegetation floating in shallow water of lakes or marshes, sometimes on muskrat houses or on solid ground. *Eggs*, usually 2 or 3; buffy or olive, marked (usually heavily) with browns or blackish brown. Incubation 21 to 22 days (R.E. Goodwin), by both sexes.

Range. Breeds widely in the Northern Hemisphere of both the New and Old Worlds. In North America from much of interior-southern Canada south to south-central California, northern Nevada, Colorado, Nebraska, Kentucky, Pennsylvania, western New York, and Maine. Winters coastally from Panama to Peru and to Surinam.

Subspecies. *Chlidonias niger surinamensis* (Gmelin).

Remarks. This graceful inhabitant of inland lakes and marshes, while in Canada, feeds on grasshoppers, dragonflies, beetles, flies, moths, and other insects, most of which it catches on the wing.

Subfamily **Rynchopinae:** Skimmers

Large, long-winged tern-like birds of tropical and subtropical coasts, with webbed front toes and a strange, thin, knifelike, laterally compressed bill, the lower mandible much longer than the upper, comprise this family (Figure 70).

Black Skimmer

Bec-en-ciseaux noir
Rynchops niger Linnaeus
Total length: 40.5 to 51 cm
Figure 70

Unmistakable. A long-winged bird of Atlantic coasts with peculiar thin knifelike bill, the lower mandible of which extends far beyond the upper one. Forehead, sides of head below eye, and under parts white. Rest of head, hind-neck, back, and upper side of wings black. Tips of secondaries and inner primaries white, giving a conspicuous white hind-edge to wing. Tail white mixed with brown, forked. Basal half of bill red, terminal half black.

Range. Breeds along the Atlantic and Gulf of Mexico coasts from Massachusetts to Yucatan; northern and eastern South America; and on the Pacific Coast from northern Mexico to southern South America.

Subspecies. *Rynchops niger niger* Linnaeus.

Figure 70
Black Skimmer

Status in Canada. Casual in Nova Scotia (Cole Harbour, Cape Sable, August 1924, large numbers, as a result of a hurricane; again in 1968, numbers varying from singles to about 200, 22 October to 1 November on the south shore after a hurricane) and New Brunswick (Grand Manan: August 1879, large groups; also three taken there in October 1924. Kent Island: 50 counted, 15 September 1944). Accidental in Newfoundland (between 30 September and 10 October 1958, numbers appeared near Burgeo, St. Alban's, Boxey, Brigus Junction, Milltown, Placentia, Heart's Content, Happy Adventure, Gaultois, and other localities); southwestern Quebec (Lake Saint-Pierre: specimen, 26 October 1938); and Ontario (photo record: one at Whitby Harbour, November 1977; sight record near Point Pelee, 6 July 1978 and Erieau, 14 September 1981). Sight record only for Prince Edward Island (three at Wood Island, 19 August 1967). Occurrences in Canada usually a result of hurricanes.

Family **Alcidae**:
Auks, Murres, and Puffins

Number of Species in Canada: 17

Birds of this family frequent salt water and come ashore only to breed. They are expert swimmers and divers. All species are short-necked and stout-bodied, and most are mainly black and white. The short narrow wings beat very rapidly in flight. Legs are short and are set far back near the end of the body, thus accounting for an upright posture on land; hind toe absent or vestigial, front toes fully webbed. The bill is short but highly variable in shape. Small fishes and marine invertebrates are the staple foods.

Dovekie

Mergule nain
Alle alle (Linnaeus)
Total length: 19 to 23 cm
Plate 40

Range in Canada. Not known to breed in Canada, although perhaps might do so (has been found ashore in suitable habitat on Hans Island near Colin Archer Fiord). Occurs commonly as a migrant, winter resident, or summer non-breeder along the coasts of Baffin Bay and Davis Strait; Jones Sound, Lancaster Sound, Hudson Strait, and northern Hudson Bay; rarely west to Melville Island, western Victoria Island (Holman region), and northeastern Mackenzie (Perry River), and north to northern Ellesmere Island (Parr Inlet) and Axel Heiberg Island (Smith Fiord). Winters in northern Hudson Bay and Hudson Strait (probably also farther north) and southward off the coast of Labrador, southeastern Quebec, Newfoundland, and the Maritimes. Accidental inland, sometimes in large numbers, because of storms, very rarely west to the Great Lakes and Manitoba (Warren Landing).

A diminutive sea diver of eastern waters with stubby bill; short thick neck; black-and-white coloration. Small size readily distinguishes it from other eastern Canadian sea divers. In winter plumage it somewhat resembles some West Coast species but does not normally come into contact with them (see Ancient Murrelet, and Cassin's and Least auklets).

Measurements *(A. a. alle). Adult male*: wing, 111–116.5 (114.3); tail, 31.3–37.5 (34.3); exposed culmen, 12.9–16 (14.3); tarsus, 19.5–21.3 (20.5). *Adult female*: wing, 108–114 (112) mm.

Field Marks. (Small size, stubby (approximately 1 cm) bill, and markings distinguish it from our other eastern sea divers.

Habitat. Marine. In winter offshore salt water, edges of pack-ice, openings in drift-ice. Occasionally numbers are storm-blown inland or to inshore waters. For nesting (not known in Canada) talus of rocky cliffs near the sea.

Nesting. (Unknown in Canada but should be looked for in the eastern Arctic near Greenland.) In colonies, often immense. The single egg is laid on a rock crevice or among rock rubble of talus of arctic cliffs near the sea. *Egg*, one, is pale bluish, usually unmarked. Incubation period said to be 24 days.

Range. Breeds from northern Greenland, Jan Mayen, Spitsbergen, Novaya Zemlya, and Franz Josef Land south to southern Greenland, Iceland, and Bear Island. Winters from within the breeding range in suitable open water south to New Jersey and to the Azores, Canary Islands, France, and the Baltic Sea; irregularly farther south.

Subspecies. *Alle alle alle* (Linnaeus).

Common Murre

(Atlantic or California Murre)

Marmette de Troïl
Uria aalge (Pontoppidan)
Total length: 42 to 45.5 cm
Plate 40

a   b

Figure 71
Field marks of
a) Thick-billed Murre
b) Common Murre

Breeding Distribution of Common Murre

Range in Canada. Breeds on Atlantic and
Pacific coasts: British Columbia (Cleland,
Sartine, Triangle islands); Labrador (locally
north to Nunarsuk Island); southeastern
Quebec (north shore of the Gulf of St.
Lawrence: Fog Island to Brador Bay; Anticosti
Island, Bonaventure Island, Rochers aux
Oiseaux); Newfoundland (Funk, Baccalieu,
Green islands; Cape St. Mary's); Nova Scotia
(formerly at least: Bird Islands); and southern
New Brunswick (Machias Seal Island).

Winters on offshore waters from northern
Newfoundland southward; also along the coast
of British Columbia. Casual in inland Quebec
(Lake Saint-Jean).

Bill long (for an alcid), rather slender, pointed, all black. Breeding
plumage as illustrated, but in Atlantic populations some individuals
have a white eye-ring and a white line extending backwards from it.
These variants were once thought to indicate a distinct species, and it
was named "Ringed Murre," *Uria ringvia*. Bill characters, size, and
markings distinguish the Common Murre from most other members of
the family. In breeding plumage, however, it is very similar to the
Thick-billed Murre, from which it differs in its more slender, longer bill
and in lacking a bare pale line (bluish white in life) along the cutting
edge of the upper mandible near the gape. The "Ringed Murre" variation has no counterpart in the Thick-billed Murre. Winter adults and
immatures of the two species of murres are easily distinguished (see
Field Marks).

Measurements *(U. a. aalge). Adult male*: wing, 192–200 (196.5);
tail, 39.3–50.6 (45.4); exposed culmen, 40.8–43.5 (42.3); tarsus,
37.2–38.7 (38.1). *Adult female*: wing, 194.5–204 (199.9) mm.

Field Marks. The relatively long, slender, pointed bill as well as
the size and the markings distinguish it from most species of the family.
In breeding plumage, it is very similar to the Thick-billed Murre, from
which it differs by having the white of the breast meet the black of the
fore-neck in a less distinct peak (in the Thick-billed Murre the white on
breast forms a distinct peak at the junction with the black of the fore-
neck: Figure 71), the longer slenderer bill, and the lack of a pale line
along cutting edge of upper mandible near gape. Adults and immatures
in winter plumage have a spur of dark colour extending backwards from
the eye region, quite different from the Thick-billed.

Habitat. Strictly marine. In winter, offshore coastal waters
(between 8 km from shore and the edge of the continental shelf). In
breeding season, the vicinity of sea cliffs or rocky islands.

Nesting. In colonies, sometimes immense, often with other species.
Egg is laid on bare rock of cliff ledge or rocky island. *Egg*, one only;
pear-shaped, pale greenish to bluish, variously spotted, blotched, and
scrawled with browns or black. Incubation, by both sexes, period variable 28 to 35 days (various authors), but probably rarely less than
30 days.

Range. Breeds along coasts and islands of the North Pacific and
North Atlantic from Bering Strait south to northern Japan (perhaps
eastern Korea) and to central California; and from western Greenland,
Iceland, Bear Island, and Novaya Zemlya south to Nova Scotia and to
northern France and Portugal.

Subspecies. (1) *Uria aalge aalge* (Pontoppidan) is the subspecies of
the Atlantic coast. (2) *U. a. inornata* Salomonsen is the only subspecies
known to occur in British Columbia.

Thick-billed Murre

(Brünnich's Murre)

Marmette de Brünnich
Uria lomvia (Linnaeus)
Total length: 43 to 48 cm
Plate 40

Breeding Distribution of Thick-billed Murre

Range in Canada. Breeds in northwest Mackenzie (locally: Cape Parry); and in the eastern
Arctic (Coburg, southeast Cornwallis, Prince
Leopold, and Bylot islands, eastern Baffin
Island, Coats Island, Digges Sound, and Akpatok Island); the Labrador coast, Newfoundland, Madeleine Islands (Rochers aux Oiseaux);
and Saint-Marie Islands on outer north shore
of Gulf of St. Lawrence. Recently a small
breeding colony was discovered in coastal
British Columbia (Triangle Island). Recorded
without evidence of breeding north to Ellesmere
Island (Eureka).

Winters in offshore waters within the breeding range (where open water permits) and
southward, commonly on the Grand Banks,
and in smaller numbers off Nova Scotia, New
Brunswick, and Prince Edward Island. Casual,
usually in late autumn, sometimes in numbers,
in southern Ontario and southwestern Quebec
(upper St. Lawrence, Great Lakes, Ottawa
River); recorded once in interior southern
Keewatin (Edehon Lake). Rare migrant in
northern Yukon (Herschel Island). Casual on
coastal British Columbia (Ladner).

Similar to Common Murre but bill heavier and plumage markings
somewhat different (see preceding species and Field Marks below).

Measurements *(U. l. lomvia). Adult male*: wing, 194.9–215 (207.6);
tail, 44.5–53 (48.9); exposed culmen, 30.3–37.2 (33.7); tarsus, 34.7–37.8
(35.6). *Adult female*: wing, 195–212.5 (204.8) mm.

Field Marks. Very similar to Common Murre, differing from it as
follows (breeding plumage): presence of a pale line along the cutting
edge of the upper mandible near the gape and by a more acute-angled
peak of white from the breast into the dark fore-neck. Adult in winter
plumage and immature: black of crown extends down uniformly over
the ear region (in Common Murre the ear region, if whitish, with a dark
spur extending back across it from the eye). Although in all seasons the
bill is thicker and shorter, this is often very difficult to discern and is
not always a reliable criterion in immature birds.

Habitat. Marine. In breeding season, sea cliffs and nearby cold
turbulent water. In winter, offshore waters. Has slightly less tolerance
for warmish waters than the Common Murre.

Nesting. In colonies, often immense, frequently with other birds.
No nest, the egg being laid on bare rock of cliff ledge or on flat top.
Eggs one only; usually pear-shaped, extremely variable in colour but
most often bluish green irregularly spotted, scrawled, and blotched with
browns, sometimes clouded with lilac. Incubation period variable, 30 to
35 days (L.M. Tuck), by both sexes.

Range. Breeds on islands and coasts in the Arctic of North Amer-
ica and Eurasia and south to the Commander, Aleutian, and Kodiak
islands, the Gulf of St. Lawrence, southern Greenland, Iceland, and Jan
Mayen; also in Spitsbergen, Bear Island, Franz Josef Land, Novaya
Zemlya, Murmansk coast of northern Russia, Severnaya Zemlya, New
Siberian Islands, and Wrangel Island. Winters on salt water within
much of the breeding range and somewhat south of it, in North
America south to southeastern Alaska and Delaware.

Subspecies. (1) *Uria lomvia lomvia* (Linnaeus) is the subspecies
inhabiting the eastern Arctic and the Atlantic Coast. Birds taken in the
southern interior of Ontario and southwestern Quebec are of that race.
(2) *U. l. arra* (Pallas) is the only race known to visit the coast of British
Columbia and the coast of Yukon. Probably the population breeding on
Cape Parry, Mackenzie District, is referable to it (no specimens
available).

Razorbill

(Razor-billed Auk)

Petit Pingouin
Alca torda Linnaeus
Total length: 40 to 47 cm
Plate 40

Breeding Distribution of Razorbill

Range in Canada. Atlantic coasts and islands. Breeds in extreme southeastern Baffin Island (Harper Islands south of Loks Land— V.G. Wynne-Edwards, in litt.); Digges Island, N.W.T., off northwestern Quebec; Labrador coast, southeastern Quebec (north shore of the Gulf of St. Lawrence, Pèlerin Islands and also on island near Saint-Jean-Port-Joli on lower St. Lawrence River, Anticosti Island, Bonaventure Island, Madeleine Islands); Newfoundland; northeastern Nova Scotia (Ciboux and Hertford islands); and southern New Brunswick (Yellow Ledge, south of Grand Manan; Machias Seal Island).

Winters mostly in offshore waters from southern Labrador and Newfoundland southward. Accidental in southern Ontario (Toronto, Hamilton, Upper Rideau Lakes) and southwestern Quebec (Lake Saint-Louis, Lake Saint-François).

Bill laterally compressed (deep and thin), grooved with white line (absent in young) across it; tail pointed, central tail feathers somewhat elongated. Winter plumage similar to breeding plumage, but throat and sides of neck are white, and the white line from eye to base of bill is obscure or lacking, although the one crossing the bill remains. Young in first autumn are similar to winter adults, but bill is smaller, shallower, without grooves or a white line; thus it somewhat resembles winter murres, but in the hand the more laterally compressed bill and pointed tail distinguish the Razorbill.

Measurements *(A. t. torda). Adult male*: wing, 186.2–204 (196.4); tail, 73.9–89 (81.7); exposed culmen, 32–37.4 (34.8); tarsus, 31.8–35.5 (33.5). *Adult female*: wing, 196–201 (197.9) mm.

Field Marks. A black-and-white sea diver the size of a small duck but with deep, laterally compressed bill entirely different from that of any duck. Most likely to be confused with the murres, but the Razorbill's much deeper bill (with strongly arched culmen) with white line across it, is very different from the slender, pointed, unmarked bill of murres. In breeding plumage, the Razorbill has a narrow white line from eye to base of bill. Autumn immatures, with small unmarked black bill, are more difficult to distinguish from winter Thick-billed Murres, but usually the deeper, more rounded bill profile is evident. Winter Common Murres are readily separable also by their well-defined dark spur extending backward from the eye. Young Atlantic Puffins have enough of the characteristic puffin face-pattern to identify them; also they are smaller, chunkier, and lack white tips to the secondaries.

Habitat. Marine. In winter, mostly offshore waters of the ocean. In nesting season, sea cliffs on coasts or islands, boulder-strewn shores near salt water.

Nesting. In colonies, sometimes with murres, on sea cliffs or among boulders and rocks. No nest is constructed, the egg being laid in natural crevices, holes, or under rocks or overhangs. *Eggs*, usually one only; strongly tapered and elongated, buffy to greenish white, spotted and blotched with browns or blacks. Incubation, by both sexes, 33 to 36 days (Keighley and Lockley); averages 36 days (W.J. Plumb).

Range. Breeds along coasts from western Greenland, Iceland, Norway, and northern Russia, south to Maine, northern France, and southern Finland. In winter ranges south to South Carolina (rarely) and the Canary Islands.

Subspecies. *Alca torda torda* Linnaeus.

Great Auk

Grand Pingouin
Pinguinus impennis (Linnaeus)
Total length: 71 to 76 cm
Figure 72

Figure 72
Great Auk

Range in Canada. Extinct. Formerly bred in Newfoundland (Funk Island; possibly elsewhere) and perhaps also on the Madeleine Islands (Rochers aux Oiseaux), Quebec. Its former occurrence in southern New Brunswick (shores of the Bay of Fundy, Nantucket Island), Nova Scotia (Port Joli, St. Margarets Bay, Mahone Bay), and Labrador (Avayalik Island) is indicated by bones found in Indian shell heaps, but evidence of breeding is lacking. The supposed reference in the diaries of Champlain to breeding on Mud Island, Nova Scotia, seems to be based on erroneous translation from the French and doubtless refers to the Gannet. It probably wintered more or less commonly in waters off the East Coast and in numbers on the Grand Banks of Newfoundland.

A big auk with large, laterally compressed, much-grooved bill, rudimentary wings too small for flight. Upper parts black, becoming dark brown on sides of head and neck and on throat. Large white patch in front of eye. Secondaries tipped white. Under parts (except head and neck) white. Bill black with whitish grooves.

Measurements. *Adult male*: wing, about 146; tail, about 76; exposed culmen, 80–89; tarsus, 42.16 mm (Ridgway).

Habitat. Coastal waters of the north Atlantic, nesting on rocky coasts and islands.

Nesting. In large colonies on rocky islands and coasts. The single *egg* was laid on bare rock. It was pale buff with brown, black, or grey scrawls and blotches, and about 12.6 cm long.

Range. Extinct. Last definite record on 3 June 1844, on Eldey Rock off Iceland. Bred along coasts on both sides of the north Atlantic: eastern Canada, Iceland, the outer Hebrides (St. Kilda); probably the Orkneys; possibly Greenland, the Faeroe Islands, and Lundy. Wintered on salt water from southern Greenland south to Florida and southern Spain.

Black Guillemot

Guillemot à miroir
Cepphus grylle (Linnaeus)
Total length: 30.5 to 35.5 cm
Plate 40

Breeding Distribution of Black Guillemot

Range in Canada. Breeds on suitable coasts and islands near the sea from northern Elles-mere Island south through Somerset (Port Leopold), Devon, and Bylot islands, eastern and southern Baffin Island, Melville Peninsula, Southampton Island, Hudson and James bays, Hudson Strait, Ungava Bay, Labrador, south-ern Quebec (north shore of Gulf of St. Lawrence, St. Lawrence River west at least to Saguenay River and Pèlerin Islands, Anticosti and Madeleine islands, Gaspé Peninsula), New-foundland, New Brunswick, Prince Edward Island, and Nova Scotia; also in northern Yukon (Herschel Island). Summer sight records of single birds: Banks Island, western Victoria Island (Holman), and Adelaide Peninsula, N.W.T.

Winters off the breeding places, as open water permits, north at least to Igloolik, Baffin Bay, and Davis Strait, and southward along the entire Atlantic Coast of Canada; also near Southampton Island, and in Hudson Bay and Hudson Strait. Accidental in interior Mackenzie (Fort Good Hope), southern Manitoba (Morris 12 November 1966), and southern Ontario (Hamilton, Toronto; sight record for Kingston).

Bill rather long, straight, pointed, black in colour. *Breeding plumage*: All black except large white wing patch and white under wing coverts and red legs. *Winter adults*: Wings and tail as in breeding plumage; head, neck, and under parts mainly white, more or less mixed with black; crown and back black variously mixed with white. *Young*: Resemble winter adults but are less extensively whitish; white wing patch mottled with blackish. Its large white wing patches differ from any other alcid of eastern Canada but are very much like those of the Pigeon Guillemot of the West Coast (see Pigeon Guillemot).

Measurements *(C. g. ultimus)*. *Adult male*: wing, 155.2–164.1 (160.7); tail, 46–51 (49.3); exposed culmen, 24–30 (27.6); tarsus, 30–33 (31.5). *Adult female*: wing, 154.0–170.2 (158.8) mm.

Field Marks. A teal-sized sea-diver with slender pointed bill and large white wing patch. Not likely to be confused with any other species of the Atlantic Coast or eastern Arctic. The White-winged Scoter is larger with an entirely different bill. The Pigeon Guillemot of coastal British Columbia is very similar, but the Black Guillemot is not known to have occurred in British Columbia. *Voice*: Vague, weak, shrill whistles. Usually a silent bird.

Habitat. Marine (also rarely brackish water). In nesting season, the rocky coasts where cliffs, talus slopes, fractured rocks, and rock rubble provide nesting places. In winter, offshore waters; edges and leads of pack-ice; also to some extent, where open water permits, inshore waters. Forages in waters of various depths.

Nesting. Nests in colonies, frequently small, or in single pairs, in crevices and crannies of talus slopes and rock rubble, in cliff faces, even in soft red clay bluffs (the birds perhaps excavating holes themselves), often at no great height above high tides, but also up to considerable height on cliffs. *Eggs*, usually 2, sometimes 1; white to greenish or buffy, spotted and blotched, often handsomely, with various browns and purplish grey. Incubation 27 to 33 days, usually 28 (H.E. Winn), by both sexes.

Range. Almost circumpolar. Breeds in the Arctic of both the New and Old Worlds (but very locally in western arctic Canada) south to northern Alaska (probably), James Bay, Maine, southern Greenland, Iceland, Scotland, southern Scandinavia, and northern Siberia. Slightly farther south in winter.

Subspecies. *Cepphus grylle atlantis* Salomonsen breeds from south-ern Labrador (where it intergrades with the following subspecies), the Gulf of St. Lawrence, and Newfoundland southward. *C. g. ultimus* Salomonsen occupies the remainder of the known breeding range in Canada from the high Arctic south to James Bay and northern Labrador. *C. g. mandtii* (Mandt) has recently been found breeding in northern Yukon (Herschel Island).

Pigeon Guillemot

Guillemot du Pacifique
Cepphus columba Pallas
Total length: 32 to 37 cm
Plate 40

Breeding Distribution of Pigeon Guillemot

Range in Canada. Breeds commonly on the coast of British Columbia wherever suitable conditions are found. Winters off the breeding grounds.

A West Coast species very similar to the Black Guillemot of the Canadian Arctic and the Atlantic Coast, differing by (1) brownish-grey under wing coverts (but sometimes mixed with considerable white), (2) a black bar or spur cutting part way across the white patch (extent of white often greatly reduced) on upper side of wing, and (3) somewhat larger size.

Measurements *(C. c. columba). Adult male*: wing, 167–180.9 (174.1); tail, 46.5–53.2 (49.1); exposed culmen, 31–34.9 (31.7); tarsus, 33.2–36.7 (35.1). *Adult female*: wing, 166.8–175 (171.7) mm.

Field Marks. Pacific Coast. Adults are readily distinguishable from all but the Black Guillemot, which is not known to visit the Pacific Coast. The black bar part way across white wing patch of adults (unreliable in immatures) and the brownish under wing coverts, when they can be seen, would distinguish the Pigeon Guillemot. In immatures the white wing patch is often heavily obscured, and the dark of the under wing coverts is more or less mixed with white.

Habitat and Nesting. Similar to Black Guillemot. Birds sometimes excavate own burrows. Incubation said to be 30 days (Drent and Guiguet). *Eggs*, usually 2; slightly larger and more heavily marked than in Black Guillemot.

Range. North Pacific. Breeds from the Chukotski Peninsula, islands in Bering Sea (except the Pribilofs), and the Aleutian Islands south to the Kurile Islands and California (Santa Barbara Islands).

Subspecies. *Cepphus columba columba* Pallas is the breeding and common permanent resident of coastal British Columbia. Dickinson (1953) has assigned a specimen from Lund, British Columbia, to *C. c. kaiurka* Portenko, which breeds in the western Aleutian Islands.

Marbled Murrelet

Alque marbrée
Brachyramphus marmoratus (Gmelin)
Total length: 24 to 26.5 cm
Plate 40

Range in Canada. Permanent resident along the coast of British Columbia. Although the nest is not certainly known, the bird obviously breeds commonly along virtually all the coast of that province as attested by (1) eggs taken from oviduct of adult females (Harrison Lake; off Mitlenatch Island; Swanson Bay); (2) the finding of flightless young (Vancouver, Masset, and elsewhere); (3) the finding of an adult with a broken partly incubated egg in debris of a felled tree (Masset); and (4) numerous observations of adults carrying food inland.

Accidental in Quebec (specimen: Oka, 11 November 1979).

Bill slender, pointed. *Breeding plumage*: Upper parts dusky, the back feathers with rusty-brown tips; under parts mottled brown and white. *Winter plumage*: Blackish above, feathers of back tipped with bluish, narrow white band (often incomplete) on back of neck, scapulars mixed with white, under parts white. *Autumn immatures* similar to winter adults, but white under parts are finely barred with dusky.

Measurements *(B. m. marmoratus). Adult male*: wing, 122–130 (128.1); tail, 30–34 (32.9); exposed culmen, 16.5–20 (17.6); tarsus, 16.9–17.9 (17.3). *Adult female*: wing, 121.5–128.6 (125.8) mm.

Field Marks. In breeding plumage, small size and colour. In winter plumage, its white stripe above the folded wing distinguishes it from the similar Ancient Murrelet.

Habitat. Mainly coastal salt water but, according to Munro and Cowan (1947), sometimes larger lakes on the coast of British Columbia are used. Nesting habitat not known but is inland, perhaps at times as much as 40 km from the sea.

Nesting. Poorly known. Nest is placed either in a tree or on the ground. *Egg*: one; pale olive-green with irregular brownish-black spots. Incubation by both parents. For an account of the evidence available in British Columbia, see R.H. Drent and C.J. Guiguet (1961. Occasional Papers, British Columbia Provincial Museum, No. 12). Nests inland within 40 km of the sea, probably usually much nearer.

Range. Breeds on or near the Pacific Coast from Alaska south to central California; also in Siberia. The few known nests have been found in Alaska, California, and Siberia. Winters off shore in most of its summer range.

Subspecies. (1) *Brachyramphus marmoratus marmoratus* (Gmelin) is the subspecies breeding in Canada. (2) *B. m. perdix* (Pallas), of eastern Siberia, has been recorded once in Quebec (Oka).

Xantus' Murrelet

Alque à dos noir
Synthliboramphus hypoleucus (Xantus)
Total length: 20 to 21 cm

Status in Canada. Accidental. One collected
after flying aboard a vessel at sea about 90 km
southeast of Moresby Island, British Columbia,
on 25 October 1971.

Adults summer and winter: Upper parts *solid* blackish-slate. Wing
linings white. Under parts mainly immaculate white, including throat,
and not extending upward on neck as in winter Ancient and Marbled
murrelets.

Field Marks. Resembles a tiny winter plumaged murre. Uniform
blackish back, white chin and throat, no white extending up sides of
neck combine to separate it from Canadian similar species.

Range. Breeds from southern California to central Baja California.

Subspecies. Above specimen not examined by the writer and its
subspecies is not known by me.

Ancient Murrelet

Alque à cou blanc
Synthliboramphus antiquus (Gmelin)
Total length: 24 to 26.5 cm
Plate 40

Breeding Distribution of Ancient Murrelet

Range in Canada. Breeds in north coastal
British Columbia (north and west coasts of
Graham Island; Langara Island, Moresby
Island). Winter resident and transient along the
entire coast of British Columbia. Accidental in
the interior of British Columbia (Swan Lake in
Okanagan valley, 26 October 1939); Yukon
(Pelly Lake, November 1951); Alberta (Edmon-
ton, 25 October 1975); Manitoba (Winnipeg,
8 October 1953; also Lake Winnipeg, autumn
1975); Ontario (Toronto, 18 November 1901;
Lake Erie, 15 November 1908); and Quebec
(Montréal, 13 April 1913).

Measurements. *Adult male*: wing, 130.2–140.2 (134); tail, 32.7–38.8
(35.3); exposed culmen, 13–14.9 (14.2); tarsus, 25.7–28.9 (27.2). *Adult
female*: wing, 132.9–141.2 (135.7) mm.

Field Marks. A small alcid of the West Coast. *Breeding plumage*:
black bib contrasts with white breast, sides of neck, and pale bill; white
stripe over eye extends backward onto nape. *Winter plumage*: similar to
Marbled Murrelet but lacks white line along scapulars.

Habitat. Marine. Nests on coastal islands.

Nesting. In colonies. Nest of dried grasses in burrows (or crevices)
beneath stones, roots, or fallen logs on grassy or wooded slopes of
coastal islands. *Eggs*, usually 2; often elongate and surprisingly large for
size of bird, variable from bluish milky-white through creams and buffs,
marked with different shades of brown and bluish greys. Incubation
about 35 days (S.G. Sealy), by both sexes. Young leave nesting burrows
when very small (variously estimated at one to four nights after
hatching) and scramble down to join adults on the sea at night.

Range. North Pacific. Breeds from the Aleutian, Sanak, and
Kodiak islands to the Queen Charlotte Islands, British Columbia, and
casually to Carroll Island, Washington; also from the Commander
Islands and Kamchatka to Amurland, Sakhalin, the Kurile Islands,
Korea, and Dagelet Island. Ranges farther south in winter, in North
America to northern Baja California.

Cassin's Auklet

Alque de Cassin
Ptychoramphus aleuticus (Pallas)
Total length: 20 to 22.5 cm
Plate 40

Breeding Distribution of Cassin's Auklet

Range in Canada. Breeds on coastal islands of British Columbia: Queen Charlotte Islands, Queen Charlotte Strait (Tree Islets, Pine Island), the Scott Islands, and Solander Island (off Cape Cook). Winters, apparently in very small numbers, off Vancouver Island (Barclay Sound).

A small sea-diver, without much plumage change seasonally and lacking breeding plumage adornments. Adults blackish slate above with dull brownish-grey throat and fore-neck, sides mixed with grey; breast and abdomen white; small white spot above and below eye; bill blackish, the basal third of lower mandible yellowish or flesh; iris white (as in other auklets, but not murrelets). Immatures similar to adults but with more white on throat.

Measurements. *Adult male*: wing, 109.5–129 (120.7); tail, 28–34.5 (31.4); exposed culmen, 18.5–20 (19.3); tarsus, 23.5–25 (24.6). *Adult female*: wing, 120–122 (121) mm (Ridgway).

Field Marks. Pacific Coast. Smaller than Marbled and Ancient murrelets. On water (when white abdomen is hidden) looks all dark with, at close range, a tiny white spot over eye and a pale area at base of lower mandible. There is little seasonal change (young have more white on the throat), and in winter plumage it is the only *small* sea-diver with dark fore-neck; however, Ancient Murrelet often retains black bib until late autumn. Rhinoceros Auklet is obviously larger.

Habitat. Marine. Nests on coastal islands.

Nesting. In colonies. Nest, an accumulation of plant rubbish in burrows similar to those of Ancient Murrelet. *Egg*, one only; dull white, sometimes tinged with bluish or greenish, is unmarked. Incubation by both parents. The young, like other burrow-inhabiting alcids except the Ancient Murrelet, remain in the burrows until fledged. The incubation period is 38 days (D.A. Manuwal).

Range. Breeds on the Pacific Coast of North America from Sanak Islands (formerly), Shumagin and Kodiak islands, Alaska, south to Baja California (San Geronimo and San Martin islands) and Guadalupe Islands. Winters from Vancouver Island to northern Baja California.

Subspecies. *Ptychoramphus aleuticus aleuticus* (Pallas).

Parakeet Auklet

Figure 73
Head of Parakeet Auklet

[**Parakeet Auklet**. Alque perroquet. *Cyclorrhynchus psittacula* (Pallas). Figure 73. Total length: 25 cm. Bill peculiar: stubby, deep, laterally compressed, the *lower mandible strongly upturned*, red in adults, more brownish in young. Breeding adults have the upper parts and throat black; under parts and a narrow plumelike line extending back from eye, white. In winter adults and immatures the throat is more or less white and the white plumes are absent.

Measurements. *Adult male*: wing, 144.5–152 (148); exposed culmen, 14.5–16.5 (15.2); greatest depth of bill, 13–15.5 (14.4); tarsus, 26.5–31 (29.2). *Adult female*: wing, 140.5–152 (145.8); greatest depth of bill, 13–15.5 (14.2); tarsus, 28–30 (28.8) mm (Ridgway).

Field Marks. Peculiar stubby, *reddish* bill with strongly upturned lower mandible, combined with plumage details mentioned above.

Habitat. Marine.

Range. Breeds from northeastern Siberia and islands in Bering Sea south to the Aleutians and Chirikof Island, southwest of Kodiak Island, Alaska. Winters south to the coast of California.

Status in Canada. Hypothetical. Almost certainly a regular winter visitor to waters off the coast of British Columbia. Convincing sight records of three singles, one of which came aboard ship, on 24 February 1971, approximately 25 km off Vancouver Island, British Columbia, but was not collected or photographed. Other sight records off Vancouver Island. Data on an old specimen allegedly from Franklin Bay, N.W.T. are unsatisfactory.]

Least Auklet

Alque minuscule
Aethia pusilla (Pallas)
Total length: ca. 15 to 16.5 cm

Status in Canada. Accidental in northwestern Mackenzie (Kittigazuit: specimen found on bare ice of small lake, January 1927).

The tiniest alcid. Breeding plumage blackish above with white patch in scapulars, narrow white tips to secondaries; forehead and face in front of and below eye, streaked with narrow white feathers, these extending backward across ear; chin blackish, rest of under parts white, irregularly spotted or mottled with dusky; bill stubby, with a little knob near base of culmen. Winter plumage similar but under parts (except blackish chin) unmarked white and knob on bill lacking.

Measurements. *Adult male*: wing, 90–97.5 (92.9); tail, 25.5–29 (27.1); exposed culmen, 8–9 (8.6); tarsus, 17–19.5 (18.3). *Adult female*: wing, 88.5–96 (93.6) mm (Ridgway).

Habitat. Marine.

Range. Breeds from the coast of Chukotski Peninsula, Diomede Islands, and Cape Lisburne, Alaska, south on islands in Bering Sea to the Aleutian and Shumagin islands.

Crested Auklet

Alque panachée
Aethia cristatella (Pallas)
Total length: 23 to 25 cm
Figure 74

Figure 74
Head of Crested Auklet

Status in Canada. One record for British Columbia (specimen collected by a sealer off Vancouver in the winter of 1892–1893).

Adults in summer: Upper parts plain slaty-black; under parts unmarked dark grey. On head a slaty-black recurved frontal crest and a narrow white facial line extending from the eye posteriorly to the side of the neck. Bill reddish orange, iris white or pale yellow. In winter the bill is smaller and dull brown instead of reddish orange.

Measurements. *Adult male*: wing, 125–143 (134.8); tail, 33–38 (35.7); exposed culmen, 10–12 (11.2); tarsus, 24–28 (26.4). *Adult female*: wing, 131–137 (134) mm.

Field Marks. Resembles Parakeet Auklet but possesses a crest, has a dark (not white) abdomen.

Habitat. Marine.

Range. Breeds in western Alaska (Bering Sea islands), the Aleutian Islands, and in eastern Siberia.

Rhinoceros Auklet

Macareux rhinocéros
Cerorhinca monocerata (Pallas)
Total length: 35.5 to 39.5 cm
Plate 40

Breeding Distribution of Rhinoceros Auklet

Range in Canada. Breeds on coastal islands of British Columbia: Queen Charlotte Islands (Langara, Hengesen, Lihou, and Kunghit islands), Chatham Sound (Lucy Island), Triangle and Pine islands. Variable numbers summer off southern Vancouver Island. Winters in small numbers off southern Vancouver Island and in Strait of Georgia.

Measurements. *Adult male*: wing, 175–183 (177.8); tail, 42.5–60.5 (55); exposed culmen, 32.5–36 (34); tarsus, 27–30 (28.2). *Adult female*: wing, 169–181 (175.6) mm (Ridgway).

Field Marks. A largish West Coast alcid (between murrelets and murres in size), blackish brown above; with greyish-brown cheeks, throat, fore-neck, sides, and flanks; whitish belly; side of head with two lines of white plumelike feathers (shorter in winter) extending backward, one from above the eye, the other from the corner of the mouth. In breeding season only, the yellowish bill is equipped with a vertical knob at the base of the culmen; hence the name Rhinoceros Auklet. Immatures similar to winter adults, but head plumes are lacking; bill is much smaller and more dusky. Adults are easily identified, but immatures resemble immature Tufted Puffins although with smaller bill and whiter belly. Immatures are similar also in colour to Cassin's Auklet but are obviously larger.

Habitat. Marine. Nests on coastal islands.

Nesting. In colonies. Nests in a chamber at the end of a long burrow in the ground of wooded islands. The egg is laid on a small heap of miscellaneous grasses, twigs, and leaves. *Egg*, one only, is dull white, sometimes immaculate, but usually spotted with lavender, grey, or light brown; sometimes rather heavily spotted with darker browns. Incubation period is 39 to 45 days (Summers and Drent). Young remain in the burrow until fledged.

Range. Breeds from southeastern Alaska (Saint Lazaria and Forrester islands) south to northwestern Washington (Destruction Island), formerly to California (Farallon Islands); also from the Kurile Islands south to northern Honshu and Korea. Winters from southern part of breeding range to Baja California and to Korea and Japan.

Tufted Puffin

Macareux huppé
Fratercula cirrhata (Pallas)
Total length: 36.5 to 39.5 cm
Plate 40

Breeding Distribution of Tufted Puffin

Range in Canada. Breeds along the coast of British Columbia: Queen Charlotte Islands, Moore Islands, Queen Charlotte Strait (Pine and Storm islands), Scott Islands, Vancouver Island (Solander, Clark, Cleland, and Mandarte islands). Winter records for Victoria, but apparently most of the population winters at sea.

Bill is unmistakable as that of a puffin. The dark-grey under parts distinguish it from the Horned and Atlantic puffins.

Measurements. *Adult male*: wing, 189.5–208 (197.5); tail, 60.0–64.2 (62.6); exposed culmen, 58.1–62.8 (59.8); tarsus, 34.8–36 (35.4). *Adult female*: wing, 183.5–197.8 (191.2) mm.

Field Marks. Pacific Coast. Puffin bill, dark grey-brown under body and straw-coloured head tufts are unmistakable. In winter the bill is much smaller, the face is mostly dusky, and the head tufts are missing. The under parts are always darker than the white under parts of the Horned Puffin (although in young birds they are light greyish).

Habitat. Marine. Breeds on coastal islands.

Nesting. In colonies. Nests either in burrows in the soil of higher grassy slopes of coastal islands or in natural crevices and cavities in rock; occasionally on the ground surface. Nest, whether in burrows or in rock crevices, is usually an accumulation of grass and leaves. *Egg*, one only, is dull white, and many are marked with greys or light brown. Incubation is by both parents.

Range. Breeds from the Kolyuchin Islands and East Cape, Siberia, and the Diomede Islands south to Kamchatka, Commander and Kurile islands, Sea of Okhotsk, Sakhalin, and Hokkaido; from Cape Lisburne, Alaska south to southern California; and islands in Bering Sea south to the Aleutians.

Atlantic Puffin

(Common Puffin)

Macareux moine
Fratercula arctica (Linnaeus)
Total length: 29 to 34.5 cm
Plate 40

Breeding Distribution of Atlantic Puffin

Range in Canada. Breeds along the coast of Labrador (Negro Island southward); southeastern Quebec (north shore of the Gulf of St. Lawrence west to Betchouane; Anticosti, Bonaventure, and Madeleine Islands); northern and eastern Newfoundland (St. John Bay, Walham Islands, Funk Island, Witless Bay, Baccalieu Island); Nova Scotia (very locally: Hertford and Ciboux islands, Pearl Island; formerly Seal Island); and southwestern New Brunswick (Machias Seal Island). Recently found nesting in small numbers on Digges Islands, N.W.T., off the northwest tip of Quebec. Reports of nesting on Resolution Island, N.W.T., require investigation. Wanders, perhaps regularly, to Canadian eastern Arctic (Bylot and Prince Leopold islands, Cape Adair. Photo record: Cape Hay, Bylot Island, 26 August 1978, Wayne Renaud).

Winters from Newfoundland southward in Atlantic waters. Accidental in Ontario (Ottawa, late October 1881) and southwestern Quebec (Lake Saint-Pierre).

The grotesque, triangular, laterally compressed, and highly coloured bill makes this bird unmistakable as a puffin, the only puffin of normal occurrence on the East Coast. Winter adults and immatures have the bill much reduced in size and a darker face, but the characteristic face and other puffin markings are evident enough.

Measurements *(F. a. arctica)*. *Adult male*: wing, 157–166.5 (160.8); tail, 47–52.2 (50.6); exposed culmen, 47.5–53.2 (50.5); tarsus, 26.9–29 (28.3). *Adult female*: wing, 157–161.8 (155.5) mm.

Field Marks. East Coast. Adults in breeding plumage unmistakable as a puffin, the only puffin of our East Coast. Winter adults and immatures have much smaller and duller bills, and the sides of the head are darker than in breeding birds. However, usually the characteristic puffin colour pattern (black band around fore-neck, paler throat and sides of head), as well as the big head and thick short neck will be evident. Shows no white anywhere on upper side of wing (other *East* Coast alcids have either a white line along the ends of the secondaries or a white wing patch).

Habitat. Marine. For nesting, coastal islands or sea cliffs.

Nesting. In colonies. Nest, either in a chamber at the end of a burrow in the ground or in a crevice or cranny in the rock of a cliff. *Egg*, usually one, is most often plain dull white but sometimes is somewhat spotted with browns and lilac. Incubation 40 to 43 days (R.M. Lockley), the greater part by the female. Young remain in the burrows until fledged.

Range. Breeds from Greenland, Jan Meyen, Spitsbergen, and Novaya Zemlya south to Maine, Iceland, the British Isles, northern France, Norway, and northwestern Russia. Winters south to Massachusetts and the western Mediterranean Sea.

Subspecies. (1) *Fratercula arctica arctica* (Linnaeus) is the only subspecies known to breed in Canada and is the common winter resident. (2) *F. a. grabae* (Brehm), a slightly smaller subspecies, is known as a winter visitor from Europe to Newfoundland (two specimens banded at St. Kilda, British Isles, were taken, one at Herring Neck, the other on Bonavista Bay, in December 1939). (3) *F. a. naumanni* Norton, larger than *F. a. arctica*, breeds in Greenland and probably birds found in the Canadian Arctic are referable to it.

Remarks. There is a comical solemnity about the puffin with its serious facial expression and oversized, brightly coloured bill. Its parrot-like appearance has given it the names "sea parrot" and "perroquet." Much of the bulk and bright colour of the bill are shed after the breeding season; consequently this is much less impressive during autumn and winter.

Puffins are usually unwary, often even curious. At their nesting places they walk with a dignified gait, standing up on the toes unlike other alcids that shuffle more awkwardly with the tarsi pressed flat on the ground for support. On the water they are excellent swimmers and divers. Under water they use their wings for propulsion. Unless a wind is blowing, they have difficulty in becoming airborne, often splashing over the water surface for considerable distances. Once in the air, however, their little rapidly beating wings propel them swiftly with frequent side-to-side swaying, usual in the alcids.

Fishes, caught by underwater pursuit, are the main food of puffins. They are carried to the young in the parent's bill. The slippery fish are held crosswise in the beak, and it is surprising how many can be carried at one time.

Like other birds that nest in burrows in the ground, puffins are vulnerable to such mammal predators as cats, rats, dogs, and foxes. Consequently they choose islands for nesting purposes. Colonies quickly disappear, even from islands, once mammal predators have gained access to them. Numbers of the Atlantic Puffin have declined in recent years, especially near settled areas.

Horned Puffin

Macareux cornu
Fratercula corniculata (Naumann)
Total length: 37 cm
Plate 40

Range in Canada. Breeds in small numbers on the coast of northern British Columbia (south probably to Triangle Island. Wanders farther south to Victoria). Accidental in Northwest Territories (specimen: Basil Bay, Mackenzie District, 24 August 1973).

A North Pacific species resembling the Atlantic Puffin but with the black band across the fore-neck extending forward completely to the chin; a somewhat differently shaped and coloured bill; and overall larger size especially the tail. Its pure-white abdomen and lower breast distinguish it from adult Tufted Puffins. Immature Tufted Puffins may be pale greyish below but not pure white and they have a very much smaller bill.

Measurements. *Adult male*: wing, 170–187.5 (181.4); tail, 60–68 (64.1); exposed culmen, 46–55 (50.6); tarsus, 27–30 (27.9). *Adult female*: wing, 168–185 (177.9); tail, 61–68 (63.5) mm (Ridgway).

Habitat. Marine.

Nesting. In colonies. Nests in burrows, in natural crevices, or in rocky cavities of sea cliffs. The single egg is dull white, usually faintly marked with purplish grey, buff, or olive. Incubation by both sexes.

Range. Breeds in northeastern Siberia, coastal Alaska (Cape Lisburne southward), north coastal British Columbia, islands in the Bering Sea and southward to the Aleutian Islands. Winters in the breeding range and southward to British Columbia, more rarely to Washington, Oregon, and California.

Order **Columbiformes:**
Sandgrouse, Pigeons, and Doves

Family **Columbidae:**
Pigeons and Doves

Number of Species in Canada: 6

Pigeons and doves resemble in a general way the familiar domesticated pigeon or Rock Dove and are not difficult to recognize. The head is small in proportion to body size; the bill is soft and fleshy basally, with a horny tip; legs short; toes four, the hind toe on the same level as the others. Tail is variable, short to long. The family is poorly represented in Canada, but it is a large one with greatest diversity in tropical parts of the world. About 290 species are recognized. The names "dove" and "pigeon" are not based on trenchantly different taxonomic characters and consequently do not represent two distinct groups. The Rock Dove, for example, in captivity is called "domestic pigeon."

Rock Dove

(Domestic Pigeon)

Pigeon biset
Columba livia Gmelin
Total length: 28 to 34 cm
Plate 41

Range in Canada. Introduced by establishment of feral domestic stock. Permanent resident in cities and farmland in southern Canada from coast to coast.

In addition to the normal wild plumage (Plate 41), selective breeding has produced many variations in colour and form. In Canada it is not likely to be confused with any living species except the Band-tailed Pigeon of western British Columbia, but the Rock Dove's two dark wing bars, reddish legs, dark bill, and, in flight, white rump patch readily distinguish it. Occasionally the Rock Dove is mistaken by the novice for the extinct Passenger Pigeon, but regardless of colour variations the squarish tail of the Rock Dove is entirely different from the long, pointed tail of the Passenger Pigeon.

Habitat. In Canada, mainly in cities, towns, and farms; nesting in or on buildings and foraging in cultivated fields, barnyards, garbage dumps, railway yards, and streets. Usually avoids extensive forest but occasionally perches in trees.

Nesting. Nest, a shallow, slightly hollowed accumulation of twigs and straws placed (in Canada) usually inside or outside a building or cliff. *Eggs*, usually two; white and glossy. Incubation 17 to 19 days (Witherby et al.), by both sexes. Young at first are fed "pigeon milk" (a substance produced within the crop of the parents), later on regurgitated grain. Two or three broods are raised annually, as nesting may be attempted even in winter.

Range. Native to the Old World from islands in the eastern Atlantic eastward across southern Europe to parts of China and across northern Africa. Now widely established by feral domestic stock in North, Central, and South America, the Hawaiian Islands, parts of the West Indies, Australia, New Zealand, and in other scattered parts of the world.

Subspecies. North American populations are derived from several Old World subspecies, and consequently this mongrel stock can be referred to species only.

Band-tailed Pigeon

Pigeon à queue barrée
Columba fasciata Say
Total length: 36.5 to 39.5 cm
Plate 41

Breeding Distribution of Band-tailed Pigeon

Range in Canada. Breeds in southwestern British Columbia (De Horsey Island, Saltspring Island, Victoria, Coquitlam. Species has been recorded inland as far as Mount Robson Provincial Park and Lytton, and north to Terrace). Winters in Victoria and in small numbers in Vancouver; more rarely farther north.

Casual visitant to Alberta (specimen: Leduc, 27 July 1967; sight records: Lethbridge, Seebe, Hanna, Jasper); Saskatchewan (sight records: near Rosetown, 6 August 1970; Saskatoon, 30 September 1970); Manitoba (photo: one at Dauphin, April 1982, seemed tame and was possibly an escapee); and Ontario (specimen: Port Hope, 8 October 1970; photo record: Dorion, 20 October 1978; sight records: Rondeau Provincial Park, Pickering, Long Point). Accidental in Nova Scotia (photo record: Seal Island, 19 October 1974) and New Brunswick (photo: Fredericton, 1–15 February 1981).

A large pigeon, in Canada found west of the Coast Range. Adult female similar to but duller than adult male. Immatures lack the narrow white band across back of neck; head, neck, and breast are brownish grey; and the feathers of the chest and smaller wing coverts have narrow pale margins (see Field Marks).

Measurements *(C. f. fasciata). Adult male*: wing, 209–228.5 (218.5); tail, 133.8–155.9 (146.2); exposed culmen, 17.5–21 (19.8); tarsus, 26.5–30 (28.2). *Adult female*: wing, 209.9–219.5 (215.8) mm.

Field Marks. A large pigeon of western British Columbia, always distinguishable from the smaller Mourning Dove and the extinct Passenger Pigeon by its squarish or slightly rounded (not pointed) tail. Most likely to be confused with Rock Dove (domestic pigeon), which also has squarish tail, but Band-tailed Pigeon differs in (1) broad pale band across end of tail with narrow dark band anterior to it, (2) yellowish feet and base of bill, (3) lack of black band across wing coverts, (4) uniformly coloured lower back and upper tail coverts (therefore no white patch shows in flight), (5) adults having narrow white band across back of neck (but absent in young), and (6) frequently alighting in trees (Rock Dove infrequently does so). *Voice*: two or three notes, the first pigeon-like; the others lower, and somewhat suggesting the voice of a Great Horned Owl.

Habitat. More open woodland (both coniferous and deciduous) and edges. In spring and autumn it visits grainfields, but it may be found in various situations where foods like elderberry, cherries, cascara, arbutus, and acorns are available. It especially likes tall trees, including dead ones, for perching.

Nesting. Nest, a loose, often frail, platform of twigs on a horizontal branch of a coniferous or deciduous tree, at various heights between 2.4 and 12 m or more. *Egg*, usually one, rarely two; white, slightly glossy. Incubation period probably 18 to 20 days (C.E. Bendire), by both sexes.

Range. Breeds from southern British Columbia, Utah, and north-central Colorado south to Baja California (Cape region), the Mexican tableland, and the mountains of Guatemala, Honduras, El Salvador, and northern Nicaragua. Winters from southwestern United States (north to British Columbia) southward.

Subspecies. *Columba fasciata monilis* Vigors.

Ringed Turtle-Dove

[**Ringed Turtle-Dove**. Tourterelle rieuse. *Streptopelia risoria* (Linnaeus). Total length: 30.5 cm. Size of Mourning Dove but coloration pale tan (not brown), tail squarish (not pointed), and with a narrow black band across the back of the neck.

Status in Canada. Observations of this cage bird are reported in various parts of the country and it is known to have nested in southern Ontario. These individuals are escapees from captivity. There is no evidence of permanent establishment of this bird in the wild in any part of Canada.]

White-winged Dove

Tourterelle à ailes blanches
Zenaida asiatica (Linnaeus)
Total length: 28 to 31 cm

Status in Canada. Accidental in British Columbia (specimen: Sheringham Point, Vancouver Island, July 1918); Ontario (specimen: Fort Albany, 17 June 1942; photo: Belleville, 14–19 December 1975); New Brunswick (photo: North Head, Grand Manan, 22 May 1984; sight records: Marys Point and Campobello Island, both in July 1977); Nova Scotia (photo: Seal Island, 27 August 1979; sight record: Sable Island, 10 August 1979; Stellarton, 8–23 May 1982). Both specimens (not examined by the writer) have been referred to *Z. a. mearnsi* (Ridgway).

Similar to Mourning Dove in size and general coloration but has greater wing coverts largely white (forming a conspicuous white bar); secondaries narrowly tipped white; tail roundly and broadly white-tipped except central feathers. In the field, looks like a Mourning Dove with white wing patch, and tail as described.

Mourning Dove

Tourterelle triste
Zenaida macroura (Linnaeus)
Total length: 28 to 33 cm
Plate 41

Breeding Distribution of Mourning Dove

Range in Canada. Breeds in southern British Columbia (commonly in southern interior north at least to Prince George; very locally and in small numbers on the coast: Victoria, New Westminster); central and southern Alberta (Jasper, Lesser Slave Lake, Milk River); south-central and southern Saskatchewan (Carlton, Prince Albert, Nipawin, Cypress Hills, Regina, Yorkton); southern Manitoba (Garland, Shoal Lake, Aweme, Hillside Beach); southern Ontario (north to Sioux Lookout, Cochrane; range has expanded northward in recent times); southwestern Quebec (Montréal, Amos region, Rimouski; reports of nesting at Fort-George and east of Fort-George are at hand but lack documentation); southern New Brunswick (rarely: Glenwood, Saint John); locally in Nova Scotia (Gaspereau, Avonport, Starrs Point, probably elsewhere in recent years); and recently Prince Edward Island.

Tail long, pointed when closed, the central feathers longest. Female similar to male but duller with shorter tail. Late summer and early autumn immatures are duller than adult females and lack the black spot under the ear; the feathers of fore-neck, scapulars, and wing coverts have paler margins. The pointed tail distinguishes it from all other living Canadian doves and pigeons (the extinct Passenger Pigeon also had a long pointed tail but was much larger and never possessed a black spot below the ear).

Measurements *(Z. m. marginella). Adult male*: wing, 141–153.5 (146); tail, 119.9–149.1 (135.4); exposed culmen, 13–15.3 (14.1); tarsus, 18.9–21.4 (20.1). *Adult female*: wing, 139.2–147 (143.3) mm.

Field Marks. A small slender brown bird with obviously pigeon-like head and motions, a long pointed tail; at close range the adults show a small black spot under the ear. Rises with a twittering whistle of the wings and in flight exposes much white in outer tail feathers. *Voice*: A mournful slow *Oh-woe-woe-woe*.

Habitat. Open woods, groves, and woodlots of both deciduous and coniferous trees. Forages in a variety of situations, such as weedy wasteland, cultivated fields and stubble, grassland, roadsides, beaches, and gravel pits.

Nesting. Usually single pairs; sometimes colonies. Nest, a fragile platform of twigs in coniferous (preferred) or deciduous trees, most often 4.5 to 7.6 m up; also, especially on the prairies, on the ground. Sometimes the nest is placed on an old nest of another species. *Eggs*, usually 2; pure white. Incubation 15 days (O.L. Austin), by both parents. Young in nest are fed first on "pigeon milk," then on regurgitated seeds. Usually two broods annually.

Range. Breeds from southern Canada (and possibly southeastern Alaska) south to Panama and the West Indies. Northernmost populations move farther south to winter.

Isolated breeding has been convincingly reported, but without supporting data, north to Fort-George, Quebec; 209 km east of Fort-George on Fort George (Grande) River; and on Big River, Labrador.

Wanders widely outside breeding range, especially in autumn: northern British Columbia and Yukon (Dawson, Teslin, Carcross); southern Mackenzie (sight records: Reliance, Norman Wells, Hay River); northern Manitoba (Brochet, Churchill); northern Ontario (Winisk, Attawapiskat); southern James Bay (Ship Sands Island); central and eastern Quebec (Cabbage Willows Bay, Pointe-des-Monts, Sept-Îles, Johan-Beetz Bay, Anticosti and Madeleine islands, Gaspé Peninsula); Labrador (Nain, Red Bay, Spotted Islands, Battle Harbour); and Newfoundland (very numerous autumn records).

Winters in southern Ontario (north to Ottawa), southwestern Quebec (Montréal), and in small numbers in southern British Columbia (Okanagan Landing, Victoria), Nova Scotia, and rarely Prince Edward Island and Newfoundland (St. John's).

Subspecies. (1) *Zenaida macroura marginella* (Woodhouse) is the breeding bird of western Canada eastward through Manitoba. (2) *Z. m. carolinensis* (Linnaeus), with slightly darker, less greyish coloration and slightly smaller size, breeds from southern Ontario eastward. Breeding specimens from western Ontario (Thunder Bay) have not been examined, and their affinities are uncertain.

Passenger Pigeon

Tourte
Ectopistes migratorius (Linnaeus)
Total length: 38 to 45.5 cm
Plate 41

Status in Canada. Extinct. Details of former breeding range poorly known. In Alberta, bones have been excavated from the site of Fort George on North Saskatchewan River; its presence was reported by early travellers as far west as Edmonton but there is no evidence of its breeding there. Bred in central-eastern Saskatchewan: Cumberland House (Thomas Drummond, 1830. Botanical Miscellany 1, pp. 180–181). Twenty-one observations of the species in Saskatchewan and two in Manitoba are summarized by C.S. Houston (1972. Blue Jay, vol. 30, no. 2, pp. 77–83). Manitoba: Probably nested widely, abundantly in southern parts, and wandered north to Churchill and York Factory; known breeding colony at Waterhen River between Lakes Manitoba and Winnipegosis; last known Manitoba specimen taken at Winnipegosis, 13 April 1898. Ontario: Bred in great numbers in southern parts; also west to northern Lake of the Woods and north to Moose Factory. M.H. Mitchell (1935. Contributions Royal Ontario Museum Zoology 7, pp. 1–181) has presented an excellent history of the species in Ontario and includes breeding records for 45 of the 55 Ontario counties and districts. Last known Ontario specimen taken was at Sherkston, near Niagara, mid-September 1891; last reliable sight record was at Penetanguishene, 18 May 1902. Quebec: Formerly southwestern parts, north rarely to perhaps Fort-George and east probably to Gaspé Peninsula; species

A large extinct pigeon with long, pointed, much-graduated tail feathers. Adult male as illustrated. Adult female much duller, browner above; fore-neck, breast, and abdomen greyish brown; tail shorter. Juvenal similar to adult female but feathers of head, neck, upper breast, and scapulars tipped with whitish. The long, pointed tail distinguished it from Rock Dove and Band-tailed Pigeon. It differed from the Mourning Dove in its much larger size, different coloration, especially of adult male, and lack of a black spot under the ear in adults of both sexes.

Measurements. *Adult male*: wing, 196.5–214.5 (204.9); tail, 173–211 (193.5); exposed culmen, 15–18 (16.7); tarsus, 26–29 (27.4). *Adult female*: wing, 175–210 (198.1) mm (Ridgway).

Field Marks. Unnecessary as the species is extinct.

Nesting. Usually in colonies, sometimes incredibly immense; occasionally in single pairs. Nest a frail platform loosely made of sticks and twigs on a branch of a deciduous (preferred) or coniferous tree at heights from 2.4 to 15 m. A single white *egg* (sometimes two) was laid. Incubation about 14 days, by both sexes (A.C. Bent). Two or more broods annually, sometimes only one.

Range. Extinct. The last individual died in captivity in Cincinnati, Ohio, 1 September 1914. Last known specimen taken in the wild at Sargento, Ohio, 24 March 1900. Formerly bred from central Montana, North Dakota, southern Manitoba and southeastern Canada south to eastern Kansas, Oklahoma, Mississippi, and Georgia. Wintered in southeastern United States.

recorded east to Pointe-des-Monts and Anti-costi Island. New Brunswick: Was abundant in summer with breeding records for Scotch Lake, Grand Falls, and possibly Grand Manan; last known specimen killed at Scotch Lake, 1899. Nova Scotia: Former breeder and transient; last definite record about 1857. Prince Edward Island: Apparently it was common and probably bred.

West of Saskatchewan there is no definite evidence of breeding, although it may have done so. It is known to have occurred in British Columbia (specimen: Chilliwack, 29 June 1859); Alberta (west at least to McLeod River, west of Edmonton); and Mackenzie District (formerly wandered down the Mackenzie valley to Forts Simpson, Norman, and Good Hope). Accidental on Baffin Bay, 31 July 1829.

Remarks. Probably no other medium-sized North American bird existed in such vast numbers as did the Passenger Pigeon. In migration great flocks darkened the sky; in roosting places, limbs of trees crashed under the sheer weight of its numbers; largest nesting colonies occupied hundreds of square miles. Its habit of concentrating in immense flocks facilitated its mass slaughter. Trainloads were shipped from favoured areas. It laid only one or two eggs to a clutch, and its reproductive potential was therefore inadequate to cope with the vast drain on its numbers. It was gunned, trapped, and clubbed off the face of the earth. Today the Passenger Pigeon, whose myriads not so long ago were one of the wonders of this continent, is gone forever. We, and all who follow us, will never see a living one.

Common Ground-Dove

Colombe à queue noire
Columbina passerina (Linnaeus)
Total length: 15 to 17 cm

Status in Canada. Accidental. One found dead on 29 October 1968 near Red Rock, Ontario. Specimen in Royal Ontario Museum.

A tiny, short-tailed dove with considerable chestnut coloration in the primaries and wing linings. Tail with the two central feathers plain greyish-brown, the others dull black, the outermost with a trace of whitish near the tips.

Measurements. *Adult male*: wing, 84–89 (86); tail, 59–65 (62); exposed culmen, 11–12 (11.5); tarsus, 15–17 (16). *Adult female*: wing, 85–88 (86.5); tail, 55–63 (60); exposed culmen, 11.5–12 (11.7); tarsus, 15–17 (15.8) mm (Ridgway).

Field Marks. Tiny size (little larger than a sparrow); chestnut areas in spread wing; and short dark tail. Separable from the Ringed Turtle-Dove *(Streptopelia risoria)*, a cage bird that occasionally escapes from captivity, by darker (not sandy) coloration, lack of a black crescent on the nape, and short dark tail.

Range. Resident from southern California, central Arizona, southern Texas, and South Carolina, south to Costa Rica, northeastern South America and the Greater and Lesser Antilles.

Order **Psittaciformes:**
Parrots and Allies

Family **Psittacidae:**
Lories, Parakeets, Macaws, and Parrots

Number of Species in Canada: hypothetical

Carolina Parakeet

[**Carolina Parakeet**. Conure de Caroline. *Conuropsis carolinensis* (Linnaeus). Hypothetical. Three small bones (premaxilla, proximal half of the left carpometacarpus, and pygostyle) of the extinct Carolina Parakeet were recently discovered by archaeologists on the Calvert site (a Glen Meyer Indian site dating to about 1100 A.D.) near London, Ontario (Rosemary Prevec. 1984. Kewa, Newsletter of the London Chapter, Ontario Archaeological Society, no. 84-7, pp. 4–8). The species is known to have ranged northward as far as central New York and might have occasionally straggled into southern Canada. There is the possibility, however, that this individual was transported by man to southern Ontario to serve some ceremonial function.]

Order **Cuculiformes:**
Cuckoos and Plantain-eaters

Family **Cuculidae:**
Cuckoos, Roadrunners, and Anis

Number of Species in Canada: 3

The cuckoo family containing 125 or more species is represented in the tropical and temperate parts of all the continents of the world. The North American species build fragile nests, but many of the Old World species are parasitic, laying their eggs in the nests of other birds.

Although the species of the world vary greatly in appearance, the two species that breed in Canada are very similar. Long slender birds, plain brown above, plain white below, with long graduated tails, slightly downcurved bills, and zygodactylous (two toes in front, two behind) feet. Economically, cuckoos are extremely valuable because they devour vast numbers of insects and have a particularly voracious appetite for caterpillars.

Black-billed Cuckoo

Coulicou à bec noir
Coccyzus erythropthalmus (Wilson)
Total length: 28 to 32 cm
Plate 41

Breeding Distribution of Black-billed Cuckoo

Range in Canada. Breeds in central-eastern and southeastern Alberta (Athabasca, Duhamel, Camrose, Sullivan Lake, Castor); southern Saskatchewan (Cypress Hills, Somme, Yorkton, Regina); southern Manitoba (Riding Mountain National Park, Hartney, Hillside Beach, Indian Bay, Shoal Lake, probably Cedar Lake); southern and central Ontario (commonly in the south; in small numbers north at least to Sioux Lookout, Kearns, and Matheson); southwestern Quebec (probably Lake Abitibi, Montréal, Chambly, Hatley, Québec, Rivière-du-Loup); New Brunswick; Prince Edward Island; and Nova Scotia.

Sexes similar (for distinctions from Yellow-billed Cuckoo, see Field Marks). Young resemble adults, but white tips of tail feathers are less distinct, the eye-ring is not red, the primaries are often lightly edged with rufous, and there is a pale area near the base of the lower mandible.

Measurements. *Adult male*: wing, 132.9–140.9 (136.5); tail, 147.4–159.8 (152.6); exposed culmen, 20.2–23.9 (21.9); tarsus, 21.1–24.1 (22.9). *Adult female*: wing, 130.4–148.9 (141.1) mm.

Field Marks. Longer than American Robin. Long graduated tail, slender outline; brown upper parts, plain-white under parts, and down-curved bill mark it as a cuckoo. Mainly black bill, red eye-ring, narrower much less sharply defined white tips to the tail feathers, and in flight lack of a *conspicuous* cinnamon-rufous area in the wing separate it from Yellow-billed Cuckoo. *Caution*: First-autumn birds may show just enough rufous in the spread wing to cause confusion with Yellow-billed Cuckoo. Consequently, identification should not be based on wing coloration alone. *Voice*: Hollow wooden clucks, tending to phrases of three or four clucks, with a slight pause between phrases.

Habitat. More open woodland; tangles of willow, alder, vines, and similar cover.

Nesting. Nest is of twigs. It usually is fragile but often is more substantially made than that of the Yellow-billed Cuckoo and is usually better lined with soft vegetable material. It is placed most often 0.6 to 2.1 m above the ground (occasionally more or less) on a branch in a low bush or tree, either deciduous or coniferous. *Eggs*, 2 to 4, usually 3; blue-green, averaging slightly smaller and darker than those of the Yellow-billed. Incubation, by both sexes, requires 10 or 11 days (Ruth Spencer), 14 days (other authors). Occasionally lays in nests of other birds including that of the Yellow-billed Cuckoo.

Recorded in summer north to north-central Ontario (Moosonee) and in Quebec to Lake Waswanipi and eastern Gaspé Peninsula (Sandy-Beach, Percé). Accidental in Newfoundland (St. John's, 12 October 1955 and various other records including one sight record at Cape Onion). There are sight records for interior British Columbia.

Yellow-billed Cuckoo

Coulicou à bec jaune
Coccyzus americanus (Linnaeus)
Total length: 28 to 32 cm
Plate 41

Breeding Distribution of Yellow-billed Cuckoo

Range in Canada. Breeds in southern Manitoba (rarely: Selkirk); southern Ontario (commonly in Lake Erie region but rarely north to Manitoulin Island, Sudbury, and Ottawa); rarely in extreme southwestern Quebec (Montréal region, Old-Chelsea, Lennoxville, Ulverton); and southern New Brunswick (Saint John). Reported to have nested in southwestern British Columbia (Victoria, Pitt Meadows).

Casual or accidental owing mainly to autumn storms, in Nova Scotia (many records September–December); Prince Edward Island (Brackley Point, Mount Stewart); Newfoundland (St. John's region: specimens, 12 October 1954, and 15 November 1955); north shore of the Gulf of St. Lawrence (Moisie River, Quebec, 6 October 1953); and Labrador (Hamilton River). Notable was October 1954, when large numbers appeared in Nova Scotia and New Brunswick, and small numbers in Newfoundland. Accidental in Alberta (specimen: Edmonton, 14 September 1968; photo record: Rocky Mountain House, 25 July 1971) and in Manitoba (specimen: Stony Mountain, 24 August 1969).

Range. Breeds from southern Canada (Alberta east), south to eastern Wyoming, Nebraska, Kansas, Tennessee, and South Carolina (Mount Pleasant). Winters in northwestern South America.

Sexes alike (see Field Marks). Young resemble adults but are duller; the black of the lateral tail feathers is much greyer, and the white tips are less of a contrast.

Measurements *(C. a. americanus). Adult male*: wing, 137–142 (139); tail, 140.2–143.9 (141.1); exposed culmen, 23.9–26.1 (24.9); tarsus, 26.3–26.9 (26.6). *Adult female*: wing, 140–156.5 (148.1) mm.

Field Marks. Plain-brown upper parts, unmarked greyish-white under parts, downcurved bill, long graduated tail, and slender outline mark it as a cuckoo. The yellow lower mandible, broad white tips to the otherwise black outer tail feathers (best observed from below as they are concealed from above by brown central tail feathers), and a cinnamon-rufous area in the primaries (conspicuous in flight) separate it from adult Black-billed Cuckoo but see *Caution* under Black-billed Cuckoo. *Voice*: A long series of hollow wooden clucks, characteristically becoming slower near the end.

Habitat. Open woodland; willow and alder tangles; thickets.

Nesting. The nest, a frail flat loose structure of twigs sparsely lined with soft plant material, is placed usually 1 to 2.7 m above ground in shrubbery or a low tree. The three or four light greenish-blue *eggs* are said to be incubated by both sexes but mainly by the female. Incubation period about 14 days. Rarely it lays eggs in other birds' nests, including that of the Black-billed Cuckoo.

Range. Breeds in southern Canada (locally) south to northern Mexico and parts of the West Indies. Winters in South America.

Subspecies. (1) *Coccyzus americanus americanus* (Linnaeus) breeds from Ontario eastward; probably the small Manitoba breeding population also is referable to it, but no specimens were examined by me.
(2) *C. a. occidentalis* Ridgway, averaging somewhat larger in size, is the subspecies breeding in British Columbia.

Groove-billed Ani

Ani à bec cannelé
Crotophaga sulcirostris Swainson
Total length: 30 to 33 cm
Figure 75

Figure 75
Groove-billed Ani

Status in Canada. Accidental in Ontario (one found dead at Lake Bernard, Sundridge, Parry Sound District, on 27 October 1978. Another was found dead at Rosslyn on 1 November 1983. Sight record of one at Stromness on 12 October 1969).

Adults (sexes alike): A black bird with a long loose-jointed tail and a large laterally compressed bill with a high curved ridge and several indistinct grooves parallel with the curve of the culmen. General coloration black faintly glossed with purplish. Feathers of head and neck broadly but indistinctly edged with purplish or purplish bronze. Iris brown. Legs and feet black. Readily separable from blackbirds by its high peculiar bill.

Measurements. *Adult male*: wing, 128–157 (142.5); tail, 160–197 (180.2); culmen, 25–30 (28.1); tarsus, 31–36 (34.1). *Adult female*: wing, 128–142 (133.9); tail, 160–182 (167.7) mm (Ridgway).

Range. Resident in southern Texas, southern Baja California, Central America, and southward on both coasts of South America to Guyana and northern Chile and in northwestern Argentina.

Subspecies. *Crotophaga sulcirostris sulcirostris* Swainson.

Order **Strigiformes:**
Owls

This order has a worldwide distribution. Owls have a large head, more or less flattened in front, with broad facial disc. Eyes are large and are directed forward. Bill is strongly hooked; the toes are armed with sharp, curved talons. The outer toe is reversible. The legs are feathered in most species. Plumage is extremely soft and fluffy facilitating silent flight.

Most owls hunt at night, but some, like the Snowy and Short-eared owls and the Northern Hawk-Owl, hunt in daylight or at dusk. Even the nocturnal owls have excellent vision in daylight except when brought suddenly from darkness into strong light. Rodents, particularly mice and rats, are the staple food of most of these interesting birds of prey. Their great value in keeping rodent numbers in check would be difficult to overestimate.

Family **Tytonidae:**
Barn-Owls

Number of Species in Canada: 1

Face, long and triangular or heart-shaped; eyes rather small for an owl. Legs are long and are covered with short scanty feathers, the toes with a sparse covering of bristles, the middle toenail pectinate on inner edge. Structurally these owls differ greatly from other owls, but their general habits are similar.

Common Barn-Owl

Effraie de clochers
Tyto alba (Scopoli)
Total length: 37 to 44.5 cm
Plate 42

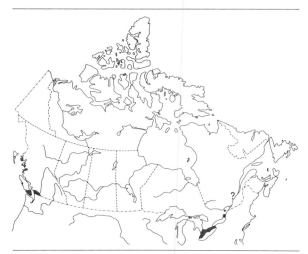

Breeding Distribution of Common Barn-Owl

Range in Canada. Breeds in extreme southwestern British Columbia (Victoria, Crescent Beach, Ladner), and southern Ontario (Kingsville, Chatham, Strathroy, Blenheim, Queenston, Kingston; very rarely northeastward to Winchester where four young were raised in 1980). Reports of breeding in Quebec are not acceptable. Winters in breeding range.

Wanders casually north to southern Alberta (photo: Lethbridge, 8 July 1979); southern Saskatchewan (Kindersley, Regina, Aylesbury); southern Manitoba (La Rivière, Whitewater Lake, Sainte-Anne-des-Chênes); southern

Head rather large without ear tufts, facial disc distinctly heart-shaped, eyes black and not large, lower legs and toes scantily feathered. Adults of both sexes and immatures similar in coloration. Upper parts mainly buffy, back to top of head frosted over with greyish and spotted with blackish and greyish; under parts variable from tawny to white, without any bars or stripes, but finely spotted or speckled with black.

Measurements. *Adult male*: wing, 314–345 (328.6); tail, 126–152.5 (138.1); culmen (from cere), 21–24 (22.1). *Adult female*: wing, 320–360 (336.9) mm (Ridgway).

Field Marks. A medium-sized, slender-bodied, pale, generally buffy owl with long heart-shaped face, black eyes, no ear tufts, and no stripes or bars on the finely spotted under parts. The Short-eared Owl, another buffy owl of about the same size, is easily distinguished from it by striped under parts, well-feathered legs and toes, yellow eyes, and very differently shaped facial disc. *Voice*: hisses and rasping cries and a variety of weird notes.

Habitat. Forages over fields and similar open places particularly where small rodents abound. Roosts and nests in buildings, hollow trees, and cavities in cliffs and banks.

Nesting. In dark sheltered places, such as hollows in trees or cliffs, barn lofts, towers of abandoned or less disturbed buildings. No nest is made, but as the site is used year after year, piles of rodent fur and bones accumulate. *Eggs*, usually 5 to 8; white. Incubation period 30 to 34 days (Niethammer). Young fed by both parents, but incubation by the female.

Range. Nearly cosmopolitan. In the New World from extreme southern Canada (locally) south to southern South America and the West Indies.

Ontario (Sault Ste. Marie, Ottawa); and
Quebec (Montréal, Berthierville, Cap-
Tourmente). Accidental in New Brunswick
(Cape Tormentine); Nova Scotia (Tusket, River
Bourgeois, Canso, Lower Argyle); and New-
foundland (St. Anthony, 29 November 1957).

Subspecies. Although many subspecies of the Common Barn-Owl
are found in various parts of the world, *Tyto alba pratincola*
(Bonaparte) is the only one known from North America.

Family **Strigidae**: Typical Owls

Number of Species in Canada: 15

A large family including all the owls except the barn-owls and represented in most parts of the world. Face more rounded, less triangular,
than in the Tytonidae; eyes usually larger, ear tufts often present. It
differs also in numerous structural details.

Flammulated Owl

(Flammulated Screech Owl)

Petit-duc nain
Otus flammeolus (Kaup)
Total length: 16 to 19 cm
Plate 42

Range in Canada. Very rare and local breeder
in southern British Columbia. On 12 June
1962, a nest was located in a ponderosa pine
felled by a logger about 35 km west of Penticton. On 23 August 1947, a dying juvenal was
photographed at Summerland. On 15 July 1977
a young bird, being fed by its parents, was
photographed 6 km northwest of Penticton;
breeds also near Kamloops.

Other records, all in British Columbia:
Penticton (one found dead, November 1902);
Kamloops (one collected on 11 August 1935, at
Lac du Bois); Invermere (one found dead in
September 1977).

Suggests a screech-owl but is smaller and has dark instead of yellow
eyes and shorter ear tufts and quite naked toes.

Measurements. *Adult male*: wing, 128–138 (132.9); tail, 58–63.5
(59.7); culmen (from cere), 8.5–10 (9.5). *Adult female*: wing, 128.5–144
(135.2) mm (Ridgway).

Field Marks. Looks like a small screech-owl with dark-brown eyes
(instead of yellow).

Habitat. Pine, Douglas fir, and other coniferous woodland.

Nesting. In a woodpecker hole or similar tree cavity. *Eggs*, usually
3 or 4; white.

Range. Breeds from southern British Columbia south through the
mountains west of the Great Plains to the highlands of Mexico and
Guatemala.

Subspecies. *Otus flammeolus flammeolus* (Kaup). Some authors
regard the Flammulated Owl as a subspecies of the Old World *Otus
scops*.

Eastern Screech-Owl

Petit-duc maculé
Otus asio (Linnaeus)
Total length: 18 to 24 cm
Plate 42

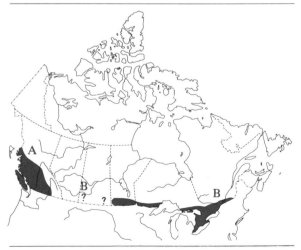

Breeding Distribution of
A) Western Screech-Owl
B) Eastern Screech-Owl

A small eared owl with yellow eyes, thus very similar to Western
Screech-Owl. In eastern Canada any small (folded wing chord 180 mm
or less) owl with well-developed ear tufts is probably this species. The
Eastern Screech-Owl has two well-marked plumage colour phases (grey
and rufescent) regardless of sex or age. In British Columbia two owls
very similar to this one are found (see Western Screech-Owl and
Flammulated Owl).

Measurements *(O. a. naevius)*. *Adult male*: wing, 145.5–170.5
(160.2); tail, 68–82.5 (76.4); culmen (from cere), 13–15.5 (14.9). *Adult
female*: wing, 160–176 (166); tail, 72.5–83 (79.2); culmen (from cere),
14.5–16 (15.3) mm (Ridgway).

Field Marks. A small nocturnal owl with prominent ear tufts and
yellow eyes. Plumage either grey or rusty brown. In eastern Canada and
in eastern parts of the prairies this is the only species likely to be
encountered, but in British Columbia its place is taken by two other
very similar species, the Western Screech-Owl and the Flammulated
Owl. The Long-eared and Great Horned owls also have prominent ear
tufts but are so much larger that there should be no confusion.
(*Caution*: Young birds may lack ear tufts.) *Voice*: A tremulous low
whistle descending rapidly toward the end.

Range in Canada. Resident in southern Manitoba (Lyleton, Aweme, Riding Mountain, Oak and Whitewater lakes, Red and Assiniboine river valleys); southern Ontario (commonly in south and northward at least to North Bay and Ottawa; presence of species reported north to Lake Nipissing, Thunder Bay, and Lake of the Woods); and extreme southwestern Quebec (Chelsea, Montréal). Probably breeds sparsely in southeastern Saskatchewan (perhaps Yorkton or Moose Jaw Creek valley). Possibly breeds in extreme southwestern New Brunswick (Grand Manan, but definite evidence lacking).

Recorded without evidence of breeding in Alberta (Flatbush, Kinuso, Cardston, Belvedere); Saskatchewan (west to Cypress Hills and northwest to Saskatoon); and New Brunswick (mostly sight records in southwest). Accidental in Nova Scotia (Indian Lake, September 1892).

Habitat. Open woodlands, groves, orchards, shade trees, sometimes roosting on buildings.

Nesting. In holes in trees (old woodpecker holes, natural cavities) and bird boxes at heights varying from 2 to 24 m. *Eggs*, usually 4 or 5; white. Incubation requires about 26 days (A.R. Sherman) mostly, if not entirely, by the female.

Range. Resident from southeastern Saskatchewan (probably), southern Ontario, southern Quebec, and southwestern Maine south to northeastern Mexico and Florida and west to eastern Montana, northeastern Wyoming, and Kansas.

Subspecies. (1) *Otus asio naevius* (Gmelin) with well-marked grey and rusty colour phases, is the breeding bird of Ontario and Quebec. (2) *O. a. swenki* Oberholser, a much paler race with two colour phases, is the bird of western Manitoba (Aweme, Oak Lake), tending through darker coloration toward *naevius* at Winnipeg and Whitemouth.

Western Screech-Owl

Petit-duc des montagnes
Otus kennicottii (Elliot)
Total length: 19 to 25.5 cm
Plate 42

Range in Canada. Permanent resident in western and southern interior British Columbia (coast of mainland, Vancouver and Goose islands; southern interior: Okanagan valley and north rarely to Vanderhoof region).

A small *eared* owl with yellow eyes, thus very similar to Eastern Screech-Owl, but differing in having more prominent dark streaking on both upper and under parts and in slightly larger size. The nominate (West Coast) race has much heavier and more extensive pigmentation generally (with corresponding reduction of white, the abdominal areas and legs tawny rather than white). Although in United States populations the Western Screech-Owl differs from the Eastern Screech-Owl in having a black bill, this distinction does not hold in Canadian populations.

Measurements *(O. k. kennicottii). Adult male*: wing, 170.5–190.5 (176.5); tail, 82–98.5 (89); culmen (from cere), 14.5–16.5 (15.1). *Adult female*: wing, 170.5–187.5 (179.2); tail, 85.5–93 (89.2); culmen (from cere), 14.5–16.5 (15.5) mm (Ridgway).

Field Marks. Very difficult to distinguish in the field from the Eastern Screech-Owl (except by voice). However, any small owl with conspicuous ear tufts and yellow eyes found in British Columbia is likely to be this species. Flammulated Owl is very similar but has dark eyes. *Voice*: Differs from the descending call of the Eastern Screech-Owl: A series of hollow (lower in pitch) whistles with a somewhat wooden quality and delivered on an even scale, the notes speeding up until they run into each other.

Habitat. Open woodlands, especially deciduous ones.

Nesting. Similar to Eastern Screech-Owl.

Range. Resident from extreme southern Alaska (Juneau) south through western British Columbia to Baja California and Sinaloa; and in the interior east to Okanagan valley, British Columbia, Idaho, Utah, New Mexico, southeastern Colorado, western Texas (Juno), southeastern Coahuila, and Mexico City.

Subspecies. (1) *Otus kennicottii kennicottii* (Elliot) a heavily pigmented race, is the bird of coastal British Columbia. (2) *O. k. macfarlanei* (Brewster), much paler than the nominate race, inhabits the southern interior of British Columbia (Okanagan valley).

Great Horned Owl

Grand-duc d'Amérique
Bubo virginianus (Gmelin)
Total length: male, 46 to 58.5 cm;
female, 56 to 63 cm
Plate 42

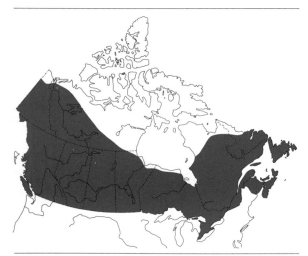

Breeding Distribution of Great Horned Owl

Range in Canada. Resident throughout most wooded parts north to the limit of trees in Yukon, Mackenzie, British Columbia (except Queen Charlotte Islands), Alberta, Saskatchewan, Manitoba, Ontario, Quebec (north at least to Kuujjuaq, but apparently not recorded from Madeleine Islands), Labrador (north to Okak), Newfoundland, New Brunswick, Prince Edward Island, and Nova Scotia.

Recorded without evidence of breeding in Keewatin (mainly in winter: Windy River; mouth of Thlewiaza River. Casual at Chesterfield Inlet: specimen, 10 June 1935). Winters within breeding range including northern parts, and sometimes probably also north of breeding range; for example, in Keewatin and perhaps elsewhere where winter ptarmigan abound. Individuals wander over long distances, perhaps in all directions but mainly southward.

A large owl, the only Canadian owl over 40.5 cm in total length with prominent ear tufts. Sexes similarly coloured, but populations are geographically variable in colour (see Subspecies).

Measurements *(B. v. virginianus). Adult male*: wing, 337–380.5 (356.9); tail, 193–223.5 (209.9); culmen (from cere), 27–31.4 (29.8). *Adult female*: wing, 357.5–395.5 (380.8) mm.

Field Marks. Large size and prominent ear tufts. *Voice*: a series of deep *hoo* notes, often five, which are less varied and deeper than the Barred Owl's; also a scream.

Habitat. Both deciduous and coniferous woods varying from extensive heavy forests to isolated groves, woods of city parks, and, on the prairies, wooded coulees and river valleys.

Nesting. Nest, usually in an old nest of a hawk, crow, or squirrel in trees; sometimes in a cavity in a tree or on a cliff ledge. *Eggs*, usually 2 or 3; white. Incubation 30 days (A.K. Gilkey et al.).

Range. North and South America from the northern limit of trees south (except the West Indies) to the Straits of Magellan. There is limited migration and wandering.

Subspecies. (1) *Bubo virginianus virginianus* (Gmelin), medium dark coloration with distinctive amount of redness in the plumage: southern Ontario, southern Quebec, New Brunswick, Prince Edward Island and Nova Scotia (tends towards *heterocnemis* in northern Cape Breton Island). (2) *B. v. heterocnemis* (Oberholser), very dark: Newfoundland, Labrador, central and northern Quebec. (3) *B. v. subarcticus* Hoy *(wapacuthu* of the *A.O.U. Check-list*, Fifth Edition), extremely pale, extensively white: Mackenzie (status in extreme northwestern part uncertain), central-eastern British Columbia (Peace River parklands), Alberta (except mountains), Saskatchewan, Manitoba, western and northern Ontario (however, western and northern Ontario populations have recently been considered separable and named *scalariventris* Snyder, 1961, Royal Ontario Museum, Contributions 54, p. 5. As I have examined little pertinent breeding material, I cannot express an opinion as to the validity of *scalariventris*. Also, birds of southern parts of the Prairie Provinces are referred to *occidentalis* in *A.O.U. Check-list* (Fifth Edition) but our large series from the southern parts of the Canadian prairies is not separable from *subarcticus* from farther north). (4) *B. v. lagophonus* (Oberholser), much darker than *subarcticus*, usually less tawny than *virginianus*: the Yukon, interior British Columbia (except Peace River parklands), and southwestern Alberta (mountains); possibly extreme western Mackenzie (but only one non-breeding specimen available). (5) *B. v. saturatus* Ridgway, darker than *lagophonus* and less tawny: Humid coastal parts of British Columbia. Outside breeding season individuals wander considerably, often widely.

Remarks. The Great Horned Owl is savage and powerful. It preys on a wide variety of birds and small mammals, notably rabbits, rats, mice, grouse, ducks, crows, poultry, and skunks. Occasionally it even attacks a porcupine. It is our only owl that is considered really destructive. Small animals are eaten entire. The indigestible bones, fur, and feathers are regurgitated as pellets, as is usual in owls.

It hunts mostly at night or at dusk. The daylight hours are spent dozing in the branches of a tree. Crows detest it. When a sharp-eyed crow spots an owl, the crow lets out a peculiarly intonated *caw*, which soon tells every other crow within hearing that an owl is in the vicinity. Crows quickly gather in numbers about the dozing owl, and, perching as near as they consider expedient, all *caw* at the top of their voices. When the owl seemingly can stand it no longer, it flies but is closely followed by the noisy black mob, and several such attempts to get away may be necessary before the owl is finally able to shake off its tormentors.

Snowy Owl

Harfang des neiges
Nyctea scandiaca (Linnaeus)
Total length: 56 to 68.5 cm
(female larger than male)
Plate 42

Breeding Distribution of Snowy Owl

Range in Canada. Breeds from Prince Patrick Island (probably) and northern Ellesmere Island (Cape Sheridan) south through the Arctic Archipelago to northern Yukon (Herschel Island); northern Mackenzie (Baillie Island, Perry River, and probably inland for an undetermined distance); Keewatin; northern Manitoba (Churchill); Southampton Island; Hudson Bay (Belcher Islands); northern Quebec (Povungnituk, Kogaluc River, Kuujjuaq); and northern Labrador (south to Okak, possibly to Nain).

Winters within parts of the breeding range, but probably south of the zone of 24-hour winter darkness, and south in irregular numbers to southernmost parts of all the provinces. Largest flights to southern localities occur about every four years, these being correlated with periodic low points in numerical fluctuations of small mammals in the Arctic, especially lemmings, which are a staple arctic food.

A large owl, as large as the Great Horned but lacks ear tufts; general coloration white, more or less barred and spotted with dark brown; eyes yellow; legs and toes very heavily feathered. Adult male is mainly white (occasionally immaculate). Adult female is more heavily marked than adult male, and immatures are more profusely (often heavily) marked than adult females.

Measurements. *Adult male*: wing, 375.5–407.5 (396.4); tail, 210–219.5 (214.1); culmen (from cere), 24.7–29 (27). *Adult female*: wing, 415–438.5 (414.9) mm.

Field Marks. A large, bulky, very white owl (often heavily barred and spotted with dark brown) with round head lacking ear tufts. Unlikely to be confused with anything but whitish races of the Great Horned Owl, but lack of ear tufts distinguishes it. It is active in daylight and frequents open places.

Habitat. For nesting, low or high-arctic tundra, preferably hummocky or rolling. In migration and winter in the south, open places such as fields, prairies, marshes, coasts, shores of lakes and large rivers. Perches on the ground, fence posts, straw stacks, trees, radio towers, and buildings.

Nesting. On the ground, a slight depression often thinly lined with moss or grass in a high spot on rolling tundra. *Eggs*, 5 to 7, occasionally more or less; white. Incubation 32 to 33 days (Witherby et al.), by the female.

Range. Circumpolar; arctic tundras of the world. Winters within breeding range and south to central Europe, central Asia, and northern United States; occasionally south to southern United States.

Remarks. The hardy Snowy Owl is a winter visitor to the settled southern parts of Canada. Its luxurious feather coat is ideal for a life in the cold. Its feet are densely feathered to the tips of the toes, and the bill is almost hidden in the warm feathers of the face. Only the searching yellow eyes are fully exposed. It spurns the protection of heavy forest and frequents instead more open expanses where winter's bitterest blasts blow unimpeded. Unlike many other owls, this one is active during the daylight hours.

In the Arctic, this owl depends for food on lemmings and other rodents and, to some extent, on birds and fishes. Lemmings tend to fluctuate violently in numbers periodically, building up to great abundance every four years or so, then suddenly dying off. In the resulting periods of lemming scarcity the owls must wander southward to find adequate food. Thus in southern Canada relatively large numbers of Snowy Owls appear, usually during one winter in four. Sometimes flights will occur in two successive winters, the second involving smaller numbers.

Northern Hawk-Owl

Chouette épervière
Surnia ulula (Linnaeus)
Total length: 36.5 to 43 cm
Plate 44

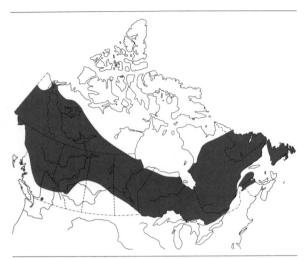

Breeding Distribution of Northern
Hawk-Owl

Range in Canada. Breeds (north to tree limit)
from northern Yukon (Lapierre House, Old
Crow); northwestern and central Mackenzie
(Mackenzie Delta, Anderson River, Great Slave
Lake); northern Saskatchewan (Lake Athabasca); northern Manitoba; northern Ontario;
northern Quebec (Kuujjuaq, Hutte sauvage
Lake); central Labrador, (Okak, Udjuktok
Bay), and Newfoundland south locally to
southern British Columbia (Atlin, Peace River
region, south to Tod Mountain, situated 40 km
northeast of Kamloops, and Manning Provincial Park); south-central Alberta (near Banff,
probably Red Deer); central-eastern Saskatchewan (Hudson Bay Junction); southern Manitoba (Riverton, Kalevala near Mulvihill);
Ontario (Sutton Ridges, Thunder Bay, Parry
Sound, Ottawa; perhaps Cameron); southern
Quebec (Lochaber, Gaspé Peninsula); and New
Brunswick (rarely: Tabusintac).

Winters from northernmost parts of breeding range (Mackenzie Delta, Hutte sauvage
Lake) south irregularly and in variable numbers
to southern parts of all provinces.

A medium-sized slender owl without ear tufts; tail longish, decidedly
graduated, its feathers tapering toward tip. Sexes alike in colour. Upper
parts dark brown spotted with white. Chest and abdomen sharply and
regularly barred with brown; greyish-white facial disc with black outer
border, the border extending down to sides of breast. Eyes and exposed
part of bill, yellow. The sharply barred chest, sides, and abdomen, and
the long tail are distinctive.

Measurements. *Adult male*: wing, 210–231 (222.4); tail, 167–187
(177.9); culmen (from cere), 18.6–19.8 (19). *Adult female*: wing,
223–235.5 (228.6) mm.

Field Marks. A medium-sized, slender, long-tailed owl (often flicks
tail) with sharply barred under parts and without ear tufts. Black outer
margin of facial disc extends down to sides of chest. Active in daylight.
Often perches on tree tops. Long slender tail gives it a hawk-like
appearance. Flight, swift and hawk-like with rapid wing-beats, occasionally hovers. *Voice*: A series of *kip, kip,* or *kleep, kleep*; a rising
skree-e-e-e-e-yip, the *yip* emphatic.

Habitat. Open coniferous or mixed woodland, muskeg, or burntland with standing stubs.

Nesting. Nests in hollow top of a dead tree stub, in an old woodpecker hole, or in an old hawk or crow nest. *Eggs*, usually 3 to 7;
white. Incubation period 25 to 29 days.

Range. Holarctic. Breeds in the northern coniferous belts, north to
tree limit, across Eurasia and North America. Winters in the breeding
range and somewhat farther south, in North America south to southern
Canada and northern United States.

Subspecies. *Surnia ulula caparoch* (Müller).

1 Black-billed Cuckoo,
p. 304
a) adult
b) first-autumn plumage showing
wing and bill coloration extremes,
which may cause confusion with
Yellow-billed Cuckoo)

1b

1a

3 Belted Kingfisher, p. 341
adult male

3

2 Yellow-billed Cuckoo, p. 305
adult

2

6 Band-tailed Pigeon, p. 299

6

4 Mourning Dove,
p. 300

4

5

7 Rock Dove, p. 298

7

5 Passenger Pigeon, p. 301

Crosby '63

42

1 Great Horned Owl, p. 310

2 Long-eared Owl, p. 325

3a

4 Western Screech-Owl,
p. 309

3b

3 Eastern Screech-Owl, p. 308
a) grey phase
b) red phase

5 Common Barn-Owl, p. 307

7 Flammulated Owl, p. 308

6 Snowy Owl, p. 311

Crosby

2 Great Gray Owl, p. 324

1 Spotted Owl, p. 322

3 Barred Owl, p. 323

Crosby

4 Short-eared Owl, p. 326

1 Northern Hawk-Owl, p. 312

1

2 Northern Saw-whet Owl,
p. 328

2

3

3 Northern Pygmy-Owl, p. 321

4

4 Burrowing Owl, p. 321

5

5 Boreal Owl, p. 327

Crosby

1 White-throated Swift, p. 336

2 Black Swift, p. 334

3 Vaux's Swift, p. 336

4 Chimney Swift, p. 335

5 Common Poorwill, p. 331

6 Common Nighthawk, p. 330

7 Whip-poor-will, p. 332

Crosby

46

1 Black-chinned
Hummingbird, p. 338
adult male

3a

4a

2a

3b

4 Calliope Hummingbird, p. 339
a) adult male
b) female

4b

2b

5

2 Ruby-throated
Hummingbird, p. 337
a) adult male
b) female

3 Rufous Hummingbird, p. 340
a) adult female
b) adult male

6 Red-bellied Woodpecker, p. 345
male

7a

5 Anna's
Hummingbird,
p. 338
adult male

6

9a

7 Yellow-bellied Sapsucker, p. 345
a) adult male
b) adult female

8

7b

9b

8 Red-breasted
Sapsucker, p. 346
adult (*ruber* race)

9 Williamson's Sapsucker, p. 347
a) adult male
b) adult female

Crosby

1a 1b

1 Downy Woodpecker,
p. 348
a) adult male
b) adult female

2

2 Hairy Woodpecker,
p. 349
adult male

4a

4b

4 Black-backed Woodpecker, p. 352
a) adult male
b) adult female

5

5 Pic tri 5 Three-toed
Woodpecker,
p. 351
adult male

3 Red-headed Woodpecker, p. 344
a) first-autumn immature
b) adult

3b

3a

6 Lewis's Woodpecker, p. 343

6

7

7 Pileated Woodpecker, p. 354
adult male

8 Northern Flicker, p. 352
a) "Red-shafted" races,
adult male
b) "Yellow-shafted" races,
adult female
c) "Yellow-shafted" races,
adult male

8c

8a

8b

Crosby
/65

48

1

2 Western Wood-Pewee, p. 356

2

4

4 Great Crested Flycatcher, p. 367

1 Eastern Wood-Pewee, p. 357

3

3 Olive-sided Flycatcher, p. 355

5 Eastern Kingbird, p. 370

5

6

6 Western Kingbird, p. 369

8

7 Eastern Phoebe, p. 365

7

8 Say's Phoebe, p. 366

Crosby

Northern Pygmy-Owl

Chouette naine
Glaucidium gnoma Wagler
Total length: 16 to 18.5 cm
Plate 44

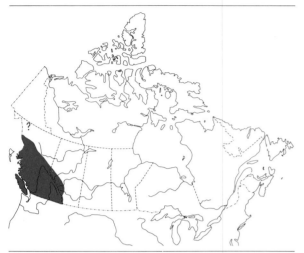

Breeding Distribution of Northern
Pygmy-Owl

Range in Canada. Found in British Columbia
(permanent resident breeding in southern and
central parts including Vancouver Island.
Recorded, but without evidence of breeding,
northwest to Atlin and Driftwood River.
Absent from Queen Charlotte Islands and
probably from the northeastern corner of the
province) and Alberta (probably breeds in
mountains of southwest near Banff and Jasper,
but definite evidence is needed. Wanders in
winter farther east: to Nordegg, Peers, Fort
Assiniboine, Phoenix, Sedgewick, McLeod
River valley, Calgary, and Alexo).

A tiny western owl, smaller even than the Saw-whet Owl, with small
head and no ear tufts. Sexes alike. Upper parts greyish to reddish
brown, finely spotted with buffy white especially top of head, scapulars,
and wings; around back of neck a narrow half-collar of mixed black
and white. Lower breast and abdomen, white striped with dark brown.
Tail dark brown with six or seven white cross-bars. Eyes yellow. Distinguished from other Canadian owls by very small size and black-and-
white half-collar on back of neck. Young similar to adults but top of
head dark grey with only a few spots on forehead.

Measurements *(G. g. swarthi). Adult male*: wing, 87.3–93.3 (89.6);
tail, 57.5–65 (62.2); culmen (from cere), 10.6–11.9 (11.2). *Adult female*:
wing, 90.9–96 (92.8) mm.

Field Marks. A bluebird-sized western owl with small head, no ear
tufts, and rather longish tail often held quite high. Might be confused
with the Saw-whet Owl, which is slightly larger. The Pygmy's sharper,
darker stripes on the under parts, the black-and-white half-collar on
hind neck, the small head, and the often slightly elevated tail distinguish
it. The Pygmy is active during the day, especially early morning and
evening. *Voice*: A series of hollow, low, whistled, spaced *ook* notes,
which are easily imitated.

Habitat. Open or broken coniferous and mixed woodland, edges
and openings of coniferous forest.

Nesting. In abandoned woodpecker holes in trees, either deciduous
or coniferous. *Eggs*, 2 to 7, usually 3 or 4; white, almost spherical.
Incubation, by female, lasts about 28 days.

Range. Southeastern Alaska and northwestern and central British
Columbia south through the Rockies and California to Guatemala.

Subspecies. There is considerable disagreement on the subspecies
and their nomenclature. The *A.O.U. Check-list* (Fifth Edition) recog-
nizes three races in British Columbia: (1) *Glaucidium gnoma swarthi*
Grinnell (Vancouver Island), (2) *G. g. grinnelli* Ridgway (western mainland), and (3) *G. g. californicum* Sclater (interior of British Columbia
and western Alberta). However, see Munro and Cowan (1947) and
Jewett, Taylor, Shaw, and Aldrich (1953). A study of critical material
from both Canada and United States is needed.

Burrowing Owl

Chouette des terriers
Athene cunicularia (Molina)
Total length: 23 to 25.5 cm
Plate 44

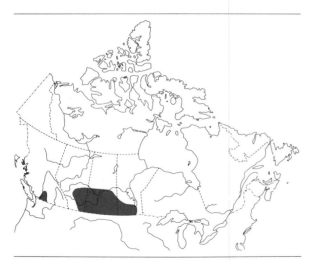

Breeding Distribution of Burrowing Owl

A smallish round-headed owl with no ear tufts, poorly developed facial
disc, long slim legs (tarsi unfeathered except sparsely in front), and
short tail. Adults, above greyish brown, thickly spotted with whites and
buffs; eyebrows and throat white, the lower throat crossed by a dark-
brown half-collar; breast and abdomen whitish, barred with brown; eyes
yellow. Young for a short time lack brown bars on under parts. Size,
sandy coloration, and long, slim, almost-bare legs and toes make the
species unmistakable.

Measurements *(A. c. hypugaea). Adult male*: wing, 166–176
(171.5); tail, 77–84.5 (81.6); culmen (from cere), 13.9–15 (14.4). *Adult
female*: wing, 169–178.5 (172.5) mm.

Field Marks. A smallish sandy-coloured owl with short tail and
long, slim, almost-bare legs. Active both day and night, mostly at dusk.
Usually seen on the ground, or on a low fence post, in open country.
Has bobbing motion when disturbed. Short-eared Owl also is found in
similar open places but is much larger, is differently shaped, and has
striped instead of barred under parts.

Habitat. Drier open short-grass treeless country.

Range in Canada. Breeds in southern interior British Columbia (Kamloops; Similkameen and Okanagan valleys); southern Alberta (southern plains north to Munson and Provost); southern Saskatchewan (southern plains north to Livelong, Saskatoon, and Nipawin); southwestern and central-southern Manitoba (Whitewater Lake, Virden, Emerson, Winnipeg vicinity).

A few winter in extreme southwestern British Columbia (Comox; Trail and Snake islands; rarely Victoria and Vancouver). Casual in Ontario (specimen: Ajax, 15 October 1963; sight records at Aldershot, Erieau, Kleinberg, and Manitoulin Island). Accidental in southern Quebec (specimen: Matagami, 10 May 1971; photo record: Arvida, September 1959). Sight record for New Brunswick: Sackville, 18–28 June 1978.

Nesting. Nests at the end of a (1.5 to 3 m) ground burrow, dug and abandoned by a mammal. *Eggs*, 6 to 10; white, often nest-stained.

Range. Plains and treeless areas from southern parts of western Canada through western United States (west from Minnesota, Iowa, Oklahoma, and rarely Louisiana) to Honduras, central and southern Florida, the West Indies, Central America, and much of South America. In winter, it retreats from its northernmost breeding grounds.

Subspecies. *Athene cunicularia hypugaea* (Bonaparte).

Spotted Owl

Chouette tachetée
Strix occidentalis (Xantus)
Total length: 42 to 48.5 cm
Plate 43

Breeding Distribution of Spotted Owl

Range in Canada. Scarce permanent resident in extreme southwestern mainland British Columbia (north to Alta Lake, east to Hope and Manning Provincial Park). Not known to occur on Vancouver Island.

A largish round-headed hornless owl with black eyes. Most closely resembles the Barred Owl but averages slightly smaller; browns are much darker and richer; top of head and hind-neck are spotted (instead of barred) with whitish; and abdomen is barred instead of striped. Sexes alike.

Measurements. *Adult male*: wing, 310–326 (320.5); tail, 210–220 (215.8); culmen (from cere), 21–22 (21.3). *Adult female*: wing, ca. 328 mm (Ridgway).

Field Marks. A largish dark-brown hornless owl with black eyes, found in forests of southwestern British Columbia. Our only other owls with black eyes are the Barred Owl and the obviously different Common Barn-Owl. The Spotted is easily distinguished from the Barred by the former's lack of stripes on the abdomen and by its darker, richer coloration.

Habitat. Dense forests, mainly coniferous, wooded ravines.

Nesting. Little known in Canada. In a tree cavity or crevice in a cliff. *Eggs*, 2 or 3; plain white.

Range. Permanent resident from southwestern British Columbia southward in coastal forests to southern California; and in the southern Rocky Mountains, from central Colorado south through eastern Arizona, New Mexico and western Texas to central Mexico.

Subspecies. *Strix occidentalis caurina* (Merriam).

Barred Owl

Chouette rayée
Strix varia Barton
Total length: 45.5 to 58 cm
Plate 43

Breeding Distribution of Barred Owl

Range in Canada. Permanent resident in woodlands of British Columbia (scarce: Liard Crossing; Hart Lake, about 80 km north of Prince George; near Likely; Birch Creek; Salmon River, northwest of Vernon; probably Cortes Island); central and western Alberta (Edmonton, Smoky River, north of Jasper; and northward in wooded country at least to Lesser Slave Lake region and probably McMurray); central Saskatchewan (Klogei, Madge, and Emma lakes, Cumberland House); south-central and southeastern Manitoba (woodland north to Reader Lake near The Pas); central and southern Ontario (north at least to Sandy Lake and Moose Factory); southern Quebec (north to Lake Waswanipi; Lake Paterson, Mistassibi watershed; Godbout); New Brunswick, Prince Edward Island; and Nova Scotia. Winters throughout breeding range.

Rare visitant to Vancouver Island (photos: Victoria, 26 November 1969 and 5 and 7 April 1979) and Vancouver (photo: winter 1977–1978).

A largish brown-and-white round-headed owl without ear tufts. Sexes alike. Upper parts greyish brown, barred on head, neck, tail and flight feathers, and spotted elsewhere, with buffy white. Under parts whitish, the chest closely barred, the abdomen striped with brown; eyes blackish; bill yellowish. The combination of barred breast and striped abdomen distinguishes it.

Measurements *(S. v. varia). Adult male*: wing, 310.5–330 (320.1); tail, 209–230.5 (218.6); culmen (from cere), 21.5–25 (23.6). *Adult female*: wing, 320.5–334 (328.5) mm.

Field Marks. A largish brown-and-white, nocturnal, round-headed owl with no ear tufts. It has black eyes, a barred breast, and a striped abdomen. Resembles Great Gray Owl and also the Spotted Owl of western British Columbia. The Barred Owl's barred breast, black eyes, and smaller size exclude the Great Gray. Striped abdomen and paler coloration separate it from the Spotted Owl. *Voice*: Hooting is less deep and more varied than that of the Great Horned Owl, closing with an extra syllable. Sounds like, *"Who cooks for yo-all?"*

Habitat. Denser darker forests, woodlands, even isolated woodlots of maturer trees (apparently prefers coniferous or mixed woods to deciduous), especially near lakes, streams, swamps, or marshes.

Nesting. Usually in hollows in trees (either deciduous or coniferous) but also in deserted tree nests of hawks or crows. *Eggs*, 2 or 3; plain white.

Range. Southern wooded Canada (from eastern British Columbia east to Nova Scotia) southward through the United States (east of the Rocky Mountains), and the mountains of Mexico to western Guatemala and Honduras.

Subspecies. *Strix varia varia* Barton.

Great Gray Owl

Chouette lapone
Strix nebulosa Forster
Total length: 63.5 to 84 cm
Plate 43

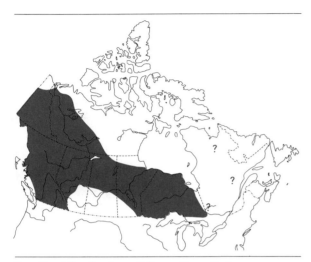

Breeding Distribution of Great Gray Owl

Range in Canada. Definite breeding data relatively few. Breeds sparsely in wooded country from northern Yukon (Old Crow, Lapierre House); northwestern and central Mackenzie (Lockhart River, Great Slave Lake); Saskatchewan (Pasquia Forest, Fort-à-la-Corne Game Reserve, and Flat Creek in Prince Albert National Park; probably Lake Athabasca); northern Manitoba (The Pas); and northern Ontario (probably Severn River, Moose Factory); south through southern Yukon and interior British Columbia (probably south at least to Hulcar, 22.5 km north of Vernon); northern and central Alberta (Fort Chipewyan, Whitemud Lake, Belvedere, Edson, Rocky Mountain House, Jasper, possibly to Sundre and Calgary); Manitoba (Dauphin Lake, South Junction); and central Ontario (Atikokan, Nipissing District; Pickle Lake). Probably Quebec but breeding evidence lacking (reported in summer at Fort-Mackenzie; Vauquelin River; just north of Lake Saint-Jean; and Gatineau Park).

Winters throughout breeding range (north to Mackenzie Delta) and in irregular numbers south of it in wooded parts of southern Canada and southeastward casually to New Brunswick and Nova Scotia (Pictou County). An exceptionally heavy southward movement in winter 1978–1979 when up to 34 were counted on small Amherst Island, near Kingston, Ontario.

A very large (our largest), grey round-headed, hornless owl with very large facial disc, yellow eyes, and long tail. Sexes alike. Most closely resembles Barred Owl but is much larger, more greyish (less brownish) in coloration, lacks distinct bars on back of neck and breast, has yellow eyes.

Measurements. *Adult male*: wing, 396–437.5 (416.3); tail, 295.5–305 (299.1); culmen (from cere), 22.5–25.3 (24.3). *Adult female*: wing, 417–461.5 (433.4) mm.

Field Marks. An extremely large grey hornless owl with very large facial disc, yellow eyes, long tail, and indistinctly striped under parts. Below the bill is a black area, which divides a narrow but surprisingly conspicuous white throat patch. Distinguished from Barred Owl by bright-yellow eyes, unbarred breast, conspicuous white throat-markings, and much more definite concentric rings on facial disc. It usually is quite tame. Frequently forages in daylight.

Habitat. Boreal forests, either coniferous or deciduous; spruce-tamarack bogs. While wintering in settled parts of the country, various woodland types, frequently deciduous. Often hunts meadow mice in open fields or bushy clearings using fence posts, low trees, shrubbery, and wood edges as lookouts.

Nesting. In an abandoned nest of hawk or crow, 4.5 to 15 m up in either a broadleafed or coniferous tree. *Eggs*, 2 to 5 or more, most often 3; dull white, rather small for the size of the bird and less rounded, more oval, than is usual in owls.

Range. Northern coniferous belt across North America and Eurasia. In North America breeds from near tree limit in central Alaska and Canada south in the western mountains to California (Madera County), northern Idaho, western Montana, Wyoming, northern Minnesota, and south-central Ontario. Winters within breeding range and irregularly south of it.

Subspecies. *Strix nebulosa nebulosa* Forster.

Remarks. Although our largest owl, its food is primarily mice and other small mammals.

Long-eared Owl

Hibou moyen-duc
Asio otus (Linnaeus)
Total length: 33 to 41 cm
Plate 42

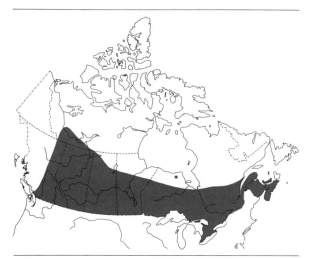

Breeding Distribution of Long-eared Owl

Range in Canada. Breeds in woodlands in southern Mackenzie (Fort Simpson, Fort Providence); southern British Columbia (Nulki Lake, Lulu Island, Vaseux Lake, possibly Comox where young male was collected in August 1933); Alberta; Saskatchewan; central and southern Manitoba (Shoal Lake, Aweme; probably north to The Pas and Herb Lake; recorded in summer north to Churchill); central and southern Ontario (north to Sutton Ridges (rarely) and James Bay); southern Quebec (north to Saint-Félicien and Rimouski: probably to Gaspé Bay; recorded in summer north to Grande rivière de la Baleine and Lake Guillaume-Delisle); New Brunswick (Saint John, St. Stephen; probably Saint-Léonard), Nova Scotia (Wolfville); and Prince Edward Island (Rustico Island). In winter withdraws from northern colder parts of the range but winters in warmer parts (British Columbia, southern Ontario, and the Maritimes); one record for Labrador (Red Bay, 8 December 1930) and Yukon (specimen: Dempster Highway, Mile 65, 19 May 1977).

Ear tufts long, conspicuous. Sexes similar (female larger and slightly darker). Upper parts dark brown, mixed with tawny and speckled and mottled with greyish white. Face tawny. Abdomen and sides white, boldly striped and narrowly cross-barred with brown. Eyes yellow. Canada has four owls with conspicuous long ear tufts, one very large (Great Horned), two small (screech-owls), and one medium-sized (Long-eared) (see also Field Marks).

Measurements *(A. o. wilsonianus). Adult male*: wing, 269.5–295 (286.7); tail, 141.5–153.5 (148.1); culmen (from cere), 15–17.7 (17.1). *Adult female*: wing, 274.8–300 (283.6) mm.

Field Marks. A not large (crow-sized) owl with long ear tufts, which are usually visible when it is at rest. Great Horned and screech-owls also have conspicuous ear tufts. Long-eared Owl's much smaller size, slenderer build, position of ear tufts nearer centre of head, and stripes on abdomen distinguish it from the Great Horned Owl; and its larger size and tawny face separate it from the grey-phased screech-owls. In flight when the ear tufts are flattened, its greyer (less buffy) general coloration distinguishes it from the Short-eared Owl. It is nocturnal, whereas the Short-eared Owl is active during the day as well as at night.

Habitat. Denser parts of woods (not necessarily extensive) and copses, probably preferring coniferous or mixed wood when available but in the Prairie Provinces regularly uses deciduous types also. Hunts over open country as well as in woodland. Often roosts gregariously.

Nesting. Nests in woodland, 3 to 9 m up in a tree, usually using a nest of a hawk, crow, or magpie; occasionally on the ground. *Eggs*, 3 to 7; white. Incubation period about 28 days (E.L. Summer), mainly by the female.

Range. Holarctic. Breeds in woodland across Eurasia and south to northwest Africa, and across North America. In North America from southern Canada south to northwest Baja California, southern Arizona, Oklahoma, Arkansas, and Virginia.

Subspecies. (1) *Asio otus wilsonianus* (Lesson) breeds across eastern Canada intergrading with the following subspecies in southwestern Manitoba. (2) *A. o. tuftsi* Godfrey, a paler western subspecies, breeding from extreme southwestern Manitoba (Whitewater Lake), and Saskatchewan westward (no material examined from Mackenzie District or northern Alberta).

Remarks. Dozing away the daylight hours deep in tangles of prairie coulees or in coniferous or alder thickets in the East, this owl is not often seen. Mice and other small rodents are its staple food. Although usually silent, its calls include soft hoots, mews, and shrieks.

Short-eared Owl

Hibou des marais
Asio flammeus (Pontoppidan)
Total length: 33 to 43 cm
Plate 43

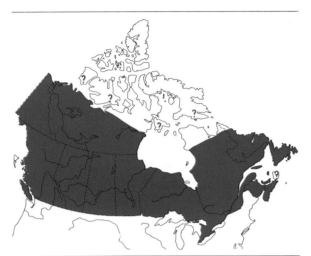

Breeding Distribution of Short-eared Owl

Range in Canada. Breeds from northern Yukon, northern Mackenzie (Franklin Bay, Coronation Gulf), central Keewatin (Schultz Lake), southern coasts of Hudson Bay, James Bay, northern Quebec (Feuilles River, Kuujjuaq), and northern Labrador (Ramah), south through southern Yukon to southern British Columbia (except Queen Charlotte and Vancouver islands), Alberta, Saskatchewan, Manitoba, Ontario, Quebec, the Maritimes, and Newfoundland. Perhaps breeds north to southern Banks Island, and southern Victoria Island, where the species has been reliably reported in summer. Perhaps also on southern Baffin Island (old breeding reports at the Greater Kingwah and Kingnait Fiord require confirmation).

Winters in southern British Columbia, southern Ontario, occasionally in the Maritimes, Newfoundland, and Madeleine Islands, Quebec; rarely and precariously elsewhere.

Ear tufts very short, scarcely discernible. A medium-sized buffy-white owl, the upper parts broadly but softly streaked, the abdomen narrowly and more sharply streaked with brown. Flight feathers and tail barred with brown. Eyes yellow, framed by a small poorly defined blackish area on facial disc.

Measurements. *Adult male*: wing, 283.5–307.5 (302.9); tail, 135.5–149.5 (146); culmen (from cere), 16–18.2 (16.8). *Adult female*: wing, 291–315 (302) mm.

Field Marks. A crow-sized brown-streaked buffy owl (ear tufts usually not perceptible), active in daylight, especially at dusk, and inhabiting open places (not a woodland owl). Like the Long-eared Owl, it shows in flight a black patch near the wrist on the underside of the wing, but the more buffy general colour and complete lack of any cross-barring on the abdomen of the Short-ear should distinguish it. The Rough-legged Hawk shows a similar black wrist mark in flight, but the owl has a very different big-headed silhouette and lighter, more buoyant flight. Northern Harriers, inhabiting similar open areas, have a conspicuous white rump patch, which the owl lacks.

Habitat. Open grassland, grassy or bushy meadows, fresh and salt marshes, bogs, low-arctic tundra.

Nesting. On ground in open places, a depression often sparsely lined with grasses and similar material, sometimes sheltered by a clump of grass or weeds. *Eggs*, 4 to 9, usually 5 to 7; white. Incubation period 24 to 28 days (J. Vincent, *in* Witherby).

Range. Europe, Asia, North and South America, Hawaiian Islands. Withdraws in winter from northernmost parts of range.

Subspecies. *Asio flammeus flammeus* (Pontoppidan).

Remarks. With easy buoyant wingbeats, the Short-eared Owl quarters marsh and meadow. Now and then it pauses to pounce on any unwary mouse. It is most often observed in the evening, but it is more or less active also at other times of the day or night. Like most of our owls, it is a valuable and efficient destroyer of rodent pests.

Boreal Owl

(Richardson's Owl)

Nyctale boréale
Aegolius funereus (Linnaeus)
Total length: 21.5 to 26.5 cm
Plate 44

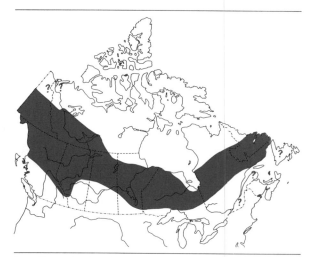

Breeding Distribution of Boreal Owl

Range in Canada. Breeds (details of full breeding range not well known) in woodland from central Yukon (Forty Mile; possibly north to Old Crow), Mackenzie (Fort Simpson; probably north to Lake Hardisty and possibly even to Mackenzie Delta where early autumn occurrence has been reported); northern Saskatchewan (Lake Athabasca); northern Manitoba (probably York Factory and Cape Churchill); northern Ontario; central Quebec (probably Paul Bay; possibly Lake Aulneau); and Labrador (Hopedale); south to northern British Columbia (Flood Glacier; probably Laurier Pass); central Alberta (Belvedere, Jasper, Banff, and lower Kananaskis valley); central-eastern Saskatchewan (Nipawin); southern Manitoba (near Winnipeg, Shelley); central Ontario (Kenora, Mildred, Kapuskasing); southern New Brunswick (Grand Manan); and Madeleine Islands, Quebec. Probably breeds also in Newfoundland, but evidence is inconclusive.

Winters within breeding range and southward: north at least to northern British Columbia (Atlin); southern Mackenzie (Fort Simpson); central Manitoba (Herb Lake); south-central Quebec (Lake Mistassini); and southern Labrador; south in irregular (occasionally substantial) numbers to southern parts of all the provinces including the Maritimes and Newfoundland.

A small owl lacking ear tufts. *Adults (sexes similarly coloured)*: Upper parts chocolate brown spotted with white, thickly so on forehead; under parts white, blotchily streaked with brown; greyish-white facial disc has a narrow dark-brown or blackish outer border. Eyes yellow. Bill yellowish.

Measurements. *Adult male*: wing, 159.5–173.5 (165.9); tail, 88–102.5 (96.5); culmen (from cere), 13.2–16 (14.4). *Adult female*: wing, 164.8–179.9 (173.6) mm.

Field Marks. A smallish nocturnal (diurnal in northernmost part of range) dark brown-and-white owl without ear tufts. Separable from the Saw-whet Owl by larger size, yellowish bill, and round white spots on forehead (instead of narrow streaks). Round hornless head distinguishes it from the screech-owls, which are of similar size. *Voice*: In breeding season a monotonous *tu-tu-tu-tu* with a hollow quality a little reminiscent of winnowing of a snipe.

Habitat. Coniferous and mixedwood forests. When it wanders into settled country in winter, it may roost in a variety of situations including isolated deciduous trees as well as coniferous woodland, sometimes buildings, and even on a haystack.

Nesting. Nests in cavities in trees (abandoned nests of larger woodpeckers or in natural cavities). The tree may be either broadleaf or conifer. *Eggs*, 3 to 7, usually 4 to 6; white. Incubation probably largely, if not entirely, by female. Incubation period 27 days (A. Norberg).

Range. Breeds in boreal woodlands across Eurasia and North America. In North America from Alaska eastward across the coniferous forest belt of Canada. In winter, south irregularly to northern United States.

Subspecies. *Aegolius funereus richardsoni* (Bonaparte).

Northern Saw-whet Owl

Petite Nyctale
Aegolius acadicus (Gmelin)
Total length: 18 to 21.5 cm
Plate 44

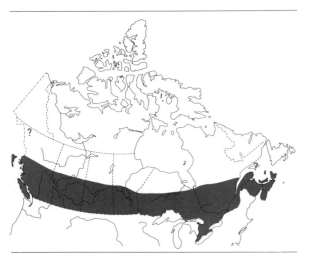

Breeding Distribution of Northern Saw-whet Owl

Range in Canada. Permanent resident where woodland habitat is available all across extreme southern Canada from Vancouver Island, British Columbia, to Cape Breton Island, Nova Scotia, and north to central British Columbia (northern Queen Charlotte Islands, Topley, Nulki Lake; possibly northwest to Atlin where twice taken in winter); central Alberta (Big Mouth Creek on Athabasca River and near Valleyview); central Saskatchewan (Prince Albert, Nipawin); central Manitoba (Cedar Lake); central Ontario (Red Lake, Lake Nipigon, Moose Factory); southern Quebec (La Vérendrye Park, Gaspé Peninsula, Madeleine Islands, possibly to Fort-George and Anticosti Island); New Brunswick; Prince Edward Island; and Nova Scotia (Sydney, Cape North).

Winters within breeding range, but many individuals move to more southern points, occasionally in incursion numbers. Casual in Newfoundland (specimens: Colinet, April 1940; Saint John's, 5 April 1980).

Our smallest *eastern* owl, only the Pygmy-Owl of the West being smaller. No ear tufts. Adults most similar to Boreal Owl but smaller; browns (especially of under parts) more reddish; crown with narrow white *streaks* instead of spots; outer sides of facial disc tinged buffy and marked with dusky lines radiating outward; bill black. Juvenal plumage (worn only a short time after leaving nest) is solid brown above (but wings white-spotted as in adults), a brown band across breast, plain cinnamon-buff abdomen and sides; facial disc blackish brown, except whitish space between and over eyes.

Adults easily distinguished from Pygmy-Owl by their larger size, softer more luxuriant plumage, well-feathered toes (sparsely feathered in young), larger head, lack of spots on sides.

Measurements *(A. a. acadicus). Adult male*: wing, 127–139.2 (133.2); tail, 66.9–74 (70.3); culmen (from cere), 11.6–12.9 (12.4). *Adult female*: wing, 131.5–144.9 (140.3) mm.

Field Marks. A very small hornless nocturnal owl. Black bill, forehead streaked instead of spotted, and smaller size distinguish it from the Boreal Owl. Separable from Pygmy-Owl of the West by broader more diffuse reddish-brown abdominal streaks (dark, sharply defined in Pygmy), larger size and heavier build, larger head. Unlike the Pygmy-Owl, the Saw-whet is not active in the daytime (but both hunt at dusk). *Voice*: Various calls, but the commonest is a long-continued series of monotonous, short, evenly spaced, low whistles.

Habitat. Coniferous and deciduous woodlands, especially moister ones; also dense alder thickets and cedar and tamarack bogs.

Nesting. Nests in old woodpecker holes or other cavities in trees. *Eggs*, 4 to 7, usually 5 or 6; white. Incubation period variously reported from 21 to 28 days. At least 26 days (L.M. Terrill).

Range. Breeds from southeastern Alaska and across southern Canada south to southern California, Arizona, Mexico (Oaxaca, Puebla, Veracruz), Oklahoma, Missouri, Ohio, West Virginia, and Maryland.

Subspecies. (1) *Aegolius acadicus acadicus* (Gmelin) is the breeding bird of all Canada except Queen Charlotte Islands, British Columbia. (2) *A. a. brooksi* (Fleming), a more heavily pigmented subspecies, is confined to Queen Charlotte Islands, British Columbia.

Remarks. One misty evening in early September on northern Cape Breton Island, I was setting out a line of mouse traps in an alder thicket. There came a soft flutter of wings, and quite suddenly a Sawwhet Owl was sitting on an alder branch not more than 3 m from my face. It seemed overcome with curiosity. Its contortions were comical as its head twisted sideways and up and down until sometimes its chin almost rested on its feet as its wide round eyes strove to get a better look at me. After a few minutes of this, it fluttered off into the fast-gathering dusk, its flight suggesting that of a woodcock.

Tameness is a characteristic of this tiny owl. Perched motionless and silent in shadowy woodlands during the day, it is readily overlooked. It is active at night, and in the dusk and during spring it is often quite vocal. It derives its name from one of its calls, which sounds like the filing of a saw. Its ringing, metallic, one-syllabled call-notes may be delivered monotonously for a considerable time, with only short pauses between, during the darker hours and in the evening and morning dusk, mostly in spring.

The Saw-whet Owl's food consists mainly of mice, but it takes also bats, shrews, young squirrels, insects, and the occasional small bird. In the severest parts of the winter, especially if the snow is very deep, Saw-whets seem to have difficulty securing adequate food, and at such times they may suffer considerable mortality.

Order **Caprimulgiformes:**
Goatsuckers, Oilbirds, and Allies

Family **Caprimulgidae:**
Goatsuckers

Number of Species in Canada: 5

Plumage soft and coloured in mixture of wood browns, buffs, white, and black. Head rather flattened; bill tiny; mouth enormous, opening back under the ears; feet small and weak, the middle toenail with comb-like serrations on its edge. The name "goatsucker" was long ago derived from an erroneous belief that these birds with their large mouths sucked milk from goats in pastures. Doubtless the birds flew about over the pastures only to feed on the insects attracted or stirred up by the animals. Birds of this family are extremely beneficial as their food is mostly insects taken on the wing. They have nearly noiseless flight, large eyes, and nocturnal vision. Their soft plumage closely resembles that of the owls, their nearest relatives. They build no nest, the eggs being laid on the ground.

Lesser Nighthawk

Engoulevent minime
Chordeiles acutipennis (Hermann)
Total length: 23 cm
Figure 76

Very similar to the somewhat larger Common Nighthawk but with the pale wing bar (white in male, buffy in female) closer to tip of wing.

Measurements. *Adult male*: wing, 173–192 (183.4); tail, 104–119 (111.6); culmen, 5–6.8 (5.9); tarsus, 13–15 (14). *Adult female*: wing, 168.5–180 (175); tail, 102–110 (106.1); culmen, 5.1–7 (6); tarsus, 12.5–15.2 (13.5) mm (Ridgway).

Field Marks. Very similar to Common Nighthawk but pale wing bar situated closer to wing tip. In females wing bar is buffy instead of white (although the males have the wing bar white as in the Common Nighthawk). Wing tips more rounded, less pointed. Usually flies lower. Does not execute long steep dives. Does not have the *peent* call of the Common Nighthawk and does not produce a booming noise in flight. Produces trills, whinnying, and winnowing sounds.

Range. Breeds from central California, southwestern Utah, Arizona, southern New Mexico, and southern Texas south to northern Chile and southern Brazil. Winters from northern Mexico southward.

Figure 76
Lesser Nighthawk

Status in Canada. Accidental in Ontario (Point Pelee National Park, 29 April 1974, one individual, apparently a female. Several photos support this unusual record).

Common Nighthawk

Engoulevent d'Amérique
Chordeiles minor (Forster)
Total length: 21 to 25.5 cm
Plate 45

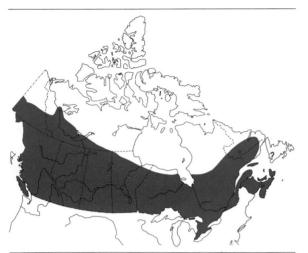

Breeding Distribution of Common Nighthawk

Range in Canada. Breeds all across southern Canada from Vancouver Island, British Columbia east to Cape Breton Island, Nova Scotia; and north through British Columbia (but apparently not recorded for Queen Charlotte Islands) to southern Yukon (Faro, Mile 40 Canol Road, Kathleen River), north through Alberta to southern Mackenzie (Nahanni National Park, Fort Simpson, probably Norman Wells–Fort Norman areas of Mackenzie valley), and to northern Saskatchewan (Lake Athabasca, Black Lake area); northern Manitoba (Lynn Lake, Bird; probably Churchill and Lac Brochet); northern Ontario (north to the coastal lowlands and western James Bay coast); south-central Quebec (north to Fort-George; Lake Mistassini; the inner north shore of the Gulf of St. Lawrence, east probably to about Natashquan; Anticosti Island; eastern Gaspé Peninsula); New Brunswick; Prince Edward Island; and Nova Scotia. Scarce summer resident in interior southern Labrador (Goose Bay, Churchill Falls, Sawbill). Rare summer visitor to Newfoundland (Bonavista Bay, Bay of Islands, Channel-Port aux Basques; no evidence of breeding).

Casual in northern Yukon (Lapierre House; sight record on the arctic coast of Bloomfield Lake, 12 September 1973) and coastal Labrador (Makkovik). Accidental on Melville Island, N.W.T.

Wings long. Tail slightly forked. No bristles on sides of mouth. Very small bill and enormous mouth mark it as a goatsucker. White wing patch, pronounced barring of abdomen and sides, slightly forked tail, lack of buffy bars on primaries, and lack of bristles on sides of mouth distinguish it from other goatsuckers that occur in Canada. *Adult male*: Upper parts blackish, marbled and spotted irregularly with greys, white, and buffs; a conspicuous white patch across the middle of four or five wing primaries; a white bar across tail near its tip; a white band across throat extending backward to below ear coverts; abdomen and sides whitish, regularly barred with blackish. *Adult female*: Similar but broad white patch across tail wanting (although several narrow bars are present); white patches in primaries smaller; throat band often more buffy white. *Juvenals* resemble adult female, but white throat band absent or faintly indicated; primaries with narrow white margins at tips.

Measurements *(C. m. minor)*. *Adult male*: wing, 189–208.5 (198.3); tail, 103.5–120 (101.7); exposed culmen, 6.2–7.5 (6.8); tarsus, 13.3–15.9 (14.9). *Adult female*: wing, 184.2–208 (194.4) mm.

Field Marks. Most often seen on summer evenings (but sometimes at other times of day), high in the air over city or country. The long, slender, pointed wings show a characteristic conspicuous white patch, and the tail is slightly forked (male shows a white tail bar near the tip). Flight graceful, wing beats often erratic. Occasionally it nose-dives, the wings producing a hollow booming sound at the bottom of the dive. Spends day perched lengthwise on a tree branch, on a fence post, on the ground, or on a flat roof of a building. When at rest it resembles the Whip-poor-will, from which it is distinguishable by a white wing patch (often not visible in folded wings), longer wing (reaching to or beyond tip of tail), slightly different position of white throat band (nearer base of bill), slightly forked tail, and decidedly barred sides and abdomen, but no bars on primaries. *Voice*: Mostly in flight, a single harsh nasal *peent*.

Habitat. Forages in the air over city or wilderness. Roosts in trees in open woodlands, fence posts in open areas, or on the ground in woodland openings and clearings, natural open areas, burntlands, flat tops of buildings.

Nesting. No nest is made, the eggs being laid on the ground on sand, gravel, or rock in open places such as woodland openings, clearings, burntlands, prairies and plains, and flat (preferably gravelled) roofs of buildings. *Eggs*, 2; variable in colour, creamy white to pale olive-grey or olive buff, speckled with greys, browns, and black. Incubation 19 days (H. Mousley, A.O. Gross) by female, but some authors doubtfully report assistance by male.

Range. Southern Canada south to southern California; central Nevada; Arizona; northeastern Sonora, Chihuahua, Tamaulipas and Durango, Mexico; Bahama Islands; Jamaica; and Puerto Rico. Winters in South America.

Subspecies. (1) *Chordeiles minor minor* (Forster) is the breeding bird of all eastern Canada and the greater part of western Canada except the dry belt of extreme southeastern British Columbia (Trail, Cranbrook, Elko, Flathead), which is occupied by (2) *C. m. hesperis* Grinnell, a somewhat paler race; and southeastern Alberta (Milk River, Cypress Hills), southern Saskatchewan (Cypress Hills, Davidson), and extreme southwestern Manitoba (Whitewater Lake), which is occupied by (3) *C. m. sennetti* Coues, the palest and most greyish race in Canada. Specimens from extreme southwestern Alberta (south of Banff), not examined by me but said to be intermediate between *hesperis* and *sennetti*.

Remarks. Most people easily recognize the Common Nighthawk with a white spot on each of its long wings as it courses back and forth high in the air on summer evenings. Its nasal *peent*, and the deep booming sound produced by its wings as it pulls out of a steep dive are common sounds over city and country.

It feeds almost entirely on insects, which it captures on the wing. Its mouth is so large that it opens back under the ear and is ideal for this kind of insect catching. As many as 500 mosquitoes have been found in the stomach of a single nighthawk. Another, accidentally killed, had 2175 flying ants in its stomach. Many kinds of beetles are eaten voraciously. When the bird flies close to the ground, it often takes grasshoppers. Although called "Nighthawk" it is not related to the hawks at all, its small soft beak and weak feet being entirely different. Needless to say, it is illegal to molest this valuable and interesting bird at any time.

Common Poorwill

Engoulevent de Nuttall
Phalaenoptilus nuttallii (Audubon)
Total length: 18 to 21.5 cm
Plate 45

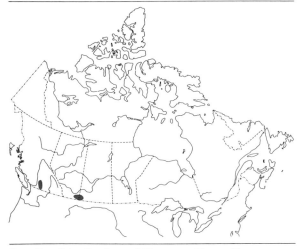

Breeding Distribution of Common Poorwill

Range in Canada. Breeds in southern interior British Columbia (commonly in semi-arid parts: Okanagan valley; Kamloops; Ashcroft, Fraser valley; about 30 km south of Lillooet; Hope; recorded north to Riske Creek where specimen was found dead on 8 September 1968); southern Alberta (locally: Cypress Hills); and southwestern Saskatchewan (Cypress Hills, Great Sand Hills).

Casual in central-eastern Alberta (Lindbergh, 22 October 1971). Accidental in northern Ontario (specimen: North Point, 4 June 1982).

Small bill, immense mouth, and general coloration mark it as a goatsucker. Upper parts finely mottled with greys and browns and sharply marked with black. Tail short, rounded, the outermost three feathers tipped with white (more narrowly in female); cheeks, throat, and upper breast blackish, the throat crossed by a white band. Its small size and short tail distinguish it from our other goatsuckers. From the Common Nighthawk it is distinguished further by its rounded (instead of slightly forked) tail, bristles on sides of mouth, and lack of any white patch on the wings. The white of tail is *at* the tip; in Nighthawk (male only) the white is a bar *near* the tip.

Measurements. *Adult male*: wing, 141–151 (144.4); tail, 84.6–90.2 (87.9); exposed culmen, 7.6–10.6 (9.3); tarsus, 16.8–18.2 (17.4). *Adult female*: wing, 137.5–141 (139.5) mm.

Field Marks. In Canada the only goatsucker normally found in the range of the Poorwill is the Common Nighthawk. Poorwill shows no white patch in the spread wing, is smaller with shorter wing and shorter rounded tail (which, when spread, may show small white tips to the outer feathers). Male Nighthawk shows a white band on tail but not a white tip. Poorwill's voice is an emphatic and far-carrying *poor-will* (accent on second syllable), at close range *poor-will-uck*, usually heard at dusk or at night.

Habitat. Semi-arid sagebrush benchlands or grassy openings in dry open woodland of the Canadian southwest.

Nesting. Eggs laid on bare ground or on a rock, often partly shaded by a bush. The two eggs are pinkish white.

Range. Breeds from southern interior British Columbia, southern Alberta, northwestern South Dakota, and southwestern Iowa south (on the Pacific Coast from central California to southern Baja California) and through eastern Kansas and central Texas to central Mexico. Winters from southwestern United States southward.

Subspecies. *Phalaenoptilus nuttallii nuttallii* (Audubon).

Chuck-will's-widow

Engoulevent de Caroline
Caprimulgus carolinensis Gmelin
Total length: 28 to 33 cm

Status in Canada. Breeds in extreme southern Ontario (nest discovered at Point Pelee on 5 June 1977). Presence of a pair there had been noted two years previously. Probably has nested also at Prince Edward Point where the species was present in 1978 and in two previous years.

Accidental visitant to New Brunswick (specimen: Saint John, 20 May 1916); Nova Scotia (specimens: Pictou, late October, about 1890; Canso, 1 June 1905; Freeport, early May 1963; photo: Outer Island, 1 November 1981); and Quebec (photo: Westmount, 3 May 1983).

The largest goatsucker known to occur in Canada. Similar to Whip-poor-will but decidedly larger and readily distinguishable from it in the hand by differences in the long bristles on sides of mouth. These bristles have fine branches near their base, while those of the Whip-poor-will are bare, unbranched. Adult male Chuck-will's-widow also differs from the male Whip-poor-will by brown instead of black throat; less conspicuous white in the tail, the white there confined to the *inner* webs of three outer tail feathers (in the male Whip-poor-will, white occupies both webs of the three outer tail feathers). Females and immatures are similar to those of Whip-poor-will but much larger size and branched mouth bristles are always diagnostic.

Measurements. *Adult male*: wing, 206.5–225 (213.9); tail, 138.5–151 (144.1); exposed culmen, 9–14.5 (12.5); tarsus, 17.5–19 (18.4). *Adult female*: wing, 201.5–215 (209) mm (Ridgway).

Field Marks. More often heard than seen and voice distinguishes it from the Whip-poor-will. Call is *chuck-will-widow* (four syllables with strongest accent on second to last syllable compared with the Whip-poor-will's *three* syllabled *whip-poor-will* with strongly accented last syllable). Chuck-will's-widow is overall more brownish, with brown instead of black throat, shows less white in the tail, and is somewhat larger in dimensions.

Habitat. Woodlands and woodland patches, deciduous, coniferous, or mixed.

Nesting. *Eggs* (2) are cream or whitish, handsomely blotched and spotted with browns underlaid with purplish greys. Eggs are placed on the ground usually on dead leaves. Incubation period about 20 days.

Range. Breeds from southern New Jersey, southern Ontario, southern Illinois, and eastern Kansas south to southern Florida, the Gulf Coast, and central Texas. Winters from Florida south through the Greater Antilles, southern Mexico, Central America, to Colombia.

Whip-poor-will

Engoulevent bois-pourri
Caprimulgus vociferus Wilson
Total length: 23 to 25.5 cm
Plate 45

Breeding Distribution of Whip-poor-will

Range in Canada. Breeds in central Saskatchewan (rarely: Nipawin; probably Prince Albert, Yorkton, and Anglin Lake); southern Manitoba (Gypsumville, Shoal Lake, Sprague); central-southern and southern Ontario (Off Lake, Nipigon, Kapuskasing); southern Quebec (Lake

Bill small, mouth enormous. Wings long, tail rounded. Sides of mouth with long black bristles. Colours somewhat variable. *Adult male* coloured in browns, greys, and mottled with black, the top of head streaked with black; throat blackish with narrow white band across lower part; large white area on both webs of the three outermost tail feathers extending to tips. *Adult female* similar but throat band narrower and more buffy; white areas lacking in tail, the three outermost feathers broadly tipped with buff.

Measurements. *Adult male*: wing, 154–167.5 (161.9); tail, 112.5–134.5 (128.2); exposed culmen, 8–11.5 (10.1); tarsus, 15.5–18.5 (17.3). *Adult female*: wing, 148.6–158.5 (152.7) mm.

Field Marks. Perches on the ground or lengthwise on a horizontal branch. A longish Robin-sized bird with tiny down-bent bill. Similar to the Nighthawk when perched, but the Whip-poor-will's wing tips do not reach the tip of the *rounded* tail (in Nighthawk they reach to or beyond the slightly forked tail tip), its sides and abdomen are never obviously regularly barred. In flight it shows no white wing patch and never flies at any great height as the Nighthawk does. *Voice*: Far-carrying *whip-poor-will*, the last syllable accented and loudest, repeated tirelessly at dusk and during the night in spring and early summer. (See also Chuck-will's-widow.)

Habitat. Ungrazed woodlands of various developments, especially those with openings; woodland edges; woodlots. Perhaps prefers mixed-wood or deciduous types, but open coniferous woods sometimes harbour good numbers too.

Simard, southern La Vérendrye Park, Wakefield, Montréal, Brompton Lake, Coleraine, Québec); New Brunswick (Scotch Lake, Saint John), and rarely Nova Scotia (Waverley Game Sanctuary, Frog Lake). Rare visitant to Gaspé Peninsula, Saint-Gédéon, and Saint-Félicien, Quebec. Accidental on outer north shore of the Gulf of St. Lawrence (23 km west of Harrington-Harbour, 11 June 1936).

Nesting. Eggs are laid on bare ground or leaf litter, usually on the outer fringes of ungrazed woodland. *Eggs*, 2; white, small-blotched and spotted irregularly with grey and some browns. Incubation 19 to 21 days (G.S. Raynor), mainly by the female.

Range. Breeds in woodlands from southern Canada (Saskatchewan to Nova Scotia) south (east of the Great Plains) to northeastern Oklahoma, northeastern Texas, northern Louisiana, northwestern South Carolina, and eastern Virginia; also from central Arizona, New Mexico, and southwestern Texas to Honduras. Winters from southeastern United States and northern Mexico south to El Salvador and Honduras.

Subspecies. *Caprimulgus vociferus vociferus* Wilson.

Order **Apodiformes:**
Swifts and Hummingbirds

It surprises many to learn that swifts and hummingbirds are classified in the same order. Although their bills, mouths, and some aspects of their appearance are very different, many important anatomical features are similar. Obvious external similarities common to both swifts and hummingbirds include long, narrow wings (because of very long primaries and very short secondaries) and very small feet.

Family **Apodidae:**
Swifts

Number of Species in Canada: 4

Small, long-winged, mostly dull-coloured birds with very small bill and very large mouth; small but strong feet, the hind toe reversible; primaries very long, stiff, somewhat bowed, reaching when closed well beyond tip of tail; plumage (in all Canadian species) rather hard and stiff. On the wing they somewhat resemble swallows, but their wing action is very different. The wings of swifts buzz and twinkle and often seem, erroneously, to beat alternately. There are frequent short glides on stiff bowed wings. All are insect eaters and feed entirely on the wing.

Black Swift

Martinet sombre
Cypseloides niger (Gmelin)
Total length: 16.5 to 18.5 cm
Plate 45

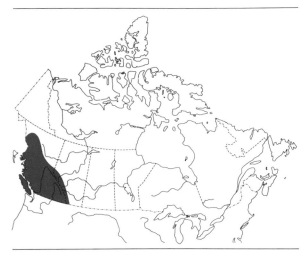

Breeding Distribution of Black Swift

Range in Canada. Summer resident, breeding in British Columbia (throughout southern parts including Vancouver Island and northwestward at least to Telegraph Creek; near Kleena Kleene, Clinton, and at Chilliwack); also in southwestern Alberta (Banff and Jasper national parks).

A sight record of one at Digges Island, N.W.T., on 9 August 1980, is supported by a photo taken by Bruce Lyon.

Our largest swift, but only slightly larger than the differently coloured White-throated Swift. Large size and lack of spines on the tips of the tail feathers distinguish it from the Chimney and the Vaux's swifts. *Adult male*: Very dark sooty, almost black, above and below, slightly paler on head and neck; forehead and crown feathers with narrow pale margins; small black area in front of eyes; tail slightly forked and lacking spines on feather tips. *Adult female*: Similar, but feathers of abdomen and under tail coverts more likely to be tipped with white; tail even less forked (almost truncate).

Measurements *(C. n. borealis). Adult male*: wing, 160.3–170 (164); tail, 56–64.9 (61.5); exposed culmen, 6–7 (6.5); tarsus, 12.5–13.9 (13). *Adult female*: wing, 155.5–171 (164.7) mm.

Field Marks. Large size for a swift, all-black appearance, and slightly forked tail. Vaux's Swift (also Chimney Swift, which is unknown in Black Swift's range in Canada) is obviously smaller, with greyish under parts, and short rounded tail. The White-throated Swift, another large swift with forked tail, has extensive white on throat, breast, and mid-abdomen. The Purple Martin might be confused with it but for its typical swallow outline and flight, very different from that of swifts.

Habitat. Forages in the air in mountain country at various heights. In fair weather high in the air, often at great heights; in dull, threatening, or rainy weather near the ground or low over water. For nesting, walls of mountain canyons.

Nesting. Relatively few nests have been discovered. Nest is of mosses, bits of ferns and grasses, in a crevice in the wall of a mountain canyon or cliff, or sea cliff. Nests found have usually been in moist places, often near waterfalls. *Egg*, one only, is dull white.

Range. Breeds in mountains or sea cliffs from southeastern Alaska, northern British Columbia, and southwestern Alberta south to Costa Rica; also in the West Indies and in British Guiana. Winters probably in tropical America.

Subspecies. *Cypseloides niger borealis* (Kennerly).

Chimney Swift

Martinet ramoneur
Chaetura pelagica (Linnaeus)
Total length: 12 to 14.4 cm
Plate 45

Figure 77
Tail of Chimney Swift

Breeding Distribution of Chimney Swift

Range in Canada. Breeding summer resident in central-eastern Saskatchewan (Nipawin); southern Manitoba (Dauphin, St. Laurent, Selkirk, Winnipeg, Indian Bay); southern and south-central Ontario (north to about Sandy Lake, Cochrane); southern Quebec (north to Amos, Senneterre, Lake Saint-Jean, Percé; recorded rarely in summer on Anticosti and Madeleine islands); New Brunswick; Prince Edward Island; and Nova Scotia (including Cape Breton Island). Possibly breeds also in southwestern Newfoundland (numerous summer records of occurrence, especially at Codroy where observed in several summers, but breeding evidence lacking). Casual on the north shore of the Gulf of St. Lawrence (Matamec, Harrington-Harbour).

Our only eastern (Saskatchewan eastward) swift. Its very long wings (longer than the bird itself and extending far beyond the tail) and short tail with the feather shafts projecting as spines beyond the webs (Figure 77) distinguish it from other eastern birds. Upper parts dark sooty-brown (slight gloss), palest on rump, blackish on wings; abdomen dark like the back, paling to brownish grey on throat. Smaller size and spiny tail distinguish it from the Black and the White-throated swifts. It is very similar, however, to Vaux's Swift, but its somewhat larger size and darker under parts identify it in the hand.

Measurements. *Adult male*: wing, 124–131.6 (127.8); tail, 40.5–44 (42.3); exposed culmen, 4.7–5.9 (5.2); tarsus, 11.9–13.9 (12.2). *Adult female*: wing, 124.5–131.5 (128.4) mm.

Field Marks. Any swift in eastern Canada and west to Saskatchewan is almost certainly this one. Usually seen in flight, often high in the air. A small sooty bird, likely to be mistaken for a swallow but readily distinguished from swallows by its cigar-shaped body (seems to lack a tail, unless the short rounded tail is spread), long, narrow, pointed wings, its silhouette bowed slightly backward, quick jerky flight (sometimes giving the illusion of alternating wing beats), often interspersed with short glides. The voice, once learned, also distinguishes it from swallows. Not safely separable in the field from Vaux's Swift, a slightly smaller swift of the western mountains with somewhat paler under parts, but the ranges of the two in Canada are widely separated. *Voice*: A far-carrying, sharp, staccato *chit-chit-chit*, at times running together into a prolonged chittering.

Habitat. Forages in the air, often at considerable heights in fair weather but tending to fly lower during threatening or rainy weather, then often preferring the air over open water or open land. Nested and roosted originally in hollow trees, but most have now adapted to man's chimneys. Highly gregarious.

Nesting. Nested formerly inside hollow trees or in crevices of rock cliffs. Now most have adapted to the interior of chimneys and, less often, the interior of old buildings. In remote areas a few still nest in hollow trees. Nest is of twigs glued together and to the chimney wall by the bird's saliva to form a shallow bracket-like structure. *Eggs*, usually 4 or 5; white. Incubation averages 19 days, but variable, by both parents (R.B. Fischer).

Range. Breeds from southern Canada (Saskatchewan east to Nova Scotia) south to southeastern Texas, the Gulf States, and central Florida. Winters in the upper Amazon River drainage of South America.

Remarks. Swifts are well named, for they are indeed fast flyers. On calm summer evenings they may fly so high as to be mere specks in the sky, and their voices, like the clicking of knitting needles, drift faintly down to earth. In cloudy weather they fly low. They always seem in a hurry, and as they zigzag across the sky their wings seem almost to twinkle. This bird does not intentionally alight on the ground. It feeds on flying insects, taken on the wing. When thirsty it can skim close to the water, touching the surface lightly with its bill. Nesting twigs are snapped off as the bird hovers at a tree branch. It sleeps clinging to the vertical wall of a chimney or hollow tree.

Vaux's Swift

Martinet de Vaux
Chaetura vauxi (Townsend)
Total length: 10 to 11.4 cm
Plate 45

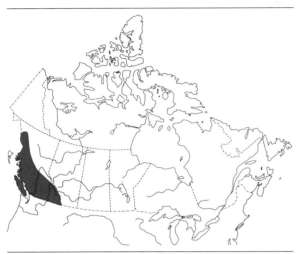

Breeding Distribution of Vaux's Swift

Range in Canada. Breeding summer resident in British Columbia (across southern parts, Vancouver Island east to Elko and northwestward through Horsefly to Telegraph Creek; perhaps to Mile 45 Haines Road; apparently not recorded on Queen Charlotte Islands).

Our smallest swift. Similar to Chimney Swift (including spiny tail) but decidedly smaller (wing about 11.4 cm or under) and paler, especially the under parts, the throat being greyish white.

Measurements. *Adult male*: wing, 107.9–112.8 (111.6); tail, 34.9–37.7 (36.1); exposed culmen, 4.1–5 (4.6); tarsus, 11–11.3 (11.1). *Adult female*: wing, 105–116.5 (111.5) mm.

Field Marks. A small swift of the western mountains with greyish under parts and no obvious tail (unless spread, when it looks short and rounded). Black and White-throated swifts are obviously larger with different under parts, and definite, slightly forked tails. Probably not safely separable in the field from the Chimney Swift, but the ranges of the two in Canada are well separated.

Habitat. Forages in the air at various heights and over many different types of country. When flying low, appears to favour the vicinity of water, woodland openings, burntlands, flats, river valleys. For nesting, hollows in trees, sometimes in chimneys.

Nesting. Nest, a narrow bracket of twigs, weed stems, or conifer needles, cemented together and to the inside of a hollow tree or, less often, chimney interior. Has adapted less readily to using man's chimneys than has the Chimney Swift. *Eggs*, usually 4 to 6; dull white. Incubation period 18.5 to 20 days (Baldwin and Zaczkowski) by both sexes.

Range. Southeastern Alaska and northern British Columbia south to central California (mainly west of the Cascades and Sierra Nevada); also Mexico to Panama and in northern Venezuela. Winters mainly from southern Mexico southward.

Subspecies. *Chaetura vauxi vauxi* (Townsend).

White-throated Swift

Martinet à gorge blanche
Aeronautes saxatalis (Woodhouse)
Total length: 15.2 to 17.8 cm
Plate 45

Breeding Distribution of White-throated Swift

Range in Canada. Breeds in central-southern British Columbia (on cliffs in and near Okanagan valley: Osoyoos Lake, Summerland, White Lake, Vaseux Lake, Okanagan Falls, Rutland, Vernon); also near Fairmont Hot Springs; Armstrong; Robson; near Castlegar; and near Williams Lake; probably Spences Bridge.

Sight records for southern Vancouver Island but without evidence of breeding.

A large western swift, only slightly smaller than the Black Swift. Wings long; tail ample, decidedly forked, lacking spine-like projections. Upper parts brownish black or sooty brown; line over eye, tips of secondaries, patch on either side of rump, the throat, breast, and median part of abdomen, white; sides blackish. The only Canadian swift with extensive patches of white.

Measurements *(A. s. saxatalis)*. *Adult male*: 137–145.5 (141.9); tail, 50.5–61 (58.9); exposed culmen, 5.5–6.2 (5.9); tarsus, 10.7–11.4 (11.1). *Adult female*: wing, 136.2–145.1 (141.5) mm.

Field Marks. White throat, breast, and middle of abdomen contrast with dark sides, and there is a conspicuous white patch on either side of rump. No other Canadian swift has extensive white patches. Beginners might confuse it with the Violet-green Swallow because of the white patches on the sides of the rump, but the swallow's outline and flight action are very different.

Habitat. Forages widely over various types of mountain country, roosting and nesting on mountain cliffs and canyon walls.

Nesting. Nest, usually in a crevice in a wall of a cliff (often inaccessible), is a shallow cupped bracket of feathers and often grass and other plant material, glued together and to the rock by the bird's saliva. *Eggs*, usually 4 or 5; white.

Range. Breeds from central-southern British Columbia south in the mountains to Guatemala and El Salvador. Winters from central California and southwestern New Mexico southward.

Subspecies. *Aeronautes saxatalis saxatalis* (Woodhouse) is the subspecies inhabiting central-southern British Columbia. If the species is eventually found in Alberta, specimens should be examined for the possibility of a larger race, *sclateri*.

Family **Trochilidae**: Hummingbirds

Number of Species in Canada: 5

This very large family, which contains the smallest of birds, is confined to the New World. Most of the more than 300 species are found in the tropics, but the family is represented from Alaska to Patagonia. Hummingbirds are easily recognized by their diminutive size, brilliant iridescent colours, especially in the males, and by the darting, hovering (even backward) flight, which is accompanied by a characteristic humming sound. The wings are long, slender, and pointed; the feet small and weak; the bill is slender and in Canadian species straight (but the shape is extremely variable elsewhere). The long extensile tongue is ideal for reaching nectar and tiny insects deep inside flowers.

Ruby-throated Hummingbird

Colibri à gorge rubis
Archilochus colubris (Linnaeus)
Total length: 7.5 to 9.4 cm
Plate 46

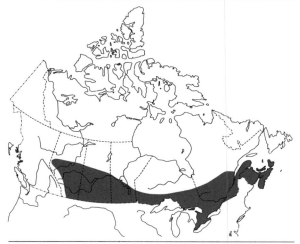

Breeding Distribution of Ruby-throated Hummingbird

Range in Canada. Breeds in central and southeastern Alberta (Lesser Slave Lake, Belvedere, Elk Island National Park, Brooks); central Saskatchewan (Flotten Lake, Prince Albert, Nipawin, Buchanan); southern Manitoba (The Pas: 32 km north; Swan River, Lake St. Martin, Red River, Hillside Beach, Indian Bay; probably Overflowing River); southern and south-central Ontario (north to about Lake of the Woods, Wabigoon, Lake Nipigon, Kapuskasing, perhaps Lake Abitibi); southern Quebec (north to La Vérendrye Park, Lake Saint-Jean, and eastern Gaspé Peninsula, but not on Madeleine Islands); New Brunswick; Prince Edward Island; and Nova Scotia (including Cape Breton Island).

Casual in northern Manitoba (Churchill); northern Ontario (Moose Factory, Attawapiskat); north shore of the Gulf of St. Lawrence (Sept-Îles, Johan-Beetz Bay); and Newfoundland (Avalon Peninsula, St. Anthony). Accidental in central Labrador (Davis Inlet, 17 July 1882).

Adult male: Tail forked, its feathers tapering toward tips; upper parts glossy green; throat bright metallic-red changeable in different positions to dull blackish); breast and middle of abdomen greyish white; sides greyish brown mixed with glossy green. *Adult female*: Similar to adult male but throat greyish white; tail not forked, feather tips more rounded, the outer three tail feathers tipped with white. *Young*: Similar to adult female, but young males have throat streaked with dusky, sometimes showing traces of red.

Measurements. *Adult male*: wing, 39.9–43.2 (40.9); tail, 26.4–30.4 (28); exposed culmen, 14.2–16.7 (15.2). *Adult female*: wing, 44.3–48 (45.7) mm.

Field Marks. The only hummingbird to be expected from eastern Alberta eastward. Small size and buzzing insect-like flight distinguish it as a hummingbird.

Habitat. Gardens, orchards; woodland clearings and edges; almost anywhere flowers provide tiny insects and nectar and not too far from trees or tall shrubbery for perching, shelter, and nesting. Feeds at flowers of many kinds, both wild and cultivated; often takes insects flycatcher-fashion; occasionally feeds at sapsucker borings.

Nesting. Nest, a neat little cup saddled on a limb of a tree. It is composed of bud scales and plant down, the outside covered with bits of lichen and held together by spider silk. *Eggs*, 2; white. Incubation 16 days (A.F. Skutch), by female alone.

Range. Breeds from southern Canada (Alberta eastward to Nova Scotia) south to the Gulf States and west in the United States to eastern North Dakota, central Nebraska, central Oklahoma, and east-central Texas. Winters from northern Mexico and southern Texas south to Costa Rica; also in southern Alabama and southern Florida.

Remarks. Hummingbirds feed on minute insects and nectar which they obtain from flowers. Their tiny wings move so rapidly in flight that they produce a characteristic humming sound, hence the name. They are capable of rapid direct flight, of remaining perfectly stationary in the air as they feed at flowers, and of even flying backwards for short distances.

The males take no part in nesting duties and leave the drudgery of incubating the eggs and raising the young entirely to the females. They quarrel frequently among themselves, and when so engaged their squeaky, high-pitched voices are incessantly audible.

The Ruby-throated has the widest distribution in Canada of all hummingbirds and is the only species found in the eastern part of the country. Beginners sometimes confuse it with large hawk moths, which also feed at flowers.

Black-chinned Hummingbird

Colibri à gorge noire
Archilochus alexandri (Bourcier and Mulsant)
Total length: 7.5 to 9.5 cm
Plate 46

Range in Canada. Scarce breeder in southern interior British Columbia (Chilliwack east to Creston, north to Grindrod and Nicholson).

Casual visitant to Alberta (specimen: Calgary, 25 June 1979). Hypothetical in Saskatchewan (unsupported but convincing sight record at Regina, 1 June 1970).

Adult male: Above, metallic green; chin and upper throat black, lower throat iridescent purplish violet (but changeable: black in some positions); breast whitish, median abdomen greyish, sides and flanks darker overlaid with green. *Adult female*: Above, metallic green, forehead and crown duller and more greyish brown; tail rounded, outer three tail feathers tipped with white; under parts dull white (more purely so on abdomen). From Rufous Hummingbird, the Black-chinned is easily distinguished by its lack of any rufous coloration in body plumage or at base of tail; from the Calliope by larger size, solid dark throat in male, and complete lack of rufous in the female.

Measurements. *Adult male*: wing, 43.8–45.3 (44.4); tail, 23.5–28.7 (26.7); exposed culmen, 16.5–18.3 (17.4) mm.

Field Marks. *Adult male*: Throat patch looks black, but in certain positions the shiny violet lower throat can be seen. Female differs from Rufous and Calliope by lack of buffy on sides. *Caution*: Throats of some other hummingbirds may look black in certain lights.

Nesting. Nest, of vegetable downs held together with cobwebs, is saddled on a tree branch. *Eggs*, 2; white. Incubation period 16 days (S.R. Demaree) by the female.

Range. From southern British Columbia and northwestern Montana south to northern Baja California, northwestern Mexico, and northwestern Texas. Winters from southeastern California south to southwestern Mexico.

Anna's Hummingbird

Colibri d'Anna
Calypte anna (Lesson)
Total length: 9 to 10.2 cm
Plate 46

Range in Canada. In recent years has become a rare breeder and a regular autumn-winter visitant to southern British Columbia, mainly coastal (Victoria, Saanich, Vancouver, Langley, Comox, Campbell River) and more rarely in the interior (Okanagan Falls, Penticton, Kelowna). Has nested recently near Terrace. Casual visitant to Alberta (photo record: one carefully observed at Calgary on 6 October 1976).

Somewhat larger than other hummingbirds found in Canada. Adult male has both crown and throat patch iridescent red or purplish red. Throat patch elongated laterally onto sides of neck (but not projecting behind neck as in Costa's). Rest of upper parts mainly greenish; sides and flanks duller green. The reddish or purplish-red crown (caution: both it and throat patch may appear blackish in certain lights) readily distinguishes the adult male from other hummingbirds known to occur in Canada (Costa's has a decidedly purple or violet crown and throat).

Range. Breeds in southern British Columbia and Washington west of the higher mountains and south to northwestern Baja California.

Costa's Hummingbird

[**Costa's Hummingbird**. Colibri de Costa. *Calypte costae* (Bourcier). Total length: 7.5 to 8.8 cm. Adult male has a purple or violet crown, throat, and gorget, the last projecting backward *past* the sides of the neck. Compare Anna's Hummingbird.

Range. Breeds from central California, southern Nevada, and southwestern Utah to northwestern Mexico.

Status in Canada. Hypothetical. Sight record of an adult male by several very competent observers near Cadboro Bay, Victoria, British Columbia, 14–17 April 1972.]

Calliope Hummingbird

Colibri calliope
Stellula calliope (Gould)
Total length: 7.2 to 8.4 cm
Plate 46

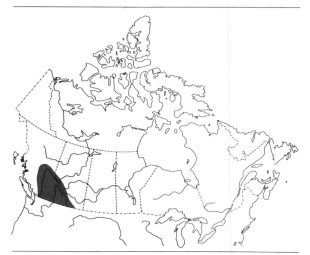

Breeding Distribution of Calliope Hummingbird

Range in Canada. Breeds in interior British Columbia (Princeton, Okanagan valley, Elko, north to Prince George region; possibly northwest to Topley) and in mountainous southwestern Alberta (Waterton Lakes, Jasper, and Banff national parks and eastward to Exshaw and Longview). Casual in southwestern Saskatchewan (Shaunavon). Scarce visitant to the coast of British Columbia (Vancouver, Kerrisdale).

Our smallest hummingbird. *Adult male*: Above, iridescent green; throat with long narrow purple feathers (elongated on sides of throat and extending down side of neck) forming distinct streaks on whitish background. *Adult female*: Above, iridescent bronzy green; throat whitish, usually more or less faintly streaked with dusky; breast and middle of abdomen white merging into cinnamon on sides and flanks; tail with three outermost feathers tipped white, cinnamon coloration restricted to very narrow margins near the base of some of the feathers. The adult male's decidedly purple, heavily streaked throat with elongated feathers down sides of neck is unmistakable. Females and young are more difficult but are distinguishable from Ruby-throated and Black-chinned in similar plumages by decidedly cinnamon flanks. Closely resembles female and young Rufous, but in the hand the Calliope is seen to have much less cinnamon in the base of the tail (very narrow margins, not extending to middle pair of feathers).

Measurements. *Adult male*: wing, 37.6–43.5 (39.1); tail, 18.7–23 (20.9); exposed culmen, 13–14.9 (13.8). *Adult female*: wing, 41.3–45 (43.1) mm.

Field Marks. Adult male with heavy purple streaks on throat (these feathers elongated laterally thus extending down sides of neck) is very distinct. Females and young show considerable cinnamon on the flanks, which distinguishes them from Ruby-throated and Black-chinned hummingbirds; but they are so similar to female Rufous that they cannot ordinarily be safely distinguished in the field.

Habitat. In mountains: openings in woodland, glades, burntlands, flowery meadows; for nesting, open woodland either coniferous, deciduous, or mixedwood.

Nesting. Typically saddled on a sloping branch (various heights) of a coniferous or deciduous tree, often beneath another protecting overhanging branch. Nest, a firm neat cup of plant downs, lichens, and mosses, bound together with cobwebs. *Eggs*, 2; white. Incubation period 16 days (D.F. Brunton et al.) by the female.

Range. Breeds in mountainous country from south-central British Columbia and southwestern Alberta south to northern Baja California and east to western Colorado. Winters in Mexico.

Remarks. This is the tiniest bird in Canada. Its average weight is about 2.5 g. Yet it does not hesitate to dive-bomb birds much larger than itself. A mother bird, with half-grown young in the nest, has been known to chase a squirrel from the nest tree. Even large hawks are occasionally "attacked."

As in other hummingbirds, its food is nectar, tiny insects, and little spiders, most of which it finds in flowers. Most brightly coloured flowers attract it, but red ones appear to be preferred. Often it takes insects on the wing, flycatcher-fashion.

Rufous Hummingbird

Colibri roux
Selasphorus rufus (Gmelin)
Total length: 8.1 to 9.5 cm
Plate 46

Breeding Distribution of Rufous Hummingbird

Range in Canada. Breeds in British Columbia (commonly across the southern part, including Vancouver Island, northward through Queen Charlotte Islands and Vanderhoof, and north-westward at least to Dokdaon Creek. Found in summer, possibly breeds, northwest to Chilkat Pass and Atlin. Probably absent from north-eastern corner), and southwestern Alberta (Waterton Lakes, Banff, and Jasper national parks). Scarce summer visitant in southwestern Yukon (Carcross, Marsh Lake, Whitehorse). Wanders eastward occasionally to east-central Alberta (Red Deer, Edmonton, Little Fish Lake) and rarely to southwestern Saskatchewan (Eastend).

Accidental in Ontario (specimen: Winisk, 8 September 1966; sight record: Wheatley, August 1972). Sight records for Manitoba (Churchill, Treesbank; photo: one at Selkirk, early September to 18 October 1979) and Nova Scotia (Bedford, 8-9 August 1967).

Adult male: Upper parts cinnamon-rufous, glossy green on crown and often more or less on back; throat patch metallic scarlet (changeable to greenish or dark brown); sides, flanks, tail coverts, and much of tail feathers, cinnamon-rufous paling to whitish on breast. *Adult female*: Upper parts bronze-green; tail with much cinnamon-rufous basally, largely blackish terminally, but three outermost feathers tipped white; throat, breast, and median abdomen whitish; many of the throat feathers tipped with scarlet to greenish (sometimes forming a patch); sides, flanks, and under tail coverts pale cinnamon-rufous.

The adult male's rufous coloration and flaming extensive throat patch distinguish it from all others of regular occurrence in Canada (but individuals showing green speckling on the back might be mistaken for the smaller, decidedly green-backed Allen's Hummingbird with narrower outer tail feathers, which is found farther south in the United States). Adult females and young resemble Calliope Hummingbirds of similar sex and age, but in the hand they are obviously larger and have much more cinnamon-rufous in the base of the tail than Calliopes. Ruby-throated and Black-chinned in all plumages lack cinnamon-rufous colouring everywhere (an occasional young bird may have just a suggestion of buffy on the flanks but never in the tail or elsewhere).

Measurements. *Adult male*: wing, 40.2–42.8 (41.3); tail, 27.2–30 (28.8); exposed culmen, 15.5–16.9 (16.1). *Adult female*: wing, 43.3–45.3 (44.2) mm.

Field Marks. As given above. Females and young difficult to distinguish from Calliope of similar sex or age.

Habitat. Forages over a great variety of habitats, mainly where flowers are available, from seacoast, coastal islands, and valley bottoms to meadows above timberline.

Nesting. In a variety of trees, bushes, and vines. Probably favours a low sloping branch of a conifer. Nest, a firm cup of plant downs and mosses, with lichens on the outside, held together by cobwebs. *Eggs* 2; white. Incubation by female alone.

Range. From southeastern Alaska, southwestern Yukon, east-central British Columbia, and southwestern Alberta south through Washington and Oregon to northwestern California and southern Idaho. Winters in Mexico.

Allen's Hummingbird

[**Allen's Hummingbird**. Colibri d'Allen. *Selasphorus sasin* (Lesson). Hypothetical. Photographic evidence of a male in Victoria, British Columbia, in spring, 1971, does not eliminate the possibility of confusion with the very similar Rufous Hummingbird.]

Order **Coraciiformes:**
Kingfishers, Motmots, Rollers, and Allies

Family **Alcedinidae:**
Kingfishers

Number of Species in Canada: 1

Figure 78
Foot of Belted Kingfisher

Stocky birds with rather large heads, which are crested in many species; heavy, straight, pointed bills; very short legs; middle and outer toes joined together *for over half their length* (Figure 78). The North American species are all fish eaters and are usually seen in the vicinity of water. The family is widely distributed in warmer parts of the world, especially in the Australian region.

Belted Kingfisher

Martin-pêcheur d'Amérique
Ceryle alcyon (Linnaeus)
Total length: 28 to 37.5 cm
Plate 41

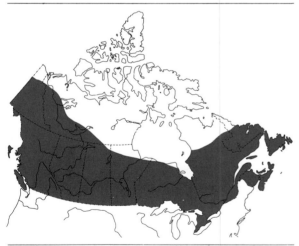

Breeding Distribution of Belted Kingfisher

Range in Canada. Breeds through the southern parts of all provinces and northward through British Columbia (including Queen Charlotte and Vancouver islands) to central Yukon (Eagle River at Dempster Highway Mile 237); through Alberta to western and northwestern Mackenzie (Fort Good Hope, Norman Wells; possibly to

Head large, crested. Bill straight, tapering to a point. Legs short; feet small, three of the four toes directed forward, the two outermost joined for basal half of their length. *Adult male*: Upper parts greyish blue with wide white collar around neck; white spot in front of eye; under parts white, except sides, flanks, and a broad band across breast, blue. *Adult female*: Similar to adult male, but sides, flanks, and a second breast band (below the blue one) cinnamon-rufous. *Young*: Resemble adults but bill shorter and breast bands much-mixed with reddish brown. Some young males show vestiges of a red second breast band.

Measurements *(C. a. alcyon)*. *Adult male*: wing, 151.3–159.5 (156.7); tail, 82–90 (86.7); exposed culmen, 48–52.9 (50.4); tarsus, 10.6–12 (11.2). *Adult female*: wing, 147–163.5 (155.4) mm.

Field Marks. Larger than a robin, with large crested head, blue back, very short legs, rather long pointed bill. Male with one blue band across white breast; female with an additional reddish band below the blue one. Usually seen near water, often perches motionless for long periods, dives with resounding splash, sometimes hovers over water on rapidly beating wings. *Voice*: A loud, harsh rattle. Blue Jay also is a crested blue-backed bird but is easily distinguished by its *black* necklace (which extends right up sides of neck), longer legs, and much longer tail.

Habitat. The vicinity of fish-inhabited water (preferably clear) either fresh or salt: lakes, ponds, rivers, streams, salt water near shore or islands and not too far from elevated perching places such as trees, posts, telephone wires. For nesting, steep earth banks (when obtainable), not necessarily in the immediate vicinity of water. Breeding populations in rocky areas limited by availability of nesting sites. Sometimes utilizes man-made cutbanks of roads and railways, gravel pits, sawdust piles (often unsuccessfully); rarely even wheel tracks through earth mounds; occasionally an earth-filled root of an upturned tree.

Fort McPherson and Anderson River where it has been noted in summer); northern Saskatchewan (Lake Athabasca, Wollaston Lake); central Manitoba (north to about Thicket Portage, Oxford Lake; probably Gillam and Missi Falls); Ontario (north to Winisk and Sutton rivers, Moose Factory); central Quebec (north at least to Grande rivière de la Baleine, Lake Mistassini, the north shore of the Gulf of St. Lawrence, Schefferville region, Anticosti and Madeleine islands); and from New Brunswick, Prince Edward Island, and Nova Scotia north to northern and eastern Newfoundland and Labrador (Hopedale).

Winters in coastal and southern interior British Columbia (regularly on the coast; occasionally and locally in the interior) and extreme southern Ontario. Occasional individuals sometimes present in winter in southern Quebec, Nova Scotia, Prince Edward Island, and southern Newfoundland.

Nesting. Nests in a circular chamber at the end of a burrow excavated by both sexes in the face of a steep earth bank. Burrow, usually 0.9 to 2.1 m long, rarely considerably longer, is horizontal or slightly upslanting. Usually (not always) near the top of the bank. *Eggs* are laid on bare chamber floor in which a lining of fish bones gradually accumulates. *Eggs*, 5 to 8, usually 6 or 7; white, somewhat glossy. Incubation 23 to 24 days (H. Mousley), mainly by female, but the male at least sometimes assists.

Range. Breeds from central Alaska and across much of forested Canada south to southern United States (including southern California, southern Texas, and southern Florida). Winters from southeastern Alaska, southern British Columbia, Wyoming, Nebraska, Illinois, extreme southern Ontario, Vermont, New Hampshire, and Maine south through much of Central America and the West Indies to Panama, Curaçao, and Trinidad.

Subspecies. (1) *Ceryle alcyon alcyon* (Linnaeus) breeds throughout eastern Canada and extends westward to Yukon Territory (Teslin Lake), northeastern British Columbia (Peace River, Liard River), and Alberta east of the foothills. (2) *C. a. caurina* Grinnell, of somewhat larger size occupies extreme southwestern Alberta (Waterton Lakes, MacLeod), southern and coastal British Columbia, and perhaps extreme southwestern Yukon. Because of the lack of suitable study material, areas of intergradation with the nominate race are not well understood.

Remarks. The tousle-headed silhouette of the kingfisher is a familiar sight to all who frequent Canadian waters. On one of its numerous favourite perches it patiently watches for fishes in the water below. It may dive either from a perch or from the air. Sometimes it hovers in the air for a moment and then hits the water with a resounding splash. If successful in catching a fish, it carries it out of the water in its bill. Although the kingfisher feeds mainly on small fishes, it sometimes eats beetles, grasshoppers, crickets, and even frogs. Most of the fishes taken are of little economic value. Some are actually harmful destroyers of young trout. At fish hatcheries kingfishers can be destructive, but screens placed over pools will protect the young fish.

Ordinarily, kingfishers are wary and difficult to approach closely. Often they would go unseen were it not for their harsh rattle, which draws attention to them as they disappear around a bend in the river. Swift, graceful, and picturesque, the Belted Kingfisher adds colour to the scene.

Order **Piciformes:**
Woodpeckers, Jacamars, Toucans, and Barbets

Family **Picidae:**
Woodpeckers and Wrynecks

Number of Species in Canada: 14

Figure 79
a) Extensile tongue of Pileated Woodpecker
b) Detail of tongue tip

Woodpeckers are highly specialized for climbing the trunks and branches of trees and for digging out wood-boring insects. The bill is hard, straight, and chisel-like, ideal for digging holes in either dead or living wood; the tongue is slender, fitted with a horny spear at its tip (Figure 79), and is capable of being extended far beyond the bill tip to impale and withdraw insect larvae from deep cavities. The skull is extremely thick and heavy, enabling it to withstand the shock of using the head as a hammer. The legs are short; the three or four toes, usually four, with two in front and two behind, are fitted with sharp claws for climbing. The tail is very stiff and is well fitted for bracing against tree trunks.

Most species feed mainly on insects, and as their diet includes a high proportion of wood-boring species the importance of these avian tree surgeons is great.

Lewis's Woodpecker

Pic de Lewis
Melanerpes lewis (Gray)
Total length: 26.5 to 29 cm
Plate 47

Breeding Distribution of Lewis's Woodpecker

Range in Canada. Breeds in southern British Columbia (but is now much reduced on Vancouver Island; north at least to Williams Lake) and southwestern Alberta (Jasper National Park to Waterton Lakes). Winters in southern British Columbia (southern coast, Okanagan valley, and rarely southern Vancouver Island).

Adults (sexes similar): Upper parts glossy greenish-black except narrow grey collar; face dull dark-red; breast grey (black feather bases sometimes show through) shading into rose on abdomen, sides, and flanks. Feathers of under body rather hairlike. *Young* are similar to adults but lack red face and grey collar; rose on under body duller.

Measurements. *Adult male*: wing, 159.3–174.9 (169.9); tail, 83.5–101 (91.9); exposed culmen, 28.2–30.9 (29.6); tarsus, 23.7–26.2 (25.2). *Adult female*: wing, 153.8–171 (163) mm.

Field Marks. Adults with solid-black upper parts, narrow grey collar around back of neck, grey breast, rose-tinted abdomen. Flight not undulating like that of other woodpeckers, often glides; wings solid black and rather broad. Frequently catches insects in the air, flycatcher-fashion. *Voice*: Rather silent but in breeding season a harsh *krar*.

Habitat. Open areas with scattered trees, such as burntlands with standing dead wood, logged-over places, wooded roadsides, open woodland.

Nesting. Nest in an excavated tree cavity, typically a dead tree. *Eggs*, usually 6 or 7; dull white. Incubation is by both sexes.

Wanders irregularly north to central British Columbia (rarely as far as Masset and Takla Lake) and east to central and southeastern Alberta (Lesser Slave Lake, Belvedere, Camrose, Sullivan Lake, Brooks). Rare visitor in Saskatchewan (Herschel, Tisdale, Saltcoats, Eastend, Tuxford, Regina, Qu'Appelle valley), Manitoba (Winnipeg, Churchill), and casual in Ontario (photo record: Windsor, February 1973; also two sight records for Emo; one for Point Pelee).

Red-headed Woodpecker

Pic à tête rouge
Melanerpes erythrocephalus (Linnaeus)
Total length: 22 to 25 cm
Plate 47

Breeding Distribution of Red-headed Woodpecker

Range in Canada. Breeds in southern Saskatchewan (very rarely and locally: Cypress Hills; formerly Moose Jaw; recently Lumsden); southern Manitoba (Dauphin, Winnipeg Beach, Sprague); southern Ontario (northward in diminishing numbers to about Kenora, Wawa, Sault Ste. Marie, Pembroke, North Bay, Ottawa); southwestern Quebec (Breckenridge, Hudson-Heights, Lachine, Hatley); and formerly, at least, in southern New Brunswick (Saint John). Range somewhat less extensive than formerly.

Irregularly wanders westward to British Columbia (photo record: Vernon, 11 July 1965); southern Alberta (Waterton Lakes, Foremost, Calgary, Elk Island Park); and eastward uncommonly to Nova Scotia (Ketch Harbour, Windsor and many sight records in recent years). Winters in southern Ontario (rarely) and very rarely southern Manitoba (St. Vital, Balmoral).

Range. Breeds from southern British Columbia, southwestern Alberta, Montana, and southwestern South Dakota, south to California, Arizona, and New Mexico.

Adults (sexes alike) characterized by solid, unspotted masses of red, white, and black. Whole head, neck, and upper breast crimson red; back, scapulars, and wing coverts black; rump, secondaries, upper tail coverts, and under body (lower breast to under tail coverts) white. *Young* differ from adults in having head and neck mostly greyish brown to blackish, the throat streaked; feathers of back and scapulars tipped with grey; and the white secondaries are crossed by one or two black bars, the tertials often by three or more. The basic patterns of the young (particularly the large white wing patch formed by the white secondaries) are so similar to those of adults that there is no mistaking them.

Measurements *(M. e. erythrocephalus). Adult male*: wing, 131.8–142 (136.4); tail, 71.6–79.9 (73.9); exposed culmen, 21.2–28.7 (25.9); tarsus, 19.2–23.5 (21.6). *Adult female*: wing, 131–138 (134.9) mm.

Field Marks. The completely red head and neck, contrasting masses (unspotted) of black and white on the body, especially the large white patch on the wing, can be mistaken for nothing else that occurs within the Red-headed Woodpecker's range. Young have blackish-brown head and dusky-streaked throat (little or no red), and there are some black bars on the mainly white wing patch, but their basic patterns are so suggestive of those of adults (especially the large white wing patch) that there should be no difficulty in distinguishing them. (Note: The Red-breasted Sapsucker *(Sphyrapicus ruber)* has the whole head and neck red but is otherwise very different. Its range and that of the Red-headed Woodpecker are widely separated.)

Habitat. Open woods, burntlands, groves, and scattered large trees in open places.

Nesting. Nests in a cavity excavated in dead wood of a tree, telephone pole, or fence post. *Eggs*, 4 to 7; white. Incubation said to be about 14 days (A.C. Bent), by both sexes.

Range. Breeds from southern Canada (Saskatchewan to New Brunswick) south to northern New Mexico, central Texas, the United States Gulf Coast, and Florida. Somewhat migratory in northernmost part of range.

Subspecies. *Melanerpes erythrocephalus caurinus* Brodkorb occupies the western part of the breeding range east to western Ontario. *M. e. erythrocephalus* (Linnaeus), slightly smaller in size, breeds from southern Ontario eastward.

Remarks. There is a common tendency in Canada to misapply the name ''Red-headed Woodpecker'' to any of the various woodpeckers that show a red mark on the head. Anyone who has seen the real Red-headed Woodpecker, however, is unlikely to mistake it.

This species takes insects on the wing, flycatcher-fashion, more frequently than do most other woodpeckers. It eats also fruits and nuts in some quantities and is not above taking eggs and young of other birds on occasion. Except in extreme southern Ontario, it is nowhere a common bird in Canada.

Red-bellied Woodpecker

Pic à ventre roux
Melanerpes carolinus (Linnaeus)
Total length: 22.2 to 25.4 cm
Plate 46

Range in Canada. Rare and local permanent resident in extreme southern Ontario, breeding in Middlesex County; but formerly north to Wellington County and east to Halton County. Occasionally observed in other parts of southern Ontario (north to Sault Ste. Marie and east to Kingston and Ottawa).

Very rare in southern Saskatchewan (specimen: Regina, 26 May 1959; also several sight records, one north to Saskatoon); Manitoba (specimen: Stonewall, 23 January 1971; sight records: Winnipeg, Sanford, Brandon, possibly has nested); Quebec (photo record: Saint-Augustin, Portneuf County, 2 November 1969 to 30 March 1970; also sight records at Montréal, Alcove near Hull); and Nova Scotia (specimen: Brier Island, 24 June 1969; photo records: Middleton, 15 November 1961 to 5 May 1962, and Kentville, 8 January 1968; sight record: Crousetown, early December 1968 to 2 March 1969).

Adult male with whole back, scapulars, and wings (except primaries), black barred with white; whole top of head, nape, and back of neck, bright red; under parts (including throat), brownish grey with more or less red in middle of abdomen. *Female* is similar to male but top of head grey, red coloration being confined to nape, back of neck, and forehead; red of mid-abdomen more restricted.

Measurements. *Adult male*: wing, 123.5–139 (131); tail, 72.5–85 (77.7); exposed culmen, 28–33 (29.8); tarsus, 20–23 (21.9). *Adult female*: wing, 122–133 (128.3) mm (Ridgway).

Field Marks. Extensive black-and-white zebra-like barring of back and wings, combined with red on the head, distinguishes it from other Canadian woodpeckers. Males have the whole top of head, nape, and back of neck red; females have a grey crown, but the nape and back of neck are like those of the male. The red suffusion on the belly is hard to see in both sexes. A noisy bird. One of its calls, a harsh *chur-r-r-r* is suggestive of the voice of the tree frog *(Hyla versicolor)*.

Habitat. Varies from mature timber to dooryard trees. Too rare in Canada for generalization but is known to nest in mature deciduous woodland in southern Ontario.

Nesting. The usually 4 or 5 white *eggs* are laid in a cavity in a tree, often a dead one, excavated by the birds at heights up to 12 m. Incubation, by both parents, 12 to 13 days.

Range. Breeds from southeastern Minnesota, extreme southern Ontario, western New York, and Delaware south to southern Texas and southern Florida.

Subspecies. *Melanerpes carolinus zebra* (Boddaert).

Yellow-bellied Sapsucker

Pic maculé
Sphyrapicus varius (Linnaeus)
Total length: 19.5 to 22 cm
Plate 46

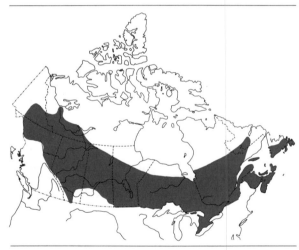

Breeding Distribution of Yellow-bellied Sapsucker

Range in Canada. Breeds in wooded areas from southern Yukon (sparsely); western Mackenzie (Fort Simpson, Great Slave Lake, north to Fort Norman); northwestern and central-eastern Saskatchewan (Milliken Lake, Wollaston Lake); central Manitoba (Thicket Portage); north-central Ontario (Ney Lake, Attawapiskat); southern Quebec (Lake Mistassini, Gaspé

Adult male: Crown red, bordered by black; from nasal tufts backward across side of neck, a white band; back black copiously marked with white; throat red with black border expanding into a posteriorly rounded black patch on breast; rest of under body yellowish white with black V-marks down sides and flanks; upper surface of wing black with a conspicuous longitudinal white patch along wing coverts, a row of white spots along outer edge of primaries and secondaries. *Adult female*: Similar to adult male but throat white instead of red; red of crown often reduced and quite often completely replaced by black. *Young in juvenal plumage*: Little or no red on head; no black patch on breast; breast and sides brownish or olivaceous, the former cross-barred with dusky. Wings similar to adult.

Measurements *(S. v. varius)*. *Adult male*: wing, 119–127 (122.5); tail, 59–78.1 (69.7); exposed culmen, 21.2–25 (22.9); tarsus, 18.9–21.5 (20.3). *Adult female*: wing, 119.2–125.3 (121.8) mm.

Field Marks. White longitudinal patch on side of folded wing marks it as a sapsucker. East of the Rockies it is distinguished readily from other woodpeckers. Adult male has a red crown and throat patch; adult female has usually a red crown (occasionally all black) and a white throat; both sexes have a black breast patch and yellowish-white abdomen. Young in juvenal plumage resemble adults but are more brownish, lack black breast patch, have little or no red on the head, but like adults have the long white sapsucker wing patch (see also Red-breasted Sapsucker and Williamson's Sapsucker).

Habitat. In breeding season prefers deciduous or deciduous-coniferous woodlands, particularly when poplars and birches are important components.

Nesting. Nest in a hole excavated by the birds in a tree (usually dead or partly so) at various heights. Incubation, by both sexes, lasts 12 to 13 days.

Peninsula, Anticosti Island); interior Labrador (Churchill River); and central Newfoundland (east at least to Swift Current) south to northern British Columbia (Telegraph Creek, Dease Lake, Peace River Parklands, Trapper Creek near Pine Pass on Hart Highway); Alberta (east of the Rockies); south-central Saskatchewan (Wingard, Good Spirit Lake, Moose Mountain, rarely Cypress Hills); southern Manitoba; southern Ontario; and throughout New Brunswick, Nova Scotia, and Prince Edward Island.

Range. Breeds in woodlands from southern Yukon, northern British Columbia (mostly east of the mountains), and southern Canada, southeastern South Dakota, central Illinois, northern Ohio, northern New York, and central New England, south in the Alleghenies to Tennessee, North Carolina, and northern Georgia. Winters from southwestern and central United States south to western Panama, the Gulf Coast, Florida, and in small numbers in the West Indies.

Range. Southern and southeastern British Columbia, southwestern Alberta, and western Montana south to east-central California, central Arizona, southern New Mexico, and extreme western Texas.

Red-naped Sapsucker

Pic à nuque rouge
Sphyrapicus nuchalis Baird
Total length: 19.6 to 22.2 cm

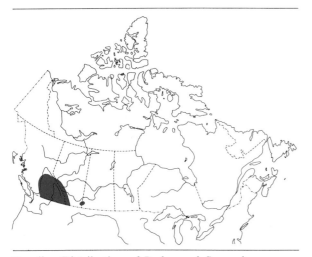

Breeding Distribution of Red-naped Sapsucker

Range in Canada. Southern and southeastern British Columbia (Kersley, Kleena Kleene, Princeton, Okanagan valley, Creston, Fernie, Flathead valley), southwestern Alberta (Rocky Mountains), and the Cypress Hills of Alberta and Saskatchewan. Winters in southwestern United States and Mexico.

Adults resemble Yellow-bellied Sapsucker but red coloration more extensive on head, that of crown extending posteriorly onto the nape. In adult males the red of throat extends farther posteriorly onto black breast patch and laterally onto the malar region. Adult females have at least the lower part of the throat red. White areas of back are reduced in both sexes and the wings and tail average slightly longer. Juvenals resemble those of the Yellow-bellied Sapsucker but are darker.

Field Marks. White longitudinal patch on side of folded wing makes it a sapsucker. It is so similar to Yellow-bellied Sapsucker that it can be certainly distinguished in the field only under close observation conditions. See description above.

Nesting. In a hold in a tree at various heights. Similar to Yellow-bellied Sapsucker.

Range. Southern and southeastern British Columbia, southwestern Alberta and western Montana south to east-central California, central Arizona, southern New Mexico, and extreme western Texas.

Remarks. So similar to Yellow-bellied Sapsucker that until very recently it was treated as being conspecific with it.

Red-breasted Sapsucker

Pic à poitrine rouge
Sphyrapicus ruber (Gmelin)
Total length: 20 to 22.5 cm
Plate 46

Adults (sexes similar): Head, neck, and breast poppy red; nasal tufts and a bar extending backward under the eye, whitish. Back, wings, and tail resemble those of Yellow-bellied Sapsucker but the white areas are greatly reduced (although the longitudinal white wing patch is obvious). *Juvenals* resemble those of the Yellow-bellied Sapsucker but head and breast are darker and the breast more uniform; white areas of back much restricted. Often (but not always) there is a reddish suffusion on crown, throat, and breast.

Measurements *(S. r. ruber). Adult male*: wing, 118–127.5 (123.1); tail, 71.5–77 (74.6); culmen, 23–25.5 (24.2); tarsus, 20–22 (20.7). *Adult female*: wing, 120–125.5 (122.8); tail, 71–79 (75.1); culmen, 22–25 (23.8); tarsus, 19–21 (20.1) mm (Ridgway).

Field Marks. A long white patch down the side of folded wing indicates a sapsucker. Adult Red-breasted Sapsuckers have the whole head, neck, and breast red and they lack a black breast patch. Immatures in autumn are similar to those of the Yellow-bellied, but are darker and some show a diagnostic reddish suffusion over throat, breast, and crown.

Breeding Distribution of Red-breasted Sapsucker

Range in Canada. Breeds in British Columbia (coast and coastal islands mostly west of the Cascades in the south; but north of latitude 53°, extends far eastward to vicinity of Pine Pass, Tupper Creek, Indianpoint Lake; northwest at least to Dokdaon Creek; and southeast to Kersley). Winters on the Pacific coast of British Columbia.

Habitat. Either deciduous or coniferous woodlands.

Nesting. Similar to Yellow-bellied Sapsucker.

Range. Breeds in Pacific coast woodlands from southwestern Alaska south through western British Columbia, western Washington, western Oregon, northwestern California, the Sierra Nevada, and higher mountains to southern California. Extends east of the Cascades at points in Oregon, Washington, and British Columbia.

Subspecies. *Sphyrapicus ruber ruber* (Gmelin) is the subspecies found in Canada. Another race occurs in western United States.

Williamson's Sapsucker

Pic de Williamson
Sphyrapicus thyroideus (Cassin)
Total length: 22.5 to 24.8 cm
Plate 46

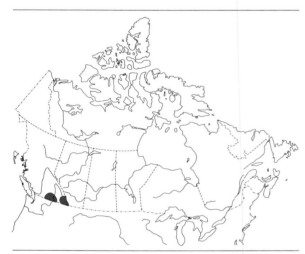

Breeding Distribution of Williamson's Sapsucker

Range in Canada. Breeding summer resident in extreme southern interior British Columbia: Manning Provincial Park, Okanagan region (mountains on International Border from Similkameen east to Midway and north to Schoonover Mountain), and East Kootenay (Cranbrook, Newgate).

Accidental in Saskatchewan (specimen: one of two in Moose Mountain Provincial Park was collected on 30 May 1965. Sight record: Saskatoon, 23 August 1977).

Adult male: Upper parts black. Rump patch, spots on flight feathers, and conspicuous longitudinal wing patch (along wing coverts) white; sides of head with two white stripes; throat and breast black with narrow red median throat patch. Belly yellow. *Adult female*: Very different. Back, scapulars, and wing coverts barred black and whitish; head brown with black streaks; rump patch white; throat brown (occasionally a trace of red); breast and sides barred black and whitish, middle of breast usually with black patch; belly yellowish. *Young male*: Resembles adult male but is duller, median throat patch white. *Young female*: Resembles adult female but is duller, belly whitish, no black breast patch.

Measurements *(S. t. nataliae)*. *Adult male*: wing, 131.6–139 (135.7); tail, 76.9–90 (83.5); exposed culmen, 23.2–27 (24.9); tarsus, 20.3–23.5 (21.9). *Adult female*: wing, ca. 135 mm.

Field Marks. Adult male, a black-backed woodpecker with white rump and conspicuous long white patch on wing coverts; head black with two white stripes on each side and a narrow red throat patch (white in juvenal). Female is entirely different and lacks a white patch in the wing. The extensive regular barring of upper parts combined with white rump distinguishes her from other Canadian woodpeckers.

Habitat. Open coniferous woodland (especially western larch, Douglas fir, and yellow pine), sometimes burntlands, in the mountains of interior southern British Columbia.

Nesting. Nest, a cavity excavated by the birds in a tree, often dead or partly dead. *Eggs*, usually 5 or 6; white. Incubation by both parents.

Range. Breeds in the mountains from southern interior British Columbia and western Montana south to southern California, central Arizona, and northern New Mexico.

Subspecies. (1) *Sphyrapicus thyroideus thyroideus* (Cassin) breeds in the Okanagan region of British Columbia east to Midway. (2) *S. t. nataliae* (Malherbe) breeds in the East Kootenay of British Columbia. The latter has a shorter, more slender bill.

Downy Woodpecker

Pic mineur
Picoides pubescens (Linnaeus)
Total length: 16 to 18.5 cm
Plate 47

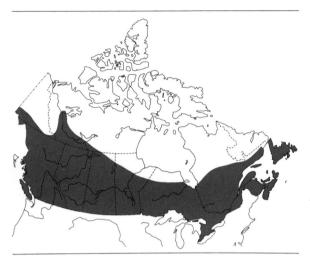

Breeding Distribution of Downy Woodpecker

Range in Canada. Breeds from southern Yukon (probably Dezadeash Lake); southwestern Mackenzie (Carcajou River west of Fort Norman; Fort Simpson; Nahanni National Park; Wood Buffalo National Park); northern Alberta; northwestern and central-eastern Saskatchewan (Lake Athabasca, southern Reindeer Lake); north-central Manitoba (Thicket Portage); western and northern Ontario (Severn Lake, Fort Albany); southern Quebec (Lake Mistassini, Matamec, Anticosti Island, Petit Mécatina River, Saint-Augustin, Madeleine Islands); and Newfoundland, south through the International Boundary through British Columbia (including Vancouver Island but not Queen Charlotte Islands), Alberta, Saskatchewan, Manitoba, Ontario, southern Quebec, and through New Brunswick, Prince Edward Island, and Nova Scotia. Winters within most of the breeding range north at least to southern Mackenzie, northwestern Saskatchewan, and Lake Mistassini, Quebec.

A small black-and-white woodpecker with broad white stripe down middle of back, rather short bill (shorter than head), and in the adult male a small bright-red bar on back of head. Young only shortly out of the nest often have red, yellow, or white spots on the crown. South coastal British Columbia populations have the white under parts tinged with smoky brown (see Subspecies). Colour and markings like Hairy Woodpecker, but very much smaller size and much shorter bill (shorter than head) easily distinguish it in the hand. Our smallest woodpecker.

Measurements *(P. p. medianus)*. *Adult male*: wing, 92.1–98.7 (94.7); tail, 50.6–61 (57.7); exposed culmen, 14.4–18.1 (16.2); tarsus, 15.9–17.1 (16.8). *Adult female*: wing, 92–98.7 (95.2) mm.

Field Marks. A small black-and-white woodpecker, the male with a small red bar on the back of the head. A broad white stripe down the middle of the black back distinguishes it from other woodpeckers except the Hairy, which it very closely resembles. Much smaller size of the Downy is often hard to judge, and the best field mark is the short bill of Downy (much shorter than head). In most parts of Canada the presence of black spots on the white outer tail feathers distinguishes the Downy from the Hairy (however, on the west coast of British Columbia and in Newfoundland this is useless as many Hairy Woodpeckers have similar markings). The Three-toed Woodpecker has the sides and flanks heavily barred.

Habitat. Open deciduous or mixed deciduous and coniferous woodland and tall shrubbery, and in various situations from wilderness areas to city parks and shade trees, farm groves, woodlots, and orchards. Forages in trees, shrubbery, and sometimes, especially in winter, on non-woody plants in fields. Prefers deciduous trees and tall shrubbery.

Nesting. In an excavated cavity in a dead tree or dead part of a living one, at heights varying from a few to 18 m above the ground. *Eggs*, usually 4 or 5; white. Incubation reported as 12 days (F.L. Burns), by both sexes.

Range. Breeds in woodlands from southeastern Alaska and across southern Canada (see below) south to southern California, central Arizona, south-central Texas, and along the Gulf Coast from Louisiana to Florida.

Subspecies. (1) *Picoides pubescens nelsoni* (Oberholser): southern Mackenzie, northern and northeastern British Columbia, Alberta (except extreme southwest but south to Banff), Saskatchewan, Manitoba, (intergrading in south with *medianus*), and probably northwestern Ontario (intergrades with *medianus* in Rainy River district). In whiteness of under parts and white spotting on wings it is similar to *medianus* but averages slightly larger with perhaps less black barring on white of tail (very variable), whites a little purer. A poorly characterized race. As size variation is a cline, delimitation of range, apart from that of *medianus*, is arbitrary. (2) *P. p. medianus* (Swainson): southern and eastern Ontario, Quebec, Newfoundland and the Maritimes. Averages slightly smaller than *nelsoni*. (3) *P. p. leucurus* (Hartlaub): central and southern British Columbia (except southwestern coast and southern Vancouver Island) and extreme southwestern Alberta (Waterton Lakes National Park). Similar in size to *nelsoni*, but wing coverts with white spots reduced and white of under parts not so pure. (4) *P. p. gairdnerii* (Audubon): southern coastal British Columbia and Vancouver Island. Like *leucurus* in reduced white spotting of wing coverts but under parts decidedly tinged with smoky brown; size averages smaller. (5) *P. p. glacialis* (Grinnell): extreme north coast of British Columbia; has wandered once to Queen Charlotte Islands, 24 August 1920.

Remarks. This is our smallest woodpecker and in many parts of the country our commonest. It is a confiding bird and is more likely to come closer to our dwellings than would most of its relatives. In winter it is easily attracted by a supply of suet to the backyard feeding shelf.

In appearance it is almost a counterpart of the larger Hairy Woodpecker. The males of both species have a little red bar on the nape and, for that reason, are often mistaken for the very different Red-headed Woodpecker.

Insects constitute over 75 per cent of the food of this woodpecker. Almost all insects eaten are economically harmful and include some wood-boring species. An interesting study of the effects of the Downy and Hairy woodpeckers on the coddling moth has been made in Nova Scotia by C.R. MacLellan (1958. The Canadian Entomologist, vol. 90, no. 1, p. 21). In the years 1950 to 1956 he found that these woodpeckers reduced the overwintering population of the coddling moth on his study area by 52 per cent!

Hairy Woodpecker

Pic chevelu
Picoides villosus (Linnaeus)
Total length: 21.5 to 26.5 cm
Plate 47

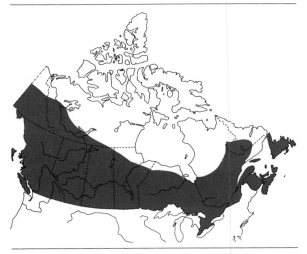

Breeding Distribution of Hairy Woodpecker

Range in Canada. Breeds in wooded areas from central Yukon (Forty Mile); southwestern and central-southern Mackenzie (Forts Providence and Simpson, Nahanni National Park, Wood Buffalo National Park; probably northwest to Fort Norman); northern Saskatchewan (Lake Athabasca, Hasbala Lake); north-central Manitoba (Bird); northern Ontario (Severn Lake, Sutton Narrows); southern Quebec (Eastmain, Lake Saint-Jean, Moisie River, Anticosti Island); interior Labrador (Churchill River, possibly Schefferville region); and Newfoundland southward through British Columbia (including Queen Charlotte and Vancouver islands), Alberta, Saskatchewan, Manitoba, Ontario, southern Quebec, New Brunswick, Prince Edward Island, and Nova Scotia (including Cape Breton Island). Winters north to southern Mackenzie and northern Newfoundland.

A black-and-white (but on West Coast whites are tinged with sandy brown) four-toed woodpecker, with broad white stripe down middle of back and bill nearly as long as head. Varies geographically (see Subspecies). Adult male with bright-red bar (often divided into two spots) on nape but lacking in female. Young not long out of the nest often show reddish or yellowish spots on crown, but young male does not have red on nape. A large edition of the common Downy Woodpecker but decidedly larger with much longer bill.

Measurements *(P. v. septentrionalis). Adult male*: wing, 127–137.5 (131); tail, 71.5–92.1 (81.9); exposed culmen, 29–38.6 (33.6); tarsus, 22–26.3 (24.3). *Adult female*: wing, 119–138.1 (127.8) mm.

Field Marks. A black-and-white woodpecker with a broad white stripe down middle of back, the adult male with a small bar of red on the nape. Closely resembles the Downy Woodpecker but is larger. However, size is hard to judge unless the two are together. The best distinction is the Hairy's relatively much longer bill (nearly as long as head), that of the Downy being more stubby and obviously shorter than the head. Another distinction valid in most parts of the continent (except the Pacific Coast region and Newfoundland) is the immaculate (no black spots or bars) white outer tail feathers of the Hairy. The Three-toed Woodpecker has heavily barred sides and flanks.

Habitat. In nesting season more mature woodlands and forests but in heavy forests prefers more open parts, edges or openings; also burns and logged-over areas. Inhabits deciduous, coniferous, or mixedwood forests but over most of its range prefers at least an admixture of deciduous trees. Tends to be less tolerant than the Downy Woodpecker of young, smaller tree growth. In winter inhabits a wide variety of trees, often visiting ornamental trees and tall shrubbery even in urban areas.

Nesting. In a cavity excavated by the birds in a living or dead tree. *Eggs*, 3 to 5; white. Incubation reportedly 14 days (F.L. Burns), by both sexes.

Range. Breeds in wooded areas from central Alaska and across Canada south to Panama and the Bahamas. Winters mainly within breeding range, although there may be some migratory movement, especially in more northern populations.

Subspecies. (1) *Picoides villosus septentrionalis* (Nuttall): Yukon, northern and central British Columbia (including Peace River Parklands, Chezacut), southern Mackenzie, Alberta (east of the Rocky Mountains), Saskatchewan, Manitoba, western and central Ontario (Kapuskasing), Quebec (Abitibi County). A large race with copiously white-marked black upper parts, all-white under body, including sides and flanks. (2) *P. v. villosus* (Linnaeus): southern Ontario, southern Quebec (including Gaspé Peninsula and Anticosti Island), New Brunswick, Prince Edward Island and Nova Scotia. Similar to (1) but averaging smaller. (3) *P. v. terraenovae* (Batchelder): Newfoundland. Similar to (2) but whites in upper parts reduced; sometimes whiter outer tail feathers with black spots and occasionally lightly dark-barred flanks. (4) *P. v. monticola* (Anthony): interior southern and south-central British Columbia, southwestern Alberta (southern mountains intergrading northward with (1) in Jasper National Park); similar to (1) but white spotting of wing coverts reduced. (5) *P. v. sitkensis* (Swarth) is doubtfully separable from *harrisi*: northern coast region of British Columbia (but not Queen Charlotte Islands) south to Calvert Island and Rivers Inlet: like (4) in reduction of white spotting on wings but white of under parts more tinged with brownish. (6) *P. v. harrisi* (Audubon): southern coast and Vancouver Island of British Columbia. Differs from (5) in still darker, more smoky under parts. (7) *P. v. picoideus* (Osgood): Queen Charlotte Islands, British Columbia. The most heavily pigmented of all the races. White spotting on wings sparse and small, white stripe down back, brownish and often spotted or barred with black, white outer tail feathers often spotted or broadly barred with black; flanks often barred, and sides streaked with black; under parts more heavily smoky brown than in (6). (8) *P. v. orius* (Oberholser): extends northward into Canada in the Cascades, a short distance north of the International Boundary in British Columbia.

White-headed Woodpecker

Pic à tête blanche
Picoides albolarvatus (Cassin)
Total length: 23 to 24 cm

Range in Canada. Rare but regular permanent resident in the Okanagan, Similkameen, and Kettle valleys of British Columbia. Active nests have been discovered near Vaseux Lake (two) and on Anarchist Mountain. (See W.C. Weber and S.R. Cannings, Syesis, vol. 9, pp. 215–220.)

Adults are all black, except white head, fore-neck, patch on primaries of the wing, and, in the male only, a red bar across the nape. Young are similar to adults, but black is duller.

Field Marks. Unmistakable, as described above.

Habitat. Favours open ponderosa pine forest.

Range. Southern British Columbia, eastern Washington, and northern Idaho south to southern California and western Nevada.

Subspecies. *Picoides albolarvatus albolarvatus* (Cassin).

Three-toed Woodpecker

(Northern Three-toed Woodpecker)

Pic tridactyle
Picoides tridactylus (Linnaeus)
Total length: 20.3 to 24.5 cm
Plate 47

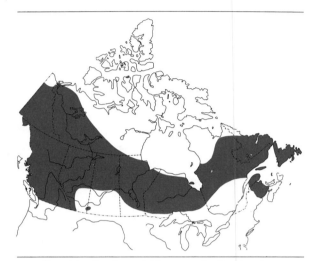

Breeding Distribution of Three-toed Woodpecker

Range in Canada. Breeds from near tree limit in northern Yukon (Old Crow); northwestern and central Mackenzie (Mackenzie Delta, Fort Anderson, Great Slave Lake); northern Saskatchewan (Lake Athabasca, Charcoal Lake); northern Manitoba (Churchill; perhaps Sandhill Lake); northern Ontario (probably Severn River); northern Quebec (Lake Guillaume-Delisle, Kuujjuaq); northern Labrador (Saglek Bay); and Newfoundland south through southern British Columbia (but not on Queen Charlotte and Vancouver islands); southwestern and central-eastern Alberta (Battle River region); central Saskatchewan (Nipawin; locally Cypress Hills); southern Manitoba (Riding Mountain, Whitemouth); central Ontario (Thunder Bay; near Chapleau; Abitibi Lake; one isolated successful nesting at Lake Opinicon); Quebec (south at least to Lake Mistassini, Pointe-des-Monts, Anticosti Island; probably Gaspé Peninsula; southern limits poorly known); and New Brunswick (rarely and locally south to Fundy National Park).

Casual in southwestern Keewatin (Windy River). Winters within the breeding range, but individuals move south of the breeding range irregularly into southern Ontario and southwestern Quebec. Very rare visitor to Nova Scotia (photo: Ingonish, February 1973; also sight records). Sight records only for Prince Edward Island.

Three instead of four toes distinguish it from the other woodpeckers except the Black-backed Woodpecker. The present species differs from the Black-backed in having white bars on the back (in western populations the white bars are sometimes coalesced into a longitudinal white stripe down the back) and is somewhat smaller in size. As in the Black-backed, the male has a yellow crown-patch, which is lacking in the adult female. In female Three-toed Woodpeckers there is usually (not always) white spotting on the black crown.

Measurements *(P. t. bacatus). Adult male*: wing, 111.2–119 (114.1); tail, 64.9–77.3 (71.5); exposed culmen, 25.5–29 (27); tarsus, 20.1–22.3 (21.3). *Adult female*: wing, 109.8–115 (112.1) mm.

Field Marks. Large yellow crown patch identifies male Three-toed and Black-backed woodpeckers, and white areas in the middle of the back (usually white bars) denote the present species. Females of this species, lacking a yellow crown patch and with white down the middle of the back (usually at least some barring can be detected) might be confused by beginners with female Hairy Woodpecker. In eastern populations especially, the Three-toed has obvious white barring on the back instead of a solid white longitudinal stripe, but in some western individuals the whites are more extensive and occasionally are fused into a solid white stripe. The sides and flanks of the Three-toed Woodpeckers are heavily barred; those of the Hairy Woodpecker *over most of its range* are plain white. (Caution: On the West Coast and in Newfoundland, Hairy Woodpeckers often have slightly barred *flanks*, but the barring does not include the sides. The Queen Charlotte Islands Hairy, however, often has black streaks on the sides *and* barred flanks.)

Habitat. Coniferous woodlands and burntlands (or similar stands of dead trees); muskegs.

Nesting. Similar to Black-backed Woodpecker.

Range. Breeds north to tree limit in North America, Europe, and Asia. In North America: northern Alaska and across Canada (see Range in Canada) south to southern Oregon, Arizona, New Mexico, Minnesota, central Ontario, northern New York (Adirondack Mountains), northern Vermont (Green Mountains), northern New Hampshire (White Mountains), and Maine.

Subspecies. (1) *Picoides tridactylus bacatus* Bangs: Manitoba eastward. White bars on back narrower but usually quite distinct, rarely very few and indistinct. (2) *P. t. fasciatus* Baird: Yukon, Mackenzie, British Columbia, Alberta, western Saskatchewan. Similar to *bacatus* but with more white on back, white bars larger and often partly, occasionally completely, coalesced forming a more or less unbroken longitudinal patch; white spots on forehead larger.

Black-backed Woodpecker

(Black-backed Three-toed Woodpecker)

Pic à dos noir
Picoides arcticus (Swainson)
Total length: 23 to 25.5 cm
Plate 47

Breeding Distribution of Black-backed
Woodpecker

Range in Canada. Breeds in coniferous woodland from southern Yukon (Sixmile River;
north probably to Snag and the southern
Ogilvie Mountains); central-western and
southern Mackenzie (Norman Wells, Fort
Simpson, Great Slave Lake); northern Saskatchewan (Lake Athabasca, Hasbala Lake);
northern Manitoba (Bird, York Factory);
northern Ontario (Sutton Lake, southern James
Bay); south-central Quebec (southern James
Bay, Lake Mistassini, north shore of the Gulf
of St. Lawrence, Anticosti Island); central
Labrador (Hamilton Inlet, Sandgirt Lake); and
Newfoundland south through British Columbia
(east of the Cascades); central and southwestern
Alberta (Battle River region); central Saskatche-
wan (Prince Albert, Saskatchewan River);
southern Manitoba (High Lake); western and
southern Ontario (south to Pancake Bay,
Algonquin Provincial Park); southern Quebec
(Lake Trente et un Milles, Inlet, Lake Trois
Saumons, Gaspé Peninsula); New Brunswick;
Prince Edward Island; and Nova Scotia.

Winters mainly in the breeding range, but
individuals wander south irregularly in small
numbers. In certain years, irregularly spaced,
relatively large numbers move southward.

Three instead of four toes distinguish it from other woodpeckers except
the Three-toed. *Adult male*: Above, bluish black (including whole back)
except yellow crown patch, white spots on flight feathers, and mainly
white outer tail feathers; sides of head with narrow white line (sometimes absent) running back from eye and a broad white stripe below
eye; under parts mostly white, the sides and flanks heavily barred black
and white. *Adult female*: Like adult male but crown black without
yellow patch. *Young*: Resemble adult male, there being a smaller yellow
crown patch in the young male and frequently young females too have
yellow feathers in the crown.

Measurements. *Adult male*: wing, 126.1–132 (128.6); tail, 73.8–84.6
(79.4); exposed culmen, 31–34 (32.2); tarsus, 22.5–24.9 (23.8). *Adult
female*: wing, 121–132 (126.3) mm.

Field Marks. Solid-black back, yellow crown patch in male (lacking in female), white under parts, the sides and flanks extensively barred
with black. All-black back distinguishes it from Three-toed. Williamson's Sapsucker male, of southern British Columbia, has white patch on
sides of wings, white rump, and mostly black breast and should be
easily distinguishable.

Habitat. Coniferous woodlands and burned areas with standing
dead trees.

Nesting. In an excavated cavity in a dead or living tree, usually
(not always) coniferous. Generally at no great height, 0.6 to 6.0 m, but
exceptionally (mainly in the West) up to 24 m. Incubation said to be
14 days (A.C. Bent), by both sexes.

Range. Breeds from central Alaska and across Canada (see Range
in Canada) south to central California, western Nevada, northwestern
Wyoming, southwestern South Dakota, northern Minnesota, Upper
Peninsula of Michigan, northern New York (Adirondack Mountains),
Vermont (Green Mountains), New Hampshire (White Mountains), and
Maine.

Northern Flicker

(Yellow-shafted and Red-shafted flickers)

Pic flamboyant
Colaptes auratus (Linnaeus)
Total length: 30.5 to 35 cm
Plate 47

The Yellow-shafted and Red-shafted flickers are now treated as
subspecies of a single species called Northern Flicker.

Eastern and northwestern races *Colaptes auratus luteus* Bangs and
C. a. borealis Ridgway (formerly collectively called Yellow-shafted
Flicker): *Adult male*: Crown and back of neck grey, a scarlet crescent
across nape; back, wing coverts, and most of secondaries olive brown
barred with black; rump white; sides of head, throat, and upper breast
vinaceous brown; ''moustache'' patches and large crescent across breast

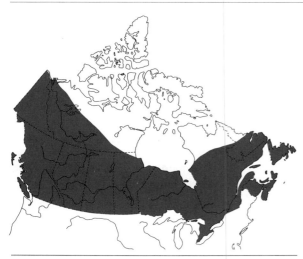

Breeding Distribution of Northern Flicker

Range in Canada. Breeds from coast to coast in southern parts and northward to near tree limit in northern Yukon (Firth River); northwestern and central Mackenzie (Mackenzie Delta, Anderson River, Fort Enterprise and Reliance); northern Manitoba (Kasmere River, Churchill); northern Ontario; north-central Quebec (Grande rivière de la Baleine, Schefferville); south-central Labrador (Kaipokok Bay, Goose Bay), and Newfoundland.

Winters in southern Ontario (Plover Mills, Hamilton, Toronto; rarely Ottawa), and in very small numbers in southwestern Quebec (Montréal region), southern Newfoundland, southern New Brunswick, Nova Scotia, and British Columbia (regularly on the coast, small numbers in southern interior). Casual in northern Quebec (Cape Wolstenholme, July 1925; Ungava Bay, October 1882).

black; rest of under body brownish white to yellowish white, heavily spotted with black; shafts of flight feathers, underside of wing, and much of underside of tail yellow. *Adult female*: Similar to adult male but lacks black "moustache" patches. *Young in juvenal plumage* (worn for only a short time while in and after leaving nest): Similar to adult male, but both sexes have black "moustache" patches (sometimes poorly indicated); often there is some reddish on the forehead, and the throat is more greyish.

Southwestern races, *Colaptes auratus cafer* (Gmelin) and *C. a. colaris* Vigors (formerly collectively called Red-shafted Flicker): Similar to above but yellow is replaced by red on the shafts of the flight feathers, underside of wings, and underside of tail. Top of head is brown, throat grey, and the male has red (not black) "moustache" patches (lacking in female or only faintly indicated by brown). In juvenal plumage only the male has red "moustache" patches, these brownish and inconspicuous in the female. (Note: In areas where these forms intergrade, e.g., Cypress Hills of Alberta and Saskatchewan, various combinations of these two colour types are found.)

Measurements *(C. a. luteus)*. *Adult male*: wing, 150.9–164 (157.4); tail, 98.7–111.5 (105.9); exposed culmen, 31.3–39 (34.3); tarsus, 25.9–30.8 (28.7). *Adult female*: wing, 152.1–166.9 (156.9) mm.

Field Marks. A rather large brown woodpecker with a broad white rump patch conspicuous in flight. Often feeds on the ground. *Voice*: a loud far-carrying series of *yucks*; a more deliberate *flicker-flicker-flicker*.

Habitat. This wide-ranging and adaptable species inhabits a variety of habitat but prefers moderately open situations including open woodland of all kinds; farmland, burntland, pastures and similar open places with, or not too far from, trees. Forages on the ground (especially where ants are present) as well as in trees. Uses trees also for cover, roosting, drumming, and nesting. On treeless plains or prairie, telephone poles or fence posts may serve to some extent instead of trees; or it may nest in a building, rarely even in a haystack, earth bank, or other strange place.

Nesting. A cavity, excavated by both sexes, most often in a tree, frequently a dead one, at heights from 0.6 to 18 m; often in a telephone pole or fence post, sometimes in a building and more rarely in a variety of other situations. Bird boxes are sometimes used. *Eggs*, usually 6 to 9; glossy white. Incubation 11 to 12 days (Althea Sherman), by both sexes.

Range. From about tree limit in Alaska and across Canada south to southern Texas, the Gulf Coast of United States, Florida Keys, Cuba, and Grand Cayman Island, Mexican mainland south to the Isthmus of Tehuantepec.

Subspecies. (1) *Colaptes auratus luteus* Bangs is the breeding bird of eastern Canada. (2) *C. a. borealis* Ridgway, of slightly larger average size, is generally understood to include the northern part of the breeding population from Alaska east to Labrador. Birds from Ontario eastward, however, are best referred to *luteus*. There is a slight increase in size northwestward, and if *borealis* is recognized it should be restricted to western populations, east perhaps to Manitoba but boundaries are rather arbitrary. (3) *C. a. cafer* (Gmelin) is the breeding bird of coastal British Columbia west of the Cascades. (4) *C. a. collaris* Vigors, paler and more greyish, slightly larger, breeds in southern British Columbia (east of the Cascades), southern Alberta, and southwestern Saskatchewan.

Pileated Woodpecker

Grand Pic
Dryocopus pileatus (Linnaeus)
Total length: 40.5 to 49.5 cm
Plate 47

Breeding Distribution of Pileated Woodpecker

Range in Canada. Breeds in forested regions from southern Mackenzie (Fort Simpson, Upper Buffalo River) south through northeastern, central, and southern British Columbia (Vancouver Island, Elko, Thutade Lake, Fort Nelson River); Alberta (except southeastern corner); northwestern and central Saskatchewan (Lake Athabasca, southern Reindeer Lake, Big Gully Creek, Nipawin, Good Spirit Lake); central and southern Manitoba (north to about Thicket Portage and Herb Lake); central and southern Ontario (north to Sandy Lake and southern James Bay); southern Quebec (north at least to Lake Waswanipi, Lake Saint-Jean, Gaspé Peninsula; possibly Anticosti Island); New Brunswick; Nova Scotia (including Cape Breton Island); and formerly Prince Edward Island (now extirpated).

Winters mostly in the breeding range, but perhaps withdrawing from northernmost parts.

By far our largest woodpecker. Patterned in broad masses of black and white and with a conspicuous bright-red pointed crest (not just a red bar across nape). Males have the whole forehead and a patch behind the base of the bill red also.

Measurements *(D. p. abieticola). Adult male*: wing, 230.4–246.8 (236); tail, 148.5–163 (157); exposed culmen, 50–58.8 (55.2); tarsus, 33.5–37.8 (35.3). *Adult female*: wing, 220.2–238 (228.5) mm.

Field Marks. Unmistakable. A crow-sized woodpecker with conspicuous bright-red crest; rest of plumage mainly black with white stripe on side of head and down sides of neck; white areas in and under the wings show prominently in flight. *Voice*: Commonly a *cuk-cuk-cuk*, a little like that of a flicker, but more deliberate, lower-pitched, more powerful.

Habitat. Mature woodlands of various kinds, especially those containing some standing dead trees. Although it probably prefers, especially in the breeding season, more extensive wilder forests, these are not essential. Where unmolested, it also inhabits woodlots, parks, and other less extensive stands of mature trees. Sometimes, especially in winter, it forages close to dwellings in city suburbs if maturer trees are present.

Nesting. Nests in a cavity excavated by the birds, 4.5 to 21 m up in a dead or, less often, living tree, either deciduous or coniferous. *Eggs*, 3 to 4; white. Incubation 18 days (J.S.Y. Hoyt), by both sexes.

Range. Resident in forested parts of Canada and the United States south to central California, central Texas, the United States Gulf Coast, and southern Florida.

Subspecies. (1) *Dryocopus pileatus picinus* (Bangs): British Columbia (area of intergradation with the following race not well understood). (2) *D. p. abieticola* (Bangs), average larger size and paler coloration, occupies the remainder of the range in Canada from Mackenzie and western Alberta eastward.

Order **Passeriformes:**
Perching Birds

The passerine or perching birds make up by far the largest avian order, containing, as it does, almost half of the more than 8000 species of the world's living birds. All species have four toes, three in front, one behind, the hind toe well developed and on the same level as the others. The feet are ideal for grasping limbs in perching. Most have well-developed songs. All are land birds, and the open sea has no useful place in their existence; indeed, it is just another migration hazard for many species.

Family **Tyrannidae:**
Tyrant Flycatchers

Number of Species in Canada: 26

This large family of 360 species, more or less, is confined to the Western Hemisphere with its centre of abundance in the tropics. The bill is typically flattened, broad at the base, slightly hooked at the tip, and has stiff bristles at its base. Legs and feet are weak but ideal for perching. Song is less well developed than in other families of this order. Flycatchers usually perch with alert upright posture, occasionally to frequently jetting the tail. Passing insects are taken by a short quick flight and a snap of the bill, after which the bird resumes perching to watch for other insects.

Olive-sided Flycatcher

Moucherolle à côtés olive
Contopus borealis (Swainson)
Total length: 18 to 19.8 cm
Plate 48

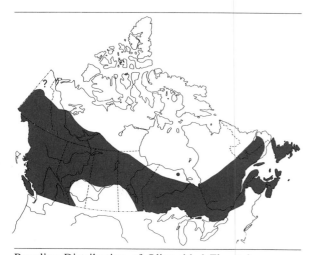

Breeding Distribution of Olive-sided Flycatcher

Range in Canada. Summer resident, breeding from central-western and southern Yukon (north to Yukon River, Ogilvie Mountains; species recorded north to Old Crow and Richardson Mountains); central-western and southern Mackenzie (north to southern Great Slave Lake and Snowdrift; and in the upper Mackenzie valley north probably to Fort Norman); northern Saskatchewan (Lake Athabasca, Patterson Lake); north-central Manitoba

Adults (sexes similar): Upper parts dull greyish-olive, darkest on crown; sides of rump with a patch of white feathers (often concealed by folded wings); wings and tail dusky, the wing coverts with paler tips, the secondaries and tertials narrowly edged whitish; sides of breast, sides, and flanks dark greyish-olive; throat, centre of breast, and belly whitish or pale yellowish (contrasting with sides of breast). Bill blackish above, pale brownish below becoming dusky toward tip.

Measurements. *Adult male*: wing, 103.2–112.4 (106.9); tail, 67.5–75 (70.9); exposed culmen, 16.8–17.9 (17.4); tarsus, 13.5–15.5 (14.6). *Adult female*: wing, 98.6–105.1 (101.9) mm.

Field Marks. A stout, short-necked flycatcher with very erect posture, larger than the pewees, smaller than kingbirds. The dark sides of the breast extend well down on the sides of the abdomen and contrast with the white belly. Often the fluffy white tufts on either side of the rump partly show from under the folded wings (they are quite noticeable as the bird flies away). Usually perches well up, near or at the top of a tree (often in dead one). *Voice* is unmistakable; an emphatic whistled *Come right here* or *Quick-three beers*; also commonly when even mildly excited, *pip-pip-pip* in threes, slightly descending.

Habitat. Perches high in trees, often dead ones or those with high dead branches or living trees with slender tops. Burntlands with standing dead trees, bogs, lakeshores with water-killed trees, lumbered areas and other clearings in woodland; sometimes tall trees about farmland, occasionally orchards (Nova Scotia).

Nesting. Nest is placed well out on a branch of a conifer (less often a deciduous tree, rarely even an apple tree) ordinarily at considerable height but may rarely be as low as 2 m. It is made of twigs, rootlets, lichens, and mosses and lined with fine grasses and rootlets. *Eggs*, 3 or 4; are handsome: creamy to light buff with a broad wreath around the larger end of brighter browns and more or less purplish-grey in spots and blotches. Incubation 16 to 17 days (L.H. Walkinshaw).

Range. Breeds in wooded regions from central Alaska east to Newfoundland and south to northern Baja California, central Arizona, northern New Mexico, central Minnesota, northern Michigan, and Massachusetts; and in the mountains south to North Carolina and Tennessee. Winters in South America.

(Thicket Portage, Bird); northern Ontario (Sutton Ridges, Favourable Lake, southern James Bay); south-central Quebec (Lake Mistassini, Lake Méchant); southern Labrador (Goose Bay); and Newfoundland south through British Columbia (including Vancouver Island but not Queen Charlotte Islands); through northern, central, and southwestern Alberta (south in the mountains and foothills to Waterton Lakes and to the edge of wooded country in central-eastern parts: Pigeon and Battle lakes; absent from the southeastern plains); south-central Saskatchewan (south to about Nipawin; absent from the plains); southern Manitoba (Duck Mountains, Whitemouth); southern Ontario (south to about Mount Forest, Holland Swamp, Lindsay, Sharbot Lake); southern Quebec (south to Gatineau Park, Hatley, Gaspé Peninsula, Anticosti and Madeleine islands); and through New Brunswick, Prince Edward Island, and Nova Scotia.

Remarks. Although the Olive-sided Flycatcher is usually a forest recluse, this is not always so. When the writer was a boy in Wolfville, Nova Scotia, this fine flycatcher summered regularly on the edge of that town and sometimes nested in apple orchards.

Western Wood-Pewee

Pioui de l'Ouest
Contopus sordidulus Sclater
Total length: 15 to 17 cm
Plate 48

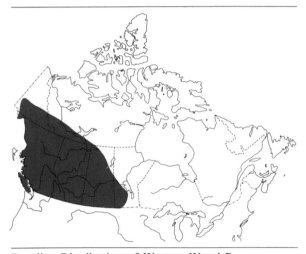

Breeding Distribution of Western Wood-Pewee

Range in Canada. Summer resident, breeding from southern Yukon (north at least to Little Salmon River and Lapie River); southern Mackenzie (Hill Island Lake, Nahanni National Park; also sight records north to Fort Good Hope); northern Alberta; northwestern and central-eastern Saskatchewan (Lake Athabasca, Kazan Lake, Cumberland House); and south-central Manitoba (northwestern Lake Winnipegosis, Lake St. Martin) south through southern British Columbia (including Vancouver Island; not recorded from Queen Charlotte Islands); southern Alberta (locally: Milk River, Waterton Lakes); southern Saskatchewan (locally: Regina region, probably Cypress Hills); and southwestern Manitoba (east to Delta where outnumbered by *virens*). Three records for Ontario: two on the basis of song (Point Pelee in May 1968 and May 1969) and a specimen (North Point, 20 June 1984).

Very similar to Eastern Wood-Pewee but upper parts a little more greyish; olive greyish of under parts darker and more extensive; lower mandible usually darker.

Measurements *(C. s. veliei). Adult male*: wing, 83.7–87.1 (85.5); tail, 62–68 (65.7); exposed culmen, 12.1–13.2 (12.7); tarsus, 12.5–14.5 (13.7). *Adult female*: wing, 79.1–86.1 (82.1) mm.

Field Marks. *Voice* is the only field distinction from Eastern Wood-Pewee. Fortunately its harsher nasal *pe-ear* is very different from the calls of the Eastern Wood-Pewee. Its larger size, much darker coloration, and lack of an eye-ring readily separate it from the *Empidonax* flycatchers.

Habitat. More open woodland (mixed, deciduous, or coniferous) openings and edges; trees and tall shrubbery along coulées and rivers; orchards.

Nesting. Nest, usually saddled on a horizontal limb (deciduous or coniferous). It tends to be a bit larger and deeper than that of the Eastern Wood-Pewee, and lichens are apparently not so often used in its exterior. *Eggs*, 2 to 4, usually 3; similar to those of the Eastern Wood-Pewee.

Range. Breeds from central-eastern Alaska and western Canada (east to central-southern Manitoba) south to western Panama. Winters from Panama to Venezuela and Bolivia.

Subspecies. Two races in Canada are recognized in the *A.O.U. Check-list* (1957): (1) *Contopus sordidulus veliei* Coues, breeding in all the Canadian part of the range except western British Columbia; (2) *C. s. saturatus* Bishop, characterized by average slightly darker coloration, inhabiting western British Columbia; areas of intergradation with *veliei* vaguely understood. Several authors, perhaps with good reason, regard *saturatus* as a synonym of *veliei*. Certainly, the extent of individual variation in breeding populations is great.

Eastern Wood-Pewee

Pioui de l'Est
Contopus virens (Linnaeus)
Total length: 15 to 17 cm
Plate 48

Breeding Distribution of Eastern Wood-Pewee

Range in Canada. Summer resident, breeding in southern and southwestern Manitoba (Coulter Park, Gainsborough Creek, Delta, Shoal Lake, Whitemouth; probably Lake St. Martin); western and southern Ontario (north to about Sioux Lookout, Mildred, Agawa, Timagami, Kirkland Lake); southern Quebec (north to about Ville-Marie, Blue-Sea-Lake, Québec, Lake Saint-Jean, Rivière-du-Loup, Matapédia valley); New Brunswick (Saint-Léonard, Fredericton; probably Campbellton and Bathurst); Prince Edward Island; and Nova Scotia (including Cape Breton Island). Probably breeds in southeastern Saskatchewan (summer records for Good Spirit Lake, Runnymede, Fort San, Grenfell; recorded regularly in the Qu'Appelle valley). Recorded rarely in summer in eastern Gaspé Peninsula (Grande-Grève, Percé).

Accidental at sea (320 km off Hopedale, Labrador, 31 August 1929).

Larger than any of our *Empidonax* flycathers, wing much longer, coloration darker, greyer (much less greenish), lacks eye-ring. Pale lower mandible, wing bars, and somewhat smaller size distinguish it from Eastern Phoebe. *Adults (sexes alike)*: Upper parts dark greyish-olive; crown feathers rather long with dark centres; wing and tail dusky; wing bars pale greyish, edging on secondaries and tertials whitish; breast and sides greyish olive; throat whitish, abdomen pale yellowish-white; bill brownish black above, pale yellowish or whitish below with dusky tip. *Young*: Buffy wing bars and often the pale area of the lower mandible is more restricted, sometimes mainly dusky.

Measurements. *Adult male*: wing, 80.8–86.8 (84.1); tail, 63–68 (65.5); exposed culmen, 12.2–13.1 (12.9); tarsus, 12.5–14 (13.7). *Adult female*: wing, 78.3–86.2 (82.1) mm.

Very similar to Western Wood-Pewee but upper parts more olivaceous (less greyish), under parts less extensively olive-greyish, this colour paler, lower mandible usually paler.

Field Marks. Between the Eastern Phoebe and the *Empidonax* flycatchers in size. It is much darker and less greenish than the *Empidonax* flycatchers and lacks an eye-ring, and its longer wing extends halfway down the tail. Its obvious wing bars and lack of the tail-wagging habit distinguish it from the Eastern Phoebe; also at close range its pale lower mandible, smaller size, smaller bill, and less definite breast patches distinguish it from the Olive-sided Flycatcher. Its planitive lazy whistled *pee-a-wee*, the second syllable lowest, the third rising, distinguishes it from all others. Also *pee-wee* dropping in pitch.

Habitat. Prefers maturer open deciduous woodland and openings; forests, woodlots, tall shade trees in towns, old orchards, mixed woods. Sometimes more open coniferous woodland.

Nesting. Nest, of grasses, plant fibres, and similar material, is covered on the outside with lichens. It is saddled on a horizontal branch (most often deciduous) at heights from 2.4 to 18 m. *Eggs*, 2 to 4, usually 3; creamy white with a ring of brown dots, spots, and blotches around the large end. Incubation 12 to 13 days, by the female (*in* Bent).

Range. Breeds from southern eastern Canada (southern Manitoba east to Cape Breton Island) south to central and southwestern Texas, the Gulf Coast of United States, and central Florida. Winters from Costa Rica, Colombia, and Venezuela south to Peru.

Yellow-bellied Flycatcher

Moucherolle à ventre jaune
Empidonax flaviventris (Baird and Baird)
Total length: 12.7 to 14.7 cm
Plate 49

Breeding Distribution of Yellow-bellied Flycatcher

Range in Canada. Summer resident in southern Yukon (probably breeding near Coal Creek and Yukon River); breeding in central-western and southern Mackenzie (Fort Norman, Soulier Lake, Nahanni National Park); northern British Columbia (Dease Lake, Atlin, Muskwa River, Trutch, and McDonald Creek); northern and central Alberta (south at least to Glenevis; also unconfirmed June reports in the Calgary area); northern and central Saskatchewan (south at least to Nipawin); Manitoba (north probably to Churchill); Ontario (Fort Severn south at least to Algonquin Provincial Park and Ottawa; also locally on Amherst Island in northeastern Lake Ontario); central and southern Quebec (Schefferville region south to Hatley and the Madeleine Islands); southern Labrador (Goose Bay, Chateau Bay); Newfoundland; New Brunswick; Prince Edward Island; and Nova Scotia.

Adults (sexes alike): Upper parts greenish olive; tail deep greyish-brown; wings blackish, the middle and greater coverts tipped with pale yellowish or whitish (forming two wing bars), and the secondaries margined with same; eye-ring pale yellow; under parts, including throat, pale yellow, the chest decidedly tinged with olive; wing linings pale yellowish, decidedly yellow on bend of wing. *Young*: Similar to adults but wing bars slightly buffy, yellow of under parts paler, the upper parts duller.

Measurements. *Adult male*: wing, 62.5–70.9 (67.2); tail, 51.0–56.0 (53.5); exposed culmen, 9.9–11.3 (10.5); tarsus, 16.0–17.5 (16.8). *Adult female*: wing, 61.2–68.2 (63.7) mm.

The uniformly yellow under parts *including throat and chin* distinguish it from all other small Canadian flycatchers except the Western. Differs from the Western in more greenish (less brownish or greyish) upper parts, chest less buffy or brownish; bend of wing *yellow* instead of buffy; the outermost (tenth) primary is usually longer than the fifth, instead of shorter.

Field Marks. A small greenish flycatcher, with two whitish wing bars and *yellowish under parts including throat*. The yellow under parts separate it from other *eastern* flycatchers of similar size (sometimes in autumn others show a yellowish tinge below, but in only the present species does the yellow cover the throat). *Voice*: *Chelek* (more liquid than the *chebec* of Least Flycatcher); a plaintive *pe-wheep*, second syllable rising, with slight suggestion of the *pee-wit* of Semipalmated Plover. The Western Flycatcher (of western and southern British Columbia and southwestern Alberta) is very similar in appearance but its voice is different.

Habitat. Shady, moss-floored thickets and woodland; alder-willow shrubbery often mixed with conifers; bogs; wooded streams. Forages mainly in shady lower stratum of woodlands but on breeding grounds sometimes uses perches 9 to 12 m high in the sunny top of either a coniferous or deciduous tree for singing (*chelek* song).

Nesting. Nest of rootlets, grass, and moss is usually placed on the ground (often sunk in moss) or sometimes in the roots of a fallen tree. *Eggs*, 3 to 5; white, sparingly spotted with browns. Incubation 12 to 14 days (E.H. Forbush), by the female.

Range. Breeds from southern Canada (east of the Rockies) south locally to northern parts of North Dakota, Wisconsin, northeastern Pennsylvania (Pocono Mountains), and New York (Adirondack and Catskill mountains). Winters from eastern Mexico south to eastern Panama.

Acadian Flycatcher

Moucherolle vert
Empidonax virescens (Vieillot)
Total length: 14 to 16 cm
Plate 49

Breeding Distribution of Acadian Flycatcher

Range in Canada. Breeds in extreme southern Ontario (Rondeau, Hamilton, Pickering; summer records in Prince Edward County at Prince Edward Point).

Accidental in Quebec (specimen: Point Natashquan, 22 June 1928. Sight record: Lake Sergent, 22-24 July 1984) and in British Columbia (specimen: Leonie Lake, 9 June 1934).

Similar to Traill's Flycatcher but upper parts olive green (less brownish or greyish); upper mandible (in skins) usually more brownish (less blackish). Wing tip longer: from end of secondaries to tip of longest primary averages in males 19.3 mm; in females 17.3 (compared with 14.2 and 12.8 for Traill's). (See L.L. Snyder, 1953. Contributions Royal Ontario Museum of Zoology, No. 35, pp. 1–26.)

Measurements. *Adult male*: wing, 71–80.5 (74.3); tail, 55–61.5 (59.3); exposed culmen, 11.5–13 (12.6); tarsus, 14.5–16 (15.5). *Adult female*: wing, 67.5–75.5 (70.2) mm (Ridgway).

Field Marks. In appearance practically indistinguishable from Traill's Flycatcher and often from Least Flycatcher. Voice and habitat are the best characters. *Voice*: *Ka-zeep*, second syllable higher; also commonly *peep*. In breeding plumage, the under parts are only faintly tinged with yellowish, and the throat is white, thus distinguishing it from the Yellow-bellied Flycatcher. In autumn plumage, however, some individuals are very yellowish below, this extending onto the throat, and the two are then not safely distinguishable. In Canada, however, the Acadian has a very restricted range.

Habitat. Shady maturer woodland, especially beech. Frequents lower levels well below the treetops. Does not ordinarily leave woodlands in the nesting season.

Nesting. Nest, a rather untidy shallow structure, *suspended* hammock-wise from the fork of a branch, usually 2.4 to 4.5 m above ground, frequently near a stream. *Eggs*, usually 3; white sparingly dotted, mostly near larger end, with browns. Incubation period 13 to 15 days (Walkinshaw).

Range. Breeds mainly from southeastern North Dakota, northern Iowa, southern Michigan, extreme southern Ontario, southern New York, and southwestern Connecticut south to central Texas, the Gulf Coast, and central Florida. Winters from Costa Rica to northern South America.

Traill's Flycatcher Complex

The A.O.U. Check-list Committee (1973. Auk, vol. 90, no. 2, pp. 415–416) has decided to divide Traill's Flycatcher into two sibling species: *Empidonax traillii* (Audubon) and *Empidonax alnorum* Brewster, with vernacular names Willow Flycatcher and Alder Flycatcher, respectively. As the two species can be distinguished in the field only by voice, many cannot be identified and for these the old, more comprehensive name Traill's Flycatcher may still be used. The two-species concept is based on the studies of R.C. Stein (1963. Proceedings American Philosophical Society, vol. 107, no. 1, pp. 21–50) to which those who aspire to the sure identification of birds either in the field or in the hand are referred.

Alder Flycatcher

Moucherolle des aulnes
Empidonax alnorum Brewster
Total length: 13.3 to 17 cm
Plate 49

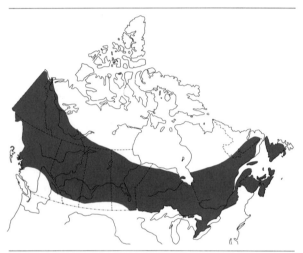

Breeding Distribution of Alder Flycatcher

Range in Canada. Breeds in northern Yukon (upper Babbage River); northwestern and central-southern Mackenzie (Fort McPherson, Fort Norman, Fort Resolution); northern Alberta; northern Saskatchewan (Lake Athabasca); northern Manitoba (Ilford); northern Ontario (Fort Severn); southern Quebec (Lake Mistassini, Matamec, Havre-Saint-Pierre; possibly Piagochioui River near northern James Bay); southern Labrador (Goose Bay); and southern Newfoundland (Bay of Islands, Doyles) south to south-central and southern British Columbia (Bella Coola, Williams Lake, Mount Robson); southern Alberta (except the mountains in the southwest); southern Saskatchewan (locally); southern Manitoba; southern Ontario; southern Quebec; New Brunswick; Prince Edward Island; and Nova Scotia.

Accidental in District of Franklin (specimen: Resolute Bay, Cornwallis Island, 10 June 1982).

Tail not forked. Sexes similar. Upper parts greenish olive (darker and less pure green than in Acadian Flycatcher); eye-ring and wing edging whitish; wing bars buffy whitish; throat and chin white; breast and sides greyish olive; belly, flanks, and under tail coverts whitish usually more or less (sometimes decidedly) suffused with yellow. *Young*: similar to adults but wing bars decidedly buff, upper parts browner.

Measurements. *Adult male*: wing, 68.5–76.5 (72.07); tail, 55.0–63.6 (58.73); bill (from anterior nostril to tip), 7.6–9.3 (8.52). *Adult female*: wing, 65.8–70.5 (68.63); bill, 8.0–9.0 (8.5) mm (R.C. Stein).

Field Marks. One of the larger members of the small *Empidonax* flycatchers, but size is often confusing. Best identified by voice and habitat. A widely distributed species found in alders, willows, and similar thickets in moist (but sometimes drier) situations. Distinguishable in the field from Willow Flycatcher only by advertising song, a raspy *fee-bee-o* (Willow Flycatcher song is *fitz-bew*). However some skeptics claim to have heard one individual singing both song types. Other vocalizations: *pit* and *wee-oo*.

Habitat. Typically, alder or willow thickets usually along streams, lakes, ponds, bogs or swamps; damp cut-over or burned areas growing up in alders and similar thickets; bushy upland field (parts of Nova Scotia).

Nesting. Nest of grasses, weed stalks, fibres, often untidy externally because of hanging grasses but with nest cup-lining of fine grasses. It is placed in an upright crotch of a bush. *Eggs*, 3 to 4; usually more or less finely spotted with browns, mostly near larger end. Incubation usually 12 days but up to 14 days (R.C. Stein) by the female.

Range. Breeds from central Alaska and across the boreal forests of Canada south to central British Columbia, northern Michigan, New York, and New England and in the Appalachian Mountains at least to western Maryland (adapted from Stein). Recently reported south to North Carolina and Tennessee! Winters from southern Mexico to Argentina.

Willow Flycatcher

Moucherolle des saules
Empidonax traillii (Audubon)
Total length: 13.3 to 17 cm

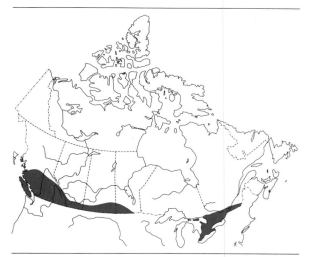

Breeding Distribution of Willow Flycatcher

Range in Canada. Southwestern Quebec (reported in breeding season at Montréal, Granby, Eastern Townships and north to Piedmont); southern Ontario (north at least to Sudbury and Ottawa); southwestern Manitoba; southern Saskatchewan (north probably to Qu'Appelle valley); southwestern Alberta; and southern British Columbia (Vancouver Island, Bella Coola, Mount Robson). Species has been reported from New Brunswick (Turtle Creek Dam, 8 June 1983). Nova Scotia (one breeding record at Indian Point Cove, on Mahone Bay, in 1980—voice was taped).

Practically identical to Alder Flycatcher, but with relatively slightly longer bill and more rounded wings; in colour tends to have relatively slightly paler, less greenish back. However, there is considerable overlapping of these characters and some specimens apparently are not certainly identifiable even in the hand. Voice is the best distinction between the two (see Field Marks).

Measurements. *Adult male*: wing, 67.5–74.5 (70.55); tail, 56.3–63.9 (59.01); bill (from anterior nostril to tip), 8.0–10.3 (9.12). *Adult female*: wing, 64.4–70.2 (67.01); bill, 8.4–9.5 (8.85) mm (R.C. Stein).

Field Marks. Distinguishable from the Alder Flycatcher in the field only by voice. Advertising song sounds like *fitz-bew* (that of the Alder is *fee-bee-o*).

Habitat. Tends to inhabit shrubbery along streams and lake edges in *grassland* rather than in woodland (latter preferred by Alder Flycatcher). Said to prefer willow and rose to other shrub types whereas the Alder shows no such preference.

Nesting. Nest is similar to that of Alder Flycatcher but is said to be more compact and cottony (similar to that of a Yellow Warbler) while that of the Alder is bulkier, more loosely built (more like that of a Song Sparrow).

Range. Breeds in continental United States (except Alaska) and indefinitely northward into southern Canada.

Remarks. A large proportion of these flycatchers observed in the field will be silent and therefore unidentifiable. In such cases the more comprehensive name "Traill's Flycatcher" may still be used.

Least Flycatcher

Moucherolle tchébec
Empidonax minimus (Baird and Baird)
Total length: 12.5 to 14 cm
Plate 49

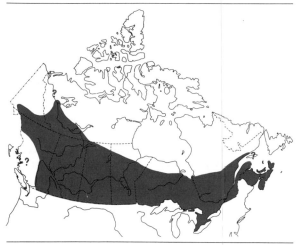

Breeding Distribution of Least Flycatcher

Range in Canada. Summer resident, breeding from southwestern and southern Yukon (Haines Junction, Watson Lake); central-

The smallest Canadian flycatcher. *Adults*: Very similar to Willow and Alder flycatchers but averaging slightly paler and usually a bit more greyish, under parts more whitish (less yellowish), wing bars and edging more whitish, tail very slightly forked; bill rather broad. *Young*: Similar to adults but wing bars dull buff, upper parts slightly more brownish.

Measurements. *Adult male*: wing, 60.6–68.5 (64.3); tail, 51.8–59.3 (55.9); exposed culmen, 9.4–10.5 (9.9); tarsus, 15.5–16.5 (16.1). *Adult female*: wing, 56.5–64.5 (60.6) mm.

Field Marks. Although it averages whiter underneath and is slightly smaller than other small flycatchers in Canada, these points are seldom very helpful in the field. Its emphatic, often-repeated *chebec* identifies it instantly in spring and early summer.

Habitat. More open deciduous or mixed woodland, forest edges and openings, deciduous second growth, woodlots, copses, orchards, suburban shade trees, city parks, alder thickets.

Nesting. Nest, a neat thin-walled cup usually set deep in an upright crotch of a branch, either deciduous or coniferous, or on a horizontal branch supported by upright twigs; sometimes in alder or other tall shrubbery. Nest usually 1.6 to 7.5 m above ground. *Eggs*, 3 to 6 (usually 4); creamy white. Incubation 12 days (O.W. Knight), by the female.

Range. Breeds from southern Canada (but rare in much of British Columbia) south to Montana, northeastern Wyoming, southwestern Missouri, northern Ohio, and western North Carolina. Winters from north-central Mexico to Panama.

western and central-southern Mackenzie (Norman Wells, Fort Simpson, southern Great Slave Lake; perhaps Rae); northern Alberta; northern Saskatchewan (Lake Athabasca, Stony Rapids); north-central Manitoba (Thicket Portage, Oxford Lake); northern Ontario (Big Trout Lake, Fort Albany); southwestern and central-southern Quebec (Baie-du-Poste, Matamec, Percé, probably Madeleine Islands, perhaps Anticosti Island); and northern Nova Scotia south through British Columbia (locally: Dease Lake, Lower Post, Fort Nelson, Trutch, Peace River parklands, Indianpoint Lake; Murtle Lake; near 100 Mile House; near Clinton and Penticton; and very locally Victoria); southern Alberta (including the southwestern mountains south to Waterton Lakes National Park); southern Saskatchewan; southern Manitoba; southern Ontario; southern Quebec; and throughout New Brunswick, Prince Edward Island, and Nova Scotia. Sight record for Newfoundland (Gros Morne National Park, 1 to 6 July 1974).

Remarks. This, our smallest flycatcher, is one of several closely related species that look so much alike that many people despair of identifying them. Fortunately most of them have distinctive voices in spring and early summer. The Least Flycatcher's emphatic *chebec* is easily recognizable. Like other small flycatchers it is an avid eater of insects, and as it inhabits our orchards and gardens much more often than the others, its usefulness is enhanced.

Hammond's Flycatcher

Moucherolle de Hammond
Empidonax hammondii (Xantus)
Total length: 12.5 to 14.5 cm
Plate 49

Breeding Distribution of Hammond's Flycatcher

Range in Canada. Breeds in southwestern Yukon (probably Selwyn River; also Mile 100 Dempster Highway); much of British Columbia (throughout the south and northward through Fort St. James, Prince George, and northwestward to Atlin; not known in Peace River parklands and the northeastern corner); and southwestern Alberta (mountains: Jasper, Banff, and Waterton Lakes national parks).

Bill rather narrow. Tail definitely emarginate. *Adults (sexes alike)*: Upper parts greyish olive (most greyish on head); outer web of outer tail feathers more or less greyish; eye-ring dull white; breast and sides pale olive-grey, throat paler grey; abdomen and under tail coverts yellowish to whitish. *Young*: Similar to adults but wing bars buffy, upper parts more brownish.

Measurements. *Adult male*: wing, 64.5–73.0 (69.9); tail, 53.5–63.0 (58.2); exposed culmen, 9.3–10.3 (9.8); tarsus, 16.0–17.5 (16.8). *Adult female*: wing, 66.0–70.4 (67.5) mm.

Similar to Dusky Flycatcher but tenth (outermost) primary usually longer than fifth; difference between length of wing and tail greater: 10.0–14.8 mm (average 11.9) in Hammond's; 5.0–8.6 mm (average 7.2) in Dusky; throat grey (less whitish), outer web of outer tail feather greyish (less whitish). From Least Flycatcher it is distinguished by longer wing and tail (tail more decidedly emarginate), relatively narrow bill, and decidedly darker under parts; from Willow and Alder flycatchers by emarginate tail, narrower bill, and darker under parts; and usually the lower mandible is darker than that of Least, Willow, or Alder.

Field Marks. A small flycatcher of the western mountains. Extremely difficult and often impossible to distinguish from Dusky Flycatcher in the field. Hammond's has slightly more uniformly dingy under parts, and the tail is a little shorter, but these points are of little help without considerable field experience with the two. The voices too are very similar. Song, usually in three parts *sweép, tsurp, seep* (the last rising), is very similar to that of the Dusky Flycatcher. The song of Hammond's tends to be more emphatic than that of the Dusky and the second part more burred. Habitat differences are often helpful.

Habitat. Typically mature coniferous or mixed forests of the western mountains up to near timberline with much of its activity in the higher forest strata.

Nesting. Nest, a cuplike structure of plant fibres, lined with grasses and hairs. It is usually placed in the fork of a horizontal branch, most often of a conifer, and usually 7.6 to 18.2 m up; a few nests have been reported at much lower levels, however. *Eggs*, usually 3 or 4; white and generally immaculate, but some have small brown spots. Incubation period 15 days (D.E. Davis) by the female.

Range. Breeds from southern Alaska, northern British Columbia, southwestern Alberta, central-southern Montana, and northwestern Wyoming south to northwestern and central-eastern California, Utah, western Colorado, and central-northern New Mexico. Winters in southeastern Arizona, the western mountains and central plateau of Mexico, and south in the highlands to Nicaragua.

Dusky Flycatcher

(Wright's Flycatcher)

Moucherolle sombre
Empidonax oberholseri Phillips
Total length: 13 to 15.2 cm
Plate 49

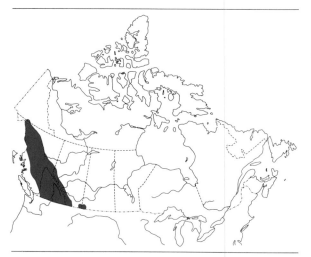

Breeding Distribution of Dusky Flycatcher

Range in Canada. Summer resident, breeding in southwestern Yukon (Carcross); British Columbia (the southern half, apparently mainly east of the Coast and Cascade ranges, and northwestward through the Vanderhoof and Prince George regions to Telegraph Creek and Atlin; unknown in the northeastern corner and Peace River parklands); southwestern and (locally) southeastern Alberta (Jasper, Banff, and Waterton Lakes national parks and east to Beauvais Lake, Bragg and Silver creeks; also Cypress Hills); and extreme southwestern Saskatchewan (Cypress Hills). Uncommon migrant on the coast of British Columbia and rarely noted there in summer but without evidence of breeding.

Similar to Hammond's Flycatcher, but tenth (outermost) primary usually shorter than fifth; difference between length of wing and length of tail less, averaging 7.2 mm (extremes 5.0–8.6 mm); colour of anterior under parts paler and less uniform (throat whitish, instead of grey, contrasting more with grey of breast); outer web of outer tail feathers more whitish; bill averages longer, and lower mandible is more variable in colour, blackish to flesh (usually blackish in Hammond's).

Measurements. *Adult male*: wing, 68.4–72.8 (70.1); tail, 59.5–65.5 (62.8); exposed culmen, 10.1–12.0 (11.1); tarsus, 17.5–19.5 (18.4). *Adult female*: wing, 60.0–73.0 (65.7) mm.

Field Marks. (See Hammond's Flycatcher, which is extremely similar.) Song sounds to the writer like *sewéep, hreek, seep* (sometimes with a fourth part) and is very similar to that of Hammond's (but very different from that of Willow, Alder, or Least flycatchers). Habitat is often useful in helping to distinguish it from Hammond's.

Habitat. Usually stands of tall shrubbery (such as willows) among which are trees, either deciduous or coniferous; open deciduous or mixed woodland in drier situations. It is not a bird of extensive mature damp coniferous forests, such as are preferred by Hammond's. Usually forages and nests at lower levels than Hammond's but sometimes perches in the tops of fair-sized trees 12 m or so high.

Nesting. Nest, a neat cup of vegetable fibres and grasses, is most often placed in an upright crotch of a willow, alder, aspen, or similar tree (less often in a conifer) at heights between 0.9 and 2.1 m (rarely up to 6 m). *Eggs*, 3 or 4; dull white. Incubation period 12 to 15 days (Howsley *in* Bent); 14 days (N.K. Johnson).

Range. Breeds from southwestern Yukon, northwestern and central-eastern British Columbia, southwestern Alberta, southwestern Saskatchewan, and Wyoming south to southern California, central Arizona, and central-northern New Mexico. Winters from southeastern Arizona and northern Mexico south to southern Mexico.

Gray Flycatcher

Moucherolle gris
Empidonax wrightii Baird
Total length: 14 to 15.5 cm

Status in Canada. Accidental in Ontario: One netted in the Toronto Islands, Toronto, on 11 September 1981 was examined in detail in the hand and photographed by R.D. James.

One of several similar small flycatchers with white eye-ring and wing bars. Adults similar to Dusky Flycatcher but upper parts paler and greyer; under parts whitish or greyish; bill relatively longer, the lower mandible flesh colour at base, usually dark anteriorly. Outer web of outer tail feather paler (white or nearly so).

Measurements. *Adult male*: wing, 68.5–76.5 (72.6); tail, 57.5–64 (60.8); exposed culmen, 12–13.5 (12.9); tarsus, 17–20.5 (18.3). *Adult female*: wing, 66–74.5 (69.1); tail, 56.5–62 (58.9); exposed culmen, 10.5–13 (12.9); tarsus, 16.5–19 (18.8) mm (Ridgway).

Range. Breeds from central Oregon, southwestern Idaho, southwestern Wyoming, and central Colorado south mostly in the Great Basin to central eastern California, southern Nevada, central Arizona, and western New Mexico.

Western Flycatcher

Moucherolle obscur
Empidonax difficilis Baird
Total length: 14 to 15 cm
Plate 49

Breeding Distribution of Western Flycatcher

Range in Canada. Summer resident, breeding in British Columbia (commonly on the coast and coastal islands including Queen Charlotte and Vancouver islands; in southern interior: Coldstream in Okanagan valley and northward at least to within 16 km of Dease Lake; Pass Lake ca. 180 km east-northeast of Prince George), and southwestern Alberta (Gorge Creek in Turner valley; Bragg Creek, Banff National Park). Apparently breeds sympatrically with the similar *E. flaviventris* in the Dease Lake region of British Columbia and perhaps also in southwestern Alberta.

Resembles Yellow-bellied Flycatcher in extensive yellow of under parts (including throat) but differs as follows: outermost (tenth) primary shorter than fifth, wing bars duller, contrasting less with other feathers of the wing, olive of upper parts more brownish or greyish (less greenish), bend of wing buffy instead of yellow, breast and sides more brownish-olive; tail averages slightly longer. The extensively yellow under parts (including throat) distinguish it from similar species other than the Yellow-bellied.

Measurements *(E. d. difficilis)*. *Adult male*: wing, 63.1–71.8 (66.9); tail, 56–63 (58.5); exposed culmen, 10.5–11.7 (11.1); tarsus, 16–18 (17.3). *Adult female*: wing, 60.4–63.5 (61.8) mm.

Field Marks. A western species. The extensively yellow under parts *including throat* separate it from most small flycatchers in its range. Other small western mountain flycatchers (except Yellow-bellied) show some yellow on the under parts but not on the throat. Probably indistinguishable by appearance alone in the field from the Yellow-bellied Flycatcher, but the voices of the two are very different. *Voice*: Song is often *pseet, ptsick, seet* (the last highest).

Habitat. Shady, more open areas below the tree crowns of woodland, deciduous or coniferous, especially about depressions and similar moist parts, ravines, bottoms, and stream courses. However, dense thickets of tall shrubbery, such as those preferred by the Willow and Alder flycatchers, are not much frequented by the present species.

Nesting. Nest, a cup made of plant fibre, mosses, rootlets, and sometimes feathers or hair, is placed in a variety of situations such as rock ledges on streams, in the roots of an upturned tree, in a small tree, on a stump or building. *Eggs*, 3 or 4; white lightly to moderately spotted and blotched with reddish browns. Incubation period about 15 days (Laidlaw Williams).

Range. Breeds from southern Alaska, southern British Columbia, southwestern Alberta, and western Montana, northern Wyoming, and southwestern South Dakota south in the highlands to Baja California, Honduras, and western Texas. Winters from northern Mexico southward.

Subspecies. *Empidonax difficilis difficilis* Baird is the breeding bird of most of British Columbia. *E. d. hellmayri* Brodkorb inhabits southwestern Alberta and probably contiguous parts of extreme southeastern British Columbia.

Black Phoebe

Moucherolle noir
Sayornis nigricans (Swainson)
Total length: 16 to 17.5 cm
Plate 50

Status in Canada. Accidental in British Columbia (specimen: Vancouver, 11 November 1936; photo: Vancouver, 26–27 April 1980). The specimen represents the subspecies *Sayornis nigricans semiatra* (Vigors).

Dull black except white abdomen; edges of secondaries and outer web of outer tail feathers whitish; under tail coverts white, frequently streaked with dusky. The only Canadian flycatcher with a black breast.

Range. California, southwestern Utah, southern New Mexico, and central Texas south in the highlands to Argentina.

Eastern Phoebe

Moucherolle phébi
Sayornis phoebe (Latham)
Total length: 16 to 18 cm
Plate 48

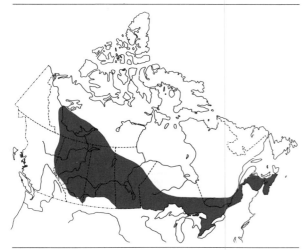

Breeding Distribution of Eastern Phoebe

Range in Canada. Summer resident, breeding from central-western and southern Mackenzie (Norman Wells, Fort Simpson, Rae, Fort Resolution); northern Saskatchewan (Lake Athabasca, Stony Rapids, Reindeer River); northern Manitoba (Bird; recorded in summer north to Churchill); and central Ontario (Sandy Lake, Lake Nipigon, Lake Abitibi); south to central-eastern British Columbia (Peace River parklands); southern Alberta (Jasper National Park, Gorge Creek, Cypress Hills, Brooks); south-central and southeastern Saskatchewan (Cochin; St. Louis; Moose Mountain; Yorkton region); southern Manitoba, and through southern Ontario; also southwestern Quebec (Blue-Sea-Lake, Montréal, Hatley, Québec, Rivière-du-Loup; western Chaleurs Bay, probably north to Amos); western New Brunswick (Saint-Léonard, Woodstock, Fredericton); and in recent years, Nova Scotia (Shelburne, Yarmouth, and Kings counties).

Casual visitant to southeastern Quebec (Moisie River, 9 May 1953). Probably of casual occurrence also (sight records only but by competent observers) in southwestern Yukon (Pine Creek); central-western Quebec (Grande rivière de la Baleine); and Newfoundland (Witless Bay). Sight records only for Prince Edward Island.

Adults (sexes similar): Top and sides of head and back of neck blackish brown (darker than back); back and scapulars greyish olive; wings and tail mostly dark brown; edges of wing coverts slightly paler but not forming conspicuous wing bars; under parts white with yellowish tinge (in autumn decidedly yellowish); sides of breast pale greyish-olive; bill black above and *below*. *Young*: Similar to autumn adults, but upper parts more brownish, two buffy wing bars present.

Measurements. *Adult male*: wing, 80.7–90.3 (85.3); tail, 70–76 (73.1); exposed culmen, 13.8–15.4 (14.7); tarsus, 17–19 (18). *Adult female*: wing, 80.1–87.8 (83.7) mm.

This is one of the larger of the small dull-coloured flycatchers. Most similar to the pewees, but its dark *underside* of bill, lack of *distinct* white wing bars, larger stouter legs, and less-pointed wings distinguish it.

Field Marks. A bluebird-sized dull-coloured flycatcher, the top of the head more blackish than the back. Its lack of *conspicuous* white wing bars (young have buffy wing bars), its habit when perched of frequently wagging the tail, its black *lower* mandible, and its voice distinguish it from pewees and other similar small flycatchers. *Voice: Fee-be* with accent on first syllable (very different from the drawn-out call of the Eastern Wood-Pewee); also a sharp *chip*.

Habitat. In nesting season, often the vicinity of streams and lakes where rocky walls or bridges provide nesting places, and trees or shrubbery furnish foraging places, also frequently the vicinity of buildings often remote from water.

Nesting. Nest, rather bulky, of mud (not always used), moss, grasses, rootlets, lined with fine grasses, hair, and plant fibres, is placed on ledges of rock, under bridges, culverts, and overhangs of buildings. *Eggs*, usually 5; white (occasionally a few spots of brown). Incubation apparently variable: 14, 16, 17 days (W.P. Smith); 13 days (Knight); 15 to 20 days (L. deK. Lawrence); by the female.

Range. Breeds from Canada (see Range in Canada) south to southwestern South Dakota and eastern New Mexico, central and northeastern Texas, central Alabama, western South Carolina, and North Carolina. Winters mainly from Virginia south through the states on the Atlantic Coast and west through states on the Gulf Coast and south to southern Mexico.

Say's Phoebe

Moucherolle à ventre roux
Sayornis saya (Bonaparte)
Total length: 17 to 20 cm
Plate 48

Breeding Distribution of Say's Phoebe

Range in Canada. Breeds from northern Yukon (Babbage River, Komakuk); western Mackenzie (Mackenzie Delta, McTavish Arm, Fort Norman; occurs at least in migration at Fort Simpson and other southern Mackenzie localities, but evidence of breeding at these southern localities is not known to the writer); central Alberta (Athabasca district, possibly Dixonville); and central Saskatchewan (Kazan Lake, probably Carlton House) south through southern British Columbia (east of Cascade and Coast ranges); southern Alberta; southern Saskatchewan; and southwestern Manitoba (Oak Lake, Lyleton, Aweme). (Note: Definite evidence of breeding is needed for a very large area comprising southern Mackenzie, northern Alberta, and northeastern British Columbia.)

Scarce transient in coastal British Columbia (Victoria, Chilliwack). Quebec (Godbout; also a sight record at Percé). Accidental in Ontario (photo record: London: 32 km northwest; specimen: North Point, 4 August 1976; sight records: Haileybury, Dryden) and Nova Scotia (specimen: Seal Island, 24 September 1966; photo records: Sable Island, 19 September 1974 and Seal Island, 20 May 1981; sight records for Dartmouth and Ingonish).

Adults (sexes similar): Upper parts brownish grey (darkest on top and sides of head); tail black; breast greyish, becoming very pale on throat and with buffy wash; abdomen and under tail coverts cinnamon; wings dark brownish-grey, the inner secondaries and ends of greater wing coverts edged with dull whitish. *Young*: Similar to adults but middle and greater wing coverts tipped with cinnamon (forming two cinnamon wing bars).

Measurements *(S. s. saya)*. *Adult male*: wing, 104.0–108.5 (106.1); tail, 80.0–85.0 (83.0); exposed culmen, 14.3–16.8 (15.4); tarsus, 20.0–21.5 (20.6). *Adult female*: wing, 95.0–104.0 (100.3) mm.

Field Marks. A bluebird-sized flycatcher of the West. Its cinnamon belly and black tail identify it. *Voice*: A plaintive *pee-urr*.

Habitat. Open, usually dry places where bushes, fences, buildings, or even low rocks and earth hummocks provide look-out perches. For nesting, rocky walls, buildings, bridges, and similar locations that provide a place for the nest with, preferably, at least some overhang above.

Nesting. Nest a flattish structure of grasses, plant fibres, wool, and hair, placed on a sheltered ledge, in natural situations or man-made structures, or similar situations. *Eggs*, usually 4 or 5; white, sometimes with a few brownish spots. Incubation two weeks (I.G. Wheelock), by the female.

Range. Breeds from central Alaska, Yukon, western Mackenzie, and the Prairie Provinces of Canada to northern Mexico. Winters from California and southern Texas south to Mexico.

Subspecies. M.R. Browning (1976. Auk, vol. 93, no. 4, pp. 843–846) concludes that *Sayornis saya yukonensis* is a synonym of nominate *saya*. I agree. All Canadian populations are best referred to *Sayornis saya saya* (Bonaparte).

Vermilion Flycatcher

Moucherolle vermillon
Pyrocephalus rubinus (Boddaert)
Total length: 14 to 16.5 cm
Plate 50

Status in Canada. Accidental in southern Ontario (Toronto, 29 October 1949; sight records for Renfrew and Prince Edward counties).

Adult male: Crown and under parts bright red (under parts somewhat paler and sometimes tinged with orange); sides of head and upper parts greyish brown; wings and tail mainly dusky or blackish; bill brownish black. *Adult female*: Upper parts brownish grey; under parts whitish, the breast, sides, and flanks distinctly but narrowly streaked with dusky, belly pale salmon to buffy.

Range. Southwestern United States south to Guatemala and Honduras; also South America.

Subspecies. *Pyrocephalus rubinus mexicanus* Sclater.

Ash-throated Flycatcher

Tyran à gorge cendrée
Myiarchus cinerascens (Lawrence)
Total length: 20.2 to 21.5 cm
Plate 50

Status in Canada. Casual visitant to British Columbia (specimen record: Marpole, Vancouver, 7 October 1953; another was captured, banded, and released at the same locality on 11 October 1953; also several additional sight records) and Ontario (photo: Whitby, 29 October 1982; sight records: Point Pelee, November 1962; Prince Edward Point, 7 November 1982; Fort Erie, 6 June 1983); Quebec (sight record: Franquelin).

Similar to Great Crested Flycatcher, but upper parts browner (less greenish), under parts very much paler, the throat and belly sometimes nearly white; bill smaller.

Range. Breeds from southwestern Oregon (probably rarely eastern Washington), southern Idaho, southwestern Wyoming, Colorado, and northern and central Texas south to Guerrero, Mexico, and southern Baja California.

Subspecies. *Myiarchus cinerascens cinerascens* (Lawrence).

Great Crested Flycatcher

Tyran huppé
Myiarchus crinitus (Linnaeus)
Total length: 20.2 to 23 cm
Plate 48

Breeding Distribution of Great Crested Flycatcher

Range in Canada. Summer resident, breeding in central-eastern Alberta (Two Hills region; Ministik Lake); southeastern Saskatchewan (High Hill, Moose Mountain, Indian Head; pairs noted north to near Cumberland House); southern Manitoba (Aweme, Lake St. Martin, Hillside Beach, Whitemouth); southwestern and southern Ontario (north at least to Maclennan, Lake Nipissing, Petawawa; also Rainy River); southwestern Quebec (Montréal, Hatley, Blue-Sea-Lake, Québec, Sainte-Anne-de-la-Pocatière, possibly farther east); southwestern New Brunswick (Woodstock); and recently Nova Scotia (near Halifax; Milton; Kejimkujik National Park).

Sight record for Newfoundland (near Channel-Port aux Basques, 17 July 1974).

Accidental at Coppermine, N.W.T. (semi-mummified specimen found on 26 June 1980 by Wayne E. Renaud).

About the size of the Eastern Kingbird. Upper parts olive brown, the feathers of crown with darker centres (but crown never has a concealed red patch); inner webs of tail feathers (except central pair) cinnamon rufous; throat and breast grey; belly, sides, flanks, and under tail coverts yellow; wings greyish brown, the secondaries and wing coverts edged with white (forming two wing bars), the edges of the primaries tinged with chestnut.

Measurements *(M. c. boreus)*. *Adult male*: wing, 102.5–111 (106.5); tail, 91–98.5 (93.9); exposed culmen, 18.8–21.5 (20.1); tarsus, 21–22.5 (21.6). *Adult female*: wing, 97–103.5 (99.7) mm.

Field Marks. A large (about kingbird size) flycatcher, typically of woodlands, with yellow belly, grey throat and upper breast, *much rufous in tail* (especially underside) and a little in the wings, and two white wing bars. The only other flycatcher of regular occurrence in Canada that closely resembles it is the Western Kingbird (both occur regularly in Manitoba and eastern Saskatchewan). The Great Crested Flycatcher's rufous tail, white wing bars, different habitat, and voice will prevent confusion between the two. *Voice*: Varied. A loud harsh whistled *kweep* is characteristic and common, often followed by several *wick-wick-wick*'s.

Habitat. More mature woodlands, preferring deciduous or mixed-wood types; maturer woodlots, groves of taller trees, orchards near woodland. Usually frequents the upper branches.

Nesting. In a cavity in a dead or living tree, most frequently a deciduous one. The cavity may be a natural one or a woodpecker hole. Bird boxes are used also. Nest, often bulky, an accumulation of leaves (including pine needles), hair, feathers, moss, twine, miscellaneous litter, and often one or more cast snake skins. (However, snake skins are by no means always used, even in areas where snakes are common.) *Eggs*, most often 4 to 6; creamy white to buffy, heavily and handsomely blotched, lined, and streaked with browns and sometimes a little grey or lavender. Incubation, variously given by authors, 13 to 15 days, by the female.

Range. Southern Canada (eastern Saskatchewan east to Nova Scotia) south to western Oklahoma, central Texas, the Gulf Coast of United States, and Florida. Winters from Florida and eastern and southern Mexico south to Colombia.

Subspecies. *Myiarchus crinitus boreus* Bangs.

Remarks. There has been considerable speculation as to why the Great Crested Flycatcher so frequently places a piece of cast-off snake skin in its nest. A popular belief is that the snake skin acts as a scarecrow to repel would-be nest intruders. However, the snake skin is often buried deep under other nesting materials, or it may be replaced by something similar such as cellophane or onion skins. Perhaps the truth of the matter is that snake skin is used simply because it makes good nesting material and because its shininess attracts the flycatcher's attention.

Beetles, bees and wasps, flies, bugs, grasshoppers and crickets, butterflies and moths including their caterpillars, dragonflies, and spiders constitute the bulk of its food. A few berries are eaten also.

Erect and alert, it perches on a high branch. Every so often it dashes out and snaps up a passing insect. Like most of its relatives, it is aggressive toward other birds that venture too close to its nest.

Brown-crested Flycatcher

[**Brown-crested Flycatcher**. Tyran de Wied. *Myiarchus tyrannulus* (Müller). Plate 50. Hypothetical. Sight record of one at Reifel Sanctuary, south of Vancouver, British Columbia, on 22 and 25 September 1976.]

Tropical Kingbird

Tyran mélancolique
Tyrannus melancholicus Vieillot
Total length: 20.2 to 24.0 cm

Status in Canada. Casual or accidental in British Columbia (specimen: French Beach, Renfrew District, southern Vancouver Island, February 1923. Photographic record: Victoria, 16 to 22 October 1972; and near Metehosin, 20 November 1982. Sight record: Colwood, Vancouver Island, 26 to 30 October 1977).

Similar to Western Kingbird but tail uniform dusky-brown (instead of black with white outer margin) and slightly forked; has dark area through eye and across ear, and larger bill. Its reddish-orange crown patch (adults), slightly forked tail, and attenuated outer primary tips distinguish it from the Great Crested Flycatcher.

Range. Southeastern Arizona, northern Mexico, and southern Texas south to Bolivia and Argentina.

Subspecies. The one Canadian specimen is referable to *Tyrannus melancholicus occidentalis* Hartert and Goodson.

Cassin's Kingbird

Tyran de Cassin
Tyrannus vociferans Swainson
Total length: 22.2 to 23 cm

Status in Canada. Accidental in Ontario (specimen collected 5 June 1953, at Achray, Grand Lake, northeastern Algonquin Provincial Park; sight records for Ottawa and Point Pelee).

Another large flycatcher with a yellow belly, but its black tail distinguishes it from all other Canadian flycatchers but the Western Kingbird. Closely resembles Western Kingbird and, like it, has a black tail, but the outer margins of the tail in Cassin's are not conspicuously white (at most only a suggestion of white or pale brown) and the grey of head and breast is darker.

Range. Central California and southern Montana south to Guerrero, Mexico. Farther south in winter.

Subspecies. *Tyrannus vociferans vociferans* Swainson.

Thick-billed Kingbird

Tyran à gros bec
Tyrannus crassirostris Swainson
Total length: 22.5 cm

Status in Canada. Accidental: British Columbia (immature male at Qualicum Beach, 20 October to 11 November 1974. Found dead on 12 November 1974).

Not to be expected in Canada. A heavy-billed kingbird with a dark-brown head (with concealed yellow crown patch), greyish-brown upper parts, slightly notched solid dark-grey tail, yellowish (sometimes whitish) breast and belly. General "bull-headed" appearance. Usually noisy.

Measurements. *Adult male*: wing, 132–136 (134); tail, 99.5–103.5 (101.4); exposed culmen, 24.5–28 (26.7); tarsus, 19.5–21 (20.2). *Adult female*: wing, 126–135 (130); tail, 94.5–100 (97.6); exposed culmen, 23.5–25.5 (24.8); tarsus, 19–20.5 (19.7) mm (Ridgway).

Range. Western and southern Mexico, Guatemala; very locally southern Arizona.

Western Kingbird

(Arkansas Kingbird)

Tyran de l'Ouest
Tyrannus verticalis Say
Total length: 20.2 to 23.5 cm
Plate 48

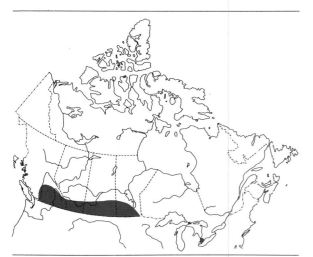

Breeding Distribution of Western Kingbird

Range in Canada. Summer resident, breeding in southern interior British Columbia (Okanagan valley, Williams Lake, southern Wells Grey Provincial Park, Cranbrook); southern Alberta (north at least to Scollard and Bodo, west at least to Calgary); southern Saskatchewan (Cypress Hills region, Davidson, Simpson, Melville); southern Manitoba (Oak Lake, Winnipeg, Whitemouth); and very rarely in extreme southern Ontario (Port Alma in 1943).

Rare visitant to Vancouver Island (Ucluelet, etc.). Rarely but regularly wanders east of breeding range in autumn in southern Ontario (mainly in migration); southeastern Quebec (Cap-Tourmente, 1 September 1969; Moisie River, 22 September 1958; various sight records including Madeleine Islands); New Brunswick (Machias Seal Island; Sackville vicinity; etc.); Nova Scotia (West LaHave, 17 November 1940 to 26 January 1941, and many other records); and Newfoundland (Cappahayden, 5 November 1957; Bay of Exploits, 7 August 1890). Sight record for Prince Edward Island (Dalvay).

Accidental on Bathurst Island, N.W.T. (specimen, 2 August 1973) and Cape Dalhousie, N.W.T. (sight record, 15 June 1972).

Adults: Head, neck, and breast pale grey (whitish on chin); top of head with concealed orange-red patch; through eye to ear, a suggestion of a faint dusky patch; belly yellow; tail black except contrasting white outer web of outermost feather on each side; tips of outer primaries of the wing narrowed to a point (less so in female). *Young in juvenal plumage*: Similar to adults but crown patch lacking, colours duller and paler, tips of outer primaries more rounded, only outermost tending to be pointed.

Measurements. *Adult male*: wing, 125.5–133.5 (129.4); tail, 88.5–96.5 (93); exposed culmen, 20.5–22.5 (21.7); tarsus, 18.5–19.5 (19.1). *Adult female*: wing, 118.5–127.0 (123.5) mm.

Field Marks. A large flycatcher, primarily western in distribution, with yellow belly, pale-grey head and breast (sometimes whitish on throat), black tail with narrow white outer edges (white edges sometimes hard to see because of wear). Of birds occurring regularly in Canada, the Great Crested Flycatcher is most likely to be confused with it, but the Western Kingbird's *black tail* and lack of definite white wing bars (if such bars are present in the kingbird, it is only a suggestion of them) distinguish it. *Voice*: Various shrill twitters and squeaks; or a series of harsh notes; often a single *kip*. Voice usually lower pitched than that of Eastern Kingbird.

Habitat. Open situations such as prairies but in the vicinity of at least one or two trees, shelter belts, telephone poles, or houses for perching and nesting; and in the mountains open areas among scattered trees.

Nesting. In trees and shrubs and on telephone poles and buildings. It is a rather bulky structure of grasses, hair, wool, and various fibrous materials. *Eggs*, 3 to 5, usually 4; very similar to Eastern Kingbird. Incubation period is given variously by authors as 12 to 14 days.

Range. Breeds from southern western Canada (interior southern British Columbia east to southern Manitoba; rarely extreme southern Ontario) south to northern Baja California, northwestern Mexico, and west-central Texas, and east to northwestern Ohio and (rarely) north-central Missouri. Winters mainly from Mexico south to Nicaragua; in small numbers in coastal southeastern United States (South Carolina to Florida).

Eastern Kingbird

Tyran tritri
Tyrannus tyrannus (Linnaeus)
Total length: 19.5 to 22 cm
Plate 48

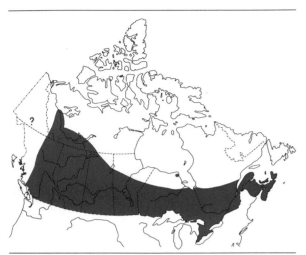

Breeding Distribution of Eastern Kingbird

Range in Canada. Summer resident, breeding
from north-central British Columbia (Nulki
Lake, Bouchie Lake, Peace River parklands;
recorded in summer, possibly breeds, north to
near Trutch and Muskwa); central-western
Mackenzie (Norman Wells, Nahanni National
Park); northwestern and central-eastern Saskatchewan (Lake Athabasca, Cree Lake);
central Manitoba (Thicket Portage); central
Ontario (Sandy Lake, Kapuskasing, Moose
Factory, rarely north to 54°44'; 82°25'); southern Quebec (Lake Saint-Jean, Rivière-du-Loup,
Rimouski, Gaspé Peninsula); south through
southern parts of British Columbia (but very
rarely, if ever, on Vancouver Island; possibly
formerly in Comox region), Alberta, Saskatchewan, Manitoba, Ontario, Quebec, and through
New Brunswick, Prince Edward Island, and
Nova Scotia (including Cape Breton Island).
Possibly breeds rarely in southern Yukon
(reported feeding young at Snafu Lake).

Casual in southern Yukon (Champagne);
central Quebec (Moar Bay; north shore of the
Gulf of St. Lawrence: Mingan, Natashquan,
Baie des loups; Anticosti Island); and New-
foundland (St. Andrew's, Tompkins, Cappa-
hayden). Accidental on Bathurst Inlet, northern
Hudson Bay (Coats Island); Southampton
Island (Coral Harbour); Baffin Island (Cape
Dorset); and Labrador (Killinek, Hopedale).

Adults: Upper parts blackish slate, the top and sides of head black with
a concealed orange to scarlet patch in centre of crown; tail black with
white tip; under parts white, the breast shaded with grey. *Young (in
juvenal plumage)*: Like adults but without orange-red crown patch,
upper parts duller, the head little if any darker than the back.

Measurements. *Adult male*: wing, 115–126.5 (119.2); tail, 82–92.5
(86.3); exposed culmen, 18.3–20.6 (19.0); tarsus, 17.5–19.5 (18.6). *Adult
female*: wing, 109.5–118.5 (113.9) mm.

Field Marks. A large flycatcher; blackish above, white below, the
black tail tipped with white. Usually seen perched on a fence or tree in
open places. Posture erect, alert. Flies with rapid, quivering wing
strokes. *Voice*: Commonly a single strident *dzeet* and a more prolonged
shrill twittering in which *kitter* sounds are frequent.

Habitat. More open places: fields, pastures, and prairies (with
trees, shrubbery, or fence posts for perching and nesting), parklands,
scattered trees, orchards, wood edges, farmland, standing drowned trees
on rivers, lakes, and bogs.

Nesting. At various heights, usually 2.5 to 6.0 m, on a branch of a
tree or bush, occasionally on a fence post or tree stump. Nest, a rather
bulky structure of twigs and grasses lined with animal hair, rootlets, dry
grasses, and plant fibre. *Eggs*, usually 3 or 4; white—spotted, dotted,
and blotched with browns and often some greys. Incubation 12 to 13
days (F.L. Burns), 13 days (O.W. Knight), by the female.

Range. Breeds from southern Canada south to northeastern California, northern Nevada, northern Utah, northeastern New Mexico,
central Texas, the Gulf Coast of United States, and southern Florida.
Winters in South America.

Remarks. Eastern Kingbirds are pugnacious and will not tolerate
the presence of any large bird near their nesting territory. A crow,
hawk, heron, or other large bird passing nearby is immediately and
ignominiously driven off by the fury and agility of the kingbird's
attack.

Kingbirds are flycatchers and therefore are insect eaters. The Eastern Kingbird perches with erect posture on a post or tree in an open
place and alertly watches for passing insects. With a short dash and an
audible snap of the bill, it picks off its prey in mid-air and nonchalantly
returns to its perch to await another insect.

Gray Kingbird

Tyran gris
Tyrannus dominicensis (Gmelin)
Total length: 20 to 23.5 cm

Status in Canada. Accidental. A specimen was taken at Cape Beale, Vancouver Island, British Columbia, on 29 September 1889. Ontario (photos: Ottawa, Hay Bay; sight records for Kingston, Point Pelee); New Brunswick (Rothesay); and Nova Scotia (Sable Island).

Similar to Eastern Kingbird but upper parts paler (ashy grey); ear coverts dusky; tail lacks white tip; bill decidedly larger and longer; size somewhat larger.

    Measurements. *Adult male*: wing, 111–122 (116.2); tail, 82–100 (90.3); exposed culmen, 24.5–28 (26.1); tarsus, 17.5–19.5 (18.5). *Adult female*: wing, 107.5–120 (113.2) mm (Ridgway).

    Range. Breeds in coastal southeastern United States (South Carolina, Georgia, Florida) and the West Indies south to northern Venezuela.

    Subspecies. *Tyrannus dominicensis dominicensis* (Gmelin).

Scissor-tailed Flycatcher

Tyran à longue queue
Tyrannus forficatus (Gmelin)
Total length: 30 to 38 cm (including long tail)
Plate 50

Status in Canada. Scarce visitant: British Columbia (photo records for Vancouver Island and Revelstoke; also sight records); Alberta (sight records); Saskatchewan (photo: near Saskatoon, September 1980; also sight records at Milestone, Lumsden, Tugaske, Rosthern); Manitoba (York Factory, 1880; also 2 October 1924; Portage la Prairie, 31 October 1884; Delta, 20 October 1951); Ontario (specimen: Red Rock, 30 October 1978; photo records: Streetsville, 17 May 1970; Ferndale, November 1972. Also numerous sight records); Quebec (Noranda, 30 October 1938; Pointe-des-Monts, 14 August 1894; Sept-Îles, 10 May 1955; near Caniapiscau, 16 July 1982); New Brunswick (Clarendon Station, 21 May 1906; Alma, 20 June 1907; Grand Manan, 26 October 1924); and Nova Scotia (photo record: Cape Sable, 19 November 1978).

Tail extremely long, forked, 20 to 25 cm in males. *Adult male*: Upper parts light grey, the crown with a concealed patch of orange-red; wings blackish, their coverts and secondaries edged in white; middle tail feathers blackish, the outer three on each side white (often with pinkish tinge) with black ends; throat whitish, shading to pale grey on breast; sides, flanks, and under tail coverts salmon; wing linings pale pinkish; axillars and patch on under wing coverts red. *Adult female*: Similar to adult male but duller, crown patch small or wanting, tail shorter. *Young*: Similar to adult female but crown patch always absent, greys more brownish; pinkish of under wings paler, the sides more buffy than pink.

    Range. Breeds from eastern New Mexico, southeastern Colorado, western Oklahoma, central Kansas, western Arkansas, and western Louisiana south to southern Texas.

Fork-tailed Flycatcher

Tyran à queue fourchue
Tyrannus savana Vieillot
Total length: 33 to 40.5 cm
Figure 80

Figure 80
Head of Fork-tailed Flycatcher

Status in Canada. Accidental in Nova Scotia (photo records: Near Dartmouth, 26 September 1970; Seal Island, 24 to 26 August 1976) and Ontario (photo record: Dorion, 29 October 1977). Sight record for Quebec (first-year bird on Bonaventure Island, 30 June 1982) and New Brunswick (Grand Bay, late October to 15 November 1977).

A medium-sized flycatcher with extremely long (20 to 25 cm) tail, thus similar in shape to Scissor-tailed Flycatcher but adults differ as follows: top and sides of head and nape black; crown patch (usually hidden) yellow; tail black (except narrow outer edge of outermost rectrix white); under parts white (not conspicuously marked with salmon pink). Immatures are similar to adults but black of head is replaced by dark brown and there is no yellow crown patch.

    Measurements. *Adult male*: wing, 104–120 (111.1); tail, 230–303 (264.9); exposed culmen, 14–17 (15.4); tarsus, 16–18.5 (17.2). *Adult female*: wing, 100–107 (103.3); tail, 173–220.5 (201.7); exposed culmen, 15–16.5 (15.8); tarsus, 16.5–17.5 (17.1) mm.

    Range. Southern Mexico south through Central America and South America to central Argentina.

    Subspecies. Not determinable from photos.

Family **Alaudidae**:
Larks

Number of Species in Canada: 2

Larks are ground birds that run instead of hopping. The hind toenail is very long and sharp. The tarsus is scutellate (scaled) and is rounded behind (not sharply ridged as in most passerines). Wings are rather long and pointed and have nine primaries. Bill rather slender, rather short, and pointed. Many larks have an impressive flight song. They eat large numbers of weed seeds and also a considerable number of insects. The family is primarily an Old World one. North America has only one native species, the Horned Lark. The famous Skylark of Europe has been introduced into southern Vancouver Island, British Columbia, and is established there. The so-called meadowlark is not a lark at all but belongs to the subfamily Icterinae.

Eurasian Skylark

Alouette des champs
Alauda arvensis Linnaeus
Total length: 17.5 to 19 cm
Plate 55

Range in Canada. Introduced to southern Vancouver Island, British Columbia, but dates given by authors vary by a few years. Two introductions seem to have been made, the first in 1902 or 1903, from which there appear to have been some survivors. In 1908 or 1913, a second introduction was made and the species became well established on Saanich Peninsula, southern Vancouver Island, British Columbia. In March 1962, the total population was estimated by D. Stirling and R.Y. Edwards at about one thousand. Recently it has become greatly reduced by a combination of severe winter weather and loss of habitat to human housing.

Bill slender, feathers of hind crown longish, hind toenail much elongated. *Adults*: Upper parts buffy brown to greyish brown, heavily streaked with blackish brown; line over eye buffy white; ear coverts brown streaked with dusky; outer two-thirds of outermost tail feathers mostly white, the next with white outer web; throat whitish with short brown streaks; breast buffy brown, heavily streaked with blackish brown, sides and flanks more lightly streaked; belly and tail coverts plain white.

Measurements. *Adult male*: wing, 109.5–116 (113.3); tail, 68.5–73 (70.4); exposed culmen, 11–13.5 (12.2); tarsus, 24–26 (24.8). *Adult female*: wing, 98–111 (104.2) mm (Ridgway).

The much elongated hind toenail distinguishes it from most birds of similar colour, except longspurs, pipits, and the Horned Lark. The slender bill separates it from longspurs; its much larger size from our pipits; its different head and breast markings from the Horned Lark.

Field Marks. Somewhat larger than a sparrow. A streaky brown bird with short crest and white outer tail feathers. It is usually seen either on the ground or in flight. Spends up to three or four minutes in continuous song on the wing at considerable heights, often with sustained hovering. Slender bill separates it from sparrows; stouter body and less slender bill from our pipits; and different head and breast markings from the Horned Lark (which has similar habits).

Habitat. Open sparsely vegetated ground: airfields, pastures, cultivated land, golf courses. Avoids narrow valleys and small fields bordered by trees.

Nesting. Nest of grasses in a depression on the ground. *Eggs*, usually 3 or 4; greyish white, thickly spotted with brown. Incubation 11 days, by the female (*in* Witherby).

Range. Eurasia and northern Africa. Has been introduced and established in some other parts of the world.

Subspecies. *Alauda arvensis arvensis* Linnaeus.

Horned Lark

Alouette cornue
Eremophila alpestris (Linnaeus)
Total length: 17.2 to 20 cm
Plate 55

Bill slender, pointed, shorter than head; hind toenail much elongated, nearly straight. The elongated hind toenail, large black patch on upper breast, and narrow black face patch curving from the bill backward under the eye are a combination that identifies Horned Larks. Tail mostly black except central feathers, which are brown like back, and outer web of outermost feathers, which is white. In addition, the male has a black band across the front of the crown, which extends backward narrowly to join a pair of slender black "horns" (erectile feathers). Juvenal plumage (worn only a short time) lacks these black areas and has white spots on the upper parts.

Measurements (*E. a. alpestris*). *Adult male*: wing, 108–118 (111.5); tail, 66.5–75 (71.8); exposed culmen, 11–13 (12.2); tarsus, 22–25 (24). *Adult female*: wing, 101–109 (103.8) mm (H.C. Oberholser).

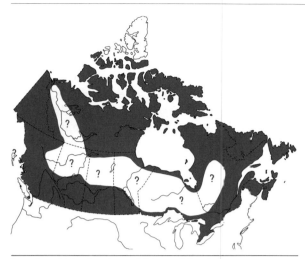

Breeding Distribution of Horned Lark

Range in Canada. Breeding range governed by availability of suitable habitat, therefore absent or extremely local in a broad belt of unsettled forested non-mountainous country stretching from Alberta to Quebec. Breeds from the arctic islands (Prince Patrick, Melville, Bathurst, Devon, and northern Baffin) southward through Yukon, Mackenzie (but apparently absent from Mackenzie valley above the delta), Keewatin (including Southampton Island); through British Columbia (locally: status on Vancouver and Queen Charlotte islands uncertain but breeds at least near Victoria); central and southern Alberta (absent or very local in northern half but perhaps breeds about Lake Athabasca; breeds commonly from about Athabasca southward in mountains and plains); northwestern and southern Saskatchewan (Lake Athabasca, and from Nipawin and Prince Albert southward); Manitoba (Churchill and Hudson Bay coast, and in the southern part from about Swan River and Lake St. Martin southward); Ontario (coasts of James and Hudson bays; also the southern parts from about Sudbury and Ottawa southward; locally on north shore of Lake Superior: Rossport and Peninsula; also locally in extreme west: Emo); northern, central, and southern Quebec (south to Hatley, Gaspé Peninsula, and Madeleine Islands; local in forested interior where barren higher parts of mountains provide habitat); Labrador; Newfoundland; New Brunswick; Prince Edward Island (recently—apparently since early 1900s); and Nova Scotia (recently: probably first established about 1918; now fairly common and widespread).

Winters in southern parts of most provinces: British Columbia, Alberta, Saskatchewan, Manitoba, Ontario (rarely north to Ottawa), Quebec (rarely north to Anticosti Island), Newfoundland (rarely: Argentia), New Brunswick, Nova Scotia, and probably Prince Edward Island.

Field Marks. A brown-backed, slender-billed ground bird, larger than a sparrow, usually seen in companies or flocks. The black breast-shield and black face patch curving downward from bill to below the eye are easily recognized. The tiny black "horns" are often difficult to see. Runs or walks instead of hopping. Flight somewhat undulating; overhead, the black of tail contrasts with white under parts. *Voice*: At all seasons sibilant high-pitched notes, one to three to a series, given especially when flushing or in flight. In the breeding season the tinkling wiry song is given either in flight or from the ground.

Habitat. Open terrain with a minimum of ground cover. In the East, ploughed or sparsely vegetated fields, airports, upper beaches, and barren shores; on the prairies, shortgrass plains, sparse sagebrush flats; in the mountains, grasslands, meadows, and sparsely vegetated places above and below timberline; in the Arctic, gravel ridges, hills, plateaus, rock desert, raised beaches—mostly drier situations. In winter, various types of open terrain, especially where weeds protrude above the snow or where weed seeds or grain are available, such as weedy fields, grain stubbles, and weedy shores.

Nesting. In a hollow of the ground in drier open places. Nest, usually composed of grasses and similar available vegetation, lined with plant down, hair, or feathers. *Eggs*, 3 to 5; greyish, thickly speckled with pale brown; speckling sometimes confluent and occasionally forming a wreath of solid brown around larger end. Incubation (by the female) 11 days (G.B. Pickwell) in Illinois and New York, perhaps varies somewhat in other parts of the vast range of the species.

Range. Alaska and arctic Canada south to southern Mexico, with an isolated population in Colombia, South America; also northern Eurasia south to northern Africa. In North America it winters from southern Canada southward.

Subspecies. (1) *Eremophila alpestris arcticola* (Oberholser): Yukon, Mackenzie Delta, and high mountains of British Columbia and southwestern Alberta. (2) *E. a. hoyti* (Bishop): arctic islands south to northeastern Alberta, northwestern Saskatchewan, northeastern Manitoba, extreme northwestern Ontario (Fort Severn). (3) *E. a. alpestris* (Linnaeus): northern Quebec and northern Labrador south to southern James Bay, southeastern Quebec (Gaspé Peninsula, Madeleine Islands), and Newfoundland. (4) *E. a. leucolaema* Coues: southern Alberta (east of the mountains), southwestern Saskatchewan. (5) *E. a. enthymia* (Oberholser): central-eastern Alberta (Tofield, Clyde), central Saskatchewan, southern Manitoba, extreme western Ontario (Emo)—affinities of (4) and (5) require study. (6) *E. a. praticola* (Henshaw): southern Ontario, southwestern Quebec (Gatineau Point, Lake Saint-Jean basin), New Brunswick, Prince Edward Island, and Nova Scotia. (7) *E. a. strigata* (Henshaw): southwestern British Columbia west of Cascade Mountains. (8) *E. a. merrilli* (Dwight): intermontane valleys of southern British Columbia.

Remarks. On open prairie, arctic tundra, the seacoast, or on man's cultivated fields, there the Horned Lark thrives, for it has no use for trees. Its foraging is done on the ground. Weed seeds make up the bulk of its food, although many insects are eaten also. Many Horned Larks remain in the southern parts of Canada during the winter months. In some parts of the country just north of the usual winter range, such as Ottawa, Ontario, the Horned Larks are the earliest spring arrivals, as a rule before mid-February. While the snow is still deep, many congregate along the bare shoulders of roads and highways in companies and flocks. They also seek food in other open places where weed stalks protrude above the snow. When a flock alights, its members disperse, running hither and thither in their energetic search for weed seeds. When they have worked over one weed patch, away they fly to another, leaving behind an intricate lacework of tiny tracks in the snowy field.

Family **Hirundinidae:**
Swallows

Number of Species in Canada: 8

Swallows are found in both hemispheres of the world. They have long pointed wings, a more or less forked tail, slender body, short neck, flattish head, a small flat bill, which broadens at the gape to form a wide mouth, and small weak feet. Their food is insects, which are taken on the wing. Swallows are not outstanding singers, but their pleasant twitterings, graceful flight, and gentle ways have earned them a high place in the affection of man. Barn and Cliff swallows use our buildings for nesting. Tree Swallows and Purple Martins take advantage of the nesting boxes we provide for them.

Purple Martin

Hirondelle noire
Progne subis (Linnaeus)
Total length: 18.5 to 21.5 cm
Plate 51

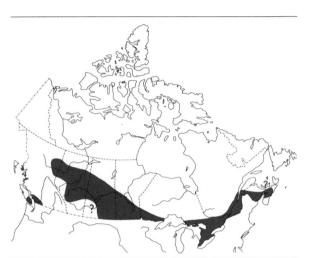

Breeding Distribution of Purple Martin

Range in Canada. Summer resident, breeding locally in extreme southwestern and central-eastern British Columbia (in two widely separated areas: southern Vancouver Island, Vancouver; Peace River parklands); Alberta (Calgary, Sylvan Lake and Penhold eastward and north to McMurray and the Peace River District: Dixonville); north-central and southern Saskatchewan (Kazan Lake, Cumberland House, Moose Mountain; perhaps absent from southwestern corner); southern Manitoba (The Pas southward); western and southern Ontario (Minaki, Kenora, Thunder Bay; and from about Wawa, Mattawa, and Ottawa southward); southern Quebec (Montréal, Québec, Kénogami, Sainte-Anne-de-la-Pocatière, Trois-Pistoles, Sherbrooke); southern New Brunswick (Pointe-du-Chêne, Hampton, Fredericton); Nova Scotia (Amherst; formerly Windsor, Truro, Oxford); and perhaps Prince Edward Island.

Accidental in southern Yukon (two sight records only).

Tail distinctly, but not deeply, forked; upper mandible slightly hooked at tip. Our largest swallow. *Adult male*: Above and below dark glossy purplish-blue; wings and tail dull blackish. *Adult female and young in first spring*: Upper parts mixed dark blue and grey, often with grey collar across back of neck and greyish forehead; throat, breast, sides, and flanks greyish brown, the feathers with grey margins, paling to whitish on belly and under tail coverts but with dark shaft streaks. Young males resemble adult females during the first year.

Measurements. *Adult male*: wing, 145.0–152.5 (149.5); tail, 71.5–78.5 (75.1); exposed culmen, 10.3–12.5 (11.4); tarsus, 14.5–15.5 (15.1). *Adult female*: wing, 141.0–152 (144.0) mm.

Field Marks. Our largest swallow. The adult male, uniformly *dark above and below* (looks black in some lights) is unlike any other swallow. At a distance in gliding flight, the Starling might be confused with it, but the slender bill of the Starling is usually apparent. Females and young have grey throats and breasts, whitish bellies. *Voice* is a good means of identification when learned. It is rather loud and pleasing and contains characteristic chirruping notes and gurgles that are easily recognized.

Habitat. The vicinity of suitable nesting boxes in open places on country farms, in towns and cities. In uninhabited areas, open parts of woodland, woodland openings and edges, and burntlands with hollow dead trees for nesting. Forages both high and low over open water, marshes, and open terrain. Tends to be locally distributed, and many apparently suitable areas are not inhabited by this swallow.

Nesting. Varies from single pairs to large communities. Today most nest in man-provided bird houses of various sizes from singles to ornate many-compartment houses placed on tall poles of 4.5 to 6 m in open places. Occasionally openings or cavities in buildings are used. Formerly nested in hollow trees, woodpecker holes, and cavities in cliffs before man provided nesting boxes, and does so today in remoter and uninhabited country. Nest is loosely made of grasses, twigs, feathers, and often fresh leaves and a little mud. *Eggs*, usually 4 or 5; dull white. Incubation usually 15 to 17 days (Allen and Nice), mainly, if not entirely, by the female.

Range. Breeds (locally, absent from extensive areas) from southern Canada south to Baja California and central Mexico, the Gulf of Mexico coast, and southern Florida. Winters in South America.

Subspecies. *Progne subis subis* (Linnaeus).

Remarks. By erecting suitable nesting houses, we can induce these fine swallows to spend the summer in our gardens. Their graceful flight, pleasant voices, gentle ways, and economically beneficial food habits make them a real asset to have about. Starlings and House Sparrows compete with them for nesting sites, and that is why martin houses should be taken down in the autumn and not be put up until the Purple Martins return in spring.

The food of the Purple Martin is almost entirely insects, which it catches on the wing.

Tree Swallow

Hirondelle bicolore
Tachycineta bicolor (Vieillot)
Total length: 12.5 to 15.7 cm
Plate 51

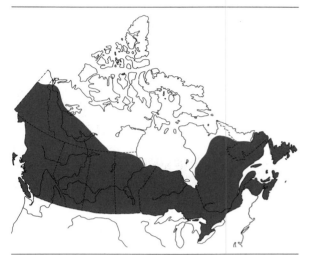

Breeding Distribution of Tree Swallow

Range in Canada. Breeds from northern Yukon (Old Crow); northwestern and southern Mackenzie (Fort Norman, Great Slave Lake; probably Aklavik); northern Alberta; northern Saskatchewan (Lake Athabasca, Stony Rapids); northern Manitoba (Churchill); northern Ontario (Cape Henrietta Maria); northern Quebec (Schefferville region, Kuujjuaq); central Labrador (Goose Bay, Ashuanipi Lake; recorded north to Davis Inlet without evidence of breeding); and Newfoundland south throughout southern Canada from western British Columbia (Queen Charlotte and Vancouver islands) east to eastern Nova Scotia (Cape Breton Island), and Newfoundland, but locally absent in parts of southeastern Alberta and southern Saskatchewan where nest sites are few.

Casual or accidental on Banks Island (specimen: Sachs Harbour, 15 June 1964; photo record: Cape Prince Alfred, 28 June 1968); Seymour Island (specimen: 7 June 1975); Boothia Peninsula (Levesque Harbour); and Keewatin (Chesterfield, Southampton Island, Windy River, Pelly Bay).

Tail slightly forked. *Adult male*: Upper parts glossy steel blue, with greenish reflections, this extending down on sides of head well below the eye; under parts white. *Adult female*: Similar to adult male but upper parts usually duller, often mainly dusky greyish-brown with only the feather tips bluish. *Young*: Upper parts dull brownish-grey, this extending down on sides of head to well below the eye and more sharply cut off from the white of the under parts than in young Violet-green Swallow.

Measurements. *Adult male*: wing, 114–125 (118.3); tail, 52–60 (55.8); exposed culmen, 6–7.8 (6.7); tarsus, 11.5–13 (12.5). *Adult female*: wing, 109–124 (113.5) mm.

Field Marks. All-white under parts and steel-blue upper parts separate it from all other swallows in the East. In the West another species has all-white under parts (see Violet-green Swallow). Young have brownish-grey upper parts (as do some adult females) and often show a greyish wash on the breast, but this is never so dark nor so well defined as the breast band of the Bank Swallow. Unlike the Rough-winged Swallow, the young Tree Swallow has a pure-white throat.

Habitat. Forages in the air, preferably over water or moist ground; lakes, ponds, sloughs, dams, larger streams, fresh and brackish marshes, wet meadows, and bogs. In nesting season availability of suitable nesting places governs numbers. Flooded places such as beaver dams or those made by man, flooded shores, and similar places with numerous standing dead trees near water attract concentrations.

Nesting. In a cavity in a tree, either natural or made by a woodpecker, sometimes in buildings; uses bird boxes where available. Nest, a collection of grass and similar material lined with feathers. *Eggs*, usually 4 to 6; white. Incubation period 13 to 16 days (Austin and Low), by both sexes.

Range. Breeds from north-central Alaska and across Canada (north to near tree limit) south to southern California, western Colorado, northeastern Kansas, northeastern Louisiana, and Virginia. Winters from southern United States (in the East occasionally north to Massachusetts) south to Honduras, Nicaragua, and Cuba.

Violet-green Swallow

Hirondelle à face blanche
Tachycineta thalassina (Swainson)
Total length: 12.5 to 14 cm
Plate 51

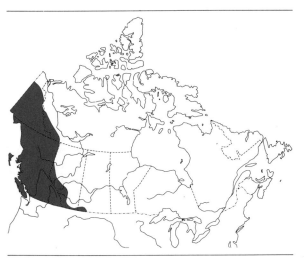

Breeding Distribution of Violet-green Swallow

Range in Canada. Summer resident, breeding in Yukon (north to Old Crow); southwestern Mackenzie (Nahanni National Park); throughout British Columbia (except perhaps parts of the northeast); southwestern Alberta (mountains from Jasper south to Waterton Lakes; also near Red Deer and along Milk River); and very locally in southwestern Saskatchewan (Val Marie, perhaps east to near Constance).

Accidental in Manitoba (Sandilands, April 1945).

Tail not deeply forked. *Adult male*: Crown and back green with bronze tint, especially on crown; rump and upper tail coverts violet or purplish (white of under parts extends up onto sides of rump); under parts white, extending up over cheeks to the eye. *Adult female*: Similar to male but much duller, crown and nape often mostly brownish, this colour extending down much of cheeks. *Young*: Upper parts greyish brown, darkest on back where faintly glossed purplish; under parts white but breast often tinged with brown.

Adults with green and violet coloration are unmistakable. Young resemble young Tree Swallows, but throat is less pure white, and the brown on sides of face is not sharply cut off from the white.

Measurements. *Adult male*: wing, 111–118.5 (114.6); tail, 44.0–47.0 (45.7): exposed culmen, 4.7–5.4 (5.0); tarsus, 10.5–11.5 (11.2). *Adult female*: wing, 106.0–111.0 (109.2) mm.

Field Marks. The green and violet upper parts are distinctive at close range. In flight a small white patch on each side of the rump distinguishes it from other swallows (see White-throated Swift), although this is sometimes suggested in the Tree Swallow (in which the pair of spots are much more widely spaced). In the adult male the cheeks are white up to and around the back of the eye. Young have greyish-brown upper parts and resemble young Tree Swallows, but brown on top of head is less sharply cut off from the white below on the face.

Habitat. Forages over various terrain, open country, water, and above forest tops and at various heights depending on weather factors affecting height of flying insects.

Nesting. In cavities and crevices of cliffs (often at great heights), in woodpecker holes, cavities in buildings, in bird boxes, even rarely in piled lumber. Nesting material consists of grasses and small twigs with a lining of feathers. *Eggs*, 4 to 6; white. Incubation period about 15 days (J.M Edson).

Range. Breeds from Alaska, Yukon, southwestern Alberta, central Montana, and southwestern South Dakota south to northern Baja California and Sonora, Mexico, and through Colorado, New Mexico, and western Texas to southern Mexico. Winters mainly in Mexico and northern Central America.

Subspecies. *Tachycineta thalassina lepida* Mearns.

Northern Rough-winged Swallow

Hirondelle à ailes hérissées
Stelgidopteryx serripennis (Audubon)
Total length: 12.8 to 14.5 cm
Plate 51

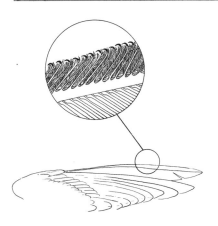

Figure 81
Wing of Northern Rough-winged Swallow showing hooklets (much magnified) on outer edge of outer primary

Adults have outer web of outer primary furnished with fine recurved hooklets (Figure 81), difficult to see but readily felt by passing the finger along the edge of the wing toward the tip. *Adults (sexes similar)*: Resemble Bank Swallow but whole throat, breast, and sides brownish grey, paling gradually to white on abdomen; brown of upper parts slightly paler than in Bank Swallow. *Young*: Similar to adults but wing coverts and tertials tipped with pale cinnamon, the throat and upper breast more or less tinged with same; hooklets on outer web of outer primary lacking or nearly so.

Measurements. *Adult male*: wing, 103.2–114.3 (110.8); tail, 47.0–51.5 (50.5); exposed culmen, 6.0–6.8 (6.4); tarsus, 11.0–11.5 (11.1). *Adult female*: wing, 99.0–108.0 (103.5) mm.

Field Marks. A brown-backed swallow resembling the Bank Swallow but whole throat and breast are plain greyish (instead of white with sharply defined dark breast-band). Young Tree Swallows often show a vague greyish suffusion on the breast but have a white throat and dull-grey upper parts.

Habitat. In the breeding season the vicinity of suitable nesting places (see Nesting), foraging over both water and dry land (even the driest parts of semi-arid plains).

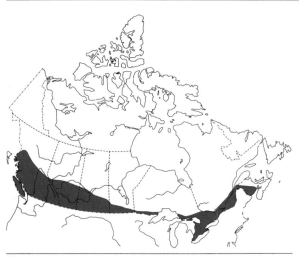

Breeding Distribution of Northern Rough-winged Swallow

Range in Canada. Summer resident, breeding in southern and central British Columbia (Hazelton, Prince George, Kleena Kleene, Victoria, Creston); southern Alberta (north to Jasper and Edmonton), southern Saskatchewan (north to near Saskatoon); southern Manitoba (Indian Bay); western and southern Ontario (Rainy River District; and from the extreme southern part north to Sault Ste. Marie, Sudbury, Ottawa); southwestern Quebec (Lac Simon, Batiscan, Lachine, Lennoxville, Rivière-du-Loup); and southwestern New Brunswick (Woodstock, Browns Flat).

Scarce visitor to Nova Scotia (Seal and Sable islands).

Nesting. Often singly, not so highly colonial as is the Bank Swallow. In burrows in banks of sand, clay, or gravel, excavated by the swallows themselves, or in deserted kingfisher burrows, natural cavities, holes in cement walls, bridges, culverts, and similar situations. Nest of grasses, rootlets, leaves, and similar material depending on locality. *Eggs*, usually 6 or 7; white. Incubation period, 16 days (W.A. Lunk), mainly, if not entirely, by the female.

Range. Breeds from southern Canada (locally) south to Peru, Paraguay, and Argentina; not in the West Indies. Winters from southern United States southward, but only small numbers in the West Indies.

Bank Swallow

Hirondelle de rivage
Riparia riparia (Linnaeus)
Total length: 12 to 14 cm
Plate 51

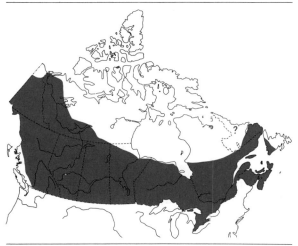

Breeding Distribution of Bank Swallow

Range in Canada. Summer resident; breeding where suitable nesting sites are available, from northern Yukon (Old Crow); northwestern and central-southern Mackenzie (beyond tree limit on Mackenzie Delta, Kittigazuit, Fort Ander-

Tail somewhat forked. Upper parts greyish brown (some feathers with paler edges), darkest on head and extending down over ear coverts; under parts white with well-defined greyish-brown band across breast.

Measurements. *Adult male*: wing, 97.4–106.7 (101.4); tail, 45–50.5 (47.7); exposed culmen, 5.9–6.9 (6.3); tarsus, 10.5–11.0 (10.9). *Adult female*: wing, 95.1–105.9 (101.3) mm.

Field Marks. A brown-backed smallish swallow with a *clearly defined dark breast band* on otherwise white under parts. Rough-winged Swallow also has brown upper parts, but the whole throat and breast are greyish with no clearly defined breast band. *Voice*: A harsh twitter.

Habitat. Forages over water and open land. Breeding populations are rather locally distributed, being confined to the general vicinity of suitable nesting places (see Nesting) and usually at no great distance from water.

Nesting. In colonies. A long tunnel is excavated by the birds in steep banks (tunnels tend to be concentrated near the top) of sand, sandstone, clay, gravel, and in similar softer earths in gravel pits, railway and road cuts, riverbanks, and shores. Nest, of grass and feathers, is placed in a chamber at the end of the tunnel. *Eggs*, 4 to 6; white. Incubation 14 to 16 days (Dayton Stoner), by both sexes.

son, Slave River); northern Alberta; northern Saskatchewan (Lake Athabasca); northern Manitoba (Herchmer, possibly Wolverine River); northern Ontario (Severn River, Winisk); central Quebec (Roggan River, Moisie River, Mingan River, Havre-Saint-Pierre; possibly lower Rivière à la Baleine, Koksoak River near Kuujjuaq); southern Labrador (Goose Bay, perhaps near Hopedale); and southwestern Newfoundland (Highlands, Swift Current) south through southern Yukon (Burwash Landing; Canyon); through southern interior British Columbia, southern Alberta, southern Saskatchewan (locally), southern Manitoba, southern Ontario, southern Quebec (including Gaspé Peninsula and Madeleine Islands), New Brunswick, Prince Edward Island, and Nova Scotia. Scarce migrant on Vancouver Island (Victoria, Mitlenach Island).

Accidental in Franklin District (at Cambridge Bay, Victoria Island, 6 June 1966, and Igloolik, 23 May 1979 (specimens). Sight record for Melville Island, 12 June 1820).

Range. Breeds in North America (north-central Alaska east to northern Quebec and Newfoundland and south to southern United States) and across Eurasia. North American populations winter in South America.

Subspecies. *Riparia riparia riparia* (Linnaeus).

Cliff Swallow

Hirondelle à front blanc
Hirundo pyrrhonota Vieillot
Total length: 12.5 to 15 cm
Plate 51

Breeding Distribution of Cliff Swallow

Range in Canada. Summer resident, breeding from northern Yukon (coastal plain); northern Mackenzie (Mackenzie Delta, Lockhart and Anderson rivers, Coppermine and Kendall rivers); Keewatin (Nueltin Lake, South Henik Lake, probably Back River below Macdougall Lake); northern Manitoba; northern Ontario (Fort Severn); and southern Quebec (Lac Simard, Sept-Îles, Anticosti Island) south through southern British Columbia (but not recorded from Queen Charlotte Islands), southern Alberta, southern Saskatchewan, southern Manitoba, southern Ontario, southwestern and central-southern Quebec (Montréal, Hatley, Gaspé Peninsula), New Brunswick, Prince Edward Island, and Nova Scotia (including

Tail relatively short, almost square or very slightly forked. *Adults*: Forehead pale buff to whitish; crown dark glossy-blue, the back similar but streaked with white; collar around back of neck greyish; rump cinnamon buff; throat and sides of head rich chestnut with small patch of black on lower throat; breast, sides, and flanks pale greyish-brown; belly white or whitish. *Young*: Resemble adults somewhat but upper parts mostly dark brown; throat and sides of head dusky, sometimes mixed with dull chestnut. The buffy rump patch distinguishes both adults and young from other swallows.

Measurements *(H. p. pyrrhonota)*. *Adult male*: wing, 105.5–111.5 (109.4); tail, 47.0–51.0 (48.8); exposed culmen, 6.4–7.3 (6.8); tarsus, 12–13 (12.3). *Adult female*: wing, 105–112 (108.8) mm.

Field Marks. Most like Barn Swallow in general coloration but chunkier, with much shorter *squarish* tail, a *buffy rump patch*, and a whitish forehead patch. *Voice*: Rather soft but tends to be more squeaky than that of other swallows.

Habitat. Forages over water, marshes, and open land. In breeding season the vicinity of suitable nesting places (see Nesting), ideally within cruising distance of open water for drinking and foraging, and mud for nesting material.

Nesting. Highly colonial, sometimes in hundreds and rarely in thousands, usually in much smaller numbers. Nest is made of pellets of mud gathered by the birds. It is usually roofed over and often has a more or less downward protruding neck forming the entrance. Nest chamber is scantily lined with grass and feathers. Nests are close together and are plastered to the vertical walls of cliffs and canyons; but especially in the East this swallow, adopting man-made structures, has placed its nest on buildings, particularly under the eaves, on concrete bridges, and under culverts. *Eggs*, usually 4 or 5; white to creamy, variously dotted and spotted with light and dark browns. Incubation period 12 to 14 days (reported by various authors) mainly by the female. House Sparrows frequently destroy the eggs and occupy the nests of this swallow.

Range. Breeds from central Alaska and Canada south through the United States (except South Carolina, Florida, and the eastern Gulf States) to southern Mexico. Winters in South America.

Subspecies. (1) *Hirundo pyrrhonota pyrrhonota* Vieillot: Manitoba (except southwestern part) eastward; also extreme southwestern British Columbia. (2) *H. p. hypopolia* (Oberholser) (paler less rusty breast,

Cape Breton Island). Numbers of this swallow have declined in many areas in recent years, especially in the East.

Cave Swallow

Hirondelle à front brun
Hirundo fulva Vieillot
Total length: 14 cm

Figure 82
Head of
a) Cliff Swallow
b) Cave Swallow

Status in Canada. Casual or accidental in Nova Scotia (a desiccated specimen found dead on Sable Island on 21 June 1968, was probably one of nine reported seen there a month or more earlier. Also on Sable Island, up to three were carefully identified in the period 14 to 30 June 1969. On Seal Island, Yarmouth County, a male was collected on 15 or 16 May 1971 by Dr. Ian McLaren. Sight records near Louisbourg, 9 July 1982).

usually paler rump patch, average larger size): Yukon, Mackenzie, British Columbia (except extreme southwest, but west at least to Okanagan valley), Alberta, Saskatchewan, and extreme southwestern Manitoba (Whitewater Lake).

Very similar to the Cliff Swallow (Figure 82) but throat and sides of head much paler (cinnamon or buff instead of rich chestnut); no black throat patch; forehead much darker, dark chestnut, and not sharply marked off posteriorly from crown; rump darker (chestnut). Size smaller.

Measurements *(H. f. fulva). Adult male*: wing, 101–108 (103.5); tail, 42–47 (45.0). *Adult female*: wing, 101–106 (103.7); tail, 44–48 (45.7) mm.

Range. Southeastern New Mexico, south-central Texas, northeastern Mexico (Coahuila to southern Tamaulipas, and Yucatan) and the Greater Antilles.

Subspecies. The two Nova Scotian specimens are referable to the Greater Antilles race, *Hirundo fulva fulva* Vieillot.

Barn Swallow

Hirondelle des granges
Hirundo rustica Linnaeus
Total length: 14.8 to 19.5 cm
Plate 51

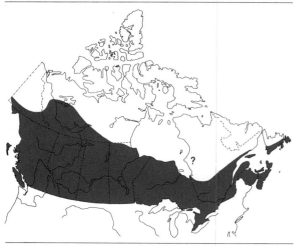

Breeding Distribution of Barn Swallow

Range in Canada. Summer resident, breeding from southern Yukon (Whitehorse, perhaps Burwash Landing); western Mackenzie (Fort

Tail deeply forked, the outer feathers decidedly elongated. *Adult male*: Forehead chestnut; rest of upper parts dark steel-blue; each tail feather (except central pair) with a patch of white on inner web; throat and middle breast chestnut, bordered on sides of neck and sides of breast by an extension downward of the blue of upper parts; rest of under parts cinnamon-rufous to cinnamon (sometimes quite pale). *Adult female*: Usually duller above and paler below than adult male; tail shorter. *Young*: Much duller above and paler below than adults; tail shorter.

Measurements. *Adult male*: wing, 116.0–122.0 (119.1); tail, 82.0–108.0 (89.5); exposed culmen, 7.2–7.8 (7.5); tarsus, 10.5–11.5 (11.3). *Adult female*: wing, 116.0–122.0 (118.3) mm.

Field Marks. Our only swallow with a *deeply* forked tail or with white in the tail feathers. The combination of blue upper parts and chestnut throat also separates it from all but the Cliff Swallow. The Barn Swallow has a uniformly blue back and rump (no brownish rump patch). The cinnamon abdomen, visible in flight at considerable distances, and long tail will distinguish it from other swallows. Young Barn Swallows have less deeply forked tail than adults, but nevertheless it is usually more deeply forked than in other swallows. *Voice*: Song a pleasant bubbly chatter, occasionally punctuated with a little, slightly rising, grating trill; also, especially in the air, *kvick, kvick*.

Norman, Fort Franklin, Great Slave Lake); northwestern and central-eastern Saskatchewan (Lake Athabasca, southern Wollaston Lake); central Manitoba (north to Thompson; also an isolated breeding record near Churchill); western and central Ontario (Malachi, Sioux Lookout, Hearst, South Porcupine, Moosonee; local nesting at Cape Henrietta Maria and Winisk); southern Quebec (Cabbage Willows Bay, Lake Saint-Jean, Anticosti Island; possibly Lake Waswanipi); and southern Newfoundland (Codroy valley, Shoal Harbour) south through British Columbia (including Queen Charlotte and Vancouver islands), Alberta (but scarce in the Peace River District), southern Saskatchewan, southern Manitoba, southern Ontario, southern Quebec (including Madeleine Islands), New Brunswick, Prince Edward Island, and Nova Scotia. Reports of local breeding in Labrador lack confirmation.

Rare on north shore of the Gulf of St. Lawrence. Casual in southern Keewatin (Eskimo Point: 40 km south), and southern Labrador (Hopedale, St. Mary's River). Accidental on Victoria Island (Cambridge Bay, Holman), Cornwallis Island (Resolute Bay: specimen, 24 June 1969), and Mansel Island, N.W.T., 14 June 1980.

Habitat. In the breeding season the vicinity of a suitable nesting site (see Nesting) and within cruising radius of water for drinking, foraging, and providing mud for nest building. Forages over water, marshes, and open land; often low but also at great heights in fair weather.

Nesting. Either in single pairs or small colonies. In protected places such as inside buildings of various kinds, under bridges, in caves, and under rocky overhangs of cliffs. Nest is of mud, bonded with grasses and lined with fine grasses, hair, and feathers, often on a beam in a building, on a ledge, or plastered against a wall. *Eggs*, usually 4 to 6; white, variously dotted or spotted with bright reddish-browns and duller browns. Incubation 14 to 15 days (W.P. Smith), mainly by the female with some irregular assistance from the male.

Range. Holarctic. Breeds from north-central Alaska and across much of Canada (see Range in Canada) south to central Mexico and western Florida; also across Eurasia from near the northern edge of the tree belt south to northern Africa, Egypt, Asia Minor, northwestern India, and northern China. New World populations winter in South America.

Subspecies. *Hirundo rustica erythrogaster* Boddaert is the breeding subspecies over all of Canada. An Asiatic race, *H. r. gutturalis* Scopoli, is accidental 145 km west of Tasu Sound, Queen Charlotte Islands, British Columbia, where an emaciated specimen was captured on 15 July 1960.

Family **Corvidae**: Jays, Magpies, and Crows

Number of Species in Canada: 11

A large family of conspicuous birds, which is found in much of the world but not in New Zealand. Size medium to large, including the largest of passerine birds. Bill is stout, tapering, usually about as long as the head. Nostrils are covered with stiff, bristlelike feathers. Tarsi are scutellate in front, plain behind. Primaries ten. The crows are black, black and white, or dull-coloured; the wings longer than the tail; and on the ground, instead of hopping, they walk. Jays are usually smaller than crows and are often brightly coloured. Many jays are crested and have long tails. Instead of walking on the ground, they hop.

Birds of this family are of uncertain economic status. They are valuable as scavengers and destroyers of insects, but, on the other hand, they eat cultivated fruits and grains and sometimes destroy the eggs and young of other birds.

Gray Jay

(Canada Jay)

Geai du Canada
Perisoreus canadensis (Linnaeus)
Total length: 27.5 to 30.5 cm
Plate 52

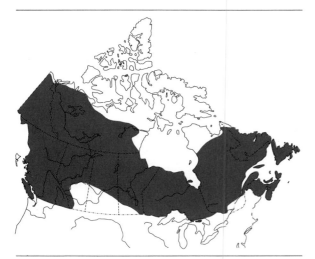

Breeding Distribution of Gray Jay

Range in Canada. Permanent resident, breeding (north to about tree limit) from northern Yukon (British Mountains); northern Mackenzie (wooded parts of Mackenzie Delta, Anderson River, lower Horton River, Thelon River); southwestern Keewatin (Windy River); northern Manitoba (Sandhill Lake, Churchill); northern Ontario; northern Quebec (Kuujjuaq, Rivière à la Baleine, George River, Koroc River); northern Labrador (wooded parts); and Newfoundland south through British Columbia (including Vancouver Island, but absent from Queen Charlotte Islands); central and southwestern Alberta (south in the mountains and foothills to Waterton Lakes National Park, and east of the mountains south to the edge of heavy woods: Pigeon and Battle lakes, and formerly, at least, to wooded country near Red Deer, Penhold, and Innisfail; absent from the southern and southeastern plains); central Saskatchewan (Prince Albert, Nipawin); southern Manitoba (except southwestern corner); south-central Ontario (Manitoulin Island, Round Lake in Renfrew County; Algonquin Provincial Park; Lake Nipissing; rarely Ottawa region); southern Quebec (La Vérendrye Park, Laurentides Park, Rimouski, Gaspé Peninsula, Anticosti Island); New Brunswick; Prince Edward Island; and Nova Scotia (including Cape Breton Island).

Winters mostly within breeding range, north to northwestern Mackenzie (Mackenzie Delta) and northern Quebec (Kuujjuaq). Also wanders somewhat south of the breeding range in winter, some years in considerable numbers; in small numbers to Madeleine Islands. Accidental on Sable Island, Nova Scotia.

Plumage loose and fluffy. Head without a crest. Bill rather short. Extent and depth of greys varies somewhat geographically but not enough to cause confusion as to species. *Adults (P. c. canadensis)*: Head white with blackish-slate cap on hind crown and nape, this dark colour extending narrowly forward to encircle eyes; back, wings, and tail slaty, the flight feathers and tail feathers tipped with white; abdomen, sides, and flanks plain grey (paler than black) paling to whitish near tail; bill and legs black. *Juvenal*: All blackish-grey above and below, darkest on top of head, palest on lower abdomen toward tail; tips of wing and tail feathers brownish white; bill partially light-coloured (see Subspecies).

Measurements *(P. c. canadensis). Adult male*: wing, 138.0–148.5 (143.2); tail, 142.0–150.5 (144.4); exposed culmen, 20.6–21.8 (21.3); tarsus, 33.0–37.0 (35.6). *Adult female*: wing, 136.5–146.5 (139.5) mm.

Field Marks. A grey crestless jay, typically of coniferous forests, with fluffy plumage, short bill, and longish tail. The dark hind-neck, eye, and bill are conspicuous against the otherwise white head. It is very curious, often very bold. It frequently visits backwoods camps and picnic grounds for scraps. Young in juvenal plumage (first summer) are uniformly dark (in moulting, white areas of the adults often show, especially as white moustache-marks); usually they are accompanied by adults. *Voice*: Extremely varied consisting of harsh chatter, whistles (frequently *quee-oo*, dropping rapidly in pitch), soft chuckles, and many other notes, and including the mimicking of other birds. Said to have a soft, prolonged, warbling song.

Habitat. Coniferous and mixedwood forests, forest openings, and bogs.

Nesting. Nest, in a tree, usually (not always) a conifer, and most often between 1.2 and 4.5 m above the ground. Nest is made of twigs, bark, leaves, grass, moss, and caterpillar cocoons with a substantial lining of hair, feathers, fine grass, and sometimes pine needles. Its foundation of coarse twigs makes it rather bulky. *Eggs*, 2 to 6, usually 3 to 4; greyish, quite evenly dotted and fine-spotted with olive-buff. Incubation 16 to 18 days, by the female (O.B. Warren).

Range. Breeds from near tree limit in north-central Alaska and across Canada, and south to northern California, central Arizona, northern New Mexico, South Dakota (locally: Black Hills), northern Minnesota, northern Michigan, south-central Ontario, northeastern New York, northern parts of Vermont and New Hampshire, and Maine. Winters mostly in breeding range.

Subspecies. The following sketch of the subspecies is tentative pending further study with more adequate material: (1) *Perisoreus canadensis pacificus* (Gmelin): Yukon, northwestern Mackenzie, northern and central British Columbia, southwestern Alberta (Banff, Jasper); (2) *P. c. canadensis* (Linnaeus): northern Manitoba, Ontario, southern Quebec (Lake Mistassini, Anticosti Island), New Brunswick; (3) *P. c. nigricapillus* Ridgway: northern Quebec, Labrador; (4) *P. c. sanfordi* Oberholser: Newfoundland, Nova Scotia, Prince Edward Island, eastern New Brunswick; (5) *P. c. albescens* Peters: Alberta (east of the mountains), Saskatchewan, western Manitoba, southern Mackenzie; (6) *P. c. bicolor* Miller: interior southern British Columbia, extreme southwestern Alberta (Waterton Lakes National Park); (7) *P. c. arcus* Miller: Rainbow Mountains, British Columbia; (8) *P. c. griseus* Ridgway: southern coastal British Columbia, north to Kimsquit.

Steller's Jay

Geai de Steller
Cyanocitta stelleri (Gmelin)
Total length: 30.5 to 34 cm
Plate 52

Breeding Distribution of Steller's Jay

Range in Canada. Permanent resident in western and southeastern British Columbia (Stikine River, Poison Mountain about 96 km north of Hazelton, eastward at least to within 100 km east of Prince George, and southward including Queen Charlotte and Vancouver islands) and southwestern Alberta (Jasper and Waterton Lakes national parks).

Individuals occasionally wander eastward in Alberta (Glenevis, Whitecourt, Swan Hills, Cochrane). Casual in eastern Saskatchewan (Indian Head, Saltcoats, Yorkton, and near Borden). Accidental in Quebec (Cap-Rouge, 8 November 1926; subspecies: *annectens*). One sight record for Yukon (near Kathleen Lake, 1 July 1944).

Head crested. *Adults*: Head, neck, upper back, and upper breast blackish, the forehead usually streaked with blue, the throat more or less streaked with grey; wings, tail, lower back, rump, and under parts (posterior to upper breast) deep blue, the wings and tail usually with some black bars. Interior birds *(annectens)* often have a whitish spot above the eye. *Young*: Have blue wings and tail, but back, rump, and the under parts are blackish.

Measurements *(C. s. stelleri)*. *Adult male*: wing, 144.0–150.0 (147.7); tail, 137.0–149.5 (141.4); culmen, 29.3–32.3 (30.3); tarsus, 42.0–47.5 (45.5). *Adult female*: wing, 139.0–150.0 (143.3) mm.

Field Marks. A dark blue-and-black prominently crested bird somewhat larger than a Robin. A much darker jay than the Blue Jay and *with dark under parts. Voice*: A harsh *shack-shack-shack, wek-wek-wek*, and various other calls, even a warbled song.

Habitat. Coniferous and mixedwood forests, either extensive or broken; also many other types of treed places, often including orchards and gardens.

Nesting. Most frequently in a conifer (often Douglas fir). Nest is a rather bulky but well-made structure of twigs, frequently plastered with mud, and lined with rootlets, grass, pine needles, or other soft material. *Eggs*, 3 to 5; greenish or bluish, fairly evenly dotted or spotted with browns or olive. Incubation, 16 to 17 days, by the female.

Range. Resident from southern Alaska, western and southern British Columbia, and southwestern Alberta south through southern California and Mexico to El Salvador and the highlands of Nicaragua; east to southwestern Texas.

Subspecies. (1) *Cyanocitta stelleri stelleri* (Gmelin): coastal British Columbia (lower Stikine River, Vancouver Island). (2) *C. s. carlottae* Osgood, a darker race averaging somewhat larger: Queen Charlotte Islands, British Columbia. (3) *C. s. annectens* (Baird), with paler coloration than *stelleri*, much paler than *carlottae*, and often with a whitish area above to the eye: southwestern Alberta and interior British Columbia. Possibly, as some authors assert, its breeding range in the Skeena River region extends to the coast (Porcher Island) interrupting that of *stelleri*, but material known to be breeding is needed to establish this. (4) *C. s. paralia* Oberholser: extreme southwestern mainland of British Columbia west of the Cascades (Munro and Cowan 1947; Aldrich *in* Jewett et al. 1953. On the other hand, this population is included in the nominate race in the *A.O.U. Check-list*, 1957).

Blue Jay

Geai bleu
Cyanocitta cristata (Linnaeus)
Total length: 28 to 31.5 cm
Plate 52

Unmistakable. (See Field Marks.)

Measurements. *Adult male*: wing, 133.5–143.0 (137.9); tail, 127.0–143.5 (134.2); exposed culmen, 23.8–28.4 (26.6); tarsus, 34.5–36.5 (35.6). *Adult female*: wing, 127.0–136.0 (130.8) mm.

Field Marks. A crested bird, slightly longer than a Robin, with blue upper parts, grey-white under parts with a black necklace, and white spots in wings and tail. The only bird likely to be confused with it is Steller's Jay (of the western mountains), which also has a crest but differs in having all-blue under parts (black in young) and in showing no white in wing or tail. Bluebirds are very much smaller birds without any crest. *Voice*: Extremely varied. A loud *jay, jay* call and a whistled *too-wheedle, too-wheedle* are familiar to most people. It has a variety of other notes including a scream like a Red-shouldered Hawk, various chattering and conversational notes, and a soft pleasing but infrequently heard song.

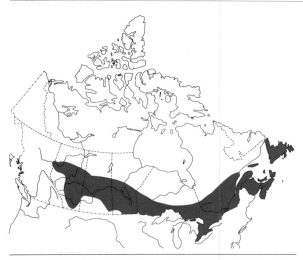

Breeding Distribution of Blue Jay

Range in Canada. Has expanded westward in recent years in western parts of its range. Permanent resident breeding in extreme central-eastern British Columbia (Clayhurst); central Alberta (east of the mountains: Peace River District and McMurray south to Calgary, Beynon, recently Lethbridge); central Saskatchewan (Smoothstone Lake, Kazan Lake, Yorkton, Moose Mountain, Qu'Appelle valley); south-central and southern Manitoba (Thicket Portage, Clear Lake, Whitemouth); central and southern Ontario (Sioux Lookout, and Kapuskasing southward); southern Quebec (La Vérendrye Park, Lake Saint-Jean, Gaspé Peninsula, perhaps Anticosti Island southward including Madeleine Islands); Newfoundland; New Brunswick; Prince Edward Island; and Nova Scotia.

Occasionally wanders south on the prairies to southern Alberta (Craigmyle, Brooks), southern Saskatchewan (Ravenscrag, Regina), and in recent years westward into British Columbia (Victoria, Vancouver, Kimberley; Pacific Rim, Mount Revelstoke and Yoho national parks). Rare vagrant at Churchill, Manitoba (one reported on 19 June 1940).

Habitat. Mixed and deciduous woodland of various types, especially where beech and oak are present; shade trees about towns and cities.

Nesting. In a tree, most often coniferous, and usually 2.4 to 7.5 m up. Nest is rather bulky and is made of sticks, moss, and lichens, grasses, wool, paper, and various soft items, and lined with grass, rootlets, and feathers. *Eggs*, usually 4 to 6; buffy to greenish or bluish with small spots and blotches of brown or olive. Incubation period 17 to 18 days (Arnold *in* Bent), by the female.

Range. Southern Canada (Alberta eastward) and United States recently west to Oregon (Union) south to southeastern Texas, the Gulf of Mexico coast, and southern Florida.

Subspecies. *Cyanocitta cristata bromia* Oberholser. The Newfoundland population has been described as *C. c. burleighi* Bond, but the writer has not examined any Newfoundland specimens and therefore can offer no comment on the validity of this proposed new subspecies.

Remarks. The Blue Jay is handsome, noisy, mischievous, and inquisitive. It adds life to the woodlands at any time of the year, especially in winter when so many other birds have moved to warmer climates. Its raucous calls are heard at all times of the year, but it is often noisiest in the quiet of autumn when most birds are silently hurrying south. It is practically omnivorous, eating fruits, insects, grains, acorns, and, unfortunately, sometimes the eggs and nestlings of other birds. Although economically of dubious value, it is surely one of the most beautiful and interesting of birds.

Scrub Jay

Geai à gorge blanche
Aphelocoma coerulescens (Bosc)
Total length: 28 to 33 cm
Figure 83

Figure 83
Scrub Jay

A crestless jay. *Adults*: Upper parts mostly blue; back greyish brown; narrow superciliary line, white; cheeks blackish; chin, throat, and middle chest white vaguely streaked with bluish; sides of breast blue, thus forming a blue border to the white throat patch; remainder of under parts greyish white, but under tail coverts often tinged bluish.

Measurements *(A. c. californica)*. *Adult male*: wing, 125.5–132 (129.3); tail, 137–147 (142.7); exposed culmen, 24.9–27.4 (26.4); tarsus, 40.4–45 (41.1). *Adult female*: wing, 115.6–127 (121.7); tail, 124.5–137 (130.2); exposed culmen, 20.8–26 (24.4); tarsus, 37.6–46 (41) mm (Ridgway).

Field Marks. In Canada, most like the Blue Jay but Scrub Jay lacks a crest, has a brownish back, narrow white superciliary line, blackish cheeks, and blue (instead of black) border to the white throat patch. No white areas in wings or tail.

Status in Canada. Accidental in British Columbia: One photographed at Langley on 8 November 1981 by Wayne Campbell.

Range. Resident in extreme southwestern Washington, Oregon, southeastern Idaho, southwestern Wyoming, Colorado, and central Texas south to southern Mexico.

Pinyon Jay

[**Pinyon Jay**. Geai des pinèdes. *Gymnorhinus cyanocephalus* Wied. Hypothetical. Sight record near Eastend, Saskatchewan, 16 September 1910—L.B. Potter, 1943. Canadian Field-Naturalist, vol. 57, no. 4 and 5, p. 70.]

Clark's Nutcracker

Casse-noix d'Amérique
Nucifraga columbiana (Wilson)
Total length: 31 to 33 cm
Plate 52

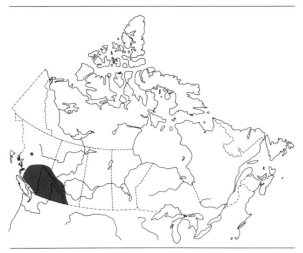

Breeding Distribution of Clark's Nutcracker

Range in Canada. Permanent resident, breeding in southern and central British Columbia (east of the coast but west to Alta Lake, and northward to Mount Cronin and the Bulkley valley) and in the mountains of southwestern Alberta.

Wanders west to Vancouver and Queen Charlotte islands, British Columbia; north to southern Yukon (Robinson, Sheep Mountain, Rancheria River); and east of the mountains in Alberta (Porcupine Hills, Beaverlodge, Belvedere, McMurray); southern Saskatchewan (Cypress Hills, Moose Jaw, Saskatoon region); southern Manitoba (Winnipeg, Margaret); and Ontario (photo record: Dryden, 18 April 1973; Caribou Island, 9 May 1981; also sight records in Paipoonge and Aubrey townships, November 1972).

Adults (sexes alike): Head, neck, and body, pale smoky-grey, whitish on forehead, throat, and about eye; wings black, the secondaries with broadly white ends; tail mostly white, the central feathers black; under tail coverts white; bill and feet black. *Young*: Similar to adults but paler and duller.

Measurements. *Adult male*: wing, 186–198 (191.1); tail, 109–122 (113.4); exposed culmen, 33.4–48.5 (39.8); tarsus, 34–37.5 (35.7). *Adult female*: wing, 177.5–194 (185.5) mm.

Field Marks. A stout grey bird with longish pointed black bill, black wings with a white patch, and white outer tail feathers. Usually found in the western mountains. Reminds one of a cross between a crestless jay and a woodpecker. The Gray Jay shows no contrasting blacks and whites in wing or tail and has a shorter bill and a longer tail. Shrikes are smaller, show a black patch through the eye, and have a shorter blunter bill. Nutcrackers are usually noisy with harsh grating calls like *char-r-r* or *kra-a-a*, repeated two or three times.

Habitat. Typically, open or broken coniferous woods, clearings, edges, and burntlands at higher altitudes of the western mountains, descending to valleys in winter. Although largely dependent on conifer seeds (especially those of the whitebark pine, *Pinus albicaulis*) for food, it eats many other foods and may forage in various situations. In winter it may visit camps or farmyards for scraps.

Nesting. In coniferous trees at various distances from the ground. Nest is of twigs lined with dry grass, shredded bark, conifer needles, and hair. *Eggs*, usually 2 to 4; pale greenish with small spots of pale brown or olive. Incubation probably 16 or 17 days (C.E. Bendire), by both sexes.

Range. Breeds from about central British Columbia, southwestern Alberta, central and western Montana, and western and southeastern Wyoming south through the mountains to northern Baja California, eastern Arizona, and western New Mexico.

1 Least Flycatcher, p. 361

2 Alder Flycatcher, p. 360

3 Yellow-bellied Flycatcher, p. 358

4 Acadian Flycatcher, p. 359

5 Hammond's Flycatcher, p. 362

6 Western Flycatcher, p. 364

7 Dusky Flycatcher, p. 363

Crosby

1 Scissor-tailed Flycatcher, p. 371

2 Vermilion Flycatcher, p. 366
a) adult male
b) adult female

3 Black Phoebe, p. 365

4 Ash-throated Flycatcher, p. 367

5 Brown-crested Flycatcher, p. 368

1 Bank Swallow, p. 377
a) adult
b) flying

1a

1b

2 Northern Rough-winged Swallow, p. 376
a) adult
b) flying

2a

2b

3 Violet-green Swallow, p. 376
a) adult
b) juvenal

3a

3b

4 Cliff Swallow, p. 378

4

5 Barn Swallow p. 379

5

6 Tree Swallow, p. 375
a) adult male
b) juvenal

6a

6b

7 Purple Martin, p. 374
a) adult male
b) female

7a

7b

Crosby

1 Blue Jay, p. 382

1

3

4 Gray Jay, p. 381

4

3 Black-billed Magpie, p. 393

2

5

2 Steller's Jay, p. 382

5 Clark's Nutcracker, p. 384

6

6 Northwestern Crow, p. 395

8

8 Common Raven, p. 396

7 American Crow, p. 394

7

Crosby

3 Chestnut-backed Chickadee, p. 401

53

2 Siberian Tit, p. 400

1 Mountain Chickadee, p. 399

4 Boreal Chickadee, p. 400

5 Black-capped Chickadee, p. 398

6 Bushtit, p. 403

7 Red-breasted Nuthatch, p. 404

8 Pygmy Nuthatch, p. 406

9 Tufted Titmouse, p. 402

Crosby

10 White-breasted Nuthatch, p. 405

1 Bewick's Wren, p. 410

2 Rock Wren, p. 408

3 Carolina Wren, p. 409

6 Brown Creeper, p. 406

5 House Wren, p. 410

4 Winter Wren, p. 412

7 American Dipper, p. 415

8 Marsh Wren, p. 414

9 Sedge Wren, p. 413

Crosby

1 Northern Mockingbird, p. 433

2 Gray Catbird, p. 432

3 Brown Thrasher, p. 434

4 Sage Thrasher, p. 434

5 Red-throated Pipit, p. 436

6 Water Pipit, p. 437
a) summer
b) autumn

6b

6a

8

8 Sprague's Pipit, p. 438

7

9

Crosby

7 Eurasian Skylark, p. 372

9 Horned Lark, p. 372

56

1 Northern Wheatear, p. 420
adult male in summer

2 Townsend's Solitaire, p. 423
adult

3 Hermit Thrush, p. 427

4 Veery, p. 424

5 Gray-cheeked Thrush,
p. 425

7 Swainson's Thrush, p. 426

6 Wood Thrush, p. 428

Crosby

Black-billed Magpie

Pie bavarde
Pica pica (Linnaeus)
Total length: 45.5 to 56 cm
Plate 52

Breeding Distribution of Black-billed Magpie

Range in Canada. Permanent resident, breeding in southern Yukon (Canyon, Carcross; probably Forty Mile); interior British Columbia (Chilkat Pass, Prince George region, Okanagan valley, Roosville); Alberta (north at least to Peace River District and Hay Lake); Saskatchewan (north at least to Beaver River, Carlton, and Nipawin); southern Manitoba (north to Pikwitonei, Mile 213 Hudson Bay Railway, southeast probably to Piney); and extreme southwestern Ontario (Rainy River District).

Winters mainly within the breeding range, but there is an apparently regular movement north and east of it. Wanders to southern Mackenzie (Wrigley, Dubawnt River, Fort Resolution, Fort Smith); southern Keewatin (Windy River); northern Saskatchewan (Lake Athabasca, Reindeer Lake); northern Manitoba (Churchill); and coastal British Columbia; rarely to eastern Ontario (western James Bay, Timmins, Toronto, Point Pelee, Odessa). Casual in western Quebec (Eastmain, also various sight records, some of which may have been escaped captives). Hypothetical in Labrador (Davis Inlet, where one was reported to L.M. Tuck, in litt., as having been shot on 2 September 1957, but not preserved). Sight records for the Maritimes.

Accidental in Franklin (specimen: Banks Island: Sachs Harbour, 13 May 1972).

Its breeding range has expanded eastward and northward within the past half century, and reports indicate more regular winter occurrence eastward and northward of the breeding range.

Tail very long (making up more than half the bird's total length), graduated. Head, neck, back, tail coverts, throat, and breast black; scapulars, belly, sides, and flanks white; inner webs of primaries largely white; wings glossy greenish-blue; tail glossy green with more or less purple or bronze toward tip; upper rump greyish white; bill and legs black.

Measurements. *Adult male*: wing, 196.0–223.5 (207.5); tail, 242.0–343.5 (280.8); exposed culmen, 32.2–35.9 (33.5); tarsus, 46.0–50.5 (48.3). *Adult female*: wing, 187.0–202.0 (195.4) mm.

Field Marks. Unmistakable. A largish black-and-white bird with very long tail and flashing white patches in the wing tips when flying. *Voice*: A harsh rapid *yak yak yak yak yak*; often a querulous *yak* or two.

Habitat. Thickets and scattered trees in open places rather than heavy forest; shrubbery and trees along coulees, shelter belts on the prairies; streamside and canyon shrubbery, tree patches, edges and openings of woodland.

Nesting. Nest, in a tall bush or tree, is a domed-over mass of sticks, often thorny ones, with one or more entrances in the side leading to an inside cup of mud, which is lined with rootlets, fine grass, and hair. *Eggs*, usually 6 to 9; greenish grey heavily blotched with browns. Incubation 16 to 18 days (C.E. Bendire), by the female.

Range. Both New and Old Worlds. In North America, from southern and central coastal Alaska and western Canada south to central-eastern California, Nevada, Kansas, Nebraska, and South Dakota. Also across Eurasia and in northwestern Africa.

Subspecies. *Pica pica hudsonia* (Sabine).

Jackdaw

Choucas des tours
Corvus monedula Linnaeus
Total length: 31 to 34 cm
Figure 84

Status in Canada. Accidental. In spring of 1984, single individuals appeared in Nova Scotia, one on Brier Island on 5 May, one on Outer Island 20–21 May. One was photographed. (Just prior to this, between 23 March and 6 April 1984, three Jackdaws visited the village of Miquelon, in the French islands of St. Pierre and Miquelon, south of Newfoundland. One appeared to be exhausted and was captured by a child and released.) How these birds reached North America is unknown at the time of writing.

Figure 84
Jackdaw

A very small, stubby-billed crow with a whitish eye. Crown, front of face, back, wings, and tail black. Cheeks and nape dark silvery grey. Abdomen greyish black. Bill, legs, and feet black. Irides greyish white. Characteristic call *chak*.

Range. Eurasia eastward to Ussuriland.

American Crow

Corneille d'Amérique
Corvus brachyrhynchos Brehm
Total length: 43 to 53 cm
Plate 52

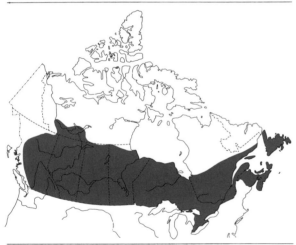

Breeding Distribution of American Crow

Range in Canada. Breeds from north-central interior British Columbia (east of the coast: Hazelton, Fort Connolly, Babine Lake, and Peace River District); southwestern Mackenzie (Fort Simpson, Latham Island, Fort Smith); northern Alberta; northern Saskatchewan (Lake Athabasca); northern Manitoba (Churchill);

Similar to Common Raven but much smaller; feathers of throat not elongated or pointed; tail not wedge-shaped. *Adults*: All black with violet or greenish-blue gloss strongest on back, wings, and tail. *Juvenal plumage* (worn only a short time after leaving nest): Dull brownish black, only wings and tail glossy.

Measurements *(C. b. brachyrhynchos)*. *Adult male*: wing, 303.0–328.0 (316.9); tail, 170.0–200.0 (183.3); exposed culmen, 46.0–52.0 (48.5); tarsus, 58.0–63.0 (60.5). *Adult female*: wing, 300.0–321.5 (310.4) mm.

Field Marks. Large size, all black coloration, and familiar caw. Its longish bill separates it from black hawks. See Common Raven and, on the Pacific Coast, Northwestern Crow, both similar to the American Crow.

Habitat. Highly adaptable and resourceful, and with an appetite for a vast range of vegetable and animal foods, the crow is capable of occupying a correspondingly great variety of habitats. It prefers open places for foraging and wooded areas for nesting, resting, and roosting. Agricultural areas with their woodlots and broad cultivated fields are ideal for its requirements, and greatest populations are found in such habitats. Obviously the American Crow is one of the minority of species that have profited most from extensive land use by man. It flourishes also in coastal areas. Extensive heavy forest has smaller populations, and these are mainly in the vicinity of lakes, rivers, marshes, meadows, and bogs. Winter populations in deep-snow regions usually concentrate about garbage dumps of towns and cities. Tidal shores support large winter flocks even in deep-snow areas. In many places, winter flocks have greatly declined with the passing of the old slaughterhouses.

northern Ontario; central Quebec (Lake Mistassini, Havre-Saint-Pierre, Chevery near Harrington-Harbour); and Newfoundland (except the northern peninsula) south through southern British Columbia (east of the coast), Alberta, Saskatchewan, Manitoba, Ontario, Quebec (including Anticosti and Madeleine islands), New Brunswick, Prince Edward Island, and Nova Scotia.

Winters in southern British Columbia (Okanagan valley, Nulki Lake); southern Saskatchewan (Regina); southern Ontario; southern Quebec (Hull, Montréal, Québec, Arvida, Île-Verte, Gaspé Peninsula); southern Newfoundland; New Brunswick; Prince Edward Island; and Nova Scotia.

Casual in eastern Keewatin (Eskimo Point).

Nesting. Usually in trees, both coniferous and deciduous, and at various heights, sometimes in low bushes or on the ground. Nest is a durable structure of sticks, lined mainly with various soft materials such as grass, moss, leaves, bark, rootlets, hair, or rags. *Eggs*, usually 4 to 6; greenish, variously blotched and spotted with browns. Incubation 17 to 20 days, by both sexes (O.W. Knight).

Range. Breeds across southern Canada (except the West Coast) and south to northern Baja California, central Arizona, central Texas, the Gulf of Mexico, and southern Florida. Winters from parts of southern Canada southward.

Subspecies. (1) *Corvus brachyrhynchos brachyrhynchos* Brehm: southwestern Mackenzie, northern Alberta, northern Saskatchewan, Manitoba, Ontario, Quebec, Newfoundland, New Brunswick, Prince Edward Island, and Nova Scotia. (2) *C. b. hesperis* Ridgway, averaging smaller and with relatively smaller and more slender bill: interior British Columbia, central and southern Alberta, southern Saskatchewan.

Remarks. It has been said that if the average person were asked to name four birds, one of them would probably be the American Crow. Although it is familiar to everyone, very few have much good to say for it. It is omnivorous and eats practically anything edible. It is destructive to crops, particularly corn, and it often takes the eggs and young of more desirable birds. On the other hand, it destroys large numbers of insects.

It is generally conceded, however, that the harm it does outweighs the good. Consequently no laws protect it. Despite constant persecution, the American Crow is an extremely resourceful bird, well able to look after itself and maintain its numbers. Probably it has actually profited and increased as a result of its contacts with man and his agriculture.

Northwestern Crow

Corneille d'Alaska
Corvus caurinus Baird
Total length: 42 to 44.5 cm
Plate 52

Breeding Distribution of Northwestern Crow

Range in Canada. Permanent resident on the coast and islands of British Columbia (including Queen Charlotte and Vancouver islands and inland at least to Chilliwack).

Like American Crow but smaller with relatively smaller feet.

Measurements. *Adult male*: wing, 274.5–292.5 (283.5); tail, 152.0–170.5 (163.0); exposed culmen, 43.5–49.0 (47.0); tarsus, 46.0–53.0 (51.0). *Adult female*: wing, 256.5–284.5 (272.0); tail, 144.5–162.5 (153.0); exposed culmen, 41.5–47.5 (45.0); tarsus, 45.0–51.0 (48.0) mm (Ridgway).

Field Marks. Its voice is the best distinction in the field from the American Crow, the *caw* of the Northwestern being a higher-pitched, more nasal, and rather flat *kaah*. In flight, wing beats noticeably more rapid.

Habitat. Usually not far from salt water. Primarily a beach-comber, foraging on coastal shores, beaches, and tide flats; also agricultural areas. Coastal woodlands for nesting and roosting.

Nesting. Nest, a mass of sticks and twigs lined with softer materials like grass, hair, and bark fibre. Usually in a coniferous tree but sometimes on the ground under bushes, windfalls, or boulders. *Eggs*, usually 4 or 5; similar to those of American Crow but slightly smaller.

Range. Coasts and islands from southern Alaska south to Washington.

Remarks. Additional studies are needed to ascertain beyond doubt whether this crow is really a separate species or merely a subspecies of the American Crow.

Fish Crow

Corneille de rivage
Corvus ossifragus Wilson
Total length: 37 to 44.5 cm

Status in Canada. Casual visitor to Ontario
(Point Pelee: 15 May 1978 and 21 April 1982;
also Long Point) and Nova Scotia (Sable
Island, 12 January 1967; Cape Sable, 23 February
1966).

Very similar to American Crow but decidedly smaller than eastern populations, somewhat glossier, the gloss more greenish blue on the under parts. In the hand, the back is seen to be more uniform (that of American Crow is faintly squamate). Call a high-pitched *kar*, thus different from the *caw* of the American Crow adult, but confusingly similar to the voice of young American Crows; thus voice is not a reliable distinction in early summer.

Measurements. *Adult male*: wing, 264.5–300 (278); tail, 148–176.5 (158.5); exposed culmen, 40.5–45 (43); tarsus, 45.5–50 (48). *Adult female*: wing, 264.5–282.5 (271.5); tail, 137.5–165 (152); exposed culmen, 39–42 (40.5); tarsus, 44.5–47 (46) mm (Ridgway).

Range. Eastern United States from New York and Massachusetts southward on the Atlantic Coast to southern Florida, and westward on the Gulf Coast to southern Texas; also inland on major waterways to eastern Oklahoma, southern Illinois, southwestern Kentucky, and central Virginia.

Chihuahuan Raven

[**Chihuahuan Raven**. Corbeau à cou blanc. *Corvus cryptoleucus* Couch. Total length: 48 to 52 cm. Similar to Common Raven but much smaller, with relatively longer nasal plumes, and with the concealed basal part of the feathers of neck and breast white instead of grey.

Range. Southeastern Arizona, southern New Mexico, south-central Nebraska, south to central Mexico.

Status in Canada. Hypothetical. A specimen was captured, minutely examined, banded, and released at Long Point, Ontario, 14–15 May 1976, by D.J.T. Hussell. This specimen was probably an escapee as the species is often kept in captivity in the United States.]

Common Raven

Grand Corbeau
Corvus corax Linnaeus
Total length: 56 to 67 cm
Plate 52

Figure 85
Head of Common Raven showing elongated pointed throat feathers

Somewhat similar to American Crow but much larger and with very much heavier bill; feathers of throat elongated and pointed (Figure 85); tail somewhat wedge-shaped. *Adults (sexes similar)*: All black with purplish or violet lustre. *Young in juvenal plumage* (worn only a short time after leaving nest): Similar to adults but head and body dull brownish-black and feathers of throat not elongated or pointed.

Measurements *(C. c. principalis)*. *Adult male*: wing, 417.0–445.0 (427.9); tail, 228.0–258.5 (244.5); exposed culmen, 72.0–78.0 (74.4); tarsus, 62.0–67.5 (64.9). *Adult female*: wing, 398.0–437.0 (421.4) mm.

Field Marks. In Canada, likely to be confused only with the American Crow. Although much larger than the American Crow, size is often deceptive in the field, unless the two are seen together. The Common Raven shows a definitely rounded or wedge-shaped spread tail (easily noted in flight overhead); on take-off from the ground the Raven often takes two or three hops to become airborne, whereas the Crow jumps directly into the air; in flight the Raven's longer neck and bill extend farther ahead of the wings. Ravens glide and soar more frequently, and often do barrel-rolls, dives, and tumbles. *Voice*: is one of the best distinctions. The Raven's commonest call is a hoarse, far-carrying, rather wooden croak or *kwawk* (very different from the American Crow's *caw*). It has a variety of other notes including a bell-like one. Young Common Ravens are often very noisy, with higher-pitched, more prolonged calls than adults, which are easily distinguishable from those of young crows.

Breeding Distribution of Common Raven

Range in Canada. Permanent resident, breeding from high-arctic islands (locally, depending on cliffs for nesting: Prince Patrick Island, southern Ellesmere Island) south through Yukon, Mackenzie, Keewatin, and southern Baffin Island to southern British Columbia (including coastal islands); northern Alberta (south to Winagami Lake and in the mountains to near Waterton Lakes); central Saskatchewan (Flotten Lake, Nipawin); central-western and southern Manitoba (northwestern Lake Winnipegosis, Rennie); western and south-central Ontario (Manitoulin Island, Bruce Peninsula, Iron Bridge, Algonquin Provincial Park; probably VanKoughnet); southern Quebec (near Aylmer, Lake Lyster, Cap-Tourmente, Rivière-du-Loup, Percé, Madeleine Islands, formerly Montréal); Labrador; Newfoundland; New Brunswick; Prince Edward Island; and Nova Scotia. Wanders north to northern Ellesmere Island, but evidence of breeding there is lacking.

Winters mainly within breeding range north at least to Melville Island and northern Baffin Islands, N.W.T.; also somewhat south of the breeding range in Alberta, Saskatchewan, and rarely extreme southern Ontario.

Habitat. Most often mountainous and wilder hill country and sea-coasts in both arctic and forested regions. Breeding distribution in the Arctic is governed by presence of cliffs for nesting, often those used by seabird colonies. In wooded regions, trees are frequently used as nesting sites permitting nesting in flatter lowlands. Largely a scavenger, it forages over a wide variety of terrain but is partial to shores of lakes, rivers, and the sea; and in settled country, roadsides and town garbage-dumps. Assertions that it shuns civilization are not necessarily true, for it prospers in numerous well-settled parts of the Maritimes (notably the heavily farmed Annapolis valley) and visits regularly subarctic towns and villages within its breeding range in the north country, perching on buildings and scavenging at garbage dumps, often becoming quite tame where not persecuted. Its preferred habitat and that of man do not overlap to a great extent.

Nesting. In single pairs on cliff ledges and cavities and in trees (mostly conifers). Nest, a large mass of sticks lined with various soft materials, depending on availability, such as moss, grass, seaweed, and hair. *Eggs*, usually 3 to 5; similar to those of American Crow but usually larger. Incubation 20 to 21 days (*in* Witherby et al.) in the British Isles; 20 days (R.C. Harlow) in Pennsylvania, by the female.

Range. Both New and Old Worlds. In the New World from subarctic Alaska, arctic Canada, and Greenland, south through western United States and Mexico to Nicaragua and in eastern North America south to Minnesota, northern Michigan, Maine and, in the Appalachian Mountains, south to northern Georgia. In the Eastern Hemisphere from northern Eurasia south to northern Africa, Asia Minor, northwest India, and Japan.

Subspecies. (1) *Corvus corax principalis* Ridgway: all Canada except southern interior British Columbia. (2) *C. c. sinuatus* Wagler, characterized by average smaller size and slightly longer tarsus: southern interior British Columbia: specimens examined from Okanagan valley, Horsefly River, Yahk, Revelstoke.

Family **Paridae**:
Titmice

Number of Species in Canada: 7

Small birds of woods and thickets with short but usually quite robust bills; nostrils hidden by tufts of stiff feathers; short rounded wings, and soft fluffy plumage. Except in the nesting season they are usually seen in small companies and are often accompanied by kinglets, nuthatches, and woodpeckers.

Black-capped Chickadee

Mésange à tête noire
Parus atricapillus Linnaeus
Total length: 12.3 to 14.5 cm
Plate 53

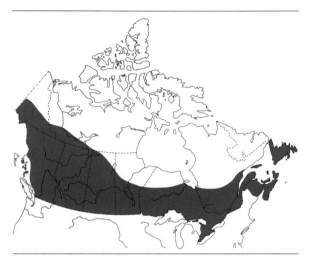

Breeding Distribution of Black-capped Chickadee

Range in Canada. Permanent resident, breeding from southern Yukon (southern Ogilvie Mountains, Burwash Landing, Carcross, Dezadeash Lake; probably Lapie River); southwestern Mackenzie (Nahanni National Park, Fort Simpson, Fort Resolution); northern Saskatchewan (Lake Athabasca, Stony Rapids); north-central Manitoba (Thicket Portage); north-central Ontario (Favourable Lake, Fort Albany); southern Quebec (southern James Bay, Lake Saint-Jean, Matamec, Anticosti Island); and Newfoundland south through southern British Columbia (except coastal islands and north coast), Alberta, Saskatchewan, Manitoba, Ontario, Quebec (including Madeleine Islands), New Brunswick, Prince Edward Island, and Nova Scotia (including Cape Breton Island).

Plumage soft and loose. *Adults (sexes similar)*: Crown and back of neck black; back olive-grey (more or less mixed with buffy, especially in winter); wings and tail blackish slate, the secondaries and greater wing coverts edged with greyish white, the tail feathers edged with grey or white; chin and throat black; sides of head, sides of neck, and under body white, sides and flanks tinged with buff; bill black; legs dark bluish-grey. *Young in juvenal plumage* are similar to adults but duller.

Measurements *(P. a. atricapillus)*. *Adult male*: wing, 64.6–68.6 (66.1); tail, 58.0–73.0 (63.4); exposed culmen, 8.8–9.7 (9.1); tarsus, 15.9–16.8 (16.4). *Adult female*: wing, 60.0–65.4 (62.7) mm.

Field Marks. Familiar to almost everyone, and one of the easiest of birds to attract to the backyard feeding shelf. A fluffy, confiding, unstreaked little bird with a black cap and bib, which contrast with the white on sides of head. Usually in small loose companies often associating with other woodland birds. *Voice*: Its clearly pronounced *chicka-dee-dee-dee* is frequently given at all times of the year. Its sweet whistled *fee-bee* (first part higher) is most often heard in late winter and spring. In Canada the only other chickadee with a jet-black cap is the Mountain Chickadee of the West, which has a white eyebrow line.

Habitat. Forages in dry or wet deciduous or mixed woodlands of various age and extent, woodland openings and edges, tall thickets such as willows and alder, woodlots and wood patches, ornamental shrubbery and trees about houses, occasionally on weeds in open fields (see also Nesting).

Nesting. In a cavity, usually low, in a soft decaying stump, generally excavated by the birds, taking turns; sometimes in an old woodpecker hole, a natural cavity, or a bird box. Soft materials such as moss, vegetable fibres, hair, and feathers are carried inside the cavity to form the nest. *Eggs*, usually 6 to 8; dull white, spotted with reddish brown. Incubation about 13 days (E.P. Odum) by the female.

Range. Central Alaska and southern Canada, south to northwestern California, central Utah, northern New Mexico, northeastern Oklahoma, central Missouri, southern Ohio, eastern Tennessee, western North Carolina, western Maryland, and northern New Jersey.

Subspecies. (1) *Parus atricapillus atricapillus* Linnaeus: eastern Canada (except Newfoundland) west to western Ontario and southwestern Manitoba (Winnipeg). (2) *P. a. bartletti* (Aldrich and Nutt), darker and browner than (1): Newfoundland. (3) *P. a. septentrionalis* Harris, paler than (1) with longer tail and wing: southern Yukon, southwestern Mackenzie, northern British Columbia (south to Vanderhoof and Hazelton), Alberta, Saskatchewan, western and central Manitoba (The Pas, Thicket Portage, Oak Lake). (4) *P. a. fortuitus* (Dawson and Bowles), very similar to (1) but slightly paler: southern British Columbia (north at least to Lillooet and Revelstoke, east to Flathead valley). (5) *P. a. occidentalis* Baird, darker and browner even than (2): extreme southwestern mainland British Columbia (Vancouver, Chilliwack).

Remarks. Whoever saw a dejected chickadee? Even on the greyest day of midwinter, when the thermometer remains below zero and the snow lies deep over the land, the chickadee is the personification of cheerfulness and good nature. Chickadees rove through the woods in small loose companies, constantly pausing to scrutinize the leafless branches for the insect eggs they relish so much. Indeed, insects make up the greater part of their food throughout the year, these including some of the worst crop and orchard pests. Seeds and small wild fruit also are eaten.

This chickadee is one of the easiest of birds to attract to a backyard feeding shelf. Even nothing more than a piece of suet attached to the bark of a tree will provide a winter-long attraction for a small company.

Carolina Chickadee

Mésange minime
Parus carolinensis Audubon
Total length: 11.5 cm

Status in Canada. Accidental in Ontario (immature female collected at Long Point on 18 May 1983 is in the Royal Ontario Museum). There are two sight records: Toronto, April 1914; Rondeau Provincial Park, July 1960, this latter identification based on vocalizations.

Very similar to the Black-capped Chickadee but smaller with relatively shorter tail. All of the pale edging of the wing feathers is narrower and greyer, giving a more uniform grey coloration to the wing. Black throat patch more sharply defined posteriorly against the breast. Chickadee note is higher and more rapid. The *fee-bee* whistle of the Black-capped is usually four-noted in the present species.

Measurements *(P. c. extimus)*. *Adult male*: wing, 64.3; tail, 54.9; tarsus, 16.2. *Adult female*: wing, 61.2; tail, 53.3; tarsus, 15.4 mm.

Range. Southeastern Kansas, central parts of Missouri, Illinois, Indiana, Ohio, southern Pennsylvania, and central New Jersey south through eastern Texas, the Gulf Coast, and central Florida.

Mountain Chickadee

(Gambel's Chickadee)

Mésange de Gambel
Parus gambeli Ridgway
Total length: 12.5 to 14.5 cm
Plate 53

Breeding Distribution of Mountain Chickadee

Range in Canada. Permanent resident, breeding in the mountains of northwestern, central, and southern interior British Columbia (Vancouver area, Kleena Kleene, Atlin, Topley, Vander-hoof, Lillooet, Okanagan Landing, Cranbrook, Waldo) and southwestern Alberta (Jasper, Banff, and Waterton Lakes national parks).

Has wandered northward to southern Yukon (Dezadeash Lake, Whitehorse) and eastward in Alberta (Edmonton, Calgary, and Lethbridge) and to southwestern Saskatchewan (in winter of 1966–1967 to Piapot and Maple Creek).

Similar to Black-capped Chickadee but with a white eyebrow stripe, the sides and flanks much less buffy.

Measurements. *Adult male*: wing, 66.4–69.9 (68.6); tail, 59–63 (60.9); exposed culmen, 9.5–11.6 (10.2); tarsus, 16.5–18.5 (17.5). *Adult female*: wing, 63.6–67.5 (65.4) mm.

Field Marks. The *black cap* distinguishes it from all other Canadian chickadees except the Black-capped. A white eyebrow line separates it from all others including the Black-capped. *Voice*: The chickadee call is harsher than that of the Black-capped and more variable, thus *chickadeer-deer, cha-dee-dee-dee*, and so on. The whistled call is *fee-bee-bee* (usually three or four syllables but occasionally only two; first note always highest). It also has lisping *sssp* calls like those of the Black-capped.

Habitat. Coniferous forests, up to near timberline in western mountains, especially more open types but foraging often includes deciduous woods and thickets. It forages in tree crowns to a much greater extent than the Black-capped.

Nesting. In a natural cavity or woodpecker hole in a tree, occasionally in a bird box. Moss, grass, plant fibres, fur, feathers, and almost any other available soft material make up the nest. *Eggs*, 6 to 12; dull white sometimes immaculate but usually spotted with reddish brown in various extents. Incubation 14 days (I.G. Wheelock).

Range. Mountains of western North America from northern British Columbia and southwestern Alberta south to northern Baja California, Arizona, New Mexico, and southwestern Texas.

Subspecies. *Parus gambeli grinnelli* (van Rossem).

Siberian Tit

(Gray-headed Chickadee)

Mésange lapone
Parus cinctus Boddaert
Total length: 13.6 to 15 cm
Plate 53

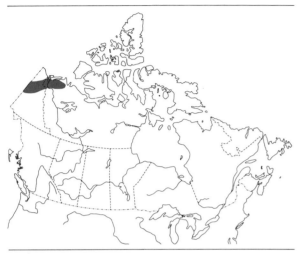

Breeding Distribution of Siberian Tit

Range in Canada. Permanent resident in the northern limits of woodland in northern Yukon (Old Crow) and northwestern Mackenzie (Aklavik, Fort Anderson).

Somewhat similar to Boreal Chickadee but general coloration much paler and greyer; crown and back much greyer (less brownish), sides and flanks pale brownish-buff (instead of rich cinnamon-brown), wing tertials broadly edged with whitish, sides of neck white (instead of clear grey), size somewhat larger.

Measurements. *Adult male*: wing, 69–70 (69.8); tail, 65.5–68 (66.5); exposed culmen, 9–11 (10.1); tarsus, 15.5–16.5 (15.7). *Adult female*: wing, 65.5–69.5 (67.6); tail, 63–69 (67.3); exposed culmen, 9–10.6 (9.8); tarsus, 16–16 (16) mm.

Field Marks. Distinguishable from Boreal Chickadee by white (instead of clear-grey) sides of neck, pale-buff (instead of reddish-brown) sides and flanks, and whitish margins of tertials. The colour of flanks and the whitish edgings of tertials suggest the Black-capped Chickadee but the greyish-brown crown characterizes the Siberian Tit. *Voice*: A complaining *dee-deer, chee-ee*, or *pee-vee* (O. Murie); slightly hoarser than that of the Boreal (S.D. MacDonald).

Habitat. Broken coniferous or aspen woods and willow thickets near the northern edges of tree limit.

Nesting. A cavity in a tree stump. Nest of mammal hair and moss. *Eggs*, 6 to 9; white, finely spotted with reddish brown.

Range. From northern Norway eastward across northern Eurasia and in Alaska, northern Yukon, and northwestern Mackenzie.

Subspecies. *Parus cinctus lathami* Stephens.

Boreal Chickadee

(Hudsonian or
Brown-headed Chickadee)

Mésange à tête brune
Parus hudsonicus Forster
Total length: 12.5 to 14 cm
Plate 53

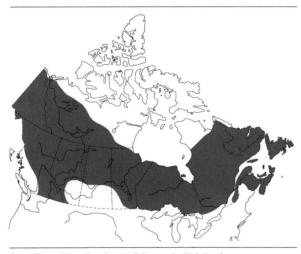

Breeding Distribution of Boreal Chickadee

Range in Canada. Permanent resident in the coniferous belt from northern Yukon (middle Firth River); northwestern and western Mackenzie (Mackenzie valley north to the Delta, Great Bear Lake, Great Slave Lake); northern Saskatchewan (Lake Athabasca, Newnham

Adults: Crown and hind-neck brown; back brownish olive to hair-brown; wings and tail dark slate with paler grey edges; cheeks whitish merging into pale grey on auricular region and becoming dark grey on sides of neck; chin and throat black; medial under parts white, slightly greyish on sides of chest; sides and flanks between cinnamon-brown and russet.

Measurements *(P. h. hudsonicus)*. *Adult male*: wing, 63.2–66.2 (65.8); tail, 59–65.9 (63.2); exposed culmen, 7.6–9.8 (8.9); tarsus, 16–17.5 (16.9). *Adult female*: wing, 58.7–64.1 (62.8) mm.

Field Marks. The brown cap, reddish (instead of pale-buffy) flanks, and more brownish (less greyish) general coloration distinguish it from the Black-capped Chickadee. It resembles the Chestnut-backed Chickadee of the West but lacks the red back of that species (see also Siberian Tit). *Voice*: Commonly *sickaday-day*, slower and a little more highly pitched than the *chicka-dee* of the Black-capped; easily recognizable.

Habitat. Primarily coniferous and mixed woodland but forages to some extent also in deciduous trees and thickets.

Nesting. In a natural cavity, woodpecker hole, or a cavity excavated by the chickadees in a tree or stump not often over 3 m above ground. Nest is of moss, shreds of bark, and mammal hair. *Eggs*, usually 5 to 7; white, sparingly fine-spotted with reddish brown.

Range. Resident in the coniferous forest belt from the northern limit of trees in continental Alaska and across Canada south to central-northern Washington, northwestern Montana, northeastern Minnesota, northeastern New York, northern Vermont, northern New Hampshire, and Maine.

Lake); northern Manitoba (Cochrane River, Churchill); northern Ontario (Severn River); northern Quebec (Kuujjuaq, George River, Koroc River); Labrador (Okak southward); and Newfoundland south through southern British Columbia (east of the Coast Ranges); southwestern and central Alberta (Banff, Astotin Lake); central Saskatchewan (Flotten Lake, Prince Albert, Nipawin); southern Manitoba (Clear Lake, Spruce Woods Forest Reserve, Sprague; absent from extreme southwestern corner); south-central Ontario (Atikokan, Maclennan, Algonquin Provincial Park); southern Quebec (Campbell's-Bay, Lake Monroe, Lavaltrie, Baldwin-Mills, Saint-Aubert, Percé, Anticosti and Madeleine islands; absent or very local in most of extreme southwestern corner); New Brunswick; Prince Edward Island; and Nova Scotia.

Recorded west to Stuie, British Columbia. Winters mainly within breeding range north to northwestern Mackenzie (Mackenzie Delta); northern Saskatchewan (Stony Rapids); southwestern Keewatin (Windy River); and northern Quebec (George River). There is a more or less regular movement of individuals to areas somewhat south of the breeding range and apparently sometimes even northward as in southwestern Keewatin (Mowat and Lawrie 1955, p. 111). Irregularly, irruptive autumn movements take large numbers to extreme southern Ontario and beyond.

Subspecies. (1) *Parus hudsonicus hudsonicus* Forster: eastern Manitoba (Churchill, East Braintree), Ontario, northern and central Quebec (south to about Lake Saint-Jean, the north shore of the Gulf of St. Lawrence, Anticosti Island), Labrador, Newfoundland. (2) *P. h. littoralis* Bryant, averaging slightly smaller and browner than *hudsonicus*: southern Quebec, New Brunswick, Prince Edward Island, and Nova Scotia. (3) *P. h. farleyi* Godfrey, a pale, brown-backed race with grey on sides of neck pale and restricted: Alberta (except mountains), southern Mackenzie (probably Fort Simpson, Reliance); Saskatchewan; western Manitoba (The Pas, Clear Lake). (4) *P. h. evura* Coues, a pale-grey or olivaceous-backed bird with grey sides of neck often nearly as pale as in *farleyi*: northern Yukon (Old Crow), northwestern Mackenzie (Mackenzie Delta). (5) *P. h. columbianus* Rhoads, darker and less brownish than *hudsonicus*, much darker than *evura* or *farleyi*: British Columbia and southwestern Alberta. *P. h. cascadensis* Miller is not considered separable.

Chestnut-backed Chickadee

Mésange à dos marron
Parus rufescens Townsend
Total length: 11.3 to 12.5 cm
Plate 53

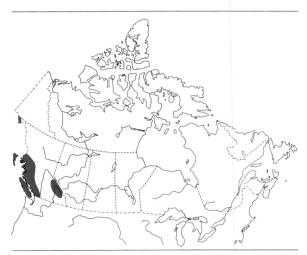

Breeding Distribution of Chestnut-backed Chickadee

Range in Canada. Permanent resident, breeding commonly in western British Columbia (coastal slopes and islands including Vancouver, the Queen Charlotte Islands, and other islands; in Skeena River valley east to Hazelton; frequently recorded in the southern interior; probably breeding locally in Wells Gray and Mount Revelstoke parks; probably breeds also in Klehini valley in the extreme northwest near the Alaskan boundary). Rare visitor to Alberta (Waterton Lake).

Crown and back of neck dark brown; throat brownish black; cheeks and sides of neck white; back and rump chestnut; breast and median under parts white; sides and flanks chestnut.

Measurements. *Adult male*: wing, 60.1–64.3 (61.9); tail, 48–52.5 (49.9); exposed culmen, 8.9–9.6 (9.3); tarsus, 14.5–16.5 (15.9). *Adult female*: wing, 56.5–66.8 (59.9) mm.

Field Marks. A chickadee of the West. Because of its brown head and chestnut sides it is likely to be confused mostly with the Boreal Chickadee. The Chestnut-back has a rich chestnut back, the white of face extends backwards onto sides of neck (instead of becoming grey), and the flanks are of a deeper red like the back. *Voice: tsick-a-dee-dee*, shriller and more rapid than in other chickadees; also various high-pitched lisping notes suggesting those of a Brown Creeper or Golden-crowned Kinglet.

Habitat. Mostly coniferous woods but also deciduous trees and thickets, even burntlands. Forages well up in trees as well as at lower levels.

Nesting. In a cavity in a dead tree or dead part of a living tree, either excavated by the chickadees or in a woodpecker hole or natural cavity. Nest is of various soft materials like hair or feathers with a moss foundation. *Eggs*, commonly 6 or 7; white, sparingly and lightly dotted with browns.

Range. Pacific Coast and islands from central-southern Alaska south to central California and for various distances inland in the mountains of British Columbia, Washington, Idaho, and northwestern Montana.

Subspecies. *Parus rufescens rufescens* Townsend.

Tufted Titmouse

Mésange bicolore
Parus bicolor Linnaeus
Total length: 15.3 to 16.5 cm
Plate 53

Range in Canada. Scarce permanent resident in southern Ontario. Known to have bred at Hamilton, Sarnia, Welland, London, and Lorne Park near Toronto. It has been recorded north to Owen Sound and east to Kingston and there is a sight record (many observers) at a feeder in Ottawa. A recent arrival, it was first observed in Canada at Point Pelee on 2 May 1914. Increase in numbers has been very slow.

Casual visitant to Quebec (photo record: North-Hatley, December 1978; sight record: Lennoxville, late October 1980 and 5 November 1981; also Brossard, Stanstead, and Rock Island) and New Brunswick (photo: Fredericton, 24 December 1983).

A large crested chickadee *without* a black bib. Upper parts plain slate-grey, the forehead blackish; under parts whitish with pale-rusty flanks. Bill rather heavy, black.

Measurements. *Adult male*: wing, 74.5–83 (79.8); tail, 65–75 (68.5); exposed culmen, 11–13 (12.1); tarsus, 19.5–22 (20.4). *Adult female*: wing, 72–79.5 (76.7); tail, 61.5–71 (66.8); exposed culmen, 11–13 (12); tarsus, 19–21.5 (20.2) mm (Ridgway).

Field Marks. A crested small bird with plain bluish-grey upper parts, rusty flanks, and blackish forehead. The dark eye is conspicuous in the greyish-white face. Other crested birds are very different (see Blue Jay, waxwings). *Voice*: A whistled *peto* repeated several times; a hoarse *dee dee dee*.

Habitat. Deciduous and mixed woodland and patches in rural areas; and in residential areas where there is adequate tree growth as in parks and cemeteries. Visits feeding trays about houses.

Nesting. In a natural cavity in a tree, or in an abandoned woodpecker hole, or in a bird box at various heights. Leaves, bark, moss and grass are used to fill up excess cavity space, and the nest cup is made of various soft materials like hair, rags, and string. Often the nest contains a cast snake skin. *Eggs*, most often 5 or 6; white, finely spotted with browns. Incubation 12 to 13 days, by the female.

Range. Permanent resident from southeastern Nebraska, southern Wisconsin, southern Ontario, southern New York, and southwestern Connecticut south to eastern Texas, the Gulf Coast of United States, and central Florida. Has spread northward in recent years.

Family **Aegithalidae**:
Long-tailed Tits and Bushtits

Number of Species in Canada: 1

The Bushtit, formerly included in the true titmouse family Paridae, is currently placed in this otherwise Old World family. It is the only North American species in the family and its affinities are not too clear. It is tiny, obscurely coloured, with longish somewhat graduated tail, and stubby bill. Although in the Bushtit the irides of both adult males and the young are brown, those of the adult female are pale cream colour. Bushtits differ further from true titmice in building intricately woven bag-like nests.

Bushtit

Mésange buissonnière
Psaltriparus minimus (Townsend)
Total length: 10 to 11.4 cm
Plate 53

Range in Canada. Permanent resident in extreme southwestern British Columbia (Vancouver region; and Vancouver Island: Victoria northward on east side at least to Campbell River). It is a recent arrival on Vancouver Island. The first nest for the island was found near Victoria, where now common, in 1937.

Bill deeper than broad, its depth at base more than half the length of exposed culmen. Tail slender, longish (longer than wing), and somewhat graduated. Top of head brown; back and rump brownish grey; under parts brownish white, darkening to brown on sides and flanks. No wing bars or other conspicuous marks.

Measurements. *Adult male*: wing, 46.5–47 (46.7); tail, 51–54 (52.6); exposed culmen, 7.5–8.1 (7.9); tarsus, 16–16 (16.0). *Adult female*: wing, 47.3–48.4 (47.9) mm.

Field Marks. A tiny nondescript brownish-grey bird of southwestern British Columbia with stubby bill and rather long tail. Moves actively about exploring the branches in all positions, often upside down, with frequent high-pitched call-notes. Lack of any definite markings, such as wing bars, eye-ring, and eyebrow line, as well as its longer tail, distinguishes it from kinglets. *Voice*: Frequent high-pitched *tsit-tsit*'s, lisping notes, and a shrill quavering trill.

Habitat. Deciduous and mixed more open woodland and edges; thickets and patches of deciduous shrubbery in both rural and residential areas; logged-over areas growing up in bushes.

Nesting. Nest is amazingly large and intricately woven for such a tiny bird: a bag-like structure, 17 to 25 cm long and 7.5 to 10 cm wide, suspended from a branch and beautifully woven of mosses, lichens, spider webs, plant down, and insect cocoons. The entrance is at the side and usually near the top. *Eggs*, usually 5 to 7; dull white. Incubation about 12 days (A.B. Addicott), by both sexes.

Range. Southwestern British Columbia, southeastern Oregon, southwestern Wyoming, and western Colorado south to southern Baja California, Sonora, and western and central Texas.

Subspecies. *Psaltriparus minimus minimus* (Townsend).

Family **Sittidae**: Nuthatches

Number of Species in Canada: 3

Nuthatches forage on the trunk and branches of trees and characteristically work down the trunk head-first. They are small birds with straight, slender, tapering bills; rather long and pointed wings; short tails, and rather long toes, three in front, one behind, and all with laterally compressed claws. The name "nuthatch" comes from the habit of inserting nuts in bark crevices and hammering them with the bill until the shell is broken.

Red-breasted Nuthatch

Sittelle à poitrine rousse
Sitta canadensis Linnaeus
Total length: 10.2 to 12.4 cm
Plate 53

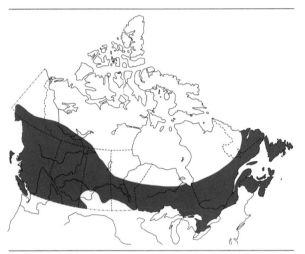

Breeding Distribution of Red-breasted Nuthatch

Range in Canada. Permanent resident in most of breeding range, breeding from southern Yukon (Fort Selkirk, Kathleen River); southwestern Mackenzie (Fort Simpson, Tazin River); northwestern Saskatchewan (Lake Athabasca, southern Reindeer Lake); central Manitoba (Reader Lake); north-central Ontario (Big Trout Lake, Moose Factory); south-central Quebec (Lake Mistassini, Anticosti Island, north shore Gulf of St. Lawrence: Lake Allard, probably Saint-Augustin; recorded in two summers at Lourdes-de-Blanc-Sablon); Labrador (Goose Bay, Makkovik); and Newfoundland (throughout) south to southern British Columbia (including Queen Charlotte and Vancouver islands); Alberta (but very locally in the southeast); southwestern and south-central Saskatchewan (Cypress Hills, Nipawin, rarely Saskatoon and Indian Head); southern Manitoba; southern Ontario (Wasaga Beach, Erindale, St. Williams); southern Quebec (Aylmer, Hatley, Gaspé Peninsula, Madeleine Islands); New Brunswick; Prince Edward Island; and Nova Scotia.

Casual north to northern Manitoba (Churchill) and central-eastern James Bay (Paint Hills Islands).

Winters mostly within breeding range, but many individuals move somewhat farther south in irregular, sometimes irruptive, numbers.

Adult male: Top of head and back of neck black; face white with black line through eye, creating a long white eyebrow line; back, rump, and wing coverts greyish blue or bluish grey; central tail feathers bluish grey, others black with considerable white toward tips; chin whitish passing into buff or ochraceous buff of under parts. *Adult female*: Similar to male but black of crown replaced by dark greyish-blue and under parts paler. *Young* resemble adults of their respective sexes but are paler.

Measurements. *Adult male*: wing, 65.8–68.8 (67.3); tail, 34.5–42.5 (37.7); exposed culmen, 13.5–14.4 (13.9); tarsus, 15–16.5 (15.7). *Adult female*: wing, 63.8–67.9 (65.7) mm.

Field Marks. Smaller than the White-breasted Nuthatch. Our only nuthatch with a white eyebrow stripe. The reddish under parts are diagnostic when well developed, but some individuals show very little buffy underneath. *Voice*: A nasal *nyak nyak nyak*, higher in pitch than that of the White-breasted; also similar *hit* notes.

Habitat. Coniferous and mixedwood forests are preferred, but foraging is done also in deciduous trees to some extent.

Nesting. In a cavity usually excavated by the birds in the soft wood of a decaying tree, stump, or post, and at various heights usually among or near coniferous trees (occasionally 185 m from coniferous trees). The cavity entrance is smeared with pitch, but the function of this is not understood satisfactorily. Nest is composed of materials such as shredded bark, grasses, and rootlets, often lined with hair. Sometimes the eggs are laid on wood chips on the cavity floor. *Eggs*, 4 to 7; white, variously spotted or dotted with reddish browns. Incubation 12 days (F.L. Burns).

Range. Breeds in coniferous forests from southeastern Alaska east to Newfoundland and south in the mountains to southern California, southeastern Arizona, Wyoming, and South Dakota, also to central Minnesota and northern Michigan, and in the Appalachian Mountains to eastern Tennessee and western North Carolina, southern New York, and Massachusetts. Winters within breeding range and somewhat south of it.

White-breasted Nuthatch

Sittelle à poitrine blanche
Sitta carolinensis Latham
Total length: 13 to 15.5 cm
Plate 53

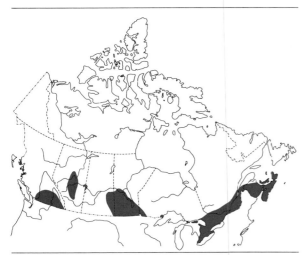

Breeding Distribution of White-breasted Nuthatch

Range in Canada. Permanent resident, breeding in interior southern British Columbia (Lillooet, Okanagan valley, Canal Flats, Waldo); Alberta (Rocky Mountain House and Athabasca south to Calgary. Has increased recently in the province); east-central Saskatchewan (Prince Albert, Moose Mountain, Qu'Appelle valley, perhaps Prince Albert); southern Manitoba (Swan River, Lake St. Martin, Winnipeg, Hillside Beach); western Ontario (Rainy River; Thunder Bay); southern Ontario (Manitoulin Island, North Bay, Ottawa southward); southwestern Quebec (Blue-Sea-Lake, Québec, Montréal, Hatley, Cap-Tourmente; recorded in April north to Arvida without evidence of breeding); New Brunswick (Saint-Léonard, Saint John); Prince Edward Island (Harmony Junction); and Nova Scotia (including Cape Breton Island).

Casual on Vancouver Island (Comox, Victoria).

Bill straight or slightly uptilted, slender, pointed; tail short, as in other nuthatches. Top of head and back of neck black (in females, black of crown usually more or less mixed with grey); back and rump pale bluish-grey; two central tail feathers plain bluish-grey, others black with much white toward tips; sides of head (to above eye), sides of neck, and under parts white; with chestnut on thighs and on under tail coverts.

Measurements *(S. c. cookei). Adult male*: wing, 88.4–94.1 (90.6); tail, 44.5–50 (47.3); exposed culmen, 18.1–20 (19.1); tarsus, 17.5–19.5 (18.6). *Adult female*: wing, 88.5–90.4 (89.5) mm.

Field Marks. A short-tailed small bird working down a tree trunk upside-down is likely to be a nuthatch. The White-breasted Nuthatch, our largest species, forages on tree trunks and larger branches. Its plain-white face (no black line through the eye) is the best distinction from the Red-breasted, for the latter's rusty breast is difficult to see in some individuals. Its black crown readily separates it from the little Pygmy Nuthatch of the West. *Voice*: Commonly a nasal *yank yank yank*; frequently soft notes that sound like *hit hit*; song, a hollow whistled *tew tew tew tew*.

Habitat. In the East, primarily maturer deciduous woodlands and mixedwoods, woodlots, orchards, shade trees of residential areas. In British Columbia, ponderosa pines are favoured.

Nesting. In a hole in a tree at various heights, a natural cavity, woodpecker hole, a cavity excavated by the nuthatches themselves, or in a bird box. Bark shreds, twigs, grass, and leaves are used as cavity fillers, and there is a lining of fur and feathers. *Eggs*, 5 to 9, white, rather evenly spotted with various browns and often a little lavender. Incubation 12 days (A.A. Allen) by the female.

Range. Resident from southern Canada south to southern Mexico (Oaxaca) and central Florida. Absent from much of the Great Plains.

Subspecies. (1) *Sitta carolinensis cookei* Oberholser: eastern Canada westward to Alberta. (2) *S. c. tenuissima* Grinnell, with longer, slenderer bill and darker-grey upper parts: interior southern British Columbia. (3) *S. c. aculeata* Cassin, smaller and paler above than *tenuissima*, less purely white below; casual in southwestern British Columbia according to the *A.O.U. Check-list* (1957). The writer has seen no Canadian specimens of *aculeata*.

Pygmy Nuthatch

Petite Sittelle
Sitta pygmaea Vigors
Total length: 9.4 to 11.3 cm
Plate 53

Breeding Distribution of Pygmy Nuthatch

Range in Canada. Permanent resident in southern interior British Columbia (Okanagan valley, Grand Forks, Newgate). Casual on the coast: Vancouver Island (near Comox, October 1931) and near Vancouver.

Top of head greyish brown; on nape usually a vague area of whitish; rest of upper parts mostly bluish grey; two central tail feathers bluish grey with basal half white, rest of tail feathers blackish with considerable white toward tips; under parts and cheeks (to below eye) pale buffy; the flanks more or less bluish-grey.

Measurements. *Adult male*: wing, 59.5–64.1 (62.2); tail, 30–35 (31.9); exposed culmen, 12.9–14.4 (13.9); tarsus, 14–15 (14.5). *Adult female*: wing, 58.7–65 (61.5) mm.

Field Marks. Our smallest nuthatch. A western species distinguished from our other nuthatches by its greyish-brown crown. At closer range a whitish area on the nape is often discernible. *Voice*: Utterly unlike our other two nuthatches, a very high-pitched, not nasal *te-dee, te-dee*, more like certain notes of the American Goldfinch than a nuthatch's; various cheeping notes. Members of the flocks call frequently.

Habitat. Mainly open ponderosa-pine woodlands.

Nesting. In a cavity in a dead tree, usually excavated by the nuthatches themselves, but sometimes in an old woodpecker hole. *Eggs*, most often 6 to 8; white flecked with reddish browns. Incubation by the female.

Range. Resident in the mountains from southern British Columbia, western Montana, and southwestern South Dakota south to northern Baja California, Arizona, and the central plateau of Mexico south to Morelos and Puebla.

Subspecies. *Sitta pygmaea melanotis* van Rossem.

Family **Certhiidae**:
Creepers

Number of Species in Canada: 1

Most species of creepers are found in the Old World. The one North American species forages on the trunks of trees, advancing up the bark by jerky hitches. It has a stiff, slender, graduated tail, the feather tips of which are sharply pointed. The toenails are relatively large, curved, and sharp, that of the hind toe as long as the toe itself. Its food is mainly insects.

Brown Creeper

Grimpereau brun
Certhia americana Bonaparte
Total length: 12.5 to 14.5 cm
Plate 54

a

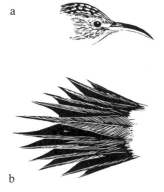

b

Figure 86
Brown Creeper
a) head
b) tail

Bill slender, downcurved, sharp-pointed. Tail rather longish, graduated, the feathers stiffened and sharp-pointed (Figure 86). *Adults (sexes similar)*: Upper parts, deep brown streaked with greyish white, becoming tawny on rump and upper tail coverts: wings mainly dark brown with a patch of pale buff across middle of primaries and secondaries; outer webs of tail feathers pale brown, inner webs dusky; sides of head brown with whitish eyebrow line; under parts white, the flanks and under tail coverts tinged buffy.

Measurements (*C. a. americana*). *Adult male*: wing, 62.4–67.6 (65.0); tail, 49–67.3 (60.6); exposed culmen, 13.3–15.9 (14.4); tarsus, 14.5–15 (14.8). *Adult female*: wing, 61.6–66.5 (63.3) mm.

Field Marks. A small bird with brown white-streaked upper parts, usually seen creeping up a tree trunk with longish tail pressed against the bark. When it reaches the top of a tree, it flies to the bottom of another, the wings showing a pale-buffy patch in flight. At close range the down-curved bill can be seen. *Voice*: At all seasons a very high-pitched *seep*, the pitch similar to that of Golden-crowned Kinglet's *seet seet seet* but only one syllable, more prolonged, and less emphatic. Song, heard in spring, a short wiry warbler-like song: usually about three high-pitched rolling warbles preceded by a slightly longer, shriller note. It is similar to one of the songs of the Blackburnian Warbler.

Breeding Distribution of Brown Creeper

Range in Canada. Breeds in British Columbia (Queen Charlotte Islands, Stikine River, Dease Lake, Tetana Lake, Indianpoint Lake southward, including Vancouver Island); central and southwestern Alberta (Athabasca, Edmonton, Lac la Nonne, Pigeon Lake, Jasper, Banff); central Saskatchewan (Flotten Lake, Big River, Nipawin; probably Kazan Lake and 60 km north of La Ronge); central and southern Manitoba (The Pas, High Portage, Otter Falls); central and southern Ontario (north to Wetigo Hills, Sutton Ridges, Favourable Lake, Lake Attawapiskat, Fort Albany; south to Middlesex, Welland, and Essex counties); southern Quebec (Lake Mistassini, Moisie Bay, Natashquan, Anticosti Island southward); Newfoundland; New Brunswick; Prince Edward Island; and Nova Scotia.

Summer sight records for southern Yukon (Dezadeash Lake, Tagish Lake) and northern Saskatchewan (Wollaston Lake).

Winters mainly within breeding range with some withdrawal probably from higher latitudes. Some move south to and through southern Alberta and southern Saskatchewan (areas in which it is not known to breed).

Habitat. Primarily mature woodland either coniferous or deciduous but forages, especially in winter, in various situations including shade trees in residential areas and has even been seen on the wall of a tall building in the heart of a large city.

Nesting. Usually the nest is under a piece of loose bark of a tree but is reported occasionally in a natural cavity or old woodpecker hole. When built under loose bark, the nest is a crescent-shaped structure of twigs, bark shreds, moss, spiderwebs, and feathers. *Eggs*, 4 to 8, usually 5 or 6; white, sparsely marked with dots of reddish brown. Incubation 14 to 15 days, by the female.

Range. Widely distributed in the Northern Hemisphere of both the New and Old Worlds. In North America from southeastern Alaska east to Newfoundland and south through the western mountains and through Mexico to Nicaragua; in eastern United States to southern Wisconsin and Massachusetts and in the Appalachian Mountains to eastern Tennessee and western North Carolina.

Subspecies. (1) *Certhia americana americana* Bonaparte: eastern Canada to Manitoba. (2) *C. a. montana* Ridgway, less buffy, with purer whites and average slightly larger size than *americana*: Saskatchewan, Alberta, interior British Columbia (east of Cascade and Coast ranges). (3) *C. a. occidentalis* Ridgway, brownest of the races: coasts and coastal islands of British Columbia.

Family **Troglodytidae**: Wrens

Number of Species in Canada: 8

Canadian species are small mostly brownish birds, often barred or spotted on wing, tail, and flanks. Wings short, rounded, with ten primaries. Bill slender, slightly downcurved. They are energetic and inquisitive, rarely still a moment. Usually they carry the tail high, often cocked up over the back. Habitat varies, depending on species, from woodland thickets to marshes, arid canyons, and rock piles. They feed mainly on insects.

Rock Wren

Troglodyte des rochers
Salpinctes obsoletus (Say)
Total length: 13.2 to 15.5 cm
Plate 54

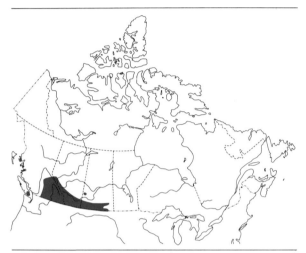

Breeding Distribution of Rock Wren

Range in Canada. Summer resident, breeding in southern British Columbia (Cache Creek, Kamloops, Okanagan valley, Elko, very locally on Vancouver Island: Duncan; species has been recorded without evidence of breeding north to Hanceville, Indianpoint Lake, Mount Robson Provincial Park); southern Alberta (Jasper, Frank, Red Deer River, Milk River); and southern Saskatchewan (Cypress Hills, Pilot Butte, Unity area, northern Last Mountain Lake).

Casual in Ontario (Port Weller, St. Catharines, Ear Falls).

Accidental in Nova Scotia (photo record: Seal Island, 4–8 October 1980).

There are three extraordinary but convincing summer sight records: near Stanton, northwestern Mackenzie (E.O. Höhn); Fort Chipewyan, northern Alberta (Francis Harper); and Churchill, Manitoba (J.A. Crosby and Eva Beckett), with suggestion of possible nesting at the last locality!

Adults: Upper parts greyish brown or brownish grey, finely speckled with black and whitish; rump cinnamon; tail with two central feathers greyish brown barred with dusky, the others broadly tipped with cinnamon-buff and crossed by a subterminal band of black; under parts whitish tinged with pinkish buff on sides and flanks, throat and upper breast more or less finely streaked with dusky. *Young*: Similar to adults but upper parts only faintly dotted with black (white flecks lacking); under parts without streaking of any kind.

Measurements. *Adult male*: wing, 65.3–73.7 (70.3); tail, 49–55 (51.9); exposed culmen, 16.2–19 (17.1); tarsus, 20–22 (21.2). *Adult female*: wing, 66.4–69.3 (68.2) mm.

Field Marks. A large pale greyish-brown wren of rocky places in the West (see Habitat). Spread tail shows buffy tips and subterminal black bar on all but two middle feathers. Adults show dusky throat-streaks (absent in young) or otherwise plain-whitish under parts (see Canyon Wren, which also inhabits rocky places). *Voice*: Song is variable but with many couplets, often a contralto *tra-lee tra-lee tra-lee tra-lee*; also frequent trills.

Habitat. Rocky outcrops, broken cliff faces, talus slopes, canyons, even hard earth banks, often in dry hot situations in mountains and on the western plains.

Nesting. In crevices and crannies in and among rocks (see Habitat). Entrance to nest is often paved with small flat stones. Nest is made of grass, weeds, and rootlets; lined with fine grass, hair, and feathers. *Eggs*, 4 to 8, usually 5 or 6; white sparingly fine-spotted with reddish browns.

Range. Breeds from interior southern British Columbia, southern Alberta, southern Saskatchewan, and northwestern North Dakota south to southern Baja California and through the highlands and deserts of Mexico and Central America to Costa Rica. Winters from Oregon, Montana, and Wyoming southward.

Subspecies. *Salpinctes obsoletus obsoletus* (Say).

Canyon Wren

Troglodyte des canyons
Catherpes mexicanus (Swainson)
Total length: 13.2 to 14.5 cm
Figure 87

Figure 87
Canyon Wren

Range in Canada. Very local permanent resident in southern interior British Columbia (southern Okanagan valley from Osoyoos north to Penticton, perhaps to Naramata; summer sight records reported for the Nelson region).

Bill relatively long and slender. *Adults*: Top of head, nape, and upper back greyish brown changing to chestnut on lower back and rump, the upper parts dotted with black and white; tail rusty, narrowly barred with black; throat and upper breast white, rest of under parts chestnut, barred or dotted with black and flecked with white.

Measurements. *Adult male*: wing, 56.5–61.5 (59.7); tail, 51–54 (52.4); exposed culmen, 19–22.5 (20.5); tarsus, 17.5–18.5 (18.1). *Adult female*: wing, 55–60.5 (57.2) mm (Ridgway).

Field Marks. In Canada to be expected only in interior southern British Columbia. The plain-white throat and upper breast contrasting with chestnut abdomen make it easy to identify. *Voice*: Song is an impressive whistle on a descending scale varying in speed and duration: *dee-ah dee-ah dee-ah dah-dah-dah*. Also *check*.

Habitat. Canyon walls (especially along water), cliff faces, and rockslides.

Nesting. In crevices of rocks or caves. *Eggs*, usually 5 to 6; white with sparse dots of reddish brown.

Range. Resident from interior southern British Columbia, northern Idaho, southeastern Montana, and southwestern South Dakota south through western United States and Mexico to the Isthmus of Tehuantepec and southern Baja California.

Subspecies. *Catherpes mexicanus conspersus* Ridgway.

Carolina Wren

Troglodyte de Caroline
Thryothorus ludovicianus (Latham)
Total length: 13.2 to 15 cm
Plate 54

Breeding Distribution of Carolina Wren

Range in Canada. Permanent resident in southern Ontario (breeding from Point Pelee to Loretto and Canton. Nesting was first recorded in Ontario in 1905 at Point Pelee). Recently recorded nesting in southwestern Quebec (Chambly: one brood raised in 1975).

Rare non-breeding wanderer to Ottawa and Longlac, Ontario; southern Manitoba (Delta, 20 October 1938; Winnipeg, 31 August 1925; Hargrave, 14 November 1972); and New Brunswick (St. Andrews, 8 November 1974 to 4 February 1975; also sight records). Accidental on Madeleine Islands (specimen: 19 August 1971). Sight records for Nova Scotia.

Adults: Upper parts reddish brown, with broad whitish eyebrow stripe, rump with concealed white spots; wings and tail duller brown than back and barred with dusky; under parts mostly buffy, palest on throat (whitish), darkest on breast, sides, and flanks; under tail coverts barred with black.

Measurements. *Adult male*: wing, 54.5–64 (60.4); tail, 45.5–55.5 (50.6); exposed culmen, 15–18 (16.6); tarsus, 20–22.5 (21.5). *Adult female*: wing, 55–59.5 (56.9) mm (Ridgway).

Field Marks. A large reddish-brown wren with a conspicuous whitish eyebrow stripe and buffy under parts, especially the flanks and breast. *Song*: A loud rich whistled *tea-kettle, tea-kettle, tea-kettle*. It sings in all seasons.

Habitat. Thickets and tangles in open woodland, often along streams, either in the country or in residential areas.

Nesting. In various kinds of cavities and crannies either in woodlands or about human habitations. Nest is of twigs, leaves, moss, bark fibres, and is lined with softer materials such as feathers, hair, fine rootlets, and fine grass. *Eggs*, usually 4 to 6; white or buff, usually heavily spotted with browns. Incubation said to be 12 to 14 days (Bent), by the female.

Range. Resident from southeastern Nebraska east to southeastern Massachusetts and south through central and coastal Texas to northeastern Mexico, the Gulf Coast, and southern Florida.

Subspecies. *Thryothorus ludovicianus ludovicianus* (Latham).

Bewick's Wren

Troglodyte de Bewick
Thryomanes bewickii (Audubon)
Total length: 12.5 to 14 cm
Plate 54

Breeding Distribution of Bewick's Wren

Range in Canada. Permanent resident in southwestern British Columbia (Victoria, Comox, Vancouver, Chilliwack, Howe Sound) and in extreme southern Ontario (Point Pelee; recorded in summer north to York and Grey counties. A recent arrival in Ontario, first recorded in 1898; first nest found 1950). Casual at Deep River, Ontario (photo record: 26 June 1971).

Adults: Upper parts brown, with a conspicuous whitish line over eye; flight feathers with more or less dusky barring; central two tail feathers brown barred with dusky, outer ones blackish brown, their outer web with white markings and broadly tipped with greyish white; under parts greyish white, the sides and flanks tinged with brown, under tail coverts barred with blackish.

Measurements *(T. b. calophonus). Adult male*: wing, 51.5–56.5 (54.2); tail, 51–57 (52.7); exposed culmen, 14.6–17.2 (15.9); tarsus, 19.5–20.5 (20.1). *Adult female*: wing, 48.8–52.1 (50.9) mm.

Field Marks. Its conspicuous whitish eyebrow streak distinguishes it from the House Wren. Its *less reddish*-brown upper parts, greyish (no buffy or rusty wash) breast and belly, and slenderer build separate it from the Carolina Wren. When the white edge of the tail can be seen, this distinguishes it from both. Its tail is noticeably longer too. *Voice*: song is variable and far-carrying, often a little like that of a Song Sparrow. Also has a buzzing scold note.

Habitat. Thickets and brushy places in farming country, urban areas, or open woods.

Nesting. In various kinds of cavities about the habitations of man, including bird boxes. Also in old woodpecker holes, in knotholes in fallen trees, and even in dense brush piles. Sticks, leaves, straw, and other debris are used as nest cavity fillers, and this is lined with feathers or similar soft material.

Range. Southwestern British Columbia, central Washington, southern Utah, southern Nebraska, southern Michigan, extreme southern Ontario, central Pennsylvania, and Virginia, south to southern Baja California and southern Mexico (Oaxaca) and to northern parts of the Gulf states.

Subspecies. (1) *Thryomanes bewickii calophonus* Oberholser: southwestern British Columbia. (2) *T. b. altus* Aldrich: southern Ontario.

House Wren

Troglodyte familier
Troglodytes aedon Vieillot
Total length: 11.4 to 13.5 cm
Plate 54

Tail short, bill slightly downcurved and pointed, as is typical of wrens. *Adults (sexes similar)*: Upper parts dull greyish-brown, the rump brighter and often with a few dusky bars and with concealed white spotting; tail brownish, narrowly barred with blackish; sides of head pale grey or buffy with a barely perceptible light eyebrow line; under parts dingy, more whitish medially, the breast tinged with buffy grey, the sides and flanks pale brown, more or less faintly barred with dusky.

Measurements *(T. a. parkmanii). Adult male*: wing, 49.6–53.3 (51.7); tail, 40–46.5 (43.6); exposed culmen, 12–13 (12.4); tarsus, 16.5–18.5 (17.5). *Adult female*: wing, 47.6–51.4 (49.9) mm.

Field Marks. Small size, brown upper parts, and stubby, often cocked-up tail indicate a wren. The House Wren is recognizable by its lack of definite markings, even the eyebrow stripe is usually invisible. Lacks the usually definite eyebrow stripe and heavily barred sides of the smaller Winter Wren and has a less stubby tail; lacks the eyebrow line and white tail spots of Bewick's Wren. Usually habitat separates it from the two marsh wrens; but the Carolina, Canyon, and Rock wrens all have distinctive markings. *Voice*: Sings with great frequency, over long periods of the day, a rapid, chattering, rather unmusical, but pleasant song, which rises in pitch at the beginning and falls off toward the end. It is easily recognized when heard a few times. Also a scolding, grating chatter.

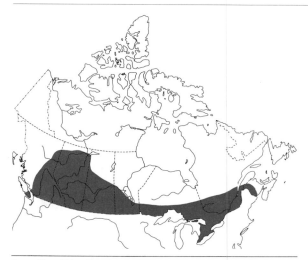

Breeding Distribution of House Wren

Range in Canada. Summer resident, breeding across southern, and in central-eastern, British Columbia (Comox, Prince George, Kamloops, Okanagan valley, Cranbrook; also Peace River parklands; probably Fort Nelson. Recorded in spring at Clearwater); northern, central, and southern Alberta (Keg River and Murdock Creek southward, but scarce in the southwestern mountainous corner); central and southern Saskatchewan (Dorintosh, Emma Lake, Nipawin, Cypress Hills, Regina. Recorded in summer at Kazan Lake); southern Manitoba (The Pas, Brandon, Lake St. Martin, Emerson, Sprague); central and southern Ontario (Malachi, Sioux Lookout, Lake Nipigon, Lake Abitibi southward); southwestern Quebec (Amos, Arvida, Rivière-du-Loup, Hull, Montréal, Hatley); and New Brunswick (Fredericton, Grand Falls).

Scarce visitor to Nova Scotia (Gasper eau, Wolfville, Bridgetown, Liverpool, Sable Island) and Prince Edward Island, but breeding evidence lacking. Casual at Hazelton, British Columbia, and Churchill, Manitoba. Casual visitor to Newfoundland (sight record: one at St. John's, 6–9 December 1983).

Habitat. Deciduous thickets and shrubbery in various situations in woodland openings and open woodland, along prairie coulees and shelter belts, in mountain valleys, burntlands, and especially near human habitations on farmland and in residential areas. In breeding season a cavity suitable for nesting must be in the vicinity.

Nesting. In cavities of extremely varied types but usually a hole in a tree or a bird box. It is extremely adaptable, however, and has been known to use various objects (such as pockets in clothing, an old shoe, even a cow skull), which have been left hanging on trees, posts, or in sheds; in cavities in houses and in farm machinery or old automobiles, and behind the loose bark of a dead tree. The nest is a mass of twigs and rubbish as cavity filler, with a lining of soft materials like hair or feathers. *Eggs*, most often 6 to 8; pinkish white, thickly dotted with reddish brown. Incubation 13 to 14 days (Baldwin and Kendeigh), by the female.

Range. Breeds from southern Canada south to northern Baja California, southeastern Arizona, northern Texas, northern Arkansas, Tennessee, and northern Georgia. Winters from the southern part of the breeding range south to southern Mexico, the Gulf Coast, and southern Florida.

Subspecies. (1) *Troglodytes aedon aedon* Vieillot: New Brunswick, possibly extreme central-southern Quebec (Hatley). (2) *T. a. baldwini* Oberholser, allegedly somewhat darker and less rufescent than *aedon* but poorly marked: Quebec, southern Ontario (north to Bigwood, Lake Nipissing, Algonquin Provincial Park). (3) *T. a. parkmanii* Audubon, paler and greyer, slightly larger than *baldwini*: British Columbia, Alberta, Saskatchewan, Manitoba, western and central Ontario (Malachi, Sioux Lookout, Lake Abitibi). Areas of intergradation of the respective races in the East require refinement because of lack of adequate material from critical areas.

Remarks. As its name implies, the House Wren often summers near houses where the grounds provide suitable bushy cover and a nesting cavity. A bird box with a 2.5 cm entrance is often accepted. House Wrens seem to be forever fussing and scolding over nothing at all. The male sings tirelessly from dawn to dusk, and in the lazy quiet of the noonday heat its energy is completely anomalous. Insects make up most of its menu.

As mentioned above, under Nesting, this wren utilizes a wide variety of cavities for nesting. Sometimes these are unwisely chosen. Once a House Wren attempted for some days to fill the bottomless space between the roof and fly of the writer's tent. It deposited over a peck of sticks on the ground below, before it abandoned the attempt. Another pair nested in the door of an old discarded automobile. On sunny afternoons the heat within the metal door was intolerable, and the female remained inside for less than a minute at a time, emerging panting with open bill. Eventually the nest was abandoned, and the eggs were found to be baked hard.

Two broods, sometimes three, are raised in a season. House Wrens do not remain mated permanently or even throughout a whole year. In fact, they change mates between two nesting periods in the same season, and there is evidence that males sometimes practise polygamy.

Winter Wren

Troglodyte des forêts
Troglodytes troglodytes (Linnaeus)
Total length: 10 to 11.4 cm
Plate 54

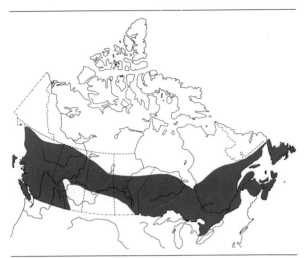

Breeding Distribution of Winter Wren

Range in Canada. Breeds in British Columbia (commonly on the coast and coastal islands and north at least to Stikine River and Dease Lake, probably to Haines Road near the Alaska border; locally in the interior: Driftwood River, Likely, Okanagan Landing, Lytton, Rocher Déboulé, Mount Revelstoke National Park, probably Tupper Creek; apparently absent from much of the drier more sparsely wooded southern parts); northern and northwestern Alberta (south to Athabasca and in the mountains: Jasper, Banff, Waterton Lakes national parks); central Saskatchewan (Cross, Island, Cree, and McLennan lakes); Manitoba (Overflowing River, Hillside Beach); central and southern Ontario (Big Trout Lake, Fort Albany; Middlesex, Waterloo, and Prince Edward counties and northward to the Hudson Bay lowlands); southern Quebec (Lake Mistassini, Lake Sainte-Anne, Natashquan, Saint-Augustin, Belles Amours Bay, Anticosti Island; Aylmer, Montréal, Percé, Madeleine Islands); southern Labrador (L'Anse-au-Loup); Newfoundland; New Brunswick; Prince Edward Island; and Nova Scotia.

Winters in small numbers in British Columbia, southern Ontario, southwestern Quebec, New Brunswick, Nova Scotia, and rarely Newfoundland.

Recorded in summer in southern Yukon (Sheldon Lake, August 1944) and in southern Mackenzie (upper Buffalo River).

Smaller than the House Wren; tail much shorter. *Adults (T. t. hiemalis)*: Upper parts reddish brown; the back, scapulars, and rump lightly barred with dusky; rump with concealed white spots; wings and tail mostly brown, barred with dusky; narrow buffy line over eye; under parts pale brownish, the abdomen and flanks darker and more or less barred and speckled with dusky. *Young* darker below, the eyebrow stripe indistinct.

Measurements *(T. t. hiemalis). Adult male*: wing, 45.5–49.1 (47.4); tail, 26.5–30.5 (29.5); exposed culmen, 11.3–12.3 (11.9); tarsus, 17.5–18.5 (18.1). *Adult female*: wing, 41.6–50 (45.0) mm.

Field Marks. A tiny wren, with reddish-brown upper parts and very stubby cocked-up tail, usually seen in woodlands and woodland tangles. Smaller and darker than the House Wren and with distinctly barred flanks, usually an eyebrow line (but often not perceptible in young), and shorter tail. Has a habit of bobbing. *Voice*: Very different from that of the House Wren. Song an amazing performance for such a small bird, a sustained (up to eight or nine seconds), loud, and extremely varied procession of rapid notes, occasionally interspersed with a trill or a slight pause, after which the song goes on again, the notes tumbling over one another. Alarm note, a double *kip-kip* (but often only one *kip*), suggests a little the Song Sparrow's *chimp* (which is usually single) but is sharper.

Habitat. In the nesting season mostly maturer coniferous woodland, typically in shadowy moist forests where the floor is strewn with brushy tangles and fallen trees, especially along streams and lakes; also brush and slashing in smaller forest openings. Forages in the low forest stratum, but much of the singing is done also in the tops of tall conifers. In migration both coniferous and deciduous woodlands are frequented, especially those with brush-strewn floors.

Nesting. Very often in a cavity in the earthy roots of an upturned tree, in and under old stumps and brush piles, in mossy banks and in other less common situations. The nest is rather bulky and is made of twigs, moss, and grasses with an entrance on the side leading to the interior, which is lined with feathers or fur. *Eggs*, most often 5 or 6; white, dotted (usually sparingly) with reddish brown. Incubation 14 to 17 days, by the female.

Range. Northern Hemisphere of both the New and Old Worlds. In North America from the Aleutian Islands and southeastern Alaska eastward to Newfoundland, and south to central California, central Idaho, the Great Lakes, western and central Massachusetts, and in the Appalachian Mountains to northern Georgia. Also in Iceland and much of Eurasia. In winter retreats from the colder more northern parts of its range in Canada.

Subspecies. (1) *Troglodytes troglodytes hiemalis* Vieillot: central-eastern British Columbia (Peace River parklands) and Alberta (except the Rocky Mountains) eastward through Saskatchewan, Manitoba, Ontario, Quebec, Newfoundland, New Brunswick, Prince Edward Island, and Nova Scotia. (2) *T. t. pacificus* Baird, darker with less distinctly barred upper parts: British Columbia (except Peace River parklands) and the mountains of southwestern Alberta.

Sedge Wren

(Short-billed Marsh Wren)

Troglodyte à bec court
Cistothorus platensis (Latham)
Total length: 10 to 11.4 cm
Plate 54

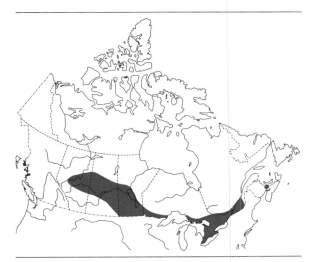

Breeding Distribution of Sedge Wren

Range in Canada. Breeds in central-eastern Alberta (Cold Lake, Gainford; probably Bonnyville and Glenevis); southern Saskatchewan (Laura, Saskatoon, Nipawin, Quill Lakes, Qu'Appelle valley, Regina); southern Manitoba (The Pas, Norway House, Lyleton, Lake St. Martin, Sprague); western Ontario (Indian Bay, Wabigoon, Kenora, Thunder Bay region); southern Ontario (north to Sault Ste. Marie, Lake Nipissing, Ottawa); extreme southwestern Quebec (Perkins, Lanoraie bog, Hatley, Sorel, Cap-Tourmente); and southern New Brunswick (Midgic).

Casual visitant to Nova Scotia (specimen: Seal Island, 2 October 1967).

A very small wren with streaks on top of head and on back. *Adults*: Upper parts brown streaked with blackish and white; rump, upper tail coverts, and tail barred with dusky; sides of head buffy with usually a faint narrow dusky line through eye and without any *distinct* light eyebrow stripe; under parts white with buffy wash across breast, and on sides, flanks, and under tail coverts.

Measurements. *Adult male*: wing, 43.4–46.2 (44.6); tail, 32.5–41 (37.9); exposed culmen, 10.3–11.6 (10.9); tarsus, 15.5–17 (16.3). *Adult female*: wing, 41.5–45.1 (43.5) mm.

Field Marks. The Sedge and Marsh wrens both have streaked backs. The Sedge Wren, compared with the Marsh Wren, has top of head streaked (instead of plain blackish-brown) and a scarcely visible buffy eyebrow stripe (Marsh Wren has a well-marked white one). Habitat often helps to distinguish the two; the Sedge Wren inhabits marsh grass rather than cattails. *Voice*: Song, an unmusical effort, begins with two or more dry *tsips* (like the sound produced by hitting two small stones together), followed by rapid unmusical notes on a descending scale and often a little trill at the end.

Habitat. Moist grass and sedge marshes, bogs, and damp meadows, often with a scattering of low bushes and often bordering willows or alders. It does not ordinarily inhabit cattails.

Nesting. In grassy marshes. Nest, a ball of grass well hidden in the upright grass or sedge to which it is attached and with an entrance at the side. Usually several dummy nests are made in the vicinity. *Eggs*, 4 to 8, usually 7, white. Incubation 12 to 14 days (L.H. Walkinshaw).

Range. Breeds from southeastern Saskatchewan east to eastern New Brunswick and south to Arkansas and southeastern Virginia; also from southern Mexico south through Central America and south to southern South America.

Subspecies. *Cistothorus platensis stellaris* (Naumann).

Marsh Wren

(formerly Long-billed Marsh Wren)

Troglodyte des marais
Cistothorus palustris (Wilson)
Total length: 10 to 13.2 cm
Plate 54

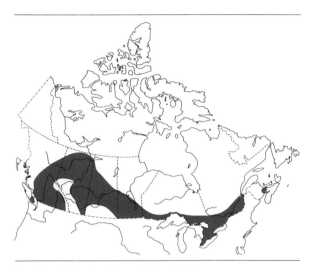

Breeding Distribution of Marsh Wren

Range in Canada. Breeds in suitable marshes in central and southern British Columbia (Vanderhoof region, Kleena Kleene, Duncan, Vancouver, Okanagan valley, Columbia River); Alberta (Lake Athabasca southward to Red Deer and locally at Lake Newell, Pakowki Lake, probably Cypress Hills. Not known in the mountains of the southwest); central Saskatchewan (Kazan Lake, Emma Lake, Nipawin, Devil's Lake, Regina, Moose Mountain, Gainsborough); southern Manitoba (Riding Mountain, Lake St. Martin, Lyleton, Whitemouth); western Ontario (Indian Bay, Wabigoon, Sibley Provincial Park); southern Ontario (north at least to Nipigon, Kapuskasing, and Ottawa; probably Manitoulin Island and Lake Nipissing; one exceptional record north to the vicinity of North Point on southern James Bay); southwestern Quebec (Buckingham, Montréal, Magog, Sorel, probably Cap-Tourmente); and southern New Brunswick (Midgic, Red Head Marsh).

Winters in southern British Columbia; rarely in southern Ontario (Point Pelee). Scarce migrant or casual visitant in Nova Scotia (Port Joli Harbour, Wallace, Wolfville).

Adults: Top of head plain blackish-brown; on back a triangular blackish-brown patch streaked with white; rest of upper parts mostly brown, the tail barred dusky; white stripe over eye; under parts whitish, the sides and flanks plain buffy-brown, the breast often lightly tinged with same.

Measurements *(C. p. dissaeptus)*. *Adult male*: wing, 49–55.8 (51.1); tail, 35.5–43 (40.5); exposed culmen, 14.1–15.5 (14.6); tarsus, 20.5–21.5 (21.3). *Adult female*: wing, 47.2–51.6 (49.1) mm.

Field Marks. Any wren deep in a wet cattail marsh is probably this one. The Marsh Wren is larger, has no streaks on the dark crown, shows a *well-defined* white line over the eye, and occurs in wetter marshy places than the Sedge Wren. *Voice*: Song is rather low-pitched but vigorous, bubbly, and staccato.

Habitat. Cattail, tule, and bulrush shallow-water marshes.

Nesting. In cattail, tule, and bulrush marshes. The nest is a largish ball of marsh vegetation with side entrance and is attached to upright marsh plants. The exterior is of long, coarse vegetation, and the inner lining is of soft materials such as cattail down and feathers. In addition to the nest used to house the eggs and young, which is built by the female, there are also several incomplete extra nests built by the male. The males of most wrens make such dummy nests, the function of which is not satisfactorily known. *Eggs*, most frequently 5 or 6, are dull brown (thus different from other wrens), finely dotted or spotted with darker browns. Incubation 13 days (W.A. Welter), by the female.

Range. Breeds from southern Canada south to northern Baja California, central New Mexico, the Gulf Coast (Texas to Florida) and to central Florida on the Atlantic Coast.

Subspecies. (1) *Cistothorus palustris dissaeptus* Bangs: Breeds in southern Ontario, southwestern Quebec and New Brunswick. (2) *C. p. iliacus* (Ridgway) (paler and more brownish than *dissaeptus*): western Ontario (Indian Bay) and Manitoba. (3) *C. p. laingi* (Harper) (much paler and buffier than *iliacus*): Alberta (east of the Rockies), Saskatchewan. (4) *C. p. plesius* Oberholser (much less rufescent than *laingi*): central and southern interior British Columbia. (5) *C. p. paludicola* Baird, compared with *plesius*, darker and less greyish: southwestern British Columbia (Duncan, Vancouver, Huntingdon).

Also (6) *C. p. palustris* (Wilson) of the U.S. coast (Rhode Island to Virginia) is a casual visitant to Nova Scotia (Port Joli Harbour), and (7) *C. p. waynei* (Dingle and Sprunt), of the U.S. coast (southeastern Virginia and North Carolina) is accidental in New Brunswick (Grand Manan, Fairville).

Family **Cinclidae:**
Dippers

Number of Species in Canada: 1

Compactly built aquatic birds that dive and swim well, can walk on water bottom, but have unwebbed toes. Plumage dense; bill straight, short, laterally compressed; tail square or slightly rounded; wings short.

American Dipper

Cincle d'Amérique
Cinclus mexicanus Swainson
Total length: 17.5 to 21.5 cm
Plate 54

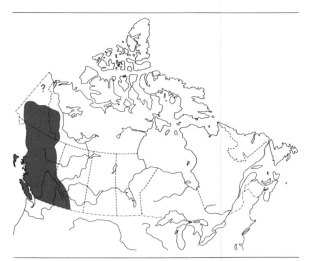

Breeding Distribution of American Dipper

Range in Canada. Permanent resident along mountain streams in central and southern Yukon (Coal Creek, Ogilvie Mountains, Canyon Lake, Rose River. Perhaps north to the Old Crow region where reported in April), southwestern Mackenzie (Vermilion Creek, Nahanni National Park) throughout British Columbia (including Queen Charlotte and Vancouver islands), and southwestern Alberta (Jasper, Banff, and Waterton Lakes national parks). Winters within most of breeding range including Yukon and southwestern Mackenzie (Nahanni National Park).

Casual in southern Mackenzie (Buffalo River near Great Slave Lake) and in southwestern Saskatchewan (Cypress Hills region: several sight records).

Bill laterally compressed (deeper than wide), tail short, plumage compact and dense. Whole body slaty grey, the head and neck tinged with brown, top of head darkest; narrow white mark on upper and lower eyelids.

Measurements. *Adult male*: wing, 83.1–94.6 (91.1); tail, 42.5–52 (49.1); exposed culmen, 18.5–20.1 (18.9); tarsus, 27.5–31 (29.1). *Adult female*: wing, 83.3–93.9 (87.4) mm.

Field Marks. Unmistakable. A chunky short-tailed all-grey bird, smaller than a robin, found about western mountain streams. When standing, it has a habit of rapidly raising and lowering its body by bending the legs; hence the name "dipper." Feeds in and under water at all seasons. Flight is buzzy, usually follows the stream, not far above the water; shows no distinctive markings in wings or tail. *Voice*: A clear melodious song is given at all seasons and in all kinds of weather. Alarm note *tzeet*, often repeated.

Habitat. Mountain streams at various elevations up to timberline; usually fast-moving streams that remain open in winter but sometimes mountain ponds or lakeshores.

Nesting. On a ledge, rocky niche, or crossbeam under a bridge or similar support along a stream, sometimes near or behind a waterfall. Nest, a bulky dome-shaped structure with an outer shell of moss and some grass. There is an entrance hole on the side leading to an inner bowl of grass. *Eggs*, usually 4 or 5; white. Incubation by the female only, about 16 days (H.W. Hann; G.J. Bakus).

Range. From the Aleutian Islands and north-central Alaska, north-central Yukon, southwestern Alberta, north-central Montana, and southwestern South Dakota (Black Hills) south to southern California and through the highlands of Mexico and Central America to western Panama.

Subspecies. *Cinclus mexicanus unicolor* Bonaparte.

Family **Muscicapidae**: Old World Warblers, Kinglets, Gnatcatchers, Old World Flycatchers, Thrushes, Babblers, and Allies

Number of Species in Canada: 22

This is a vast assemblage of ten-primaried songbird taxa, several of them former families, now downgraded to subfamilies. Most of the groups have Old World affinities, only two of its subfamilies being represented in Canada.

Subfamily **Sylviinae**: Old World Warblers, Gnatcatchers, and Kinglets

A very large subfamily, most species of which are confined to the Old World. It is represented in Canada by three resident species and one accidental. The kinglets are tiny arboreal birds.

Arctic Warbler

Pouillot boréal
Phylloscopus borealis (Blasius)
Total length: 12 cm
Plate 61

Status in Canada. Accidental on Prince Patrick Island (Mould Bay, 21 July 1949), N.W.T. The specimen, too large for the Alaska race *kennicotti*, is referred to *P. borealis borealis* (Blasius).

Suggests a small vireo but bill tip sharp, never slightly hooked. Much duller than autumn Tennessee Warbler, decidedly less yellowish below, larger with decidedly heavier bill. *Adults*: Upper parts greyish olive; line over eye pale yellowish or whitish; very narrow whitish wing bar (obscure in worn plumage); under parts plain whitish tinged with yellow, the sides and flanks tinged with greyish olive.

Golden-crowned Kinglet

Roitelet à couronne dorée
Regulus satrapa Lichtenstein
Total length: 9 to 10 cm
Plate 58

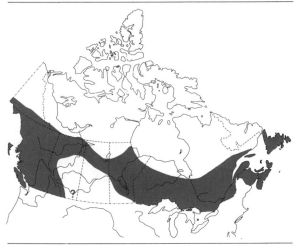

Breeding Distribution of Golden-crowned Kinglet

Range in Canada. Breeds in coniferous woodland in southern Yukon (Kathleen River, Canyon Mountain near Whitehorse, and Kluane Game Sanctuary); throughout British Columbia (including coastal islands); northern and southwestern Alberta (Mile 110 Mackenzie Highway, Wood Buffalo National Park, Fort Chipewyan, Swan Hills, and the Rocky Mountains of the southwest; probably the Cypress Hills); central Saskatchewan (sparsely: 65 km north of Lac La Ronge, Waddy Lake, Crean Lake region, Doré Lake, Fort-à-la-Corne Forest Reserve); northern, central, and southeastern Manitoba (Churchill, Overflowing River, Duck Mountain, Julius); Ontario (Big Trout Lake, Sutton Ridges, Fort Albany; south rarely to York County, London; possibly to Niagara Peninsula); southern Quebec (Lake Mistassini, Lake Méchant, Gaspé Peninsula, Anticosti Island southward, perhaps east to Petit Mécatina River); Newfoundland; New Brunswick; Prince Edward Island; and Nova Scotia.

Possibly breeds in extreme southwestern Mackenzie (summer sight-records in Nahanni National Park).

Winters in southern and coastal British Columbia, southern Alberta, southern Saskatchewan (Nipawin, Regina), southern Manitoba, southern Ontario, southern Quebec, the Maritime Provinces, and Newfoundland.

A very small bird with fine-pointed bill. *Adult male*: Centre of crown orange with outer border yellow, this in turn bordered (on forehead and sides of crown) by black; line over eye dull white; back of neck greyish, changing to greenish olive on back (brightening on rump); wings and tail dusky, the feathers edged with yellowish; two whitish wing bars; under parts whitish tinged with buffy olive. *Adult female*: Similar to adult male, but centre of crown all yellow (no orange). *Young* for a short time after leaving nest lack the crown patch, texture of body plumage is looser, coloration is more brownish-olive. White eyebrow line distinguishes them from Ruby-crowned Kinglet.

Measurements *(R. s. satrapa)*. *Adult male*: wing, 54.3–58.8 (57.1); tail, 41.5–45 (43.3); exposed culmen, 6.3–8.5 (7.7); tarsus, 16.5–17.5 (17.2). *Adult female*: wing, 52.7–56 (54.8) mm.

Field Marks. Kinglets are tiny olive-green and grey birds, smaller and shorter-tailed than warblers. Both species are very active in the tree branches and have a characteristic and frequent habit of flicking the wings. The yellow crown with black border and the white eyebrow stripe distinguish this species from the Ruby-crowned Kinglet. The voices of the two are very different. *Voice*: A call frequently given at all times of the year is a hurried high-pitched lisping *tsee-tsee-tsee*; also a single *tsee*, similar to the call of the Brown Creeper but less prolonged. Song very high-pitched, the first parts like the call-notes and ending in an unmusical twitter.

Habitat. Coniferous forests and groves, mixedwoods with a preponderance of conifers. In migration and winter, also deciduous trees or bushes.

Nesting. Usually well up in a coniferous tree (but sometimes low). Nest of green mosses, lichens, strips of bark, rootlets; lined with feathers. Nest is spherical with the opening at the top. It is usually suspended or partly so from twigs but sometimes is placed on a limb. *Eggs*, 5 to 10, usually 8 or 9; whitish or creamy with pale-brown dots or spots.

Range. In coniferous woodland from southeastern Alaska east across southern Canada to Newfoundland and south to southern California and Arizona (also the highlands of southern Mexico and Guatemala), central Minnesota, northern Michigan, southern Ontario, northern New York, southern Maine, and in the mountains south to Tennessee and western South Carolina. Winters north to southern Canada.

Subspecies. (1) *Regulus satrapa satrapa* Lichtenstein: eastern Canada and west to northeastern Alberta. (2) *R. s. amoenus* van Rossem (upper parts brighter and less greyish than in *satrapa*): interior British Columbia and mountains of Alberta. (3) *R. s. olivaceus* Baird (darker, more brownish above than *amoenus*, under parts average more dusky): coastal British Columbia, west of the Cascade Mountains.

Remarks. It seems surprising to find these feathered mites happily wintering in Canada when many larger species have gone south to warmer climates. In dim coniferous trees that shelter them from the wind, they flit about so actively that it is often hard to see them clearly. They feed almost entirely on insects (including the spruce-bud moth) and spiders. They glean insects, their eggs, and hidden larvae, from branches and bark and also are skilful flycatchers.

Ruby-crowned Kinglet

Roitelet à couronne rubis
Regulus calendula (Linnaeus)
Total length: 9.5 to 11.3 cm
Plate 58

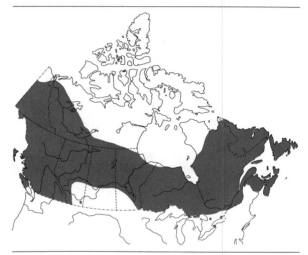

Breeding Distribution of Ruby-crowned Kinglet

Range in Canada. Breeds in Yukon (widely in the south; recorded in late May north to Old Crow); Mackenzie (Aklavik, Norman Wells, Nahanni Mountains, Fort Simpson, upper Grandin River, northern Wood Buffalo National Park); northern Saskatchewan (Lake Athabasca, Hasbala Lake); northern Manitoba (Churchill, Herchmer); northern Ontario; northern Quebec (Lake Guillaume-Delisle, Feuilles River, Koroc River, Hutte sauvage Lake); central Labrador (Attikamagen Lake, Goose Bay, Cartwright; perhaps north to Okak); and Newfoundland south through British Columbia; northern, central, and southwestern Alberta (south to edge of the parklands and through the mountains of the southwest; Cypress Hills; only a migrant on the prairies); central Saskatchewan (Waskesiu Lake, Nipawin); southern Manitoba (Duck Mountain, Lake St. Martin, Whitemouth, Julius; but only a migrant in extreme southwestern corner); southern Ontario (south very locally to Guelph, Kingston, Sandbanks Provincial Park, and near Fort Erie); southern Quebec (Montréal, Lac Auger, Lake Fraser, Woburn, Biencourt, Gaspé Peninsula, Madeleine Islands); New Brunswick; Prince Edward Island; and Nova Scotia.

Winters in southwestern British Columbia.

Similar in form and colour to Golden-crowned Kinglet but differs in head markings. *Adult male*: Top of head with a patch of vermilion; rest of upper parts greyish olive, brightening on rump and edges of flight feathers (flight feathers dusky); two whitish wing bars; edges of tertials whitish; sides of head plain greyish, except whitish eye-ring; under parts plain pale-buffy grey, the flanks more yellowish. *Adult female*: Similar to adult male but without crown patch. *Young* (for a short time after leaving nest) lack a crown patch in both sexes but can be distinguished from young Golden-crowned Kinglets by lack of a pale eyebrow stripe.

Measurements *(R. c. calendula)*. *Adult male*: wing, 55.9–61.1 (57.8); tail, 42–46.5 (43.5); exposed culmen, 7.7–9.4 (8.7); tarsus, 18.5–19.5 (19.0). *Adult female*: wing, 53.4–57.6 (55.7) mm.

Field Marks. Kinglets are olive green above and grey below, tiny active birds of tree branches, smaller than warblers, and with a characteristic habit of nervously flicking the wings. The Ruby-crowned Kinglet's whitish eye-ring and complete lack of any stripes over the eye easily separate it from the Golden-crowned Kinglet. The ruby crown-patch of the male is often hard to see. *Voice*: Song, the last parts of which are surprisingly loud for so small a bird, is variable but usually in three parts: *tee tee tee, chur chur chur, teedadee teedadee teedadee*. Scold notes: *churr* or *cheater*. Also a husky *did-it* (sometimes only a single note), which readily distinguishes the species.

Habitat. In nesting season, coniferous forests, woodlands, muskegs, also mixedwoods. In migration, all kinds of woodland; also thickets of tall shrubbery such as alder and willow.

Nesting. In coniferous trees at almost any height but most often well up. Nest and *eggs*, usually 5 to 11 to a clutch, are very similar to those of the Golden-crowned Kinglet.

Range. Breeds in coniferous woodland from northwestern Alaska east across Canada to southern Labrador and Newfoundland and south to Guadalupe Island off Baja California, central Arizona, central New Mexico, central Saskatchewan, northern Michigan, southern Ontario, northern Maine, and Nova Scotia. Winters from southern British Columbia and northern interior United States south to Guatemala, the Gulf Coast of United States, and Florida.

Subspecies. (1) *Regulus calendula calendula* (Linnaeus): Yukon, northern British Columbia, Alberta (except southwestern mountains), Saskatchewan, Manitoba, Ontario, Quebec, Labrador, Newfoundland, New Brunswick, Prince Edward Island, Nova Scotia. (2) *R. c. cineraceus* Grinnell (greyer and paler than *calendula*): interior southern and south-central British Columbia, southwestern Alberta (Waterton Lakes and Banff national parks). (3) *R. c. grinnelli* Palmer (darker than the preceding two subspecies): British Columbia coast and coastal islands.

Blue-gray Gnatcatcher

Gobe-moucherons gris-bleu
Polioptila caerulea (Linnaeus)
Total length: 10 to 12.5 cm
Plate 58

Breeding Distribution of Blue-gray Gnatcatcher

Range in Canada. Breeds in southern Ontario
(Tobermory: 19 km south; London; Point
Pelee; Turkey Point; Port Colborne; Oshawa;
Kingston; Chaffey's Locks; possibly Carlsbad
Springs) and southwestern Quebec (Montréal,
Saint-Bruno, Oka).

Rare in migration north to Ottawa, Ontario;
Lake Saint-Jean, Quebec (photo 17 May 1975);
New Brunswick (Grand Manan); Nova Scotia
(photo: Seal Island, 25 May 1975 and various
sight records east to Louisbourg); and Prince
Edward Island (photo: Diligent Pond,
30 September 1978).

Accidental in British Columbia (photo
record: Victoria, 10 November 1964) and
Newfoundland.

Bill slender, tail rather long (nearly same length as wing), outermost primary very small. *Adult male*: Upper parts mainly greyish-blue; across forehead a narrow line of black, this extending backward over eye; wings slaty, tertials margined whitish; tail mainly black, the outermost feather white, the next mainly white, and the third (from outside) tipped with white; sides of head pale grey; under parts white, the breast and sides with a bluish-grey wash. *Adult female*: Similar to adult male but upper parts less decidedly bluish and without the black lines on forehead and sides of crown.

Measurements. *Adult male*: wing, 49–54.5 (52.1); tail, 48–54 (50.3); exposed culmen, 9–11 (9.9); tarsus, 16.5–18 (17.2). *Adult female*: wing, 50–52 (50.9) mm.

Field Marks. A slender tiny bird with greyish-blue upper parts, white eye-ring, longish black tail with white outer borders. Often cocks and flits tail. Common call, a high-pitched, thin complaining *chee*.

Habitat. Open mature woodland, tall shade trees, brushy thickets with scattered trees. Although it is found most often well up in mature trees, it may be found also in low thickets and small growth.

Nesting. Usually in tall trees, infrequently in a sapling, anywhere from 3 to 18 m above ground but usually high. Nest is saddled on a limb or placed in the fork of a branch. It is compact and similar to a hummingbird's, being made of various soft plant materials held together with spider web and ornamented on the outside with lichens. *Eggs*, usually 4 or 5; pale blue to whitish with small spots of different browns. Incubation about 13 days (Bent).

Range. Northern California, Utah, eastern Nebraska, southern Wisconsin, extreme southern Ontario, central-western New York, and southern New Jersey, south through Mexico to Guatemala, the Gulf Coast of United States, and the Bahama Islands. Winters from southern United States southward.

Subspecies. *Polioptila caerulea caerulea* (Linnaeus).

Subfamily **Turdinae:** Thrushes, Bluebirds, and Solitaires

A large subfamily widely distributed in the world. There is much variation in the appearance of the many species but the young in juvenal plumage (and the adults of many species as well) are spotted. Thrushes have undivided tarsi and ten primaries (the outermost is often small or spurious). The family contains some of the world's finest singers, notably the Nightingale of Europe and the Hermit Thrush of North America.

Siberian Rubythroat

Calliope de Sibérie
Luscinia calliope (Pallas)
Total length: 14 cm
Figure 88

Figure 88
Siberian Rubythroat

Status in Canada. Accidental in Ontario. An adult male found dead on 26 December 1983 near Milton is in the Royal Ontario Museum.

Adult male: Upper parts plain dark olive-brown; wings and tail brown, the remiges and large wing coverts edged with lighter brown; superciliary stripe and malar stripe white; chin and throat glossy bright red; lores, cheeks, and narrow border of red throat, black; breast grey often becoming light brown on abdomen; under tail coverts white; flanks brown. *Adult female*: Resembles male but facial markings much less distinct, throat white (but occasionally showing speckles of red).

Range. Breeds from Siberia (Urals east to southern slopes of Anadyr Range and Kamchatka) south to Mongolia and Japan.

Subspecies. *Luscinia calliope camtschatkensis* (Gmelin).

Bluethroat

Gorgebleue
Luscinia svecica (Linnaeus)
Total length: 14 cm

Status in Canada. Accidental. A singing adult male was photographed beside Babbage River, Yukon Territory, on 9 June 1973. Sight record of two in northern foothills of British Mountains, Yukon, 14 June 1980.

A small brown-backed thrush. Male in spring and summer is unmistakable with a bright-blue throat patch with (in North American populations) a chestnut patch in the centre and a chestnut border below. In the female the blue throat patch is replaced by a white one. Both male and female show a pale eyebrow stripe. In all plumages the dark-brown tail has a *rufous base*. The tail is flirted frequently, is moved both vertically and laterally, and is often spread.

Range. Breeds widely in Eurasia, reaching North America mainly in arctic Alaska. Winters mainly in Africa and India.

Subspecies. *Luscinia svecica svecica* (Linnaeus).

Stonechat

Traquet pâtre
Saxicola torquata (Linnaeus)
Total length: 12.5 to 13.2 cm
Figure 89

Figure 89
Stonechat

Status in Canada. Accidental. One was photographed at Castalia Marsh, Grand Manan, New Brunswick, on 1 October 1983. Species identification is well established by photo of apparently a first autumn female, and apparently belonging to one of the Siberian subspecies!

A plump little bird with a habit of spreading and flirting its tail and flicking its wings. *Adult male*: Head, back, and throat black. Rump white, the feathers tipped with chestnut. Collar patch on sides of neck, white. Breast chestnut. Wings blackish except for patch of white. Tail plain black (some eastern races show a little white at base). *Female*: Upper parts mostly brown with blackish streaks, wing patch whitish, rump tawny, tail blackish brown, breast much paler than in male.

Range. Breeds widely in the Old World across Eurasia, and south as far as southern Africa.

Northern Wheatear

Traquet motteux
Oenanthe oenanthe (Linnaeus)
Total length: 14 to 15.5 cm
Plate 56

Breeding Distribution of Northern Wheatear

Range in Canada. Breeds in Yukon (Cache Creek on arctic coast, King Point, Old Crow, Ogilvie Mountains, Tepee Lake, Kluane Game Sanctuary) and northwestern Mackenzie (Richardson Mountains on western edge of Mackenzie Delta); Keewatin (Rankin Inlet, Coats Island); also in northeastern Canada from Ellesmere Island (near Slidre Fiord) and probably Axel Heiberg Island south through Baffin Island to White Island (Cape Frigid); northern Quebec (Erik Cove); Port Burwell, N.W.T.; and along the coast of Labrador (south at least to Grady Island).

Has been recorded without evidence of breeding on Boothia Peninsula (Felix Harbour, 2 May 1830) and on Bathurst Island (specimen: 15 June 1970).

Winters in the Old World, but occasional individuals occur in migration seasons in British Columbia (rarely: photo record: Victoria, 10 October 1970); Manitoba (sight records, mostly at Churchill but a sight record of one at Oak Hammock, 14 April 1982); southern Ontario (Thunder Bay, Albany River, Beaumaris, Chatham, Trenton; sight records at Hainsville, Prescott, Manotick, Ridgeway); southern Quebec (Godbout, lower Moisie River; sight records at Natashquan and on Anticosti Island); New Brunswick (Indian Island); and Nova Scotia (photo records: Seal Island, 27 September 1975; Sable Island, June 1977). Sight records for Newfoundland.

Adult male: Upper parts grey, becoming white on forehead and abruptly white on upper tail coverts; wings mostly black; tail with middle two feathers blackish, the rest with basal two-thirds white and terminal third black; across face a black patch passing under eye and with a whitish line above; throat and breast buffy; rest of under parts white, more or less tinged buffy. *Adult female*: Similar to adult male but upper parts more brownish, no black patch across face. *Young (first autumn)*: Similar to adult female but much browner above; under parts pinkish buff darkening to cinnamon buff on breast.

Measurements *(O. o. leucorhoa). Adult male*: wing, 100.5–106.5 (103.8); tail, 54.5–60.5 (58.3); exposed culmen, 13–15 (13.9); tarsus, 27–30.5 (28.9). *Adult female*: wing, 97–103.5 (99) mm (Ridgway).

Field Marks. A restless ground bird, which in all plumages shows a distinctive white rump patch and a black-and-white tail pattern (two centre feathers black, rest with basal two-thirds white, terminal third black). Adult male has black patch across face. Wheatears frequently bob, spread the tail, and move it up and down. *Voice*: A strong *chack-chack*. Song a short pleasant warble in which melodious notes are mixed with harsher ones.

Habitat. Open terrain. Stony tundra, shrub tundra, and other wastelands of the Arctic; rocky slopes, scree, and alpine meadows above timberline in the mountains.

Nesting. In crevices in rocks, cliffs, buildings, holes in the ground or under stones. Nest rather loosely made of grasses and sometimes moss; lined with grass, hair, feathers, and woolly material. *Eggs*, usually 5 to 7; pale blue. Incubation 13 to 14 days (Hantzsch) by both sexes but mainly by the female.

Range. In North America breeds in eastern arctic Canada, Labrador, and Greenland; also in Alaska, Yukon, and western Mackenzie. In the Old World breeds in Iceland, Jan Mayen, Spitsbergen, the British Isles, northern Norway, Finland, northern Russia, and northern Siberia, south to northern Africa, Asia Minor, and central Asia. New World populations winter in the Old World.

Subspecies. (1) *Oenanthe oenanthe oenanthe* (Linnaeus): Yukon, southwestern Mackenzie. (2) *O. o. leucorhoa* (Gmelin) (averages larger, with more strongly buffy under parts in autumn plumage): eastern Canada.

Eastern Bluebird

Merle-bleu de l'Est
Sialia sialis (Linnaeus)
Total length: 16.5 to 19.5 cm
Plate 57

Breeding Distribution of Eastern Bluebird

Range in Canada. Breeds in southern Saskatchewan (locally: Cypress Hills, Moose Mountain, Regina, Indian Head, Okla; near Saskatoon a female Eastern and male Mountain paired and raised five young in 1974; reports of breeding near Prince Alberta require confirmation); southern Manitoba (Lyleton, Oak Lake, Riding Mountain, Lake St. Martin, Sprague); central and southern Ontario (north to about Sandy Lake, Hearst, Lake Abitibi); southern Quebec (Blue-Sea-Lake, Montréal, Québec, Lake Trois Saumons, Rivière-du-Loup, Godbout; recorded in summer, perhaps breeding, at Senneterre, Saint-Félicien, Tadoussac, and on Gaspé Peninsula); New Brunswick; and Nova Scotia (locally: Lochbroom, Gaspereau, Yarmouth; not known on Cape Breton Island). Rare visitor to Prince Edward Island (near Charlottetown), but evidence of breeding is wanting. Casual at Havre-Saint-Pierre, Anticosti Island, and Schefferville, Quebec.

Winters occasionally in southern Ontario (Point Pelee, Toronto, Port Hope).

Casual visitor to Alberta (photos: Calgary, June 1977; sight record: Beynon, 29 September 1959).

Adult male: Bright deep-blue above, including sides of head and most of wings and tail; throat, breast, sides, and flanks reddish brown; belly and under tail coverts white. *Adult female*: Similar to adult male but very much duller above and below. *Juvenal*: Crown and back brownish grey, the back spotted with white; flight feathers and tail mostly blue but duller than the adults; under parts soiled white, streaked and spotted with brown.

Measurements. *Adult male*: wing, 93.7–101.9 (97.8); tail, 57–67 (62.8); exposed culmen, 12–14 (13.1); tarsus, 19–21 (20.0). *Adult female*: wing, 93.6–96.8 (94.9) mm.

Field Marks. The bright-blue upper parts, combined with reddish-brown breast, distinguish it from other eastern birds. Blue Jay and Indigo Bunting have much blue in the plumage but are otherwise very different. The Mountain Bluebird of the Prairies and western mountains has a blue breast. The Western Bluebird, of southern British Columbia, closely resembles the Eastern Bluebird, except that the adult male Western has an all-blue throat and the female a bluish-grey one. *Voice*: Low, short, pleasing warbles.

Habitat. Open and sparse woods, woods edges, burntland with old standing trees, orchards, farmland; in the nesting season a suitable nesting cavity must be in the vicinity.

Nesting. In tree cavities, old woodpecker holes, and bird boxes at heights from 0.9 to 9.1 m. Nest is of grass often with an admixture of leaves, twigs, rootlets, feathers, and hair. *Eggs*, 3 to 7, usually 4 to 6; pale blue, rarely white. Incubation period about 16 days (Amelia R. Laskey), but closer to 12 days (other authors), the male assisting the female.

Range. Breeds from southeastern Arizona and southern Canada (Saskatchewan east to Nova Scotia) south through Mexico to Nicaragua, the United States Gulf Coast, and southern Florida. Winters mainly from north-central United States southward.

Subspecies. *Sialia sialis sialis* (Linnaeus).

Western Bluebird

Merle-bleu de l'Ouest
Sialia mexicana Swainson
Total length: 16.5 to 19 cm
Plate 57

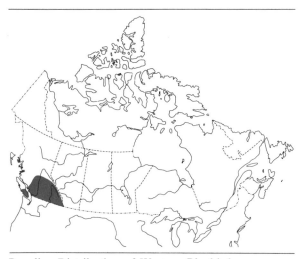

Breeding Distribution of Western Bluebird

Range in Canada. Breeds in southern British Columbia (Vancouver Island, Alta Lake, Huntingdon, Lac la Hache, Okanagan valley, Fort Steele, Newgate).

Winters in small numbers in southern British Columbia (Victoria, Comox, Chilliwack, Okanagan valley).

Adult male: Upper parts bright blue (deeper than in Eastern Bluebird), sides of head and entire throat duller blue; often more or less chestnut on back and scapulars; breast, sides, and flanks reddish brown; abdomen and under tail coverts pale bluish-grey. *Adult female*: Similar to male but very much duller, the back often brownish but not chestnut; throat greyish with bluish tinge. *Juvenal*: Similar to that of Eastern Bluebird but blue of wings and tail deeper.

Measurements. *Adult male*: wing, 100.9–107.9 (104.5); tail, 62–68 (65); exposed culmen, 12–14 (13.2); tarsus, 20–22.5 (20.8). *Adult female*: wing, 97–103.1 (100.5) mm.

Field Marks. A little larger than the House Sparrow. Similar to the Eastern Bluebird but with a blue throat in the male (sometimes chestnut on the back also can be discerned), a grey throat in the female. When reddish back patch is present, this is diagnostic. Its reddish-brown breast and darker-blue upper parts separate it from the Mountain Bluebird. Male Lazuli Bunting is similarly coloured but is smaller, with a stubby sparrow bill and two white wing bars, which bluebirds never have.

Habitat. Sparse woodland, burntland, and logged areas where there are dead trees and stubs to provide nesting cavities and lookout posts; sometimes orchards.

Nesting. Nesting similar to Eastern Bluebird. *Eggs*, usually 4 to 6; pale blue.

Range. Southern British Columbia and central Montana south through the mountains to Baja California, Michoacan, Puebla, and Veracruz, southern Mexico.

Subspecies. *Sialia mexicana occidentalis* Townsend.

Mountain Bluebird

Merle-bleu azuré
Sialia currucoides (Bechstein)
Total length: 16.5 to 19 cm
Plate 57

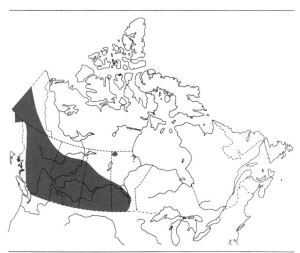

Breeding Distribution of Mountain Bluebird

Range in Canada. Breeds in southern Yukon (Dawson, Lapie River, Canyon); British Columbia (Atlin, Muncho Lake south through the interior; also on the south coast: Horseshoe Lake, Coquitlam); north-central and southern Alberta (Lesser Slave Lake and McMurray southward); central and southern Saskatchewan (Kazan Lake, La Ronge region); and Manitoba

Adult male: Upper parts bright cerulean-blue (paler than in Eastern or Western bluebirds); sides of head, throat, breast, and sides blue but duller and paler than on upper parts; abdomen and under tail coverts white. *Adult female*: Upper parts smoky grey, often tinged with blue; rump, tail, and much of wings pale bluish; under parts pale brownish or buffy grey, becoming white on abdomen and under tail coverts. *Juvenal*: Similar to that of Eastern and Western bluebirds, but distinguishable from both by paler blue on wings, tail, and rump.

Measurements. *Adult male*: wing, 108.8–120.2 (113.8); tail, 67.5–76.5 (71.9); exposed culmen, 12.2–15 (13.9); tarsus, 21.5–23 (22.3). *Adult female*: wing, 105.6–112.6 (109.8) mm.

Field Marks. Male, an all-blue bird a bit larger than a House Sparrow. The lack of any reddish brown on the breast distinguishes it from other male bluebirds. The adult female is greyish brown, but enough blue can usually be seen in wings, rump, and tail to distinguish it as a bluebird. The blue is paler than in other female bluebirds. Other birds with blue coloration are easily distinguishable: Blue and Steller's jays (conspicuous crests, much larger size), and Indigo Bunting (much smaller than a bluebird and with a stubby sparrow bill). The Mountain Bluebird has a habit of hovering frequently. *Voice*: A low *turr*. Song a short warble.

Habitat. Open country with well-spaced trees; woodland openings and edges; burntlands, lumbered areas; farmland.

Nesting. In natural cavities in trees, in abandoned woodpecker holes, on buildings, in bird boxes, or in rock crevices. *Eggs*, usually 5 or 6; pale blue, very rarely white. Incubation mainly by the female with assistance from male, 13 to 14 days; 13 days (H.W. Power).

(Garland, Spruce Woods Forest Reserve; also in the extreme northern part: Kasmere Lake, see Mowat and Lawrie 1955; and possibly Churchill, see Taverner and Sutton 1934).

Recorded in Mackenzie (Fort Resolution, Fort Franklin, Hawk Rapids on upper Back River). Casual on Queen Charlotte Islands, British Columbia, and in Ontario (specimen: Point Pelee, 4 December 1965; also sight records for Point Pelee, Thunder Bay, Atikokan).

Winters rarely or casually in southern British Columbia (Comox, Okanagan Landing).

Townsend's Solitaire

Solitaire de Townsend
Myadestes townsendi (Audubon)
Total length: 20 to 24 cm
Plate 56

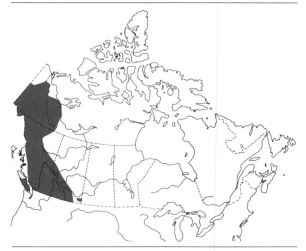

Breeding Distribution of Townsend's Solitaire

Range in Canada. Breeds from southern Yukon (Dawson, Carcross, Lapie River; probably north to the southern Richardson Mountains) and southwestern and central-western Mackenzie (mouth of Nahanni River; probably Carcajou River near Canol Road, and Fort Norman region), south through British Columbia (mostly east of the coast: Chilkat Pass, Telegraph Creek, Nulki Lake, Chilliwack, Wardner; locally on Vancouver Island), southern Alberta (mountains and foothills: Jasper, Banff, and Waterton Lakes national parks; Gorge Creek, Cypress Hills), and extreme southwestern Saskatchewan (Cypress Hills: recently in 1979).

Winters in southern British Columbia (Victoria, Okanagan valley, Moyie Valley).

Wanders east of the breeding range in migration in Alberta (Clyde, Elk Island National Park, Camrose, Sullivan Lake, Rosebud, Beynon, Brooks) and to Saskatchewan (Burnham, Lake Johnstone, Saskatoon, Regina, Yorkton, Nipawin; has wintered in Regina several times). Casual in Manitoba (Stonewall, Brandon). Occasional in Ontario (Point Pelee, 8 March 1962, and Toronto, 10 December 1975; also sight records). Casual in New Brunswick (Woodstock, 15 January to 6 April 1952);

Range. Breeds from central Alaska and western Canada south to California, Nevada, Arizona, southern New Mexico, Colorado, South Dakota (Black Hills), and northeastern North Dakota. Winters from southern British Columbia (rarely) and Montana south to Mexico and southern Texas.

Bill rather short, broad and flattened at base; tail rather long, its feathers somewhat tapered. *Adults*: Brownish grey above and below, but under parts decidedly paler; eye-ring dull white; wings with tawny patch (partly hidden by wing coverts); outermost two or three feathers of tail tipped white, the outer margin of outermost feathers white. *Young*: Wings (except coverts) and tail as in adults, but head and body feathers and wing coverts spotted with pale buff or whitish and margined with blackish.

Measurements. *Adult male*: wing, 109.1–119.7 (114.8); tail, 96.5–106.5 (100.8); exposed culmen, 11.2–13.0 (12.3); tarsus, 20.5–22 (21.3). *Adult female*: wing, 105.6–115.5 (112.1) mm.

Field Marks. A slender brownish-grey bird with short bill, longish tail, white eye-ring, and in flight a buffy wing patch and white outer edge of tail. Young have similar wings and tails to those of adults, but the head and body have pale spots. From female bluebirds, the Solitaire's longer tail and lack of any blue in wings or tail distinguish it. Its white eye-ring, buff wing patch, and darker-grey under parts separate it from the Mockingbird. *Voice*: Song is sustained and delightful, parts suggesting that of the Purple Finch. A monotonous metallic *pink*.

Habitat. Open and broken forests, spaced trees, and burntlands on slopes and rougher mountain country.

Nesting. On or near the ground (often protected by an overhang for shelter or concealment); often in cutbanks along roads and trails; in cavities at the base of trees, under overhanging banks or tree roots (including roots of an upturned tree), and under rocks. *Eggs*, 3 to 5, usually 4; entirely different from those of other thrushes: dull white, more or less uniformly spotted and finely blotched with various browns; sometimes spots are restricted, forming a loose ring.

Quebec (photo: Québec, 30 December 1981; sight records: Sherbrooke, Cap-Tourmente, Aylmer, Montréal); Nova Scotia (specimen: Wolfville, 28 December 1975; photo record: Halifax); and Newfoundland (photo: St. John's, 24 November 1983).

Range. Breeds from central-eastern Alaska, southern Yukon, southwestern Mackenzie, southwestern Alberta, and southwestern South Dakota south in the western mountains to southern California and northern Mexico (Durango). Winters at lower altitudes north to southern British Columbia.

Subspecies. *Myadestes townsendi townsendi* (Audubon).

Veery

Grive fauve
Catharus fuscescens (Stephens)
Total length: 16.5 to 19.5 cm
Plate 56

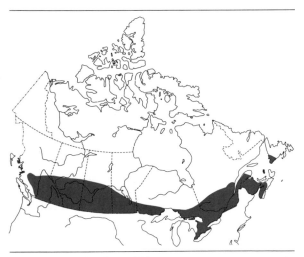

Breeding Distribution of Veery

Range in Canada. Summer resident, breeding in interior British Columbia (Kimsquit, Kleena Kleene, Quesnel, Williams Lake Indian Reserve No. 13, Okanagan Landing, Richter Pass, Trail; reported in summer north to Skeena River); central and southern Alberta (Edmonton, Athabasca, Waterton Lakes National Park, Cypress Hills); central and southern Saskatchewan (Meadow Lake, Prince Albert, Nipawin, Cypress Hills, Moose Mountain); southern Manitoba (Swan River, Lake St. Martin, Hillside Beach southward); western Ontario (Malachi, Kenora, Sioux Lookout, Thunder Bay, perhaps Rossport); southern Ontario (Sault Ste. Marie, Lake Nipissing, Mildred, New Liskeard southward); southern Quebec (Dorval in central La Vérendrye Park, Lake Saint-Jean, Hatley, Québec, Lake Trois Saumons, Anse Saint-Denis, Lake Baker, Lake Rimouski, Biencourt, Matapédia, Madeleine Islands); southwestern Newfoundland (Codroy and Humber river valleys); New Brunswick; and central and southern Nova Scotia (Annapolis Valley, Stewiake, Yarmouth). Reports of breeding on Anticosti Island and extreme eastern Gaspé Peninsula require confirmation.

Rare visitor to Prince Edward Island (photo: Dalvey Beach, 25–26 May 1973). Rare visitor to southern coast of British Columbia (North Vancouver).

Decidedly tawny upper parts and very light and sparse spotting on breast distinguish it from other similar thrushes. *Adults*: Upper parts tawny brown; no obvious eye-ring; breast strongly suffused with buff and only lightly spotted with tawny brown, this spotting running up along sides of throat; sides and flanks are suffused with paler greyish-brown; rest of under parts white.

Measurements *(C. f. fuscescens). Adult male*: wing, 98.5–104.6 (99.9); tail, 69.1–77.5 (73.7); exposed culmen, 12.4–14.6 (13.4); tarsus, 27–31.9 (29.2). *Adult female*: wing, 92.6–100.8 (96.5) mm.

Field Marks. The faintly and sparsely spotted breast and tawny upper parts distinguish it from other similar thrushes. Song, too, is easily recognized. *Voice*: Song a rolling *whee-u, whee-u, re-a, re-a*, on a descending scale. Call *phew* or *whee-u*, downslurred.

Habitat. Deciduous or deciduous-coniferous woodland, especially where more open with an understory of deciduous shrubbery; second growth, willow or alder shrubbery along lakes, streams, and coulees.

Nesting. On or near the ground. Nest is of twigs, grass, weeds, and is lined with fine grass, dry leaves, rootlets, and hairs. *Eggs*, 3 to 5, usually 4; greenish blue. Incubation 11 to 12 days (O. Annan), 12 to 13 days (L. de K. Lawrence), by the female.

Range. Breeds from interior British Columbia east to Newfoundland and south to northeastern Arizona, northeastern South Dakota, southeastern Minnesota and in the Alleghenies south to Georgia and on the Atlantic Coast south to Washington, D.C. Winters from Central America south to Colombia and central and northeastern Brazil.

Subspecies. (1) *Catharus fuscescens fuscescens* (Stephens): Nova Scotia, New Brunswick, southwestern Quebec (but not Madeleine Islands), southern Ontario (intergrading with *salicicola* in northern part of its Ontario range, Rossport east to Lake Nipissing). (2) *C. f. salicicola* (Ridgway) (duller, less tawny, more olivaceous than *fuscescens*): British Columbia, Alberta, Saskatchewan, Manitoba, western Ontario (east to Rossport, intergrading in northern periphery of range east to Lake Nipissing with *fuscescens*). (3) *C. f. fuliginosus* (Howe) (a poorly characterized race, browner than *salicicola*, darker than *fuscescens*, but many individuals are not separable): Newfoundland, Madeleine Islands, Quebec.

Gray-cheeked Thrush

Grive à joues grises
Catharus minimus (Lafresnaye)
Total length: 16.5 to 20 cm
Plate 56

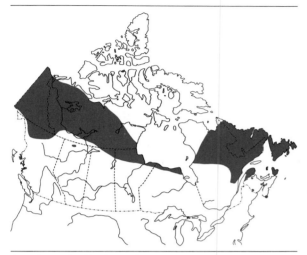

Breeding Distribution of Gray-cheeked Thrush

Range in Canada. Breeds from northern Yukon (Arctic coastal plain); northern Mackenzie (Mackenzie Delta, Horton River, Bathurst Inlet); southern Keewatin (Angikuni Lake, Tha-anne River); northern Quebec (Kuujjuaq, Koroc River); Labrador (Okak, Peter Lake, Nain, Cartwright); and Newfoundland south to northwestern British Columbia (Haines Road Mile 85; recorded in the breeding season from Driftwood Mountains and Bulkley Lake east of Telegraph Creek); southern Mackenzie (junction of South Nahanni and Flat rivers, Great Slave Lake; probably Hill Island Lake); northern Alberta (Caribou Mountains); northeastern Saskatchewan (Hasbala Lake, Milton Lake, perhaps northern Reindeer Lake); northern Manitoba (Sandhill Lake, Churchill, Herchmer, York Factory); northwestern Ontario (Fort Severn, Hawley Lake); central-western and southeastern Quebec (Kinglet Lake; 145 km south of Schefferville; north shore of the Gulf of St. Lawrence westward at least to Havre-Saint-Pierre; Chic-Choc Mountains; Percé; probably Mount Mégantic and Laurentides Park; the Madeleine Islands); New Brunswick (locally: Devil's Elbow Brook, Fundy National Park); Nova Scotia (Seal and Mud islands; probably French Mountain on Cape Breton Island). Probably breeds also in northern Alberta (Caribou Mountains).

Transient in all of extreme southern Canada west to western Alberta.

Adults: Upper parts (including tail) uniform greyish-olive (or greyish), eye-ring greyish white; cheek olive, narrowly streaked with greyish white; under parts mostly white, the breast faintly buffy and spotted with blackish, this spotting running narrowly up sides of throat; sides and flanks pale greyish-olive.

Measurements *(C. m. aliciae). Adult male*: wing, 92.3–106.4 (100.9); tail, 65.5–73 (69.5); exposed culmen, 12.6–15 (14.1); tarsus, 29–32 (30.0). *Adult female*: wing, 95.5–105 (99.9) mm.

Field Marks. Distinguished from the Veery by heavy instead of very light breast spots and by much greyer (not tawny) general coloration; from Hermit Thrush by dull-olive instead of reddish tail; from Wood Thrush by uniform dark-grey upper parts (no tawny on back of neck) and much less heavy and more restricted spotting of under parts; and from Swainson's Thrush by greyish (instead of buffy) eye-ring and cheeks. *Voice*: Song suggests that of the Veery but usually rises in pitch near the end. Alarm note *whee-u* suggesting a similar call of the Veery.

Habitat. In breeding season prefers coniferous woods, denser stands near tree limit, dense stunted spruce on coastal islands and near timberline of mountains. In migration, various types of woodland and roadside shrubbery.

Nesting. Low in trees (up to 7.6 m) or bushes or on the ground. *Eggs*, usually 3 to 5; greenish blue dotted (sometimes faintly) with browns. Incubation 13 to 14 days (G.J. Wallace) by the female; 12 days (J.K. Jehl and D.J.T. Hussell).

Range. Breeds from northeastern Siberia, northern Alaska, and from near tree limit across Canada south to northwestern British Columbia, north-central Saskatchewan, southeastern New York, and northwestern Massachusetts. Winters from southern Mexico and the West Indies south to Peru, northwestern Brazil, and Guyana.

Subspecies. (1) *Catharus minimus minimus* (Lafresnaye): Newfoundland, Gaspé Peninsula. (2) *C. m. bicknelli* (Ridgway) (resembles *minimus* in more brownish coloration but is smaller): Nova Scotia. (3) *C. m. aliciae* (Baird) (more greyish or olivaceous than the two other subspecies, averages larger than *bicknelli*): all of the North American mainland west and north of the north shore of the Gulf of St. Lawrence. (Note: Racial affiliations of populations inhabiting the north shore of the Gulf of St. Lawrence, Quebec, are unknown.)

Swainson's Thrush

(Olive-backed Thrush)

Grive à dos olive
Catharus ustulatus (Nuttall)
Total length: 16 to 19.5 cm
Plate 56

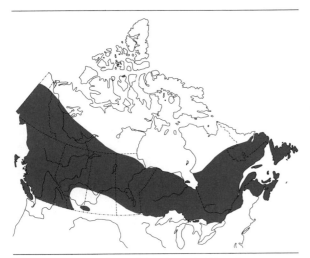

Breeding Distribution of Swainson's Thrush

Range in Canada. Breeds from northern Yukon (Old Crow, Lapierre House); western Mackenzie (Fort Good Hope, Fort Norman, Fort Simpson, Fort Resolution); northern Saskatchewan (Lake Athabasca, Hasbala Lake); northern Manitoba (Thicket Portage, probably York Factory); northern Ontario (Fort Severn, Winisk); central Quebec (Fort-George, Schefferville region); southern Labrador (upper Hamilton River, Goose Bay, Cartwright); and Newfoundland south to southern British Columbia (including coastal islands); southern Alberta (but locally in south: Cypress Hills and through the Rocky Mountains); southwestern and central Saskatchewan (Cypress Hills, Melfort); southern Manitoba (Riding Mountain, Whitemouth, Rennie); southern Ontario (southern Georgian Bay, Haliburton, Barrie, Cumberland); southern Quebec (Gatineau Park, Montréal, Magog, Gaspé Peninsula, Anticosti Island, Madeleine Islands); New Brunswick; Prince Edward Island; and Nova Scotia.

Accidental on Meighen Island, N.W.T. (specimen: 16 July 1960).

Adults: Upper parts olive brown or olive grey; eye-ring and line from eye to base of bill buff; cheeks buffy streaked with dusky; breast and sides of throat spotted with dusky; sides suffused with olive brown; rest of under parts white.

Measurements *(C. u. swainsoni). Adult male*: wing, 94.1–101.8 (99.1); tail, 65.5–76 (70.4); exposed culmen, 12.7–15 (13.5); tarsus, 27–30 (28.4). *Adult female*: wing, 89.5–98.4 (93.8) mm.

Field Marks. Breast is much more heavily spotted than that of Veery; lacks reddish-brown tail of Hermit Thrush; buffy eye-ring and face distinguish it from the Gray-cheeked Thrush. *Voice*: Song less impressive than that of the Hermit or Wood Thrush, but still very musical and pleasing. Each phrase rises higher than the preceding one, rolling upward. Calls include a *wick* and a high-pitched *queep*.

Habitat. Deciduous tall shrubbery; also coniferous woods, often with an admixture of thickets of alder, willow, or other tall shrubs; and second growth of burntlands and logged-over areas.

Nesting. Usually in a low evergreen tree or bush, sometimes a deciduous one. Nest of various materials including twigs, grass, weed stems, leaves, moss, and lichens. *Eggs*, usually 3 or 4; blue, rather evenly marked with pale browns. Incubation about 12 days, by the female.

Range. Breeds from central Alaska eastward across forested Canada to Newfoundland and south to California, Colorado, southern Ontario, central New Hampshire, and Maine; farther south in the Appalachian Mountains. Winters from Mexico south to Peru, northern Paraguay, western Brazil, and Guyana.

Subspecies. (1) *Catharus ustulatus swainsoni* (Tschudi): south-central and northeastern Alberta (Lac la Nonne, Wood Buffalo National Park), Saskatchewan, Manitoba, Ontario, Quebec, Labrador, Newfoundland, New Brunswick, Prince Edward Island, Nova Scotia. (2) *C. u. incanus* (Godfrey) (averages even greyer than *almae*): Yukon, western Mackenzie (Fort Norman, Fort Simpson), northern British Columbia (Dease Lake, Summit Lake on Alaska Highway), north-central Alberta (Grimshaw, Joussard). (3) *C. u. almae* (Oberholser) (averages somewhat greyer than *swainsoni*): southern and central interior British Columbia. (4) *C. u. ustulatus* (Nuttall), with brownish upper parts: coastal British Columbia.

Hermit Thrush

Grive solitaire
Catharus guttatus (Pallas)
Total length: 16 to 19 cm
Plate 56

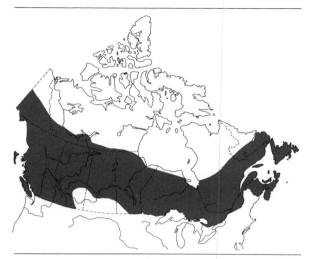

Breeding Distribution of Hermit Thrush

Range in Canada. Breeds from southern Yukon (southern Ogilvie Mountains, Little Salmon River, Donjek River, Haines Junction, Nisutlin River); southern Mackenzie (Fort Simpson, Yellowknife, Buffalo River, Soulier Lake; singing males reported north to Norman Wells); northern Saskatchewan (Lake Athabasca, Hasbala Lake); northern Manitoba (Herchmer, Bird, perhaps Churchill); northern Ontario (Big Trout Lake; Hawley Lake, Sutton Ridges); central Quebec (Moar Bay; Lake Mistassini; 145 km south of Schefferville); southern Labrador (Goose Bay, Cartwright); and Newfoundland south to southern British Columbia (including coastal islands); central and southwestern Alberta (Lac la Nonne; Athabasca; Jasper, Banff, and Waterton Lakes national parks; perhaps rarely Red Deer); central Saskatchewan (Prince Albert, Nipawin); southern Manitoba (Garland, Hillside Beach, Whitemouth); southern Ontario (Mount Forest; Madoc; Junetown in Leeds County); southern Quebec (Kingsmere, Montréal, Hatley, Madeleine Islands); and throughout New Brunswick; Prince Edward Island; and Nova Scotia.

Winters in small numbers in south coastal British Columbia (Comox, Victoria) and occasionally in southern Ontario (Toronto, Hamilton, Ottawa).

Accidental in the Arctic: Southampton Island, N.W.T., 4 October 1929; Seymour Island, summer 1974.

Reddish-brown tail contrasts with olive-brown back, distinguishing it from similar thrushes. *Adults (C. g. faxoni)*: Upper parts olive brown becoming reddish brown on rump and tail; eye-ring whitish; under parts whitish with pale-buff suffusion across breast, the breast with large wedge-shaped spots of blackish brown; sides of throat with narrow streaks of blackish brown; sides and flanks pale brownish-grey.

Measurements *(C. g. faxoni)*. *Adult male*: wing, 89.3–95 (92.2); tail, 67–73.5 (69.6); exposed culmen, 13–15.2 (14.1); tarsus, 28–31 (29.8). *Adult female*: wing, 82–96 (87.6) mm.

Field Marks. A brown-backed thrush with a well-spotted breast and a distinctive *reddish tail*. Often slowly raises the tail after alighting or when disturbed, and frequently flicks wings. Beginners might confuse it with the Fox Sparrow because of the red tail, but the Fox Sparrow has a conical stubby bill. *Voice*: Many consider it the finest singer in North America. A clear, ethereal, bell-like song made up of phrases with considerable pauses between. The phrases are similar in form but in various pitches. The lower phrases are extremely beautiful. The first note of each phrase is lower and longer than the rest of the notes. Also a soft *chuck* and several other calls.

Habitat. Mixed deciduous-coniferous or pure coniferous woodlands varying from wooded bogs and swamps to dry sandy and sparse jack pine; second growth of burntlands and logged-over clearings with standing dead trees, which are favoured as singing perches. Inhabits forest floor and lower stratum of woodlands.

Nesting. Usually on the ground; rarely in a low bush or sapling. Nest usually composed of twigs, bark fibre, ferns, and moss, lined with rootlets and pine needles. *Eggs*, 3 to 6, usually 3 or 4; plain greenish-blue (rarely with a few spots). Incubation 12 days (Gross *in* Bent), by the female.

Range. Breeds from central Alaska eastward across much of forested Canada to Newfoundland and south to southern California, northern New Mexico, central Minnesota, central Pennsylvania, and western Maryland. Winters from southern parts of the breeding range south to Baja California, Guatemala, and southern Florida.

Subspecies. Much disagreement exists among authors concerning the number of valid subspecies and the allocation of names. Until adequate material is available to clarify the matter, the *A.O.U. Check-list* (1957) may be followed. (1) *Catharus guttatus guttatus* (Pallas): southwestern Yukon south to south-central interior British Columbia (but not northeastern part). (2) *C. g. nanus* (Audubon): coast and coastal islands of British Columbia. (3) *C. g. auduboni* (Baird): southern interior British Columbia. (4) *C. g. faxoni* (Bangs and Penard): central Yukon, northeastern British Columbia, Mackenzie, Alberta, Saskatchewan, Manitoba, Ontario, central and southern Quebec, New Brunswick, Prince Edward Island, Nova Scotia. (5) *C. g. crymophilus* (Burleigh and Peters): Newfoundland.

Remarks. The Hermit Thrush is considered by many to be the finest singer of all North American birds. Its ethereal music, with its clear bell-like tones, is especially effective in the quiet of a north woods on a summer evening.

Wood Thrush

Grive des bois
Hylocichla mustelina (Gmelin)
Total length: 19 to 21.5 cm
Plate 56

Breeding Distribution of Wood Thrush

Range in Canada. Has expanded its breeding range in recent years. Breeds in southern Manitoba (locally: Riding Mountain); southern Ontario (north to Iron Bridge, Sudbury, Eau Claire); southwestern Quebec (Gatineau Park, Lake Tremblant, Château-Richer, Cap-Tourmente, probably Rivière-du-Loup); southwestern New Brunswick (St. Stephen, St. Andrews, Woodstock, Juniper); and Nova Scotia (locally: Kejimkujik National Park).

Rare visitant to Saskatchewan (sight records: Saskatoon, Biggar, Regina, Cadillac, Colgate).

A large brown-backed thrush. Upper parts mostly brown, the crown and hind-neck russet or cinnamon brown, the upper tail coverts and tail tinged with greyish olive; eye-ring white; ear coverts streaked with white and dusky; under parts mostly white, with buffy suffusion across breast, and with large black or dark-brown spots on breast, sides, and flanks.

Measurements. *Adult male*: wing, 104.5–113 (109.0); tail, 67–77.5 (71.5); exposed culmen, 16–19 (17.1); tarsus, 30–33 (31.6). *Adult female*: wing, 103–109.5 (105.6) mm.

Field Marks. A large brown-backed thrush with back of neck *more tawny than the back*, the heavy round spotting of under parts *extending to sides and flanks*. *Voice*: A clear unhurried beautiful song, often with bell-like qualities and typically in three syllables, the first high, the second lower, the third a high trill, thus *cedar-lee*. Shorter than the songs of our *Catharus* thrushes. Alarm note *quirt* or a sharp *pit pit*.

Habitat. The lower strata of maturer deciduous woodland.

Nesting. In a tree or sapling, usually 1.5 to 4.5 m up. Nest is of grasses, weed stems, and trash, with a middle layer of mud, a few dead leaves in the bottom, and a lining of rootlets. *Eggs*, greenish blue, slightly smaller than those of the American Robin and a bit more pointed. Incubation 13 to 14 days, by the female (Weaver *in* Bent).

Range. Breeds from southeastern South Dakota, central Wisconsin, southern Ontario, southwestern Quebec, southwestern Maine and probably southwestern New Brunswick south to southeastern Texas, the Gulf Coast of United States, and northern Florida. Winters mainly from northern Mexico to Panama.

Eurasian Blackbird

Merle noir
Turdus merula Linnaeus
Total length: 24 to 27 cm

Status in Canada. Accidental in southern Quebec (specimen: Outremont, island of Montréal, 23 November 1970). Sight record for Ontario (Erieau, 12 April 1981).

Similar in size and shape to American Robin. Adult male is uniformly black with an orange-yellow bill and eye ring. Adult female has uniformly dark-brown upper parts, paler (more reddish) brown under parts; chin and throat pale greyish with vague brownish streaks; bill brown. Immatures resemble adult female but are more brownish.

Range. Eurasia south to the Mediterranean region, northwestern Africa, India, and China.

Subspecies. *Turdus merula merula* Linnaeus.

Fieldfare

Grive litorne
Turdus pilaris Linnaeus
Total length: 24 to 26.5 cm
Plate 57

Status in Canada. Casual visitor to Northwest Territories (Jens Munk Island, Foxe Basin; skin in possession of an Eskimo in 1939); Ontario (photo record: Long Point, 24 May 1975; sight record: Ottawa, January 1967; Toronto, January and February 1981); Quebec (photo: Rigaud, 4 January to 14 March 1976); Nova Scotia (sight records: Louisbourg, October 1971 and 1972); and Newfoundland (photo record: St. John's, January 1973).

Head, neck, and rump bluish grey; back mostly brown; tail blackish; throat and breast, buffy brown streaked with black; sides and flanks, heavily marked with blackish or blackish brown; rest of under parts white.

Range. Northern Eurasia (Scandinavia east to south-central Siberia). In 1937 a small colony became self-established in southern Greenland (Julianehaab District).

Redwing

Grive mauvis
Turdus iliacus Linnaeus
Total length: 21 cm
Plate 57

Status in Canada. Accidental in Newfoundland (photo record: St. Anthony, 25 and 26 June 1980).

Adults (sexes similar): Upper parts olive-brown; a conspicuous buffy-white superciliary stripe. Under parts white, the throat, breast, and flanks heavily streaked *(not spotted)* with olive brown. Flanks, under wing coverts, and axillars rich chestnut or rufous. Iris brown. Bill mainly brownish, but base of lower mandible flesh colour. Legs greyish brown.

Field Marks. Slightly smaller than the American Robin. A thrush with *streaked* (not spotted) breast, a buffy stripe over the eye, and chestnut flanks. In flight the chestnut under wing coverts and axillars are visible.

Range. Breeds across northern Eurasia from Iceland eastward to the lower Kolyma River. Winters in Europe, the Mediterranean countries, and the Middle East.

Subspecies. Not apparent in photographs.

American Robin

Merle d'Amérique
Turdus migratorius Linnaeus
Total length: 23 to 27.5 cm
Plate 57

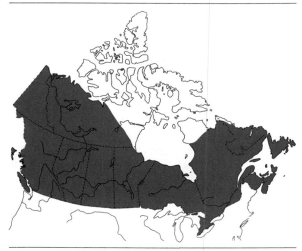

Breeding Distribution of American Robin

Range in Canada. Breeds from the limit of trees, or slightly north of it, in northern Yukon (Babbage River, Old Crow, Lapierre House); northern Mackenzie (Kittigazuit, Fort Anderson, Coppermine, Thelon River); southern Keewatin (Windy River, Angikuni Lake); northern Manitoba (Churchill); northern Ontario (Fort Severn); James Bay (Akimiski and Twin islands); northern Quebec (Feuilles and Koroc rivers, Lake Minto); Labrador; and Newfoundland south through southern Canada from Vancouver and Queen Charlotte islands, British Columbia, to Cape Breton Island, Nova Scotia.

Winters in southwestern and southern British Columbia; southern Ontario (north rarely to Thunder Bay, Wawa, and Ottawa); southwestern Quebec (Montréal, Québec; north

Adult male (T. m. migratorius): Top of head, sides of head, and nape, black but with small white areas about the eye; rest of upper parts mostly dark-grey, becoming blackish on wings and tail; outer tail feathers tipped white; throat streaked black and white; breast, sides, flanks, and upper abdomen cinnamon-rufous; lower abdomen and under tail coverts white; eye brown; bill yellow. *Adult female*: Similar to adult male but paler; black of head duller and more restricted; breast paler, many feathers edged with white. *Juvenal*: Somewhat like adults but feathers of back with white or buffy mesial streaks and black tips; wing coverts with white or buffy streaks; throat white; breast, upper abdomen, sides, and flanks reddish brown (often mainly whitish on breast) conspicuously spotted with black.

Measurements *(T. m. migratorius). Adult male*: wing, 126–133 (129.9); tail, 95–105 (101.2); exposed culmen, 19–22.1 (20.9); tarsus, 32–35 (34.1). *Adult female*: wing, 120–132.5 (126.9) mm.

Field Marks. Familiar to almost everyone. Size, brick-red breast, dark-grey back, and yellow bill are a combination that distinguishes adults. Young have black spots on the breast (showing relationship to the thrush family) and pale streaks on the back, but they otherwise look much like the adults that usually accompany them. *Voice*: Song a procession of two- or three-syllable phrases that suggests *cheer-up* or *cheerily* with variations in pitch and often continued for long periods through spring and summer. There also are various alarm and scold notes as well as a very high-pitched lisping whistle of alarm.

Habitat. In country farmland, woodlots and thickets provide cover and nesting places, and open fields furnish ideal foraging; and in residential areas, ornamental trees and shrubbery, together with grassy lawns, provide equally well for the Robin's needs. It also favours open and broken woodlands, second growth of cut-over forest areas and burntlands, forest openings and edges. In general it is much less common in heavily forested areas than in areas inhabited by man, and doubtless the Robin is one of the minority of species that have benefited by the coming of the white man.

Nesting. Usually in trees or bushes (either coniferous or deciduous), most frequently 1.5 to 4.5 m up but often much higher and occasionally on the ground. Often in recesses and nooks of building exteriors, sometimes inside buildings. Nest, a substantial structure of twigs, weed stems, and grass with base and walls of mud, lined with fine grasses and similar soft material. *Eggs*, usually 4 (in Newfoundland usually 3); plain blue. Incubation 11 to 14 (usually 12 to 13) days, by the female, with more or less assistance from the male.

rarely to Arvida and Pointe-des-Monts); New Brunswick (Saint John, Fredericton); Prince Edward Island (Souris); Nova Scotia (Wolfville, Pictou); and southern Newfoundland (regularly on Avalon Peninsula); also rarely and precariously in southern Alberta, southern Saskatchewan (Regina), and southern Manitoba (Winnipeg).

Casual on Herschel Island, Yukon; and at Frobisher Bay, Baffin Island.

Range. Breeds from the limit of trees in Alaska and across Canada south to southern Mexico and the Gulf Coast of the United States and central Florida. Winters from southern Canada southward to Guatemala and southern Florida.

Subspecies. (1) *Turdus migratorius migratorius* Linnaeus: Yukon, Mackenzie, Keewatin, north and central British Columbia (Atlin, François Lake, Tupper Creek), northern and central Alberta, Saskatchewan (except southwestern corner), Manitoba, Ontario, southern Quebec (Blue-Sea-Lake, Québec, Lake Saint-Jean, Gaspé Peninsula), New Brunswick, Prince Edward Island, Nova Scotia. (2) *T. m. nigrideus* Aldrich and Nutt, adult males with black of head and nape extending to upper back, averaging darker generally than *migratorius*: northern and central Quebec (south to Moar and Paul bays, Lake Mistassini, and the outer north shore of the Gulf of St. Lawrence), Labrador, Newfoundland. (3) *T. m. propinquus* Ridgway, averaging paler and slightly larger than *migratorius*, white tip of outer tail feathers absent or much reduced: southern interior British Columbia (Indianpoint Lake, Lillooet, Wardner), southern Alberta (Banff, Red Deer River), and southwestern Saskatchewan (Cypress Hills, possibly somewhat farther east but no material available for examination). (4) *T. m. caurinus* (Grinnell), darker and slightly smaller than *propinquus*; lacks decided white spots on tips of outer tail feathers: coastal British Columbia (Queen Charlotte and Vancouver islands; Vancouver).

Remarks. The American Robin is probably familiar to more people in Canada than any other bird. Its vast distribution, its pleasing song and personality, and its fondness for the trees and lawns about our dwellings make it a bird that is not likely to be overlooked. It arrives in most parts of the country early in the spring when the first patches of bare ground are beginning to show through the snow, and it is unquestionably our favourite harbinger of spring.

Our robin was given its name by the early settlers who noted its reddish breast, which reminded them of the European Robin. However, our bird is very much larger, and aside from the colour of its breast it is not similar to the Old World bird.

The American Robin has a varied menu, but insects, worms, and fruits make up the bulk of it. Indeed its fondness for fruits occasionally gets it into trouble with growers of small cultivated fruits. On open grassy areas, such as lawns, it eagerly seeks earthworms.

Varied Thrush

Grive à collier
Ixoreus naevius (Gmelin)
Total length: 22.5 to 25.5 cm
Plate 57

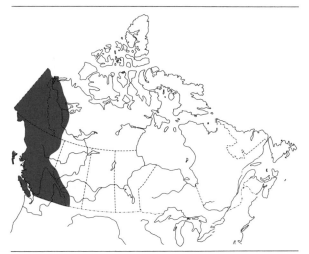

Breeding Distribution of Varied Thrush

Range in Canada. Breeds in Yukon (north to near the arctic coast: Babbage River) northwestern and western Mackenzie (Mackenzie Delta, Fort Norman, Fort Franklin, Wrigley, Nahanni National Park); British Columbia (throughout, including Queen Charlotte and Vancouver islands, but not Peace River Parklands); and southwestern Alberta (Jasper, Banff, and Waterton Lakes national parks).

Winters in western and southern British Columbia (Departure Bay, Vancouver, Queen Charlotte Islands, Okanagan Landing).

In migration it wanders east of the mountains occasionally: to Alberta (Belvedere, Edmonton, Castor, Rosebud, Camrose, Sullivan Lake, Calgary, Red Deer); Saskatchewan (specimen records: Valley Centre, 22 September 1968; Luseland, 25 September 1975; various sight records at Regina, Saskatoon, Rosetown); Manitoba (specimen record: Brandon, December 1965; also sight records); Ontario (specimen: Toronto, 7 January 1964; sight records: Thunder Bay, Maple, Norland, Ottawa, Braeside); Quebec (specimen: Manicouagan, 28 August 1890; photo records: Lachute, January 1973; Calumet, January and February 1975); New Brunswick (specimen: Stanley, 25 March 1960—had wintered there; sight records: Marysville, November 1965 to 15 January 1966; and Sackville, 6 January 1968); and Nova Scotia (photo record: Liverpool, January 1978; South Maitland, 12 January to 19 February 1977; also various sight records at Middleton, North Range, and Sable Island).

Adult male: Upper parts slate grey; sides of face blackish; over eye and back to neck, an orange-brown line; tail with small white tip to outermost feathers; two wing bars, much edging of flight feathers, and much of the under parts orange-brown; a broad black band across breast; spread wing shows a white band across inner webs of flight feathers. *Adult female*: Similar in pattern to adult male, but much paler and duller, upper parts brownish olive, breast band similar to back or paler.

Measurements *(I. n. meruloides)*. *Adult male*: wing, 122–129 (125.8); tail, 86–94.5 (90.1); exposed culmen, 19.8–21 (20.6); tarsus, 29.5–32.5 (31.7). *Adult female*: wing, 120.5–130 (125.6) mm.

Field Marks. Resembles American Robin in size, shape, and orange-brown breast, but broad black band (grey in female) across breast, orange-buff line above and behind eye, orange-brown wing bars and wing patches readily distinguish Varied Thrush. *Voice*: Song is an eerie resonant whistle in various pitches, often in a minor key, and is like the echo of a bell, prolonged at the same pitch and dying away.

Habitat. In breeding season, forests and woodland from coastal to subalpine, shady damp forests preferred. Forages in lower strata, especially on the forest floor.

Nesting. Usually 1.5 to 4.5 m above ground in a tree. Nest is made of twigs, grass, weed stems, and moss, more or less reinforced with mud and lined with grass. *Eggs*, usually 3 to 4; blue (somewhat paler than the American Robin's), sparsely marked with small spots of brown.

Range. Breeds from north-central Alaska, northern Yukon, and northwestern Mackenzie south to northwestern California, northern Idaho, and northwestern Montana. Winters from southern British Columbia to northern Baja California.

Subspecies. (1) *Ixoreus naevius naevius* (Gmelin); coastal islands and west slope of the Coast and Cascades ranges in British Columbia. (2) *I. n. meruloides* (Swainson); adult female greyer and paler than *naevius*: Mackenzie, Yukon, northern interior British Columbia. (Like Dickinson 1953, I find little consistent difference between coastal and southern interior British Columbia material. However, the limited Mackenzie material I examined is more greyish above, and I am reluctant to draw conclusions at present on the validity of *meruloides*.)

Family **Mimidae**:
Mockingbirds and Thrashers

Number of Species in Canada: 4

This family, which is restricted to the Western Hemisphere, is in many ways intermediate between the wrens and the thrushes. Compared with wrens, thrashers are larger, have longer tails, and possess rictal bristles. They have longer tails than thrushes, somewhat downcurved bills, and scutellate tarsi. They are delightful singers, and several species are famous for their ability as mimics.

Gray Catbird

Moqueur chat
Dumetella carolinensis (Linnaeus)
Total length: 21 to 24 cm
Plate 55

Breeding Distribution of Gray Catbird

Range in Canada. Summer resident, breeding in southern British Columbia (Bella Coola, Huntingdon, Lillooet, Williams Lake, Cranbrook. Breeding unknown on Vancouver Island); central and southern Alberta (north at least to Athabasca region, Cold Lake; recorded in summer north to Lesser Slave Lake); central and southern Saskatchewan (north at least to Meadow Lake and Nipawin); southern Manitoba (Overflowing River, Oak Lake, Lake St. Martin, Sprague); south-central and southern Ontario (north to about Kenora, Sault Ste. Marie, Lake Nipissing, Kearns); southwestern Quebec (Blue-Sea-Lake, Montréal, Baldwin-Mills, Québec, Île aux Coudres, Rivière-du-Loup, Saint-Gédéon; probably Forillon National Park and Percé); New Brunswick (scarce in northern parts); Nova Scotia (including rarely Cape Breton Island); and Prince Edward Island (rarely).

Casual on Vancouver Island (Comox); Sept-Îles, Quebec; on North Twin Island in James Bay (specimen: 5 June 1973); and sight records for Newfoundland (Ramea, St. Andrews, Terra Nova National Park).

Mostly dull slate-grey, slightly paler underneath; top of head blackish; under tail coverts mostly chestnut; tail blackish.

Measurements. *Adult male*: wing, 88–96.1 (91.6); tail, 90–101.5 (96.1); exposed culmen, 15.1–18 (16.8); tarsus, 26–28 (27.4). *Adult female*: wing, 85.7–94.4 (89.7) mm.

Field Marks. A slate-grey bird of thickets, smaller and longer-tailed than a robin, and with blackish cap and chestnut under tail coverts. Frequently flicks its longish black tail. *Voice*: A complaining catlike mewing is a common and unmistakable call; also an explosive stony *kak kak kak*. Song is sustained and made up of various phrases punctuated by short pauses, some phrases very musical, others discordant, and often including imitations of other bird songs and sounds. Although the song is similar to that of the Brown Thrasher and the Mockingbird, the Catbird does not ordinarily repeat its phrases; thus it is easy to distinguish Catbird songs from those of its two near relatives.

Habitat. Low, dense deciduous thickets (occasionally coniferous) along streams, ponds, roadsides, woodland edges, and prairie coulees; also commonly in bushes and shrubbery of gardens.

Nesting. In thick shrubbery, usually between 0.9 and 2.4 m above ground. The nest, rather bulky, is made of twigs, weed stems, grass, and leaves with a neat inner cup of fine rootlets and shreds of bark. *Eggs*, usually 3 to 5; glossy deep greenish-blue, unmarked. Incubation 12.8 days (R.D. Slack), by the female.

Range. Southern Canada (interior British Columbia east to Cape Breton Island) south to eastern Oregon, central Arizona, Texas, central parts of the Gulf states, and southern Florida. Winters mainly from southeastern United States and eastern Mexico through Central America to Panama and on islands in the Caribbean Sea.

Northern Mockingbird

Moqueur polyglotte
Mimus polyglottos (Linnaeus)
Total length: 22.8 to 28 cm
Plate 55

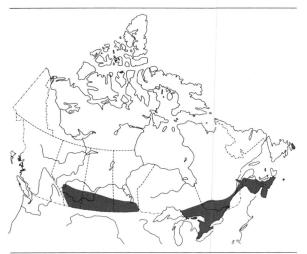

Breeding Distribution of Northern Mockingbird

Range in Canada. Very local permanent resident, spreading northward into Canada slowly and recently nesting irregularly in given localities. It is known to have nested in southern Alberta (Didsbury); Saskatchewan (Dundurn); Ontario (Amherstburg, Toronto, Manitoulin Island, Sudbury, Kapuskasing, Ottawa); southwestern Quebec (Como, Chicoutimi, Tadoussac, Guyenne, Montréal, Rimouski); southern New Brunswick (Burnt Church, Moncton, Fredericton); Nova Scotia (Halifax, Sable Island, probably Debert); Newfoundland (St. John's); and probably Manitoba (Delta Beach: juvenal with natal down adhering to head and nape). Has attempted nesting in southwestern British Columbia (Victoria) but to date unsuccessfully.

Rare or casual visitor in southern British Columbia (Duncan, Springhouse, Wells Gray Provincial Park), and Prince Edward Island (Deroche Pond, Souris); also the northern Gulf of St. Lawrence region (Sept-Îles, Anticosti Island, Bonaventure Island; sight records for Harrington-Harbour and Madeleine Islands). Accidental in southern Keewatin (McConnell River: 20 June 1960, specimen). Sight records for northern Manitoba (Churchill).

Adult male: Upper parts brownish grey; wings and tail blackish slate edged with greyish; greater and middle wing coverts tipped white, forming two white wing bars; conspicuous patch of white at base of primaries; tail with three outermost feathers mainly white; under parts pale grey; legs and bill blackish; eye pale yellowish.

Measurements. *Adult male*: wing, 106–120 (111.4); tail, 110–134 (119.9); exposed culmen, 17–18.5 (17.9); tarsus, 29.5–34 (32.5). *Adult female*: wing, 100–111.5 (104.8) mm (Ridgway).

Field Marks. A slender, long-tailed bird, grey above, greyish white below; with two white wing bars, a white patch in the wings (conspicuous in flight), and mainly white outer tail feathers. Canadian shrikes are similar but have a black face mask. Townsend's Solitaire, of the West, also is similar but has a whitish eye-ring, dark-grey under parts (not much paler than upper parts), and usually much buff in the wing patch. *Voice*: The Mockingbird's song is long, loud, usually very melodious, but includes various harsh sounds and imitations of other bird songs. A distinctive feature is that a phrase is often repeated *three* or more times before a new one is taken up (Brown Thrasher frequently uses paired phrases).

Habitat. Shrubbery and tangles, hedgerows, various kinds of ornamental shrubbery about buildings.

Nesting. Usually between 1 and 6 m up in a shrub, tree, or vine. Nest is rather bulky, a loosely woven but durable cup of twigs, moss, bark strips, grass, leaves, and trash, lined with rootlets and dried grass. *Eggs*, usually 4 or 5; pale bluish or greenish blotched and spotted with browns. Incubation approximately 12 days, by the female (Amelia Laskey).

Range. Resident from northern and north-central United States and parts of southern Canada (very locally), south to southern Mexico (Isthmus of Tehuantepec), Jamaica, and the Virgin Islands.

Subspecies. (1) *Mimus polyglottos polyglottos* (Linnaeus): The breeding bird of eastern Canada west through Manitoba. The Duncan, British Columbia, specimen has been referred to this race but has not been seen by the writer. (2) *M. p. leucopterus* (Vigors) averages slightly larger with relatively shorter tail, upper parts slightly paler-grey, more buffy above and below, white in wings a little more extensive: Saskatchewan to British Columbia presumably, but no western breeding material is available for examination.

Sage Thrasher

Moqueur des armoises
Oreoscoptes montanus (Townsend)
Total length: 20 to 22.5 cm
Plate 55

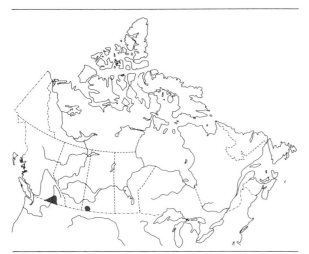

Breeding Distribution of Sage Thrasher

Range in Canada. Very local summer resident, breeding in southern British Columbia (Osoyoos, White Lake, Similkameen valley near International Boundary) and southwestern Saskatchewan (Eastend, Govenlock). Rare straggler to Alberta (Calgary, Walsh, Orion). Accidental in Ontario (specimen: Welland, 20 October 1966; photo record: Point Pelee, 12 May 1965).

Bill rather thrush-like; tail short for a thrasher. Upper parts greyish brown, the crown and back faintly streaked with dusky shade; a poorly defined pale eyebrow line; two narrow pale wing bars; outer tail feathers tipped white; under parts buffy white, more or less heavily streaked with brown; eye yellow.

Measurements. *Adult male*: wing, 95–103 (98.7); tail, 87–95 (90.8); exposed culmen, 14.5–17.5 (16.4); tarsus, 28.5–31.5 (30.4). *Adult female*: wing, 94–100 (96.2) mm (Ridgway).

Field Marks. A bird of semi-arid sagebrush plains, slightly smaller than the Robin, with brownish-grey upper parts, heavily streaked under parts, white tips to the outer tail feathers, two narrow white wing bars. *Voice*: Song is sustained (has been timed up to 2.5 minutes), energetic, and pleasing. It contains the usual thrasher repetition of phrases, but, unlike the song of the Brown Thrasher, there are no well-marked pauses between phrases. There is a little suggestion of the Catbird, but without the pauses.

Habitat. Dry sagebrush plains and thickets on arid hillsides.

Nesting. Usually in sagebrush or other bushes, sometimes on the ground. Nest is rather bulky, often partly arched over. It is made of coarse twigs and lined with grass and rootlets. *Eggs*, 4 or 5; greenish blue, spotted and blotched with reddish browns.

Range. Breeds from southern interior British Columbia, central Montana, and southwestern Saskatchewan south in the interior to central-southern California, northern New Mexico, northwestern Texas, and western Oklahoma. Winters from southern parts of the breeding range south to southern Baja California and in northern mainland Mexico.

Brown Thrasher

Moqueur roux
Toxostoma rufum (Linnaeus)
Total length: 26.5 to 30.5 cm
Plate 55

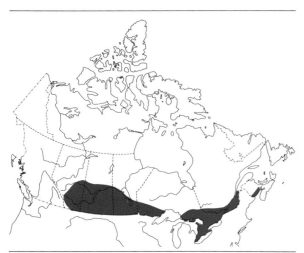

Breeding Distribution of Brown Thrasher

Range in Canada. Summer resident, breeding in southeastern Alberta (Cold Lake, Edmonton, Hardisty, Calgary, Medicine Hat, Milk River); central and southern Saskatchewan (Prince Albert, Cypress Hills, Regina); southern Manitoba (Dauphin, Brandon, Shoal Lake, Winnipeg, Sprague); western Ontario (Emo, Kenora);

Upper parts reddish brown; two white wing bars (buffy in autumn); under parts buffy white (palest on throat and abdomen), the breast, sides, and flanks heavily streaked with dark brown; eye yellow.

Measurements *(T. r. rufum)*. *Adult male*: wing, 98.1–110.4 (103.6); tail, 119.5–138.5 (127.6); exposed culmen, 23.8–27.6 (25.9); tarsus, 33–35 (34.1). *Adult female*: wing, 100.4–105.5 (102.7) mm.

Field Marks. Slightly larger and much longer-tailed than the Robin. Its bright reddish-brown upper parts and heavily streaked under parts perhaps suggest a thrush, but the Brown Thrasher's long tail, yellow eye, conspicuous white wing bars, and larger size should eliminate confusion. *Voice*: Song is loud and musical and is made up of a long procession of phrases punctuated by slight pauses. Many of the phrases are repeated and are thus given in pairs: *Drop-it-drop-it; cover it up-cover it up; pull it up-pull it up*. The paired phrases are an easy way to distinguish the song from that of the Catbird, which is otherwise similar. Also a powerful throaty *chip*.

Habitat. Deciduous thickets, bushy fields, woodland edges, and young second growth.

Nesting. In thickets and shrubbery, especially thorny types; sometimes on the ground. Nest is rather loosely constructed of twigs, sticks, weed stems, and strips of bark, and is lined with rootlets. *Eggs*, usually 4 or 5; pale bluish-white, rather uniformly covered with small brown spots. Incubation 11 to 14 days (W.G. Erwin), by both sexes.

southern Ontario (north to about Bigwood and Lake Nipissing; species reported north to Gogama); southwestern Quebec (Aylmer, Montréal, Sainte-Foy; rarely Rivière-du-Loup; recorded in the breeding season in the Lake Saint-Jean basin); and southern New Brunswick rarely (Grand Manan, Penniac, Pennfield).

Casual in southern British Columbia (Vancouver, Long Beach, Penticton); eastern Gaspé Peninsula (Sandy Lake) and on lower Moisie River (specimen: 15 June 1952); and Nova Scotia (Brier Island; also sight records by several competent observers). Accidental in southeastern Hudson Bay (Belcher Islands); North Twin Island in James Bay (specimen: 28 May 1973); Newfoundland (Cappahayden); and northern Manitoba (Churchill).

Range. Breeds from southern Canada (southeastern Alberta east to southwestern Quebec) and southwestern Maine south to eastern Colorado, northern and eastern Texas, the Gulf states, and southern Florida. Most individuals withdraw from the northern part of the range for the winter.

Subspecies. (1) *Toxostoma rufum rufum* (Linnaeus); southern Quebec. (2) *T. r. longicauda* (Baird), averaging very slightly larger: western Ontario (Kenora), southern Manitoba, southern Saskatchewan, southeastern Alberta.

Bendire's Thrasher

[**Bendire's Thrasher**. Moqueur à bec droit. *Toxostoma bendirei* (Coues). Total length: 29 cm. Hypothetical. Two sight records by competent observers of single individuals of this desert species: Saskatchewan (Dundurn, 27 May 1972) and Manitoba (Grand Beach, 14 May 1974). No photos or specimens were taken.]

Family **Motacillidae**: Wagtails and Pipits

Number of Species in Canada: 4

Terrestrial birds of open country with longish tails; slender bills; wings with nine primaries and with the inner secondaries elongated, often as long as the longest primaries; hind toe longish with long hind toenail. Instead of hopping on the ground they habitually walk and have a habit of wagging the tail up and down.

Yellow Wagtail

Bergeronnette printanière
Motacilla flava Linnaeus
Total length: ca. 16.5 cm
Plate 74

Breeding Distribution of Yellow Wagtail

Range in Canada. Breeds in northern Yukon (locally common on the coastal plain: Firth and Babbage rivers) and in extreme northwestern Mackenzie (probably Turnunuk Point). Sight record of one individual on Old Crow River, 6 August 1973.

Bill slender, sharp pointed; tail long; hind toenail elongated. *Adults (breeding season)*: Top of head, nape, and face dark ashy-grey; whitish line over eye; back olive green, often somewhat shaded with brown and brightening on rump; wings brown, the tertials edged with greenish white, the wing coverts margined with same, thus forming two yellowish-white wing bars; middle tail feathers blackish brown, outermost mainly white; under parts greenish yellow. *Young*: Wing and tail similar to adults but upper parts brown, under parts plain dingy brownish-white or buffy white, the throat white with blackish border.

Measurements *(M. f. tschutschensis)*. *Adult male*: wing, 74–82 (77.4); tail, 65–71 (67.5); exposed culmen, 11–12 (11.7); tarsus, 23–26.5 (24.5). *Adult female*: wing, 73–77 (74.6) mm (Ridgway).

Field Marks. A slender greenish-yellow bird with light eyebrow line, and a longish tail (which it flirts up and down and sideways). Outer tail feathers white. Adults have greenish-yellow under parts. Young are brown above and buffy white below with a whitish throat bordered by blackish blotches. Young somewhat resemble Water Pipit but lack stripes on the under parts.

Range. Eurasia, Alaska, and northern Yukon Territory.

Subspecies. *Motacilla flava tschutschensis* Gmelin.

White Wagtail

a

b

Figure 90
a) White Wagtail
b) Black-backed Wagtail

Black-backed Wagtail

[**White Wagtail**. Bergeronnette grise. *Motacilla alba* Linnaeus. Figure 90. Hypothetical. L.M. Turner's (1885. Proceedings U.S. National Museum, vol. 8, no. 5, p. 236) report of four (supposedly two parents and two young of the year) on 29 August 1883, near Kuujjuaq, Quebec, is only a sight record, a secondhand one at that, for the observation was made by two employees of the Hudson's Bay Company and later reported to Turner. One travelled on a ship from Ireland to the coast of Labrador in 1939 (C.P. Martin, 1939. Canadian Field-Naturalist, vol. 53, no. 8, p. 121).

There are sight records for British Columbia (Coquitlam River near its confluence with the Fraser River, 2 to 21 March 1973, one seen by many observers; and one in Pacific Rim National Park on 24 May 1977). No photos or specimens.]

[**Black-backed Wagtail**. Bergeronnette lugubre. *Motacilla lugens* Gloger. Figure 90. Hypothetical. Very similar to White Wagtail but the adult male, as its name suggests, is readily separable by its black back. Such a black-backed individual was observed in West Vancouver in April 1982 but unfortunately there is no photograph or specimen record. Perhaps additional British Columbia records listed under White Wagtail may refer to this species but diagnostic details are not available. For a useful treatment of the identification and affinities of these two similar taxa see Joseph Morlan (1981. Continental Birdlife, vol. 2, no. 2, pp. 37–50).]

Red-throated Pipit

Pipit à gorge rousse
Anthus cervinus (Pallas)
Total length: 14.5 to 15.2 cm
Plate 55

Status in Canada. Accidental in northern Yukon (specimen: Stokes Point, male, 23 June 1980 (*vide* Henri Ouellet); sight record: upper Babbage River, 9 June 1973).

In all plumages is more boldly and more extensively streaked than the Water and Sprague's pipits. Streaks much darker and extending *over the rump*. In the hand, the Red-throated Pipit's very dark (almost blackish) centres of the upper tail coverts differ from those of the Water Pipit. Males in breeding plumages have throat, breast, and superciliary line rusty to vinaceous pink. Legs brownish-flesh colour.

Field Marks. Male in breeding plumage is readily separable from Water and Sprague's pipits by its pinkish breast and superciliary line. At all seasons its bolder streaking (on upper parts expanding almost to blackish blotches) differs noticeably from both Sprague's and Water pipits. Its obviously paler legs distinguish it from Water Pipit.

Range. Breeds across northern Eurasia from northern Scandinavia east to the Chukotski Peninsula; also in western Alaska (Bering Sea islands and coastal regions and northward to Cape Lisburne). Winters in northern Africa, southern Eurasia, and the Philippine Islands.

Water Pipit

(American Pipit)

Pipit spioncelle
Anthus spinoletta (Linnaeus)
Total length: 15 to 17.5 cm
Plate 55

Breeding Distribution of Water Pipit

Range in Canada. Breeds in suitable arctic barrens, alpine treeless areas, and similar situations from northern Banks Island (Mahogany Point), Bylot Island, and northern Baffin Island south through Yukon (including Herschel Island) to southern British Columbia and southwestern Alberta (Rocky Mountains); south-central and southeastern Mackenzie (mountains near Norman Wells; Nahanni National Park; Manitou Island on Great Bear Lake; Dubawnt River); southern Keewatin (Nueltin Lake); northern Manitoba (Meades Lake, Churchill); northern Ontario (Little Cape, Cape Henrietta Maria); southern Quebec (Moar Bay, Schefferville, Blanc-Sablon, Ouapitagone Harbour, Middle (Galibois) Island; locally Mount Albert on Gaspé Peninsula); southern Labrador; and Newfoundland.

Migrates through all southern Canada. Small numbers winter in southern British Columbia (Victoria, Lulu Island).

Casual visitant to Bathurst Island, N.W.T. (specimen: 17 June 1971).

Bill slender, short, pointed; hind toe elongated. *Adults (breeding plumage)*: Upper parts greyish brown, the top of head and the back streaked with dusky; buffy-white superciliary line; wings dusky brown with buffy edging; tail mainly dusky brown, the outermost feather on each side largely white, with less white on the next, and on only the tip (if any white is present) of third from outside; under parts pinkish buff, the upper breast, sides, and flanks narrowly streaked with dusky. Legs blackish brown. *Adults and young (autumn)*: Upper parts much browner and more olive; breast, sides, and flanks more heavily streaked with dusky. Legs blackish brown.

Measurements *(A. s. rubescens)*. *Adult male*: wing, 76.9–86.2 (82.8); tail, 61–66 (63.3); exposed culmen, 12.3–13.5 (12.8); tarsus, 21–23 (21.7). *Adult female*: wing, 75.5–84 (79.3) mm.

Field Marks. A sparrow-sized, brownish, thin-billed bird with dark breast-streaks. Feeds on the ground often in flocks, walks instead of hopping; frequently wags tail. In flight shows white outer tail feathers. Although the Vesper Sparrow and some longspurs show white in the outer tail feathers, the slim bill of the Water Pipit separates it from them and other sparrows. It most closely resembles Sprague's Pipit of the prairies, but the Water Pipit's blackish (instead of flesh-coloured) legs distinguish it. *Voice*: At any time of year a sharp *tsip-tsip* (usually given in twos) or *tsip it*, especially when flushing or in flight. This note is much sharper than a similar one given by the Horned Lark. On the breeding grounds a tinkling flight song is common.

Habitat. For nesting in the Arctic, vegetated, usually sloping, rocky ground; in the mountains, rocky situations and alpine meadows mostly above timberline. In migration, open areas with low or no vegetation; shores, beaches, mud flats, ploughed or moist fields, gravel pits, sand dunes.

Nesting. On the ground. Under or near a rock, under low vegetation, on a mossy hummock, or in a cavity in a rock pile. Nest mainly of grasses and twigs. *Eggs*, 4 to 7, usually 4 or 5; greyish or buffy white, thickly spotted with various browns, often so thickly that the background colour is nearly or quite obscured. Incubation probably close to that of the Old World nominate race, about 14 days, by the female.

Range. Breeds in Eurasian and North American tundra and mountains. In North America from northern Alaska east to western Greenland and south in the western mountains to Oregon, Utah, northern Arizona, and northern New Mexico; also south locally to Maine (Mount Katahdin). Canadian populations winter mainly in the United States and south to Guatemala.

Subspecies. (1) *Anthus spinoletta rubescens* (Tunstall) is the breeding bird of all Canada except British Columbia and southwestern Alberta. (2) *A. s. pacificus* Todd (paler coloration): British Columbia (north at least to Dease Lake), southwestern Alberta. No breeding material for southwestern Yukon examined.

Sprague's Pipit

Pipit des Prairies
Anthus spragueii (Audubon)
Total length: 15 to 17.5 cm
Plate 55

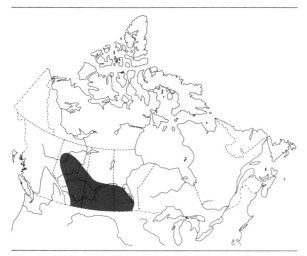

Breeding Distribution of Sprague's Pipit

Range in Canada. Breeds in suitable grassland in north-central, central, and southern Alberta (from Dixonville in Peace River District and Athabasca south to the International Boundary, and west to the foothills, e.g., Yaha Tinda prairies just east of Banff National Park); central and southern Saskatchewan (Prince Albert region, Nipawin southward); and central-western and southern Manitoba (The Pas, Lake St. Martin, Aweme, Hillside Beach southward). Recorded in breeding season at Rainy River, Ontario, but no definite evidence of nesting.

Sight records north to Churchill, Manitoba, and east to Kent County, Ontario.

Hind toenail longer than that of Water Pipit; crown and upper parts decidedly streaked, feathers margined with buffy often giving lower back a somewhat scaly appearance; legs pale. *Adults*: Crown and upper parts decidedly streaked buffy and dusky; tail dusky, the two outer feathers largely white; cheeks and under parts buffy white, the breast sharply (but not profusely) streaked with dusky; legs pale brown, flesh, or pale yellowish-brown.

Measurements. *Adult male*: wing, 78.5–84.9 (82.0); tail, 53–60 (56.7); exposed culmen, 12–13.8 (12.7); tarsus, 21–23 (22.2). *Adult female*: wing, 77.2–83.5 (78.6) mm.

Field Marks. A buffy-brown, slender-billed sparrow-sized bird of the western prairies; shows white outer tail feathers in flight. Its slender bill separates it from the sparrows (including the longspurs), lack of black areas on head or upper breast from the Horned Lark. Resembles Water Pipit but has pale legs, buff-striped upper parts, and generally paler coloration. *Voice*: Song is given in series of seven or eight tinkling double notes on a descending scale, usually as the bird circles high in the air: *sewee, sewee, sewee.*

Habitat. Prairie grasslands and short-grass plains, preferably unploughed and unburned.

Nesting. On the ground and often overarched with grass. Nest is mainly of grasses with some weed stems and coarser grasses in the outer bowl. *Eggs*, 4 to 7; greyish white, spotted with olive brown or purplish brown.

Range. Breeds from the prairies of Canada south to Montana, North Dakota, and northwestern Minnesota. Winters from southern Arizona, Texas, southern Louisiana, and northwestern Mississippi to southwestern Mexico.

Family **Bombycillidae**: Waxwings

Number of Species in Canada: 2

Figure 91
Secondary feather from wing of Bohemian Waxwing showing waxlike appendage at tip

Crested arboreal birds, their short bills broad at the base and slightly hooked at the tip; wings, rather long, pointed, have ten primaries (outermost much reduced); the tips of some of the secondaries often have small, red, waxlike appendages (Figure 91), but these are not always present, and their presence is not correlated with age, sex, or season. Tail moderate, tail coverts long. Plumage sleek. Fruits and berries make up the bulk of their food, but insects also are taken, often flycatcher fashion.

Bohemian Waxwing

Jaseur boréal
Bombycilla garrulus (Linnaeus)
Total length: 19 to 22 cm
Plate 58

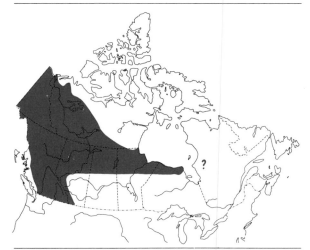

Breeding Distribution of Bohemian Waxwing

Range in Canada. Breeds in Yukon (Old Crow, Forty Mile, Burwash Landing, Carcross; found in summer north to upper Babbage and Firth rivers); Mackenzie (Mackenzie Delta, Anderson River, Great Bear Lake, Reliance, Fort Smith); interior British Columbia (Atlin, Telegraph Creek, Pouce Coupé, Vancouver region, Carpenter Mountain in the Cariboo District, Moose River in Yellowhead Pass region, Alta Lake); northern and western Alberta (south to about Athabasca River and in the mountains and foothills to Banff); northern Saskatchewan (Lake Athabasca, Kazan Lake); and northern Manitoba (Churchill, Cochrane River, Thicket Portage).

Breeds in northern Ontario (summer records in three different years near junction of Sutton and Warchesku rivers, collected birds showing evidence of having bred). Present in mid-June in central-western Quebec (Grande rivière de la Baleine, 14 June 1971, and through June at Lac Vincellotte on La Grande River where a collected male was in breeding condition.

Winters from central British Columbia (Puntchesakut Lake, François Lake), southwestern Mackenzie (Fort Liard), central Alberta (Edmonton, Elk Island National Park), central Saskatchewan (Prince Albert National Park), and southern Manitoba (Lake St. Martin) southward; irregularly in southern Ontario (Sault Ste. Marie, Lake Nipissing, Cochrane, Ottawa southward), and southwestern Quebec (Hull, Montréal, Québec; rarely Arvida); very rarely in New Brunswick (Grand Manan, Saint John, Fredericton), and Nova Scotia (Halifax, Pictou, Baddeck). Winter sight records for Prince Edward Island (Charlottetown), and Newfoundland (L'Anse-aux-Meadows, St. Anthony, St. John's, Clarenville).

Head crested, bill short, flattened toward base; plumage sleek. *Adults*: Soft brownish-grey generally, brownest (cinnamon) on head, greyish on rump and abdomen; narrow mask through eye and patch on throat black; secondaries with white tips to outer webs and with bright-red (rarely yellow) appendages like sealing wax, sometimes absent; primaries and primary coverts blackish, the coverts tipped white, the primaries with tips of yellow and/or white; tail becoming blackish near end and with broad yellow tip; under tail coverts chestnut. *Young in juvenal plumage* (worn only a short time): Similar to adults but much duller, crest smaller, red appendages to secondaries fewer or absent; under parts dark olive-grey streaked with white, middle of abdomen whitish; no black bib.

Measurements. *Adult male*: wing, 109.6–118.9 (113.9); tail, 64.5–69 (66.1); exposed culmen, 12.1–14 (12.9); tarsus, 19.5–21 (20.2). *Adult female*: wing, 108.7–117.5 (112.7) mm.

Field Marks. Crest, brownish coloration, black patch through eye, and yellow tail tip make it a waxwing. Usually seen in flocks. Tiny red appendages on secondaries are often absent, and when present they are difficult to see. Similar to Cedar Waxwing but larger, *with chestnut instead of whitish under tail coverts*, small white patches in wing. Young birds are duller with smaller crest, no black on throat, and the olive-brown under parts are streaked with white. Chestnut under tail coverts and wing pattern (white and yellow patches) distinguish them from Cedar Waxwing of similar age. *Voice*: Similar to that of Cedar Waxwing but lower in pitch, more buzzy.

Habitat. In breeding season coniferous (sometimes mixedwood) woodlands and muskegs; also burntlands. In winter various types of berry- and fruit-producing trees and shrubs, often about dwellings.

Nesting. On a branch 1.2 to 15 m up in a coniferous tree. Nest of twigs, grass, *Usnea* lichen, and lined with fine grass, plant fibres, or conifer needles. *Eggs*, 4 to 6; pale blue and well marked with blackish dots and often a few fine lines. Incubation 13 to 14 days, by the female.

Range. Breeds widely in Eurasia and in northwestern North America. In North America from western Alaska east to Manitoba and south to central Washington, northern Idaho, northwestern Montana, and southern Alberta.

Subspecies. *Bombycilla garrulus pallidiceps* Reichenow.

Cedar Waxwing

Jaseur des cèdres
Bombycilla cedrorum Vieillot
Total length: 16.5 to 20 cm
Plate 58

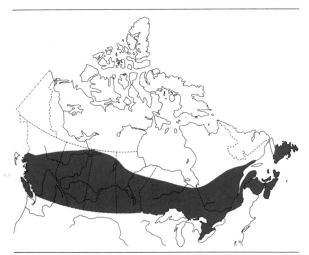

Breeding Distribution of Cedar Waxwing

Range in Canada. Breeds across southern Canada north to north-central British Columbia (Skeena River valley, Tetana Lake, Tupper Creek); northern Alberta (Lake Athabasca, Peace River District); northern Saskatchewan (Stony Rapids); central Manitoba (Thicket Portage); northern Ontario (Sandy Lake, Moose Factory, perhaps north to Sutton Ridges); south-central Quebec (Lake Mistassini, inner north shore of the Gulf of St. Lawrence: Matamec, Natashquan; recorded in summer in August east to 35.5 km inland from Saint-Augustin—specimen; and to Grande rivière de la Baleine; specimen 14 June 1971. Recorded rarely on Anticosti Island without evidence of nesting); New Brunswick; Prince Edward Island; Nova Scotia; and Newfoundland.

Casual in southwestern Mackenzie (Fort Simpson, 18 June 1958—specimen) and northeastern Manitoba (Churchill). Scarce migrant on Queen Charlotte Islands.

Winters in southern British Columbia (Victoria, Vancouver, Okanagan Landing); Alberta (north to Edmonton); southern Ontario (Thunder Bay, Huntsville, Ottawa southward); southwestern Quebec (Montréal, Québec); southern New Brunswick; southern Nova Scotia; and irregularly elsewhere (north occasionally to Saskatoon, Saskatchewan).

Similar to Bohemian Waxwing but smaller; lacks white or yellow on the wing and has no chestnut on under tail coverts. *Adults*: Narrow band across forehead and back over eyes black; chin blackish passing into brown on throat; rest of head, neck, breast, and back cinnamon brown passing into grey on rump and blackish toward end of tail (which has a broad yellow tip); wings slaty grey, the secondaries with tiny red appendages like sealing wax (but sometimes lacking); abdomen, sides, and flanks pale greenish-yellow; under tail coverts whitish. *Young in juvenal plumage*: Similar to adults but much greyer; crest shorter; no black behind eye or on throat; breast and sides olive brown streaked with white; middle of abdomen whitish, red appendages to secondaries either lacking or poorly developed.

Measurements. *Adult male*: wing, 90.6–98 (95.4); tail, 57.5–63.5 (59.5); exposed culmen, 10.1–11.3 (10.6); tarsus, 15.5–16.5 (15.9). *Adult female*: wing, 89.5–96.9 (94.1) mm.

Field Marks. A crested brownish bird with a yellow-tipped tail is a waxwing. Sits erect, usually is seen in flocks or companies. Similar only to the Bohemian Waxwing, from which the following points separate it: under tail coverts white (never chestnut); no white or yellow patches in wings; abdomen, sides, and flanks pale yellowish (instead of soft grey). *Voice*: A high-pitched whistled hiss, similar to that of the Bohemian Waxwing but higher-pitched and less buzzy.

Habitat. Extremely varied, open and sparse woodlands either deciduous or coniferous, sparse second growths, trees and shrubbery about dwellings, orchards, edges of dams, lakes, rivers, marshes, bogs, and burntlands where standing dead trees provide lookout perches; the vicinity of berry and small-fruit-bearing trees and bushes.

Nesting. In the horizontal branches of trees or tall shrubs, either deciduous or coniferous, 1.2 to 12 m up. Nest is bulky, made of twigs, bark strips, plant fibres, fine rootlets, *Usnea* lichen, paper, rags, or twine; lined with fine similar materials. *Eggs*, 3 to 5; pale bluish-grey or greenish blue, with usually well-spaced small spots or dots of black or blackish brown. Incubation period averages 11.7 days (R.B. Lea), 12 to 14 days (authors), by the female.

Range. Breeds from extreme southeastern Alaska east to Newfoundland and south to northern California, northern Utah, northwestern Oklahoma, southern Illinois, northern Alabama, and northern Georgia. Winters from northern United States (and locally southern Canada) south to Panama.

Remarks. The Cedar Waxwing is attired in soft, harmonious colours. Its silky plumage seemingly never has a feather out of place. It has a friendly nature and generally is seen in flocks. The bulk of its food is made up of small fruits, mostly wild kinds. About orchards of ripe cherries, however, it can be destructive. It devours quite a variety of insects also, often catching them flycatcher-fashion.

1 Eastern Bluebird, p. 421
a) adult male
b) adult female

1a

1b

2b

2 Mountain Eluebird, p. 422
a) adult male
b) adult female

2a

3 Redwing, p. 429

3

4 Fieldfare, p. 428

4

5 Varied Thrush, p. 431
adult male

5

6a

6 Western Bluebird,
p. 422
a) adult male
b) adult female

6b

7 American Robin, p. 429
a) juvenal
b) adult male

7a

7b

58

1 Golden-crowned Kinglet,
p. 416
a) adult female
b) adult male

2 Ruby-crowned Kinglet, p. 417
a) adult male
b) adult female

3 Blue-gray Gnatcatcher,
p. 418

4 Loggerhead Shrike,
p. 451

5 Northern Shrike,
p. 450

7 Cedar Waxwing, p. 440
a) juvenal
b) adult

6 Bohemian Waxwing,
p. 439

1 Yellow-throated Vireo, p. 456

3 White-eyed Vireo, p. 454

2 Hutton's Vireo, p. 456

5 Bell's Vireo, p. 454

4 Solitary Vireo, p. 455

7 Warbling Vireo, p. 457

6 Philadelphia Vireo, p. 458

8 Red-eyed Vireo, p. 459

Crosby

1a

1 Northern Parula, p. 465
a) adult male
b) adult female
c) autumn immature

1b

2b

2 Yellow Warbler, p. 466
a) adult male
b) adult female

2a

1c

5a

3 Brewster's Warbler, p. 461
hybrid Golden-winged
× Blue-winged Warbler

4

3

5b

4 Blue-winged Warbler, p. 460
adult male in breeding plumage

5 Golden-winged Warbler, p. 461
a) adult female
b) adult male

8 Black-and-white Warbler, p. 483
a) adult male in breeding plumage
b) autumn immature

6

8a

6 Worm-eating Warbler, p. 485

7

8b

7 Prothonotary Warbler,
p. 484
adult male

Crosby.

1a

2 Arctic Warbler, p. 416

2

3a

1b

3b

1 Tennessee Warbler, p. 462
a) male in breeding plumage
b) autumn immature

3 Orange-crowned Warbler, p. 463
a) adult male in breeding plumage
b) autumn immature

4a

4b

5

6a

4 Nashville Warbler, p. 464
a) adult in breeding plumage
b) autumn immature

5 Virginia's Warbler, p. 464

7a

7 Cape May Warbler, p. 469
a) adult male in breeding plumage
b) adult female in
   breeding plumage
c) autumn immature female

7b

6b

6 Magnolia Warbler, p. 468
a) adult male in breeding plumage
b) autumn immature

8 Kirtland's Warbler, p. 477
adult male in breeding plumage

8

7c

Crosby

62

1 Townsend's Warbler, p. 473
a) adult female in breeding plumage
b) autumn immature
c) adult male in breeding plumage

2 Yellow-rumped Warbler, p. 470
a) "Myrtle" Warbler subspecies:
autumn
b) "Myrtle" Warbler subspecies:
male in breeding plumage
c) "Myrtle" Warbler subspecies:
female in breeding plumage
d) "Audubon's" Warbler subspecies:
male in breeding plumage

4 Black-throated Green Warbler, p. 474
a) male in breeding plumage
b) female in breeding plumage
c) autumn immature

5 Hermit Warbler, p. 472
male in breeding plumage

3 Black-throated Gray Warbler, p. 472
male in breeding plumage

6 Black-throated Blue Warbler,
p. 470
a) female
b) male in breeding plumage

7 Cerulean Warbler, p. 482
a) female in breeding plumage
b) male in breeding plumage

Crosby

1 Blackpoll Warbler, p. 481
a) female in breeding plumage
b) male in breeding plumage
c) autumn immature

2 Bay-breasted Warbler, p. 480
a) male in breeding plumage
b) male in autumn plumage
c) female in breeding plumage
d) autumn female

4 Chestnut-sided Warbler, p. 467
a) autumn immature
b) male in breeding plumage

3 Blackburnian Warbler, p. 475
a) autumn
b) male in breeding plumage
c) female in breeding plumage

6 Pine Warbler, p. 476
a) female
b) adult male

5 Yellow-throated Warbler, p. 476
male in breeding plumage

Crosby

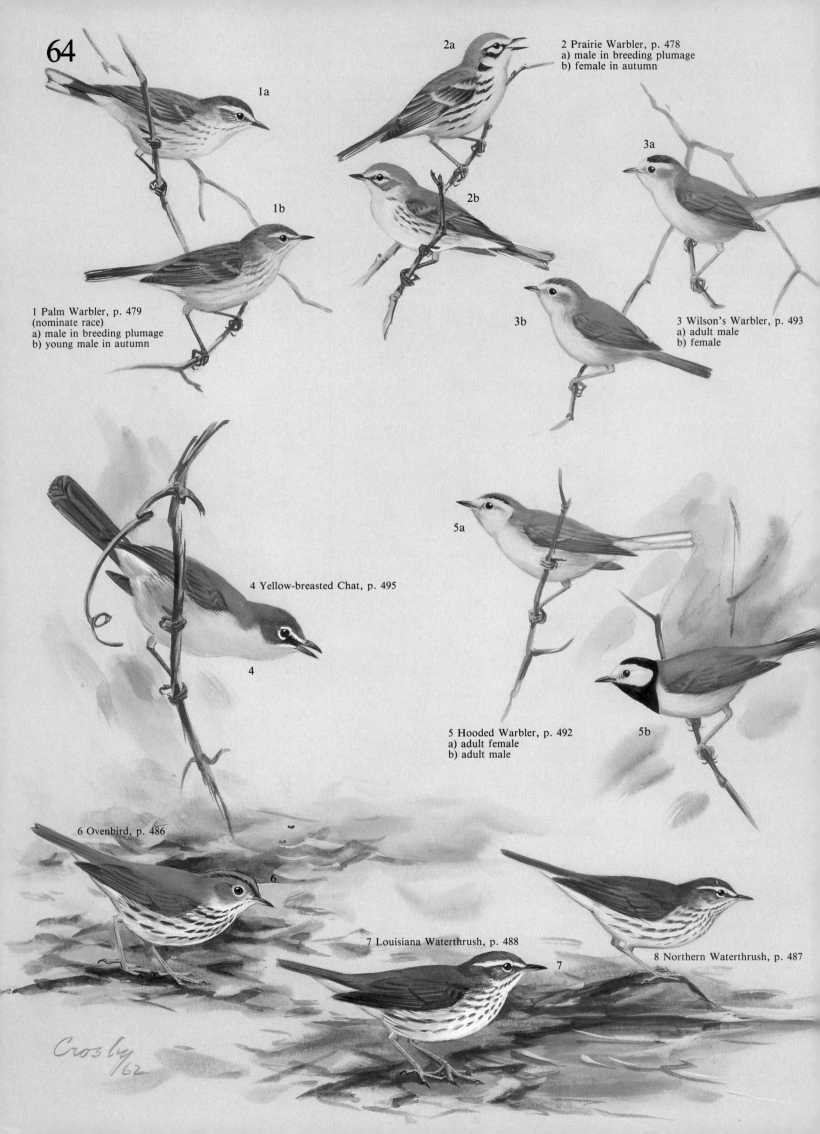

64

1a

1b

1 Palm Warbler, p. 479
(nominate race)
a) male in breeding plumage
b) young male in autumn

2a

2 Prairie Warbler, p. 478
a) male in breeding plumage
b) female in autumn

2b

3a

3b

3 Wilson's Warbler, p. 493
a) adult male
b) female

4 Yellow-breasted Chat, p. 495

4

5a

5 Hooded Warbler, p. 492
a) adult female
b) adult male

5b

6 Ovenbird, p. 486

6

7 Louisiana Waterthrush, p. 488

7

8 Northern Waterthrush, p. 487

Crosby
'62

Family **Ptilogonatidae:** Silky-Flycatchers

Number of Species in Canada: 1

This New World family containing four species is closely related to the waxwings and is treated as a subfamily of the Bombycillidae by some authors. Like waxwings the members of this family have a crest, silky plumage and a fondness for berries and insects, the latter taken on the wing flycatcher fashion. They have shorter wings and longer tails than waxwings and adult males and females are differently attired.

Phainopepla

Phénopèple
Phainopepla nitens (Swainson)
Total length: 17 to 19.5 cm

Status in Canada. Accidental in southern Ontario (Wallacetown, 26 December 1975 to 21 January 1976). Photographs. Subspecies not determinable from photos.

Adult male. A crested bird, uniformly glossy-black in coloration except white patches in the wings. Iris red. Female and immature are crested, body coloration plain darkish-grey, wings and tail somewhat darker, the wing coverts margined with pale grey or white, forming inconspicuous wing patches.

Measurements. *Adult male*: wing, 90–99 (94.6); tail, 91–105 (96.1); exposed culmen, 10–12 (10.8); tarsus, 16–19.5 (17.6). *Adult female*: wing, 86–96 (90.5); tail, 83–96 (89.7); tarsus, 17–19 (18.2) mm.

Field Marks. Adult male is a slender black bird with conspicuous crest and white wing patches, which are very evident in flight. The female and immature birds might be confused with waxwings (also crested) but waxwings show a yellow tail-band and brown (rather than grey) general coloration.

Range. Central California, southern Utah, and western Texas south to central Mexico.

Family **Laniidae:** Shrikes

Number of Species in Canada: 2

Figure 92
Head of Loggerhead Shrike

Medium-sized birds with robust, strongly hooked bills, the upper mandibles with a notch and a toothlike projection near the tip (Figure 92). The feet are suitable for perching but are not fitted for grasping or holding prey. Perhaps because the feet are relatively weak, prey is impaled on thorns or barbed wire to hold it. The family is a large one that originated in the Old World and reaches its best development there. Shrikes subsist on animal food, such as insects, small birds, and small mammals.

Northern Shrike

Pie-grièche grise
Lanius excubitor Linnaeus
Total length: 22.5 to 27.5 cm
Plate 58

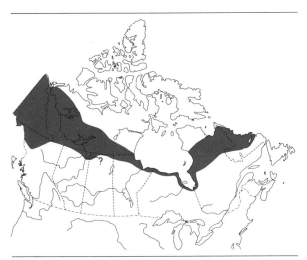

Breeding Distribution of Northern Shrike

Range in Canada. Breeds from Yukon (lower Blow River, Forty Mile, Ogilvie Range, probably north to Old Crow where recorded in spring); northern Mackenzie (Mackenzie Delta, Fort Anderson, Great Slave Lake, and near junction of Hanbury and Thelon rivers); southwestern Keewatin (probably Windy River); northern Quebec (Feuilles River, Koroc River); and northern Labrador (Okak) south to northern British Columbia (Atlin, Mile 80 Haines Road, Dease Lake); northern Alberta (Lake Athabasca); northern Manitoba (Churchill, York Factory); central Quebec (Grande rivière de la Baleine, Schefferville region and locally south to Cabbage Willows Bay); and southern Labrador (Sandwich Bay). Recently found breeding in northern Ontario (Sutton Ridges; there are old summer records at Fort Severn, Winisk, Cape Henrietta Maria, and Moosonee).

In migration and winter all across settled southern Canada: southern British Columbia (including Vancouver Island), Alberta, Saskatchewan, Manitoba, Ontario, southern Quebec, Newfoundland, New Brunswick, Prince Edward Island, and Nova Scotia.

Upper mandible hooked. *Adults (female often duller with less white in wings and tail)*: Crown, nape, and back light bluish-grey paling to white on rump, with ends of scapulars, the lower forehead, and a line back over eyes white also; black mask from base of bill to ear coverts; wings mostly black with a white patch at base of primaries; secondaries and tertials narrowly tipped white; tail mostly black but outer feather on either side mainly white with rapidly diminishing extent of white on each more inward feather; under parts white with more or less fine wavy dusky barring (but sometimes nearly or quite absent). *Young (first year)*: Resemble adults but grey areas very much browner; face patch usually confined to behind eye, brownish and veiled; under parts more brownish and much more heavily barred with dusky.

Measurements *(L. e. borealis)*. *Adult male*: wing, 108.4–116.3 (112.9); tail, 104–115 (110.0); exposed culmen, 18.3–19 (18.7); tarsus, 25.5–28 (26.3). *Adult female*: wing, 109.8–113.2 (111.9) mm.

Field Marks. A grey-and-black robin-sized bird with a *black mask* through the eye and a hooked bill is a shrike. Flight is undulating, and the white patch in the wing flashes conspicuously. When perched, it flicks its tail frequently. The Northern Shrike closely resembles the Loggerhead Shrike, but in settled parts of southern Canada only the Loggerhead is likely to be encountered in summer and only the Northern in winter. The Northern Shrike is a larger bird, usually shows more barring on the breast, most (not all) lack any black on the forehead, often show a more extensive pale area at the base of the bill in autumn and winter. Breeding adults of both species have an all-black bill. Young of the year are more easily confused, but those of the Northern are more brownish above and below than young Loggerheads and have much more heavily barred under parts. In all plumages the Northern has a heavier, longer, more heavily hooked bill. *Voice*: Song a disjointed but musical medley of warbled notes, whistles, imitations of other bird songs, interspersed with various harsh notes. The performance is usually given from a treetop and is often of long duration. Alarm note is a harsh *sheck sheck*.

Habitat. On the breeding grounds, open sparse woods, thickets, bogs; also low growth near or above timberline of mountains. In winter, various types of more open situations where trees, hedges, wood patches, shade trees, or telephone poles provide lookout perches (habitat often similar to that occupied in summer by the Loggerhead Shrike).

Nesting. In a branch of a tree or bush. Nest is bulky, made of twigs and lined with rootlets, wool, hair, lichens, and feathers. *Eggs*, usually 4 to 7, sometimes up to 9. Eggs greyish white, spotted and blotched with olive brown or dull olive and usually some spots of purplish grey. Incubation 15 to 16 days mainly, if not entirely, by the female.

Range. Eurasia, northern Africa, and northern North America. In North America breeds from Alaska across the northern mainland of Canada to Labrador; winters south to northern California, central Arizona, central Missouri, central Ohio, and Maryland.

Subspecies. (1) *Lanius excubitor borealis* Vieillot: eastern Canada. (2) *L. e. invictus* Grinnell (paler and larger): Manitoba (Churchill, York Factory) westward.

Remarks. From some vantage point like a treetop, post, or wire, the Northern Shrike patiently watches for its prey. It eats mice, small birds, and, when available, large insects. It often impales its prey on a thorn or fence-wire barb, or wedges it into a fork in a branch. Although a predator, it is a songbird with weak untaloned feet. Its heavy hooked beak serves as a weapon to deliver a blow, to hold and shake its prey, or to tear off pieces of flesh for eating. Never abundant, it has no great effect on its prey species.

Loggerhead Shrike
(Migrant Shrike)

Pie-grièche migratrice
Lanius ludovicianus Linnaeus
Total length: 22 to 24.5 cm
Plate 58

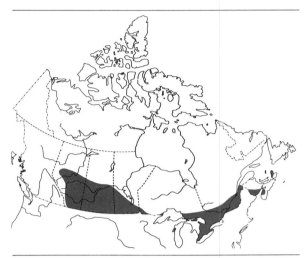

Breeding Distribution of Loggerhead Shrike

Range in Canada. Breeds in north-central, central, and southern Alberta (east of the mountains, from Fairview and Lesser Slave Lake southward); central and southern Saskatchewan (Meadow Lake, Nipawin southward); southern Manitoba (Swan River, Lake St. Martin, Deer Lodge; said to have nested once at Churchill (L.I. Grinnell and R.S. Palmer, 1941. Canadian Field-Naturalist, vol. 55, no. 4, p. 52)); western Ontario (Emo, Rainy River, Thunder Bay); southern Ontario (Sault Ste. Marie, Lake Nipissing, Ottawa southward); southwestern Quebec (Hull, Montréal, Hatley, Québec, Saint-Pacôme, Kamouraska); New Brunswick (Upper Woodstock, Sussex, Fairville); and rarely Nova Scotia (Chipmans Corner, Petit Étang).

Rare visitor to southern British Columbia (Chilliwack, Osoyoos, Edgewood, Okanagan Landing). Casual in northern Manitoba (Churchill).

Similar to Northern Shrike but smaller; *adults* with darker grey upper parts, unbarred (or nearly so) under parts, black face bar more extensive, usually reaching narrowly across lower forehead. *Young* Loggerhead Shrikes in juvenal plumage, however, have no black on the forehead and show fine barring on breast and sides, but this barring is much finer and less conspicuous than in the Northern Shrike.

Measurements *(L. l. migrans). Adult male*: wing, 94.8–100.9 (97.9); tail, 88.5–100 (95.3); exposed culmen, 14.8–16.6 (15.5); tarsus, 25.5–28.5 (26.4). *Adult female*: wing, 90.5–98.1 (95.1) mm.

Field Marks. A grey-and-black robin-sized bird with a black bar through the eye is a shrike. The Loggerhead, though very similar to the Northern, is smaller with relatively stubbier bill. Adults have unbarred under parts and the black of face bar usually extends narrowly across the lower forehead. Young Loggerheads are very lightly barred with dusky on breast and sides but are more greyish (not brownish). A shrike found in settled southern Canada in summer is probably a Loggerhead, in winter probably a Northern (see Mockingbird). *Song*: A mixture of pleasing and harsh notes; usually of shorter duration than the song of the Northern.

Habitat. Open country with hedgerows, copses, scattered trees or tall shrubs, telephone poles and wires, and fence posts where adequate lookout posts and nesting sites are present.

Nesting. From 1.5 to 6 m up in a tree or shrub (especially a thorny one). Nest is rather bulky and is made of twigs lined with rootlets, plant fibres, soft cottony or woolly materials, hair, feathers, rags, or paper. *Eggs*, 4 to 6; greyish white, spotted and blotched with greys and browns. Incubation period 13 to 16 days (O.W. Knight) by the female.

Range. Breeds from southern Canada (Alberta east to Nova Scotia) south through the United States to southern Mexico, the Gulf Coast of United States, and southern Florida. Winters mainly from north-central United States southward.

Subspecies. (1) *Lanius ludovicianus migrans* Palmer: southeastern Manitoba (intergrading westward with *excubitorides* in the Lake St. Martin region), southern Ontario, southern Quebec, New Brunswick, Nova Scotia. (2) *L. l. excubitorides* Swainson (averages paler, upper tail coverts and edges of scapulars more extensively whitish): central and southern Alberta, central and southern Saskatchewan, southwestern Manitoba (Swan River, Douglas). (3) *L. l. gambeli* Ridgway: the southern British Columbia visitants have been referred to this form.

Family **Sturnidae**:
Starlings

Number of Species in Canada: 2

A large Old World family, two species of which have been introduced by man into North America. One species, the European Starling, has flourished and spread rapidly across the continent. The other, the Crested Myna, has remained confined mostly to the vicinity of Vancouver, British Columbia, where it was introduced early in the century.

European Starling

Étourneau sansonnet
Sturnus vulgaris Linnaeus
Total length: 19 to 21.5 cm
Plate 67

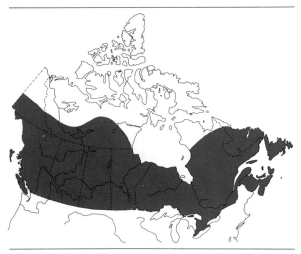

Breeding Distribution of European Starling

Range in Canada. Introduced; range still expanding. In 1978 the breeding range was approximately as follows: Across southern Canada and north through British Columbia (including Vancouver and Queen Charlotte islands) to southern Yukon (Dawson, White-horse); southern and central Mackenzie (Nahanni National Park, Lookout Point on Thelon River); northern Manitoba (Churchill); northern Ontario (Big Trout Lake, Winisk); northern Quebec (Kuujjuaq southward including Anticosti and Madeleine islands); central Labrador; and Newfoundland southward to the Maritimes (including Sable Island).

Recorded without evidence of breeding north to northern Mackenzie (Inuvik, 27 June 1968), Southampton Island (Coral Harbour, 8 August 1975), and extreme northern Quebec (Salluit, Povungnituk).

Winters in more or less diminished numbers within the more southern parts of the country, but has been observed in December at Yellow-knife, N.W.T.

Bill almost as long as head, tapering to a point. Tail short, square. Feathers of breast in adults with pointed tips, long and attenuated in adult males. *Adult male (breeding plumage: midwinter, spring, early summer)*: Glossy blackish with purple and green reflections; wings and tail blackish edged with buff; some buffy spots on back usually retained from winter plumage; bill mainly yellow, but base of lower mandible dark grey or bluish, iris brown, legs reddish brown. *Adult male (winter plumage: late summer–early winter)*: Similar to adult male in breeding plumage but upper parts with numerous buffy spots, under parts with many white spots; bill mainly dusky. *Adult female*: Similar to respective plumages of adult male but feathers of breast with shorter, less attenuated tips, iris with a yellowish outer edge; in breeding plumage the base of the lower mandible is creamy or pinkish (instead of dark grey or bluish). *Young (juvenal plumage)*: Upper parts dark greyish-brown; wings and tail with buffy edges; throat whitish; rest of under parts greyish brown, the middle of abdomen streaked whitish.

Measurements. *Adult male*: 121.5–130.5 (127.2); tail, 61–64 (62.6); exposed culmen, 25.9–29.1 (27.7); tarsus, 27–30 (29.3). *Adult female*: wing, 120–126.5 (122.9) mm.

Field Marks. Looks black, thus resembles a blackbird but with short stubby tail. From midwinter to midsummer its yellow bill separates it from any Canadian blackbird. When in late summer the bill turns dusky, the plumage becomes white-spotted, unlike any of our blackbirds. In flight it has a characteristic short-tailed triangular outline, and at a distance the underside of the spread wings looks brownish against the black body. Ordinary flight is swift and direct. Usually seen in flocks, often very large. As it frequents buildings of cities, towns, and farms, it is familiar to most people who live in southern Canada. Although the young are mouse-brown, they have the same stubby tail and characteristic outline as the adults. *Voice*: Song, a rambling procession of whistles, warbles, squeaks, chirps, clicks, gurgles, and often imitations of other bird voices. Calls include various whistles and other notes. Flocks gathered for roosting keep up a continuous twittering chorus.

Habitat. Extremely variable. Frequents city, town, country. For nesting, it requires cavities in trees, building crevices, and similar situations; for roosting, trees, bushes, cattail marshes, buildings, and cliffs; for feeding, open places such as pastures, fields, gardens, lawns, garbage dumps, marshes, and shores.

Nesting. In woodpecker holes and natural cavities in trees; in cavities about buildings or cliffs; and in bird boxes; often in country mailboxes. Sticks, straw, weed stems, grass, and trash are used to fill the cavity, and there is a lining of finer grasses and feathers. *Eggs*, usually 4 or 5, often 6; rarely more. They are pale bluish or greenish white, rarely white. Incubation 11 to 14 days (various authors), by the female assisted by the male.

Range. Iceland, northern Norway, northern Finland, northern Russia, and southern Siberia (east to about Lake Baikal) south to the Canary Islands, Palestine, Iraq, Iran, central India, and northeastern China.

Introduced into North America (New York City, 1890) and now breeding all across southern Canada and in much of the United States. More northern populations partly migratory.

This Old World species has spread into Canada from the United States where it was first introduced at New York City in 1890. It was first recorded in the provinces of Canada approximately as follows: Ontario: Niagara Falls, autumn, 1914; Nova Scotia: Halifax, 1 December 1915; Quebec: Betchouane, April 1917; New Brunswick: Grand Manan, autumn, 1924; Prince Edward Island: Tignish, late 1930 or early 1931; Manitoba: York Factory, 11 May 1931; Alberta: Camrose, late 1934; Saskatchewan: Tregarva, spring, 1937; Newfoundland: Tompkins, 9 June 1943; British Columbia: Williams Lake, winter, 1945–1946; Yukon: Whitehorse, June 1970.

Subspecies. *Sturnus vulgaris vulgaris* Linnaeus.

Remarks. The unfortunate introduction of the Starling into North America is an example of the inevitable blunders inherent in tampering with the delicate balance of nature by persons equipped with little more than good intentions. The modest numbers of Starlings liberated in New York City in 1890 have now grown to millions that have spread and are still spreading over the greater part of the United States and southern Canada.

The Starling's food habits are mainly beneficial, for insects make up the bulk of its menu. It has an appetite for small fruits, however, and sometimes does serious damage in the cherry orchard.

Much more serious is its habit of usurping the nesting cavities used by many of our native birds. Doubtless it is a major factor in the recent widespread decline of the Red-headed Woodpecker and probably the Eastern Bluebird also. Its nesting and roosting in large numbers on buildings poses another serious problem involving many thousands of dollars' worth of damage annually.

Crested Myna

Martin huppé
Acridotheres cristatellus (Linnaeus)
Total length: 22.8 to 26.5 cm
Plate 67

Range in Canada. Introduced into Vancouver, British Columbia, in the 1890s. Common (but numbers fluctuate) in the Vancouver region including Lulu Island, Ladner, and western parts of the Fraser Delta; also small numbers have been recorded locally on southern Vancouver Island (Nanaimo; has been observed from Courtenay south to Victoria).

Nasal plumes, erect and well developed, form a low crest over base of bill. *Adults (sexes similar but female with smaller nasal crest)*: Plumage mainly blackish, the under parts washed with grey; wings black, the base of the primaries and outer secondaries white, forming a large white wing patch; tail and under tail coverts black, tipped with white; eye orange to yellow; bill pale yellowish, rose-coloured at base; legs orange-yellow. *Young*: Resemble adults but plumage is dark brown, crest lacking, and there are no white tips to tail or under tail coverts.

Measurements. *Adult male*: wing, 129–141 (134); tail, 71–84 (77.9); exposed culmen, 21.1–26.7 (24.2); tarsus, 38.5–40 (39.4). *Adult female*: wing, 129–132.5 (130.8) mm.

Field Marks. A black, chunky, short-tailed, robin-sized bird with yellowish bill and a peculiar crest (much less developed in females than in adult males) at the base of the bill covering the nostrils. A white patch in the wing is very conspicuous in flight and can sometimes be partly seen when the bird is perched. Young for a short time after leaving the nest are much browner than adults, and the crest is not developed; but their silhouette otherwise resembles that of the adults, and they show a light bill and a white patch in the spread wing.

Habitat. Forages in open agricultural areas: fields, gardens, orchards, pastures with the cattle; and in garbage dumps. Roosts usually in flocks on city buildings and in trees.

Nesting. In woodpecker holes and other cavities in trees; in crevices, cavities, holes, and pipes of buildings; and in bird boxes. The nest cavity is filled with trash, like grass, weeds, paper, feathers, rootlets, and cast snake skins. *Eggs*, 4 to 7, usually 4 or 5; greenish blue. Incubation 14 days (Mackay and Hughes).

Range. East Pakistan, northern Burma, and southern China south to southern Burma, Indochina, Hainan, and Taiwan. Introduced in the Philippines, Japan, and British Columbia.

Subspecies. *Acridotheres cristatellus cristatellus* (Linnaeus).

Remarks. Unlike the European Starling, the Crested Myna has not spread significantly in the 90 years since it was introduced. V.M. Mackay and W.M. Hughes (1963. Canadian Field-Naturalist, vol. 77, no. 3, pp. 154–162) place its numbers in the Vancouver area at between 2000 and 3000, a decline in the latest 35 years. In the 1978 Christmas Bird Count, 270 were recorded in the Vancouver area.

Family **Vireonidae**: Vireos

Number of Species in Canada: 8

Small plain woodland birds without conspicuous patterns, usually dull greenish-olive above, white below. Bill rather short, rather thick, slightly hooked. Wings with ten primaries, the outermost very short or vestigial. These birds are arboreal and resemble some of the duller-coloured warblers, but usually the heavier bill and more sluggish movements of the vireos will distinguish them. Economically they are very beneficial, since they consume large numbers of insects including both hairy and hairless caterpillars. The family is confined exclusively to the Western Hemisphere. The name vireo, derived from Latin, indicates green coloration and refers to the colour of the upper parts.

White-eyed Vireo

Viréo aux yeux blancs
Vireo griseus (Boddaert)
Total length: 11 to 14 cm
Plate 59

Range in Canada. Nests rarely and locally in southern Ontario (Rondeau: nested unsuccessfully in 1971 and again in 1973; in 1979, young were being fed at Rondeau and Point Pelee. Reported to have nested in Toronto in 1898).

Occasional visitant to southern Ontario (Point Pelee, Woodstock, Listowel, Erie Beach, Toronto, Ottawa) and Nova Scotia (photo record: Outer Island, one mistnetted on 9 October 1976; Sable Island, 15 November 1977; sight records: Seal Island, 13 October 1975, 20 September and 11 October 1976, 7 October 1977). Very rare visitant to southern Quebec (photo record: Montréal, 27 April to 31 May 1977; sight record: Lucerne, 31 October 1971; Cap-Tourmente, 12 May 1980). Sight record for Manitoba (Winnipeg, 3–4 July 1981).

A small vireo with rather heavy bill. Upper parts olive green, the neck more greyish; broad yellow streak from base of bill back over and almost around the eye; wings and tail dusky brown edged with olive green; wings with two yellowish-white wing bars; under parts mostly white, the sides and flanks yellow, this colour extending to the shorter under tail coverts; iris white; legs greyish blue.

Measurements. *Adult male*: wing, 60–65 (61.4); tail, 46–54 (49.0); exposed culmen, 9.5–11 (10.1); tarsus, 18–20 (19.5). *Adult female*: wing, 57–63 (60.5) mm (Ridgway).

Field Marks. A small vireo with two wing bars, yellow eye-ring, and yellow bar from base of bill back to eye; whitish throat and breast. The white eye is diagnostic but usually cannot be seen in the field. The Yellow-throated is another vireo with yellow eye-ring, but it has a yellow throat and breast. The Solitary Vireo has a light eye-ring and bar in front of eye, but these are white, not yellow. *Song*: Unlike that of other vireos. It usually contains five to seven emphatic notes beginning and ending with a *chick* or *tick*.

Habitat. Thickets, especially on moist ground.

Nesting. Nest is a pensile cup usually placed low in thickets or shrubbery. *Eggs*, 3 to 5, are white very finely speckled with blackish brown. Incubation 12 to 15 days.

Range. Eastern Nebraska, southern Wisconsin, central Ohio, southern Ontario, and Massachusetts (probably) south to central Mexico, the Gulf Coast of United States, and southern Florida; also Bermuda.

Subspecies. *Vireo griseus noveboracensis* (Gmelin).

Bell's Vireo

Viréo de Bell
Vireo bellii Audubon
Total length: 11 to 13 cm
Plate 59

Status in Canada. Rare visitant to southern Ontario (specimen: Point Pelee, 23 June 1970. Several sight records, mostly in May, north to Presqu'ile Provincial Park).

A small, very plain vireo. Crown dull greyish-brown; rest of under parts dull greyish-olive. Narrow eye-ring, supraloral stripe, and indistinct wing bars dull white. A small dusky area in front of eye. Under parts dull white becoming yellow on sides and flanks, a faint yellowish wash across chest.

Measurements. *Adult male*: wing, 52–58.5 (55.5); tail, 41.5–46.5 (44.7); exposed culmen, 9–10 (9.8); tarsus, 18–19 (18.6). *Adult female*: wing, 52–56.2 (55.1) mm.

Range. Breeds from northern California, central Arizona, central Nebraska, and northwestern Indiana south to central Texas and Guatemala. Winters from northern Mexico south to Nicaragua.

Solitary Vireo

(Blue-headed Vireo)

Viréo à tête bleue
Vireo solitarius (Wilson)
Total length: 12.5 to 15 cm
Plate 59

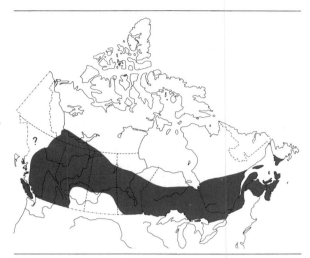

Breeding Distribution of Solitary Vireo

Range in Canada. Breeds in British Columbia (across the southern part including Vancouver Island and north on the mainland at least to the Vanderhoof region and Peace River parklands; perhaps north to Dease Lake; specimen taken 22 June 1962; and near Clarke Lake); southwestern Mackenzie (Little Buffalo and Sass rivers probably to Fort Simpson); northern and central Alberta (Grimshaw, Wood Buffalo National Park, Athabasca, Glenevis, and Jasper but very scarce in the mountains); northwestern and central Saskatchewan (Lake Athabasca, southern Reindeer Lake, Prince Albert, Nipawin); central and southern Manitoba (Thicket Portage, Duck Mountain, Clandeboye Bay on southern Lake Manitoba, Rennie; probably north to Gillam); central Ontario (Big Trout Lake, Fort Albany, Port Sydney, Algonquin Provincial Park, Howdenvale, Bracebridge); southwestern Quebec (Mount Plamondon, Waswanipi–Bell River area, Lake Saint-Jean, Sainte-Marguerite River, Grande-Grève, and Anticosti Island southward; probably southern Lake Mistassini; status on Madeleine Islands uncertain); southwestern Newfoundland (Doyles); New Brunswick; Prince Edward Island; and Nova Scotia.

In migration across all southern Canada.

Top and sides of head and hind-neck dark slaty-grey; eye-ring and lores white; back, rump, and upper tail coverts olive green; two white or yellowish wing bars; tail blackish with olive-green edging except the outermost feather on each side, which has narrow white edging; under parts mostly white, the sides and flanks yellow mixed with olive green; under tail coverts usually with yellowish suffusion; iris brown; legs blue-grey.

Measurements *(V. s. solitarius)*. *Adult male*: wing, 69.6–74.8 (72.7); tail, 50.5–54.0 (52.2); exposed culmen, 9.6–11.6 (10.7); tarsus, 17–19 (18.0). *Adult female*: wing, 72.2–74.6 (73.2) mm.

Field Marks. A vireo with two whitish wing bars, dark-grey sides of head (contrasting with white throat), white eye-ring and lores. *Voice*: Song a series of spaced short phrases similar to those of the Red-eyed Vireo but with longer pauses between and, especially in the western mountains, shriller. Sometimes the phrases are run together producing a continuous rich warble. Nasal scolding notes.

Habitat. More open mixed coniferous and deciduous woods.

Nesting. In a tree, usually a conifer, and ordinarily not more than 4.5 m above the ground (although much higher nests are quite often seen). *Eggs*, 3 to 5, usually 4; white, spotted and dotted sparsely (mostly near the large end) with light and dark browns.

Range. Southern Canada south in the mountains to southern Baja California, Guatemala, and El Salvador; and to North Dakota (locally), central Minnesota, central Michigan, southern Ontario, and northern New Jersey; in the mountains to northern Georgia. Winters from southern United States southward to Nicaragua and Cuba.

Subspecies. (1) *Vireo solitarius solitarius* (Wilson): northeastern British Columbia (Peace River parklands), southwestern Mackenzie, northern central Alberta, Saskatchewan, Manitoba, Ontario, Quebec, Newfoundland, New Brunswick, Prince Edward Island, and Nova Scotia. (2) *V. s. cassinii* Xantus (duller coloration): southern British Columbia (Indianpoint Lake, Nulki Lake, Comox, Waldo); migrant in southwestern Alberta (Canmore, 27 May 1891) but not known to breed there.

Yellow-throated Vireo

Viréo à gorge jaune
Vireo flavifrons Vieillot
Total length: 12.5 to 15 cm
Plate 59

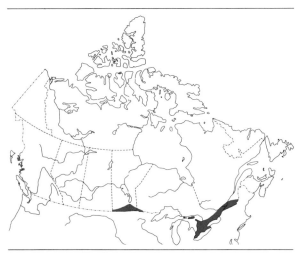

Breeding Distribution of Yellow-throated Vireo

Range in Canada. Breeds in southern Manitoba (Winnipeg, Fort Garry, rarely Melita; probably Emerson and Turtle Mountain Provincial Park); southern Ontario (Peterborough and Ottawa southward, rarely Manitoulin Island); and southwestern Quebec (Hull, Montréal, Bolton, Hatley; probably Sherbrooke).

Recorded rarely, without definite evidence of breeding, in Saskatchewan (Madge Lake, Nipawin, Qu'Appelle valley, Moose Mountain), and western Ontario (Kenora). About 12 sight records for New Brunswick. Rare in Nova Scotia (two specimens: Indian Harbour, 9 April 1958, and Brier Island, 3 September 1979. Sight records for Sable River, Sable Island, Seal Island, and near Halifax).

Bill rather stout. Our only vireo combining white wing bars with a *bright-yellow throat* and breast. *Adults*: Top and sides of head, back of neck, and upper back yellowish olive; eye-ring and lores yellow; lower back and rump slaty grey; wings with two prominent white bars; tail blackish with greyish-white edging; throat and breast bright yellow; rest of under body chiefly white, becoming greyish on flanks; iris brown; legs bluish grey.

Measurements. *Adult male*: wing, 74–80 (77.1); tail, 47.5–52 (49.2); exposed culmen, 10.5–12 (11.5); tarsus, 18–20 (19.3). *Adult female*: wing, 72–78 (75) mm (Ridgway).

Field Marks. No other Canadian vireo has a combination of two white wing bars and a bright-yellow throat and breast. It might be confused with the Pine Warbler, but the vireo has a thicker, blunter bill and lacks the Pine Warbler's white tail patches. The Philadelphia Vireo has a yellowish breast but no wing bars. *Song*: Similar to the Red-eyed Vireo's but lower pitched, more deliberate, more musical.

Habitat. Chiefly open stands of mature deciduous trees, often in residential areas, foraging in the upper stratum.

Nesting. Nest is suspended from a fork in a tree branch. Much spider web is used in the construction of the deep, well-made nest, which is beautifully decorated with lichens and egg cases of spiders. *Eggs*, 3 to 5, usually 4; white, well spotted on the larger end with various browns; usually somewhat more heavily marked than in other vireos.

Range. Breeds from southern Manitoba, central Wisconsin, central Michigan, southern Ontario, southwestern Quebec, northern New Hampshire, and southwestern Maine (locally) south to central and eastern Texas, the Gulf Coast of United States, and central Florida. Winters mainly from southern Mexico south to Panama.

Hutton's Vireo

Viréo de Hutton
Vireo huttoni Cassin
Total length: 11 to 12 cm
Plate 59

Breeding Distribution of Hutton's Vireo

A very small nondescript vireo with white wing bars. Upper parts dull olive, becoming greenish olive on rump; incomplete eye-ring and poorly defined streak from base of bill to eye whitish; wings and tail dusky with olive edging, the wings with two white bars; under parts dull buffy-olive becoming whitish on abdomen.

Measurements. *Adult male*: wing, 59.5–63 (60.9); tail, 47–50 (48.6); exposed culmen, 8.5–9 (8.7); tarsus, 18.5–20 (19.0). *Adult female*: wing, 59–62 (60.2) mm (Ridgway).

Field Marks. A small nondescript vireo of the south coast of British Columbia with two white wing bars, a whitish incomplete eye-ring, and whitish stripe from base of bill to eye. In general, its colour somewhat resembles the Ruby-crowned Kinglet, but the bill is thicker and the head larger. *Song: Chee-ah* or *chee-wee* frequently repeated, the accent may be either on first or second syllable.

Habitat. Deciduous and mixed woodland and shrubbery.

Nesting. Nest is suspended from a fork in a branch of a tree (deciduous or coniferous) or tall shrub. *Eggs*, 3 to 5, usually 4; white with scattered small spots and dots of browns, mostly near the larger end. Incubation probably 14 to 16 days.

Range. Permanent resident from southwestern British Columbia south along the Pacific Coast to southern Baja California and from central Arizona, southwestern New Mexico, and western Texas south to Guatemala.

Range in Canada. Permanent resident in south-western British Columbia (Vancouver Island and the southwest coast of the mainland north at least to Kingcome Inlet).

Warbling Vireo

Viréo mélodieux
Vireo gilvus (Vieillot)
Total length: 12.5 to 15 cm
Plate 59

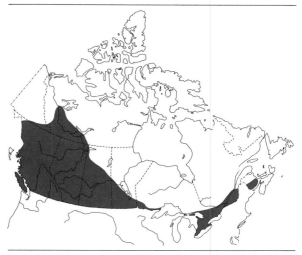

Breeding Distribution of Warbling Vireo

Range in Canada. Breeds in central-western and southwestern Mackenzie (Fort Norman, Nahanni National Park, Fort Simpson, Fort Smith); British Columbia (all across south including Vancouver Island and northward on the mainland to Atlin, Trutch, and Lower Liard Crossing); Alberta (throughout, but scarce in southeast); central and southern Saskatchewan (southern Prince Albert National Park, Codette, Regina, Yorkton); southern Manitoba (Duck Mountain, Dauphin, Fairford, St. Vital, Whitemouth); western Ontario (Kenora, Thunder Bay); southern Ontario (Manitoulin Island, North Bay, Sudbury, Mildred, Ottawa southward); southwestern Quebec (Gatineau Park, Montréal, Hatley, Québec; possibly slightly farther east as a single singing individual has been taken at Lac Trois Saumons, and a single singing individual recorded from Cacouna); and New Brunswick (sparsely: Hammond River).

Rare visitant to Nova Scotia (specimens: Seal Island, 1 September 1971; Sable Island, 13 June 1967; also sight records). Sight records for Prince Edward Island and Newfoundland.

Subspecies. (1) *Vireo huttoni huttoni* Cassin: mainland of southwestern British Columbia. (2) *V. h. insularis* Rhoads (darker in colour): Vancouver Island.

Top of head and back of neck smoke grey, the back and rump similar but tinged with olive green; white stripe over eye less distinct than in Red-eyed or Philadelphia vireos; wings and tail brownish grey with pale edges; no wing bars; under parts mostly white, the sides and flanks lightly tinged with pale yellow or pale buff; eye brown; legs bluish grey.

Measurements *(V. g. gilvus). Adult male*: wing, 67.1–74.8 (70.1); tail, 50–57 (51.9); exposed culmen, 10.2–12.5 (11.1); tarsus, 17–18.5 (17.9). *Adult female*: wing, 64.6–71.1 (68.0) mm.

Field Marks. It has no white wing bars and no eye-ring; thus it is similar to the Red-eyed and Philadelphia vireos. Its white (not yellowish) breast separates it from the Philadelphia Vireo. Smaller size and much less distinct head markings distinguish it from the Red-eyed. Its song is entirely different from that of our other vireos. Its heavier bill and more leisurely motions distinguish it from warblers. *Voice*: Its song is not broken up into disconnected phrases as in our other common vireos. It is a continued musical warble, usually gradually rising in pitch and intensity; similar to the song of the Purple Finch but much less energetic and less loud.

Habitat. Mature deciduous trees, usually well up in the leafy canopy. Open woodland both deciduous and mixed, woodland edges, shade trees in towns and cities, orchards, parks, prairie groves, alder and willow thickets.

Nesting. Usually high in a deciduous tree. Nest is a well-made cup, suspended by its rim from a fork of a twig, frequently near the end of the branch. *Eggs*, 3 to 5; dull white sparsely dotted with browns, mostly near the large end. Incubation reported to be 12 to 14 days (O.W. Knight), by both sexes.

Range. Breeds from southern Canada, south to Baja California and central-northern Mexico, central Texas, southern Louisiana, northern Alabama, western North Carolina, and Virginia. Winters from Mexico to Guatemala and El Salvador.

Subspecies. (1) *Vireo gilvus gilvus* (Vieillot): southeastern Alberta (east of the mountains), Saskatchewan, Manitoba, Ontario, Quebec. (2) *V. g. swainsonii* Baird (coloration darker than in *gilvus*, size smaller): British Columbia, southwestern Mackenzie, northern and southwestern Alberta.

Philadelphia Vireo

Viréo de Philadelphie
Vireo philadelphicus (Cassin)
Total length: 11 to 12.5 cm
Plate 59

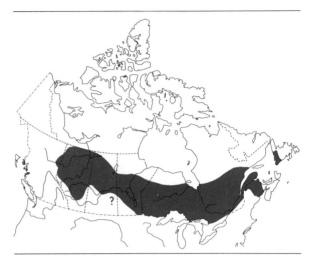

Breeding Distribution of Philadelphia Vireo

Range in Canada. Breeds in central-eastern British Columbia (Peace River parklands); northern, central, and south-central Alberta (Wood Buffalo National Park, south to Cold Lake, Sundre, Red Deer, Swan Hills, Bistcho Lake); northwestern and central Saskatchewan (Fond du Lac, Kazan Lake, Flotten Lake, Somme; reports of breeding in extreme south-east are not completely satisfactory); central and southern Manitoba (Thicket Portage, Swan River, Duck Mountain, Whitemouth); north-central, central, and southern Ontario (Big Trout Lake, southern James Bay south to Rainy River, Bruce Peninsula, Washago, Buckshot Lake, nearly to Madoc); south-central and southwestern Quebec (Eastmain, Baie-du-Poste, Lake Saint-Jean, Moisie Bay, Québec, Gaspé Peninsula); New Brunswick (Tabusintac, probably Edmundston and Anagance); and probably southwestern Newfoundland (female with brood patch at Tompkins, 12 July 1943). Rare in Nova Scotia (specimens: Norwood, 9 July 1904 and Cape Sable, 7 October 1974; also various sight records).

Crown grey (in autumn often tinged with olive); rest of upper parts greyish olive-green; over eye a dull greyish-white stripe and through eye a dusky streak (head markings similar to Red-eyed Vireo but much less distinct); wings and tail dark greyish-brown with olive-green edging; no wing bars; breast and sides pale yellow, usually becoming whitish on throat and abdomen; eyes brown; legs bluish grey.

Measurements. *Adult male*: wing, 65.4–70 (68.2); tail, 45–52 (48.9); exposed culmen, 9–11 (10.2); tarsus, 16–17 (16.9). *Adult female*: wing, 63.7–68.8 (66) mm.

Field Marks. No wing bars and no eye-ring, thus differing from all vireos of regular occurrence in Canada except the Red-eyed and Warbling. It is smaller with less distinct head markings than the Red-eyed. Its pale yellow (instead of white) breast distinguishes it from both the Red-eyed and Warbling vireos. Lack of white wing bars separates it from the Yellow-throated. Resembles Tennessee and Orange-crowned warblers, but the vireo's thicker, blunter bill is very different from the slender, pointed warbler bill. *Voice*: Song similar to that of the Red-eyed Vireo but higher-pitched and with longer pauses between phrases.

Habitat. Open mixed and deciduous woodland, woods edges, aspen parklands, second growth on burntlands and logged areas, thickets of alder and willow.

Nesting. In a deciduous tree or tall shrub, 3 to 13.7 m up. Nest suspended in usual vireo fashion. Bark strips, plant down, and *Usnea* lichen are likely to be part of the nest exterior, and there is a lining of grasses, pine needles, and sometimes animal hair. *Eggs*, 3 to 5; white, sparsely spotted (near the large end mostly) with browns. Incubation 14 days or a little less, by both sexes (H.F. Lewis).

Range. Breeds mainly in Canada (see Range in Canada) but also south to central-northern North Dakota, northern New Hampshire, and central Maine. Winters from Guatemala south to Panama and north-western Colombia.

Red-eyed Vireo

Viréo aux yeux rouges
Vireo olivaceus (Linnaeus)
Total length: 13.5 to 16.5 cm
Plate 59

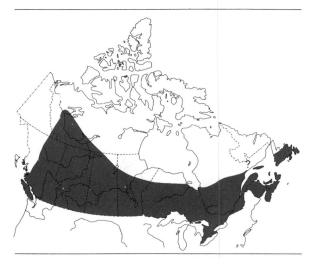

Breeding Distribution of Red-eyed Vireo

Range in Canada. Breeds in southwestern Mackenzie (Norman Wells; Forts Norman, Simpson, and Resolution; Yohin Lake); eastern and southwestern British Columbia (Lower Liard Crossing, Trutch, Peace River parklands, Vanderhoof area, Hagensborg, Chilliwack, Hope, Okanagan Landing, Cranbrook; Vancouver Island); throughout Alberta; northwestern, central, and southern Saskatchewan (Lake Athabasca, Dead Lake on Churchill River southward); central and southern Manitoba (Thicket Portage southward); north-central and southern Ontario (Big Trout Lake, North Point, southern James Bay southward); south-central and southwestern Quebec (Baie-du-Poste, Lake Saint-Jean, Îlets Jérémie, Tadoussac, Grande Baie Lake, Anticosti Island, Aylmer, Montréal, Hatley, Gaspé Peninsula, Madeleine Islands); New Brunswick; Prince Edward Island; Nova Scotia (including Cape Breton Island); and Newfoundland (Corner Brook, Topsail, Clarenville).

Migrates through southern Canada.

Our only vireo with a red eye. The largest of our vireos lacking white wing-bars. *Adults*: Crown mouse-grey, bordered on either side by a narrow dusky line; rest of upper parts dull olive-green; over eye a broad greyish-white stripe and a dusky stripe through the eye; wings and tail dusky with yellowish-green edging; no wing bars; under parts white, the flanks tinged with yellowish olive, the wing linings pale sulphur-yellow, and the under tail coverts with a yellowish suffusion; eye red; legs bluish grey.

Measurements. *Adult male*: wing, 79.2–82.7 (80.5); tail, 53–57 (55.2); exposed culmen, 12–14.4 (13.2); tarsus, 17–18.5 (17.5). *Adult female*: wing, 76.8–79.7 (77.9) mm.

Field Marks. Lacks white wing bars, therefore most likely to be confused with Warbling and Philadelphia vireos. Its white eyebrow stripe, bordered above and below by a black line, is decidedly more definite than that of the other two. Its grey crown contrasts more strongly with its green back. Its breast is white, that of the Philadelphia yellowish. Its larger size is not always apparent, and its red eye is hard to see in the field. Its song is completely different from that of the Warbling Vireo. *Voice*: Short, similar phrases with slightly rising inflection and delivered tirelessly for long periods of the day in the breeding season. Alarm note, a complaining nasal *quee*.

Habitat. Primarily deciduous trees and tall shrubbery: parklands; shade trees; more open woodland; shrubbery, such as alder and willow, along streams and lakes; second growth of burntlands and logged areas; open mixedwoods.

Nesting. In a tree or bush most often 1.5 to 3 m above ground, but varying from 0.9 to 16.7 m, usually in a deciduous tree, occasionally in a conifer. Nest, a well-made cup, suspended by its rim from the fork of a branch. The outside of the nest is made of bits and strips of bark, paper from wasp nests, moss, lichens, leaves, plant fibres, bound together with spider webs. It is lined with grasses, rootlets, pine needles, sometimes hair. *Eggs*, usually 3 or 4; dull white marked mostly near the large end with dots or small spots of reddish brown, dark brown, or blackish. Incubation period 12 to 14 days, by the female (L. de K. Lawrence); some authors assert that incubation is by both sexes.

Range. Breeds from southern Canada (see Range in Canada) south to northern Oregon, northern Idaho, Wyoming, eastern Colorado, western Oklahoma, central Texas, the United States Gulf Coast, and central Florida. Winters from Colombia and Venezuela to eastern Peru and western Brazil. Other races breed in Central and South America south to central Argentina, Bolivia, and eastern Peru.

Subspecies. *Vireo olivaceus olivaceus* (Linnaeus) is the breeding subspecies throughout Canada and most of the United States. *V. o. flavovirides* (Cassin) is of accidental occurrence in Canada (specimen taken) at Godbout, Quebec, on 13 May 1883). It was formerly considered a separate species, *V. flavovirides*, Yellow-green Vireo.

Remarks. All through the warm summer days, the Red-eyed Vireo's song goes on and on as the bird searches leisurely among the leafy branches for its insect food. Its songs are short phrases punctuated with pauses. Many have a rising inflection that sounds as though the bird were asking questions and answering them itself. Vast numbers of insects are destroyed by vireos, and some berries are eaten also.

Family **Emberizidae**:
Wood-Warblers, Tanagers, Cardinals, Sparrows, Buntings, Meadowlarks, Blackbirds, and Orioles

Number of Species in Canada: 106

This vast and complex family comprises a great assemblage of small to medium-sized birds that are mostly New World in their affinities. It contains the subfamily Parulinae (the wood-warblers, formerly the family Parulidae); the subfamily Thraupinae (the tanagers, formerly the family Thraupidae); the subfamily Cardinalinae (cardinals, grosbeaks, and allies, formerly the subfamily Richmondeninae of the family Fringillidae); the subfamily Emberizinae (buntings, sparrows, and allies); the subfamily Icterinae (blackbirds, orioles, and allies, formerly the family Icteridae); and it includes also the subfamily Coerebinae (bananaquits, which are not represented in Canada).

Subfamily **Parulinae**:
Wood-Warblers

The wood-warblers are confined to the Western Hemisphere and are well represented during the summer months in Canada. They are small and frequently brightly coloured. Most have slender sharp-pointed bills, wings with nine primaries, and rather even tails. The adult males and females in breeding plumage are often coloured differently, while in autumn the adults may be very different again; the autumn immatures and juvenals just out of the nest are still different. These various plumages in the same species, combined with the fact that warblers are among the most active of birds, often foraging high in the leafy tree-tops, make field identification of the many species an intriguing challenge. The beginner would probably be well advised to confine himself at first to the adult males in spring.

Although called warblers, they do not warble. Many of the songs are not particularly musical, but they are energetic, pleasing, and distinctive enough to be useful aids in identification. The food of our warblers is mostly insects, but occasionally a few seeds or a little fruit is eaten. They are numerous in summer and collectively destroy vast numbers of insects.

Blue-winged Warbler

Paruline à ailes bleues
Vermivora pinus (Linnaeus)
Total length: 11.4 to 12.7 cm
Plate 60

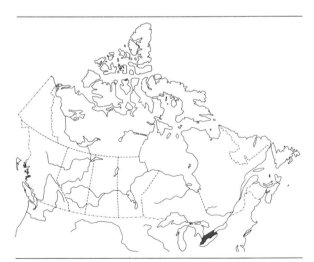

Breeding Distribution of Blue-winged Warbler

Range in Canada. Breeds rarely in extreme southern Ontario (north to Toronto).

It has wandered north, rarely, to Wasaga Beach and Ottawa, Ontario. Accidental in Saskatchewan (specimen: Regina, 9 November 1965) and Nova Scotia (specimen: Brier Island, 3 September 1979; photo record: Seal Island, 24 August 1971; sight records for Outer Island

Adult male: Top of head and under parts lemon-yellow except whitish under tail coverts; narrow black stripe through eye; back, scapulars, rump, and upper tail coverts olive green; wings mostly dusky, but bluish grey coverts and edging give them a bluish look when folded; two white or yellowish-white wing bars; tail bluish grey, the inner webs of outer feathers with much white; bill blackish in spring, paler in autumn. *Adult female*: Similar to adult male but duller, the olive green more extensive, covering most of top of head.

Measurements. *Adult male*: wing, 57.7–63.2 (60.2); tail, 43.4–48.3 (46); exposed culmen, 10.4–11.4 (10.7); tarsus, 17–18 (17.3). *Adult female*: wing, 56.1–59.2 (57.7) mm (Ridgway).

Field Marks. A yellow warbler with very narrow blackish stripe through the eye, two white wing bars. *Song*: Commonly an unhurried buzzy two syllable *zee-bee*, the second syllable usually (not always) lower, a little suggestive of a sigh.

Habitat. Brushy neglected fields and pastures, woodland openings and edges, thickets along streams and swamps.

Nesting. On or very near the ground, usually among vegetation. *Eggs*, 4 to 7, usually 5 or 6; white, sparsely spotted or speckled with browns and purplish grey. Incubation 10 to 11 days by the female.

Range. Breeds from eastern Nebraska, southeastern Minnesota, southern Michigan, northern Ohio, extreme southern Ontario (rarely), southern New York, and southwestern Massachusetts, south to north-

and Halifax). Sight records for Quebec (Montréal, 22 May 1976) and New Brunswick (Machias Seal and Kent islands).

western Arkansas, southern Illinois, northern Alabama, northern Georgia, North Carolina, and Delaware. Winters from southern Mexico south to Nicaragua and Panama.

Golden-winged Warbler

Paruline à ailes dorées
Vermivora chrysoptera (Linnaeus)
Total length: 12.4 to 13.5 cm
Plate 60

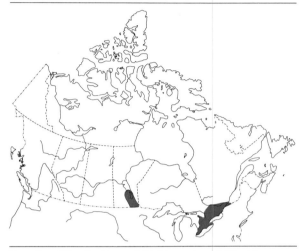

Breeding Distribution of Golden-winged Warbler

Range in Canada. Local summer resident, breeding in southern Manitoba (Vivian; Little George Island, Lake Winnipeg; Menisino; probably Riding Mountain National Park); southern Ontario (north at least to Torrance and to Canoe Lake, north of Kingston; probably north to Algonquin Provincial Park where it is more or less regularly present in June); and in southwestern Quebec (Philipsburg; Lake Philippe. Summer records north more or less regularly to Mont Tremblant).

Casual in Nova Scotia (specimen: Brier Island, 3 September 1979; male banded on 17 May 1961, Outer Island. Sight record: Seal Island, 24 September 1966). Sight records for Saskatchewan (Regina) and New Brunswick (Chamcook Lake, Kent Island, Grand Manan).

Adult male: Top of head lemon yellow; rest of upper parts bluish grey; sides of head whitish with broad black patch from base of bill to ear coverts; middle and greater wing coverts yellow, producing a conspicuous yellow patch on the wing; outer three tail feathers on each side with much white toward tips; throat patch black; rest of under parts whitish becoming greyish on sides of breast, sides, and flanks; bill blackish; eyes brownish. *Adult female*: Similar to adult male but duller; the black of throat and sides of head replaced by grey.

Measurements. *Adult male*: wing, 59.7–65 (62.2); tail, 43.2–47.5 (46.2); exposed culmen, 10.4–11.4 (10.7); tarsus, 17–18 (17.5). *Adult female*: wing, 57.7–63.5 (59.9) mm (Ridgway).

Field Marks. Male is a black-throated warbler with a yellow wing patch. Female similar but blacks replaced by grey. *Song*: A buzzy *zee bz bz bz*, the first syllable highest.

Habitat. Shrubby wastes, old bushy pastures, bushy edges and openings in deciduous woodland, shrubby borders of streams.

Nesting. On the ground, or very near it. Nest, usually on dead leaves or in ferns or weed stalks, is rather bulky and is made of strips of bark, grass, and leaves and lined with finer grass and shreds of bark. *Eggs*, 4 to 7; white, variously marked with browns and purplish grey. Incubation 10 to 11 days by the female.

Range. Breeds from southern Manitoba, central-eastern Minnesota, northern Michigan, southern Ontario, and eastern Massachusetts south to southeastern Iowa, northern Indiana, southern Ohio, northern Georgia, northwestern South Carolina, and southeastern Pennsylvania. Winters from Guatemala and Nicaragua south to central Colombia and northern Venezuela.

Hybrids. In areas where both Golden-winged and Blue-winged warblers breed, the two sometimes hybridize. Hybridization produces two main phenotypes, which were thought to be separate species and were called, respectively, Brewster's Warbler (Plate 60) and Lawrence's Warbler. Lawrence's, the rarer of the two, is not illustrated but has yellow under parts, black throat, and black patch on side of head. A male of the Brewster type was collected near London, Ontario, on 14 May 1956. There are various sight records in southern Ontario of Brewster's, but only a few of Lawrence's. In 1956, a female Golden-winged paired with a male Blue-winged at Milton Heights, Ontario, and raised a brood of four young. For a discussion of the genetics of Brewster's and Lawrence's warblers, see K.C. Parkes, 1951. Wilson Bulletin, vol. 63, no. 1, pp. 5–15.

Tennessee Warbler

Paruline obscure
Vermivora peregrina (Wilson)
Total length: 11.4 to 12.7 cm
Plate 61

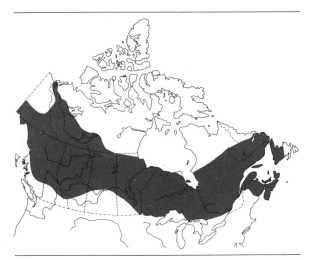

Breeding Distribution of Tennessee Warbler

Range in Canada. Summer resident, breeding from southern Yukon (Pine Creek, Kathleen Lake, Hutshi Lakes, Watson Lake); northwestern, central-western, and southern Mackenzie (Inuvik, Fort Good Hope, Brackett Lake, Norman Wells, Rae, Reliance); northern Saskatchewan (Lake Athabasca, Hasbala Lake); northern Manitoba (Churchill); northern Ontario, (Favourable Lake, Lake Attawapiskat, Fort Albany); north-central Quebec (Schefferville); southern Labrador (Goose Bay, Cartwright, Sawbill); and western Newfoundland (Gaff Topsail, Doyles) south to southern British Columbia (mainland only: Kimsquit, Chezacut, Indianpoint Lake, probably 158 Mile House and Kootenay National Park); southwestern and south-central Alberta (Banff National Park, Red Deer, Camrose); south-central Saskatchewan (Cochin, Prince Albert, Nipawin, Somme); southern Manitoba (Duck Mountain, Hillside Beach, Whitemouth); south-central Ontario (Sudbury, North Bay, Algonquin Provincial Park); southern Quebec (Amos, Stoneham, Rivière-du-Loup, Gaspé Peninsula, inner north shore of the Gulf of St. Lawrence, Anticosti Island, and probably Madeleine Islands); New Brunswick; Prince Edward Island; and Nova Scotia (Wolfville, Albany; Cape Breton Island).

Male in breeding plumage: Top of head and hind-neck bluish grey; line over eye whitish; narrow line through eye dusky; back, scapulars, wing coverts, and rump olive green; wings and tail with olive-green edging; no wing bars; outer tail feathers usually with an inconspicuous small greyish-white patch; under parts plain greyish white; legs dark bluish-grey or brownish-grey. *Female (breeding plumage)*: Similar to adult male but grey of head mixed with olive green; the pale line over eye and on under parts tinged with yellow. *Adult male (autumn)*: Crown mixed with olive green; under parts more greenish than in breeding plumage. *Adult female (autumn)*: No grey on head; upper parts all olive-green, under parts washed with yellow. *Young (first autumn)*: No grey on crown; upper parts all olive-green; line over eye and under parts yellow, becoming more whitish on belly and under tail coverts (which sometimes are decidedly yellowish, however); some show a poorly defined light wing bar.

Measurements. *Adult male*: wing, 62.6–67.5 (64.9); tail, 41–45 (42.6); exposed culmen, 10–11.5 (10.5); tarsus, 16.2–17.4 (16.7). *Adult female*: wing, 56.3–63.3 (60.5) mm.

Field Marks. Spring adults with grey top of head, white line over eye, and dark line through eye. Beginners might confuse it with Philadelphia, Red-eyed, or Warbling Vireo, but the warbler's slender sharp-pointed bill and quicker actions should eliminate confusion. The autumn Tennessee resembles the Orange-crowned Warbler, but the under parts of the Tennessee are never streaked; its eye stripes are more definite; it usually has white under tail coverts, but the Orange-crowned always has yellow ones. However, many Tennessee Warblers also have yellowish under tail coverts. Their song is suggestive of that of the Nashville Warbler but is louder, more staccato, and usually in three instead of two parts.

Habitat. Coniferous, mixed, and deciduous woodlands, bogs, alder and willow thickets, burntlands, more open deciduous second growth. In migration all types of woodland.

Nesting. On the ground often in bogs but sometimes on dry hillsides. Nest often in sphagnum and sometimes arched-over by moss or grass. The nest is of grasses. *Eggs*, 4 to 7; white, dotted or spotted with reddish browns.

Range. Breeds widely in forested Canada (see Range in Canada) and south to northwestern Montana, northern Minnesota, northern Wisconsin, northern Michigan, northeastern New York, southern Vermont, central New Hampshire, and southern Maine. Winters from southern Mexico and Guatemala south to Colombia and Venezuela.

Orange-crowned Warbler

Paruline verdâtre
Vermivora celata (Say)
Total length: 12.2 to 13.4 cm
Plate 61

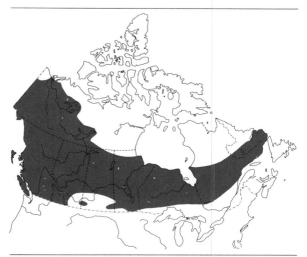

Breeding Distribution of Orange-crowned Warbler

Range in Canada. Summer resident, breeding in Yukon (Old Crow southward); western and central-southern Mackenzie (Mackenzie Delta; Forts Anderson, Norman, Simpson; Hill Island Lake); British Columbia (throughout, including coastal islands); Alberta (throughout north, centre, and in mountains of southwest; local in southeast: Red Deer and Bow Rivers, Cypress Hills); Saskatchewan (Lake Athabasca, Charcoal Lake, Flotten Lake, Prince Albert National Park, Nipawin; locally in the south: Cypress Hills, Qu'Appelle valley); Manitoba (Lynn Lake, Churchill, Duck Mountain, Aweme); northern and central Ontario (Fort Severn, Favourable Lake, Lake Attawapiskat, Big Piskwamish Point, Lake Nipigon, Kapuskasing, Mildred, Genier); central Quebec (Grande rivière de la Baleine, Lake Albanel, Moisie Bay); and southern Labrador (Goose Bay).

Uncommon migrant south of the breeding range in southern Ontario, and scarce migrant in southwestern Quebec (Montréal, Québec, Hatley). Casual in Nova Scotia (specimen: Halifax, January to 8 February 1951; also several sight records) and at Hope Point, Bernard Harbour on Dolphin and Union Strait, and Belcher Islands, N.W.T.

Adult male: Upper parts dusky olive green, brightening on rump; a partly concealed crown patch of dull orange; eyelids and line over eye yellowish; a narrow, poorly defined streak of dusky through eye; wings and tail without white patches; under parts including under tail coverts and wing linings greenish yellow, the breast and sometimes the throat indistinctly streaked with olive green; bill dark grey; legs olive grey. *Adult female*: Very similar to adult male, sometimes indistinguishable, but usually duller and more greyish in colour, the orange crown patch more restricted or absent. *Young in autumn*: Similar to adults but duskier, the crown patch either very small or wanting.

Measurements *(V. c. celata)*. *Adult male*: wing, 56.9–62.5 (59.8); tail, 46–51.5 (48.6); exposed culmen, 10–11.2 (10.6); tarsus, 16.5–18.5 (17.5). *Adult female*: wing, 55–59.2 (56.8) mm.

Field Marks. A dingy greenish-yellow warbler with no distinct markings, the crown patch rarely visible. Its vaguely streaked and usually more extensively yellow under parts distinguish it from autumn Tennessees. The Nashville Warbler also has a reddish crown patch but shows a white eye-ring against more greyish sides of the head; it has brighter yellow unstreaked under parts. *Song*: A colourless trill, dropping slightly in pitch near the middle, and weakening near the end.

Habitat. Brushy and open deciduous woods, the deciduous elements of mixedwoods, second growths in clearings or burntlands, various brushy thickets and stands of tall shrubbery.

Nesting. On the ground, sometimes in a low bush. Nest, of grass, shreds of bark, and moss, lined with fine grass, hair, and feathers. *Eggs*, 4 to 6; white, finely dotted around the larger end with reddish browns and often a little purplish grey.

Range. Breeds in central Alaska and much of forested Canada (see Range in Canada) and south to Baja California, southern Arizona, and western Texas. Winters from southern United States south to Guatemala and southern Florida.

Subspecies. (1) *Vermivora celata celata* (Say) (palest and greyest race): northern central, southeastern Yukon, Mackenzie, northern and central Alberta (except mountains and Cypress Hills); northern and central Saskatchewan (except Cypress Hills), Manitoba, Ontario, Quebec. (2) *V. c. orestera* Oberholser (similar to *celeta* but larger, more yellowish): southwestern Yukon (Kluane Lake, Carcross); interior British Columbia (east of the coast), southern Alberta (southwestern mountains, Cypress Hills), southwestern Saskatchewan (Cypress Hills). (3) *V. c. lutescens* (Ridgway) (brighter yellow in colour than either *celata* or *orestera*, smaller than the latter): British Columbia coast and islands.

Nashville Warbler

Paruline à joues grises
Vermivora ruficapilla (Wilson)
Total length: 11.4 to 12.7 cm
Plate 61

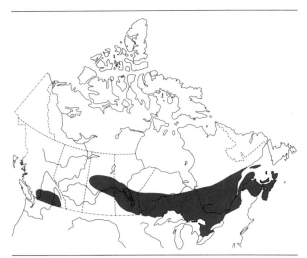

Breeding Distribution of Nashville Warbler

Range in Canada. Summer resident, breeding in southern interior British Columbia (Pemberton, Lillooet, Clearwater, Revelstoke, Pitt Lake, Trail); southwestern Alberta (rarely: Link Creek); central Saskatchewan (sparsely: Kazan Lake, Montreal River, Prince Albert National Park); central and southern Manitoba (Moose and Cedar lakes, Duck Mountain, Hillside Beach, Rennie); central and southern Ontario (Favourable Lake and Moosonee, southward, but very local in extreme south, reportedly to Middlesex County); southern Quebec (Taschereau, Amos, Lake Saint-Jean, Lake Sainte-Anne on Toulnustouc River, perhaps Mingan, Piashti Bay, and Anticosti Island, southward including Madeleine Islands); New Brunswick; Prince Edward Island; and Nova Scotia (including Cape Breton Island). Summer sight records for southwestern Newfoundland.

Rare migrant on Vancouver Island.

Adult male: Top of head, cheeks, hind-neck, and sides of neck bluish grey; chestnut patch on top of head, but usually somewhat obscured by grey; eye-ring white; narrow streak from base of bill to eye greyish white; rest of upper parts olive green; wings and tail with no white bars or patches; under parts, including under tail coverts, bright yellow becoming whitish on lower belly. *Adult female*: Similar to adult male but duller in colour and with chestnut crown patch smaller or absent. *Young (first autumn)*: Duller than adults, the grey of head more brownish, crown patch of male smaller or absent, almost always absent in female.

Measurements *(V. r. ruficapilla). Adult male*: wing, 56–61.7 (59.2); tail, 40–47 (44.2); exposed culmen, 9.3–10.9 (10.1); tarsus, 16–17 (16.6). *Adult female*: wing, 53.3–57.6 (56.3) mm.

Field Marks. Bright plain-yellow under parts and grey head, white eye-ring. The grey, which extends down low on cheeks and sides of neck, is sharply cut off from bright-yellow throat. No white wing bars or tail patches. In autumn the grey of head is more brownish, but yellow of throat is still sharply cut off from it. *Song*: Resembles somewhat that of Tennessee Warbler but has less carrying power and is in two instead of three (usually) parts: *see it, see it, see it, ti-ti-ti-ti-ti*, the second part lower than the first and much more rapid.

Habitat. Sparse immature deciduous or mixed woods, especially where aspen or birch is a component, with low bushes, on either dry or moist land: second growths on old clearings, burntlands, sparsely treed bogs.

Nesting. On the ground, usually well concealed by shrubs or in a mossy hummock; nest of moss, grass, bark strips, leaves; lined with fine grass or hair. *Eggs*, 4 or 5; white, speckled with reddish browns usually mainly about the large end. Incubation mostly, if not entirely, by the female.

Range. Breeds from southern Canada south to central California, northern Utah, southern Minnesota, southern Michigan, northeastern West Virginia, and western Maryland. Winters from northern Mexico, southern Texas, and southern Florida south to Guatemala.

Subspecies. (1) *Vermivora ruficapilla ruficapilla* (Wilson): Manitoba, Ontario, Quebec, New Brunswick, Prince Edward Island, Nova Scotia, probably Saskatchewan. (2) *V. r. ridgwayi* van Rossem (rump brighter, more yellowish, lower abdomen more extensively whitish): southern British Columbia.

Virginia's Warbler

Paruline de Virginia
Vermivora virginiae (Baird)
Total length: 10.9 to 12 cm
Plate 61

Status in Canada. Casual in southern Ontario (specimen: Point Pelee, 16 May 1958. Photo record: Pelee Island, 10 May 1974. Sight record: Point Pelee, May 1975). Its breeding range is in southwestern United States from central Nevada, southeastern Idaho, northeastern Utah, and central northern Colorado southward.

Adults: Upper parts grey except chestnut patch on crown and bright olive-green rump and upper tail coverts; eye-ring white; no wing bars or tail patch; under parts greyish white with yellow patch on middle of breast (sometimes extending to throat), and bright-yellow under tail coverts.

Northern Parula

Paruline à collier
Parula americana (Linnaeus)
Total length: 10.9 to 12.5 cm
Plate 60

Breeding Distribution of Northern Parula

Range in Canada. Summer resident, breeding locally in southeastern Manitoba (Waugh, Lac du Bonnet); central and southern Ontario (Off Lake, Timmins, Lake Abitibi, Long Point); southern Quebec (Lake Waswanipi, Blue-Sea-Lake, Québec, Lake Rimouski, Percé, Hatley, Lake Trois Saumons; probably Madeleine Islands); New Brunswick; Prince Edward Island; Nova Scotia (including Cape Breton Island).

Occurs in summer north to Lake Saint-Jean and Anticosti Island, Quebec. Scarce visitor to Saskatchewan (Emma Lake, Fort Qu'Appelle, Moose Mountain, McLean, Sovereign). Casual in Alberta (specimen: 24 km west of Turner Valley, 6 June 1958. Sight records at Calgary, Wayne, and Rosedale).

Adult male: Upper parts mainly greyish-blue, this extending down over face and sides of breast; upper and lower eyelids partly white; in middle of back, a large patch of greenish yellow; two prominent white wing bars; two or three outermost tail feathers on each side with large white patch near tip; throat and much of breast yellow; yellow of throat separated from that of breast by a blackish band and behind that band some spots of reddish brown; sides usually tinged with chestnut; abdomen and under tail coverts white. *Adult female*: Resembles adult male but is duller; band across breast either absent or very much restricted, but often there are a few brownish feather tips on upper breast. *Young in autumn*: Blue of upper parts much obscured by greenish; breast band lacking or only faintly indicated.

Measurements. *Adult male*: wing, 58.1–64.7 (61.1); tail, 41–45.5 (43.5); exposed culmen, 9.9–11 (10.4); tarsus, 16–17 (16.5). *Adult female*: wing, 53.7–59 (56.2) mm.

Field Marks. This and the Canada Warbler are our only two bluish-backed warblers with yellow under parts. The Parula's two white wing bars and tail patches, greenish-yellow patch on the back, different face pattern, and (when present) different breast band readily separate it from the Canada. The Parula's greenish-yellow back patch separates it from other warblers, and the breast of the male is very distinctive. *Song*: Although there are variations, the usual pattern is a buzzy rising trill ending in an abrupt emphatic *zip* or *wip*.

Habitat. Either deciduous or coniferous woods and openings, particularly in moister places where the lichen *Usnea* (old man's beard moss) grows. Forages most often at medium heights and up to upper branches. In migration various types of woodland and tall shrubbery.

Nesting. Nest is hollowed out in a hanging bunch of *Usnea* lichen, often without lining or with only a few pieces of grass or other plant material or a few horse hairs. Where *Usnea* is scarce, a hanging cluster of hemlock or spruce may be used and some *Usnea* added. *Eggs*, usually 4 or 5; white, speckled and spotted with browns and drab. Incubation 12 to 14 days, by the female (R. and J. Graber).

Range. Breeds from southeastern Manitoba east to Nova Scotia and south to the Gulf Coast from eastern Texas to central Florida. Winters from Mexico south through Central America to Nicaragua and from Florida south through the Greater and Lesser Antilles to Barbados.

Remarks. This is one of the smallest and prettiest of the wood-warblers. It often forages high in the treetops where it may best be located by its song. It is widely but unevenly distributed in summer, its numbers being influenced by the availability of the lichen *Usnea*, which it prefers as a nesting site. The name "parula," which means *little titmouse*, refers to its occasional tendency to cling upside-down to a branch or cluster in chickadee-fashion.

Yellow Warbler

Paruline jaune
Dendroica petechia (Linnaeus)
Total length: 12 to 13.3 cm
Plate 60

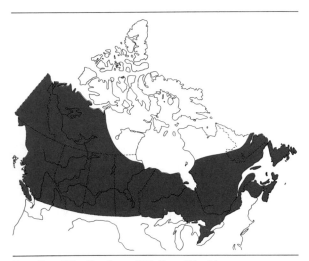

Breeding Distribution of Yellow Warbler

Range in Canada. Summer resident, breeding from northern Yukon (the arctic coast, Old Crow, Lapierre House); northwestern and central Mackenzie (Mackenzie Delta, Richards Island, Fort Anderson, Bathurst Inlet, Reliance); northern Saskatchewan (Lake Athabasca, Black Lake area, Reindeer Lake); northern Manitoba (Lynn Lake, Churchill); northern Ontario (throughout); central Quebec (Lake Guillaume-Delisle, mouth of Grande rivière de la Baleine, Lake Mistassini, Schefferville, north shore of the Gulf of St. Lawrence; recorded in summer north to headwaters of Swampy Bay River); southern Labrador (Grand Falls, Holton Harbour, Goose Bay); and Newfoundland south through southern coastal and interior British Columbia (except perhaps Queen Charlotte Islands); and through southern parts of Alberta; Saskatchewan; Manitoba; Ontario; Quebec (including Madeleine Islands); New Brunswick; Prince Edward Island; and Nova Scotia (including Cape Breton Island).

Accidental on Southampton Island, N.W.T. (specimen: August 1951) and Baffin Island (specimen: Pond Inlet, 7 October 1978).

Inner webs of tail with large *yellow* patches, thus differing from other Canadian warblers of generally yellow coloration. *Adult male*: Upper parts mostly yellowish olive-green, becoming yellow, sometimes with an orange tinge, on crown; wings dark with yellow edging; tail with large patches of *yellow on inner webs*; sides of head and the under parts rich yellow, the breast, sides, and flanks striped with chestnut. *Adult female*: Similar to adult male but duller, slightly more greenish above, paler yellow below and with few or no chestnut stripes. *Young (first autumn)*: similar to adult female but less yellow above; under parts unstreaked pale dusky-yellow; yellow patches in tail smaller and paler.

Measurements *(D. p. aestiva)*. *Adult male*: wing, 59.2–64.3 (62.1); tail, 43–47 (45.2); exposed culmen, 9.1–11 (10.2); tarsus, 17.5–18.5 (18.1). *Adult female*: wing, 56.7–63.2 (59.0) mm.

Field Marks. The common yellow warbler in much of Canada, often nesting in ornamental shrubbery in gardens. Adult male's reddish breast streaks are readily seen at close range, but in females and young the streaks are faint or absent. In any plumage the *yellow* patches in the tail are diagnostic. Female Wilson's Warbler closely resembles female and young Yellow Warbler, but it has no light patches in the tail. The eastern race of the Palm Warbler has reddish streaks on a yellow breast, but the Palm Warbler constantly wags its tail (which has white instead of yellow patches). The Yellow Warbler and the American Goldfinch are both sometimes called "yellow bird," but the slender bill and yellowish instead of black wings easily distinguish the warbler. *Song*: Lively, cheerful, but variable. Many songs sound like *tzee tzee tzee tzee setta wee see*. Many people confuse it with that of the Chestnut-sided Warbler.

Habitat. Thickets, especially those of alder and willow, in moister areas like the edges of streams, lakes, bogs, marshes; garden shrubbery is almost equally popular.

Nesting. In bush or tree, most often 0.9 to 2.4 m up but rarely as high as 12 m. Nest is firmly fastened to a fork of a branch and is composed of plant fibres, grasses, shredded bark, sometimes twine or cotton wool. Although often bulky externally, the cup is neat and is lined with fine grasses, hairs, and plant down. *Eggs*, usually 4 or 5; white to bluish white, spotted mostly around the large end, with various browns and purplish greys. Incubation, by the female, is reported to average 11 days (F.G. Schrantz).

Range. Breeds from north-central Alaska, and from near tree limit across Canada south to southern Baja California, central Peru, coastal Venezuela, Trinidad, the Antilles, Bahamas, and Florida Keys. Winters from Mexico and the Bahamas south to Peru and Brazil.

Subspecies. (1) *Dendroica petechia aestiva* (Gmelin) (the palest Canadian race): southeastern Alberta, southern Saskatchewan, extreme southern Manitoba, southern Ontario (Off Lake, North Bay), southern Quebec (Québec, Gaspé Peninsula), New Brunswick, Prince Edward Island, and Nova Scotia (but on Cape Breton Island intergrading with and closer to *amnicola*). (2) *D. p. amnicola* Batchelder (darker, more olivaceous above than *aestiva*): Yukon, Mackenzie, northeastern British Columbia (Peace River District), northern and central Alberta, northern and central Saskatchewan, northern and central Manitoba, northern and central Ontario, central Quebec (Lake Saint-Jean, Anticosti Island, north shore Gulf of St. Lawrence; also Madeleine Islands), southern Labrador, and Newfoundland. (3) *D. p. rubiginosa* (Pallas) (darker above than *amnicola*, the forehead more extensively olivaceous): western British Columbia (Atlin, Hazelton, Victoria). (4) *D. p. morcomi* Coale: interior southern British Columbia (Okanagan Landing, Newgate). The subspecies of the Yellow Warbler are in need of study.

Remarks. Because the Yellow Warbler, more often than most warblers, frequents the ornamental shrubbery about our dwellings all across the country, it is probably seen more often by the average person than any other warbler. Many know it as "yellow bird." Its spritely, if not particularly melodious, song is rendered with enthusiasm, especially in May and June. One male has been credited with 3240 songs in a day at the height of the singing season. Insects are its main food.

Chestnut-sided Warbler

Paruline à flancs marron
Dendroica pensylvanica (Linnaeus)
Total length: 12 to 14.4 cm
Plate 63

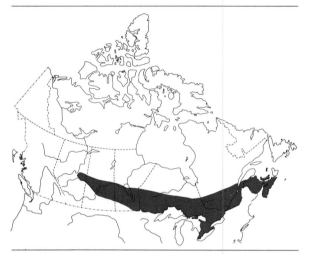

Breeding Distribution of Chestnut-sided Warbler

Range in Canada. Summer resident, breeding in central-eastern Alberta (reported to have bred in 1934 at Boyle; no other breeding records although there are occurrences in the breeding season, apparently regularly in the Cold Lake–Ethel Lake region); central Saskatchewan (Carlton, Emma Lake, Candle Lake, Nipawin; probably Flotten Lake); central and southern Manitoba (The Pas, Riding Mountain, Duck Mountain, Portage la Prairie, Hillside Beach, Indian Bay); central and southern Ontario (Pickle Lake, Lake Abitibi, southward; recorded north to Moosonee where perhaps breeding); southern Quebec (Lake Chicobi in Amos region, Lake Saint-Jean, Tadoussac, Lake Rimouski; Hull, Montréal, Hatley, Baker Lake, Madeleine Islands; recorded rarely on Gaspé Peninsula, but evidence of breeding is lacking); New Brunswick; Prince Edward Island; and Nova Scotia (except Cape Breton Island).

Rare visitor to British Columbia (photo: Mount Robson Provincial Park, 22 June 1971. Sight record: Reifel Refuge, 29 September 1964).

Adult male (breeding plumage): Crown bright greenish-yellow bordered by black; back and scapulars streaked black and greenish yellow; region in front of eye black, this extending in a broad narrowing patch down to jaw and also joining black stripe above eye; ear region and sides of neck white; two yellowish wing bars; three outer tail feathers with white patch; under parts plain white, except broad chestnut stripe extending from near black jaw patch backward along sides and flanks. *Adult female (breeding plumage)*: Similar to adult male but black and chestnut areas reduced; yellow crown duller, more greenish. *Adult male (autumn)*: Upper parts mainly bright greenish-yellow, sparsely streaked or spotted with dusky on back and rump; sides of head plain grey without black; under parts plain white with well-marked chestnut stripe along sides. *Adult female and young in autumn*: Similar to adult male in autumn but with very little or no chestnut on flanks.

Measurements. *Adult male*: wing, 61.6–65.8 (63.8); tail, 47–51 (49.7); exposed culmen, 9.9–10.6 (10.2); tarsus, 17–18 (17.6). *Adult female*: wing, 58.6–61.5 (60.1) mm.

Field Marks. *Breeding plumage*: Easily recognized by the chestnut sides, yellow crown, yellowish wing bars, and plain-white under parts. Golden-winged Warbler also has a yellow crown and yellow wing bars but it shows a black or grey throat and decidedly yellow (not yellowish) wing bars. *Autumn plumages*: Plain-grey face (no black), greenish-yellow upper parts, yellow wing bars; adults usually with more or less chestnut on sides, young lack it. The Bay-breasted, the only other warbler with chestnut sides, is in breeding plumage so different otherwise that there is little chance of confusion. Sometimes the Bay-breast also shows chestnut on the sides in autumn, but the Chestnut-sided Warbler's plain-grey face (sharply cut off from the yellow top of head), lack of a dusky eye streak, and decidedly white under parts mark it. *Song*: Rather loud and emphatic. Has two common songs, one of which suggests that of the Yellow Warbler but has a distinctive ending, the next-to-last syllable strongly accented. To some it sounds like *very, very pleased to meetcha*.

Habitat. Open bushy second growth and thickets, deciduous or mainly so, on both dry and moist ground.

Nesting. In a sapling, low bush, or vine, usually 0.3 to 0.9 m up. Nest is constructed of shredded bark, grass, fine weed stalks, and frequently some plant down and is lined with fine grass and often some hair. *Eggs*, 3 to 5, generally 4; white-spotted, speckled, or blotched with browns and some greys. Incubation 12 to 12.5 days, by the female (Louise de K. Lawrence).

Range. Breeds from central-eastern Alberta east to Nova Scotia and south to eastern Nebraska, southern Wisconsin, northern Ohio, central New Jersey, and in the Appalachians to northern Georgia and northwestern South Carolina. Winters from southern Nicaragua to Panama.

Magnolia Warbler

Paruline à tête cendrée
Dendroica magnolia (Wilson)
Total length: 10.2 to 13 cm
Plate 61

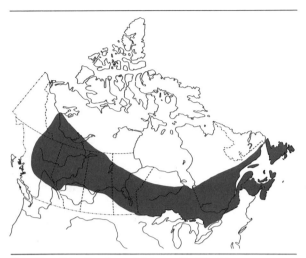

Breeding Distribution of Magnolia Warbler

Range in Canada. Summer resident, breeding in central-western and southwestern Mackenzie (Fort Norman, western Great Slave Lake); northeastern, central, and south-central British Columbia (Trutch, Liard Crossing, Driftwood valley, Little River P.O., Hazelton, Quesnel, Indianpoint Lake); northern and central Alberta (south to about Banff, Edson, Edmonton); northwestern and central Saskatchewan (Lake Athabasca, Meadow Lake, Nipawin); central and southern Manitoba (Gillam, Oxford House, Riding Mountain, Hillside Beach); central and southern Ontario (Big Trout Lake, Fort Albany, Off Lake, Thunder Bay, Wasaga Beach, Sharbot Lake, Guelph, probably north to Aquatuk Lake); south-central and southern Quebec (Eastmain, Lake Mistassini, north shore of the Gulf of St. Lawrence east at least to Saint-Augustin, Anticosti Island, Low, Hatley, Gaspé Peninsula, Madeleine Islands; formerly Montréal region, Bury); southern Newfoundland; New Brunswick; Prince Edward Island; and Nova Scotia (including Cape Breton Island); probably Labrador (Hamilton River).

Accidental in southern Davis Strait, N.W.T. (62°55′N, 60°23′W) (sight record: an immature came aboard a ship on 15 September 1976).

Broad white band on tail separates it in all plumages from other Canadian warblers. *Adult male (breeding plumage)*: Top of head and nape bluish grey; line back from eye white; sides of head black; back and scapulars black; rump patch yellow; tail mostly black, with a broad white band across its middle (but not across two centre feathers); wings with two white wing bars; under parts mostly bright yellow, the breast, sides, and flanks heavily streaked with black, the under tail coverts white. *Adult female (breeding plumage)*: Similar to adult male but top of head duller; back olive green with black spots; white wing bars narrower; black streaks on under parts narrower and duller. *Young and adults in autumn*: Resemble adult females in breeding plumage, but top and sides of head greyish; back olive green, sometimes spotted with black (adult male); under parts mostly plain yellow, more or less faintly streaked on sides and flanks.

Measurements. *Adult male*: wing, 58.7–61.5 (60.5); tail, 47–51.5 (49.1); exposed culmen, 9.1–11 (9.8); tarsus, 17.5–18.5 (17.9). *Adult female*: wing, 54.1–59.8 (57.1) mm.

Field Marks. A yellow-breasted, yellow-rumped warbler with distinctive tail markings. In any plumage the tail from below appears white at the base with a very broad black band across the end (see Cape May Warbler). *Song: Wisha wisha wisha witsy*, rising slightly. Also a distinctive call-note, *tlep*.

Habitat. On breeding grounds, mostly young or low coniferous woods or open mixedwood and edges. In migration, various types of woodland and thickets.

Nesting. Usually (not always) low in a small conifer. Nest is of grass and weeds, lined with hair and fine rootlets. *Eggs*, 3 to 5, usually 4; white variably marked with reddish browns and purplish grey, especially on larger end. Incubation 11 to 13 days, by the female (A.C. Bent).

Range. Breeds in Canada (see Range in Canada) and south in the United States to northeastern Minnesota, central Wisconsin, central Michigan, and locally to central West Virginia, western Virginia, northeastern Pennsylvania, northwestern New Jersey, and northern Massachusetts. Winters from central Mexico through Central America to Costa Rica and the West Indies.

Cape May Warbler

Paruline tigrée
Dendroica tigrina (Gmelin)
Total length: 11.8 to 14 cm
Plate 61

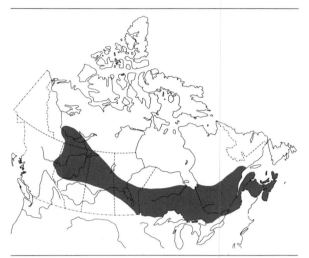

Breeding Distribution of Cape May Warbler

Range in Canada. Summer resident breeding in southwestern and central-southern Mackenzie (Fort Simpson, Slave River); central-eastern British Columbia (Peace River parklands); northern and central Alberta (Grimshaw, Wood Buffalo National Park, Fort Assiniboine, Lac la Nonne, Glenevis. An isolated breeding record at Brooks, in 1951, seems unlikely to be repeated); Saskatchewan (Lake Athabasca, Montreal River, Kazan Lake, Prince Albert National Park); central and southeastern Manitoba (Thicket Portage, Duck Mountain, Julius); north-central and central Ontario (Lac Seul; Sandy Lake; Moose Factory; Dorcas Bay in Bruce County; Algonquin Provincial Park); southern Quebec (Eastmain, Lake Saint-Jean, Sainte-Marguerite River, Lake Trois Saumons, Gaspé Peninsula, Blue-Sea-Lake, Ulverton, Madeleine Islands); New Brunswick; Prince Edward Island; and Nova Scotia (rather rare but including Cape Breton Island). Possibly breeds sparsely in Yukon (sight record of a pair with at least one young at Toobally Lake, summer 1983).

Recorded without evidence of breeding on Anticosti Island and at mouth of Natashquan River, Quebec.

Casual in Newfoundland (specimen: St. Andrew's, 25 August 1959).

Adult male (breeding plumage): Top of head and narrow line through eye black or blackish; patch of chestnut on sides of face sometimes interrupting yellow above eye; sides of neck yellow; back and scapulars yellowish green spotted or streaked with black; rump yellow; tail blackish with large white patches on outer feathers near tip (decreasing extent of white inward); patch of white on wing coverts; under parts yellow fading to white on lower abdomen; throat, breast, sides, and flanks streaked with black often with a tinge of chestnut on throat. *Adult female (breeding plumage)*: Much duller than adult male, the top of head olive streaked with dusky; sides of head pale yellow with olive ear coverts; rump patch and sides of neck yellowish; two faint white wing bars; under parts whitish, the whitish more or less tinged with yellow; throat, breast, and sides streaked with dusky. *Adult male (autumn)*: Similar to adult male in spring but upper parts tinged with grey, under parts lightly frosted with white. *Adult female (autumn)*: Similar to female in breeding plumage but a bit more decidedly yellow on breast and rump, streaks of under parts veiled by white. *Young (autumn)*: Resemble adults, in autumn, of their respective sexes, but white of tail more restricted; male with no chestnut on face and no black cap; female with less or no yellow on under parts, but with a faint tinge of yellow always present on sides of neck.

Measurements. *Adult male*: wing, 65.4–71.3 (67.2); tail, 45.5–50.5 (47.9); exposed culmen, 9.9–11 (10.5); tarsus, 17–18.5 (17.8). *Adult female*: wing, 61.3–67 (63.4) mm.

Field Marks. Adult male's chestnut cheeks, white patch on wing coverts, and yellow black-streaked under parts are a combination that is unmistakable. Female lacks chestnut cheeks and is of much duller general coloration but shows a yellow rump and a yellowish area on sides of neck. Young female in autumn is extremely dull coloured (Plate 61) but has a yellowish rump and a small yellowish patch on sides of neck. This yellowish neck patch, although sometimes obscure, is characteristic of the Cape May, regardless of how dull the bird may be otherwise, and distinguishes it from other similar warblers such as the Yellow-rumped (which has a more definite yellow rump patch) (see also Magnolia and Palm warblers). *Song*: a high-pitched sibilant *seep seep seep seep*, four or more times in the same high pitch.

Habitat. On breeding grounds, coniferous woods and mixedwoods, especially more open types and edges. Sings and nests mainly in the upper branches. In migration various kinds of woods and thickets.

Nesting. Usually near the top of a conifer, 9 to 18 m up. Nest of moss, grass, small twigs, and plant down, lined with fine grass, hair, and feathers. *Eggs*, 4 to 9; white, spotted, mostly near the large end, with reddish browns and a little purplish grey.

Range. Breeds in Canada (Alberta east to Nova Scotia) and south in the United States to northeastern North Dakota, northern and central-eastern Minnesota, northern Wisconsin, northern Michigan, northeastern New York, central-eastern Vermont, and southern Maine. Winters in the West Indies.

Black-throated Blue Warbler

Paruline bleue à gorge noire
Dendroica caerulescens (Gmelin)
Total length: 12 to 14 cm
Plate 62

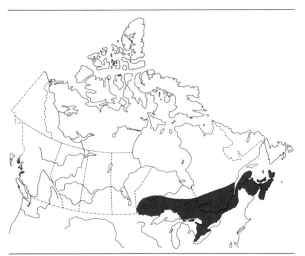

Breeding Distribution of Black-throated Blue Warbler

Range in Canada. Summer resident, breeding in central and southern Ontario (Lac Seul, Kapuskasing, Lake Abitibi, southward); southern Quebec (La Vérendrye Park, Mount Plamondon, Lake Saint-Jean, Tadoussac, Gaspé Peninsula, Chelsea, Hatley, Lake Trois Saumons); New Brunswick, Prince Edward Island; and Nova Scotia (including Cape Breton Island). Recorded in summer at Mingan, Anticosti Island, and Madeleine Islands, Quebec; Indian Bay, southeastern Manitoba; and Emma Lake, central Saskatchewan. Recorded in migration seasons in western Manitoba (Treesbank); southern Saskatchewan (Fort Qu'Appelle, Percival, Moose Jaw, Regina). Casual in Alberta (specimens: Edmonton, Tofield, Rosebud, and near Nordegg). Accidental in British Columbia (photo: a male at Creston, on 22 September 1984).

Adult male: Upper parts mainly dark greyish-blue, occasionally with some black spots on back; a small white patch at the base of the primaries; no wing bars; outer feathers of tail with large white patches reaching to near ends; sides of head, throat, upper breast, and sides black; rest of under parts white. *Adult female*: Very different from male. Upper parts and cheeks uniform dull-olive or olive green, often with a trace of blue on crown, upper tail coverts, and edging of tail; at base of primaries a small whitish spot, smaller than that of adult male and sometimes concealed; no wing bars; whitish stripe over eye; lower eyelid partly white; outer tail feathers with or without inconspicuous greyish patches; under parts plain pale greenish-yellow. *Young (autumn)*: Like adult of their respective sexes; male with blue of upper parts duller and somewhat mixed with olive; black below with grey feather tips; and posterior white under parts tinged with yellow.

Measurements. *Adult male*: wing, 64–67.1 (64.9); tail, 50–53 (51.2); exposed culmen, 9.2–11 (10.1); tarsus, 18–18.5 (18.3). *Adult female*: wing, 57.6–62.8 (60.7) mm.

Field Marks. The male with blue upper parts, black face, throat, and sides, and a small white spot near base of primaries is unmistakable. Females are plain, unstreaked, olive green and look like several other warblers, especially female Tennessees. Usually the small white wing spot at the base of the primaries, which marks the Black-throated Blue, can be seen. When this mark cannot be discerned, the solidly dark cheeks separate it from the Tennessee, and the lack of wing bars from the female Cerulean. *Song*: Very distinctive. A lazy *zwee-a zwee-a zwee-a zwee*, the last upslurred. A junco-like *chip*.

Habitat. In the breeding season, deciduous and mixed woodland where there is an understory of shrubs or saplings; often old clearings and logged-over areas.

Nesting. From 0.3 to 0.9 m above ground in a sapling, shrub, or small tree. Nest rather bulky, composed of bark shreds, leaves, rotten wood and lined with rootlets, fine grasses, or hair. *Eggs*, 3 to 5, usually 4; spotted, blotched, or clouded with browns. Incubation 12 days, by the female (Louise de K. Lawrence).

Range. Breeds from southeastern Canada (western Ontario east to Nova Scotia) south to central-eastern Minnesota, northern Wisconsin, central Michigan, western and northeastern Pennsylvania, southeastern New York, Rhode Island, and Massachusetts and in the Appalachian Mountains to northeastern Georgia. Winters mainly in the West Indies.

Subspecies. *Dendroica caerulescens caerulescens* (Gmelin).

Yellow-rumped Warbler

(Myrtle Warbler; Audubon's Warbler)

Paruline à croupion jaune
Dendroica coronata (Linnaeus)
Total length: 12 to 15.5 cm
Plate 62

Yellow-rumped Warbler is the name assigned by the A.O.U. Check-list Committee (1973. Auk, vol. 90, no. 2, p. 417) to a combination into one species of what were formerly thought to be two species called "Myrtle Warbler" and "Audubon's Warbler."

Eastern and northwestern populations, formerly known as "Myrtle Warbler," are described as follows: *Adult male (breeding plumage)*: Upper parts mostly bluish-grey, streaked with black and with a patch of bright yellow on crown and another on rump; streak over eye and small spot on upper and lower eyelid white; across face a broad black patch; three outer tail feathers with a white patch on inner web; two white wing bars; under parts mainly white, the breast, sides, and flanks heavily streaked with black, and with a yellow patch on either side of breast. *Adult female (breeding plumage)*: Similar to adult male but duller; more brownish above, black streaking narrower below, cheek patch duller. *Young and adults in autumn*: Upper parts and sides of head mainly brownish, the back and scapulars streaked with black, crown patch partly or quite concealed by brown feather tips; conspicuous yellow rump patch; under parts mostly dingy white; the breast,

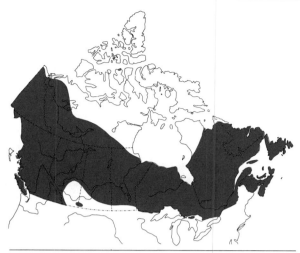

Breeding Distribution of Yellow-rumped Warbler

Range in Canada. Breeds from northern Yukon (Old Crow, Lapierre House); northwestern and central Mackenzie (Mackenzie Delta, Fort Anderson, southeastern Great Bear Lake, Reliance, and near junction of Hanbury and Thelon rivers); southwestern Keewatin (probably: Windy River); northern Manitoba (Sandhill Lake, Churchill); northern Ontario (Fort Severn, Fort Albany); northern Quebec (Feuilles River, Koroc River); north-central Labrador (Tikkoatokak Bay, Angutausugevik); and Newfoundland south through British Columbia; central and southwestern Alberta (Jasper National Park, Bow valley, Battle River region, also Cypress Hills); central and southern Saskatchewan (Flotten Lake, Prince Albert, Nipawin, Fort Qu'Appelle, locally Cypress Hills); southern Manitoba (Duck Mountain, Spruce Forest Reserve, Hillside Beach); southern Ontario (Bruce, Simcoe, Frontenac, and Leeds counties); southern Quebec (Gatineau Park, Hatley, Gaspé Peninsula, Anticosti and Madeleine islands, north shore of Gulf of St. Lawrence); New Brunswick; Prince Edward Island; and Nova Scotia (including Cape Breton Island). Migrates through southern Canada.

Winters in southern Nova Scotia (locally in small numbers: Wolfville, Yarmouth, Port Mouton) and in southwestern British Columbia (Victoria, Vancouver).

Casual on King William Island, Baker Lake, Chesterfield Inlet, and Southampton Island, N.W.T. Sight record on Prince Leopold Island, N.W.T. (a male, 20 June 1975).

sides, and flanks streaked with dusky, and with a faint yellow patch usually on either side of breast but sometimes absent in young females.

Populations breeding in central and southern British Columbia, the mountains of southwestern Alberta, and the Cypress Hills, formerly called "Audubon's Warbler" are very similar to the above but differ as follows: *Adults in breeding plumage*: Throat bright yellow instead of white, but yellow is less extensive in females; cheeks mostly bluish-grey, not solid black; white areas in tail usually more extensive and present on four or five (instead of two or three) outermost feathers; and in the adult male the white of wing bars is more extensive, often forming a patch. *Adults in autumn* are similar to eastern populations but have yellow on throat and more white in the tail. *Young in autumn* are very similar to eastern birds but some show yellow on the throat. In all cases there is more white in the tail feathers.

Measurements (*D. c. coronata*). *Adult male*: wing, 70.2–74.3 (72.7); tail, 55–58.5 (57.0); exposed culmen, 10–10.9 (10.4); tarsus, 18–19.5 (18.5). *Adult female*: wing, 67.7–72 (69.7) mm.

Field Marks. Although other warblers like the Cape May, Magnolia, and Palm have a yellowish rump patch, it is not so bright nor so well marked as that of the Yellow-rumped. This, in combination with a yellow patch on either side of the breast, distinguishes the Yellow-rumped from other warblers. *Song*: A tinkling trill like the rattle of a small chain, either rising or falling near the end. The ordinary call-note *chep* is distinctive.

Habitat. Coniferous and mixed woodlands, especially in more open situations. In migration, various types of woods, thickets, roadside trees, gardens.

Nesting. Usually in a coniferous tree (infrequently deciduous), 0.3 to 15 m above ground, most often about 3 to 4.5 m, very rarely on the ground. Nest, rather loose and bulky, is made of twigs, grass, rootlets, and moss and is lined with hair and often feathers. *Eggs*, generally 4 or 5; white, spotted and blotched with various browns and often some underlying grey. Incubation 12 to 13 days (O.W. Knight), by the female.

Range. Breeds from north-central Alaska and across Canada south through the mountains to northern Mexico (northern Baja California, Durango) and east of the mountains to central Alberta, northern Minnesota, central Michigan, eastern New York, eastern Pennsylvania, and Massachusetts. Winters from southwestern British Columbia, northern and north-central United States and Nova Scotia south to central Panama and the Greater Antilles.

Subspecies. (1) *Dendroica coronata coronata* (Linnaeus): A white-throated subspecies breeding in north-central Alberta (Grimshaw, Lesser Slave Lake), Saskatchewan (except Cypress Hills), Manitoba, Ontario, Quebec, Labrador, Newfoundland, New Brunswick, Prince Edward Island and Nova Scotia. (2) *D. c. hooveri* McGregor (white throated like *D. c. coronata* but slightly larger): Yukon, Mackenzie, northwestern British Columbia. (3) *D. c. auduboni* (Townsend): a yellow-throated race breeding in coastal British Columbia. (4) *D. c. memorabilis* Oberholser (yellow throated like *auduboni* but averaging slightly larger): southeastern and central British Columbia, southern Alberta, southwestern Saskatchewan (Cypress Hills).

Remarks. This species might well be the most numerous of the wood-warblers in Canada. It breeds over vast parts of the country, and its numbers, especially in autumn migration, are often most impressive. Although primarily an insect eater, the Yellow-rumped is one of few warblers that can subsist on berries and seeds over protracted periods. I have several times seen Yellow-rumped Warblers wintering in Nova Scotia despite the cold and deep snow, usually in the vicinity of bayberry bushes, the berries of which they were eating eagerly. Checks later on showed that they wintered successfully.

Black-throated Gray Warbler

Paruline grise à gorge noire
Dendroica nigrescens (Townsend)
Total length: 10.2 to 13 cm
Plate 62

Breeding Distribution of Black-throated Gray Warbler

Range in Canada. Local summer resident, breeding in southwestern British Columbia (Stuie and Hagensborg in Bella Coola valley southward, and east as far as Lillooet, and recently on Vancouver Island).

Accidental in Saskatchewan (specimen: Regina, 3 May 1965); southern Ontario (photo records: Toronto, 7 December 1952 and 5 May 1962. Sight records: Point Pelee, September 1955; Toronto, May 1969), and Nova Scotia (photo record: Seal Island, 10 October 1972; sight records: Sable and Brier islands). Sight records for Alberta (Banff, Calgary).

Adult male (breeding plumage): Crown and sides of head black; small narrow yellow spot between bill and eye and a white line back from eye to side of nape; back bluish grey streaked with black; outer three tail feathers with inner webs largely white; two white wing bars; throat black, separated from black of cheek by a broad white stripe; sides and flanks streaked with black; rest of under parts white. Bill and legs black. *Adult female (breeding plumage)*: Similar to adult male but much duller, crown greyish, throat mainly white, more or less blackish on lower throat or upper breast, streaks on sides more greyish-black. *Young and adults in autumn*: Resemble adults in spring but upper parts largely brownish, streaks on back vague or lacking; under parts whitish with brownish tinge, the throat and sides with more or less blackish or dusky.

Measurements. *Adult male*: wing, 58.7–63.4 (61.3); tail, 47–52 (49.3); exposed culmen, 9.3–10.8 (10.2); tarsus, 17–18 (17.5). *Adult female*: wing, (four only) 58.1–59 (58.6) mm.

Field Marks. Adult male is a black-throated warbler with grey upper parts and white under parts, the only yellow a narrow spot between eye and bill (often hard to see). Its solid black cheeks and black-streaked sides distinguish it from chickadees. Females and young lack a black throat patch but have dark cheeks, which distinguish them from Black-and-white and Blackpoll warblers, with which they might otherwise be confused. The Blackpoll has pale-brown legs; the Black-throated Gray has black legs. *Song*: Low lisping *weezy weezy weezy wee-zee*, the end accented and slurred up or down.

Habitat. More open coniferous and mixedwoods, especially with bushy undergrowth; openings and edges.

Nesting. In coniferous or deciduous trees or shrubbery generally at lower elevations but sometimes quite high. Nest is of plant fibre, grass, small weed stalks, and is lined with hair and feathers. *Eggs*, 3 to 5, usually 4; white, speckled with reddish browns and some underlying purple, mostly on large end.

Range. Breeds from southwestern British Columbia and northwestern and central Colorado south in the mountains to northern Baja California, Arizona, and New Mexico. Winters from central California and southern Arizona to southern Mexico.

Townsend's Warbler

Paruline de Townsend
Dendroica townsendi (Townsend)
Total length: 11.4 to 12.5 cm
Plate 62

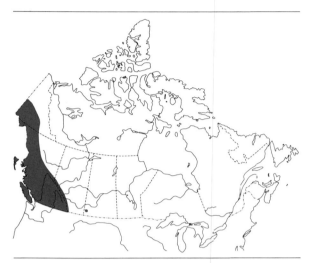

Breeding Distribution of Townsend's Warbler

Range in Canada. Breeds from central Yukon (southern Ogilvie Mountains, Rose and Lapie rivers; probably Marsh Lake); British Columbia (including Queen Charlotte and Vancouver islands, but apparently absent from northeastern corner); southwestern Alberta (Rocky Mountains); and very recently one breeding record in southwestern Saskatchewan (Cypress Hills).

Wanders east of Rocky Mountains rarely: in southern Alberta (Neutral Hills, Calgary, Edmonton, Rosebud).

Accidental in Ontario (photo record: Point Pelee, 10 May 1972; sight record: Point Pelee, 1 May 1966), Nova Scotia (photo record: Sable Island, 9–10 June 1973), and Newfoundland (photo: one at St. John's, 16 November to 13 December 1983).

Adult male (breeding plumage): Crown, cheeks, and throat black; broad stripe over eye, small patch under eye, broad stripe between cheeks and throat, and the sides of the neck yellow; back, scapulars, and rump olive green spotted or streaked with black; outer two tail feathers with inner webs mainly white, the next with less white; two white wing bars; breast yellow (but black of throat extends to upper breast); sides yellowish streaked with black; belly and under tail coverts white. *Adult female (breeding plumage)*: Similar to adult male in breeding plumage but crown with much olive; cheeks olive instead of black; throat mostly yellow, breast striped with black. *Young and adults in autumn*: Similar to adult female in breeding plumage but upper parts with little or no streaking; the throat and breast yellow, the sides lightly streaked with dusky.

Measurements. *Adult male*: wing, 63.1–69.9 (66.5); tail, 47.1–54 (51.5); exposed culmen, 9.9–10.8 (10.2); tarsus, 18.1–19 (18.5). *Adult female*: wing, 59.4–64.8 (62.5) mm.

Field Marks. Yellow on head and breast combined with black throat, crown, and face patch in male; olive face patch in female and young. It differs from other extreme western warblers so much that little confusion is likely. Resembles Black-throated Green Warbler but has a definite cheek patch. *Song*: Lazy and buzzy, the quality suggestive of that of the Black-throated Green Warbler but usually more sibilant or lisping at the end.

Habitat. In breeding season, coniferous forest, often foraging and singing high in the treetops. In migration various kinds of woodland and shrubbery.

Nesting. In a coniferous tree. *Eggs*, 3 to 5; white, speckled and spotted with browns.

Range. Breeds from southern Alaska and southern Yukon south on the coast and islands to northwestern Washington and in the interior to central Oregon, northern Idaho, central-southern Montana, and northwestern Wyoming. Winters in west-central and southern California and from central Mexico south to Nicaragua.

Hermit Warbler

Paruline à tête jaune
Dendroica occidentalis (Townsend)
Total length: 11 to 14 cm
Plate 62

Status in Canada. Accidental in Nova Scotia (female photographed on Sable Island, 26–27 May 1975; a different female photographed there on 4 June 1975). Ontario (one immature killed by flying into tower near Bath on 10 September 1978; photo record: Point Pelee, 2–7 May 1981). Sight record for Quebec (Westmount, a bright male, 13 May 1982). Sight record for British Columbia (near Lost Lake: a male on 15 May 1946).

Similar to Black-throated Green and Townsend's warblers but forehead and crown mainly yellow. Face plain yellow with little or no darker postocular area. Back mainly grey. In the hand, the feathers of the crown are seen to be yellow basally.

Measurements. *Adult male*: wing, 63–69 (66.1); tail, 49–52 (50.5); exposed culmen, 9.5–11 (10.1); tarsus, 18–21 (19.4). *Adult female*: wing, 62–63 (62.3) mm (Ridgway).

Range. Breeds mainly from southwestern Washington south to northwestern and central eastern California. Winters from central Mexico south to Nicaragua.

Black-throated Green Warbler

Paruline verte à gorge noire
Dendroica virens (Gmelin)
Total length: 11 to 13.4 cm
Plate 62

Breeding Distribution of Black-throated
Green Warbler

Range in Canada. Breeds in extreme central-eastern British Columbia (probably Chetwynd–Moberly Lake region); northern and central Alberta (Chenal des Quatre Fourches, Peace River District, Athabasca, Belvedere, Glenevis); central Saskatchewan (Kazan Lake, Emma Lake); central and southern Manitoba (Moose and Cedar lakes, Duck Mountain, Julius); central and southern Ontario (Sandy Lake, Moosonee southward); south-central and southern Quebec (Baie-du-Poste; north shore of Gulf of St. Lawrence east at least to Saint-Augustin: 35 km north; Anticosti Island; Gatineau Park; Hatley; Gaspé Peninsula; Madeleine Islands); southern Labrador (Goose Bay); Newfoundland; New Brunswick; Prince Edward Island; and Nova Scotia (including Cape Breton Island).

Scarce migrant in southern Alberta and southern Saskatchewan.

Adult male (spring plumage): Upper parts yellowish olive-green, the back with or without small spots of black; often a small yellow area in centre of forehead; sides of head and sides of neck yellow with narrow dusky streak through eye; two white wing bars; two outermost tail feathers mainly white, the third and often others with tip of inner web white; throat and breast black; belly and under tail coverts white (often tinged with yellow); sides streaked with black. *Adult female (breeding plumage)*: Similar to adult male but duller generally, with less white in tail; chin and throat yellow, the upper breast blackish with white feather tips. *Adult male (autumn)*: Like adult male in breeding plumage but has black throat and breast feathers with whitish tips. *Young male and female in autumn*: Similar to adult male in autumn but throat and breast yellowish, often with some black on upper breast.

Measurements. *Adult male*: wing, 60.5–65.5 (63.4); tail, 47–52.5 (50.1); exposed culmen, 10–10.9 (10.4); tarsus, 17–18.5 (17.7). *Adult female*: wing, 59.3–63.8 (61.0) mm.

Field Marks. The yellow sides of the head with the black throat and upper breast of the adult male and the blackish upper breast of the adult female easily distinguish it. Young often show no black on the upper breast or throat, but the yellow cheeks separate it from otherwise similar warblers. Its range does not overlap that of the Townsend's Warbler (which has a dark cheek patch). *Song* is a pleasing, lazy *zee zee zee zoo zee* on an even pitch, except that the second syllable from the last is lowest.

Habitat. In breeding season, more open coniferous and mixed-woods. Conifers with an admixture of birch or aspen are ideal; edges and second growths. In migration, various kinds of woodland and thickets.

Nesting. Usually (not always) in conifers, both small and large and at various heights. Nest is of grasses and shredded bark, lined with fine vegetable material, hair, and feathers. *Eggs*, usually 4 or 5; white, speckled and spotted with reddish browns, and some underlying purplish grey. Incubation from 12 (C.J. Stanwood) to 13 (L. de K. Lawrence) days, by the female.

Range. Breeds from Alberta east to Newfoundland and in the United States south to central-eastern Minnesota, central Michigan, eastern Ohio, Pennsylvania (locally), and northern New Jersey, and in the mountains south to Alabama and northern Georgia. Winters from southern Texas and southern Florida south to the Greater Antilles and Panama.

Subspecies. *Dendroica virens virens* (Gmelin).

Remarks. The unhurried song of the Black-throated Green Warbler has pleasant connotations with the scent and shade of evergreen woodlands on warm summer days. This bird is more often heard than seen, for much of its foraging is done in the medium to higher levels of the trees. It is rather tame, however, and especially when feeding in the lower branches it is an easy bird to observe. It is a persistent singer, and its song is easy to recognize. Insects, gleaned from the branches and foliage of trees, make up the bulk of its diet.

Blackburnian Warbler

Paruline à gorge orangée
Dendroica fusca (Müller)
Total length: 11.4 to 14 cm
Plate 63

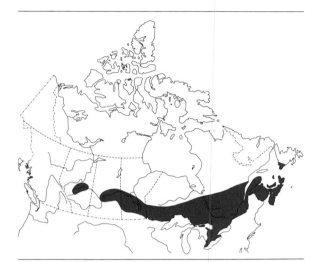

Breeding Distribution of Blackburnian Warbler

Range in Canada. Summer resident, breeding in central Alberta (Glenevis, probably Skeleton Lake, Grand Centre, Cold Lake, and near Edmonton); central Saskatchewan (Crean and Emma lakes, Prince Albert, Cumberland House, Candle Lake); central and southern Manitoba (Overflowing River, Riding and Duck mountains, Hillside Beach, Rennie); central and southern Ontario (northern limits uncertain but north at least to Lac Seul, Lake Nipigon, and Lake Abitibi, and southward to near Long Point, Toronto, and Leeds County); southern Quebec (Waswanipi–Bell River area, Lake Saint-Jean, Pointe-des-Monts, Lake Sainte-Anne on Toulnustouc River; Gatineau Park, Hatley, Lake Rimouski, Gaspé Peninsula, Madeleine Islands); New Brunswick; Prince Edward Island; Nova Scotia (including Cape Breton Island); and southwestern Newfoundland (Pasadena).

Recorded without evidence of breeding north to Trout Lake and Fort Severn, Ontario; and to Lake Albanel and Natashquan, Quebec.

Adult male: Above, mostly black, a narrow yellow patch on crown and two whitish stripes down back; line over eye, sides of neck, throat, and breast bright orange; cheeks black; large white patch on wing coverts; inner webs of outer two to four tail feathers with much white; under parts behind orange breast, whitish tinged with orange; sides and flanks streaked with black. *Adult female*: Resembles adult male but yellow replaces orange; upper parts olive green streaked with black and a little whitish; cheek patch olive; two white wing bars. *Young (autumn)*: Closely resemble adult female but even duller, yellows paler; centre patch of crown much obscured.

Measurements. *Adult male*: wing, 65.5–69.3 (67.8); tail, 46–49.5 (48.1); exposed culmen, 10.4–11.3 (10.7); tarsus, 16.5–18 (17.3). *Adult female*: wing, 61.9–66.4 (64.1) mm.

Field Marks. Adult male with bright-orange breast and black upper parts is unmistakable. In females and young, yellows replace the orange of the adult male, and dark olive-green replaces the blacks; however, the dark cheek patch is clearly outlined against the yellow of eyebrow and throat. *Song*: Very high-pitched and wiry, often ending in a readily recognizable high buzz, *zip zip zip zip zeeeeee*; also a rolling high-pitched *chickety chickety chickety chick*.

Habitat. In nesting season, coniferous and mixed woodland, both mature and well-developed second growth, foraging most often among higher branches. In migration various types of woods and thickets.

Nesting. Usually in a branch of a coniferous tree, 1.5 to 26 m up. Nest is of small twigs, dry grasses, soft plant down or *Usnea* lichen, lined with rootlets, hair, and fine grass. *Eggs*, usually 4 or 5; white, spotted and blotched with reddish browns and often some underlying purplish greys. Incubation 12 to 13 days, by the female (Louise de K. Lawrence).

Range. Breeds from central Saskatchewan east to Gaspé Peninsula and Nova Scotia, and south to central Minnesota, central Wisconsin, central Michigan, northeastern Ohio, Massachusetts, and in the Appalachian Mountains to northern Georgia and south Carolina. Winters from Guatemala south to central Peru and Venezuela.

Remarks. In full sunlight, against a background of dark coniferous trees, the flame-coloured breast of the Blackburnian Warbler is impressive. The male is one of our most brilliant warblers, but his wiry little song is rather unmusical. Like other warblers this one is mainly insectivorous, its diet high in forest insects that are destructive to trees.

Yellow-throated Warbler

Paruline à gorge jaune
Dendroica dominica (Linnaeus)
Total length: 12 to 14.5 cm
Plate 63

Status in Canada. Rare visitant to southern
Ontario (specimen record: Long Point, 25 May
1970; also one captured and released there on
12 May 1970. Photo records: Hamilton, 2 May
1974; Point Pelee, 2 May 1976; Moosonee,
autumn 1982. Also various sight records north
to London and Ottawa); southern Quebec
(photo record: Philipsburg, 30 October to
13 November 1971); New Brunswick (photo:
Machias Seal Island, 11 August 1976); Nova
Scotia (photos: Sable Island, 22 August 1968;
Seal Island, 7 September 1969 and 26 September
1971). Accidental in Newfoundland (specimen:
St. John's, 11 November 1953; photo: one of
three in St. John's, 14–25 November 1983).
Sight record only for Saskatchewan (Weyburn,
16 May 1970).

Adults (sexes similar but female usually has less black on top of head
and sides of throat and neck): Upper parts bluish grey, the forehead
and sides of crown black; white line over eye (may be either yellow or
white in front of eye) joining white patch on side of neck; a tiny white
spot on mid-forehead and another under eye; broad black patch on
sides of head, extending down side of neck and breaking up on sides of
breast to form black streaks along sides and flanks; throat and breast
lemon yellow, abdomen and under tail coverts white; two white wing
bars; two or three outermost tail feathers with large white patches.
Young in autumn: Similar to adults but more brownish above and
below.

    Field Marks. To be identified in Canada with caution. A grey-
backed warbler with lemon-yellow throat and upper breast, white stripe
above eye (may be yellow in front of eye) and white patch on side of
neck; two white wing bars. Perhaps female or young Blackburnian
Warblers might be mistaken for it. The Blackburnian has a similar dark
cheek patch, but its eyebrow stripe and patch on side of neck are
yellow. The Yellow-throated Warbler creeps along the branches.

    Range. Breeds from Nebraska east to southeastern New York and
southwestern Connecticut and south to eastern Texas, the United States
Gulf Coast, central Florida, and the northern Bahamas.

    Subspecies. The Newfoundland and the Long Point, Ontario,
specimens have been subspecifically determined as *Dendroica dominica
albilora* Ridgway; the Moosonee bird as *D. d. dominica*.

Pine Warbler

Paruline des pins
Dendroica pinus (Wilson)
Total length: 12.5 to 14.5 cm
Plate 63

Breeding Distribution of Pine Warbler

Range in Canada. Summer resident, breeding in
southern Manitoba (Julius, Sprague); western
Ontario (Off Lake, Malachi); central and
southern Ontario (north to Wawa); and locally
in southwestern Quebec (Hull, Thurso,
Chambly).

    Occurs in Alberta rarely but status uncertain
(Castor, 5 June 1924; Athabasca: sight records
of singing males in July). Rare migrant in
southern New Brunswick (Saint John, Grand
Manan); Nova Scotia (specimens: Gaspereau,
Seal Island, Outer Island; also sight records);

Adult male: Upper parts unstreaked yellowish olive green; cheeks similar
to upper parts; obscure yellowish line over eye; two white wing bars;
two outer tail feathers on each side with large white patches; throat,
breast, and upper abdomen yellow usually faintly streaked with olive;
lower abdomen and under tail coverts white. *Adult female*: Similar to
but much duller than male; upper parts tinged brownish, nape often
greyish; cheeks greyish; under parts dingy white, more or less yellowish
on breast; flanks tinged brownish. *Young female in autumn*: Upper
parts still browner than adult female in autumn, often without decided
green above or yellow below.

    Measurements. *Adult male*: wing, 68.9–72.8 (70.9); tail, 52.9–56
(54.1); exposed culmen, 9.9–11.6 (10.7); tarsus, 17.2–18.7 (18.0). *Adult
female*: wing, 66.6–70.5 (68.4) mm.

    Field Marks. Males have a decidedly yellow breast, often faintly
streaked; two white wing bars; large white patches in outer tail feathers,
and no other conspicuous markings. Females and young in autumn are
extremely nondescript, brownish or greyish above, dingy white below
often with a buffy or yellowish tinge to the breast, white wing bars,
white under tail coverts. The Pine Warbler's dark legs usually distinguish it from autumn Blackpolls, its white under tail coverts from
autumn Bay-breasts, its plain unstreaked back from both. The Pine
Warbler's creeping habits, frequent association with pine trees, and song
also assist in identifying it. *Song*: Very much like the trill of a Chipping
Sparrow but usually a little more musical and often somewhat slower.
Speed is variable, however.

    Habitat. In nesting season, usually pine woodlands. In migration
various kinds of trees are used for foraging.

    Nesting. In the branches of a pine tree (various species) from 3 m
upwards from the ground. Nest is made of weed stalks, shreds of bark,
pine needles, and lined with hair, feathers, and pine needles. *Eggs*, 3 to
5, usually 4; white, speckled and blotched with browns and some greys.

and Saskatchewan (specimen: Regina, 6 May 1964; various sight records). Casual vagrant to Newfoundland (photos: one about 16 November to 26 December 1983; one immature, 27 November to 13 December 1983. Both in St. John's).

Range. Breeds in pine woodland from southern Manitoba east to southern Quebec and south to the Gulf Coast of the United States, southern Florida, the Bahamas, and Hispaniola. Winters mainly from Arkansas, Tennessee, and South Carolina southward in the breeding range.

Subspecies. *Dendroica pinus pinus* (Wilson).

Remarks. This warbler is well named, for it prefers to live in pine trees of various species. It has a habit of creeping about the branches or even on the trunks of trees. Insects are its favourite food, but it eats many pine seeds, wild fruits, and berries if insects are not available.

Kirtland's Warbler

Paruline de Kirtland
Dendroica kirtlandii (Baird)
Total length: 14.5 cm
Plate 61

Status in Canada. Formerly bred very locally in southern Ontario (Petawawa. See Paul Harrington, 1939. Jack Pine Warbler, vol. 17, no. 4, pp. 95–97). A very rare visitant to southern Ontario (old specimen records for Toronto, Point Pelee, and Parry Sound; also over 20 sight records northward to Georgian Bay, Petawawa, and Kingston). Casual visitor to southwestern Quebec (photo record: Kazabazua, 27 May 1978. This was an apparently unmated singing male, which had been banded previously in Michigan).

A large warbler. *Adult male*: Upper parts bluish grey with black stripes (coarse on back, fine on top of head); cheeks blackish with spot of white on upper and lower eyelids; outer two tail feathers on each side with white patch on inner web; under parts pale yellow; the sides of breast lightly streaked with black, the sides of body heavily so; under tail coverts white. *Adult female*: Resembles adult male but is duller, nape and rump more brownish grey; cheeks grey; yellow of under parts paler, the breast more extensively speckled with black.

Measurements. *Adult male*: wing, 67.4–71.8 (70.2); tail, 58–62 (60.2); exposed culmen, 10–11.3 (10.8); tarsus, 20–22 (20.9). *Adult female*: wing, 64–71 (66.7) mm.

Field Marks. A large tail-wagging warbler, bluish grey above, yellow below. Might be confused with Canada Warbler, but the Kirtland's black-streaked sides, black-streaked back, dark legs, and habit of pumping the tail up and down should distinguish it. The young Magnolia Warbler looks a little like the Kirtland's but has a yellow rump patch, a distinctive tail pattern, and lacks the tail-wagging habit. In nesting season, Kirtland's Warbler is confined to immature jack pine woodlands.

Nesting. Nest on the ground in stands of young jack pine. *Eggs*, usually 4 or 5, are white, speckled, blotched, and spotted with browns. Incubation 13 to 16 days by the female.

Range. Breeds in central Michigan. Winters in the Bahama Islands.

Remarks. The Kirtland's Warbler is a critically endangered species whose world numbers in 1978 were thought to be just under 400.

Prairie Warbler

Paruline des prés
Dendroica discolor (Vieillot)
Total length: 10.9 to 13.2 cm
Plate 64

Breeding Distribution of Prairie Warbler

Range in Canada. Breeds locally in southern Ontario (Lambton County up the shore of Lake Huron and southern Georgian Bay; Cross Lake, Frontenac County; Mazinaw Lake; and between Westport and Kingston). Recorded in June rarely north to Manitoulin Island, Lake Nipissing, and in migration seasons at Ottawa, Eganville, and Lake Doré, Ontario.

Rare visitant to Quebec (photo: Montréal, 17 May 1976; also sight records); New Brunswick (specimens: Machias Seal Island, 19 August 1951 and August 1967; Kent Island, 25 August 1967; also sight records); Nova Scotia (specimens: Seal Island, 6 September 1970, Outer Island, 12 October 1980; photo records: Seal and Sable islands; also several sight records); and Newfoundland (photo: one adult, 16 November to 2 December 1983 at St. John's).

A small warbler. *Adult male*: Upper parts yellowish olive-green, the back with chestnut spots (partly concealed in autumn); two yellowish wing bars; three outer tail feathers on each side with very large white areas, the outermost mainly white on both webs; sides of head yellow with narrow black line through eye and a broader black patch down over jaw; under parts bright yellow, the sides of breast and sides of body broadly streaked black; legs dark olive-brown. *Adult female*: Similar to adult male but usually duller, the chestnut spots on back faint or absent, the blacks on sides of head replaced by grey; black streaks on sides of body more obscure. *Young females*: Upper parts plain greyish olive-green, cheek grey, wing bars obsolete; streaks on sides faint.

Measurements. *Adult male*: wing, 54.4–58.2 (56.5); tail, 47.5–50.5 (49.0); exposed culmen, 9–10.2 (9.7); tarsus, 17–19 (18.2). *Adult female*: wing, 51–57 (53.8) mm.

Field Marks. A small tail-wagging warbler with bright-yellow under parts, black streaks confined to sides of head and body, the males with *two distinct face stripes*, and chestnut spots on back (the last often hard to see). Females and young are duller with black of head replaced by greenish grey. *Song*: Easily recognizable once learned. A series of distinct notes rising gradually higher in pitch to the end.

Habitat. Not grassy prairies as its name erroneously suggests. Instead, dry scrubby areas, brushy second growths, and, in sand dune country, pine and ground juniper.

Nesting. In bushes or saplings usually 0.6 to 1.5 m above ground, sometimes considerably higher. Its compact nest is made of plant down, grass, and leaves and lined with rootlets, hair, feathers, and cottony plant materials. Incubation 12 to 13 days (L.H. Walkinshaw), by the female.

Range. Breeds from southeastern South Dakota east to southern New Hampshire and south to eastern Oklahoma, southern Louisiana, northern Mississippi, southeastern Alabama, and the Florida Keys. Winters from central Florida south through the West Indies and in islands off Mexico and Central America.

Subspecies. *Dendroica discolor discolor* (Veillot).

Palm Warbler

Paruline à couronne rousse
Dendroica palmarum (Gmelin)
Total length: 12.5 to 14.5 cm
Plate 64

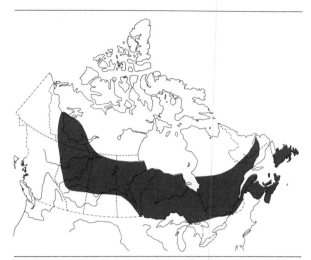

Breeding Distribution of Palm Warbler

Range in Canada. Breeds from central-western Mackenzie (Kelly Lake; Forts Norman, Providence, and Resolution); northwestern Saskatchewan (Lake Athabasca, Stony Rapids; probably Milton Lake); northern Manitoba (Bird, Churchill); northern Ontario (Fort Severn, Attawapiskat River mouth, Moosonee); south-central Quebec (Fort-George, Baie-du-Poste, Sept-Îles, Mingan); southern Labrador (Goose Bay); and Newfoundland south to northeastern British Columbia (Trutch); central Alberta (Niton, Glenevis, Elk Island National Park); central Saskatchewan (Roddick, probably Nipawin); southern Manitoba (Overflowing River, Indian Bay); central and southern Ontario (Lake of the Woods, formerly near Ottawa); southern Quebec (Lanoraie; Matane County); New Brunswick; Prince Edward Island; and Nova Scotia (including Cape Breton Island).

Accidental at Bernard Harbour, Dolphin and Union Strait, Mackenzie, N.W.T., 28 September 1915; sight records on Prince Leopold Island, N.W.T. (singles on 17 June, 15 July, and 6 August 1975). Casual at Vancouver and on Vancouver Island, British Columbia.

There are two subspecies, one eastern, one western, different enough to be recognizable in the field.

Dendroica palmarum palmarum: Adults (sexes similar) in breeding plumage: Crown chestnut with narrow yellowish line in middle of forehead; back and scapulars greyish olive-brown, narrowly streaked darker; lower rump and upper tail coverts yellowish olive; two indistinct buffy wing bars; two outer tail feathers on each side with white patch at end of inner web, occasionally a small white spot on third; yellow stripe over eye; cheeks and sides of neck greyish brown; throat, breast, and under tail coverts bright yellow, the sides of throat, breast, and sides of body narrowly streaked with brown; abdomen whitish or faintly yellowish; legs olive brown. *Adults in autumn*: Similar to breeding adults but crown with little or no chestnut, stripe over eye white, under parts whitish (except yellow under tail coverts), only faintly tinged with yellow and streaked with dusky. *Young in autumn*: Like adults in autumn but browner above, buffy white below, the breast and sides lightly streaked with brownish, under tail coverts yellow.

Dendroica palmarum hypochrysea (eastern Ontario eastward): Similar to above but entire under parts yellow, even in autumn and immature plumages; streaks on under parts more chestnut than brown; upper parts more olive; size averages slightly larger.

Measurements *(D. p. hypochrysea). Adult male*: wing, 61.7–68.8 (65.2); tail, 48–56.5 (53.0); exposed culmen, 9.6–10.5 (10.1); tarsus, 19–21 (19.9). *Adult female*: wing, 59.4–64.5 (61.5) mm.

Field Marks. A tail-wagging warbler, which even in dullest plumages has bright-yellow under tail coverts and, greenish-yellow rump (noticeably paler than back). In breeding plumages a dull-red cap is diagnostic. The eastern race (eastern Ontario eastward) has the entire under parts yellow in breeding plumage, yellowish in autumn. The western race has less extensively yellow under parts in breeding plumage (Plate 64), and in autumn young, buffy-white under parts (except yellow under tail coverts). Kirtland's and Prairie warblers also are tail-waggers. *Song*: A simple, flat-toned trill, a little like that of the Chipping Sparrow but less energetic.

Habitat. In nesting season, bogs or barrens or similar situations on either dry or wet ground where trees are scattered and where there is ground shrubbery.

Nesting. On or near the ground, often concealed by shrubby vegetation or under a seedling; occasionally in a low conifer sapling. Nest is of weed stalks, grass, shreds of bark, and moss, and is lined with fine grass, rootlets, and feathers. *Eggs*, 4 or 5; white, speckled with browns and sometimes a little lavender, mostly around the large end. Incubation 12 days (F.L. Burns).

Range. Breeds in Canada from northern Alberta and western Mackenzie east to Newfoundland and in northern United States south to northeastern Minnesota, central Michigan, central New Hampshire, northern and eastern Maine. Winters from Louisiana east to North Carolina and south to the Yucatan Peninsula, northern Honduras, the Greater Antilles, the Bahamas, and Bermuda.

Subspecies (described above): (1) *Dendroica palmarum palmarum* (Gmelin): western and central Canada east to Moosonee and Kapuskasing, Ontario. (2) *D. p. hypochrysea* Ridgway: eastern Canada west to Lake Mistassini, Quebec and Ottawa, Ontario.

Bay-breasted Warbler

Paruline à poitrine baie
Dendroica castanea (Wilson)
Total length: 12.5 to 15.3 cm
Plate 63

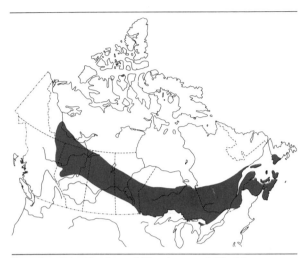

Breeding Distribution of Bay-breasted Warbler

Range in Canada. Summer resident, breeding in southwestern Mackenzie (probably: Wrigley, Nahanni National Park, Fort Simpson, Sass River); northeastern and central-eastern British Columbia (probably Peace River District and at Miles 335–336 Alaska Highway; perhaps Lower Liard Crossing; recorded in breeding season once at Indianpoint Lake, Yoho National Park, Tetana Lake); northern Alberta (Lesser Slave Lake, Wood Buffalo National Park south to Skeleton Lake, Boyle, Athabasca); central Saskatchewan (southern Reindeer Lake south to Flotten Lake; probably Kazan Lake and Cumberland House); central and southern Manitoba (The Pas, Oxford House, Duck Mountain, Hecla Island, Indian Bay; rarely and exceptionally south to Delta Beach Ridge); central and southern Ontario (Sandy Lake, Fort Albany; Off Lake, Dorcas Bay in Bruce County, Algonquin Provincial Park); south-central and southern Quebec (Baie-du-Poste, Lake Saint-Jean, Sainte-Marguerite River; Blue-Sea-Lake, Hatley, Gaspé Peninsula, Anticosti and Madeleine islands); New Brunswick; Prince Edward Island; Nova Scotia (including Cape Breton Island); and southwestern Newfoundland (sight records in the breeding season north to Gros Morne National Park). Limits of the breeding range may fluctuate considerably depending upon food availability, especially the spruce budworm.

Recorded in June on the inner north shore of the Gulf of St. Lawrence (Matamec, Johan-Beetz Bay, mouth of Big Natashquan River).

Adult male (breeding plumage): Crown chestnut; forehead and sides of head black; patch on sides of neck buffy; back and rump, grey streaked with black; two white wing bars; two or three outer tail feathers with a white patch; throat, upper breast, sides, and flanks rich chestnut but chin often blackish; rest of under parts white with slight buffy tinge. *Adult male (autumn)*: Very different. Upper parts mostly olive green with some black streaks; usually traces of chestnut on crown; wing bars with slightly yellowish tinge; under parts yellowish or greenish on throat, pale buffy on abdomen and under tail coverts; more or less chestnut on sides. *Adult female (breeding plumage)*: Essentially like adult male in breeding plumage but chestnut of crown sparse and streaked with black; black of cheeks mixed with grey; chestnut of throat and sides sparse, patchy, paler. *Young and adult female (autumn)*: Similar to adult male in autumn but usually without (or just a trace of) chestnut on sides.

Measurements. *Adult male*: wing, 71.7–74.9 (73.1); tail, 51–54 (52.7); exposed culmen, 10–11.1 (10.7); tarsus, 18.5–19 (18.9). *Adult female*: wing, 69.4–71.9 (70.5) mm.

Distinctions. *Autumn specimens closely resemble corresponding plumages of Blackpoll Warbler*. When traces of chestnut are present on the sides, this eliminates the Blackpoll Warbler (but see Chestnut-sided Warbler). When no chestnut is present on the sides, such Bay-breasts are separable from Blackpolls by their pale-buffy (instead of white) under tail coverts and usually unstreaked (instead of faintly but definitely streaked), less greenish-yellow under parts, and usually darker legs.

Field Marks. Adults in breeding plumage, with chestnut on throat and sides and a buffy patch on sides of neck, are readily identified. In autumn, adults and young are very different from breeding adults, being olive green above, buffy white below; thus they closely resemble autumn Blackpoll Warblers. Some individuals of the Bay-breast have traces of chestnut on the sides, which quickly eliminates the Blackpoll (but see Chestnut-sided Warbler, autumn). Bay-breasts with no chestnut on the sides can usually be distinguished from autumn Blackpolls by their buffish under tail coverts (pure white in Blackpoll), usually unstreaked and less greenish under parts, and usually darker legs (Plate 63). The buffish under tail coverts and streaked back distinguish them in autumn from duller-coloured individuals of the Pine Warbler. *Song*: Very high and sibilant: *zee-a, zee-a, zee-a, zee* in much the same pitch.

Habitat. In breeding season, coniferous woods, often with an admixture of deciduous trees; wood edges and openings; second growths.

Nesting. Usually 1.5 to 6 m up in a coniferous tree. Nest is of fine twigs and grass, lined with rootlets and hair. *Eggs*, 4 to 7, most often 5; white, spotted and blotched with browns and underlying spots of grey. Incubation slightly over 12 days (H.L. Mendall), by the female.

Range. Breeds from Alberta east to Nova Scotia and south in the United States to northeastern Minnesota, northern Wisconsin, northeastern New York, and southern Maine. Winters from Panama to northern Colombia and western Venezuela.

Remarks. In many parts of the country the Bay-breasted Warbler is uncommon and handsome enough to elicit a second look from most observers. It is one of the later arrivals in spring migration and it often passes through quickly, but occasionally good numbers remain about for a few days. It is at once the wonder and the despair of many how this and the Blackpoll Warbler can look so different in spring plumage and yet so much alike in autumn dress.

Blackpoll Warbler

Paruline rayée
Dendroica striata (Forster)
Total length: 12.5 to 14.5 cm
Plate 63

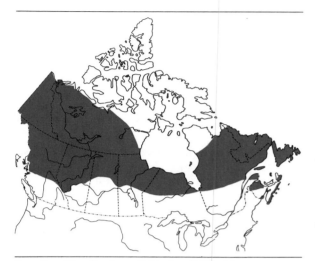

Breeding Distribution of Blackpoll Warbler

Range in Canada. Summer resident, breeding from near tree limit in northern Yukon (Old Crow); northern Mackenzie (northern Mackenzie Delta, Fort Anderson, Bathurst Inlet, Artillery Lake, Thelon River); southern Keewatin (Nueltin Lake, Tha-anne River); northern Manitoba (Churchill); northern Ontario (Fort Severn); northern Quebec (Lake Guillaume-Delisle, Feuilles River, Alluviaq Fiord); northern Labrador (Port Manvers, Nain); and Newfoundland south to south-central interior British Columbia (Mosher Creek, Indianpoint Lake); central and southwestern Alberta (North Saskatchewan River and south in the mountains and foothills to Banff and Bragg Creek); north-central Saskatchewan (Kazan and Reindeer lakes); central Manitoba (The Pas, Thicket Portage); north-central Ontario (Favourable Lake, Moosonee); southern Quebec (Baie-du-Poste, Anticosti Island, Stoneham, Gaspé Peninsula, Madeleine Islands; probably Mount Orford); coastal New Brunswick (Kent Island, Tabusintac; perhaps locally in the northern interior); and Nova Scotia (Cape Fourchu, islands off the south shore, Cape Breton Island).

A regular spring and autumn migrant in most parts of the country south of its breeding range except extreme southwestern British Columbia.

Accidental on Cornwallis Island, N.W.T. (photo: Resolute Bay, 23 May 1971).

Adult male (spring): Top of head down to eyes black; sides of head white; back, scapulars, and rump grey or olive grey streaked with black; two white (or yellowish) wing bars; outer two or three tail feathers with a white spot on inner web; under parts white; sides of throat, sides of breast, and sides of body streaked with black; legs pale brown. *Adult male (autumn)*: Very different from spring, Upper parts olive green (no black cap), streaked with dusky; sides of head olive yellow with faint pale line over eye; under parts yellowish, very much less profusely streaked than in spring; under tail coverts white. *Adult female (spring)*: Upper parts greenish grey streaked with black; wings and tail, similar to adult male in spring but wing bars more yellowish; pale stripe over eye; under parts whitish suffused with yellow and finely streaked with black on sides of throat, sides of breast, and sides of body. *Young and adult female in autumn*: Similar to adult male in autumn but more faintly streaked below.

Measurements. *Adult male*: wing, 70.1–75.3 (73.2); tail, 48–53 (50.8); exposed culmen, 10.1–11 (10.5); tarsus, 18.5–20 (19.2). *Adult female*: wing, 66.5–72.8 (69.2) mm.

Distinctions (see Bay-breasted and Pine warblers).

Field Marks. Male in spring and early summer, a black-capped warbler with plain *white cheeks*, which distinguish it from the Black-and-white and the Black-throated Gray warblers. Lack of a black bib separates it from the Black-capped Chickadee. In autumn it is very much like autumn Bay-breasted Warbler, but tail coverts are always white (see Bay-breasted Warbler). Autumn birds may be confused with some Pine Warblers, but the Blackpoll has light-brown legs (instead of blackish) and some streaking on the upper parts (the Pine has plain upper parts). *Song*: An extremely high-pitched *tsit tsit tsit tsit tsit* in the same pitch, rising in volume toward the middle, falling off toward the end; thus easy to recognize.

Habitat. Coniferous woods, especially spruce, frequently stunted, also mixedwood edges, logged and burned areas, alder thickets, frequently on moist ground. In migration both deciduous and coniferous trees.

Nesting. Usually low in a spruce, rarely on the ground. Nest is of grasses, lichens, fine mosses, and twigs; lined with feathers, hairs, and fine grasses. *Eggs*, generally 4 or 5; white, speckled and blotched with browns and some greys.

Range. Breeds across Canada in northern coniferous forests (see Range in Canada) and south in northeastern United States to eastern New York, northwestern Massachusetts, central New Hampshire, and southern Maine; also in Alaska. Winters in South America from Colombia to eastern Peru, western Brazil, and Chile.

Cerulean Warbler

Paruline azurée
Dendroica cerulea (Wilson)
Total length: 10 to 12.5 cm
Plate 62

Breeding Distribution of Cerulean Warbler

Range in Canada. Breeds in southern Ontario (Walkerton, Bruce County; Toronto; Kingston southward) and southwestern Quebec (Mount Saint-Hilaire, Mount Yamaska). Casual in southwestern Manitoba (specimen: Whitewater Lake, 2 June 1924). Sight records only for Nova Scotia and New Brunswick. Sight records north of its breeding range in Ontario (Manitoulin Island, Ottawa) and Quebec (Gatineau Park).

Adult male: Upper parts and cheeks bright blue, the back streaked with black; tail with small white patch on inner web of all feathers except middle pair; two white wing bars; under parts mainly white with a narrow blue-black band across upper breast; sides and flanks streaked with blue-black. *Adult female*: Upper parts pale bluish to olive greenish, unmarked; sides of head whitish with narrow dusky streak through eye, pale stripe above eye; wings and tail similar to those of adult male; under parts whitish more or less tinged yellowish; sides and flanks usually with suggestion of streaking. *Young (first autumn)*: Resemble adult female but more greenish above, more yellowish below.

Measurements. *Adult male*: wing, 62–67.6 (65.5); tail, 43.2–47.7 (45); exposed culmen, 9.4–10.2 (9.9); tarsus, 15.7–17 (16.5). *Adult female*: wing, 58.2–62.7 (61.2) mm (Ridgway).

Field Marks. Adult male with blue upper parts, white under parts, narrow blackish band across upper breast, and two white wing bars is easily recognized. Females and young are much more obscure. Presence of wing bars and lack of a small white spot at base of primaries separate them from the female Black-throated Blue. From young Blackpoll Warblers they can be distinguished by paler (less deep yellow) under parts and by lack of any streaks or spots on the back. *Song*: It resembles the buzzy song of the Northern Parula, but the last syllable is prolonged and rising in pitch.

Habitat. In nesting season usually mature deciduous woodland, foraging and singing high in the trees. Sometimes coniferous trees.

Nesting. In a branch of a deciduous or, less often, coniferous tree usually 7.5 to 18 m up. Nest is rather shallow but is neatly made of bark shreds, grass, or small weed stalks and is lined with hair and rootlets. *Eggs*, 3 to 5, usually 4; white or whitish, speckled or blotched with browns.

Range. Breeds from southeastern Nebraska east through extreme southern Ontario to southeastern New York and south to eastern Texas, southeastern Louisiana, central Alabama, and North Carolina. Winters in South America (Colombia and Venezuela to Peru and Bolivia).

Black-and-white Warbler

Paruline noir et blanc
Mniotilta varia (Linnaeus)
Total length: 11 to 14 cm
Plate 60

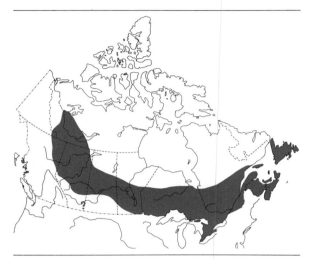

Breeding Distribution of Black-and-white Warbler

Range in Canada. Summer resident breeding in central-western and southwestern Mackenzie (Fort Norman, Fort Simpson, Fort Smith; probably Nahanni National Park); central-eastern British Columbia (Peace River parklands, Fort Nelson); Alberta (Peace River District, Wood Buffalo National Park, south at least to Belvedere and Camrose; possibly Cypress Hills where presence in July is recorded); central and southeastern Saskatchewan (Kazan Lake, Nipawin, probably Madge Lake and Qu'Appelle valley); central and southern Manitoba (Thicket Portage, The Pas, Riding Mountain, Portage la Prairie, Shoal Lake, Hillside Beach, Rennie); north-central and southern Ontario (Sandy Lake, Lake Attawapiskat, Moose Factory, perhaps Wetigo Hills southward); southern Quebec (Val-d'Or, Lake Saint-Jean, Mingan, Anticosti Island, Aylmer, Hatley, Montréal, Gaspé Peninsula, Madeleine Islands; species recorded east to Nétagamiou River and Saint-Augustin); Newfoundland; New Brunswick; Prince Edward Island; and Nova Scotia (including Cape Breton Island).

There are sight records for southwestern British Columbia (Reifel Island, May 1972, etc.) and for northeastern Manitoba (Churchill, 15 June 1966).

Culmen somewhat convex. *Adult male*: Boldly striped black-and-white above and below, except belly, which is plain white; a broad white stripe down centre of otherwise black crown; two white wing bars; outer tail feathers with white areas on inner webs. *Adult female*: Similar to adult male but duller, the whites tinged with buff; under parts more extensively white, the dusky stripes confined mainly to sides and flanks.

Measurements. *Adult male*: wing, 67.2–71.5 (68.6); tail, 45.5–54 (49.6); exposed culmen, 10.4–12.1 (11.7); tarsus, 16.5–17 (16.8). *Adult female*: wing, 64.5–67.8 (66.4) mm.

Field Marks. A black-and-white striped warbler with a white stripe down middle of crown. Other black-and-white warblers (Black-throated Gray and Blackpoll) have no white stripe through middle of crown. Its distinct white eyebrow stripe also separates it from the Blackpoll. The Black-and-white has a distinctive habit of creeping along the branches and trunks of trees. *Song*: High pitched and rolling, usually made up of a number of double syllables, thus *weetsy weetsy weetsy weetsy weetsy weetsy*.

Habitat. Deciduous and mixed woodlands of various types, especially in moister situations. Forages in lower or middle branches, also in willow or alder shrubbery on edges of coniferous woodland.

Nesting. On the ground in a slight depression, often at the base of a tree, shrub, or stump, or beside a log or stone. Occasionally in a low stump or in the roots of an overturned tree. Nest is of grass, bark strips, leaves, moss, and rootlets; lined with hair. *Eggs*, 4 or 5, rarely 6; white, speckled or blotched with reddish browns and often some purplish grey. Incubation 13 days (Hatch *in* Forbush), by the female.

Range. Breeds from Canada south to eastern Montana, central Texas, southeastern Louisiana, central Alabama, central Georgia, and southeastern North Carolina. Winters from northern Mexico, southern Texas, central Florida, and the Bahamas south through the West Indies and Central America to Ecuador, Colombia, and northern Venezuela.

American Redstart

Paruline flamboyante
Setophaga ruticilla (Linnaeus)
Total length: 12 to 14.5 cm
Plate 65

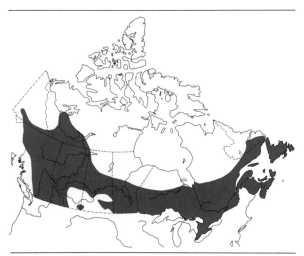

Breeding Distribution of American Redstart

Range in Canada. Summer resident, breeding from southern Yukon (Sheep Creek, Watson Lake, Teslin); northern British Columbia (Atlin, Liard Crossing); central-western and central-southern Mackenzie (Nahanni National Park, Fort Norman, Fort Resolution); north-central Saskatchewan (Kazan Lake, La Ronge); north-central Manitoba (Cormorant Lake, Thicket Portage); north-central Ontario (Favourable Lake, Moose Factory); central Quebec (Eastmain, Baie-du-Poste; north shore of the Gulf of St. Lawrence; Saint-Augustin River: 35 km inland; Anticosti Island); southern Labrador (Goose Bay); and Newfoundland south through southern interior British Columbia (Pemberton eastward); southern Alberta (but in extreme southeast only locally: Cypress Hills); south-central Saskatchewan (south to Saskatoon and locally in Qu'Appelle valley, Moose Mountain and Cypress Hills); southern Manitoba; southern Ontario; southern Quebec (including Madeleine Islands); New Brunswick; Prince Edward Island; and Nova Scotia (including Cape Breton Island).

Casual on the coast of British Columbia (Reifel Island). Accidental on Banks Island, N.W.T. (Sachs Harbour, 19 September 1952) and at Port Burwell, N.W.T.

Bill broad at base for a warbler. Wings rather long and pointed. *Adult male*: Head, neck, back, throat, and upper breast black; central tail feathers black, the others orange or salmon pink with a broad terminal band of black; wings black with substantial orange patch at the base of the flight feathers; sides of breast and under wing coverts orange; belly white, the sides tinged with orange. *Adult female*: Crown, hind-neck, and sides of head grey, passing into olive on back and rump; wings and tail patterned as in adult male but patches yellow instead of orange; throat and breast dull greyish-white; rest of under parts white with patch of yellow on either side of breast; mid-breast, sides, and flanks often tinged yellowish. *Young (first autumn)*: Similar to adult female. *Young male (first spring)*: Similar to adult female but with irregular black markings appearing about head and on under plumage.

Measurements *(S. r. tricolora).* *Adult male*: wing, 61.7–65.5 (63.5); tail, 55–58.5 (56.8); exposed culmen, 8–9.1 (8.7); tarsus, 17–18.5 (17.5). *Adult female*: wing, 57.1–62.4 (59.4) mm.

Field Marks. A distinctively marked warbler with a habit of frequently drooping its wings and spreading its tail. The adult male with its black and orange pattern is unmistakable. The adult female and young, although grey above, have wing, tail, and breast pattern like that of the adult male, but the patches are yellow instead of orange. *Song*: High-pitched, lisping, but variable: *tsee tsee tsee tsee-o* (slurred downward at end) or *teetsy teetsy* and other songs.

Habitat. More open parts of deciduous and mixed woodlands, second growths, woodlots, tall shrubbery.

Nesting. Usually in a deciduous (rarely coniferous) tree or tall shrub generally 1.8 to 7.6 m up. Nest is often in a crotch or group of upright branches. It is neatly and firmly made of grasses, plant down, and shreds of bark and is lined with hair, grass, rootlets, or feathers. *Eggs*, 3 to 5, usually 4; white, spotted and speckled with browns and a little purplish grey. Incubation 12 days, by the female (A.C. Bent).

Range. Breeds from southeastern Alaska east to southern Labrador and Newfoundland, and south to eastern Oregon, northern Utah, northern Colorado, southeastern Oklahoma, southeastern Louisiana, and central Georgia. Winters from Mexico, Cuba, and Puerto Rico south to Ecuador and northern Brazil.

Subspecies. (1) *Setophaga ruticilla tricolora* (Müller): All of Canada except extreme southern Ontario. (2) *S. r. ruticilla* (Linnaeus) (adult females and immature males slightly darker above): extreme southern Ontario (Hamilton southward).

Remarks. This is one of the handsomest and most active of our warblers. Rarely still a moment, it flits from branch to branch, darts after flying insects, or snatches up insect larvae from twigs and foliage. It has a characteristic habit of drooping its wings and fanning its tail, thus displaying the contrasty orange patches located there. It is a common summer resident in much of its extensive range.

Prothonotary Warbler

Paruline orangée
Protonotaria citrea (Boddaert)
Total length: 13.4 to 14.7 cm
Plate 60

Bill longish, sharp-pointed. *Adult male*: Head, neck, and under parts (except white under tail coverts) bright orange-yellow; back yellowish olive-green; rump and wing coverts bluish grey; no wing bars; tail blackish except that most of the inner webs of all but innermost feathers are white with black tips; bill blackish; legs dark bluish. *Adult female*: Similar to adult male but duller, the yellowish olive-green of back extending over back of neck to top of head.

Measurements. *Adult male*: wing, 71.1–74.2 (72.9); tail, 46.2–49.8 (48); exposed culmen, 12.9–13.7 (13.2); tarsus, 18.3–19.8 (19). *Adult female*: wing, 65.5–69.1 (67.3) mm (Ridgway).

Breeding Distribution of Prothonotary Warbler

Range in Canada. Local summer resident, breeding only in extreme southern Ontario (Rondeau Provincial Park, Port Rowan, Turkey Point, Point Abino, Hamilton, Ridgeway; sight records north to North Bay).

Casual in New Brunswick (Milltown, 31 October 1862; also sight records at Kent and Machias Seal islands; St. Andrews), and Nova Scotia (specimen records: Cape Sable, 21 September 1962 and 1 October 1967; Sable Island, 10 August 1970; and Bridgetown, 13 October 1979; also sight records off Halifax, and at Cape Sable, Sable Island, Seal Island, and Louisbourg). Quebec (sight record: Saint-Rose Lake, 17 to 18 June 1977; photo record: Montréal, 20 May 1981) and Saskatchewan (Regina, 17 May 1969, and 13 September 1978).

Field Marks. A golden-yellow warbler with plain bluish-grey wings (no wing bars) and white areas in tail. Separable from the Yellow Warbler by dark (instead of yellow) wings, and white (instead of yellow) areas in tail. It lacks the Blue-winged Warbler's white wing bars and black line through eye. *Song*: A loud ringing *tweet tweet tweet tweet tweet*.

Habitat. Usually the vicinity of flooded or swampy woodlands.

Nesting. Usually in a woodpecker hole or natural cavity in a tree, rarely more than 4.5 m up. Sometimes on man-made buildings, bridges, or in bird boxes. *Eggs*, usually 4 to 6; boldly spotted and blotched with browns and purplish greys. Incubation period 12 to 14 days (L.H. Walkinshaw) by the female.

Range. Breeds from southern Minnesota, southern Michigan, southern Ontario, central New York, and New Jersey south to eastern Texas, the Gulf Coast of United States, and central Florida. Winters from southern Mexico south through Central America to Colombia and northern Venezuela.

Worm-eating Warbler

Paruline vermivore
Helmitheros vermivorus (Gmelin)
Total length: 12.5 to 14.5 cm
Plate 60

Status in Canada. Occasional visitant to southern Ontario (London, 28 May 1908; Long Point, 4 May 1960; also, individuals were banded at Bradley's Marsh and Long Point, spring 1961; also sight records north to Ottawa) and Nova Scotia (specimens: Sable Island, 3 October 1902; Seal Island, 14 October 1978. Photo record: Seal Island, 10 May 1975. Sight record: Sable Island, 7 June 1978). Sight records for Quebec (Montréal region: 27 May 1957; 21 May 1966; May 1974; and 9 May 1979) and Saskatchewan (Saskatoon, 19 May 1979, one carefully observed by experienced observers).

Bill rather large for a warbler. Sexes similar. Head buffy with broad black stripe on either side of crown and a narrower one through the eye; rest of upper parts greyish olive-green; no wing bars or patches in the tail; under parts plain buffy; bill and legs brownish.

Measurements. *Adult male*: wing, 66.3–72.9 (69.3); tail, 47.7–51 (49.3); exposed culmen, 12.9–14.5 (13.7); tarsus, 17.3–18.3 (18.0). *Adult female*: wing, 64.8–67.1 (65.8) mm (Ridgway).

Range. Breeds from northeastern Kansas, central Ohio, and southeastern Massachusetts south to northeastern Texas, central-southern Louisiana, northern Georgia, and northeastern North Carolina. Winters from Mexico south to Panama and in the West Indies.

Swainson's Warbler

Paruline de Swainson
Limnothlypis swainsonii (Audubon)
Total length: 12.5 to 15.5 cm

Status in Canada. Accidental in Nova Scotia
(specimen: immature female at Seal Island,
9 October 1972). Sight records only for Ontario
(Point Pelee, May 1968).

A plain large-billed warbler. Crown plain brown somewhat more rusty
than the back; over eye a dull-whitish stripe; under parts plain dull
yellowish-white becoming olive grey on sides; legs and feet flesh.

Measurements. *Adult male*: wing, 67.3–72.1 (69.6); tail, 46.5–49.8
(48.3); exposed culmen, 14.7–16.0 (15.5); tarsus, 17.5–18.3 (18.0). *Adult
female*: wing, 69.3–70.6 (70.1); exposed culmen, 15–15.7 (15.5) mm
(Ridgway).

Field Marks. A very plain large-billed warbler; brown above, the
crown more rusty than the back and with a whitish eyebrow stripe. No
eye-ring, no wing bars, and no stripes on either upper or under parts.
Lacks the conspicuous crown stripes of the Worm-eating Warbler. Has
a much larger bill than the female Black-throated Blue Warbler and
lacks the latter's white wing spot.

Range. Breeds from northeastern Oklahoma, southern Illinois,
southern Ohio, and southeastern Maryland south to southeastern
Louisiana, southern Alabama, and northern Florida. Winters in Cuba,
Jamaica, Yucatan, and British Honduras.

Ovenbird

Paruline couronnée
Seiurus aurocapillus (Linnaeus)
Total length: 14 to 16.5 cm
Plate 64

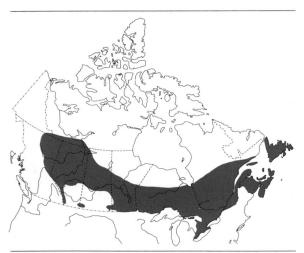

Breeding Distribution of Ovenbird

Range in Canada. Summer resident, breeding in
northeastern British Columbia (Liard Hot
Springs, Fort Nelson, Muskwa, Peace River
parklands, Prince George); southern Mackenzie
(Fort Resolution; probably Nahanni National
Park); northern and central Alberta (south to
about Edmonton and in the mountains south to
Waterton Lakes; also locally in extreme south-
east: Cypress Hills); central and, very locally,
southern Saskatchewan (Kazan Lake, southern
Reindeer Lake, Cumberland House, Nipawin;
locally Cypress Hills, Moose Mountain,
Qu'Appelle valley, and Ekapo Lake); central
and southern Manitoba (The Pas, Thicket
Portage, Norway House, Riding Mountain,
Turtle Mountains, Rennie); central and south-
ern Ontario (Favourable Lake, North Point,
Moosonee southward); south-central and south-
ern Quebec (Baie-du-Poste, Mingan, Anticosti
Island southward, including Madeleine Island);

Adults (sexes similar): Top of head with two blackish stripes extending
backward from forehead to nape, these stripes bordering an area of
brownish orange; rest of upper parts, sides of head, and sides of neck
plain olive-green; eye-ring whitish; wings and tail with no white markings; under parts white, spotted or streaked with blackish on breast and
sides and with a line of same on either side of throat; legs flesh-
coloured.

Measurements *(S. a. aurocapillus)*. *Adult male*: wing, 72.8–77.4
(75.5); tail, 53–56 (54.1); exposed culmen, 11.4–12.4 (12.0); tarsus,
21–22.5 (21.9). *Adult female*: wing, 69.8–76.1 (72.8) mm.

Field Marks. A large warbler with unmarked olive-green upper
parts, wings, and tail; white under parts heavily streaked with black on
breast and sides; whitish eye-ring, and a dull-orange crown bordered by
two black stripes. Usually seen *walking* on the ground or on a low
branch in deciduous woodland. Waterthrushes are somewhat similar but
have a pale line over the eye and an unmarked crown. Beginners might
confuse the Ovenbird with small thrushes, but the black marks in its
under parts are stripes rather than spots, especially on the sides. *Song*:
Unmistakable. Sounds like *teacher* repeated five to fifteen times, each
repetition becoming louder.

Habitat. Deciduous closed-canopy woodlands, preferably with not
too much underbrush and a good carpet of leaf litter; occasionally
mixedwoods. Sometimes open jack pine woodland or rarely even white
spruce forest (Amos, Quebec, region).

Nesting. On the ground, usually in more open parts of the forest
floor. Nest is arched over, often by leaf litter, like a Dutch oven (hence
the name Ovenbird). Nest is of grass, weed stems, rootlets, leaves, and
moss, with a lining of fine grasses and hair. *Eggs*, 3 to 6; white, spotted
with reddish browns and some purplish grey, generally forming a wreath
around the large end. Incubation 11 days and 12 hours to 14 days,
averaging 12 days, 5.6 hours (H.W. Hann), by the female.

Range. Breeds from southern Mackenzie east to Newfoundland
and in the United States south to eastern Colorado, southeastern
Oklahoma, northern Alabama, and northern Georgia. Winters from the
Gulf of Mexico coast and southern South Carolina south to Panama,
northern Colombia, northern Venezuela, and the Lesser Antilles.

Subspecies. (1) *Seiurus aurocapillus aurocapillus* (Linnaeus): Most
of the Canadian part of the breeding range except Newfoundland and
extreme southeastern Alberta and southwestern Saskatchewan (Cypress
Hills). However, limited material available from northern Alberta
tends toward *cinereus* and perhaps should be referred to that race.

Newfoundland; New Brunswick; Prince Edward Island; and Nova Scotia (including Cape Breton Island).

(2) *S. a. cinereus* Miller (averages paler and more greyish above than *aurocapillus*): extreme southeastern Alberta and southwestern Saskatchewan (Cypress Hills). (3) *S. a. furvior* Batchelder (darker above with more brownish-orange crown patch, heavier crown stripes): Newfoundland.

Northern Waterthrush

Paruline des ruisseaux
Seiurus noveboracensis (Gmelin)
Total length: 12.5 to 15 cm
Plate 64

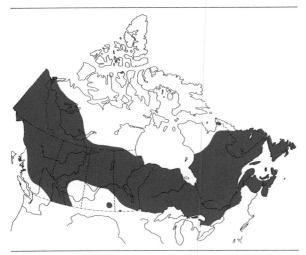

Breeding Distribution of Northern Waterthrush

Range in Canada. Summer resident, breeding from northern Yukon (Old Crow; recorded in summer north to the coastal plain); northwestern Mackenzie (Mackenzie Delta, McTavish Arm); northern Saskatchewan (Lake Athabasca, Black Lake region, Cochrane River); northern Manitoba (Churchill); northern Ontario (Fort Severn, Moose Factory); northern Quebec (Lake Guillaume-Delisle, Koroc River); central Labrador (Davis Inlet southward; perhaps north to Angutausugevik); and Newfoundland south to south-central and southeastern British Columbia (Stuie, Horse Lake, Flathead valley); Alberta (south to the Edmonton region and in the southwestern mountains to Waterton Lakes National Park); central Saskatchewan (Flotten Lake, Nipawin, Cumberland House; and south locally to Qu'Appelle valley, Ekapo Lake, and Moose Mountain); southern Manitoba (Dauphin, Indian Bay; probably Turtle Mountain); southern Ontario (Hamilton); southern Quebec (Gatineau Park, Hatley, Lake Rimouski, Percé); and throughout New Brunswick; Prince Edward Island; and Nova Scotia. Recorded in summer in southwestern Keewatin (Windy Bay).

Accidental in Franklin (Banks Island, 11 September 1914).

Adults and young: Above uniform olive (varying among individuals between brownish and greyish olive); buffy line over eye; sides of head dusky olive; wings and tail without any conspicuous light areas; under parts pale yellow to white, the throat dotted, the breast and sides liberally streaked with sooty olive; legs brownish flesh.

Measurements *(S. n. notabilis)*. *Adult male*: wing, 72.7–76.9 (75.3); tail, 51.5–55.5 (53.1); exposed culmen, 12.6–13.9 (13.3); tarsus, 20.5–22.5 (21.5). *Adult female*: wing, 70–74 (72.2) mm.

Field Marks. This thrush-like warbler, heavily streaked below, has a prominent buffy eyebrow stripe and a habit of constantly teetering its body like a Spotted Sandpiper. Its small size, teetering motions, and streaked (instead of spotted) under parts separate it from real thrushes. Extremely similar to Louisiana Waterthrush (rare in Canada), but the Northern's more yellowish under parts, buffy instead of white eyebrow stripe, and, best of all, its spotted throat (immaculate in Louisiana Waterthrush) will mark it. *Song*: Loud, spirited, almost staccato, usually ending in a characteristic *chew chew chew*.

Habitat. Shrubby thickets, notably alder and willow, near water along streams, ponds, and lakes, swamps, bogs and wet parks of woodlands with shallow pools of water.

Nesting. In the roots of an upturned tree, or in a cavity of a bank or stump. Nest is of mosses, leaves, grasses, and twigs and is lined with hair and blossom stalks of mosses. *Eggs*, generally 4 or 5; white, blotched and spotted with browns and often some purplish greys. They are usually more heavily marked than those of the Ovenbird. Incubation 12 days, by the female (S.W. Eaton).

Range. Breeds from north-central Alaska east across Canada to Newfoundland and south to northern Idaho, western Montana, northern North Dakota, northern Wisconsin, northern Michigan, northeastern Ohio, northern Pennsylvania, and Massachusetts. Winters from Mexico, Cuba, and the Bahamas south to Ecuador, northeastern Peru, southern Venezuela, and the Guianas.

Subspecies. (1) *Seiurus noveboracensis noveboracensis* (Gmelin): eastern Quebec (Schefferville, Moisie Bay, Rivière-du-Loup), Labrador, Newfoundland, New Brunswick, Prince Edward Island, Nova Scotia. (2) *S. n. notabilis* Ridgway, more greyish, less greenish upper parts; less yellowish under parts: Yukon, Mackenzie, northern British Columbia (Atlin, Fort Nelson), Alberta, Saskatchewan, Manitoba, Ontario, western Quebec (Baie-du-Poste, Lake Saint-Jean, Gatineau Park). (3) *S. n. limnaeus* McCabe and Miller, with darker upper parts than *notabilis*, under parts intermediate in yellow between *noveboracensis* and *notabilis*, size (except tarsus) small: central and southeastern British Columbia.

Remarks. Waterthrushes are really wood-warblers, not thrushes. The name "water warbler" would be a more suitable one, for they do prefer the vicinity of water. Like the Ovenbird, they walk instead of hopping; but unlike it, they have a habit of almost constantly teetering the body like a Spotted Sandpiper. They spend most of their time on or near the ground, but not infrequently a male will select a perch high in a tree for singing purposes. The Northern Waterthrush eats insects and other small animal material.

Louisiana Waterthrush

Paruline hochequeue
Seiurus motacilla (Vieillot)
Total length: 15 to 16 cm
Plate 64

Range in Canada. Breeds locally in extreme southern Ontario (London, Hamilton, Websters Falls, and Kingston).

Casual in western Quebec (specimen: Cascades, 24 May 1974; sight record: Aylmer, 25 May 1975) and Nova Scotia (photo record: Sable Island, 9 August 1970; one reportedly found dead at Cape Sable, 28 July 1976; also sight records).

Very similar to Northern Waterthrush but averages larger, especially bill; under parts usually much whiter; line over eye white; throat virtually unspotted. *Adults and young*: Upper parts uniform greyish-olive; broad *white* stripe over eye; no white patches in wings or tail; under parts white, heavily streaked with brownish, except throat, which is immaculate or at most with mere flecks of brown; a narrow line on either side of throat; legs flesh-coloured.

Measurements. *Adult male*: wing, 75.7–84.3 (80.3); tail, 49.5–55.4 (51.8); exposed culmen, 12.4–13.5 (13.2); tarsus, 21.6–22.9 (22.3). *Adult female*: wing, 79.9–81 (78.7); exposed culmen, 12.9–14.2 (13.5) mm (Ridgway).

Field Marks. Extremely similar in appearance and habits to Northern Waterthrush but has a white (instead of buffy or yellowish) eyebrow stripe, lacks any yellowish in the white of under parts; has an *unspotted* throat. *Song*: Similar to that of Northern Waterthrush but the last part more variable, lacking the *chew chew chew* ending, which is so frequent in the Northern's song.

Habitat. Wooded ravines with running streams, woodland swamps.

Nesting. Similar to Northern Waterthrush. *Eggs*, 4 to 6; white, speckled and blotched with browns and greys. Incubation 12 to 14 days, by the female (S.W. Eaton).

Range. Breeds from eastern Nebraska, southern Michigan, southern Ontario, central New York, and Rhode Island south to eastern Texas, the United States Gulf Coast, and South Carolina. Winters from northern Mexico, Cuba, and the Bahamas south to northern South America.

Kentucky Warbler

Paruline du Kentucky
Oporornis formosus (Wilson)
Total length: 12.5 to 14.7 cm
Plate 65

Status in Canada. Rare visitor to southern Ontario (Point Pelee, Strathroy, Bryanston, Bradford, Rondeau Provincial Park; also various sight records). Casual visitor to Nova Scotia (specimens: Sable Island, 1 September 1902; Brier Island, 1 September 1975; Cape Sable, 6 September 1969. Photo record: Seal Island, 16 May 1976; also sight records). Accidental in Newfoundland (specimen: Bonavista Cove, 4 September 1971). Sight record for Quebec (Montréal, 18 May 1974 and 27 May 1979) and Saskatchewan (Moose Jaw, 25 September 1971).

Adult male: Crown black, some feathers tipped with grey; line over eye and almost encircling eye, yellow; cheek patch and band down sides of neck black; rest of upper parts, wings, and tail plain olive-green; under parts, including under tail coverts, bright yellow. *Adult female*: Similar to adult male but duller, the blacks of head replaced by dusky are more restricted.

Measurements. *Adult male*: wing, 65–74.7 (70.1); tail, 49–52.3 (51); exposed culmen, 11.4–12.7 (11.9); tarsus, 20.8–23.4 (22.3). *Adult female*: wing, 62.7–66.8 (65) mm (Ridgway).

Distinctions. Canada Warbler also has a yellow eye-ring and eyebrow line but differs in its blue-grey upper parts, markings on breast, and white (instead of yellow) under tail coverts. The Hooded Warbler shows some white in the tail.

Range. Breeds from southeastern Nebraska, central Indiana, southern Pennsylvania, and southwestern Connecticut south to central Texas, southern Mississippi, and central Georgia.

Connecticut Warbler

Paruline à gorge grise
Oporornis agilis (Wilson)
Total length: 13 to 15.2 cm
Plate 65

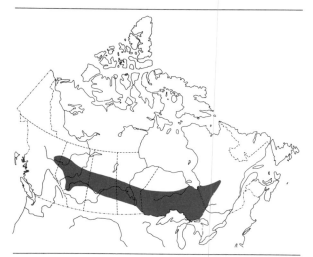

Breeding Distribution of Connecticut Warbler

Range in Canada. Breeds in central-eastern British Columbia (Tupper Creek); north-central and central Alberta (Peace River District, Cold Lake, Belvedere, Sundre); central Saskatchewan (Kazan Lake, Prince Albert, and near Roddick); central and southern Manitoba (The Pas, Riding Mountain, Whitemouth, Sprague); north-central to south-central Ontario (Sandy Lake, southern James Bay, Thunder Bay, Hearst, Cochrane, Manitoulin Island); and central-western Quebec (Rupert-House; Amos region; probably east to Lake Mistassini).

Uncommon migrant in southern Alberta, southern Saskatchewan, and southern Ontario (Erie Beach). Rare spring and autumn visitor to Nova Scotia (specimen record: Brier Island, 15 October 1979; also sight records). Sight records only for New Brunswick.

Wing longer than in Mourning Warbler. Wing length usually 19 mm or more greater than tail length. Eye-ring complete regardless of sex or age. *Adult male*: Head, throat, and upper breast slaty grey, palest on throat; complete white eye-ring; rest of upper parts, wings, and tail plain olive-green; abdomen and under tail coverts yellow; sides and flanks pale olive-green; legs brownish-flesh colour. In autumn the top of head is brown. *Adult female*: Similar to adult male but duller and more brownish; the slate of head, neck, and breast is replaced by brownish olive or greyish olive; throat brownish buff or buffy white. *Young*: Similar to adult female but breast darker and more olivaceous; eye-ring slightly buffy.

Measurements. *Adult male*: wing, 68.8–73.5 (71.2); tail, 47.5–52.5 (49.5); exposed culmen, 11.7–12.9 (12.2); tarsus, 20–22.5 (21.3). *Adult female*: wing, 67.5–71.8 (69.3) mm.

Field Marks. Adult male most closely resembles male of Mourning and MacGillivray's warblers but has a complete white eye-ring (incomplete in MacGillivray's, absent in Mourning) and lacks any black on the throat or breast. Adult females and young in autumn have the breast more brownish, a complete and more conspicuous eye-ring, and longer under tail coverts than corresponding plumages of Mourning and MacGillivray's (both of which have usually incomplete eye-rings). However, many young in autumn are difficult to distinguish. Novices often mistake the Nashville Warbler for the Connecticut, but the Nashville is much smaller and has a yellow throat, which is sharply marked off from grey cheeks. *Song*: *Chuckety chuckety chuckety chuck* and various similar renditions of repeated syllables.

Habitat. For nesting, frequently spruce and tamarack bogs; also, especially in central Alberta, dry ridges, knolls with open poplar woods. In the Amos, Quebec, region it uses open immature jack pine.

Nesting. On the ground often at the base of a small sapling or weed. Nest is of grasses, plant fibres, sometimes a few leaves. *Eggs*, 4 or 5; white, variously marked with browns.

Range. Breeds from central-eastern British Columbia east to north-central Ontario and central-western Quebec and south to northern Minnesota, northern Wisconsin, northern Michigan, and south-central Ontario. Winters from northern Venezuela to central Brazil.

Mourning Warbler

Paruline triste
Oporornis philadelphia (Wilson)
Total length: 12 to 14 cm
Plate 65

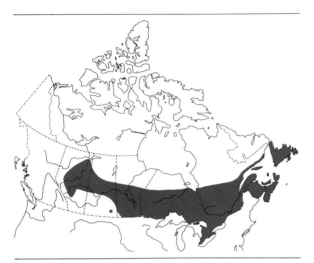

Breeding Distribution of Mourning Warbler

Range in Canada. Breeds in northeastern British Columbia (Peace River District; recorded in summer at Fort Nelson, Steamboat Mountain, Parker Lake); Alberta (east of the mountains and foothills: Lesser Slave Lake, Chipewyan south to Red Deer and Rocky Mountain House where hybridization with *O. tolmiei* reportedly occurs); central Saskatchewan (Kazan Lake, Montreal River, Emma Lake, Roddick, Cumberland House, Nipawin; locally in Qu'Appelle valley and Moose Mountain); central and southern Manitoba (Cormorant and Cross lakes southward); central and southern Ontario (Favourable Lake, southern James Bay southward); south-central Quebec (Eastmain, Baie-du-Poste, Anticosti Island, and probably east to mouth of Little Mécatina River, and southward including Madeleine Islands); Newfoundland; New Brunswick; Prince Edward Island; and Nova Scotia (including Cape Breton Island). Sight records of this species in northeastern British Columbia (Fort Nelson region) require confirmation and more study.

Wing decidedly shorter than that of Connecticut Warbler; wing usually over 11 (but less than 19) mm longer than tail; under parts usually brighter yellow. *Adult male*: Head and neck slate grey, eye-ring absent, the feathers of upper breast mostly black, those of throat mostly black with grey tips; rest of upper parts olive green; no wing bars or tail spot; under parts from lower breast to under tail coverts bright yellow, darkening on sides and flanks to olive green. In autumn, the black of upper breast is much veiled with grey. *Adult female*: Similar to adult male but entire hood grey without black on upper breast or throat and often with a faint whitish eye-ring, which usually is not quite complete. *Immatures in autumn*: Faint eye-ring present but usually is broken. Upper parts uniform dark olive-green. Under parts mostly yellow, usually including throat, the upper breast usually tinged with olive, grey, and often some buff; and in young males often a few concealed black feathers are present.

Measurements. *Adult male*: wing, 58.6–64.4 (61.5); tail, 45.5–53 (49.3); exposed culmen, 11–12.6 (11.6); tarsus, 20–21.5 (20.4). *Adult female*: wing, 55.4–60.4 (58.1) mm.

Field Marks. Adult male is separable from that of Connecticut Warbler by black of upper breast and by lack of a white eye-ring; from adult male of MacGillivray's by lack of white on eyelids. Adult female has hood and upper breast grey (brownish in Connecticut) and often has a *broken* white or whitish eye-ring, thus easily confused with Connecticut unless the break in the eye-ring can be discerned. The autumn immature Mourning Warbler has a pale eye-ring but usually a yellowish throat (autumn immature of Connecticut has a brownish upper breast without yellow on throat). In all these plumages the Mourning Warbler has much brighter yellow under parts. The autumn Mourning Warbler also resembles the female Common Yellowthroat, but the uniformly yellow under parts of the former (belly whitish or buffy in Yellowthroat) distinguish it. *Song*: A rolling *churry churry churra churra* with variations.

Habitat. Shrubbery and bushes of young second growth on burntlands and clearings: woodland edges and sunny openings; margins of bogs and marshes.

Nesting. Usually on the ground, often in tangles of briery shrubs or other low vegetation; occasionally in a low bush. Nest rather bulky and made of dead leaves and grasses, lined with rootlets, hair, and fine grasses. *Eggs*, 3 to 5; white, spotted and blotched mostly at large end with reddish browns and some purplish grey. Incubation, by the female, lasts 12 to 13 days.

Range. Breeds from central Alberta east to Newfoundland and south to northeastern South Dakota, northeastern Illinois, northern Ohio, southeastern New York, and Massachusetts; and in the Appalachian Mountains to West Virginia and northwestern Virginia. Winters from southern Nicaragua and Costa Rica south to northern Ecuador, central Colombia, and western Venezuela.

Remarks. When Alexander Wilson first discovered this bird, he named it Mourning Warbler because of the black areas on its breast. Wilson never saw more than one specimen. Had he known the bird better, he doubtless would have given it a more suitable name. There is nothing about its behaviour or loud cheerful song to suggest mourning.

MacGillivray's Warbler

Paruline des buissons
Oporornis tolmiei (Townsend)
Total length: 12 to 14 cm
Plate 65

Breeding Distribution of MacGillivray's Warbler

Range in Canada. Breeds in extreme southwestern Yukon (Haines Road: Miles 98 and 113); British Columbia (Haines Road: Mile 45, Dease Lake, Lower Liard Crossing, and Tupper Creek southward including Vancouver Island); southern Alberta (Rocky Mountains and foothills; and very locally east of the mountains: Red Deer River valley, Cypress Hills); and extreme southwestern Saskatchewan (Cypress Hills). Recorded eastward in Saskatchewan to Wood Mountain (specimen: 11 June 1895). Accidental in Ontario (specimen: Hamilton, 20 May 1890).

Wing usually less than 8 mm longer than tail. Under parts usually brighter yellow than Connecticut Warbler. *Adult male (breeding plumage)*: Top and sides of head and sides of neck bluish slate deepening to blackish in front of eye and with a white spot on both upper and lower eyelid; rest of upper parts plain olive-green; no wing bars or tail patches; throat and upper breast blackish, the feathers tipped with grey. *Adult female (breeding plumage)*: Similar to adult male but throat and breast without any black, the throat sometimes almost whitish; head paler grey without any black in front of eye; white spots on upper and lower eyelids present but usually less prominent.

Measurements. *Adult male*: wing, 57.6–62.2 (59.6); tail, 50.5–54.5 (52.3); exposed culmen, 10.5–12.1 (11.3); tarsus, 20–22 (20.9). *Adult female*: wing, 53.2–60.2 (56.6) mm.

Field Marks. (See Connecticut and Mourning Warblers, both of which are more eastern in distribution.) However, autumn immatures of MacGillivray's Warbler are not safely separable in the field from those of the Mourning Warbler. Autumn birds somewhat resemble female and autumn Common Yellowthroats but have a more uniformly yellow abdomen and often a suggestion of a hood showing down to the upper breast. *Song*: Three or four quick notes in the same pitch, followed by several lower notes: *see it, see it, see it, peachy, peachy*.

Habitat. Brush and thickets on logged-over areas, forest edges and openings, bushy mountainsides, and similar tall shrubbery on either moist or dry ground.

Nesting. In a bush or weed usually 0.3 to 1.8 m from the ground, rarely higher. Nest of weed stalks and grasses, lined with fine grasses, rootlets, and hair. *Eggs*, usually 3 to 5; white, spotted and blotched with browns and some grey.

Range. Breeds from southeastern Alaska, northern British Columbia, southern Alberta, and southwestern Saskatchewan south to central California, central Arizona, and central New Mexico. Winters from northern Mexico south to Panama.

Subspecies. *Oporornis tolmiei tolmiei* (Townsend).

Common Yellowthroat

(Maryland Yellow-throat)

Paruline masquée
Geothlypis trichas (Linnaeus)
Total length: 12 to 14 cm
Plate 65

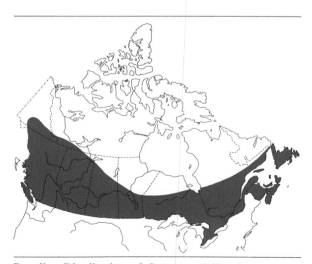

Breeding Distribution of Common Yellowthroat

Wings rather short, rounded; tail only slightly shorter than folded wing; tarsus over one-third as long as wing. *Adult male (breeding plumage)*: Forehead and sides of head black, forming a mask, which is margined narrowly above and behind by greyish; rest of upper parts, wings, and tail olive green; no wing bars or tail patches; throat and breast yellow; abdomen whitish to pale buff; sides and flanks brownish olive. In autumn, the black mask feathers are tipped with grey. *Adult female*: Differs from adult male in having no black mask; crown and sides of head greyish olive, the forehead often tinged with brown; pale eyebrow line and inconspicuous pale eye-ring. *Young in autumn*: Resemble adults in autumn but are duller and browner, the male with black mask only partly developed and lacking its grey border.

Measurements (*G. t. brachidactyla*). *Adult male*: wing, 52–58.4 (55.0); tail, 48.5–53.5 (50.9); exposed culmen, 10.6–11.6 (11.0); tarsus, 19.5–21.5 (20.1). *Adult female*: wing, 49.3–57.9 (52.6) mm.

Field Marks. A warbler of low shrubbery and with wrenlike motions. The adult male, with broad black mask and yellow throat, is unmistakable. Young males in autumn often show enough of the telltale black mask to identify them. Females have no mask but usually (not always) show some yellowish on throat, and in any case the throat is pale and is sharply cut off from the dark cheeks. Might be confused with Connecticut, Mourning, or MacGillivray's in autumn plumages, but the Common Yellowthroat has a whitish or dull-buffy abdomen; in the other three it is yellow. *Voice*: Song is distinct, sounding like *witchery witchery witchery*, but is variable both individually and geographically. Its *chip* has a peculiar husky quality that identifies it.

Range in Canada. Breeds in southern Yukon (Hutshi Lake, Pelly River at Canol Road; probably near Dempster Highway); extreme southwestern Mackenzie (Nahanni National Park, Sass River); British Columbia (Atlin, Lower Liard Crossing southward including Vancouver Island); Alberta (throughout); central and southern Saskatchewan (Kazan Lake, La Ronge southward); central and southern Manitoba (Cormorant Lake, Cross Lake southward; possibly Gillam); north-central and southern Ontario (Sioux Lookout, southern James Bay southward); south-central and southern Quebec (Lakes Mistassini and Albanel, outer north shore of the Gulf of St. Lawrence southward including Anticosti and Madeleine islands); Newfoundland; New Brunswick; Prince Edward Island; and Nova Scotia.

Casual occurrences north to Churchill, Manitoba, and once on Kugong Island, N.W.T.

Habitat. Low bushes and thickets bordering streams, ponds, roadsides, and wood edges; bushy pastures and old fields; cattails and bulrushes of marshes and similar situations, most frequently on moist ground but often in dry bushy places as well.

Nesting. On or very near the ground among low vegetation. Nest of weed stalks, grasses, and leaves is rather bulky and has a lining of fine grasses and often hair. *Eggs*, 3 to 5, usually 4; white, marked mostly at the large end with browns, some black, and often underlying grey. Incubation 12 days, by the female (P.B. Hofslund).

Range. Breeds from southeastern Alaska east to Labrador and Newfoundland and south to southern Mexico, the Gulf Coast of United States, and southern Florida. Winters from southern United States south to Panama and Puerto Rico.

Subspecies. (1) *Geothlypis trichas brachidactyla* (Swainson): eastern Canada from eastern Ontario (Amyot, Fort Albany) east to Newfoundland and Nova Scotia. (2) *G. t. campicola* Behle and Aldrich (similar to *brachidactyla* but upper parts lighter, yellow of under parts richer and more extensive): western Ontario (Lac Seul), Manitoba, Saskatchewan, Alberta, and southern and central British Columbia (east of the coast). (3) *G. t. yukonicola* Godfrey (similar to *campicola* but upper parts distinctly greyer): southern Yukon, northwestern British Columbia (Dease Lake). (4) *G. t. arizela* Oberholser (very similar to *campicola* but upper parts more yellow-green, less greyish): coastal British Columbia (Vancouver Island, Chilliwack).

Remarks. The male, with his bright-yellow throat and jet-black mask, is one of the easiest of birds to recognize. Most vegetation tangles, especially those near moist places, have at least one pair of these interesting warblers. They are very active birds, peering and posturing with wrenlike energy when intruders enter their domain. They seem more irritated than alarmed, however, and repeatedly utter a characteristically husky *tscick* of disapproval.

Hooded Warbler

Paruline à capuchon
Wilsonia citrina (Boddaert)
Total length: 12.5 to 14.5 cm
Plate 64

Range in Canada. Breeds only in extreme southern Ontario (Orwell, Tillsonburg, Mansewood, Newbury).

Wanders somewhat farther northward in Ontario (sight records to Ottawa and Manitoulin Island). Scarce visitor to Nova Scotia (specimen records: Cape Sable, 30 September 1962; Sable Island, 16 October 1975; Outer Island, 9 October 1979. Photographic record: Seal Island: 28 April to 3 May 1975. Also various sight records). Southern Quebec (photo: Otterburn Park, 5-6 May 1983; sight records: Montréal, Sainte-Anne-de-Bellevue, Aylmer), and New Brunswick (Cape Spencer). Casual in Manitoba (specimen: Churchill, 10 June 1952; also sight records for southern part) and Newfoundland (sight record: St. John's, 8-16 November 1983).

Adult male: Forehead and sides of head bright yellow; rest of head, neck, throat, and upper breast black; remainder of upper parts yellowish olive-green; no wing bars; two outer tail feathers on each side with inner webs extensively white, the next with a white patch; under parts from black of hood to tail bright yellow. *Adult female*: Similar to adult male but with either mere traces of black suggesting part of the male's hood, or no black at all. The white in the tail distinguishes it from similar mostly yellow warblers without white wing bars.

Measurements. *Adult male*: wing, 65.5–69.1 (67.6); tail, 55.4–59.7 (57.7); exposed culmen, 9.9–11.2 (10.7); tarsus, 19–20.1 (19.7). *Adult female*: wing, 60.2–66.8 (63.0) mm (Ridgway).

Field Marks. Adult male, with its black hood and yellow mask, is unmistakable. Adult females and young females in autumn are olive green above, yellow below, and show only traces, if any, of the male's black hood. The white in the tail of the Hooded distinguishes it from similar yellow warblers without white wing bars, e.g., Wilson's Warbler. *Song*: *Weeta-weeta-wee-tee-o* suggests that of the Magnolia Warbler but is much louder.

Habitat. Favours mature deciduous forest, particularly along stream bottoms and ravine edges and where saplings and shrubbery grow on the forest floor. Inhabits the lower forest stratum.

Nesting. Nest site averages about 0.6 m above ground in the fork of a seedling, bush, or grape tangle. Nest is of dead leaves and bark strips, held together by spider silk and lined with fine shreds of bark and grasses. *Eggs*, usually 3 or 4; white, speckled or blotched with browns, mostly around the large end. Incubation 12 days; young remain in nest about eight days after hatching (A.B. Williams).

Range. Breeds from northeastern Nebraska east to Rhode Island and south to southeastern Texas, the United States Gulf Coast, and northern Florida. Winters from southeastern Mexico south to Costa Rica and rarely Panama.

Wilson's Warbler

Paruline à calotte noire
Wilsonia pusilla (Wilson)
Total length: 10.5 to 13 cm
Plate 64

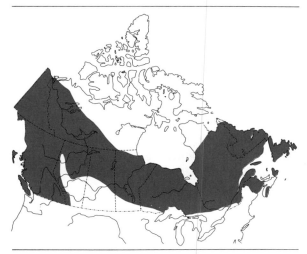

Breeding Distribution of Wilson's Warbler

Range in Canada. Summer resident, breeding from northern Yukon (north coastal plain); northwestern and central-eastern Mackenzie (Mackenzie Delta, Fort Anderson, Artillery Lake); northwestern Saskatchewan (Lake Athabasca, Hasbala Lake); northern Manitoba (Churchill, York Factory); northern Ontario (Fort Severn, Lake Attawapiskat, Fort Albany); northern Quebec (Lake Guillaume-Delisle, Feuilles River, Koroc River); central Labrador (Makkovik, Cartwright); and Newfoundland south through British Columbia (including Vancouver Island, Queen Charlotte Islands); southwestern and central-eastern Alberta (Banff and Waterton Lakes national parks; formerly to Nevis); central Saskatchewan (Kazan Lake, Nipawin); southern Manitoba (Lake St. Martin); south-central Ontario (Sudbury); southern Quebec (Guérin, north shore of the Gulf of St. Lawrence; Anticosti Island, Campbell's Bay; Gaspé, Cachée River, formerly Montréal); New Brunswick (locally, Tabusintac, St. Stephen, Saint John); and locally in Nova Scotia (Deerfield, Harrigan Cove; probably Cape Breton Island). Migrant in Prince Edward Island, but possibly breeds rarely. Accidental in northern Baffin Island (Arctic Bay, July 1954).

Migrates through southern Canada.

Bill short, rather wide at base; bristles about mouth extending forward beyond nostrils. *Adult male*: Crown black; forehead and stripe over eye, yellow; rest of upper parts olive green, this extending forward over ear coverts; rest of sides of head yellow; no wing bars or white patches in tail; under parts lemon yellow including under tail coverts, the sides and flanks tinged with olive green. *Adult female*: Similar to adult male but black cap usually restricted and much hidden by olive. *Young in first autumn*: Similar to adults but males with cap more broadly tipped with olive, females with cap concealed or absent.

Measurements *(W. p. pusilla). Adult male*: wing, 52–56.6 (54.3); tail, 46.5–50 (49.0); exposed culmen, 8.4–9.2 (8.8); tarsus, 17–18 (17.4). *Adult female*: wing, 49.8–53.4 (51.8) mm.

Field Marks. A yellow warbler without wing bars or pale patches in the tail. Adults with a black cap (smaller in female), a bright-yellow stripe over eye. The dark eye stands out on an otherwise featureless face. Young Yellow Warblers have yellow wing bars and yellow patches in the tail. Female and young Hooded Warblers show white in the tail. Male American Goldfinch is a yellow bird with a black cap, but its thick sparrowlike bill and black wings quickly distinguish it. *Song*: A series of rapid, almost staccato, chattering notes, dropping in pitch toward the end.

Habitat. In nesting season frequents shrubbery, such as alder, willow, and dwarf birch in moist open places especially along streams, ponds, and bogs; and at various elevations in the mountains in shrubbery of valley bottoms, mountainsides, and alpine meadows.

Nesting. On the ground, often at the base of a shrub or small tree or in a grass hummock. Nest is bulky and is made of grasses, small leaves, and mosses, and is lined with grasses and hair. *Eggs*, 4 to 6, usually 5; white, finely spotted and speckled with reddish browns. Incubation, by the female, lasts 11 to 13 days.

Range. Breeds from northern Alaska east to Labrador and Newfoundland, and south to southern California, central Nevada, northern Utah, and northern New Mexico, northern Minnesota, northern Vermont, and central Maine. Winters from northern Mexico and southern Texas south to Costa Rica and western Panama.

Subspecies. (1) *Wilsonia pusilla pusilla* (Wilson): Mackenzie (Fort Anderson, Artillery Lake), northern and eastern Alberta (north and east of mountains and foothills), Saskatchewan, Manitoba, Ontario, Quebec, Labrador, Newfoundland, New Brunswick, and Nova Scotia. (2) *W. p. pileolata* (Pallas) (coloration above and below brighter than in *pusilla*): southern Yukon (no northern material examined, but Old Crow specimens are referred to *pusilla* by Irving 1960), British Columbia (interior), and northwestern Alberta (mountains and foothills). (3) *W. p. chryseola* Ridgway (brighter above and below than *pileolata*): southwestern coastal British Columbia (Victoria, Vancouver).

Remarks. This bright little bundle of animation goes about its daily chore of securing food with zest and excitement. It darts after flying insects and takes them with an audible snap of its bill. It has a habit of nervously twitching its tail. Even on migration, preference for bushy moist places like those on its nesting grounds is still marked, but it is then much more tolerant of other types, including dry ones.

Canada Warbler

Paruline du Canada
Wilsonia canadensis (Linnaeus)
Total length: 12.5 to 14.5 cm
Plate 65

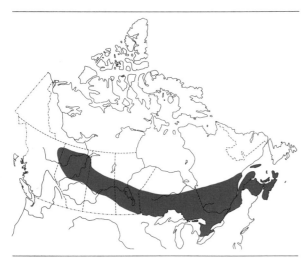

Breeding Distribution of Canada Warbler

Range in Canada. Summer resident, breeding in northeastern British Columbia (Peace River District; probably: Fort Nelson region); northern and central Alberta (Wood Buffalo National Park south to Glenevis and Cold Lake; and west to Belvedere and Joussard; probably Grimshaw); central Saskatchewan (Flotten Lake, Carlton, Cumberland House, Nipawin); central and southwestern Manitoba (The Pas, Moose and Cedar lakes, Lake St. Martin; probably Island Lake); north-central and southern Ontario (Favourable Lake, Moose Factory; south, at least formerly, to Middlesex County); south-central and southern Quebec (Baie-du-Poste, Matamec, Anticosti Island, Montréal, Hatley, Gaspé Peninsula); New Brunswick; Prince Edward Island; and Nova Scotia (including Cape Breton Island). Sight record for southern Mackenzie (Fort Liard, 6 July 1975). Uncommon migrant in southern Saskatchewan and southern Alberta.

Mouth bristles well developed. Wings rather long and pointed. *Adult male*: Forehead and much of crown black, the feathers much edged with grey, and sometimes a pale narrow line in mid-forehead; rest of upper parts bluish grey; no wing bars or tail patches; narrow streak from base of bill to eye and eye-ring, yellow; area in front of eye extending back under eye to side of neck black; under parts bright yellow except a necklace of black spots and white under tail coverts. *Adult female*: Similar to adult male but duller. Forehead with little or no black, crown often tinged yellow-olive; black of face replaced by olive grey; spotting across breast sparser, spots dusky or olive instead of black. *Young in autumn*: Similar to adult female, but breast markings are still fainter, and the upper parts are often lightly washed with olive brown.

Measurements. *Adult male*: wing, 61.9–67.8 (64.8); tail, 53.5–58.5 (56.2); exposed culmen, 10–11.4 (10.7); tarsus, 18–19.5 (18.9). *Adult female*: wing, 60.1–62.6 (61.6) mm.

Field Marks. A black necklace (but faint and greyish in females and young) on otherwise unmarked bright-yellow under parts. Plain-grey upper parts, yellowish eye-ring and thin line from bill to eye, white under tail coverts. *Song*: Is preceded by a single *chip* (sometimes two) and a very slight pause, then the quick slightly staccato song, which often contains characteristic *ditchety* phrases.

Habitat. Shrubbery undergrowths of woodlands, tall shrubbery such as alder and willow along streams, swamps, and similar moist places.

Nesting. On or near the ground under a sapling, in a mossy hummock, on a mossy stump or log, in a bank cavity, or among the roots of an overturned tree. Nest rather bulky and made of weeds, grasses, leaves, and bark shreds, and lined with fine plant fibres, rootlets, and often hair. *Eggs*, 3 to 5; white, well speckled with chestnut.

Range. Breeds in Canada from Alberta east to Nova Scotia and south in the United States to central Minnesota, central Michigan, northern Ohio, and in the Appalachians to eastern Tennessee, northwestern Georgia, western North Carolina, and to northern New Jersey. Winters from Colombia and Venezuela south to central Peru.

Painted Redstart

Paruline à ailes blanches
Myioborus pictus (Swainson)
Total length: 12.5 to 14 cm
Plate 65

Status in Canada. Accidental in Ontario: an individual appeared in Pickering Township on 4 November 1971, and was captured there on 9 November; also in British Columbia (West Vancouver, 4 November 1973, where one was closely observed by several competent observers).

Adults (sexes similar): A strikingly beautiful bird. Head, neck, upper chest, sides, back, rump, wings, and tail black. Wings with large white patch. Tail with three outer feathers largely white. Breast bright red.

Measurements. *Adult male*: wing, 68–75 (71.9); tail, 61–68 (63.3); exposed culmen, 8–9 (8.6); tarsus, 16–17 (16.6). *Adult female*: wing, 67–70 (68.7) mm (Ridgway).

Field Marks. Unmistakable among warblers, this one has a habit of spreading the tail and wings. A beginner might possibly confuse it with the male Rose-breasted Grosbeak, a very much larger bird with a heavy bill (quite unlike the slender bill of a redstart).

Range. Breeds from northern Arizona, southwestern New Mexico, and western Texas south to northern Nicaragua. Winters from northern Mexico southward.

Subspecies. Specimen not examined by the writer but probably *Myioborus pictus pictus* Swainson.

Yellow-breasted Chat

Paruline polyglotte
Icteria virens (Linnaeus)
Total length: 17 to 19 cm
Plate 64

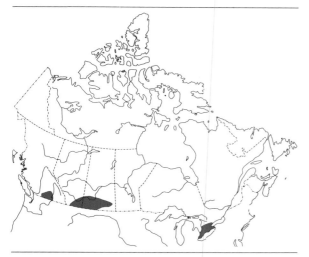

Breeding Distribution of Yellow-breasted Chat

Range in Canada. Breeds in southern British Columbia (Okanagan and Similkameen valleys); Alberta (Steveville, Empress, Milk River valley, Cypress Hills, rarely north to Rosebud and Drumheller); southern Saskatchewan (Frenchman River valley, Maple Creek, Regina, Fort San, Tregarva vicinity, rarely north to near Saskatoon); and southern Ontario (north to Peel regional municipality).

Casual in Quebec (specimens: Chicoutimi, 12 September 1971; Limoilou, 20 October 1976; also sight records); New Brunswick (specimens: Grand Manan, Machias Seal Island, St. Andrews); Nova Scotia (specimens: Brier Island, Port Mouton); and Newfoundland (specimens: Cappahayden, St. John's). Sight records for Manitoba and Prince Edward Island. Most of these East Coast records are for autumn or winter.

Size very large for a warbler. Bill shorter than head, stout, its ridge decidedly convex. Wings and tail nearly equal in length (the tail often a trifle longer) and both somewhat rounded. *Adult male*: Upper parts, including wings and tail, greyish olive-green (often quite greyish in worn plumage); no wing bars or tail patches; stripe from bill back over eye, spot under eye, and stripe from base of bill back over jaw, white; rest of sides of head greyish green becoming slaty or blackish in front of eye; throat, breast, and under wing coverts bright yellow; rest of under parts white, tinged on sides and under tail coverts with buffy grey. *Adult female*: Similar to adult male but usually duller in colour, the yellows less bright, the dark area in front of eye more greyish. *Autumn adults and young*: Similar to summer adults but upper parts more decidedly green, flanks more buffy.

Measurements *(I. v. auricollis). Adult male*: wing, 75.5–83.9 (79.3); tail, 74–88 (81.1); exposed culmen, 13.1–16.7 (14.8); tarsus, 25.5–28 (26.6). *Adult female*: wing, 73–80 (77.6) mm.

Field Marks. Large size, bright-yellow breast, two white stripes on side of head, no wing bars, and longish tail make good field marks. Habitat and song also are helpful. *Song*: Very varied, a series of disjointed noises: *cuks, quits*, and harsh nasal laughing notes, often interspersed with a series of whistles somewhat suggesting a man whistling to a dog.

Habitat. Thickets and tangles of tall shrubbery beside streams or ponds, in old overgrown bushy clearings and in similar situations where it can keep out of sight.

Nesting. In a small tree, sapling, or bushy tangle usually 0.6 to 1.5 m above ground. Nest is bulky and is composed of coarse materials like leaves, shreds of bark, coarse straws, and weed stalks, and lined with fine grasses. *Eggs*, 3 to 5; white, spotted usually over the entire egg with browns and purplish grey. Incubation 11 days by the female (Petrides); probably longer.

Range. Breeds from southern Canada (very locally) and northern United States south to north-central Mexico, the United States Gulf Coast, and northern Florida. Winters from Mexico and southern Texas south to western Panama.

Subspecies. (1) *Icteria virens virens* (Linnaeus): southern Ontario. (2) *I. v. auricollis* (Deppe) (more greyish upper parts, white of malar region more extended, yellow of under parts deeper): British Columbia, Alberta, Saskatchewan.

Subfamily **Thraupinae:** Tanagers

Smallish, nine-primaried, mostly arboreal, the tanagers are one of the most brightly coloured groups in the world. All of the more than 200 species are tropical and only three species range northward as far as Canada.

Summer Tanager

Tangara vermillon
Piranga rubra (Linnaeus)
Total length: 17.5 to 19.5 cm
Plate 66

Status in Canada. Occasional visitant to southern Ontario (north to Thunder Bay, Manitoulin Island, Ottawa); southern New Brunswick (Grand Manan); and Nova Scotia (Yarmouth, Annapolis Royal, Wolfville, Halifax, West Middle Sable, Seal Island).

Rare visitant to southwestern Quebec (photo: Philipsburg; also sight records).

Bill similar to that of Scarlet Tanager but somewhat larger and with "tooth" obsolete. *Adult male (summer and winter)*: Plain dull-red all over but somewhat paler below; flight feathers brown, edged with dull red; no wing bars. *Adult female*: Upper parts plain yellowish olive-green; flight feathers brownish, edged with yellowish olive-green; no wing bars; a vague yellowish eye-ring and obscure yellowish streak from base of bill to eye; under parts dull yellow, brighter on under tail coverts. *Young in first autumn*: Resemble adult female, but the young male is more richly coloured.

Measurements *(P. r. rubra). Adult male*: wing, 92.5–99.6 (95.5); tail, 71.1–74.7 (72.4); exposed culmen, 16.8–19.3 (17.5); tarsus, 18.3–19.8 (19.3). *Adult female*: wing, 88.9–95.8 (91.9) mm (Ridgway).

Accidental in Manitoba (specimen: The Pas, 25 May 1966; near Brandon, 13 June 1981) and Saskatchewan (photo record: Frontier, 7 May 1976).

Field Marks. Adult male is all rose-red without black on wings or tail, thus differing from Scarlet Tanager. Female is more yellowish, especially below, than female Scarlet. Lack of pronounced wing bars always separates it from the Western Tanager.

Range. Breeds from southeastern California, New Mexico, Nebraska, Iowa, central Ohio, Maryland, and Delaware south to northern Mexico and southern Florida. Winters from northern Mexico south to Bolivia and Brazil.

Subspecies. *Piranga rubra rubra* (Linnaeus).

Scarlet Tanager

Tangara écarlate
Piranga olivacea (Gmelin)
Total length: 16.5 to 19 cm
Plate 66

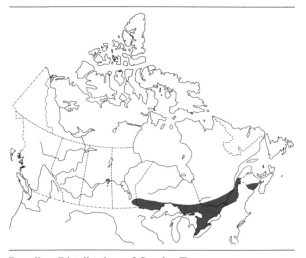

Breeding Distribution of Scarlet Tanager

Range in Canada. Summer resident, breeding in southeastern Manitoba (Whitemouth, Indian Bay; summer records for Turtle Mountain Provincial Park); southern Ontario (Sioux Lookout, Thunder Bay, Mildred southward); southwestern Quebec (Lake Témiscamingue, Rivière-du-Loup, Old-Chelsea, Montréal, Hatley; recorded but not breeding at Lake Saint-Jean and Forillon National Park); and New Brunswick (sparingly: Fredericton; near Saint John). Various sight records in southeastern Saskatchewan and an observation of one of a pair carrying food near Nipawin suggest possible breeding there.

Casual in Nova Scotia (Wolfville, Pictou, Seal Island, Westport, Yarmouth, Halifax); Newfoundland (Ferryland, Colinet Island in Placentia Bay, Funk Island, St. John's); and Prince Edward Island (sight records). Accidental in British Columbia (specimen: Comox, 14 November 1926); Alberta (specimen: Calgary, November 2, 1964; sight record: 2 May 1981); and northern Ontario (specimen: North Point, 14 August 1977).

Bill shape similar to that of Western Tanager. *Adult male (breeding plumage)*: Bright scarlet with all-black wings and tail. *Adult male (autumn and winter)*: Yellowish olive-green except black wings and tail. *Immature male (first spring)*: Similar to adult male in breeding plumage but red usually duller, the primaries and secondaries brownish instead of black. *Adult female*: Upper parts olive greenish; wings and tail dark greyish-brown (not black), edged with olive green; under parts dull pale-yellow, becoming brighter on under tail coverts. *Young (first autumn)*: Similar to adult female, but young males have some of the wing coverts and scapulars black.

Measurements. *Adult male*: wing, 91–97.9 (95.0); tail, 62.7–70 (67.1); exposed culmen, 13.3–16.1 (14.8); tarsus, 18.5–20.1 (19.2). *Adult female*: wing, 88.8–96 (91.3) mm.

Field Marks. The male in breeding plumage, a scarlet bird with *black* wings and *tail*, is not likely to cause any recognition difficulty. The male Summer Tanager has the reds duller and no black on wings or tail. Scarlet Tanager lacks *prominent* wing bars shown by Western Tanager and orioles, although some Scarlet Tanagers show narrow whitish or yellowish wing bars, which may cause difficulties. Female is more greenish, less yellowish below than female Summer Tanager. *Voice*: Song resembles that of the American Robin but with a hoarse quality that readily identifies it. Common call-note is a raspy *chip-kurr*.

Habitat. Prefers mature deciduous woodland but often frequents mixedwoods and pine woods.

Nesting. Well out on a horizontal branch of a tree, 3 to 15 m up. Nest is a rather shallow and loosely built structure of twigs, rootlets, and grasses with a lining of grasses and rootlets. *Eggs*, 3 to 5, usually 4; bluish or greenish, spotted or speckled with browns. Incubation period 13 to 14 days, by the female (L.S. Kohler).

Range. Breeds from southeastern Manitoba east to New Brunswick and south to eastern Oklahoma, central Alabama, and northern Georgia. Winters in South America from Colombia to Bolivia.

Western Tanager

Tangara à tête rouge
Piranga ludoviciana (Wilson)
Total length: 17.5 to 19.5 cm
Plate 66

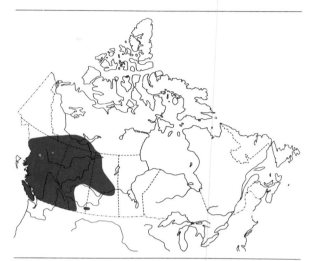

Breeding Distribution of Western Tanager

Range in Canada. Summer resident, breeding in northern, central, and southern British Columbia (upper Stikine River, Peace River District, and southward including Vancouver Island but not Queen Charlotte Islands); southern Mackenzie (Fort Liard, Fort Smith; perhaps Fort Simpson where several times recorded in summer); Alberta (northern parts south to about the North Saskatchewan River and in the mountains to Waterton Lakes; sparsely in the Cypress Hills); and central Saskatchewan, (Lake Athabasca, Kazan Lake, Big River, Nipawin; locally: Cypress Hills).

Recorded in summer in southern Yukon (Kluane; Rancheria River; between Morley River and Teslin).

Accidental in Ontario (photo records: Cooksville, Port Hope; several sight records elsewhere); southern Quebec (specimen: Kamouraska, 10 June 1938; also sight records); and Nova Scotia (specimen: Digby, 20 November 1957; also a sight record). Sight records for southwestern Manitoba.

Bill stout but somewhat elongated, shorter than head, its ridge down-curved; upper mandible slightly toothed near middle of cutting edge. *Adult male (breeding plumage)*: Head red, palest on throat; rest of under parts, neck, rump, and upper tail coverts yellow; back, wings, and tail mostly black; two pale-yellow wing bars. *Adult male (autumn)*: Similar, but head mostly greenish olive with some red on forehead and chin. *Immature male (first spring)*: Similar to adult male in spring but duller, the flight feathers more brownish. *Adult female*: Crown, cheeks, hind-neck, rump, and upper tail coverts greenish olive; back olive grey; wings and tail greyish brown; two whitish or pale-yellow wing bars; under parts yellow. *Young in first autumn*: Similar to adult female but males have yellow of under parts brighter, the females duller.

Measurements. *Adult male*: wing, 91–97.9 (94.8); tail, 67–75.5 (70.0); exposed culmen, 13.9–16 (14.9); tarsus, 19–21.4 (20.1). *Adult female*: wing, 88.3–94.9 (92.3) mm.

Field Marks. The only Canadian tanager with *well marked* yellow or whitish wing bars. Caution: some Scarlet Tanagers show a narrow, usually poorly defined whitish wing bar (see Scarlet Tanager), and may be mistaken for Western Tanagers! Females somewhat resemble female orioles but have stouter, less sharply pointed bills; greener, less orange plumage; and the tanager is usually decidedly more sluggish. *Voice*: Song somewhat suggests that of an American Robin but is so much hoarser and lower that it is easily recognizable. It is very similar to the Scarlet Tanager's song. Common call-note, a querulous *purty*.

Habitat. Open coniferous and mixed woodland.

Nesting. In a branch of a coniferous (less often deciduous) tree at various heights. Nest is rather loosely constructed of twigs, rootlets, and grasses and is lined with hair and fine rootlets. *Eggs*, usually 3 to 5; pale blue, speckled and spotted with browns over most of their surface. Incubation, by the female, is of 13 days' duration (I.G. Wheelock).

Range. Breeds from southern Alaska, northern British Columbia, central-southern Mackenzie, northeastern Alberta, and central Saskatchewan south to northern Baja California, northern Sonora, southwestern New Mexico, and western Texas. Winters from Baja California and central Mexico through Guatemala and El Salvador to Costa Rica.

Subfamily **Cardinalinae:**
Cardinals, Grosbeaks, and Allies

A relatively small group of medium to small-sized New World species. They are characterized by sexual dimorphism and many are colourful with reds, yellows, or blues prominent in their plumage. The Painted Bunting, Rose-breasted Grosbeak, and Northern Cardinal are examples of colourful representatives.

Northern Cardinal

Cardinal rouge
Cardinalis cardinalis (Linnaeus)
Total length: 19 to 23.5 cm
Plate 68

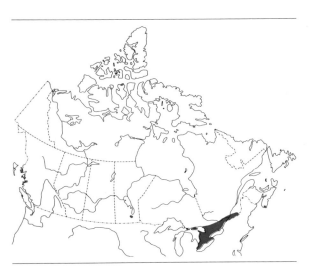

Breeding Distribution of Northern Cardinal

Range in Canada. Breeds and resides throughout the year in southern Ontario (north to Manitoulin Island, Ottawa); southwestern Quebec (Hull, Hudson, Montréal region, Sherbrooke); rarely Nova Scotia (very recently and locally: Pubnico, Yarmouth); and southern Manitoba (rarely and irregularly: Winnipeg). Has greatly expanded its breeding range in Canada. First known nesting in Canada was at Point Pelee, Ontario, in 1901.

Wanders occasionally north of its breeding range in Ontario (Thunder Bay, New Liskeard); Quebec (Québec, Madeleine Islands, Chicoutimi). Rare visitant to Saskatchewan (specimen: Craven, 29 December 1960; also sight records northwest to Saskatoon) and New Brunswick (photo record: Fredericton; various sight records). Sight record for Newfoundland (Sally's Cove).

Head crested; bill heavy and grosbeak-like; wings short, rounded; tail rather long. *Adult male*: Mainly vermilion red, the back and rump darkest and with greyish feather edges; bib and narrow area around base of bill black; bill red or orange-red. *Adult female*: Wings and tail dull red, the feathers broadly edged with greyish olive; crest also dull red, tipped and mixed with greyish olive; rest of upper parts greyish olive; under parts tawny or buffy, the breast often with a little red; bill reddish or pinkish.

    Measurements *(C. c. cardinalis). Adult male*: wing, 91–98.2 (94.1); tail, 96–108.7 (102.2); total culmen, 18.3–20 (19.2); tarsus, 23.9–26 (24.6). *Adult female*: wing, 88.1–96 (90.9) mm.

    Field Marks. A Catbird-sized bird with prominent crest and heavy reddish bill, the male red with black on throat and near base of bill; the female brownish with dull-red wings, tail, crest, and bill. *Voice*: Various clear whistled notes, often *hurry, hurry, hurry*. Call-note a thin *tsip*, rather weak for the size of the bird.

    Habitat. Deciduous or coniferous thickets, bushy tangles, and hedges on woodland edges, borders of old fields, clearings, streamside shrubbery, and bushy areas about dwellings.

    Nesting. In tall shrubbery or small trees, usually 1.5 to 2.4 m up; very rarely on a building. Nest is loosely constructed of twigs, shredded bark, weed stems, rootlets, and grasses and is lined with grasses, rootlets, or hair. *Eggs*, 3 or 4; white to greyish or greenish white and variously spotted and blotched with browns. Incubation about 12 to 13 days, by the female (Amelia Laskey).

    Range. Permanent resident from southeastern South Dakota east through extreme southern Ontario and Nova Scotia, south to the Gulf of Mexico coast and southern Florida; and from southeastern California, central Arizona, southern New Mexico, and northern Texas south to southern Mexico and British Honduras.

    Subspecies. *Cardinalis cardinalis cardinalis* (Linnaeus).

Rose-breasted Grosbeak

Cardinal à poitrine rose
Pheucticus ludovicianus (Linnaeus)
Total length: 17.5 to 21.5 cm
Plate 68

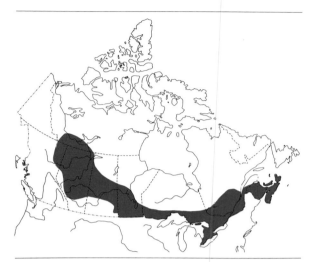

Breeding Distribution of Rose-breasted Grosbeak

Range in Canada. Summer resident, breeding in northeastern British Columbia (Tupper Creek, Fort Nelson; rarely near Kamloops: in 1977 a pair nested but photos do not eliminate the possibility that the female may have been *P. melanocephalus*); southwestern and central-southern Mackenzie (Fort Simpson, Buffalo River, perhaps Nahanni National Park); northern, central, and southeast-central Alberta (south, east of the mountains, to Rocky Mountain House and Red Deer); central and southeastern Saskatchewan (Kazan Lake, Churchill River, Yorkton, Qu'Appelle valley, Moose Mountain); southern Manitoba (The Pas, Lake St. Martin, Turtle Mountain Provincial Park, Lyleton, St. Vital); western Ontario (Malachi, Sioux Lookout, Thunder Bay); southern Ontario (New Liskeard, Washagami, Lake Nipissing southward; recorded in summer north to Lake Nipigon and Lake Abitibi but without evidence of breeding); southwestern Quebec (southern La Vérendrye Park, Lake Saint-Jean, Lake Trois Saumons, Cabano, and probably Matapedia valley southward); New Brunswick (Saint-Léonard, McAdam, Waterford); Prince Edward Island; and Nova Scotia (but scarce on Cape Breton Island).

Casual in southwestern Alberta (Banff); south-central Quebec (Moisie River, Anticosti Island, Grande-Grève); northern Ontario (Winisk); and Newfoundland (Doyles, Tompkins, St. John's). Sight record for southwestern British Columbia (Victoria) and northern Manitoba (Churchill).

Bill heavy and large, the ridge of upper mandible curved. *Adult male (breeding plumage)*: Head, neck, throat, most of back, and most of wings black; middle wing coverts, tips of secondaries and tertials, and base of primaries white; tail feathers black, the outer three on each side with large white areas on inner webs; wing linings, breast, and narrow extension down centre of breast carmine red; rest of under parts white. *Adult male (autumn and winter)*: Wings and tail similar to adult male in breeding plumage: head, neck, back, and scapulars brown streaked with black; stripe down middle of crown, another over eye, and one on cheek buffy white; under parts, including throat, mostly whitish, the breast with traces of red and washed with buffy; breast and sides streaked with dusky; wing linings reddish. *Immature male (first breeding plumage)*: Similar to adult male in breeding plumage but flight feathers brown instead of black, and red of breast usually paler. *Young male (first autumn)*: Similar to adult male in winter but wings and tail greyish brown, wings with two white or buffy bars and with no (or very little) white in tail; on breast a flush of pink, which is veiled by buff; wing linings pink. *Adult female*: Similar to young male in first autumn but no pink on breast; wing linings yellow; wing bars always white. (Note: In all above plumages, males have pink wing linings, females yellow.)

Measurements. *Adult male*: wing, 99–109.8 (104.4); tail, 70.1–78.5 (74.6); exposed culmen, 15.4–18.2 (16.9); tarsus, 22–24 (22.5). *Adult female*: wing, 99.1–105 (102.5) mm.

Field Marks. The contrasting black and white, the flashing white-spotted wings, and the red breast patch of the adult male in breeding plumage are easily recognized. Females and young look a little like the female Purple Finch but are obviously much larger. In the West, the female is easily confused with that of the Black-headed Grosbeak but is more whitish underneath (less brownish), and the breast is more heavily streaked. *Immature males* have reddish wing linings (which are diagnostic when they can be discerned); the Black-headed always has yellow ones. *Voice*: Song suggests that of the American Robin, but it is more energetic and richer and is more rapidly delivered. Although its song is also similar to that of the Scarlet Tanager, it is much more energetic and completely lacks the characteristic harshness of the Tanager's song. Alarm note, a high-pitched *tick*. The voice distinguishes it from all but the Black-headed Grosbeak.

Habitat. Deciduous and mixed woodlands, ideally where larger trees grow not too far from tall shrubbery, such as along streams, lakes, ponds, and marsh edges; often second growths.

Nesting. In tall shrubbery or a tree, usually 1.5 to 4.5 m above ground. Nest is a fragile flattish structure, loosely made of twigs, strips of bark, rootlets, fine grasses, and sometimes conifer needles. *Eggs*, 3 to 5; variable, pale greenish, bluish, or greyish, spotted and blotched with reddish brown, dark brown, and purplish. Incubation 12 to 13 days (H.R. Ivor), by both sexes.

Range. Breeds from northeastern British Columbia eastward across southern Canada to Nova Scotia and south to south-central Alberta, northern North Dakota, eastern Kansas, southwestern Missouri, eastern Tennessee, northern Georgia, western North Carolina, and central New Jersey. Winters from southeastern and southern Mexico south through Central America to Ecuador, Colombia, and Venezuela.

Black-headed Grosbeak

Cardinal à tête noire
Pheucticus melanocephalus (Swainson)
Total length: 17.5 to 21.5 cm
Plate 68

Breeding Distribution of Black-headed Grosbeak

Range in Canada. Summer resident, breeding in southern British Columbia (Hagensborg, Horseshoe Lake, lower Quinsam Lake, Victoria, Chilliwack, Grand Forks, Newgate. Species recorded in migration at Lower Arrow Lake and Shuswap Falls); southern Alberta (Taber, Medicine Hat, Waterton Lakes National Park; occurred formerly north to High River); and southern Saskatchewan (Maple Creek and apparently rarely and locally at Last Mountain Lake).

Wanders occasionally elsewhere in Saskatchewan (Lake Johnstone, Regina, Estevan, and near Armley). Casual in southern Manitoba (near Delta; Treesbank, Winnipeg, and near Pierson).

Casual in Ontario (photo: Dundas, 22 December 1973; sight record near Kenora) and Nova Scotia (photo: Barrington Passage, November 1973).

Bill shaped as in Rose-breasted Grosbeak. *Adult male (breeding plumage)*: Head, neck, chin, back, wings, and tail, mostly black; band across back of neck, rump, streaks on back (and often stripe behind eye and median crown stripe) cinnamon brown; wings with two white bars, base of primaries white, forming a white patch; large white patch on outermost three tail feathers; under parts cinnamon brown, becoming yellow in middle of belly and on under wing coverts; lower mid-abdomen whitish. *Adult male (autumn and winter)*: Similar to above but upper parts more cinnamon or buffy. *Adult female*: Upper parts dark brown streaked with buffy or white, especially the middle of crown and on back; wings and tail greyish brown, the white areas on wings much restricted, those on tail absent or nearly so; wing linings yellow as in male; stripe over eye, chin, and sides of throat whitish; breast mostly cinnamon-buff; abdomen pale yellow or white; sides and flanks streaked with dusky but streaks sparse or absent on breast (decidedly fewer than on breast of Rose-breasted Grosbeak). *Young (first autumn)*: Similar to adult female but under parts paler, with little or no yellow; upper parts more spotted, head stripes more whitish, better defined; wing lining yellow in both sexes. *Immature male (first breeding plumage)*: Similar to adult male in breeding plumage but duller and with brown (instead of black) flight feathers. (Note: Female Rose-breasted Grosbeaks have saffron yellow wing linings, while those of the Black-headed Grosbeak are paler (lemon yellow).)

Measurements *(P. m. maculatus)*. *Adult male*: wing, 97.4–103.5 (99.4); tail, 73.5–82.1 (77.8); exposed culmen, 15.4–17 (16.4); tarsus, 22–23.8 (23.1). *Adult female*: wing, 97–101 (99.0) mm.

Field Marks. Adult male with black head, white-patched black wings, cinnamon breast, sides, and rump, and heavy bill, is easily recognized. Female is extremely similar to female Rose-breasted Grosbeak, but the Black-head's more buffy (less whitish) and almost unstreaked breast is a help. *Voice*: Similar to that of Rose-breasted Grosbeak.

Habitat. More open woodlands (deciduous or mixedwood), especially where there is an admixture of tall shrubbery as along streams, ponds, and lake edges, woodland openings and margins; open second growths and bushy places.

Nesting. In tall bushes or in trees (usually deciduous) often near water, 1.2 to 6 m above ground. Nest is loosely constructed of twigs, weed stems, rootlets, and grass. Sometimes it is very flimsily made. *Eggs*, 2 to 5, usually 3 or 4; pale greenish or bluish, spotted and blotched with browns. Incubation 12 days (H.G. Weston, Jr.), by both sexes. As is true with the Rose-breasted Grosbeak, the male sometimes sings while incubating the eggs.

Range. Breeds from southern British Columbia, southern Alberta, and central Nebraska south to southern Mexico. Winters in Mexico.

Subspecies. (1) *Pheucticus melanocephalus maculatus* (Audubon): coastal southwestern British Columbia (Victoria, Chilliwack). (2) *P. m. melanocephalus* (Swainson), which averages slightly larger in size: interior southern British Columbia, southern Alberta, southwestern Saskatchewan.

Blue Grosbeak

Passerin bleu
Guiraca caerulea (Linnaeus)
Total length: 16.5 to 19 cm
Plate 68

Status in Canada. Occasional visitant to southern Ontario (Long Point; also various sight records: Chatham, Bowmanville, Toronto, Cliff Lake, North Bay); New Brunswick (Grand Manan); and Nova Scotia (Sable River, Halifax; also various sight records especially in spring 1961, when observed at West Middle Sable, Waverley, Princess Lodge, Lydgate). Sight records only for Quebec (Saint-Paul-du-Nord, Port-au-Saumon, Laurentides), and Saskatchewan (near Saskatoon, 26 May 1974).

Bill heavy, conical. *Adult male*: Mainly rich purplish-blue; wings with two chestnut bars; under tail coverts more or less tipped white. *Adult female*: Upper parts olive brown, more or less tinged with tawny, the back and scapulars vaguely streaked; wings and tail dusky brown, the wings with brown edgings and two tawny bars, the tail edged with greyish blue; under parts brownish buff, palest on throat and abdomen; head, rump, and wing coverts with more or less bluish. *Young (first autumn)*: Resemble female.

    Measurements. *Adult male*: wing, 82–90 (86.4); tail, 63.5–67 (66.0); exposed culmen, 14.7–17.5 (16.3); tarsus, 19.8–20.8 (20.5). *Adult female*: wing, 78–84 (81.5) mm.

    Field Marks. Much larger size, heavier bill, and chestnut wing bars separate it from the male Indigo Bunting. It is much larger with relatively massive bill compared with female Indigo and Lazuli buntings.

    Range. Breeds from central California, central South Dakota, southern Ohio, and southeastern Pennsylvania south to the Gulf States and through Mexico and Central America to Costa Rica.

    Subspecies. *Guiraca caerulea caerulea* (Linnaeus).

Lazuli Bunting

Passerin azuré
Passerina amoena (Say)
Total length: 12.9 to 14.5 cm
Plate 68

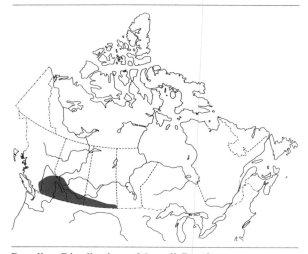

Breeding Distribution of Lazuli Bunting

Range in Canada. Breeds in southern British Columbia (Lillooet, Williams Lake Indian Reserve No. 1, Okanagan Landing, Elko; singing males reported north to near Chetwynd); southern Alberta (Jasper, Banff, and Waterton Lakes national parks, Gorge Creek and east locally to Castor, Beynon, and Brooks); and southern Saskatchewan (Shaunavon, Moose Jaw, Moose Mountain, Qu'Appelle valley, probably Estevan, perhaps rarely Regina where a pair summered). Hybridizes with *P. cyanea* in southwestern Saskatchewan.

    Scarce visitor to coastal British Columbia (Vancouver Island) and Manitoba (Treesbank, Pinawa, Winnipeg, Cranberry Portage). Accidental in southern Mackenzie (Fort Providence, 4 July 1903) and Ontario (photo: Pickle Lake, 10 May 1979; sight record: Point Pelee, 23 May 1983).

    The possibility that this bird may be conspecific with *P. cyanea* requires more investigation.

Adult male: Head, neck, throat, and rump light cerulean blue; back and scapulars darker blue; wings and tail blackish edged with bluish; two white wing bars; breast cinnamon, this colour extending to sides; abdomen and under tail coverts white. *Adult female*: Upper parts greyish brown, the rump greyish blue; back often indistinctly streaked with dusky; wings and tail, dusky edged with greenish blue; two dull-buffy or whitish wing bars; throat, breast, and sides buffy (breast darkest); abdomen and under tail coverts dingy white. *Young (first autumn)*: Similar to adult female but without bluish tinge on rump and usually with fine dusky streaks on breast. *Immature male (first breeding plumage)*: Like adult male but blue of upper parts is usually mixed with brown.

    Measurements. *Adult male*: wing, 70.5–74 (72.2); tail, 52.9–57.9 (56.2); exposed culmen, 9–10 (9.7); tarsus, 15.9–17.9 (16.9). *Adult female*: wing, 66.2–72.4 (68.7) mm.

    Field Marks. About the size of a Chipping or Clay-colored Sparrow. The adult male, with bright-blue upper parts and throat, cinnamon breast, and two white wing bars, is easily recognized. The female is a small plain-brownish sparrow with a ruddy breast and a suggestion of blue on wings, rump, and tail edging; it has somewhat more definite wing bars than the female Indigo Bunting. Bluebirds are coloured somewhat similar to Lazuli Bunting, but the bunting's stubby bill is entirely different from the slender bluebird bill. *Voice*: Song, which is variable but quite loud and strident, is a little suggestive of the Indigo Bunting's. It is made up of two to four groups of notes in different pitches, e.g., *swip swip swip, zu zu ee, see see, sip see see*. Call-note *tsip*.

    Habitat. Bushy country, burntlands, and clearings.

    Nesting. In a bush or coarse weed. Nest is a cup constructed of grass, plant fibres, and weed stems and is lined with fine grass and hair. *Eggs*, 3 or 4; bluish white (occasionally with small dark spots). Incubation period 12 days (F.L. Burns).

    Range. Breeds from southern British Columbia east to southern Saskatchewan and northeastern South Dakota, south to northwestern Baja California, southern Nevada, central Arizona, and western Oklahoma. Winters from southern Baja California and southern Arizona south to south-central Mexico.

Indigo Bunting

Passerin indigo
Passerina cyanea (Linnaeus)
Total length: 13.4 to 14.5 cm
Plate 68

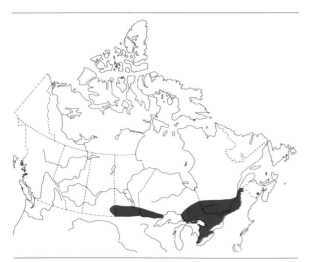

Breeding Distribution of Indigo Bunting

Range in Canada. Summer resident, breeding in southeastern Saskatchewan (Moose Mountain and Qu'Appelle valley where it hybridizes with *P. amoena*, probably Estevan); southern Manitoba (Turtle Mountain National Park, Portage la Prairie, Grand Beach; Hillside Beach); central and southern Ontario (Kenora, Thunder Bay, Cochrane southward); southwestern Quebec (southern La Vérendrye Park, Québec, Cabano, Gatineau Park, Montréal, Hatley; recorded in summer at Lake Saint-Jean); and New Brunswick (rarely: Woodmans Point, Cambridge Narrows, Hampton, probably also at St. Stephen and Petitcodiac).

Casual in British Columbia (summer sight records: South Slocan, Agassiz, Vancouver, Spences Bridge, Shuswap Lake, Trail); Alberta (Lac la Nonne, Turner Valley, Elkwater Lake); Nova Scotia (numerous records mostly for southern peninsula, mainly April and May, one in June; recorded also from Sable Island); and Newfoundland (South Island, La Poile, Calvert, Portugal Cove).

Sight records for Prince Edward Island (Marshfield).

Bill conical, its ridge convex. *Adult male (breeding plumage)*: Blue all over, the head more purplish; wings and tail dusky edged with blue. No wing bars. *Adult male (winter plumage)*: Somewhat like adult female, the blue colour concealed by brown feather edges but showing on primaries, tail, rump, and wing coverts. *Adult female*: Upper parts olive brownish, the back sometimes lightly streaked, the rump sometimes with a greenish-grey tinge; wings and tail dusky, narrowly edged with greenish; greater wing coverts and tertials edged with cinnamon-buff; under parts dull buffy-whitish with some olive-buff on breast and sides, the breast faintly streaked with dusky greyish-brown. Some individuals have a few blue feathers in the plumage. *Young in first autumn*: Resemble adult female. *Immature male (first breeding plumage)*: Similar to adult male in breeding plumage but blues lighter, less pure; wing coverts with some brown.

Measurements. *Adult male*: wing, 66.7–69.5 (68.0); tail, 50.9–53.6 (52.1); exposed culmen, 9.9–11.5 (10.6); tarsus, 16.9–18.3 (17.5). *Adult female*: wing, 62.7–66.5 (63.7) mm.

Field Marks. Adult male obviously smaller, with much less robust bill, than the rare Blue Grosbeak, lacks the Grosbeak's chestnut wing bars. Female is a brown finch, characterized by its lack of stripes, or well-marked wing bars. Upper mandible is seen to be decidedly convex at close range. It resembles female Lazuli Bunting of the West but has less obvious wing bars. *Voice*: Song, a bit goldfinch-like but much more leisurely, the notes well spaced: *zwee zwee zwee, zorry zorry, tsu tsu*, finishing *diminuendo*. Alarm note a sharp *chip*.

Habitat. Likes a combination of bushy ground cover for nesting, and trees for singing: deciduous woodland edges and openings, old clearings, second growths, abandoned farms and old pastures, shrubby roadsides, streamsides, lake edges. Sings commonly high in a tall tree.

Nesting. In a shrub or bush not far above the ground. Nest, a cup-shaped structure of twigs, weeds, grass, bark shreds, and often a few leaves; lined with fine grasses and often hair. *Eggs*, 3 or 4; bluish white. Incubation 12 days (F.L. Burns), mainly by the female.

Range. Breeds from South Dakota and southern Manitoba east to Maine and south to southwestern Oklahoma, southeastern Texas, the Gulf Coast of United States, and northern Florida. Winters mainly from central Mexico, Cuba, and the Bahamas south to central Panama.

Painted Bunting

Passerin nonpareil
Passerina ciris (Linnaeus)
Total length: 13 to 14 cm

Status in Canada. Accidental (some of the records were undoubtedly escapees as this bird is occasionally kept in captivity although this is illegal). Ontario (photo records: Port Huron, 2 May 1973; Long Point, 21 May 1978. Banding record: one netted and banded in Toronto, late autumn 1978. Sight record: Rideau Ferry, bird present in three-week period July to August 1966). Nova Scotia (sight record: Sable Island, 31 July 1965). New Brunswick (sight record: Seal Cove, 7 May 1983).

The colourful adult male, combining red under parts with a blue head, is unmistakable if clearly seen. The female's bright yellowish-green plumage is unlike that of other North American birds in its size range (see female tanagers).

Range. Southeastern United States.

Dickcissel

Dickcissel
Spiza americana (Gmelin)
Total length: 15 to 17.5 cm
Plate 68

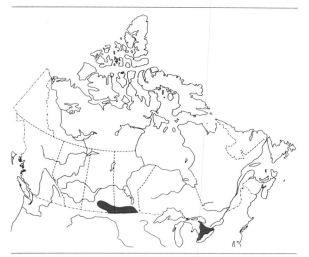

Breeding Distribution of Dickcissel

Range in Canada. Breeding is extremely sporadic in most of its Canadian breeding range. Breeds in southern Saskatchewan (formerly at least: Bred in Regina, and probably Lake Johnstone, in 1933 and 1934. No recent definite breeding records, but species was observed in Saskatoon on 4 July 1973); southern Manitoba (Whitewater Lake, Oak Lake, Winnipeg. In the early part of the 1973 nesting season, species was present from Lyleton east to Sprague in alfalfa fields mostly. Most nesting attempts were thwarted by harvesting of the alfalfa. See S.G. Sealy, 1976. Canadian Field-Naturalist, vol. 90, no. 4, pp. 464–466); southern Ontario (formerly at least: Point Pelee, Lake St. Clair, London. In 1972 nested at Melbourne).

Casual in southern British Columbia (Vaseux Lake, Victoria, Tofino); southern Alberta (Walsh, Brooks); eastern Ontario (Ottawa); southern Quebec (Moisie Bay, Johan-Beetz Bay, Anticosti Island, Montréal, Cape Gaspé); Prince Edward Island; Nova Scotia (Halifax, mouth of Bay of Fundy, Brier Island, Stewiake; also numerous sight records mostly in autumn); and Newfoundland (Terra Nova, Burgeo; sight record: St. Anthony). Several sight records for southern New Brunswick. Almost all of the many East Coast records are for autumn.

Middle tail feathers narrow and pointed. *Adult male*: Crown, hind-neck, and ear region grey; stripe over eye pale yellowish; back and scapulars greyish brown striped with black; rump paler than back, unstreaked; wing coverts chestnut; bend of wing yellow; no wing bars; lower throat with black bib (obscure or absent in autumn); upper throat white; breast bright yellow, often extending down middle of abdomen; rest of under parts white; bill bluish with dusky sides; legs greyish brown. *Adult female*: Somewhat similar to adult male but much duller; crown and ear patch grey; crown and rump narrowly streaked with dusky; stripe over eye whitish; chestnut on wing narrowly reduced or absent; throat white without black bib but margined on either side by a narrow dusky streak; breast tinged with yellow and narrowly streaked with dusky; flanks streaked somewhat with dusky; rest of under parts whitish. *Young in autumn*: Similar to adult female but much tinged with buffy, the male with rich chestnut wing coverts, yellowish eyebrow stripe.

Measurements. *Adult male*: wing, 79–84.8 (81.1); tail, 54.2–61 (58.9); exposed culmen, 13.2–15 (14.3); tarsus, 22.6–24.5 (23.3). *Adult female*: wing, 74.7–77.5 (75.7) mm.

Field Marks. The adult male in breeding plumage (black bib on yellow breast) might suggest a tiny meadowlark, but it is only half as large as a meadowlark and its stubby bill is entirely different. The female resembles a female House Sparrow but usually shows a trace of yellow on the breast and has a more distinct eyebrow stripe and paler general coloration. Female also resembles female Bobolink, but the general coloration is much greyer (less yellowish) and the Dickcissel has no pale median crown stripe or heavy line back from eye. *Voice*: song has good volume, a somewhat staccato *chup-chup-klip-klip-klip* or *dick, dick, dickcissel*.

Habitat. Open situations such as grassy, clover, alfalfa, weedy, and brushy fields, meadows, and prairies.

Nesting. On or near the ground, sometimes in shrubs or in a tree. Nest, a rather bulky cup made of grass, weed stalks, and leaves, lined with grass and rootlets. *Eggs*, 3 to 5; pale blue. Incubation 11 to 13 days, by the female.

Range. Breeds from eastern Montana, southern Saskatchewan, and southern Ontario south to central Colorado, central-southern Texas, southern Louisiana, and central Georgia; formerly, now sporadically, east to the Atlantic Coast and north to Massachusetts. Winters from south-central Mexico to Colombia, Venezuela, and the Guianas.

Remarks. This bird appears often as a stray on the southeastern coast of Canada, sometimes north to Newfoundland and the north shore of the Gulf of St. Lawrence. In one small clearing on lower Moisie River, Quebec, it was recorded during three successive autumns, 1950 to 1952.

Subfamily **Emberizinae:** Buntings and Sparrows

The New World "sparrows" and the Old World buntings (genus *Emberiza*) form the bulk of this large subfamily of smallish birds with cone-shaped bills, the cutting edge of the lower mandible abruptly angled downward near the base. The Snow Bunting and the Lapland Longspur are found regularly in northern parts of both hemispheres and form a connecting link. The subfamily's representation in species is far greater and more diversified in the Western Hemisphere and it probably originated here and spread later to the Old World.

Green-tailed Towhee

Tohi à queue verte
Pipilo chlorurus (Audubon)
Total length: 16.5 to 17.8 cm

Status in Canada. Casual or accidental in Saskatchewan (Tregarva, 6 June 1929, and Dollard, 18 May 1944, are supported by specimens; also sight record: Tregarva, 28 June 1935); Ontario (photo records: London, 30 March 1954; Terra Cotta, 24 November 1956. Sight records: Welland, Whitby); southern Quebec (Saint-Augustin west of Québec, 31 October 1957: specimen); and Nova Scotia (specimen: Cape Sable Island, 14 May 1955; photo records: Seal Island, 18 May 1974 and Sable Island, 10 June 1974).

Bill conical but not heavy; tail quite long (longer than wing), the outer feathers shortest. *Adult male*: Top of head reddish brown; rest of upper parts olive grey; wings and tail mostly yellowish olive-green; edge of wing near bend and the under wing coverts yellow; no wing bars; throat white, forming a large white patch, which is sharply defined against deep grey of breast and sides of head; abdomen white; sides and flanks brownish grey; spot between eye and base of bill (supraloral region) white. *Adult female*: Usually slightly duller than adult male.

Measurements. *Adult male*: wing, 76.4–83.3 (80.0); tail, 79.5–87.2 (83.8); exposed culmen, 12.2–12.9 (12.7); tarsus, 22.6–25.4 (24.1). *Adult female*: wing, 71.1–78.7 (75.9) mm (adapted from Ridgway).

Distinctions. A long-tailed greyish-green bird with large reddish-brown cap and large white throat patch sharply defined against the deep-grey breast and sides of head.

Range. Breeds from central Oregon, southwestern Montana, and Wyoming south through the mountains to southern California, central Arizona, and southern New Mexico.

Rufous-sided Towhee

(Eastern, Red-eyed, or Spotted Towhee)

Tohi à flancs roux
Pipilo erythrophthalmus (Linnaeus)
Total length: 19 to 22 cm
Plate 71

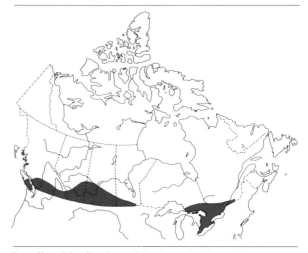

Breeding Distribution of Rufous-sided Towhee

Range in Canada. Breeds in southern British Columbia (Comox, Lillooet, Okanagan Landing, Elko); southern Alberta (Lethbridge, Calgary, Morrin, Rosebud; sporadically north to Coronation, Camrose, and Wainwright); southern Saskatchewan (Cypress Hills, Elbow, Carlton); southern Manitoba (Treesbank, Winnipeg); southern Ontario (north to Sudbury, North Bay, Ottawa); and extreme southwestern Quebec (Ormstown, Lucerne, Rigaud, Saint-Bruno, Mont Shefford).

Tail rather long (longer than wing); bill conical. Western populations have more white in wing coverts and back; females are much darker brown than in eastern populations. *Adult male (P. e. erythrophthalmus* of eastern Canada): Head, neck, upper parts, and upper breast black, the black of upper breast sharply cut off from the white lower breast and abdomen; sides and flanks chestnut, this extending to the under tail coverts, where paler; wings black with a small white patch, formed by the white basal parts of the outer webs of the outermost four or five primaries; tertials with some white outer edges; tail black with large mass of white on terminal part of several outer feathers on each side. Eye red. *Adult female*: Similar to adult male, but black is replaced by brown. *Young* (for a short time after leaving the nest) are streaked with dusky above and below.

Western races have the wing coverts, scapulars, and back spotted with white, but white is more restricted on the primaries; western females have the head, neck, and upper parts much darker than in the eastern nominate race (a very dark greyish-brown or greyish black instead of the more cinnamon brown of eastern birds).

Measurements *(P. e. erythrophthalmus)*. *Adult male*: wing, 82–90.5 (86.5); tail, 88–98.2 (93.4); exposed culmen, 12.5–14.2 (13.4); tarsus, 25.6–29 (27.7). *Adult female*: wing, 77.3–89.1 (81.9) mm.

Field Marks. Instantly recognizable. Catbird size with long tail and sparrow-type bill. Black (in male) or brown (in female) head and upper parts, strikingly reddish-brown sides, white abdomen sharply cut off from dark breast, large amount of white in the ends of the outer tail feathers. Western populations with more white in back and in wing coverts than eastern birds, and the western females have much darker brown (almost blackish) heads and upper parts. In the East the common call is *to-whee*, second syllable higher; song is two notes followed by a trill and is often thought to sound like *drink your teeéeea*. Voice of western populations is somewhat different but includes a whining nasal alarm note and a song that ends in a buzzy trill (often at a distance only the trill is audible).

Habitat. Bushy areas and thickets with an accumulation of leaf litter on the ground: brushy fields, willow-alder patches, woodland edges and openings. On the prairies, shrubbery along coulees and streams. In the mountains bushy shrubbery on mountainsides and valleys, and on the West Coast shrubbery tangles.

Nesting. On the ground or near it in a low bush. Nest is rather loosely made of weed stalks, strips of bark, twigs, and grasses and is

Scarce visitant in northern Ontario (Fort Severn); southeastern Quebec (Québec, Île aux Basques, and lower Moisie River); New Brunswick (Irishtown, Fredericton, Gannet Rock); Nova Scotia (Northport, Greenfield, Sable Island); Newfoundland (Corner Brook); and Prince Edward Island. Records in the Maritimes more numerous in recent years.

lined with fine grasses and rootlets. *Eggs*, 4 to 6; white, speckled with reddish brown and a little lavender. Incubation 12 to 13 days (C.E. Heil) by the female.

Range. Breeds from southern Canada (British Columbia east to southwestern Quebec), northern Vermont, central New Hampshire, and southwestern Maine south through Mexico to Guatemala, northern Oklahoma, central-southern Louisiana, the eastern Gulf Coast of the United States, and southern Florida. Winters north to southern British Columbia, extreme southern Ontario, and in small numbers, the Maritime Provinces.

Subspecies. (1) *Pipilo erythrophthalmus erythrophthalmus* (Linnaeus), described above: Manitoba, Ontario, Quebec. (2) *P. e. arcticus* (Swainson) (resembles *erythrophthalmus* but wing coverts, scapulars, and back spotted with white; females with head and upper parts blackish brown): Alberta, Saskatchewan. (3) *P. e. curtatus* Grinnell (similar to *arcticus* but blacks purer, less olivaceous): interior southern British Columbia (Lillooet, Elko). (4) *P. e. oregonus* Bell (similar to *curtatus* but coloration darker): coastal southwestern British Columbia (Comox, Chilliwack).

Bachman's Sparrow

Bruant des pinèdes
Aimophila aestivalis (Lichtenstein)
Total length: about 14.5 cm
Plate 72

Status in Canada. Casual in southern Ontario (specimens: Point Pelee, 16 April 1917; Long Point, 6 May 1928; photo record: Point Pelee, 14 May 1961; also sight records at Point Pelee).

Wing short, rounded; tail equal to or longer than wing; tail decidedly graduated, the outer feathers much the shortest, tail feathers rather narrow with rounded tips. *Adults*: Upper parts grey or buffy grey, heavily streaked with chestnut brown (becoming mostly greyish on the rump); sides of head buffy grey with thin dark line extending backward from the eye; bend of wing pale yellow; no white in wings or tail; breast, sides, and flanks buffy, the flanks sometimes streaked with brown; belly greyish white.

Measurements *(A. a. bachmani)*. *Adult male*: wing, 58.4–63.5 (61.2); tail, 60.9–66.5 (64.0); exposed culmen, 10.9–13.2 (12.2); tarsus, 18.3–20.3 (19.3). *Adult female*: wing, 57.9–60.4 (59.2) mm (adapted from Ridgway).

Field Marks. A brown-backed sparrow with buffy unstreaked breast. A little like the Field Sparrow but bill not pink.

Range. Breeds from southern Missouri, central Ohio, and central Maryland south to southeastern Texas, the Gulf Coast of United States, and central Florida.

Subspecies. *Aimophila aestivalis bachmani* (Audubon).

Cassin's Sparrow

Bruant de Cassin
Aimophila cassinii (Woodhouse)
Total length: about 14.5 cm
Figure 93

Figure 93
Cassin's Sparrow

Status in Canada. Accidental in Ontario (Point Pelee, 13 May 1967) and Nova Scotia (Seal Island, 18 to 20 May 1974). Both records are supported by identifiable photographs. Sight record of one at Marathon, Ontario, 28 September 1981.

Adults: Similar to Bachman's Sparrow but upper parts paler and greyer, the back more spotted or barred than streaked, the middle two tail feathers more or less barred, the flanks more heavily streaked.

Measurements. *Adult male*: wing, 59.6–67.3 (64.2); tail, 60.9–71.6 (67.0); exposed culmen, 10.2–11.7 (10.9). *Adult female*: wing, 60.9–64.2 (62.7); tail, 63.5–69.8 (66.2); exposed culmen, 10.2–11.9 (10.9) mm.

Range. Breeds from central Colorado, western Kansas, western Oklahoma, and central and western Texas south to northern Mexico. Winters in southeastern Arizona, south-central Texas, and Mexico.

American Tree Sparrow

Bruant hudsonien
Spizella arborea (Wilson)
Total length: 14.5 to 16.4 cm
Plate 72

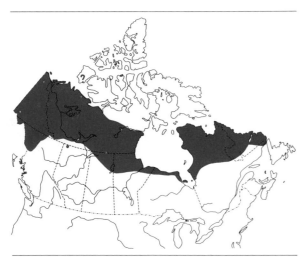

Breeding Distribution of American Tree Sparrow

Range in Canada. Breeds from northern Yukon (Herschel Island, Firth River); northern Mackenzie (Mackenzie Delta, lower Anderson River, Coppermine, Bathurst Inlet, Thelon River); central-interior Keewatin (Beverly Lake); northern Manitoba (Churchill); northern Ontario (Fort Severn, Little Cape, Cape Henrietta Maria); southern James Bay (Paint Hills Islands, South Twin Island); northern Quebec (Povungnituk River, Deception Bay, Feuilles River, Kuujjuaq, Koroc River, Alluviaq Fiord); Labrador (Saglek Bay, Battle Harbour); south to northwestern British Columbia (Dease Lake); southeastern Yukon (Sheldon Lake); central-western and southern Mackenzie (Nahanni National Park, Little Dal Lake, Fort Franklin, Hill Island Lake); extreme northwestern Alberta (Cameron Hills); northern Saskatchewan (Reindeer Lake, perhaps Fond-du-Lac); northern Manitoba (Herchmer, Cape Tatnam); northern Ontario; central Quebec (Bienville Lake, Schefferville, Brador). Possibly breeds on Banks Island, N.W.T. (May and June records at De Salis Bay, Cape Kellett, Sachs Harbour). Casual visitant to Victoria Island, N.W.T. (specimen: Cambridge Bay, 5 June 1962).

Winters in southern British Columbia, southern Alberta (in small numbers north to Camrose), southwestern Saskatchewan (Cypress Hills region), southern Ontario (North Bay, Ottawa southward), southwestern Quebec (Aylmer, Montréal, rarely north to Québec), New Brunswick, Prince Edward Island, and Nova Scotia.

Transient in Newfoundland.

Adults: Top of head, streak extending back from eye to small ear patch, and (usually) small streak across jaw, chestnut; rest of head and neck grey, hind-neck tinged with rusty; rest of under parts greyish white, unstreaked but with a dusky spot in centre of breast, a small chestnut patch on each side of breast, sides buffy brown; back and scapulars streaked with black, buffy, and brown; rump plain brown; wings with two conspicuous white bars; tail plain dusky with outer edge of outermost feather greyish white; upper mandible and tip of lower mandible dusky, rest of lower mandible yellow; legs pale brownish; feet blackish. *Juvenal plumage* (worn for a short time after leaving nest): Top of head brown with dusky streaks; breast and sides buffy with dusky streaks; otherwise similar to adults.

Measurements *(S. a. arborea). Adult male*: wing, 72.1–76.8 (74.8); tail, 63.4–69 (66.7); exposed culmen, 9.5–11 (10.4); tarsus, 19.6–21.6 (20.7). *Adult female*: wing, 69.1–72.1 (70.4) mm.

Field Marks. In settled parts, a winter visitor or spring and autumn migrant. Has red cap, single dusky spot in middle of unstreaked breast, two white wing bars, and usually a little yellow on the lower mandible. The similar Field Sparrow differs in its pink bill and lack of breast spot. The Chipping Sparrow has a black line through the eye and no breast spot. The Swamp Sparrow is darker and duller above and lacks conspicuous white wing bars (but sometimes has a small dusky breast spot). *Voice*: The spritely but modest song begins with two or more higher notes and ends in a warble. When feeding, a musical *teelit* or *teelwit*. Call-note *tseet*, different enough from the *chips* of other birds to be recognizable.

Habitat. In nesting season, open woody shrubbery such as willow, dwarf birch, and alder, sometimes scrub conifers along streams, in bogs, and above timberline in the western mountains, and on some of the low-arctic tundra. Also in winter and migration, weedy fields, gardens, and similar open places that provide weed seeds.

Nesting. On the ground or more rarely in a low shrub or tree, rarely up to 1.5 m above ground, and usually under a woody shrub. Nest is a cup made externally of heavy grass and weed stalks, rootlets, bits of moss, lichen, or bark, and lined with feathers, hairs, sometimes sporophytes of moss. *Eggs*, 4 to 6, usually 5; pale bluish to pale greenish, speckled with browns. Incubation 12 to 13 days, by the female (A.M. Baumgartner).

Range. Breeds in Alaska and across central Canada (Yukon east to Labrador). Winters from southern Canada south to northern California, central Arizona, central Texas, Arkansas, Tennessee, and North Carolina.

Subspecies. (1) *Spizella arborea arborea* (Wilson): Breeds from eastern Mackenzie (Coppermine), Keewatin, and northern Saskatchewan, east to Labrador and eastern Quebec. (2) *S. a. ochracea* Brewster (coloration paler, size slightly larger than in *arborea*): Breeds in Yukon, northwestern British Columbia and northwestern Mackenzie (Mackenzie Delta, Anderson River, Fort Franklin).

Remarks. In the autumn, when the Tree Sparrows come down to southern Canada, we know that winter is near. In loose flocks they rustle about in the half-bare shrubbery, and their call-notes possess an icy tinkle. The Tree Sparrow is valuable as a destroyer of weed seeds.

Chipping Sparrow

Bruant familier
Spizella passerina (Bechstein)
Total length: 12.5 to 14.5 cm
Plate 72

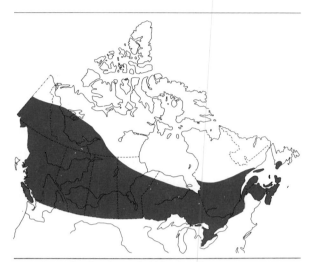

Breeding Distribution of Chipping Sparrow

Range in Canada. Breeds from central Yukon (Dawson); central Mackenzie (Fort Good Hope, Reliance, Dickson Canyon reportedly north to km 510–590 Dempster Highway); northern Alberta; northern Saskatchewan (Lake Athabasca, Reindeer Lake); northeastern Manitoba (Bird, Ilford); central Ontario (Big Trout Lake, Fort Albany); southern Quebec (Fort-George, Baie-du-Poste, Sept-Îles, Mingan, Anticosti Island; recorded in summer at Natashquan); and southwestern Newfoundland (Codroy valley) south throughout extreme southern Canada: southern British Columbia (but not on Queen Charlotte Islands); Alberta; Saskatchewan (local in south); Manitoba; Ontario; southwestern Quebec (also Madeleine Islands); New Brunswick; Prince Edward Island; and Nova Scotia (including Cape Breton Island).

Casual at Churchill, Manitoba, and northern Newfoundland (St. Anthony).

Occasional in winter in Nova Scotia (Gaspereau, Wolfville, Port Mouton) and southern Ontario (Toronto).

Adult male: Crown chestnut, forehead grey and black; back and scapulars light brown streaked with black; rump grey; broad stripe over eye, also chin and throat whitish; through eye a narrow black stripe; rest of sides of head and remainder of under parts plain grey; wings with two inconspicuous whitish bars; tail dusky with no white patches; bill blackish in spring but with base of lower mandible paler, in autumn lower mandible mostly flesh colour; legs pale brown or flesh. *Adult female*: Similar to adult male but often duller and frequently with the crown more or less streaked with black. *Adults in autumn*: Colours duller, less contrasting, chestnut of crown usually partly hidden by buffy feather tips. *Young in first autumn*: Resemble adults but much duller, the top of head brown streaked with black; line over eye as well as wing bars buffy; breast and sides of head strongly tinged buffy; bill dark brown above, flesh colour below. *Juvenal*: Similar above to autumn young but breast and sides with dusky streaks.

Measurements *(S. p. passerina)*. *Adult male*: wing, 66.6–72.5 (70.1); tail, 55.6–60.2 (58.5); exposed culmen, 9–9.9 (9.4); tarsus, 16–17.8 (16.7). *Adult female*: wing, 66.2–70.5 (67.5) mm.

Field Marks. Spring and summer adults, with plain-grey breast, red cap, black streak through eye and a broad white stripe over it, are not likely to be mistaken. Autumn birds, however, are very similar to autumn Clay-colored Sparrows. The cheek patch of the Clay-colored usually shows a dark margin, which the Chipping Sparrow lacks. Under good conditions, the grey rump of the Chipping Sparrow distinguishes it from the Clay-colored (which has a buffy-brown rump) (see also Brewer's Sparrow). *Voice*: Song a simple dry trill made up of a procession of rapidly uttered *chips*. A single *chip*.

Habitat. Openings and edges of woodlands; scattered trees; thickets and trees bordering open grassy places; orchards, gardens, shrubbery, and lawns about dwellings.

Nesting. In a deciduous or coniferous tree, bush, or vine, usually 0.9 to 3 m up, but seldom up to 7.6 m, or rarely on the ground. Nest is a cup, composed externally of grass stems and often some weed stems, and is lined with hair, fur, or rootlets. *Eggs*, 3 to 5; blue, spotted with dark brown, blackish, reddish brown, sometimes some lavender, mostly around the large end; rarely immaculate. Incubation 11 to 13 days, by the female.

Range. Breeds from eastern Alaska and British Columbia east to Newfoundland and south to northern Baja California, Nicaragua, the United States Gulf Coast, and northern Florida. Winters from southwestern and central United States southward.

Subspecies. (1) *Spizella passerina passerina* (Bechstein): southern and eastern Ontario, southern Quebec, southwestern Newfoundland, New Brunswick, Prince Edward Island, Nova Scotia. (2) *S. p. boreophila* Oberholser (larger, more greyish than *passerina*): Yukon, Mackenzie, British Columbia, Alberta, Saskatchewan, Manitoba, western Ontario (west of the Great Lakes, perhaps east to the foot of James Bay).

Clay-colored Sparrow

Bruant des plaines
Spizella pallida (Swainson)
Total length: 12.5 to 14 cm
Plate 72

Breeding Distribution of Clay-colored Sparrow

Range in Canada. Breeds in interior British Columbia (Fort Nelson, Minaker River, Charlie Lake; sparsely farther west and farther south to Nulki Lake, Fifty-nine Mile House, Okanagan Landing); southern Mackenzie (Norman Wells, Yellowknife, Fort Resolution; recorded in summer at Fort Simpson and Nahanni National Park); northern, central, and southern Alberta; northwestern, central, and southern Saskatchewan (Lake Athabasca, Cumberland House southward; recorded in summer north to Stony Rapids and Hasbala Lake); central-western and southern Manitoba (The Pas, Hillside Beach southward); western Ontario (Kenora, Thunder Bay); southern Ontario (Sault Ste. Marie, Sudbury, Craigleith, Camp Borden, Ayr, Trafalgar, Ottawa, Kingston, rarely and recently north to Moosonee and North Point); and southwestern Quebec (sparsely and recently: La Sarre, North-Hatley, probably Saint-Placide and Saint-Colomban).

Casual visitant to Nova Scotia (photo records: Seal Island, 18 May and 2 November 1975). Sight records for southern Yukon (near Dawson, Sheldon Lake, Teslin), northern Manitoba (Churchill), northern Ontario (Fort Severn), New Brunswick (Grand Manan, Fredericton), and Newfoundland (photo: one overwintered at a feeder in St. John's, 15 November 1983 to 25 April 1984).

Adults: Crown with buffy-grey median stripe, sides of crown brown streaked with black; hind-neck and sides of neck plain greyish; back and scapulars buffy brown streaked with black; rump brownish or greyish brown; tail brown, narrowly edged with grey; two faint whitish or pale-buffy wing bars; broad stripe over eye buffy white; ear patch buffy brown with narrow dark-brown border above and below; under parts whitish, somewhat tinged with pale-greyish buff on breast and sides; bill dusky above and at tip, otherwise flesh colour; legs brownish flesh. *Young (first autumn)*: Similar to adults but much more buffy; the crown not much darker than the back, its median stripe less distinct than in adults; breast strongly tinged buffy. *Juvenal*: Quite similar to young in autumn but breast and sides with dusky streaks.

Measurements. *Adult male*: wing, 58.1–62.8 (60.7); tail, 57–61.7 (58.9); exposed culmen, 8.6–10 (9.5); tarsus, 16.7–18.5 (17.6). *Adult female*: wing, 56.4–63.5 (59.4) mm.

Field Marks. A small sparrow with a plain breast, somewhat resembling a Chipping Sparrow, but adult Clay-color differs in having a plain-grey hind-neck and a more distinct brown ear patch bordered above and below by a narrow dark-brown line, and in lacking a definite black line through the eye. Autumn Chippies and Clay-colors both show a brown ear patch, but in the Chipping this patch is not bordered by a dark line above and below; also the Chipping has a grey rump (never brown), but the rump of the autumn Clay-colored is usually buffy brown (see also Brewer's Sparrow). *Voice*: Song is two to four insect-like buzzes and is readily recognizable. Also a weak *chip*.

Habitat. Woody shrub patches and thickets, such as willow, alder, wolfberry, and rose, along streams, edges of ponds, lakes, or swamps; tall shrubbery on meadows; areas where aspen groves are interspersed with woody shrubbery; brushy openings, edges, and burns of woodland (either deciduous or coniferous).

Nesting. Low, up to 2.1 m, in deciduous bushes or small conifers; occasionally on the ground. Nest is outwardly of grass and weed stems and is lined with fine grass and hair. *Eggs*, 3 to 5; greenish blue, spotted and speckled with various browns or black, mostly around the large end. Incubation period 11 to 11.5 days (L.H. Walkinshaw).

Range. Breeds from interior British Columbia east to southern Ontario and south to central Montana, southeastern Wyoming, southeastern Colorado, northern Texas (very locally), northern Iowa, southern Wisconsin, and central Michigan. Winters in southern Texas and Mexico.

Brewer's Sparrow

Bruant de Brewer
Spizella breweri Cassin
Total length: 12.5 to 13.7 cm
Plate 72

Breeding Distribution of Brewer's Sparrow

Range in Canada. Breeds in southwestern Yukon (Kluane region); interior British Columbia (Chilkat Pass, Atlin, Similkameen and Okanagan valleys, Midway, Elko); central-western and southern Alberta (Jasper, Banff, and Waterton Lakes national parks; Milk River, Cypress Hills region); and southwestern Saskatchewan (Cypress Hills region).

Has wandered farther east in Saskatchewan to Old Wives Lake (Lake Johnstone; sight records to Elbow and Regina).

Adults: Upper parts pale greyish-brown streaked with black, but rump only indistinctly streaked; two poorly defined buffy-white wing bars; tail dark brown narrowly edged with grey; inconspicuous greyish-brown cheek patch has faint darker narrow line above and below it; poorly defined pale streak over eye; under parts dull white, the breast and sides lightly washed with greyish buff (sometimes very faintly streaked); bill dusky above, brownish flesh below; legs brownish flesh. *Young in first autumn*: Similar to adults but more buffy above; wing bars buffy and more distinct. *Juvenal*: Similar to young in first autumn but breast and sides with dusky streaks.

Measurements *(S. b. breweri). Adult male*: wing, 59.6–64.5 (61.8); tail, 56.9–63.2 (59.7); exposed culmen, 8.7–10 (9.2); tarsus, 16.5–17.9 (17.4). *Adult female*: wing, 57.5–62.2 (60.2) mm.

Field Marks. A slender pale-greyish sparrow with plain breast and streaked upper parts. Perhaps most likely to be confused with Clay-colored Sparrow but lacks the median crown stripe of the Clay-color, has the sides of head more uniform, and is without conspicuous grey on the hind-neck. *Voice*: Song is surprisingly varied and sustained with numerous abrupt changes in pitch and tempo, combining buzzes and canary-like trills. Various nervous *lisps* and *chips*.

Habitat. Open country with low bushy shrubbery on the plains, on mountain meadows above timberline, and in open parts of mountain valleys.

Nesting. In a sagebrush bush or other low shrub. Nest is a compact cup of grass and weed stems and is lined with hair and fine grasses. *Eggs*, 3 or 4; greenish blue speckled with reddish browns.

Range. Southwestern Yukon, central-western southern Alberta, southwestern Saskatchewan, and southwestern North Dakota south to southern California, central Arizona, and northwestern New Mexico. Winters in southwestern United States and northwestern Mexico.

Subspecies. (1) *Spizella breweri breweri* Cassin: southern Alberta (east of the mountains), southwestern Saskatchewan; also central-southern British Columbia (White Lake, Midway). (2) *S. b. taverneri* Swarth and Brooks (darker above, slightly larger than *breweri*): southwestern Yukon, northwestern, central, and southeastern British Columbia (southeast to Elko).

Field Sparrow

Bruant des champs
Spizella pusilla (Wilson)
Total length: 12.6 to 15 cm
Plate 72

Breeding Distribution of Field Sparrow

Adults: Top of head, back, and scapulars rusty brown, the back and scapulars streaked with blackish but head and neck not streaked; rump plain light-brown; wings with two whitish bars; tail dark brown with narrow grey edging; sides of head grey with pale eye-ring and touches of rusty behind eye and on ear coverts; under parts whitish with buffy wash across breast and on sides and flanks; bill reddish or pink; legs brownish-flesh colour. *Juvenal*: Similar to adults but duller, the crown brown instead of rusty, the breast and sides with light-dusky streaks.

Measurements *(S. p. pusilla). Adult male*: wing, 62.7–67.8 (64.9); tail, 62–68.4 (65.9); exposed culmen, 8.7–9.8 (9.1); tarsus, 17.6–18.9 (18.3). *Adult female*: wing, 60–63.3 (62.9) mm.

Field Marks. Has rusty upper parts, white wing bars, and unstreaked breast, thus resembling the Tree Sparrow, but the present species has a pinkish bill and lacks a dusky spot on the breast. *Voice*: The pleasing song begins with two or more slow sweet whistles, then speeds up to a trill at the end. Call-note, *tsip*.

Habitat. Neglected brushy fields, old grown-up pastures, areas of thorn scrub, burntlands, wood edges, sparse second growths, and areas where small trees are interspersed with brambles and grasses.

Range in Canada. Breeds in southern Manitoba (locally: near Winnipeg); southern Ontario (Wasaga Beach, Deep River, Ottawa southward); southwestern Quebec (Aylmer, Rigaud, Montréal, Hatley, Mont Shefford); and southern New Brunswick (Fredericton).

Casual elsewhere in eastern Quebec (lower Moisie River, 24 April 1959; Madeleine Islands, 8 July 1887); Nova Scotia (photo record: Seal Island, 8 November 1971; also various sight records); northern Ontario (Cape Henrietta Maria); and Saskatchewan (photo: one near Meyronne, 17 and 19 December 1983).

Rare in winter in southern Ontario (Toronto).

Nesting. In a low bush or scrubby small tree or on the ground. Nest of grasses, weed stems, and rootlets is lined with fine grasses, hair, and sometimes bark fibre. *Eggs*, 2 to 5; greyish white to bluish, spotted and speckled with reddish browns. Incubation, 11 to 12 days (L.H. Walkinshaw), by the female.

Range. Breeds from southeastern Montana east across northern United States and through southern Ontario and southwestern Quebec to southern Maine and south to central Texas, Louisiana, and southern Georgia. Winters from Kansas east to Massachusetts and south to northeastern Mexico, southern Texas, the United States Gulf Coast, and central Florida.

Subspecies. *Spizella pusilla pusilla* (Wilson).

Vesper Sparrow

Bruant vespéral
Pooecetes gramineus (Gmelin)
Total length: 14 to 17 cm
Plate 71

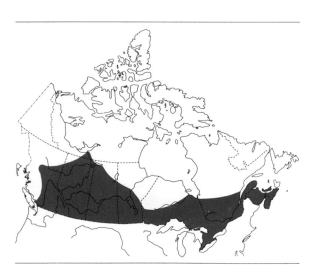

Breeding Distribution of Vesper Sparrow

Range in Canada. Summer resident, breeding in central and southern British Columbia (mostly east of the coast: François Lake, Peace River parklands southward; rarely on Vancouver Island: Victoria); southern Mackenzie (probably Fort Smith, Fort Simpson); Alberta; central and southern Saskatchewan (Lake Athabasca, probably Wollaston Lake southward); central and southern Manitoba (Thompson, Lynn Lake, The Pas, Lake St. Martin, Hillside Beach southward); central and southern Ontario (Malachi, Sioux Lookout, Lake Nipigon, and Moose Factory southward); southern Quebec (La Sarre, Amos, Lake Saint-Jean and Gaspé Peninsula southward but status on Madeleine Islands uncertain); New Brunswick; Prince Edward Island; and Nova Scotia (but occurrence on Cape Breton Island hypothetical).

Occasionally winters in Nova Scotia and extreme southern Ontario.

Casual on inner north shore of the Gulf of St. Lawrence (specimen: lower Moisie River, Quebec, 24 April 1959).

Bill conical. *Adults* (slightly paler in breeding season than in winter): Upper parts greyish brown or brownish grey, streaked with dusky; eye-ring whitish; cheek patch brownish; lesser wing coverts reddish brown; two vague buffy wing bars; tail mostly dark brown, the outermost feather on each side and one feather, sometimes two, next to it with some white; under parts dull white; the side of throat, breast, sides, and flanks streaked with dusky, sometimes tinged with buffy; bill mostly dusky or brownish above, flesh colour below; legs flesh colour.

Measurements *(P. g. gramineus)*. *Adult male*: wing, 79.6–83.1 (81.7); tail, 54.3–64.2 (60.9); exposed culmen, 11.1–12.1 (11.6); tarsus, 20.3–21.2 (20.7). *Adult female*: wing, 75.3–82.3 (78.5) mm.

Field Marks. A streaked brownish-grey sparrow with *white outer tail feathers conspicuous in flight*. Face has a noticeable cheek patch and a narrow white eye-ring. The reddish-brown lesser wing coverts (near bend of wing) are diagnostic when they can be seen. Juncos also have white outer tail feathers, but their dark-slate upper parts distinguish them at a glance. Pipits, with similar tails, are slender-billed tail waggers, and they walk instead of hopping (see also longspurs). *Voice*: Song begins with two similar clear unhurried whistles, followed by higher ones and then by a descending jumble of twitters and trills.

Habitat. Grassy and weedy fields, pastures, prairies, clearings, roadsides, gravel pits, and similar open, weedy, fairly dry situations. Much activity is on or near the ground. Bushes, weeds, fence posts, and trees are used as singing posts and retreats.

Nesting. On the ground either hidden by a tuft of grass or a weed, or in the open. Nest is of grasses, rootlets, occasionally some weed stems, and is lined with fine grasses or horse hair. *Eggs*, usually 3 to 5; whitish, speckled and scrawled, sometimes thickly, with various browns and sometimes a little purplish grey. Incubation period 11 to 13 days (Knight, Burns), 13 to 14 days (Bryant); mainly, if not entirely by the female.

Range. Breeds from interior British Columbia east to Nova Scotia and south to central-eastern California, central Arizona, central New Mexico, central Missouri, Tennessee, and North Carolina. Winters from southwestern United States, southern Illinois, West Virginia, southern Pennsylvania, and Connecticut south to southern Mexico, the Gulf of Mexico coast, and central Florida.

Subspecies. (1) *Pooecetes gramineus gramineus* (Gmelin): eastern Ontario, Quebec, New Brunswick, Prince Edward Island, Nova Scotia. (2) *P. g. confinis* Baird (averages paler and greyer than *gramineus*): British Columbia, Alberta, Mackenzie, Saskatchewan, Manitoba, western Ontario (Wabigoon, Rainy River).

Lark Sparrow

Bruant à joues marron
Chondestes grammacus (Say)
Total length: 14.5 to 17 cm
Plate 71

Breeding Distribution of Lark Sparrow

Range in Canada. Summer resident, breeding in southern interior British Columbia (Okanagan and Similkameen valleys, north at least to Kamloops; possibly has nested west to Chilliwack); southeastern Alberta (Calgary, Lethbridge, Steveville, Medicine Hat, Milk and Lost rivers, Chin Coulée, and north to Big Valley, Cadogan, and Czar); in southern Saskatchewan (Cypress Hills region, Swift Current, Regina, sporadically north to Nipawin and Battleford); southern Manitoba (Oak Lake, Winnipeg); and southern Ontario (Point Pelee, Walsingham, Toronto, Kingston, Sudbury).

Occurrence records north to Puntchesakut Lake, British Columbia; Prince Albert, Saskatchewan; Lake St. Martin, Manitoba; Hornepayne, Chapleau, and Moosonee, Ontario.

Casual or accidental in southeastern Quebec (lower Moisie River, 25 May 1955, a specimen of the western race *strigatus*; sight record at Aguanish, 25 August 1934). Casual visitor to New Brunswick (Grand Manan: three specimens of *strigatus*, one of *grammacus*); Nova Scotia (Sable Island, Upper Granville. Over 30 sight records for Grand Desert, West Middle Sable, Outer Island, Brier Island, Sable Island, etc. The Upper Granville specimen was identified by the writer as *grammacus*, the eastern race); and Prince Edward Island (specimen: Montague, January 1978). Very rare visitant to Vancouver Island, British Columbia.

Accidental in Newfoundland (photo: Cape Roy, 21 September 1980).

Bill conical; wings longish, pointed; tail rounded, rather long but shorter than wing. *Adults (sexes similar)*: Top of head chestnut, divided by a whitish median stripe, the chestnut becoming blackish on forehead; rest of upper parts greyish brown, the back and scapulars streaked with dark brown; sides of head white with a chestnut ear patch, a thin black line through the eye, a black line joining ear patch with base of bill and another along side of throat; two inconspicuous buffy wing bars; tail brownish to blackish, all feathers except the middle pair tipped with white, the white tips increasing in extent outwardly and with the outer web of the outermost feather white to the tail coverts; under parts plain white with black spot in centre of breast; breast and sides often lightly tinged with greyish brown; bill dull bluish-dusky, paler below; legs flesh colour. *Juvenals* resemble adults, but crown and ear patch are greyish brown, the breast streaked or spotted with dusky.

Measurements *(C. g. strigatus). Adult male*: wing, 86.4–95.7 (91.4); tail, 69.5–76.7 (73.9); exposed culmen, 12–13.1 (12.7); tarsus, 19.1–21.9 (20.7). *Adult female*: wing, 81.9–87.4 (84.5) mm.

Field Marks. A little larger than a Song Sparrow. The chestnut, black, and white head markings, white-margined tail (white-tipped, thus different from that of Vesper Sparrow), and plain-white under parts with black breast spot make it unmistakable. *Voice*: Song is long, variable, and melodious, beginning with loud clear double notes followed by a series of short trills, runs, pauses, and *churs*. Also a weak *chip*.

Habitat. Open country with scattered trees or bushes; prairies, wood edges, roadsides, abandoned cultivated areas, often about farms or villages. Badlands of Red Deer River south of Morrin, Alberta, are much favoured.

Nesting. On the ground, usually under a weed, or in a bush. Nest is of grass and weed stems with a lining of finer grasses, rootlets, and long hairs. *Eggs*, 3 to 5; white, spotted and scrawled with blackish and often some purplish. They are quite distinctive. Incubation period 11 days (Ross Hardy) to 13 days (other authors), by the female.

Range. Breeds from southern interior British Columbia, southern parts of the Prairie Provinces, central Minnesota, southern Michigan, southern Ontario, western New York, and central Pennsylvania south to southern California, northern Mexico, Louisiana, central Alabama; rarely to Virginia and central North Carolina. Winters in southern United States and south to southern Florida, southern Mexico, and El Salvador.

Subspecies. (1) *Chondestes grammacus grammacus* (Say): Breeds in southern Ontario. A rare visitor to Nova Scotia and New Brunswick. (2) *C. g. strigatus* Swainson (upper parts paler, streaks on back narrower): Breeds in British Columbia, Alberta, Saskatchewan, Manitoba. Accidental visitor east to southeastern Quebec (lower Moisie River) and southern New Brunswick (Grand Manan).

Black-throated Sparrow

(Desert Sparrow)

Bruant à gorge noire
Amphispiza bilineata (Cassin)
Total length: 12 to 13.3 cm
Plate 71

Status in Canada. Accidental in British Columbia (specimen: Murtle Lake, Wells Gray Provincial Park, 8 June 1959; sight record: one near Osoyoos on 27 June 1981). An undocumented sight record for Alberta (Barrhead, 14–18 May 1979).

Adults: Plain grey above, the back tinged with brown; conspicuous line over eye and another on jaw, white; ear patch dark grey; area in front of eye black; chin, throat, and middle of breast jet black; rest of under parts white becoming greyish on sides and flanks; no wing bars; tail blackish, the outermost feather on each side with white outer web and tipped white, and often the second and third feather from outside also white-tipped; bill bluish dusky, legs brownish black.

Measurements *(A. b. deserticola). Adult male*: wing, 64.0–70.6 (67.3); tail, 60.9–68.3 (64.3); exposed culmen, 9.9–10.7 (10.2); tarsus, 18.0–19.8 (19.1). *Adult female*: wing, 62.2–66.0 (64.5) mm.

Field Marks. A grey, black-throated sparrow with a conspicuous white line over the eye and another along the jaw and some white in the outer tail feathers. Harris's Sparrow also has a black throat but is a much larger sparrow with very different face pattern and no conspicuous white in the tail.

Range. Breeds from northeastern California, southwestern Wyoming, northwestern Oklahoma, and central-northern Texas south to southern Baja California and north-central Mexico (Jalisco, Hidalgo). Winters from United States deserts southward.

Subspecies. *Amphispiza bilineata deserticola* Ridgway.

Sage Sparrow

Bruant de Bell
Amphispiza belli (Cassin)
Total length: 13.3 to 15.5 cm
Figure 94

Figure 94
Sage Sparrow

Status in Canada. Casual in southwestern British Columbia (specimen: Lulu Island, 2 October 1930; sight records: near Osoyoos, 3 May 1970 and Pitt Meadows, 27 April 1982).

Adults: Upper parts and sides of head greyish brown or brownish grey, the back decidedly brown and usually more or less streaked with dusky; spot in front of eye and narrow eye-ring white; sides of throat with a few fine dark streaks leaving a white malar stripe; rest of under parts white, usually with a dusky spot in middle of breast; the sides buffy and streaked with dusky; wings and tail blackish with pale brown edging; outer tail feathers with outer web and narrow tip white; bill pale greyish-blue.

Measurements *(A. b. nevadensis). Adult male*: wing, 77.47–81.28 (79.25); tail, 70.61–78.49 (74.68); exposed culmen, 9.4–10.41 (10.16); tarsus, 20.83–22.61 (21.59). *Adult female*: wing, 72.39–80.01 (75.69) mm (Ridgway).

Field Marks. A greyish-brown sparrow, white below with an inconspicuous dark spot in middle of breast, a few fine dark streaks on sides of throat, and a few streaks on the sides. The tail is often flicked upward when the bird is alarmed, and when spread it shows narrow white outer edges.

Range. Breeds from interior central Washington, southern Idaho, and northwestern Colorado south to central Baja California, southern Nevada, and northwestern New Mexico.

Subspecies. *Amphispiza belli nevadensis* (Ridgway).

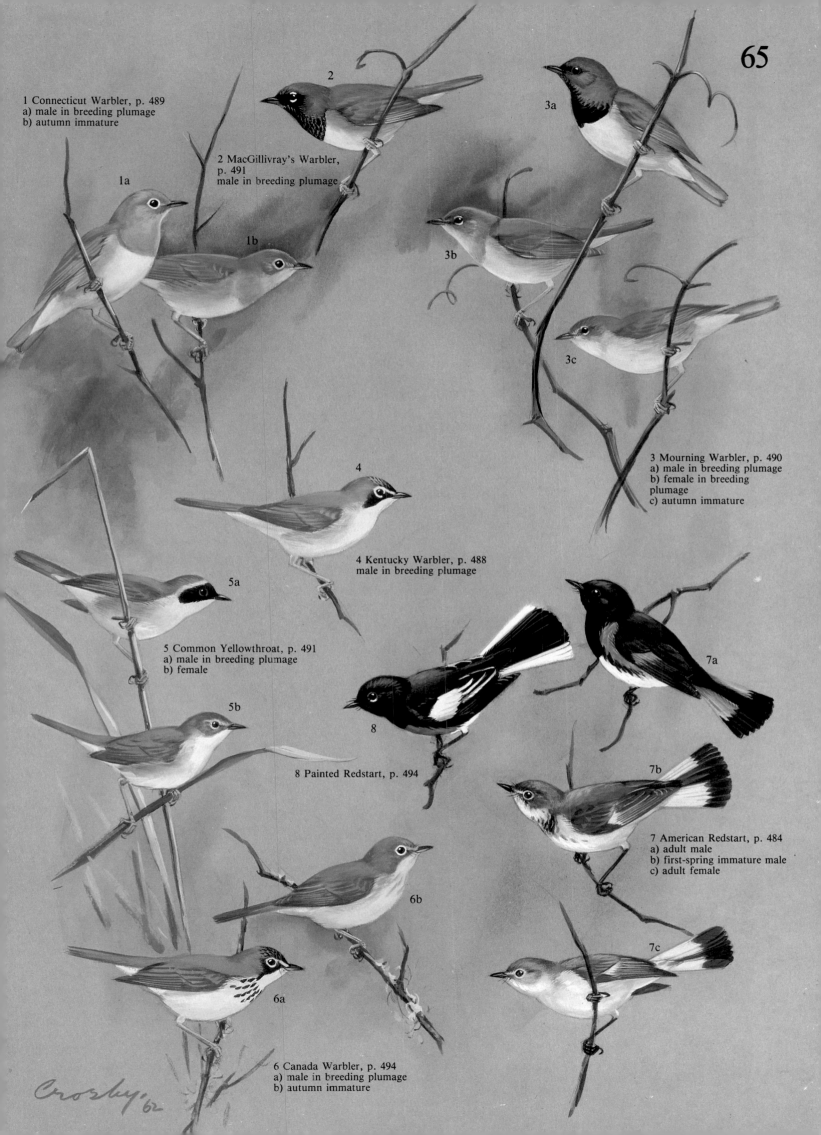

1 Connecticut Warbler, p. 489
a) male in breeding plumage
b) autumn immature

2 MacGillivray's Warbler,
p. 491
male in breeding plumage

3 Mourning Warbler, p. 490
a) male in breeding plumage
b) female in breeding
plumage
c) autumn immature

4 Kentucky Warbler, p. 488
male in breeding plumage

5 Common Yellowthroat, p. 491
a) male in breeding plumage
b) female

8 Painted Redstart, p. 494

7 American Redstart, p. 484
a) adult male
b) first-spring immature male
c) adult female

6 Canada Warbler, p. 494
a) male in breeding plumage
b) autumn immature

Crosby '62

1a

1 Western Tanager, p. 497
a) male in breeding plumage
b) female

1b

2a

2b

2 Summer Tanager,
p. 495
a) male in
breeding plumage
b) female

3a

3b

3 Scarlet Tanager, p. 496
a) male in breeding plumage
b) female

4a

4b

4c

4 Orchard Oriole, p. 567
a) male in breeding plumage
b) first-spring immature male
c) female

5c

5 Northern Oriole,
p. 558
a) "Baltimore" (eastern) race:
male in breeding plumage
b) "Baltimore" (eastern) race:
female
c) "Bullock's" (western) race:
male in breeding plumage
d) "Bullock's" (western) race:
female

5a

5b

5d

7

8

8 Western
Meadowlark,
p. 550

6a

6b

6 Bobolink, p. 547
a) male in
breeding plumage
b) female

7 Eastern Meadowlark, p. 549

Crosby

1 Rusty Blackbird, p. 552
a) first-autumn immature male
b) male in breeding plumage

2 Brewer's Blackbird, p. 553
a) male in breeding plumage
b) female

3 Yellow-headed Blackbird, p. 551
a) adult male
b) female

4 Red-winged Blackbird, p. 548
a) adult male
b) female

5 Common Grackle, p. 555

6 Brown-headed Cowbird, p. 556
a) adult male
b) female

7 European Starling, p. 452
a) winter plumage
b) breeding plumage

8 Crested Myna, p. 453
adult male

Crosby

68

1 Northern Cardinal, p. 498
a) adult male
b) adult female

1a

1b

2 Black-headed Grosbeak, p. 500
a) adult female
b) adult male

2a

2b

4 Rose-breasted Grosbeak, p. 499
a) male in breeding plumage
b) female

4a

4b

3 Indigo Bunting, p. 502
a) female
b) male in breeding plumage

3a

3b

5 Lazuli Bunting, p. 501
a) male in breeding plumage
b) female

5a

5b

6 Dickcissel, p. 503
a) adult female
b) male in breeding plumage

6a

6b

7 Blue Grosbeak, p. 501
a) male in breeding plumage
b) female

7a

7b

8 House Sparrow, p. 574
a) female
b) male in breeding plumage

8a

8b

Crosby

1a

2

2 Lesser Goldfinch,
p. 571
(*hesperophila* race)
adult male

3b

3a

1b

3 Evening Grosbeak,
p. 572
a) adult male
b) female

1c

1 American Goldfinch, p. 571
a) male in breeding plumage
b) male in winter plumage
c) female in breeding plumage

5 Hoary Redpoll, p. 569   5

4

4 Common Redpoll,
p. 568

6 Pine Siskin, p. 570

7a

6

7 Pine Grosbeak, p. 561   7b
a) adult male
b) female

9

8 Brambling, p. 560
winter male   8

Crosby

9 Common Chaffinch, p. 560
male in breeding plumage

70

1 Red Crossbill, p. 565
a) adult male
b) female

1a

1b

2a

2 White-winged Crossbill, p. 567
a) adult male
b) juvenal

2b

4 Cassin's Finch, p. 564
a) adult male
b) female

3a

3 Purple Finch, p. 563
a) female
b) adult male

3b

4b

4a

5 Henslow's Sparrow, p. 527

6 House Finch, p. 564
a) adult male
b) female

5

6a

6b

7

7 Le Conte's Sparrow,
p. 528

11

8

10 Seaside Sparrow, p. 529

11 Baird's Sparrow,
p.525

8 Grasshopper
Sparrow, p. 526

10

9

9 Sharp-tailed Sparrow, p. 529

Crosby

1 Black-throated Sparrow, p. 512
male in breeding plumage

2 Lark Sparrow, p. 511
adult

3 Harris's Sparrow, p. 538
a) autumn immature
b) adult in breeding plumage

5 Lark Bunting, p. 523
a) male in breeding plumage
b) female

4 Savannah Sparrow, p. 523
a) adult, most races
(variable)
b) "Ipswich" Sparrow
race: adult

6 Vesper Sparrow, p. 510

7 Rufous-sided Towhee, p. 504
a) adult male (western races)
b) female (eastern race)
c) adult male (eastern race)

crosby

1a

1e

1b

1 Dark-eyed Junco, p. 539
a) "Oregon" Junco races: autumn immature
b) "Oregon" Junco races: adult male
c) "Slate-colored" Junco races: autumn immature
d) "Slate-colored" Junco races: adult male
e) "Gray-headed" Junco race *(J. h. caniceps)*

2 American Tree Sparrow, p. 506

2

3 Field Sparrow, p. 509

1c

3

1d

4 Bachman's Sparrow, p. 505

4

5 Brewer's Sparrow, p. 509

5

7a

6a

7b

6b

6 Clay-colored Sparrow, p. 508
a) adult
b) autumn immature

7 Chipping Sparrow, p. 507
a) adult
b) autumn-immature

Crosby

1 White-crowned Sparrow, p. 536
a) adult (*gambelii* race)
b) adult (*leucophrys* race)
c) autumn immature

2a

2b

2 Golden-crowned Sparrow, p. 536
a) adult
b) autumn immature

1a

1c

1b

3 White-throated Sparrow, p. 535
a) adult
b) autumn immature

3a

3b

4a

4 Swamp Sparrow, p. 533
a) adult
b) autumn immature

4b

5

5 Lincoln's Sparrow, p. 532
adult

6b

7

6a

7 Song Sparrow,
p. 531
adult
(eastern race)

6 Fox Sparrow, p. 530
a) adult (eastern race)
b) adult (*townsendi* race)

Crosby

1 Rosy Finch, p. 561
a) adult male (*littoralis* race)
b) adult male (*tephrocotis* race)

2 Yellow Wagtail, p. 435
male in breeding plumage

3 Smith's Longspur, p. 543
a) male in breeding plumage
b) female

4 Chestnut-collared Longspur, p. 543
a) female
b) male in breeding plumage

5 McCown's Longspur, p. 540
a) female
b) male in breeding plumage

7 Snow Bunting, p. 545
a) winter plumage
b) male in breeding plumage

Crosby

Lark Bunting

Bruant noir et blanc
Calamospiza melanocorys Stejneger
Total length: 15 to 19 cm
Plate 71

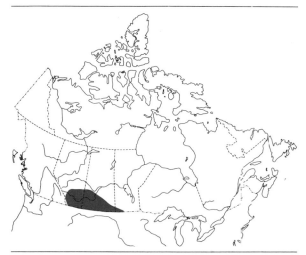

Breeding Distribution of Lark Bunting

Range in Canada. Breeds in southern Alberta (east of the Rockies: west to Calgary and Fort MacLeod; north to about Sibbald, Castor, and Youngstown); southern Saskatchewan (Crane Lake, Regina, Indian Head, Kindersley, northward sporadically to Clavet, situated about 23 km southeast of Saskatoon); and southwestern Manitoba (Lyleton, Brandon). There is a tendency for the breeding range to expand temporarily during periods of dry summers.

Scarce visitant to southern British Columbia (Oak Bay, Vancouver, Okanagan Landing, Ootsa Lake, Kootenay National Park); Ontario (specimen: Low Bush, 5 June 1925; photo records: London, Point Pelee; also various sight records in the south and northward to Moosonee). Casual visitant to Quebec (specimen: Ferme-Neuve, 13 May 1970; sight records: Sept-Îles, Saint-Fulgence); New Brunswick (Nantucket Island, 15 August 1910; also sight records); and Nova Scotia (specimen: Brier Island, 27 May 1967; photo record: Seal Island, 5 September 1970; several sight records).

Bill quite large, deeper than broad at its base. *Adult male (summer)*: Mostly plain black, the middle and greater wing coverts white, forming a contrasting patch; tertials edged with white; some white on tips of inner webs of some tail feathers; bill bluish grey. *Adult female*: Upper parts greyish brown streaked with dusky; wings and tail dusky, wing patch much smaller and more buffy than that of the male; white spot near tip of inner web of some tail feathers; sides of head with pale line over eye and brownish ear patch; under parts white, the breast and sides streaked with dusky and with a blackish line down either side of throat. *Adult male (winter)*: Similar to adult female, but wing patch larger, with traces of black showing through, especially on breast or throat. *Juvenal* (shortly after leaving nest): Similar to adult female but feathers of upper parts more buffy and paler, the back more scaly, the under parts with finer streaks.

Measurements. *Adult male*: wing, 84.7–90.6 (87.9); tail, 64.8–68 (66.2); exposed culmen, 11.6–15 (13.5); tarsus, 22.9–26 (24.8). *Adult female*: wing, 81.8–85 (83.3) mm.

Field Marks. Adult male in summer, a black bird of the western prairies (slightly larger than the House Sparrow) with a conspicuous white patch in the wing. Could be confused only with the Bobolink, but the latter has white on the back but not in the wings. Females, young, and winter males are brown-and-white-streaked sparrows with a pale line over the eye. They look a little like the female Purple Finch but usually show a white or buff patch in the wing, which distinguishes them from the Purple Finch and other similar birds. Habitat preferences, too, are very different from those of the Purple Finch. *Voice*: Song is delightful and varied, containing whistles, trills, and some repetitions of *wack wack wack*. It is given either when the singer is perched, or when the bird half-floats to the ground with peculiar slow flaps of fully extended wings.

Habitat. Drier treeless plains and prairies, especially where the grasses have a considerable admixture of sagebrush.

Nesting. On the ground, often under a small shrub or tuft of grass. Nest is rather loosely constructed of grass and rootlets. *Eggs*, 4 to 6; pale blue, usually unmarked.

Range. Breeds from southern Alberta, southern Saskatchewan, southwestern Manitoba, and southwestern Minnesota south (east of the Rockies) to southeastern New Mexico, western Oklahoma, and Kansas. Winters from southern California, central Arizona, and north-central Texas to central Mexico.

Savannah Sparrow

(includes Ipswich Sparrow)

Bruant des prés
Passerculus sandwichensis (Gmelin)
Total length: 13.3 to 16.5 cm
Plate 71

Bill conical but rather slender; culmen nearly straight; wings longer than tail; tail very slightly forked, tail feathers with more or less pointed tips (except when worn). *Adults (sexes similar)*: Upper parts brown, the top of head and back streaked with whitish, buffy and black; narrow median crown-streak yellowish white; a yellow stripe over and in front of eye; cheeks brownish; wings and tail dusky with light-brown edges but without any white areas; bend of wing yellowish; under parts white, the sides of throat, breast, sides, and flanks streaked sharply with blackish brown and medium brown; a buffy or whitish stripe across jaw (malar region) bordered above and below by a blackish line; bill dusky, pale at base of lower mandible; legs flesh colour. *Young (first winter plumage)*: Similar to adults but decidedly more buffy. *Juvenal plumage*: Resembles adults but much more strongly buffy or yellowish. See also Subspecies.

Breeding Distribution of Savannah Sparrow

Range in Canada. Breeds from northern Yukon (Herschel Island); northern Mackenzie (Richards Island, Coronation Gulf, lower Perry River); northern Keewatin (Back River, Chesterfield Inlet); northern Manitoba (Churchill); northern Ontario (Fort Severn, Cape Henrietta Maria); islands in James Bay, northern Quebec (Salluit, mouth of Koksoak River, Alluviaq Fiord); northern Labrador; and Newfoundland south through southern British Columbia (including Vancouver Island), Alberta, Saskatchewan, Manitoba, Ontario, Quebec (including Anticosti and Madeleine islands), New Brunswick, Prince Edward Island, and Nova Scotia (including Sable Island).

Winters in small numbers in southwestern British Columbia, extreme southern Ontario, and Nova Scotia.

Casual on Southampton Island and Pelly Bay, N.W.T. Accidental on Cornwallis Island (specimen: Resolute Bay, 4 September 1954), Victoria Island (specimen: Albert Edward Bay, 30 June 1972) and Seymour Island (specimen: 16 June 1975), N.W.T.

Measurements *(P. s. savanna)*. *Adult male*: wing, 68.3–73.2 (70.5); tail, 49.9–54.8 (51.9); exposed culmen, 9.8–11.3 (10.6); tarsus, 20.1–21.8 (20.9). *Adult female*: wing, 62–68.1 (65.2) mm.

Field Marks. A streaked sparrow of open places, especially grassy fields. Resembles the Song Sparrow but has a yellowish line over the eye; a narrow yellowish-white streak in centre of crown; a much shorter, slightly forked tail (Song Sparrow has a rounded tail); and more pinkish legs. One eastern subspecies, *P. s. princeps*, is decidedly larger, paler, and much greyer and is usually separable from other races of the Savannah Sparrow in the field. In the Prairie Provinces see Baird's Sparrow. *Voice*: Song is a lisping *tsip tsip tsip tsip tse-wheeeeeeeeee-you* (the *wheeee* is trilled, the final *you* abrupt and much lower). Alarm note *tsip*.

Habitat. Open areas, especially moist grasslands such as hayfields and meadows; marshes (either fresh or salt), bogs, grassy sand dunes, and grassy streamsides. Areas with herbaceous plants or clumps of shrubbery are popular, but extensive tree cover is avoided.

Nesting. On the ground, in a hollow scratched out by the birds, usually sheltered by grass, a shrub, or a small tree. Nest is of grass and plant stems, occasionally some moss, and is lined with fine grasses. *Eggs*, usually 4 to 6; whitish, variously spotted and splashed with browns and often a little purplish. Sometimes the browns hide most of the ground colour. Incubation period averages 12 days (R.S. Palmer) by the female (reports of incubation by the male require confirmation).

Range. Breeds from northern Alaska east to northern Labrador and Newfoundland and south to southern Baja California, southern Mexico, and Guatemala; and in eastern United States south to Missouri, Indiana, Ohio, West Virginia, western Maryland, and southeastern Pennsylvania. Winters from southern Canada south to Cuba and Guatemala.

Subspecies. (1) *Passerculus sandwichensis labradorius* Howe, coloration dark and brownish: Newfoundland, Labrador, northern Quebec (Ungava Bay south at least to southern James Bay, Lake Saint-Jean, and the north shore of the Gulf of St. Lawrence), northern Ontario (south to Biscotasing, North Bay). (2) *P. s. savanna* (Wilson), paler than either *labradorius* or *oblitus*, browner than *oblitus*: breeds in Nova Scotia, Prince Edward Island and New Brunswick, Madeleine Islands. (3) *P. s. princeps* Maynard, formerly considered a separate species named Ipswich Sparrow, much paler, greyer, and larger than any other eastern race, breeds on Sable Island, Nova Scotia. (4) *P. s. mediogriseus* Aldrich, darker and somewhat more brownish than *savanna*: southern Ontario (Bigwood southward), southern Quebec (Eastern Townships, Gaspé Peninsula). (5) *P. s. oblitus* Peters and Griscom, coloration dark, more greyish (less brownish) than *savanna* and *labradorius*: Keewatin, Manitoba, western Ontario. (6) *P. s. brooksi* Bishop, smallest of the races, intermediate in colour between *anthinus* and *nevadensis*: northwestern coastal British Columbia (Vancouver Island, Sumas, Rainbow Mountains). (7) *P. s. anthinus* Bonaparte, bill slenderer than in eastern races, somewhat more brownish than *oblitus*: northern Yukon, northern Mackenzie (east to Perry River, Thelon River) and south to interior south-central British Columbia (Mile 149 Cariboo Road, Nulki Lake). (8) *P. s. nevadensis* Grinnell, very pale and grey, bill slender: southern interior British Columbia (where not typical), central-eastern British Columbia (Peace River parklands), Alberta, Saskatchewan, southwestern and central-western Manitoba (The Pas, Lake St. Martin, Whitewater Lake). (9) *P. s. sandwichensis* (Gmelin), migrant and winter visitor to southwestern British Columbia (Vancouver Island, Vancouver) from breeding grounds in Alaska.

Remarks. In hayfields all across the country this is often the commonest sparrow. It is primarily a ground bird. It feeds and nests on the ground, but perches on fence posts, wires, bushes, and trees as well.

Its flight is low, swift, slightly undulating, and it terminates typically with the bird dropping suddenly back into the grass. The weak insect-like song may be given at any daylight hour but is especially frequent in the dusk of a calm summer evening. The Savannah Sparrow devours large quantities of weed seeds and insects and is a valuable bird to have about the farm.

Baird's Sparrow

Bruant de Baird
Ammodramus bairdii (Audubon)
Total length: 12.5 to 14.7 cm
Plate 70

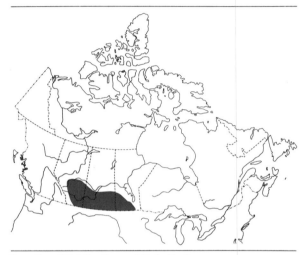

Breeding Distribution of Baird's Sparrow

Range in Canada. Breeds in southeastern Alberta (North to Beaverhill Lake, west to Calgary); southern Saskatchewan (Maple Creek, Regina, Saskatoon, head of Last Mountain Lake, Qu'Appelle valley; observed in summer north to Manito Lake, Redberry Lake, and Nipawin); and southern Manitoba (Swan River, Lake St. Martin, Winnipeg, Whitemouth).

Casual at Grand Rapids, Manitoba. Unsubstantiated sight records only for Ontario (Toronto, Emo) and British Columbia (Richmond, 4 June 1981).

Adults (female somewhat duller than male): Head suffused with buffy or ochraceous, deepest on crown and nape, palest (often white) on throat; top of head streaked with black, mostly on sides of crown leaving a rich buffy median stripe (less obvious in female); sides of head with two narrow black lines, one across lower jaw, one on side of throat; rest of upper parts light brown with blackish spots and streaks and with much feather edging of buff and white; wings greyish brown edged with buff or pale rufous; tail mostly dark brown edged with pale buff, the outer feather on each side buffy white terminally (less extensive in female); under parts white with buffy wash across breast and often on throat, and with sharply defined but well-spaced streaks of black or dark brown on breast (forming a sparse necklace) and sides; bill flesh colour, dusky near tip; legs brownish flesh. *Juvenals* resemble adults, but the feathers of the back are margined with white giving a scaly appearance; streaks on breast less sharply defined.

Measurements. *Adult male*: wing, 70–73.4 (71.6); tail, 49–53.8 (50.7); exposed culmen, 10.6–12 (11.4); tarsus, 20.9–22.3 (21.6). *Adult female*: wing, 66.3–70.5 (68.3) mm.

Field Marks. A sparrow of the prairies, somewhat suggesting a pale Savannah Sparrow. The strong buffy coloration of crown and nape and much sparser breast streaks distinguish it from the Savannah. The outer tail feathers, especially those of the male, often look whitish, particularly in flight. *Voice*: Song is two, three, or more *zips* followed by a musical little trill on a lower pitch.

Habitat. Dry grassy areas where the grass is fairly long and often where scattered low shrubs are present for singing perches; weedy fields, wheat fields, and in dry years on the bottom of dried-out sloughs.

Nesting. On the ground among grass, either under grass or a low shrub or without overhead protection. Nest is of grass lined with finer grasses and occasionally hairs or setae of mosses. *Eggs*, 4 to 6; white, spotted and blotched with reddish brown, mostly about the larger end. Incubation period about 11 days, by the female (Cartwright, Shortt, and Harris).

Range. Breeds from southern Alberta east to southern Manitoba and south to Montana, central South Dakota, southeastern North Dakota, and central-western Minnesota. Winters from southern Arizona and New Mexico south to northern Mexico.

Grasshopper Sparrow

Bruant sauterelle
Ammodramus savannarum (Gmelin)
Total length: 12.3 to 13.7 cm
Plate 70

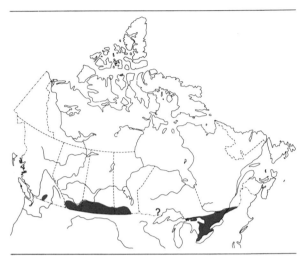

Breeding Distribution of Grasshopper Sparrow

Range in Canada. Breeds in central-southern British Columbia (Okanagan valley, northward to near Vernon); southern Alberta (Lost River valley, Calgary); southern Saskatchewan (25 km north of Maple Creek; Regina, Asquith, Earl Grey, Qu'Appelle valley; summer sight records north to Saskatoon); southern Manitoba (Whitewater Lake, West Shoal Lake, Winnipeg); southern Ontario (north to Sudbury and Ottawa; perhaps Thunder Bay); and southwestern Quebec (Aylmer, Chambly Basin, Huntingdon).

Scarce visitant near Québec, Quebec; New Brunswick (specimens: Waweig, Grand Manan); Prince Edward Island (8 km northeast of St. Peters); Newfoundland (Rose Blanche, Cape Race); Nova Scotia (specimens: Seal Island, Cape Sable, Conrad Beach; photo record: Cape Breton Highlands National Park; various sight records); and British Columbia (Vancouver Island, photo record: Saanich).

Bill relatively heavier than in Savannah Sparrow; lesser wing coverts greenish yellow, thus different from other Canadian sparrows; tail feathers somewhat pointed. *Adults (breeding plumage)*: Top of head mostly blackish, finely streaked with buffish or greyish and with a broad median stripe of greyish buff; rest of upper parts mixed greyish, buffy, chestnut, and black, the black most apparent on back and scapulars; hind-neck greyish, streaked with chestnut; wings dusky, edged with buffy grey; lesser wing coverts greenish yellow; bend of wing bright yellow; tail dusky, edged with buffy grey, the outer tail feathers paler than the inner ones; sides of head buffy, yellowish in front of eye, with a narrow dark streak extending backward from eye; under parts buff, paling to whitish on abdomen; bill pale bluish with dusky ridge; legs flesh colour. *Adults (winter)*: Similar to breeding adults but brighter, the upper parts with more chestnut and less black, the under parts more buffy, the breast sometimes lightly streaked with reddish brown. *Juvenal plumage*: Scapulars tipped with russet spots; under parts dull buffy-white, the breast distinctly streaked with dusky; no yellow over eye or on edge of wing.

Measurements *(A. s. pratensis)*. *Adult male*: wing, 60–63.4 (61.6); tail, 43–47 (44.7); exposed culmen, 11–12.4 (11.6); tarsus, 17.8–21 (19.3). *Adult female*: wing, 58.4–62.7 (60.2) mm.

Field Marks. A small, rather short-tailed grass sparrow, the adults with buffy unstreaked breasts and unstreaked sides. Other similar sparrows of open fields have definite streaks on sides. It has a peculiar flat-headed appearance. *Voice*: Two main songs: (1) a short (one to three seconds) insect-like buzz, which is preceded by one or two *chips*, (2) a sustained song, a jumble of squeaky, wiry notes. Singing is most frequent in early morning and late evening.

Habitat. Old fields, hayfields, and prairies with clumps of grass and weeds (preferably with last year's grass still standing). Situations are usually drier than those chosen by Savannah Sparrow.

Nesting. On the ground, the nest well hidden in grass or other vegetation and often arched over. Nest is made of grass and lined with fine grasses and hairs. *Eggs*, usually 4 or 5; white, spotted with reddish brown mainly about the larger end. Incubation 11 to 12 days, by the female.

Range. Southern Canada (interior southern British Columbia east to southwestern Quebec), northern Vermont, central New Hampshire, and Maine south to southern California, Arizona, Colorado, central Texas, Arkansas, central Gulf States, and Florida; also from southern Mexico to central Panama, western Colombia, and Ecuador, Jamaica, Puerto Rico, Curaçao, and Bonaire. Winters from southern United States southward.

Subspecies. (1) *Ammodramus savannarum pratensis* (Vieillot): southern Ontario, southwestern Quebec. (2) *A. s. perpallidus* (Coues), with paler coloration, wing and tail longer, bill smaller: southern British Columbia, southern Alberta, southern Saskatchewan, southern Manitoba.

Henslow's Sparrow

Bruant de Henslow
Ammodramus henslowii (Audubon)
Total length: 11.8 to 13.5 cm
Plate 70

Breeding Distribution of Henslow's Sparrow

Range in Canada. Breeds locally in southern Ontario (sporadically but sometimes commonly north to Barrie and Ottawa, probably Manitoulin Island; east at least to Morrisburg). Has been recorded in Quebec (Hull, Eccles-Hill, Montréal). In northernmost parts of its range (e.g., Ottawa) the species may nest commonly for a period of years then disappear completely over the next period, only to appear again years later.

Accidental in Nova Scotia (photo record: Seal Island, 12 to 24 October 1976).

Bill rather stout; tail feathers narrow and pointed. *Adults*: Top of head, hind-neck, and sides of neck pale olive-greenish; two blackish stripes on crown on either side of a pale median crown stripe; back and scapulars chestnut and black, the feathers narrowly edged with white; rump chestnut brown with blackish feather centres; wings and tail tinged with chestnut brown and with blackish feather centres; bend of wing yellow; a narrow dark streak back from eye, another back from base of bill across jaw, and a narrow one on either side of throat; a dark area on ear region; under parts whitish, the breast, sides, and flanks decidedly buffy and streaked with blackish; bill brownish paling to flesh colour below; legs flesh.

Measurements *(A. h. henslowii)*. *Adult male*: wing, 50.3–54.5 (52.9); tail, 46.1–51 (49.2); exposed culmen, 10.9–12.5 (11.6); tarsus, 16–17 (16.4). *Adult female*: wing, 49–55.4 (52.6) mm.

Field Marks. Another short-tailed flat-headed sparrow, this one frequenting upland fields. Its streaked breast, greenish hind-neck, and more chestnut wings distinguish it from the Grasshopper Sparrow. Its greenish hind-neck distinguishes it also from other similar sparrows such as Baird's, Le Conte's, and Sharp-tailed. Its song is the best means of recognizing it. *Voice*: Song, unlike that of any other Canadian bird, is ridiculously short and unmusical, a simple *tse-slick* with the accent on the second syllable. It sings most often at dusk; also regularly at night and on cloudy days; less often in the heat of sunny midday.

Habitat. Open fields and meadows in which the grass is interspersed with weeds (usually unmowed fields are preferred). Frequently the fields are damp and low-lying.

Nesting. Often in small loose colonies. Nest is most often on the ground, sheltered by a tuft of grass or a weed; occasionally 15 to 50 cm above ground in a weed or clump of grass. Nest is a loosely woven cup of grasses, often arched-over with grass. Incubation period 10 to 11 days, by the female (A.S. Hyde).

Range. Breeds locally from eastern South Dakota, central Minnesota, central Michigan, southern Ontario, southern Vermont, and New Hampshire south to eastern Kansas, southern Illinois, northern Kentucky, and North Carolina. Winters from southeastern Texas east to Florida and on the Atlantic coastal plain from South Carolina to central Florida.

Subspecies. *Ammodramus hensiowii henslowii* (Audubon).

Le Conte's Sparrow

Bruant de Le Conte
Ammodramus leconteii (Audubon)
Total length: 11.4 to 13.5 cm
Plate 70

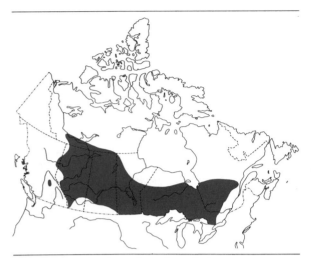

Breeding Distribution of Le Conte's Sparrow

Range in Canada. Breeds in southwestern and central-southern Mackenzie (Fort Simpson, Little Buffalo River, pair reported north to 64°15′N, 127°22′W); central-eastern British Columbia (Peace River parklands; probably in the Cariboo: 115 Mile, Westwick Lakes, and Kootenay District: Columbia valley); Alberta (south to Lethbridge and Brooks, but local in the south; and west to near Jasper); northwest-central, and very locally, in southern Saskatchewan (Lake Athabasca, Churchill River, David-son, Indian Head, Moose Mountain); central and southern Manitoba (The Pas, Lake St. Martin, Lyleton, Hillside Beach southward); north-central to southern Ontario (Attawapiskat, Big Piskwamish Point, East Point; Bradford, probably Toronto and Ottawa. Irregular and local in the south; recorded in summer north to Fort Severn and Winisk); and Quebec (Cabbage Willows, Amos region; Saint-Fulgence).

Recorded in migration at Beaupré, Quebec (21 May 1935) and very rarely in Nova Scotia.

Bill rather slender; tail feathers narrow and sharply pointed. *Adults*: Top of head blackish and brown on either side, with a pale-buff stripe down the middle of the crown; hind-neck striped with chestnut and buffy grey; back and scapulars black mixed with brown, the feathers edged with pale buff, pale grey, or whitish; broad stripe over eye buffy yellow; narrow line extending back from eye blackish; ear patch greyish, malar region buffy yellow; no wing bars; no white in tail; bend of wing white or whitish; breast, sides, and flanks buffy; sides and flanks (but not breast) streaked with blackish; bill bluish; legs dusky flesh colour. *Juvenal*: Similar to adults but more buffy yellowish, hind-neck with little or no chestnut, instead mostly yellowish; breast streaked with blackish.

Measurements. *Adult male*: wing, 50–55.3 (52.3); tail, 44.8–51 (48.1); exposed culmen, 9.6–11.5 (10.7); tarsus, 17–19.1 (18.0). *Adult female*: wing, 47.7–54.3 (50.8) mm.

Field Marks. A small short-tailed grass sparrow with very buffy eyebrow stripe; greyish ear region, plain-buffy breast, but with the sides streaked with black. Most like the Sharp-tailed Sparrow but median crown stripe pale buff (instead of grey), hind-neck pinkish (instead of plain dark-grey). Its sharply streaked sides and grey ear region (some-times obscure and hard to see) separate it from the Grasshopper Sparrow. *Voice*: A short insect-like buzz: *tse bzzzzz*, about one second long.

Habitat. Moist grass and sedge meadows, damp thickly matted grass and shrub tangles on edges of marshes and bogs, areas of tall rank grass either moist or dry.

Nesting. On the ground or a few inches above it in a clump of dead grass and usually concealed by a tangle of vegetation. *Eggs*, 4 or 5; greenish white speckled with browns mainly at the larger end. Incubation period 13 days, by the female (L.H. Walkinshaw).

Range. Breeds from southern Mackenzie east to western Ontario and south to north-central Montana, North Dakota, Minnesota, north-ern Michigan, and southern Ontario. Winters south of the breeding range in central and southern United States.

Sharp-tailed Sparrow

Bruant à queue aiguë
Ammodramus caudacutus (Gmelin)
Total length: 12.8 to 14.8 cm
Plate 70

Breeding Distribution of Sharp-tailed Sparrow

Range in Canada. Summer resident, breeding (very locally) in southern Mackenzie (south-western Great Slave Lake); central-eastern British Columbia (Peace River parklands); northern and south-central Alberta (Dixonville, southern Slave River, and southward to about Red Deer but not in the mountains); central and southern Saskatchewan (Emma Lake, Cypress Lake, Davidson, Qu'Appelle valley, perhaps Regina and Moose Mountain); central and southern Manitoba (The Pas, Riding Mountain, Lyleton, Caliento, Sprague, recorded in summer at Churchill); northern Ontario (coast of James Bay west to Winisk); central-western and central-southern Quebec (in three widely disjunct areas—coast of James Bay: north at least to Eastmain; lower St. Lawrence River: Île aux Grues, Saint-Germain, Île-Verte, Cap-Tourmente, and locally near Percé; also Madeleine Islands); and along the coasts of New Brunswick, Prince Edward Island, and Nova Scotia (including Cape Breton Island).

Migrant in southern Ontario and southwestern Quebec (Lochaber). Summer sight records in northern Manitoba (Churchill).

Bill slender for a sparrow; tail rather short (shorter than folded wings), its feathers narrow and sharply pointed. *Adults*: Top of head with broad median stripe of brownish grey, this bordered on either side by a blackish-brown stripe; rest of upper parts olive grey, the back and scapulars conspicuously striped with blackish brown and a little white; sides of head rich buff with grey ear patch, a narrow blackish line back from the eye; no wing bars or tail patches; bend of wing yellow; under parts whitish but breast, sides, and flanks buffy and streaked with dusky; bill bluish dusky; legs pale brownish. *Juvenal*: General colour rich buff, broadly streaked above with blackish and narrowly on sides and flanks, sometimes on breast.

Measurements *(A. c. subvirgatus)*. *Adult male*: wing, 57.8–60.4 (59.1); tail, 48.4–54.6 (50.3); exposed culmen, 11.7–12.3 (12.0); tarsus, 20.8–22.1 (21.6). *Adult female*: wing, 53.7–59 (56.0) mm.

Field Marks. A small, short-tailed sparrow with very buffy face, greyish ear patch, dark-grey centre of crown, grey hind-neck, black and white stripes on back, lightly striped buffy breast (see Subspecies). The broad dark-grey centre of crown and more contrastingly striped (with black and white) back distinguishes it from similar species like Henslow's, Grasshopper, Le Conte's, and Baird's sparrows. Also it frequents wetter habitats. Flight is buzzy and slow, the short wings beating rapidly. The Sharp-tailed Sparrow most closely resembles the Le Conte's but has a dark-*grey* middle crown, *grey* hind-neck, and lightly streaked breast. *Voice*: Song is a short *te-sheeeeeeeeee*; the *sheee*-part highest pitched, bubbly, and ending abruptly.

Habitat. On the coast, salt and brackish marshes (including wet *Spartina* areas), grassy meadows in the vicinity of salt water. In the western interior, margins of pools, lakes, and marshes, usually preferring a wetter habitat than that of the Le Conte's Sparrow.

Nesting. In loose colonies. On the ground in tall grass. Nest is made of grasses with a lining of finer grasses. *Eggs*, 4 to 6; pale greenish or bluish white, speckled thickly with browns. Incubation is by the female and lasts about 11 days (N.P. Hill).

Range. Breeds locally from southern Mackenzie and central Manitoba south to central Alberta, North Dakota, northeastern South Dakota, and northwestern Minnesota; also on southern James Bay; lower St. Lawrence River; and from northern New Brunswick south on the coast to North Carolina. Winters on the Atlantic Coast from New York south to southern Florida and on the Gulf of Mexico coast from southern Texas east to Florida.

Subspecies. (1) *Ammodramus caudacutus subvirgatus* Dwight: lower St. Lawrence River and Madeleine Islands, Quebec; also New Brunswick, Prince Edward Island and Nova Scotia. (2) *A. c. alterus* (Todd) (more richly coloured than *subvirgatus* but less so than *nelsoni*; intermediate between the two): eastern and western coast of James Bay. (3) *A. c. nelsoni* Allen (more richly coloured than *alterus*, buffs more intense, back more brownish, general coloration darker): southern Mackenzie, central-eastern British Columbia, Alberta, Saskatchewan, Manitoba.

Seaside Sparrow

Bruant maritime
Ammodramus maritimus (Wilson)
Total length: 13.4 to 16.5 cm
Plate 70

Status in Canada. Casual visitant to Nova Scotia (specimen: West Lawrencetown, 5 February 1962; photo record: West Lawrencetown, 14 January 1974; also sight records) and New Brunswick (specimen: Fundy National Park, 18 August 1966; also autumn sight records).

A salt-marsh sparrow. Form similar to that of the Sharp-tailed Sparrow but larger (especially bill), much duller and greyer (little or no buff anywhere); yellow line in front of eye and often extending back over it; pale streak across jaw; back not conspicuously streaked.

Range. Atlantic coastal marshes from Massachusetts south to northern Florida and from central peninsular Florida along the Gulf of Mexico coast to southern Texas.

Subspecies. The Nova Scotian specimen is referable to *Ammodramus maritimus maritimus* (Wilson).

Fox Sparrow

Bruant fauve
Passerella iliaca (Merrem)
Total length: 17 to 19 cm
Plate 73

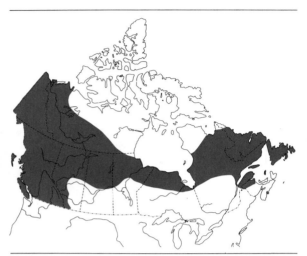

Breeding Distribution of Fox Sparrow

Range in Canada. Breeds from northern Yukon (Babbage River, Cache Creek); northwestern and central-eastern Mackenzie (Mackenzie Delta, Anderson, Artillery Lake); southwestern Keewatin (Nueltin Lake); northern Manitoba (Churchill); northern Ontario (Fort Severn, Winisk); northern Quebec (Lake Guillaume-Delisle, Kuujjuaq, Koroc River); and northern Labrador (Nachvak) south to southern British Columbia (including Queen Charlotte and Vancouver islands but locally in the interior); southwestern and central-eastern Alberta (Waterton Lakes National Park, Red Deer); central Saskatchewan (Nipawin, probably Meadow Lake); central Manitoba (Ilford; an old report of breeding at Duck Mountain requires confirmation); northern Ontario (Big Trout Lake, Moose Factory); southeastern and central-southern Quebec (Schefferville, Pélerins and Basques islands; Gaspé Peninsula; Anticosti and Madeleine islands; very local in the interior and apparently absent from large areas); northwestern New Brunswick (locally); south coastal Nova Scotia (Guilford Island); and southern Newfoundland.

Migrates throughout southern Canada.
Sight records for Banks Island, N.W.T.
Winters in southwestern British Columbia and rarely in southern Ontario, southwestern Quebec, New Brunswick, Nova Scotia, and southern Newfoundland.

A large, sturdily built sparrow, extremely variable geographically in colour, eastern populations mostly rusty red, west coast birds entirely different, mostly sooty brown (see Subspecies). *Adults (P. i. iliaca)*: Rusty brown and grey in various proportions, the rusty brightest on wings, tail, and upper coverts, much mixed with grey on top of head and on back (but top of head and back often mostly grey); two inconspicuous whitish wing bars; under parts white with broad stripes, blotches, and arrow-shaped spots of rusty and chestnut on sides of throat, breast, sides, and flanks; bill dusky above, yellowish below; legs flesh to clay colour. *Juvenal*: Similar to adults but much duller above, white of under parts less pure, streaks on breast narrower (less blotched); plumage texture looser.

Measurements. *Adult male*: wing, 84.6–91.4 (87.8); tail, 69.2–75.6 (72.9); exposed culmen, 11.2–13.8 (12.4); tarsus, 23.8–24.9 (24.5). *Adult female*: wing, 80.8–86.4 (83.9) mm.

Field Marks. A large robust sparrow, its coloration varying greatly geographically (see Subspecies). East of the Rockies and in the northwest it is characterized by its fox reds (especially the tail); the under parts white, heavily blotched and arrow-marked with rusty or chestnut. In interior southern British Columbia it is dark grey above; and on the west coast it is a sooty-brown colour. Much foraging is on the ground where the birds scratch noisily among the leaf litter. *Voice*: The delightful but short song begins with two or three somewhat slurred whistles and closes with more rapid notes, which descend in pitch.

Habitat. Woodland thickets and edges, scrubby woods either coniferous or deciduous, stunted conifers on the coasts, burntlands, and cutover land, streamside shrubbery.

Nesting. On the ground under a bush or tree or low in a tree or shrub. Nest is of grass, twigs, moss, and rootlets, and is lined with grass, hair, and often wool or feathers. *Eggs*, usually 4 or 5; bluish white or greenish white, speckled and spotted with reddish browns.

Range. Breeds from northern Alaska east to Labrador and Newfoundland and south to northwestern Washington on the Pacific Coast of United States and in the mountains to southern California and to central parts of Nevada, Utah, and Colorado. Winters from southern Canada (locally) and northern United States to southern United States.

Subspecies. (1) *Passerella iliaca iliaca* (Merrem), (a rusty-brown race): Breeds in northern Ontario, Quebec, Labrador, Newfoundland, and Nova Scotia. (2) *P. i. zaboria* Oberholser (similar to *iliaca* but averages darker and more greyish): Yukon, Mackenzie, northern British Columbia (south to Dease Lake, Peace River parklands), northern and central Alberta (but not southwestern mountains), northern Saskatchewan, northern Manitoba. (3) *P. i. altivagans* Riley (similar to *zaboria* but browns less rufescent and upper parts more vaguely streaked): Breeds from interior central and southeastern British Columbia (Thutade Lake, Mount Revelstoke), and southwestern Alberta (Jasper National Park intergrading southward in Banff toward *schistacea*). (4) *P. i. schistacea* Baird (head and back dark grey, little streaked): extreme southeastern British Columbia and southwestern Alberta (Waterton Lakes National Park). (5) *P. i. olivacea* Aldrich (averages slightly darker and more olivaceous than *schistacea*): southwestern and south-central interior British Columbia (Mount McLean, Nelson). (6) *P. i. fuliginosa* Ridgway (the darkest and sootiest of the races): southwestern British Columbia (coast including Vancouver Island but not Queen Charlotte Islands). (7) *P. i. townsendi* (Audubon) (similar to *fuliginosa* but somewhat brighter and less sooty): Queen Charlotte Islands, British Columbia.

In addition, the following races that breed in Alaska winter in southwestern British Columbia: (8) *P. i. unalaschensis* (Gmelin); (9) *P. i. insularis* Ridgway; (10) *P. i. sinuosa* Grinnell; (11) *P. i. annectens* Ridgway.

Song Sparrow

Bruant chanteur
Melospiza melodia (Wilson)
Total length: 15.3 to 17.7 cm
Plate 73

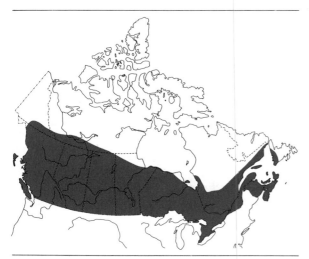

Breeding Distribution of Song Sparrow

Range in Canada. Breeds from central-southern Yukon (Squanga Lake); central-southern Mackenzie (Nahanni National Park, southern Great Slave Lake; perhaps Fort Simpson); northern Saskatchewan (Lake Athabasca, Stony Rapids, Wollaston Lake); northern Manitoba (Herchmer, Lynn Lake; probably Churchill); northern Ontario (Fort Severn, Fort Albany); southern Quebec (Fort-George, Lake Saint-Jean, north shore of the Gulf of St. Lawrence east to Blanc-Sablon); and southwestern Newfoundland (Parsons Pond, Codroy valley); south through British Columbia (including Vancouver and Queen Charlotte islands), Alberta, Saskatchewan, Manitoba, Ontario, Quebec (including Anticosti and Madeleine islands), New Brunswick, Prince Edward Island, and Nova Scotia (including Cape Breton Island).

Winters in coastal and southern British Columbia, southern Ontario (north rarely to Thunder Bay, Manitoulin Island, and Ottawa), and in small numbers in southwestern Quebec (Montréal, rarely to Québec), southern New Brunswick, Prince Edward Island, and Nova Scotia; rarely in Newfoundland (Mobile, St. John's).

Casual in southeastern Keewatin (mouth of McConnell River). Accidental on Banks Island (De Salis Bay), N.W.T.

Wings short and rounded; ninth (outermost) primary shorter than or equal to fourth; tail longish and rounded at tip. The species is extremely variable geographically, west coast populations being darker than more eastern populations (see Subspecies). *Adults (M. m. melodia)*: Top of head brown, narrowly streaked with black and with a narrow grey median stripe; back and scapulars brown streaked with black and with a little greyish feather edging; rump olive brown lightly streaked with dusky; upper tail coverts with a median streak of dark brown; two inconspicuous whitish wing bars; tail brown, the two central feathers with a dusky median line; broad whitish or greyish line over eye; sides of head buffy or greyish with three dark narrow stripes: one behind eye, one along lower edge of cheek, the third bordering sides of throat; sides of neck greyish, lightly streaked with brown; under parts white, the breast, sides, and flanks distinctly streaked with dark brown or black with usually a central breast spot; bill dusky above, paler below; legs pale brownish. *Juvenal*: Resembles adult, but white and grey areas are replaced by yellowish white or buffy; breast streaks finer and usually not forming a breast spot; plumage texture looser. Very similar to juvenal Lincoln's and Swamp sparrows but (when wing fully developed) outermost (ninth) primary shorter than fourth in the Song, longer in Lincoln's. In the flesh, the juvenal Swamp Sparrow has the inside of mouth yellowish, thus separating it from juvenal Song Sparrow.

Measurements *(M. m. melodia). Adult male*: wing, 62.4–69.9 (65.8); tail, 63.1–71 (66.9); exposed culmen, 11.5–13.1 (12.2); tarsus, 20.9–22.3 (21.8). *Adult female*: wing, 60–64.5 (61.9) mm.

Field Marks. A common bird about garden shrubbery all across southern parts of the country. A brown-backed sparrow (in British Columbia very dark and sooty), its whitish under parts heavily streaked with brown and usually with a dark central breast spot. Flies with a pumping action of the longish tail. Several other sparrows have a conspicuously streaked breast, but the Song Sparrow lacks white outer tail feathers shown by the Vesper; it is smaller and much less heavily streaked below than the Fox Sparrow; it has a longer tail than the Savannah and never shows any yellow in front of the eye; adults lack the buffy suffusion on the breast shown by the Lincoln's. In addition, the Song Sparrow's frequently uttered call-note instantly separates it from any of these. *Voice*: The spritely sweet song is a characteristic spring and summer sound in most of southern Canada. It begins with two or three loud notes, which sound like *sweet, sweet, sweet*, followed by a trill, then several short notes that run down to the end of the song. The common call-note is *chimp* with a peculiar quality unlike that of any similar sparrow.

Habitat. Bushy shrubbery along the margins of ponds, lakes, and streams; bushy openings and edges of woods; farmland thickets; shrubbery about buildings; hedgerows; bushy pastures. Not a bird of closed-canopy mature forest.

Nesting. Either on the ground or in a bush or small tree. Early nests are most often on the ground. Nest, composed externally of grasses, weeds, bark and leaves, is lined with finer grasses, roots, and hair. *Eggs*, 3 to 5; pale bluish to greyish green, speckled and blotched with browns and reddish browns. Incubation, by the female alone, requires slightly over 12 to 13 days, rarely 14 to 15 days (Margaret M. Nice).

Range. Breeds from southern Alaska (including the Aleutian Islands) eastward across much of southern Canada to Newfoundland, and south to Mexico, northern New Mexico, northern Arkansas, southeastern Tennessee, northern Georgia, and northwestern South Carolina. Winters from southern Alaska and parts of southern Canada south to southern United States and Mexico.

Subspecies. (1) *Melospiza melodia melodia* (Wilson): southeastern Ontario (Muskoka District), Quebec, Newfoundland, New Brunswick, Prince Edward Island, Nova Scotia. (2) *M. m. euphonia* Wetmore (upper parts duller than *melodia*): southern Ontario (Bruce County, Hamilton). (3) *M. m. juddi* Bishop (upper parts more greyish, the back feathers with more contrasting blackish centres): central-eastern British Columbia (Peace River), Mackenzie, Alberta (except southwestern mountains), Saskatchewan, Manitoba, and western Ontario (east to James Bay). (4) *M. m. merrilli* Brewster (much darker than *juddi* and more uniformly coloured above): southern interior British Columbia (Alta Lake, Shuswap Falls, Newgate), extreme southwestern Alberta (Waterton Lakes National Park). (5) *M. m. morphna* Oberholser (very dark coloration): southwestern British Columbia (Vancouver Island, Chilliwack). (6) *M. m. rufina* (Bonaparte), even darker and sootier than *morphna*, averages larger: northern coastal British Columbia (Queen Charlotte, Porcher, and Spider islands). (7) *M. m. inexspectata* Riley (very similar to *morphna* but more greyish or sooty, less rufescent): southern Yukon, interior northern and central British Columbia (Atlin southeast through interior British Columbia to about latitude 51°, but not Peace River parklands). (8) *M. m. caurina* Ridgway (similar to *rufina* but larger): Migrant on the coast of British Columbia.

Remarks. This sparrow is one of the commonest and most widely distributed in southern Canada. It is also one of the most desirable. Although absent from many parts of Canada during the winter, it is one of the very earliest to return in spring. From the first day of its arrival until well after most birds have ceased singing in late summer, its sweet, pleasing song is heard all over the countryside. Weed seeds bulk large in its diet, although it eats insects also. P.A. Taverner estimated, conservatively, that in the southern cultivated parts of Ontario alone Song Sparrows destroy over 11,000 tonnes of weed seeds annually.

Lincoln's Sparrow

Bruant de Lincoln
Melospiza lincolnii (Audubon)
Total length: 13.5 to 15.3 cm
Plate 73

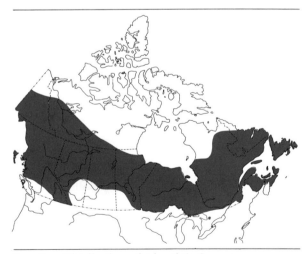

Breeding Distribution of Lincoln's Sparrow

Range in Canada. Breeds from central Yukon (Forty Mile); central-western and southeastern Mackenzie (Forts Good Hope, Simpson, and Resolution; Hill Island Lake; summer sight records north to Inuvik); northern Saskatchewan (Lake Athabasca, Wollaston Lake); northern Manitoba (Churchill); northern Ontario (Fort Severn, Attawapiskat); northern Quebec

Ninth (outermost) primary longer than fourth. *Adults*: Top of head light brown streaked with black and divided by a median stripe of grey; back, scapulars, rump, and upper tail coverts olive brown streaked with black, most heavily on the back; edges of flight feathers rusty brown; tail greyish brown, the two central feathers with a dusky median stripe; stripe over eye and sides of neck greyish; cheek patch margined above and below by a narrow dark-brown streak; malar region buffy; band across breast, sides, and flanks, buffy streaked with black; throat and abdomen white; bill dusky above, bluish below, also often a little yellowish; legs brownish flesh. *Young (first autumn)*: Closely resemble adults. *Juvenals*: Similar to adults but colours more suffused, white of throat and abdomen much less pure, no pure-grey median crown stripe, plumage texture looser. Juvenals very closely resemble those of Swamp Sparrow but have the roof of the mouth greyish brown instead of yellow; and when the wing is well developed, the ninth (outermost) primary is longer than the fourth.

Measurements *(M. l. lincolnii)*. *Adult male*: wing, 61.2–65.3 (63.5); tail, 54.1–60 (56.7); exposed culmen, 10.3–11.3 (10.8); tarsus, 19.9–22.6 (21.7). *Adult female*: wing, 54.6–63 (58.9) mm.

Field Marks. The broad, buffy, black-streaked band across the breast and down the sides distinguishes it from adults of other sparrows. Juvenal Song and Swamp sparrows are very similar to juvenal Lincoln's, being almost impossible to separate in the field. Adult Lincoln's, however, have whiter throat and abdomen and a characteristic sleekness that is very different from the loose texture of the plumage of juvenal Song and Swamp sparrows.

The Lincoln's Sparrow is a skulker, adept at keeping out of sight. On the breeding grounds it can often be recognized by its nervous, almost frenzied, rapid *chips* when an intruder appears. Meanwhile the

(Grande rivière de la Baleine, Kuujjuaq, Hutte sauvage Lake); central Labrador (Nain); and Newfoundland south to southern British Columbia (including Queen Charlotte Islands but perhaps not Vancouver Island; and on the mainland south at least to Chilcotin Lake, Clinton: 9.6 km south, Carpenter Mountain); southwestern and south-central Alberta (Waterton Lakes National Park, Calgary, Red Deer, Camrose); central Saskatchewan (Prince Albert, Nipawin); southern Manitoba (Duck Mountain, Whitemouth, Julius); southern Ontario (Algonquin Provincial Park, Luther Marsh; Alfred Bog, Mer bleue; very locally south to Wainfleet); southern Quebec (very locally: Lac des Loups, Baldwin Mills, Québec, Biencourt, Gaspé Peninsula, Woburn, Anticosti and Madeleine islands); New Brunswick; Prince Edward Island; and Nova Scotia (locally, mostly in eastern localities).

Migrates through southern Canada.

Casual in northern Yukon (Old Crow, Clarence Lagoon).

bird is never still, bobbing, turning, flitting the wings and tail constantly with each *chip*. *Voice*: Song is easily recognizable, a pleasing but hurried melody with some of the bubbling qualities of the House Wren and some characteristics of the Purple Finch's song. The *chip* alarm note is variable even in the same individual.

Habitat. In the breeding season, bogs, moist meadows with patches of alder and willow or stunted conifers, and similar moist and bushy places are favoured. In migration various types of thickets, brush piles, hedges, roadsides, and often weedy or grassy open places near bushes or wood edges.

Nesting. On the ground. Nest is of coarse grasses lined with finer grasses and rootlets. *Eggs*, 4 or 5; whitish or greenish white, blotched and speckled with browns. Incubation period 13 days (J.M. Speirs and R. Andoff) by the female.

Range. Breeds from northwestern Alaska east to central Labrador and south in the western mountains to southern California and northern New Mexico, and in the east to northern Minnesota, northern Michigan, northern New York, and central Maine. Winters from southern United States south to Guatemala and El Salvador.

Subspecies. (1) *Melospiza lincolnii lincolnii* (Audubon): Ontario, Quebec, Labrador, Newfoundland, New Brunswick, Prince Edward Island, Nova Scotia. (2) *M. l. gracilis* (Kittlitz): coastal British Columbia (Queen Charlotte and Vancouver islands; Khutze Inlet). (3) *M. l. alticola* (Miller and McCabe): Yukon, Mackenzie, British Columbia (except coast), Alberta, Saskatchewan, Manitoba.

Remarks. In a low tree or bush on the nesting grounds, the Lincoln's Sparrow reveals its presence by its bubbling song. If an intruder approaches, the sparrow stops singing and slips away. A few minutes later it may sing again from shrubbery farther on. In migration it is usually silent, and because it is extremely adept at keeping out of sight, most of the population slips through unobserved.

Swamp Sparrow

Bruant des marais
Melospiza georgiana (Latham)
Total length: 12.7 to 14.7 cm
Plate 73

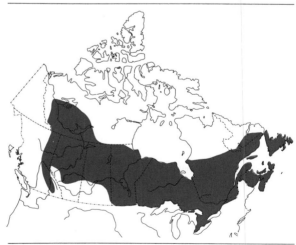

Breeding Distribution of Swamp Sparrow

Range in Canada. Breeds in central-western and southern Mackenzie (Nahanni National Park, Norman Wells, Keith Arm, Hill Island Lake); eastern British Columbia (Minaker River, Nulki Lake, Peace River parklands, Nelson; probably Watson Lake); northern and south-central

Ninth (outermost) primary shorter than fourth. *Breeding plumage*: Top of head variable. Commonly, crown is chestnut, forehead black divided by a narrow grey line, but often top of head is dark brown streaked with black and with a grey median line from base of bill to nape; back and scapulars reddish brown, broadly streaked with black and narrowly with white; rump olive brown, upper tail coverts brown; most of exposed parts of closed wing chestnut; tail brown edged with rusty, the two centre feathers with a blackish median stripe; sides of head and sides of neck mostly grey, cheeks slightly brownish, bordered above by a narrow, dark postocular streak and below usually by another reaching back from gape; throat and abdomen whitish; a broad pale-grey band across breast extending to sides where it joins the brown of sides and flanks; breast often finely streaked darker and often with a vague dusky spot; bill dusky above, paler below; legs pale brownish. *Adults in autumn and winter*: Resemble breeding birds but top of head often more heavily streaked with black and with more buffy general coloration. *Young in first autumn*: Like adults in autumn but eyebrow stripe buffy or even, rarely, yellow instead of pure grey, and as a rule more buffy generally. *Juvenal*: Very similar to juvenal Lincoln's Sparrow but usually darker above with darker chestnut wing edging. The usually (not always) yellowish inside of mouth distinguishes juvenals in the flesh from those of both the Lincoln's Sparrow and the Song Sparrow.

Measurements (*M. g. georgiana*). *Adult male*: wing, 58.9–62.7 (60.7); tail, 53–60 (56.1); exposed culmen, 9.9–12 (11.1); tarsus, 20.9–22.3 (21.6). *Adult female*: wing, 54.5–61.4 (57.6) mm.

Alberta (south to Battle River region and Red Deer); northern and central Saskatchewan (Lake Athabasca, Churchill River, Emma Lake, Nipawin); northern, central, and southern Manitoba; northern, central, and southern Ontario; central and southern Quebec (Grande rivière de la Baleine, Lake Mistassini, the north shore of the Gulf of St. Lawrence east to Blanc-Sablon at least, and southward including Anticosti and Madeleine islands); southern Labrador (Goose Bay); Newfoundland; New Brunswick; Prince Edward Island; and Nova Scotia (including Cape Breton Island).

Migrates through most of southern Canada but only rarely in western British Columbia.

Casual in north-central Quebec (near Redmond Lake).

Occasional in winter in extreme southern Ontario, southwestern Quebec, New Brunswick, Prince Edward Island, and Nova Scotia.

Field Marks. A rather dark-backed sparrow of wetlands, for the most part showing chestnut on the wing edgings and a chestnut cap; whitish throat and plain-grey breast (often there is a vague dusky breast spot). Chipping and Tree sparrows also have red caps, but the Tree Sparrow, a winter bird in settled southern parts of Canada, has prominent white wing bars and a *well-defined* breast spot instead of a vague one, or none at all. The Chipping Sparrow is a slenderer bird with all-grey (instead of brownish) flanks; the dark line through the eye extends forward to the base of the bill, not just behind the eye; and it has very different habitat preferences. *Voice*: Song is a trill a little like that of the Chipping Sparrow but more musical, slower, and louder. Call-note, a metallic *chink*.

Habitat. In the breeding season, wetlands. Margins of ponds, lakes, and streams with tall emergent vegetation such as cattails, or woody shrubbery like alder and willow; freshwater marshes with tangles of vegetation. In migration it favours this type of habitat but frequents also weedy fields near water or even dry thickets on wood edges and openings.

Nesting. In a tussock of marsh vegetation or low in a bush. Nest is composed outwardly of coarse grasses or grasslike vegetation and is lined with fine grasses. *Eggs*, usually 4 or 5; variable in coloration but usually pale bluish-green, blotched and speckled with various shades of brown. Incubation period about 13 days (O.W. Knight); by the female.

Range. Breeds from Mackenzie and northeastern British Columbia east to southern Labrador and Newfoundland and south in the United States to eastern Nebraska, northern Missouri, northern Indiana, central Ohio, south-central West Virginia, and Delaware. Winters from eastern Nebraska, Iowa, southern Wisconsin, and extreme southern parts of eastern Canada (locally and rarely) south to southern Texas, the Gulf Coast of the United States, and southern Florida.

Subspecies. (1) *Melospiza georgiana ericrypta* Oberholser: British Columbia, Alberta, Saskatchewan, Manitoba, northern Ontario (Rainy River District, Chapleau), central and southern Quebec (south to Lake Saint-Jean, Gaspé Peninsula), Labrador, Newfoundland, extreme northern New Brunswick. (2) *M. g. georgiana* (Latham), characterized by darker, duller upper parts: southern Ontario (Biscotasing, Eganville, southward), southwestern Quebec (Kazabazua, Québec southward), central and southern New Brunswick, Prince Edward Island, and Nova Scotia.

White-throated Sparrow

Bruant à gorge blanche
Zonotrichia albicollis (Gmelin)
Total length: 16 to 18 cm
Plate 73

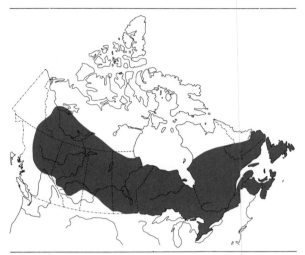

Breeding Distribution of White-throated Sparrow

Range in Canada. Breeds from southeastern Yukon (Watson Lake); western-central and southern Mackenzie (Norman Wells, Nahanni National Park, central-northern Great Slave Lake); northern Saskatchewan (Stony Rapids, Hasbala Lake); northern Manitoba (Churchill, Bird, Herchmer, Fort Nelson); northern Ontario (Fort Severn, Attawapiskat); north-central Quebec (Grande rivière de la Baleine, Schefferville); southern Labrador (Goose Bay, Cartwright); and Newfoundland south to central-interior British Columbia (commonly in northeast; and westward sparingly to Kispiox valley and Nulki Lake); central Alberta (south to about Red Deer and Nevis); central and southeastern Saskatchewan (Prince Albert, Sheho, Qu'Appelle valley and Moose Mountain region) and through southern Manitoba (except extreme southwest); southern Ontario; southern Quebec (including Anticosti and Madeleine islands); New Brunswick; Prince Edward Island; and Nova Scotia.

In migration occurs sparingly south of the breeding range in southern British Columbia (rarely west to Vancouver Island), southern Alberta, and southern Saskatchewan.

Winters rarely in southern Ontario, south-western Quebec, southern parts of the Maritimes, and southern British Columbia. Very rarely elsewhere.

Accidental in southern Baffin Island (West Foxe Islands, 3 July 1955). Summer sight records for Coats Island, N.W.T.

Adults (variable; see J.K. Lowther, 1961. Canadian Journal of Zoology, vol. 39, no. 3, pp. 281–292): Top of head with two broad lateral stripes varying from all black to dark chestnut brown; median crown stripe varying from white to grey or tan; back and scapulars chestnut brown striped with black; rump plain pale-brown; two white wing bars; bend of wing pale yellow; tail dark brown narrowly edged with pale brown; broad pale stripe over eye, yellow in front, white to buffy behind eye; narrow line from eye to nape, black to brown; cheeks and upper breast, grey (often more or less streaked with dusky); throat patch white, sharply cut off from surrounding grey and framed on each side by a thin line of black; sides and flanks grey mixed with brown; abdomen white; bill dark brown above, paler and more bluish grey below; legs pinkish flesh or pale brown. *Juvenal*: Upper parts mostly chestnut brown streaked with black; median crown stripe and stripe over eye buffy grey; line extending from eye to nape brown; wing bars buffy; sides of throat, breast, and sides buff streaked with blackish brown; throat greyish white (but not sharply cut off in a patch); abdomen dull white tinged with buff. Juvenals of the White-throat are readily distinguished from juvenal White-crowns by much more rusty coloration in the upper parts of the former.

Measurements. *Adult male*: wing, 72–77.8 (73.9); tail, 68–77 (73.2); exposed culmen, 10–12 (11.4); tarsus, 23–24.1 (23.6). *Adult female*: wing, 65.4–73.9 (69.3) mm.

Field Marks. A largish sparrow. Its striped head is most like that of the White-crowned Sparrow, but the present species has a white throat patch well defined against the grey of breast, a yellow spot in front of eye, and a dark bill (instead of pinkish or yellowish). *Voice*: The plaintive whistled song begins with two clear leisurely notes, followed by a three-note phrase, repeated two or three times. Canadians often paraphrase it *I-love-Canada, Canada, Canada*. It also has a lisping call-note, *tseet*.

Habitat. Bushy openings in or edges of woodlands (mostly coniferous or mixedwood), burntlands, clearings cluttered with slashing, open young woodlands and thickets.

Nesting. Usually on the ground beneath a shrub or in a clump of grass. Nest is a cup composed externally of grass, twigs, chips of rotten wood, mosses, conifer needles and lined with fine grasses, rootlets, hair, sometimes pine needles. *Eggs*, 3 to 5, usually 4; greyish, bluish, or greenish white, variously blotched and speckled with browns and sometimes some purplish grey. Incubation period 11 to 14 days (J.K. Lowther).

Range. Breeds from wooded parts of Canada (southern Yukon and interior British Columbia east to Newfoundland) south in the United States to northern North Dakota, central Minnesota, central Michigan, northern Ohio, northern West Virginia, southeastern New York, and Massachusetts.

Remarks. The unhurried, clearly whistled song of the White-throated Sparrow is one of the delightful summer sounds of the north woods. Except in the extreme West, this sparrow is numerous as a summer resident or as a spring and autumn migrant. It eats insects, weed seeds (including seeds of ragweed), and wild fruits.

Golden-crowned Sparrow

Bruant à couronne dorée
Zonotrichia atricapilla (Gmelin)
Total length: 15 to 18.3 cm
Plate 73

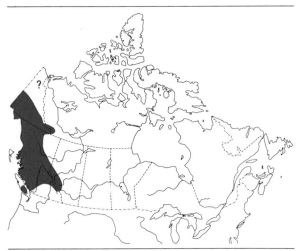

Breeding Distribution of Golden-crowned Sparrow

Range in Canada. Breeds from central Yukon (southern Ogilvie Mountains, Kluane Game Sanctuary, Rose River, Sheldon Lake, probably north to Bell River where reported in breeding season) and southwestern Mackenzie (Nahanni National Park) southward to southern British Columbia (mainly Coast Ranges and eastward: Alta Lake, Tonquin Pass; rarely southern Vancouer Island: Saanich), and southwestern Alberta (Jasper and Banff national parks east to Mountain Park).

In migration southern British Columbia including Queen Charlotte and Vancouver islands. Winters in small numbers in southwestern British Columbia (Victoria, Vancouver, Okanagan Landing).

Casual east of the Rockies in Alberta (Red Deer, Calgary), Saskatchewan (Regina, Indian Head), and northwestern Mackenzie (Tuktoyaktuk). Accidental in Ontario (photo: one immature at Gosport, 3–20 January 1982) and Nova Scotia (photo record: Caledonia, 8–11 May, 1977; sight record: Sable Island, 9 October 1967).

Adults: Top of head black with a broad median stripe of yellow, which becomes abruptly grey posteriorly; back and scapulars olive brown, broadly streaked with blackish brown; rump plain olive-brown; two white wing bars; tail plain brown; sides of head, sides of neck, throat, and breast greyish or brownish grey; sides and flanks brownish; abdomen whitish; bill brownish or dusky above, pale below; legs pinkish brown to greyish brown. *Young (first autumn)*: Similar to adults but without the broad black crown stripes. Instead, the forehead is yellowish olive, the posterior part of crown greyish brown, both flecked or narrowly streaked with dusky. *Juvenal*: Resembles young in first autumn but yellowish olive is lacking on forehead; sides of throat, breast, sides, and flanks are streaked with dusky. Any trace of yellow in the crown separates the young from young White-crowns.

Measurements. *Adult male*: wing, 77.3–84 (81.1); tail, 76–81.3 (78.6); exposed culmen, 11.2–12.1 (11.9); tarsus, 23.1–25.2 (24.4). *Adult female*: wing, 75.2–79.5 (77.5) mm.

Field Marks. A large sparrow somewhat like the White-crowned, but adults lack white stripes on head. Instead, the Golden-crown has a broad yellow median crown stripe, bordered on each side by a broad black stripe, and has a mostly dark bill instead of a yellowish or pinkish one. Young in autumn might be confused with the White-crowned but lack the well-defined brown and buffy head stripes of the White-crown and usually show yellow on the forehead (which the White-crown never has). *Voice*: Song is usually three or four whistled notes on a descending scale and is usually in a minor key.

Habitat. In the nesting season, thickets of shrubbery, mostly above or at timberline in the western mountains, recumbent and dwarf conifers near timberline, shrubbery along streams. In migration and in winter it favours brushy situations similar to those inhabited by the White-crown.

Nesting. On the ground or low in a shrub or dwarfed tree. *Eggs*, usually 4 or 5; pale greenish or pale buffy speckled with browns.

Range. Breeds from western coastal Alaska and south-central Yukon south to southern British Columbia and southwestern Alberta; also extreme northeastern Siberia. Winters from southern British Columbia southward (mostly west of the Cascades and Sierra Nevada) to northern Baja California.

White-crowned Sparrow

Bruant à couronne blanche
Zonotrichia leucophrys (Forster)
Total length: 16.5 to 19 cm
Plate 73

Geographically variable (see Subspecies). *Adults (Z. l. leucophrys)*: Top of head with two broad stripes of black, separated by a broad median stripe of white; black of crown reaches down to cover upper half of lores (but not in most western races; see Subspecies); a narrow black line extends from eye to back of nape with a broader band of white above it; rest of face, sides of neck, and breast plain grey becoming whitish on throat and abdomen and becoming greyish buffy on sides and flanks; back and scapulars light grey broadly streaked with brown; rump and upper tail coverts pale brownish; wings with two white bars; tail dark brown; bill reddish or pinkish brown (but see Subspecies); legs flesh colour to brown. *Young (first autumn)*: Similar to adults but more brownish (less greyish); the dark head stripes brown instead of black, the light head stripes buffy instead of whitish. *Juvenal*: Similar to young in first autumn but breast and sides profusely streaked with dusky; streaks of the back and scapulars black instead of brown.

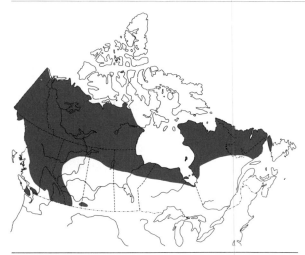

Breeding Distribution of White-crowned Sparrow

Range in Canada. Breeds from northern Yukon (upper Babbage River); northern Mackenzie (Mackenzie Delta, mouth of Anderson River, Coppermine, Bathurst Inlet); central Keewatin (Back River); northern Manitoba (Lynn Lake, Churchill); northern Ontario (Fort Severn); northern Quebec (Déception Bay, Kuujjuaq); Port Burwell, N.W.T.; and northern Labrador south through southern British Columbia (including southern Vancouver Island but evidently absent from the north coast and Queen Charlotte Islands, sparsely and locally in extreme southern interior mountains); northern, western, and southeastern Alberta (Peace River, Dixonville, Lake Athabasca; Jasper, Banff, and Waterton Lakes national parks eastward to Nordegg and Calgary; also Cypress Hills); northern and extreme southwestern Saskatchewan (Lake Athabasca, Reindeer Lake; also in the Cypress Hills); northern Manitoba (Brochet, Ilford); northern Ontario (Fort Albany, Moose Island, and inland to Big Trout and Sutton lakes); James Bay (Akimiski Island, Paint Hills Islands); south-central Quebec (Paul Bay, Schefferville, Sawbill, the outer north shore of the Gulf of St. Lawrence from about Johan-Beetz Bay eastward); and northern Newfoundland (Flowers Cove, St. Anthony).

Spring and autumn transient through most of Canada south of the breeding range but uncommon in New Brunswick, rare and irregular in Nova Scotia and Prince Edward Island.

Casual in Franklin District: Banks Island (Sachs Harbour), Victoria Island, Somerset Island (Union River), Bathurst Island (specimen: 30 July 1984), Melville Peninsula (Elizabeth Point), and southern Baffin Island (Dorset, Taverner Bay, Lake Harbour). Accidental on Fletcher's Ice Island (82°37′N, 99°50′W) 16 June 1957. Sight records on Prince Leopold Island (singles seen in June, July, and August 1975).

Measurements (*Z. l. leucophrys*). *Adult male*: wing, 76.8–83 (79.9); tail, 72–76.3 (74.1); exposed culmen, 10.9–12.2 (11.8); tarsus, 22.1–24 (23.2). *Adult female*: wing, 73.1–79 (75.4) mm.

Field Marks. The conspicuous black and white stripes on the otherwise grey head distinguish this largish sparrow from others except the White-throated Sparrow. However, the White-crown's pinkish or yellowish (instead of mostly dusky) bill, lack of a yellow spot in front of eye, and absence of a sharply defined white throat patch are points that distinguish it. The White-crown's paler (pinkish or yellowish) bill and lack of any yellow on the crown distinguish it from the Golden-crowned Sparrow. Young White-crowns in their first autumn have reddish-brown and buff head stripes but otherwise closely resemble the adults. The geographic races differ considerably and under good conditions can sometimes be distinguished in the field (see Subspecies). *Voice*: Song is rather short and a little melancholy. It begins with one or two leisurely whistles followed by quicker notes ending in two or three rapidly descending notes. It is much less impressive than that of the White-throated Sparrow.

Habitat. Throughout its vast breeding range it is primarily a bird of woody shrubbery and thickets in more open situations: dwarf birch and dwarf willow patches on tundra edge or along streams and depressions; in recumbent or stunted spruce on wind-swept coasts; also bushy edges of woodlands, openings, old burns, and mountainside shrubbery.

Nesting. On the ground or near the ground in a bush or stunted tree. Nest is rather bulky, composed externally of twigs, coarse grass, shreds of bark, often moss and lichen, and is lined with fine grasses and rootlets or hair. *Eggs*, usually 4 or 5; pale greyish white to pale greenish-blue, thickly blotched and speckled with reddish browns. Incubation period averages 12 to 12.5 days and up to 14 days (B.D. Blanchard), by the female.

Range. Breeds from northern Alaska eastward across much of the northern mainland of Canada to Labrador and northern Newfoundland and south in the United States to south-central California, Nevada, central Arizona, and northern New Mexico. Winters from southern British Columbia, southern Idaho, Kansas, Kentucky, and western North Carolina south to central Mexico, the Gulf Coast of United States, and Cuba.

Subspecies. (1) *Zonotrichia leucophrys leucophrys* (Forster), white stripe above eye cut off in front by a black bar; bend of wing usually white; bill pinkish: Breeds in Ontario (intergrading with *gambelii* at Fort Severn), Quebec, Labrador, Newfoundland. (2) *Z. l. gambelii* (Nuttall), resembles *leucophrys*, but white line over eye not cut off anteriorly but extends forward unbroken to base of bill; bill yellowish or pinkish brown: Yukon, Mackenzie, Keewatin south to northwest and central-southern British Columbia (intergrading with *oriantha* at Elko), southwestern Alberta (intergrades with *oriantha* from Banff southward), northern Saskatchewan, northern Manitoba (intergrading with *leucophrys*), and northwestern Ontario (intergrades with *leucophrys* at Fort Severn). (3) *Z. l. oriantha* Oberholser (white stripe over eye interrupted by black bar, thus resembling *leucophrys* but back coloration paler): southwestern and southeastern Alberta (Waterton Lakes National Park, Cypress Hills), southwestern Saskatchewan (Cypress Hills), also southeastern British Columbia (Elko). (4) *Z. l. pugetensis* Grinnell (white stripe over eye not cut off in front of eye by a black bar, thus resembling *gambelii* but coloration above and below darker and duller, bend of wing consistently yellow, size slightly smaller): southwestern British Columbia (Vancouver Island, Vancouver).

Harris's Sparrow

Bruant à face noire
Zonotrichia querula (Nuttall)
Total length: 17.5 to 19.6 cm
Plate 71

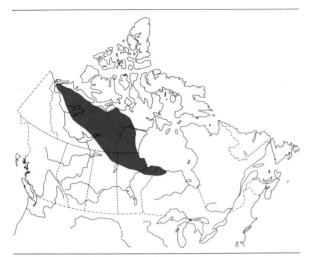

Breeding Distribution of Harris's Sparrow

Range in Canada. Breeds in Mackenzie (eastern Mackenzie Delta, head of Great Bear River, Bathurst Inlet, eastern Great Slave Lake, Thelon River); southern Keewatin (Aberdeen Lake, Nueltin Lake, Tha-anne River); northeastern Saskatchewan (Hasbala and Milton lakes); northern Manitoba (Cochrane River, Churchill, Bird); and northeastern Ontario (Fort Severn). Possibly breeds in northeastern Yukon (lower Bonnet Plume River).

Common spring and autumn transient in Saskatchewan and Manitoba; scarce transient in British Columbia (but recorded west to Vancouver Island), Alberta, and western Ontario (Thunder Bay).

Rare transient in southern and central Ontario (London, Strathroy, Etobicoke, Rossport, Kirkland Lake, Ottawa, Hornepayne) and southwestern Quebec (Saint-Laurent, Val d'Or, Charlesbourg, Rimouski), accidental on Banks Island (photo Nelson Head, 15 June 1974) and Jenny Lind Island (specimens 1 and 5 June 1966), N.W.T., and in Nova Scotia (photo: Seal Island, 29 September 1973; photo record: Wilmot, 16 December 1981 at least to 23 February 1982).

Winters sparingly in southern British Columbia (Victoria, Sumas, Lillooet).

Adults (spring and summer): Top of head, nape, front of face, chin, and throat, black, which extends as streaks or spots to the mid-breast; sides of head behind eye mostly grey with small black patch just behind ear region; remainder of upper parts brown, the back and scapulars streaked with black; two white wing bars; tail greyish brown, its outer feathers often narrowly tipped with white; under parts (except black throat and mid-breast) white, the sides and flanks buffy, streaked with black and dusky; under tail coverts buffy with grey-brown centres; bill pinkish brown; legs pale brown. *Adults (autumn and winter)*: Similar to adults in spring but cheeks and sides of neck buffy, spot behind ear region brown, blacks somewhat obscured. *Young (first autumn)*: Similar to adults in autumn but throat white, bordered on either side by a narrow blackish stripe; crown feathers black centrally and much margined with greyish buff giving crown a scaly appearance; a necklace of blackish brown on upper breast. *Juvenal*: Greyish buff above, streaked with dusky, heavily (almost blackish) on crown, but stripes on rump paler and sparser; sides of breast buffy finely streaked dusky; under parts whitish, the breast and sides streaked dusky; throat with dusky stripe on each side; wing bars buffy.

Measurements (breeding birds). *Adult male*: wing, 83–89.4 (85.7); tail, 79.1–86 (81.7); exposed culmen, 12–13.4 (12.9); tarsus, 23–25 (24.2). *Adult female*: wing, 78.9–83.5 (81.0) mm. (Specimens in fresh autumn plumage average slightly larger in wing and tail.)

Field Marks. A large sparrow. Adult in spring and summer with black throat, face, and crown; grey cheeks; pinkish bill; in autumn with buffy cheeks and the blacks somewhat obscured. First autumn immature has the throat white, a heavy necklace of blackish brown, and buffy cheeks. *Voice*: The song is whistled, begins with one to several notes on the same pitch in a minor key usually; these are followed by other notes, which may be either higher or lower. Has a loud metallic *chip*; also musical twitters, often interspersed with harsh notes.

Habitat. In the nesting season patches of stunted trees and woody shrubbery in the ecotone between forest and tundra. In migration and winter, various thickets, edges of woodland, and hedgerows.

Nesting. On the ground in the shelter of a shrub or stunted tree. Nest is composed externally of twigs, weed stems, mosses, and lichens, and is well lined with fine grasses. *Eggs*, 3 to 5; pale greenish or greyish (variously blotched, often heavily) and speckled with reddish browns. Incubation period at least 13.5 days (J.R. Jehl and D.J.T. Hussell).

Range. Breeds in Mackenzie, Keewatin, and northern Manitoba. Winters from southern British Columbia, northern Utah, northern Nebraska, and central Iowa to southern California, central Arizona, south-central Texas, and Tennessee.

Dark-eyed Junco

(formerly Slate-colored Junco;
includes Oregon and Gray-headed juncos)

Junco ardoisé
Junco hyemalis (Linnaeus)
Total length: 14.5 to 16.5 cm
Plate 72

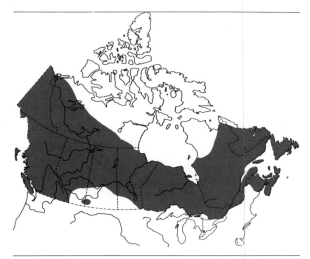

Breeding Distribution of Dark-eyed Junco

Range in Canada. Breeds from northern Yukon
(except narrow coastal plain); northwestern and
central Mackenzie (Mackenzie Delta, Fort
Anderson, Reliance); southern Keewatin
(Windy River); northern Manitoba (Churchill);
northern Ontario (Shagamu River); southern
James Bay (Charlton and Paint Hills islands,
probably Akimiski Island); northern Quebec
(Lake Guillaume-Delisle, Koroc River, Kopaluk
near Kangiqsualujjuaq, Kuujjuaq); Labrador
(Nain, Makkovik, Goose Bay, Cartwright); and
Newfoundland south through British Columbia;
south-central Alberta (Nevis, Jasper, Cypress
Hills); south-central Saskatchewan (Roddick,
Nipawin; locally Cypress Hills, and the
Qu'Appelle valley); southern Manitoba (Riding
Mountain, Winnipeg, Rennie); southern Ontario
(locally south to Barrie, formerly at least to
London); southern Quebec (Gatineau Park,
Hatley, Gaspé Peninsula, Anticosti and Madeleine
islands); and throughout New Brunswick;
Prince Edward Island; and Nova Scotia.
Migrates abundantly in southern Canada.

Winters in small numbers in southern
British Columbia, north on the coast to Queen
Charlotte Islands, southern Alberta (north
to Edmonton), southern Saskatchewan (north
to Nipawin), southern Manitoba (Winnipeg),
southern Ontario (Huntsville, Ottawa southward), southwestern Quebec (Aylmer, Montréal, Québec), New Brunswick, Prince Edward
Island, Nova Scotia, and Newfoundland
(Avalon Peninsula, Tompkins, Ship Cove).

Casual on Banks Island (specimens: Sachs
Harbour, 23 and 30 May 1953); Baillie Island;
Bernard Harbour, Mackenzie, 8 June 1916;
Repulse Bay; Southampton Island; and south-
ern Baffin Island (Lake Harbour, 2 June 1931).
Sight records for Prince Leopold Island,
N.W.T. (June and August 1975).

The Slate-colored Junco and the Oregon Junco are now considered one
and the same species and are combined under the name Dark-eyed
Junco, *Junco hyemalis* (1973. Auk, vol. 90, no. 2, p. 418).

Varies greatly geographically, especially in colour (see Subspecies).
Junco hyemalis hyemalis of eastern North America: *Adult male*: Head,
neck, back, rump, wings, breast, sides, and flanks plain dark-slate
colour, darkest (almost black) on head; lower breast, abdomen, and
under tail coverts plain white sharply cut off from slaty parts; central
tail feathers slaty black, the two outermost tail feathers white, the third
partly slate, partly white; bill pinkish or flesh colour, often tipped with
dusky especially in autumn and winter; legs brownish-flesh colour.
Adult female: Similar to adult male but paler grey and usually (not
always) with some dusky in second from outermost tail feather. *Young
in first autumn and winter*: Similar to adults, but males somewhat
tinged with brown, the females decidedly so, the slaty areas washed with
brown, the tertials edged with brown. *Juvenal*: Head, neck, back, rump,
breast, sides, and flanks greyish brown streaked with dusky; abdomen
white; tail similar to that of adult.

Junco hyemalis oreganus of coastal British Columbia: *Adult male*:
Head, neck, and upper breast black, thus forming a hood, which is well
defined both above and below, the black *not* extending onto sides; sides
and flanks pinkish cinnamon; back and scapulars rich dark brown;
rump slaty grey; abdomen white contrasting sharply with black breast;
no wing bars; tail blackish, its outermost feathers white or nearly so,
the second mostly white, the third with a little white toward tip; bill
pinkish flesh and often dusky at tip; legs pale brownish. *Adult female*:
Similar to adult male but head, neck, and breast dull slate; top of head,
hind-neck, and back brown; sides and flanks duller and less pinkish.
Juvenal: Upper parts brown streaked with black; throat, breast, and
sides buffy streaked with black; otherwise similar to adults.

Measurements *(J. h. hyemalis)*. *Adult male*: wing, 76.4–79.8 (78.4);
tail, 64.1–70.1 (67.2); exposed culmen, 10.2–11.5 (10.8); tarsus,
20.2–21.8 (20.9). *Adult female*: wing, 70.2–76 (73.4) mm.

Field Marks. Sparrow-size birds showing white outer tail feathers,
conspicuous in flight. Adults have solid dark slate-coloured head and
breast (no streaks), the dark breast sharply cut off from white abdomen. Upper parts and sides are slaty but showing more or less reddish
brown on sides and back (this varies according to subspecies and sex).
Vesper Sparrow has similar white outer tail feathers but its *streaked*
breast and upper parts readily separate it from *adult* juncos (no
streaks). Juncos in juvenal plumage (worn briefly in late summer) are
streaked but the streaks are dull and much less contrasty, the overall
appearance darker and duller, than in Vesper Sparrows. *Voice*: Song is
a trill somewhat like that of the Chipping Sparrow but more musical;
also a soft rambling combination of twitters, warbles, and *chips*. Its
alarm note, a *chip* with a characteristic snapping ring to it.

Habitat. In the nesting season, coniferous and mixed woodlands,
especially openings and edges; burntlands, occasionally gardens. In
winter and migration, various weedy places; fields, roadsides, gardens,
and similar situations not too far from cover of trees or thickets.

Nesting. On or near the ground, the nest usually concealed under
vegetation, behind tree roots or under a fallen tree; often in a cavity in
a steep slope; sometimes in the roots of an upturned tree or in a crevice
in a stump; exceptionally on the verandah of a house. Nest is a cup,
outwardly constructed of rootlets, grass, and moss, and lined with fine
grasses, rootlets, hairs, moss stems, rarely porcupine quills. *Eggs*,
usually 4 or 5, rarely 6; whitish or pale bluish-white, speckled (occasionally somewhat blotched) with reddish browns and often a little purplish
grey. Incubation 11 to 12 days (F.L. Burns), usually by the female but
according to T.S. Roberts (1932) rarely assisted by the male. Two
broods annually.

Range. Breeds from northwestern Alaska east to Labrador and Newfoundland and much of forested Canada (see Range in Canada) and south to northern Baja California, and in the United States south to coastal California, western Nevada, southern Idaho, northern Wyoming, South Dakota, central Minnesota, Wisconsin, central Michigan, northeastern Ohio, northern and western Pennsylvania, New York, and Connecticut, and in the Appalachian Mountains to northern Georgia. Winters from southern Canada south to northern Mexico and southern United States.

Subspecies. (1) *Junco hyemalis hyemalis* (Linnaeus): Breeds in northern and central Yukon, Mackenzie, southern Keewatin, Alberta (except mountains), Saskatchewan, Manitoba, Ontario, Quebec, Labrador, Newfoundland, New Brunswick, Prince Edward Island, and Nova Scotia. (2) *J. h. cismontanus* Dwight (similar to *hyemalis* but hood more blackish, often noticeably darker than back; back more brownish; females with sides more mixed with pinkish brown): southwestern Yukon, northern and central British Columbia (northeast at least to Muncho and Summit lakes where intergrading with *hyemalis*), southwestern Alberta (Jasper National Park); intergrades with *montanus* where the ranges of the two come together. (3) *J. h. oreganus* (Townsend) with very dark head, sides, and back; very ruddy back and sides (see description above): coastal British Columbia (south to Calvert Island). (4) *J. h. shufeldti* Coale with greyer, less reddish back, less blackish head, than *oreganus*: southwestern British Columbia (west slopes of the Coast Range, intergrading with *oreganus* on Vancouver Island). (5) *J. h. montanus* Ridgway, similar to *shufeldti* but wings and tail averaging shorter: central and south interior British Columbia, southwestern Alberta. (6) *J. h. mearnsi* Ridgway, paler grey hood, paler more pinkish sides than in any of the above-listed races: southeastern Alberta and southwestern Saskatchewan (Cypress Hills). (7) *J. h. caniceps* (Woodhouse) lacks well-defined hood; has blackish lores, a rufous-red patch on upper back; very pale ashy-grey head, neck, sides, and under parts: accidental in British Columbia (near Qualicum Beach, 9 November 1975) and in Manitoba (St. Vital, 26 January 1963 until March 1964). Photos support both records.

McCown's Longspur

Bruant à collier gris
Calcarius mccownii (Lawrence)
Total length: 14 to 16 cm
Plate 74

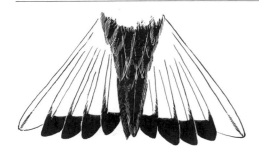

Figure 95
Tail of McCown's Longspur

Bill rather stout; hind toenail long and slender. *Adult male (breeding plumage)*: Top of head black, becoming mixed with brownish grey on nape and grey on back of neck; back and scapulars pale buffy-brown broadly streaked with dusky; rump more greyish, less heavily streaked; wings with patch of chestnut formed by some of the lesser and middle coverts; tail with two dusky central feathers, the rest mostly white and tipped with brownish black (but black much reduced or absent on outermost); sides of head grey with broad white line over eye and a black one from base of bill backward across jaw; under parts mostly white with a broad black crescent across breast; bill bluish black; eyes dark brown. *Adult male (autumn and winter)*: Similar but black areas obscured by brownish or buffy feather tips. *Adult female*: Upper parts pale buffy-brown streaked with dusky; middle wing coverts usually with a trace of chestnut; tail as in adult male; sides of head pale buff with a narrow dark-brown line extending back from eye and one from base of bill backward across jaw; under parts whitish, the breast feathers tipped with buff and sometimes some grey.

Measurements. *Adult male*: wing, 87–95.9 (90.3); tail, 51.5–58.5 (54.8); exposed culmen, 10.9–12.5 (11.9); tarsus, 19–20.4 (19.7). *Adult female*: wing, 81.7–86.2 (84.5) mm.

Breeding Distribution of McCown's Longspur

Range in Canada. Breeds in southeastern Alberta (east of the mountains: north to Youngstown, west to Calgary) and southern Saskatchewan (north to Rosetown, Davidson, Regina; formerly Indian Head). Recorded in migration in southwestern Manitoba (Whitewater Lake and near Lyleton).

Casual in southern British Columbia (Chilliwack, Newgate) and north-central Alberta (Lesser Slave Lake).

Field Marks. Adult male in spring and summer is easily recognizable by the black crescent on the breast and black top of head (Horned Lark also has a black crescent on the breast, but its thin bill and face markings are quite different). Female McCown's Longspur is a brown sparrow with unstreaked breast. It is most like the female Chestnut-collared Longspur, but the McCown's unstreaked under parts and peculiar tail pattern (spread tail forms an inverted dark "T" on an otherwise white background, Figure 95) are helpful in separating the two (see Chestnut-collared Longspur). *Voice*: Song is an exuberant and pleasing series of warbles and twitters, usually given as the bird floats slowly downward to the ground with spread tail and wings.

Habitat. Short-grass plains; occasionally cultivated fields.

Nesting. In a small depression on the ground. Nest is mostly of coarse grasses and is lined with finer grasses. *Eggs*, 3 to 5, rarely 6; white to pale greenish, speckled, scrawled, and lined with browns and a little purplish grey. Incubation requires 12 days (F.W. Mickey), probably entirely by the female.

Range. Breeds from southern Alberta, southern Saskatchewan and central-northern North Dakota, south to southeastern Wyoming, northeastern Colorado, northwestern Nebraska, and central North Dakota. Winters from Arizona, Colorado, and Kansas south to northwestern Mexico and southeastern Texas.

Lapland Longspur

Bruant lapon
Calcarius lapponicus (Linnaeus)
Total length: 15.2 to 17.6 cm
Plate 74

Figure 96
Tail of Lapland Longspur

Hind toenail long, as long as or longer than hind toe. *Adult male (breeding plumage)*: Head and breast black, except a broad white or buffy stripe behind eye, this stripe extending downward on sides of neck and sides of breast; hind-neck chestnut; back and scapulars buffy, heavily striped with black; tail mostly blackish brown, the outermost feathers on each side largely white terminally, the next feather with only a little white near the tip; under parts, posterior to black breast, white, the sides and flanks streaked with black; bill yellow with dusky tip; legs blackish. *Adult female (breeding plumage)*: Somewhat like adult male but top of head brownish black streaked with buff; a broad buffy stripe over eye; ear patch brown, narrowly margined with black; variable amounts of black on lower throat and breast but mixed with white and buff (sometimes only narrowly streaked with black); hind-neck with chestnut paler, more restricted, and streaked with dusky. *Adults and young in autumn and winter*: Resemble adult females in breeding plumage but buffier above and below; males have more extensive chestnut patch on hind-neck but much obscured by buff feather tips. *Juvenal*: Upper parts yellowish buff and brown, heavily streaked with black; under parts yellowish white, the breast and sides tinged with yellowish buff and streaked with black; wings and tail of young similar to those of adults.

Measurements *(C. l. lapponicus)*. *Adult male*: wing, 92–96.4 (93.7); tail, 61–69.4 (64.3); exposed culmen, 10.5–11.8 (11.2); tarsus, 19.9–21.9 (21.0). *Adult female*: wing, 84–87.6 (86.2) mm.

Distinctions. In all plumages shows less white in the tail than McCown's and Chestnut-collared longspurs (Figure 96).

Breeding Distribution of Lapland Longspur

Range in Canada. Breeds in the Arctic from Prince Patrick Island (Mould Bay); Melville Island (Winter Harbour); Bathurst Island; and northern Ellesmere Island (Lake Hazen) south to northern Yukon (Herschel Island and the coastal plain; also farther south at high altitudes at least to Ogilvie Mountains); northern Mackenzie (Mackenzie Delta, Coppermine, Heuss Lake); southern Keewatin (Nueltin Lake); northeastern Manitoba (Churchill); northern Ontario (Little Cape, Cape Henrietta Maria); James Bay (Twin Islands); northern Quebec (Point Louis-XIV, Payne Lake, mouth of Koksoak River); and northern Labrador (south at least to Okak).

Migrates through most parts of southern Canada, being especially common in the Prairie Provinces but rather scarce in Newfoundland (sight records: St. Anthony, Ramea, Funk Island).

Winters in small numbers in southern British Columbia (Lulu Island, Okanagan Landing), southern Alberta (Milk River), southern Saskatchewan (Cypress Hills region, Regina), southern Ontario (north to about Ottawa), southwestern Quebec (Aylmer, Frelighsburg), New Brunswick, Prince Edward Island, and Nova Scotia.

Field Marks. Adult males in breeding plumage are unmistakable by black crown, face, and breast and chestnut hind-neck. Females are more nondescript but usually are accompanied by males. Males (both old and young) in autumn and winter have no black on the head but show some evidence of chestnut hind-neck. Both males and females show broad buffy streaks on the back and less white in the spread tail than do other longspurs (Figure 96). All longspurs spend much time on the ground and usually run instead of hopping. *Voice*: On the arctic breeding grounds, a short but lively, tinkling, warbling sound is given in flight, usually as the bird descends slowly to the ground. Flight-call is of two or three syllables; the second and third notes run together and are slightly lower than the first.

Habitat. In the breeding season, arctic tundra, preferring wet hummocky areas, tussocky meadows, grass and shrub cover; also sedge tundra. In migration and winter, weedy and grassy fields, grain stubbles, airfields, and shores, usually in companies or flocks, often associated with Horned Larks, Snow Buntings, or pipits.

Nesting. In a depression in the ground, in a hummock or tussock, often under shrubs. Nest is of grasses lined with fine grasses, feathers, willow cotton, and sometimes hair. *Eggs*, usually 4 to 6; greenish grey to olive brown, blotched and speckled with browns and lined and spotted with black. Incubation 10½ to 13 days (W.H. Drury), by the female; 12 days (D.F. Parmelee).

Range. Circumpolar. Breeds in much of Alaska, northern Canada, Greenland, and northern Eurasia. In North America winters from southern Canada south to northern California, northern Arizona, New Mexico, northeastern Texas, southern Louisiana, and Virginia.

Subspecies. (1) *Calcarius lapponicus lapponicus* (Linnaeus): Breeds in the Arctic Archipelago, eastern Mackenzie (Coppermine), Keewatin, northern Manitoba, northern Ontario, northern Quebec, northern Labrador. (2) *C. l. alascensis* Ridgway (upper parts paler than in *lapponicus*): Breeds in northern Yukon and northwestern Mackenzie (Mackenzie Delta).

Remarks. In southern parts of Canada we know the Lapland Longspur as a spring and autumn migrant and winter resident. It is a ground bird, inhabiting open fields and shores in winter, often in association with Horned Larks and Snow Buntings. On the ground it ordinarily runs about, but it is capable of hopping also. In its summer home in the low Arctic, the male has a delightful song which he pours out while he gently floats down to the ground on set wings.

Smith's Longspur

Bruant de Smith
Calcarius pictus (Swainson)
Total length: 14.5 to 16.5 cm
Plate 74

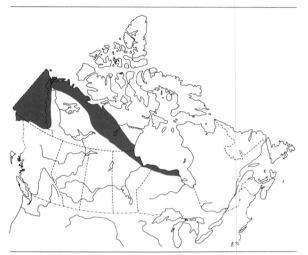

Breeding Distribution of Smith's Longspur

Range in Canada. Breeds from northern Yukon (Herschel Island); northern Mackenzie (Caribou Hills west of Mackenzie Delta, Little Carcajou Lake, Anderson River, Coppermine); south to southern Yukon (Kluane Game Sanctuary); extreme northwestern British Columbia (Chilkat Pass); central-eastern Mackenzie (Grassy Island, perhaps Nahanni National Park); southern Keewatin (Windy River); northeastern Manitoba (Churchill); and northern Ontario (Fort Severn, Cape Henrietta Maria).

Migrates mainly through Manitoba, Saskatchewan, and Alberta. Rare in central and southern British Columbia (Dease Lake, Kispiox valley, Swan Lake in Peace River District, Boundary Pass). Rare in southern Ontario (Thunder Bay; sight records for Simcoe County and Kingston).

Hind toenail elongated. *Adult male (breeding plumage)*: Top and sides of head black, bordered below by white and with a white line over eye and an elongated white spot on the ear region; back feathers and scapulars with blackish centres and broad buffy margins; back of neck and entire under parts ochraceous buff; anterior lesser wing coverts black, posterior ones white, forming a broad white bar; tail brownish black centrally, the outermost feather on each side mainly white, that next to it with a long white stripe, the third from outside with traces of white on the basal part of outer webs; bill dark brown above, paler below and often yellowish at base; legs brown. *Adult male (autumn and winter)*: Similar to breeding male but black of head replaced by streaks of buff and dusky, the breast more or less slightly streaked with dusky. *Adult female*: Somewhat like winter male. *Young in autumn and winter*: Similar to adults in winter but anterior lesser wing coverts brown instead of black and with white wing bar very narrow.

Measurements. *Adult male*: wing, 90.5–95.5 (92.7); tail, 60.5–68.3 (64.4); exposed culmen, 10–11.2 (10.7); tarsus, 19.2–20.8 (19.9). *Adult female*: wing, 84–91 (87.1) mm.

Field Marks. The adult male in breeding plumage, with black crown and cheeks and plain-buffy under parts, is easily recognizable. Females and all autumn birds are more obscure, the head streaked buffy and dusky. The under parts are buffier than those of other longspurs, and the legs, especially of the young, are paler brown.

Habitat. In the nesting season, grassy and hummocky tundra. In migration, fields, prairies, airports, and similar grassy and weedy open places.

Nesting. On the ground, often on a mossy hummock or grassy tussock. Nest is of grasses lined with finer grasses, feathers, and down. *Eggs*, usually 4 to 6; pale greenish or pale bluish, speckled with browns and lined and spotted with black (only one set seen by the writer). Incubation period 11.5 to 12 days (Jehl and Hussell).

Range. Breeds in northern Alaska and low Arctic and Subarctic of northwestern mainland Canada east to northern Ontario. Winters from Kansas and Iowa south to Oklahoma, central Texas, northwestern Louisiana, Mississippi, and Alabama; rarely Tennessee.

Chestnut-collared Longspur

Bruant à ventre noir
Calcarius ornatus (Townsend)
Total length: 13 to 16.5 cm
Plate 74

Figure 97
Tail of Chestnut-collared Longspur

Hind toenail moderately elongated. *Adult male (breeding plumage)*: Top of head, stripe behind eye, stripe on lower ear coverts, black; stripe over eye and spot on nape white; hind-neck deep chestnut; back and scapulars buff and grey thickly striped with black; lesser wing coverts black; tail with two middle feathers mostly brown, the others white basally, the two or three outermost mainly white; cheeks and throat white, the cheeks tinged with buff (occasionally throat also); breast and most of anterior abdomen black (sometimes mixed with chestnut); posterior abdomen and under tail coverts white; bill bluish grey, blackish at tip and along culmen; legs dark brown. *Adult male (autumn and winter)*: Similar to breeding plumage but black areas obscured or hidden by buffy feather tips. *Adult female*: Upper parts greyish buffy-brown with dusky streaks; under parts greyish buff, breast and anterior abdomen darkest and usually faintly streaked with dusky; throat paler and often bordered on either side by a narrow dusky streak; legs more brownish than male's. *Young (first autumn and winter)*: Similar to adults in winter but lesser wing coverts brown and buff instead of black and white.

Breeding Distribution of Chestnut-collared Longspur

Range in Canada. Breeds in southern Alberta (west to Calgary, north to Bittern Lake, irregularly to Beaverhill Lake); southern Saskatchewan (south of Biggar; Burke Lake, 24 km east of Saskatoon; and Quill Lakes southward); and southwestern Manitoba (Brandon, Winnipeg).

Casual in British Columbia (Kispiox valley, Newgate, and Vancouver Island), northern Alberta (McMurray); northern Manitoba (Churchill); and Ontario (photo record: near Sudbury, 18 April 1978; sight records for Kingston and Sault Ste. Marie). Accidental in New Brunswick (specimen: Nantucket Island) and Nova Scotia (specimen: Cape Sable, 28 May 1964; sight records at Outer Island, Cape Sable, and Port La Tour).

Measurements. *Adult male*: wing, 81.2–86.8 (84.4); tail, 55–60 (57); exposed culmen, 10–11.2 (10.7); tarsus, 18.9–20 (19.6). *Adult female*: wing, 75.9–80 (77.9) mm.

Field Marks. This and McCown's Longspur are summer residents of the prairies and are often found in the same area. In the nesting season the male Chestnut-collared has black under parts and a white or buffy face and throat, a combination that separates it from other longspurs. Females and autumn birds are more difficult to recognize, but in the Chestnut-collared the breast is faintly streaked (plain in McCown's) and the tail pattern, shown in flight, is different (Figure 97). *Voice*: The spirited and pleasing song is usually given as the bird, with spread tail, glides to the ground after a short flight. Common call-note is *til-lip* (first syllable accented), also a staccato twitter, probably of alarm.

Habitat. Short-grass plains and prairies.

Nesting. On the ground, usually in a hollow and often concealed in grass or under shrubs. Nest is composed externally of grasses and weed stems and is lined with fine grasses and sometimes hair. *Eggs*, 4 to 6; greyish white to pale buff or greenish white, spotted, speckled, and lined with browns and lavender. The incubation period is 12.5 days (A.D. DuBois), by the female.

Range. Breeds from southern Alberta east to southern Manitoba southeastward to northeastern Colorado, northern Nebraska, and southwestern Minnesota. Winters from northern Arizona, northeastern Colorado, and central Kansas south to northwestern Mexico, southern Texas, and northern Louisiana.

Rustic Bunting

Bruant rustique
Emberiza rustica Pallas
Total length: 14.5 cm
Figure 98

Figure 98
Rustic Bunting

Status in Canada. Accidental in British Columbia: Sight record of two at Queen Charlotte, Queen Charlotte Islands, 26 October 1971. Photo record: Jordan River, first observed 25 November 1983, and wintered there.

Adult male: Crown and sides of head black (but much obscured by mottled brown in winter), a white stripe extends backward from over eye toward nape; white spot in centre of nape; upper parts mostly chestnut streaked with black; under parts mainly white with showy cinnamon band across breast and on flanks. Tail brown, showing white on outer edges. Wing bars present but inconspicuous. *Adult female*: Similar to adult male but with much less black on crown and sides of head. Nape spot reduced or absent. Upper parts more brownish (less chestnut). Breast band much reduced, often broken and streaked. *Immatures* resemble adults but are duller, breast band streakier and more tawny. Wing of males, 75–81; of females, 72–76 mm.

Range. Breeds from northern Sweden eastward across northern Russia and northern Siberia to the Gulf of Anadyr and southward to north-central Russia, northern Sakhalin, and Kamchatka.

Snow Bunting

Bruant des neiges
Plectrophenax nivalis (Linnaeus)
Total length: 15 to 18.5 cm
Plate 74

Breeding Distribution of Snow Bunting

Range in Canada. Breeds from the high Arctic, Prince Patrick Island (Mould Bay), Ellef Ringnes Island (Isachsen), Axel Heiberg Island, and northern Ellesmere Island (Alert) south to Yukon (Herschel Island, the arctic coastal plain, and at high altitudes south to the southern Ogilvie Mountains, head of Stewart River in Selwyn Mountains and Kluane Game Sanctuary); northwestern British Columbia (Chilkat Pass); northwestern and central-eastern Mackenzie (Mackenzie Delta, Harrowby Bay, Clinton-Colden Lake); central and southeastern Keewatin (Beverly Lake, Chesterfield Inlet, Eskimo Point); Southampton Island; Hudson Bay (Nastapoka Islands, Belcher Islands); northern Quebec (southern Ungava Bay); and northern Labrador (Okak, perhaps Nain).

Rare summer resident, but not known to breed, on the Hudson Bay coasts of Manitoba (Churchill) and Ontario (Cape Henrietta Maria, Brant River).

Winters all across extreme southern Canada and north at least to northwestern British Columbia (Atlin); central Alberta; central Saskatchewan (Dorintosh, Cumberland House); southern Manitoba (Lake St. Martin); southern Ontario (Thunder Bay, Lake Nipissing); southern Quebec (Aylmer, Lake Saint-Jean, Gaspé Peninsula); southern Labrador (Battle Harbour); Newfoundland; New Brunswick; Prince Edward Island; and Nova Scotia; in milder winters north to northwestern Mackenzie (Aklavik).

A single Snow Bunting was recorded at the North Pole on 24 April 1979.

Bill rather small. Hind toenail rather long and slender. *Adult male (breeding plumage)*: Mostly pure white, but back, scapulars, alula, tertials, primaries (except basally) black (some individuals also have black primary coverts); four to six inner tail feathers black, the rest white; bill and legs black. *Adult male (winter)*: Similar to breeding male but upper parts, face, breast, and sides tinged with rusty brown, the blacks mostly concealed except in wings; bill yellow, tipped dusky. *Adult female (breeding plumage)*: Similar to adult male in breeding plumage but hindneck usually with some dusky streaks, top of head and often other areas of body tinged with rusty; black of back and scapulars mixed with white and often extending farther down rump; primaries with less extensive white areas, the lesser and greater wing coverts blackish with whitish margins; bill and legs black. *Adult female (winter)*: Similar to breeding female, but upper parts, sides of head, breast, and sides of body tinged with rusty; bill yellow with dusky tip. *Juvenal*: Upper parts buffy grey, the back streaked vaguely with black, the rest very lightly streaked; throat pale grey, breast and sides buffy grey (paler than back) with faint dusky streaks; abdomen yellowish white.

Measurements. *Adult male*: wing, 103.8–110 (108.2); tail, 66–74 (68.9); exposed culmen, 9.8–11.4 (10.4); tarsus, 20.3–22 (21.5). *Adult female*: wing, 98–102.3 (99.9) mm.

Field Marks. A robust ground bunting with much white in plumage. Usually runs instead of hopping. Flight undulating, flashing contrasting areas of black and white in the wing. In winter the white areas are heavily tinged with rusty, and the birds are usually in flocks. *Voice*: In flight it has a characteristic short, slightly rising, musical twitter, which often ends with an emphatic *chert*. On the breeding grounds it has a loud musical warbled song, which is given either on the ground or in flight.

Habitat. In the Arctic it favours terrain such as rocky shores and stony escarpments, mountain slopes, cliffs and their talus; hummocky moss tundra; also arctic human settlements. In migration and winter, open weedy and grassy fields, grain stubbles, shores, and roadsides.

Nesting. In crevices in rocks, cracks in cliffs (sometimes at considerable heights), under stones and rock piles, and in various other cavities and crannies. Nest is made of mosses and grasses and lined with grasses, feathers, and hair. *Eggs*, usually 4 to 7; greyish white to bluish white, blotched and speckled (often heavily) with various browns and often lavender. Incubation period 12.5 to 13 days (Sutton and Parmelee), 12 days (Wynne-Edwards); by the female.

Range. Circumpolar arctic parts of the world and more locally in subarctic areas, migrating farther south in winter. In North America breeds in Alaska (including the Aleutian Islands), arctic Canada, and Greenland. Winters from central-western and southern Alaska and southern and south-central Canada south to Oregon, northern Utah, northern New Mexico, Kansas, Indiana, Ohio, and Virginia, and southward on the Pacific Coast casually to northwestern California and on the Atlantic Coast casually to Georgia.

Subspecies. *Plectrophenax nivalis nivalis* (Linnaeus).

Remarks. In southern Canada the Snow Bunting is a sure harbinger of winter. It is well named, for it comes just prior to the first snow squalls of late autumn; it revels all winter in the snowy countryside; and it departs for the North while there is still snow in the southland.

In winter it is usually seen in flocks, sometimes large ones. It feeds on the seeds of weeds that project above the snow. When a flock alights on a weedy field, the birds lose no time in dispersing over the ground, running rapidly from one weed to another, occasionally jumping up to snatch seeds high on the bare stalks. As the flock works the field, those in the rear rise up from time to time and alight again ahead of the others. When the field has been worked over, they all take to the air. A large flock of Snow Buntings, their white and black patterns flashing, is a pretty sight as they wheel and swirl in the soft winter sunlight. Flight is somewhat undulating. As a long, loose flock flies low over a distant snowy field, the birds seem to appear and disappear alternately, depending on whether their dark or white areas are turned toward the observer. When heavy snows cover the weed tops, the birds become conspicuous at roadsides and farmyards.

For people living in the Arctic, the Snow Bunting becomes a harbinger of spring after leaving its winter range. On its northern nesting grounds it adds a delightful song to the already long list of its pleasing attributes.

McKay's Bunting

Bruant blanc
Plectrophenax hyperboreus Ridgway
Total length: 15.8 to 19 cm
Figure 99

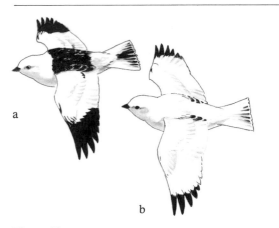

Figure 99
a) Snow Bunting
b) MacKay's Bunting

Status in Canada. Accidental in British Columbia (photo: one at Wickaninnish Beach, Pacific Rim National Park, 12 February 1980).

Like the Snow Bunting, but much more extensively white. In breeding male, the back and primary coverts are white and only the most posterior scapulars are black. Wings more extensively white basally. Female tends to be slightly more mottled than male but is always much whiter than female Snow Bunting. In winter, there is some rusty about the head, neck, and rump but bird is always conspicuously whiter than Snow Bunting. As in Snow Bunting, the bill is black in summer, yellowish with dusky tip in winter.

Measurements. *Adult male*: wing, 109.7–118.6 (114.3); tail, 65.5–74.7 (70.6); exposed culmen, 11.2–12.7 (12.2); tarsus, 21.1–23.6 (22.4). *Adult female*: wing, 104.1–109.5 (107.2); tail, 64.0–68.6 (66.8); exposed culmen, 10.7–11.7 (11.2); tarsus, 20.8–23.1 (21.8) mm (Ridgway).

Range. Breeds on islands in the Bering Sea (Hall, St. Matthew, St. Paul, and St. Lawrence).

Subfamily **Icterinae:**
Bobolink, Blackbirds, Meadowlarks, Orioles, and Allies

This interesting subfamily is confined to the Western Hemisphere. Its ninety-odd species are found over much of the Americas and are notable for their diversity. They vary in colour from plain black (often with striking iridescence) through yellows, browns, reds, and orange. The bill is conical, pointed, often with the culmen in a straight line and extended backward onto the forehead. They vary in size from that of a sparrow to a crow.

Bobolink

Goglu
Dolichonyx oryzivorus (Linnaeus)
Total length: 16.5 to 20.2 cm
Plate 66

Figure 100
Pointed tail feathers of Bobolink

Breeding Distribution of Bobolink

Range in Canada. Summer resident, breeding in southern interior British Columbia (Penticton, Waldo; north locally to 150 Mile House); southern Alberta (Wainwright, Athabasca, Whitecourt, Camrose, Calgary); central and southern Saskatchewan (Midnight Lake, Saskatoon, Nipawin, Eastend, Yorkton, Regina, Moose Mountain); southern Manitoba (Garland, St. Laurent, Whitemouth); central and southern Ontario (Dryden, Thunder Bay, Chapleau southward; reported in summer, and probably breeds, north to Sioux Lookout, Kapuskasing, Missanabie, Strickland, Reesor, Cochrane, and Matheson); southwestern Quebec (Taschereau, Amos, Lake Saint-Jean, Percé southward; recently colonized Madeleine Islands); New Brunswick; Nova Scotia (including Cape Breton Island); and Prince Edward Island (Bideford, Ellerslie). It has only recently colonized Prince Edward Island.

Casual in northern Ontario (Big Trout Lake, Moose Factory); Newfoundland (Cape Broyle, 9 June 1956, and several sight records); southern Labrador (Grady Harbour, 12 September 1927); southeastern Quebec (Brador Bay, summer 1924); and Vancouver Island, British Columbia (Victoria, 4 November 1967).

Bill, short and sparrowlike; wings longish, the two outermost feathers longest; tail, rather stiff and with sharp-pointed tips (Figure 100); hind toenail much elongated. *Adult male (breeding plumage)*: Head and under parts black, some of the feathers of flanks, abdomen, and under tail coverts edged with buff; large buff patch on back of neck; upper back black streaked with buffy; rest of back, rump, upper tail coverts, and scapulars pale grey to whitish; wing and tail black with yellowish edging; bill black; legs brown. *Adult male (winter plumage)*: Similar to adult female, but often a few black feathers are still not moulted by the time it departs from Canada in autumn. *Adult female*: Upper parts, buffy olive streaked with black; top of head with central pale streak, bordered on either side by a broad blackish or brownish stripe; sides of head yellowish olive with narrow blackish streak extending backward from eye; wing and tail dusky, edged with yellowish-olive; under parts plain yellowish-olive, the sides, flanks, and under tail coverts streaked with black; bill brown, darkest near tip; legs brown. *Young in autumn plumage*: Similar to adult female but often more decidedly yellowish on under parts.

Measurements. *Adult male*: wing, 92.8–99.8 (95.8); tail, 63.5–70.5 (66.6); exposed culmen, 14.5–15.8 (15.2); tarsus, 26–28 (27.0). *Adult female*: wing, 83–88.4 (85.9) mm.

Distinctions. Adult females, autumn adults of both sexes, and young in autumn, with striped upper parts and sparrowlike bills, closely resemble sparrows. The long hind toenail of the Bobolink suggests one of the longspurs, but the Bobolink's sharp-pointed tail feathers are different from those of longspurs. Some sparrows have sharp-pointed tail feathers, but those particular species are smaller than the Bobolink, and their hind toenails are not elongated.

Field Marks. Adult male in spring and summer, with black under parts, whitish scapulars, greyish-white rump, and large buff patch on back of neck, is one of the easiest birds to recognize. In the West, the male Lark Bunting also has black under parts, but white areas are confined to patches in the wings. Females and autumn young very closely resemble sparrows but are somewhat larger and more yellowish, and they have distinctive call-notes. *Voice*: Song is a delightful, loud, bubbling performance made up of short banjo-like notes, sung as the male flies, on rapidly but shallowly beating wings, or when he is perching; also a characteristic call-note of late summer and autumn, which sounds like *pink* and helps identify the sparrowlike females and young.

Habitat. Fields and meadows of tall grass, clover, alfalfa, or grain. Also, in autumn, marshes and other open places.

Nesting. On the ground in tall grass or similar vegetation in open places. Nest is flimsily made of grasses and weed stalks with a sparse lining of fine grasses. *Eggs*, 4 to 7, usually 5 or 6; pale grey to pale brownish, irregularly blotched and spotted with various browns and purplish greys. Incubation variously reported 10 to 13 days, by the female.

Range. Breeds from southeastern British Columbia east to Nova Scotia and south to northeastern California, northern Utah, central Colorado, northeastern Kansas, central Illinois, northwestern Ohio, northern West Virginia, Pennsylvania, and central New Jersey. Winters in eastern Bolivia, western Brazil, Paraguay, and northern Argentina.

Remarks. In Canada, we know the Bobolink in summer when the male is handsomely attired in black, white, and buff. He delivers his ecstatic, banjo-like song either while perched or in slow flight with rapid shallow wing strokes. We associate him with broad fields of tall grass redolent with clover and speckled with buttercups and daisies.

In late summer, shortly before leaving Canada, the male assumes a dull sparrowlike plumage similar to that of the female, and the famous song is heard no more. Bobolinks then rove about in flocks, and the usual call becomes a metallic *pink*. In migration through southern United States they are called "rice birds" because they are sometimes destructive of grain. While in Canada, however, Bobolinks are highly insectivorous, but they eat some weed seeds as well.

Red-winged Blackbird

Carouge à épaulettes
Agelaius phoeniceus (Linnaeus)
Total length: 19 to 25.5 cm
Plate 67

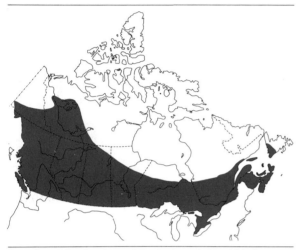

Breeding Distribution of Red-winged Blackbird

Range in Canada. Breeds from southern Yukon (Slims River, Sulphur Lake, Von Wilczek Lakes, near Mayo); central-western and central-southern Mackenzie (Gibson Gap, eastern Great Bear Lake, Fort Simpson, Slave River delta); northern Saskatchewan (Lake Athabasca, Stony Rapids, Reindeer Lake); central Manitoba (The Pas, Thompson, Oxford House); north-central Ontario (Sandy Lake, Moosonee); southern Quebec (Lake Saint-Jean, Grandes-Bergeronnes, Moisie River, Gaspé Bay, Anticosti Island: recently Madeleine Islands); and southwestern Newfoundland (Stephenville Crossing, Doyles) and southward through all extreme southern Canada (but not Queen Charlotte Islands, British Columbia).

Winters in southern British Columbia (Vancouver Island, Okanagan valley) and extreme southern Ontario (in small numbers: Point Pelee, Toronto, Chatham; rarely north to Ottawa); rarely southern Quebec (Montréal) and the Maritimes.

Casual in northern Manitoba (Churchill) and at Johan-Beetz Bay, Quebec. Accidental on Victoria Island (Cambridge Bay), N.W.T.

Adult male: Completely black except red lesser wing coverts and buffy-whitish middle wing coverts (forming a conspicuous red patch at bend of wing with buffy-whitish border). *Young male (first autumn)*: Dull black, much obscured and margined with buff and reddish brown above and with pale buff to whitish below; usually a buffy streak over eye; wing patch orange spotted with black (some individuals with little or no orange). *Young male (first spring)*: Dull black with some pale feather edges; wing patch orange spotted with black. *Adult female*: Very different from adult male. Upper parts brownish black streaked and edged with buffs, greyish, and rusty; light streak through middle of crown and another over eye; lesser wing coverts (near bend of wing) often more or less reddish or orange; under parts streaked whitish and blackish; chin and throat less heavily marked or immaculate and often pinkish, buffy, or greenish yellow.

Measurements *(A. p. phoeniceus)*. *Adult male*: wing, 115–124.5 (120.3); tail, 88–97.5 (91.2); exposed culmen, 21.7–24.7 (22.7); tarsus, 26.5–29.5 (28.6). *Adult female*: wing, 96–102.5 (98.0) mm.

Field Marks. The male is usually unmistakable, but when perched the red shoulder patch is often concealed. However, at least the buffy-white border of the red patch can be seen. The female has the *entire* breast, abdomen, and sides streaked black-and-white. *Voice*: Song is a gurgling, cheerful *konk-ke-ree*, the first syllable lowest in pitch, the third syllable highest, prolonged, and usually trilled. Common call, *chuck*. When alarmed, a down-slurred *tee-err*.

Habitat. For nesting, freshwater marshes and water edges, which have thick growths of cattails, bulrushes, sedges, and similar vegetation; bushes and small trees on water margins; occasionally dry upland fields. Forages mostly in fields and grain stubbles, ploughed land, and various open places. After nesting, flocks scatter over the countryside during the day and converge at dusk on marshes to roost.

Nesting (see Habitat). Nest, a loosely woven structure of coarse marsh vegetation lined with finer grasses. Most often it is woven into and supported by living marsh vegetation and less often in bushes and small trees on water edges; sometimes in weeds of dry upland fields; rarely in a larger tree. *Eggs*, 3 to 4, usually 4; pale bluish-green, blotched, spotted, and streaked with browns, black, grey, and purple. Incubation, 10 to 12 days, usually 11, is entirely by the female (A.A. Allen).

Range. Northwestern British Columbia east to southwestern Newfoundland and south to Costa Rica, the northern Bahamas, Cuba, and Isle of Pines.

Subspecies. (1) *Agelaius phoeniceus phoeniceus* (Linnaeus): central and southern Ontario (Sault Ste. Marie, Lake Abitibi), southern Quebec, southwestern Newfoundland, New Brunswick, Prince Edward Island, and Nova Scotia. (2) *A. p. arctolegus* Oberholser (similar to *phoeniceus* but larger): southern Yukon, Mackenzie, northern and south-central British Columbia (Williams Lake, 100 Mile House), Alberta, Saskatchewan, Manitoba, western and northwestern Ontario (Sioux Lookout, Moosonee). (3) *A. p. nevadensis* Grinnell (bill slenderer, females average a little greyer than *arctolegus*): interior southern British Columbia (Okanagan Landing, Kamloops, Newgate). (4) *A. p. caurinus* Ridgway (averages smaller than *nevadensis*; females more richly coloured): southwestern British Columbia (Vancouver Island, Vancouver).

Remarks. The male Red-winged Blackbird effervesces with energy and personality. His bright-red epaulettes flash in the sun as he flits from one perch to another, and the marshes ring with his cheerful *conkeree* song. The males arrive early in spring, often when most of the marshes are still icebound. The modestly attired females come a little later. In spring and autumn, the seeds of weeds and cereal crops make up about 90 per cent of its food. During June and July, however, insects and other animal food comprise from 70 to 100 per cent of it, the young being fed entirely on animal food. Unduly large late-summer and autumn flocks are often destructive of grains.

Eastern Meadowlark

Sturnelle des prés
Sturnella magna (Linnaeus)
Total length: 21.5 to 28 cm
Plate 66

Breeding Distribution of Eastern Meadowlark

Range in Canada. Breeds in southern Ontario (Sault Ste. Marie, North Bay, Ottawa, southward); southwestern Quebec (Blue-Sea-Lake, Stoneham, Rivière du Loup, Biencourt); southern New Brunswick (locally: Fredericton, Sussex); and Nova Scotia (very locally: near Bridgetown). Reports of breeding on Madeleine Islands, Quebec, need confirmation.

Recorded without evidence of breeding north to central Ontario (Thunder Bay, Dryden, Gogama, Cochrane, Englehart, Attawapiskat); Lake Saint-Jean, Pointe-des-Monts, Sept Îles, and Percé, Quebec. Casual in Prince Edward Island. Accidental in central-western Quebec (Eastmain, 17 November 1946) and Newfoundland (St. Shotts, 4 January 1938; sight records: L'Anse-aux-Meadows, 22–30 November 1977).

Winters in extreme southern Ontario (Point Pelee, London, Toronto, Hamilton, Kingston, casually north to Ottawa); occasionally in New Brunswick and Nova Scotia (more in autumn than any other season but with considerable winter mortality).

Bill tapering, nearly straight, pointed in side view, but in dorsal view the tip is somewhat rounded; ridge of bill extends well back on forehead; wings short; tail rather short, its feathers somewhat pointed; feet large, especially hind toe. *Adult male (breeding plumage)*: Crown with median buffy stripe, bordered on each side by a broader blackish stripe; rest of upper parts streaked with buff, black, and browns; tertials and secondaries heavily barred with black but with light-brown edges; bend of wing yellow; tail feathers brownish grey barred with black, but the outer feathers chiefly white; pale stripe from nostril back over eye is yellow in front of eye, buff behind eye; narrow blackish line extending back from eye; rest of sides of head greyish white, usually with fine streaks on ear coverts; throat, much of breast, and abdomen lemon-yellow; broad black crescent on breast, its ends extending to sides of neck; sides, flanks, and under tail coverts buffy white streaked with black. *Adult female (breeding plumage)*: Similar to adult male but obviously smaller, coloration somewhat duller, the dark stripes on crown streaked with brown; black crescent on breast smaller. *Adults and young in autumn*: Similar to adults in spring but much more brownish above and below, with buffy feather tips obscuring the black crescent and dulling the yellow parts.

Measurements. *Adult male*: wing, 116.7–125 (119.7); tail, 71–82.5 (78.1); exposed culmen, 27.5–34.6 (32.7); tarsus, 38.5–41.5 (40.3). *Adult female*: wing, 104–113.8 (107.4) mm.

Distinctions (see Western Meadowlark).

Field Marks. A short-tailed robin-sized bird with a black crescent on its bright-yellow breast. Flies with rapid beats of the short wings alternating with very short glides and showing white outer feathers in the short tail. The flicker also has a black crescent on the breast but shows a white rump patch and no white in the tail. The Western Meadowlark is the only bird with which the Eastern is likely to be confused (see Western Meadowlark). *Voice*: Song, a clear high-pitched, far-carrying whistle, often rendered as *spring o' the year*, is entirely different from that of the Western Meadowlark. A harsh chatter of alarm.

Habitat. Open fields and similar situations with adequate grassy cover. In autumn, grain stubbles are popular.

Nesting. On the ground in open grassy areas. Nest is concealed in grass and usually has dome-shaped roof. Nest is made of grasses and weed stalks and is lined with fine grasses. *Eggs*, 3 to 7, most frequently 5; white-speckled, spotted, and blotched with browns and bluish grey. Incubation 13 to 15 days, usually 14, by the female (G.B. Saunders *in* Bent).

Range. Southern Ontario east to New Brunswick and south through central and eastern United States to Arizona, New Mexico, Texas, the Gulf Coast, Cuba, and through Mexico and Central America south to Colombia, Venezuela, Guyana, and Brazil.

Subspecies. *Sturnella magna magna* (Linnaeus).

Western Meadowlark

Sturnelle de l'Ouest
Sturnella neglecta Audubon
Total length: 21.5 to 28 cm
Plate 66

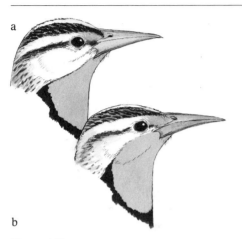

a

b

Figure 101
a) Eastern Meadowlark
b) Western Meadowlark

Breeding Distribution of Western Meadowlark

Range in Canada. Breeds in central and southern British Columbia (François Lake, Lonesome Lake, Prince George region southward including Vancouver Island); north-central and southern Alberta (Peace River southward); central and southern Saskatchewan (Meadow Lake, Amyot Lake, Nipawin southward); southern Manitoba (Swan River, Garland, Lake St. Martin, Sprague); western Ontario (Lake of the Woods, Dryden, Thunder Bay); southern Ontario (rarely and locally: Sault Ste. Marie, Rutherglen, Hamilton, Bradford, Cobourg, Napanee); and rarely southwestern Quebec (Verchères, Saint-Anicet. Québec: paired with *magna*).

Winters in southern British Columbia, and occasionally in southern Alberta, southern Saskatchewan, and southern Manitoba.

Casual in southern Mackenzie (Fort Simpson and 48 km below Fort Simpson), northern Manitoba (Churchill), and central-eastern Ontario (Moosonee, North Point).

Extremely similar to Eastern Meadowlark but *yellow of throat more extensive* (Figure 101), reaching up to lower cheeks (malar region), upper parts paler and more greyish, the feather edges paler and wider, wings and tail more sharply barred (bars not so confluent or run together as in Eastern); sides and flanks more spotted than streaked.

Measurements *(S. n. neglecta). Adult male*: wing, 121–132 (125.6); tail, 72–79 (76.0); exposed culmen, 29.9–35.8 (32.7); tarsus, 36.5–40.5 (38.0). *Adult female*: wing, 105.5–118.5 (109.9) mm.

Field Marks. Not ordinarily separable in the field by sight from the Eastern Meadowlark. Voice, however, is very different. *Voice*: The rich bubbling song is completely different from the thin high-pitched whistle of the Eastern Meadowlark. A throaty *chuck* also is unlike any utterance of the Eastern.

Habitat. Open grassy areas similar to the habitat preferences of the Eastern Meadowlark.

Nesting. Similar to that of Eastern Meadowlark.

Range. Breeds from British Columbia east to southern Ontario and south to northern Mexico, central Texas, and Louisiana.

Subspecies. (1) *Sturnella neglecta neglecta* Audubon: Alberta, Saskatchewan, Manitoba, Ontario, Quebec. (2) *S. n. confluenta* Rathbun (darker, more extensively blackish upper parts than in *neglecta*): throughout southern British Columbia (east at least to Elko).

Remarks. Meadowlarks are not larks at all. They are brightly coloured members of the blackbird subfamily. There are two species of meadowlarks in Canada, the Eastern and the Western. It amazes most people how two species can sound so different yet look so much alike.

Yellow-headed Blackbird

Carouge à tête jaune
Xanthocephalus xanthocephalus (Bonaparte)
Total length: 21.5 to 28 cm (female much
shorter than male)
Plate 67

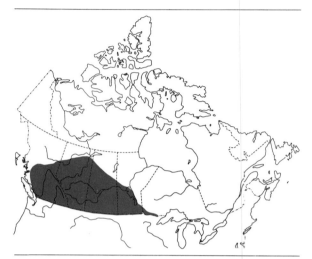

Breeding Distribution of Yellow-headed Blackbird

Range in Canada. Breeds in interior-central and southern British Columbia (Ootsa Lake, Tachick Lake, Giscome, Peace River District, Kleena Kleene, Vancouver, Okanagan valley, Wardner); Alberta (Athabasca Delta and Peace River District southward, but locally in south); north-central and southern Saskatchewan (Kazan Lake, Churchill River southward); central and southern Manitoba (Cedar and Moose lakes, La Rivière, Victoria Beach); western Ontario (Lake of the Woods, Steep Rock) and locally in southern Ontario (Lake St. Clair). Recorded in summer east to Quibell and Lake Nipigon, Ontario.

Casual in southern Mackenzie (Fort Simpson, Hay River), and northern Manitoba (Churchill). Casual in Quebec (Rupert-House, Amos, Godbout, Sainte-Anne-de-la-Pocatière, Montréal); Nova Scotia (various records: specimen record: Gaspereau, 5 January 1980. Photo records: Sable Island, May 1970 and August 1975; also various sight records); and on North Twin Island, James Bay (specimen: 5 June 1973). Sight records only for New Brunswick.

Adult male: Head, neck, and most of breast rich yellow to nearly orange, also often a few yellow feathers near vent; patch about eyes and narrow margin around base of bill black; patch on wing (primary coverts and part of greater wing coverts) white; rest of plumage black. *Adult female*: Mostly dusky brown, the wings without a white patch; stripe over eye, cheeks, and throat varies from whitish to yellowish usually becoming yellow on upper breast but sometimes mostly white also; lower breast streaked with white. *Young male (first autumn)*: Similar to adult female but larger, the yellows darker and richer; the primary coverts tipped with white, thus faintly suggesting a white wing patch. *Young male (first spring)*: Similar to young male in autumn but yellows purer, the top of head more blackish. *Young female in autumn*: Similar to adult female.

Measurements. *Adult male*: wing, 135–143.5 (139.9); tail, 95–107.5 (101.9); exposed culmen, 21.4–25.8 (23.2); tarsus, 33–35.5 (34.3). *Adult female*: wing, 112–116.5 (113.8) mm.

Field Marks. Adult male is unmistakable. Adult female and young with yellowish or whitish areas about head and breast can scarcely be mistaken for anything else. The song is a yodeling often-discordant *kleep-kloop-a-ah-oo*. Call, *chuck*.

Habitat. For nesting, deeper sloughs, wet marshes and lake edges where there is adequate emergent vegetation. Forages also on grainfields, freshly ploughed ground, barnyards, and similar places.

Nesting. In emergent vegetation usually over water, the nest attached to growing marsh plants. It is a basketlike structure, woven from dead, water-soaked vegetation. *Eggs*, 3 to 5, usually 4; whitish, quite thickly speckled over all with browns and greys. Incubation 12 to 13 days, by the female (R.W. Fautin).

Range. Breeds from central-interior British Columbia east to extreme western Ontario and northwestern Ohio, south to southern California, northeastern Baja California, southern New Mexico, northern Texas, Missouri, and northwestern Indiana. Winters from southwestern Central California, east to southern Louisiana and south to south-central Mexico.

Rusty Blackbird

Quiscale rouilleux
Euphagus carolinus (Müller)
Total length: 21.5 to 24.8 cm
Plate 67

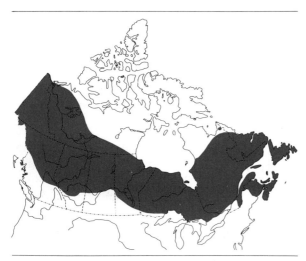

Breeding Distribution of Rusty Blackbird

Range in Canada. Breeds from northern Yukon (Blow and Firth rivers); northern Mackenzie (Mackenzie Delta, Fort Anderson, Dease Arm, Grassy Island, Finnie River); southern Keewatin (Nueltin Lake); northern Manitoba (Churchill); northern Ontario (Fort Severn, James Bay); northern Quebec (Lake Guillaume-Delisle, Kuujjuaq, Koroc River); central Labrador (Nain); and Newfoundland south to south-central interior British Columbia (east of Coast Ranges: Likely; possibly 150 Mile House); south-central and southwestern Alberta (Jasper, Banff, Okotoks, Red Deer region); central Saskatchewan (Prince Albert, Nipawin); central Manitoba (Riding Mountain National Park); western and south-central Ontario (Thunder Bay, Algonquin Provincial Park); southern Quebec (La Vérendrye Park, Petite-Rivière, Saint-François, Saint-Fabien-de-Panet, near Fort-Coulonge, Harrington-Harbour, Notre-Dame-des-Bois, Anticosti and Madeleine islands); New Brunswick; Prince Edward Island; and Nova Scotia.

Winters in small numbers in southern Ontario (Kitchener, Reaboro, Toronto, Kingston) and casually elsewhere in other southern parts of the country. Migrates through southern Canada but scarce on Vancouver Island, British Columbia.

Casual at Baker Lake, Keewatin. Accidental on Victoria Island, N.W.T. (specimen: Holman, summer, 1977).

Adult male (breeding plumage): All black with faint bluish-green gloss on body and slight violet gloss on head and neck; bill and legs black; eye yellowish white. *Adult male (winter plumage)*: Similar, but black partly veiled by rusty-brown feather tips on upper parts, and by paler-brown feather tips on sides of head and under parts. *Adult female (breeding plumage)*: Plain dull-slate, the upper parts darker and slightly glossy; bill and legs black; eye pale yellow. *Adult female (winter plumage)*: Similar to breeding plumage but washed and overlaid with rusty brown, the under parts tipped with paler brown or buff; stripe over eye buff. *Young in autumn*: Similar to adults in autumn.

Measurements. *Adult male*: wing, 110.5–117.4 (114.6); tail, 85–94.5 (88.9); exposed culmen, 19–21.9 (20.5); tarsus, 29.5–33 (31.4). *Adult female*: wing, 103.1–112.4 (107.3) mm.

Field Marks. Eyes yellow in both sexes. Very similar to Brewer's Blackbird but male in breeding plumage much less glossy, the head and neck not strongly purplish. Females in breeding plumage are dull slate in colour like female Brewer's in comparable plumage but have yellowish (not brown) eyes. Autumn Rusties are much more heavily blotched with rusty brown and pale brown than are Brewer's. Grackles are much larger and (at close range) glossier. Cowbirds have stout, sparrowlike bills and brown eyes. *Voice*: Song is short and ends in a high note that sounds like a squeaky hinge.

Habitat. Wet woods and tall shrubbery where pools of water stand on the ground; bogs, partly flooded lake and stream edges, beaver dams.

Nesting. In a low conifer or, less often, a deciduous bush, at heights usually less than 3 m, generally (not always) near water. Nest is a bulky and strongly made structure of twigs, grass, moss, and rotting vegetation (which dries very hard) and is lined with fine grasses. *Eggs*, 4 or 5; pale bluish-green, well spotted and blotched (but rarely scrawled) with various browns and a little grey. Incubation about 14 days, by the female (A.C. Bent).

Range. Breeds from northern Alaska east to Labrador and Newfoundland and south to central British Columbia, central Manitoba, northeastern New York, northern New Hampshire, central Maine, and Nova Scotia.

Subspecies. (1) *Euphagus carolinus carolinus* (Müller): Breeds in all of Canada except that occupied by the following race. (2) *E. c. nigrans* Burleigh and Peters (rusty feather edges in autumn average darker): Newfoundland, Madeleine Islands, and Nova Scotia (possibly also eastern New Brunswick).

Remarks. Before the ice is gone from the lakes and while woodland pools formed by the melting snow still abound, the Rusty Blackbird returns in spring. Its straw-coloured eyes search out favoured food morsels along shallow water edges or in moist leaf litter. If disturbed, the birds fly up and alight in the leafless branches of nearby trees, and soon the flock breaks into a squeaky cacophony of blackbird music. In most thickly settled parts of the country the Rusty Blackbird is only a spring and autumn transient.

Brewer's Blackbird

Quiscale de Brewer
Euphagus cyanocephalus (Wagler)
Total length: 20 to 26 cm
Plate 67

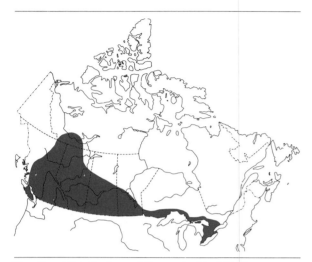

Breeding Distribution of Brewer's Blackbird

Range in Canada. Breeds in southeastern Mackenzie (Fort Simpson, Hay River); central and southern British Columbia (Smithers on Bulkley River, Fort Nelson, 46 km north of Prince George, Comox, Columbia Lake); north-central and southern Alberta (Meikle River north of Peace River and Calling Lake north of Athabasca, southward); central and southern Saskatchewan (Île-à-la-Crosse, Prince Albert, Nipawin southward); southern Manitoba (Swan River, Dauphin, Lake St. Martin, Rennie); western and south-central Ontario (Kenora, Thunder Bay, Geraldton, Sault Ste. Marie, North Bay, Sudbury, Manitoulin Island, Holland Marsh, Tay Township, Erieau). A recent arrival in eastern Ontario, it is extending its range eastward.

Recorded in autumn in Queen Charlotte Islands, British Columbia.

Winters in southern British Columbia (Vancouver Island, Vancouver, Kelowna) and rarely in south-central Alberta (Camrose) and southern Ontario.

Casual in north-central Ontario (Lake Attawapiskat, 5 June 1939). Accidental in Keewatin (Baker Lake, November 1923) and Nova Scotia (photos: Dartmouth, 18 October 1972; near Halifax, November 1975; Lockeport, 3 to 23 January 1977).

Adult male: Black, the head and neck strongly glossed with purple, the rest of plumage faintly glossed with bluish green; bill and legs black; eye pale yellowish or straw. *Young male in autumn*: Similar to adult male but feathers of head, neck, back, breast, and sides faintly tipped with greyish brown or buff. *Adult female (breeding plumage)*: Head, neck, and under parts brownish grey, very faintly glossed with greenish on under parts and with purplish on head; back, wings, and tail darker and glossier; bill and legs black; eye light brown. *Females in autumn*: Similar to female in breeding plumage but head, neck, and breast paler and more buffy grey.

Measurements. *Adult male*: wing, 121–133 (128.4); tail, 95–102.5 (99.8); exposed culmen, 20.4–24 (21.7); tarsus, 29.5–33.5 (31.7). *Adult female*: wing, 115–121 (117.4) mm.

Field Marks. Adult male, with pale-yellowish eyes, resembles that of the Rusty Blackbird, but the head and neck of the Brewer's are much more purplish. It is much smaller than the Common Grackle. The adult female looks much like a female Rusty, but the female Brewer's has brownish (instead of yellowish) eyes. Autumn Brewer's are much less rusty.

Habitat. More open areas with bushy tangles near by; hedges, roadside shrubbery, and bushy growths along streams and irrigation ditches; and on farmlands. Forages extensively in fields, pastures (often associates with cattle and sheep), golf courses, and lawns. It doubtlessly has profited by man's clearing of forests, irrigation projects, and cultivated crops.

Nesting. Often in loose colonies. Nest may be on the ground, in low bushes, or in trees. It is composed of coarse twigs and grasses, often mixed with mud and lined with fine rootlets, hair, and fine grasses. *Eggs*, most often 5 or 6; pale greenish-grey, spotted and blotched with browns, sometimes so heavily marked that the grey ground colour is hidden. Incubation reportedly 12 to 14 days, by the female.

Range. Breeds from British Columbia east to western Ontario and south to Baja California, central Arizona, New Mexico, northern Texas, Oklahoma, northern Iowa, and southwestern Michigan. Winters from southwestern Canada, Montana, Kansas, and Alabama south to southern Mexico and the Gulf Coast.

Great-tailed Grackle

Grand Quiscale
Quiscalus mexicanus (Gmelin)
Total length: male 46; female 36 cm

Status in Canada. Accidental. An adult female was photographed at Cape St. James, Queen Charlotte Islands, British Columbia, in May 1979.

Much larger than Common Grackle with relatively longer tail, the female very differently coloured. Adult males are shiny black with purplish gloss, yellow eyes. Adult females are brown, darker on back, wings, and tail; eyes yellowish. Immatures in first autumn have brown eyes. Very similar to Boat-tailed Grackle.

Measurements. *Adult male*: wing, 184.2–198.9 (189.2); tail, 195.6–235 (217.2); culmen (from base), 39.6–48 (44.7); tarsus, 47–52.8 (51.3). *Adult female*: wing, 142.2–158.5 (150.1); tail, 129–165.1 (147.8); culmen (from base), 343.8–39.4 (37.1); tarsus, 38.4–44.5 (41.1) mm (Ridgway).

Range. Resident from southeastern California, southern Utah, southeastern Colorado, southern Nebraska, southwestern Missouri, and southwestern Louisiana southward to Panama and in coastal South America from northwestern Venezuela southward to northern Peru.

Boat-tailed Grackle

Quiscale des marais
Quiscalus major Vieillot
Total length: male 42.5; female 33 cm

Status in Canada. Casual in Nova Scotia. Sight records of single birds on Sable Island, 7 May 1968; Glace Bay, 5 August 1969.

Adults very similar to Great-tailed Grackle but somewhat smaller, tail shorter and narrower, the eyes of Gulf Coast populations brown, those of the Atlantic Coast yellowish. In adult males the purplish gloss of head and neck tends to become more greenish posteriorly on back, flanks, and abdomen. Adult females are brownish thus like Great-tailed but average somewhat paler ventrally. Much larger than Common Grackle, and the female is very differently coloured.

Measurements. *Adult male*: wing, 175.8–189.2 (182.4); tail, 162.1–186.4 (170.7); culmen (from base), 41.7–46 (43.7); tarsus, 49–54.6 (51.1). *Adult female*: wing, 133.4–146.1 (142.7); tail, 124.5–135.9 (129.5); culmen (from base), 34.8–38.4 (37.1) mm (Ridgway).

Range. New York and New Jersey southward along the Atlantic Coast, Florida, and westward on the Gulf Coast of United States to southeastern Texas.

Common Grackle

(Bronzed Grackle)

Quiscale bronzé
Quiscalus quiscula (Linnaeus)
Total length: 28 to 34 cm
Plate 67

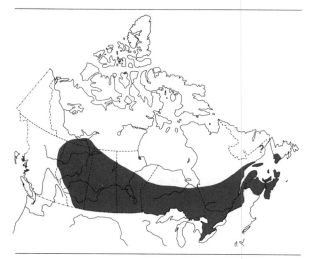

Breeding Distribution of Common Grackle

Range in Canada. Breeds in southern Macken-zie (Fort Resolution); northeastern British Columbia (Boundary Lake, Cecil Lake; near Fort Nelson, Tupper Creek); Alberta (east of the Rockies but local in northern forested areas and on the prairies); northwestern, central, and southern Saskatchewan (Lake Athabasca, Rein-deer Lake, local on southern prairies); north-ern, central, and southern Manitoba (Churchill southward); central and southern Ontario (Favourable Lake, and Moosonee southward); southern Quebec (Lake Abitibi, Amos, Lake Saint-Jean, Havre-Saint-Pierre southward including Anticosti and Madeleine islands; found in summer at Saint-Augustin); south-western Newfoundland; New Brunswick; Prince Edward Island; and Nova Scotia (including Cape Breton Island).

Wanders rarely to Reliance, Mackenzie; Jasper and Banff, Alberta; to northern and eastern Newfoundland (St. Anthony, Bay Bulls), and to Vancouver, British Columbia.

Sight record north to Rankin Inlet, Keewatin, 10 June 1970.

Small numbers winter in southern Ontario and rarely in southern Quebec, southern New Brunswick, Prince Edward Island, and Nova Scotia.

Much larger than the Rusty or Brewer's blackbirds; tail decidedly gradu-ated, the middle feathers longest. *Adult male*: Head, neck, and upper breast highly iridescent greenish blue or purple; rest of plumage uniform shiny bronze with more or less purplish reflection on wings and tail; bill and legs black; eye yellowish white. *Adult female*: Similar to adult male but smaller; coloration duller. *Young in juvenal plumage* (worn a short time after leaving nest): Dull sooty-brown with a suggestion of purplish sheen on wings and tail; eye brown. *Young in autumn plumage*: Like adults.

Measurements *(Q. q. versicolor). Adult male*: wing, 141–153 (145.1); tail, 126.5–143 (133.1); exposed culmen, 28.8–31.9 (30.4); tarsus, 35–38 (36.8). *Adult female*: wing, 128–132 (130.2) mm.

Field Marks. Our largest blackbird of regular occurrence (longer than the American Robin). At close range it is decidedly glossy with the bluish and purplish of head and neck sharply cut off from the shiny bronze remainder of the plumage; whitish eyes prominent. At a distance it looks all black. Tail is long and wedge-shaped. Flight is steadier and more level than that of most other blackbirds. Especially in spring, the spread tail is keel-shaped, turned up at the sides in a V-shape, this most apparent in flight. *Voice*: Song is short, discordant, and squeaky but is readily recognizable. Common call is a lusty *chuck*.

Habitat. Forages on the ground, especially where wet, in open places such as fields, pastures, lawns, golf courses, shores, marshes, or in wet alders and willows or open wet woodlands. Perches and nests in open woods, parks, groves, and shade trees.

Nesting. Frequently in small colonies. Usually in trees, preferably conifers; occasionally in bushes, cavities in trees; even rarely on the ground or inside buildings. Nest is a bulky but sturdy structure of sticks, weeds, and grass, these usually plastered together with mud and lined with grasses and rootlets. *Eggs*, usually 4 to 6; pale bluish or greenish and boldly blotched, scrawled, and spotted with browns or black. Incubation 14 days, by the female (A.O. Gross *in* Bent), usually 11 to 12 days (Petersen and Young).

Range. Breeds from southern Canada (Alberta east to southwest-ern Newfoundland) and southward, east of the Rockies, to central Colo-rado, central and southern Texas, the Gulf Coast of United States, and southern Florida. Withdraws in winter from most breeding areas in Canada.

Subspecies. (1) *Quiscalus quiscula versicolor* Vieillot is the only subspecies of regular occurrence in Canada. (2) *Q. q. stonei* Chapman (body plumage less uniform, the back and scapulars more or less barred with metallic blue, green, purple, and bronze): Accidental visitor to New Brunswick (Kent Island, 20 November 1931) and southwestern Quebec (Mirabel, 26 April 1973: two specimens).

Remarks. Even while the snow is still deep in shaded places, the Common Grackles make their early spring appearance. Their squeaky songs sound like unoiled wheelbarrows and, though certainly not musi-cal, are not altogether unpleasant. Grackles are gregarious and usually are seen in flocks, often including other blackbirds. They look black at a distance but at close range are really quite handsome. They have bright-yellow eyes, and the surprisingly iridescent colours of their plumage flash in the sun as the birds swagger about. Their diet includes many insects, grains, seeds, fruits, garbage, and not infrequently the eggs and young of other birds.

Brown-headed Cowbird

(Eastern or Nevada Cowbird)

Vacher à tête brune
Molothrus ater (Boddaert)
Total length: 17 to 21 cm
Plate 67

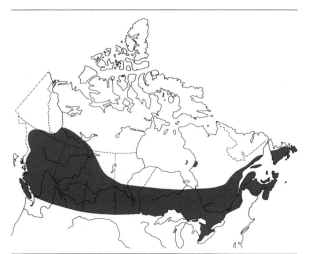

Breeding Distribution of Brown-headed Cowbird

Range in Canada. Breeds in British Columbia (Calvert Island, Dease Lake, Fort Nelson, Nulki Lake, François Lake, Swan Lake in Peace River District southward including Vancouver Island); southern Mackenzie (Nahanni National Park, Fort Simpson, Fort Resolution); Alberta; north-central and southern Saskatchewan (Kazan Lake, Cumberland House southward); southern Manitoba (The Pas, Norway House, Hillside Beach, Sprague); central and southern Ontario (Moosonee, Kenora, Hornepayne, Cochrane southward); southern Quebec (Amos, La Malbaie, Tadoussac, Harrington-Harbour, Anticosti and, recently, Madeleine islands southward; an isolated northern breeding record at Great-Whale-River (Todd 1963)); New Brunswick; Nova Scotia (Halifax, Wolfville, Wedgeport; a recent arrival in the province; first definite nesting 1929); Prince Edward Island (breeding first recorded in 1953 at Stanhope); and recently in Newfoundland.

Recorded without definite evidence of breeding in Queen Charlotte Islands, British Columbia; central-western Mackenzie (Fort Norman, Norman Wells); northwestern Saskatchewan (Lake Athabasca, Wollaston Lake); northern Manitoba (Churchill); north-central Ontario (Trout Lake, Lake Attawapiskat, Moosonee); southern Labrador (Capstan Island).

Winters sparingly in southern Ontario (north rarely to Ottawa) and, in recent years, regularly in southern Nova Scotia and southern New Brunswick. Rarely elsewhere in southern Canada.

Accidental on Bathurst Island, N.W.T. (specimen: 14 July 1975).

Bill short for a blackbird, stout and sparrowlike; tail shorter than folded wing, square at tip. *Adult male*: Head and neck brown; rest of plumage black with greenish and purplish gloss; bill and legs black; eye brown. *Adult female*: Greyish brown above, slightly glossy, the feathers with darker centres; under parts brownish grey with fine dark streaking; throat much paler and with little or no streaking; bill and legs blackish brown; eye brown. *Juvenal plumage*: Similar to adult female but feathers of upper parts margined with grey; under parts buffy or whitish streaked with greyish brown, throat paler and much less heavily streaked. Young in first winter plumage are very similar to adults.

Measurements *(M. a. ater)*. *Adult male*: wing, 107–114.6 (109.1); tail, 69.5–80.5 (75.2); exposed culmen, 16.6–18.8 (17.7); tarsus, 25–27 (25.9). *Adult female*: wing, 94–100.5 (97.9) mm.

Field Marks. A small brown-eyed blackbird with short sparrowlike bill. Male, with brown head and glossy black body (bird looks all black at a distance), is easily to recognize. Females are brownish grey, nondescript blackbirds, but the sparrowlike bill distinguishes it from female Rusties and Brewer's. *Voice*: Its song is a couple of low gurgles followed by a squeak: *glug-glug-ge-leek*. A common call is a high-pitched almost hissing whistle followed by two short lower notes: *wheeeee-tse-tse*; also a *chuck*.

Habitat. Forages in open areas such as pastures, grainfields, and other cultivated places. Often associates with cattle, horses, and other large mammals for the insects they stir up or attract. Perches in trees and bushes in various situations.

Nesting. It is parasitic, building no nest of its own. The female lays its eggs in the nests of other small birds, particularly warblers, vireos, finches, flycatchers, and thrushes. Ordinarily the individual Cowbird lays only one of its eggs in a given nest, but sometimes more than one Cowbird lays in the same nest. Sometimes the host throws the Cowbird egg from the nest or builds a new floor over the offending egg. In most cases the parasite's egg is incubated and the young Cowbird raised, often at the expense of some or all of the host's own young. The *eggs* are whitish, speckled and blotched with various browns over most of the egg's surface. The incubation period is 11 to 12 days (M.M. Nice; H.W. Hann).

Range. British Columbia east to Nova Scotia and south to northern Mexico, Louisiana, southern Mississippi, and South Carolina. Winters south to southern Mexico.

Subspecies. (1) *Molothrus ater ater* (Boddaert): eastern Ontario (Rossport eastward), southern Quebec, New Brunswick, Prince Edward Island, Nova Scotia. (2) *M. a. artemisiae* Grinnell (averages larger, with longer, relatively slenderer bill, and paler more brownish coloration in females): British Columbia, Mackenzie, Alberta, Saskatchewan, Manitoba, western Ontario (intergrades with *ater*).

Remarks. The Cowbird gets its name from its common habit of associating with cattle and other large mammals that attract and stir up insects. Indeed a very large part of the Cowbird's diet is made up of insects, including many destructive ones. Its food habits therefore are highly beneficial. The good it does, however, is doubtless more than nullified by its parasitic nesting habits (see Nesting), which certainly cause the destruction of large numbers of young insectivorous and seed-eating small birds.

Black-cowled Oriole

[**Black-cowled Oriole**. Oriole à capuchon. *Icterus dominicensis* (Linnaeus). Total length 19.5 to 21.5 cm. *Adults (sexes alike)*: Mostly black, but rump, upper wing coverts, and bend of wing bright yellow; posterior under parts usually yellowish. Resembles Scott's Oriole but has no white wing bars and the tail is all black (no yellow).

    Range. The West Indies, southern Mexico, and Central America.

    Status in Canada. Hypothetical. Sight record at Seal Island, Nova Scotia, on 24 May 1971 by Ben Doane who did detailed sketches and a good description.]

Orchard Oriole

Oriole des vergers
Icterus spurius (Linnaeus)
Total length: 15 to 18.5 cm
Plate 66

Breeding Distribution of Orchard Oriole

Range in Canada. Breeds locally in southern Saskatchewan (Fort Qu'Appelle; Buffalo Pound Lake; 20 km northwest of Saskatoon); southern Manitoba (Oak Lake, Lyleton, Cypress River, Delta); and southern Ontario (Point Pelee, Fort Erie, Chatham, Toronto; Prince Edward County; Kingston).

    Casual in southern New Brunswick (Kent Island; also various sight records), and Nova Scotia (Sable Island, Chezzetcook; also several sight records).

    Sight records for Quebec (various reports from Montréal east to Bonaventure Island) and Newfoundland (near St. John's, 10 June 1974).

Bill tapering, pointed, very slightly downcurved; tail shorter than folded wing, rounded. *Adult male*: Head, neck, back, scapulars, upper breast, and tail, black; wings mainly black with greater coverts and flight feathers edged with whitish or pale chestnut, lesser and middle coverts chestnut; lower back, tail coverts, and all under parts posterior to upper breast, rich chestnut. *Adult female*: Upper parts yellowish olive becoming greyish and duller on back and scapulars; wings greyish dusky with pale edging and two white wing bars; under parts olive yellowish. *Young (first autumn)*: Similar to adult female but male larger with more brownish back. *Young male (first spring)*: Similar to adult female but with black chin and throat and often with traces of black and chestnut elsewhere.

    Measurements. *Adult male*: wing, 75.6–80 (77.8); tail, 67.4–71.9 (69.5); exposed culmen, 15–16.9 (15.9); tarsus, 20–22.1 (21.1). *Adult female*: wing, average 74.7 mm.

    Field Marks. The adult male with its chestnut-and-black coloration is easy to recognize. First-year male in spring resembles the female but has a black bib (Northern Oriole with black throat has more orange colouring on breast). Female resembles female Northern Oriole but is smaller and has more uniform greenish-yellow under parts with no orange tinge. Somewhat similar to female Scarlet Tanager but bill much slenderer and more sharply pointed. *Song*: Less loud than that of Northern Oriole and quite different, more Robin-like; short, ending with slurred, falling, harsher notes.

    Habitat. Scattered trees about gardens, orchards, shade trees along roadsides. Avoids heavily forested regions.

    Nesting. Nest is a pouch woven of grasses and suspended from a fork in a branch of a tree or shrub 2.1 to 6 m up. It is not so deeply pouched as that of the Northern Oriole. *Eggs*, 3 to 7, usually 4 or 5; whitish, spotted and scrawled with browns and purplish grey, heaviest around large end. Incubation variable, reportedly 11 to 14 days, by the female.

    Range. Breeds from southern Manitoba, southern Ontario, and Massachusetts south to northern Mexico, southern Texas, the Gulf Coast of United States, and northern Florida, and west to central Nebraska and northeastern Colorado. Winters from southern Mexico to Colombia and Venezuela.

Northern Oriole

(includes Baltimore Oriole and Bullock's Oriole)

Oriole du Nord
Icterus galbula (Linnaeus)
Total length: 18 to 22.8 cm
Plate 66

Breeding Distribution of Northern Oriole

Range in Canada. Breeds in southern British Columbia (Langley, Courtenay, Alkali Lake, Okanagan valley, Creston); central and southern Alberta (Peace River district, Lesser Slave Lake, and Cold Lake southward); central and southern Saskatchewan (Kazan Lake, Emma Lake, Nipawin southward); southern Manitoba (northern Lake Winnipegosis, Lake St. Martin, Indian Bay southward); western Ontario (Malachi, Kenora, Thunder Bay); southern Ontario (north to Iron Bridge, Sudbury, New Liskeard); southwestern Quebec (Blue-Sea-Lake, Québec, Montmagny, Rimouski, Montréal, Hatley, Rouyn, and Baie-Saint-Paul); southern New Brunswick (Perth-Andover, Fredericton, Moncton); Nova Scotia (Berwick, Gaspereau, Digby, Mill Village); and in Prince Edward Island (very recently). Species has increased in the Maritimes in recent years.

Casual visitant to central Ontario (Chapleau, Moosonee), northern Manitoba (York Factory), and Newfoundland (Ramea, St. John's, Newfoundland Banks). Occasional in late autumn and winter in Nova Scotia and rarely elsewhere.

The Baltimore and the Bullock's orioles are considered conspecific and therefore are now combined into one species named Northern Oriole.

The eastern subspecies, *Icterus galbula galbula* (Linnaeus), formerly Baltimore Oriole, is as follows:

Form similar to that of Orchard Oriole but larger and differently coloured. *Adult male*: Head, neck, back, scapulars, and narrow extension onto upper breast, black; rest of under parts, rump, and upper tail coverts bright rich orange-yellow; wings mainly black, the flight feathers edged narrowly with white, tertials and greater wing coverts broadly edged with same, lesser and middle wing coverts yellow; tail with two middle feathers black (except concealed yellow bases), rest of tail feathers yellow at tips, the extent of yellow increasing outwardly. *Adult female*: Yellow olive above, variably spotted with black; rump dull yellow-olive to dull orange; tail similar but duller; wings dusky with two white bars and narrow whitish edging; under parts dull orange, frequently (not always) with some black on throat and occasionally elsewhere. *Young (first autumn)*: Resemble adult female but paler and without black on throat.

Measurements. *Adult male*: wing, 89.2–98.9 (93.7); tail, 70–76.5 (73.7); exposed culmen, 17.6–19.7 (19.0); tarsus, 22–24 (23.0). *Adult female*: wing, 85–92.1 (88.9) mm.

The western subspecies (breeding in southern British Columbia and southern Alberta), *Icterus galbula bullockii* (Swainson), is as follows:

Adult male: Top of head, back of neck, back, stripe down middle of throat, and line through eye black; wings mostly black, much of middle and greater coverts white, forming large white wing patch, flight feathers edged in white; middle tail feathers black (except hidden yellow bases), outer tail feathers mostly yellow and tipped blackish; rump and upper tail coverts yellow; stripe over eye, cheeks, and under parts (except black of throat) orange-yellow. *Adult female*: Crown and hindneck yellowish olive; back and rump olive greyish; upper tail coverts and tail olive yellow; two white wing bars; sides of head, vague stripe over eye, sides of neck, and breast dull orange-yellow; throat usually more whitish, sometimes blotched with black; abdomen and sides dull buffy-white; under tail coverts yellowish or yellow. *Young in autumn*: Resemble adult female but duller and with no trace of black on throat. *Young male in spring*: Resembles adult female, but chin, broad stripe down throat, and patch in front of eye black.

Measurements. *Adult male*: wing, 98.7–102.7 (101.3); tail, 77.5–81.5 (80.1); exposed culmen, 17.8–20 (18.9); tarsus, 24–26.5 (24.6). *Adult female*: wing, 91.2–98.6 (94.0) mm.

Field Marks. Adult males of the species, somewhat smaller than robin size, and with bright orange and black plumage, should not be confused with any other species of regular occurrence in Canada.

Adult males of the "Baltimore" subspecies are readily distinguished in the field from the western "Bullock's" race by the solidly black head of the former (Plate 66). Females and immatures of the two races are much more difficult to separate in the field but the "Baltimore" populations have more uniformly yellowish under parts (in "Bullock's" the abdomen and sides tend to be more whitish or greyish) (*see also* female Orchard Oriole and female tanagers). *Voice*: Song is a series of loud, clear whistles with irregular pauses between. A grating chatter of anxiety. A low whistled *tewly*.

Habitat. Scattered tall trees (in the East, elms are particularly favoured); more open deciduous woodland along streams, river valleys, and farmland.

Nesting. Nest is a curious bag-like structure up to 150 mm or more deep, suspended from a tree branch, often well up. The entrance is usually at the top. The nest is skilfully woven of plant fibres, hair, and twine. It is durable and may remain intact for several years. When the leaves have fallen, it is quite conspicuous in the bare branches. *Eggs*,

4 to 6; greyish white, with streaks, blotches, and irregular scrawls of browns, black, and a little purplish grey. Incubation, variously reported 12 to 15 days, by the female.

Range. Breeds from southern British Columbia east to Nova Scotia and south to southern California, northern Mexico, southern Texas, southeastern Louisiana, north-central Georgia, western South Carolina, central Virginia, and Delaware. Winters mainly from Mexico south to Colombia, Venezuela, and Costa Rica.

Subspecies. Described above. (1) *Icterus galbula galbula* (Linnaeus) is the breeding form from central Alberta eastward. (2) *I. g. bullockii* (Swainson) breeds in southern British Columbia and southern Alberta (lower south Saskatchewan and Red Deer rivers and in Milk River valley). There is considerable racial intergradation in eastern Milk River valley, Alberta.

Scott's Oriole

Oriole jaune-verdâtre
Icterus parisorum Bonaparte
Total length: 18.5 to 21.5 cm

Status in Canada. Accidental. An adult male was well photographed on 9 November 1975, at Silver Islet Landing, 30 km ESE of Thunder Bay, Ontario, by Arne Maki.

Adult male: Head, neck, and back uniform black; rump, upper tail coverts, under parts (posterior to chest) lemon yellow; wings black with yellow lesser coverts and a white bar; tail black with yellow conspicuous on basal half, especially the outer feathers. *Adult female*: Upper parts dull greenish (more yellowish on rump), the top of head and back streaked darker; wings dusky with two white bands; under parts yellowish olive.

Measurements. *Adult male*: wing, 98.6–106.7 (104.4); tail, 79.2–91.9 (88.4); exposed culmen, 20.8–24.6 (22.9); tarsus, 22.9–25.4 (23.9). *Adult female*: wing, 94.5–102.1 (97.8); tail, 81.3–88.4 (84.3); exposed culmen, 20.3–22.9 (21.3); tarsus, 23.4–24.9 (24.1) mm (Ridgway).

Field Marks. The extensive black and *lemon*-yellow combination of adult males distinguishes them from other orioles likely to be encountered in Canada. Similar orioles are found south of the United States but most lack either a white wing bar or any yellow in the tail. Female Scott's Orioles are more greenish yellow than most other females except the Orchard Oriole but the latter is smaller.

Range. Breeds from southeastern California, central Arizona, central New Mexico, and western Texas south to northern Mexico. Winters in Mexico.

Family **Fringillidae**: Finches

Number of Species in Canada: 15

Mainly arboreal smallish birds with conical bills suitable for extracting and eating seeds. Bill differs from that of most buntings in that the cutting edge of the lower mandible does not angle abruptly downward near its base. Most species are sexually dimorphic. Finches are found in Eurasia, Africa, and the Americas, but by far the most species are native to the Old World.

Subfamily **Fringillinae**: Fringilline Finches

Three Old World species of one genus make up this small group. They are similar structurally to the Carduelinae but differ in having no crop and they feed their young on invertebrates rather than by regurgitation of plant food.

Common Chaffinch

Pinson des arbres
Fringilla coelebs Linnaeus
Total length: 15 to 16 cm
Plate 69

Status in Canada. Accidental in Newfoundland
(photo record of a male in St. John's on
25 February 1967).

Adult male (Fringilla coelebs coelebs): Forehead black. Crown, nape, and hind neck slaty blue. Back chestnut. Rump green or greenish. Lores, cheeks, and line over eye pinkish chestnut. Under parts pinkish brown. Patch on shoulder and wing bar behind it, white. Outer tail feathers mostly white. *Adult female and immature*: Upper parts dull yellowish-olive becoming green on wings. Under parts plain brownish-grey. White areas in wing and tail similar to those of male but white not so pure.

    Field Marks. A House Sparrow-size finch with a conspicuous white shoulder patch and a white wing bar behind it, conspicuous white outer tail feathers, and a greenish rump. The adult male's coloration is unmistakable.

    Range. Breeds widely across Eurasia and south to the Mediterranean region, Asia Minor, southern Russia, and western Siberia. Winters somewhat farther south to northern Africa.

    Subspecies. Unknown. Cannot be determined from photographs.

Brambling

Pinson du Nord
Fringilla montifringilla Linnaeus
Total length: 15 cm
Plate 69

Status in Canada. Casual visitor to British Columbia (photo records: near Tlell, Queen Charlotte Islands, one at a feeder on 7 February 1971 and for four weeks thereafter; Reifel Island, 7 to 9 November 1971; Queen Charlotte, Queen Charlotte Islands, two in late November 1983; sight records: Tlell, 5 February 1972; near Sooke 20 November 1983); Manitoba (photo: East St. Paul, 22 to 28 October 1983; Winnipeg, 15 May 1984); Ontario (photo: Atikokan, 23 October 1983); and Nova Scotia (photo: Lake Echo, 18 May 1983).

Adult male: Top and sides of head and back black (much obscured in autumn and winter by buff feather tips). Patch down middle of rump white. Wing with two buffy to white bars and a small white patch on the inner primaries. Lesser wing coverts, throat, and upper breast rusty brown. Lower breast, belly, and under tail coverts white, the last more or less tinged with buff. Flanks coarsely but sparsely spotted with dusky. *Adult female and immature*: Similar to adult male but black areas of male replaced by mottled dark browns and buffs.

    Field Marks. Rusty-buff shoulder patch of the male and rusty-buff breast in both sexes in combination with white rump, conspicuous in flight.

Subfamily **Carduelinae**: Cardueline Finches

A large group containing over 120 species which are widely distributed in many parts of both the New and Old Worlds. They have conical bills, strong jaw muscles, a crop, and a powerful gizzard for digesting seeds. Many excel as singers and the group includes that famous songster the Canary *(Serinus canaria)*. Some members, such as the crossbills, Pine Grosbeak, redpolls, and siskins are noted for their irregular (but sometimes cyclical) irruptive movements.

Rosy Finch

Roselin brun
Leucosticte arctoa (Pallas)
Total length: 14.7 to 17 cm
Plate 74

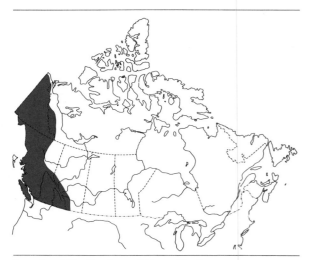

Breeding Distribution of Rosy Finch

Range in Canada. Breeds on mountain summits from northern Yukon and extreme western Mackenzie (Castle Rock in northeastern Richardson Mountains; probably Nahanni National Park); south through southern British Columbia and southwestern Alberta (Jasper, Banff, and Waterton Lakes national parks).

Winters in lowlands of southern and central British Columbia (north at least to Quesnel and Peace River District) and in southern and central Alberta (valleys and foothills of the southwestern mountains and irregularly farther east to Elk Island National Park and Brooks); also southwestern Saskatchewan (Eastend). Sporadically elsewhere in Saskatchewan (east to Regina and Indian Head, north to the Carlton area and Torch River). Casually east to Manitoba (Birtle, Erickson, Pinawa) and Ontario (photo records: all at Thunder Bay, 31 March 1963; February–March 1973; and 21 January 1975, respectively).

Adult male (breeding plumage): Nasal tufts white; crown black, bordered behind by grey, which extends down over the cheeks often to throat in one of our two subspecies *(littoralis)*, grey much more restricted in the other race *(L. a. tephrocotis)* and not extending onto cheeks; body mostly brown above and below, the back streaked with dusky; wings, rump, upper and lower tail coverts, and belly, more or less tinged with pink; bill black. *Adult male (winter)*: Similar to breeding plumage but black on crown much restricted, the brown feathers of body margined with white or buffy; bill yellowish with blackish tip. *Adult female*: Similar to adult male but somewhat duller and paler. *Young*: Somewhat like adults but mostly greyish brown without pink on the body or grey on head.

Measurements *(L. a. littoralis). Adult male*: wing, 102.7–108.9 (104.9); tail, 62–73 (68.6); exposed culmen, 11–12.1 (11.5); tarsus, 18.9–20.9 (19.9). *Adult female*: wing, 101–104 (102.5) mm.

Field Marks. Sparrow-sized ground birds of the West, usually in groups or flocks. General coloration, dark brown with pink suffusion on rump, wings, and belly; black cap on grey top of head, the grey extending down over cheeks and ear region in the race *littoralis*, but in *tephrocotis* the cheeks and ear region are brown like the body. *Voice*: Common call-notes suggest those of the House Sparrow. Song a rich goldfinch-like warble.

Habitat. In summer, for nesting, it inhabits rocks and cliffs among the glaciers and permanent snow above timberline on mountain summits. In autumn it descends to lowlands in mountain valleys, the West Coast, and foothills where it favours fields and open places, roadsides, straw stacks, farmyards, even invading the streets of towns and visiting feeding shelves.

Nesting. In crevices in cliffs or under rocks on mountain summits. The rather bulky nest is made of grass stems and rootlets and lined with grassy fibres, fine rootlets, plant down, or a few feathers. *Eggs*, 4 or 5; pure white. Incubation 12 to 14 days by the female.

Range. Islands of Bering Sea, the Aleutians, central Alaska, central Yukon, and southwestern Alberta south in the western mountains to central-eastern California, eastern Oregon, and northwestern Montana.

Subspecies. (1) *Leucosticte arctoa littoralis* Baird (grey of head extends down over cheeks and ear region): southwestern Yukon (Tepee Lake), western British Columbia (Dease Lake, Tenquille Lake, Déboulé Mountain, Vancouver Island). (2) *L. a. tephrocotis* (Swainson) (cheeks and ear region brown like body): central Yukon, south to southeastern British Columbia and southwestern Alberta.

Pine Grosbeak

Dur-bec des pins
Pinicola enucleator (Linnaeus)
Total length: 23 to 24.5 cm
Plate 69

Bill stubby, heavy, the culmen decidedly downcurved, the upper mandible slightly hooked; nasal tufts long, concealing nostrils; tail slightly forked. *Adult male*: General coloration dull red (dull pinkish-red in winter, light poppy-red in summer), the feathers with grey bases, the grey showing through in many places; nasal tufts and narrow line in front of eye blackish; back with dusky feather centres; scapulars mostly greyish; wings and tail dusky, the tertials and some secondaries edged with white; two white wing bars (often tinged reddish); abdomen, much of sides and flanks grey; under tail coverts greyish centrally with whitish margins; bill blackish, often paler at base of lower mandible; legs black. *Immature male*: Similar to adult female, but some have crown and rump reddish instead of yellowish olive. *Adult female*: General colour plain grey, the crown and rump yellowish olive to russet; hind-neck, back, and under parts more or less washed with olive; wings and tail similar to those of adult male. *Young females*: Similar to adult females.

Breeding Distribution of Pine Grosbeak

Range in Canada. Breeds from northern Yukon (Old Crow, probably upper Firth River); north-western and central Mackenzie (Mackenzie Delta, near Fort Anderson, Great Bear Lake, Reliance); northern Manitoba (Churchill, probably Sandhill Lake); northern Ontario (80 km south of Winisk); northern Quebec (Lake Guillaume-Delisle, Kuujjuaq, Hutte sauvage Lake; probably Koroc River); north-central Labrador (Okak); and Newfoundland south to southern British Columbia (including Queen Charlotte and Vancouver islands); northern Alberta (probably Wood Buffalo National Park); southwestern Alberta (mountains only: Banff and Jasper national parks); northern Saskatchewan (Tazin Lake, Hasbala Lake, probably south to central parts); north-central Manitoba (Ilford and probably farther south); central and south-central Ontario (Temagami Forest Reserve; rarely south to Sundridge, Bancroft, and probably Combermere); south-eastern and central-southern Quebec (locally: Baie-du-Poste, Biencourt, Lake Rimouski, Percé, Témiscouata County; Anticosti and Madeleine islands); New Brunswick; and Nova Scotia (including Cape Breton Island). Sight records in southwestern Keewatin (Windy River).

Winters within much of breeding range, north at least to northwestern Mackenzie (Mackenzie Delta), northwestern Saskatchewan (Lake Athabasca), south-central Quebec (Lake Mistassini), and southern Labrador; winters also in areas outside the breeding range; central and southern Alberta, southern Saskatchewan, southern Manitoba, southern Ontario, south-western Quebec, and Prince Edward Island, as well as in all southern parts of the breeding range. Winter movements are irregular, and the species may be common or abundant in a given area one winter and absent the next.

Measurements *(P. e. eschatosa). Adult male*: wing, 102.5–115.9 (110.8); tail, 85.1–95.1 (89.3); exposed culmen, 13.8–15.9 (14.6); tarsus, 19–23.1 (21.9). *Adult female*: wing, 105–110.9 (107.1) mm.

Field Marks. A large (Robin-sized) finch with heavy blackish bill. In migration and winter, frequently in small flocks. Usually tame. Motions are rather deliberate. Male Purple and Cassin's finches also are largely reddish but are much smaller and lack conspicuous white wing bars. Females and young Pine Grosbeaks are large, plain-grey finches with yellowish crown and rump and two white wing bars. The *dark* bill and lack of conspicuous white wing *patches* (other than bars) distinguish them from the Evening Grosbeak. *Voice*: Common call at all times of the year, two or three high-pitched musical whistles on a descending scale, somewhat suggesting that of the Greater Yellowlegs but less strident. The pleasing warbled song suggests that of the Purple Finch but is less energetic and usually shorter.

Habitat. In the breeding season more open coniferous forest (or less often, mixedwoods), openings and edges. In migration and winter, deciduous trees are much favoured (especially white ash, mountain ash, flowering crab), also shade trees about towns, apple orchards, and tall shrubbery as well as conifers, especially pines.

Nesting. In a coniferous tree usually not more than 3 to 4.5 m above ground but rarely up to 9 m. Nest is rather flimsily made of twigs, rootlets, grass, and moss. It is lined with such materials as fine rootlets, grasses, and hair. *Eggs*, usually 4 to 5; greenish blue with spots and dots of browns and purplish grey, mainly at the large end. Incubation 13 to 14 days, by the female.

Range. Holarctic. In North America breeds in northern forests from northern Alaska eastward across Canada to Newfoundland and south to central California, northern New Mexico, central Manitoba, central Ontario, northern New Hampshire, central Maine, and Nova Scotia; also in northern woodlands of Eurasia from Scandinavia east to northeastern Siberia, Kamchatka, and northern Japan. Winters within much of the breeding range and irregularly considerably farther south.

Subspecies. (1) *Pinicola enucleator leucura* (Müller): central Mackenzie (Great Bear Lake, Reliance), northern and central Manitoba, northern and central Ontario, northern Quebec, Labrador. (2) *P. e. eschatosa* Oberholser (smaller and darker than *leucura*): southern Quebec (including Baie-du-Poste where intergrading with *leucura*), Newfoundland, New Brunswick, Nova Scotia. (3) *P. e. alascensis* Ridgway (larger size, except bill, and paler coloration than *leucura*): Yukon, western Mackenzie (Mackenzie Delta, Fort Simpson), northeastern British Columbia. (4) *P. e. flammula* Homeyer (bill larger than in *leucura*, dusky centres of back feathers less distinct): northwestern British Columbia (Telegraph Creek, Dease Lake, Tetana Lake). (5) *P. e. carlottae* Brooks (small, especially tail, coloration dark): Queen Charlotte and Vancouver islands, and along the mainland coast of British Columbia. (6) *P. e. montana* Ridgway: southern interior British Columbia (Puntchesakut Lake, Indianpoint Lake southward) and southwestern Alberta (Jasper and Banff national parks).

Purple Finch

Roselin pourpré
Carpodacus purpureus (Gmelin)
Total length: 14 to 16 cm
Plate 70

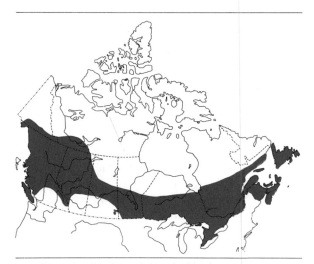

Breeding Distribution of Purple Finch

Range in Canada. Breeds in southern Yukon (Whitehorse, Carmacks); southwestern Mackenzie (Nahanni National Park, Fort Simpson); northern, central, and southwestern British Columbia (Atlin and at points along the Alaska Highway, south on the coast to Vancouver Island and in the interior to Big Bar Lake and southern Wells Gray Provincial Park); northern, central, and southwestern Alberta (Wood Buffalo National Park south to Jasper and Banff in the mountains and to Edmonton, Elk Island National Park, and probably Battle River); central and southeastern Saskatchewan (Kazan Lake, Missinipe, Prince Albert, Nipawin; locally: Moose Mountain and recently Qu'Appelle valley); south-central and southern Manitoba (The Pas, Norway House probably Island Lake southward); central and southern Ontario (Favourable Lake, and Moose Factory southward); south-central and southern Quebec (Eastmain, Lake Mistassini, Matamec, Saint-Augustin southward including Anticosti Island and probably Madeleine Islands); central and southern Newfoundland; New Brunswick; Prince Edward Island; and Nova Scotia (including Cape Breton Island).

Winters in southern British Columbia; southern Manitoba (Brandon, Winnipeg); southern Ontario (north at least to Thunder Bay, Manitoulin Island, North Bay, Ottawa); southwestern Quebec (Hull, Montréal, Québec); southern New Brunswick (Scotch Lake, Fredericton, Saint John); Prince Edward Island; Nova Scotia (Wolfville, Pictou, Antigonish, Halifax); and southern Newfoundland (St. John's).

Casual in southern Labrador (Cartwright). Accidental in eastern Franklin (off Resolution Island, 1 September 1877).

Bill heavy, short, conical; tail shorter than wing and slightly forked. *Adult male*: Upper parts, head, neck, breast, and sides variable red (duller in autumn and winter), the crown crimson to purplish red, the rump more pinkish, the back and scapulars streaked with brown; eye and ear region and patch on side of jaw often brownish; small area in front of eye greyish white; wings and tail dark brown narrowly edged with pale reddish or brownish; two faint narrow wing bars of brownish red; middle of abdomen and under tail coverts white. *Immature male (first breeding plumage)*: Similar to adult female. *Adult female*: Upper parts olive greyish streaked with dusky and also a little whitish; white line back from eye; eye and ear regions olive; wings and tail dusky, narrowly edged with pale olive; two pale wing bars; under parts white, heavily streaked with olive except middle of abdomen, the under tail coverts usually unstreaked (sometimes longer ones are lightly streaked). Occasional females show traces of red in the plumage. *Young in first winter plumage*: Similar to adult female.

Measurements (*C. p. purpureus*). *Adult male*: wing, 78.4–85 (82.3); tail, 51.5–61.5 (58.4); exposed culmen, 10.2–12 (11.3); tarsus, 17.5–18.4 (17.9). *Adult female*: wing, 74–81.8 (78.3) mm.

Field Marks. Size of House Sparrow. The red (not purple) adult male is much smaller than the (Robin-sized) red male Pine Grosbeak. Uncrossed mandibles distinguish it from crossbills. Females and young are heavily streaked, with a dusky patch on sides of head and a white line back from eye; the heavy bill distinguishes them from other streaked sparrows of the East. In the West see Cassin's and House finches. *Voice*: Song is a rich, rapid, and spirited warble, very reminiscent of that of the Warbling Vireo but much more energetic. Call, a metallic *pink*, which is quite distinctive.

Habitat. More open mixed and coniferous woodland, openings and edges, farm woodlots, even orchards. In winter various kinds of trees and tall shrubbery, orchards, parks, and gardens.

Nesting. 1.5 to 18 m up in a tree (usually coniferous but more rarely in an apple or other deciduous tree or very rarely in a hedge). Nest, which is of twigs, grasses, and rootlets, is lined with fine grasses and hair. *Eggs*, 4 to 6; blue, with fine dark-brown or blackish spots chiefly about the large end. Incubation period about 13 days (O.W. Knight), by the female.

Range. Breeds across wooded parts of Canada from British Columbia (except interior southern part) east to Newfoundland and south along the Pacific Coast to northern Baja California, and to North Dakota, central Wisconsin, northeastern Ohio, southeastern West Virginia, and southeastern New York. Winters from southern Canada (locally) south to southern United States.

Subspecies. (1) *Carpodacus purpureus purpureus* (Gmelin): eastern Manitoba (Selkirk, Rennie), Ontario, Quebec, New Brunswick, Prince Edward Island, Nova Scotia, and Newfoundland. (2) *C. p. taverneri* Rand (paler coloration especially in adult male): southwestern Mackenzie, northern and central British Columbia, Alberta, Saskatchewan, western Manitoba (Riding Mountain, The Pas). (3) *C. p. californicus* Baird (darker, with dorsal streaking in adult male more obscure): southwestern British Columbia (Comox, Kimsquit, Lillooet).

Cassin's Finch

Roselin de Cassin
Carpodacus cassinii Baird
Total length: 15 to 17 cm
Plate 70

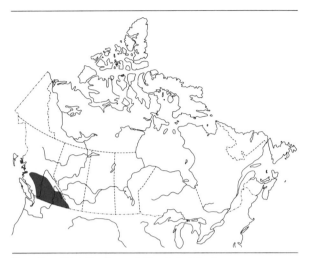

Breeding Distribution of Cassin's Finch

Range in Canada. Breeds in southern interior British Columbia (Stuie, Clinton, Mile 85 Cariboo Road, Arrow Lakes, Okanagan, Wardner) and in extreme southwestern Alberta (Waterton Lakes National Park and north about to Canmore and the Bow valley).

Winters occasionally in southern British Columbia (Okanagan Landing).

Similar to Purple Finch but larger with relatively less stubby bill and differing in colour as follows. *Adult male* with reds paler, the red of crown brighter, forming a definite cap, which contrasts with the more brownish remainder of upper parts; throat and breast paler, more pinkish; under tail coverts usually conspicuously streaked with dusky. *Females and immatures* are more greyish (less olive) than in Purple Finch, the streaks on under parts finer and sharper, the under tail coverts usually conspicuously streaked with dusky.

Measurements. *Adult male*: wing, 90.4–96.8 (93.4); tail, 61.8–66 (64.3); exposed culmen, 12–12.9 (12.5); tarsus, 18–19.1 (18.6). *Adult female*: wing, 86.3–92.6 (88.3) mm.

Field Marks. To be expected in southern interior British Columbia and extreme southwestern Alberta. It is separable, with difficulty, in the field from the Purple Finch by characters given above. It also resembles the smaller, more stubby-billed House Finch. The adult male Cassin's Finch, however, has the reds paler and less, if any, dusky streaking on the belly and sides than the male House Finch. Females and young Cassin's Finch have longer bills (with straighter culmen), darker coloration above and below, and sharper, finer, darker streaks on the under parts than the House Finch in corresponding plumages. *Song*: Similar to that of Purple Finch but call-note quite different, a two or three syllable *kee-up*, the second syllable lower.

Habitat. Open coniferous forests in the western mountains ranging up to considerable altitudes.

Nesting. In a coniferous tree at various heights above ground. Nest is of twigs, rootlets, and grasses, lined with fine grass. *Eggs*, usually 4 to 5; greenish blue, sparingly spotted with browns and purplish grey. Incubation 12 to 14 days, by the female.

Range. Breeds from southern interior British Columbia, extreme southwestern Alberta, central Montana, northern Wyoming south in the interior mountains to northwestern California, northern Baja California, northern Arizona, and northern New Mexico. Winters within much of breeding range and south to northern Mexico.

Remarks. Cassin's Finch is very closely related to the much more widely distributed Purple Finch. The two look and seem to act very much alike, but the call-note of Cassin's Finch sounds like *kee-up* (first syllable high-pitched) and differs from the metallic *pink* of the Purple Finch.

House Finch

Roselin familier
Carpodacus mexicanus (Müller)
Total length: 12.5 to 14 cm
Plate 70

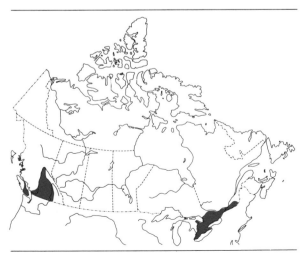

Breeding Distribution of House Finch

Bill stubby, culmen much more downcurved than in Purple or Cassin's finches. *Adult male*: Forehead, stripe over eye, and rump, red, rosy pink, or scarlet; rest of upper parts brownish grey, obscurely streaked with darker brown and often washed with reddish; wings and tail dusky with pale-greyish edging and two obscure pale wing bars; throat and upper breast reddish; lower breast, abdomen, sides, flanks, and under tail coverts whitish, thickly streaked with greyish brown. *Adult female*: Like adult male but without any red, that of the upper parts replaced by brown, that of throat and upper breast by whitish and striped with greyish brown as in the rest of the under parts; face lacks definite patterns shown in Purple and Cassin's finches. *Young*: Resemble adult female.

Measurements *(C. m. frontalis)*. *Adult male*: wing, 74.5–83.2 (78.6); tail, 57–65 (61.7); exposed culmen, 9.3–11 (10.0); tarsus, 16–18.2 (17.2). *Adult female*: wing, 74.3–78 (75.9) mm.

Field Marks. Gregarious. Resembles Purple and Cassin's finches but is smaller, and the stubbier bill has a more downcurved culmen. Adult male has the red coloration more restricted and the whole lower breast, abdomen, and sides thickly streaked with greyish brown.

Range in Canada. Breeds in southwestern and central-southern British Columbia: Vancouver Island (Victoria and north along the east coast to near Campbell River), Vancouver, Abbotsford, Chilliwack, Hope, Princeton, near Lillooet, the entire Okanagan valley, Grindrod, Kamloops, Williams Lake, and northward to Prince George.

Recently has spread into southeastern Canada from introduction by man into eastern United States. Now breeds in southern Ontario (first nested in 1978 in Niagara-on-the-Lake. In 1980 it bred at Kingston and St. Thomas; in 1981 in London; in 1982 in Hamilton, Toronto, Simcoe, Port Dover, Port Hope; in 1983 in Pembroke; in 1984 in Ottawa) and in southwestern Quebec (in 1983 nested at Sherbrooke, Philipsburg, Pointe-Claire).

Sight records for New Brunswick (Saint John); Nova Scotia (Yarmouth, Barrington Passage, Pubnico, Halifax); Manitoba (Stonewall, vicinity of Winnipeg); Saskatchewan (Regina, Saskatoon); and Alberta (specimen: Jasper National Park, 29 May 1944; photo records: Calgary, Waterton Lakes National Park). In Ontario has wandered north to Marathon (photo: 12 May 1976).

Winters in much of the breeding range.

Females and young are paler above than Purple and Cassin's finches and have no definite face patterns. Its frequent habitat in western towns, which is similar to that of House Sparrows, tends to eliminate its two near relatives. *Voice*: A spirited warbling song somewhat suggesting a cross between a Purple Finch and a Vesper Sparrow. Some of its calls sound like the chirps of the House Sparrow.

Habitat. Sunny drier areas are preferred (but with at least some water available); farmlands with thin shrubbery, trees, orchards, and buildings; towns. In many ways similar to the requirements of the House Sparrow in cultivated and urban areas.

Nesting. Various situations such as crannies on building exteriors, vines about houses, bird boxes, tree cavities, clumps of shrubs, and even in old nests of other bird species like the Cliff Swallow, the American Robin, and the Northern Oriole. Nest is made of various soft materials depending upon availability, such as grass, twigs, rootlets, cotton wool, string. *Eggs*, usually 4 or 5; bluish, sparingly spotted with blackish. Incubation period averages 14 days (Bergtold) by the female.

Range. Southwestern and central-southern British Columbia, Idaho, Wyoming, and western Nebraska south to southern Mexico. Introduced by cagebird dealers into eastern North America at Long Island, New York, in 1940 and now present in much of eastern United States and spreading into southeastern Canada.

Subspecies. *Carpodacus mexicanus frontalis* (Say). For comments on affinities of introduced eastern populations, see J.W. Aldrich and J.S. Weske (1978. Auk, vol. 95, no. 3, pp. 528–536).

Red Crossbill

Bec-croisé rouge
Loxia curvirostra Linnaeus
Total length: 14 to 16.5 cm
Plate 70

a   b

Figure 102
Bill of Red Crossbill
a) lateral view
b) dorsal view

Bill with tips somewhat elongated and crossed (Figure 102), the tip of the upper mandible bent downward, the lower upward; tail somewhat notched. No white bars on wings (in North American populations). *Adult male*: General coloration above and below, dull red; brightest on rump, dullest on back where brown feather centres show through; wings and tail blackish brown; no wing bars; middle of abdomen greyish; under tail coverts grey (the feathers with large dark centres), usually washed with reddish. *Adult female*: General coloration greyish olive, more or less striped and spotted darker, becoming yellow on rump and often on breast and sides; wings and tail plain blackish-brown with narrow pale edges. *Immature male*: Variable, some resembling adult female; many others have various mixtures of yellows, reds, and green. *Juvenals of both sexes*: When they leave the nest both sexes are pale greyish, more or less tinged with olive or yellowish and conspicuously streaked on head and body with dusky; wings and tail similar to those of adult female.

Measurements *(L. c. pusilla* from Newfoundland). *Adult male*: wing, 88.3–97.7 (91.7); tail, 53–59.4 (55.9); exposed culmen, 17–18.6 (17.7); tarsus, 16.3–17.8 (17.1). *Adult female*: wing, 87.2–92.3 (89.5) mm.

Field Marks. Large-headed, heavy-billed House-Sparrow-sized birds, usually seen in flocks in coniferous trees where they feed on the seeds of conifer cones, using both bill and feet like parrots, often hanging upside-down. Adult male reddish: female yellowish grey with yellowish rump. Often tame, sometimes allowing the crossed bill tips to be seen, which mark them as crossbills. The plain wings (no white bars) separate them from White-winged Crossbills. *Voice*: Calls *jip jip*, less harsh and more musical than calls of the White-winged Crossbill. Song loud, shorter than that of the White-winged, consists of whistled notes, more or less interspersed with warbled phrases (L. de K. Lawrence).

Breeding Distribution of Red Crossbill

Range in Canada. Permanent resident but highly nomadic, its wanderings governed to a large extent by the availability of its staple food, conifer seeds. Nesting time is as erratic as its wanderings and may occur in any month of the year. The breeding range is not well known. Its presence in an area is no guarantee that it is breeding there. Its nesting in a given area is no indication that it will nest there next year or in the next decade, or that it nested there last year. Breeds in coniferous forests of southern Yukon (Kluane, Nisutlin River); southern Mackenzie (Fort Smith, Fort Simpson); British Columbia (throughout, including coastal islands); Alberta (but in the south confined to the Rockies and foothills and the Cypress Hills); Saskatchewan (locally: Lake Athabasca, Cypress Hills, Saskatoon, Moose Jaw, probably Regina); southern Manitoba (recorded north to Echimamish River, Thompson, and Churchill but without evidence of breeding); central and southern Ontario (Lake Manitowick, northern Algoma District; Rutherglen, Algonquin Provincial Park, Pakenham, Toronto, Guelph. Species recorded north to Fort Severn and Sutton River); southern Quebec (Tadoussac, Lake Grand, Saint-Bruno; reportedly wanders to Grande rivière de la Baleine and Natashquan; recorded in summer on Anticosti and Madeleine islands); New Brunswick (Grand Manan, Scotch Lake); Prince Edward Island; Nova Scotia (Wolfville, Halifax, Seabright); and Newfoundland.

Habitat. Usually coniferous trees, the bird's movements often guided by the abundance or scarcity of the cone crop. Feeds less often on seeds or fruits of deciduous trees and shrubs, e.g., elm, flowering crab, and alder.

Nesting. The nest, which is at various heights, usually in a coniferous tree and well out on a branch, is made of twigs, shreds of bark, weed stems, grass, and is lined with moss, plant down, fur, or feathers. *Eggs*, usually 3 or 4, sometimes 5; pale bluish-green, spotted with browns and lavender, mostly at the larger end. Incubation, by the female, is between 12 and 15 days (Ross and Ross). Nesting time is erratic; it may breed any time of the year.

Range. Boreal coniferous forests across Eurasia and North America south to northern Spain, northern Africa, islands in the Mediterranean, northern India, southern China, Japan, and the northern Philippines. In North America from southeastern Alaska east to Newfoundland and south in the mountains to northern Baja California, northern Nicaragua, and in eastern United States south to northern Wisconsin, Tennessee, and North Carolina.

Subspecies. (1) *Loxia curvirostra pusilla* Gloger (larger size, general coloration darker): Breeds in Newfoundland. Wanders, mainly in winter, to Ontario, Quebec, New Brunswick, and Nova Scotia. (2) *L. c. minor* (Brehm), smaller with slenderer bill and paler coloration than *pusilla*: Breeds in Ontario, Quebec, New Brunswick, Prince Edward Island, and Nova Scotia; wanders westward, probably breeding, to southern Manitoba, central and northwestern Saskatchewan, southern Mackenzie (Fort Smith). (3) *L. c. bendirei* Ridgway (similar to *minor* but slightly larger, wing and bill longer; reds brighter, more scarlet; greys sootier): southwestern Saskatchewan (Cypress Hills), southwestern and southeastern Alberta (Rocky Mountains, Cypress Hills), interior British Columbia, southern Yukon. (4) *L. c. sitkensis* Grinnell, the smallest of our crossbills with stubby bill (culmen 13.5–15 mm): Resident in coastal British Columbia but wanders sporadically sometimes in large numbers east as far as New Brunswick. Perhaps has bred in the interior (see Ludlow Griscom, 1937. Proceedings Boston Society of Natural History, vol. 41, no. 5, pp. 77–209, for a study of the subspecies of this crossbill).

White-winged Crossbill

Bec-croisé à ailes blanches
Loxia leucoptera Gmelin
Total length: 15 to 17 cm
Plate 70

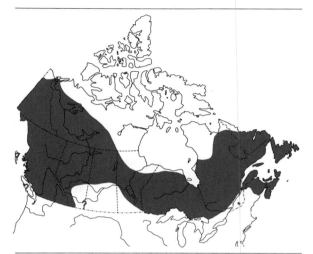

Breeding Distribution of White-winged Crossbill

Range in Canada. Resident in coniferous forests from northern Yukon (Old Crow); northern Mackenzie (Mackenzie Delta, Dease River, Thelon River); northern Saskatchewan (Lake Athabasca, Black Lake region); central Manitoba (The Pas, Grand Rapids; reported in summer without evidence of breeding north to Churchill); northern Ontario (Fort Severn, Fort Albany); northern Quebec (Grande rivière de la Baleine, Lacs des loups marins, Kuujjuaq, Hutte sauvage Lake); north-central Labrador (Okak, Hopedale); and Newfoundland south through British Columbia (but scarce on Queen Charlotte and Vancouver islands where nesting is not known); southwestern and central-eastern Alberta (perhaps also Cypress Hills); central Saskatchewan (Flotten Lake); southeastern Manitoba (Julius); southern Ontario (Michipicotin River, Head Lake); southern Quebec (La Vérendrye Park, Stoneham, Loretteville, Lake Rimouski, Gaspé Peninsula; also Anticosti and Madeleine islands; once nested on Mount Orford); New Brunswick; Prince Edward Island; and Nova Scotia. Winters within the areas included above and wanders somewhat farther south.

Scarce visitor to northern Manitoba (Churchill). Accidental in Franklin (southern Baffin Island: Lake Harbour).

Bill tips crossed as in Red Crossbill, but bill is thinner. Two white wing bars in all plumages. *Adult male*: General coloration variable red (bright scarlet or vermilion in summer, dull and pinkish in winter); scapulars, area across back, wings, and tail black, the tertials tipped with white; two conspicuous white wing bars; mid-abdomen and flanks greyish, the latter streaked with dusky; under tail coverts blackish with grey margins. *Adult female*: Wings and tail as in adult male; elsewhere mostly olive green or greyish streaked with dusky, the rump clear yellow; breast and sides washed with yellow and streaked with dusky; rest of under parts grey streaked with dusky. *Immature male (first winter)*: Somewhat resembles adult male, but reds mostly replaced by yellow mixed with more or less red. *Juvenal plumage* (worn only a short time after leaving nest): General coloration, pale greyish or brownish streaked with dusky; wings blackish with two white bars.

Measurements. *Adult male*: wing, 86.2–90.4 (88.0); tail, 57.1–63.5 (60.9); exposed culmen, 15.9–16.9 (16.2); tarsus, 15.9–17 (15.6). *Adult female*: wing, 80.5–87.1 (83.9) mm.

Field Marks. When the crossed mandibles are visible, this species could be confused with only the Red Crossbill, but the conspicuous white wing bars distinguish the White-winged in all plumages. The white wing bars separate it also from the Purple Finch, the much smaller size from the Pine Grosbeak, and the crossed bill tips distinguish it from both. *Voice*: Call *cheet cheet*, much harsher and more strident than corresponding calls of the Red Crossbill and unlike any other. When heard in chorus as from a flying flock, it becomes a characteristic, easily recognized chatter. The song is delightful, vigorous, varied, and sustained, containing frequent canary-like trills, as well as harsh rattles and pleasing warbles. The volume changes frequently. The singer perches in the top of a coniferous tree or flies in a circle on slowly flapping wings.

Habitat. Open coniferous or mixed woodlands, openings, edges, and groves. Primarily a bird of conifers, it is less inclined to feed in deciduous trees and shrubs than the Red Crossbill.

Nesting. May occur in any month of the year. Nest is placed in a coniferous tree at various heights above the ground. It is constructed of twigs, *Usnea* lichen, and bark shreds, and is lined with grasses, hair, or feathers. Incubation is by the female. Incubation period uncertain.

Range. Resident in boreal coniferous forests in Eurasia (Scandinavia east to Siberia); in northern North America; and there is an isolated resident population in Hispaniola. In North America breeds from central Alaska eastward across Canada to Labrador and Newfoundland and south in northern United States to northern Oregon, northern Minnesota, northern Michigan, northern New York, northern Vermont, New Hampshire, and Maine.

Subspecies. *Loxia leucoptera leucoptera* Gmelin.

Common Redpoll

Sizerin flammé
Carduelis flammea (Linnaeus)
Total length: 11 to 15 cm
Plate 69

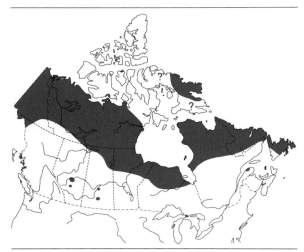

Breeding Distribution of Common Redpoll

Range in Canada. Breeds locally from northern Yukon (Herschel Island); northern Mackenzie (Mackenzie Delta, Franklin Bay, Coppermine); southern Victoria Island (Cambridge Bay); northern Keewatin (probably Perry River); northern Manitoba (Churchill); northern Ontario (Fort Severn, Little Cape, Cape Henrietta Maria); Baffin Island (Clyde Inlet, Cumberland Peninsula); northern Quebec (Salluit, Kuujjuaq); and northern Labrador (Nachvak) south to northwestern British Columbia (Atlin); southern Mackenzie (Fort Simpson, Fort Providence, Soulier Lake); central Alberta (sporadically and locally: Edmonton and Devon in 1974; Camrose in 1941; Red Deer in 1924); central Saskatchewan (Mortlach in 1960; Saskatoon in 1969); northern Manitoba (Cochrane River, Herchmer, York Factory); northern Ontario (Lake Attawapiskat; summer records at Kenora, Thunder Bay, Nakina); central and southeastern Quebec (Fort-George, Schefferville, Blanc-Sablon; rarely Madeleine Islands; locally Mount Albert); southern Labrador (Cartwright); and Newfoundland (except southwestern corner).

Winters within southern parts of the breeding range and southward (but irregularly: common to abundant in some years, rare or absent in others in a given locality) in most parts of southern Canada including British Columbia (but rarely reported on the coastal islands), Alberta, Saskatchewan, Manitoba, Ontario, Quebec, New Brunswick, Prince Edward Island, Nova Scotia (including Cape Breton Island), and Newfoundland.

Similar to Hoary Redpoll but much darker, the rump not plain white but heavily streaked with dusky; under tail coverts with heavier dusky streaks; proportions also differ, depending somewhat on races concerned. *Adult male (breeding plumage)*: Cap bright red; rest of upper parts dark greyish-brown with indistinct dark streaks and some of greyish white; rump greyish white (often pinkish), heavily streaked with dusky; wings and tail dark greyish-brown; two narrow white wing bars; chin blackish; cheeks, breast, and sides often tinged with red or pink; rest of under parts white, the sides and under tail coverts streaked with dusky. *Adult male (winter)*: Similar to breeding plumage but very much paler and more buffy, rump more whitish (often pinkish), but always decidedly streaked with dusky; wing bars more or less buffy; pink of breast paler. *Adult female*: Similar to adult male, including red cap, but without red or pink on under parts.

Measurements *(C. f. flammea). Adult male*: wing, 69.8–75.3 (72.7); tail, 50.4–60.2 (55.8); exposed culmen, 8.2–10.2 (9.0); tarsus, 13.6–15.8 (14.8). The northeastern race *rostrata* is much larger: wing, 75.6–83.9 (80.5). *Adult female (C. f. flammea)*: wing, 68.3–74.8 (70.5) mm.

Field Marks. Redpolls are small stubby-billed finches with a bright-red cap, blackish chin, dark streaks on sides, the adult males often showing a pinkish suffusion on the breast. In thickly settled southern parts of the country they are winter visitants and are usually seen in twittering flocks of various sizes, feeding either in weed patches on the ground or in trees. The Common Redpoll very closely resembles the Hoary, but the former's general coloration is noticeably darker; the rump is heavily streaked like the back (not decidedly white), and at close range the bill can often be seen to be slightly longer, less stubby than that of the Hoary. *Voice*: Flight call tends to be a double-noted *zit-zit*. Flocks maintain a constant twitter of metallic notes. Song, a trill accompanied by a twitter.

Habitat. Varies somewhat with latitude. In the high Arctic, ravines and rocky slopes with some shrubby ground cover. In the Subarctic and low Arctic, patches of spruce, dwarf birch, alder and willow thickets, mats of dwarf spruce, and other thick low shrubbery. In winter in southern localities, open woodland (either deciduous or coniferous), weed patches, fields, and bushy fence rows. It is especially fond of seeds of birch and alder.

Nesting. In dwarf trees and shrubs, on the ground on sedge tussocks, or in rock crevices. Nest is of grasses and twigs and is warmly lined with cottony plant down, feathers, sometimes fur or hair. *Eggs*, usually 5 or 6; blue, dotted and spotted with reddish brown. Incubation period 10 to 11 days (L.I. Grinnell) for *flammea*; 11 days (E.M. Nicholson) for *rostrata*; by the female.

Range. Circumpolar Arctic and Subarctic. In North America from Alaska eastward across northern Canada to Greenland. Winters from the southern breeding range south to northern California, Nevada, Colorado, Kansas, Ohio, West Virginia, and South Carolina.

Subspecies. (1) *Carduelis flammea flammea* (Linnaeus) is the breeding form of Yukon (except perhaps Herschel Island, see *C. f. holboellii*), northern British Columbia, Mackenzie, Victoria Island, Keewatin, Manitoba, Ontario, Quebec, Labrador, and Newfoundland. (2) *C. f. rostrata* (Coues), larger size with thicker bill, coloration somewhat darker and browner than in *flammea*, adult males with red of under parts less extensive and less intense: Baffin Island, N.W.T. (3) *C. f. holboellii* (Brehm), of doubtful validity but supposedly intermediate in size between *flammea* and *rostrata* with slenderer bill than the latter, colour similar to *flammea*, is alleged to be the breeding form of Herschel Island, Yukon.

The common wintering form in southern Canada is *C. f. flammea*, but *rostrata* is also a winter visitant in small numbers to southern parts of the East from Ontario to Newfoundland.

Hoary Redpoll

Sizerin blanchâtre
Carduelis hornemanni (Holböll)
Total length: 11 to 15 cm
Plate 69

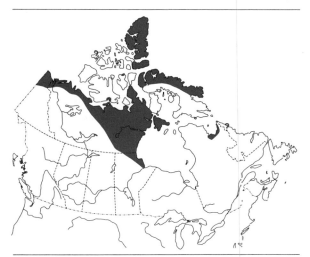

Breeding Distribution of Hoary Redpoll

Range in Canada. Breeds (locally, but range poorly known) in northern Yukon (Old Crow); northern and central-eastern Mackenzie (Mackenzie Delta, Anderson River, Bathurst Inlet, Thelon River); southern Victoria Island (Cambridge Bay); Keewatin (Adelaide Peninsula, Baker Lake, Windy River); northern Manitoba (Churchill); and from northern Ellesmere Island (Alert, Fosheim Peninsula) south through Bylot Island and Baffin Island (Clyde Inlet, Cumberland Peninsula) south to Southampton Island and northern Quebec (Kuujjuaq). Reported breeding in northern Labrador (Nachvak) requires confirmation. Summer sight records for Prince Patrick and Ellef Ringnes islands.

Winters within much of the breeding range (north at least to northern Yukon), northwestern Mackenzie, Southampton Island, and southern Baffin Island (Pangnirtung Fiord) and southward, locally and irregularly, to southern British Columbia and other southern parts of the country including Alberta, Saskatchewan, Manitoba, Ontario, and Quebec. Specimen records in the Maritime Provinces for only Nova Scotia (Gaspereau). Photo records for New Brunswick. Sight records only for Newfoundland and Prince Edward Island.

Similar to Common Redpoll but general coloration decidedly paler, the rump (except in worn breeding plumage) white or pinkish with little or no streaking, thus contrasting with the back. The subspecies *C. h. exilipes* is similar in size to *C. flammea flammea*, but *exilipes* (Hoary Redpoll) has a shorter more obtuse bill, a slightly longer tail, and the under tail coverts of *exilipes* are much more lightly streaked or immaculate.

Measurements *(C. h. exilipes). Adult male*: wing, 70.9–75.8 (74.1); tail, 56–63.7 (59.9); exposed culmen, 7–8.7 (7.9); tarsus, 13.8–15.9 (14.7). *Adult female*: wing, 68.1–72.4 (71.2) mm.

Field Marks. A very pale edition of the Common Redpoll, but rump white, contrasting with the back and tail.

Habitat Usually similar to that of the Common Redpoll. In the high Arctic, ravines and rocky slopes with some shrubby ground cover.

Nesting. In bushes or crevices in rocks. Nest is of grass stems and weeds and is lined with feathers. Nest may be used more than one year (V.C. Wynne-Edwards). *Eggs*, usually 5 or 6; blue, spotted and dotted with light brown. Incubation is by the female.

Range. Breeds across the Arctic of both the New and Old Worlds. In North America from Alaska east across arctic Canada to Greenland; in winter south to southern British Columbia, eastern Montana, South Dakota, Minnesota, Indiana, Ohio, and Maryland.

Subspecies. (1) *Carduelis hornemanni hornemanni* (Holböll), the largest and palest of the Redpolls: Northeastern Franklin (Ellesmere Island, Bylot Island, and at least northern Baffin Island—no breeding material from southern Baffin Island examined). (2) *C. h. exilipes* (Coues), smaller and slightly darker than *hornemanni*, the under tail coverts more often streaked: Yukon, Mackenzie, southern Victoria Island, Keewatin, Manitoba and Quebec.

Pine Siskin

Chardonneret des pins
Carduelis pinus (Wilson)
Total length: 11 to 13 cm
Plate 69

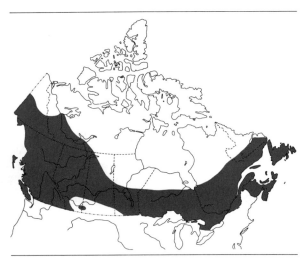

Breeding Distribution of Pine Siskin

Range in Canada. Breeds from central Yukon (Forty Mile, Kluane Lake, Watson Lake); central-southern Mackenzie (near Fort Resolution, and northward along Mackenzie valley to Fort Norman); northwestern and central-eastern Saskatchewan (Lake Athabasca, La Ronge, Nipawin); central-western and southern Manitoba (The Pas, Lake St. Martin; recorded in summer north to Thompson, southern Indian Lake, Churchill); central Ontario (Casummit-Birch lakes, Favourable Lake, Kapuskasing; probably southern James Bay); central Quebec (Lake Mistassini; Lake Sainte-Anne on Toulnustouc River; Saint-Augustin; has been recorded in summer north rarely to Grande rivière de la Baleine and Schefferville region); southern Labrador (Hamilton Inlet); and Newfoundland south through wooded parts of southern Canada in British Columbia (including Queen Charlotte and Vancouver islands); Alberta (except where suitable habitat is lacking on southeastern prairies); southern Saskatchewan (very locally: Cypress Hills, Indian Head); southern Manitoba (Spruce Woods Forest Reserve, Julius); southern Ontario (Guelph); southern Quebec (Gatineau Park, Hatley; and including Anticosti and Madeleine islands); New Brunswick; Prince Edward Island; and Nova Scotia (including Cape Breton Island).

Winters within most southern parts of its breeding range (but irregularly; common one year, perhaps absent the next in a given area) but is usually uncommon or rare in winter in Alberta and Saskatchewan.

Accidental on Bathurst Island, N.W.T. (specimen: 29 July 1973), Cornwallis Island, N.W.T. (photo record: Resolute Bay, August 1973), and Coats Island, N.W.T. (specimen: 25 July 1975).

Bill longer and more slender than that of redpolls and goldfinches. Tail slightly forked. Sexes similar in appearance. Upper parts greyish brown streaked with dusky, paler on rump; wings and tail dusky with narrow yellowish or white edging; bases of wing and tail feathers yellow (often concealed), usually showing as a small wing patch; two whitish or buffy wing bars; under parts dull white streaked (except on belly) with dusky.

Measurements. *Adult male*: wing, 68.3–76.2 (72.8); tail, 44.9–48.1 (46.5); exposed culmen, 9.8–11.1 (10.6); tarsus, 13.9–14.9 (14.3). *Adult female*: wing, 69–75.8 (71.5) mm.

Field Marks. A small heavily streaked finch with a touch of yellow on the wings and often at the base of the tail. Usually seen in groups or flocks. Its streaked breast distinguishes it from winter goldfinches. Its small yellow patch in the wings, heavily streaked breast, and longer, more pointed bill distinguish it from both species of redpolls. *Voice*: A frequently uttered call is a rather harsh *zwee-e-e-e-t*, rising in pitch. It is harsher than a similar call of the redpolls. Song is somewhat goldfinch-like but huskier and more buzzy. Has other goldfinch-like calls.

Habitat. Coniferous and mixed woods of various ages and densities, sometimes ornamental groves and shade trees about towns. Prefers conifers for nesting but forages in both conifers and deciduous trees as well as in shrubbery (especially alders) and at various heights.

Nesting. Usually in a conifer 1.8 to 12 m above ground. Nest is of twigs, shredded bark, *Usnea* lichen, grass, and rootlets, and is lined with fine rootlets, hair, or moss. *Eggs*, 3 to 6; pale blue, spotted and speckled with browns and purplish, mainly about the large end. Incubation 13 days (Weaver and West), by the female only.

Range. Breeds in woodlands from southern Alaska east to Newfoundland and south to northern Baja California, through the Mexican highlands to Guatemala, and in the central and southern United States south to Kansas, northern Pennsylvania, and Connecticut. Winters in the breeding range and south to southern Florida.

Subspecies. *Carduelis pinus pinus* (Wilson).

Remarks. The Pine Siskin is notable for its erratic comings and goings and unpredictable nesting times. It may be common and breeding in a given locality one year, completely absent the next. Togetherness is strong in their social structure, for they are almost always in flocks of various sizes, even at nesting times. They eat seeds of conifers, birch, and alder; small leaves, buds, and insects.

Lesser Goldfinch

(Arkansas Goldfinch; Green-backed Goldfinch)

Chardonneret mineur
Carduelis psaltria (Say)
Total length: 9.5 to 11.4 cm
Plate 69

Status in Canada. Casual in British Columbia (specimens: Indianpoint Lake, Huntingdon. Sight records at Vancouver). Sight record for Ontario (adult female, 10 August 1982).

Form similar to that of American Goldfinch but measurements smaller. *Adult male*: Variable geographically: either with upper parts mostly black *(C. p. psaltria)* or with black crown and rest of upper parts dull greenish-olive *(C. p. hesperophila)*; wings mostly black with white patch at base of primaries; greater wing coverts tipped white, and tertials margined with white; tail black, the inner webs of the outermost feathers white with black tips; under parts light yellow, paler on under tail coverts. *Adult female*: Olive green above (including rump); wings duller than in male and with white patch at base of primaries more restricted or absent; white in tail restricted to a small white spot on each outer feather or almost imperceptible.

Distinctions. Differs from American Goldfinch in smaller size. Adult male in summer with either black or dull-olive upper parts, instead of canary yellow (retains black cap all year); white patch at base of primaries; different tail pattern. Adult female resembles American Goldfinch, but rump is olive like the back, instead of paler.

Range. Breeds from southwestern Washington, western Oregon, northern Nevada, northern Utah, northern Colorado, and central Texas south to northwestern Peru, Colombia, and northern Venezuela.

Subspecies. *Carduelis psaltria hesperophila* (Oberholser).

American Goldfinch

Chardonneret jaune
Carduelis tristis (Linnaeus)
Total length: 11.4 to 14 cm
Plate 69

Breeding Distribution of American Goldfinch

Range in Canada. Breeds in southern British Columbia (Port Hardy, Alta Lake, Lytton, Williams Lake Indian Reserve No. 1, Okanagan valley, Cranbrook, perhaps Alkali Lake); north-central and southern Alberta (Peace River, Athabasca southward); central and southern Saskatchewan (Kazan Lake, Cumberland House southward); central-western and southern Manitoba (The Pas, Lake St. Martin, Hillside Beach southward); central and southern Ontario (Sioux Lookout, Lake Nipigon, Lake Abitibi, and probably Moose Factory southward); southern Quebec (Amos, Lake Saint-Jean, Lake Sainte-Anne on Toulnustouc River, Anticosti Island, and Gaspé southward, including Madeleine Islands); southwestern Newfoundland (Cape Anguille, Doyles); New

Adult male (summer): General colour, canary yellow; crown, forehead, space in front of eyes, and most of wings and tail, black; tail coverts, middle wing coverts, ends of greater coverts, and edging on some of the flight feathers, white; inner webs of the tail feathers whitish toward the tips; legs pale brown; bill orange-yellow darkening toward the tip. *Adult female (summer)*: Upper parts brownish olive tinged with yellowish, especially on rump and scapulars; no black cap; wings and tail similar to those of the adult male, but dusky instead of black and with no yellow on the lesser wing coverts; under parts greenish yellow but under tail coverts white; bill yellow, darkening toward tip. *Adults in winter*: Yellow is mostly replaced by brownish olive, and the black cap of the male is missing, but the male is distinguishable from the female by more blackish wings, clearer whites in wings, and bright-yellow lesser wing coverts. *Immatures in first autumn and first winter* are more brownish than adults; the whitish wing areas are more buffy, and the males throughout their first year lack the bright-yellow lesser wing coverts of adult males.

Measurements *(C. t. tristis)*. *Adult male*: wing, 69.8–74 (71.9); tail, 42.4–51.5 (48.2); exposed culmen, 9.6–11 (10.1); tarsus, 12.5–14.2 (13.5). *Adult female*: wing, 67.4–73.8 (70.5) mm.

Field Marks. The summer male is a small, bright-yellow, stubby-billed bird with black cap, wings, and tail. The Yellow Warbler, another yellow bird, has no black in the plumage and possesses a much slimmer bill. The duller female goldfinch might be confused by beginners with vireos or some warblers, but the goldfinch's stubby bill is very different. Winter goldfinches are much less distinctive (male lacks black cap), but usually they show a suggestion of yellow on head and neck; the wings and tail are blackish with whitish or buffy markings. The stubby bill marks it as a finch, and the completely unstreaked plumage is very different from that of Pine Siskins, most sparrows, the redpolls, and female Purple Finches. At any time of the year it is usually seen in groups or flocks. *Voice*: As it flies (flight is conspicuously undulating), an unmistakable *per-chic-o-ree*. Song is a sustained energetic procession of short trills and twitters with frequent querulous interjections of *sweet* or *swee*.

Habitat. Weedy fields, cultivated lands, roadsides, and similar open weedy places not too far from wood edges or patches, second growths, tall shrubs, or orchards. In nesting season requires open deciduous woods or shrubs.

Brunswick; Prince Edward Island; and Nova Scotia (including Cape Breton Island). Casual at Natashquan, Quebec, and southern Labrador (Cape Mugford).

Winters in southern British Columbia (Esquimalt, Vancouver, Chilliwack, Okanagan valley), southern Ontario, southwestern Quebec (north to Québec region), New Brunswick, and Nova Scotia.

Nesting. In a tree or shrub, 0.3 to 6 m above ground. Trees preferred are scattered ones, in open places, not in extensive forests. The cuplike nest is composed of shredded bark, plant stems, and grass, and is lined with thistledown or other plant downs. *Eggs*, 2 to 7, usually 4 or 6; pale bluish. Incubation period 12 to 14 days (L.H. Walkinshaw), by the female, fed by the male.

Range. Breeds across southern Canada (British Columbia east to southwestern Newfoundland) and south to northern Baja California, southern Colorado, northeastern Texas, northern Louisiana, central Alabama, and South Carolina. Winters from southern Canada and northern United States south to Mexico, the Gulf Coast of United States, and southern Florida.

Subspecies. (1) *Carduelis tristis tristis* (Linnaeus): Ontario, Quebec, Newfoundland, New Brunswick, Nova Scotia, Prince Edward Island, intergrading with the following race in extreme western Ontario (Ingolf). (2) *C. t. pallida* (Mearns) (adult females, winter males, and immatures in winter paler than *tristis*, size slightly larger): interior British Columbia, Alberta, Saskatchewan, Manitoba. (3) *C. t. jewetti* (van Rossem) (winter plumage darker and browner than in *pallida*): southern coastal British Columbia (Vancouver Island, Chilliwack).

Remarks. Everything the Goldfinch does seems to radiate good nature and the joy of living. Its song is lively, almost effervescent; its flight is bouncy and undulating. Many people call it "wild canary" or "thistle bird," the latter because of its fondness for thistle seeds. It also relishes various other kinds of seeds, particularly those of dandelions, and takes some insects as well.

European Goldfinch

[**European Goldfinch**. Chardonneret élégant. *Carduelis carduelis* (Linnaeus). Hypothetical. Adults, with red face, forehead, and chin; black hind crown; and black wings with very large yellow patch display a combination not shown by any native bird. The species has been introduced into parts of United States and was established in Long Island, New York, where it has recently been extirpated. A specimen collected in Toronto, Ontario, 21 May 1887, and a recent sight record in New Brunswick may represent strays from the former Long Island colony, but the possibility that they were escaped cage birds cannot be excluded.]

European Greenfinch

[**European Greenfinch**. Verdier. *Carduelis chloris* (Linnaeus). Hypothetical. Photographic record of one in Saint John, New Brunswick, 31 March to 3 April 1977. Although perhaps a natural occurrence, the possibility that it was an escapee cannot be dismissed because the species is a popular cage-bird.]

Evening Grosbeak

Gros-bec errant
Coccothraustes vespertinus (Cooper)
Total length: 17.5 to 21.5 cm
Plate 69

Bill extremely heavy, cone-shaped, the culmen very broad without a ridge. Plumage somewhat variable. *Adult male*: Forehead and stripe over eye yellow; top of head black; rest of head, also neck and upper back dark brownish-olive passing into yellow on scapulars and lower back and on posterior under parts; upper tail coverts, tail, and most of wings black, but tertials white, forming a large wing patch; bill pale yellowish-green; legs brownish or dark flesh colour. *Adult female*: Upper parts mostly grey, darkest on top of head, palest on rump; back of neck tinged greenish yellow; cheeks grey, similar to top of head; throat, abdomen, and under tail coverts whitish, with a dusky streak down each side of throat; breast, sides, and flanks buffy greyish more or less mixed with yellow; wings dull black, the tertials grey-edged or tipped with whitish; primaries (except three outermost) white at base forming a small white patch; tail black, the inner webs broadly tipped white. *Young (first winter)*: Resemble adults but young males may be separated from adult males by blackish inner margins of the white tertials.

Breeding Distribution of Evening Grosbeak

Range in Canada. Breeds locally (breeding range based largely on summer occurrences, as definite breeding data are relatively few) in north-central and southern British Columbia (Bear Lake, situated 80 km north of Takla Lake, and south through Alta Lake, Okanagan valley, Wardner, probably Vancouver Island, but apparently not recorded from Queen Charlotte Islands; noted in summer north to Smith River, 80 km south of Yukon border); northern, central, and southwestern Alberta (Athabasca Delta, Dunvegan, Lesser Slave Lake, Swan Hills, Glenevis, Belvedere, Jasper, Banff); central Saskatchewan (Somme, Nipawin, Amisk Lake); southern Manitoba (Overflowing River, Selkirk, Indian Bay); central and southern Ontario (Kenora, Elsas, Hawk Junction, Algonquin Provincial Park, Hornepayne, Kapuskasing south to Owen Sound, Brockville, Harrowsmith. Summer records north to Moosonee); southern Quebec (Amos, Mount Plamondon, Lake Saint-Jean, Anticosti Island, Lake Rimouski, Québec region, Kingsmere, Coaticook, Sainte-Anne-des-Monts; recently Madeleine Islands. Reported in summer at Godbout and Îlets-Jérémie); New Brunswick (Saint-Léonard, Grand Lake, Nashwaak, Hampton, Riley Brook); Nova Scotia (Ingonish Beach, Bedford, Allendale); and probably Prince Edward Island (Brackley Beach). Recorded once in summer in extreme southwestern Mackenzie (Buffalo River and Nahanni National Park) but without evidence of breeding.

Winters within much of the breeding range and southward and eastward to Prince Edward Island and Newfoundland (east to St. John's).

Formerly this was primarily a western species, but in recent times it has rapidly pushed its breeding range eastward. In Ontario it was first known to nest at Lake of the Woods in 1920, first in Muskoka District in 1927, and first in Algonquin Provincial Park in 1932. It has in recent years extended its breeding range east to Cape Breton Island, Nova Scotia, and Anticosti and Madeleine islands, Quebec.

Measurements *(C. v. vespertinus). Adult male*: wing, 105.4–115.3 (110.9); tail, 60–69.6 (65.2); exposed culmen, 16.2–20 (18.6); tarsus, 19.8–21.9 (20.6). *Adult female*: wing, 104.7–111.4 (108.5) mm.

Field Marks. Usually in companies or flocks. Very large conical *yellowish-white* bill, black wings with large white patches. Males have much yellow in the plumage, the females mostly grey. *Voice*: Call, a *cheep* somewhat similar to the *cheep* of a House Sparrow but louder and more strident. Song, a rather short, jerky warble.

Habitat. In breeding season mixed and coniferous woodland including second growths, occasionally even nesting in a town shade tree. In winter and migration, various types of woods, wood patches, parks, and shade trees about towns. It is particularly partial to the seeds of the Manitoba maple or box elder, *Acer negundo*, and is readily attracted to backyard feeding shelves where sunflower seeds are favourites. Salted gravel piles attract it at any time of the year.

Nesting. In either a coniferous or deciduous tree, 4.5 to 18 m up. Nest is a loosely made shallow structure of twigs, rootlets, and bark shreds and is lined with rootlets and fine twigs. *Eggs*, 3 to 5; bluish green marked with browns and greys. Incubation 12 to 14 days, by the female.

Range. Breeds in a rather narrow strip across Canada (British Columbia to Nova Scotia) and south in the mountains to central California and southern Mexico; in the East to northeastern Minnesota, northern New York, and Massachusetts. Winters from southern Canada southward irregularly to southern United States.

Subspecies. (1) *Coccothraustes vespertinus vespertinus* (Cooper): All of the breeding range in Canada east of the Rockies. (2) *C. v. brooksi* (Grinnell) (averages darker in colour, especially females): British Columbia and southwestern Alberta (Rocky Mountains).

Family **Passeridae**:
Old World Sparrows

Number of Species in Canada: 1

There are no native North American species of this Old World family of robust, plain, finchlike birds. One species, the House Sparrow, has been introduced into Canada and now flourishes in most southern parts of the country and throughout the United States.

House Sparrow

(English Sparrow)

Moineau domestique
Passer domesticus (Linnaeus)
Total length: 14.7 to 17 cm
Plate 68

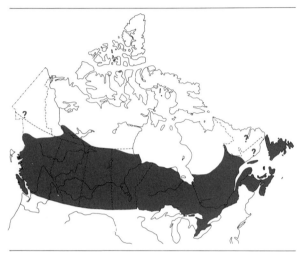

Breeding Distribution of House Sparrow

Range in Canada. Introduced and widely established (first introduced into North America in 1850 at Brooklyn, New York, and somewhat later in Québec and Halifax, Canada). Permanent resident breeding in southern Yukon (recently and locally: Whitehorse) and from central and northeastern British Columbia (Porcher Island, Stewart, Smithers, Fort Nelson, Fort St. John); southwestern Mackenzie (Fort Simpson, Yellowknife); northwestern and central Saskatchewan (Lake Athabasca, Wollaston Lake); northern Manitoba (Churchill); northern Ontario (Fort Severn, Winisk, Fort Albany, Moose Factory); southern Quebec (La Ferme, Chibougamau, Lake Saint-Jean, Schefferville, Godbout, Sept-Îles, Rivière-au-Tonnerre, Anticosti Island, Gaspé Peninsula, Madeleine Islands; recorded at Havre-Saint-Pierre); and northern Newfoundland (St. Anthony) southward all across southern Canada including Vancouver Island, British Columbia and the Maritime Provinces.

More robust generally than our native sparrows with relatively heavy strong bill. *Adult male (breeding plumage)*: Top of head, nape, and rump grey; chestnut patch from eye to nape and broadening over side of neck; small white spot behind eye; patch between eye and base of bill black; back streaked with black, buff, and chestnut; wings with white bar; tail all dark brown with narrow buffy edging; throat and middle of breast black; ear coverts grey; jaw and sides of neck whitish; rest of under parts greyish white, the sides and flanks grey or buffy grey; under tail coverts tinged with buffy brown; bill black; legs brownish. *Adult male (autumn and winter)*: Similar to adult male in breeding plumage but more brownish generally, the black of throat and breast partly hidden by grey feather tips; bill dark brown, pale toward base. *Adult female*: Upper parts dull brown, the back streaked as in the male but lacking chestnut patch behind eye and with little or no chestnut on wing coverts, no black on throat or breast; a pale buffy line from above eye back to nape; dingy wing bar present; under parts dingy grey with buffy tinge; bill as in winter male. *Young (first autumn)*: Resemble adults in autumn, but the young males have black of throat and breast even more concealed by pale feather tips.

Measurements. *Adult male*: wing, 73.9–79 (76.4); tail, 54.5–60 (57.9); exposed culmen, 12.1–13.9 (12.8); tarsus, 18.5–20 (19.3). *Adult female*: wing, 72.4–77.5 (74.7) mm.

Field Marks. The common sparrow about the buildings of cities and farms, thus familiar to everyone. Male with black bib (partly hidden in autumn and winter), chestnut patch back from eye, and white wing bar. Females, dull brown above, with a faint buffy stripe back from eye, dingy-grey under parts, and a heavier bill than that of the native sparrows. The call is diagnostic. *Voice*: A monotonous *chirp* or *chisseck*, repeated over and over *ad nauseum* and all too familiar to any city dweller; also a harsh chatter.

Habitat. The vicinity of human buildings and cultivated land: cities, farms, fields, yards, garbage dumps, streets, and roadsides.

Nesting. In cavities about buildings, dense growths of vines on buildings, bird boxes, natural and woodpecker cavities in trees, tree branches; sometimes drives Cliff Swallows from their mud nests and occasionally uses cavities in banks excavated by Bank Swallows. Cavities are filled with coarse materials such as straw, feathers, and assorted trash. When nest is built in tree branches, it is an untidy domed structure with an entrance hole in the side. *Eggs*, 3 to 7, most often 5; variable in colour, white to pale greenish or bluish, finely and rather uniformly spotted with greys and browns. Incubation 12 to 13, or even 14 days, mostly by the female but with assistance from the male (Jourdain *in* Witherby); usually 12 days (R.L. Weaver).

Range. Native to Eurasia and northern Africa. It has been introduced by man in many parts of the world, including North and South America. In North America from Canada south to southern United States and south-central Mexico (Guerrero).

Subspecies. *Passer domesticus domesticus* (Linnaeus).

Remarks. The introduction of the House Sparrow into North America was a mistake. It flourished and has spread to most settled parts of Canada and the United States. It is a pugnacious ruffian, driving away our native birds and usurping their nesting cavities. Its all too successful competition with Tree Swallows and other native cavity-nesting birds is well known to all who provide and maintain nesting boxes for our native species, and it is doubtless a major factor in the serious decline in the Cliff Swallow's numbers.

Glossary

A

Abdomen That part of the under surface of the body between the breast and the under tail coverts.

Acute Sharp-pointed.

Adult A bird that has assumed its final or definitive plumage type. (Birds wearing any immature plumage, even though breeding, are called subadult, immature, or juvenile.)

Albinism Absence or partial absence of colour in parts of animals that are normally coloured. In complete albinism the animal is all white except the iris of the eye, which is pink (see melanism).

Allopatric Refers to forms whose breeding ranges do not overlap (see sympatric).

Altricial Refers to species whose young, hatched blind and helpless, require considerable rearing before they can leave the nest (see precocial).

Alula Feathers attached to the "thumb" part of the wing.

Anterior More toward the front (see posterior).

Aquatic Water-frequenting.

Arboreal Tree-frequenting.

Asymmetrical Not symmetrical.

Attenuated As applied to feathers, tapering gradually; slender.

Auricular Pertaining to the ear.

Auriculars Feathers of the ear region.

Avian Pertaining to birds.

Axillars A group of feathers, usually more or less elongated, at the armpit between the wing and the body.

B

Bar A long marking across the body or across a feather; a transverse marking (see stripe).

Belly The under surface of the body between the breast and the under tail coverts. Here used interchangeably with "abdomen."

Belted Having a band across breast or belly.

Bend of Wing The most anterior part of the folded wing.

Booted Refers to tarsus, not divided.

C

Cere A covering, sometimes swollen, of the base of the upper mandible of the bill in some birds such as hawks, owls, and parrots.

Clutch A complete set of eggs laid by an individual female at a single nesting.

Coalesce To grow together or unite.

Commissural Line Line of contact between upper and lower mandibles when closed.

Confluent Running together.

Coniferous Applied to trees: cone-bearing, mostly evergreens.

Conspecific Belonging to one and the same species.

Contour Feathers The vaned or webbed feathers of the bird that form its main outside covering and give it its characteristic outline or contour. They include the flight feathers, but not the down or hairlike filoplumes.

Coverts Small feathers covering the base of the tail; also rows of small feathers on the wing, covering the base of the flight feathers and the wing surfaces; also short feathers covering the ear region.

Crepuscular Pertaining to twilight.

Crest Elongated feathers on top of head.

Crown Top of the head.

Culmen The ridge of the upper mandible (maxilla) of the bill.

D

Deciduous Shed periodically. Applied to the broad-leafed trees that shed their leaves seasonally. The plumes of herons that are shed early are said to be "deciduous" also.

Decurved Down-curved.

Dimorphic Having two distinct forms.

Diurnal Active in the daytime.

Dorsal Pertaining to the back.

E

Ecotone An area of transition between two major biotic communities.

Emarginate As applied to the tail, slightly forked. As applied to a wing feather, abruptly narrowed as though cut away.

Erectile Capable of being raised.

Ethology The objective study of behaviour.

Exotic Foreign.

Extensile Capable of being thrust out, as the tongue.

Extinct No longer living anywhere (see extirpated).

Extirpated Eradicated from part of its range (see extinct).

Extralimital Occurring normally beyond the geographic boundaries of the area being discussed.

F

Family A taxonomic group composed of related genera. Family names end in "idae." It is lower in rank than the order, higher than the genus.

Feral Wild. Here applied to domesticated animals that are living in the wild, independent of direct assistance from man.

Flanks The hindmost part of the sides of the body.

Form A neutral term, applicable to any taxonomic unit, and without particular nomenclatural significance.

Frontal Pertaining to the forehead.

G

Genus (plural genera) A taxonomic group of species that are more closely related to one another than to other species.

Graduated With reference to the tail: middle feathers longest, the rest becoming successively shorter.

Gregarious In flocks.

Gular Pertaining to the throat.

H

Hiatus A gap or vacant area.

Holarctic The northern parts of both the New and Old Worlds.

Hybrid An individual whose parents are of two different species.

Hypothetical As applied to status of a species, evidence of occurrence less than completely satisfactory.

I

Immaculate Without markings.

Indigenous Native to a given part of the world.

Insectivorous Insect-eating.

Intergradation Merging gradually from one form to another through a continuous series of intermediate forms.

Iris (plural irides) The coloured part of the eye surrounding the black pupil.

J

Juvenal Refers to that particular plumage succeeding the natal down (or succeeding in certain species the naked nestling stage without natal down). It is the first plumage of real contour feathers (see juvenile).

Juvenile May be applied to any immature plumage or to an immature bird.

L

Lamellate Equipped with fine plates (or lamellae) as in the sides of a duck's bill.

Lateral Pertaining to the side.

Length (Total) Of a bird, the distance in a straight line from the tip of the bill to the tip of the longest tail feather.

Lobed (of bird's toes) Possessing projecting rounded membranous flaps.

Loral Pertaining to the lores.

Lores The area between the eye and the base of the upper mandible.

M

Mandibles In plural, the two halves of the bill. In singular, the lower half of the bill (see Maxilla).

Mantle The plumage of the back and upper surface of the wings.

Maxilla The upper half of the bill; also called upper mandible.

Median or Medial Pertaining to the middle.

Melanism An abnormally dark coloration caused by an excess of dark pigment (see Albinism).

Mixedwood In reference to woodlands, composed of both coniferous and deciduous trees.

Molt or Moult Includes both the shedding and replacement of plumage.

N

Nail A horny tip of the upper mandible (or maxilla) in ducks, geese, and swans.

Nape That part of the hind-neck just below the base of the skull.

New World Pertaining to the Western Hemisphere.

Nocturnal Active at night.

Nuchal Pertaining to the nape or back of neck.

O

Old World Pertaining to the Eastern Hemisphere.

Omnivorous Eating a large variety of both animal and plant food.

Oology The study of birds' eggs, especially the shell.

Order A taxonomic group composed of related families.

Ornithology The scientific study of birds.

P

Pectinate Furnished with comblike teeth as in the middle toe of herons.

Pectoral Pertaining to the breast.

Pelagic Frequenting the ocean, away from the coasts.

Pensile As applied to nests, hanging suspended from a fork of a branch, or similar situation, and not supported below.

Periphery An outer edge or boundary.

Phase With reference to plumage, differences in colour not correlated with age, sex, race, or season.

Phenotype The individual's expressed traits, of which the most readily apparent are its visible characters.

Photographic Record A record based on an identifiable photograph.

Piebald Having contrastingly coloured patches, especially white and black.

Posterior More toward the rear (see anterior).

Postocular Behind the eye.

Precocial Refers to birds whose young hatch covered with down, able to run or swim shortly after hatching; e.g. ducks, sandpipers.

Primaries The flight feathers attached to the hand (manus) of the wing. Primaries are counted from the inside outward.

Pyriform Pear-shaped.

R

Race The same as subspecies.

Recurved Curved upward.

Reticulate With reference to the tarsus, markings resembling a network.

Rump That area of the upper parts between the back and the upper tail coverts.

S

Scapulars A group of feathers growing from the shoulders (humeral feather tracts).

Scute A horny plate or scale.

Scutellate Referring to tarsus, covered with scutes or scales.

Secondaries Those flight feathers attached to the forearm (ulna) of the wing. The innermost, when differently shaped and coloured, are often referred to as tertials but are really specialized secondaries.

Sight Record A record based wholly on observation in the field and not supported by a specimen in the hand or by an identifiable photograph.

Species Popularly thought of as a "kind" of animal or plant. A taxonomic group of similar individuals that interbreed freely among themselves (or are biologically capable of doing so) but do not normally breed with individuals of other such groups.

Speculum A patch on the wing, usually rectangular, contrasting in colour with the rest of the wing and often brightly coloured and more or less iridescent. It is especially common in ducks.

Spicule Applied here to small, hard, sharp-pointed bodies on the foot of the Osprey.

Sternum The breastbone.

Streak A slender longitudinal mark.

Stripe Elongated marking running lengthwise of the bird (see bars).

Subapical Near the tip.

Subfamily A subdivision of the family; it is composed of subordinate groupings of related tribes and genera. Subfamily names end in "inae."

Subspecies Geographically limited subdivisions of the species that are taxonomically different from other such subdivisions of the same species.

Subterminal Near the end.

Superciliary Pertaining to the eyebrow.

Sympatric Refers to two or more forms whose breeding ranges occupy the same ground or overlap more or less.

T

Tarsus That part of the foot from the base of the toes to the heel. Although popularly thought of as the "leg," it is really only part of the foot, corresponding to the human instep but with the bones fused. It is properly the tarso-metatarsus.

Taxon (plural taxa) Any taxonomic unit.

Taxonomy The classification of plants and animals according to their natural relationships.

Terrestrial Frequenting the ground.

Tertials Often used as a name for the innermost secondaries when they differ in shape and colour (also, as in loons, in moult pattern) from the rest of the secondaries.

Tribe A taxonomic group intermediate in rank between the genus and the subfamily. Names of tribes end in "ini."

Truncate Square-tipped.

U

Ulna The stouter of the two bones of the forearm on which, in birds, grow the secondaries.

V

Ventral Pertaining to the underside; opposite of dorsal.

Vermiculated Marked with fine irregularly wavy lines, suggesting the tracks of many small worms.

Vernacular Name The name of a taxonomic unit in one's own language.

Vinaceous Wine-coloured.

Z

Zygodactylous Having two toes in front and two behind.

Selected References

Some Provincial Works on Birds

Where recent comprehensive works are available, these are listed first under each province; otherwise references are cited in alphabetical order of authors' names.

Alberta

Salt, W.R., and J.R. Salt. 1978. The birds of Alberta. Edmonton: Hurtig.

Clarke, C.H.D., and I. McT. Cowan. 1945. Birds of Banff National Park, Alberta. Canadian Field-Naturalist, vol. 59, no. 3, pp. 83–103.

Cowan, I. McT. 1955. Birds of Jasper National Park, Alberta, Canada. Canadian Wildlife Service, Wildlife Management Bulletin (Ottawa), series 2, no. 8, pp. 1–67.

Erskine, A.J. 1968. Birds observed in north-central Alberta, summer 1964. Blue Jay, vol. 26, no. 1, pp. 24–31.

Godfrey, W.E. 1952. Birds of the Lesser Slave Lake–Peace River areas, Alberta. National Museum of Canada Bulletin 126, pp. 142–175.

Rand, A.L. 1948. Birds of southern Alberta. National Museum of Canada Bulletin 111, pp. 1–105.

Randall, T.E. 1933. A list of the breeding birds of the Athabasca district, Alberta. Canadian Field-Naturalist, vol. 47, no. 1, pp. 1–6.
1946. Birds of the Eastern Irrigation District, Brooks, Alberta. Canadian Field-Naturalist, vol. 60, no. 6, pp. 123–131.

Sadler, T.S., and M.T. Myres 1976. Alberta birds, 1961–1970, with particular reference to migration. Provincial Museum of Alberta, Natural History Occasional Paper 1, pp. 1–314.

Salt, W.R. 1973. Alberta vireos and wood warblers. Provincial Museum and Archives of Alberta, Publication 3, pp. 1–141.

Soper, J.D. 1942. The birds of Wood Buffalo Park and vicinity, northern Alberta and District of Mackenzie, N.W.T., Canada. Transactions Royal Canadian Institute, vol. 24, part 1, no. 51, pp. 19–97.
1949a. Notes on the fauna of the former Nemiskam National Park and vicinity, Alberta. Canadian Field-Naturalist, vol. 63, no. 5, pp. 167–182.
1949b. Birds observed in the Grande Prairie–Peace River region of northwestern Alberta, Canada. Auk, vol. 66, no. 3, pp. 233–257.

British Columbia

Munro, J.A., and I. McT. Cowan, 1947. A review of the bird fauna of British Columbia. British Columbia Provincial Museum, Special Publication 2, pp. 1–285.

Beebe, F.L. 1974. Field studies of the Falconiformes of British Columbia. British Columbia Provincial Museum, Occasional Papers, no. 17, pp. 1–163.

Campbell, R.W., H.R. Carter, C.D. Shepard, and C.J. Guiguet. 1979. A bibliography of British Columbia ornithology. British Columbia Provincial Museum, Heritage Record 7, pp. 1–185.

Campbell R.W., and A.L. Meugens. 1971. The summer birds of Richter Pass, British Columbia. Syesis, vol. 4, parts 1 and 2, pp. 93–123.

Campbell, R.W., M.G. Shepard, and R.H. Drent. 1972. Status of birds in the Vancouver area in 1970. Syesis, vol. 5, pp. 137–167.

Cowan, I. McT. 1939. The vertebrate fauna of the Peace River District of British Columbia. British Columbia Provincial Museum, Occasional Papers, no. 1, pp. 1–102 (Birds, pp. 11–66).

Drent, R.H., and C.J. Guiguet. 1961. A catalogue of British Columbia sea-bird colonies. British Columbia Provincial Museum, Occasional Papers, no. 12, pp. 1–173.

Hatler, D.F., R.W. Campbell, and Adrian Dorst. 1978. Birds of Pacific Rim National Park. British Columbia Provincial Museum, Occasional Papers, no. 20, pp. 1–192.

Munro, J.A. 1949. The birds and mammals of the Vanderhoof region, British Columbia. American Midland Naturalist, vol. 41, no. 1, pp. 1–138.
1950. The birds and mammals of the Creston region, British Columbia. British Columbia Provincial Museum Occasional Papers, no. 8, pp. 1–90.

Paul, W.A.B. 1959. The birds of Kleena Kleene, Chilcotin District, British Columbia, 1947–1958. Canadian Field-Naturalist, vol. 73, no. 2, pp. 83–93.

Swarth, H.S. 1922. Birds and mammals of the Stikine River region of northern British Columbia and southeastern Alaska. University of California Publications in Zoology, no. 24, pp. 125–314.
1924. Birds and mammals of the Skeena River region of northern British Columbia. University of California Publications in Zoology, no. 24, pp. 315–394.
1926. Report on a collection of birds and mammals from the Atlin region, northern British Columbia. University of California Publications in Zoology, no. 30, pp. 51–162.

Weeden, R.B. 1960. The birds of Chilkat Pass, British Columbia. Canadian Field-Naturalist, vol. 74, no. 2, pp. 119–129.

Franklin District

Snyder, L.L. 1957. Arctic birds of Canada. Toronto: University of Toronto Press.

Brown, R.G.B., D.N. Nettleship, P. Germain, C.E. Tull, and T. Davis. 1975. Atlas of eastern Canadian seabirds. Ottawa: Canadian Wildlife Service. (Applies also to Quebec, Labrador, Newfoundland, and the Maritime Provinces.)

Duvall, A.J., and C.O. Handley. 1946. Report on wildlife reconnaissance of the eastern Canadian Arctic. Special Report, United States Department of the Interior, Fish and Wildlife Service. Manuscript report. 138 pp.

Hussell, D.J.T., and G.L. Holroyd. 1974. Birds of the Truelove lowland and adjacent areas of northeastern Devon Island. Canadian Field-Naturalist, vol. 88, no. 2, pp. 197–212.

MacDonald, S.D. 1954. Report on biological investigations at Mould Bay, Prince Patrick Island, N.W.T. National Museum of Canada Bulletin 132, pp. 214–238.

Maltby, L.S. 1978. Birds of the coastal zone of Melville Island, 1973–1975. Canadian Field-Naturalist, vol. 92, no. 1, pp. 24–29.

Manning, T.H., E.O. Höhn, and A.H. Macpherson. 1956. The birds of Banks Island. National Museum of Canada Bulletin 143, pp. 1–144.

Manning, T.H., and A.H. Macpherson. 1961. A biological investigation of Prince of Wales Island, N.W.T. Transactions Royal Canadian Institute, no. 33 (part 2), pp. 116–239.

Parmelee, D.F., and S.D. MacDonald. 1960. The birds of west-central Ellesmere Island and adjacent areas. National Museum of Canada Bulletin 169, pp. 1–103.

Parmelee, D.F., H.A. Stephens, and R.H. Schmidt. 1967. The birds of southeastern Victoria Island and adjacent small islands. National Museum of Canada Bulletin 222, pp. 1–229.

Renaud, W.E., W.G. Johnston, and K.W. Finley. 1981. The avifauna of the Pond Inlet region, N.W.T. American Birds, vol. 35, no. 2, pp. 119–129.

Smith, T.G. 1973. The birds of the Holman Region, western Victoria Island. Canadian Field-Naturalist, vol. 87, no. 1, pp. 35–42.

Soper, J.D. 1928. A faunal investigation of southern Baffin Island. National Museum of Canada Bulletin 53, pp. 1–143. 1946. Ornithological results of the Baffin Island expeditions of 1928–1929 and 1930–1931, together with more recent records. Auk, vol. 63, no. 1, pp. 1–24; no. 2, pp. 223–239; no. 3, pp. 418–427.

Tuck, L.M., and Louis Lemieux. 1959. The avifauna of Bylot Island. Dansk Ornithologisk Forenings Tidsskrift, vol. 53, no. 3, pp. 137–154.

Wynne-Edwards, V.C. 1952. Zoology of the Baird Expedition (1950). 1. The birds observed in central and south-east Baffin Island. Auk, vol. 69, no. 4, pp. 353–391.

Keewatin District

Harper, Francis. 1953. Birds of the Nueltin Lake Expedition, Keewatin, 1947. American Midland Naturalist, vol. 49, no. 1, pp. 1–116.

Macpherson, A.H., and T.H. Manning. 1959. The birds and mammals of Adelaide Peninsula, N.W.T. National Museum of Canada Bulletin 161, pp. 1–63.

Manning, T.H. 1948. Notes on the country, birds and mammals west of Hudson Bay between Reindeer and Baker lakes. Canadian Field-Naturalist, vol. 62, no. 1, pp. 1–28.

Mowat, F.M., and A.H. Lawrie. 1955. Bird observations from southern Keewatin and the interior of northern Manitoba. Canadian Field-Naturalist, vol. 69, no. 3, pp. 93–116.

Parker, G.R., and R.K. Ross. 1973. Notes on the birds of Southampton Island, Northwest Territories. Arctic, vol. 26, no. 2, pp. 123–129.

Preble, E.A. 1902. A biological investigation of the Hudson Bay region. North American Fauna, no. 22, pp. 1–140. Washington, D.C.: United States Department of Agriculture.

Savile, D.B.O. 1951. Bird observations at Chesterfield Inlet, Keewatin, in 1950. Canadian Field-Naturalist, vol. 65, no. 4, pp. 145–157.

Sutton, G.M. 1932. The birds of Southampton Island, Hudson Bay. Memoirs of Carnegie Museum (Pittsburgh), no. 12 (part 2, section 2), pp. 1–275.

Todd, W.E.C. 1963. (See under Quebec.)

Labrador

Austin, O.L., Jr. 1932. The birds of Newfoundland Labrador. Memoirs of Nuttall Ornithological Club, no. 7, pp. 1–229.

Todd, W.E.C. 1963. Birds of the Labrador Peninsula and adjacent areas. Toronto: University of Toronto Press.

Mackenzie District

Clarke, C.H.D. 1940. A biological investigation of the Thelon Game Sanctuary. National Museum of Canada Bulletin 96, pp. 1–135.

Hanson, H.C., Paul Queneau, and Peter Scott. 1956. The geography, birds, and mammals of the Perry River region. Arctic Institute of North America, Special Publications, no. 3, pp. 1–96.

Höhn, E.O. 1959. Birds of the mouth of the Anderson River and Liverpool Bay, Northwest Territories. Canadian Field-Naturalist, vol. 73, no. 2, pp. 93–114.

MacFarlane, R. 1908. List of birds and eggs observed and collected in the North-West Territories of Canada, between 1880 and 1894. *In* Through the Mackenzie Basin, by Charles Mair. Toronto: William Briggs. (Birds, pp. 287–447.)

Preble, E.A. 1908. A biological investigation of the Athabasca–Mackenzie region. North American Fauna, no. 27, pp. 1–574.

Soper, J.D. 1942. (See under Alberta.)

Trauger, D.L., and R.G. Bromley. 1976. Additional bird observations on the West Mirage Islands, Great Slave Lake, Northwest Territories. Canadian Field-Naturalist, vol. 90, no. 2, pp. 114–122.

Weller, N.W., D.L. Trauger, and G.L. Krapu. 1969. Breeding birds of the West Mirage Islands, Great Slave Lake, N.W.T. Canadian Field-Naturalist, vol. 83, no. 4, pp. 344–360.

Williams, M.Y. 1922. Biological notes along fourteen hundred miles of the Mackenzie River system. Canadian Field-Naturalist, vol. 36, no. 4, pp. 61–66. 1933. Biological notes, covering parts of the Peace, Liard, Mackenzie and Great Bear River basins. Canadian Field-Naturalist, vol. 47, no. 2, pp. 23–31.

Manitoba

Callin, E.M. 1981. Birds of the Qu'Appelle, 1957–1979. Saskatchewan Natural History Society Special Publication 13.

Cooke, F., R.K. Ross, R.K. Schmidt, and A.J. Pakulak. 1975. Birds of the tundra biome at Cape Churchill and La Pérouse Bay. Canadian Field-Naturalist, vol. 89, no. 4, pp. 413–422.

Gardner, K.A. 1981. Birds of the Oak Hammock Marsh wildlife management area. Winnipeg: Wildlife Branch, Manitoba Department of Natural Resources.

Godfrey, W.E. 1953. Notes on birds of the area of intergradation between Eastern Prairie and Forest in Canada. National Museum of Canada Bulletin 128, pp. 189–240.

Jehl, J.R., and B.A. Smith. 1970. Birds of the Churchill region, Manitoba. Manitoba Museum of Man and Nature, Special Publication 1, pp. 1–87.

Johnson, J.W. 1970. A bird list for Thompson, Manitoba. Blue Jay, vol. 28, no. 1, pp. 14–19.

Knapton, R.W. 1979. Birds of the Gainsborough–Lyleton region (Saskatchewan and Manitoba). Saskatchewan Natural History Society, Special Publication 10, pp. 1–72.

McNicholl, M.K. 1975. Manitoba bird studies: a bibliography of Manitoba ornithology. Manitoba Department of Mines, Resources and Environmental Management.

Rogers, F.J. 1937. A preliminary list of the birds of Hillside Beach, Lake Winnipeg, Manitoba. Canadian Field-Naturalist, vol. 51, no. 6, pp. 79–86.

Shortt, T.M., and Sam Waller. 1937. The birds of the Lake St. Martin region, Manitoba. Contributions Royal Ontario Museum of Zoology, no. 10, pp. 1–51.

Soper, J.D. 1953. The birds of Shoal Lake, Manitoba. Ottawa Naturalist, vol. 32, no. 8, pp. 137–144, no. 9, pp. 157–164; also Canadian Field-Naturalist, vol. 33, no. 1, pp. 12–20. (Supplementary data by E.S. Norman, 1920. Canadian Field-Naturalist, vol. 34, no. 8, p. 154.)

New Brunswick

Squires, W.A. 1952. The birds of New Brunswick. The New Brunswick Museum, Monograph Series 4, 164 pp. (Revised edition, 1976.) The New Brunswick Museum, Monograph Series 7, 221 pp.

Pettingill, O.S., Jr. 1939. The bird life of the Grand Manan Archipelago. Proceedings of the Nova Scotian Institute of Science, vol. 18, part 4, pp. 293–372.

Newfoundland

Peters, H.S., and T.D. Burleigh. 1951. The birds of Newfoundland. St. John's: Newfoundland Department of Natural Resources. (Supplementary notes published by W.E. Godfrey, 1961. National Museum of Canada Bulletin 172, pp. 98–111.)

Tuck, L.M. 1968. Recent Newfoundland bird records. Auk, vol. 85, no. 2, pp. 304–311.

Nova Scotia

Tufts, R.W. 1961 (= 1962). The birds of Nova Scotia. Halifax: Nova Scotia Museum. (2nd ed., 1973.)

Godfrey, W.E. 1958. Birds of Cape Breton Island, Nova Scotia. Canadian Field-Naturalist, vol. 73, no. 1, pp. 7–27.

McLaren, I.A. 1981. The birds of Sable Island, Nova Scotia. Proceedings of the Nova Scotian Institute of Science, vol. 31, part 1, pp. 1–84.

Ontario

James, R.D., P.L. McLaren, and J.C. Barlow. 1976. Annotated checklist of the birds of Ontario. Royal Ontario Museum, Life Sciences Miscellaneous Publications.

Baillie, J.L., Jr. 1947. The summer birds of Sudbury district, Ontario. Contributions Royal Ontario Museum of Zoology, no. 28, pp. 1–32.

Baillie, J.L., Jr., and Paul Harrington. 1936–1937. The distribution of breeding birds in Ontario. Transactions Royal Canadian Institute, vol. 21, pp. 1–50, 199–283.

Baillie, J.L., Jr., and C.E. Hope. 1943. The summer birds of the northeast shore of Lake Superior, Ontario. Contributions Royal Ontario Museum of Zoology, no. 23, pp. 1–27.

Beardslee, C.S., and H.D. Mitchell. 1965. Birds of the Niagara frontier region. Bulletin Buffalo Society of Natural Sciences, no. 22, p. 478. (A supplement by H.D. Mitchell and R.F. Andrle was published in 1970: Bulletin Buffalo Society of Natural Sciences, no. 22, Supplement.)

Dear, L.S. 1940. Breeding birds of the region of Thunder Bay, Lake Superior, Ontario. Transactions of Royal Canadian Institute, vol. 23, pp. 119–143.

Denis, Keith. 1961. Birds of the Canadian Lakehead area. Thunder Bay Field-Naturalist Club, Supplement No. 2, pp. 1–8. Mimeographed.

Devitt, E.O. 1967. The birds of Simcoe County, Ontario. Barrie, Ont.: Brereton Field-Naturalist Club.

Fleming, J.H. 1901. A list of the birds of the districts of Parry Sound and Muskoka, Ontario. Auk, vol. 18, no. 1, pp. 33–45. (Corrections by same author, 1901. Auk, vol. 18, no. 3, pp. 276–277.)
1906–1907. Birds of Toronto, Ontario. Part 1, Water birds, Auk, vol. 23, no. 4, pp. 437–453; Part 2, Land birds, Auk, vol. 24, no. 1, pp. 71–89. (Additions by same author, 1913. Auk, vol. 30, no. 2, pp. 225–228.)

Goodwin, C.E. 1982. A bird-finding guide to Ontario. University of Toronto Press.

Kelley, A.H. 1978. Birds of southeastern Michigan and southwestern Ontario. Bloomfield Hills, Mich.: Cranbrook Institute of Science.

Lloyd, Hoyes. 1944. The birds of Ottawa, 1944. Canadian Field-Naturalist, vol. 58, no. 5, pp. 143–175. (Addenda by same author and others have appeared more recently in same journal.)

MacLulich, D.A. 1938. Birds of Algonquin Provincial Park, Ontario. Contributions Royal Ontario Museum of Zoology, no. 13, pp. 1–47.

Manning, T.H. 1952. Birds of the West James Bay and southern Hudson Bay coasts. National Museums of Canada Bulletin 125, pp. 1–114.

Nicholson, J.C. 1972. The birds of Manitoulin Island. Sudbury, Ont.: The author.

Peck, G.K., and R.D. James. 1983. Breeding birds of Ontario: Nideology and distribution. Volume 1: nonpasserines. Royal Ontario Museum Life Sciences Miscellaneous Publications.

Quilliam, H.R. 1973. History of the birds of Kingston, Ontario. 2nd rev. ed. Kingston, Ont.: Kingston Field Naturalists.

Saunders, W.E., and E.M.S. Dale. 1933. History and list of birds of Middlesex County, Ontario. Transactions of Royal Canadian Institute, no. 19, pp. 161–248.

Sheppard, R.W. n.d. (1960). Bird life of Canada's Niagara frontier. Mimeographed.

Smith, W.J. 1957. Birds of the clay belt of northern Ontario and Quebec. Canadian Field-Naturalist, vol. 71, no. 4, pp. 163–181.

Snyder, L.L. 1928a. The summer birds of Lake Nipigon. Transactions Royal Canadian Institute 16, pp. 251–277.
1928b. A faunal investigation of the Lake Abitibi region, Ontario. University of Toronto Studies, Biological Series, no. 31, pp. 1–34.

1931. A faunal survey of Long Point and vicinity, Norfolk County, Ontario. Transactions Royal Canadian Institute 18, pp. 117–227.

1938. A faunal investigation of western Rainy River district. Ontario. Transactions Royal Canadian Institute 22, pp. 157–213.

1942. Summer birds of the Sault Ste. Marie region, Ontario. Transactions Royal Canadian Institute 24, pp. 121–153. (Addenda by Fred Warburton, 1950. Canadian Field-Naturalist, vol. 64, no. 6, pp. 192–200.

1951. Ontario birds. Toronto: Clarke, Irwin.

1953. Summer birds of western Ontario. Transactions Royal Canadian Institute 30, pp. 47–95.

1957. Changes in the avifauna of Ontario. Pages 26–42 in Changes in the Fauna of Ontario, edited by F.A. Urquhart. Toronto: University of Toronto Press.

Speirs, J.M. 1973–1975. Birds of Ontario County. Parts 1, 2 and 3 (Tyrannidae through Fringillidae). Federation of Ontario Naturalists.

Sprague, Terry. 1969. Birds of Prince Edward county. Picton, Ont.: Prince Edward Region Conservation Authority.

Stirrett, George. 1973. Birds of Point Pelee National Park. Part 1 (winter); Part 2 (spring); Part 3 (summer); Part 4 (autumn). Ottawa: Information Canada.

Taverner, P.A., and B.H. Swales. 1907–1908. The birds of Point Pelee. Wilson Bulletin, vol. 19, no. 2, pp. 37–54, no. 3, pp. 82–99, no. 4, pp. 133–153; and vol. 20, no. 2, pp. 79–96, no. 3, pp. 107–129.

Todd, W.E.C. 1963. (See under Quebec.)

Tozer, R.G., and J.M. Richards. 1974. Birds of the Oshawa–Lake Skugog region, Ontario. Oshawa, Ont.: The authors.

Prince Edward Island

Godfrey, W.E. 1954. Birds of Prince Edward Island. National Museum of Canada Bulletin 132, pp. 155–213.

Anonymous. 1974. Prince Edward Island field check-list of birds. Charlottetown: Department of Environment and Tourism. (Gives brief status for 262 species.)

Quebec

Todd, W.E.C. 1963. Birds of the Labrador Peninsula and adjacent areas. Toronto: University of Toronto Press.

Ball, S.C. 1938. Summer birds of the Forillon, Gaspé County, Quebec. Canadian Field-Naturalist, vol. 52, no. 7, pp. 95–103, no. 8, pp. 120–122. (Additions by same author, 1954. Canadian Field-Naturalist, vol. 68, no. 3, pp. 103–108.)

1952. Fall bird migration on the Gaspé Peninsula. Peabody Museum of Natural History, Yale University Bulletin 7, pp. 1–211.

Brown, Peter 1967. Status of birds, Lake St. John region, Quebec. Canadian Field-Naturalist, vol. 81, no. 1, pp. 50–62.

Cayouette, Raymond, and Jean-Luc Grondin. 1972. Les oiseaux du Québec. Orsainville: La Société Zoologique de Québec, Inc.

David, Normand. 1980. Status and distribution of birds in southern Quebec. Charlesbourg: Cahiers d'ornithologie Victor-Gaboriault 4. Club des ornithologues du Québec.

Dionne, C.E. 1906. Les oiseaux de la province de Québec. Québec: Dussault and Proulx.

Gaboriault, Wilfrid. 1961. Les oiseaux aux Iles-de-la-Madeleine. Le Naturaliste canadien, vol. 88, nos. 6 and 7, pp. 166–180, nos. 8 and 9, pp. 181–224.

Godfrey, W.E. 1949. Birds of Lake Mistassini and Lake Albanel, Quebec. National Museum of Canada Bulletin 114, pp. 1–43.

Godfrey, W.E., and A.L. Wilk. 1948. Birds of the Lake St. John Region, Quebec. National Museum of Canada Bulletin 110, pp. 1–32.

Harper, Francis. 1958. Birds of the Ungava Peninsula. University of Kansas, Museum of Natural History Miscellaneous Publication 17, pp. 1–171.

Lemieux, Serge. 1978. Les oiseaux de la Réserve nationale de faune du Cap Tourmente, Québec. Le Naturaliste canadien, vol. 105, no. 3, pp. 177–193.

Lewis, H.F. 1922–1938. Notes on Labrador Peninsula birds. Auk, vol. 39, no. 4, pp. 507–516; vol. 40, no. 1, pp. 135–137; vol. 42, no. 1, pp. 74–86, no. 2, pp. 278–281; vol. 44, no. 1, pp. 59–66; vol. 45, no. 2, pp. 227–229; and Canadian Field-Naturalist, vol. 42, no. 8, pp. 191–194; vol. 44, no. 5, pp. 109–111; vol. 45, no. 5, pp. 113–114; vol. 48, no. 6, pp. 98–102, no. 7, pp. 115–119; vol. 51, no. 7, pp. 99–105, no. 8, pp. 119–123; vol. 52, no. 4, pp. 47–51.

Lloyd, Hoyes 1944. (See under Ontario.)

Manning, T.H. 1946. Bird and mammal notes from the east side of Hudson Bay. Canadian Field-Naturalist, vol. 60, no. 4, pp. 71–85.

1949. The birds of north-western Ungava. Pages 155–224 in A summer on Hudson Bay, by Mrs. Tom Manning. London: Hodder and Stoughton.

Manning, T.H., and A.H. Macpherson. 1952. Birds of the east James Bay coast between Long Point and Cape Jones. Canadian Field-Naturalist, vol. 66, no. 1, pp. 1–35.

McNeil, Raymond. 1961. Avifaune du Parc de la Vérendrye, Québec. Le Naturaliste canadien, vol. 88, no. 4, pp. 97–129.

McNeil, Raymond, Jean Boulva, Wilfrid Gaboriault, and J.C. Strauch, Jr. 1973. Observations récentes sur les oiseaux aux Iles-de-la-Madeleine, Québec. La Revue de Géographie de Montréal, vol. 27, no. 2, pp. 157–171.

Ouellet, Henri. 1969. Les oiseaux de l'île Anticosti, province de Québec, Canada. Publications in Zoology 1. Ottawa: National Museums of Canada. National Museum of Natural Sciences.

1974. Les oiseaux des collines montérégiennes et de la région de Montréal, Québec, Canada. Publications in Zoology 5. Ottawa: National Museums of Canada, National Museum of Natural Sciences.

1975. Contribution à l'étude des oiseaux d'hiver au parc National de Forillon, Québec. La Revue de Géographie de Montréal, vol. 29, no. 4, pp. 289–304.

Ouellet, Henri, and Reginald Ouellet. 1963. Bird notes from Lac Ste. Anne, Saguenay County, Quebec. Canadian Field-Naturalist, vol. 77, no. 4, pp. 146–153.

Savile, D.B.O. 1950. Bird notes from Great Whale River, Que. Canadian Field-Naturalist, vol. 64, no. 3, pp. 95–99.

Smith, W.J. 1957. (See under Ontario.)

Tanguay, René. 1964–1965. Les oiseaux des comtés de Kamouraska, L'Islet et Montmagny, P.Q. Le Naturaliste canadien, vol. 91, no. 12, pp. 309–331; vol. 92, no. 1, pp. 8–48 and no. 2, pp. 49–58.

Taverner, P.A. 1929. Bird notes from the Canadian Labrador, 1928. Canadian Field-Naturalist, vol. 43, no. 4, pp. 74–79.

Saskatchewan

Anweiler, G.G. 1970. The birds of the Last Mountain Lake Wildlife Area, Saskatchewan. Blue Jay, vol. 28, no. 2, pp. 74–83.

Belcher, Margaret. 1980. Birds of Regina. Rev. ed. Saskatchewan Natural History Society, Special Publication 12, pp. 1–151.

Callin, E.M. 1980. Birds of the Qu'Appelle, 1857–1979. Saskatchewan Natural History Society, Special Publication 13, pp. 1–168.

Godfrey, W.E. 1950. Birds of the Cypress Hills and Flotten Lake regions. Saskatchewan. National Museum of Canada Bulletin 120, pp. 1–96.

Houston, C.S. 1949. The birds of the Yorkton District, Saskatchewan. Canadian Field-Naturalist, vol. 63, no. 6, pp. 215–241.

Houston, C.S., and M.G. Street. 1959. The birds of the Saskatchewan River, Carlton to Cumberland. Saskatchewan Natural History Society Publication 2, pp. 1–205.

Mitchell, H.H. 1924. Birds of Saskatchewan. Canadian Field-Naturalist, vol. 38, no. 6, pp. 101–118.

Mowat, F.M. 1947. Notes on the birds of Emma Lake, Saskatchewan. Canadian Field-Naturalist, vol. 61, no. 3, pp. 105–115.

Nero, R.W. 1963. Birds of the Lake Athabasca region, Saskatchewan. Saskatchewan Natural History Society, Special Publication 5, pp. 1–143.
1967. The birds of northeastern Saskatchewan. Saskatchewan Natural History Society, Special Publication 6, pp. 1–96.

Nero, R.W., and M.R. Lein. 1971. Birds of Moose Mountain, Saskatchewan. Saskatchewan Natural History Society, Special Publication 7, pp. 1–55.

Potter, L.B. 1943. Bird notes from southwestern Saskatchewan. Canadian Field-Naturalist, vol. 57, nos. 4 and 5, pp. 69–72.

Randall, T.E. 1962. Birds of the Kazan Lake region, Saskatchewan. Blue Jay, vol. 20, no. 2, pp. 60–72.

Renaud, W.E., and D.H. Renaud, 1975. Birds of the Rosetown–Biggar district, Saskatchewan. Saskatchewan Natural History Society, Special Publication 9, pp. 1–120.

Soper, J.D. 1952. The birds of Prince Albert National Park, Saskatchewan. Canadian Wildlife Service, Wildlife Management Bulletin (Ottawa), series 2, no. 4, pp. 1–83.

Todd, W.E.C. 1947. Notes on the birds of southern Saskatchewan. Annals of the Carnegie Museum No. 30, pp. 383–421.

Yukon Territory

Rand, A.L. 1946. List of Yukon birds and those of the Canol Road. National Museum of Canada Bulletin 105, pp. 1–76.

Drury, W.H., Jr. 1953. Birds of the Saint Elias Quadrangle in the southwestern Yukon Territory. Canadian Field-Naturalist, vol. 67, no. 4, pp. 103–128.

Frisch, Robert. 1982. Birds by the Dempster Highway. Privately published.

Godfrey, W.E. 1951. Notes on the birds of southern Yukon Territory. National Museum of Canada Bulletin 123, pp. 88–115.

Hoefs, Manfred. 1973. Birds of Kluane Game Sanctuary, Yukon Territory, and adjacent areas. Canadian Field-Naturalist, vol. 87, no. 4, pp. 345–355.

Irving, Laurence. 1960. Birds of Anaktuvuk Pass, Kobuk, and Old Crow. United States National Museum Bulletin 217, pp. 1–409.

Birds of Some Contiguous Parts of the United States

Bull, John. 1974. Birds of New York State. Garden City, N.Y.: Doubleday/Natural History Press.

Burleigh, T.D. 1972. Birds of Idaho. Caldwell, Idaho: Caxton Printers.

Eaton, E.H. 1910–1914. Birds of New York. 2 vols. New York State Museum Memoir 12.

Forbush, E.H. 1925–1929. Birds of Massachusetts and other New England states. 3 vols. Boston: Commonwealth of Massachusetts.

Gabrielson, I.N., and F.C. Lincoln. 1959. The birds of Alaska. Washington, D.C.: Wildlife Management Institute.

Jewett, S.G., W.P. Taylor, W.T. Shaw, and J.W. Aldrich. 1953. Birds of Washington State. Seattle: University of Washington Press.

Kessel, B., and D.D. Gibson. 1978. Status and distribution of Alaska birds. Studies in Avian Biology, no. 1, pp. 1–100.

Palmer, R.S. 1949. Maine Birds. Bulletin of Museum Comparative Zoology, vol. 102, pp. 1–656.

Payne, R.B. 1983. A distributional checklist of the birds of Michigan. Museum of Zoology, University of Michigan, Miscellaneous Publications 164.

Roberts, T.S. 1932. The birds of Minnesota. 2 vols. Minneapolis: University of Minnesota Press.

Saunders, A.A. 1921. A distributional list of the birds of Montana. Pacific Coast Avifauna, no. 14, pp. 1–194.

Stewart, R.E. 1975. Breeding birds of North Dakota. Fargo, N.Dak.: Tri-College Center for Environmental Studies.

Biology of Birds

Farner, D.S., and J.R. King (editors). 1971–1975. Avian Biology. Volumes 1 to 5. New York: Academic Press.

Marshall, A.J. (editor). 1960–1961. Biology and comparative physiology of birds. 2 vols. New York: Academic Press.

Pettingill, O.S., Jr. 1970. Ornithology in laboratory and field. 4th ed. Minneapolis: Burgess.

Rand, A.L. 1967. Ornithology: an introduction. New York: W.W. Norton.

Van Tyne, J., and A.J. Berger. 1976. Fundamentals of ornithology. 2nd ed. New York: John Wiley and Sons.

Wallace, G.J. 1963. An introduction to ornithology. 2nd ed. New York: Macmillan.

Welty, J.C. 1975. The life of birds. 2nd ed. Philadelphia: W.B. Saunders.

Field Guides

Farrand, John, Jr. (editor). 1983. The Audubon Society Master Guide to birding. 3 volumes. New York: Alfred A. Knopf.

Peterson, R.T. 1980. A field guide to the birds. 4th ed. Boston: Houghton Mifflin (North America east of the Rockies.) **1961.** A field guide to western birds. Boston: Houghton Mifflin (North America west of the 100th Meridian: also Hawaiian Islands).

Robbins, C.S., B. Bruun, and H.S. Zim. 1983. Birds of North America: A guide to field identification. 2nd ed. New York: Golden Press.

Scott, S.L. (editor). 1983. Field guide to the birds of North America. Washington, D.C.: National Geographic Society.

General Reference

Bent, A.C. 1919–1968. Life histories of North American birds. United States National Museum Bulletins, 107, 113, 121, 126, 130, 135, 142, 146, 162, 167, 170, 174, 176, 179, 191, 195, 196, 197, 203, 211, and 237 (parts 1 to 3). (The authors and numerous collaborators have compiled, from a vast number of sources, information on courtship, nesting, eggs, young, immature plumages and moults, food, general behaviour, distribution, and migration and egg dates of North American birds. Although these volumes quickly went out of print, Dover reprints are available.)

Palmer, R.S. (editor). 1962–1976. Handbook of North American birds. Vols. 1–3. (loons through waterfowl). New Haven, Conn.: Yale University Press. (Other volumes of this encyclopedic treatment of North American birds are in preparation.)

Thompson, A.L. (editor). 1964. A new dictionary of birds. New York: McGraw-Hill.

Witherby, H.F. (editor). 1938–1941. The handbook of British birds. Vols. 1 to 5. London: H.F. Witherby. (Contains very detailed treatment of many North American bird species.)

Plumage Descriptions

Ridgway, Robert 1901–1919. The birds of North and Middle America, United States National Museum Bulletin 50, Parts 1 to 8.

Ridgway, Robert, and Herbert Friedmann. 1941–1946. The birds of North and Middle America. United States National Museum Bulletin 50, Parts 9 and 10.

Friedmann, Herbert. 1950. The birds of North and Middle America. United States National Museum Bulletin 50, Part 11.

Oberholser, H.C. 1974. The bird life of Texas. 2 vols. Austin: University of Texas Press. (Contains extremely detailed plumage descriptions of many bird species found also in Canada.)

Prater, A.J., J.H. Marchant, and J. Vuorinen. 1977. Guide to the identification and ageing of holarctic waders. British Trust for Ornithology, Field Guide 17.

Nomenclature and Classification

American Ornithologists' Union. 1983. Check-list of North American birds (Sixth Edition). This is the standard authority on scientific and English names.

Ouellet, Henri, and Michel Gosselin. 1983. Les noms français des oiseaux d'Amérique du Nord. Syllogeus 43. Ottawa: National Museum of Natural Sciences, National Museums of Canada.

Index

A